Placenames of the World

SECOND EDITION

Placenames of the World

Origins and Meanings of the Names for 6,600 Countries, Cities, Territories, Natural Features and Historic Sites

Second Edition

ADRIAN ROOM

McFarland & Company, Inc., Publishers
Jefferson, North Carolina, and London

Library of Congress Cataloguing-in-Publication Data

Room, Adrian.
Placenames of the world : origins and meanings of the names for 6,600
countries, cities, territories, natural features and historic sites /
Adrian Room.— 2nd ed.
p.   cm.
Includes bibliographical references.

ISBN 0-7864-2248-3 (illustrated case binding : 50# alkaline paper)

1. Names, Geographical.   I. Title.
G105.R66   2006   910'.01'4 — dc22   2005017522

British Library cataloguing data are available

Cover photograph ©2005 Stockbyte

Manufactured in the United States of America

*McFarland & Company, Inc., Publishers
Box 611, Jefferson, North Carolina 28640
www.mcfarlandpub.com*

Contents

Two or three of them got round me, and begged me for the twentieth time to tell them the name of my country. Then, as they could not pronounce it satisfactorily, they insisted that I was deceiving them, and that it was a name of my own invention. One funny old man, who bore a ludicrous resemblance to a friend of mine at home, was almost indignant. "Unglung!" said he, "who ever heard of such a name?— anglang, angerlang — that can't be the name of your country; you are playing with us." Then he tried to give a convincing illustration. "My country is Wanumbai — anybody can say Wanumbai, I'm an orang-Wanumbai; but N-glung! who ever heard of such a name? Do tell us the real name of your country, and when you are gone we shall know how to talk about you."

— Alfred Russel Wallace, *The Malay Archipelago* (1869)

Preface

The Basic Principles of Placename Study

This new edition of a dictionary first published in 1997 aims to give the origins of 6,600 of the world's most familiar placenames, ranging from from natural objects, such as oceans, seas, rivers, lakes, mountains, islands, capes, and forests, to objects built or delimited by humankind, such as towns, cities, counties, states, and the many different kinds of administrative regions that exist. Prime among all these are the world's many countries, from Afghanistan to Zimbabwe, whether naturally delimited, such as the large islands of Australia and Greenland, or with continental borders and frontiers that may well have been the cause of bitter wrangling and bloodshed, such as Mexico and Poland. Over 1,000 new entries have been added, with increased emphasis on names in countries that were to some extent underrepresented earlier, such as China, Germany, Hungary, India, Israel, and Japan, while many of the original entries have been expanded. Errors and omissions have also been corrected.

Toponymy, or placename study, is a complex discipline that basically involves three key aspects: *history*, *geography*, and *language*. These frequently intermingle to give a full enough picture for a name to be reasonably satisfactorily interpreted. From a practical point of view, it is usually the *language* that is best tackled first. Not necessarily that of the present name, but that of its earliest known form, which may be quite different from what it is now. And when the *history* of a named place is traced back also as far as possible, it may well be found that its original name was entirely different to its present one, and even in a totally different language. The third aspect of a named place, its *geography*, is its descriptive side. It may relate to a particular characteristic of a natural object, such as the color of a mountain, or the speed of a river's current, or may involve human geography, and associate the name directly to that of the people who are or were indigenous to a place, or who built or settled or conquered it.

The human side of a placename is of course paramount, since all names were given by humans in the first place. A lake may form as a result of natural processes, but it does not name itself. Humans do that, either casually or simply for practical purposes, or deliberately and even with due ceremony.

Leafing through the book, the reader will notice that many natural objects have basic names that simply describe them in general terms. This is particularly true of rivers, whose names are among the oldest we have, and which often turn out to mean simply "river." This is because the people who first come to live by a river, in any country in any era, refer to it simply as "the river." There is no need to call it anything else. Everyone knows which river is meant. Hence the common Celtic river name Avon in England. But when another river is involved, such as a tributary, or a different river to which people have moved from their original place of settlement, then it will need to be called something else, if only for purposes of differentiation. This will probably not be too difficult, since no two rivers are exactly alike. They differ in length, breadth, color, speed of current, and surrounding landscape and vegetation. Broadly, therefore, for the reasons outlined here, it is the natural objects that have the oldest names. The exception to this is the natural object that is in difficult or originally inaccessible territory, such as a remote mountain or a hidden lake. Here the name will be more recent, and likely to have been specially created by an explorer or adventurer who may not even speak the native language of the territory.

The converse is thus also broadly true, that most towns and cities have deliberate rather than casual names. Very often a personal name is involved. Many British towns and villages, for example, contain the names of Anglo-Saxon and Scandinavian landholders, while in North America and indeed most former colonial countries the settlements were frequently named for the settler, or for a family member or associate. By the same token, many colonial names are transfers of existing names from "the old country," whichever that happens to be.

Humans are diverse beings with credos and doctrines that have varied widely over the centuries. The legacies of what was once held brave or noble or sacred by a particular people remain enshrined in the placenames of today. The Americas, for example, still display the religious names ("Christian" names in a literal sense) bestowed in the 16th century by European missionaries. The name today may be a shadow of its former self (Los Angeles was originally a name four times as long) but it is still there as a reminder of the history of the place and the geographical origin of its people. In the countries of the former Soviet Union, similarly, names of political heroes still remain on the map, despite exten-

sive renaming following the collapse of Communism in the early 1990s.

Toponymy is not only a complex science. It is a difficult and at times frustrating one. It is a science beset by faint clues and blind alleys. Many names are wily and deceptive. They seem to be one thing while turning out to be another. A study of this kind is thus ready bait for the amateur angler, who thinks that armed with some fairly rudimentary tackle (a smattering of history here, a nodding acquaintance with a language there) it is possibly to net and dissect a placename to the satisfaction and admiration of all concerned. But things are not always so simple!

In studying placenames one is constantly returning to the matter of language. It would be naïve to suppose that even the longest established countries in the world, such as those of Europe, have names solely in the language of the country concerned. Thus while France has mostly French names, it also has German names and, from its history of settlement, Gaulish and Frankish names. Britain has many Celtic names. Much of eastern Germany has names of Slavic origin. The different strata of names that lie preserved in most countries of the world can be seen most clearly in the former colonial countries. The Americas have many names of Native American (i.e. non–European) origin. Australia has Aboriginal names. New Zealand has Maori names. South Africa has names in many indigenous African languages, some mutually related, some not.

Toponymy involves both living and dead languages. In many European countries some of the better known city names evolved from their Latin names, given when they were part of the Roman empire. The Romans in turn often based their names on existing ones, which in many parts of Europe are often Celtic in origin. There are thus at least three strata of names to consider here. Historically, of course, one needs to go back as early as possible and see what the Celtic names meant. Did the Celts base them on even earlier names? If so, what were they?

In studying placenames, one must remember a general principle that applies to all names. *They all originally had a meaning.* Even the modern arbitrary or artificial name must have had an origin of some sort, its arbitrariness or artificiality serving as its "meaning." It does at least make some kind of statement. The object of this dictionary is to spell out, as far as is possible, what the meaning is. And if it is not known, it will be necessary to say so, or at least to say what the name does *not* mean.

Here, once again, one comes up against the amateur interpreter, who holds firmly to a popular etymology. Such "folk" etymologies became widely current in the 19th century, when the growth of scientific knowledge generally prompted the enthusiastic toponymist to publish his favorite theories. Thus, it was claimed, England's Brighton was named for a Saxon bishop, St. Brighthelm, Scotland's Edinburgh is so called after its royal possessor, Edwin, king of Northumbria, Germany bore the name of a Roman emperor Germanicus (it is not clear which), the Red Sea was really the "Reed Sea," the Italian capital, Rome, was named for its founder, Romulus, and Holland's Zuider Zee is so called after "an eminent grazier of the name of Zuider." (This last is found in the third edition of William Pulleyn's *The Etymological Compendium, or, Portfolio of Origins and Inventions*, published in London in 1853. "Invention" is actually the appropriate term, although not all of the author's topographical entries are as wayward.) Some of these fancies are still quoted today, or are commonly held as fact. A few further examples are cited in some of the present book's entries, a prime example being that for *London*.

The Classification of Placenames

Mention has already been made of descriptive names. However, this is only one type of name, albeit one of the most common. There are other types. The American toponymist George R. Stewart has distinguished ten categories of placenames, outlined in the introduction to his *American Place-Names* and expanded and exemplified in *Names on the Globe* (see the Select Bibliography, beginning on page 431). His classification has hardly been bettered, and will serve as well for names worldwide as for names in his native United States. The ten types are: (1) Descriptive names; (2) Associative names; (3) Incident names; (4) Possessive names; (5) Commemorative names; (6) Commendatory names; (7) Folk etymologies; (8) Manufactured names; (9) Mistake names; (10) Shift names. This particular order generally reflects the chronological development of names, so that the earliest names we have historically are descriptive, associative, and incident.

Let us briefly consider each of these ten types, not necessarily restricting ourselves to Stewart's own definitions. (A few examples below were devised for illustrative purposes, but most are genuine and well known, and have their own entries in the book.)

Descriptive names can be direct, such as Whitewater, relative, such as Upper Arlington (implicitly contrasted with a Lower Arlington), indirect or metaphorical, such as Dragon Mountain (its peak is shaped like a dragon's head), subjective, such as Disappointment Bay (where explorers did not find what they sought), and habitual, such as Saturday (where a regular weekly market is held). England's most common placename is Newton, a descriptive name of the relative type, implying a settlement that arose later than another, already existing, or at least incorporating some kind of new feature. All names containing the word for a compass point, such as North, South, East, West, are also descriptive names of the relative type. Size, color, and shape are common characteristics of directly descriptive names. It is easiest of all to name an object from its appearance, since it is by sight that one first distinguishes it.

Associative names are those that link a place with something. An example is Mill Hill. The hill is associated with a nearby mill, and is named for it. In a sense, of course, such names are descriptive, but form a discrete enough category to be distinguished from that type. Many places are named for local flora or fauna, so that one has Pine Valley, Holly Ridge, and Beaver Meadow. The German city of Leipzig, named for its lime trees, is a name of this type. It should be borne in mind that a place named for associated natural objects of this kind may be named as much for their rarity as their abundance. Thus Pine Valley may be so called either for its many pines or conversely for a single pine that grows there, possibly prominent among other types of trees. Associative names may also involve human-built objects, such as bridges. Hence the many towns around the world named for this particular structure, such as America's Bridgeport, England's Cambridge, France's Pontoise, Belgium's Bruges, Germany's Zweibrücken, and Bosnia-Hercegovina's Mostar.

Incident names are given from a particular event occurring at or near a place. A classic example is Council Bluffs, Iowa, named for a historical powwow or council. Many names given by navigators and explorers are of this type, such as those bestowed by Christopher Columbus for a particular saint's day when a sighting or landing was made. Just one example of many is St. Vincent, in the West Indies, discovered by Columbus on January 22, 1498, the feast-day of St. Vincent of Saragossa. Incident names are popular with amateur toponymists, who have devised, for example, a meaning "field of corpses," referring to a fa-

mous battle, for the English city of Lichfield. That would certainly be an incident. But the Lich- of the name is not Old English *līc*, "corpse," but a Celtic word meaning "gray."

Possessive names are those denoting a particular ownership. Mention was made earlier of places named for landholders and settlers. Names of this kind usually incorporate the owner's or founder's name, such as Tennessee's Johnson City, but they may equally include a title or office. France's Abbeville is thus named for the abbot on whom it originally depended. Possessive names do not necessarily refer to a single individual. Territories named for a particular tribe or people also fall into this category, such as Greece, named for the Greeks whose land it was and is, and France, named for the Franks. (America is not a name of this type, since its people are named for the country, not the country for its people.) Within France itself, Normandy has a possessive name, as that of the Normans, the people of Scandinavian origin who invaded and settled it.

Commemorative names are those given to honor a particular person or place, or to enshrine an abstract quality or ideal. Examples of the first kind are the many places named in the New World for Christopher Colombus, including the various American cities called Columbia and Columbus itself, the South American republic of Colombia, and the Panamanian city of Colón and its suburb, Cristóbal, representing the Spanish forms of both the great explorer's names. Some names of this type commemorate a royal or aristocratic title that is itself a placename. Familiar examples are New York and New Orleans, named respectively for the English Duke of York and French duc d'Orléans. All of the names transferred from a settler's homeland are commemorative names. There are many such examples in the former British colonies, not least in North America.

Saints' names can also be included here, even if they arise as incident names, since the aim is to commemorate a particular saint. Also in the group are the biblical placenames such as Bethel, Bethlehem, and Salem, bestowed by Christian missionaries. Tasmania, Australia, has a curious cluster of transferred names commemorating British rivers. They include a Clyde, a Derwent, an Esk, a Mersey, a Tamar, and several others. Names commemorating abstractions include Concord, New Hampshire, and Peace River, Canada. But the abstractions are also incident names, since they mark an amicable agreement between two formerly warring factions.

Commendatory names are those designed to augur well for a settlement's future. They comprise and incorporate a whole range of pleasant or propitious words, or honor deities whose influence is deemed to be beneficial and favorable. Springfield and Fairfield are commendatory names found widely throughout the United States, while India's Lucknow enshrines the name of Lakshmi, the Hindu goddess of good fortune and beauty. Most countries have examples of a "bad" name changed to one felt to be "good." The United States has a Poverty Ridge that became Prosperity; Belarus has a Zagryazye ("Dirty Place") that became Bereznyanka ("Birch Trees"). (Sometimes such ameliorations are made on mistaken grounds. England's Belgrave, "beautiful grove," was renamed from an original Merdegrave in the belief that this name contained French *merde*, "shit." The offending word was actually Old English for "marten," the small animal.) A classic commendatory name is that of the Cape of Good Hope, so called because it was hoped that the sea route around it would lead to India and its riches. Not only that, but it replaced the unpropitious earlier descriptive name of Cape of Storms.

Folk etymology, or popular etymology, has had an insidious influence on place-names and their study, as has already been illustrated. It is involved especially when a name in one language is misinterpreted in another, often purely on a resemblance of sound or spelling. The derivation of the name of Canada from Spanish *cañada*, commonly found, is a typical example, since Canada's name is of Native American origin, not European. Most countries have names of this type. Thus England's Inkpen Beacon is a hill that never had an original scribal reference, and France's Saintes does not honor saints, male or female, but preserves, albeit in corrupt form, a Gaulish tribal name. There is a school of thought that attributes "the sleeve" as an interpretation of *La Manche*, the French name of the English Channel, to folk etymology. Detractors of the traditional origin claim its true meaning is "the channel," from a Celtic word that gave the name of The Minch, Scotland.

Manufactured names are among the most recent. They are those that have been artificially devised or concocted for new settlements. There are several examples in the United States, such as Tesnus, Texas, and Tolono, Illinois. The former is a reversal of "sunset." The later is a meaningless compilation of letters chosen by its deviser with the aim of creating an attractive and easily pronounceable name, rather in the manner of a trade name. (Although meaningless in the normal sense of the word, it is nevertheless meaningful in that it was created with a particular purpose. Tolono = euphony.) Many manufactured names are formed by combining elements of existing names. Thus Africa has Tanzania as a blend of the first syllables of Tanganyika and Zanzibar, with a classical-style suffix, and even Pasadena is a name similarly compiled from elements of four different Native American names. On the whole, the more recent a country's history, the more likely it is to have a representation of manufactured names. The reorganization of local government boundaries in England in 1974 resulted in few such names, chiefly as combinations of elements from existing names created for the new administrative districts. They were mostly fairly conservative. One of the more adventurous was Wychavon, combining a historic spelling of the second half of Droitwich with the river name Avon. (A government report at the time specifically stipulated that "concocted" names were best avoided.)

Mistake names are those that arose, as the term implies, from some kind of error. Most authorities agree that the name of Oregon arose as a mistake name, from a misdivision of (a French form of) its original name of Ouariconsint. Ouaricon was written on one line, and Sint on another, leaving the former word alone to evolve into the present name. Some of England's brief river names evolved as the result of a misunderstanding. They are so-called "back formations," deriving from a town name. A good example is the Cam River at Cambridge. The river was originally the Granta, and gave the town's earlier name of (in modern terms) Grantabridge. However, Granta gradually became Cam in the town's name, and this was then taken to be the actual river name. One of the best known mistake names is that of Nome, Alaska, said to represent a navigator's written query on a sea chart, "? Name." It is nicely appropriate that the cape should have a mistake name from this particular word.

Shift names are names that have been transferred from one place to another. As stated, many commemorative names are of this type. They are mostly found in more recent cultures, but also exist in older countries. Many of England's county names ending in -shire are shift names from the name of their chief town. Oxford thus gave the name of Oxfordshire, and Lincoln of Lincolnshire. The name may have been shortened or corrupted over the years, but it is still there, as in Cheshire from Chester, and Lancashire from Lancaster. Renamings often involve shift names, as when Russia's Stalingrad adopted the river name Volga to replace that of the discredited Stalin, so becoming Volgograd. It follows from this that all places named for their rivers have shift names. Cambridge, instanced above, was historically a river-based shift name, while today its river, the Cam, is a town-derived shift name. Sometimes a single named object may produce a whole cluster of shift names, whether in the form of the basic name or with an added generic. Thus Portsmouth, England, gave the names of Portsmouth, New Hampshire, Portsmouth, Ohio, Portsmouth, Rhode Island, and Portsmouth, Virginia, even if one or more of these made the shift from an existing American place of the name, not from the original. Similarly, the Missouri River gave the name of the state of Missouri as well as the two Little Missouri rivers (one is not even a tributary), Missouri City, Texas, and Missouri Valley, Iowa. A royal or aristocratic title derived from a placename can also strictly speaking serve to create a shift name, so that New York is in this category, the name of the English city being shifted across the Atlantic through the vehicle of the royal title.

Naming Patterns

Although placenames exist in every country of the world, the nature of the names, and the method of giving them, vary considerably from one part of the globe to another. The following is a bird's-eye view of the various naming patterns that can be discerned in different continents. In such a summary it is not possible to single out the particular naming characteristics of every country, but all of the major countries and regions are here, from the oldest part of the world to the newest.

1. North America. The placenames of North America are relatively easy to chart and interpret when compared to the much more complex names of, say, Asia and Africa. The majority of names are of relatively recent European colonial origin, and mostly in English, French, and Spanish. As is to be expected, many names are accordingly commemorative, and one need merely glance at a map of North America to find a whole host of familiar European names, both those of places and of people. There are also Native American names, of course, although these take up less than 10 percent of the total. Of the 67 counties of Pennsylvania, for example, barely half a dozen have Native American names, while in Kentucky a mere 90 names out of an approximate total of 30,000 are of this type. Moreover, many Native American names have been corrupted in the process of assimilation to English and other European languages, making their correct interpretation difficult.

While English names are found throughout North America, French names are mainly concentrated in eastern Canada, especially around Ottawa and in the St. Lawrence basin. Spanish names are chiefly in the southwest of the United States. Many of them are of religious (missionary) origin, so that Spanish *San* or *Santa*, "saint," begins several well known Californian names, such as San Francisco, San Diego, San Jose, Santa Barbara, Santa Ana, and Santa Cruz. A further pocket of French names is found in Louisiana, as attested by such familiar names as New Orleans, Lafayette, and Baton Rouge.

Alaska, as an "outpost" of the continental United States, has the usual spread of English names but also names of Inuit (Eskimo) and Russian origin, the latter the result of Russia's presence in the peninsula during the first half of the 19th century. (The territory was sold to the United States in 1861.)

Greenland is geographically part of North America, and it also has a large representation of Inuit names. In recent years these have gradually superseded the colonial Scandinavian names, mainly those of coastal settlements founded by Danish, Norwegian, and Swedish traders in the 18th and 19th centuries.

2. Central and South America. The extensive territory of Central and South America, from Mexico to Tierra del Fuego, is dominated by Spanish and Portuguese placenames of colonial origin. As with North America, such names are comparatively modern, so are readily researched and interpreted. Indigenous names are also present, many of them of Arawakan origin, while in Mexico itself names of Nahuatl provenance predominate. (It is thanks to Spanish contact with Native American languages in this part of the world that English now has words such as *maize, cannibal, hammock, cocoa, chocolate, tomato, coyote,* and *chilli.*)

Placenames in the West Indies are extremely varied in their language of origin. Relatively few indigenous names remain, and although the larger islands and settlements still have native names (Cuba, Havana, Haiti, and Jamaica are among the best known), the smaller islands almost all have European names. Among them are Puerto Rico, Dominica, Barbados, and Antigua. The mingling of languages is evident in the placenames of even the smallest islands. In Haiti, for instance, the western part of the island has mostly French names, while in the east they are Spanish. Here, as elsewhere in former colonial territories, it is noticeable that European names are mostly evident in coastal areas, while indigenous names are more fully preserved inland.

3. Europe. The placenames of Europe have been researched more fully than anywhere else. This is chiefly because the names of rivers, lakes, and ancient cities have been recorded in historical documents dating from the earliest times. However, this positive factor has a negative corollary: if such names were recorded early, and certainly in pre–Roman times, they already existed at the time of their recording, and so date back to an era when one can only surmise which languages were involved, let alone which peoples spoke them. As will be seen, London's name remains of uncertain origin.

Although, as mentioned, it broadly holds true that the placenames of a particular European country or region are usually in the language of its inhabitants, the overall picture has been made much more complex by the many migrations, invasions, and resettlements that have taken place. Two examples may be cited. France is named for the Franks, the Germanic people who invaded their territory, but the French themselves speak a Romance language, that of the Romans who earlier also occupied their land. Before them both, the Gauls, a Celtic race, were the indigenous inhabitants. France thus now has names of all three types. England was also at one time populated by a Celtic people, but was invaded by the Angles, Saxons, Jutes, and Scandinavians, all likewise speaking a Germanic language, so that the placenames of Britain today are similarly a meld of these . (England was also earlier invaded by the Romans, but they mostly adopted existing Celtic names, rather than devising their own, or transferring them from their native land. The Romans in fact introduced very few words to the English language, although one of them, significantly, was *street*, from Late Latin *via strata*, "paved way.")

In considering European placenames, one is thus working on several linguistic and historical levels simultaneously. The historical side is important, for unless one is aware that Spain, for example, was colonized by Phoenicians and Greeks, invaded by Vandals, and conquered by Muslims, one would be hard put to it to interpret the Latin, Germanic, and Arabic names that can be found in certain regions. Put the other way around, the placenames in these particular languages in these particular regions are witness to the fact that such colonization, invasion, and conquest took place.

Aside from the languages just mentioned, Europe also contains a notable Slavic placename presence, not just in Russia west of the Urals, but also in much of central and eastern Europe, including eastern Germany. The placenames of Russia and the countries of the former Soviet Union (many of them actually in Asia, not Europe) gained prominence for their political motivation and content. Since the demise of the Soviet Union in 1991, however, many names, even the most widely known, have reverted to their prerevoluionary, czarist forms. Leningrad is once again St. Petersburg, while Gorky has resurrected its formerly familiar name of Nizhny Novgorod.

The Greek names of Greece in southern Europe should not be overlooked, since they are in many cases ancient, dating from classical or even pre-classical times. Finally, the placenames of Albania, in a language not closely related to other Indoeuropean languages, and the names of Hungary, Finland, and Estonia, in an entirely non-Indoeuropean language, stand out linguistically among other European names. In their meanings, however, they share many common characteristics.

The variety of natural features in Europe significantly contributes to the complexity of European placenames, since different territories have different name-type frequencies. In central Europe, for example, many names include the word for bridge, ford, wood, hill, and mountain, while in northern Europe, especially Norway, names are needed for the many capes, islands, bays, inlets (fjords), and other coastal features. In places the sense of "hill" merges with that of "wood," so that Germany's Teutoburg Forest (German *Teutoburger Wald*) is actually a range of hills. The Weald, in southern and southeastern England, is now largely a tract of open land between hills, but formerly it was heavily afforested, and its name relates to German *Wald*, "wood." The same goes for The Wolds, a broad upland region of northeastern England. This is perhaps also the place to mention that the *-berg* ("hill") and *-burg* ("castle") found in many German names are linguistically related. A castle is often built on a hill, as an advantageous natural site for both defense and attack, each from a superior position above the enemy.

4. Africa. In real terms, the oldest recorded placenames of Africa are in the north of the continent, and the most recent in the south. The Mediterranean coastal lands have names that date back to the earliest times, with the Phoenicians founding their first settlements here in the 12th century BC. The names of South Africa, on the other hand, are still largely colonial. But the interior of the continent contains a wealth of indigenous names, in various African languages, with roots in an era that essentially predates the earliest recorded period. The history and languages of indigenous Africa are still today the least fully researched, although the colonial "discovery" of equatorial and southern Africa did much, at least, to define the geography of such regions.

Northern Africa contains several strata or "layers" of placenames in different languages that require careful disentanglement. Chronologically speaking, the names can be distinguished as pre–Berber, Berber, Phoenician, Greek and Latin, Arabic, Italian, Spanish, and French. Many of the latter European names, given in the 19th century, have now disappeared, and have been superseded by indigenous or at any rate earlier names. In Algeria and Tunisia, for example, the French names have almost entirely been replaced by Arabic. The Arabs themselves gave their names following their conquest of this part of Africa in the 7th century A.D.

The Portuguese were the first Europeans to navigate the African coastland. They arrived in the 15th century, and noted many of the placenames they encountered. The mutual ignorance of each others' languages by Europeans and Africans often led to misunderstandings. Banjul, Gambia's capital, thus came to have a name meaning "rope matting," since the visitors' query about the name of the place was taken as an expression of interest in what the local people were making. But while noting existing names, the colonists also gave them. Cameroon remains as a name of Portuguese legacy today. However, it was only when the period of European exploration proper began, in the 19th century, that Africa received the majority of the European names it still retains. Most are English, and in the south, as stated. But French names are still in evidence in western Africa, for instance in Gabon, although their present representation is much thinner than it was. A few German names similarly remain in southwestern Africa, in what is now Namibia.

The English and Afrikaans names of South Africa date from the late 18th century, following the arrival of English settlers, then Dutch. The abandonment of white supremacy in the late 20th century, and the outlawing of apartheid in the 1990s, did not immediately result in a reversion from colonial to indigenous names. A renaming program of this kind should logically follow, however, even if on a restricted scale.

Before leaving Africa and its placenames, mention should be made of the Malagasy placenames of Madagascar, which are in the majority in the island. Some French colonial names remain, but are insignificant in number. The names themselves are unusual, since Malagasy is an Indonesian language, not an African. Antananarivo and Fianarantsoa are typical lengthy Malagasy names, the former meaning "city of a thousand," the latter "place where one studies what is good."

5. Asia. The placenames of Asia are noticeably different in character to those of

Europe. This is chiefly because of the continent's distinctive geographical features, history, and languages. Asia is a vast territory, extending from Turkey in the east to Japan in the west, and from Siberia in the north to Indonesia in the south. This means that Asian placenames share few common characteristics. Some of the names in western Turkey are of Greek origin, as the territory here, in what is still known as Asia Minor, was part of ancient Greece before the arrival of the Turks in the 10th and 11th centuries. East of the Mediterranean, in countries such as Syria, Iraq, and Jordan, the majority of names are Arabic, as they are further south in Saudi Arabia, as the country's name implies. A notable exception is Israel, where there are mostly Hebrew names. It is here that one finds such familiar ancient biblical names as Tyre, Damascus, Bethlehem, and Jerusalem, as well as modern names introduced by Jewish immigrants to Palestine between 1878 and 1948, when the state of Israel was established. Some names arose even more recently as those of planned towns and cities. Names of smaller places include both those of "rural" type for the many kibbutzim (communal villages) and moshavim (cooperative settlements) founded during this period and those commemorating Zionist leaders and pioneers.

Arabic placenames show a considerable degree of uniformity, in whatever country they occur. The same cannot be said for the names of Iran and Afghanistan. Although Iranian (Persian) and Afghani are related languages, and the placenames of the two countries are largely in these languages, both lands have a sizable proportion of Turkic and Arabic names. Many of the Iranian names are extremely old, and have gradually undergone transformation and corruption over the centuries. The placenames of neighboring Tajikistan have many characteristics in common with those of Iran and Afghanistan.

The placenames of India and Pakistan are among the most complex in the world. Many of them are extremely old, and the convoluted histories of the two countries, coupled with the great number of races that inhabit them, makes the toponymical jigsaw a difficult one to piece together. The peoples of India do not form a single ethnic group, but speak around 170 different languages, each with its own grammar and vocabulary. To complicate the picture even further, many places, even quite well-known towns and cities, have undergone multiple renaming. Thus Ujjain, in Madhya Pradesh, one of the oldest cities in India, was known as Avanitika, Padmavati, Kushasthali, Bhagavati, Haranyavati, Kandakatringa, Kumudvati, Pratikalpa, and Vishala, before finally acquiring its present name. Even Delhi has had over ten different names. Many older names in India and Pakistan are Sanskrit in origin, especially some of the more familiar, such as Kashmir, Punjab, Gujarat, Ganges, Indus, Brahmaputra, and Srinagar. Most of the other names are Hindi, with many towns ending in -*pur*, Hindi for "town." The suffix -*abad*, also frequent in India, as well as in other Asian countries, is of Iranian origin. It means "inhabited place," and so also effectively "town."

As in India, many placenames in China have also frequently undergone renaming, chiefly as a result of a change in economic or political circumstances. Some of the older cities have been renamed six or seven times. Not only that, but sometimes one and the same place can have several different names simultaneously. This is true (as elsewhere, in fact) of rivers, so that the Yangtze has six different names for different sections from its source to its mouth. The other side of the coin is that Chinese names are relatively easy to interpret, since they consist of words (ideograms) that can be readily translated. Even so, for the meaning of a name to be interpreted correctly, one needs to understand the history and language of the country.

Many words are used in metaphorical senses, so that where a name contains "orchid" (*lán*), for example, it does not mean that the place abounds in this plant but that it is regarded as sophisticated. Most Chinese names are descriptive or associative, with such meanings as "southern capital" (Nanking) or "east of the mountain" (Shandong). The name of Shanghai means "above the sea." Many placenames in northeastern China are Manchu in origin, while there are Mongolian names in the northwest, Tibetan names in Tibet, in the southwest, and Turkic names also in the southwest.

In Mongolia itself descriptive names proliferate, although some modern names are political in nature, such as Ulan Bator, Sukhebator, amd Choybalsan. The Mongolian language is particularly rich in descriptive words for natural features, so that every mountain, every slope, and every gully has its own term. It is estimated that there are around 220 different geographical terms to describe the country's varied terrain, and these regularly appear in placenames.

Korean placenames are similar, in that they mostly describe natural features. However, many names relate to historical events. Some rivers and mountains close to the Chinese border have two names, one Korean, one Chinese. Thus the Amno River has the Chinese name of Yalu. Few Chinese names have actually encroached into North Korea, however.

The placenames of Japan are somewhat similar in nature to those of China. The names were formerly written in two forms: one using Chinese ideograms, and having the meaning that the characters themselves had, the other using another set of ideograms, of older Chinese origin, in order to indicate the pronunciation. As a result, the actual meaning of a Japanese name can be quite different from the apparent meanings of the characters used to write it. Frequently it is difficult to determine what the original meaning actually was.

The placenames of Indonesia and the Philippines are almost as complex as those of India, although they have been studied less extensively. Few maps of Indonesia exist with names in their indigenous forms, and most maps of this island country are French, English, or Dutch in origin, that is, in the languages of their European colonists. At the same time, many of the names actually given by the colonists are rarely adopted locally. It is the local names adopted instead that have proved difficult to research. The nature of the names varies from island to island. Thus in Java most names are blends of a plant or animal name with that of a river, stream, or pond.

There are still a number of Spanish colonial names in the Philippines, whose own name itself honors a Spanish king. As in Central and South America, as well as the southwestern United States, many of the names are religious in origin, bestowed by Catholic missionaries. There are also some English names. But indigenous names now generally predominate, although the names of the provinces often combine a local name with a Spanish descriptive, such as Davao del Norte or Ilocos Sur.

6. Australasia and Oceania. The placenames of Australia and New Zealand divide quite neatly into two types: indigenous and colonial. Most Australian names are English in origin, but there is also a significant proportion of Aboriginal names, many of them surviving in corrupt forms. Aboriginal names have not caught on to the degree one might expect, mainly because the Aborigines were a nomadic people, and any objects or places they named would retain the name only as long as the namers were there to preserve it and use it widely enough for it to be recorded. Moreover, the first European settlers in Australia (the English in the late 18th century) had little contact with the indigenous inhabitants, and rarely adopted their placenames, even if they knew what they were in the first place. The same is true to a lesser extent of New Zealand, although there the indigenous language is Maori. Maori names are very varied in nature. There are many incident names, marking an event such as a battle or a death that took place at one or other particular location. However, the increasing integration and interbreeding of the Maori population with the former English colonists, far greater than any integration of Aborigines in Australia, has led to the increasing use of Maori placenames in New Zealand in recent years.

The placenames of Oceania, represented by the island groupings of Melanesia, Micronesia, and Polynesia, are predominantly Polynesian, although each island group has its own particular language or languages, most of them in turn with their own dialects. The chief Polynesian languages are Hawaiian, Maori, Tahitian, Samoan, and Tuamotu. Here, too, some European names remain from the colonial past, although in rapidly diminishing numbers. Sometimes a local indigenous name replaces a European one, as Tuvalu did that of the Ellice Islands. Less commonly a European name is adopted in a local form. The name of Kiribati thus replaced that of the Gilbert Islands, so that the names are actually one and the same. The interpretation of Polynesian names can be difficult, and the very origin of the languages themselves has been the subject of intensive research. It is at least known that they are all closely related.

7. **Antarctica.** The placenames of the Antarctic differ from those of the rest of the world as sharply as does the polar continent itself. This is partly because Antarctica has never had a settled indigenous population. Antarctic placenames are moreover unique in being almost entirely commemorative. Virtually every coast, land, island, glacier, massif, or ice shelf is named for its discoverer, for a ship, for a monarch or head of state, for a family member or friend, or for some other individual, whether of personal or national significance. Unlike in the New World, there are very few names transferred from towns, cities, or countries, although Little America, Brabant Island, and Norvegia Cape are among the exceptions. The names themselves are all in European languages, most of them given in the 19th century by successive German, Norwegian, Belgian, and British explorers. Later American and Russian explorers and scientists added their own names. Antarctica itself, however, has a Greek name.

8. **Seas and oceans.** A word should be said concerning the names of the world's seas and oceans. Three main characteristics are discernible. First, there are fewer names for the seas and oceans than there are for places on land. This is not simply because permanent settlement is virtually impossible but because humans gained access to many maritime expanses only relatively recently. Second, the names of seas and oceans are international, and are usually translated into the language concerned. The Pacific Ocean is thus known to the French as *océan Pacifique*, to the Germans as *Stiller Ozean*, and to the Russians as *Tikhij okean*. The languages are different but the meaning remains the same. Third, many seas are named for their adjoining country or territory, so are associative names. Examples are the Baltic Sea, Caribbean Sea, Sea of Japan, South China Sea, Labrador Sea, and Norwegian Sea. However, there are exceptions, such as the Barents Sea, named for its discoverer, the North Sea and Mediterranean Sea, named for their locations, and the Black Sea, Red Sea, and White Sea, named for their colors, literally or figuratively. The names of straits, bays, and gulfs belong here, such as the Strait of Magellan and Hudson Bay. It can be seen that many maritime names are thus commemorative in origin.

Following a consideration of the basic principles of naming, and an overview of naming patterns in their global context, here is the point to explain what the reader may expect to find in the dictionary. This will itself serve to elucidate further the toponymical procedures involved in its compilation.

Placename Frequencies

What is the most common placename in the world? Without a complete record of all existing placenames, it is virtually impossible to say, and even then one would need to consider such factors as language differences, shades of interpretation, and the linguistic composition of the names themselves. But it is possible to give a rough guide.

A study of the index to over 200,000 names in *The Times Comprehensive Atlas of the World* (*see* Bibliography, page 431) shows that "saint" names and "new" names generally outnumber others. Considering the words for both "saint" and "new" in their different languages, as instanced in Appendix I (beginning on page 419), the count for each name numbers well over 3,000. And this in a necessarily selective index. Certain countries contain a higher proportion of "saint" names than others, notably France and the many (historically colonized) Catholic countries of South America.

"New" names, on the other hand, are found virtually all over the world. They can range from a prosaic "new place" (or the equivalent) for a recently founded settlement, which will only be "new" at the time of naming in relation to some existing place, and will eventually thus become "old," to a place with the word for "new" added to an existing name, as New London or New York. As mentioned, Britain's most common placename is Newton, now often distinguished by an added name or word, as Newton Abbot, Newton Stewart, while France has many places Châteauneuf ("new castle"), similarly distinguished.

"Saint" names and "new" names can of course vary widely in content, from England's St. Albans to Portugal's São Vicente, and Germany's Neuburg to Sweden's Nyköping.

Identical names in a particular country are frequently found for natural features, where a distinguishing addition is often not necessary. There are thus a number of lakes in Finland called Pyhäjärvi ("holy lake") and several in Sweden called Storsjön ("great lake"). On the other hand, the many inhabited places in Mexico called Rosario have a name meaning "rosary," testifying to the country's Catholic heritage, while even now there are more than a few settlements in Russia named Oktyabrsky, for the October Revolution. (Placenames preserve history, and some of the smaller places in the former Soviet Union thus continue to bear their revolutionary or Communist names.)

Running one's eye down the many columns of placenames in the *Atlas*'s index, one frequently comes across conspicuous "blocks" of identical United States names. The following occur at least ten times in their various states: Albion, Alexandria, Arlington, Ashland, Athens, Auburn, Augusta, Aurora, Albany, Bridgeport, Bristol, Buffalo, Burlington, Cambridge, Camden, Canton, Chester, Cleveland, Clinton, Columbia, Columbus, Dover, Fairfield, Fairview, Farmington, Florence, Franklin, Fulton, Georgetown, Glenwood, Greenfield, Greenville, Greenwood, Hamilton, Hampton, Hanover, Hartford, Hillsboro, Hudson, Independence, Jackson, Jamestown, Jasper, Jefferson, Kingston, Lancaster, Lebanon, Lexington, Liberty, Lincoln, Livingston, Madison, Manchester, Mansfield, Marion, Marshall, Middletown, Milford, Milton, Monroe, Monticello, Montrose, Mount Vernon, Newcastle (or New Castle), Newport, Newton, Oakland, Oxford, Perry, Petersburg, Plymouth, Princeton, Quincy, Richland, Richmond, Rochester, Salem, Sheridan, Springfield, Stanton, Taylor, Trenton, Troy, Washington, Waverly, Webster, Weston, Wilson, Winchester, Windsor.

Some of these names are adoptions of prestigious or important names elsewhere in the world, and in many cases England, as Albion, Alexandria, Athens, Bristol, Cambridge, Dover, Oxford, Richmond, Troy, Winchester, Windsor. Plymouth also belongs here, not simply as a noted name but as a historically significant one. Other names relate to the country's royalist background, as Albany, Georgetown, Hanover, Jamestown, Kingston (for King Charles II), Princeton. America's own history is reflected in the names of its presidents, statesmen, soldiers, and other major figures, as Cleveland, Clinton, Franklin, Fulton, Hamilton, Jackson, Jasper, Jefferson, Lincoln, Livingston, Madison, Marion (the "Swamp Fox"), Marshall, Monroe, Perry, Quincy, Sheriden, Stanton, Taylor, Trenton, Washington, Webster, Wilson, as well as in idealistic names such as Independence and Liberty. Columbia and Columbus are names duly honoring the discoverer of America, while Hudson commemorates a famous explorer. Other names evoke the "green and pleasant land" that their successors inherited, as Fairfield, Fairview, Farmington, Greenfield, Richland, Springfield. The *Atlas* records 20 instances of this last in as many states. (See its four entries in the dictionary.)

Unlike the names in Catholic countries mentioned above, the Puritan heritage of the USA did not produce many overtly religious names, although Salem is present to represent both peace and Jerusalem. Oakland is a common instance of the popular tree name, others being the cedar and the pine. The former may have been influenced by the biblical cedars of Lebanon, a name found in its own right, while both these trees are pleasantly fragrant. The name Waverly (*sic*) owes its popularity to the Waverley novels of Sir Walter Scott. It should not be assumed that all identical names have a sole reference, however, and some of the apparent adopted placenames may represent family names, as Chester, Dover, or New-

port. The general euphony of these popular names is notable, the majority being bisyllabic and easy to pronounce and spell. (Read the list aloud and an almost poetic cadence is heard.) It will be noticed, incidentally, that Native American names, which rarely reduplicate, are conspicuously absent from the popularity stakes.

Presentation and Arrangement of Entries

Each entry comprises three elements. First comes the name. This is usually followed by a simple identifier of the named place, such "town" or "mountain," with the name of its country and its general location in that country, such as "northern Pakistan" or "southern United States." (Capital cities, however, are designated simply as "capital.") For greater precision of location, Britain is divided into its four constituents: England, Scotland, Wales, and Northern Ireland. It should be noted that Ireland means the republic. A place in "northern Ireland" is thus not in Northern Ireland. Places in Alaska are located in the "northwestern United States," but places in Hawaii, in the northern Pacific, have their United States allegiance noted directly after their location. The identifier "port" implies a seaport. Other types of port are specified accordingly, such as "river port," "lake port."

There then begins the main entry, with the origin of the name. There may well be further locational information, especially in English-speaking countries, so that a state will be specified in the United States, and a county in England, Wales, or Northern Ireland. (Scotland now has regions, which are less frequently named.) Names of states and provinces are also respectively given for India and China, but in Japan the location is given by island. A certain amount of background history, with dates, will usually be included at this point, especially if it is relevant for the meaning of the name. Earlier names are also often mentioned, with an indication in turn of their own meanings, if known. Biblical forms of names, or their English translation, are quoted for sake of consistency from the Authorized King James Version of 1611. Space prohibits the detailed listing of *all* former names, so that their inclusion in the entry is selective. There are cross-references in many cases, or mentions of similar names elsewhere.

The names themselves are presented in their normal accepted spelling, with or without accents, diacritics, etc., as appropriate, especially in the case of European names. This does not mean that the forms are always the English conventional ones. It was necessary to strike a balance here, based partly on objective criteria, partly on subjective. For example, the name of China's capital appears under Beijing, not Peking, but the Spanish city of Zaragoza is entered as Saragossa, since that form of the name is the one still most familiar to English speakers. The French cities of Lyons and Marseilles also appear with their final *s*, although properly they should not have it. Reims, on the other hand, does have it, and is entered under this spelling, not Rheims. Within the entries, names are given in their precise transliterated form. Languages that have no capital letters will thus produce names without such letters. These include Arabic and Chinese names, the latter with their respective tone marks. With regard to Chinese names in entry headings, the dictionary generally follows the *Encyclopædia Britannica*, using a Wade-Giles–based system of romanization, even though many gazetteers and atlases now use the Pinyin form. (Illogically, *Britannica* uses Wade-Giles in its text but Pinyin in its maps, so that for example Tsingtao appears in the former but Qingdao in the latter.)

Where the name is significantly different, or still unfamiliar as a result of recent name changes, there is a separate cross-referral to the entered form. Thus Peking cross-refers to Beijing, and Burma to Myanmar. In India, the reader will find Tiruchchirappalli, however much a mouthful, rather than the outmoded and corrupt Trichinopoly. But Bombay remains, although now officially Mumbai. Cross-referrals of major places are selective, and mainly concern important or recent renamings. Ceylon thus cross-refers to Sri Lanka, and Leningrad to St. Petersburg, but there is no cross-referral from Upper Volta to Burkina Faso or from Molotovsk to Severodvinsk. In some instances the new indigenous name is not even mentioned, mainly because of its unfamiliarity. Thus in Myanmar (formerly Burma), the Irrawaddy River is now properly the Ayeyarwady. But its entry does not include this form.

The names of towns and cities in the now independent states of the former Soviet Union present a particular problem, since they were, and mostly still are, familiar in their Russian forms. Open an atlas at a map of Ukraine, for example, and one finds Kyyiv, not Kiev, Lviv, not Lvov, Kryvyy Rih, not Krivoy Rog, Mykolayiv, not Nikolayev. The same goes for Homyel in Belarus (not Gomel), Qaraghandy in Kazakhstan (not Karaganda), and Baki in Azerbaijan (not Baku). Although it would be (literally) politically correct to enter these under their (relatively) new forms, they are nevertheless given under their familiar forms, for ease of reference, but with the indigenous form regarded as an alternant. For Ukraine, however, the indigenous form is in fact usually cited in the relevant entry.

Appendices and Bibliography

The dictionary's main entries are followed by three appendices and a select bibliography. The appendices, each with its preamble, aim to augment the general information given in the main entries. They range from lists of common placename elements to foreign (non–English) name forms.

The select bibliography that closes the book lists those titles that were most of use in the course of its compilation and that are the most likely to be of service to the reader seeking further information.

Stamford, Lincolnshire, England
September 2005

The Placenames

Aachen. *City, western Germany.* The name of the city and spa refers to its springs, deriving ultimately from Old High German *aha*, "water." The French name of Aachen is *Aix-la-Chapelle*. The first word of this is of identical meaning, but evolved from related Latin *aquis*, the ablative plural form of *aqua*. The second part of the name, differentiating this town from **Aix-en-Provence** and **Aix-les-Bains**, refers to the church here in which Emperor Charlemagne is buried.

Aalborg *see* **Ålborg**

Aalen. *City, southern Germany.* The city arose around a Roman fort on the Kocher River and apparently takes its name from a tributary of this river now known as the *Al*. It is possible, however, that the tributary was named after the town, not the other way around.

Aalsmeer. *Town, western Netherlands.* The town is said to take its name from the eels found in the former lake here, from Duch *aal*, "eel," and *meer*, "lake."

Aargau. *Canton, northern Switzerland.* The canton derives its name from the River *Aar* which flows through it and German *Gau*, "district." The river's own name represents the Indoeuropean root *ar*, "river." The French name of the canton is *Argovie*.

Aarhus. *City and river port, eastern Denmark.* The city takes its name from the river on which it stands. The river's own name means simply "river mouth," from Old Danish *aa*, "river," and *os*, "mouth" (*cp.* **Oslo**). The city, whose name is also spelled *Århus*, is located at the point where the river flows into Aarhus Bay and so into the Kattegat.

Aasiaat *see* **Egedesminde**

Abadan. *City and port, southwestern Iran.* The city is named for *Abbad ibn al-Husayn*, the Arab holy man who founded it in the 8th or 9th century.

Abakan. *City, south central Russia.* The capital of Khakassia derives its name from the *Abakan* River on which it lies. The river's name,

popularly said to mean "bear's blood," from Khakas *aba*, "bear," and *kan*, "blood," actually adds *kan*, "river," to a first element of uncertain origin.

Abancay. *City, southern Peru.* The city is said to derive its name from Quechua *amankay*, the name of a flower similar to a white lily.

Abbeville. *Town, northern France.* The town arose in the 9th century as a dependency of the *abbots* of St.-Riquier. Hence its name, which means "abbot's settlement," from French *abbé*, "abbot," and *ville*, "settlement," "town."

Abbottabad. *City, northern Pakistan.* The city was founded in 1853 and named for Sir James *Abbott* (1807–1896), the first British deputy commissioner of the region.

Abenberg. *Town, southern Germany.* The name, meaning "*Abo*'s fort," was originally that of the castle below which the town arose in the 13th century.

Åbenrå. *City, southern Denmark.* The city takes its name from the fjord of the same name, at the head of which it lies. The fjord name derives from Danish *åbne*, "open," and *rade*, "road," denoting a broad river mouth where ships can anchor.

Abensberg. *Town, southern Germany.* The town arose by a 12th-century castle of the same name, meaning "height on the *Abens* River." The river name itself is based on Indoeuropean *ab*, "water."

Abeokuta. *Town, southwestern Nigeria.* The town was founded in c. 1830 as a settlement for refugees from slave hunters. The fugitives concerned originally gathered in a cave under a mass of porphyry. Hence the name, from a local phrase meaning "refuge among rocks."

Aberdeen. *City and port, northeastern Scotland.* The city has a name of Celtic origin meaning "(place at the) mouth of the *Don*." The present city stands on the Dee River, but it developed from a settlement at the mouth of the *Don*, which enters the North Sea here in the modern district of Old Aberdeen. Celtic *aber*, "mouth," is found as the first element of the names of many coastal towns in Scotland and Wales.

Aberystwyth. *Town and resort, western Wales.* The town, on Cardigan Bay, has a Celtic name meaning "(place at the) mouth of the *Ystwyth*." The present town is at the mouth of the Rheidol River, but its original location was in the valley of the Ystwyth, which now enters the sea to the south. The river's own name means "winding" (Welsh *ystwyth*, "flexible," "pliant").

Abidjan. *City and port, southern Côte d'Ivoire.* The country's former capital, on the Gulf of Guinea, was founded in 1903. The story goes that when the first French colonists arrived here they met some women and asked them where they were. The women, misunderstanding the question, replied in their own language, "*T'chan m'bi djan*," "Coming from cutting leaves." The Frenchmen noted the name and gave it to the new settlement.

Abilene. *City, southern United States.* The Texas city, founded in 1881 as the new railhead for the overland Texas cattle drives, took the name of the previous railhead, *Abilene*, Kansas. This was itself named in c. 1860 for the biblical *Abilene* (Luke 3:1), whose own name is said to mean "grassy place."

Abingdon. *Town, southern England.* The Oxfordshire town has a name meaning "*Æbba*'s hill," from the Anglo-Saxon personal name and Old English *dūn*, "hill." The hill in question is probably the one to the north of the town.

Abitibi. *River, east central Canada.* The river, in northeastern Ontario, is so named for its source in *Abitibi* Lake. The lake's name represents Algonquian *abitah*, "middle," and *nipi*, "water," referring to its location on a former canoe route between the Ottawa Valley and James Bay.

Abkhazia. *Republic, northwestern Georgia.* The republic, a self-declared sovereign state from 1999, takes its name from the *Abkhaz*, its indigenous Caucasian people. Their own name is said to derive from Georgian *apsua*, "soul," meaning "animate ones," "those speaking the same language," as distinct from the incomprehensible tongues of other peoples.

Åbo *see* **Turku**

Aboukir *see* **Abukir**

Abovyan. *City, central Armenia.* The city, founded in 1963 on the site of the former village of *Elar*, was named for the Armenian writer Khachatur *Abovyan* (1805–1848), who was born near here.

Abruzzi. *Mountains, south central Italy.* The precise origin of the name is uncertain, although it may be related to Latin *aper, apri*, "boar," or *abruptus*, "steep." The mountains are the loftiest and most rugged in the Apennines.

Abu Dhabi. *Emirate, United Arab Emirates.* The constituent state of the United Arab Emirates has an Arabic name meaning "father of *Zabi*," from *abū*, "father of," construct state of *ab*, "father," and the personal name *z̧abī*, from *z̧ab*, "gazelle." (For a construct state noun, *see* **Ramat Gan**.) The sheikhdom arose around the settlement of *Abu Zabi*, now the overall capital of the United Arab Emirates.

Abuja. *Capital of Nigeria.* Transfer of Nigeria's capital from Lagos to Abuja, a new city in the center of the country, was completed in 1991. It took its name from the historic Hausa emirate of *Abuja*, itself named for the fortified settlement founded in 1828 near Zuba by *Abu Ja* ("Abu the Red").

Abukir. *Village, northern Egypt.* The village has an Arabic name meaning "father of *Qīr*," from *abū*, "father of," construct state of *ab*, "father," and the personal name *Qīr*. (For a construct state noun, *see* **Ramat Gan**.) The name gained fame from Nelson's victory over the French off Abukir in the Battle of the Nile (1798).

Abu Simbel. *Village, southern Egypt.* The village has an Arabic name meaning "father of *Sunbul*," from *abū*, "father of," construct state of *ab*, "father," and the personal name *sunbul*, meaning "hyacinth," "lavender." (For a construct state noun, *see* **Ramat Gan**.) The name was formerly familiar as *Ipsambul*.

Abydos. *Historic city, southern Egypt.* The sacred city, a royal necropolis, has a name of uncertain origin. Its namesake, the ancient town of *Abydos* in northwestern Turkey, on the Hellespont, is said to derive its name from Greek *a-*, "not," and *buthos*, "depth," "deeps of the sea," referring to the relatively shallow waters off the coast here.

Abyssinia *see* **Ethiopia**

Acadia. *Historic territory, eastern North America.* The name of the former French territory is indigenous in origin, from the Native American word *akadi*, "fertile land." The French form of the name is *Acadie*. The suggestion of *Arcadia*, as if denoting a colonial "paradise," is purely fortuitous.

Acapulco. *City and port, southwestern Mexico.* The name of the city is Nahuatl in origin and is said to mean "conquered city," presumably referring to some early episode in its history.

Accra. *Capital of Ghana.* The city and port derives its name from the indigenous African word *n'kran*, "ant." This was the nickname used by local forest dwellers for the Nigerian tribesmen who settled here in the 16th century.

Accrington. *Town, northwestern England.* The Lancashire town has a name meaning "acorn farm," from Old English *æcern*, "acorn," and *tūn*, "farm." Accrington was formerly on the edge of Rossendale Forest and acorns from the oaks there would have been used as mast (hog fodder).

Aceh. *Province, western Indonesia.* The province, in northern Sumatra, derives its name from Malay *aci*, "beech," a tree widely found here. The name was spelled *Atjeh* before the spelling reform of 1972.

Achaea. *Historic region, central Greece.* The name is traditionally derived from *Achaeus*, the mythological ancestor of the Achaeans. It may actually have had an original sense "coastland."

Achelous. *River, central Greece.* The name of one of Greece's longest rivers is said to derive from Greek *akheō*, "I resound," "I make a noise," and *helos*, "marsh," "damp place," referring both to its turbulent course through gorges and to the alluvial deposits at its delta. In classical mythology, the name is also that of its god.

Acheron. *River, northwestern Greece.* The river, thought in ancient times to flow to Hades, has a name of uncertain origin. It may well relate to Germanic *aha*, "water," in turn from Indoeuropean *ab* in this sense.

Achim. *Town, northwestern Germany.* The town, in the Weser valley, has a meaning "settlement on the river," from Old High German *aha*, "water," "river," and *heim*, "homestead," "settlement."

Achinsk. *City, south central Russia.* The city, founded in 1621, takes its name from the *Achyg*, a Tatar people from the upper reaches of the Chulym River.

Acireale. *Town, southern Italy.* The town, in eastern Sicily, is said to derive the first part of its name from the *Acis* River of classical mythology, itself named for the shepherd *Acis*, loved by Galatea, and the second part from *real*, "royal," an epithet granted in 1642 by Philip IV of Spain. However, its Roman name was *Aquilia*, and the present name more probably evolved as a reinterpreted form of this.

Acoma. *Pueblo, southern United States.* The New Mexico pueblo, believed to be the oldest continuously inhabited place in the United States, derives its name from Keresan *ako*, "white rock," and *ma*, "people," referring to its location atop a sandstone mesa (butte).

Aconcagua. *Mountain, western Argentina.* The highest peak in the Andes has an Native

American (Araucan) name deriving from that of the river that rises in its foothills. The river's own name comes from *konka*, "sheaf of straw," and *hue*, "place abundant in," alluding to the fertility of the valley here.

Acre. *City and port, northern Israel.* The city has a name that may derive from a Hebrew word meaning "enclosed," referring to its location on the Bay of Haifa. It is mentioned in the Bible as *Accho* (Judges 1:31) and also as *Ptolemais* (Acts 21:7). The latter name comes from the Egyptian king *Ptolemy* II Philadelphus, who conquered it in the 3d century B.C. The city's indigenous name is *Akko*. The French know it as *Saint-Jean d'Acre*, since at the time of the Crusades it was held by the Knights Hospitalers (Knights of *St. John*).

Adamawa. *Plateau, west central Africa.* The volcanic upland, mainly in north central Cameroon (as *Adamaoua*), takes its name from Moddibo *Adama* (died 1848), founder of a Fulani emirate here.

Adam's Peak. *Mountain, southwestern Sri Lanka.* The mountain is so named from the belief that the biblical *Adam* stepped here, leaving his mark in a large hollow resembling the print of a human foot. The chain of shoals between India and Sri Lanka is accordingly known as *Adam's Bridge*. It is also known as *Rama's Bridge*, from the Hindu legend that the bridge was built to transport the god Rama to the island to rescue his wife, Sita, from the demon king Ravana. *See* **Rameswaram.**

Adana. *City, southern Turkey.* The city is said to take its name from Phoenician *'adan*, "pleasure," "delight," a word popularly related to the biblical *Eden*.

Addis Ababa. *Capital of Ethiopia.* The city has an Amharic name meaning "new flower," from *ăddis*, "new," and *ăbăba*, "flower." This was the propitious name given it by Empress Taitu, wife of Emperor Menelik II, when in 1887 she persuaded her husband to build a new capital near the hot springs in the center of the country, as an improvement on its predecessor, *Entoto*, which was on a cold, exposed site.

Adelaide. *City, southern Australia.* The capital of South Australia was founded in 1837 and named in honor of Queen *Adelaide* (1792–1849), wife of William IV of England.

Adélie Coast. *Region, eastern Antarctica.* The coastal region, south of Australia, was discovered in 1840 by the French explorer Jules-Sébastien-César Dumont d'Urville (1790–1842), who named it for his wife, *Adélie*. An alternate name for the region is *Adélie Land*.

Aden. *City and port, southern Yemen.* The

former capital of Yemen probably derives its name from Akkadian *edinnu*, "plain." Some scholars have related it to the biblical Garden of *Eden*, whose own name is generally accepted as having this same meaning.

Adige. *River, northeastern Italy.* The river, known to the Romans as *Atesis*, has a name that ultimately goes back to Indoeuropean *at*, "rapid," referring to its current. German speakers know the river as the *Etsch*. *See also* **Este**.

Adirondacks. *Mountain range, eastern United States.* The range, in New York State, derives its name from a Native American (Algonquian) people. Although the meaning of their own name has probably been lost, it is sometimes said to be "eaters of tree bark."

Admiralty Islands. *Island group, southwestern Pacific.* The islands, in Papua New Guinea, were so named in 1767 by the British navigator Philip Carteret in honor of the English *Admiralty*, which had financed his expedition. They were discovered in 1616 by the Dutch, who named them *The Twenty-One Islands* (although there are nearer 40). They should not be confused with the **Amirante Islands**.

Adrano. *Town, southern Italy.* The town, in eastern Sicily, originated as the ancient settlement of *Hadranon*, founded in c. 400 B.C. near a sanctuary dedicated to the Siculan god *Adranus*. Hence its name, which until 1929 was officially spelled *Adernò*.

Adrar. *Settlement, southwestern Algeria.* The palm-grove settlement derives its name from Tuareg *adrar*, plural *idraren*, "mountain." The identically named region of central Mauritania has a name of the same origin.

Adrianople *see* **Edirne**

Adriatic Sea. *Sea, southern Europe.* The sea, an arm of the Mediterranean between Italy and the Balkan Peninsula, takes its name from the Venetian port of *Adria*. Its own name probably derives from the Illyrian word *adur*, "water," "sea," although today the city is more than 12 miles (20 km) inland.

Aegean Sea. *Sea, southern Europe.* The sea, between Greece and Turkey, is traditionally said to be named for the mythical Greek king *Aegeus*, father of Theseus, who according to legend threw himself into it on learning, falsely, that his son was dead. The name has also been popularly linked with Greek *aix, aigos*, "goat." It probably dates back to pre–Hellenic times, however, representing a word *aiges*, "tides," "waves."

Aeolian Islands *see* **Eolie Islands**

Afars and Issas *see* **Djibouti**

Afghanistan. *Republic, central Asia.* The country takes its name from its indigenous people, the *Afghanis*, with the final *-stan* representing the Old Persian word for "country." The people's own name comes from *Afghana*, possibly the Persian name of an ancestor.

Africa. *Continent south of Europe.* The world's second largest continent has a name that originally applied to just a small part of it, corresponding to modern Tunisia. The name itself may relate to Arabic *'afar*, "dust," "earth," referring to the predominant desert here. This would have given an ethnic name meaning something like "desert people," which subsequently became a regional name and eventually spread south to the whole continent.

Afyon. *City, western Turkey.* The city was originally known as *Acroënus*. In the 13th century it was taken by the Seljuk Turks and renamed *Karahisar*, "black fort," for the ancient fortress atop a cone of volcanic rock here. This name was then prefixed with Turkish *afyon*, "opium," for the region's former chief product, and the word eventually became the sole name.

Agadir. *City and port, southwestern Morocco.* The city's name represents Tuareg *aggādir*, "wall," "embankment," referring to the natural slope on which the old town was built above the modern port and harbor.

Agana. *Capital of Guam.* The indigenous Chamorro form of the capital's name is *Hagåtña*, meaning "blood," in the sense "life blood." The town has always been the center of the island's government. *See also* **Guam**.

Agassiz, Lake. *Historic lake, central North America.* The former glacial lake, in southern Canada and the northern United States, was so named in 1879 for the Swiss-born American naturalist and geologist Louis *Agassiz* (1807–1873), whose specialty was glaciology.

Agde. *Town, southern France.* The town was known to the Romans as *Agatha*, a name that itself goes back to Greek *agathē*, "good," implying *agathē tukhē*, "good fortune," a mystically propitious name. Agde is one of the few French towns to have a Greek name. Two others are **Antibes** and **Nice**.

Agen. *Town, southwestern France.* The town derives its name from Gaulish *aginno*, "height," or *aganno*, "rock."

Agincourt. *Village, northern France.* The village has a name meaning "*Aizo*'s homestead." The French form of the name is *Azincourt*.

Agra. *City, north central India.* The city, in Uttar Pradesh state, is mentioned in the *Mahabharata* as *Agrabana*, a name said to mean "paradise." Ptolemy referred to it in the 2d century A.D. as *Agara*.

Agram see **Zagreb**

Ağrı. *City, eastern Turkey.* The city is named for Mt. **Ararat**, to the east, from its Turkish name of *Ağrı daği*.

Agrigento. *Town, southern Italy.* The town, in southwestern Sicily, was founded in c. 580 B.C. and has a name ultimately going back to Greek *Akragas*, traditionally said to refer to *Akragante*, daughter of Zeus, who is supposed to have built it. But her name was almost certainly devised to explain an existing name of obscure meaning. Until 1927 Agrigento was known as *Girgenti*, from an Arabic distortion of *Agrigentum*, its Roman name.

Aguascalientes. *City, central Mexico.* The city, in the state of the same name, has a name representing Spanish *aguas calientes*, "hot waters," referring to its many thermal springs.

Agulhas, Cape. *Cape, southern South Africa.* Africa's southernmost cape derives its name from Portuguese *agulha*, "needle." The reference is said to be to the magnetic needle of a compass, which shows no deviation here but points due (not magnetic) north. The name could equally apply to the needle-like rocks and reefs here, the cause of many shipwrecks.

Agung. *Volcano, southern Indonesia.* The volcano, on the island of Bali, derives its name from Indonesian *gunung agung*, "great mountain."

Ahaggar. *Plateau, southern Algeria.* The large plateau, in the north central part of the Sahara, has a Tuareg name originally denoting the members of a particular high-ranking tribe, then the tribe itself. The name is also spelled *Hoggar*.

Ahaus. *Town, northwestern Germany.* The town, near the Dutch border, has a name meaning "house on the *Aa* River." The river name, from Indoeuropean *aha*, "water," is properly that of the upper reaches of the Berkel, itself a tributary of the IJssel.

Ahlen. *Town, northwestern Germany.* The meaning of the name is uncertain, and the eel (German *Aal*) that appears in the town's coat of arms is simply a popular or punning interpretation.

Ahmadabad. *City, west central India.* The former capital of Gujarat state (1960–70) has a name meaning "*Ahmad*'s town," from the Arabic personal name *Ahmad* and Hindi *ābād*, "inhabited place." The personal name is that of Sultan *Ahmad* Shah, who founded the city in 1411.

Ahrensburg. *Town, northwestern Germany.* The town arose in the 18th century by a 16th-century castle named *Ahrensfelde*, after a nearby village. The town adopted the name, meaning

"*Arn*'s open land," substituting German *Burg*, "castle," for the original *Feld* (related to English *field*).

Ahvaz. *City, southwestern Iran.* The city was named by Muslim Arabs in the 7th century as *sūq al-ahwāz*, "market of the *Khuz*," referring to the local *Khuz* people, who gave the name of **Khuzestan**.

Ahvenanmaa. *Island group, western Europe.* The Finnish islands, in the Gulf of Bothnia, have a name meaning "land of perch," from *ahven*, "perch" (the fish), and *maa*, "land." The Swedish name of the islands is *Åland*, "land of rivers," from *å*, "river," and *land*, "land."

Aichach. *Town, southern Germany.* The town has a name meaning "oak forest," from Old High German *eich*, "oak," and the collective suffix *-ahi*, represented here by *-ach*.

Aichi. *Prefecture, central Japan.* The prefecture, in the island of Honshu, derives its name from Japanese *ai*, "to love," and *chi*, "to know."

Aigues-Mortes. *Town, southeastern France.* The name means literally "dead waters," from Latin *aqua*, "water," and *mortua*, "dead." The reference is to the town's location amid lagoons and salt pools in the Rhône estuary.

Ain. *River, eastern France.* The name derives from a pre–Latin word meaning simply "water," as for the *Inn* River at **Innsbruck**, Austria.

Aïn Beïda. *Town, northeastern Algeria.* The town is famous for its springs, the largest of which gave its name, "white spring," from Arabic *'ain*, "spring," and *baida*, feminine of *abyad*, "white."

Aisne. *River, northern France.* The name ultimately derives from pre–Latin *ax*, "river."

Aix-en-Provence. *Town, southeastern France.* The first word of the town's name is the French word that evolved from Latin *aqua*, ablative plural *aquis*, as a cognate of the Germanic word, meaning "water," which gave the name of **Aachen**. The reference is thus to the local springs. The second part of the name indicates the town's location in **Provence** and distinguishes it from Aachen itself (as *Aix-la-Chapelle*) and **Aix-les-Bains**.

Aix-la-Chapelle see **Aachen**

Aix-les-Bains. *Town, eastern France.* The first part of the name is identical to that of **Aix-en-Provence** and *Aix-la-Chapelle*, the latter being the French name of **Aachen**. The meaning is thus "water," alluding to local springs. These are more specifically identified by the second part of the name, meaning "the baths." The sulfur springs here have been known since Roman times.

Ajaccio. *Capital of Corsica.* The city's name

probably derives from Low Latin *adjacium*, "stop," "halting place," referring to its location on the Mediterranean coast. The name has been popularly linked with *Ajax*, the famous warrior of Greek mythology.

Ajaria. *Republic, southwestern Georgia.* The republic derives its name from the *Ajars*, who form part of the indigenous population. Their own name comes from that of a river here.

Ajman. *Emirate, United Arab Emirates.* The smallest state of the United Arab Emirates derives its name from Arabic *'ajman*, "foreigner," "Persian," implying that its original inhabitants differed in some way from their neighbors.

Ajmer. *City, northwestern India.* The city, in Rajasthan state, takes its name from that of *Ajayadeva*, the rajah who founded it in the 11th century.

Akashi. *City, southern Japan.* The city, in the island of Honshu, has a name meaning "shining stone," from Japanese *aka*, "shining," and *ishi*, "stone."

Aken. *Town, central Germany.* The town, a port on the Elbe River, has a name meaning "by the water" related to that of **Aachen.**

Akhdar Mountains. *Range, northeastern Libya.* The mountains derive their name from Arabic *akhḍar*, "green," referring to the relative fertility of the terrain here, by contrast with the barren Sahara, to the south.

Akhisar. *Town, western Turkey.* The town, historically the biblical *Thyatira* (Acts 16:14, etc.), derives its name from Turkish *ak*, "white," and *hisar*, "fortress."

Akhtopol. *Town and resort, southeastern Bulgaria.* The Black Sea resort arose on the site of the Greek colony of *Agathopolis*, "noble city," and its present name evolved from this.

Akita. *City, north central Japan.* The city, in the island of Honshu, has a name meaning "field of ripe rice," from *aki*, "fall," "autumn," and *ta*, "field of rice." The two ideograms that make up *aki* respectively mean "cereals," "grain," and "fire," denoting corn ripened in the fall.

Akkad. *Historic region, central Iraq.* The region derives its name from the Sumerian city of *Agde*, which (as *Acca*) is mentioned in the Bible as one of the four cities ruled by Nimrod (Genesis 10:10). The ultimate meaning of the name is uncertain.

Akmola *see* **Astana**

Akron. *City, north central United States.* The Ohio city is 1,200 ft (370 m) above sea level, at the confluence of two rivers, and when it was founded in 1825 it was given a name alluding to this lofty location, from Greek *akron*, "tip," "summit."

Akrotiri. *Peninsula, southwestern Cyprus.* The peninsula, the site of a British military base, has a name meaning simply "promontory" (classical Greek *akrōtērion*).

Akşehir. *Town, southwestern Turkey.* The town's name means "white town," from Turkish *ak*, "white," and *şehir*, "town." *Cp.* **Belgorod.**

Aksu. *City, northwestern China.* The city, in the Uighur Autonomous Region of Sinkiang, derives its name from the river here, its own name meaning "white water" (Uighur *ak*, "white," and *su*, "water").

Aksum. *Town, northern Ethiopia.* The name, also that of an early kingdom here, is of unknown origin.

Aktau. *City, western Kazakhstan.* The city arose in 1963 on the discovery of natural oil and gas here, and was named for the nearby mountain, its own name meaning "white mountain" (Kazakh *ak*, "white," and *tau*, "mountain."). From 1964 through 1991 it was renamed *Shevchenko*, for the Ukrainian poet and revolutionary Taras Shevchenko (1814–1861), exiled here in the 1850s.

Aktyubinsk. *City, west central Kazakhstan.* The city arose around a fort built here in 1869 with the name of *Ak-Tyube*, "white hilltop," from Kazakh *ak*, "white," and *tube*, "hilltop."

Akureyri. *Town and port, northern Iceland.* The town derives its name from Icelandic *akur*, "field," and *eyri*, "tongue of land," describing its location at the end of Eyja Fjord.

Alabama. *State, southern United States.* The state takes its name from the river that flows south through it. The river's own name represents that of a Choctaw people, said to be from either *alibamo*, "we stay here," alluding to a place of settlement, or *alba-aya-mule*, "we clear a way through the forest."

Alagoas. *State, northeastern Brazil.* The state's name represents Portuguese *as lagoas*, "the lakes," of which there are many here.

Åland *see* **Ahvenanmaa**

Alaska. *State, northwestern United States.* The state has an Inuit (Eskimo) name, deriving from *alakshak*, "great land." This was spelled *Alyaskat* on the first Russian maps of the territory. Russia sold Alaska to the USA in 1867.

Álava. *Province, northern Spain.* The province derives its name from Basque *araiiar*, "among the mountains," describing its location on the southern slopes of the Pyrenees.

Albacete. *City, southeastern Spain.* The city's name represents Arabic *al-basīṭa*, "the plain," from *al*, "the," and a derivative of *basaṭa*, "to extend," "to stretch." The city is on the La Mancha plateau.

Al-Bahr al-Ahmar. *Governorate, eastern Egypt.* The governorate has the Arabic name of the **Red Sea**, indicating its location between the Nile and the Red Sea coast.

Alba-Iulia. *City, west central Romania.* The first part of the name refers to the Roman fort *Apulum*, the remains of which are nearby. The second part names *Julius*, a deputy ruler of Transylvania. The Hungarian name of Alba-Iulia is *Gyulafehérvár*, "white city of *Julius*," translating the earlier Slavic name *Balgrad* (*cp.* **Belgrade**). In 1718 Prince Eugene of Savoy built a castle here and named it *Karlsburg*, "Charles's castle," for the Holy Roman emperor *Charles* VI (1685–1740). German speakers thus know the city by this name.

Albania. *Republic, southern Europe.* The country, bordering the Adriatic Sea, has a very old name, possibly deriving from a pre–Celtic word *alb*, "hill," (*cp.* **Alps**) or from an Indoeuropean root word *albh*, "white." The Albanian name for the country is *Shqipëri*, "land of eagles," from *shqipónjë*, "eagle." (The double-headed eagle on the national flag was taken from the state coat of arms.) The territory that the Romans knew as *Albania* was not the modern state but a region of Asia bordering the Caspian Sea.

[1]Albany. *City, eastern United States.* The state capital of New York was founded as a Dutch trading post in 1614. When a party of Walloons built Fort Orange nearby in 1624 the settlement around it was originally known as *Beverwyck*. Fort Orange was captured by the British in 1664 and the village was renamed as now in honor of the Duke of York and *Albany* (1633–1701), later James II. The Duke's own title derives from the poetic name for Scotland, and itself probably has the same origin as **Albion**.

[2]Albany. *City, southwestern United States.* The Georgia city was founded in 1836 and named for **[1]Albany**, New York.

Albemarle Sound. *Inlet, eastern United States.* The coastal inlet of North Carolina derives its name from the English soldier George Monck, 1st Duke of *Albemarle* (1608–1670).

Albert, Lake. *Lake, central Africa.* The lake, divided between Uganda and the Democratic Republic of Congo, was so named in 1864 by its discoverer, the British explorer Samuel Baker, for Prince *Albert* (1819–1861), consort of Queen Victoria. In 1973 it was unilaterally named *Lake Mobutu Sese Seko* by the Zairean president (1930–1997) for himself. However, its earlier name generally remains in use and is found on most maps. A local Lunyoro name for the lake

is *Ruitanzige*, "killer of locusts," presumably because swarms of these insects perish in its waters.

Alberta. *Province, western Canada.* The province was formed in 1882 and was named in honor of Princess Louise Caroline *Alberta* (1848–1939), fourth daughter of Queen Victoria and wife of the governor general, John Douglas Sutherland Campbell, Marquess of Lorne. The princess was named after her father, Prince *Albert*, so the name could also be regarded as commemorating Victoria's late husband, the Prince Consort. *Cp.* **Albert, Lake**.

Albertville. *Town, southeastern France.* The town, in Savoy, takes its name from Charles *Albert* of Savoy (1798–1849), king of Sardinia-Piedmont, who created it in its present form in 1835 by combining the village of L'Hôpital with the small town of Conflans.

Albi. *Town, southern France.* The town takes its name from the Roman personal name *Albius*, perhaps itself deriving from Latin *albus*, "white." *Cp.* **Albion**.

Albion. *Historic name of Britain.* The ancient name, applying also individually to England and Scotland, is usually derived from the Indoeuropean root *albh*, "white" (the source of Latin *albus* in the same sense), supposedly referring to the white cliffs of Dover, on the English Channel, the first natural feature seen by visitors to Britain when crossing from continental Europe. But a more likely origin is in *alb*, "world," an element related to Medieval Welsh *elfydd*, "world," "region."

Ålborg. *City and port, northern Denmark.* The city had the Medieval Latin name of *Alburgum*, suggesting an origin in Old Norwegian *áll*, "channel," "pass," and *borg*, "castle," "fort." The city, one of the oldest in Denmark, is on the southern side of the Limfjord, and this could have been the "channel."

Albret. *Region, southwestern France.* The name goes back to Latin *Leporetum*, from *lepus*, *leporis*, "hare," an animal formerly in plentiful evidence here.

Albuquerque. *City, southern United States.* The New Mexico city was founded in 1706 and named for the Spanish administrator and viceroy of Mexico, Francisco Fernández de la Cueva, Duque de *Alburquerque* (1617–1676). The place-name has omitted the first *r* of his title by confusion with the famous Portuguese soldier Afonso de *Albuquerque* (1453–1515). The Portuguese surname is Spanish in origin, however, and derives from the town of *Alburquerque*, southwestern Spain. Its own name means "white oak," ultimately from Latin *albus*, "white," and *quercus*, "oak."

Alcalá de Henares. *City, central Spain.* The city has an Arabic name meaning "the fort by the river," from *al-ḳal'a,* "the fort," and a Spanish-influenced corruption of *an-nahr,* "the river." There are various other places of the basic name, which here is distinguished from them by the addition of the second part. The river here is the *Henares,* named for it.

Alcántara. *Town, western Spain.* The town takes its name from Arabic *al-ḳanṭara,* "the bridge," this being the six-arched Roman bridge that spanned the Tagus River here. It was destroyed in the 13th century but has been rebuilt several times.

Alcatraz. *Island, western United States.* The island, in San Francisco Bay, California, was so named from the identical Spanish word for "pelican," as these birds were numerous here.

Alcázar de San Juan. *Town, central Spain.* The town was named by the Arabs *al-ḳaṣr,* "the palace." The second part of its name refers to the Knights Hospitalers of *St. John,* who conquered it in 1186, and it was the center of their order from the 14th through 16th century.

Alcazarquivir *see* **Ksar el-Kebir**

Alchevsk. *City, eastern Ukraine.* The city was founded in 1895 around an ironworks, and the settlement that developed was named for one *Alchevsky,* founder of the construction company. From 1931 through 1961 it was renamed *Voroshilovsk,* for the Soviet president Kliment *Voroshilov* (1881–1969). From 1961 through 1992 it was further renamed *Kommunarsk,* from Russian *kommunar,* "communard," a word historically related to a member of the 1871 Paris Commune.

Alcira *see* **Alzira**

Alderney. *Island, Channel Islands, western English Channel.* The third largest of the Channel Islands has a name that is probably Scandinavian in origin, from an unrecorded word *aurin,* "gravel," and the frequently found *ey,* "island." The Romans knew the island as *Riduna,* while the French name for it is *Aurigny.*

Aldershot. *Town, southern England.* The Hampshire town has an Old English name deriving from *alor,* "alder," and *scēat,* "corner of land" (literally "shoot"). Alder trees would at one time have grown in the angle of land that protrudes into the county of Surrey here.

Alençon. *City, northwestern France.* The city's name ultimately goes back to the Gaulish personal name *Alantio.*

Alentejo. *Historic region, southeastern Portugal.* The former province has a name meaning "beyond the Tagus," from Portuguese *alem,* "beyond," and the river name. The region is "be-

yond" the Tagus from the point of view of someone standing north of it.

Aleppo. *City, northern Syria.* The city's original Arabic name was *Halab,* of Semitic origin and uncertain meaning. Its Roman name was *Beraea.*

Alès. *Town, southeastern France.* The town has a name of Merovingian origin but uncertain meaning. Some trace it back to a Phoenician source meaning "industry." Until 1926 the name was spelled *Alais.*

Alessandria. *City, northwestern Italy.* The city, founded in 1168, was originally called *Civitas Nova,* "new city." It was later renamed as now for Pope *Alexander* III (c. 1100–1181), and in 1175 became a bishopric.

Aletschhorn. *Mountain, south central Switzerland.* The name means "avalanche peak," from a dialect form of Romansh *avalantse,* the source of English *avalanche* itself, and *horn,* "horn," "peak."

Aleutian Islands. *Island chain, northwestern United States.* The islands, extending west of Alaska, take their name from the *Aleuts,* their indigenous inhabitants. Their own name is of obscure origin but may mean simply "people."

Alexander Archipelago. *Island group, northwestern United States.* The islands, in southeastern Alaska, were so named in 1867 for *Alexander* II (1818–1881), czar of Russia.

Alexandretta *see* **İskenderun**

¹Alexandria. *City and port, northern Egypt.* The city takes its name from *Alexander* the Great, who founded it in 332 B.C. after his capture of Egypt.

²Alexandria. *City, southern United States.* The Louisiana city was laid out in 1810 and named for *Alexander* Fulton, on whose land grant, made by the Spanish, the original settlement was founded in 1785.

³Alexandria. *City, eastern United States.* The Virginia city was settled in 1695 and a community called *Belhaven* was founded in 1731. In 1749 it was renamed as now for John *Alexander,* to whom the land here had originally been granted.

Alexandrina, Lake. *Lake, southern Australia.* The lake, in South Australia, was crossed in 1830 by the explorer Charles Sturt, who named it for 11-year-old Princess *Alexandrina,* the future Queen Victoria (1819–1901). (Victoria's first name honored her godfather, *Alexander* I, czar of Russia.)

Alexandroúpolis. *City, northeastern Greece.* The city, founded by the Turks in 1860 as *Dedeağaç* ("grandfather's tree"), was ceded to

Greece in 1919 and renamed "*Alexander*'s city," for *Alexander* (1893–1920), king of Greece (or according to some, for *Alexander* the Great).

Alföld *see* **Great Alföld**

Algarve. *Historic region, southern Portugal.* The ancient kingdom has a name of Arabic origin representing *al-ğarb*, "the west." The allusion is to its geographical location in former Arab territory. The region is often referred to in English as *the* Algarve, as if translating the Arabic definite article: "Twelve English fans were arrested in the Algarve yesterday" (*The Times*, June 16, 2004).

Algeciras. *City and port, southwestern Spain.* The city derives its name from Arabic *al-jazīra al-ḥaḍrā'*, "the green island" (literally "the island the green"). When the Arabs landed in Spain in A.D. 711 they were struck by the greenness of the countryside, quite different from their own dry and barren land. *Cp.* **Algiers**.

Algeria. *Republic, northern Africa.* The country takes its name from **Algiers**, the city selected to be its capital in 1830, when Algeria was a French colony. The Latin-style *-ia* ending matches that of neighboring **Tunisia**, also named for its capital.

Alghero. *Town and port, northwestern Sardinia.* The name of the Italian town ultimately goes back to Latin *alga*, "seaweed," referring to the abundance of algae on and off the Mediterranean coast here.

Algiers. *Capital of Algeria.* The city and port was founded in the 10th century on the site of a Roman town. It has an Arabic name representing *al-jazā'ir*, "the islands," referring to the four islands that formerly lay off the coast here but that were joined to the mainland from 1525.

Al-Hammada al-Hamra'. *Region, northwestern Libya.* The desolate rocky region has a name meaning "the red desert," from Arabic *al*, "the," *ḥamāda*, "rocky desert," and *ḥamra*, feminine of *aḥmar*, "red." The color is that of the rocks and stones here.

Al-Hasa. *Region, eastern Saudi Arabia.* The name of the region represents Arabic *al-aḥsā'*, "the oasis," referring to the oasis, the largest in Saudi Arabia, at its center.

Alicante. *City and port, southeastern Spain.* The name of the city name evolved under Arabic influence from its original Roman name of *Lucentum*. This is probably of Iberian origin, but has been derived by some from Greek *akra leuka*, "high (and) bright," referring to Alicante's seaside location. (It may be no coincidence that the coast here is known as the *Costa Blanca*, "white coast.") The first syllable of the name falsely suggests Arabic *al*, "the," as for **Algiers** and other places.

Alice Springs. *Town, central Australia.* The town, in Northern Territory, is named for Lady *Alice* Todd, wife of Sir Charles Heavitree Todd (1826–1910), postmaster general of South Australia. The name originally applied to some springs here used as a water resource by engineers erecting the Overland Telegraph Line. Lady Alice was responsible for its construction. The name then passed to the telegraph station that opened in 1871 and subsequently to the town. When the town was gazetted in 1888, however, it was named *Stuart*, for the Scottish-born explorer John McDouall *Stuart* (1815–1866). It officially adopted the earlier and more popular name in 1933.

Al-Kaf. *Town, northwestern Tunisia.* The town is a stronghold at an altitude of 2,560 feet (780 m). Its name represents the Arabic for "the rock."

Al-Karak. *Town, west central Jordan.* The town, the biblical *Kir-haraseth* (Isaiah 16:7, etc.), has a Hebrew name meaning "wall of potsherds," referring to its steep-walled site.

Al-Kharijah. *City, central Egypt.* The city takes its name from the local oases, from Arabic *al-wāḥāt al-khārijah*, "the outer oases," referring to the two groups of oases here in the Libyan Desert. They are "outer" by comparison with the Dakhla Oasis, to the west. The Romans knew both oases by the singular name of *Oasis Magna*, "great oasis," again by comparison with the Dakhla Oasis, which is smaller.

Alkmaar. *City, northwestern Netherlands.* The city's name is said to mean "all sea," from Dutch *al*, "all," and *meer*, "sea," "pool," referring to the town's low-lying location 6 miles (10 km) from the sea.

Al-Kuwayt *see* **Kuwait**

Allahabad. *City, northern India.* The city, a center of Muslim pilgrimage in Uttar Pradesh state, has a Hindi name of Arabic origin meaning "city of *Allah*," i.e. "city of God." The name was given in 1583 by the Mughal emperor Akbar.

Allegheny Mountains. *Mountain range, northeastern United States.* The Pennsylvania range derives its name from Delaware *alleghany*, a word of uncertain origin. A meaning "endless mountains" has been suggested.

Allentown. *City, eastern United States.* The Pennsylvania city was laid out in 1762 by William *Allen*, mayor of Philadelphia, and originally named *Northampton*. In 1838 it was renamed for its founder.

Allier. *River, central France.* The name ultimately derives from the Indoeuropean root *el*, "flowing."

Allon Moreh. *Settlement, West Bank*. The settlement in the Samarian Highlands was founded in 1980 by members of the Jewish rightist organization Gush Emunim and given a Hebrew name meaning "oak of *Moreh*," referring to the "oak which was by Shechem" (Genesis 35:4) where Abraham built an altar after his vision of God on the plain of *Moreh* (12:6).

Allon Shevut. *Settlement, West Bank*. The settlement near Hebron was founded by Orthodox Jewish settlers in 1970 and given a Hebrew name meaning "return to the oak." *Cp.* **Allon Moreh**.

Alma-Ata *see* **Almaty**

Almadén. *Town, west central Spain*. The town derives its name from Arabic *al-ma'dīn*, "the mine." The reference is to the mercury mines here. Hence the town's alternate name of *Almadén del Azogue*, the latter word being Spanish for "mercury." *Cp.* **Azogues**.

Al-Mahdiyah. *Town and port, eastern Tunisia*. The town was founded in 912 by 'Ubayd Allah *al-Mahdi* ("the rightly guided one") (died 934), founder of the Fatimid dynasty, and is named for him.

Al-Marj. *Town, northeastern Libya*. The town, which arose on the ancient Greek colony of *Barca*, has an Arabic name meaning "the meadow."

Almaty. *City, southeastern Kazakhstan*. The former Kazakh capital, long familiar as *Alma-Ata*, has a name traditionally interpreted as "father of apples," from Kazakh *alma*, "apple," and *ata*, "father." However, recent research has shown that the name has been distorted from an original form *Almalyk*, meaning simply "abundant in apples." The town arose from a fort founded in 1854, and from 1885 to 1921 was known as *Verny*, from Russian *vernyj*, "true," "faithful," implying a reliable stronghold. In 1994 the Kazakh parliament voted to move the capital north to *Akmola*, renamed **Astana** in 1998.

Almería. *City and port, southern Spain*. The city has an Arabic name, from *al-mir'aya*, "the watchtower," referring to one by the coast here in former times. The Roman name of the city was *Portus Magnus*, "big harbor."

Al-Minya. *City, northeastern Egypt*. The city derives its name from that of the ancient town of *Menat Khufu*, the ruins of which lie nearby (*see* **Giza**).

Almirante Brown. *City, eastern Argentina*. The city, now a suburb of Buenos Aires, was founded in 1873 as a political subdivision of Buenos Aires and was originally named *Adroqué*, for its founder. (Its railroad station still has this name.) In 1886 a statue to the Irish-born Argentinian naval officer, *Admiral* Guillermo *Brown* (1777–1857), hero of the 1827 battle of Juncal, was erected in the central plaza and the town adopted his name and rank.

Almodóvar del Campo. *Town, south central Spain*. The town's main name represents Arabic *al-mudawar*, "the defended," "the protected," referring to a fortified place. (There is an old Moorish fort here.) The rest of the name, Spanish for "of the plain," distinguishes this town from others identically named.

Alonim. *Kibbutz, northern Israel*. The kibbutz, west of Nazareth, has a Hebrew name meaning "oaks."

Alps. *Mountain system, south central Europe*. The mountains have a name that is almost certainly pre–Celtic and possibly Ligurian, based on the same root word *alb*, "height," that may have given the name of **Albania**.

Alsace. *Historic region, eastern France*. The name has a number of possible origins. It may come from Gaulish *alisa*, "cliff," since the cliffs of the Vosges Mountains here would have impressed the Gauls when they came from southern Germany. Or it may represent Gaulish *aliso*, "alder," as these trees are common here. Some authorities propose an origin in *Illzas*, an early name of the *Ill* River, which runs through the region. Alsace was formerly a German province, and German speakers know it as *Elsaß*.

Alsdorf. *City, western Germany*. The name means "*Adal*'s village," with the personal name a short form of a name such as *Adalbert*.

Alsfeld. *Town, central Germany*. The name means "*Adalo*'s open land," the personal name being a short form of a name such as *Adalwin*.

Altai Mountains. *Mountain system, central Asia*. The mountains, between Mongolia and China, are said to derive their name from Mongolian *alt*, "gold." However, this precious metal was discovered here only in the 19th century, and the name is much older than that. Another possible origin is in Turkish *ala*, "speckled," and *dağ*, "mountain," referring to the variegated coloring of the mountains, with their white peaks, black boulders, green vegetation, and gray granite rocks.

Altamura. *Town, southeastern Italy*. The town, founded in c. 1200, derives its name from Italian *alta mura*, "high wall," referring to the medieval wall that surrounds it.

Altena. *Town, northwestern Germany*. The

name was originally that of the medieval castle here, its own name apparently deriving from a river name of pre–German origin.

Altenburg. *City, central Germany.* The city's name means "old castle," referring to the original Slav fortress here.

Altenkirchen. *Town, western Germany.* The name means "old church," referring to the original parish church of St. Martin here.

Altona. *District of Hamburg, northern Germany.* The name refers to a former inn here, recorded in 1536 as belonging to *Joachim van Lo to der Pepermolenbeeke*, "Joachim of Lo by the pepper-mill stream." For carters coming from Hamburg, this inn was *al to nā*, "all too near," or temptingly close. Hence the name, of Low German origin. (This apparent folk etymology has led some authorities to interpret the name more prosaically as German *die alte Au*, "the old meadow.")

Altoona. *City, eastern United States.* The Pennsylvania city, founded in 1849, is said to derive its name from Cherokee *allatoona*, "high lands of great worth."

Altötting. *Town, southern Germany.* The name means "old place belonging to *Oto*'s people," called "old" (*alt*) for distinction from the nearby later *Neuötting*, which was *neu* ("new").

Altyn Tagh. *Mountain range, western China.* The range has a Tatar name meaning "golden mountain," from *altyn*, "gold," and *tag*, "mountain." Its Chinese name is *aěrjěn*, as a phonetic rendering of *Altyn*.

Alvarado. *City and port, eastern Mexico.* The city takes its name from Pedro de *Alvarado* (c. 1485–1541), a lieutenant of Hernán Cortés, who landed here in 1518.

Älvsborg. *County, southwestern Sweden.* The county's name derives from Old Swedish *älv*, "river," and *borg*, "fort." There are many rivers here. The fort is the one at *Vänersborg*, the county capital.

Al-Wadi al-Jadid. *Governorate, southwestern Egypt.* The region has an Arabic name meaning "the new valley," indicating its administrative reorganization in 1958. Before this date it was known as *as-Sahra' al-Janubiya*, "the southern desert."

Al-Wahat al-Kharijah *see* **Al-Kharijah**

Alwar. *City, northwestern India.* The city, in Rajasthan state, is said to take its name from a nearby mountain. The meaning of its own name is uncertain.

Alzenau. *Town, central Germany.* The town arose in the 9th century and was originally known as *Wilmundsheim*, "*Willimund*'s village."

This name was replaced in the 14th century by the present one, originally that of a newly-built castle, which was itself presumably so called by grumpy neighbors, who found it "all too near" (German *allzu nahe*) to them. (*Cp.* **Altona**.) The town is also known as *Alzenau in Unterfranken*, for its location in *Lower Franconia* (*see* **Franconia**).

Alzira. *City, eastern Spain.* The city originated as the Iberian settlement of *Algezira Sucro*, a name of Arabic origin meaning "island of Sucro," from *al-jazīra*, "the island," and the name of the *Sucro* River. The "island" represents the city's location between two branches of this river.

Amagasaki. *City, central Japan.* The city, in the island of Honshu, derives its name from Japanese *ama*, "nun," and *misaki*, "cape."

Amalfi. *Town and port, southern Italy.* The town was founded by the Romans, who called it *Amalphis*, from Latin *ad*, "by," and the name of the *Malphe* River here.

Amarapura. *Town, central Myanmar.* The former Burmese capital, founded in 1783, has a Myanmar (Burmese) name meaning "city of immortality," from *amara*, "immortality," and *pura*, "town."

Amaravati. *Historic town, southern India.* The ancient Buddhist center, in Andhra Pradesh state, has a Sanskrit name meaning "abode of the immortals," from *amarā*, "immortal," "god," and *vatī*, "house," "abode." Amaravati was regarded as the abode of Indra, the Hindu god of the firmament and of rain.

Amarillo. *City, southern United States.* The Texas city arose in 1887 as a railroad construction camp and derives its name from Spanish *amarillo*, "yellow," apparently referring to the color of local clay deposits.

Amazon. *River, South America.* The world's largest river (by volume) has an Native American (Tupi or Guaraní) name meaning "wave," referring to the notorious bore that runs up its lower reaches. When Spanish explorers were here in the 16th century, they associated the name with the *Amazons* of classical mythology, mainly because local tribesmen were beardless and graceful and wore their hair long, like the legendary women warriors.

Amber. *Historic city, northwestern India.* The city, in Rajasthan state, dates back to before the 12th century and takes its name from *Ambarisha*, king of Ayodhya (Oudh). (His full name was *Ambarikhanera*, but this was shortened to *Ambara* or *Amber*.) The name is also spelled *Amer*.

Amberg. *City, southeastern Germany.* The city's name means "*Ammo*'s height."

Amboise. *Town, west central France.* The town's name may derive either from Gaulish *ambe*, "river," alluding to the Loire, on which it lies, or from a Gaulish personal name *Ambatius.* *Cp.* **Amiens.**

Amélie-les-Bains-Palalda. *Town and resort, southwestern France.* The spa town near the border with Spain was originally known simply as *Les Bains*, "the springs." In 1840 it added the name of Marie-*Amélie* of Bourbon (1782–1866), wife of King Louis Philippe. *Palalda* is the old town above the Tech River here, its name coming from Latin *palatium*, "palace," and the Roman personal name *Danus.*

America. *Continent between Pacific and Atlantic.* Although Columbus discovered America in 1492, and it was known to Norse navigators almost five centuries earlier, the name did not appear on any map until the German cartographer Martin Waldseemüller placed it on one in 1507. He derived it from *Americus*, the latinized forename of the Florentine (Italian) explorer *Amerigo* Vespucci (1451–1512) who had accompanied Columbus. An alternate origin in the name of Richard *Ameryk*, sheriff of Bristol, England, who financed John Cabot's voyage of 1497, is usually dismissed by traditionalists. (A fuller discussion of the name is given in two articles: M.S. Beeler, "America—The Story of a Name," and Zoltan J. Farkas, "The Challenge of the Name *America*," both in Kelsie B. Harder, comp., *Names and their Varieties*, University Press of America, 1986.) See *also* **United States of America.**

Americana. *City, south central Brazil.* The city was founded in 1868 by immigrants from the former Confederate States of *America.* Hence its name. Until 1938 it was known as *Vila Americana*, "American town."

American Samoa *see* **Samoa**

Amersfoort. *Town, central Netherlands.* The town is on the *Eem* (formerly *Amer*) River. Hence its name, denoting a *ford* (Middle Dutch *foort*) across this river.

Ames. *City, central United States.* The Iowa city was laid out in 1865 and named for Oakes *Ames* (1804–1873), a railroad financier and Massachusetts congressman.

Amherst. *Town, northeastern United States.* The Massachusetts town was founded in 1759 and named for Jeffrey *Amherst*, 1st Baron Amherst (1717–1797), British commander in North America in the French and Indian War (1754–63).

Amiens. *City, northern France.* The city, known to the Romans as *Ambianum*, derives its name from the Gaulish people known as the *Ambiani*. Their own name comes from Gaulish *ambe*, "river," referring to the Somme, on which the town stands. (*Cp.* **Amboise.**) The Celtic name of Amiens in pre–Roman times was *Samarobriva*, "*Somme* bridge."

Amirante Islands. *Island group, western Indian Ocean.* The islands, southwest of the Seychelles, have a name of Portuguese origin representing *ilhas do almirante*, "admiral's islands." The name was given in honor of the Portuguese navigator Vasco da Gama, who discovered the islands in 1502. The group should not be confused with the **Admiralty Islands.**

Amman. *Capital of Jordan.* The name pays tribute to *Ammon*, the ancestor of the ancient Semitic people known as the *Ammonites*. In the Bible, Ammon's own name is related to that of the Ammonites' city of origin, referred to as "Rabbath of the children of Ammon" (Deuteronomy 3:11), which itself amounts to little more than "city of the Ammonites."

Ammassalik. *Town, southeastern Greenland.* The town derives its name from *angmagssat*, the Greenlandic word for the capelin (a smeltlike fish used as food and bait), found off the coast here. The name is properly the Western Greenland form, and the town is now often known as *Tasiilaq*, the Eastern Greenland form. But the island on which the town lies is still known as *Ammassalik.*

Amorbach. *City, southwestern Germany.* The city arose around an 8th-century Benedictine monastery and probably derives its name from Old High German *amar*, "spelt" (a kind of cereal), and *bah*, "stream."

Amoy. *City and port, eastern China.* The name of the city, in Fukien province, is the Western form of a local dialect pronunciation of the Chinese name, *Hsia-men*, from *xià*, "summer," and *mén*, "gate."

Amritsar. *City, northern India.* The city, in Punjab state, derives its name from Sanskrit *amṛta*, "immortal," and *saras*, "lake," "pool." The actual "lake of immortality" is the sacred pool around which the town was founded in 1577. The Golden Temple that stands on an island in the pool is the principal holy place of the Sikhs.

Amstelveen. *Town, western Netherlands.* The town, now a suburb of **Amsterdam**, has a name meaning "peat bog on the *Amstel*," from the river name and Dutch *veen*, "fen."

Amsterdam. *Capital of the Netherlands.* The

city and canal port has a name meaning "*Amstel* dam," referring to the dam that was built early between dykes across the *Amstel* River here. The river name is said to derive from Germanic *ama*, "current," and *stelle*, "place." Other Dutch towns and cities have similar "dam" names, such as **Edam, Rotterdam, Schiedam.**

Amu Darya. *River, central Asia.* The river, flowing generally northwest from Afghanistan to the Aral Sea, has a name of Uzbek origin meaning simply "long river," from *amu*, "long," and *dario*, "river." The name is appropriate for a river 1,500 miles (2,400 km) in length. *Cp.* **Syr Darya.** In ancient times it was known as the *Oxus*, a name said to mean "flowing water."

Amundsen Gulf. *Gulf, northern Canada.* The gulf, an eastern extension of the Beaufort Sea in the Northwest Territories, is named for the Norwegian Arctic polar explorer Roald *Amundsen* (1872–1928), who sailed the Northwest Passage here in 1903–06.

Amur. *River, northeastern Asia.* The river, forming the border between northeastern China (Manchuria) and Russia, has a name that probably represents Mongolian *amar*, "calm," "peace," alluding to its slow current. However, the Mongolians themselves know it as *har mörön*, "black river," and the name could equally have evolved from this. *See also* **Heilungkiang, Sakhalin.**

Anaheim. *City, southwestern United States.* The California city was founded by German immigrants in 1857 and has a name meaning "*Ana* settlement," referring to the *Santa Ana* ("St. Anne") River here.

Anáhuac. *Plain, central Mexico.* The plain, in the heartland of Aztec Mexico, derives its name from Maya *anawak*, "(land) by the water," referring to five interlocking lakes formerly here.

Anantapur. *City, south central India.* The city, in Andhra Pradesh state, takes its name from *Ananda*, wife of the *dewan* (senior official) of the medieval kingdom of Vijanagar who built it, with Hindi *pur*, "town," added.

Anatolia. *Region, western Turkey.* The name, used as an alternant for Asia Minor, derives from Greek *anatolē*, "sunrise," "east," since the region is in the eastern part of Asia. *Cp.* **Asia.**

An-ch'ing. *City and port, eastern China.* The former capital of **Anhwei** province derives its name from Chinese *ān*, "peace," "calm," and *qìng*, "to celebrate," "to congratulate."

Anchorage. *City and port, northwestern United States.* The Alaska city has a self-descriptive name for its maritime role. It was founded in 1914 as the headquarters of the Alaska Railroad, which connects it with Fairbanks.

Ancona. *City and port, east central Italy.* The city, on the Adriatic Sea, was founded by Greeks from Syracuse in the 4th century B.C. Its name derives from Greek *ankōn*, "bend," "elbow," referring to the curving coastline at this point.

Andalusia. *Region, southern Spain.* The region takes its name from the *Vandals*, the Germanic people who raided Roman provinces in the 3d and 4th centuries A.D. and who settled here. Their own name means simply "wanderers," from Old German *wandjan*, "to wander." The initial *V-* has disappeared in the current name (Spanish *Andalucía*).

Andaman Islands. *Island group, Bay of Bengal.* The Indian islands have a Hindi or Bengali name ultimately deriving from Sanskrit *hanumaṅt*, "*Hanuman*," the name of the Hindu monkey god and king of Hindustan. *Cp.* **Hanumangarh.**

Andernach. *City, western Germany.* The city arose around a Roman fort called *Antunnacum*, "*Antunnus*'s place," with a Celtic personal name.

¹Anderson. *City, east central United States.* The Indiana city was founded in 1823 on the site of a Delaware village and named for William *Anderson*, the English name used by a subchief, Koktowhanund.

²Anderson. *City, eastern United States.* The South Carolina city was founded in 1826 on former Cherokee land and named for a local Revolutionary hero, General Robert *Anderson* (1805–1871).

Andes. *Mountain chain, western South America.* The mountains have a name of Quechua origin, although its exact meaning is uncertain. It may derive from *andi*, "peak," "crest," or from *anti*, "east." The latter seems unlikely, however, given the location of the chain down the continent's west coast. A third possibility is in *anta*, "copper," as this mineral is found here. *Cp.* **Antofagasta.**

Andhra Pradesh. *State, southeastern India.* The state has a name meaning "Telugu state," from Telugu *aṅdhramu*, "Telugu," and *pradesh*, "state," itself from Sanskrit *pradesha*, "place," "region." *Cp.* **Himachal Pradesh, Uttar Pradesh.**

Andorra. *Principality, southwestern Europe.* The principality, in the Pyrenees between France and Spain, probably derives its name from an indigenous (Navarrese) word *andurrial*, meaning "shrub-covered land." Its capital, of the same name, has the full name *Andorra la Vella*, "Andorra the old."

Andover. *Town, southern England.* The name of the Hampshire town was originally that of the river on which it lies, now the *Anton*. It is Celtic in origin and means "ash stream," from *onno*, "ash tree," and *dubro*, "water." (*Cp.* ¹**Dover**.) The *Anton* came to be so called in the 19th century from the river name *Antona* in the *Annals* of the 1st-century B.C. Roman historian Tacitus, itself a corrupt form of *Trisantona*, referring to a river *Trent* (identical with the northern **Trent**) or *Tarrant*.

Angara. *River, southeastern Russia*. The Siberian river bases its name on *angar*, a word of Tunguso-Manchurian origin meaning "mouth," "fissure," "gorge," describing its many rapids.

Angel Falls. *Waterfall, southeastern Venezuela*. The world's highest waterfall was discovered in 1935 and named for the American bush pilot James *Angel*, who crash-landed his plane nearby in 1937.

Angers *see* **Anjou**

Angkor. *Historic city, northwestern Cambodia*. The former capital of the Cambodian empire (from the 9th through 15th century, when it was destroyed) has a name that ultimately goes back to Sanskrit *nagara*, "city." It had two noted temple complexes: *Angkor Wat*, the latter word from Cambodian *vot*, "pagoda," "Buddhist shrine," and *Angkor Thom*, the latter word from Thai *thom*, "great." But these are really descriptive terms, and the city's actual name was *Yashodharapura*, from Sanskrit *yashodhara*, "holding fame" (from *yashas*, "fame," "glory," and *dhara*, "carrying," "holding"), and *pura*, "town."

Anglesey. *Island, northwestern Wales*. The island's name has long been popularly linked with the *Angles*, the Germanic people who gave the name of **England**. However, as for other islands around the Welsh coast, it is more likely to be of Scandinavian origin, deriving either from Old Norse *ǫngull*, "angle," and *ey*, "island," referring to the island's "angular" coastline, or from the personal name *Qngull*, so that it was "*Qngull*'s island." The Welsh name of Anglesey is *Môn*, "hill," "mountain," referring to Holyhead Mountain (*see* **Holyhead**). *See also* **Man, Isle of**.

Angola. *Republic, southwestern Africa*. The country takes its name from *N'gola*, the title of the native ruler here in the late 15th century, when the territory was colonized by the Portuguese.

Angora *see* **Ankara**

Angostura *see* **Ciudad Bolívar**

Angoulême. *City, western France*. The city's present name evolved from its Medieval Latin name of *Inculisma*. The first part of this represents a pre–Latin root element *eskol*, of uncertain meaning. The second part represents the Gaul-ish superlative suffix *-isama*, related to Latin *-issimus*. The city was thus "the most" in some respect.

Angra do Heroísmo. *City, Azores*. The former capital of the Azores, on the south coast of the island of Terceira, became a city in 1534 under the name *Angra*, Portuguese for "bay." The rest of the name, Portuguese for "of heroism," was added later to commemorate the island's resistance to Spanish invasion in 1380–82.

Angra dos Reis. *City and port, eastern Brazil*. The Portuguese explorer Gaspar de Lemos arrived in the Ilha Grande Bay here on January 6, 1502, the feast of the Epiphany, otherwise known as Three Kings Day (for the three wise men who brought gifts to the infant Jesus). Hence the city's name, Portuguese for "bay of the kings."

Anguilla. *Island, eastern West Indies*. The island was so named by Columbus when he discovered it in 1493. It is the Spanish word for "eel," and alludes to the island's elongated appearance.

Angus. *Historic region, eastern Scotland*. The former county derives its name from *Angus*, 8th-century king of the Picts. His own name means "sole choice."

Anhalt. *Historic region, east central Germany*. The former duchy takes its name from the 12th-century dukes *von Anhalt*, their own name corresponding to Middle High German *anhalt*, "reason," "grounds," and later "halt." The name thus means "stopping place," as the dukes were here to stay.

Anhwei. *Province, eastern China*. The name derives from Chinese *ān*, "peace," "calm," and *huī*, "emblem." The two parts of the name represent the first two elements of the names of two of the province's largest cities: **An-ch'ing**, its former capital, and *Hui-chou* (now *She-hsien*).

Anjou. *Historic region, northwestern France*. The name equates to that of *Angers*, one of the former province's oldest cities. This derives from the *Andecavi*, the Roman name of the Gaulish people here. Their name is of unknown origin, and the Gaulish name of Angers is also unknown. The Romans called it *Juliomagus*, "*Julius*'s market," referring to *Julius* Caesar. *Cp.* **Fréjus**.

Ankara. *Capital of Turkey*. The city probably derives its name from the same Indoeuropean root word *ang*, "bend," that gave the name of **Ancona**. This would relate to the settlement's original location in a winding gorge. It is not likely that the name derives from *anchor* in some language, as if people had come to settle or "anchor" here, although this word itself comes from the Indoeuropean root. The city's name was formerly familiar as *Angora*.

Anklam. *Town, northern Germany.* The name was originally *Tanclam*, meaning "*Taglim's* place," with an Old Polabian personal name.

Annaba. *City and port, northeastern Algeria.* The name of the city evolved from Arabic *madīnat al-'unnāb*, "town of the jujube" (a tree bearing an edible berry-like fruit). Its former French colonial name was *Bône*. This represents the city's original Roman name of *Hippo*, accusative *Hipponem*, itself from Greek *hippōn*, "stable," denoting a place where horses were fed and watered while working at the port. *Cp.* **Bizerta**.

Annaberg-Buchholz. *Town, east central Germany.* The town, in the Erzgebirge, was formed in 1949 on the amalgamation of *Annaberg*, founded in 1496 as a silver-mining settlement and named for a chapel dedicated to St. *Anne*, patron saint of mountain (*Berg*) dwellers, and *Buchholz*, "beech wood."

An-Nafud. *Desert, northwestern Saudi Arabia.* The desert has an Arabic name meaning simply "the desert."

Annam. *Historic kingdom, eastern Indochina.* When in 111 B.C. the Chinese invaded the ancient Vietnamese kingdom of *Nam Viêt* (a name equivalent to **Vietnam**), they gave it a name meaning "pacified south," from *ān*, "peace," and *nán*, "south." Not surprisingly, the name was resented by the inhabitants, who on gaining their independence in 939 named their land *Dai Viêt*, "Great *Viêt*." The name *Annam* reappeared in 1790, when the region was increasingly under French influence.

Annapolis. *City, eastern United States.* The state capital of Maryland was settled in 1649 by Puritans under the propitious name of *Providence*. On becoming capital in 1694 the settlement was renamed for Princess *Anne* (1665–1714), who as Queen Anne gave it a charter in 1708. Greek *polis* means "town."

Annapurna. *Mountain range, central Nepal.* The range takes its name from that of a Hindu goddess, her name in turn from Sanskrit *anna*, "food," and *pūrṇa*, "abundant." The mountains here were seen as favorable to agriculture in the valleys below.

Ann Arbor. *City, northeastern United States.* The Michigan city was founded in 1824 by two settlers, John Allen and Elisha W. Rumsey, who named it for their wives, both called *Ann*. Legend has it that the men trained wild grapevines into an arbor, originally calling it *Anns' Arbor*, and that this came to give the present form of the name. But it could be they actually intended a classical-style name suggesting **Annapolis**, which had been preempted.

Annecy. *Cit and port, eastern France.* The city derives its name from the Germanic personal name *Anerik*.

Annobón. *Island, southwestern Equatorial Guinea.* The island, in the Gulf of Guinea, was sighted by the Portuguese in 1471. They first landed here on New Year's Day, January 1, 1474. Hence the name, from Old Portuguese *anno bom*, "New Year" (literally "good year"). From 1973 through 1979 the island was known as *Pagalu*, a Creole name meaning "papa cockerel," from Spanish *papá*, "papa," "father," and *gallo*, "cockerel," "rooster." The cockerel was the symbol of Equatorial Guinea's dictator president Francisco Macías Nguema (1922–1979) in the presidential elections of September 1968. The island reverted to its original name following his assassination. *See also* **Bioko**.

Annweiler. *Town, western Germany.* The town's name means "*Anno*'s farmstead," probably with the personal name of a Frankish settler.

Ansbach. *City, southern Germany.* The name of the city was recorded in the 9th century as *Onoltespah*, that of a tributary of the Rezat River here. Its own name means "*Onold's* stream."

An-shan. *City, northeastern China.* The city, in Liaoning province, derives its name from Chinese *ān*, "saddle," and *shān*, "mountain," referring to the shape of a nearby mountain.

Antakya. *City, southern Turkey.* The old Syrian capital, the biblical *Antioch* (Acts 6:5, etc.), was founded in c. 300 B.C. by the Macedonian general Seleucus I Nicator, who named it for his father, *Antiochus*. The name was later taken by other eastern towns, including another biblical *Antioch* (Acts 13:14–52), now the ruined city in west central Turkey known as *Antioch of Pisidia*. *See also* **Mary**.

Antalya. *City and port, southwestern Turkey.* The city, the biblical *Attalia* (Acts 14:25), takes its name from *Attalus* II Philadelphus, king of Pergamum, who founded it in the 2d century B.C.

Antananarivo. *Capital of Madagascar.* The city's name means "city of a thousand," from Malagasy *an-*, a prefix denoting a placename, *tanàna*, "town," and *arìvo*, "thousand." The reference is to the great number of inhabitants. During the French colonial period the name was modified to *Tananarive*.

Antarctica. *Continent surrounding South Pole.* The continent has a classical-style name, from Greek *anti*, "opposite," and *arktikos*, "Arctic," referring to its location exactly opposite the **Arctic** Regions around the North Pole.

Antibes. *Town and port, southeastern France.* The name of the Mediterranean town is a corrupt form of Greek *Antipolis*, "opposite the town." Antibes faces Nice across the Baie des Anges.

Anticosti. *Island, eastern Canada.* The island, in the Gulf of St. Lawrence, is popularly said to have a name representing Spanish *ante*, "before," and *costa*, "coast." However, it is more likely to be of Native American origin. A meaning "hunting ground of the bear" has been suggested.

Antigua. *Island, eastern West Indies.* The island was discovered by Columbus in 1493 and named by him for the church of Santa Maria la *Antigua* ("St. Mary the Ancient") in Seville.

Antigua Guatemala. *City, south central Guatemala.* The city was founded in 1527 as *Santiago de los Caballeros de Guatemala*, "St. James of the knights of Guatemala," and became the capital of Spanish Guatemala. It was destroyed by a volcanic eruption, however, and the village that arose on the site was called *Ciudad Vieja*, "old city." Another capital city named *Santiago* was constructed nearby in 1542, but was demolished by an earthquake in 1773, when the capital was moved to the site of *Nueva Guatemala*, "new Guatemala," the modern *Guatemala City*. Santiago, when rebuilt, was accordingly named *Antigua Guatemala*, "old Guatemala."

Anti-Lebanon. *Mountain range, southwestern Asia.* The range, running north and south between Lebanon and Syria, has a name ultimately of Greek origin meaning "opposite **Lebanon**." The Arabic name of the range is *jabal ash-sharki*, "eastern mountain."

Antilles. *Island group, eastern West Indies.* The name of the islands was originally given in 1474 by the Florentine (Italian) cartographer Paolo Toscanelli to a hypothetical island here. Later, after the discovery of the islands by Columbus, the name was applied to the group as a whole. It has been popularly derived from Latin *ante*, "before," and *illas*, "islands," as if referring to their location off the American coast, but the true origin is probably in some older language. Some authorities have linked the name with that of the **Atlantic Ocean.**

Antioch *see* **Antakya**

Antipodes. *Island group, South Pacific.* The islands, southwest of New Zealand, have a Greek name meaning literally "opposite the feet," from *anti*, "opposite," and *pous, podos*, "foot." The reference is to their location, which is "down under," diametrically opposed to that of Green-

wich, England. (The longitude of Greenwich is 0°, and that of the Antipodes 180°.) The name is sometimes colloquially applied to Australia and New Zealand as a whole.

Antofagasta. *City and port, northern Chile.* The city derives its name from Quechua *anta*, "copper," and *pakakta*, "hidden." The allusion is to a place concealing an underground supply of copper. Antofagasta still exports copper from its mines as a major commercial activity.

Antrim. *County, northeastern Northern Ireland.* The county has a name that literally means "one house," from Irish *aon*, "one," and *treabh*, "house." This originally applied to the site of a solitary farm, with the name later spreading to the surrounding district.

Antsirabe. *Town, central Madagascar.* The town derives its name from Malagasy *an-*, the placename prefix (as for **Antananarivo**), *sìra*, "salt," and *bé*, "big," "much." The town is noted for its saline springs, the result of volcanic action, and is now a health resort.

Antsiranana. *Town and port, northern Madagascar.* The town has a Malagasy name meaning simply "the port," from *an-*, the placename prefix (as for **Antananarivo**), and *serànana*, "port." Its former name was *Diego Suárez*, a combination of the names of *Diego* Dias, the Portuguese captain who discovered Madagascar in 1500, and Hernán *Suárez*, the Spanish admiral who landed here in 1506.

Antwerp. *City and port, western Belgium.* The city has a name of Germanic origin, from *anda*, "at," and *werpum*, "wharf," denoting its location on the Scheldt River. Legend tells how a Roman warrior cut off the hands (*hand*) of a giant here and threw (*werpen*) them into the river, so that the city's coat of arms shows a castle with a pair of severed hands above. The French form of the name is *Anvers*.

Anuradhapura. *Town, northern Sri Lanka.* The ancient capital of the Sinhalese kings of Ceylon, sacred to Buddhists and traditionally founded in the 5th century B.C., is named for *Anuradha*, minister of Prince Vijaya, who arrived here from India with the first settlers then. The final *-pura* is Sanskrit "town." The prince's name means "victory."

An-yang. *City, northeastern China.* The city, in Honan province, derives its name from Chinese *ān*, "peace," "calm," and *yáng*, "light," "sun."

Anzio. *Town and port, western Italy.* The town's Roman name of *Antium* is of uncertain origin but has been popularly associated with the Greek mythological figure *Anteius*, son of Poseidon.

Aomori. *City and port, northern Japan.* The city, in the island of Honshu, has a name meaning "green forest," from Japanese *ao*, "blue," "green," and *mori*, "wood," "forest."

Aorangi *see* **Cook, Mt.**

Aosta. *City, northwestern Italy.* The city takes its name from the Roman emperor *Augustus*, its founder in 25 B.C.

Aotearoa *see* **New Zealand**

Apeldoorn. *Town, central Netherlands.* The town has a name that means simply "apple tree," from Dutch *apel*, "apple," and *door*, an old word for "tree" (now replaced by *boom*). The English villages of *Appledore* in Devon and Kent have a name of related origin and identical meaning.

Apennines. *Mountain range, central Italy.* The name is ultimately based on Celtic *penn*, "hill." *Cp.* **Pennines.**

Aphrodisias. *Historic town, southwestern Turkey.* The former capital of Caria, now in ruins, was named for *Aphrodite*, the Greek goddess of love, who was worshiped here.

Apolda. *City, east central Germany.* The city, dating from the 12th century, derives its name from Old Saxon *appul*, "apple," referring to *apple* orchards here. (The final *-da* of the name represents the collective suffix *-ede*, from Old Saxon *-ithi*, Old High German *-idi*.)

Appalachians. *Mountain system, eastern North America.* The mountains in Canada and the United States derive their name from a now extinct Native American people, the *Apalachee*, who inhabited a region corresponding to modern northwestern Florida. Their own name comes from an indigenous (possibly Hitchiti) word *apalatchi*, meaning "people on the other side."

Appenzell. *Town, northeastern Switzerland.* The town takes its name from its original Roman name of *Abbatis cella*, "abbot's cell," referring to the abbots of St.-Gall, who ruled it from the 11th century. *Cp.* **Abbeville.**

Appian Way. *Roman road, southern Italy.* The road, also known by its Roman name of *Via Appia*, runs south from Rome to Capua and then on to Brindisi. It was the first major Roman road, and is named for the Roman censor *Appius Claudius Caecus*, its initiator in the 3d century B.C.

Appleton. *City, northern United States.* The Wisconsin city was founded on the Fox River by Amos A. Lawrence (1814–1886) of Boston and originally called *Grand Chute*, for its waterpower. It was subsequently renamed for Samuel *Appleton*, Lawrence's father-in-law.

Apurímac. *River, southern Peru.* The name of the river is said to represent Quechua *apu rimak*, "the speaking lord," from *apu*, "lord," "wealthy one" and *rima*, "to speak." The "speaking" is its noisy torrential course through narrow canyons. The "lord" is its power.

Aqaba. *Town and port, southwestern Jordan.* The town derives its name from Hebrew *'aqabba*, itself from a root word meaning "heel," "lowest part" (Arabic *ka'b*, Hebrew *'aqev*), referring to a pass here. The biblical name of the town is *Ezion-geber* (1 Kings 9:26), "backbone of a giant."

Aquino. *Town, south central Italy.* The original town arose as the Roman settlement of *Aquinum*, taking its name from Latin *aqua*, "water." It was laid waste in the 6th century, and the present town arose nearby, keeping the name.

Aquitaine. *Historic region, southwestern France.* The former Roman province of *Aquitania* borders the Atlantic. Hence its name, based on Latin *aqua*, "water," with a suffix that probably means simply "land," "territory."

Arabia. *Desert region, southwestern Asia.* The great peninsula to the east of the Red Sea derives its name from its indigenous inhabitants, the *Arabs*. Their own name is usually interpreted as "tent dwellers," implying a nomadic people. The Bible states that "neither shall the Arabian pitch tent" (Isaiah 13:20), although the Hebrew word *'aravi* here translated as "Arabian" seems to mean any desert dweller. According to another theory the name relates to Arabic *ğarb*, "west," implying a people who lived in western Asia.

Arad. *Town, southern Israel.* The town was founded in 1961 near the site of the biblical town of the same name (Numbers 21:1–3). (The "king Arad" mentioned here is really "king of Arad.") The name is traditionally interpreted as "wild ass."

Arafura Sea. *Sea between Australia and New Guinea.* The sea is said to take its name from the *Alifuru*, an indigenous people of the Moluccas. Their own name may represent the local word *halefuru*, "uninhabited (region)," referring to the sparse population of many of the smaller islands.

Aragon. *Historic region, northeastern Spain.* The ancient kingdom takes its name from a river here. Its own name is ultimately based on the Indoeuropean root word *ar*, "water," found in the names of other rivers such as Italy's **Arno** or Scotland's **Ayr.** *See also* **Arles.**

Araguaia. *River, central Brazil.* The river is said to derive its name either from Tupi *ara-gua-y*, "river of the valley of parrots," or from Tupi *ara*, "day," "time," and *guaia*, "crab."

Arak. *City, west central Iran.* The city's name

appears to be a corruption of its Arabic name, *'irāk 'ajam*, "Persian bank" (*cp.* **Iraq**). Its former name was *Sultanabad*, "town of the sultan."

Arakan. *Mountain range, western Myanmar.* The name is said to be a European corruption of Sanskrit *rākshasa*, "ogre," as a term applied by early Buddhists to unconverted people.

Aral Sea. *Sea, central Asia.* The sea, between Kazakhstan and Uzbekistan, probably derives its name from a Kyrgyz or Kazakh word *aral*, meaning "island." If so, the designation is apt, since the sea contains over 1,000 islands.

Arambagh. *Town, eastern India.* The West Bengal town has a name meaning "garden of rest," from Hindi *ārām*, "rest," and *bāg*, "garden." Its former name was *Jahanabad*, as for **Jahanabad**.

Aran Islands. *Island group, western Ireland.* The three islands, in Galway Bay, derive their name from Irish *ára*, "kidney," alluding to their kidney-shaped contour. They are individually named as *Inishmore* ("big island"), *Inishman* ("middle island"), and *Inisheer* ("eastern island").

Ararat. *Mountain, eastern Turkey.* The volcanic peak was originally named *Urartu*, from the name of an ancient Assyrian kingdom. This may itself be based on an Indoeuropean root word *ar*, "mountain." The Turkish name of Ararat is *Ağrı dağı*, "mountain of sorrow," but the first word of this may actually derive from *Aqori*, a Georgian village that was buried when the volcano erupted in 1840. The Persian name of the mountain is *kūhe nūḥ*, "mountain of Noah." Where the English Bible tells of Noah's Ark resting "upon the mountains of Ararat" (Genesis 8:4), the Vulgate (Latin version) has "*super montes Armeniae*," "on the mountains of Armenia" (*see* **¹Armenia**). Among the many fanciful accounts of the name is the legend of the Armenian king Ara the Fair who spurned the love of the 9th-century B.C. Assyrian queen Sammu-ramat (Semiramis) and was defeated by her troops at the foot of the mountain.

Araucanía. *Region, southern Chile.* The region takes its name from the *Araucanian* Indians, whose territory at one time included almost the whole of Chile. Their own name is of uncertain origin. Derivations have been proposed in Guaraní *arauca*, "parrot cage," in *ara*, "sky," and *oka*, "house," and in *rag*, "clay," and *ko*, "water."

Aravalli Range. *Mountain range, northwestern India.* The name of the hill system represents Sanskrit *āra*, "outer edge," "bank," and *āvali*, "chain," "range."

Arbroath. *Town and port, eastern Scotland.* The town has a Celtic name that means "(place at the) mouth of the *Brothock*," the latter being

the stream on which Arbroath stands. The initial *Ar*- thus equates to the more common *Aber*- found in such names as **Aberdeen**. Robert Southey's poem *The Inchcape Rock* (1802) has the full form of the name:

> And then they knew the perilous rock,
> And blest the Abbot of Aberbrothok.

Arcadia. *Historic region, southern Greece.* The region's name is traditionally derived from that of the mythological Greek character *Arcas*, son of Zeus, who was supposedly its first king.

Archangel *see* **Arkhangelsk**

Arctic. *Region surrounding North Pole.* The polar region takes its name from Greek *arktos*, "bear," referring not so much to the polar bears found here but to the region's location below the constellation of the Great Bear (Ursa Major). *Cp.* **Antarctica**.

Ardabil. *City, northwestern Iran.* The city is said to take its name from its founder some time before the 7th century, *Ardabil* ben Armanin.

Ardèche. *River, southeastern France.* The first part of the river's name is probably the Indoeuropean root element *ar*, "water," although it could also be Gaulish *ardu*, "high," referring to the Cévennes Mountains in which the river rises. The rest of the name is the Gaulish suffix *-esc*.

Ardennes. *Wooded plateau, western Europe.* The elevated region of northeastern France and southeastern Belgium has a Gaulish name that is probably either based on *ardu*, "high," or represents *ar duenn*, "land of forests." England's Forest of *Arden*, famous from Shakespeare, has a similar name. *See also* **Argonne**.

Arequipa. *City, southern Peru.* The city derives its name from Aymara *ari*, "peak," and Quechua *qipa*, "behind." Arequipa is thus "behind the summit," a name describing its location at the foot of the dormant volcano El Misti.

Arezzo. *City, north central Italy.* The city was known in Roman times as *Arretium*, a name probably of Etruscan origin but uncertain meaning.

Argenteuil. *Town, northern France.* The town, now a suburb of Paris, had the Roman name of *Argentogilum*. This derives from the Gaulish personal name *Argantius*, itself based on *arganto*, "silver," and *ialo*, "clearing," "village," so essentially meaning "dweller in the bright place." The "bright place" was probably a location by the Seine River here.

Argentina. *Republic, southern South America.* Spanish explorers in South America in the early 16th century bartered goods for the silver ornaments worn by the local people, not realizing that the silver was not obtained locally. It was this precious metal that thus mistakenly gave the present country its name, from Spanish *argento*, "silver." *See also* **La Plata**.

Argonne. *Wooded plateau, northeastern France*. The plateau has a name of Celtic origin meaning either "high (place)" or "forest." *Cp.* **Ardennes**.

Argos. *City, southern Greece*. The city possibly derives its name from Greek *argos*, "bright," "shining," referring to its prominent location, although some authorities favor an origin in a pre–Hellenic word *arge*, "land," "plain."

Argyll. *Historic region, western Scotland*. The former county has a name that means "land of the *Gaels*," from Old Irish *airer*, "country," and the ethnic name. The Gaels were originally an Irish people who in the 5th century A.D. came to settle as a Scots kingdom in what was then Pictish territory.

Århus *see* **Aarhus**

Ariel *see* **Jerusalem**

Arizona. *State, southwestern United States*. The name of the state has been popularly derived from Spanish *arida zona*, "dry region." However, a more likely source is in an Native American (Papago) name *Arizonac*, from *ali*, "small," and *shonak*, "place of the spring." An origin in Basque *aritz ona*, "good oak," proposed by William A. Douglass in his article "On the Naming of Arizona" (*Names*, Vol. 27, No. 4, December 1979), seems rather far-fetched, although the presence of Basque explorers and colonizers in the region is historically attested, as is that of oak trees around *Arizonac*, the village that initially gave the name and that itself lay by a small stream in the south of the present state.

Arkansas. *State, south central United States*. The state takes its name from the river that bisects it. The river's own name comes from that of the Native American *Arkansea* people who lived by it. The meaning of their name is uncertain, although "downriver" has been suggested. The French wrote the name with a final plural *s*, falsely suggesting a link with the name of **Kansas**, to the northwest.

Arkhangelsk. *City and river port, northwestern Russia*. The city, often referred to by English speakers as *Archangel*, was so named in 1613 for its 12th-century monastery, dedicated to St. Michael the *Archangel*. It was founded by Ivan the Terrible in 1584, the year of his death, as *Novokholmogory*, "New *Kholmogory*," after a village of this name further up the same river (the Dvina). Its own name is of uncertain origin, although it came to be inappropriately associated

with Russian *kholm*, "hill," and *gora*, "mountain."

Arlberg. *Mountain region, western Austria*. The region's name is traditionally derived from *Adlerberg*, "eagle mountain." But although the second element is certainly German *Berg*, "mountain," the first part is more likely to represent German dialect *arle*, "dwarf conifer." *See also* **Vorarlberg**.

Arles. *City, southeastern France*. The city was known to the Romans as *Arelatum* or *Arelate*, probably from pre–Indoeuropean *ar-el*, "mountain," and the suffix *-ate*. An alternate origin is in Gaulish *are*, "by," a borrowing from Greek *para*, and *late*, "marsh," from Greek *platus*, "flat."

Arlington. *County, eastern United States*. The Virginia county, a suburb of Washington DC, takes its name from the estate of George Washington Parke Custis, adopted son of George Washington. He named it for Henry Bennet, 1st Earl of *Arlington* (1618–1685), who shared Charles II's grant of the colony of Virginia with Lord Thomas Culpepper. The English earl's title comes from *Harlington*, Middlesex, now a district of Greater London.

Armagh. *County, east central Northern Ireland*. The county is named for its chief town, itself with a name meaning either "height of *Macha*," from Irish *ard*, "high," and the personal name *Macha*, or "height of the plain," from *ard* and *machaire*, "plain." Macha is a goddess of Irish mythology.

Armagnac. *Historic region, southwestern France*. The region takes its name from that of a former family here. Its own name may possibly have been related, albeit remotely, to that of [1]**Armenia**.

Armavir. *City, southwestern Russia*. Although founded only in 1839, the city was named by Armenian settlers for the historic capital of the ancient Assyrian kingdom of *Urartu* (*see* **Ararat**).

[1]**Armenia**. *Republic, western Asia*. The ancient country has a name of uncertain origin. It is traditionally derived from one *Armenak*, supposedly the original ancestor of all present Armenians. A recent school of thought traces the name back to *Nairi*, "land of rivers," as the former name of a mountainous region here. The placename itself is first recorded in a rock inscription dated A.D. 521 near the Iranian city of Bakhtaran (formerly Kermanshah).

[2]**Armenia**. *City, west central Colombia*. The city was founded in 1889 and apparently named for the ancient kingdom of [1]**Armenia**, western Asia.

Armentières. *Town, northern France*. The

town's name goes back to Gallo-Roman *armentum*, "herds," "cattle." Romans kept cattle here in the 1st century B.C.

Armidale. *City, southeastern Australia.* The city, in New South Wales, was founded in 1839 by G.J. Macdonald, commissioner for crown lands, and named for his father's Scottish baronial estate at what is now *Armadale* on the Isle of Skye.

Armorica. *Historic region, northwestern France.* The ancient territory, corresponding to modern Brittany and Normandy, has a name of Gaulish origin, from *are*, "on," "at," and *mor*, "sea." The reference is to its maritime location, bounded by the English Channel to the north and the Atlantic to the west. The name is preserved in the Brittany department *Côtes-d'Armor* (until 1990 *Côtes-du-Nord*).

Arnhem. *City, eastern Netherlands.* The city's present name evolved from its Roman name of *Arenacum*. This is based on Latin *arena*, "sand," to which has been added Germanic *heim*, "abode," "village," denoting the site of the original settlement on the sandy banks of the Rhine.

Arnhem Land. *Peninsula, northern Australia.* The peninsula, in Northern Territory, was discovered in 1623 by the Dutch explorer Jan Carstensz, who named it for his ship, the *Arnhem*, itself named for **Arnhem**, in the Netherlands.

Arno. *River, central Italy.* The river derives its name from the Indoeuropean root word *ar*, "river," "water." For similar names, *cp.* **Aragon**, **Ayr**.

Arnsberg. *City, western Germany.* The name, meaning "*Arn*'s height," with an Old German personal name, was originally that of the castle around which the town arose in the 12th century.

Arnstadt. *City, east central Germany.* The city's name means "*Arn*'s settlement," with the same Old German personal name as for **Arnsberg**.

Arras. *Town, northern France.* The town derives its name from the *Atrebates*, the Gaulish people who inhabited the province of **Artois**, of which it was the capital. The name thus has the same origin.

Artashat. *Town, southern Armenia.* The town was known as *Kamarlyu* until 1945, when it was renamed as now for the ancient capital of Armenia, whose ruins are nearby. Its own name derived from the Armenian ruler *Artaxas*, who founded it in c. 176 B.C.

Arthur's Pass. *Mountain pass, southern New Zealand.* The pass, through the Southern Alps in central South Island, was named for the English-born surveyor and engineer Sir *Arthur* Dudley Dobson (1841–1934), the first white man to cross it (in 1864).

Artigas. *City, northwestern Uruguay.* The city was founded in 1852 and was originally known as *San Eugenio*, "St. Eugene." It was soon renamed as now for the revolutionary leader José Gervasio *Artigas* (1764–1850), regarded as the father of Uruguayan independence.

Artois. *Historic region, northern France.* The former province derives its name from the Gaulish people who were its original inhabitants. These were the *Atrebates*, their own name meaning simply "inhabitants," from *trebu*, "tribe." *See also* **Arras**.

Artyomovsk. *City, eastern Ukraine.* The city was originally known as *Bakhmut*, for the river here. In 1924 it was renamed *Artyom*, for the party alias used by the Communist leader and Donbass miner Fyodor Andreyevich Sergeyev (1883–1921), who headed the local defense headquarters here during the Civil War. He was killed testing a new type of passenger plane. (His party name is a pet form of the regular Russian forename *Artemy*, "Artemas.") The Ukrainian form of the name is *Artemivs'k*.

Aruba. *Island, southern West Indies.* The island, in the Lesser Antilles, is popularly said to have received its name from the words "*Oro hubo*" ("There was gold!"), uttered by the Spanish explorer Alonso de Ojeda, after his visit here in 1499. A source in Arawak *oibubai*, "guide," is more credible.

Arunachal Pradesh. *State, northeastern India.* The state has a Hindi name amounting to "land of the rising sun," from *arunachal*, "dawn," and *pradesh*, "land." (In Hindu mythology, *Aruna*, whose name properly means "reddish," is the god of the dawn.) From 1954 through 1972 the state was known as *North East Frontier Agency*.

Asahikawa. *City, central Japan.* The city, in the island of Honshu, has a name meaning "river of the rising sun," from Japanese *asahi*, "rising sun," and *kawa*, "river." The river here is the Ishikari.

Ascension. *Island, South Atlantic.* The island, a British dependency since 1815, was originally discovered by the Spanish navigator in Portuguese service João da Nova in 1501 and named *Ilha da Concepção*, "Conception Island," for the Immaculate Conception of the Virgin Mary. It was then rediscovered in 1508 on *Ascension* Day, and renamed *Ilha da Ascenção*. The name is geographically apt for its terrain, which rises (ascends) to the central peak of Green Mountain, an extinct volcano. It is also biblically appropriate, as Jesus ascended from the Mount of Olives, another "Green Mountain."

Aschaffenburg. *City, south central Germany.* The name means "fortified place on the *Aschaff*," the river's name meaning "ash stream," for the ash trees that grew by it.

Aschersleben. *City, central Germany.* The city's name, first recorded in the 9th century, means "*Askger*'s estate," with *-leben* related to English *leave* in the sense "remnant" ("thing *left* over").

Ascot. *Village, southern England.* The Berkshire village has a name found elsewhere in England meaning "eastern cottage," from Old English *ēast*, "east," and *cot*, "cottage." The original settlement may have been so called because it was east of Easthampstead, now a district of Bracknell.

Asenovgrad. *Town, southern Bulgaria.* The town arose in the 14th century as a fortified post and is name for the Bulgarian king Ivan *Asen* II (died 1241), with Slavic *grad*, "town," added to the possessive form of his name.

Ashdod. *City and port, southwestern Israel.* The present city was founded in 1956 4½ miles (7 km) from the former biblical city of this name (Joshua 15:47, etc.), known to the Greeks as *Azotos*. The name itself is of uncertain origin. A meaning "stronghold" has been suggested.

Ashdot Ya'aqov. *Kibbutz, northeastern Israel.* The kibbutz, founded in 1933 in the Jordan valley between the Jordan and Yarmuk rivers, has a Hebrew name meaning "falls of Jacob."

Asheville. *City, eastern United States.* The North Carolina city was settled in 1794 and originally named *Morristown*, for the Revolutionary financier Robert *Morris* (1736–1806). It was soon after renamed for North Carolina governor Samuel *Ashe* (1725–1813).

Ashikaga. *City, central Japan.* The city, in the island of Honshu, derives its name from Japanese *ashi*, "foot," and *ki*, "to be influential."

Ashkelon *see* **Ashqelon**

Ashkhabad. *Capital of Turkmenistan.* The city arose in 1881 as a military post on the site of the ancient settlement of *Askhabad* and adopted its name. The name itself derives from Turkmen *uskh*, "dear," and *ābād*, "inhabited place," "town," so can be understood overall to mean "place of pleasure," "abode of love." From 1919 through 1927 the town was known as *Poltoratsk*, for Pavel *Poltoratsky* (1888–1918), a revolutionary active in Turkestan who was killed in the Civil War. The name is now formally spelled *Ashgabad*.

Ashqelon. *City and resort, southwestern Israel.*

The present city arose in modern times 1½ miles (2 km) northeast of the biblical city and port of *Ashkelon* (Judges 1:18, etc.). The name is very old, and in pharaonic archives of the 14th century B.C. is recorded as *Asqaluna*. The meaning of the name is uncertain. It may be related to Hebrew *sql*, "to weigh," referring to the city's economic role.

Ashtabula. *City, east central United States.* The Ohio city takes its name from the river at the mouth of which it lies. The river's own name is Algonquian in origin and said to mean "river of many fish."

Ashur. *Historic city, northern Iraq.* The ancient religious capital of **Assyria** shares the origin of its name with that of its country.

Asia. *Continent east of Europe.* The world's largest continent has a name of disputed origin. It may represent Assyrian *aṣū*, "to rise," meaning "land of the rising sun," otherwise an eastern land as opposed to Europe, to the west. Another possible source is in Sanskrit *uṣā*, "dawn," with a similar sense. The Romans used the name *Asia* for a province in the western part of Asia Minor formed in 133 B.C. out of the kingdom of Pergamum.

Asir. *Region, southwestern Saudi Arabia.* The region of coastal plains and high mountains has a name deriving from Arabic *'asīr*, literally "captive," implying country that is hard to traverse.

Askelon *see* **Ashqelon**

Asmara. *Capital of Eritrea.* The name is Tigrinya in origin and means "flowery wood."

Asnières. *Town, northern France.* The town, now a suburb of Paris, has a name that ultimately derives from Latin *asinus*, "ass," "donkey." The place was one where donkeys were formerly bred or kept. The full name is *Asnières-sur-Seine*, denoting its location by this river.

Asperg. *Town, southern Germany.* The name means either "*Ask*'s fortified place" or "(fortified place on the) hill where ash trees grow." The latter is probably more likely.

Assam. *State, northeastern India.* The name is probably ethnic in origin, from the *Ahamiya* who invaded the region in the 13th century. They spoke *Ahom*, a Tibetan-Burmese language, and its own name may in turn represent Thai *ahom*, "invincible." According to some authorities, the name is Sanskrit, from the prefix *a-*, "without," and *sama*, "same," otherwise "(people) without equal."

Assiniboine. *River, southern Canada.* The river, a tributary of the Red River in Saskatchewan and Manitoba, derives its name from the *Assiniboin*, the Native American people formerly here. Their own name comes from an Ojibwa (Chippewa) phrase meaning "one who cooks with stones." (Hence their English nickname of "Stonies.")

Assisi. *Town, central Italy.* The town, known to the Romans as *Assisium*, has a name that may be Umbrian in origin, although the *-isium* suggests a pre–Latin provenance. Its actual meaning is obscure.

Assyria. *Historic kingdom, western Asia.* The ancient empire has a name that is identical with that of its chief city, *Assur* (*Ashur*). This in turn represents the name of the god of the Assyrians, and probably derives from Assyrian *sar*, "prince." The god's name is the basis of that of the last great Assyrian king, *Assurbanipal* ("Assur is the creator of the king"), who moved the capital of Assyria from the city of Assur to a new city which he built at Calah (Numrud). The place-name is not related to that of **Syria**.

Astana. *Capital of Kazakhstan.* The city was founded in 1830 as *Akmola*, from Kazakh *ak*, "white," and *mola*, "tomb." In 1832, when the settlement was raised to town status, this was modified to *Akmolinsk*. In 1961 the name was changed altogether to *Tselinograd*, from Russian *tselina*, "virgin land," and the familiar *-grad*, "town," referring to the extensive land reclamation then under way in this part of Kazakhstan. In 1994, when it was decided to move the capital here from Almaty, the old name was re-adopted, but in the indigenous form *Aqmola*. In 1998, as the capital, it took its present symbolic name, meaning simply "the capital."

Astorga. *City, northwestern Spain.* The city takes its name from the first word of its Roman name, *Asturica Augusta*, "grand Asturian (place)," in turn from *Asturia*, the Latin name of **Asturias**.

Astrakhan. *City, southwestern Russia.* The name is said to represent Turkish *hacı tarhan*, from *hacı*, "hajji" (a Muslim who has made a pilgrimage to Mecca), and *tarhan*, "untaxed," from *tarh*, "tax." The village of *Ashtarhan* was founded on the Volga in or before the 13th century 5 miles (12 km) from the present city, and its repute as a center of Islam could well have gained it exemption from local taxes.

Asturias. *Region, northwestern Spain.* The autonomous region and former kingdom has a name deriving from Basque *asta*, "rock," and *ur*, "water," describing its maritime location and topography.

Asunción. *Capital of Paraguay.* The city was founded by the Spanish on August 15, 1537, the feastday of the *Assumption* of the Virgin Mary. Hence its name, not to be confused with any place named **Ascension**. (The words *Assumption* and *Ascension* are closer in some European languages than they are in English, as Spanish *Asunción* and *Ascensión*, Portuguese *Assunção* and *Ascensão*.)

Aswan. *City, southeastern Egypt.* The city arose by the Nile on the site of the ancient city of *Swen*, referred to in the Bible as *Syene* (Ezekiel 29:7, etc.). Its name represents the Egyptian for "market."

Atacama. *Desert, northern Chile.* The desert region derives its name from that of a local people here. Their own name is said to represent Quechua *takama*, "black duck," presumably alluding to their totemic bird.

Athens. *Capital of Greece.* The city is traditionally said to derive its name from the Greek goddess *Athene*, whose temple here was the Parthenon. Some authorities link the name with Greek *aktē*, "shore," "maritime place," "raised place," referring to the hills of Athens (and especially the Acropolis, "high city") on the Attic plain not far from the Saronic Gulf, an inlet of the Aegean Sea. But the name is almost certainly pre–Hellenic, and remains of uncertain origin. *Cp.* **Attica**.

Athlone. *Town, north central Ireland.* The town, in Co. Westmeath, has a name representing Irish *Baile Átha Luain*, "town of the ford of *Luan*." The ford here would have been over the Shannon River. The identity of the named man is uncertain.

Athos, Mt. *Mountain, northeastern Greece.* The mountain has a descriptive name, from Greek *thoos*, "sharp," "pointed," referring to its marble summit. The Greek Orthodox Church also know it as *Hagion Oros*, "holy mountain."

Atjeh *see* **Aceh**

Atlanta. *City, southeastern United States.* The state capital of Georgia gained city status in 1845 and was given its present name then by the railroad engineer J.E. Thomson, with reference to its location at the terminus of the Western and *Atlantic* Railroad. Its original name, when founded in 1837, was actually *Terminus* itself.

Atlantic City. *City and resort, eastern United States.* The New Jersey city, a fishing village until the construction of a railroad in 1854, could hardly have any other name for its site by the **Atlantic Ocean**.

Atlantic Ocean. *Ocean separating the Americas from Europe and Asia.* The great ocean bears the name of both *Atlas*, the giant of Greek mythology, and *Atlantis*, the ancient legendary land said to have sunk beneath it to the west of southern Spain. It is hard to say which of these two is the prime source, or even if either is. More plausibly, the name relates to that of the **Atlas Mountains**, since the ocean can be thought of as "beginning" to the west of these. The name is first found in the 5th century B.C. in the writings of Herodotus, who tells of a "sea beyond the Pillars of Hercules [Strait of Gibraltar] called Atlantis."

Atlas Mountains. *Mountain system, northwestern Africa*. The mountains, in Morocco and Tunisia, are said to take their name from *Atlas*, the giant of Greek mythology who held up the sky, since that is what they appear to do. The arabicized Berber name for the mountains, however, is *Daren*, representing a shortened form of *adràr n'idràren*, "mountain of mountains" (*cp.* **Adrar**), and this more probably lies behind the name, since *atl-* and *adr-* are phonologically related. The legendary land of *Atlantis* lies to the west of the mountains, submerged in the **Atlantic Ocean** (with its related name).

Attendorn. *Town, western Germany*. The name, first recorded as *Attendarra* in 1072, is of uncertain origin.

Attica. *Historic region, eastern Greece*. The ancient region is the territory of **Athens**, and its name is generally regarded as adjectival form of this, from Greek *Attikos* or Latin *Atticus*, "of Athens." However, there may be a more direct link with Greek *aktē*, "shore," "maritime place," "raised place," referring to the many hills of the region, and its location by the Aegean Sea.

Attleboro. *City, northeastern United States*. The Massachusetts city was settled in 1669 as part of Rehoboth and in 1694 was named for the English town of *Attleborough*, Norfolk, with which presumably one or more of the settlers had a connection.

Atyrau. *City and port, western Kazakhstan*. The city was founded in 1645 as a fishing settlement named *Guryev*, for the merchant Mikhail *Guryev*. In 1992 it acquired its present name, meaning "river delta," for its location on the Ural River near its mouth on the Caspian Sea.

Atzcapotzalco. *City, central Mexico*. The city was founded in the 12th century and given a Nahuatl name meaning "anthill," referring to its teeming population.

Aubervilliers. *Town, northern France*. The town, now a suburb of Paris, has a name meaning "*Adalberht's* farm," with the Germanic personal name followed by Medieval Latin *villare*, "farm."

Auburn. *City, northeastern United States*. The Maine city was settled in 1786 and is said to have been named for "Sweet Auburn, loveliest village

of the plain" in Oliver Goldsmith's poem *Deserted Village* (1770). There are other cities of the name in Alabama, New York, and Washington, all apparently of the same origin. (Goldsmith's village has long been traditionally identified with Lissoy, Co. Westmeath, Ireland, which actually renamed itself thus, although his fictional settlement is now thought to be a composite. By coincidence, *Auburn* is a real "deserted village" in Yorkshire, England, on the North Sea coast, where it was gradually eroded by the sea from the 18th century. Its name means "stream with eels.")

Auch. *Town, southwestern France*. The original settlement here was named *Elimberrum*, from Basque *ili*, "town," and *berri*, "new." In the 4th century the town adopted a name from the Aquitanian tribe known as the *Auscii*, their own name related to Basque *euskal*, "Basque" (*see* **Basque Country**).

Auckland. *City and port, northern New Zealand*. The city, in North Island, was founded in 1840 as the capital of British colonial New Zealand and was named for George Eden, Earl of *Auckland* (1784–1849), first lord of the Admiralty. The earl inherited the title from his father, who was born near Bishop *Auckland*, Co. Durham, England.

Aue. *Town, east central Germany*. The original name of the settlement here was *Zelle*, from Medieval Latin *cella*, "cell," from a small monastery here. The name *Aue*, first recorded in the 15th century, probably referred to the land around the monastery, from Middle High German *ouwe*, "island," "land surrounded by water," referring to the site by the Zwickauer Mulde.

Auerbach. *Town, east central Germany*. The name was originally that of a river here, from Old High German *ūr*, "aurochs" (a now extinct species of wild ox), and *bach*, "stream," meaning a stream or river where this animal regularly came.

Augsburg. *City, southern Germany*. The city was founded in c. 30 A.D. around the Roman colony of *Augusta Vindelicorum*, which was linked with Italy by the road known as the *Via Claudia Augusta*, so named for the Roman emperor Caesar *Augustus* (63 B.C.–A.D. 14). The second part of the Roman name derived from the *Vindelici*, the people who inhabited the region. In due course Germanic *burg*, "fort," was added to the first part of the name, which was eventually reduced to its first syllable.

[1]**Augusta**. *Town, southern Italy*. The coastal town in eastern Sicily was founded in 1232 by Emperor Frederick II who named it *Augusta*

Veneranda, "grand (place) worthy to be revered." The present name has retained the first word of this.

²**Augusta.** *City, northeastern United States.* The state capital of Maine was so named in 1797, probably (although not certainly) for Pamela *Augusta* Dearborn, daughter of the Revolutionary general Henry Dearborn (1751–1829), marshal for the District of Maine (1789–93).

³**Augusta.** *City, southeastern United States.* The Georgia city was founded in 1735 and named for Princess *Augusta* (1719–1772), future mother (1738) of George III of England.

Augustów. *Town, northeastern Poland.* The town was founded in 1561 by Sigismund II *Augustus* (1520–1572), king of Poland, and is named for him.

Aulis. *Historic town and port, eastern Greece.* The ancient town derives its name from Greek *aulis, aulidos,* "tent," "camp."

Aurangabad. *City, west central India.* The city, in Maharashtra state, was founded in 1610 and originally known as *Khadki.* Its name was changed in honor of himself by the Mogul emperor of India *Aurangzeb* (1618–1707), who built a tomb nearby in imitation of the Taj Mahal (itself erected for his mother, Mumtaz Mahal). The final *-abad* is Hindi for "town."

Aurich. *Town, northwestern Germany.* The town's name is of uncertain origin. The second element probably represents Middle Low German *rīke,* "realm," in the sense "district," "region." The first element may represent Old High German *ouwa,* "island," "raised land by water," referring to the damp or marshy moorland where the original settlement arose.

Aurillac. *Town, south central France.* The town derives its name from the Roman personal name *Aurelius* and the Gallo-Roman suffix *-acum.*

¹**Aurora.** *City, west central United States.* The Colorado city, a suburb of Denver, was founded in 1891 and originally named *Fletcher,* for its Canadian-born founder, Donald *Fletcher.* It received its present name, that of the Roman goddess of the dawn, in 1907. The name gained considerable popularity in the USA for its favorable associations.

²**Aurora.** *City, east central United States.* The Illinois city was laid out in 1834 and named for the Roman goddess of the dawn.

Austerlitz. *Historic town, southeastern Czech Republic.* The town, famous from Napoleon's 1805 victory against the Russian and Austrians, has a name recorded in 1243 as *Nuzedliz,* "new village," corresponding to Austria's **Neusiedl.** Its

current Czech name is *Slavkov u Brna,* "*Slavkov* near **Brno.**"

Austin. *City, southern United States.* The state capital of Texas was founded in 1839 and named in honor of the Texan pioneer Stephen F. *Austin* (1793–1836).

Australasia. *Sector of Oceania, central and South Pacific.* The name is used compositely for Australia, New Zealand, and the islands of the southwestern Pacific. It was devised in the mid-18th century from a combination of Latin *australis,* "southern" (the base of **Australia**), and **Asia,** as a term to designate lands, many then still undiscovered, that lay south of Asia.

Australia. *Island continent, southern hemisphere.* From at least the 2d century A.D., travelers' tales had told of a *terra australis incognita,* "unknown southern land," believed to exist in the southern hemisphere. Australia was sighted by the Spanish in the early 17th century, and later that century was explored by the Dutch, who called it *New Holland.* (*See also* **Western Australia.**) Eventually, in 1814, Matthew Flinders (*see* **Flinders Ranges**) published his *Voyage to Terra Australis,* in which he wrote, by way of a footnote: "Had I permitted myself any innovation upon the original term [*Terra Australis*] it would have been to convert it into Australia, as being more agreeable to the ear, and an assimilation to the name of the other great portions of the earth." (He had actually wanted to include *Australia* in the title, but his patron, Sir Joseph Banks, objected.) In 1817, Governor Lachlan Macquarie (*see* **Macquarie, Lake**), who had read Flinders' footnote, recommended the name *Australia* be adopted, and thereafter used it in official correspondence.

Austrasia *see* **Austria**

Austria. *Republic, central Europe.* The country's present name is a shortened form of its Medieval Latin name, *Marchia austriaca,* "eastern borderland," so called as it was at the eastern edge of Charlemagne's former empire. Confusingly, the name happens to suggest "south," as for **Australia,** through a coincidental similarity between Latin *australis,* "southern," and the Old German name of Austria, *Ōstarrīhi* (modern *Österreich*), "eastern kingdom." This earlier Austria was "eastern" in relation to Frankish possessions west of the Rhine, which were distinguished as the *Westarrīhi* (modern *Westerreich*), "western kingdom." After these were conquered by Clovis in the 6th century, the territory was divided into *Austrasia* ("eastern kingdom") and *Neustria* ("new western kingdom"), the latter adding French *neuf* (German *neu*), "new." It was "new" as it had been colonized by the Franks since their earlier settlement in northern Gaul. These two Frankish kingdoms, *Austrasia* and *Neustria*, respectively covering present northeastern France and parts of western and central Germany on the one hand and the area of present France west of the Meuse and north of the Loire rivers on the other, remained as rivals over the next two centuries under the Merovingian kings.

Autun. *Town, east central France*. The town arose from the 1st-century B.C. Roman fort of *Augustodunum*, so named for the Roman emperor Caesar *Augustus* (63 B.C.–A.D. 14), with Gaulish *dunon*, "hill," "fort," added. Autun is just one of many European towns named for this emperor. Others include **Aosta, Augsburg, Badajoz**, and **Saragossa**.

Auvergne. *Historic region, south central France*. The region takes its name from the *Arverni*, the Gaulish people who formerly inhabited it. Their own name is of uncertain origin. It may represent *are*, "at," and *verna*, "alder," so that they lived by an alder grove.

Auxerre. *City, central France*. The city's Gaulish name is a blend of the personal name *Autesio* and *duron*, "house," "fort."

Ava. *Historic city, central Myanmar*. The name of the former city, on the Irrawaddy River by an irrigated region of rice fields, is said to be a corruption of its original Burmese name, *Inwa*, meaning "entrance to the lake."

Avellaneda. *City, eastern Argentina*. The city, just southeast of Buenos Aires, was originally a slum settlement known by the Spanish designation of *Barracas al Sur*, "huts to the south." In 1914 it was renamed in memory of Nicolás *Avellaneda* (1837–1885), former president of Argentina.

Avernus, Lake. *Lake, south central Italy*. The lake lies in the crater of an extinct volcano. Its forbidding appearance and emissions of vapors caused it to be regarded in classical times as the mouth of Hell. Hence its name, from Greek *a-*, "without," and *ornis*, "bird," from the belief that the vapors killed birds flying over it.

Avignon. *City, southeastern France*. The city ultimately bases its name on the proto–Indoeuropean root word *ab*, "water." Avignon is on the Rhône.

Ávila. *City, central Spain*. The city's name is a shortened form of its Roman name, *Albicella*, itself from Latin *alba cella*, "white cell" (in the monastic sense).

Avon. *Historic county, southwestern England*. The former county (1974–96) took its name from the river that flows through it to the Bristol Channel. There are other rivers of the name in England, and they all derive from Celtic *abona*, "river."

Awalai. *Town, central Bahrain*. The town, developed in the 1930s by the Bahrain Oil Company, has an Arabic name meaning "high places," a former name of Bahrain itself.

Ayacucho. *City, south central Peru*. The city was founded in 1539 and originally called *Huamanga*. In 1825 it was given its present name, that of the surrounding plains, itself from a Quechua word said to mean "corner of the dead." The renaming marked the gaining of Peruvian independence following the battle on these plains of December 9, 1824, when Antonio José de Sucre (*see* **Sucre**) defeated the Spanish forces of Viceroy José de la Serna.

Aydın. *City, southwestern Turkey*. The city was known in the 13th century as *Güzelhisar*, from Turkish *güzel*, "beautiful," and *hisar*, "castle." In the 14th century it was renamed as now for the ruling *Aydın* dynasty.

Ayers Rock. *Outcrop, central Australia*. The great sandstone monolith, in Northern Territory, was named in 1873 for Sir Henry *Ayers* (1821–1897), prime minister of South Australia, which then extended this far north. The rock is sacred to Aborigines, and is increasingly known by its Aboriginal name, *Uluru*, said to mean "howling."

Aylesbury. *Town, south central England*. The Buckinghamshire town has an Old English name meaning "*Ægel's* fortified place," with the personal name followed by *burh*, "fort."

Ayodhya. *City, northern India*. The ancient city, in Uttar Pradesh state, derives its name from Sanskrit *ayodhyā*, "invincible," from *a-*, "not," and *yodhya*, "to be warred against," from *yudh*, "war." As *Oudh*, pronounced to rhyme with "loud," the name is also that of a former state. (Hence Lord Dalhousie's punning dispatch, "*Vovi*," Latin for "I have vowed," i.e. "I have Oudh," referring to his annexation of Oudh in 1856, following Sir Charles Napier's earlier telegraphic quip, "*Peccavi*," "I have sinned," i.e. "I have Sind," after the British victory of Hyderabad in **Sind** in 1843.)

Ayr. *Town, southwestern Scotland*. The town takes its name from the river on which it stands. The river name derives from a pre–Celtic word *ar*, meaning simply "water." Names based on the same root word include **Aragon** in Spain and **Arno** in Italy.

Aytos. *Town, eastern Bulgaria*. The town derives its name from its medieval fortress of *Aetos*, its own Greek name meaning "eagle."

Ayutthaya. *City, south central Thailand*. The city has a name of identical origin and meaning to that of **Ayodhya**. It was founded in 1350 and was the Siamese capital until 1767, when it was destroyed by the Burmese. Its past history has given it the alternate name of *Krung Kau*, "former capital." Its full formal name is *Phra Nakhon Si Ayutthaya*, literally "lord town of the good and invincible one," from Thai *phra*, an honorific meaning "lord," "god," *nakhon*, "town," *si*, "good," and the present name.

Azamgarh. *Town, northern India*. The town, in Uttar Pradesh state, was founded in 1665 by a local chief, *Azam* Khan, and is named for him, with Hindi *garh* meaning "fortress."

Azania *see* **South Africa**

Azerbaijan. *Republic, central Asia*. The name is of disputed origin. It may derive from Old Persian *Aturpatakan*, itself from Greek *Atropatene*, from the personal name *Atropates*, that of the general who proclaimed the independence of this land in the time of Alexander the Great. But a source in local words *azer*, "fire," and *baydjan*, the latter a form of Iranian *baykān*, "guardian," seems more probable. The reference would be to the former temples of fire worshipers here.

Azogues. *City, south central Ecuador*. The city derives its name from Spanish *azogue*, "mercury," found locally. *Cp.* **Almadén**.

Azores. *Island group, North Atlantic*. The islands were discovered by the Portuguese in 1492 and named for the many goshawks here, from *açores*, plural of *açor*, the Portuguese word for this bird.

Azov, Sea of. *Sea, southeastern Europe*. The sea, between Ukraine and Russia north of the Black Sea, probably takes its name from the town of *Azov* at its eastern end. This in turn may go back to East Turkish *azak*, "low," alluding to its location, but it is popularly derived from *Azum* or *Azuf*, the name of a Polovtsian prince killed in 1067 when the town was captured.

Az-Zarqa. *City, northern Jordan*. Jordan's second largest city takes its name from the river here, a tributary of the Jordan, known in Arabic as *an-nahr az-zarqā'*, "the blue river." Its biblical name was *Jabbok* (Genesis 32:23), from Hebrew *baqoq*, "to flow," "to depopulate."

Az-Zubayr. *Town, southeastern Iraq*. The arose around a mosque dedicated to the memory of *Zubayr*, one of the companions of Muhammad, who was killed in the Battle of the Camels (658).

Baalbek. *Historic city, eastern Lebanon*. The ancient Syrian city has a name that probably derives from that of the Phoenician sun god, *Baal*, with *bakk* meaning "city." The city was a center of the worship of Baal, and was renamed by the Greeks as *Heliopolis*, "sun city."

Baba Budan Range. *Mountain range, southern India*. The range, an outlier of the Western Ghats in Karnataka state, was originally known as *Chandragiri*, "mountains of the moon." It was renamed as now in the 17th century for *Baba Budan*, the Muslim pilgrim who introduced coffee-growing to India.

Babel *see* **Babylon**

Bab el Mandeb. *Strait, southwestern Asia*. The strait, between the Red Sea and the Indian Ocean, has an Arabic name representing *bāb al-mandab*, "gate of the tears." The reference is to the hazards to navigation that the passage formerly presented.

Babenhausen. *Town, western Germany*. The name, first recorded in 1236 as *Babinhus*, means "*Babo*'s house(s)."

Babylon. *Historic city, central Iraq*. The ancient but now ruined city, formerly capital of Babylonia, derives its name from Akkadian *Bāb-ilān*, "gate of the gods." Its name is identical in origin to that of the biblical city of *Babel*, site of the "Tower of Babel," although here the Akkadian original was *Bāb-īlu*, "gate of God." *Babel* evolved from the Hebrew form of this, whereas the name *Babylon* developed under Greek influence.

Bacău. *City, east central Romania*. The city, first mentioned in 1408, arose from a customs post at a point where trade routes merged to cross the Bistriţa River here. Hence its name, based on Romanian *bac*, "ferry."

Bačka. *Historic region, northwestern Serbia*. The region, approximating to western Vojvodina, derives its name from Serbo-Croat *bač*, "shepherd," denoting an area of pastureland.

Backnang. *Town, southern Germany*. The second part of the name derives from Old High German *wang*, "field," "meadow." The first part probably represents a personal name based on Old High German *bāga*, "quarrel."

Back River. *River, northern Canada*. The river, in Nunavut, has a name that suggests it flows "back," as if in a reverse direction or one different from that expected. It is in fact named for the British explorer George *Back* (1796–1878), who helped trace the Arctic coastline of northern Canada and who discovered it in 1833 when searching for the missing British explorer John Ross. The river's alternate name is the *Great Fish River*.

Bactria. *Historic region, southwestern Asia*. The

ancient territory, represented by modern Afghanistan, Pakistan, and the countries of former Soviet Central Asia, derives its name from the village now known as *Balkh*, near Wazirabad in Afghanistan. Its own name is that of the river here, and means "marshy place" (*cp.* **Balkhash, Lake**).

Badajoz. *City, southwestern Spain.* The city, near the border with Portugal, derives its name from Arabic *badākhus*, a corruption of its original Roman name of *Pax Augusta*, "peace of *Augustus*," referring to the emperor Caesar *Augustus*, and implying a colony subservient to him.

Badakhshan. *Province, northeastern Afghanistan.* The name is traditionally explained to mean "place of rubies," from Iranian *badash*, "ruby," and although this may simply be an attempt to explain an otherwise obscure name, the region is in fact noted for its precious stones, including ruby deposits. The same name is found in the *Badakhshan* autonomous viloyat north of the border in Tajikistan.

Bad Cannstatt. *Town and resort, southwestern Germany.* The resort, now a district of Stuttgart, arose on the site of a Roman camp by an old crossing of the Neckar River. The second part of the main name is Old High German *stat*, "place," "settlement." The first part is of uncertain origin. It may represent an old German personal name *Canto* or perhaps derive from a shortened form of Celtic *Condate*, "confluence," referring to the meeting of the Nesenbach with the Neckar nearby. The first word is German *Bad*, "bath," denoting the mineral springs here.

Bad Dürkheim. *City, west central Germany.* The city, a health resort (hence *Bad*, "bath"), has a name recorded in 778 as *Turincheim*, "dwelling place of the *Thuringians*," implying that these people (*see* **Thuringia**) founded the original settlement here.

Baden. *Historic state, southwestern Germany.* The state, now part of **Baden-Württemberg**, has a name that means simply "baths," referring to the natural springs here. *Cp.* **Baden-Baden, Bath**.

Baden-Baden. *Town, southwestern Germany.* The spa town, in the Black Forest, has a name that refers both to its own natural springs (German *Baden*, "baths") and those more generally of the former state of **Baden**, in which it lies. The name specifies it as the "Baden" Baden, as distinct from any other place of this name with springs in Germany. There were Roman baths here in the 3d century A.D.

Badenweiler. *Village and resort, southwestern Germany.* The internationally famed health resort arose on the site of a Roman thermal establishment first revealed in 1784. Its name thus basically means "(place by the) baths." The second part of the name was probably influenced by nearby *Oberweiler* and *Niederweiler*, where *-weiler* means "settlement."

Baden-Württemberg. *State, southwestern Germany.* The state was formed in 1952 on the merger of three former states: *Württemberg-Baden, Württemberg-Hohenzollern* (*see* **Hohenzollern**), and **Baden**. *Württemberg* took its name from the medieval castle that was the seat of the Württemberg dynasty of counts. Their own name added Germanic *burg*, "fort," either to an Old German personal name *Wirtino* or to a Celtic placename *Virodunum*, from the Celtic personal name *Viros* and Gaulish *dunon*, "fort."

Bad Gandersheim. *City and resort, north central Germany.* The health resort (*Bad*, "bath"), with its saline springs, derives its name from a settlement (*heim*) on the nearby *Gande* River. Its own name is of uncertain origin, although it could be based on non–Indoeuropean *gand*, "scree," "gravel," as possibly for **Ghent**, Belgium.

Bad Godesberg. *Town and resort, western Germany.* The town, now a district of Bonn, arose at the foot of a hill called *Godesberg*, dedicated to the Germanic war god *Woden* (but later to St. Michael), and fortified with a castle in 1210 by the archbishop of Cologne. Mineral springs were discovered in 1790 and gave the first word of the name (*Bad*, "bath").

Bad Harzburg. *City and resort, northeastern Germany.* The city, a spa (*Bad*, "bath"), derives its name from its location on a slope of the Upper **Harz** Mountains, where it arose in the 14th century around a castle (*Burg*) built by the emperor Henry IV in 1064.

Bad Homburg. *City and resort, central Germany.* The city, below the Taunus Mountains, takes its name from the castle of *Hohenberg*, "high castle," built in the 12th century. Its full name is *Bad Homburg vor der Höhe*, where the addition, "before the height," comes from an old name of the Taunus (*die Höhe*, "the height"). The mineral springs (*Bad*, "bath") here date back to Roman times.

Bad Ischl. *Town and resort, central Austria.* The town, a noted spa (*Bad*, "bath") since 1822, lies at the confluence of the Traun and *Ischler* Ache rivers, the latter basing its name on Indoeuropean *is*, "to rush," "to race," referring to its rapid current.

Bad Kreuznach. *City and resort, west central Germany.* The city arose on the site of a Roman fortress called *Cruciniacum*, from the Romano-

Celtic personal name *Crucinus* and the suffix *-acum*. The present name evolved from this, and is not related to German *Kreuz*, "cross." The first word of the name (*Bad*, "bath") denotes the warm saline springs here, first exploited as baths in 1817.

Badlands. *Region, north central United States.* The name has been applied to many rugged and eroded areas in the United States, but especially that in southwestern South Dakota, which French-Canadian trappers called *terres mauvaises* "bad lands," when experiencing difficulty traversing it.

Bad Mergentheim. *City and resort, south central Germany.* The city, with long-existing mineral springs (*Bad*, "bath"), has a name recorded in 1058 as *Mergintaim comitatus*, "*Merginta's* countship," apparently from a female personal name based on *Maria*, referring to the Virgin *Mary*.

Bad Nauheim. *City and resort, central Germany.* The city, dating from the 13th century, has a name meaning simply "new settlement." The first word of the name (*Bad*, "bath") refers to the famous saline springs here, utilized from 1858 to treat heart and nerve diseases.

Bad Neuenahr-Ahrweiler. *Town and resort, western Germany.* The present town was formed in 1969 from the merger of *Bad Neuenahr* and *Ahrweiler*, both places taking their name from the *Ahr* River here. The former name thus means "new place on the Ahr with springs" and the latter "settlement on the Ahr." The river name itself derives from Indoeuropean *ar*, "water," "river."

Bad Oeynhausen. *City, northwestern Germany.* The city arose around saltworks opened in 1739. In 1839 the Prussian geologist and mineralogist Baron Karl von *Oeynhausen* (c.1795–1865) discovered medicinal springs there, and in 1847 the new spa (*Bad*, "bath") was named in his honor. The barons took their title from the village of *Oeynhausen* near Höxter, its own name meaning "*Ago*'s houses."

Bad Reichenhall. *City, southern Germany.* The city arose on a site where saline springs (*Bad*, "bath") had long been exploited, with salt mined since Roman times. Hence its name, meaning basically "rich salt." (*See also* **Halle.**)

Bad Salzuflen. *City, northwestern Germany.* The city and spa (*Bad*, "bath") arose in the 12th century by the saltworks (*Salz*, "salt") at a place called *Ufflen*, from an element *uf-* of uncertain meaning and the dative plural of Middle Low German *lō*, "wood" (as for **Gütersloh**).

Baffin Island. *Island, northern Canada.* The largest island of the Canadian Arctic Archipelago, in Nunavut, takes its name from the English explorer William *Baffin* (c.1584–1622), who carried out research here in 1614 in his quest for the Northwest Passage. The island was originally known as *Baffin Land*.

Baghdad. *Capital of Iraq.* The city has an ancient pre–Islamic name that probably means "gift of God," with *Bagh* related to Russian *bog*, "god," and *dad* indirectly related to English *donor*. Marco Polo, in the 13th century, recorded the name as *Baudac*. The Old French form of the name, *Baldac*, gave the name of the English town of *Baldock*, Hertfordshire, founded in the 12th century by the Knights Templars.

Bagneux. *Town, northern France.* The town, now a suburb of Paris, derives its name from Latin *balneum*, "bath." There are various places with similar names in France, such as *Bagnères*, *Bagnol*, *Bagnolet*, and the like, to serve as reminders of the Roman baths that once existed.

Baguio. *City, northern Philippines.* The former summer capital of the Philippines, in western Luzon, derives its name from Spanish *bahia*, "bay," referring to the Lingayen Gulf, above which it stands (although some distance inland).

Bahamas. *Island state, northwestern West Indies.* The islands, north of Cuba, are said to have a name deriving from Spanish *baja mar*, "low sea," referring to the shallowness of the water here. More likely, however, the name is a form of the local name *Guanahani*, of unknown origin and meaning.

Bahawalpur. *City, eastern Pakistan.* The city was founded in 1748 by Muhammad *Bahawal* Khan and is named for him, with Hindi *pur*, "town," added.

Bahçelievler. *District of Istanbul, northwestern Turkey.* The name, meaning "houses with gardens," relates to the time when the district was a village, with buildings that had their own orchards. The origin is thus in Turkish *bahçe*, "garden," *-li*, "with," and *ev*, "house," plural *evler*.

Bahia. *State, eastern Brazil.* The name represents Portuguese *baía*, "bay," referring to the *Bahía de Todos os Santos*, "All Saints' bay," that lies off the coast here. The bay is itself named for its discovery by Portuguese explorers on November 1, 1501, All Saints' Day. The state capital is **Salvador**, long known as *Bahia* for the same reason.

Bahía Blanca. *City and port, eastern Argentina.* The city takes its name, Spanish for "white bay," from the bay at the head of which it lies. This was itself named for its light-colored sands by Spanish explorers in the 18th century, but the name was not officially adopted for the city until 1895.

Bahrain. *Island group, southern Persian Gulf.* The island kingdom, east of Saudi Arabia, has an Arabic name, representing *al-baḥrayn*, "the two seas," from *al*, "the," and *baḥrayn*, the dual form of *baḥr*, "sea." Bahrain is in the middle of a bay, so that its "two seas" lie respectively east and west of it.

Bahr al-Ghazal. *River, southwestern Sudan.* The river, a tributary of the Nile, has an Arabic name meaning "river of gazelles." *Cp.* **Bahr az-Zaraf.**

Bahr az-Zaraf. *River, south central Sudan.* The river, a tributary of the Nile, has an Arabic name meaning "river of giraffes." *Cp.* **Bahr al-Ghazal.**

Bahr Yusef. *Watercourse, east central Egypt.* The former dry bed of the Nile, used for irrigation along its course, has an Arabic name meaning "river of *Joseph*," presumably from a traditional association with the biblical *Joseph*, who was sold by his brothers to merchants on their way into Egypt (Genesis 37:28).

Baia Mare. *Town, northwestern Romania.* The town's name seems to mean "big bath," from Romanian *baia*, "bath," and *mare*, "big." However, the reference is not to baths but to mines, and the city is known for its lead and zinc smelting plants. This sense is confirmed by its Hungarian name, *Nagybánya*, "big mine," from *nagy*, "big," and *bánya*, "mine." The misinterpretation resulted from confusion of the Hungarian word for "mine" with the Romanian word for "bath."

Baia Sprie. *Town, northwestern Romania.* The town seems to have a name meaning "upper bath," from Romanian *baia*, "bath," and *sprie*, "upper." But it really means "upper mine," as confirmed by its Hungarian name *Felsőbánya*, from *felső*, "upper," and *bánya*, "mine." The name relates to that of **Baia Mare**, and the two towns are only 5 miles (8 km) apart.

Baie-Comeau. *Town and river port, eastern Canada.* The town, in Quebec on the St. Lawrence River, was founded in 1937 by Col. Robert R. McCormick, owner of the *Chicago Tribune*, and named for the local geologist and naturalist Napoléon-Alexandre *Comeau*. French *baie* is "bay."

Baikal, Lake. *Lake, southern Russia.* The Siberian lake has a name of Turkic origin, representing *bol*, "rich," and *göl*, "lake." The reference is to the lake's abundance of fish, especially sturgeon, which yield caviar.

Băile Herculane. *Spa, southwestern Romania.* Romania's oldest health resort dates from Roman times, when in A.D. 105 Trajan's legions, on cam-

paign to the Dacian capital, Sarmizeguta, discovered hot springs here. The Romans subsequently built a fortified settlement here called *Media* ("middle") and used the waters for curative purposes, naming them *Ad aquas Herculi sacras ad Mediam*, "sacred waters of Hercules at Media." Hence the modern name, the first word of which is Romanian for "the baths," "the springs."

Baitoushan. *Mountain, northeastern China.* The mountain, on the border between China and North Korea, has a name meaning "white-headed mountain," referring to its snow cover, from Chinese *bái*, "white," *tóu*, "head," and *shān*, "mountain." The Korean form of the name is *Paektu-san*.

Bakersfield. *City, western United States.* The California city was founded in 1869 by Thomas *Baker*, who reclaimed swamplands here, and is named for him.

Bakhchisaray. *City, southern Ukraine.* The city, in the Crimea, has a name of Turkic origin meaning "garden palace," i.e. a palace with gardens, from words related to Turkish *bahçe*, "garden," and *saray*, "palace." The name arose in the late 15th century when Bakhchisaray became the capital of the Tatar khanate. The Ukrainian form of the name is *Bakhchysaray*.

Baku. *Capital of Azerbaijan.* The city and port has a name that may derive from Old Persian *badkuba*, "windward," referring to its location on the western shore of the Caspian Sea.

Balaklava. *Town and port, southern Ukraine.* The town, in the southwestern Crimea, has a name that is said to derive from Turkish *balık*, "fish," and *yuva*, "nest," referring to the rich stocks of fish in the Black Sea here. But the second word of this could hardly give the present name, and as for many other places in this region, the true origin may be in a Greek name such as *Palakion*, with the Turks adapting this to give an apparently appropriate meaning. A derivation in Italian *bella chiava*, "beautiful quay," is attractive but linguistically untenable.

Balassagyarmat. *City, northern Hungary.* The first part of the name is the personal name *Balassa*, a form of *Balázsa* ("Blaise"). The second part is the tribal name *Gyarmat*.

Balaton, Lake. *Lake, western Hungary.* The lake probably has a name of Slavic origin, from a word related to Russian *boloto*, "swamp." Although the largest lake in central Europe, it is shallow in places, with a maximum depth of only 36 ft (11 m).

Balboa. *Town and port, south central Panama.* The town, at the southern (Pacific) entrance to the Panama Canal, was founded in 1914 and named for the Spanish explorer Vasco Núñez de *Balboa* (1475–1519), the first European to sight the Pacific (from "a peak in Darien").

Balchik. *Town, eastern Bulgaria.* The town, on the Black Sea coast, is said to derive its name from Turkish *balçık,* "wet clay," "sticky mud."

Bâle *see* **Basel**

Balearic Islands. *Island group, western Mediterranean.* The name of the Spanish islands probably goes back to pre–Indoeuropean *bal,* "shining," "white," referring to their bright appearance. Some authorities, however, trace the name to a Phoenician word ultimately related to English *ballistic,* giving a meaning "islands of slingers." The inhabitants are said to have combated the Romans in the 2d century B.C. by hurling rocks at them.

Balkans. *Mountainous region, southeastern Europe.* The name is properly that of the Balkan Peninsula, between the Adriatic, Aegean, and Black seas, and probably derives from Turkic *balkan,* "mountain." This would itself have specifically referred to what is now **Botev Peak,** the highest mountain in the range known as the *Balkan Mountains.* This range, running across Bulgaria, is also known by the Bulgarian name of *Stara Planina,* literally "old range," with "old" implying "prime," "chief," "greatest." The range was also formerly known as *Haemus,* supposedly from the mythical character of this name, the husband of Rhodope. (*See* **Rhodope.**)

Balkh *see* **Bactria**

Balkhash, Lake. *Lake, east central Kazakhstan.* The lake probably has a name of Tatar origin meaning "marshy place," although some sources prefer an origin in a Mongolian word meaning "long lake." Either is descriptively appropriate for the lake, which is 376 miles (605 km) from west to east.

Ballarat. *City, southern Australia.* The city, in Victoria, was founded in 1852 and adopted the local Aboriginal name of the location, perhaps based on *balla,* "elbow."

Ballymena. *Town, northeastern Northern Ireland.* The town, in Co. Antrim, has a name representing Irish *An Baile Meánach,* "the middle town." Ballymena is near the center of the county at a point where many roads meet. However, its name dates back to a time before the county was established, so therefore means more generally "central place," "place where roads meet."

Baltic Sea. *Sea, northern Europe.* The sea, an arm of the Atlantic connecting with the North Sea, is said to take its name from a Lithuanian or Lettish word meaning "white" (as popularly for **Albion**), or from a Slavic word meaning "marsh" (as for Lake **Balaton**). A source in a Danish word related to English *belt* has also been proposed. This last would refer to the strait formed by the Skagerrak and Kattegat, between Sweden and Denmark, at the southwestern end of the Baltic. The German name of the Baltic is *Ostsee,* "eastern sea," by contrast with the **North Sea** to the west.

Baltimore. *City, eastern United States.* The Maryland city takes its name from Cecilius Calvert, 2d Baron *Baltimore* (1605–1675), who in 1632 received the charter that granted him the possession of Maryland. The city itself was founded in 1729. Lord Baltimore's title derives from the small port of this name in southern Ireland, where the Calverts had their family seat. Its own name represents Irish *Baile na Tighe Mór,* "townland of the big house."

Baluchistan. *Region, western Asia.* The region, comprising territory now in Iran and Pakistan, has an Urdu name meaning "*Baluchi* country." The *Baluchi* were the original inhabitants, their own name coming from Urdu *baluch,* "peak," as they were mountain dwellers. The name is also that of a province in southwestern Pakistan. The final *-stan* is as for **Pakistan** itself.

Bamako. *Capital of Mali.* The name of the city is said to represent Bambara *Bamma-ko,* "behind *Bamma,*" the latter being a personal name. Other sources derive the name from *bamma-ko,* "crocodile affair," alluding to the custom, now thankfully defunct, of annually offering a live human victim to the crocodiles of the Niger.

Bamberg. *City, south central Germany.* The name is that of the ancestral castle of the *Babenberg* family, first mentioned in 906. Their own name means "*Babo*'s castle," presumably referring to their progenitor. It is not known whether they were related to the Franconian Babenberg family who were the first margraves of Austria (976–1156).

Banat. *Historic region, east central Europe.* The region, now in Hungary and Romania, derives its name from Serbian *ban,* "lord," referring to its governor in former times.

Banda Oriental. *Region, southern Uruguay.* The name is Spanish for "eastern shore," the shore being that of the Río de la Plata. The name was used of Uruguay and the southeastern corner of Uruguay in the Spanish colonial period.

Bandar Abbas. *City and port, southern Iran.* The city, on the Strait of Hormuz, was founded in 1623 by Shah *Abbas* I to replace the city of

Hormuz, which had been captured by the Portuguese early in the 16th century. The name is thus Iranian for "port of *Abbas*."

Bandar-e Khomeyni. *Town and port, southwestern Iran.* The port, at the head of the Persian Gulf, was opened in 1932 and given a name meaning "port of the town of the shah," referring to Reza *Shah* Pahlavi (1878–1944), shah of Iran from 1925 to 1941. In 1979 the Islamic revolutionaries renamed it as now in honor of Ayatollah *Khomeini* (?1900–1989), elected head of state that year after the fall of the last shah of Iran, Muhammad Reza Shah, son of Reza Shah Pahlavi.

Bandar Seri Begawan. *Capital of Brunei.* The town, originally *Brunei Town*, was given its present name in 1970 by Hassanal Bolkiah, Sultan of Brunei, in honor of his father, Sir Omar Ali Saifuddin (1918–1986), who abdicated in 1967 in favor of his son. *Bandar* is the Malay word for "port" and *Seri Begawan* was the honorary title of the abdicating sultan, meaning "illustrious," "blessed."

Bandırma. *Town and port, northwestern Turkey.* The town's name is a corruption of its ancient Greek name *Panormos*. This means "safe anchorage," from *pan*, "all," and *ormos*, literally "cord," "chain," hence "roadstead" (as a chain of boats), "anchorage." The name implies a safe haven for all ships. *Cp.* **Palermo**.

Bandundu. *City, western Democratic Republic of Congo.* The city adopted its present Bantu ethnic name in 1966. Before this it was known as *Banningville*, for the Belgian government official Émile *Banning* (1836–1898), a participant in the creation of the Congo Free State in 1885.

Bandung. *City, southwestern Java.* The name represents Malay *bandong*, "embankment." The city was founded in 1810 on an elevated site amid volcanoes and high mountains.

Bangalore. *City, southern India.* The capital of Karnataka state derives its name from the same ethnic word that gave the names of **Bengal** and **Bangladesh**. Although some way south of present Bengal, Bangalore arose in a region formerly inhabited by *Bengali* speakers.

Bangka. *Island, western Indonesia.* The island, off the east coast of Sumatra, has a Malayan name meaning "marshy," "swampy," a description that properly applies only to its coastal regions.

Bangkok. *Capital of Thailand.* The city has a Thai name said to mean "region of olive trees," from *bang*, "region," and *kok*, "olive tree." The indigenous name of Bangkok, however, is *Krung*

Thep (pronounced "Grung Tape"), "city of gods," from Thai *krung*, "city," "capital," and *theph*, "god." This name, traditionally translated "city of angels," was earlier applied descriptively to the former capital, **Ayutthaya**. An alternate name is *Phra Nakhon*, from *phra*, "god," "lord," an honorific title, and *nakhon*, "city." The official full Thai name of Bangkok is: *krung theph phra mahanakhon amon ratanakosin mahinthara ayuthaya mahadilok phop noppharat ratchathanī burīrom udomratchaniwet mahasathan amon piman awatan sathit sakkathattiya witsanukam prasit*, which may be rendered: "city of gods, the great city, the residence of the Emerald Buddha, the impregnable city (of Ayutthaya) of the god Indra, the grand capital of the world endowed with nine precious gems, the happy city, abounding in enormous royal palaces which resemble the heavenly abode where reigns the reincarnated god, a city given by Indra and built by Vishnukarn." And who can say fairer than that?

Bangladesh. *Republic, southern Asia.* The republic, bounded mostly by India, was originally known as *East Pakistan*. Its present name, which it took in 1971, is Bengali for "Bengali country," from *bangla*, "Bengali," and *desh*, "country."

[1]**Bangor.** *City, northern Wales.* The city arose as a monastic settlement and has a name representing Welsh *bangor*, a term for the upper row of rods in a wattle fence, and hence for a monastic enclosure.

[2]**Bangor.** *Town, eastern Northern Ireland.* The town, in Co. Down, has the Irish name *Beannchar*, "horned," "peaked," from *beann*, "horn," "prong." This is the equivalent of the Welsh name of [1]**Bangor**, so has the same sense. It is uncertain whether the Irish place actually adopted the name of the Welsh one, but they both had noted monastic establishments, each founded in the 6th century.

[3]**Bangor.** *City, northeastern United States.* The Maine city was settled in 1769 and was at first called *Kenduskeag Plantation* and *Sunbury* before taking its present name in 1791. It is said to derive from *Bangor*, the favorite hymn tune of one Reverend Seth Noble.

Bangui. *Capital of Central African Republic.* The city was founded in 1889 at the top of the first great rapid on the **Ubangi** River. Hence its name, Bobangui for "rapid."

Bangweulu, Lake. *Lake, northwestern Zambia.* The shallow lake has a Bantu name meaning "large water."

Banihal Pass. *Pass, northern India.* The lofty

pass, in the Pir Panjal Range, has a Kashmiri name meaning "blizzard," referring to its frequent weather conditions. A tunnel here takes the main road from Jammu to Srinagar.

Baniyas. *Village, southwestern Syria*. The village, near the source of the Jordan, had the Greek name of *Paneias*, ultimately from the Greek god *Pan*, to whom a grotto here was dedicated.

Banja Luka. *City, northeastern Bosnia-Hercegovina*. The first word of the city's name represents the adjectival form of Serbo-Croat *ban*, "lord," the title (of Iranian origin) of the governor of a military district in Hungarian border territory. This particular *banat* was in the *luka*, "bend," of the Vrbas River.

Banjarmasin. *City and port, south central Indonesia*. The town, on an island between two rivers on the south coast of Borneo, has a Malayan name meaning "many waters."

Banjul. *Capital of Gambia*. The town and port has an indigenous name that arose from a misunderstanding. When the first Portuguese colonists came to this part of Africa in the 15th century, they asked local people what it was called. The inhabitants thought they were being asked what they were making, and replied "*Bangjulo*," "rope matting." The visitors duly transcribed this as the name of the region. The town was actually founded by British colonists in 1816, and they named it *Bathurst*, for Henry *Bathurst*, 3d Earl Bathurst (1762–1834), British colonial secretary. (*Cp.* **Bathurst**.) The present name was officially adopted in 1973, although it was in local use long before this.

Banks Island. *Island, northern Canada*. The island, in the Northwest Territories, was so named in honor of the British naturalist Sir Joseph *Banks* (1743–1820), president of the Royal Society and a member of Captain Cook's voyage around the world (1768–71).

Banks Islands. *Island group, northern Vanuatu*. The islands were discovered in 1793 by the English naval officer William Bligh, who named them for his patron, Sir Joseph *Banks* (*see* **Banks Island**).

Banská Bystrica. *Town, central Slovakia*. The first word of the name is Slovak *banská*, an adjectival form of the word for "bath," referring to the winter and summer resort here. The second word is a common Slavic river name meaning "rapid" (*cp.* **Bistriţa**). The Hungarian form of the name is *Besztercebánya* (with *bánya*, "bath"). The German name is *Neusohl*, with a different river name.

Baqubah. *City, central Iraq*. The city stands on an ancient site dating back to pre–Islamic

times. Its name represents Aramaic *bāya 'kūbā*, "*Jacob*'s house."

Bar. *Town and port, southwestern Montenegro*. The town's name represents a single syllable of its alternate name, *Antivari*, meaning "opposite **Bari**." The reference is to its location across the Adriatic Sea from that Italian city and port. Ships still ply between the two ports.

Barataria Bay. *Bay, southern United States*. The bay in the Gulf of Mexico, in Louisiana, derives its name from Spanish *baratear*, "to cheat," "to deceive," referring to its entrance, which is made through a narrow channel largely blocked by islands.

Barbados. *Island, southeastern West Indies*. The island has a Spanish name translating as "bearded," from *barbados*, plural of *barbado*. The name was given by 16th-century Spanish explorers for the beard-like leaves or trails of moss on the fig trees that grew in abundance here. The name does not thus refer to the bearded inhabitants, as sometimes said.

Barbary Coast. *Coastal region, northwestern Africa*. The region derives its name from the *Berbers* that are its indigenous people. Their own name, of uncertain origin, was assimilated to Greek *barbaros*, "foreign," "ignorant," a term used for those who spoke a different language and therefore "babbled" or were "barbarians." (It was this region that gave the name of San Francisco's notorious *Barbary Coast*.) *See also* **Berbera**.

Barcelona. *City and port, northeastern Spain*. The city is said to take its name from the Carthaginian general Hamilcar *Barca*, its traditional 3d-century B.C. founder.

Barents Sea. *Sea, northern Europe*. The sea, part of the Arctic Ocean north of Norway and Russia, takes its name from Willem *Barents* (c.1550–1597), the Dutch explorer who sought a northeast passage here between the Atlantic and the Pacific, and who perished here in his quest.

Bari. *City and port, southeastern Italy*. The city, known to the Romans as *Barium*, is believed to derive its name from Latin (and Greek) *baris*, a word of Egyptian origin meaning "boat." The reference would be to its important role as a port. *See also* **Bar**.

Barkly Tableland. *Region, northern Australia*. The region, a grassy upland mostly in Northern Territory, is named for Sir Henry *Barkly* (1815–1898), British colonial governor of Victoria (1856–63).

Bar-le-Duc. *Town, northeastern France*. The town was known in the 6th century by the Latin name of *Castrum Barrum,* "camp of *Barrum,*" the latter word deriving from pre–Celtic *barr,* "height." It became the capital of a county in 954, and in 1354 the counts of Bar assumed the higher title of *duke* (French *duc*). Hence the present name, where the addition serves to distinguish this *Bar* from others.

Barletta. *City and port, southeastern Italy.* The city, known in Roman times as *Barulum,* when it served as the port and bathing resort for Canusium (modern Canosa di Puglia), has a name meaning "little **Bari,**" for the larger port some 35 miles (56 km) down the Adriatic coast.

Barmen. *Town, western Germany.* The town probably derives its name from Low German *Berme,* "dyke wall," "embankment," referring to former defensive walls here. Barmen amalgamated with other local towns in 1929 to form the present city of **Wuppertal.**

Barmer. *Town, northwestern India.* The town, in Rajasthan state, is said to have been founded in the 13th century. It was originally named *Bahadamer,* "hillfort of *Bahada,*" for *Bahada,* a local rajah. The name was subsequently contracted as now.

Barnaul. *City, south central Russia.* The city, founded in 1738, takes its name from the *Barnaulka* River, which enters the Ob here. The river name is said to be of Ket origin, meaning "river of wolves," from *boruan,* "wolves," and *ul,* "river."

Barnsley. *Town, northern England.* The former South Yorkshire town has an Old English name meaning *"Beorn's* clearing." It is not known who *Beorn* was, but his name was probably a short form of a longer name such as *Beornmōd.*

Baroda *see* **Vadodara**

Barrackpore. *Town, northeastern India.* The West Bengal town is said to take its name from the troops stationed in *barracks* here since 1772, with Hindi *pur,* "town," added.

Barrancabermeja. *City, north central Colombia.* The city derives its name from Spanish *barrancas bermejas,* "reddish cliffs," referring to the bluffs here on the Magdalena River. *Cp.* **Barranco.**

Barranco. *City, western Peru.* The city, now a district of Lima, was founded as a beach resort in 1874. Its name is Spanish for "cliff," referring to its elevated site, 213 feet (65 m) above sea level.

Barrie. *City, southern Canada.* The city, in Ontario, was settled in 1812 and is said to be named for Commodore Robert *Barrie,* British commander of a naval squadron at nearby Kingston.

Barron. *River, northeastern Australia.* The river, in Queensland, was so named in 1870 for T.H. *Barron,* a chief police clerk.

Barrow Strait. *Strait, northern Canada.* The strait, in Nunavut, was discovered in 1819 and named in honor of Sir John *Barrow* (1764–1843), a British patron of Arctic exploration.

Barry. *Town, southeastern Wales.* The town, in the Vale of Glamorgan, derives its name from Welsh *barr,* "hill," describing Barry Island here.

Barsinghausen. *Town, western Germany.* The name, recorded in 991 as *Berchinghusen,* means "settlement of *Berko's* people." The present *s* for *k* in the personal name probably came about through so-called zetacism, a characteristic of western Old Low German.

Barta'a. *Village, Israel/West Bank.* The village was founded at the end of the 19th century and named for a sheikh buried on the hill above. The 1949 Armistice line between Israel and Jordan divided the village so that it is now half in Israel and half in the West Bank.

Bartle Frere, Mt. *Mountain, northeastern Australia.* Queensland's highest peak was named in 1873 for Sir Henry *Bartle* Edward *Frere* (1815–1884), commonly called Sir *Bartle Frere,* Welsh-born governor of Bombay.

Basel. *City, northwestern Switzerland.* The city was founded as a Roman settlement in A.D. 44, and originally had the name *Robur,* from Latin *roburetum,* "oak grove." In 374 it became the fortress of the Roman emperor Valentinian I, and was then renamed *Basilia* (*Basilea*), from Greek *basilea,* "royal," and this gave the present name. The French form of the name is *Bâle,* and an older form of this, *Basle,* is still sometimes used by English speakers.

Bashkortostan. *Republic, western Russia.* The republic has a Turkic name meaning "land of the *Bashkorts,*" these being the region's indigenous people. Their own name may derive from Turkish *baş,* "head," and *kurt,* "wolf," referring to the wolf as their totemic animal, or a representation of a wolf's head as their symbol for it. The republic was formerly familiar as *Bashkiria.*

Basilicata. *Region, southern Italy.* The region takes its name from the *basilico,* or official of the Byzantine emperor, who ruled in medieval times.

Basingstoke. *Town, southern England.* The Hampshire town has an Old English name, the *-stoke* representing *stoc,* "outlying farm," meaning a farm dependent on another. In this case it was dependent on the village now known as *Old Basing,* east of the town. Its own name means "*Basa's* people," after the Anglo-Saxon who held land here.

Basque Country. *Region, northern Spain.* The region is named for its indigenous people, the *Basques*, who inhabit an area of the western Pyrenees in northern Spain and southern France. Their own name represents Basque *euskara* or *eskuara*. This contains a basic element *-sk-* which is believed to relate to maritime people or sailors, and which is also found in the name of the *Etruscans* (*see* **Etruria**). The Basque Country is bounded on the north by the Bay of Biscay. The Romans knew the region as *Vasconia*, a Latin form of the same name. The Basque name of the region is *Euskadi*, and the Spanish name *País Vasco*.

Basra. *City and port, southeastern Iraq.* Iraq's principal port, on the Shatt-al-Arab delta, has an Arabic name representing *al-baṣra*, "the soft," referring to the soft soil here.

Basse-Terre. *Capital of Guadeloupe.* The city's name is also that of the western island of Guadeloupe, a French department in the West Indies. The meaning is "low land," describing the terrain here below the dormant volcano of Soufrière. Guadeloupe's other main island, Basse-Terre's eastern twin, is *Grande-Terre*, "big land." Despite its name, Basse-Terre is the more mountainous of the two.

Bass Strait. *Strait, southeastern Australia.* The strait, between Australia and Tasmania, was named in 1798 by the English navigator Matthew Flinders (*see* **Flinders Ranges**) for his assistant surgeon George *Bass* (1771–?1803), who was first to enter it.

Bastia. *City and port, northeastern Corsica.* The city takes its name from Low Latin *bastita*, literally "built (place)," referring to a medieval fort here.

Basutoland *see* **Lesotho**

Batalha. *Town, west central Portugal.* The town takes its name from the Dominican abbey of *Santa Maria de Vitória*, "St. Mary of the victory," or *Santa Maria de Batalha*, "St. Mary of the battle." Its name commemorates the victory in 1385 of John I of Portugal over John I of Castile at nearby Aljubarrota.

Batavia. *Historic region, southwestern Netherlands.* The ancient district, on an island at the mouth of the Rhine, takes its name from the *Batavi*, the people who at one time inhabited it. Their own name is said to derive from Old German *bata*, "better." It was *Batavia* that gave the former name of **Jakarta**.

Bat Galim. *Town, northwestern Israel.* The present residential suburb of Haifa, on the Mediterranean coast, has a Hebrew name meaning "daughter of the waves."

Bath. *City, southwestern England.* The city, in the former county of Avon (and earlier in Somerset), has a name that refers directly to its Roman baths, noted for their warm springs. The Roman name of Bath was *Aquae Calidae*, "warm waters." It then became known as *Aquae Sulis*, "waters of *Sulis*," the latter being a pagan goddess whose own name may (or may not) be related to Latin *sol*, "sun."

Bathurst. *City, southeastern Australia.* The city, in New South Wales, was founded in 1815 and named for Henry *Bathurst*, 3d Earl Bathurst (1762–1834), then secretary of state for the colonies. *See also* **Banjul**.

Bathurst *see* **Banjul**

Baton Rouge. *City, southern United States.* The state capital of Louisiana, on the Mississippi, has a French name meaning "red stick." This may have originally been the name of an Native American chief. A possibly legendary account tells how 17th-century French colonists erected a red pole here, like a totem pole, to mark the boundary between their territory and that of the Indians.

Bat Shlomo. *Village, northwestern Israel.* The Jewish village, founded in 1889 by the French philanthropist Baron Edmond de Rothschild, has a Hebrew name meaning "daughter of *Solomon* (Rothschild)."

Battle Creek. *City, northern United States.* The Michigan city, at the confluence of the Kalamazoo River and Battle Creek stream, was settled in 1831 and named for a "battle" that had taken place on the river bank between two Indians and two members of a surveying party.

Battonya. *Town, southeastern Hungary.* The site here was originally owned by the *Bot* family as part of a settlement called *Anya*. The family name may derive from Hungarian *bot*, "stick," "war hammer."

Batumi. *City and port, southwestern Georgia.* The city is said to derive its name from that of the *Bathus*, a river in the ancient country of Colchis here. Its own name could represent the Greek word for "deep," a description equally applicable to the gulf on which Batumi itself stands.

Batu Pahat. *Town and port, western Malaysia.* The town, on the Malay Peninsula, has a Malay name meaning "carved rock," describing a local natural feature.

Bat Yam. *City, western Israel.* The coastal city was founded in 1926 as a suburban development called *Bayit ve-Gan*, Hebrew words meaning "house and garden." When it became a seaside resort and a residential suburb of Tel Aviv, its name was changed as now in 1936 to mean "daughter of the sea," from Hebrew *bat*, "daughter," and *yam*, "sea"

Bauchi. *State, northeastern Nigeria.* The state is said to be named for *Baushe*, a hunter who settled in the region some time before the 19th century.

Baumann Peak. *Mountain, southwestern Togo.* The mountain is named for Oskar *Baumann* (1864–1899), an Austrian explorer here at a time when Togoland (as it then was) was a German colony.

Bautzen. *City, eastern Germany.* The city's name is a Germanic alteration of its Old Sorbian name of *Budishin*, itself from the Slavic personal name *Budish*.

Bavaria. *State, southern Germany.* The state is named for the *Boii*, a Celtic people who formerly inhabited this region, with the latter part of the name representing Germanic *warjan*, "to inhabit," "to dwell." Their own name, which also gave that of **Bohemia**, may mean "warrior." The German name of the state is *Bayern*.

Bay City. *City, northern United States.* The Michigan city was settled in the 1830s on the Saginaw River not far from its entry into Saginaw *Bay*, an inlet of Lake Huron. Hence its name.

Bayeux. *Town, northwestern France.* The town derives its name from the *Baiocasses* or *Badiocasses*, the Celtic people who inhabited this region, their own name meaning "blond ones," from *badios*, "yellow," "fair," and *-casses*, "hair." The town's original Roman name was *Augustodurum*, "fort of Augustus," from the Roman emperor *Augustus* and Gaulish *duron*, "door," "house," "fort."

Bayonne. *Town and port, southwestern France.* The town derives its name from Low Latin *baia*, "bay," and Basque *on*, "good," the reference being to the fine natural harbor here.

Bayramiç. *Town, northwestern Turkey.* The name is said to refer to the regular festivals or carnivals held here during the time of the Ottoman Empire, from Turkish *bayram*, "feast-day," "holiday," and *için*, "for." But this is almost certainly a flight of fancy.

Bayreuth. *City, southern Germany.* The town, in **Bavaria**, has a name recorded in 1194 as *Baier-rute*, from Old High German *Beira*, "Bavarian," and *riuti*, "clearing." The reference is to a place cleared in forestland by the Bavarians.

Baytown. *City, southern United States.* The Texas city takes its name from its location on Galveston *Bay*.

Beachy Head. *Headland, southern England.* The name of the East Sussex headland on the English Channel may seem to suggest a *beach*. But *Beachy* actually derives from Old French *beau chef*, "beautiful headland." The chalk cliffs here present an imposing sight as one approaches the English coast from France. The second word of the name was added when the sense of the first (which already has "head") was no longer understood.

Beagle Channel. *Strait, southern South America.* The strait, in the Tierra del Fuego archipelago, takes its name from the British ship *Beagle*, under the command of Captain Robert Fitzroy, in which he and Charles Darwin explored the region from 1828 to 1834.

Beardmore Glacier. *Glacier, central Antarctica.* The glacier, one of the world's largest, was discovered by the British explorer Sir Ernest Shackleton in 1908 and named by him for William *Beardmore*, Baron Invernairn (1856–1936), who had sponsored his expedition.

Béarn. *Historic region, southwestern France.* The region takes its name from the *Benarni*, a Gaulish tribe.

Beaufort Sea. *Sea, northwestern Canada.* The sea, in the Arctic Ocean, was named in honor of the British admiral Sir Francis *Beaufort* (1774–1857), hydrographer to the Royal Navy.

Beaugency. *Town, north central France.* The name represents the Gaulish personal name *Balgentius* and the Gallo-Roman suffix *-acum*.

Beauharnois. *Town, southeastern Canada.* The town, in Quebec province, was founded in 1819 and named for Charles, Marquis de *Beauharnois* (1670–1749), governor of New France (as Canada was then known).

Beaujolais. *Region, east central France.* The region takes its name from the village of *Beaujeu*. Its own name comes from French *beau*, "beautiful," and Latin *jugum*, "hill," influenced by *jocus*, "sport," "game."

Beaumont. *City, southern United States.* The Texas city was founded in 1825 under the name of *Tevis Bluff*. In 1835 the site was acquired by one Henry Millard, who is said to have renamed it for his brother-in-law, Jefferson *Beaumont*.

Beaune. *Town, east central France.* The town takes its name from Latin *Beleno castro*, "fort of *Belenos*," from a Gaulish god equated with Apollo.

Beauport. *City, eastern Canada.* The city, now a suburb of Quebec, was established on the St. Lawrence River in 1634 and apparently given a generally commendatory name, from French *beau port*, "beautiful harbor."

Beauvais. *City, northern France.* The city

takes its name from the *Bellovaci*, the Gaulish people who inhabited the region. Its Roman name was *Caesaromagus*, "(Julius) Caesar's market," a name bestowed on other towns in the Roman empire.

Bebek. *District of Istanbul, northwestern Turkey*. As it stands, the name of the northern district of Istanbul seems to mean "baby," from Turkish *bebek*. But this can hardly be the actual origin, unless it was the nickname of some former civil or military official.

Bechuanaland *see* **Botswana**

Beckum. *Town, northwestern Germany*. The name of the town means "settlement by the streams," from Old Saxon *beki*, "stream" (modern German *Bach*), and *heim*, "home," "abode."

Bedford. *Town, south central England*. The town, in the county of the same name, has an Old English name meaning "*Bēda*'s ford," referring to the crossing over the Ouse River here.

Beersheba. *Town, southern Israel*. The city has a Hebrew name meaning either "well of the oath" or "well of the seven," depending whether one traces the second part of the name back to *shavóa'*, "to swear," or *shéva'*, "seven." Both senses are alluded to in the Old Testament, which tells of an oath and a covenant between Abraham and Abimelech. One account has the covenant relating to a well, "therefore the name of the city is Beersheba unto this day" (Genesis 26:33), but a parallel account tells how the covenant was made when Abraham gave Abimelech seven lambs (Genesis 21:28).

Begusarai. *City, northeastern India*. The city, in Bihar state, derives its name from Urdu *begam*, "begum," "princess," and Persian *saray*, "palace," referring to a building in the center of the town.

Beijing. *Capital of China*. The city, long familiar to English speakers as *Peking*, derives its name from Chinese *bĕi*, "north," and *jīng*, "capital." It is thus historically the "northern capital," as distinct from **Nanking**, the "southern capital." Beijing has been the Chinese capital continuously from 1421 with the exception of the years 1928–49, when Nanking was. During this period, Beijing was known as *Peiping*, from *bĕi*, "north," and *píng*, "peace." It had also borne this name much earlier, from 1368 to 1416. Before that, in the 13th century, it was *Khanbalik*, "city of the khan," a name recorded by Marco Polo as *Cambaluc*.

Beira. *City and port, central Mozambique*. The city was so named by Portuguese colonists for their native province of *Beira*, central Portugal. The name itself means "riverside," from Por-

tuguese *ribeira*, "river." The Portuguese province is crossed by many rivers, including the Douro, Tagus, and Mondego. The Mozambiquan port is on the Mozambique Channel at the mouth of two smallish rivers.

Beirut. *Capital of Lebanon*. The city has a Hebrew name meaning "the wells," from *be'erōt*, the plural of *be'er*, "well" (*cp.* **Beersheba**). Wells were the only source of water in this region down to Roman times.

Bei Shan. *Mountain range, northwestern China*. The name of the range means "northern mountains," from Chinese *bĕi*, "north," and *shān*, "mountain."

Beit Oren. *Kibbutz, northwestern Israel*. The kibbutz and resort, founded in 1939, has a Hebrew name meaning "house of pine."

Beit Zayit. *Village, east central Israel*. The cooperative settlement, founded in 1949 and now a suburb of Jerusalem, has a Hebrew name meaning "house of olives," for the many olive groves here.

Beja. *City, southern Portugal*. The city's name is an eroded form of its Roman name, *Pax Julia*, "Julian peace," commemorating a victory by *Julius* Caesar or some other military leader named *Julius*.

Bejaia. *City and port, northeastern Algeria*. The name is said to be a corruption of Arabic *bakāya*, "survivors," alluding to a people who took refuge here. Under French influence (from 1833) the name became *Bougie*, and the city's manufacture and export of wax and candles gave *bougie* as the standard French word for "candle."

Bekaa. *Valley, central Lebanon*. The valley derives its name from Arabic *al-bikā'*, "the lands," from *al*, "the," and the plural of *buk'a*, "earth," "land," "country."

Békéscsaba. *City, southeastern Hungary*. The first part of the name, *Békés*, is that of the county here, originally a personal name. The second part, *Csaba*, is also a personal name, presumably that of the original landowner here. The name itself means "shepherd," "nomad."

Belarus. *Republic, eastern Europe*. The country, formerly familiar as *Belorussia*, was at one time known in the English-speaking world as *White Russia*, and this actually translates the name, from Slavic words related to Russian *belyj*, "white," and *Rus'*, "Russia." The precise import of the name is uncertain. The following have been proposed: (1) The indigenous population are mostly blond with light gray eyes and wear a national dress that is predominantly white; (2) Sands covering much of the country are very pale; (3) The indigenous people have never been conquered by the Tatars, so they are "white," i.e. free. (4) The country is to the west of "main" Russia, and "white" can mean "west" in some placenames (*cp.* **White Sea**); (5) The name arose by contrast with a neighboring territory of uncertain geographical parameters known as "Black Russia," possibly for its dark soil.

Belaya Tserkov. *City, north central Ukraine.* The city, founded in the 11th century, has a name meaning "white church." The Ukrainian form of the name is *Bila Tserkva.*

Belchen. *Mountain, southwestern Germany.* The second-highest mountain in the Black Forest has a name corresponding to Old High German *belihha*, "coot" (modern German *Bläßhuhn*, literally "pale hen"). The mountain is not named for the bird, however, but for its light, speckled appearance.

Belcher Islands. *Island group, northern Canada.* The islands, in Hudson Bay, Nunavut, were discovered by the English navigator Henry Hudson in 1610 and subsequently named for Sir Edward *Belcher* (1799–1877), leader of an expedition here in search of Sir John Franklin, missing in 1847 when searching for the Northwest Passage.

Belém. *City and river port, northern Brazil.* The city arose in 1616 as a fortified settlement that was given the formal Portuguese name *Nossa Senhora de Belém do Grão Pará*, "Our Lady of Belém of the Great Pará," and the present name is a shortening of this. *Belém* is the name of a suburb of Lisbon, Portugal, where there is a convent dedicated to St. Mary of [1]**Bethlehem**. The *Pará* is the river on which the city stands, and its name is today sometimes used as an alternant for the city name.

Belfast. *Capital of Northern Ireland.* The name is Irish in origin, representing *Béal Feirste*, "ford-mouth of the sandbank." The sandbank in question is the one where the small *Farset* River (itself named for it) formerly joined the larger Lagan, just below Queen's Bridge. At low tide it was possible to ford the river here. The ford fell out of use when Long Bridge was built over the Lagan.

Belfort. *Town, eastern France.* The fortified town has a name that translates as "fine fort." The ancient castle stands on a commanding site over the strategic pass (the Belfort Gap, or *Trouée de Belfort*) between the Vosges and Jura mountains.

Belgium. *Kingdom, western Europe.* The country takes its name from the *Belgae*, the Gaulish people who inhabited the region in Roman times. Their own name may derive from

Gaulish *volca*, "swift," "active," or else go back to an Indoeuropean root element *bhelgh* meaning "swell in anger," possibly in allusion to the people's belligerent nature. If so, the name is indirectly related to English *belly* and *billow*, and perhaps also Latin *bellum*, "war."

Belgorod. *City, western Russia.* The city has a name meaning "white city," from Russian *belyj*, "white," and *gorod*, "city." The name is found elsewhere in Slav countries, as for **Belgorod-Dnestrovsky** and **Belgrade**. A "white city" may be so called for the white stone of its fortress, the light color of its soil, or the bright water of a nearby river. The color could also be symbolic in some way.

Belgorod-Dnestrovsky. *City, southwestern Ukraine.* For the first part of the name, *see* **Belgorod**. The second part represents the Russian adjectival form of the name of the **Dniester** River, on which this particular Belgorod stands. The city formerly belonged to Moldova, when it had the equivalent name of *Cetatea albă*, "the white city," from Romanian *cetate*, "city," with the feminine definite article suffix *-a*, and the feminine form of *alb*, "white." In 1484 it was conquered by the Turks, who named it equally identically as *Akkerman*, from Turkish *ak*, "white," and *kerman*, "fort." The city had this name until as recently as 1944. The Ukrainian form of the name is *Bilhorod-Dnistrovskyy*.

Belgrade. *Capital of Serbia.* The city's name equates to that of **Belgorod** and so means "white city," from Serbian *beo*, "white," and *grad*, "city." The reference is probably to the white stone of the fortress here, although the color could be symbolic. The city's Hungarian name is *Nándor-fehérvár*, with *Nándor*, a form of *Nandi*, the German pet form of *Ferdinand*, followed by Hungarian *fehér*, "white," and *vár*, "castle."

Belize. *Country, northeastern Central America.* The country, with its former capital of the same name, was originally called **Honduras** by Spanish settlers, a name now borne by the republic to its south. The British had a presence here from the first, however (*c.*1638), hence its long familiar name of *British Honduras*. It took its present name on gaining independence in 1981. The name itself is that of the river that flows through the country, entering the sea at Belize City. Its own name is probably Native American in origin, although some claim it is a corruption of *Wallace*, the surname of a Scottish adventurer known to have been an early settler here. The present capital is **Belmopan**.

Belle-Île. *Island, northwestern France.* The island, in the Bay of Biscay off the south coast of Brittany, has a French name meaning "beautiful island." Its Breton name is different, as *ar Gerveur*, "the big town," from *ar*, "the," *kêr*, "town" (with *k* mutating as *g*), and *meur*, "big" (with *m* mutating as *v*). The island's chief town, of the same name, was important as a fortified outpost of mainland France.

¹**Belleville**. *City, southern Canada*. The Ontario city was settled some time after 1776 and originally named *Meyers' Creek*, for John *Meyers*, a gristmill operator. In 1816 it was renamed as now for *Arabella* (familiarly *Belle*) Gore, wife of Francis Gore (1769–1852), lieutenant governor of Upper Canada. The name can also be favorably interpreted as French *belle ville*, "beautiful town."

²**Belleville**. *City, east central United States*. The Illinois city was founded in 1814 and named from French *belle ville*, "beautiful city."

Bellevue. *City, central United States*. The Nebraska city, on the Missouri River, arose as a fur-trading post in the early 1800s and was named from French *belle vue*, "beautiful view."

Bellingham. *City, northwestern United States*. The Washington city is named for its location on *Bellingham Bay*, itself named by George Vancouver (*see* **Vancouver**) in 1792 for Sir William *Bellingham*, supervisor of his voyage.

Bellingshausen Sea. *Sea inlet, Antarctica*. The inlet of the South Atlantic, south of South America, is named for the Russian explorer Faddei *Bellingshausen* (1779–1852), who discovered it in 1821.

Bellinzona. *Town, southern Switzerland*. The town's name is of Celtic origin and may relate to the god *Belenos* who gave the name of **Beaune**, France.

Belluno. *Town, northeastern Italy*. The town, known to the Romans as *Bellunum*, probably has a name of Celtic origin, from the personal name *Belo* and *dunu*, "hill," "fort."

Bellville. *Town, southwestern South Africa*. The town, in Western Cape province, was founded in 1861 and named for Charles Davidson *Bell*, surveyor general of the Cape. The name has the bonus of being additionally interpreted as French *belle ville*, "beautiful town."

Belmopan. *Capital of Belize*. The name of the city, founded in 1970, is a blend of **Belize** City (the former capital, frequently damaged by hurricanes), and *Mopan*, the river on which it lies.

Belo Horizonte. *City, eastern Brazil*. The city has a Portuguese descriptive name meaning "beautiful horizon." The horizon in question is the Serro do Curral, a hilly ridge that surrounds the plateau on which Belo Horizonte was built

in 1897 as Brazil's first modern city, modeled on Washington, DC. Its original name was *Cidade de Minas*, for its location in **Minas Gerais**. It took its present name in 1901.

Beloit. *City, east central United States*. The Wisconsin city was settled in 1837 and was originally known as *Blodgett Settlement*. It was then known as *The Turtle* and *New Albany* before finally acquiring its present name, said to be based on a blend of French *bel*, "beautiful," and the name of **Detroit**, in neighboring Michigan.

Belomorsk. *Town and port, northwestern Russia*. The town, in Karelia, lies by the White Sea (Russian *Beloye more*). Hence its name. It arose in 1938 on the site of the village of *Soroka*, so called after the river here, its own name meaning "river of islands," from Finnish *saari*, "island," and *joki*, "river."

Belorussia *see* **Belarus**

Benadir. *Region, southern Somalia*. The coastal region is said to derive its name from Persian *bandar*, "port," referring to the voyages of Persian and Arab traders to eastern Africa across the Arabian Sea.

Benares *see* **Varanasi**

Bend. *City, western United States*. The Oregon city takes its name from the *bend* on the Deschutes River where it was laid out in 1904.

Bendery. *City, southeastern Moldova*. The city, on the Dnieper River, has a Turkic name meaning "harbor," from a word *bender* that was itself borrowed from Persian (*cp.* **Benadir**). Bendery was a Genoese trading center in the 12th century and when part of Bessarabia, from 1918 through 1940, was known as *Tighina*. The meaning of this is unknown.

Bendigo. *City, southeastern Australia*. The city, in Victoria, was founded in 1840 and was originally known as *Sandhurst*. In 1891 it was renamed as now to honor a local prize fighter who compared himself favorably to *Bendigo*, the name adopted by the English pugilist William Thompson (1811–1880). His own name is apparently a corruption of the biblical name *Abednego*.

Bendorf. *Town, western Germany*. The name of the town probably derives from an original form equivalent to *Badindorf*, meaning "*Bado*'s village."

Bene Beraq. *City, west central Israel*. The city, a suburb of Tel Aviv-Yafo, was founded in 1924 by Orthodox Polish-Jewish immigrants near the presumed site of the biblical city of this name, meaning "sons of *Barak*."

Benelux. *Coastal region, northwestern Europe*. The name is applied collectively to **Belgium**, the

Netherlands, and **Luxembourg**, taking the first syllable of each (and fortuitously suggesting a blend of Latin *bene*, "well," and *lux*, "light"). It was officially adopted in 1948 for the political and economic union of the three, while the states are also generally known as the *Low Countries* (*see* **Netherlands**).

Benevento. *City, southern Italy.* The city has a name of Roman origin supposedly meaning "fair wind," from Latin *bene*, "well," and *ventum*, "wind." The previous name of the city was *Maleventum*. The first part of this is of pre–Indoeuropean origin and probably means "height." However, the Romans took it to mean "bad," so changed the name to *Beneventum*, its contrasting propitious equivalent. (According to Pliny, the earlier name, meaning "rich in apples," was understood as "bad outcome," but was changed to "good outcome" after the Roman victory over Pyrrhus here in 275 B.C.)

Bengal. *Historic region, eastern India.* The former Indian province has a name that is basically the same as that of **Bangladesh**, its modern neighbor. It represents that of the *Bengalis*, the region's inhabitants. Their own name is said to derive from their primal ancestor, a chief called *Banga*.

Benghazi. *City and port, northern Libya.* The city has an Arabic name meaning "sons of the conqueror," from *banī*, the plural of *ibn*, "son," and *ğāzī*, "conqueror." *Bani Ghazi* is itself the name of a locally venerated marabout (Muslim monk) whose tomb lies to the north of the city. The Greek name of Benghazi was *Hesperides* or *Euhesperides*, for the Islands of the Blessed in Greek mythology, or for the maidens who guarded the golden apples there. Later, the city took the additional name *Berenice*, either for the wife of Ptolemy III or for the daughter of Salome and niece of Herod (or possibly even as a compliment to both).

Benguela. *City and port, western Angola.* The city, founded in 1617, is said to derive its name from a local word meaning "land of sugarcane."

Beni Isguene. *Town, central Algeria.* The town, founded in the mid–11th century, has a name of Berber origin meaning "sons of those who keep the faith."

Benin. *Country, western Africa.* The name is that of a former kingdom here, and comes from its indigenous people, the *Bini*, whose own name may be related to Arabic *bani*, "sons" (*cp.* **Benghazi**). They are now more immediately associated with neighboring Nigeria, hence the name of *Benin City* in that country. Until 1974 Benin was known as *Dahomey*. This represents the

name of another historic kingdom: that of *Dan Homé*, usually interpreted as meaning "stomach of *Dan*." The reference is said to be to the palace of King Aho, which according to local legend was built on the site where his rival Dan was buried. However, some see the name as a corruption of *Agbomi*, "inside the fort," from *agbo*, "fort," "stronghold" (literally "buffalo"), and *mi*, "inside."

Ben Nevis. *Mountain, west central Scotland.* The name of Britain's highest mountain has been popularly linked with Latin *nix, nivis*, "snow," perhaps partly by association with **Snowdon**, the highest mountain in Wales. It actually comes from a nearby river, the *Nevis*, its own name deriving from Gaelic *nemess*, "spiteful," alluding to its evil repute in local legend. The first word is Gaelic *beinn*, "mountain."

Benoni. *City, northeastern South Africa.* The city, in Gauteng province, now effectively a suburb of Johannesburg, was established as a mining camp following the discovery of gold in 1887 and given the biblical name *Ben-Oni*, meaning "son of sorrow" (Genesis 35:18), with reference to the difficulty of developing the town on poor terrain.

Bensheim. *Town, central Germany.* The name means "*Basino*'s village," with an Old German personal name.

Benue. *State, east central Nigeria.* The state takes its name from the *Benue* River here, its own name meaning "mother of waters" in a local language.

Beppu. *City, southwestern Japan.* The city, on the island of Kyushu, derives its name from the Japanese personal name *Betsu* and *fu*, "prefecture."

Berat. *City, southern Albania.* The city's name is a corruption of its Slavic name *Beligrad*, "white fort," given in the 14th century by the Serbs, perhaps as a transfer of the name of their capital, **Belgrade**.

Berazategui. *District of Buenos Aires, eastern Argentina.* The district takes its name from one of the two property owners to whom the site was sold in 1860, José Clemente *Berazategui* and Juan Etcheverry.

Berbera. *City and port, northwestern Somalia.* The city, founded in classical times by Ptolemy II Philadelphus, has a name ultimately derived from Greek *barbaros*, "foreign," "not Greek," referring to the local inhabitants. *Cp.* **Barbary Coast**.

Berchtesgaden. *Town, southwestern Germany.* The name, first recorded in 1121 as *Perehtgeresgadem*, derives from the Old German personal name *Perhtger* and Old High German *gadem*, "one-roomed house," naming the original settler here and his modest dwelling.

Berdichev. *City, west central Ukraine*. The city may derive its name from Slavic *berda*, "hill," "steep slope." But the possessive ending *-ev* suggests that the origin is actually in the personal name *Berdich*. The Ukrainian form of the name is *Berdychiv*.

Berdyansk. *City and port, southwestern Ukraine*. The city was founded in 1827 and presumably named for a landowner here. In 1939 it was renamed *Osipenko*, for Polina *Osipenko* (1907–1939), a Ukrainian airwoman born near here who lost her life in a flying accident. The town readopted its original name in 1958.

Berea. *City, east central United States*. The Ohio city, now a suburb of Cleveland, was founded in 1807 on the Rocky River and was originally known as *Watertown*. It was then renamed *Middleburgh* before gaining its present name in 1836, probably from the biblical city (Acts 17:10, etc.). Its own name is of uncertain origin but the city became associated with missionary work.

Berettyóújfalu. *Town, eastern Hungary*. The first part of the town's name is that of the *Berretyó* River here. The second part means "new village," from Hungarian *új*, "new," and *falu*, "village." The river's name is said to derive from Hungarian *berek*, "marsh with groves," and *jó*, "river."

Berezina. *River, Belarus*. The river probably derives its name from Slavic *bereza*, "birch," although some sources see a link with *Borysthenes*, the Latin name of the **Dnieper**, of which it is a tributary.

Bergama *see* **Pergamum**

Bergamo. *City, northern Italy*. The city, known to the Romans as *Bergamum*, has a name based on a Celtic or Ligurian word *berg*, "mountain" (as in Germanic languages). Bergamo lies in the foothills of the Alps.

Bergen. *City and port, southwestern Norway*. The city derives its name from Old Norwegian *Björgvin*, from *björg*, "mountain," and *vin*, "pasture."

Bergen op Zoom. *Town, southwestern Netherlands*. The town has a name meaning "(place by the) hills on the *Zoom*," the latter being the river here. Its own name means "border," as it flows along the edge of marshland.

Bergerac. *Town, south central France*. The town, in the Dordogne, has a name meaning "*Bracarius*' place." The Gallo-Roman personal name means "maker of breeches."

Bergheim. *City, western Germany*. The name means literally "hill settlement," referring to the site of the original church here by the Erft River.

Bergisch Gladbach. *City, western Germany*. The first part of the city's name refers to the county of *Berg* to which it was assigned in medieval times. The second word represents the former name of the Strunde River here, meaning "shining stream," as for **Mönchengladbach**.

Bergstrasse. *Hillside tract, western Germany*. The tract, on the western slope of the Odenwald, between Darmstadt and Heidelberg, has a name meaning literally "hill street," referring to a former major trade route here, today followed by a stretch of the Bundesstraße 3 highway. The trade route itself, an old Roman road, is first recorded in a document of 795 as *strata publica*, "public street."

Bering Sea. *Sea between Alaska and Siberia*. Both the Bering Sea and the Bering Strait that connects it with the Arctic Ocean take their name from the Danish explorer Vitus *Bering* (1681–1741), who entered the service of Peter the Great of Russia in 1724. He was the first European to sight Alaska.

Berkeley. *City, western United States*. The California city takes its name from the Irish philosopher George *Berkeley* (1685–1753). His name was selected as appropriate for the campus site that opened here for the new University of California in 1873 as a merger between the existing university and the earlier College of California founded in Oakland in 1853, the centennial year of Berkeley's death.

Berkshire. *Historic county, southern England*. The county is unusual in having a name that does not derive from that of its chief town (as *Oxfordshire* from *Oxford*, *Lancashire* from *Lancaster*). The first part of the name represents *Bearroc*, the old name of a wood here. The wood was in turn probably named for the hill on which it lay, since *Bearroc* almost certainly comes from Celtic *barro*, "hill." Local history has established that the hill was probably near Hungerford, in the west of the county.

Berlin. *Capital of Germany*. The city's coat of arms shows a bear, as if associating the name with German *Bär*, "bear," or even *Bärlein*, "bear cub." But this is folk etymology at work, and the name probably has a Slavic origin, from Old Polabian *berl-* or *birl-*, "swamp," referring to the site by the Spree River where the original settlement arose. *Cp.* **Bern**.

Bermejo. *River, northern Argentina*. The name is Spanish word for "reddish," this being the color of the silt carried by the river.

Bermuda. *Island group, northwestern Atlantic.* The name of the British colony pays tribute to the Spanish explorer Juan *Bermúdez,* who is said to have visited the islands some time after 1503. He himself originally called them (in their English equivalent) *Devil Islands,* perhaps for reasons that in modern times have been associated with the infamous Bermuda Triangle. The Bermudas were also long known as the *Somers Islands,* for Sir George *Somers* (1554–1610) and a group of English colonists, who were shipwrecked here in 1609 on their way to Virginia. (It was this shipwreck that inspired Shakespeare's play *The Tempest,* first performed in 1611, in which Ariel speaks of the "still-vex'd Bermoothes.")

Bern. *Capital of Switzerland.* As for **Berlin,** the name of *Bern* has been popularly associated with German *Bär,* "bear," in this case because the Helvetii, the Celtic people who inhabited the region in the 1st century B.C., are said to have worshiped a she-bear as their totemic animal. A more likely origin is in an Indoeuropean root word *ber,* "marshy place." One account links the name with that of **Verona,** as if Bern were a northern equivalent of that Italian city. The two are only 200 miles (320 km) apart.

Bernburg. *City, central Germany.* Although a castle *Brandanburg* is mentioned here in 961, the present city's name does not mean "burned fortress" (like **Brandenburg**) but probably derives from the short form of a personal name such as *Bernhard.* The meaning is thus "*Bern's* fortified place."

Bernkastel-Kues. *City, western Germany.* The two separate towns of *Bernkastel* and *Kues* united in 1905 to form the present city. *Bernkastel* arose on the site of a Romano-Celtic settlement named *Princastellum.* The first part of this probably represents a Celtic or pre–Celtic river name of unknown meaning. The second part is Latin *castellum,* "castle." *Kues* probably derives its name from Medieval Latin *covis,* "barn."

Berry. *Historic region, central France.* The former province has a name that is a smoothed form of the Roman name *Bituricus,* from the Gaulish people here known as the *Bituriges.* Their own name means "kings of the world," from Gaulish *bitu,* "world," and *rix,* "king." This sounds very grand, but merely meant that they held authority over their particular region. *See also* **Bourges.**

Berwick. *Town, northeastern England.* The Northumberland town, formally known as *Berwick-upon-Tweed,* for its river (*see* **Tweed**), has a name found elsewhere in England. It means "barley farm," from Old English *bere-wīc,*

a designation used for the outlying part of an estate.

Besançon. *City, eastern France.* The name ultimately comes from an Indoeuropean root element *ves,* "mountain," as possibly also for the **Vosges** mountains. Besançon lies just below the Jura range.

Bessarabia. *Region, southeastern Europe.* The region, annexed by Russia in 1812 and now divided between Moldova and Ukraine, is probably so named for the dynastic name *Basarab,* that of the princes of Wallachia, and itself based on Turkish *basar,* a derivative of *bas,* "to oppress."

¹Bethany. *Village, western Jordan.* The biblical village (Matthew 21:17, etc.) has an Aramaic and Hebrew name meaning "house of poverty," from *bēt,* "house of" (construct state of *bayit,* "house"), and *'anya,* "poverty." (For a construct state noun, *see* **Ramat Gan.**)

²Bethany. *City, south central United States.* The Ohio city was founded in 1909 as a religious colony and named for the biblical **¹Bethany.**

Bethel. *Historic city, southern Palestine.* The biblical city, mentioned frequently in the Old Testament (Genesis 12:8, etc.), has a Hebrew name meaning "house of God." The town became associated with heathen worship, and was called *Beth-aven,* "house of wickedness," by the prophet Hosea (4:15, etc.). The modern name of the site is *Baytin,* in the West Bank just north of Jerusalem.

Bethesda. *Town, northwestern Wales.* The town takes its name from the biblical *Bethesda* (Aramaic, "house of mercy" or, better, "place of flowing water"), the pool in Jerusalem believed to have healing waters (John 5:2). The name was first that of the Calvinistic Methodist chapel set up here in 1820.

¹Bethlehem. *City, south central West Bank.* The biblical town (Genesis 35:19, etc.) is generally said to derive its name from Arabic words meaning "house of meat" or Hebrew words meaning "house of bread," each referring to the former fertility of the surrounding plain. Modern scholarship prefers a meaning "house of *Lahmu* and *Lahamu,*" naming a pair of Mesopotamian agricultural deities.

²Bethlehem. *City, eastern United States.* The Pennsylvania city was founded in 1741 by Moravian missionaries and is said to be named for a Christmas carol about the biblical **¹Bethlehem** sung that year.

³Bethlehem. *City, east central South Africa.* The city, in the Free State, was founded in 1860 and named for the biblical ¹**Bethlehem**, the common link being the abundance of wheat in the locality.

Bethpage. *Town, eastern United States.* The New York town is named for the biblical village of **Bethphage**. It is so called because it arose between settlements originally known as Jericho and Jerusalem, just as the village is situated halfway between Bethany and the summit of the Mount of Olives.

Bethphage. *Historic village, northern Israel.* The biblical village (Matthew 21:1) has an Aramaic name meaning "house of unripe figs."

Bethsaida. *Historic city, northern Israel.* The biblical town (Mark 6:45, etc.) has a Hebrew name meaning "house of the hunter." The town was near the northeastern shore of the Sea of Galilee, so that the "hunter" would have been a fisherman.

Béthune. *Town, northern France.* The town had the Medieval Latin name of *Bitunia*, from the Germanic personal name *Bettun*, itself based on *bata*, "better."

Beth Yerah. *Archaeological site, northern Israel.* The ancient fortified settlement has a name of Hebrew origin meaning "house of the moon," referring to a Semitic goddess.

Bet She'an. *Town, northeastern Israel.* The ancient town, mentioned in the Bible as *Beth-shean* (Joshua 17:11) or *Beth-shan* (1 Samuel 31:10), has a Hebrew name meaning "house of quiet."

Betwa. *River, central India.* The river has a shortened form of the Sanskrit name *Vetravatī*, from *vetra*, "reed," and *vatī*, "containing."

Betws-y-Coed. *Village, northwestern Wales.* The name means "chapel in the wood," from Welsh *betws*, "chapel" (from English *bead-house*, "prayer house"), *y*, "the," and *coed*, "wood."

Beverly. *City, northeastern United States.* The Massachusetts city was settled in *c.*1626 and named for the English town of *Beverley*, in the East Riding of Yorkshire. Its own name is of Old English origin and means "beaver lodge."

Beverly Hills. *City, western United States.* The California city, a residential district of Los Angeles, was known as *Beverly* until 1911, when the second word was added. Its original name was suggested by a 1907 newspaper report that President Taft was vacationing at a place called *Beverly Farms*.

Beyrouth *see* **Beirut**

Béziers. *City, southern France.* The Roman name of the city was *Baeterrae*, from a pre–Celtic word that gave the Roman name, *Baetis*, of the Guadalquivir River in southern Spain and in turn that of the historic province of *Baetica* there.

Bhadgaon. *City, eastern Nepal.* The city's name means "country of rice," from Nepalese *bhāt*, "rice," and *gāuṅ*, "country." Its older alternate name is *Bhaktapur*, "town of devotees," from *bhakt*, "devotee," "believer," and *pur*, "town."

Bharat *see* **India**

Bharatpur. *City, northwestern India.* The city, in Rajasthan state, was founded in *c.*1733 with a name meaning "*Bharata's* town," from the same legendary hero that gave the name of **India** itself.

Bhir. *Town, western India.* The town, in Maharashtra state on a tributary of the Krishna River, is said to derive its name from Persian *bhir*, "water."

Bhopal. *City, central India.* The capital of Madhya Pradesh state is said to derive its name from Sanskrit *bhūpāla*, "king," "prince," from a root word related to modern English *be*.

Bhubaneshwar. *City, eastern India.* The capital of Orissa state, a religious and pilgrimage center dating from the 3d century B.C., has a name meaning "lord of the universe," from Sanskrit *bhuvana*, "universe," and *īshvara*, "supreme deity."

Bhutan. *Kingdom, southeastern Asia.* The state has a Hindi name deriving from Sanskrit *bhoṭa*, the name of **Tibet**, and *anta*, "end." This describes the location of Bhutan at the southern extremity of Tibet. The local Dzongkha name of Bhutan is *Druk Yul*, "land of the dragon."

Biafra. *Region, eastern Nigeria.* The region takes its name from the Bight of *Biafra*, on which it lies on the Niger delta. The name of the bight is a European rendering of the ethnic name *Mafra*.

Białystok. *City, northeastern Poland.* The city's name means "white river," from Polish *biały*, "white," and *stok*, "river," "confluence." The river here is itself the *Biały*, "white," so named for its waters.

Biarritz. *Town and resort, southwestern France.* The town, near the Spanish border, has a Basque name meaning either "place of two rocks" or "place of two oaks" from *bi*, "two," and *harri*, "rock," or *haritz*, "oak." The Basque form of the name is *Miarritze*.

Biberach an der Riss. *Town, southwestern Germany.* The town was founded in 1170 on the site of the former estate of the local lords *Bibra*, their name deriving from a river name based on Old High German *bibar*, "beaver," and *aha*, "water." The rest of the name refers to the town's location on the *Riss* River, its own name deriving from the Indoeuropean root *reus*, "fast-flowing."

Biddeford. *City, northeastern United States.* The Maine city was settled in 1630 and named for the settlers' English home town of *Bideford*, Devon, whose own name was then sometimes spelled thus.

Biedenkopf. *Town, central Germany.* The town takes its name from a nearby hill, its own name meaning effectively "lookout hill."

Bielefeld. *City, western Germany.* The city takes its name from an original field name, from Middle High German *bīhel*, "ax" (presumably from the shape of the field), or *bīl*, "peak," and *feld*, "open land," "field." Bielefeld is on the hilly edge of the Teutoburg Forest.

Bielsko-Biała. *City, southern Poland.* The city was formed in 1950 when the town of *Bielsko* joined the town of *Biała* across the river of this name, itself meaning "white."

Bietigheim-Bissingen. *City, southwestern Germany.* The city was formed in 1975 on the amalgamation of the towns of *Bietigheim* and *Bissingen*, the former name meaning "abode of *Buodo*'s people," the latter meaning "(settlement of) *Buzzo*'s people."

Biggleswade. *Town, southeastern England.* The Bedfordshire town has an Old English name meaning "*Biccel*'s ford." The second part of the name is Old English *wæd* (related modern *wade*), denoting a point on the river where the water is shallow enough for people and animals to walk across. Biggleswade is on the Ivel River.

Big Sur. *Region, western United States.* The coastal region in western California extends southward from Monterey and has a Spanish name to match, from *el sur*, "the south."

Bihar. *State, northeastern India.* The state takes its name from its city of *Bihar* (not its capital), itself having a Hindi name, from Sanskrit *vihāra*, "monastery." The town was formerly surrounded by Buddhist monasteries.

Bijapur. *City, southern India.* The name of the city, in Karnataka state, is an altered form of its original name, *Vijayapura*, "city of victory," from Sanskrit *vijaya*, "victory," and *pur*, "town."

Bikaner. *City, northwestern India.* The city, in Rajasthan state, has a name meaning "settlement of *Bika*," referring to its founder, the Rajput chieftain *Bika* (died 1504).

Bikini. *Atoll, western Pacific.* The atoll, in the Marshall Islands, is named *Pikinni* in the local language, said to be from *pik*, "surface," and *ni*, "coconut," although this derivation remains uncertain.

Bilbao. *City and port, northern Spain.* The city's present name evolved as a corrupt form of its Roman name. This was *Bellum Vadum*, "beautiful ford," referring to its location on the Bay of Biscay at the mouth of the Nervión River.

Billings. *City, northwestern United States.* The Montana city was founded in 1882 by the Northern Pacific Railway and named for the company's president, Frederick K. *Billings* (1823–1890).

Biloxi. *City, southern United States.* The Mississippi city is named for a local Native American people. Their own name is said to mean "broken pot."

Bingen. *City, southwestern Germany.* The city has a name recorded in the 1st century A.D. as *Bingium*, that of the Roman fort around which it arose. Its own name is of unknown meaning but probably Celtic origin.

Bingerville. *Town and port, southern Côte d'Ivoire.* The town is named for the French explorer and colonial administrator, Louis-Gustave *Binger* (1856–1936), first governor of the Ivory Coast (in 1893).

Binghamton. *City, eastern United States.* The New York city was settled in 1787 and was originally known as *Chenango Point*. It was subsequently renamed commmemoratively for the Philadelphia banker and land developer William *Bingham* (1752–1804).

Bingöl. *City, eastern Turkey.* The city's name means "thousand lakes," from Turkish *bin*, "thousand," and *göl*, "lake." The reference is to the many small lakes in the mountains to the northeast.

Binyamina. *Township, western Israel.* The township was founded in 1922 and named for the French philanthropist Baron Edmond Rothschild (1845–1934), promoter of Jewish colonization in Palestine, who was his father's youngest son, like the biblical *Benjamin*.

Bioko. *Island, western Equatorial Guinea.* The island, in the Gulf of Guinea, takes its name from *Bioko*, one of the two sons of the former king Moka, his other son giving the name of **Malabo**. Until 1973 the island was known as *Fernando Po*, representing the name of *Fernão do Pó*, the Portuguese navigator who discovered it in 1472. (He himself called it *Formosa*, "beautiful.") From 1973 through 1979 the island was known as *Macías Nguema Biyogo*, for Francisco *Macías Nguema Biyogo* Negue Ndong (1922–1979), Equatorial Guinea's dictator president (from 1968). The present name was adopted following his execution on charges of treason and genocide. *See also* **Annobón**.

Bir Hacheim. *Village, northeastern Libya.* The village takes its name from an oasis here, its own name representing Arabic *bi'r ḥakīm*, "well of the sage."

[1]**Birmingham.** *City, central England.* Britain's second largest city has an Old English name that could be that of any small village. It means "homestead at the place named after *Beorma*." It is not known who *Beorma* was, but his name is a shortened form of *Beornmund*.

[2]**Birmingham.** *City, southern United States.* Alabama's largest city was founded in 1871 for its industrial potential, with substantial coal and iron ore deposits, and was named accordingly for [1]**Birmingham**, then England's leading industrial city and center of iron and steel production.

Birobidzhan. *City, southeastern Russia.* The Siberian city, capital of the Jewish autonomous oblast, has a name of Yiddish origin representing two rivers here, the *Bira* and the *Bidzhan*. Their own names are of uncertain origin.

Bir Zeit. *Township, central West Bank.* The Arab township, with a name meaning "well of olives," is believed to have arisen on the site of the biblical *Beth-zaith*, "house of olives."

Biscay, Bay of. *Bay, southwestern Europe.* The wide arm of the Atlantic, to the west of France and Spain, has a name of Basque origin, representing *biskar*, "mountain country." The reference is to the Pyrenees, the mountains dividing France from Spain.

Bisceglie. *Town, southeastern Italy.* The town's name is a corruption of its Roman name, *Vigiliae*, from Latin *vigilia*, "watch," "guard." There were watchtowers here to guard the Adriatic coast.

Bischofswerda. *Town, eastern Germany.* The town derives its name from words related to modern German *Bischof*, "bishop," and *Werder*, "river island," denoting land along the Elbe River held in medieval times by the bishops of Meissen. *Cp.* **Werdau.**

Bishkek. *Capital of Kyrgyzstan.* The city was founded by the Russians in 1862 on the site of a fortress named *Bishkek* built a few years earlier by the Uzbek khans of Kokand. The Russians mistakenly called it *Pishpek*, and the town was known by this name until 1926, when it was renamed *Frunze*, for the Bolshevik revolutionary hero Mikhail *Frunze* (1885–1925), who was born here. In 1991 the city reverted to its original name, this time correctly. The name itself is of uncertain meaning.

Bismarck. *City, northern United States.* The state capital of North Dakota was so named in 1873 in honor of the German chancellor, Otto von *Bismarck* (1815–1898), in recognition of the investment of German bondholders in the railroad here.

Bismarck Archipelago. *Island group, southwestern Pacific.* The archipelago was proclaimed a German protectorate in 1884 and was named for the German chancellor Otto von *Bismarck* (1815–1898). It has retained his name although now part of Papua New Guinea.

Bissau *see* **Guinea-Bissau**

Bistriţa. *City, northern Romania.* The city, founded in the 12th century, has a common Slavic river name based on *bystr*, "rapid," referring to its fast current.

Bithynia. *Historic district, northwestern Turkey.* The district is named for its inhabitants, the *Bithynians*, a Thracian people, whose own name is conventionally traced to their mythical progenitor, *Bithynus*, son of Zeus (Jupiter).

Bitola. *City, southern Macedonia.* The city was formerly noted for its monastery. Hence its name, from Slavic *obitel'*, "monastery," literally "abode." (When the meaning of the name was no longer understood, it lost its initial *o*, as if it were a prefix.) Hence also the city's alternate Turkish name of *Monastir*.

Bitterfeld. *City, eastern Germany.* The city's name means "bitter field," although the precise significance of this is uncertain.

Biwa, Lake. *Lake, central Japan.* Japan's largest freshwater lake, in the island of Honshu, derives its name from Japanese *biwa*, the word for a type of short-necked lute that it resembles in shape.

Biysk. *City, southern Russia.* The city takes its name from the *Biya* River on which it lies. The origin of the river's name is uncertain, but it probably comes from a local word meaning simply "river."

Bizerta. *City and port, northern Tunisia.* The city has an Arabic name that is a corrupt form of Low Latin *Hippo Zarytus*. This is itself a distortion of Classical Latin *Hippo Diarrhytus*, in turn from Greek *hippōn*, "stable," and *diarrhutos*, "flowing through." The reference is to a halting place for horses by a running stream. Bizerta is on the Mediterranean at the mouth of a channel from Lake Bizerte, and was originally a Phoenician outpost before it became a Carthaginian town and Roman colony. The name is now also spelled *Bizerte* and *Banzart*. *Cp.* **Annaba.**

Black Forest. *Wooded region, western Germany.* The mountainous region consists predominantly of pine trees, and these give it the general dark color for which it is named. The Romans knew the forest as *Silva Nigra*, while its German name is *Schwarzwald*, both having the same meaning.

Black Hills. *Mountain region, north central United States.* The mountainous region in South Dakota is so named for the dark appearance of its rounded hilltops and tree-covered slopes.

Black Mountains. *Mountain range, southeastern Wales.* The range, in Carmarthenshire and Powys, is so named because the mountains appear dark when seen from the southern or eastern side.

Blackpool. *Town and resort, northwestern England.* The former Lancashire resort takes its name from a pool of water here at one time, about half a mile from the sea. By the end of the 18th century the surrounding area had been turned into meadowland, and the stream that issued from the pool became the town's main sewer. The pool's dark color arose from its peaty water.

Black Sea. *Sea, southern Europe.* The sea, between Russia and Turkey, has a name that probably describes its dark appearance when its waters are whipped up during storms. In bright or clear weather it is as blue as the Mediterranean. It is actually notorious for its sudden storms, and the Old Persian word used to describe it was *akhshaēna,* "dark." This was adopted without being translated by the Greeks, who called it *Pontos Axeinos, pontos* meaning "sea." But *Axeinos* came to be interpreted as *Axenos,* "inhospitable," so that it was the "inhospitable sea." Later, perhaps through superstition, the Greeks altered this unpropitious name to the conversely propitious *Pontos Euxenos,* "hospitable sea," and English adopted this name, also without translating it, as *Euxine Sea.* One theory claims the name refers not to color but to geographical location, on the grounds that some Asiatic languages use color words for the points of the compass. On this basis, the Black Sea is the "north sea," just as the **Red Sea**, according to this concept, is the "south sea," and the **White Sea** the "west sea."

Blagoevgrad. *Town, southwestern Bulgaria.* The town was so named in 1950 for Dimitŭr *Blagoev* (1856–1924), founder of the Bulgarian Communist Party. From 1396 through 1878 it was under Turkish occupation, and was known as *Dzhumaya* (later, *Gorna Dzhumaya*).

Blagoveshchensk. *City and port, southeastern Russia.* The Siberian city, a port on the Amur River, was founded as a military post in 1856. Two years later the Church of the Annunciation was built. Hence the city's name, from Russian *Blagoveshcheniye,* "Annunciation."

Blaj. *Town, central Romania.* The town derives its name from the Hungarian personal name *Balázs* ("Blaise"). Its Hungarian name is *Balázsfalva,* "*Balázs'* village," and its German name *Blasendorf.*

Blankenburg am Harz. *City, east central Germany.* The city, a health resort at the foot of the **Harz** Mountains, has a name meaning "white castle," from an early fort built on a steep chalk cliff here.

Blantyre. *City, southern Malawi.* The city was founded in 1876 as a Scottish mission station and named commemoratively for the Scottish missionary and explorer David Livingstone (1813–1873), who was born at *Blantyre,* southeast of Glasgow. Its own name represents Gaelic *blaen tir,* "top land," "end land," which the missionaries may have taken into account for the African settlement, in the Shire Highlands at the southern end of what was then Nyasaland.

Blaubeuren. *Town, southern Germany.* The original settlement was simply known as *Beuren,* "by the houses." The first part of the name is that of the river here, itself meaning "blue," from the color of the clear blue water at its source.

Blenheim. *Town, central New Zealand.* The town, in northeastern South Island, was founded in 1847 and named for the Battle of *Blenheim* (1704), in which the Duke of Marlborough defeated the French. *See* ²**Marlborough.**

Blida. *City, northern Algeria.* The city, founded in 1553, derives its name from a diminutive form of Arabic *balad,* "town."

Blieskastel. *City, western Germany.* The name means "castle on the *Blies* River," after the original Frankish castle here. The river name appears to derive from a Romance word meaning "ravine," "narrow valley."

Bloemfontein. *City, central South Africa.* The capital of Free State province has a name that can be literally understood as "fountain of flowers," from Afrikaans *bloem,* "flower," and *fontein,* "fountain." However, it could equally pay tribute to one Jan *Bloem,* a local farmer. The name was originally that of the farm on which the town was founded in 1846. The indigenous (Sotho) name of Bloemfontein is *Mangaung,* "place of cheetahs."

Blois. *Town, central France.* The town has a name of pre–Celtic origin and uncertain meaning. Its Medieval Latin name was *Blesis.*

Bloomfield. *Town, eastern United States.* The New Jersey town, now a suburb of Newark, was settled in 1660 and originally known as *Ward-sesson*. In 1796 it was renamed as now for the Revolutionary general Joseph *Bloomfield* (1753–1823).

Bloomington. *City, east central United States.* The site of the Illinois city was settled in 1822 and originally known as *Keg Grove*. This name was then changed to *Blooming Grove* and in 1831, when the town was laid out, to *Bloomington*.

Bluefields. *City, eastern Nicaragua.* The city takes its name from a Dutch pirate, Abraham *Blauvelt*, who made his base here in the 1630s.

Blue Mountains. *Mountain range, southeastern Australia.* The mountains, in New South Wales, are part of the Great Dividing Range. Their name alludes to the bluish haze visible over them in clear weather. The color is also attributable to the blue eucalyptus forests that traverse the mountains.

Blue Nile *see* **Nile**

Blumenau. *City, southeastern Brazil.* The city was founded in 1850 by Dr. Hermann *Blumenau* from Rudolstadt, Germany, together with 17 others. His name appropriately means "flowery meadow."

Boa Vista. *City, northwestern Brazil.* The city, on the Rio Branco, has a Portuguese name meaning "good view."

Bobingen. *Town, southern Germany.* The name means "(settlement of) *Bobo*'s people."

Böblingen. *City, southwestern Germany.* The city's name is a High German alteration of the original form *Beblingen*, "(settlement of) *Babilo*'s people."

Bobo Dioulasso. *City, southwestern Burkina Faso.* The city was so named by the French in 1897 for the two main peoples that form its inhabitants, the *Bobo* and the *Dyula*. The earlier name of the city was *Sya*, "island," referring to the forest clearing by a stream where it arose in the 15th century.

Bobruysk. *City, central Belarus.* The city takes its name from the small *Bobruyka* River here, a tributary of the Berezina. Its own name is based on Russian *bobr*, "beaver."

Boca Raton. *City, southeastern United States.* The Florida city derives its name from Spanish *boca de ratón*, "mouse's mouth," referring to one of a number of sharply pointed rocks off the coast here that were a danger to shipping. (They would "gnaw" ships' cables, like a mouse.)

Bocholt. *City, northwestern Germany.* The name means "beech wood," from Old High German *buohha*, "beech," and *holz*, "wood," referring to the area where the city arose, near the Dutch border.

Bochum. *City, northwestern Germany.* The city has a name meaning "settlement among beeches," from Old High German *buohha*, "beech," and *heim*, "house," "abode." Beech woods were extensive here near the Dutch border, and Bochum and **Bocholt** are less than 40 miles (65 km) apart.

Bodensee *see* **Constance, Lake**

Bodh Gaya. *Town, northeastern India.* The holy Buddhist site, in Bihar state, derives its name from Sanskrit *bodha*, "awakening," "consciousness," and *gayā*, the name of a region and its people. It was here, under the sacred Bo tree, that Gautama (Prince Siddhartha) attained enlightenment and became the *Buddha*, his title from the same Sanskrit root.

Bodrum. *Town, southwestern Turkey.* The town arose around a castle built by the Knights Hospitalers in 1502 on the site of the ruins of ancient **Halicarnassus**. They called their stronghold *Petronium*, "castle of St. *Peter*" (whose name means "rock"), and the present name evolved from this.

Boeotia. *Historic district, eastern Greece.* The name is said to derive from a Pelasgian word meaning "fighters," from Indoeuropean *bhei*, "to fight."

Boğazköy. *Historic city, north central Turkey.* The site of the ancient Hittite capital has a name meaning "village of the gorge," from Turkish *boğaz*, "throat," "gorge," and *köy*, "village," referring to its location on a mountain slope between two deep streambeds.

Bognor Regis. *Town and resort, southern England.* The first word of the West Sussex resort's name means "*Bucge's* flat-topped hill," from the Old English female personal name *Bucge* and *ōra*, "flat-topped hill," probably referring to one of the low hills behind the town. The second word is Latin *regis*, "of the king," and was added following the convalescence of George V nearby in 1929.

Bogong, Mt. *Mountain, southeastern Australia.* Victoria's highest peak has an Aboriginal name meaning "high plains."

Bogor. *City, southern Indonesia.* The city, in western Java, has a Sunda name meaning "carpet," referring to its textile industry. It was founded by the Dutch in 1745 as the residence of the governor general and became a colonial hillside resort. As such, it was formerly called *Buitenzorg*, the Dutch equivalent of French *Sans Souci*, "without care," the name of the palace at Potsdam, east central Germany, built in 1745 by Frederick the Great, who is quoted as saying (in French): "*Quand je serai là, je serai sans souci*"

("When I am there [i.e. in the tomb], I shall be without care").

Bogotá. *Capital of Colombia.* The city was founded in 1538 by the Spanish conquistador Gonzalo Jiménez de Quesada, who named it *Santa Fé de Bacatá*, after *Santa Fé*, his birthplace in Spain, and *Bacatá*, the main settlement of the Chibcha Indians here. The latter was later corrupted to *Bogotá*.

Bohemia. *Historic region, central Europe.* The region, corresponding to the modern Czech Republic, takes the first part of its name from the *Boii*, its former indigenous inhabitants. Their own name, which also gave that of **Bavaria**, may mean "warriors." The second part of the name represents Indoeuropean *haimoz*, "home," giving an overall sense "homeland of the Boii."

Boise. *City, northwestern United States.* The state capital of Idaho has a name given by French-Canadian trappers in the early 19th century. It represents French *boisé*, "wooded," referring to the tree-lined river that provided shade for travelers crossing the arid Snake River Plain. The city thus stands on the river of the same name.

Bojador, Cape. *Cape, western Western Sahara.* The cape is said to derive its name from Portuguese *bojar*, "to jut out." However, it is almost certainly a corruption of its earlier Arabic name, *abu khaṭar*, "father of danger," referring to the dangerous reefs off the coast here.

Bokhara *see* **Bukhara**

Boksburg. *City, northeastern South Africa.* The city, in Gauteng province, and effectively a suburb of Johannesburg, was established in 1887 on the site of gold diggings. It was named for Willem E. *Bok* (1846–1904), Dutch-born state secretary of South Africa at the time.

Bolesławiec. *Town, southwestern Poland.* The town is named for the Silesian duke *Bolesław*, who built a fortress here in the 12th century. The German form of the name is *Bunzlau*.

Bolivia. *Republic, west central South America.* The state takes its name from the nationalist leader Simón *Bolívar* (1783–1830), who fought the Spanish colonial forces in many South American countries, including his native Venezuela. On his liberation of Upper Peru in 1825, that country changed its name to the present *Bolivia* in his honor. His name is also borne by a number of other places in South America, among them a department in northern Colombia, a province in central Ecuador, and a state in southeastern Venezuela. The capital of this last is **Ciudad Bolívar**.

Bologna. *City, northern Italy.* The city may derive its name either from Gaulish *bona*, "foundation," "fortress," as for **Bonn**, or else from the *Boii*, the Gaulish people who occupied it in the 4th century B.C. and who gave the name of **Bohemia**. Its Roman name was *Bononia. See also* **Boulogne**.

Bolton. *Town, northwestern England.* The town near Manchester has a name found elsewhere in the north of England. It comes from Old English *bōthl*, "building," and *tūn*, "settlement," so that the overall literal sense is "village with buildings," otherwise the main residential part of an Anglo-Saxon settlement, as distinct from outlying farms.

Bolu. *City, northwestern Turkey.* The city arose on the Roman settlement of *Claudiopolis*, "*Claudius*'s town," for one of the Roman emperors of this name. The personal name was then lost, leaving just the *-polis* to give the present form of the name.

Bombay. *City and port, western India.* The capital of Maharashtra state has a name that is popularly derived from Portuguese *bom baía*, "good bay" (although *bom* is a masculine adjective and *bahía* a feminine noun). It is probably a shortening of *Mumbadevi*, "goddess *Mumba*," referring to a Hindu deity worshiped here. It was the Portuguese, even so, who apparently introduced the European form of the name, perhaps by association with *bom*, as for **Annobón**. Since 1995 Bombay has been officially known as *Mumbai*, the Marathi form of its name.

Bondi Beach. *Resort beach, southeastern Australia.* The surfing beach, a suburb of Sydney, New South Wales, derives its name from Aboriginal *boondi*, an expressive word representing the sound of waves breaking on the beach.

Bône *see* **Annaba**

Bonifacio, Strait of. *Strait, northern Mediterranean Sea.* The strait, between Corsica and Sardinia, takes its name from the fortified town of *Bonifacio* on the southern Corsican coast, itself named for *Bonifacio* (*Boniface*) I, duke of Tuscany, who built a fort here in 838 as a defense against pirates.

Bonin Islands. *Island group, western Pacific.* The islands, south of (and belonging to) Japan, have a name that is a European alteration of Japanese *munin*, "no man," from *mu*, "no," "none," and *nin*, "man." Japanese explorers here found the islands uninhabited. The Japanese themselves know the islands as *Ogasawara*, from the name of the Japanese explorer who discovered them in 1593.

Bonn. *City, western Germany.* The former

capital of West Germany derives its name from Gaulish *bona*, "foundation," "city." *Cp.* **Boulogne, Regensburg, Vienna.** Bonn dates from the 1st century A.D.

Bonyhád. *Town, southern Hungary.* The town derives its name from the Turkic personal name *Bonyha*.

Boothia Peninsula. *Peninsula, northern Canada.* The peninsula, in Nunavut, was discovered in 1829 by the Scottish polar explorer Sir James Ross (*see* **Ross Dependency**), who named it *Boothia Felix*, for Sir *Felix Booth* (1775–1850), the English distiller who had financed his expedition. (The name puns on the Roman *Arabia Felix*, in the Arabian Peninsula.) *Felix* was later replaced by *Peninsula*.

Bophuthatswana. *Historic homeland, northern South Africa.* The territory was the homeland of the *Tswana* people, as the latter part of the name indicates. The first part represents Tswana *bo-*, a prefix for abstract nouns, and *phutha*, "to gather." The overall sense is thus "place where the Tswana gather." *Cp.* **Botswana.**

Boppard. *City, western Germany.* The city arose by the Rhine on the site of a Celtic settlement and the Roman camp of *Baudobriga*, "*Bouduos*'s fortified place," which gave the present name.

Bora-Bora. *Island, central South Pacific.* The volcanic island, one of the Society Islands, French Polynesia, has a Tahitian name said to mean "first-born."

Bordeaux. *City and port, southwestern France.* The city's present name evolved from its Roman name of *Burdigala*, comprising two Aquitanian words, *burd* and *gala*, both of uncertain meaning. They may represent the name of a people who once inhabited the region.

Borders. *Region, southeastern Scotland.* The name, officially *Scottish Borders*, refers to the *border* between Scotland and England. The name is not new, since the territory that straddles the English-Scottish border has long been known as "the Borders." This name almost certainly originated in Scotland rather than England, since to the Scots the border would have been solely with England, whereas in England the term could equally apply to the border with Wales. *Cp.* **Marches.**

Bordighera. *Town and port, northwestern Italy.* The town, on the Gulf of Genoa, derives its name from Genoese *burdiga*, a term for the thickly reeded border of a lagoon.

Borgu. *Historic region, western Africa.* The former kingdom, now part of northern Benin and northwestern Nigeria, probably derives its name from the grass known as *borgu*, used for cattle food.

Borisoglebsk. *City, southwestern Russia.* The city, founded in 1646 as a fortress dedicated to St. Peter, takes its name from the church built here in 1704 and dedicated to the 10th-century saints *Boris* and *Gleb*, sons of the Kievan prince Vladimir Svyatoslavich.

Borken. *City, western Germany.* The origin of the name is uncertain. A suggested derivation from Old Scandinavian *burkn*, "fern," is unlikely, as this word has no correspondences in Old Saxon or Middle High German.

Borkum. *Island, western Germany.* The name of the westernmost of the East Frisian islands, recorded by Pliny in the 1st century A.D. as *Burchana*, probably relates to Old Scandinavian *burkn*, "fern," Icelandic *burkni*, "brambles."

Borneo. *Island, eastern Malay Archipelago.* The largest island in the archipelago derives its name from a Portuguese alteration of the name of **Brunei**, located on it.

Bornholm. *Island, southern Baltic Sea.* The original name of the Danish island was *Burgundarholm*, from Old Danish *Burgundar*, "Burgundians," and *holm*, "island." It was from Bornholm that the Burgundians emigrated to France in the 5th century A.D. to give the name of **Burgundy.**

Bornu. *Historic kingdom, northeastern Nigeria.* The name of the former emirate is of uncertain origin. It has been traditionally derived from Arabic *barr nūḥ*, "land of Noah," as Noah's Ark is said to have landed here after the Flood. But this is probably the fancy of some Arabist.

Borromean Islands. *Island group, northern Italy.* The four small islands in Lake Maggiore were so named by the Milanese nobleman Count Vitalio *Borromeo* (died 1690), who in 1630 transformed their bare and rocky terrain into magnificent parks and gardens. The individual islands are: *Bella* (for Countess *Isabella* Borromeo), *Madre* ("mother"), *San Giovanni* ("St. John"), and *Pescatori* ("fishermen"), the latter occupied by a fishing village.

Bosnia-Hercegovina. *Republic, southeastern Europe.* The country derives its name from the two provinces that united under Austria-Hungary in 1878. *Bosnia* takes its name from the *Bosna* River here, itself perhaps from an Indoeuropean root word *bhog*, "current." *Hercegovina* has a name denoting its original status as a duchy, from Old Serbian *herceg*, "duke" (modern German *Herzog*), with the possessive ending *-ov*, and the suffix *-ina*, meaning "country."

Bosporus. *Strait, southwestern Black Sea.* The

strait, which joins the Black Sea with the Sea of Marmara, has a name traditionally derived from Greek *bous*, "ox," and *poros*, "passage," "ford." Its Turkish name is *Karadeniz Boğazı*, "Black Sea strait." The name is sometimes spelled in English as *Bosphorus*, either from a fancied origin in *bous* and Greek *-phoros*, "bearing," or by confusion with *Phosphoros* ("light-bringer"), the Greek name for the planet Venus. The name was also that of the Cimmerian Bosporus, now the Kerch Strait, connecting the Sea of Azov with the Black Sea. In Greek mythology, this was the strait that Io swam after she had been changed into a heifer by Zeus.

¹**Boston.** *Town, eastern England.* The Lincolnshire town has a name that is popularly understood to mean "*Botolph*'s stone," on the basis that its main church is dedicated to St. *Botolph*, and that this saint's "stone" was the place where he preached. The interpretation may be theoretically valid, but Botolph (Bōtwulf) was probably simply the name of the Anglo-Saxon landowner here.

²**Boston.** *City, northeastern United States.* The state capital of Massachusetts, founded in 1630, is named for the English town of ¹**Boston**, Lincolnshire, the home of some of its Puritan settlers, and itself having a strong Puritan tradition.

Botany Bay. *Inlet, eastern Australia.* The inlet of the Tasman Sea, in New South Wales, is so named from the many unfamiliar botanical species found here in 1770 by the English navigator Captain Cook, who wrote in his May 6 diary entry that year: "The great quantity of New Plants &ca. Mr. Banks and Dr. Solander found in this place occasioned my giving it the name of Botany Bay."

Botev Peak. *Mountain, central Bulgaria.* The highest mountain in the Balkans was so named in 1950 for the Bulgarian revolutionary and poet Khristo *Botev* (1849–1876), killed in the mountains here by the Turks. The peak's earlier name was *Yumrukchal*, "punch," from Turkish *yumruk*, "fist," "blow," and before that, *Ferdinandov Vruh*.

Bothnia, Gulf of. *Region of Baltic Sea, western Europe.* The northern arm of the Baltic Sea, between Sweden and Finland, derives its name from Swedish *botten*, "bottom." The reference is to the former region of Scandinavia called in what is now Sweden *Westerbotten*, "western (valley) bottom" (*see* **Västerbotten**) and what is now Finland *Osterbotten*, "eastern (valley) bottom." The Finnish name of the Gulf of Bothnia is *Pohjanlahti*, from *pohja*, "bottom," and *lahti*, "bay," "gulf."

Botoşani. *City, northeastern Romania.* The city probably derives its name from the personal name *Botoş*, although the suffix *-ani* appears to point to an ethnic name. If so, it could derive either from the same personal name or from Romanian *botoşi*, a term for a type of peasant shoe, itself indirectly related to English *boot*.

Botswana. *Republic, southern Africa.* The country is named for the people who are its indigenous inhabitants, the *Tswana*, with *bo-* the Tswana prefix for abstract nouns. (*Cp.* **Bophuthatswana**.) The people's own name is said to be a Bantu word meaning "like," "similar," referring to a group who had remained behind while the rest had emigrated. If so, the name presumably emphasizes the similarity of the two groups rather than their difference, as is more usual in ethnic names. Before 1966, when the country gained independence, it was known as *Bechuanaland*, the first part of this being an English corruption of *Botswana*.

Bottrop. *City, northwestern Germany.* The city's name was recorded in the late 11th century as *Borgthorpe*, probably combining a former district name with Old High German *dorf*, "village."

Bouaké. *City, central Côte d'Ivoire.* The name is that of the Baule king *Gbweke*, who founded the town in 1865.

Bougainville. *Island, western Pacific.* The largest of the Solomon Islands derives its name from that of the French navigator Louis Antoine de *Bougainville* (1729–1811), who discovered it in 1768.

Bouira. *Town, north central Algeria.* The town has an Arabic name meaning "small wells," from a derivative of *bi'r*, "well."

Boulder. *City, west central United States.* The Colorado city was settled by miners in 1858 and named for the many *boulders* in the area.

Boulogne. *City and port, northern France.* The city derives its name from Gaulish *bona*, "foundation," "fortress," "city," as perhaps also does **Bologna** and more certainly does **Bonn**. It seems unlikely, however, that the Roman emperor Constantine named Boulogne directly for the Italian city, as has been claimed. The city's full name is *Boulogne-sur-Mer. See also* **Boulogne-Billancourt**.

Boulogne-Billancourt. *Town, northern France.* The town, now a suburb of Paris, was originally two separate towns named respectively *Boulogne-sur-Seine* and *Billancourt*. *Boulogne-sur-Seine* was so named because its church was founded by pilgrims from **Boulogne**. (Its suffix differentiates it from that city, whose full name is *Boulogne-sur-*

Mer, "Boulogne-on-sea.") *Billancourt* has a name meaning "*Billa's* enclosure," with the Germanic personal name followed by Latin *cors, cortis,* "enclosure" (English *court*). It was Boulogne-sur-Seine that gave the name of the *Bois de Boulogne,* the Paris park that was formerly a forest.

Bountiful. *City, west central United States.* The Utah city was settled in 1847 and originally named *Sessions' Settlement,* for Perigrine *Sessions,* a Mormon pioneer. In 1855 it was renamed as now with reference to its abundant harvests.

Bounty Islands. *Island group, South Pacific.* The islands, southeast of (and administered by) New Zealand, were discovered and named in 1788 by Captain William Bligh of the English ship *Bounty.*

Bourbonnais. *Historic region, central France.* The former province probably takes its name from *Borbo* or *Borvo,* a Celtic god associated with warm springs. The god's name in turn has been associated with Gaulish *borvo,* "foam," "froth."

Bourges. *City, central France.* The city takes its name from the *Bituriges,* the Gaulish people whose capital it was. For the meaning of their own name, *see* **Berry.**

Bournemouth. *City and resort, southern England.* The Dorset city has a descriptive name referring to its location at the mouth of the small *Bourne* River, its own name meaning simply "stream" (Scottish *burn*). The present resort arose in the early 19th century.

Bou Saâda. *Town, north central Algeria.* The town, a true oasis in barren desert country, has long been a trading and resting center for Arabs and Berber nomads. Hence its name, Arabic for "place of happiness."

Bouvet Island. *Island, South Atlantic.* The island, a possession of Norway southwest of the Cape of Good Hope, is named for the French navigator Jean-Baptiste-Charles *Bouvet* de Lozier (1705–1786), who discovered it in 1739.

Bowling Green. *City, eastern United States.* The Kentucky city was settled in 1780 by Robert and George Moore and is said to be named for their sport of *bowling* wooden balls over the *green* here.

Boyne. *River, eastern Ireland.* The river takes its name from Irish *bo bhán,* "white cow." The reference is not to an actual animal but to the traditional symbol of good fortune in Irish folklore. The river was thus regarded as propitious.

Brabant. *Province, central Belgium.* The name of the province is of Old High German origin, from *brahha,* "newly-broken land," and *bant,* "region." This originally applied to the much

larger region here, settled by the Franks in the 5th century A.D.

Bradenton. *City, southeastern United States.* The Florida city is named for Joseph *Braden,* the first permanent settler here in 1854.

Bradford. *City, northern England.* There are many places of the name in England, with the former West Yorkshire city the best known. The meaning is "broad ford," which in this case meant a crossing over what is now the small Bradford Beck, in the city center. In most other Bradfords, the river is more prominent (as in the Wiltshire town of *Bradford-on-Avon*).

Braga. *City, northern Portugal.* The city, probably founded in the 3d century B.C., was known to the Romans as *Bracara Augusta,* from the *Bracarii,* a Celtic tribe, who thus ultimately gave the name.

Braganza. *City, northeastern Portugal.* The city known to the Portuguese as *Bragança* derives its name from Celtic *briga,* "height," referring to its location in the Culebra Mountains.

Brahmaputra. *River, southeastern Asia.* The river, a tributary of the Ganges, has a Hindi name meaning literally "son of *Brahma,*" from *Brahma,* the creator god in Hinduism, and *putra,* "son."

[1]**Braintree.** *Town, southeastern England.* The Essex town has an Old English name meaning "*Branca's* tree." The tree itself could have been an actual prominent one or a "built" one, perhaps as a form of cross. Either kind could have served as a meeting place for an assembly of some sort.

[2]**Braintree.** *Town, northeastern United States.* The Massachusetts town was settled in 1634 and originally bore the Native American name of *Monoticut,* said to mean "abundance." It was part of Boston until 1640 when it was separately incorporated and named as now for the English town of [1]**Braintree.**

Brampton. *City, southeastern Canada.* The Ontario city, just west of Toronto, arose in c.1830 and was named for the English town of *Brampton,* Cumbria, the birthplace of its founder, John Elliott.

Bramsche. *Town, northwestern Germany.* The name means "arable land where broom grows," from a combination of Middle Low German *bräm,* "broom," and *esch,* "cropland."

Branco, Rio *see* **Rio Branco**

Brandenburg. *City, eastern Germany.* The name, also that of a historic region here, is traditionally said to be of Slavic origin, from an original form *Branibor,* meaning "defense forest." However, it has more convincingly been derived from a Germanic source meaning "burned fortress," from words corresponding to modern German *Brand*, "burning," and *Burg*, "fortress," "city." A third possibility is an origin in a Celtic personal name such as *Brando*.

Brandon. *City, southern Canada*. The Manitoba city was founded after the arrival of the Canadian Pacific Railway in 1881 and named for *Brandon* House, a Hudson's Bay Company trading post set up here in 1793. It was itself named for Archibald Douglas, 9th duke of Hamilton, who in 1782 became also duke of *Brandon*, Suffolk.

Braniewo. *Town, northeastern Poland*. The name evolved from German *Braunsberg*, originally *Brunsberg*, that of the castle here built in 1241 by the Teutonic Knights on land cleared by burning (Old High German *brinnen*, "to burn").

Brantford. *City, southeastern Canada*. The Ontario city was founded in 1784 when the site was granted to the Mohawk chieftain Joseph *Brant* (1742–1807), original name Thayendanegea, for the settlement of the Six Nations Indians after the American Revolution.

Brasília. *Capital of Brazil*. The city, made capital in 1960, has a name that is simply the New Latin form of the name of **Brazil** itself.

Brașov. *City, central Romania*. The name of the city represents Hungarian *Brassó*, itself possibly a form of the Turkish name *Borasugh*, "clean water," although this interpretation is disputed. It has also borne the German name *Kronstadt*, "crown city," and from 1950 through 1960 was known as *Stalin* or *Orașul Stalin*, "the town of *Stalin*," for the Soviet head of state (died 1953).

Bratislava. *Capital of Slovakia*. The city derives its name from that of a former Slav colony that was itself probably named for its head or its founder. Its earlier German name, dating from the 9th century, was *Pressburg*, an eroded form of the Slavic name with *Burg*, "fort," added. *Cp.* **Wrocław**.

Bratsk. *City, southern Russia*. The city is named for the indigenous Mongoloid *Buryat* people of this region. The form of the name has been influenced by Russian *brat*, "brother."

Braunau. *Town, northern Austria*. The town, also known as *Braunau am Inn*, for its location on the *Inn* River (*see* **Innsbruck**), derives its name from Old High German *brün*, "brown," in the sense "swampy," "marshy," and *auwa*, "island," "land by water."

Braunschweig *see* **Brunswick**

Brazil. *Republic, east central South America*. The country takes its name from that of the *brazil* tree, found widely here, and valued for its red dye wood. This is not the same as the tree that yields Brazil nuts, alhough that also grows in Brazil, as its name implies.

Brazzaville. *Capital of Congo*. Unusually, the city has retained its colonial name, unlike many major other places in Africa, which have adopted or revived a native name. It is that of the French explorer Pierre Savorgnan de *Brazza* (1852–1905), who founded the town in 1883. He was born an Italian count, and his own name comes from the Adriatic island of *Brazza*, now *Brač*, Croatia.

Brecon Beacons. *Mountain range, southern Wales*. The range, in Powys, takes its name from the town of *Brecon* here, its own name coming from that of *Brychan*, a 5th-century Welsh prince. The mountain summits are called *beacons* as they were used as sites for signal fires in medieval times.

Breda. *City, southern Netherlands*. The name represents Old Dutch *brede*, "broad," and *a*, "river." Breda lies at the confluence of the Merk and the Aa, the latter name meaning simply "river."

Bregenz. *Town and resort, western Austria*. The town, at the eastern end of Lake Constance, derives its name from Celtic *briga*, "height," referring to its location at the foot of the Pfänder Mountain. *See also* **Constance, Lake**.

Breisach. *City, southwestern Germany*. The city, formally *Breisach am Rhein* for its location by the **Rhine**, was known to the Romans as *Brisiacum*, meaning "*Brisios*'s settlement," with a Gaulish personal name. The present form of the name has been influenced by names in *-ach*, as **Andernach**.

Breisgau. *Historic region, southwestern Germany*. The region, between the Rhine and the Black Forest, derives its name from its chief town, **Breisach**, and German *Gau*, "district."

Bremen. *City and river port, northwestern Germany*. The name goes back to Old Saxon *bremo*, "edge" (related to English *brim*), referring to the site where the city arose on the right bank of the Weser River. *See also* **Bremerhaven**.

Bremerhaven. *City and port, northwestern Germany*. The city, founded in 1827 at the mouth of the Weser River, has a name meaning "port for **Bremen**," with the latter city 43 miles (69 km) further inland.

Bremerton. *City and port, northwestern United States*. The Washington city is named for William *Bremer*, who laid out the site in 1891 and promoted the establishment of the Puget Sound naval shipyard here.

Bremervörde. *Town, northwestern Germany.* The town, on the Oste River, arose by an ancient river crossing where an early 11th-century castle became the residence of the archbishop of **Bremen**. Hence the name, literally "Bremen ford."

Brenner Pass. *Mountain pass, southern Austria.* The pass, on the Austrian-Italian border, takes its name from the *Breuni*, the people who at one time inhabited the region. Their own name may be of Celtic origin and mean "mountain dwellers." An alternate sense "charcoal burners" is less likely.

Brescia. *City, northern Italy.* The city, in the Alpine foothills, was known to the Romans as *Brixia*, a name that perhaps derives from Celtic *briga*, "height."

¹Brest. *City and port, northwestern France.* The city, in Brittany, has a Celtic name deriving from *bre*, "hill." Brest lies on two hills divided by the Penfeld River.

²Brest. *City, southwestern Belarus.* The city, on the Polish border, takes its name from Slavic *berest*, "elm," a tree found widely here. It passed to Lithuania in 1319 and from then until 1921 was known as *Brest-Litovsk*, "Lithuanian Brest."

Brest-Litovsk *see* **²Brest**

Bretten. *Town, southwestern Germany.* The name of the town was recorded in 767 as *Breteheim*, probably meaning "broad settlement," from an early dialect form of modern German *breit*, "wide," and Old High German *heim*, "house," "abode."

Briançon. *Town, southeastern France.* The Alpine town derives its name from Ligurian or Celtic *briga*, "height."

Bridgeport. *City, eastern United States.* The Connecticut city, on Long Island Sound, was settled in 1639 and at first called *Newfield*, then *Stratfield*. In 1800 it was incorporated as a borough and given its present name, marking the opening of the first drawbridge over the mouth of the Pequonnock River.

Bridgeton. *City, eastern United States.* The New Jersey city was founded in 1686 and originally named *Cohansey Bridge*, for a *bridge* that spanned *Cohansey* Creek here. It was then called *Bridgetown* and finally, as now, *Bridgeton*.

Bridgetown. *Capital of Barbados.* The town and port was founded in 1628 and originally called *Indian Bridge*, from the *bridge* built here beside Carlisle Bay. It was then known as *St. Michael's Town* until the 19th century, when the present name came into favor.

Brie. *Historic district, northeastern France.* The region east of Paris derives its name from Gaulish *briga*, "hill," "height."

Brighton. *City and resort, southern England.* The former East Sussex resort has an Old English name meaning "*Brihthelm's* estate." As recently as the 19th century the town was known as *Brighthelmstone*, representing the full form of the original name.

Brindisi. *City and port, southeastern Italy.* The city, known to the Romans as *Brundisium*, derives its name from Messapic *brendion*, "stag's head," referring to the antler-shaped inner harbor here.

Brisbane. *City, eastern Australia.* The capital of Queensland is named for Sir Thomas Makdougall *Brisbane* (1773–1860), the Scottish general who was governor of New South Wales (which then extended this far north) from 1821 to 1825. The name was actually given in 1834, when the original convict settlement here, laid out in 1824, became a town.

Bristol. *City and port, southwestern England.* The city, in the former county of Avon (and earlier Somerset) has a name of Old English origin meaning "assembly place by the bridge," i.e. as if *Bridgestow*. The bridge in question was probably where Bristol Bridge is now, across the Floating Harbour. The final *-l* of Bristol's name is due to a local peculiarity of pronunciation, in which words ending in a vowel have this letter added. The woman's name Monica is thus pronounced "Monical." (A fuller discussion of the name and its peculiarity is given in C.L. Wrenn, "The Name Bristol," in Kelsie B. Harder, comp., *Names and their Varieties*, University Press of America, 1986.)

Britain. *Kingdom, western Europe.* The country takes its name from its original Celtic inhabitants, the *Britons*. Their own name was recorded by the Greeks in the 4th century B.C. as *Prittanoi*, explained as meaning "figured folk," "tattooed people," referring to their habit of decorating their bodies, as the (Ancient) Britons still did with woad when the Romans were in Britain. The Roman name of Britain, *Britannia*, was later adopted for the female figure who personified the country, which came to be known as *Great Britain* by contrast with the smaller "Little Britain" that is **Brittany**. (*North Britain* and *South Britain* were at one time respective names for Scotland and England, while *West Britain* has been facetiously applied to Ireland. *Greater Britain* is a name first recorded in 1868 for the former British Empire, or Great Britain and the colonies.)

British Columbia. *Province, western Canada.* The province was established as a British crown colony in 1858, and its name was officially proclaimed then, from the ¹**Columbia** River, which rises here. It was originally planned to name the colony *New Caledonia*, for the Roman name of Scotland, but this was rejected in favor of *British Columbia*, apparently by Queen Victoria herself, in order to avoid confusion with the French island of **New Caledonia**.

Brittany. *Region, northwestern France*. The region, called *Bretagne* in French, has a name that relates directly to that of **Britain**. It arose in the 5th century A.D. when Britons inhabiting southern Britain fled across the English Channel to escape the invading Germanic tribes of Angles, Saxons, and Jutes. Hence Britain's formal name of *Great Britain*, by contrast with this new "Little Britain."

Brive-la-Gaillarde. *Town, south central France*. The first word of the town's name derives from Gaulish *briva*, "bridge," referring to a bridge over the Corrèze River here. The rest of the name means "the vigorous," rendering Latin *Curretia*, the Roman name of the river, with its strong currents. Hence also the name of the *Corrèze* itself.

Brno. *City, southeastern Czech Republic*. The city, formerly known by its German name of *Brünn*, has a name that may derive from Old Czech *brn*, "clay," referring to the damp, muddy location here, at the confluence of the Svratka and Svitava rivers. An alternate origin in German *Brunnen*, "fountain," "well," has also been proposed, as has a Celtic source in a word related to modern Welsh *bryn*, "hill." According to Ptolemy, however, the name of the Roman settlement here was *Eburodunum*, from Gaulish *eburos*, "yew," and *dunum*, "fort," and the name could actually have evolved from this.

Broads. *Area of lakes and rivers, eastern England*. The Broads, or *Norfolk Broads*, are a group of about 12 lakes in Norfolk (and partly Suffolk) famous for their boating facilities. The name relates to the wider waters of the lakes, compared with the relatively narrow channels of the rivers that join them.

Brocken. *Mountain, central Germany*. The highest peak of the Harz Mountains, famous as the legendary meeting place of the Witches' Sabbath, probably derives its name from Middle High German *brocke*, "broken-off piece," presumably referring to the many granite rocks strewn over it.

Brockton. *City, northeastern United States*. The Massachusetts city grew out of a farming community that was originally part of Bridgewater and accordingly named *North Bridgewater*. It was renamed for the Canadian town of

Brockville, Ontario, in 1874. This was itself named for Major General Sir Isaac *Brock* (1769–1812), British administrator in Canada.

Broken Hill. *City, southeastern Australia*. The New South Wales city was founded in 1883 when minerals such as lead, zinc, and silver were extracted from a humpbacked range of hills named *Broken Hill* by the explorer Charles Sturt, who first visited the site in 1844.

Bronx. *Borough, eastern United States*. The New York City borough derives its name from Jonas *Bronck*, a Swedish sea captain from the Netherlands who settled here in 1639 with a group of servants and subsequently built a farm. People came to speak of going to "the *Bronks*," and the present form of the name developed from this.

Brooklyn. *Borough, eastern United States*. Dutch farmers arrived in the region of the present New York City borough in 1636 and founded a number of settlements, one of which, in 1646, was named for the Dutch village of *Breukelen*, near Amsterdam. (Its own name ultimately derives from Old High German *bruoh*, "moor," "marshland.") The name was later anglicized to *Brooklyn*, as if for a *brook*.

Brooks Range. *Mountain range, northwestern United States*. The range, across northern Alaska, is named for the American geologist Alfred Hulse *Brooks* (1871–1924), who surveyed and mapped it from 1903 through 1924.

Brownsville. *City, southern United States*. The Texas city had its beginnings in March 1846 when a fort was constructed here named Ft. *Brown*, for Major Jacob *Brown*, killed a few weeks later when defending it from Mexican attacks. The present city arose when the railroad arrived in 1904.

Bruchsal. *City, southwestern Germany*. The first part of the city's name derives from Old High German *bruoh*, "marshland," "moor." The second part probably represents Old High German *sal*, "hall," "one-roomed house."

Bruges. *City, northwestern Belgium*. The city has a name representing Flemish *brug*, "bridge," or rather the plural of this (as in its Flemish name of *Brugge*), referring either to the many bridges over the canals here or to the fact that the town arose by a particular bridge. *Cp.* **Zeebrugge**.

Brühl. *City, northwestern Germany*. The city, near the Rhine, derives its name from Old High German *broil*, "manorial meadow," "enclosed game park," referring to the site where it arose.

Brunei. *Sultanate, northwestern Borneo*. The sultanate has a Hindi name that probably derives ultimately from Sanskrit *bhūmi*, "land," "region." It was Brunei that gave the name of the whole island of **Borneo** on which it lies. The sultanate's full official name is *Brunei Darussalam*, "Brunei, abode of peace" (*cp.* **Dar es Salaam**).

Brunswick. *City, north central Germany*. The present name, also that of a historic region here, is an anglicized form of the German name *Braunschweig*. This means "*Bruno*'s settlement," supposedly from *Bruno*, son of Duke Ludolf of Saxony, who is said to have founded the city in c.861, and Old Saxon *wīk*, "village" (from Latin *vicus*, "village").

Brussels. *Capital of Belgium*. The city's name is of Germanic origin, from *broca*, "marsh," and *sali*, "room," "building," the latter word being a borrowing from Latin *cella* (English *cell*). Brussels is low-lying, and arose in the 6th century as a fortress on a small island in the Senne River, a tributary of the Scheldt.

Bryan. *City, southern United States*. The Texas city was founded in 1855 and named for William J. *Bryan*, who inherited the site here from his uncle, Stephen F. Austin (*see* **Austin**).

Bryansk. *City, western Russia*. The city's name was recorded in the 12th century in the form *Debryansk*, apparently from Old Russian *debr'*, "thicket," alluding to the many trees that then grew here. The first part of this name was subsequently dropped.

Bubastis. *Historic city, northern Egypt*. The ancient city, in the Nile River delta, derives its name from Egyptian *Per-Bastet*, "house of Bastet," from *per*, "house," and the name of the cat-headed goddess *Bastet* (also known as *Bast*). The city is mentioned in the Bible as *Pi-Beseth* (Ezekiel 30:17).

Bucharest. *Capital of Romania*. The city is traditionally said to take its name from a shepherd called *Bucur*, who supposedly founded it in 1457. But there was almost certainly a settlement here earlier than this. Even so, the name may represent the personal name of an early landowner.

Bückeburg. *Town, western Germany*. The town arose in 1300 around a castle belonging to the counts of Schaumburg, who named their residence after a recently ruined castle nearby. The name itself derives from Middle High German *gebucke*, a word for a protective hedge made of platted branches, and Old High German *burg*, "castle."

Buckingham. *Town, south central England*. The town, in the county of the same name, has a name that essentially means "land in the river bend of *Bucc's* people," the personal name being

that of an Anglo-Saxon. The *-ham* represents Old English *hamm*, a term for "hemmed-in" land, for example in the bend of a river, as here. Buckingham lies in a bend of the Ouse.

Budapest. *Capital of Hungary*. The present city was formed in 1872 from the merger of two separate towns, *Buda*, on the right bank of the Danube, and *Pest*, on the left. *Buda* is said to derive its name from that of its founder, *Buda* or *Budda*, although it is more likely to comes from some word meaning simply "water." *Pest* derives its name from a Slavic word meaning "furnace," "oven" (modern Russian *pech*), perhaps with reference to a cave where fires burned or to a local limekiln. *Cp.* **Pécs**.

Budaun. *City, northern India*. The city, in Uttar Pradesh state, is said to have been founded in the early 10th century by *Buddh*, a Hindu rajah.

Buenos Aires. *Capital of Argentina*. The Spanish name literally means "good breezes." This is all that remains from the original name, which was *Nuestra Señora Santa María de los Buenos Aires*, "Our Lady St. Mary of the favorable winds," a propitious name for a port. The town, as distinct from the port, was founded on May 23, 1536, Trinity Sunday, and was originally named *Ciudad de la Santissima Trinidad*, "City of the Most Holy Trinity." The name of the port has now become the name of the city, and has been colloquially shortened even further to *Baires*.

Buffalo. *City, eastern United States*. New York's second largest city has a name of disputed origin. It is most likely to derive from the name of an Native American chief who lived by the creek now known as Buffalo Creek, although an alternate origin has been suggested in a corruption of French *beau fleuve*, "beautiful river," referring to this same creek. Buffalo (bison) did not in fact inhabit this region.

Bug. *River, eastern Europe*. The river in Ukraine and Poland, also known as the *Western Bug* for distinction from the *Southern Bug* in southern Ukraine, has a name of disputed origin. Some authorities see a different origin for each river. Thus the *Southern Bug* has been linked with Slavic *beg*, "current," and German *Bach*, "stream," while the *Western Bug* has been derived from Indoeuropean *bheugh*, "to turn," "to twist" (the source of German *biegen*, "to bend," and English *bow*), referring to its winding course. But these etymologies are tentative at best.

Buganda. *Historic kingdom, eastern Africa*. The former kingdom, in what is now Uganda, took its name from the *Ganda* or *Buganda* people here, as does **Uganda** itself.

Bühl. *City, southwestern Germany.* The city derives its name from Old High German *buhil*, "hill," "height," describing its location at the foot of the Black Forest.

Buin. *Town, central Chile.* The town was founded in 1844 and named in honor of the Battle of *Buin* River, Peru, won by the Chilean army.

Bukhara. *City, southern Uzbekistan.* The name, of uncertain origin, is traditionally derived from Sanskrit *vihāra*, "monastery," testifying to the increasing influence of Buddhism in Central Asia. The true origin may be in an ethnic name of unknown meaning.

Bukovina. *Historic region, east central Europe.* The region, formerly an Austrian crownland, has a name meaning "land of beeches," based on Slavic *buk*, "beech."

Bulandshahr. *City, northern India.* The city, in Uttar Pradesh state, has a name meaning "elevated town," from Hindi *buland*, "high," and Persian *shahr*, "town." The reference is to the city's location on high ground.

Bulawayo. *City, southwestern Zimbabwe.* The name is of Ndebele origin, from *bulawa*, "slaughter," with the locative suffix *-yo*. The "place of slaughter" was a fort burned by the Ndebele chief Lobengula in 1893 when the town was founded. In 1894 it moved to its present site nearby.

Bulgaria. *Republic, southeastern Europe.* The name is said to derive from Turkic *bulga*, "mixed," referring to the mixed race that the Bulgarians represent. This seems likely, since the Bulgarians are believed to have originated as a Turkic people of Central Asia, traveling west of the Volga to integrate with the Slavs of the Black Sea coast.

Bundaberg. *City and port, eastern Australia.* The Queensland city is named for the local *Bunda* tribe of Aborigines.

Bünde. *City, northwestern Germany.* The earliest record of the name is *Buginithi* in 1039, apparently from Middle Low German *bügen*, "to bend," and the Old Saxon collective suffix *-ithi*. The name presumably has some local topographical reference.

Bundi. *City, northwestern India.* The city, in Rajasthan state, is said to be named for *Bunda*, a 13th-century chieftain.

Burdur. *City, southwestern Turkey.* The city was known in medieval times by the Greek name of *Polydorion*, "many gifts," and its present name is a corruption of this.

Büren. *Town, northwestern Germany.* The name represents the dative plural of Old High German *būr*, "(little) house," so the meaning is "(place) by the houses."

Burg. *City, central Germany.* The city arose in the 12th century by a 10th-century fort. The name thus derives from Old High German *burg* in its early meaning of "walled fort," "fortified settlement." The full form of the name is *Burg bei Magdeburg*, for its proximity to **Magdeburg**.

Burgas. *City and port, eastern Bulgaria.* The city was founded in the 15th century on the site of the medieval fortified settlement of *Pyrgos*, so named from Greek *purgos*, "tower."

Burgdorf. *Town, northwestern Germany.* The town arose in the 13th century around a castle belonging to the bishops of Hildesheim. The name thus refers to this, and derives from Middle Low German *borch*, "castle," and Old High German *dorf*, "village."

Burgenland. *State, eastern Austria.* The name of the state means "land of castles," from the plural of German *Burg*, "castle," and *Land*, "land." Burgenland is on the Hungarian border, and the three castles for which it is named are now actually across the border in Hungary.

Burgos. *City, western Spain.* The city, capital of the former kingdom of Castile, has a name of Germanic origin, from *burg*, "fortress." The reference is to the fort built here in 884 as a defense against Arab invaders.

Burgundy. *Historic region, central France.* The former kingdom derives its name from the *Burgundi*, a Germanic people who settled here in the 4th or 5th century A.D., many of them coming from **Bornholm**. Their own name may go back to a Gothic word *baurgjans*, "fort dwellers," implying those who lived in a well-protected region.

Burkina Faso. *Republic, western Africa.* The republic, known until 1984 as *Upper Volta* (for the **Volta** River), has a native name meaning "land of the worthy men," from *burkina*, "worthy," and *faso*, "land," literally "father village," from Dyula *fa*, "father," and *so*, "village." The country is now often known simply as *Burkina*, on the grounds that *Faso* is effectively a generic term meaning "republic."

[1]**Burlington.** *City, southeastern Canada.* The city, in Ontario, was settled in c.1810 and named for the English town of *Burlington*, now *Bridlington*, East Riding of Yorkshire.

[2]**Burlington.** *City, northeastern United States.* The Vermont city was chartered in 1763 and named for the *Burling* family, who were pioneer landowners here.

Burma *see* Myanmar

Burnaby. *City, southwestern Canada.* The British Columbia city, now a suburb of Vancouver, developed in the late 19th century and was named for Robert *Burnaby* (1828–1878), a prominent local businessman.

Burnie. *Town and port, southeastern Australia.* The town, in northern Tasmania, was established in 1829 by the Van Diemen's Land Company as *Emu Bay Settlement*, taking this name from that of the *Emu* River here. It was subsequently renamed as now for William *Burnie*, a company director.

Bursa. *City, northwestern Turkey.* The city is named for *Prusias* I, the Bithynian king who founded it in the late 3d century B.C.

Burscheid. *Town, western Germany.* The town had its beginnings in the 9th century as the church belonging to a royal Frankish castle (Old High German *buruc*). The church stood on a ridge, so that the second half of the name, related to modern German *scheiden*, "to divide," "to separate," should here be understood as "watershed." (English *watershed* actually derives from German *Wasserscheide*.)

Burundi. *Republic, east central Africa.* The name comes from the local Bantu people, the *Rundi* or *Barundi*, with *Ba-* the prefix for the people, and *Bu-* that for the country. Burundi was part of German West Africa before World War I, and after it passed as mandated territory to Belgium as *Urundi*, the Swahili form of the name. The present name dates from 1966, when the country gained independence.

Buryatia. *Republic, southeastern Russia.* The republic is named for its indigenous *Buryat* people. Their own name was given them by their Mongol neighbors and means "forest dwellers."

Bury St. Edmunds. *Town, eastern England.* The Suffolk town has a basic name found fairly commonly in England. It derives from Old English *burh*, "fort," "town" (modern *borough*). The rest of the name relates to *St. Edmund*, king of the East Angles, killed by the Vikings in 869 and revered as a saint and martyr. His remains were buried here, and a monastery founded to safeguard them.

Bushehr. *City and port, southwestern Iran.* The city, founded in 1734, is said to have a name meaning "father of towns," from Arabic *abu*, "father," and Persian *shahr*, "town." The name is also spelled *Bushire*.

Busiris. *Historic city, northern Greece.* The ancient city, in the Nile River delta, derives its name from Egyptian *Per-Usir*, "house of *Usir*," from *per*, "house," and *Usir*, better known as

Osiris, the Egyptian god of the underworld. The town itself gave the name of the mythical Egyptian king *Busiris*, who figured in Greek mythology as the son of Poseidon and Lysianassa.

[1]Butterworth. *Town, western Malaysia.* The town, in the Malay Peninsula just east of Penang, is named for William T. *Butterworth*, governor of Singapore and Malacca from 1843 to 1855.

[2]Butterworth. *Town, southeastern South Africa.* The town, in Eastern Cape province, arose from a missionary station set up in 1827 and is named for the missionary society's former treasurer, Joseph *Butterworth*.

Buxtehude. *Town, northern Germany.* The name, recorded in the 12th century as *Buchstadihude*, derives from Old High German *buohha*, "beech," and *stado*, "bank," "shore," and, as a later addition, Middle Low German *hüde*, "(waterside) store." (The *chs* of the recorded name evolved to the present *x*.) The town arose in the 10th century as a trading center between river and road.

Byblos. *Historic city and port, western Lebanon.* The name of the ancient Mediterranean port is probably a Greek corruption of its Canaanite name *Gubla*, "mountain," whose consonants *gbl* were vocalized in biblical Hebrew as *Gebal* (Ezekiel 27:9). (Its modern name is *Jebeil*.) As papyrus was shipped through the port, or even made there, its name gave Greek *byblos* as the word for "papyrus," "paper," then "scroll," "book," and hence ultimately the name of the *Bible*. But it is also possible that the place was named from the Greek word, which might then itself be of Egyptian origin.

Bydgoszcz. *City, north central Poland.* The city derives its name from Indoeuropean *bredahe*, "marsh." The town is near the confluence of the *Brda* and Vistula rivers, the former having a name of identical origin. The city was known under Prussian rule as *Bromberg*, from a reduced form of the original name with Germanic *berg*, "fortress," added.

Byelorussia *see* Belarus

Bytom. *City, southwestern Poland.* The city, chartered in 1254, ultimately derives its name from Slavic *byt*, "settlement" (indirectly related to English *booth*). The German name of the city is *Beuthen*.

Byzantium *see* Istanbul

Caacupé. *City, central Paraguay.* The city, founded in 1770, derives its name from Guaraní *caaguycupé*, "beyond the mountain," describing the town's location in a valley of the Cordillera de los Altos.

Cabinda. *Town and port, northwestern Angola.*

The town, like the enclave in which it lies, almost certainly derives its name from the indigenous *Cabinda* people, although a popular account takes it from the final syllable of *mafuka*, a local term for the trade representative of the king of Ngoyo (now a region in the south of Cabinda), who was responsible for all commercial negotiations, including those with European delegates, and the personal name of this functionary, *Binda*.

Cabot Strait. *Strait, southeastern Canada.* The strait, between Newfoundland and Cape Breton Island, Nova Scotia, is named for the Italian navigator John *Cabot* (c.1450–c.1499), who explored this region in the late 15th century.

Cáceres. *City, western Spain.* The city's name evolved from its Roman name of *Castra Caecilii.* This means "camp of *Caecilius*," referring to the Roman consul Quintus *Caecilius* Metellus, who founded it in 74 B.C.

Cádiz. *City and port, southwestern Spain.* The city was founded as a Phoenician trading colony in c.1100 B.C., and its name goes back to Phoenician *gadir*, "fort," "enclosure." This designation originally applied not to the town or even to the fort, but to the rock on which the latter was built. (According to Pliny, it was one of the summits of Atlantis.)

Caen. *City, northwestern France.* The city has a Gaulish name meaning "battlefield," from *catu*, "battle," and *magos*, "field," "plain." The reference is to the town's strategic site on the Orne River, long making it a focus of military interest. As recently as World War II it was one of the main objects of the Allied invasion.

Caerleon. *Town, southeastern Wales.* The town, near Newport, has a name that is half Welsh, half Latin, meaning "fort of the legion," from Welsh *caer*, "fort," and Latin *legionis*, "of the legion." Caerleon is the site of a Roman camp that was the station of the Second Legion, who moved here from *Glevum* (Gloucester) in A.D. 75. The Roman name of Caerleon was *Isca legionis*, the first word of this being the Roman name of the *Usk* River, on which the town stands.

Caernarfon. *Town, northwestern Wales.* The Gwynedd town has a Welsh name meaning "fort in *Arfon*," from *caer*, "fort," and the name of the district here, meaning "opposite Anglesey," Welsh *ar Fôn*, from *ar*, "over," and *Fôn*, the mutated form of *Môn*, the Welsh name of **Anglesey**. Caernarfon stands on the Menai Straits overlooking Anglesey. The name was formerly spelled less accurately as *Carnarvon*, a form preserved in the title of the Earls of *Carnarvon* (dating from 1793). *See also* **Carnarvon Range**.

Caerphilly. *Town, southeastern Wales.* The town, near Cardiff, has a Welsh name meaning "*Ffili*'s fort," from Welsh *caer*, "fort," and the personal name. It is not known who Ffili was. The present spelling of the name is an anglicized form influenced by *Phillip*. The proper Welsh spelling is *Caerffili*.

Caesarea. *Historic city and port, western Israel.* The name is that of various ancient towns and cities in the former Roman Empire, and in each case derives from one or other of the emperors called *Caesar*. The Caesarea identified here, the modern *Qisarya*, south of Haifa, was founded by Herod the Great in c.22 B.C. and named for his patron, the emperor *Caesar* Augustus. It was the Roman capital of Palestine, and is mentioned in the Bible (Acts 8:40, etc.). It is sometimes identified as *Caesarea Palaestinae* or *Caesarea Maritima* to distinguish it from **Caesarea Philippi**. *See also* **Kayseri**.

Caesarea Philippi. *Historic city, southwestern Syria.* The ancient city is one of several places named for a *Caesar* in the former Roman Empire. This one has a temple built by Herod the Great and was enlarged in c.3 B.C. by his son *Philip* the Tetrarch, who changed its name from *Paneas* (modern *Banias*) to *Caesarea* in honor of *Caesar* Augustus, adding his own name to distinguish it from the **Caesarea** founded by his father on the Mediterranean coast. Like its namesake, it is mentioned in the Bible (Matthew 16:13, etc.). *See also* **Kayseri**.

Cagliari. *City and port, southern Sardinia.* The Italian city, known to the Romans as *Caralis*, has a name of Phoenician origin but uncertain meaning.

Caguas. *City, east central Puerto Rico.* The city was founded in 1775 and named for a local Native American chief who was an early Christian convert.

Cahokia. *Village, east central United States.* The Illinois village, founded in 1699 by Quebec missionaries, is named for a local Native American people, their own name said to mean "wild geese."

Cahors. *Town, southern France.* The town, known to the Romans as *Cadurcum*, derives its name from the *Cadurci*, a local people, whose own name has been explained as meaning "boars of battle." An earlier Roman name for the town was *Devona*, from a Gaulish word meaning "holy well."

Cairngorms. *Mountain group, east central Scotland.* The mountains take their name from their highest peak, *Cairn Gorm*, its Gaelic name meaning "blue rock," from *carn*, "rock," and *gorm*, "blue." The name is properly accented on the second syllable ("Cairn-*gorm*"), as it is the color that is stressed.

Cairns. *Town and port, northeastern Australia.* The Queensland town takes its name from Sir William Wellington *Cairns* (1828–1888), British governor general of Australia from 1875 to 1877. The town was founded in 1873 as a government customs collection point.

Cairo. *Capital of Egypt.* The name derives from Arabic *al-kāhira*, "the strong," in turn from *al-kāhir*, "the victorious." The latter was an epithet of the planet Mars, which was in the ascendant at the precise time when construction of the new city began, on Tuesday (French *mardi*, "Mars-day") July 6, 969. The name was given in 972. The Egyptian name of the original town was *Khere-ohe* or *Kheri-aha*, "place of combat," referring to the legendary battle between the gods Horus and Seth, said to have taken place here. This settlement was captured in 641 by a general of the caliph Omar I, who founded a new town on the site with the name of *Fostat* or *Fustat*. This means "military camp," and is an arabicized form of Latin *fossatum*, "entrenched," from *fodere*, "to dig." The name was later applied to what is now Old Cairo, to the south of the city center. *See also* **Egypt.**

Caithness. *Historic region, northern Scotland.* The former county has a name meaning "headland of the *Cat* people," with Old Norse *nes*, "promontory," added to the Celtic ethnic name. It is not known why the people were so called.

Calabria. *Region, southern Italy.* The name comes from that of the people who once inhabited this region, from a pre–Indoeuropean root word *kalabra* or *galabra*, "rock." *Cp.* **Calais.**

Calais. *City and port, northern France.* The city takes its name from the *Caleti*, the Gaulish people who formerly inhabited the region. Their own name may derive either from a pre–Indoeuropean root word *kal*, "rock," or possibly from a later Celtic word *cul*, "channel." If the latter, the reference would be to the English Channel, by which Calais lies, and which here, on the Strait of Dover (French *Pas de Calais*), is almost at its narrowest point.

Calatayud. *Town, northeastern Spain.* The town has a name of Arabic origin, from *kal'at ayyūb*, "fort of *Ayyub*," the latter being the name (identical with the biblical *Job*) of a Moorish prince. Calatayud was founded in the 8th century and is famous for its ruins of Moorish forts.

Calcutta. *City, northeastern India.* The present capital of West Bengal and former (1773–1912) capital of British India derives its name

from that of *Kali*, the Hindu goddess of the dead. Calcutta was only a small village when a trading post was set up here in 1690 by the East India Company. The city's name now appears in many atlases in its indigenous form *Kolkata*.

Caldas da Rainha. *Town and resort, west central Portugal.* The town's Portuguese name means "hot springs of the queen," referring to Queen Leonor (1458–1525), wife of John II, who founded a hospital here in 1485.

Caldas de Reyes. *Town and resort, northwestern Spain.* The resort, with its mineral springs, was known to the Romans as *Aquis Celenis*. Its present name, Spanish for "hot springs of the kings," dates from the 12th century, when it was so called in honor of Alfonso VII (c.1105–1157), king of Castile and León.

Caledonia *see* **Scotland**

Calexico. *City and river port, southwestern United States.* The California city is separated from **Mexicali**, Mexico, only by a fence. Hence its name, from *California* and *Mexico*.

Calgary. *City, southwestern Canada.* The Alberta city was so named in 1876 by Colonel James Macleod (1836–1894) of the Royal Canadian Mounted Police, in memory of his home village of *Calgary*, on the Scottish island of Mull.

Calicut. *City and port, southwestern India.* The city, in Kerala state, has a name that is a corruption of Tamil *kojīkode*, said to mean "fort of *Kalliai*." Ptolemy mentions the name in the 2d century A.D. in the form *Kalaikaris*. The name now often appears in the more precise form *Kozhikode*.

California. *State, southwestern United States.* The precise origin of the name remains uncertain. There are two traditional theories to account for it: (1) It was given by Hernán Cortés, the Spanish conqueror of Mexico, for a mythical Greek island reigned over by a queen called *Caliphia*; (2) It evolved from Spanish *caliente fornalla*, "hot furnace," alluding to the great heat of the sun here. But the second explanation may well have arisen to account for the first, and the name may have no real meaning. It is that of an imaginary realm in *Las sergas de Esplandián* ("The exploits of Esplandián") (1510), by the Spanish writer Garci Ordóñez de Montalvo, a sequel to his famous romance *Amadís de Gaula*, and it is now thought likely that this is the probable source of the name. *Cp.* **Patagonia.**

Caltagirone. *City, southern Italy.* The city, in southwestern Sicily, is said to derive its name from Arabic *kal'at al-jiran*, "fortress of the caves." *Cp.* **Caltanissetta.**

Caltanissetta. *City, southern Italy.* The city,

in central Sicily, is said to derive its name from Arabic *kal'at an-nisa*, "fortress of the women." *Cp*. **Caltagirone**.

Calumet City. *City, east central United States.* The Illinois city was settled in 1868 and at first called *West Hammond*. In 1924 it was renamed as now, for its location between the Little *Calumet* and Great *Calumet* rivers and its proximity to Lake *Calumet*. These waterways are themselves named for the *calumet*, the peace pipe of the Native Americans.

Calvados. *Region, northwestern France.* The Normandy department takes its name from a group of rocks here, their own name possibly representing Latin *caballi dorsum*, "horse's back," or *calvum dorsum*, "bald back." It is unlikely that the name comes from the *Salvador*, a ship of the Spanish Armada wrecked off the coast here in 1588, as this is too recent.

Calvary *see* **Golgotha**

Calw. *Town, southwestern Germany.* The name, originally that of the medieval castle here, means "bald place," describing the site on which the castle was built.

Camagüey. *City, eastern Cuba.* The city was founded as a port town in 1514 with the Spanish name *Santa María del Puerto del Príncipe*, "St. Mary of the port of the prince." It moved to its present site in 1528 and in 1903, following the end of Spanish rule, adopted its present name, that of a Native American village on the site, itself said to derive from *camagua*, the name of a shrub believed to possess magical properties.

Camargue. *Region, southern France.* The marshy region, in the Rhône delta, has a name of uncertain origin. It was first recorded in 869 as *Camaria*. It may be related to Spanish *comarca*, "country," "region," although the precise reference of this is not clear. Some derive the name from Provençal *camp marca*, "frontier field."

Cambodia. *Republic, southeastern Asia.* The country derives its name from *Kambu*, a legendary ancestor of the Cambodian people, who are said to have been spawned from his union with the nymph Mera. From 1970 to 1976 Cambodia was known as the *Khmer Republic*, and from 1976 to 1989 as *Kampuchea*. The former name relates to the same people, and supposedly blends the names of *Kambu* and *Mera*. The latter is a more accurate form of *Cambodia* given to the country by the Khmer Rouge, the Communist regime then in power (French *rouge*, "red").

Cambrai. *City, northern France.* The city is

so called from the personal name *Camarus*, itself apparently from Latin *cammarus*, "crawfish," "prawn" (*cp*. **Cameroon**). It is not known who this was.

Cambria *see* **Wales**

[1]**Cambridge**. *City, eastern England.* The city, in the county of the same name, is on the *Cam* River, although this is not the origin of the name, since the river is named for the city. The name was recorded in the 8th century as *Grantaceastir*, as if "Grantachester," from the earlier name of the river, the *Granta*, and Old English *ceaster*, "camp," a borrowing from Latin *castrum* in the same sense. Over the centuries, and mainly through Norman influence, *Granta-* was smoothed to *Cam-*, while the second part of the name was replaced by *-bridge*. The alternate river name *Granta* is still in use today in some contexts, as in the former student magazine *Granta*, now a literary quarterly.

[2]**Cambridge**. *City, southeastern Canada.* The Ontario city was created in 1973 as an amalgamation of existing towns and townships. One of the latter was Preston, whose original name (to 1830) was *Cambridge* Mills, for [1]**Cambridge**, England. Hence the new name.

[3]**Cambridge**. *City, northeastern United States.* The Massachusetts city was settled in 1630 and was originally named *New Towne*. It was organized as a town in 1636 when it became the site of Harvard College, founded by the English clergyman John Harvard, a graduate of [1]**Cambridge** University. The town was renamed for the English city in 1638.

Camden. *City, eastern United States.* The New Jersey city was laid out in 1783 and named for Charles Pratt, 1st Earl *Camden* (1714–1794), whose opposition to British taxation policies made him popular with the American colonists.

Cameron Highlands. *Highland region, western Malaysia.* The resort region, on a plateau in the Malay Peninsula, is named for the British government surveyor William *Cameron*, who stumbled on the area in 1885 but did not record his discovery.

Cameroon. *Republic, western Africa.* The country takes its name from what is now the Wouri River estuary. This was named *Rio dos Camarões*, "river of prawns," by 16th-century Portuguese explorers, for the abundance of these crustaceans in its waters.

Camilo Cienfuegos. *Town, western Cuba.* The town, originally known as *Hershey*, was renamed as now for the Cuban revolutionary *Camilo Cienfuegos* (1934–1959), killed in an airplane crash.

Camino Real. *Historic highway, northern Spain.* The 16th-century highway, with a Spanish name meaning "royal way," connected Gijón, on the north coast, with León and Madrid. The name was later adopted for other important routes in Spain. A route called *El Camino Real* was built in California during the Spanish period (1542–1841) and eventually ran from San Diego to Sonoma.

Campania. *Region, southern Italy.* The name refers to the basic topography of the region and means simply "plain," from Latin *campus*. *Cp.* **Champagne.**

Campbelltown. *City, southeastern Australia.* The city, now a suburb of Sydney, New South Wales, was founded in 1810 and was originally known as *Airds*. In 1820 it was renamed as now by Governor Lachlan Macquarie for his wife Elizabeth, née *Campbell*.

Camp David. *Rural retreat, eastern United States.* The presidential retreat, near Thurmont, Maryland, was built in 1939 and originally called *Hi-Catoctin*, for its location in *Catoctin* Mountain Park. Franklin D. Roosevelt later dubbed it *Shangri-La*, for the hidden Buddhist lama paradise in James Hilton's 1933 novel *Lost Horizon*. Dwight D. Eisenhower finally renamed it as now in 1953 for his grandson, *David* (born 1947).

Campeche. *City, southeastern Mexico.* The city, founded in 1540, derives its name from Maya *kam*, "grass snake," and *peque*, "tick" (the small parasitic insect), as these creatures are or were found here.

Campina Grande. *City, northeastern Brazil.* The city, founded on the site of a Native American village, was originally known as *Porta do Sertão*, Portuguese for "gateway to the hinterland." It became a village in 1766 and when raised to city status in 1864 was renamed as now, the name meaning "great grassland."

Campinas. *City, southeastern Brazil.* The city was originally known by the Portuguese name of *Nossa Senhora da Conceição de Campinas de Mato Grosso*, "Our Lady of the (Immaculate) Conception of the grasslands of the Mato Grosso." This was later understandably shortened as now. *See also* **Mato Grosso.**

Campobasso. *City, south central Italy.* The city was originally on a hill, but in 1732 moved down to a lower plain. The name describes this location, from Italian *campo*, "field," and *basso*, "low."

Campo Grande. *City, southwestern Brazil.* The city's Portuguese name means "big field," alluding to the extensive scrubland where it arose.

Campos. *City, eastern Brazil.* The city derives its name from Portuguese *campos*, "fields," "plains," describing the terrain here by the Atlantic seaboard.

Câmpulung. *Town, south central Romania.* The name means "long field," from Romanian *câmp*, "field," and *lung*, "long."

Câmpulung Moldovenesc. *Town, northern Romania.* The second word of the town's name means "Moldovan," to distinguish it from the identically name **Câmpulung.** The town lies on the *Moldova* River, which gave the neighboring country of **Moldova** its name.

Cana. *Historic village, northern Israel.* The biblical village, also known as *Cana of Galilee*, has a name that is ultimately of Hebrew origin, from either *qen*, "nest," or *qanō*, "to envy." It is the site of the modern Arab township *Kafr Kanna*, from Arabic *kafr*, "village," and the ancient name.

Canaan. *Historic region, Palestine.* The name of Israel, before its conquest by the Hebrews, is of Hebrew origin, perhaps from a conjectural Semitic root *kn'*, meaning "to bow down." The name is traditionally derived from a Semitic word meaning "purple," referring to the crimson dye produced in the region or to the wool made with it. This interpretation is disputed, but the territory of the "Promised Land" extended from southern **Phoenicia**, a name also said to mean "purple," to the Negev Desert. In the Old Testament, *Canaan* is the son of Shem and grandson of Noah (Genesis 9:18).

Canada. *Country, northern North America.* The country has an indigenous Native American name, from Huron or Iroquois *kanata*, "camp," "village." When sailing up the St. Lawrence in 1536, the French explorer Jacques Cartier noticed that local people referred to their settlements as *kanata*, and the French assumed that this was the name of the entire country. Among the names suggested for the proposed confederation in 1867 were: *Albertsland* (*see* **Alberta**), *Albionora* (*see* **Albion**), *Borealia* ("northern land," from Greek *Boreas*, god of the north wind), *Britannia* (*see* **Britain**), *Cabotia* (*see* **Cabot Strait**), *Colonia* (Latin, "colony"), *Efisga* (an acronym of England, France, Ireland, Scotland, Germany, and Aboriginal lands), *Norland* ("northern land"), *Superior* (*see* **Superior, Lake**), *Transatlantia* (*see* **Atlantic Ocean**), *Tuponia* (from letters in *United Provinces of North America*), and *Victorialand* (*cp.* ¹**Victoria**). The indigenous name fortunately won the day. The French name for their possessions in Canada to 1763, when they passed to the British, was *Nouvelle France* ("New France").

Çanakkale. *City, northwestern Turkey.* The city arose from a 15th-century fort called *Kale-i Sultaniye,* "fort of the sultan." By the 18th century the town had gained a reputation for its pottery. Hence its present name, from Turkish *çanak,* "pot," and *kale,* "fort."

Canary Islands. *Island group, North Atlantic.* The islands, off the coast of northwestern Africa, became known to the Romans through Juba II, king of Mauritania, whose account of an expedition there in c.40 B.C.was recorded by Pliny with a mention of the *Canariae insulae,* based on Latin *canis,* "dog," for the large dogs that the explorers had seen or heard. In mythology the Canaries were known as the *Fortunatae Insulae,* "Fortunate Islands," as the fabulous islands of the Western Ocean that were the home of the blessed dead. The local (Guanche) name of the islands, before their Spanish possession, was *Tamaran,* "land of the strong."

Canaveral, Cape. *Headland, southeastern United States.* The Florida cape has a name of Spanish origin meaning "canebrake," alluding to the abundance of this plant here discovered by Spanish explorers in the 16th century. In 1964 the cape was renamed *Cape Kennedy,* as a tribute to the assassinated U.S. president John F. Kennedy (1916–1963). The earlier name was re-adopted in 1974.

Canberra. *Capital of Australia.* The name is probably of Aboriginal origin, from *nganbirra,* "meeting place." Despite its somewhat unpropitious location, Canberra was chosen as capital in 1913, when the two largest settlements, Melbourne and Sydney, were both rivals for the honor, and neither could be advantageously selected over the other.

Cancún. *City and resort, southeastern Mexico.* The city, on the northeast coast of the Yucatán Peninsula, was originally a Maya settlement named *Cancúne,* said to mean "vessel at the end of the rainbow."

Candia *see* **Heraklion**

Cangas de Narcea. *City, northwestern Spain.* The second part of the city's name is that of the *Narcea* river on which it lies. The meaning of its own name is uncertain. The first part of the name represents a local word meaning "town."

Caniapiscau. *River, eastern Canada.* The river, in northern Quebec province, has a Native American name meaning "rocky point."

Cannes. *City and port, southern France.* The city has a name of pre–Indoeuropean origin, from *kan,* "height." The old part of the city lies at the foot of low hills.

Cantabrian Mountains. *Mountain chain,* northern Spain. The mountains derive their name from a Mediterranean root word *kanto,* "rock," "stone." The same word also lies behind **Cantal.**

Cantal. *Department, south central France.* As for Spain's **Cantabrian Mounains,** the name derives from the Mediterranean root word *kanto,* "rock," "stone." The reference here would be to the Massif Cantal, the volcanic mass that lies in the center of the region.

[1]**Canterbury.** *City, southeastern England.* The name of the Kent city relates directly to that of its county. It means "fortified place of the *Kent* dwellers," with *Cant-* representing **Kent,** *-er-* all that remains of Old English *-ware,* "dwellers," and *-bury* from Old English *burh,* "fort." The Roman name of Canterbury was *Durovernum,* "walled town by the alder marsh."

[2]**Canterbury.** *Region, southeastern New Zealand.* The local government region, in South Island, derives its name from the *Canterbury* Association, a Church of England colonizing organization established in 1848 to found an Anglican settlement in New Zealand. It was itself named for [1]**Canterbury,** England. *See also* **Christchurch.**

[1]**Canton.** *City and port, southeastern China.* The name of the city is a europeanized form of **Kwangtung,** the province of which it is the capital. The Chinese name of Canton, now found on most maps, is *Guangzhou,* from *guǎng,* "wide," and *zhōu,* "region."

[2]**Canton.** *City, east central United States.* The Ohio city was laid out in 1805 and apparently named for the *Canton* estate in Baltimore, Maryland, itself founded on trading profits from [1]**Canton,** China.

Cap-de-la-Madeleine. *City, eastern Canada.* The city, on the St. Lawrence River in Quebec, was originally known by the French name of *Cap-des-Trois-Rivières,* "cape of the three rivers." The site was renamed *Cap-de-la-Madeleine* by the French priest Abbé La Ferté, of Sainte-Marie-*Madeleine*-de-Châteaudun, in the diocese of Rouen, when land here was granted him in 1636. Hence the name of the present city, incorporated as a town in 1918.

Cape Breton Island. *Island, eastern Canada.* The island, in eastern Nova Scotia, was assigned to France in 1632 and was apparently named by Basque fishermen from the coastal locality of *Capbreton,* southwestern France, a name that itself means "Breton's chief estate." The apparent sense of "Breton cape" is thus misleading.

Cape Cod. *Cape, northeastern United States.* The long sandy peninsula in Massachusetts takes its name from the cod that abound off its shores. It was the English navigator Bartholomew Gosnold (died 1607) who recorded in his journal entry of May 15, 1602: "Near this cape we came to anchor in fifteen fathoms, where we took great store of codfish ... and called it Cape Cod."

Cape Horn *see* **Horn, Cape**

Cape of Good Hope *see* **Good Hope, Cape of**

Cape Province. *Historic province, southwestern South Africa.* The province was named for the *Cape of Good Hope* (*see* **Good Hope, Cape of**) that was its chief natural feature. In 1994 it was divided into the three new provinces of *Eastern Cape*, *Northern Cape*, and *Western Cape*. The original province was formed in 1910 from the former *Cape Colony*.

Capernaum. *Historic town, northern Israel.* The biblical town (Matthew 4:13, etc.), on the northwest shore of the Sea of Galilee, has a name of Hebrew origin meaning "village of *Nahum*," from *kefar*, "village," and the personal name (identical with that of the biblical prophet).

Cape Town. *City and port, southwestern South Africa.* The city is named for the *Cape of Good Hope* (see **Good Hope, Cape of**), on which it was first settled in 1652.

Cape Verde. *Island republic, North Atlantic.* The islands takes their name from the cape in Senegal to the west of which they lie. The cape was named *Cabo Verde*, "green cape," by 15th-century Portuguese explorers, who noted the green palm trees here contrasting with the barren, sandy coast. The republic name is really half English, half Portuguese.

Cape York *see* **York, Cape**

Cap-Haïtien. *City and port, northern Haiti.* The former capital of colonial Haiti, also called simply *Le Cap*, was founded in 1670 by the French and originally named *Cap-Français*, "French cape." Its present name, "Haitian cape," relates more directly to its geographical location in **Haiti**.

Cappadocia. *Historic region, central Turkey.* According to one account, the region takes its name from the people who at one time inhabited it, their own name deriving from Assyrian *Katpa Tuka*, "*Tuka*'s side," for their ancestor or chief, with *katpa* related to Hebrew *katef*, "side," "shoulder." But another theory traces the name to Persian *Hvaspadakhim*, "land of fine horses." Cappadocia was renowned for its breeding of horses.

Capraia. *Island, northwestern Italy.* The island, in the northern Tyrrhenian sea between Italy and Corsica, derives its name from Italian *capra*,

"goat," referring to the wild goats that are found here.

Capri. *Island, southwestern Italy.* The island's name is of uncertain origin. It has been associated not very convincingly with Greek *kapra*, "boar," Latin *capra*, "goat," and Etruscan *capra*, "burial place."

Caprivi Strip. *Region, northeastern Namibia.* The region arose as a band of territory obtained from the British in 1893 by the German chancellor Count Leo von *Caprivi* (1831–1899). Hence the name. The aim of the acquisition was to link what was then German South-West Africa (modern Namibia) to Germany's possessions in eastern Africa.

Capua. *Town, southern Italy.* The town, north of Naples, is said to take its name from Etruscan *capys*, "marsh," referring to its site on the Volturno River. The Romans knew it as *Casilinum*.

Carabobo. *State, northwestern Venezuela.* The state is named for the Battle of *Carabobo* (1821) in the Latin-American wars of independence, in which South American patriots won victory over Spanish royalists. The village itself has a tribal name perhaps from Guaraní *cari*, "man," and *mbovo*, "to share."

Caracas. *Capital of Venezuela.* The city was founded on the site of a razed village of the Native American *Caracas* people on July 25 (St. James's Day), 1567 by the Spanish conquistador Diego de Losada, who named it *Santiago de León de Caracas*, "St. James of León of Caracas." The name of the people itself is of uncertain origin.

Carbondale. *City, east central United States.* The Illinois city was founded in 1852 following the arrival of the railroad and is named for the local coalfields. It is a *dale* in so far as it is located at the edge of the Ozarks.

Carcassonne. *City, southern France.* The city's name of is pre–Indoeuropean origin, from a root word *kar*, "rock," "stone," and *kasser*, "oak."

Cardiff. *Capital of Wales.* The city, in the south of the principality, has a name that is an anglicized form of its Welsh name, *Caerdydd*, "fort on the *Taff*," from *caer*, "fort," and the name of the river on which Cardiff stands, itself probably meaning simply "water."

Cardigan. *Town, western Wales.* The town's name is an anglicized form of *Ceredigion*, "*Ceredig*'s land," the historic name of the former county of Cardiganshire, now readopted as that of a unitary authority. Ceredig was one of the sons of the 5th-century ruler Cunedda, whose own name is said to have given that of **Gwynedd**. It is unusual for a town to take its name from the surrounding territory like this. Usually it is the other way around, with a territory named for an important town or settlement.

Caria. *Historic region, southwestern Turkey.* The name is based on the pre–Indoeuropean root element *kar* or *kal*, "rock," "stone," "mountain." *Cp.* **Carcassonne**, **Carinthia**, **Carniola**, **Chartres**. The region has many mountains.

Caribbean Sea. *Sea, western North Atlantic.* The sea takes its name from an old name of the island group now known as the Lesser Antilles, formerly familiar in English as the *Caribbees*. This itself comes from the name of the indigenous people, the *Caribs*, whose own name ultimately derives from Arawak *kalinago* or *kalino*, "brave ones." The Spanish name of the islands, *Caribale*, gave English *cannibal*, from the people's supposed custom of consuming their captives.

Carinthia. *Region, southern Austria.* The province takes its name from its original indigenous inhabitants, their own name ultimately going back to pre–Indoeuropean *kar*, "rock," "stone," as they were mountain dwellers. The German name of Carinthia is *Kärnten*.

Carletonville. *Town, northeastern South Africa.* The town, in Gauteng province, was originally an unplanned settlement of the 1930 to 1950s. In 1959 it was officially designated a town and named for Guy *Carleton* Jones, a local mining director.

Carlisle. *City, northwestern England.* The Cumbria city has a name representing Celtic *cair*, "fort," added to a much reduced form of the Roman name of the fort itself. This was *Luguvalium*, from the Celtic personal name *Luguvalos*, meaning "strong as *Lugus*," the latter being a Celtic god. The spelling of the name has apparently been influenced by Old French *l'isle*, "the island" (*cp.* **Lille**), and the original fort here was in fact built on an "island" of raised land by the Eden River.

Carlow. *County, southeastern Ireland.* The name represents Irish *Ceatharlach*, "four lakes." There is no sign of the lakes now, but at one time they may have been at the point where the Burren and Burrow rivers meet.

Carlsbad. *City, southwestern United States.* The California city was settled in the 1870s and originally called *Frazier's Station*. It was renamed in 1883 when its mineral waters were compared to those at *Carlsbad*, Bohemia (now **Karlovy Vary**, Czech Republic).

Carmarthen. *Town, southwestern Wales.* The town derives its name from Celtic *cair*, "fort," and the personal name *Myrddin*, itself probably meaning "seaside fort," as also in the town's Roman name of *Maridunum* or *Moridunum*. If so, the name is something of a tautology, since it includes "fort" twice.

Carmel, Mt. *Mountain, northern Israel.* The mountain, near the Mediterranean coast, has a Hebrew name, from *karmel*, "garden," "fertile field." The region's abundant vegetation is the result of mild summers and above-average annual rainfall.

Carnac. *Village, northwestern France.* The Brittany village, noted for its megalithic monuments, has a name representing Breton *Karnag*, itself probably based on *karn*, "tumulus" (English *cairn*), with the Gallo-Roman suffix *-acum. See also* **Karnak**.

Carnarvon Range. *Mountain range, eastern Australia.* The range, a section of the Great Dividing Range, Queensland, is named for Henry Herbert, 4th Earl of *Carnarvon* (1831–1890), British colonial secretary in the 1860s and 1870s. *See also* **Caernarfon**.

Carniola. *Region, northwestern Slovenia.* The mountainous region, known in Slovene as *Kranj*, takes its name from the *Carni*, the people who at one time inhabited it. Their own name is probably based on the pre–Indoeuropean root element *kar*, "rock," as for **Caria**.

¹Carolina. *States, eastern United States.* North and South Carolina were originally a single territory, named in 1564 by French colonists *Caroline*, in honor of *Charles* IX of France (1550–1574), whose Latin name was *Carolus*. This name then fell into disuse, and when *Charles* I of England (1600–1649) granted the territory to the English colonist Robert Heath in 1629 it was under the name *Carolana*. In 1663 *Charles* II (1630–1685) regranted the region to nine proprietors under the name *Carolina*, which was as appropriate for him as it had been for his father. North and South Carolina were officially distinguished in 1710.

²Carolina. *Town, northeastern Puerto Rico.* The town was founded in 1816 and was originally known as *Trujillo Bajo*, "lower *Trujillo*," for **¹Trujillo**, Spain. In 1857 it was renamed *San Fernando de la Carolina*, for *Charles* II of Spain (1661–1700), whose Latin name was *Carolus*.

Caroline Islands. *Island group, western Pacific.* The islands were named *Islas Carolinas* by the Spanish in 1686 in honor of their king, *Charles* II (1661–1700). When originally discovered in 1528, they were called *Islas de los Barbudas*, "islands of the bearded ones," alluding to the Polynesians who formed the indigenous population.

Carpathians. *Mountain range, eastern Europe.*

The name of the mountains, in the Czech Republic and Poland, may be based on the Indoeuropean root word *ger*, "to turn," referring to a peak or summit where a mountain slope forms an angle or otherwise "veers." But a Slavic source in a word related to Russian *khrebet*, "mountain chain," as for **Croatia**, is also a possibility, and a kinship with Albanian *karpë*, "cliff," "rock," better still.

Carpentaria, Gulf of. *Inlet, northeastern Australia.* The inlet of the Arafura Sea was so named in 1623 by the Dutch navigator Jan Carstensz for the governor general of the Dutch East Indies, Pieter de *Carpentier* (1588–1659).

Carpentras. *City, southeastern France.* The name ultimately goes back to Gaulish *carbanton*, "cart," and *rate*, "fort." The fort served as a lookout post for the passage of carts over a ford across the Auzon River here.

Carrara. *Town, northwestern Italy.* The town derives its name from Latin *quadraria*, "quarry," referring to the local quarries that furnish the famous Carrara marble.

Carrickfergus. *Town, northeastern Northern Ireland.* The town, in Co. Antrim, has the Irish name of *Carraig Fheargais*, "*Fergus*'s rock," alluding to King *Fergus*, said to have been shipwrecked off the coast here in the early 4th century. The *rock* is the one on which the town's Norman castle stands.

Carson City. *City, western United States.* The state capital of Nevada was founded in 1858 on the site of *Eagle Station* and at first bore that name. It was renamed in honor of the frontiersman, trapper, and soldier Kit *Carson* (1809–1868), many of whose exploits were in this region.

Cartagena. *City and port, southeastern Spain.* The city was founded in the 3d century B.C. by the Carthaginian general Hasdrubal. It later became known to the Romans as *Carthago Nova*, "new **Carthage**," and its present name evolved from this. Both cities are on the Mediterranean, virtually due east and west of each other.

Carthage. *Historic city, northern Tunisia.* The city's name is of Phoenician origin, and represents *qart khadash*, "new town," an accurate enough description when it was founded in the 8th century B.C. *Cp.* **Chalcedon**, and *see also* **Cartagena**.

Casablanca. *City and port, western Morocco.* The city has a Spanish name meaning "white house," translating its earlier name, *Casa Branca*, given by the Portuguese in 1515 to the town they founded on the site of the former village of *Anfa*. Many of the city's buildings are still noticeably white today. The city's Arabic name, *Dar el Beida*, translates this, in full *ad-dār al baydā'*, from *al*, "the," *dār*, "house," and *baydā'*, feminine of *abyaḍ*, "white."

Casa Grande. *City, southwestern United States.* The Arizona city takes its name from the *Casa Grande*, Spanish, "big house," a tall watchtower here built by Native Americans in the 14th century. *Cp.* **Casas Grandes.**

Casamance. *Region, southern Senegal.* The region was formerly the territory of the *mansa* (Mandinka, "king") of *Kasa*. Hence the name.

Casas Grandes. *Town, northern Mexico.* The town was settled by the Spanish in 1661 and given a name, meaning "big houses," that refers to the extensive ruins nearby of a pre–Columbian town.

Cascade Range. *Mountain chain, western United States.* The chain, a continuation of the Sierra Nevada range, was so named in 1820 for the *cascades* (waterfalls) on the Columbia River, which crosses it in a deep gorge near the Washington-Oregon border.

Caserta. *City, southern Italy.* The city derives its name from a castle serving as a summer residence here, known in Latin as *Casa Hirta*, "house on the steep slope." The old town of Caserta, founded in the 8th century, lies on hills, while the modern city grew up below it in the 18th century.

Cashmere *see* **Kashmir**

Casper. *City, west central United States.* The Wyoming city arose around *Fort Caspar* here, itself named for Lieutenant *Caspar* Collins, killed by Native Americans when attempting to rescue a stranded wagon train. The present form of the name is due to the misspelling of the railroad clerk who filed the plat.

Caspian Sea. *Sea between Europe and Asia.* The great lake between Russia and Iran takes its name from the people known to the Roman as the *Caspii*, who lived on its shores and who came here from a region of the Caucasus. Their name may mean "white."

Castel Gandolfo. *Town, central Italy.* The town, with its former papal palace, takes its name from a historic castle here that belonged to the ducal *Gandolfi* family in the 12th century.

Castellammare. *City and resort, southern Italy.* The city arose around a "castle by the sea" built here in the 13th century by the Holy Roman emperor Frederick II.

Castellón de la Plana. *City, eastern Spain.* The city arose as a fortified settlement (Latin *castellum*, Spanish *castillo*, "castle") on a nearby hilltop. In 1251, on the petition of its inhabitants, it was moved from this exposed location to its present site on a fertile *plain*. Hence the second part of the name

Castile. *Historic region, central Spain*. The former kingdom is famous for its castles. Hence its name, representing Low Latin *castilla*, from Classical Latin *castella*, the plural of *castellum*, "castle."

Castres. *Town, southern France*. The town derives its name from Latin *castra*, the plural of *castrum*, "encampment." There was a Gallo-Roman camp here.

Castrop-Rauxel. *City, northwestern Germany*. The present city was formed in 1926 on the amalgamation of the town of *Castrop* with nearby *Rauxel* and other communities. *Castrop* is based on Old Saxon *thorp*, "village," while *Rauxel* derives from Old Saxon *seli*, "hall," "one-roomed building." The first part of each name is unexplained.

Çatalca. *Town, northwestern Turkey*. The town derives its name from Turkish *çatal*, "fork," alluding to its location at the point where the road divides to Istanbul, to the west, and the Sea of Marmara, to the south. The traditional form of the name is *Chatalja*.

Çatal Höyük. *Archaeological site, south central Turkey*. The Neolithic site derives its name from Turkish *çatal*, "fork," and *höyük*, "mound," "tumulus."

Catalonia. *Historic region, northeastern Spain*. The region is named for its indigenous *Catalan* population. The people's own name is of Celtic origin and probably means "chiefs of battle." *Cp.* **Châlons-en-Champagne**. The Spanish name of the region is *Cataluña*.

Catamarca. *City, northwestern Argentina*. The city, on a river between two hill spurs, takes its name from Guaraní *qata*, "slope," "incline," and *marka*, "region."

Catania. *City and port, southern Italy*. The city in eastern Sicily has a name of disputed origin. It may derive from a local word meaning "bowl," referring to the town's location among hills. Some authorities trace the name back to Phoenician *qaṭon*, "little," relating Catania to larger and more important Syracuse.

Catanzaro. *City, southern Italy*. The city derives its name from its Byzantine Greek name of *Katantzarion*, perhaps representing *kata*, "on," "near," and Arabic *anjār*, "terrace." The city is at an altitude of 1,125 feet (343 m) overlooking the Gulf of Squillace, an inlet of the Ionian Sea.

Cathay *see* **China**

Catherine, Mt. *see* **Katherina, Gebel**

Catskill Mountains. *Mountain range, eastern*

United States. The New York range has a name of Dutch origin meaning "*Kat's* stream," with *kil*, "stream," following the personal name. Popular etymology links the name with the wildcats found here.

Caucasus. *Mountain range, southeastern Europe/southwestern Asia*. The range, between the Black Sea and Caspian Sea, probably derives its name from a Pelasgian word *kau* meaning simply "mountain." Pliny proposed a Scythian origin, from a word meaning "snow-white."

Cavalla. *River, western Africa*. The river, forming part of the border between Liberia and Côte d'Ivoire, has a name that is Portuguese for "horse mackerel," a fish that early explorers found at its mouth.

Cavan. *County, northern Ireland*. The county is named for the town here, its own name representing Irish *An Cabhán*. The town lies in a hollow, above which rises a round, grassy hill. Irish *cabhán* can mean either "hollow" or "hill," one being a mirror image of the other, so that either sense is appropriate.

Cawnpore *see* **Kanpur**

Caxias. *City, northeastern Brazil*. The city, in the state of Maranhão, originally had the Portuguese name *São José das Aldeias Altas*, "St. Joseph of the high hamlets." It was renamed as now in honor of Luis Alves de Lima e Silva, duque de *Caxias* (1803–1880), soldier and patron of the Brazilian army and governor of Maranhão from 1837. *Cp.* **Duque de Caxias**.

Çaycuma. *Town, northwestern Turkey*. The town is said to derive its name from Turkish *çay*, "stream," "river," and *cuma*, "Friday," denoting a regular Friday market here.

Cayenne. *Capital of French Guiana*. The city's name is a French form of the name of **Guyana**, so that its origin and meaning are the same. *See also* **French Guiana**.

Cayman Islands. *Island group, northwestern West Indies*. The islands, northwest of Jamaica, were sighted by Christopher Columbus in 1503 and originally named by the Spanish as *Las Tortugas*, "the turtles," for the abundance of these reptiles here. By 1530 they had been renamed as now, from Spanish *caimán*, "alligator," apparently in mistaken reference to the islands' indigenous iguanas.

Ceará. *State, northeastern Brazil*. The state is said to take its name from Guaraní *ceara*, "shouting."

Cedar Falls. *City, central United States*. The Iowa city was settled in 1845 on the *Cedar* River and named for it. The river was itself named for the *cedar* trees along its banks. *Cp.* **Cedar Rapids**.

Cedar Rapids. *City, central United States.* The Iowa city was settled in the 1830s and originally called *Rapids City*, for the surging *rapids* on the Cedar River here that were a source of abundant waterpower. The settlement was renamed for the river as now when incorporated as a town in 1849. *Cp.* **Cedar Falls**.

Cefalù. *Town and port, southern Italy.* The town, in northern Sicily, had the Roman name *Cephalaedium*, a form of its Greek name *Kephaloidion*, a diminutive of *kephaloeidēs*, from *kephalē*, "head," and *eidos*, "shape," referring to the nearby promontory on which the original town arose. The present town was founded at its foot in 1131. *Cp.* **Cephalonia**.

Celebes *see* **Sulawesi**

Celldömölk. *Town, western Hungary.* The first part of the town's name, meaning "cell," was adopted from **Mariazell** in neighboring Austria. The second part is a pet form of the personal name *Dominicus*.

Celle. *City, north central Germany.* The city was founded in 1292 by Duke Otto dem Strengen von Lüneburg on an island between the Aller and Fuhse rivers. His method of founding was to move the location of a castle and town 2 miles (3 km) upstream called *Altencelle* to the present site, as being more suitable for tolls and trade. The name of the new town was thus at first *Neu-Celle*, while *Celle*, common to both, comes from Old High German *kella*, "ladle," meaning a fishing pool in the river.

Celtic Sea. *Sea, southwestern British Isles.* The sea area was designated by the British Government on June 18, 1974, as that bounded by Ushant (France), Land's End, Hartland Point, St. Govan's Head, and Rosslare. The area thus lies between Brittany, Cornwall, Wales, and Ireland, all Celtic lands.

Cenis, Mt. *Mountain and pass, southeastern France.* The pass over the French Alps to Italy is named for the massif here, its own name perhaps from Latin *cenistus*, "cinder gray," referring to the predominant color of its slopes. The French name of the pass is *Mont Cenis*, the Italian *Monte Censio*.

Central African Republic. *Republic, central Africa.* The descriptive name refers to the country's location in the African continent as a whole. It was originally part of French Equatorial Africa, and until 1958 was known as *Ubangi-Shari*, for the **Ubangi** and **Shari** rivers. It then became the *Central African Republic*, but in 1977 was renamed *Central African Empire* by its self-styled emperor, Bokassa I. In 1979 it reverted to its previous name. Unusually, it replaced an indigenous name by a europeanized one, while most other former African colonies did the reverse on gaining independence.

Cephalonia. *Island, western Greece.* The island, in the Ionian Sea, has a name based on Greek *kephalē*, "head," in the sense "mountain," referring to its predominant topography.

Cernavoda. *Town and port, southeastern Romania.* The town takes its name from the river on which it lies, as a tributary of the Danube. Its own Slavic name means "black water."

Cēsis. *Town, central Latvia.* The name is said to derive from Baltic *kesoi*, "fallow field." The German name of the town is *Wenden*, from the Slav people known as the *Wends*.

České Budějovice. *City, southwestern Czech Republic.* The main word of the city's name derives from the adjectival form of the Slavic personal name *Budivoj*, so that the name itself means "settlement of *Budivoj*'s people." The first word is Czech for "Czech," for distinction of nationality. (It was formerly in Bohemia, as part of the Austrian Empire, and its German name was simply *Budweis*.)

Ceuta. *City and port, northern Morocco.* The city, a Spanish military station on the Strait of Gibraltar, is traditionally said to derive its name from Latin *septem fratres*, "seven brothers," referring to the seven hills visible from the north here. The Arabic form of the name is *Sebta*.

Cévennes. *Mountain range, south central France.* The name probably originates from a pre–Celtic root word *kem* or *kam*, meaning "rounded height." *Cp.* **Chamonix**.

Ceylon *see* **Sri Lanka**

Chaco. *Province, northeastern Argentina.* The province forms part of the **Gran Chaco**. Hence its name. It was renamed *Presidente Juan Perón* in 1950 but resumed its original name following the revolution of 1955.

Chad. *Republic, north central Africa.* The country takes its name from Lake *Chad*, from a local word meaning "large expanse of water," otherwise simply "lake."

Chaillu Massif. *Mountain range, south central Gabon.* The massif is named for the French-born American explorer Paul du *Chaillu* (1831–1903), who is said to have discovered it during his African travels of 1855–65.

Chalcedon. *Historic town and port, northwestern Turkey.* The ancient town derives its name from a Phoenician word meaning "new town" (*cp.* **Carthage**). Its modern name is *Kadıköy*, "village of the judge," from Turkish *kadı*, "(Muslim) judge," and *köy*, "village." It is now a district of Istanbul.

Chalcis. *City, east central Greece.* The ancient city, on the island of Euboea, derives its name from Greek *khalkos*, "copper," "brass," from the historic bronze workings in the vicinity. *Cp.* **Cyprus.**

Chaldea. *Historic region, southwestern Asia.* The name is that of the region's indigenous people, the *Chaldeans* or *Chaldees*, themselves part of a Babylonian population. Hence "Chaldean" in the Bible as a synonym for "Babylonian" (except in Daniel where it amounts to "astrologer"). Their own name is of uncertain origin, but could come from an Assyrian root meaning "conquer." This appears to be supported by the biblical description of the Chaldeans as a "bitter and hasty nation" who are "terrible and dreadful" (Habakkuk 1:6–7). The eponymous ancestor of the Chaldeans is traditionally regarded as *Chesed*, one of the twelve sons of Nahor (Genesis 22:22). *See also* **Ur.**

Chaleur Bay. *Bay, southeastern Canada.* The bay, an inlet of the Gulf of St. Lawrence, was navigated by the French explorer Jacques Cartier in 1534 and named by him, from French *chaleur*, "heat," for the high temperatures he experienced here.

Châlons-en-Champagne. *Town, northeastern France.* The town takes its name from the *Catalauni*, the tribe who formerly inhabited the region. Their own name probably comes from Gaulish *catu*, "battle," and *vellaunos*, "chief," implying their prowess as warriors. The second part of the name refers to the town's location in **Champagne.** Until 1995 it was known as *Châlons-sur-Marne*, from its location on the **Marne** River, distinguishing it from **Chalon-sur-Saône.**

Chalon-sur-Saône. *City, east central France.* The Roman name of the city was *Cabillonum*, suggesting an origin either in a Latin or Gaulish personal name such as *Cabilus* or else in the source of this name, Gaulish *caballos*, "horse," "steed" (Latin *caballus*, French *cheval*). The name of the **Saône** River was added for distinction from places with similar names, such as **Châlons-en-Champagne.**

Chambéry. *City, southeastern France.* The city had the Medieval Latin name of *Camberacium*, deriving from Gaulish *cambo*, "bend," "curve," and the Gallo-Roman suffix *-acum*. The reference is to the town's location on a bend of the Leysse River, between the massifs of Beauges and La Grande Chartreuse.

Chamonix. *Town and resort, southeastern France.* The name of the mountain resort, in the Alps at the foot of Mont Blanc, derives from a pre–Celtic, possibly Ligurian root word *kam*, meaning "rounded height." *Cp.* **Cévennes.**

Champagne. *Historic region, northeastern France.* The region almost certainly derives its name from Latin *campus*, "plain," describing its prevailing topography. *Cp.* **Campania.** However, a source in Celtic *kann pan*, "white country," has also been proposed, in allusion to the chalk seen everywhere and the limestone escarpments at the region's eastern edge.

Champaign. *City, east central United States.* The Illinois city adjoins Urbana, so that the two together are often called *Champaign-Urbana*. Champaign itself was earlier *West Urbana* but in 1860 was reincorporated and renamed for its county, itself named for *Champaign* County in Ohio. The Ohio county's name arose as a form of what is now French *campagne*, "country," "plain." *Cp.* **Champagne.**

Champlain, Lake. *Lake, eastern United States.* The lake, on the American-Canadian border, is named for the French explorer and founder of Quebec, Samuel de *Champlain* (1567–1635), who discovered it in 1609.

Chan-chiang. *City and port, eastern China.* The city, in Kwangtung province, derives its name from Chinese *zhàn*, "deep," "clear," and *jiāng*, "river."

Chandernagor. *City and port, northeastern India.* The West Bengal city has a name meaning "moon town," from Hindi *chandra*, "moon," and *nagar*, "town." The name, also spelled *Chandannagar*, relates to a former cult of the moon here. *Cp.* **Chandrapur.**

Chandigarh. *City, northern India.* The joint capital of Punjab and Haryanah states derives its name from *Chandi*, one of the names of the Hindu goddess Devi, consort of Shiva, itself from Sanskrit *chandā*, "cruel," "violent," and Sanskrit *garh*, "fort."

Chandrapur. *City, western India.* The city, in Maharashtra state, has a name meaning "moon town," from Hindi *chandra*, "moon," and *pur*, "town." The name relates to a former cult of the moon here. *Cp.* **Chandernagor.**

Ch'ang-chi. *City, eastern China.* The city, in Shansi province, derives its name from Chinese *cháng*, "long," and *zhì*, "to rule," "to govern."

Chang-chia-k'ou *see* **Kalgan**

Ch'ang-chou. *City, eastern China.* The city, in Kiangsu province, derives its name from Chinese *cháng*, "ordinary," "common," and *shú*, "ripe," "cooked."

Ch'ang-ch'un. *City, northeastern China.* The capital of Kirin province derives its name from Chinese *cháng*, "long," and *chūn*, "springtime."

The name relates to the fertile grazing ground by the original village here in the 18th century. (The same ideographs give an alternate interpretation "eternal youth," lending a figurative sense to the factual.) In 1932, following the Japanese seizure of Manchuria (in northeastern China), the city was made the capital of Japan's puppet state, Manchukuo, and until 1945 was known as *Hsin-ching*, from Chinese *xīn*, "new," and *jīng*, "capital."

Ch'ang-pai Mountains. *Mountain range, northeastern China*. The range, forming the border between China and North Korea, derives its name from Chinese *cháng*, "long," and *bái*, "white." As in English, *cháng* can mean "long" in a spatial or temporal sense, so that an alternate interpretation is "ever white." Either way, the reference is to the mountains' long-lasting snow cover.

Ch'ang-sha. *City, southeastern China*. The capital of Hunan province derives its name from Chinese *cháng*, "long," and *shā*, "sand," referring to an island in the Hsiang River here.

Ch'ang-shu. *City, eastern China*. The city, in Kiangsu province, derives its name from Chinese *cháng*, "ordinary," "common," and *zhōu*, "state," "department."

Ch'ang-te. *City, east central China*. The city, in Hunan province, derives its name from Chinese *cháng*, "ordinary," "invariable," and *dé*, "virtue," "kindness."

Channel Islands. *Island group, western English Channel*. The islands, off the northwest coast of France, have a name describing their location in the English *Channel*. The islands are not strictly part of the United Kingdom, but have a special relationship with it. The French know them as *îles Anglo-Normandes*, "Anglo-Norman islands," as they originally formed part of the duchy of **Normandy**.

Chantilly. *Town, northern France*. The Medieval Latin name of the town was *Chantileium*, representing the Gallo-Roman personal name *Cantilius* with the Gallo-Roman suffix *-acum*.

Chao Phraya. *River, northern Thailand*. Thailand's principal river has a name representing Thai *chao*, "king," "royal," "sacred," and *phraya*, an honorific meaning "general," "chief."

Chardzhou. *City, southeastern Turkmenistan*. The city, arising in the 1880s as a military post, derives its name from Turkic *chor*, "four," and *dzhou*, "stream," referring to the confluence of three small rivers with the great Amu Darya here. The name was originally spelled *Chardzhuj* but in 1940 was adjusted to reflect the actual pronunciation. It now often appears in atlases as *Chärjew*.

Charente. *River, western France*. The river derives its name from proto–Indoeuropean *karantono*, "sandy," from *karanto*, "sand," describing the nature of its banks for some of its course.

Charleroi. *Town, southwestern Belgium*. The town arose on the site of a village originally named *Charnoy*. In 1666 it was renamed as now by the Spanish governor general of the Low Countries, the Marquess de Castel Rodrigo, in honor of his king, *Charles* II (1661–1700). The opaque placename *Charnoy* was thus modified to a transparent *Charleroi*, as if French *Charles roi*, "Charles (the) king."

Charles, Cape. *Cape, eastern United States*. The Virginia cape, north of the entrance to Chesapeake Bay, was so named in 1608 by Captain John Smith for 8-year-old Prince *Charles*, the future Charles I of England (1600–1649). He was the younger brother of Prince *Henry*, whose name had been given the previous year to Cape *Henry*, south of the entrance. (*See* **Henry, Cape**.)

Charlesbourg. *City, eastern Canada*. The city, just northwest of Quebec, was founded in 1659 and originally known as *Bourg Royal*, French for "royal borough." It was then renamed as now for its patron saint, *Charles* Borromée (Charles Borromeo) (1538–1584), archbishop of Milan.

[1]Charleston. *City and port, southeastern United States*. The South Carolina city was founded in 1670 and named for *Charles* II of England (1630–1685). The name was originally *Charles Town*, but the spoken form of the two words soon coalesced to give the present unified form.

[2]Charleston. *City, eastern United States*. The state capital of West Virginia was named by George Clendenin, who founded it in 1794, for his father, *Charles* Clendenin. The name was originally two words, *Charles Town*, but these were combined as a single word in 1818.

Charleville-Mézières. *City, northeastern France*. The name is that of the city formed on the Meuse River in 1966 from the twin towns mentioned, together with some smaller communes. *Charleville* was so named for *Charles* de Gonzague, duke of Nevers, who built it in 1606. *Mézières* derives its name from Latin *maceria*, "masonry," "enclosing wall," referring to its ramparts.

Charlotte. *City, eastern United States*. The North Carolina city was settled in c.1750 and named for Princess *Charlotte* Sophia (1744–1818), future wife (1761) of George III of England. *Cp.* **Charlottesville, Charlottetown**.

Charlotte Amalie. *Capital of Virgin Islands of the United States.* The town was established as a Danish colony in 1672 and named for *Charlotte Amalia* (1650–1714), queen of Denmark, wife of Christian V. The name was changed to *St. Thomas* in 1921, but reverted to its original in 1936.

Charlottenburg. *Historic city, northeastern Germany.* The former city, now a district of Berlin, took its name from the palace (*Burg*) built in 1696 by Prince (later King) Frederick I of Prussia for his second wife, Sophia *Charlotte* (1668–1705), whom he married in 1684 (when he was 27 and she 16).

Charlottesville. *City, eastern United States.* The Virginia city was settled in the 1730s and subsequently named for Princess *Charlotte* Sophia (1744–1818), future wife (1761) of George III of England. *Cp.* **Charlotte.**

Charlottetown. *City, eastern Canada.* The capital of Prince Edward Island was founded in c.1720 as a French settlement named *Port la Joie.* When the island passed to th British in 1763 it was renamed as now for Queen *Charlotte* (1744–1818), wife of George III. *Cp.* **Charlotte.**

Chartres. *City, north central France.* The city takes its name from the *Carnutes,* a Gaulish people for whom the settlement was a sacred place. The people's own name is based on the pre–Indoeuropean root element *kar,* "rock," "stone." *Cp.* **Caria.**

Châteauroux. *City, central France.* The city is named for its medieval castle (French *château*), built in the 10th century by *Raoul* le Large, prince of Déols. His name been modified to French *roux,* "russet," as if referring to the color of the castle.

Château-Thierry. *Town, north central France.* The town's name means "*Thierry*'s castle." The castle (French *château*) was built on the Marne River in 718 by Charles Martel, grandfather of Charlemagne, as a royal residence for the Merovingian king *Thierry* IV (701–737). At the time of the French Revolution the name was temporarily changed to *Égalité-sur-Marne,* for Louis-Philippe-Joseph, duc d'Orléans (1747–1793), known as Philippe *Égalité* ("Philip Equality"), who supported the Revolution and voted for the death of his cousin, Louis XVI.

Chatham. *Town and port, southeastern England.* The former Kent town has a name meaning "settlement by a wood," from the Celtic root element *ceto-,* "wood," and Old English *hām,* "settlement." The country to the south of Chatham is still well wooded.

Chatham Islands. *Island group, South Pacific.*

The islands, east of (and belonging to) New Zealand, were discovered in 1791 by Lieutenant William R. Broughton, who named them for his ship, the *Chatham,* itself named for its home port of **Chatham,** England.

Chattahoochee. *River, southeastern United States.* The river, forming part of the boundary between Georgia and Alabama and Georgia and Florida, is said to derive its name from that of an early Native American village, the name itself meaning "cornmeal" or "pounded rock."

Chattanooga. *City and port, eastern United States.* The Tennessee city probably takes its name from the Native American (Creek) name for what is now nearby Lookout Mountain, itself said to mean "rock rising to a point."

Chaumont. *Town, eastern France.* The town, on the edge of a plateau, is said to derive its name from Latin *calvus mons,* "bald mountain." However, its Medieval Latin name was *Chalmunt,* and this seems to represent Low Latin *calmis,* itself from pre–Indoeuropean *kal,* "rock," and *mons, montis,* "mountain," which perhaps better suits the topography.

Chaux-de-Fonds, La *see* **La Chaux-de-Fonds**

Cheb. *City, western Czech Republic.* The city, on the Ohře River, has a Slavic name meaning "bend," referring to the river here. Its German name is *Eger,* also a river name, from the Indoeuropean root *ag,* "to flow."

Cheboksary. *Capital of Chuvashia, western Russia.* The city, on the Volga, has a name of uncertain origin. It may have originally been that of a stream that enters the Volga here. It was earlier recorded as *Chebak.* The present Chuvash form of the city's name is *Shupashkar.*

Chechnya. *Republic, southwestern Russia.* The republic is named for its indigenous people, the *Chechen.* Their own name comes from that of the mountain village of *Chechen* north of the Caucasus here. Its own name is of unknown origin. The Chechen people's name for themselves is *Nakhchuo,* from *nakh,* "people."

Cheddar. *Town, southwestern England.* The Somerset town has a name that is probably based on Old English *cēodor,* "ravine." The reference would be to Cheddar Gorge here.

Cheektowaga. *Town, eastern United States.* The New York town, incorporated in 1839, is said to derive its name from Native American *ji-ik-do-wah-gah,* "land of the crabapple."

Cheju. *Island, northern East China Sea.* The island, a province of South Korea, derives its name from Korean *che,* "end," and *chu,* "region," "province." The reference is to its location south of South Korea.

Chekiang. *Province, eastern China*. The province derives its name from that of its principal river, from Chinese *zhè*, "crooked," and *jiāng*, "river."

Chełm. *City, eastern Poland*. The city derives its name from a Slavic word meaning "hill" (Russian *kholm*).

Chelmsford. *City, southeastern England*. The Essex city's name means "*Cēolmǣr*'s ford," the latter being a crossing over the Chelmer River here, itself named for the town.

Chelsea. *District of London, southeastern England*. The district, by the Thames, has an Old English name meaning "chalk landing place," from *cealc*, "chalk," and *hȳth*, "landing place." Chalk would have been unloaded from boats here.

Cheltenham. *Town, west central England*. The Gloucestershire town has a name of uncertain origin. Its final element is almost certainly Old English *hamm*, "river meadow," describing the site of the original settlement here by the Chelt River, itself named for the town. The first part of the name has been linked with that of the **Chiltern Hills**, with possibly a basic sense of "hill" for both. In the case of Cheltenham, the reference would be to Cleeve Hill, which overlooks the town to the northwest.

Chelyabinsk. *City, west central Russia*. The town arose in 1736 as a fort in a forest called *Chelyabi-Karagay*, and takes its name from the first part of this. The forest's name represents Turkic *karagay*, "pinewood," and *chelyabi*, "ancestor," giving an overall sense "ancestral forest."

Chemnitz. *City, eastern Germany*. The city arose in the 12th century around a monastery founded in 1143 by a trading route to Bohemia that crossed the *Chemnitz* River here. The river's own name derives from Old Sorbian *kamen*, "rock," "stone." In the 19th century, as a highly industrialized city, Chemnitz became a center of the German labor movement, and this led to its renaming from 1953 through 1990 as *Karl-Marx-Stadt*, "*Karl Marx* town," for the German founder of Communism. (Marx did not live here, and the year of renaming simply marked the 135th anniversary of his birth.)

Chen-chiang. *City and port, eastern China*. The former capital of Kiangsu province was a garrison commanding the entrance to the Yangtze River. Hence its name, meaning "guard the river," from Chinese *zhèn*, "guard," "garrison," and *jiāng*, "river."

Cheng-chou. *City, eastern China*. The capital of Honan province derives its name from Chinese *zhèng*, "solemn," and *zhōu*, "region."

Ch'eng-te. *City, northeastern China*. The city, in Hopeh province, derives its name from Chinese *chéng*, "to bear," "to undertake," and *dé*, "virtue." It is also known as *Jehol*, from the name of the *Je Ho* River on which it lies. The river's name means "hot river," referring to the warm springs that enter it near the city.

Ch'eng-tu. *City, south central China*. The capital of Szechwan province derives its name from Chinese *chéng*, "to become," "to accomplish," and *dū*, "capital," "big city."

Chennai. *City and port, southeastern India*. The capital of Tamil Nadu state, long familiar as *Madras*, was founded in 1639 when the British built a fort and trading post here on the site of the fishing village of *Madraspatnam*, "*Madras* town." The name *Madras* is said to represent Sanskrit *maṅdarāṣṭra*, "kingdom of *Manda*," from *maṅda*, a god of the underworld, and *rāṣṭra*, "kingdom." However, some authorities take it from Arabic *madrasa*, "school," as what is now a Muslim institution of higher education, itself from *darasa*, "to study," while a case has also been made for a source in Portuguese *madre de Deus*, "mother of God." *St. Thomé*, now a part of the city, was founded earlier by the Portuguese in 1504. In 1996 the city adopted the short form of its Tamil name, *Chennapatnam*, "*Chenna*'s town," for a Telugu chief.

Chepstow. *Town, southeastern Wales*. The Monmouthshire town is near enough to the English border to have an Old English name. It means "market place," from *cēap*, "market," and *stōw*, "place." Chepstow was an important local trading center. Its Welsh name is *Cas-Gwent*, "castle in **Gwent**."

Cherbourg. *City and port, northwestern France*. The city's Roman name was *Coriallum* or *Coriovallum*, from Gaulish *corios*, "army," and Latin *vallum*, "fortification," as for **Heerlen**. The present name appears to derive from a Germanic translation of this, from *hari*, "army," and *burg*, "fort," in its French form *Cherbourg*. The precise sense was "army quarters," "barracks," from a word related to modern German *Herberge*, "inn," "hostel," and thus to French *auberge*, "inn."

Cherepovets. *City, northwestern Russia*. The name, first recorded in the 15th century, is of uncertain origin. The second part may derive from Old Finnish *vesi*, "water," referring to the Sheksna River here. The first part has yet to be satisfactorily explained.

Cherkassy. *City, central Ukraine*. The city is named for the *Cherkess* or *Circassian* people who came from the northern Caucasus to settle here in the 13th century. The Ukrainian form of the name is *Cherkasy. See also* **Circassia, Novocherkassk.**

Chernigov. *City, northern Ukraine.* The name was originally that of a medieval principality here. It probably derives from Old Russian *cherniga,* "chernozem," referring to the dark, fertile earth here. The Ukrainian form of the name is *Chernihiv.*

Chernobyl. *City, northern Ukraine.* The name derives from Russian *chernobylnik,* "mugwort" (*Artemisia vulgaris*), a plant that must have grown here. The city was abandoned following the nuclear reactor disaster of 1986. The Ukrainian form of the name is *Chornobyl.*

Chernovtsy. *City, southwestern Ukraine.* The city, formerly familiar under the German name of *Czernowitz,* probably derives its name from a personal name based on Slavic *chernyj,* "black." The Ukrainian form of the name is *Chernivtsi.*

Chernyakhovsk. *City, western Russia.* The city was originally known by the German name *Insterburg,* for its location at the mouth of the *Instruch* River. In 1946 it was renamed as now for the Red Army general Ivan Danilovich *Chernyakhovsky* (1906–1945), commander of the third Byelorussian front, who was killed near here after recapturing key cities taken by the Germans.

Chersonese *see* **Kherson**

Chesapeake Bay. *Inlet, eastern United States.* The largest inlet of the Atlantic has an indigenous Native American name, either from Delaware *kcheseipogg,* "great salt water," or Algonquian *chesipoc,* "to the big river." The only certain element is the initial *che-,* "big," which the bay certainly is, as the drowned estuary of the Susquehanna River.

Cheshire. *County, northwestern England.* The county takes its name from its chief town of **Chester,** so that the name is effectively *Chestershire.*

Chester. *City, northwestern England.* The city derives its name from Old English *ceaster,* "Roman fort," a borrowing from Latin *castrum,* "camp." Unusually, the name's original first element has disappeared (*cp.* ¹**Manchester, Winchester**). It is known what the missing element was, however, since the Venerable Bede referred to Chester in the 8th century as *Legacæstir,* the first part of which represents Latin *legionum,* "of the legions." The Welsh name of Chester translates this, as *Caerlleon,* "fortress of the legions" (*cp.* **Caerleon**). The Roman fort itself, headquarters of the 20th Valeria Victrix Legion, was called *Deva,* from the **Dee** River on which the city stands. *See also* **Cheshire.**

Chesterfield. *Town, north central England.* The Derbyshire town has an Old English name meaning "open land near a Roman fort," from *ceaster,* "fort" (*cp.* **Chester**), and *feld,* "open land." The name of the fort itself is unknown.

Chester-le-Street. *Town, northern England.* The Co. Durham town has the same basic name as **Chester,** denoting that it was a Roman fort. The addition, for distinguishing purposes, refers to the Roman road here, since English *street* ultimately derives from Latin *via strata,* "paved way." (The middle *-le-* is French "the," short for *en le,* "on the.")

Cheviot Hills. *Hill range between England and Scotland.* The range takes its name from a single hill here called *The Cheviot,* recorded in the 12th century as *Chiuiet.* The meaning of this is uncertain, but it may be based on Old English *geat,* "gate," referring to a gap in the hills here.

Cheyenne. *City, west central United States.* The state capital of Wyoming takes its name from the Native American people here, their own name coming from a Dakota word *shaia* meaning "talkers," implying a group speaking a language that is unintelligible to others. The name was originally proposed for Wyoming itself when the state was created in 1868. It was rejected, however, and given to the city instead when it was made capital the following year.

Chhatarpur. *Town, central India.* The town, in Madhya Pradesh state, was founded in 1707 by *Chhatrasal,* a local king, and is named for him, with Hindi *pur,* "town," added.

Chhattisgarh. *State, east central India.* The state, created in 2000, has a name meaning "thirty-six forts," from Hindi *chhatta,* "six," *tis,* "thirty," and *garh,* "fort," as originally applied to a protected territory here.

Chia-i. *City, western Taiwan.* The city derives its name from Chinese *jiā,* "good," "beautiful," and *yì,* "justice."

Chia-mu-ssu. *City, northeastern China.* The city, in Heilungkiang province, derives its name from Chinese *jiā,* "good," "beautiful," *mù,* "tree," and *sī,* "this."

Chiang Mai. *City, northern Thailand.* The city, founded in 1292, has a name meaning "new town," from Thai northern dialect *chiang,* "town," and *mai,* "new." The city was formerly the capital of the kingdom of this name, and as such was known as *Lan Na. See* **Laos.**

Chiba. *City, eastern Japan.* The city, in the island of Honshu east of Tokyo, derives its name from Japanese *chi,* "thousand," and *ha,* "leaf," "foliage."

Chicago. *City, north central United States.* The

Illinois city has an Algonquian name probably meaning "place of garlic," referring to the wild onion plants that originally grew in the meadows here by Lake Michigan. The name was first applied to the river, then to the town built on it in the early 19th century.

Chichén Itzá. *Historic city, eastern Mexico.* The ancient Maya city arose near two wells in an otherwise arid region. Hence its name, "mouths of the wells of the *Itzá*," the latter being a tribal name.

Chichester. *City, southern England.* The West Sussex city has an Old English name meaning "*Cissa*'s Roman fort," with *ceaster*, "fort," added to the name of *Cissa*, traditionally identified as one of the three sons of Ælle, first king of the South Saxons in the 6th century. The Roman name of Chichester was *Noviomagus*, "new place." *Cp.* **Longjumeau, Nijmegen, Noyon.**

Chidambaram. *Town, southeastern India.* The town, in Tamil Nadu state, derives its name from Tamil *citt*, "wisdom," and *ampalam*, "atmosphere." The reference is to the Hindu temple here dedicated to the god Shiva in his role as Nataraja, the cosmic dancer.

Chiemsee. *Lake, southeastern Germany.* The lake, between the Inn and Salzach rivers, derives its name from the village of *Chieming* on its eastern shore, with Old High German *sēo*, "lake" (modern German *See*), added. The village's own name means "settlement of *Chiemo*'s people."

Ch'ih-feng. *Town, northeastern China.* The town, in Inner Mongolia, derives its name from Chinese *chì*, "red," and *fēng*, "peak," "summit." The reference is to the red-colored peak that overlooks the town from the northeast.

Chi-hsi. *City, northeastern China.* The city, in Heilungkiang province, derives its name from Chinese *jī*, "chicken," "rooster," and *xī*, "west."

Chihuahua. *City, northern Mexico.* The city has a Native American name meaning "dry place." It was founded in 1709 and originally had the Spanish name *Villa Real de Minas*, "royal town of mines." It adopted the present name in 1718.

Chile. *Republic, southwestern South America.* The country's name is of uncertain origin. It may derive from a Native American word meaning either "land's end" or "cold," "winter." Despite the latter sense, the name is quite unconnected with English *chilly*.

Chililabombwe. *Town, north central Zambia.* The town's name derives from local words meaning "croaking frog," from the prevalence of these creatures here. The town was founded in 1955 and until the late 1960s was known as *Bancroft*,

for the Canadian-born geologist Joseph *Bancroft* (1882–1957), who worked in Zambia for the Anglo-American Corporation and who opened a copper mine here.

Chi-lin. *City, northeastern China.* The city has a name of the same origin as that of **Kirin**, the province in which it lies.

Chilliwack. *City, southwestern Canada.* The city, in British Columbia, has a Native American (Salish) name said to mean "valley of many streams."

Chilpancingo. *City, south central Mexico.* The city has a Nahuatl name said to mean either "little place of wasps," from *chilpan*, "wasps' nest," *tzin*, "little," and *co*, "place," or "place of little red flags," from *chilli*, "chilli pepper," "reddish," *pan*, "flag," *tzin*, denoting a diminutive, and *co*, a locative indicator. The latter would refer to some kind of red-colored medicinal plant. Its full name is either *Chilpancingo de los Bravos*, honoring Nicolás, Leonardo, and Victor *Bravo*, three local heroes in the war against Spain, or more commonly *Chilpancingo de los Bravo*, for Nicolás alone, as the most prominent of the three.

Chiltern Hills. *Hill range, south central England.* The hills, in Oxfordshire and Buckinghamshire, have a name of pre–Celtic origin that may mean simply "high ones."

Chi-lung. *City and port, northern Taiwan.* The city derives its name from Chinese *jī*, "base," "foundation," and *lóng*, "grand," "prosperous."

Chimborazo. *Mountain, west central Ecuador.* The extinct volcano takes its name from the *Chimbo* River here, itself from Quechua *chimpa*, "opposite," to which Peruvian *rasu*, "snow," has been added. The river is thus "opposite" or facing the volcano, which is permanently snow-capped.

Chimkent. *City, southern Kazakhstan.* The city, dating from at least the 12th century, derives its name from Kazakh *chim*, "turf," and *kent*, "town." The implication is that it arose on a grassy site.

China. *Republic, eastern and central Asia.* The name is traditionally derived from the *Ts'in* dynasty which reigned from 221 to 206 B.C. But the territory was already recorded as *Tsinstan* in the 4th century B.C., at a time when Alexander the Great was conquering Persia and India. The actual source of the name thus appears to be in the central province of *Shaanxi* or **Shensi**, with its capital of *Xi'an* or **Sian**, around which the present country gradually arose. The country thus gave the name of the dynasty, not the other way around. A former English name for China was *Cathay*, introduced by Marco Polo in the 13th century. It comes from the *Khitan*, a semi-nomadic Mongol people who conquered northern China in the 10th century and held it for the next two centuries. A form of this is still used in some countries as a standard name of China, such as Russian *Kitaj*. The Chinese name of China is *zhōngguó*, "middle country," from *zhōng*, "middle," and *guó*, "country," or else *zhōnghuá*, "middle flower," from *zhōng*, "middle," and *huá*, "magnificent," "flourishing." The Japanese name of China is *chūgoku*, from the first of these with *ku*, "country."

Chi-nan. *City, eastern China.* The capital of Shantung province lies south of the *Chi* River. Hence its name, from Chinese *jì*, the river name, itself meaning "to save," "to help," and *nán*, "south."

Chingleput. *Town, southeastern India.* The town, in Tamil Nadu state, has a Tamil name meaning "town of red lotuses."

Ching-te-chen. *City, southeastern China.* The city, in Kiangsi province, derives its name from Chinese *jìng*, "view," "scenery," *dé*, "virtue," and *zhèn*, "garrison post," "town."

Chinhoyi. *Town, north central Zimbabwe.* The town has a name that is said to be that of a local chief, *Tshinoyi*, who settled near caves here in the 19th century. The name was spelled *Sinoya* until 1980.

Ch'in-huang-tao. *City and port, northeastern China.* The city, in Hopeh province, derives its name from Chinese *qín*, the old name of Shensi province, *huáng*, "emperor," and *dǎo*, "island."

Chinnereth *see* **Galilee**

Chinon. *Town, northwestern France.* The town was known to the Romans as *Cainum*, from the personal name *Catinus*, itself presumably from the identical Latin word meaning "bowl," "pot."

Chioggia. *Town and port, northern Italy.* The town was known to the Romans as *Fossa Clodia*, "*Clodius*'s ditch," referring to a canal here, and the present name evolved from the personal name.

Chios. *Island, eastern Greece.* The name of the Aegean island is of uncertain origin. It has been derived by some from Greek *khiōn*, "snow," for the snow that sparkles on the island's mountains in winter.

Chişinău *see* **Kishinev**

Chiswick. *District of London, southeastern England.* The district has an Old English name meaning "cheese farm," from *cīese*, "cheese," and *wīc*, "special place," "dairy farm."

Chita. *City, eastern Russia.* The city takes its name from that of the river on which it stands. The river's own name represents Evenki *chita*, "clay."

Chitradurga. *City, southern India.* The city, in Karnataka state, has a name meaning "red fort."

Chittagong. *City and port, southeastern Bangladesh.* The city's name means "white village," from Hindi *chittā*, "white," and *gānv*, "village."

Chittaurgarh. *City, northwestern India.* The city, in Rajasthan state, has a name meaning "*Chitrang*'s fort," from the name of a Rajput chieftain, with Sanskrit *garh*, "fort."

Chmielnik. *Town, southeastern Poland.* The town has a name meaning "hop field," from Polish *chmiel*, "hop."

Choctawhatchee. *River, southeastern United States.* The river, in southeastern Alabama and northwestern Florida, takes its name from that of the *Choctaw* Native Americans, with *hatchee* meaning "stream." The people's own name is said to come from Spanish *chato*, "flat," referring to their custom of flattening male babies' heads.

Chogori *see* **K2**

Cholet. *Town, western France.* The town had the Medieval Latin name of *Caulletum* or *Coletum*, apparently from Latin *caulis*, "cabbage," with reference to the local growing of this vegetable.

Cholula. *City, central Mexico.* The city has a Nahuatl name meaning "place of springs."

Chomolangma *see* **Everest, Mt.**

Chomo Lhari. *Mountain, western Bhutan.* The Himalayan peak, on the border of Bhutan and Tibet, has a name meaning "divine goddess of the mountains," from Tibetan *chomo*, "goddess," *lha*, "god," "divine" (as for **Lhasa**), and *ri*, "mountain."

Chomolönzo. *Mountain, southern Tibet.* The Himalayan peak derives its name from Tibetan *chomo*, "goddess," *lhun*, "mass," and *tse*, "summit."

Chomutov. *City, northwestern Czech Republic.* The name probably means "*Chomut*'s place," with the personal name followed by the Slavic possessive suffix -*ov*. And although *khomut* could also mean "deep river bend," it is not clear which river would be referred to here. The German form of the name is *Komotau*.

Ch'ongjin. *City, northeastern North Korea.* The city derives its name from *Ch'ong*, a Manchurian dynasty, and Korean *chin*, "resin," "rubber."

Ch'ongju. *City, central South Korea.* The city

derives its name from Korean *chŏn*, "all," "whole," and *chu*, "region."

Cho Oyu. *Mountain, southern Tibet.* The Himalayan peak, on the border between Tibet and Nepal, has a name meaning "goddess of the turquoises," from Tibetan *cho*, "highest," "goddess," and *gyu*, "turquoise."

Chorzów. *City, southern Poland.* The city arose in 1869 on the site of a mining settlement known in German as *Königshutte* and in Polish as *Królewska Huta*, "royal iron and steel works." The works then passed to state ownership and the growing industrial city adopted the name of an existing village here.

Chosen *see* **Korea**

Chott ech-Chergui. *Lake, northern Algeria.* The name represents Arabic *shaṭṭ ash-sharḳi*, "eastern chott," from *shaṭṭ* (*see* **Shatt al-Arab**), and *sharḳ*, "east."

Chott el-Djerid. *Lake, western Tunisia.* The name represents Arabic *shaṭṭ al-jarīd*, "chott of the palm trees, " from *shaṭṭ* (*see* **Shatt al-Arab**), and *jarīd*, plural of *jarīda*, "palm tree."

Chou-k'ou-tien. *Archaeological site, eastern China.* The Palaeolithic "Peking Man" site, near Beijing, derives its name from Chinese *zhōu*, "around," "circuit," for the *Chou* dynasty, reigning from the 11th through 3d century B.C., *koǔ*, "mouth," and *diàn*, "shop," "inn."

Chou-shan Archipelago. *Island group, eastern China.* The group, off the northern coast of Chekiang province, takes its name from its largest island, so called because it was thought to resemble a boat, from Chinese *zhōu*, "boat," and *shān*, "mountain." The island is steep and rugged, with a highest peak rising to 1,640 ft (500 m).

Choybalsan. *City, eastern Mongolia.* The city was founded in the 19th century as a monastery called *San Beise*. In 1931 it was renamed *Bayan Tumen*. Its present name dates from 1946, and honors the Mongolian premier Khorloghiyin *Choybalsan* (1895–1952), a hero of the 1921 Mongolian Revolution.

Chrissie, Lake. *Lake, northeastern South Africa.* South Africa's largest natural lake, in Mpumalanga, lies in a region settled in c.1866 by Alexander McCorkindale. He named the lake for *Christina* (familiarly *Chrissie*) Pretorius, daughter of Marthinus Wessel Pretorius (1819–1901), then president of the South African Republic. (He was the son of Andries Pretorius, for whom **Pretoria** is named.)

Christchurch. *City, eastern New Zealand.* The South Island city was founded in 1851 by John Godley of the Church of England Canterbury Association, who named it for his Oxford college of *Christ Church*. The name is doubly appropriate for the model Anglican settlement, since Canterbury is the seat of the Church of England and the cathedral there is also Christ Church.

Christiania *see* **Oslo**

Christmas Island. *Island, eastern Indian Ocean.* The island, an Australian possession, was named by the Dutch captain Willem Mynors, who sighted it on December 25, *Christmas* Day, 1653. It was already known to European navigators, however.

Christmas Island *see* **Kiritimati**

Ch'üan-chou. *City and port, eastern China.* The city, in Fukien province, derives its name from Chinese *quán*, "spring," and *zhōu*, "region."

Chubu. *Region, central Japan.* The region, in the island of Honshu, has a name meaning "middle department," from *chu*, "middle," "center," and *bu*, "department," "division."

Chu-chou. *City, eastern China.* The city, in Hunan province, derives its name from Chinese *zhū*, "tree trunk," and *zhōu*, "continent."

Chudskoye, Lake *see* **Peipus, Lake**

Ch'ü-fu. *Town, northeastern China.* The town, in Shantung province, and famous as the birthplace of Confucius, derives its name from Chinese *qǔ*, "music," "song," and *fù*, "mound."

Chugoku Range. *Mountain range, southwestern Japan.* The range, in the island of Honshu, has a name meaning "middle country," from Japanese *chū*, "middle," and *koku*, "country." *Cp.* **China.**

Chukchi Sea. *Sea between Russia and North America.* The sea, part of the Arctic Ocean, is named for the indigenous people of northeastern Siberia. Their name is a Russian alteration of *Chetko*, their own name for themselves, meaning simply "people," "men."

Chula Vista. *City, southwestern United States.* The California city, on the eastern shore of San Diego Bay, was laid out in 1888 and named for its "pretty view," from Spanish *chulo*, "pretty," "attractive," and *vista*, "view."

Ch'unch'on. *City, northern South Korea.* The city, in the basin of the North Han and Soyang rivers, has a name meaning "river of spring," from Korean *ch'un*, "spring" (*cp.* **Ch'ang-ch'un**), and *ch'ŏn*, "river" (*cp.* **Szechwan**).

Chungking. *City and river port, south central China.* The city, on the Yangtze River, has a name meaning "double joy," "twice blessed," from Chinese *chóng*, "to repeat," and *qìng*, "to celebrate."

Chur. *Town, eastern Switzerland.* The town,

known in French as *Coire*, derives its name from the first word of its Roman name *Curia Rhaetorum*, "meeting place of the *Raetians*," referring to its role as capital of the Roman province of **Raetia**.

¹Churchill. *Town and port, central Canada*. The Manitoba town, on Hudson Bay, takes its name from the river at the mouth of which it stands. This was itself named for John *Churchill*, 1st Duke of Marlborough (1650–1722), governor of the Hudson's Bay Company from 1685 to 1691.

²Churchill. *River, eastern Canada*. The Newfoundland river was originally the *Hamilton* River, so named in 1821 for Sir Charles *Hamilton* (1767–1849), first governor of Newfoundland. In 1965 it was renamed as now to commemorate the British prime minister Sir Winston *Churchill* (1871–1965).

Churu. *Town, northwestern India*. The town, in Rajasthan state, was founded in c.1620 by *Churru*, a local chieftain, and is named for him.

Chuvashia. *Republic, western Russia*. The republic takes its name from its indigenous people, the *Chuvash*, whose own name has been linked with Turkish *su*, "water."

Cicero. *City, east central United States*. The Illinois city, now a suburb of Chicago, was settled in the 1830s and named for *Cicero*, New York, itself named for the 1st-century B.C. Roman statesman at a time (the 1790s) when classical names were in vogue.

Ciénaga. *City and port, northern Colombia*. The city was founded in 1518 and originally had the Spanish name of *Aldea Grande*, "big village." It was subsequently renamed as now, for the nearby *Ciénaga Grande*, "big swamp," of Santa Marta, an inlet of the Caribbean.

Cienfuegos. *City, central Cuba*. The city was founded in 1819 by French colonists as *Fernandina de Jagua*. It was destroyed by a storm in 1825, but was rebuilt and named for one of the original founders.

Cieplice Śląskie Zdrój. *Town and resort, southwestern Poland*. The resort, with its mineral springs, is one of the oldest in Poland. It was originally known by the German name of *Bad-Warmbrunn*, "bath of the warm springs." The Polish name translates this.

Cieszyn. *City, southern Poland*. The name, recorded in 1365 as *Stagissce*, means "place of cattle stalls." The city's German name, *Teschen*, gave that of a former principality in eastern Europe.

Cilicia. *Historic region, southern Turkey*. The ancient district of Anatolia, mentioned in the Bible as the home country of St. Paul (Acts 21:39, etc.), is traditionally said to have been founded by *Cilix*, in Greek mythology a son of the Phoenician king Agenor.

Cincinnati. *City, north central United States*. The Ohio city was so named in 1790 by General Arthur St. Clair in honor of the Revolutionary War officers' Society of the *Cincinnati*, a hereditary military and patriotic organization founded in 1783, itself named for the 5th-century B.C. Roman statesman Lucius Quinctus *Cincinnatus*, famous for his strict morals and selfless devotion to the republic in times of crisis. An earlier name was *Losantiville*, from *L*, the initial of Licking Creek, *os*, Latin for "mouth," *anti*, Greek for "opposite," and French *ville*, "town." The settlement was thus the "town opposite the mouth of *Licking Creek*," this last being the river here.

Circassia. *Region, southwestern Russia*. The region, on the northeast coast of the Black Sea, takes its name from its indigenous people, known more accurately as the *Cherkess*. Their own name is said to represent an Ossetian word *charkas* meaning "eagle." The Circassians' own name for themselves is *Adygei*, from Abkhazian *adi*, "water." They are thus the "water dwellers," living by the Black Sea. *See also* **Cherkassy, Novocherkassk**.

Circeo, Mt. *Promontory, southwestern Italy*. The promontory, on the Tyrrhenian Sea, looks like an island when seen from the sea and is traditionally said to have actually been one. Hence its name, derived from that of *Circe*, the sorceress of classical mythology who was believed to live on an island off the west coast of Italy.

Cirencester. *Town, west central England*. The Gloucestershire town has a name that denotes its origin in a Roman fort, with the latter part from Old English *ceaster*, a borrowing from Latin *castrum*, "camp." The first part of the name represents *Corinium*, that of the Roman station here. Its meaning is obscure.

Ciskei. *Historic homeland, southern South Africa*. The former Bantu homeland has a name denoting its geographical location. It means "this side of the *Kei* (River)," from Latin *cis*, "on this side," and the name of the river that enters the sea to the east of it. *Cp*. **Transkei**.

Citlaltépetl *see* **Orizaba**

Ciudad Bolívar. *City and river port, eastern Venezuela*. The city was founded in 1764 as *San Tomás de la Nueva Guayana de la Angostura*, "St. Thomas of New Guayana of the strait" (*see* **Ciudad Guayana**), a name later shortened to *Angostura*, the strait in question being a narrowing of the Orinoco River here. In 1846 it was given its present name, meaning "city of *Bolívar*," for the Venezuelan-born nationalist leader Simón *Bolívar* (1783–1830), who also gave the name of **Bolivia**.

Ciudad del Este. *City and river port, eastern Paraguay.* The city was founded in 1957 and was originally named *Puerto Presidente Stroessner*, "port of *President Stroessner*," for Alfredo *Stroessner* (born 1912), president of Paraguay from 1954 to 1989. After his overthrow it was renamed as now, the Spanish name meaning "city of the east."

Ciudad Guayana. *City and river port, eastern Venezuela.* The city, on the Orinoco River, was founded in 1961 with a name meaning "*Guayana* city," deriving from the historic region of northeastern South America where the modern countries of **Guyana** and **French Guiana** are located. The city incorporates the earlier Spanish settlement of *Santo Tomé de Guayana*, "St. Thomas of Guayana," and this is now the city's full official name.

Ciudad Juárez. *City, northern Mexico.* The city was founded in the latter part of the 17th century and for over 200 years was known as *El Paso del Norte*, "the pass of the north." In 1888 it was renamed as now in memory of the Mexican president, Benito Pablo *Juárez* (1808–1872), who made his base here in 1865 during the struggle against the French.

Ciudad Obregón. *City, northwestern Mexico.* The city is named for Álvaro *Obregón* (1880–1928), the Mexican general and president who was born locally.

Ciudad Real. *City, south central Spain.* The city was founded in the mid–13th century by King Alfonso X as *Villa Real*, "royal town." In 1420 it was granted the status of a city (Spanish *ciudad*) and its name was modified accordingly.

Ciudad Rodrigo. *City, western Spain.* The city is named for Count *Rodrigo* González, who founded it in 1150.

Ciudad Victoria. *City, east central Mexico.* The city was founded in 1750 and in 1825 was named for the first president of Mexico, Guadalupe *Victoria* (1789–1843). (This was his assumed name; his original name was Manuel Félix Fernández.)

Cividale del Friuli. *Town, northeastern Italy.* The town was founded in Roman times as *Forum Julii*, "market of *Julius*," for *Julius* Caesar. It then gave its name to, and was capital of, **Friuli**. Hence its present name, with *cividale* evolving from Latin *civitas*, *civitatis*, "city."

Civitavecchia. *Town and port, western Italy.* The town was founded by the Romans in the 2d century A.D. and was originally known as *Trajani Portus*, "*Trajan's* port," for the Roman emperor *Trajan* (53–117). When it was destroyed by the Saracens in 828, the inhabitants fled to the mountains. They later returned, however, to the "old city," Medieval Latin *civitas vetus*, Italian *città vecchia*.

Clackmannan. *Town, central Scotland.* The town and former county have a name that literally means "stone of *Manau*," the latter being a district name. The stone (Gaelic *clach*) is an ancient glacial rock in the middle of the town, where it stands next to the Town Cross and the Tolbooth.

Clare. *County, western Ireland.* The county's name represents Gaelic *clar*, "board," "plank," applied figuratively to describe a plain or level district.

Clarksville. *City, east central United States.* The Tennessee city was settled in 1784 and named for the Revolutionary soldier and frontiersman General George Rogers *Clark* (1752–1818).

Clearwater. *City, southeastern United States.* The Florida city, on the bay of the same name, arose in the 1840s as a fishing settlement called *Clear Water Harbor*, so named for the clear, sulfate springs that bubbled up offshore. The present form of the name evolved in due course.

Cleethorpes. *Town and resort, eastern England.* The name of the Lincolnshire town means "*Clee* hamlets," with the second half of the name from Old Norse *thorp*, "outlying farm." *Clee* is a local placename meaning "clayey place."

Clermont-Ferrand. *City, south central France.* The dual name arose in 1630 on the union of the two separate towns of *Clermont* and *Montferrand*. *Clermont* has a name meaning "clear mountain," i.e. one discernible from a distance. *Montferrand* means "*Ferrand's* mountain," the personal name denoting a man with "iron-gray" hair. The latter town dropped its initial *Mont-* on merging with *Clermont* in order to avoid repetition.

¹**Cleveland.** *Historic county, northeastern England.* The former county (1974–96) took its name from the *Cleveland* Hills here, their own name meaning literally "cliff land," describing a hilly district.

²**Cleveland.** *City and port, east central United States.* The Ohio city was so named in 1796 for Moses *Cleaveland* (1754–1806) of the Connecticut Land Company, who laid it out. In 1832 the middle *a* of his name was dropped to make it simpler.

Cloppenburg. *Town, northwestern Germany.*

The name was originally that of the 13th-century castle here, itself probably from Middle Low German *kloppen*, "to knock," "to hit," and Old High German *burg*, "castle," describing its military potential for laying siege to another castle.

Cluj. *City, northwestern Romania.* The city had the Medieval Latin name of *Castrum Clus.* The latter word represents Latin *clusum*, "enclosed," referring to the location of the town, which is surrounded by hills. Its Hungarian and German names were respectively *Kolozsvár* and *Klausenburg*, both basically the same name but with *vár* and *Burg* meaning "fort." In the mid–1970s Cluj was joined with neighboring Napoca to become *Cluj-Napoca.*

Clutha. *River, southern New Zealand.* The longest river in South Island was given a historic form of the name of the **Clyde** River, Scotland.

Clwyd. *Historic county, northeastern Wales.* The former county (1974–96) took its name from the river here. Its own name is the Welsh word for "hurdle," probably because hurdles were used to ford it or to make a causeway over it in early times. The name has a parallel in that of *Baile Átha Cliath*, the Irish name of **Dublin.**

Clyde. *River, southern Scotland.* The river's name means something like "cleansing one," from a conjectural Celtic root element *clouta*, related to Latin *cloaca*, "sewer." *See also* **Clutha.**

Cnidus. *Historic city, southwestern Turkey.* The ancient Greek city in southwestern Anatolia is said to derive its name from Greek *knizō*, "I tease," "I chafe," referring to the Temple of Aphrodite here, excavated in 1970 by (the appropriately named) Iris C. Love.

Coachella Valley. *Desert region, southwestern United States.* The valley, part of the Colorado Desert in southern California, was named either for the *Cahuilla* Native Americans who inhabited the region, or from Spanish *conchilla*, "small shell," with reference to the many fossil shells locally. The present form of the name could have evolved either as a blend of these or as a miscopying of the Spanish word.

Coast of Death *see* **Costa de la Muerte**

Coats Land. *Region of Antarctica.* The region, along the south coast of the Weddell Sea, was discovered in 1904 by the Scottish explorer William S. Bruce and named by him for the financial backers of his expedition, the brothers James *Coats* (1841–1912) and Andrew *Coats* (1862–1930), of the Scottish firm of J. and P. *Coats*, Ltd. The name has been wrongly (but understandably) recorded as *Coast Land* on some charts.

Cobán. *City, north central Guatemala.* The city was founded in c.1538 and named for *Cobaóu*, a local Native American chief.

Cóbh. *Town and port, southern Ireland.* The town, in Co. Cork, has a name that is an Irish spelling of English *cove*. The reference is to Cork Harbour. From 1849 through 1922 the town was known as *Queenstown*, in honor of *Queen* Victoria, who paid an official visit here in the former year. The old name was readopted when Ireland was granted dominion status as the Irish Free State.

Coblenz *see* **Koblenz**

Coburg. *City, central Germany.* The second part of the city's name is Old High German *burg*, "fort," but the first part is of uncertain origin. A source in Old High German *kō*, "cow," is unlikely. Nor is the uncertainty helped by a document of 1217 referring to *Choburg quod antiquitus dicebatur Trufalistat*, "Coburg, called in antiquity Trufalistat."

Cochabamba. *City, central Bolivia.* The city was founded in 1574 by the Spanish conquistador Sebastián Barba de Padilla with the name of *Villa de Oropeza*, for one or other of the Spanish towns *Oropesa*. It was renamed as now when raised to city status in 1786. The name is a hispanicized form of *Khocha Pampa*, "plain of small lakes," the Quechua name of the region.

Cochin. *Town and port, southwestern India.* The town, in Kerala state, has a Tamil name that may represent *koñcham*, "little," referring to the small river where the town was originally built.

Cochin China. *Historic region, southern Vietnam.* The former French colony has a name that arose as a Portuguese corruption of its local name *Ko-chen*, of uncertain meaning. *China* was added to this to distinguish it from **Cochin** in India. The Vietnamese name of the region in precolonial days was *Nam-Ky*, "southern administrative area."

Cochiti. *Pueblo, northern Mexico.* The Pueblo Indian village was named in 1598 by the Spanish explorer Juan de Oñate after hearing the word *kotyete*, meaning "stone kiva." (A kiva is an underground chamber used for religious ceremonies by the Pueblo Indians.)

Cocos Islands. *Island group, eastern Indian Ocean.* The islands are named for their abundance of *coconut* trees. They are still sometimes known by their alternate name *Keeling Islands*, for Captain William *Keeling* (died 1620) of the East India Company, who discovered them in 1609.

Cod, Cape *see* **Cape Cod**

Cognac. *Town, southwestern France.* The town's present name evolved from its Medieval

Latin name of *Comniacum*, from the personal name *Cominius* with the Gallo-Roman suffix *-acum*.

Coimbra. *City, west central Portugal.* The city's name is based on the two Celtic words *cun*, "height," and *briga*, "fort." The original "fort on a height" was some 8 miles (13 km) to the southwest of the present town, at the location now named *Condeixa*.

Coín. *City, southern Spain.* The city, which dates from pre–Roman times, was taken by the Arabs in 813 and named by them *Cohine*, "pleasant paradise," the basis of the present name.

Colchester. *City, southeastern England.* The Essex city has the distinctive *-chester* that shows it to have been a Roman station, from Old English *ceaster*, "Roman fort," a borrowing from Latin *castrum*, "camp." The first part of the name is that of the *Colne* River on which the city stands, with the river's own name of Celtic origin and meaning simply "water." The actual name of the Roman station here was *Camulodunum*, "Camulos' fort," from the Celtic war god *Camulos*.

Colchis. *Historic region, western Georgia.* The ancient region, at the eastern end of the Black Sea, took its name from the *Colchians* who were its native inhabitants. Their own name is probably of Egyptian origin, but uncertain meaning.

Coleraine. *Town, northern Northern Ireland.* The town, in Co. Londonderry, has the Irish name *Cúil Raithin*, "recess of ferns." The name is found in variant forms elsewhere, such as *Cooleraine*, *Coolrainy*, etc.

College Station. *City, southern United States.* The Texas city arose around the Texas Agricultural and Mechanical University, founded in 1876 as a *college*. Hence the first word of the name. The college was a flag *station* (where trains are halted by a flag signal) on the railroad here. Hence the second word.

Colmar. *Town, northeastern France.* The town may derive its name either from the Germanic personal name *Galamar* or from Latin *columbarium*, "dovecote."

Cologne. *City, western Germany.* A Roman fortified settlement was founded on the site of the present city in 38 B.C. and was known as *Oppidum Ubiorum*, for the local *Ubii* people. The settlement was the birthplace of Agrippina the Younger (A.D. 15–59), wife of the emperor Claudius, and at her request the title of colony (*colonia*) was conferred on the town in A.D. 50. As such, it was endowed with the full name *Colonia Claudia Ara Agrippinensium*, "colony of Claudius with the altar of Agrippina's people."

This long name was shortened in 332 to *Colonia Agrippina*, and eventually in 450 to just *Colonia*. This is the origin of the present name, a French form adopted by English speakers. The German form of the name is *Köln*.

Colombes. *Town, northern France.* The town, now an industrial suburb of Paris, derives its name from Latin *columba*, "dove," referring to the former breeding of doves or pigeons here.

Colombia. *Republic, northwestern South America.* The only American nation that is named for Christopher *Columbus* began its history in the 16th century as part of the Spanish colonial territory of *New Granada* (*Nueva Granada*) (*see* **Granada**). In 1810 the territory began its revolt against Spain, and in 1819 gained independence under Simón Bolívar (*see* **Bolivia**), forming with what are now the separate countries of Panama, Venezuela, and Ecuador the republic of *Greater Colombia* (*Gran Colombia*). In 1830 Venezuela and Ecuador seceded from the union, and until 1850 the remaining territory was known (again) as *New Granada*. It was then reorganized as the *Grenadine Confederation* in 1858, the *United States of New Granada* in 1861, the *United States of Colombia* in 1863, and finally the *Republic of Colombia* in 1886. (Panama revolted from Colombia in 1903.)

Colombo. *Executive capital of Sri Lanka.* The city and port, on the island's west coast, has a name that is apparently of Sinhalese origin but uncertain meaning. One proposed derivation is from *kola*, "leaves," and *amba*, "mango," referring to mango trees here. Another is from *Kalantotta*, "Kelani ferry," after the *Kelani* River here. Whatever the case, the original name was corrupted to *Kolambu* by Arab traders, then in the 16th century to *Colombo* by Portuguese settlers, who may well have associated the name with Christopher *Columbus*. (The famous navigator never came here, but he did make his base in Portugal.)

Colón. *City and port, north central Panama.* The city, at the entrance to the Panama Canal, was founded in 1850 and originally named *Aspinwall*, for William Henry *Aspinwall* (1807–1885), U.S. promoter of the Panama Railway. In 1890 it was given its present name, in honor of Christopher *Columbus* (1451–1506), whose name in Spanish is *Cristóbal Colón*. The city thus bears his surname, and its twin port of *Cristóbal* his first name.

Colorado. *State, west central United States.* The state is named for its river, whose own name represents Spanish *colorado*, "colored," "reddened." The reference is to the reddish hue of its waters caused by the clay washed down from the canyons through which it passes.

Colorado Springs. *City, west central United States.* The **Colorado** city stands at the confluence of Monument and Fountain creeks, and when founded in 1871 was called *Fountain Colony*. It was soon after renamed for the nearby Manitou mineral springs.

¹Columbia. *River, western North America.* The river, rising in British Columbia, Canada, then flowing generally south and west to enter the Pacific in Oregon, USA, was visited by the Boston trader Robert Gray in 1792 and named for his ship, the *Columbia*, itself named for Christopher *Columbus*.

²Columbia. *Federal district, eastern United States.* The District of Columbia was formed in 1791 and named for the discoverer of America, Christopher *Columbus*, who was regarded as a hero at a time when America was breaking her colonial ties. This particular classical form of the name is found in many parts of the United States. *See also* **¹Columbus.**

³Columbia. *City, southeastern United States.* The state capital of South Carolina was laid out in 1786 to replace Charleston as capital and named for Christopher *Columbus*.

¹Columbus. *City, east central United States.* The state capital of Ohio was laid out in 1812 and named for Christopher *Columbus* (1451–1506), discoverer of America.

²Columbus. *City, southeastern United States.* The Georgia city was founded in 1827 and named for Christopher *Columbus*.

Communism, Peak. *Mountain, northeastern Tajikistan.* The peak, known in Russian as *pik Kommunizma* ("peak of Communism"), is the highest in the former Soviet Union. Hence its name. It was discovered in 1928 by a team from the Academy of Sciences of the USSR and its height correctly calculated at 7,495 m (24,590 feet). By mistake, however, the data were attributed to Mt. *Garmo*, 12 miles (20 km) to the south. The error was detected in 1932 and the mountain named *Stalin Peak*. In 1952, following the demotion of Stalin, the peak was renamed as now. *Cp.* **Victory, Peak.**

Como, Lake. *Lake, northern Italy.* The lake takes its name from the city at its southwestern end. This was known to the Romans as *Comum*, from Celtic *cumba*, "valley" (English *coomb*), describing its location in a valley enclosed by hills.

Comodoro Rivadavia. *City and port, southeastern Argentina.* The city was founded in 1901 and named in memory of *Comodoro* (Com-modore) Martín *Rivadavia* (1852–1901), of the Argentine navy.

Comorin, Cape. *Cape, southern India.* The cape at India's southern extremity, in Tamil Nadu state, has a name meaning "virgin girl," from Hindi *kanyā*, "girl," and *kumāri*, "virgin," as a byname of the Hindu goddess Durga, wife of Shiva. The town of **Kanniyakumari**, on the cape, contains an ancient temple dedicated to Shiva.

Comoros. *Island republic, western Indian Ocean.* The island group, northwest of Madagascar, has a name based on Arabic *ḳamar*, "moon." This was the Arabs' astronomical name for the Magellanic Clouds. Those galaxies represented the southern hemisphere, and the Arabs gave their name to all islands in the southern latitudes here, including Madagascar itself. Some authorities also link the name with the legendary *Mountains of the Moon*, said to be located somewhere in Equatorial Africa, not all that far from the Comoros. *See also* **Ruwenzori.**

Compiègne. *Town, northern France.* The town's name evolved from its Roman name of *Compendium*, meaning "short cut." This referred to the Roman route (if not Roman road) that ran across the Oise River here between Beauvais and Soissons.

Compostela. *Town, western Mexico.* The town, founded in 1535, is named for the Spanish city of **Santiago de Compostela.**

Comtat-Venassin. *Historic region, southeastern France.* The region, together with Avignon, was a papal possession from 1274 through 1791. Hence its name, from Latin *Comitatus Venaissini*, from *comitatus*, "court," "palace," and *Avenio*, the Roman name of **Avignon**, seat of the papacy from 1309 to 1377.

Conakry. *Capital of Guinea.* The city and port derives its name from a local African word *konakri* meaning "over the water," referring to Conakry's location on a peninsula which is equally visible from north or south.

Concepción. *City, south central Chile.* The city was founded in 1550 and has the full Spanish name *Concepción de la Madre Santisima de la Luz*, "(Immaculate) Conception of the Most Holy Mother of Light."

Conception Bay. *Bay, eastern Canada.* The bay, in southeastern Newfoundland, has a name translating that given by the Portuguese explorer Gaspar Côrte-Real when he arrived here on December 8, 1500, the feastday of the Immaculate *Conception*.

Concord. *City, northeastern United States.* The state capital of New Hampshire was founded in

1725 and at first named *Pennycook*, from an Algonquian word meaning "descent." It was renamed *Concord* in 1763, for the town of this name in neighboring Massachusetts, itself settled in 1635 and probably so called to mark a peaceful settlement between two warring factions, or else simply as a general commendation. There are other places of the name in the United States.

Coney Island. *Historic island, eastern United States.* The former island, in southern Brooklyn, New York City, was known to the Dutch as *Konijn Eiland*, "rabbit island," for the wild rabbits that abounded here in the 17th century, and the present name is a corrupt English form of this.

Congo. *Republic, western Africa.* The country takes its name from the river that flows through it. The river's own name is of Bantu origin and means "mountains," i.e. "river that flows from the mountains." The country is also known as *Congo-Brazzaville*, for its capital, **Brazzaville**, for distinction from the *Democratic Republic of Congo*, formerly **Zaire**, which borders it to the east.

Connacht. *Historic region, western Ireland.* The ancient province takes its name from the *Connachta* people who once inhabited this part of Ireland. Their own name is said to derive from *Conn*, a legendary hero who is claimed to have founded Connacht as the first kingdom of Ireland. The traditional English spelling of the name is *Connaught*.

Connaught *see* **Connacht**

Connecticut. *State, eastern United States.* The state takes its name from the river that flows south through it, its own name coming from Algonquian *kuenihtekot*, "beside the long river." The middle *c* of the name, which is not pronounced, was probably added by association with English *connect*.

Connemara. *District, western Ireland.* The west coastal region of Co. Galway has a name meaning "sea district of *Conmac*'s people," with *Conmac* traditionally identified as the son of the Ulster hero Fergus mac Róich (Fergus McRoy) and the legendary queen Medb (Maeve).

Constance, Lake. *Lake, central Europe.* The lake, on the border between Germany, Austria, and Switzerland, takes its name from the German town of *Constance* (*Konstanz*) that stands on its shore. The town was named for a Roman fort here, itself named in honor of the early 4th-century Roman emperor *Constantius* Chlorus or, according to some authorities, for *Constantine* the Great, his son. Cp. **Constanța**. The lake's German name is *Bodensee*, possibly deriving from Old German *bodam*, "meadow," or more probably from an Indoeuropean root word meaning "water." Its Roman name was *Brigantinus lacus*, from *Brigantium*, modern **Bregenz**, at its eastern end.

Constanța. *City and port, southeastern Romania.* The city takes its name from the Roman emperor *Constantine* the Great, who rebuilt it in A.D. 311 and named it for himself. The earlier town here was known as *Flavia Nea*, a name given by the Roman emperor Titus in honor of his father *Flavius* Vespasianus, the second word being Greek *nea*, "new."

Constantine. *City, northeastern Algeria.* The city takes its name from the Roman emperor *Constantine* the Great, who rebuilt it in A.D. 313. The original town here was known as *Cirta*, from Punic *qart*, "town." The modern name now often appears on maps in the arabicized spelling of *Qacentina*.

Constantinople *see* **Istanbul**

Cooch Behar. *Town, northeastern India.* The West Bengal town takes its name from the former princely state here. The first word represents the tribal name *Koch*, the people who founded the state in the 16th century. The second word represents Hindi *vihār*, "(Buddhist) monastery," presumably commemorating a particular one. The name is now often spelled *Koch Bihar*.

Cook, Mt. *Mountain, southwestern New Zealand.* New Zealand's highest mountain, in southwestern South Island, was named in 1851 for the English navigator Captain James *Cook* (1728–1779), who charted all of New Zealand in 1770. Its indigenous Maori name is *Aorangi*, traditionally said to mean "cloud piercer," although really "cloud in the sky." (Mt. *Aoraï*, Tahiti, has a name of identical origin.)

Cook Islands. *Island group, South Pacific.* The islands, belonging to New Zealand, take their name from the English navigator Captain James *Cook* (1728–1779), who discovered them in 1773.

Coolgardie. *Town, southwestern Australia.* The former boom town, in Western Australia, was founded in 1892 on the discovery of gold. It was successively named *Gnarlbine*, *Bayley's Find*, and *Fly Flat* before gaining its present Aboriginal name, said to mean "hollow surrounded by mulga trees."

Copacabana. *Resort beach, southeastern Brazil.* The district of Rio de Janeiro derives its name from Quechua *copac*, "blue," and *cabana*, "observation post," denoting a lookout post by the sea. The name is found elsewhere, as for the Bolivian town by Lake Titicaca.

Copenhagen. *Capital of Denmark.* The city

and port has a name that means "merchants' port," from Danish *køber*, "merchant" (literally "buyer"), and *havn*, "port," "harbor." Copenhagen remains Denmark's leading commercial city today.

Copperbelt. *Province, central Zambia.* The earlier name of the province was *Western*, not entirely appropriately for its geographical location. In 1969 this was changed as now to denote the rich copper deposits here.

Coptos. *Historic city, eastern Egypt.* The name of the city, on the east bank of the Nile, is a Greek form of its Arabic name *Qift*, itself from *Aegyptos*, the Greek form of the name of **Egypt**. The name of the *Copts*, Christian descendants of the ancient Egyptian people, is of the same origin.

Coral Sea. *Sea, southwestern Pacific.* The sea, northeast of Australia, has a self-descriptive name referring to its many coral reefs.

Corcovado, Mt. *Peak, southeastern Brazil.* The rocky peak with a statue of Christ the Redeemer overlooking Rio de Janeiro is named for its shape, from the Portuguese word for "hunchback."

Cordilleras. *Mountain ranges, western North and South America.* The ranges take their basic name from Old Spanish *cordillera*, "cord," "little rope," since they run down the continents like a continuous cord. Individual ranges or groups of ranges have their own names, such as the *Cordillera Central* in Colombia and the *Cordillera Blanca* ("white") and *Cordillera Negra* ("black") in Peru. The last two are so called for their respective presence and absence of snow.

¹Córdoba. *City, southern Spain.* The former capital of Moorish Spain derives its name from Phoenician *qorteb*, "oil press."

²Córdoba. *City, north central Argentina.* Argentina's second largest city was founded in 1573 by the Spanish conquistador Jerónimo Luis de Cabrera (1528–1574), who named it *Córdoba de la Nueva Andalucía*, "*Córdoba* of the New Andalusia," for **¹Córdoba**, his wife's birthplace in Spain.

Corfu. *Island, western Greece.* The island, in the Ionian Sea, is said to derive its name from an Italian corruption of Greek *koruphai*, "summits," referring to twin mountain peaks here. The modern Greek name of the island is *Kérkira*, from an Indoeuropean root word *kerk*, "bend," presumably describing the undulating coastline, and its chief city is now known by this name.

Corinth. *City, southeastern Greece.* The city derives its name from Pelasgian *kar*, "point," "peak," referring to its location on the Isthmus of Corinth. The Greek form of the name is *Korinthos*. The *-nthos* of this is not Indoeuropean in origin but represents an unidentifed Mediterranean language.

Cork. *City and port, southern Ireland.* The city, in the county of the same name, has an English form of its Irish name *Corcaigh*, representing *corcach*, "marsh." Cork was founded on marshland in the 7th century and its streets were intersected by muddy streams as recently as the 18th century.

Çorlu. *Town, northwestern Turkey.* The town is said to derive its name from Turkish *zorlu*, "strong," "powerful," denoting its resistance at a time when the Ottoman Empire was nearing its end. But its ancient name was *Syrollum*, and the present name is almost certainly a corruption of this.

Cornwall. *County, southwestern England.* The county bases its name on that of the *Cornovii*, a Celtic people who at one time inhabited the region. Their name means "horn people," from a word related to Latin *cornu*, "horn," referring to the long peninsula or "horn" that Cornwall is. The Anglo-Saxons added Old English *walh* to this, meaning "stranger," "foreigner," implying a people who spoke an alien, Celtic language, quite different from their own. *Cp.* **Wales**.

Coro. *City, northwestern Venezuela.* The city was founded in 1527 as *Santa Ana de Coriana*, "St. Anne of *Coriana*," the latter name deriving from the *Coros* Indians, who inhabited the region. Their name was later used alone for the settlement that grew up.

Coromandel Coast. *Region, southeastern India.* The name of the coastal region, in Tamil Nadu state, is a corruption of Sanskrit *cholamandala*, literally "circle of *Chola*," indicating its possession by an early dynasty. The Portuguese changed the first *l* of this to *r*, the Italians then rendered the *ch* as *c*, and finally the French altered the ending to give the present form of the name.

Corpus Christi. *City and port, southern United States.* The Texas city was founded in 1838 and in 1846 named for the bay on which it lies. The bay is said to have been named by the Spanish navigator Alonso Álvarez de Pineda, who visited it in 1519 on the feastday of *Corpus Christi* (the first Thursday after Trinity Sunday), but there is evidence that the name was actually given by the first settlers, who arrived here from the lower Rio Grande valley in the 1760s.

Corregidor Island. *Island, northwestern Philippines.* The island, at the entrance to Manila Bay, was fortified by the Spanish in the 18th century. It was the point where the maritime registrar (Spanish *corregidor*) would record particulars of ships entering the bay. Hence the name.

Corrientes. *City, northeastern Argentina*. The city arose in 1588 when Juan Torres de Vera y Aragón, governor of the Río de la Plata viceroyalty, built a fort here, partly named for himself, called *San Juan de Vera de las Siete Corrientes*. The last two words of this mean "seven currents," referring to the seven rapids upstream from here. The present name is the final word of the original.

Corsica. *Island, northwestern Mediterranean Sea*. The French island has a name of uncertain origin. A source in Phoenician *horsi*, "wooded," has been suggested, since the Phoenicians built their boats from pinewood of Corsican origin. The French form of the name is *Corse*.

Cortina d'Ampezzo. *Town and resort, northern Italy*. The first word of the town's name means "little court," as a diminutive of Italian *corte*, "court." The rest of the name is that of the valley here, the *Val d'Ampezzo*, from Italian *in pezzo*, "in the piece (of land)." The town and its valley are surrounded by mountains.

Cortona. *City, central Italy*. According to some sources, the city derives its name from Phoenician *qart dannu*, "fortified town," but an origin in Celtic *gord*, "fortified height," is also possible. The town is on the southern slope of San Egidio hill.

Corunna *see* **La Coruña**

Cosenza. *City, southern Italy*. The city was known to the Romans as *Consentia*, a name representing Latin *Consentes dii*, "counselor gods," the Roman equivalent of the twelve Greek gods that formed the council of Olympus.

Costa Alegre. *Coastal region, western Mexico*. The section of Pacific coast between Puerto Vallarta and Manzanillo has a Spanish name meaning "bright coast."

Costa Balsamo. *Coast region, southwestern El Salvador*. The section of Pacific coast between Acajutla and La Libertad has a Spanish name meaning "balsam coast," for the Peruvian Balsam (*Myloxyron pereirae*) here, a tree that yields balsam as a medicinal resin.

Costa Bela. *Coastal region, southwestern Portugal*. The stretch of south-facing Atlantic coast west of Setúbal has a Portuguese name meaning "beautiful coast."

Costa Blanca. *Coastal region, southeastern Spain*. The section of Mediterranean coast between the **Costa del Azahar** and **Costa Cálida** has a Spanish name meaning "white coast," referring to the white sands here.

Costa Brava. *Coastal region, northeastern Spain*. The section of Mediterranean coast between the French border and Barcelona has a Spanish name meaning "wild coast," referring to the rugged seaboard here. *Cp.* **Wild Coast**.

Costa Cálida. *Coastal region, southeastern Spain*. The section of Mediterranean coast southwest of Cartagena has a Spanish name meaning "hot coast," for the generally warm climate here.

Costa da Prata. *Coastal region, western Portugal*. The section of Atlantic coast centered on Oporto has a Portuguese name meaning "silver coast," a counterpart to the **Costa Dourada** further south.

Costa de la Luz. *Coastal region, southwestern Spain*. The section of Atlantic coast between the **Costa del Sol** and the Portuguese border has a Spanish name meaning "coast of light," referring to its sparkling sea and the silvery-white sand of its beaches.

Costa de la Muerte. *Coastal region, northwestern Spain*. The section of rocky coast centering on Cape Finisterre has a Spanish name meaning "coast of death" for the many ships and lives lost here. The English name is more usually found than the Spanish.

> For the Romans this was the edge of the world, for the Celts a place of legend, and for the sailors buffeted by the Atlantic waves a place to fear. Hundreds of shipwrecks litter the seabed, a testimony to the dangers of the rocks hidden beneath the waves and the origins of the name of the region [*The Rough Guide to Spain*, 2004].

Costa del Azahar. *Coastal region, northeastern Spain*. The section of Mediterranean coast, between the **Costa Blanca** and **Costa Dorada**, has a Spanish name meaning "orange-blossom coast."

Costa del Sol. *Coastal region, southern Spain*. The section of Mediterranean coast east of Gibraltar has a Spanish name meaning "sunny coast." The name is touristic, like many of those above and below, and the region is in fact no sunnier than anywhere else on the Spanish coast.

> This is the Costa del Sol, variously known as the Coca Cola Coast and the Costa Mierda, for which a genteel translation would be the Coast of Dung [Kenneth Tynan, "The Rising Costa del Sol," *Tynan Right and Left*, 1967].

Costa Dorada. *Coastal region, northeastern Spain*. The section of Mediterranean coast, between the **Costa del Azahar** and **Costa Brava**, has a Spanish name meaning "golden coast," referring to the golden sands of the beaches here. *Cp.* **Costa Dourada**.

Costa Dourada. *Coastal region, southwestern Portugal.* The section of Atlantic coast, between Sétubal and the Sagres, has a Portuguese name meaning "golden coast," for its golden sands. *Cp.* **Costa Dorada.**

Costa Mesa. *City, southwestern United States.* The California city was laid out as the town of *Harper* in 1906. In 1921 it was renamed as now for its location on a plateau overlooking the Pacific, from Spanish *costa*, "coast," and *mesa*, "tableland." The new name was the result of a contest, in which one Alice Plummer won $20 for her suggestion.

Costa Rica. *Republic, southern Central America.* The country has a Spanish name translating as "rich coast." This is not a touristic name, but one given in 1502 by Columbus, referring to the region's abundance of vegetation and water. He also called it *Costa del Oro*, "gold coast," perhaps alluding to the gold ornaments worn by local people.

Costa Smeralda: *Coastal region, northeastern Sardinia.* The stretch of Mediterranean coast, between the bays of Arzachena and Cugnana, has an Italian name meaning "emerald coast," referring to the bright green color of land and sea here.

[1]**Costa Verde.** *Coastal region, northern Spain.* The section of Atlantic coast, on the Bay of Biscay between Gijón and Bilbao, has a Spanish name meaning "green coast," for its general verdure.

[2]**Costa Verde.** *Coastal region, southeastern Brazil.* The section of Atlantic coast between Rio de Janeiro and Parati has a Portuguese name meaning "green coast," referring either to the emerald-green sea here, or to the verdure of the rainforest below the Serra do Mar, or to the combined effect of both.

Coswig. *Town, eastern Germany.* The name probably goes back to Old Sorbian *kos*, "blackbird," giving a sense "place where blackbirds are seen." There is a smaller town with an identical name of the same origin in central Germany.

Côte d'Azur. *Coastal region, southeastern France.* The "azure coast" is better known to English speakers as the French **Riviera**, and is the stretch of Mediterranean coastline between Cannes and Menton or Cannes and La Spezia, Italy. The color referred to is that of the sea and sky.

This is the most familiar of France's coastal names. Others are *Côte d'Albâtre*, "alabaster coast," between Le Havre and Dieppe, *Côte d'Amour*, "coast of love," on the Atlantic seaboard around La Baule, *Côte d'Argent*, "silver coast," on the Bay of Biscay between the Gironde and the Spanish border, *Côte de Beauté*, "coast of beauty," from La Rochelle to the Gironde on the Bay of Biscay, *Côte d'Émeraude*, "emerald coast," in the region of Dinard and Saint-Malo (*cp.* **Costa Smeralda**), *Côte de Grâce*, "coast of grace," between Trouville-sur-Mer and Honfleur along the southern shore of the Seine estuary (the name refers to **Le Havre**, originally *Havre-de-Grâce*), *Côte de Granit Rose*, "coast of pink granite," along the coast of northern Brittany, *Côte de Jade*, "jade coast," around the estuary of the Loire, *Côte de Nacre*, "pearl coast," to the west of Le Havre, *Côte d'Opale*, "opal coast," from the mouth of the Somme to the Belgian frontier, *Côte Fleurie*, "flowery coast," between Honfleur and Cabourg, *Côte Sauvage*, "wild coast," along the Atlantic-facing coast of the Quiberon Peninsula (*cp.* **Wild Coast**), and *Côte Vermeille*, "vermilion coast," from Collioure to the Spanish border.

Côte d'Ivoire. *Republic, western Africa.* The country's French name translates as *Ivory Coast*, as which it was officially known until 1986. The trade in ivory here was initiated by Portuguese colonists in the 16th century. The republic is still named *Ivory Coast* (or the vernacular equivalent) in some modern gazetteers and atlases, such as *Philip's Great World Atlas* (2001), but: "Since 1986, Côte d'Ivoire has requested that the French form of the country's name be used as the official protocol version in all languages" (*Britannica Book of the Year*, 2004).

Côte d'Or. *Region, east central France.* The French name means "golden ridge," and refers to the range of hills here, noted for their vines. "Golden" refers both to the color of the grapes and to their richness in quality and quantity. (This is not a touristic name, and *côte* does not mean "coast.")

Cotonou. *City and port, southern Benin.* The city has a name of local origin, and is properly *Ku Tonu*, from *ku*, "dead person," and *tonu*, "lagoon." A legend tells how the souls of the dead were borne down the Ouémé River into the sea. The legend may have arisen from the fact that the trees around the lagoon are reddish, and were believed to be stained with the blood of corpses.

Cotopaxi. *Volcano, north central Ecuador.* The active volcano has a Quechua name meaning "shining mountain," from *kotto*, "mountain," and *paksi*, "shining."

Cotswolds. *Hill range, west central England.* The Gloucestershire hills have an Old English name meaning "*Cōd's* forest," referring to the high forestland ("weald") here that belonged to an Anglo-Saxon named *Cōd*.

Cottbus. *City, eastern Germany*. The city, near the Polish border, arose around a 10th-century castle built on the site of an Old Sorbian fort and bases its name on the Old Sorbian personal name *Chotebud*.

Council Bluffs. *City, north central United States*. The Iowa city is named for a site by the Missouri called *Council Hill* or *Council Bluff* where the American explorers Meriwether Lewis and William Clark held a powwow (*council*) in 1804 with Native Americans. The city itself was settled in 1846.

Courbevoie. *Town, northern France*. The town, now a suburb of Paris, had the Medieval Latin name of *Curba Via*, "curved way," describing the curve here either in the Roman road that ran from Paris to Rouen or in the Seine River.

Courland. *Region, western Latvia*. The region, on the Baltic seacoast, derives its name from the *Curonians*, a people here in medieval times. The origin of their own name is uncertain.

Courtrai. *Town, northwestern Belgium*. The Romans knew the site here as *Cortracum* or *Curtracum*, a name of Celtic origin meaning "enclosure," and this gave the present name. Its Flemish form is *Kortrijk*.

Coventry. *City, central England*. The former Warwickshire city has an Old English name meaning "*Cofa*'s tree." It is not known who Cofa was, nor is the site of his "tree" known. It probably served as an assembly point or boundary marker of some kind. The name is still sometimes popularly explained as "convent town," usually in connection with the titillating tale of Lady Godiva, whose husband, Leofric, founded a Benedictine priory here in 1043.

Cowes. *Town and resort, southern England*. The Isle of Wight town takes its name from two sandbanks off the mouth of the Medina River here. They were called "the Cows," as if the main island were the "bull."

Cox's Bazar. *Town and port, southeastern Bangladesh*. The town is named for Captain Hiram *Cox*, a British army officer, who in 1799 arranged the settlement here of Muslim refugees from Burma.

Coyoacán. *City, central Mexico*. The city, now a suburb of Mexico City, has a Nahuatl name meaning "place of coyotes."

Cracow *see* **Kraków**

Craigavon. *Town, east central Northern Ireland*. The town, in Co. Armagh, was founded as a New Town in 1965 and named for James *Craig*, 1st Viscount *Craigavon* (1871–1940), the first prime minister of Northern Ireland. He took his title from his father's home at *Craigavon*, Co. Down.

Crailsheim. *City, southwestern Germany*. The city, originally a Frankish village dating back to the 6th century, has a name of uncertain meaning. The second part is the familiar Old High German *heim*, "house," "abode" (English *home*). The first part may represent a personal name such as *Krawel* or derive from Old High German *krouwil* (modern German *Kräuel*), a type of pick with curved ends. The city's coat of arms shows three pothooks, as used for an open fireplace, and these may have originally been called *Kräuel*. But the depiction, as often, could be simply an attempt to explain the name.

Craiova. *City, southwestern Romania*. The city, built on the site of a Roman settlement, has a name based on Slavic *krai*, "border," testifying to the longstanding presence of a Slav population here.

Cranston. *City, northeastern United States*. The Rhode Island city, originally part of Providence, became a separate town in 1754 and was named for Samuel *Cranston* (1659–1727), governor of Rhode Island from 1698 to 1727.

Cremona. *City, northern Italy*. The city was founded by the Romans in 218 B.C. on the site of a village of the *Cenomani*, the Gaulish people who also gave the name of **Le Mans**, France. Hence its name, apparently, although a source in a Celtic word meaning "garlic" (Old Irish *crim*, Welsh *craf*) is also possible, referring to the presence of this plant here.

Crete. *Island, southern Greece*. The island, in the eastern Mediterranean, is traditionally said to derive its name from *Krus*, the mythical ancestor of the Cretans. The true origin is probably in an ethnic name.

Crewe. *Town, northwestern England*. The Cheshire town has a name directly related to Welsh *cryw*, "creel." This is literally a fish basket, but here it came to have the sense "stepping stones," probably because such stones would have been laid alongside a wickerwork fence or "basket" placed across a river to trap fish. The stones in question would have been over one or more of the many streams here.

Crikvenica. *Town and resort, western Croatia*. The town, on the Adriatic coast, takes its name from Croatian dialect *crikva*, "church" (Serbo-Croat *crkva*), referring to the church by which it arose, that of a Pauline monastery founded in 1422.

Crimea. *Peninsula, southern Ukraine*. The Black Sea peninsula has a name of uncertain origin. It has been derived by some from Greek *krēmnos*, "steep bank," by others from Mongolian *kherem*, "strength," by others again from Russian *kremen'*, "flint," and by still others from Russian *kroma*, "edge," "border." But the last two of these are at best fanciful. The name is not ancient, and in classical times the Crimea was known as *Taurida*, from the native *Tauri*, whose own name may come from Celtic *tauro*, "mountain." The Russian and Ukrainian form of the name is *Krym*. See *also* **Kherson**.

Crimmitschau. *City, east central Germany.* The city's name probably derives from a Slavic personal name *Krimas*, giving a meaning "*Krimas*'s settlement."

Cristalina. *Town, central Brazil.* The town is a noted rock-*crystal* mining center. Hence the name.

Cristóbal *see* **Colón**

Croatia. *Republic, southeastern Europe.* The country has a Slavic name that is probably related to Russian *khrebet*, "mountain chain," referring to the mountains by the Adriatic coast here.

Crotone. *Town and port, southern Italy.* The town is of Greek origin and takes its name from Greek *krotōn*, "castor-oil plant" (*Ricinus communis*). From medieval times until 1928, when it was corrected to its original form, the name was spelled *Cotrone*.

Croydon. *Town, southeastern England.* The former Surrey town has an Old English name meaning "saffron valley," from *croh*, "saffron" (modern *crocus* is related), and *denu*, "valley." The valley is that of the Wandle River. Saffron was a herb used for dyeing and medicinal purposes in past times.

Crozet Islands. *Island group, southern Indian Ocean.* The islands were discovered in 1772 by the French naval commander Nicolas-Thomas Marion-Dufresne, who named them for one of his officers, Julien Marie *Crozet* (1728–1780).

Csongrád. *City, southern Hungary.* The city has a Slavic name meaning "black fortress," referring to the 11th-century defensive post here.

Csorna. *Town, western Hungary.* The town derives its name from a personal name of Slavic origin meaning "black."

Csurgó. *Town, southwestern Hungary.* The name is that of a stream here, itself meaning "trickling one," from Hungarian *csurog*, "to flow."

Cuba. *Island republic, western West Indies.* The island has a Native American name of unknown origin and meaning. A possible sense "region" has been suggested, but the language that gave

the name is extinct, and this is merely a conjecture.

Cuchilla Grande. *Hill range, eastern Uruguay.* The range of granite hills has a Spanish name meaning literally "big knife," referring to its sharp, angular rocks.

Cuddalore. *City, southeastern India.* The city, in Tamil Nadu state, derives its name from Tamil *kūṭṭal-ūr*, "junction town," referring to its location at the confluence (junction) of the Ponnaiyar River with its tributary, the Gadilam.

Cuddapah. *City, southern India.* The city, in Andhra Pradesh state, derives its name from Telugu *kaḍapa*, "gate," as it is the gateway from the north to the sacred hill pagoda at Tirupati.

Cuenca. *Town, east central Spain.* The town derives its name from Medieval Latin *concha*, "shell." The reference is to the town's "bowl-like" location, on a hill surrounded by mountains above the confluence of two rivers.

Cuernavaca. *City, south central Mexico.* The city's present name was introduced in 1521 by the Spanish conquistador Hernán Cortés as a form of the original indigenous name, *Cuauhnáhuac*, meaning "eagle's nest."

Cumae. *Historic city, southwestern Italy.* The ancient Greek city may derive its name from Greek *kuma*, "wave."

Cumberland *see* **Cumbria**

Cumberland Gap. *Pass, eastern United States.* The pass, through the *Cumberland* Mountains, was explored in 1750 by the land speculator Dr. Thomas Walker who named it for William Augustus, duke of *Cumberland* (1721–1765), son of George II, famous for his victory at Culloden in 1746.

Cumbria. *County, northwestern England.* The county has resurrected the Roman name for the region here, itself so called for the *Cymry*. This was the name, meaning "fellow countrymen," that the Britons used for themselves, and that today is the Welsh name for the Welsh (*see* **Wales**). The present county was formed in 1974 and comprises the former counties of *Cumberland* ("land of the *Cymry*") and **Westmorland**.

Cuneo. *City, northwestern Italy.* The city, near Turin, stands on a plateau in the wedge (Italian *cuneo*) formed at the confluence of the Stura di Demonte and Gesso rivers.

Curaçao. *Island, southern West Indies.* The Caribbean island was discovered by the Spanish explorer Alonso de Hojeda in 1499 and originally named *Isla de los Gigantes*, "island of giants," for its tall Native American inhabitants. The story then goes that a group of Spanish sailors suffering from malaria were later abandoned on the island, but were subsequently discovered to be completely cured. The island was thus renamed *Curación*, "cure," which under Portuguese influence became *Curaçao*. But the true origin is almost certainly less colorful, and is probably in some Native American name.

Cush. *Historic region, northeastern Africa.* The region, corresponding to modern Nubia, south of Egypt, has a name of Egyptian origin but uncertain meaning. The region is mentioned in the Bible (Isaiah 11:11, etc.) and is often translated "Ethiopia," as in Genesis 2:13, where the reference is probably to Babylon, which was occupied by the ancient people known as Kassites in the first millennium B.C. (In Genesis 10:6–8, Cush is cited as a son of Ham and father of Nimrod.)

Cuttack. *Town, eastern India.* The town, in Orissa state, was founded in the 13th century and is said to derive its name from Sanskrit *kataka*, "army," "camp."

Cuvette. *Region, north central Congo.* The region takes its name from French *cuvette*, "basin," referring to the depression in the western section of the Congo River basin that extends here from the mountains and plateaux in the west to the river itself in the east.

Cuxhaven. *City and port, northwestern Germany.* The second part of the name is an early form of modern German *Hafen*, "harbor," "port," The first part represents Low German *Koog*, "polder," referring to the embanked or dyked area of land at the mouth of the Elbe estuary.

Cuzco. *City, south central Peru.* The former capital of the Inca empire, dating from the 12th or 13th century, derives its name from a Quechua word meaning "navel," "center."

Cwmbran. *Town, southeastern Wales.* The town, near Newport, has a name meaning "valley of the *Brân*," from Welsh *cwm*, "valley," and the name of the river here, itself meaning "raven," referring to the dark color of its waters.

Cyclades. *Island group, Aegean Sea.* The Greek islands form a ring around Delos. Hence their name, from Greek *kuklos*, "circle." There may be an intentional contrast with the name of the **Sporades.**

Cynopolis. *Historic city, east central Egypt.* The name is Greek for "city of the dog," referring to the ancient temple here of Anubis, the Egyptian dog-headed god of the dead.

Cyprus. *Island republic, eastern Mediterranean Sea.* The Greek name of the island is *Kupros*, probably representing Sumerian *kabar* or *gabar*, "copper," "bronze." Copper mines were known

here in early times, and the English word *copper* derives from the island name.

Cyrenaica. *Historic region, eastern Libya.* The region takes its name from the ancient Greek city of *Cyrene* here. Its own name is said to come from that of *Cyrene*, the nymph of Greek mythology. But this is likely to be a folk etymology.

Czechoslovakia *see* (1) **Czech Republic**; (2) **Slovakia**

Czech Republic. *Republic, central Europe.* The country takes its name from the people who are its indigenous inhabitants. Their own name is said to come from an ancestral chief, although some derive it from Czech *četa*, "army." The present republic was formed in 1992 when *Czechoslovakia* was divided into two separate states. For the other state, *see* **Slovakia.**

Częstochowa. *City, southern Poland.* The city, founded in the 13th century, appears to have a name representing Polish *częstokół*, "palisade," referring to an enclosure that at one time protected it from invasion. The German form of the name in World War II was *Tschenstochau*.

Dacca *see* **Dhaka**

Dachau. *Town, southern Germany.* The town derives its name from Old High German *dāha*, "clay," and *ouwa*, "island," "raised ground by water," describing its location by the Amper River.

Dacia. *Historic region, central Europe.* The region, approximating to modern Romania, takes its name from Phrygian Greek *daos*, "wolf," referring not to the animal but to the predatory nature of the former indigenous inhabitants.

Dagestan. *Republic, southwestern Russia.* The republic, in the eastern Caucasus, has a name meaning "mountain country," from Turkish *dağ*, "mountain," and Old Persian *stān*, "country" (as for **Afghanistan** and elsewhere).

Dahna. *Desert, central Saudi Arabia.* The desert's name represents Arabic *ad-dahna*', "the desert."

Dahomey *see* **Benin**

Dairen. *City and port, northeastern China.* The city, in Liaoning province, was founded by the Russians in 1898 on the site of a fishing village called *Dalian*, from Chinese *dà*, "big," and *lián*, "to join." The reference is to a place of lively commerce. The Russians themselves called the new port *Dal'nij*, meaning "far" (an appropriate name for a new possession in the Far East), but this was clearly influenced by the existing name. The Japanese gained control of the peninsula following the Russo-Japanese War of 1904–05 and pronounced the name *Dairen*, a form that became generally used in the West. The city has now merged with the port of **Lü-shun**, so that it is commonly known as *Lü-Ta*, a combination of the first elements of this name and of *Ta-lien*, the local form of its own name.

Dakar. *Capital of Senegal.* The city and port has a name of Wolof origin, from *n'dakar*, "tamarind tree." The story goes that when European explorers questioned local people about the name of their settlement, the Africans thought they were being asked about a prominent tamarind tree on the coast nearby, and named it instead.

Dakota. *States, northern United States.* The neighboring states of North and South Dakota were formed in 1889 from the earlier unified Dakota Territory. It takes its name from a Native American word *dakota* or *lakota*, meaning "friends." This was the name of a local people who had formed an alliance with the Sioux.

Dalarna *see* **Dalecarlia**

Da Lat. *City, southern Vietnam.* The city was founded in the 19th century and named for the *Da* (now Cam Ly) River on which it stands and for its *Lat* population.

Dalecarlia. *Region, west central Sweden.* The name is an obsolescent form of the region's Swedish name *Dalarna*. This means "the valleys," from Swedish *dalar*, the plural of *dal*, "valley" (English *dale*), and *-na*, the form of the definite article ("the") suffix used after plural nouns.

Dalhousie. *Town, northwestern India.* The town, in Himachal Pradesh state, is named for James Ramsay, 10th earl of *Dalhousie* (1812–1860), British governor general of India from 1847 to 1856.

Dallas. *City, southern United States.* The Texas city, first settled in 1841 and platted in 1846, is named for George M. *Dallas* (1792–1864), vice president of the United States from 1845 to 1849.

Dalmatia. *Historic region, southern Croatia.* The region derives its name from the Indoeuropean root word *dhal*, meaning "young animal," perhaps with reference to the mountain pastures here.

Daloa. *Town, west central Côte d'Ivoire.* The original settlement here was founded by two Africans, *Gboto* and *Dalo*, and takes its name from the latter.

Daly. *River, northern Australia.* The river, in Northern Territory, was explored in 1865 and named for Sir Dominick *Daly* (1798–1868), then governor of South Australia.

Damanhur. *City, northern Egypt.* The city derives its name from ancient Egyptian *timinhor*, "city of *Horus*," referring to the sun god

of Egyptian mythology, who was worshiped here.

Damaraland. *Historic region, north central Namibia.* The region takes its name from the *Damara*, a Khoisan (Hottentot) people, with English *land* added. Their name is said to be the dual feminine form of the insulting name *Daman*, applied to them by the English. This could itself come from a San (Bushman) word *dama*, "child," or perhaps mean "riches," as in the local expression *gamocha-daman*, "rich in oxen." Another theory derives *Damara* from Malay *damar*, the name of a coniferous tree of Southeast Asia that yields a dark resin. The implication is that Dutch colonists in Africa would have been familiar with the Malay word and adopted it to describe the skin color of the Namibian people. The name is most unlikely to have originated in that of the biblical character *Damaris* (Acts 17:34), as has been proposed by some, on the grounds that Damaris was a female convert to Christianity and that the Africans were similarly converted. The Damara people's own name for themselves is *Herero*, said to be an onomatopoeic word representing the sound of a spear in flight.

Damascus. *Capital of Syria.* The city has an ancient, pre–Semitic name of unknown origin, the Western form of it representing Arabic *dimashk*. The colloquial Arabic name of Damascus is *ash-shām*, "the northern" (as seen from Arabia), which is also used for **Syria** itself and which may have led to the false association between that name and **Assyria**.

Damietta. *City and port, northern Egypt.* The city's name is an Italian alteration of Arabic *dumyāṭ*, itself a corruption of the original Coptic name *Tamiati*. The meaning of this is uncertain, although *tam-* almost certainly means "city."

Dâmrei Mountains. *Mountains, southwestern Cambodia.* The name is short for Khmer *Chuŏr Phnum Dâmrei*, meaning "mountains around which clouds turn." The French knew the mountains as *Chaîne de l'Éléphant*, "elephant range," for their appearance.

Dan. *Kibbutz, northern Israel.* The kibbutz was founded in 1939 and named after the biblical *Dan*, the northernmost point of the kingdom of Israel, itself originally known as *Laish* ("lion") but renamed by the Danites for their ancestor, as described in the Bible (Judges 18:29).

Da Nang. *City and port, central Vietnam.* The city has a Cham name meaning "big river," "main estuary." Its French colonial name, *Tourane*, was a corruption of this.

Danao. *City and port, south central Philippines.* The city, in eastern Cebu Island, derives its name from the local word *danawam*, "shallow lagoon."

Danbury. *City, northeastern United States.* The Connecticut city was settled in 1685 and in 1687 named for the English village of *Danbury*, Essex, presumably because one or more of the settlers had connections there.

Dandakaranya. *Region, east central India.* The region derives its name from the *Dandak* Forest (the abode of the demon *Dandak*) in the Hindu epic the *Ramayana*.

Dandarah *see* **Dendera**

Dandenong Ranges. *Mountain ranges, southeastern Australia.* The ranges, in Victoria, derive their name from the Aboriginal word *tanjenong*, "lofty." The name is properly that of the ranges' highest peak, Mt. *Dandenong*.

Dandong. *City and port, northeastern China.* The city, in Liaoning province, takes its name from the protectorate general set up here in the 7th century by the *Tang* dynasty, with Chinese *dōng* meaning "east." It was known until 1965 as *An-tung*.

Danube. *River, central Europe.* Europe's second longest river is said to derive its name from Sarmatian *dānu-avi*, "river of sheep," implying a river that flows through good pastureland. The first part of this is also seen in the river name **Don**. The second part is related to Latin *ovis*, "sheep." The German name of the Danube is *Donau*, the Hungarian *Duna*, and the Russian *Dunaj*.

Danville. *City, eastern United States.* The Virginia city, chartered in 1793, takes its name from the *Dan* River on which it lies. Its own name is probably of Native American origin.

Danzig *see* **Gdańsk**

Dardanelles. *Strait between Europe and Asia.* The strait between the Aegean Sea and the Sea of Marmara takes its name from the ancient Greek city of *Dardanus* on its Asian shore. The city is traditionally said to take its own name from *Dardanus*, ancestor of the kings of Troy in classical mythology. (Troy itself lies just to the south of the Dardanelles in western Turkey.) In classical times the strait was known as the *Hellespont*, representing Greek *Hellespontos*, "*Helle*'s sea," alluding to *Helle*, in Greek mythology the daughter of King Athamas, who fell from a ram into its waters when fleeing her father and cruel stepmother with her brother Phrixus. Pragmatists prefer to regard the Dardanelles as a "narrow opening," from Turkish *dar*, "narrow," and *delik*, "hole."

Dar el Beida *see* **Casablanca**

Dar es Salaam. *Capital of Tanzania.* The city and port has a name of Arabic origin, from *dār as-salām*, "house of peace." The appellation may have originally applied to the palace of the Sultan of Zanzibar, Seyyid Majid, who founded the city in 1866, or have implied that the town was a place where merchants could trade freely. The name is sometimes interpreted as "haven of peace," as if from Hindi *bandar*, "harbor," "port," although no early records contain this word and it is unlikely that *bandar*, stressed on the first syllable, would have reduced to *dar*.

Darfur. *Region, western Sudan.* The name derives from Arabic *dār*, "house," and the ethnic name *Fur*, that of the region's Negroid inhabitants.

Darjeeling. *Town, northeastern India.* The name of the West Bengal town derives from Tibetan *dojeling*, "diamond island," from *doje*, "diamond," and *ling*, "island." The reference is to the form of Buddhism known as Vajrayana (literally, "vehicle of the diamond"), otherwise Tantric Buddhism. The "island" is the raised site of Darjeeling, which is a hill station with one of the finest views in the world.

Darling. *River, southeastern Australia.* The river was named in 1829 by the Australian explorer Charles Sturt for Sir Ralph *Darling* (1775–1858), governor of New South Wales from 1825 to 1831.

Darlington. *Town, northern England.* The former Co. Durham town has an Old English name meaning "estate associated with *Dēornōth*," with the *n* of the personal name becoming *r* under Norman influence. It is not known who the named Anglo-Saxon was.

Darmstadt. *City, west central Germany.* The name of the city was recorded in the 11th century as *Darmundestat*, "*Darmund*'s place," denoting the habitation of the named man. The similarity of the second element of his name to German *Mund*, "mouth," came to suggest a "town at the mouth of the *Darm*." But the name of the Darm River that flows through the city is not recorded earlier than 1759, and clearly evolved from the town's name itself.

Dartford. *Town, southeastern England.* The Kent town has a name meaning "ford over the *Darent*," for the river here, its own Celtic name meaning "river where oak trees grow."

[1]**Dartmouth**. *Town and port, southwestern England.* As its name implies, the Devon town takes its name from its location at the mouth of the *Dart* River. The river's own name means "oak stream," from a Celtic word that also gave the name of the **Derwent**.

²**Dartmouth**. *City and port, southeastern Canada*. The Nova Scotia city is said to be named either for the English ¹**Dartmouth** or for William Legge, 2d Earl of *Dartmouth* (1731–1801), who played a significant part in events leading to the United States War of Independence.

Darwin. *Town and port, northern Australia*. The harbor of what is now the capital of Northern Territory was discovered in 1839 and named *Port Darwin* for the English naturalist Charles *Darwin* (1809–1882), who visited the coast here in 1836. The town was founded in 1869 and originally named *Palmerston* for the British prime minister, Viscount *Palmerston* (1784–1865), as for **Palmerston North**, New Zealand. In 1911, however, control of the Northern Territory was transferred from South Australia to that of the Commonwealth of Australia, and the name reverted to that of the port.

Dashhowuz. *City, northern Turkmenistan*. The city, founded in the early 19th century as a fortress, and long known as *Tashauz*, is said to have evolved its name from an original Turkmen form *Dash-hauz*, representing *dash*, "stone," and *hauz*, "reservoir." Dashhowuz is in an oasis not far from the Amu Darya River. The present corrected form of the name dates from 1994.

Dasht-e-Kavir. *Salt desert, central Iran*. The name derives from Iranian *dasht*, "rocky plain," and *kavir*, "salt marsh." *Cp.* **Dasht-e-Lut**.

Dasht-e-Lut. *Desert plateau, east central Iran*. The name derives from Iranian *dasht*, "rocky plain," and *lut*, "barren desert." *Cp.* **Dasht-e-Kavir**.

Datia. *City, central India*. The city, in Madhya Pradesh state, takes its name from *Dantavakra*, a mythological demon ruler of the region.

Datteln. *Town, western Germany*. The first part of the town's name is of uncertain origin. The second part derives from Old High German *lōh*, "copse," "grove," as for **Gütersloh**.

Daugavgrīva. *Port, northern Latvia*. The fortified outer port of Riga, some 7 miles (11 km) north of the capital, is near the mouth of the *Daugava*, the Latvian name of the Western **Dvina** River. Hence its name, meaning "*Dvina* mouth." Its German name of *Dünamünde* and former Russian name of *Ust'-Dvinsk* have the same sense.

Daugavpils. *City, southeastern Latvia*. The city's name means "*Daugava* castle," from *Daugava*, the Latvian name of the Western **Dvina** River. The city was founded in 1278 with the original German name of *Dünaburg*, "fort on the *Dvina*." The Russians later knew it as *Dvinsk*, for this same river.

Daulatabad. *Village, western India*. The ancient city, in Maharashtra state, was founded in the late 12th century and originally known as *Devagiri*, "hill of the gods," for its location atop a conical rock. In 1327 it came under the rule of the Delhi sultanate and was renamed as now, "town of riches," from Hindi *daulat*, "wealth," "riches," and *ābād*, "populated (place)."

Dauphiné. *Historic region, southeastern France*. The nucleus of the former province was the countship of Viennois, which was originally part of the kingdom of Arles and a fief of the Holy Roman Empire. The southern part of the countship was enfiefed in the 11th century to Guigues I, count of Albon, who extended his domain to include other parts of the kingdom of Arles. His grandson, Guigues IV, count from 1133 to 1142, bore the additional name *Dauphin*, "dolphin," from the heraldic fish on his coat of arms. This became a hereditary title of later counts of Albon, and passed from them to the province in the 13th century. In 1349 the future Charles V of France was made Dauphin of Viennois and Dauphiné was ceded to him. He became king in 1364, and in 1368 granted Dauphiné to his son, the future Charles VI, so establishing the precedent whereby the eldest son of the king of France, the heir apparent, bore the title *Dauphin*. The tradition continued until 1830.

Daura. *Town, northern Nigeria*. The name is that of an ancient settlement and kingdom here, and is said to derive from the Tuareg word meaning "blacksmith."

Davenport. *City, east central United States*. The Iowa city takes its name from Colonel George *Davenport* (1785–1845), to whom the site was sold after the Black Hawk Treaty of 1832.

Davis Strait. *Strait between Canada and Greenland*. The strait is named for the English navigator John *Davis* (1550–1605), who discovered it in 1585 when searching for the Northwest Passage.

Davos. *Town, eastern Switzerland*. The mountain resort derives its name from Romansh *davous*, "behind." The reference is to the valley in which Davos lies. This turns to the north behind the town and so shelters it from the wind.

Davutlar. *Town and resort, western Turkey*. The resort was originally a village called *Davut-köyü*, "*Davut's* village," for a local revered person *Davut* (David). It then became a town and took its present name, adding the Turkish plural suffix *-lar* to his name to give a sense "(place of) *Davut's* people."

Dawson. *City, northern Canada*. The former

Yukon capital, originally *Dawson City*, was founded in the Klondike gold rush of 1896 and named for the Canadian explorer George M. *Dawson* (1849–1901).

Dax. *Town, southwestern France.* The name of the town and spa is really *d'Ax*, or in modern French terms *d'eaux*, "of (the) waters." The reference is to the saline springs here. *Cp.* **Aix-les-Bains.**

Dayr al-Bahri. *Historic site, northeastern Egypt.* The archaeological site, in the necropolis of Thebes, has an Arabic name meaning "monastery of the river," from *dayr*, "monastery," and *bahri*, the adjectival form of *bahr*, "river." The site is on the west bank of the Nile.

Dayr al-Madinah. *Historic site, northeastern Egypt.* The ancient site, at Thebes, has an Arabic name meaning "monastery of the town," from *dayr*, "monastery," and *madīna*, "town." The "town" was a village for laborers working on the royal tombs in the nearby Valley of the Kings.

Dayr az-Zawr. *Town, eastern Syria.* The town probably derives its name from the historic city of *Auzara* or *Azuara* nearby. The meaning is "monastery of the grove," from Arabic *dayr*, "monastery," and *zawr*, literally "tamarisk."

Dayton. *City, east central United States.* The Ohio city was founded in 1796 and takes its name from one of its founders, the Revolutionary army captain and House of Representatives speaker Jonathan *Dayton* (1760–1824).

Daytona Beach. *City and resort, southeastern United States.* The Atlantic resort in northeastern Florida is named for Mathias *Day*, who founded it in 1870. His surname was suffixed with the common *-ton*, meaning "town," and the *-a* that ends many American town names.

Dead Sea. *Sea, southwestern Asia.* The sea (properly a lake) between Israel and Jordan is so named because it contains no living organisms as a result of its high salinity. The name was first recorded in Greek as *thalassa nekra*, then in Latin as *Mare Mortuum*. In the Bible it has several names (though never Dead Sea), one being "the salt sea" (Genesis 14:3), as a translation of Hebrew *yām hammelah*. Elsewhere in the Old Testament (it does not appear in the New Testament) it is named as "the sea of the plain" (Deuteronomy 3:17) and as "the east sea" (Ezekiel 47:18). Its Arabic name is either *al-bahr al-mayyit*, "the dead sea," or *bahr lūt*, "sea of Lot," the latter with reference to Lot's wife, who was changed into a pillar of salt here (Genesis 19:26).

Dean, Forest of. *Woodland, west central England.* The Gloucestershire woodland lies between the Severn and Wye rivers, and the *Dean* of the name is simply the Old English word *denu*, "valley." The valley in question is specifically that of Cannop Brook, which flows into the Severn.

Dearborn. *City, northeastern United States.* The Michigan city, settled in 1795, was named for the Revolutionary War hero General Henry *Dearborn* (1751–1829).

Death Valley. *Desert valley, western United States.* The valley, in eastern California and western Nevada, is the lowest, hottest, and driest region in North America. Its name relates to the extreme conditions experienced by a party of immigrants when crossing it in 1849, with some fatalities.

Deauville. *Town and resort, northwestern France.* The name means "town of the damp plain," from French *d'*, "of," Germanic *auwa*, "damp plain" (itself based on *aha*, "water"), and Latin *villa*, "settlement," "town." The resort lies at the mouth of a river on the Seine Estuary.

Debrecen. *City, eastern Hungary.* The city probably bases its name on the Slavic root word *debr*, "ravine," "escarpment," referring to a local feature, although some derive it from a personal name.

Decapolis. *Historic region, southwestern Asia.* The name is Greek for "ten towns," and applies to a region of ancient Palestine, east of the Jordan, where a league of cities of this number existed in the 1st century B.C. The most important of the ten was Damascus. The region is mentioned in the Bible (Matthew 4:25).

Decatur. *City, north central United States.* The Illinois city was founded in 1829 and named in honor of the American naval hero Stephen *Decatur* (1779–1820), killed in a duel.

Decazeville. *Town, southern France.* The town was named in 1829 for Élie *Decazes*, duc de Decazes et de Glücksberg (1780–1860), the French politician who developed the coalmines here from 1826.

Deccan. *Peninsula, southern India.* The name derives from Hindi *dakkhin*, meaning simply "south."

Děčín. *City, northern Czech Republic.* The city, founded in the 12th century, derives its name from the Slavic personal name *Deka*, itself literally meaning "child," implying a descendant (Serbo-Croat *dečak*, "boy," Russian *ditya*, "child"). The German form of the name is *Tetschen*.

Dee. *River, western England.* The river between Wales and England has a name of Celtic origin representing *deva*, "goddess." Hence its

Roman name of *Deva* (*see* **Chester**). Rivers were often personified or deified by the Celts.

Deggendorf. *City, southeastern Germany.* The city, on the Danube, has a name meaning "*Daggo*'s village." The *a* of this personal name became *e* in the genitive form (*Deggen*).

Dehradun. *City, northeastern India.* The capital of Uttaranchal state, founded in 1699, derives its name from Hindi *ḍerā*, "camp," and *dūn*, "valley," the latter referring to the region here between the Himalayan foothills and the Siwalik range.

Delagoa Bay. *Bay, southeastern Mozambique.* The name is probably a corruption of an original Portuguese name *Baía da Lagoa*, "bay of the lagoon."

Delaware. *State, eastern United States.* The state is named for Thomas West, 3d Baron *de la Warr* (1577–1618), the English soldier and colonist who was appointed governor of Virginia in 1610.

Delbrück. *Town, northwestern Germany.* The name, recorded in 1219 as *Thelebrugge*, means "plank bridge," probably referring to planks laid over marshland. The English village of *Thelbridge*, Devonshire, has a name of identical meaning.

Delft. *Town, southwestern Netherlands.* The town takes its name from Old Dutch *delf* (related to English *delve*), "ditch," "canal." Delft is located on the Schie Canal.

Delfzijl. *City, northeastern Netherlands.* The city has a name meaning "canal lock," referring to its location at the northeastern end of the Eems Canal.

Delhi. *Capital of India.* The city's name is of unknown origin, although Hindi *dehlī*, "threshold," has been suggested. This would refer to the location of Delhi on a "threshold" between the Indus and the Ganges. The city is now divided into *Old Delhi*, a walled city reconstructed in 1639 on the original site, and *New Delhi*, to the south, chosen in 1911 as capital in place of Calcutta.

Delitzsch. *City, eastern Germany.* The city derives its name from Old Sorbian *del'c*, "hill," referring to the Slavic hilltop fort around which the town arose.

Delmenhorst. *City, northwestern Germany.* The city arose some time before 1285 around a castle in the valley of the *Delme* River, and this gave the first part of the name. The second part represents Old High German *hurst*, "scrubland." The origin of the river name is unknown.

Delos. *Island, southeastern Greece.* The island, in the Cyclades, derives its name directly from Greek *dēlos*, "clear," "visible," alluding to its prominent position. *See also* **Cyclades**.

Delphi. *Town, central Greece.* The ancient town has a name representing Greek *delphos*, "dolphin." In Greek mythology, Apollo assumed the form of a dolphin, a creature symbolic of water and transformation, when he founded his shrine or oracle here, on the slopes of Mt. Parnassus.

Delray Beach. *City, southeastern United States.* The Florida city was laid out in 1896 and originally named *Linton*, for Congressman William S. *Linton*, who had bought the maritime site for development. It was renamed as now in c.1901 for *Delray*, a district of Detroit.

Del Rio. *City, southern United States.* The Texas city, on the *Rio* Grande, arose from the Spanish mission of *San Felipe del Rio*, "St. Philip of the river," set up here in c.1675. This was the name of the city until 1833, when it was shortened as now to avoid confusion with *San Felipe de Austin* in the same state.

Delta. *State, southern Nigeria.* The state, created in 1991, is named for the *Delta* of the Niger River here. *Cp.* **Rivers**.

Demavend. *Mountain, northern Iran.* The highest peak in Iran, an extinct volcano with a snow-capped cone, derives its name from Sanskrit *himavant*, "snowy mountain." *Cp.* **Himalayas**.

Demirci. *Town, western Turkey.* The town derives its name from Turkish *demir*, "iron," referring to iron-ore deposits in the mountains here.

Denali *see* **McKinley, Mt.**

Denbigh. *Town, northern Wales.* The Denbighshire town has a name meaning "little fortress," from Welsh *din*, "fortress," and *bych*, a form of *bach*, "little." The original fortress would have been where the 12th-century castle stands today, on Castle Hill to the south of the town.

Dendera. *Historic city, eastern Egypt.* The city, on the left bank of the Nile, has a name that evolved through Coptic and Greek from the second word of *Iunit Tentōre*, itself a corruption of the original name *Iunit ta Netert*, "*Iunit* of the goddess." *Iunit* is based on Egyptian *iun*, "column," while *ta Netert*, from *netert*, "goddess," was added to distinguish this city from another of the name, now known as **Heliopolis**. The deity in question was Hathor, goddess of creation. The name is also spelled *Dandarah*.

Dendermonde. *Town, northern Belgium.* The name means "mouth of the *Dender*," denoting the town's location at the confluence of this river with the Scheldt. The French form of the name is *Termonde*.

Denizli. *City, southwestern Turkey*. On the face of it, the name appears to mean "(place) by the sea," from Turkish *deniz*, "sea." It actually evolved from the name of the *Tonguzlu* tribe, who established a city here that inherited the economic role hitherto played by the nearby ancient city of **Laodicea**, which by the 14th century had become known as *Ladik*.

Denmark. *Kingdom, northwestern Europe*. The country is named for its inhabitants, the *Danes*, and their border territory (Danish *mark*, English *march*). Their own name is of uncertain origin. It has been derived by some from Old High German *tanar*, "sandbank," but others have associated it with German *Tanne*, "fir." They are thus either the "sandbank dwellers" or the "forest people." The former seems more likely, in view of Denmark's topography, with many miles of coasts and islands.

Denton. *City, southern United States*. The Texas city was settled in 1857 and named for John B. *Denton*, a Texas frontiersman.

D'Entrecasteaux Islands. *Island group, western Pacific*. The islands, in Papua New Guinea, were visited in 1793 by the French navigator Joseph Antoine Bruni, chevalier *d'Entrecasteaux* (1737–1793), and are named for him.

Denver. *City, west central United States*. The state capital of Colorado was founded in 1858 as a gold-mining center named *Auraria*, "golden." The following year it was renamed in honor of General James W. *Denver* (1817–1892), governor of the territory at the time.

Deoghar. *Town, eastern India*. The town, in Jharkand state, famous for its numerous Buddhist ruins and its temples dedicated to the Hindu god Shiva, has a Hindi name meaning "fort of the gods."

Dera Ghazi Khan. *Town, central Pakistan*. The town was founded in the late 15th century by *Ghazi Khan*, son of a Baluchi chieftain, and is named for him. (The first word is Hindi *ḍerā*, literally "camp.")

Dera Ismail Khan. *Town, north central Pakistan*. The town is named for *Ismail Khan*, son of the Baluchi chieftain who founded it in 1469. *Cp.* **Dera Ghazi Khan**.

Dera Nanak. *Town, northern India*. The town, in Punjab state, is a religious settlement built in honor of Guru *Nanak* (1469–1539), the founder of Sikhism, who lived nearby. *Cp.* **Dera Ghazi Khan**.

Derbent. *City, southwestern Russia*. The city, in Dagestan, was founded in A.D. 438 as a fortress to guard a major caravan route between Asia and Europe. It derives its name from Iranian *der*, "door," "pass," and *bend*, "obstacle," referring to the narrow gap here between the Caspian Sea and the Caucasus. The pass itself is known in some languages as "Iron Gate," for example Turkish *Demirkapıcı* and Arabic *bāb el-ḥadīd*.

Derby. *City, north central England*. The city, in the county named for it, originally had the Old English name of (in modern form) *Northworthy*, "northern enclosure." When the Danes settled here in the 9th century, they renamed it "deer village," from Old Norse *djúr*, "deer," and *by*, "village." The original enclosure may have been called "northern" because it lay to the north of Tamworth. Derby is on the *Derwent* ("oak tree") River, but there is no reason to link the two names.

Derry *see* **Londonderry**

Derventa. *Town, northern Bosnia-Hercegovina*. The town takes its name from the river on which it lies. The river's own name is probably based on Slavic *drev*, "tree," denoting its tree-lined course. Further west a Celtic source meaning "oak" could be considered, as for the **Derwent** in England.

Derwent. *River, northwestern England*. The Cumbria river has a Celtic name meaning "oak river," from the root word *deruenta* that also gave the name of the *Dart* at **Dartford**, among other rivers. There are several other rivers and places with names of the same origin, attesting to the many oaks formerly in Britain. (The tree came to symbolize English "rootedness" and steadfastness.)

Descartes. *Town, west central France*. The town is named for the French philosopher René *Descartes* (1596–1650), who was born here. At the time of his birth it was known as *La Haye-en-Touraine*, "the (place by the) hedge in **Touraine**." This was changed to *La Haye–Descartes* in 1802 and abbreviated as now in 1967 when the town merged with the nearby village of Balesmes.

Dese. *Town, central Ethiopia*. The town has an Amharic name said to mean "my joy."

Deseret *see* **Utah**

Desio. *Town, northern Italy*. The town derives its name from Latin *ad decimum*, "at the tenth," referring to its location at the tenth Roman mile from Milan on the road north to Como. A Roman mile was a thousand paces (4,860 ft/1,482 m).

Des Moines. *City, north central United States*. The state capital of Iowa takes its name from the *Rivière des Moines*, the river on which it arose around the fort built here in 1843. The river's own name is traditionally derived from French *des moines*, "of the monks," referring to French Trappist monks who settled here. It is more likely, however, to be a name of Native American origin, recorded in a 1673 text as *Moinguena*. Recent research has interpreted this as Miami-Illinois *mooyiinkweena*, meaning "shitface," from *mooy*, "excrement," *iinkwe*, "face," and the suffix *-na*, a humorous (or abusive) nickname used by the Peoria Indians for their Illinois-speaking neighbors.

Dessau. *City, eastern Germany*. The city may derives its name from Slavic *tis*, "yew tree," although Middle High German *dieze*, "rapid," is also possible, referring to the Mulde River here. A more likely origin is in a Slavic personal name *Dysh* or *Desh*, with final *-au* the Slavic possessive suffix *-ov*.

Detmold. *City, northwestern Germany*. The city's name dates at least from the 8th century, when it was recorded as *Theotmall*, meaning "people's assembly," from Old High German *thiot*, "folk," "people," and *mahal*, "assembly place." The city thus arose on or near the site of a legislative assembly of local people, similar to an Anglo-Saxon moot in England.

Detroit. *City, northeastern United States*. The Michigan city was founded by French colonists in 1701 as the fortified site of *Fort Pontchartrain du Détroit*. The last word of this is French for "strait," referring to the narrow sound between Lake St. Clair and Lake Erie on which the fort was built. The fort itself was named for the Comte de *Pontchartrain*, Louis XIV's minister of state who was the patron of the city's founder proper, Antoine de la Motte, sieur de Cadillac (1658–1730). The settlement that arose around the fort soon came to be called by the final word alone of the original name.

Deutsch-Wagram *see* **Wagram**

Deutz. *District of Cologne, western Germany*. The name was recorded in Roman times as *Divitia*, supposedly from a Romano-Celtic personal name *Divitius*. But no Celtic settlement is known here, and the origin may instead be in Latin *divitiae*, "wealth," from *dives*, "rich," as a propitious name for a future flourishing community.

Deux-Sèvres. *Department, western France*. The department's name means "two *Sèvres*," referring to the two rivers that rise here, respectively the *Sèvre Nantaise*, "**Nantes** Sèvre," and *Sèvre Niortaise*, "**Niort** Sèvre." For the origin of the basic river name, *see* **Sèvre**.

Deventer. *City, east central Netherlands*. The name, recorded in the 6th century as *Daventria*,

is of uncertain origin and meaning. It probably derives from a personal name.

Devizes. *Town, southern England*. The Wiltshire town derives its name from Old French *devises*, "boundaries," itself from Latin *divisae*, "divisions." The town is at the boundary between two historic hundreds (county subdivisions), one held by the king, the other by the bishops of Salisbury. The boundary passed through the former castle here.

Devon. *County, southwestern England*. The county ultimately takes its name from the *Dumnonii*, the Celtic people who once inhabited the region, their own name either meaning "deep ones," because they were valley dwellers, or deriving from their god, *Dumnonos*, whose name perhaps means "mysterious one." The county is also known as *Devonshire*.

Dezful. *City, southwestern Iran*. The city has an Iranian name meaning "*Dez* bridge," referring to its location on the *Dez* River. The bridge is said to have been built by Shapur II, 3d-century king of Persia.

Dezhnyov, Cape. *Cape, eastern Russia*. Russia's easternmost point was so named in 1898 by the Swedish Arctic navigator Baron Adolf Erik Nordenskjöld and the Russian Geographical Society for the Russian explorer Semyon Ivanov *Dezhnyov* (c.1605–1673), who first rounded it in 1648.

Dhaka. *Capital of Bangladesh*. The city is said to derive its name either from the *dhak*, a local tree (*Butea frondosa*) whose flowers yield a yellow dye, or from *Dhakeswari* ("hidden goddess"), the Hindu deity whose shrine is here. The former conventional Western spelling of the name was *Dacca*.

Dhaulagiri, Mt. *Mountain, west central Nepal*. The Himalayan massif, with its snow- and glacier-covered peaks, has a Hindi name meaning "white mountain," from Sanskrit *dhavala*, "white," and *giri*, "mountain."

Diablo Range. *Mountain range, southwestern United States*. The range, a section of the Pacific Coast Ranges in California, derives its name from Spanish *Monte del Diablo*, "devil's woods," the name of a Native American *ranchería* near the ridge.

Diamantina. *City, eastern Brazil*. The city is named for its *diamond* industry, which has flourished here since 1729.

Diamond Head. *Cape, northwestern Hawaii, United States*. The cape, in southeastern Oahu Island, was so named in the early 19th century when British sailors mistook some volcanic crystals here for diamonds.

Diaoyu Dao. *Islands, East China Sea*. The islands, midway between Okinawa and the China coast, have a name meaning "fishing islands," from Chinese *diàoyú*, "fishing," and *dǎo*, "island."

Dieppe. *Town and port, northern France*. The town's name is of Germanic origin and relates directly to English *deep*, referring to the depth of the water here in the English Channel at the mouth of the Arques River.

Dijon. *City, eastern France*. The city derives its name from Latin *Divio, Divionis*, representing the personal name *Divius*, meaning "divine," "godly."

Dikson. *Town and port, northern Russia*. The world's northernmost town was so named in 1875 by the Swedish Arctic explorer Nils Nordenskjöld for the Swedish merchant (of Scottish origin) Oskar *Dickson*, who had financed his expedition.

Dillenburg. *Town, western Germany*. The town takes its name from the *Dill* River on which it lies. The river's own name is of unknown origin and meaning.

Dillingen. *Town, western Germany*. The name means "(settlement of) *Dullo*'s people," with an Old German personal name. There is a smaller town of the same name on the Danube in southern Germany, but the personal name there is *Dillo*.

¹**Dimitrovgrad**. *Town, south central Bulgaria*. The town was founded in 1947 on the amalgamation of three villages and named for the Bulgarian Communist leader Georgi *Dimitrov* (1882–1949).

²**Dimitrovgrad**. *City, western Russia*. Originally called *Melekess*, a name of uncertain origin, the city was renamed as now in 1972 for the Bulgarian Communist leader Georgi *Dimitrov* (1882–1949).

Dimona. *Town, southern Israel*. The town arose in 1955 when a residential center was set up for workers at the Dead Sea Plant in Sedom (Sodom). It is named for the biblical city of *Dimonah*, one of those "of the tribe of the children of Judah toward the coast of Edom southward" (Joshua 15:21–22).

Dinan. *Town, northwestern France*. The town derives its name from Gaulish *divos*, "holy," and *nanto*, "valley," the latter being that of the Rance River. *Cp*. **Dinant**.

Dinant. *Town, southern Belgium*. The town derives its name from Gaulish *divos*, "holy," and *nanto*, "valley," the latter being that of the Meuse River. *Cp*. **Dinan**.

Dinard. *Town, northwestern France*. The town

in Brittany has a Breton name representing *din*, "hill," and perhaps *arzh*, "bear," the latter either describing the outline of the hill or denoting its northern location (like that of the **Arctic**).

Dinaric Alps. *Mountain range, western Croatia*. The range, running parallel to the Dalmatian coast, takes its name from the *Dinara*, a mountain group here. The origin of this name is unknown. The range is part of the Eastern **Alps**.

Dindigul. *City, southeastern India*. The city, in Tamil Nadu state, derives its name from Tamil *tiṇṭu kal*, "pillow rock," referring to the bare hill that overlooks it.

Dinkelsbühl. *City, southern Germany*. The second part of the city's name is Old High German *buhil*, "hill." The first part is either a personal name such as *Dingolt* or else derives from Old High German *dinkil*, "spelt" (a type of wheat). The name describes the site by the Wörnitz River where the city arose.

Dinslaken. *City, western Germany*. The second part of the name represents Old High German *lahha*, "puddle," meaning a body of standing water remaining from a river (English *lake*). The first part relates to Old High German *dinsan*, "to spread," so that the name means "place by the spreading pool," referring to the city's location in the marshy valley of the Rotbach River, a tributary of the Rhine.

Dire Dawa. *Town, east central Ethiopia*. The town arose on the edge of dry fields that yield little cultivation. Hence its name, from Amharic words meaning "empty plain."

Discovery Bay. *Bay, southern Australia*. The inlet of the Indian Ocean, at the boundary between Victoria and South Australia, is named for the ship *Discovery* that the Scottish explorer Thomas Mitchell found waiting for him here in 1836 following his journey down the Glenelg River.

Dithmarschen. *Region, northern Germany*. The name of the region between the Elbe and Eider rivers means "great marshland," from Old Saxon *thiad*, "many" (literally "people"), and *mersc*, "marsh."

Divinópolis. *City, southeastern Brazil*. A church dedicated to the Holy Spirit was built on the site of the present city in 1767 and the settlement that grew up around it was initially named *Espírito Santo da Itapecerica*, for the Native American village here. A railroad station was built in 1890 by Henrique Galvão and the town that developed was named for him in 1911, the year regarded as that of the founding of the city, which the following year was renamed as now, "heavenly city," from Portuguese *divino*, "heavenly" and the Greek-derived *polis*, "city." The name relates to the city's elevated site, 2,205 feet (672 m) above sea level, and presumably also to the original name.

Dixon Entrance. *Strait, western North America*. The strait, between southeastern Alaska, USA, and British Columbia, Canada, was named in 1788 by the English naturalist Joseph Banks for Captain George *Dixon* (c.1755–c.1800), the English navigator who sailed through it in 1787.

Diyarbakır. *City, southeastern Turkey*. The city derives its name from Turkish *diyar*, "country," "district," and the name of the *Bakr*, a nomadic tribe who settled in the region.

Djibouti. *Republic, eastern Africa*. The country takes its name from its capital, whose own name is said to derive from an Afar word *gabouri*, "plate." The reference is to a plate woven from doum palm fibers and raised on a pedestal for ceremonial purposes.

Dneprodzerzhinsk. *City, east central Ukraine*. The city derives the first part of its name from the **Dnieper** River on which it lies. It was originally known as *Kamenskoye*, "stony place," from Russian *kamen'*, "rock," "stone." In 1936 it was renamed as now for the Russian revolutionary and Communist leader Feliks *Dzerzhinsky* (1877–1926). The Ukrainian form of the name is *Dniprodzerzhyns'k*. *Cp.* **Dzerzhinsk**.

Dnepropetrovsk. *City, east central Ukraine*. The city takes the first part of its name from the **Dnieper** River on which it lies. The second part honors the Soviet Communist official Grigory *Petrovsky* (1878–1958), who worked in the city's factories and became a revolutionary leader there. This name was given in 1928. The town was founded in 1783 as *Yekaterinoslav*, "*Catherine's* glory," in honor of *Catherine* the Great (1729–1796). From 1796 through 1802 it was known as *Novorossiysk*, a name now in use for another city (*see* **Novorossiysk**). The Ukrainian form of the name is *Dnipropetrovsk*.

Dnieper. *River, western and southwestern Russia*. The river is said to derive its name from Avestan *dānu*, "river" (*cp.* **Danube**, **Don**), and *apara*, "far," meaning a river that was remote. *See also* **Dniester**.

Dniester. *River, southern Ukraine*. The river probably takes its name from Avestan *dānu*, "river" (*cp.* **Danube**, **Don**), and *nazdyō*, "near," meaning a river that was relatively close. There may well have been an implied contrast with the **Dnieper**, because when the two rivers are considered from a region to the west of the Black Sea, into which they both flow, the Dniester would be the "near" river and the Dnieper the "far" one. The ancient Greek name of the Dniester was *Tyras*, from a Scythian word meaning "swift." *See also* **Tiraspol**.

Döbeln. *City, east central Germany*. The name means "*Dobl's* settlement," with the Old Sorbian personal name followed by the possessive suffix *-in*.

Dobre Miasto. *Town, northeastern Poland*. The name is Polish for "good town," denoting a settlement in a fertile locality. The town's German name of *Guttstadt* has the same meaning.

Dobrich. *Town, northeastern Bulgaria*. The town was under Turkish rule from the 15th century to 1878, and during this period was known as *Bazardzhik*, from Turkish *bazar*, "market" (*cp.* **Pazardzhik**). Its alternate name from the 17th century was *Dobrich*, as now, said to be for one Ivanko, the son of a local landowner named *Dobrichev*. (The Turks knew him as *Dobrichoglu*, the suffix meaning "son of," corresponding to the Slavic *-ev*.) In 1949 it was renamed *Tolbukhin*, in honor of the Soviet marshal Fyodor Ivanovich *Tolbukhin* (1894–1949), commander of the 3d Ukrainian front, whose forces captured it from the Germans in 1944. It reverted to the earlier name in 1991.

Dobruja. *Historic region, eastern Europe*. The region, in southeastern Romania and northeastern Bulgaria, was founded as a principality in the 14th century by the Bulgarian boyar Balik and is named for his successor, *Dobrotitsa* (1354–1386).

Dodecanese. *Island group, southeastern Greece*. The group, in the southeastern Aegean Sea, has a Greek name meaning "twelve islands," from *dōdeka*, "twelve," and *nēsos*, "island." There are many more than twelve, but the main ones (with their Italian names in parentheses) are: Astipálaia (Stampalia), Kálimnos (Calino), Kárpathos (Scarpanto), Kásos (Caso), Khálki (Calchi), Kos (Coo), Léros (Lero), Lipsói (Lipso), Nísíros (Nisiro), Pátmos (Patmo), Sími (Simi), and Tílos (Piscopi).

Dodge City. *City, central United States*. The Kansas city, laid out in 1872, takes its name from the American soldier Richard I. *Dodge* (1827–1895), commander of nearby Fort *Dodge*, established in 1864.

Dodoma. *Capital designate of Tanzania*. The city takes its name from that of a mountain nearby. The meaning of the name is uncertain.

Dogger Bank. *Sandbank, North Sea*. The submerged sandbank off the east coast of England takes its name from the *doggers*, or Dutch fishing vessels, that formerly worked here.

Doha. *Capital of Qatar.* The name represents Arabic *ad-dawha,* "the big tree." The reference is to a prominent tree that must have stood at the site where the original fishing village arose, on the east coast of the Qatar Peninsula.

Dollart. *River basin, northwestern Germany.* The broad estuary of the Ems River has a distinctive name representing Frisian *dullart,* "sandbank."

Dolomites. *Mountain range, northeastern Italy.* The mountains take their name from the French geologist Déodat de Gratet de *Dolomieu* (1750–1801), who discovered the mineral *dolomite* here.

Dolores Hidalgo. *City, central Mexico.* The city's full name was *Ciudad Dolores Hidalgo Cuna de la Independencia Nacional,* "City of Sorrows of Hidalgo, Cradle of National Independence," for the Mexican priest and revolutionary Miguel *Hidalgo* y Costilla (1753–1811), who initiated Mexico's struggle for independence in his parish of *Dolores* here in 1810. Its own name may have commemorated the sorrows of St. Francis.

Dombóvár. *City, southwestern Hungary.* The city's name means "castle in the oak grove," from a Slavic word related to Russian *dub,* "oak" (*cp.* **Dubrovnik**), and Hungarian *vár,* "castle."

Dominica. *Island republic, eastern West Indies.* The island was discovered by Columbus on Sunday, November 3, 1493, and was named by him for that day of the week (Spanish *Domingo,* from Latin *dominica dies,* "Lord's day"). *Cp.* **Dominican Republic.**

Dominican Republic. *Island republic, northern West Indies.* The republic, which occupies two thirds of the island of Hispaniola, has a name that is a latinized form of Spanish *Santo Domingo,* "holy Sunday," given the island as a whole in 1697 with reference to its original settlement by the Spanish on a Sunday in 1496. (*See also* **Hispaniola, Santo Domingo.**)

Domrémy-la-Pucelle. *Village, northeastern France.* The village was known to the Romans as *Dompnum Remigium,* from Latin *domnus,* a variant of *dominus,* "lord," and *Remigius,* or *Rémi,* the name of the 6th-century bishop of **Reims.** This gave the main part of the name. The village is said to be the birthplace of Joan of Arc. Hence the second part of the name, meaning "the maid," "the virgin." (French *pucelle* is related to Latin *puella,* "girl.")

Don. *River, western Russia.* The river probably derives its name from Avestan *dānu,* "river," "water." The English river of the same name (*see* **Doncaster**) has a Celtic name of identical meaning and ultimately related origin.

Donauwörth. *City and port, southern Germany.* The city, at the confluence of the Danube and Wörnitz rivers, derives its name from the site of its origin, on an island (Old High German *warid*) on the **Danube** (German *Donau*).

Doncaster. *City, north central England.* The former South Yorkshire city has a name that shows it to have been a Roman station, with the second part representing Old English *ceaster,* "Roman fort," a borrowing from Latin *castrum,* "camp." The first part of the name is that of the *Don* River on which it lies. Its own name is Indoeuropean in origin and means "flowing one." (*Cp.* **Don.**) The Roman name of the station here was actually *Danum.*

Donegal. *County, northern Ireland.* The county is named for its town, whose Irish name is *Dún na nGall,* "fort of the foreigners," from *dún,* "fort," and *gall,* "foreigner," "stranger" (*cp.* **Galloway**). The "foreigners" were the Danes, who captured a primitive fort here in the 10th century.

Donetsk. *City, eastern Ukraine.* The city is the main industrial center of the *Donbass,* and takes its name from the full Russian form of this abbreviated name, which is *Donetskiy ugol'nyj bassejn,* "Donets coal basin," for the *Donets* River in which it is located. (The river name has the same basic meaning as that of the **Don.**) The original name of Donetsk, which arose from a group of mining villages in the early 1860s, was *Yuzovka,* for the Welsh entrepreneur John *Hughes* (1814–1889), who established the first ironworks here in 1869. From 1924 through 1961 the city was known as *Stalino,* for the Soviet dictator Joseph *Stalin* (1879–1953).

Dorchester. *Town, southern England.* The name of the Dorset town is probably based on a Celtic word meaning "fist," to which modern Welsh *dwrn* in this sense is related. The reference would have been to a place covered in fist-sized stones, or even to fist fights held here (as a form of pugilism). The remainder of the name represents Old English *ceaster,* "Roman station," a borrowing from Latin *castrum,* "camp." It was Dorchester that gave the name of **Dorset** itself.

Dordogne. *River, southwestern France.* The river's name derives ultimately from an Indoeuropean root word *dur* or *dor,* "stream," "river," and *anun,* "deep."

Dordrecht. *City and river port, southwestern Netherlands.* The city derives its name from *Thyre,* a former river name, and Old Dutch *drecht,* "channel." Dordrecht stands in the Rhine delta at the confluence of four rivers.

Doris. *Historic district, central Greece.* The

district took its name from the *Dorians* who were its inhabitants. Their own name is traditionally derived from *Dorus*, their mythical ancestor.

Dormagen. *City, western Germany.* The Roman name of the original settlement here was *Durnomagus*, from Gaulish *durnos*, "fist," and *magos*, "field," denoting a site for boxing contests.

Dorset. *County, southern England.* The county has a name meaning "*Dorn* settlers," with *Dorn*, the basic original name of **Dorchester**, followed by Old English *sǣte*, "settlers." *Cp.* **Somerset.**

Dorsten. *City, western Germany.* The city, dating from Roman times, has a name of uncertain origin.

Dortmund. *City, western Germany.* At first sight the name seems to denote a place at the mouth (German *Mund*) of a river called "Dort." But this is misleading, and the name has some other origin. It was recorded in the 9th century as *Throtmanni*, from an obscure first element and an Old Saxon root word meaning "water" perhaps related to Latin *manare*, "to flow."

Dos Hermanas. *Town, southern Spain.* The town was founded by Ferdinand III of Castile in 1248, when he conquered Seville. He named it from Spanish *dos hermanas*, "two sisters," for the sisters of his lieutenant, Gonzalo Nazareno.

Dothan. *City, southeastern United States.* The Alabama city was settled in 1858 and originally named *Poplar Head*. It was renamed as now in 1911 for the biblical town of *Dothan* (Genesis 37:17). The name had been unofficially current in the form *Dothen* for some years before this.

Douai. *City, northern France.* The city derives its name from the Gaulish personal name *Dous* and the Gallo-Roman suffix *-acum*.

Douala. *City and port, western Cameroon.* The city takes its name from that of the indigenous Bantu people here. Their own name probably comes from one of their ancestors. The town was so named in 1907, having originally been known as *Kamerun*, a legacy of the region's history as a German protectorate from 1884.

Douarnenez. *Town, northwestern France.* The town, in Brittany, has a name meaning "St. *Tutuarn*'s island," with the personal name followed by Breton *enez*, "island." The named saint founded a monastery on a small island off the coast here.

Doubs. *River, eastern France.* The river, a tributary of the Saône, derives its name from Gaulish *dubus*, "dark," "black," describing the color of its waters. The Romans knew the river as the *Dubis*.

Douglas. *Capital of Isle of Man, Irish Sea.* The town's name represents Gaelic *Dubhghlais*, "black stream," referring to a river here. A nearby river was named *Fionnghlais*, "white stream," by way of contrast, and the two rivers later had their names shortened respectively as *Dhoo* and *Glass*, coincidentally comprising the elements that make up the town's own name.

Dourados. *City, southern Brazil.* The site here was first settled in the 18th century by prospectors on their way to the Cuiabá gold mines. Hence the city's name, Portuguese for "gilded ones."

Douro. *River, Spain and Portugal.* The river derives its name from the Indoeuropean root word *dur* or *dor*, "water," "river." The same element gave the names of the **Dordogne** and **Durance**, among other rivers.

¹Dover. *Town and port, southeastern England.* The Kent town takes its name from the *Dour* River that enters the sea here. Its own name is of Celtic origin and means simply "water." *Cp.* **Douro.**

²Dover. *City, eastern United States.* The state capital of Delaware was laid out in 1717 on the order (in 1683) of William Penn, who named it for **¹Dover**, England.

Down. *County, southeastern Northern Ireland.* The county takes its name from Irish *dún*, "fort," meaning the one that gave the name of its chief town, **Downpatrick.**

Downpatrick. *Town, southeastern Northern Ireland.* The town's name means "St. *Patrick*'s fort," from Irish *dún*, "fort," and the saint's name. The fort probably stood where St. Patrick's cathedral is today. The personal name was added to the basic name in the 12th century, when relics said to be those of the saint were discovered here. *See also* **Down.**

Drachenfels. *Mountain, western Germany.* The mountain, in the Siebengebirge, derives its name from Old High German *trahho*, "dragon," and *felisa*, "cliff." The peak is the legendary scene of Siegfried's triumph over the dragon, but the date of origin of this tale is unknown.

Draguignan. *Town, southeastern France.* The town derives its name from the Roman personal name *Draconius*, itself based on Latin *draco, draconis*, "dragon."

Drakensberg. *Mountain range, southeastern South Africa.* The range has a name meaning "dragon mountain," from Middle Dutch *drake*, "dragon," and *berg*, "mountain." The mountains are wild and dangerous, as a dragon is supposed to be.

Drake Passage. *Strait, southern South America.* The strait between the South Atlantic and

South Pacific is so named for the English circumnavigator Sir Francis *Drake* (1540–1596). Drake actually sailed from the Atlantic to the Pacific in 1578 by passing through the Strait of Magellan, further north, but his ship, the *Golden Hind*, was blown back into the northern part of the passage by a storm, so to that extent he was familiar with its waters.

Drenthe. *Province, northeastern Netherlands.* The name derives from Germanic *thrija-hantja*, "three lands," from *thrija*, "three," and *hantja*, "land."

Dresden. *City, eastern Germany.* The city is far enough east to have a name of Slavic origin, from Old Sorbian *drezga*, "forest." The name is implicitly habitative, "(place of the) forest dwellers."

Dreux. *Town, north central France.* The town ultimately derives its name from the *Durocasses*, a Gaulish people here. The origin of their own name is uncertain, although the first part may represent Indoeuropean *dur*, "current," referring to one or other of the rivers here. Dreux itself is on the Blaise, and it is in the department of Eure-et-Loir, named for two other rivers.

Drobeta-Turnu Severin. *City, southwestern Romania.* The city, on the Danube, was originally known as the Dacian town of *Drobeta*, a name of uncertain meaning. The rest of the name, originally that of a separate town, means "tower of *Severus*," from Romanian *turn*, "tower," and the name of the Roman emperor Septimius *Severus* (146–211), who built a tower here to commemorate a victory.

Drogheda. *Town, northeastern Ireland.* The town, in Co. Louth, has the Irish name *Droichead Átha*, "bridge of (the) ford," referring to a bridge that replaced an earlier ford over the Boyne River here.

Drôme. *Department, southeastern France.* The department is named for the river here. Its own name goes back to a proto-Indoeuropean root word *drawa* or *druna*, meaning simply "flowing," "current."

Druzhba *see* **Sveti Konstantin**

Dry Tortugas. *Island group, southeastern United States.* The islands, in the Gulf of Mexico west of southern Florida, were originally named *Tortugas*, "turtles," by the Spanish explorer Ponce de León when he discovered many of these creatures here in 1513. Later, English-speaking mariners added the adjective *dry*, describing their terrain. *Cp.* **Tortuga Island**.

Dubai. *Emirate, United Arab Emirates.* The name of the emirate is of uncertain meaning. Proposed origins include: (1) It represents Farsi

words meaning "two" and "brother," referring to early twin settlements; (2) It evolved as a diminutive form of a market called *Daba*, so that it was a "little market" by comparison; (3) It derives from a word meaning "money," as its people were prosperous traders.

Dublin. *Capital of Ireland.* The city's name means "black pool," from Irish *dubh*, "black," and *linn*, "pool." The reference is to the dark color of the Liffey River on which Dublin stands. The official Irish name of Dublin is *Baile Átha Cliath*. This means "town of the hurdle ford," and alludes to the hurdles of woven withies that were used to ford the Liffey in early times.

Dubnica nad Váhom. *City, western Slovakia.* The name means "oak grove on the *Váh* River," from Slavic *dub*, "oak," and the river name, itself probably of Germanic origin and meaning "flowing one." The Hungarian name of the city, *Vágtölgyes*, has the same meaning, from Hungarian *tölgy*, "oak."

Dubno. *City, western Ukraine.* The name means "place of oaks," from Slavic *dub*, "oak."

Dubrovnik. *Town and port, southern Croatia.* The name of the Adriatic port is based on Slavic *dubrova*, "oak wood." The town was founded in the 7th century as *Rausa* or *Ragusa* by Roman refugees fleeing the invasion of Epidaurus by Avars and Slavs. The meaning of this name is unknown.

Dubuque. *City, east central United States.* The Iowa city is named for the French trader Julien *Dubuque* (1762–1810), who in 1788 persuaded the Fox Indians here to grant him lead-mining rights.

Dufourspitze. *Mountain, southwestern Switzerland.* The second-highest mountain in the Alps, near the border with Italy, is named for General Guillaume-Henri *Dufour* (1787–1875), the Swiss officer who headed the survey that fixed the positions of many peaks here. German *Spitze* means "point."

Dugi Otok. *Island, northeastern Adriatic Sea.* The Croatian island, off the west coast of Dalmatia, has a Croat name meaning "long island." Its Italian name, *Isola Longa*, has the same sense. The island is 27 miles (43 km) long.

Duisburg. *City and river port, western Germany.* The name of the town may mean "*Diu*'s fort," from the name of a Germanic god related to the *Tiw* of *Tuesday* and ultimately to the Greek god *Zeus*.

Duluth. *City, northern United States.* The Minnesota city takes its name from the French explorer Daniel Greysolen, sieur *du Luth* (1649–1710), who visited the area in 1678.

Dulwich. *District of London, southeastern England*. The name means "dill marsh," from Old English *dile*, "dill," and *wisce*, "marshy meadow." The second part of the name has been influenced by the *-wich* of names such as **Greenwich** or **Woolwich**. Dill has long been cultivated as a medicinal herb.

Dumbarton. *Town, west central Scotland*. The town's name refers to the historic Rock of Dumbarton, an ancient stronghold that still stands at its center. It means "fort of the Britons," from Gaelic *dùn*, "fort," and *Breatann*, "of the Britons," referring to the occupation of the fort by the British from the 5th century. The Britons themselves called their fortress *Alclut*, "fort by the *Clyde* (River)."

Dumdum. *Town, east central India*. The West Bengal town, now a suburb of Calcutta, takes its name from Persian *damdama*, a term for a raised mound or battery. The arsenal here was the first to manufacture what came to be known as *dumdum* bullets.

Dumfries. *Town, southern Scotland*. The town has a Gaelic name, from *dùn*, "fort," and *preas*, "copse." This gives an overall sense "wooded stronghold." The fort was probably in the oldest part of the town, now known as Mid Steeple.

Dumyat *see* **Damietta**

Dunaföldvár. *Town, central Hungary*. The town derives its name from the **Danube** (Hungarian *Duna*), the river on which it lies, and Hungarian *földvár*, "earth castle," describing the material from which the original fortress here was built.

Dunakeszi. *City, north central Hungary*. The city derives its name from the **Danube** (Hungarian *Duna*), the river near which it lies, and the tribal name *Keszi*.

Dunaújváros. *City, west central Hungary*. The history of the city's name is tortuous. It begins with a landowner named *Pentelén* ("Pantaleon"), who gave his name to a former village here. Its inhabitants saw the name as a suffixed form, in the Hungarian manner, so that it meant something like "in *Pentele*," and accordingly shortened it to *Pentele*. In the late 19th century, so as to distinguish this village from the nearby village of *Sárpentele*, the official name became *Dunapentele*, prefixed with *Duna*, the Hungarian name of the **Danube**, the river on which the village lay. In 1951 the two villages combined as a new "socialist town" called *Sztálinváros*, "Stalin's town," a name complementing that of *Lenínváros*, now **Tiszaújváros**. In 1961, on the demise of the cult of personality, the city was renamed as now, with Hungarian *új*, "new,"

and *város*, "town," added to *Duna* as the river name.

Dunbar. *Town and port, southeastern Scotland*. The town's name means "fort on a height," from Gaelic *dùn*, "fort," and *barr*, "height." The "height" is the rocky headland above the harbor where the ruins of Dunbar Castle now stand.

Dundalk. *Town and port, northeastern Ireland*. The town, in Co. Louth, has the Irish name *Dún Dealgan*, "*Dealga*'s fort." The name relates to Castletown Hill, to the west of the town, where the fort is said to have been built by the chieftain *Dealga*.

Dundas *see* **Thule**

Dundee. *City and port, eastern Scotland*. The city is on the *Tay* River, and its name is traditionally interpreted for that reason as "fort on the Tay," from Gaelic *dùn*, "fort," and the river name (the *-dee*). A more likely meaning is "fort of *Daigh*," from a Celtic personal name. It is not known who Daigh was, but his name means "fire" (Gaelic *daig*).

Dunedin. *City and port, southeastern New Zealand*. The city, in southeastern South Island, was founded in 1848 by Scottish Presbyterian settlers who originally planned to name their settlement *New Edinburgh* (*see* **Edinburgh**). Sir William Chambers, mayor of Edinburgh, instead suggested they name their colony *Dunedin*, from the historic name of Edinburgh. This was a purely Celtic name and therefore appropriate for a place of Scottish foundation.

Dunfermline. *Town, eastern Scotland*. The Fife town has a name of uncertain origin. The first syllable is undoubtedly Gaelic *dùn*, "fort," but the rest of the name has so far defied meaningful interpretation. A document dated 1251 has the name exactly as now.

Dungarpur. *Town, northwestern India*. The town, in Rajasthan state, was founded in the 14th century and named for *Dungaria*, a local chieftain, with Hindi *pur*, "town," added.

Dunkirk. *City and port, northern France*. The name means "dune church," from Middle Dutch *dune*, "dune," and *kerke*, "church." The reference is to the church of St. Éloi that was built on the dunes here by the Strait of Dover in the 7th century. The French form of the name is *Dunkerque*.

Dún Laoghaire. *Town and port, eastern Ireland*. The Dublin suburb has an obviously Irish name meaning "fort of *Laoghaire*," from *dún*, "fort," and the personal name. The identity of Laoghaire is uncertain. According to some accounts, he was a high king of Ireland and a disciple of St. Patrick. From 1821 through 1921 the town was known as *Kingstown*, for George IV, who passed through the port on his return to England from Dublin in the former year. The name is pronounced "Dunleary," and actually appeared on maps in this spelling before 1821.

Dunstable. *Town, south central England.* The Bedfordshire town has an Old English name meaning "*Dunna*'s post," with the Anglo-Saxon personal name followed by *stapol*, "post," "pillar." The post in question was probably a waymark, since Dunstable stands at the intersection of Watling Street and Icknield Way, two ancient routes.

Duque de Caxias. *City, southeastern Brazil.* The city, now a suburb of Rio de Janeiro, was known as *Meriti Station* until 1931 and from then until 1943 as *Caxias*, after which it was given its present name. The reference is to Luis Alves de Lima e Silva, *duque de Caxias* (1803–1880), soldier and patron of the Brazilian army. *Cp.* **Caxias.**

Durance. *River, southeastern France.* The river derives its name from the Indoeuropean root element *dur* or *dor*, meaning simply "water," "current." *Cp.* **Douro.**

Durango. *City, north central Mexico.* The city has a Native American name said to mean "beyond the river," referring to the Mezquital, to the west of which it lies.

Durazno. *City, central Uruguay.* The city was founded in 1821 with the name *San Pedro de Durazno*, still its full formal name today. The first part of the name, Spanish for "St. Peter," relates specifically to Dom *Pedro* de Alcántara (1798–1834), prince regent of Brazil. The second part is Spanish *durazno*, "peach tree," alluding to the local fruit trees.

Durban. *City and port, eastern South Africa.* The KwaZulu-Natal city takes its name from Sir Benjamin *D'Urban* (1777–1849), governor of Cape Colony at the time the town was founded in 1824. It was originally called *Port Natal*, for its province, but was then renamed for the governor, at first in the spelling *D'Urban* but from c.1870 as *Durban*. The Zulu name of Durban is *eThekwini*, "at the bay."

Düren. *City, western Germany.* The city may derive its name from an old name of the Ruhr River on which it stands. If so, it is probably related to the **Douro** of Spain and Portugal and the *Thur* of Switzerland (*see* **Thurgau**), and so mean simply "water," "river." The name of the Roman settlement of *Marcodurum* here is quite unrelated, deriving from Celtic words meaning "horse town."

Durg. *Town, east central India.* The town, in

Madhya Pradesh state, derives its name from Hindi *durga*, "fort." There are remains of an ancient fortress here.

Durgapur. *City, northeastern India.* The name of the West Bengal city means "town of *Durga*," the latter being the Hindu goddess who was the wife of Shiva.

¹Durham. *City, northern England.* The city, in the county of the same name, has a name that is a combination of Old English *dūn*, "hill," and Old Norse *holmr*, "island." Durham is on a lofty hill in a bend of the Wear River, the hill being the "island." The present form of the name evolved under Norman influence, without which it might have remained as *Dunholm* or *Dunham*.

²Durham. *City, eastern United States.* The North Carolina city was settled in c.1750 and originally called *Prattsburg*, for William *Pratt*, a local landowner. When he refused to give land for a railroad station, four acres were donated by Bartlett S. *Durham* (1822–1858), and the settlement was renamed for him.

Durmitor. *Mountain massif, northern Montenegro.* The name represents Balkan-Romance *dormitor*, "sleeping" (English *dormitory*). The reference is not to a dormant volcano but to a folk belief that the mountain could at any time "awake." There are mountains with similar names in the former Yugoslavia, such as the *Visitor* ("dreaming") and *Cipitor* ("slumbering").

Durrës. *City and port, western Albania.* The Adriatic port was founded by Greeks in the 7th century B.C. under the name *Epidamnos*. The Romans later called it *Dyrrhachium*, from the name of the headland here, and this apparently gave the present name. The precise meaning of these names is uncertain, although the latter has been derived from Greek *rhakhia*, "surf." The Italian form of the name is *Durazzo*.

Dursunbey. *Town, northwestern Turkey.* The name dates from the time of the Ottoman Empire, when Orhan Gazi (c.1288–c.1360), the second Ottoman sultan, appointed Emir *Dursun* as commander of this town. It accordingly took the name *Dursunbey*, with *bey* added as a title of respect.

Dushanbe. *Capital of Tajikistan.* The city's name represents Tajik *dushanbe*, "Monday," this word itself coming from *du*, "two," and *shanbe*, "Saturday" (literally "Sabbath"), i.e. a day two days after Saturday. The reference is to a regular Monday market. From 1929 through 1961 the city was known as *Stalinabad*, "Stalin's town."

Düsseldorf. *City and river port, western Germany.* The name means "*Düssel* village," from the *Düssel* River on which the city stands. The river name derives from a Germanic source *thusila*, related to modern German *tosen*, "to roar," "to thunder," so that the river is a "roaring water."

Dvina. *Rivers, eastern Europe*. The name is that of two lengthy rivers: the Northern *Dvina*, in northwestern Russia, and the Western *Dvina*, further south (but also further west, as the name states) in Belarus and Latvia. The common name may derive either from Finnish *vieno*, "gentle," referring to a slow current, or Estonian *väin*, "channel," denoting a river with many narrow stretches. The Western Dvina gave the name of both **Daugavgrīva** and **Daugavpils** in Latvia.

Dvůr Králové nad Labem. *City, northern Czech Republic*. The city's name means "queen's court on the *Elbe*," referring to the founding of the town by King Wenceslas II of Bohemia in the late 13th century and his gift of it to his *queen*, Elisabeth. The city's German name is *Königinhof an der Elbe*, with the same meaning. *See also* **Elbe**.

Dwarka. *Town, west central India*. The name of the town, in Gujarat state, is a shortened form of its Sanskrit name *Dvaravati*, "(city of) many gates," denoting its importance as a place of Hindu pilgrimage.

Dyfed. *Historic county, southwestern Wales*. The name of the former county (1974–96) is an old one, going back to the *Demetae*, a Celtic people who inhabited this part of Wales at the time of the Roman occupation. The meaning of their name is unknown.

Dzerzhinsk. *City, western Russia*. The city, formed in 1929 from the union of the town of *Rastyapino*, its suburb *imeni Sverdlova* (*see* **Yekaterinburg**), and *Chernorechenskiy Zavod*, was named for the Bolshevik leader Feliks *Dzerzhinsky* (1877–1926).

Dzhalal-Abad. *City, southwestern Kyrgyzstan*. The city derives its name from Arabic *jalāl*, "greatness," "glory," and *ābād*, "inhabited place," "town." *Cp.* **Jalalabad**.

Dzhezkazgan. *City, central Kazakhstan*. The city has a Kazakh name meaning "place where copper is mined." The copper mines here are among the largest in the world.

Dzierżoniów. *City, southwestern Poland*. The city was founded in the 12th century with the German name of *Reichenbach*, from words corresponding to modern German *reich*, "rich," "powerful," and *Bach*, "stream," referring to the Piława River, which has a strong current. The town retained this name until 1945, when it was renamed for the Polish priest and apiculturist Jan *Dzierżon* (1811–1906).

Dzungaria. *Region, western China*. The region derives its name from Mongolian *züün*, "left," and *gar*, "hand." This describes its geographical position from the point of view of someone facing north in China or Mongolia.

Ealing. *Borough of London, southeastern England*. The borough has an Old English name meaning "(settlement of) *Gilla*'s people," with the Anglo-Saxon personal name followed by *-ingas*, "people of," "followers of" (the named person).

East Anglia. *Historic region, eastern England*. The name of the region, which comprises the counties of Norfolk and Suffolk, together with parts of adjacent counties, is a latinized form of the Old English group name *Estangle*, "East Angles." These were the people who inhabited the former Anglo-Saxon kingdom here, and were so named because they were *east* of the Middle Angles, whose kingdom occupied a region roughly corresponding to the present East Midlands.

Eastbourne. *Town and resort, southern England*. The East Sussex town has a name literally meaning "eastern stream." The stream in question is the one that rises near St. Mary's Church and that followed a course now marked by Bourne Street. It is so named as it is "east" of *Westbourne*, a village some 50 miles (80 km) to the west in West Sussex.

Easter Island. *Island, South Pacific*. The island, belonging to Chile, is so named as it was discovered by the Dutch navigator Jakob Roggeveen on April 6, 1722, *Easter* Monday. It had been visited earlier, in 1695, by the English pirate Edward Davis, but he had only cursorily noted the event and had apparently not logged any name. The island's indigenous Polynesian name is *Mata-kite-ran*, "eyes that watch the stars," referring to the ancient stone heads here, and in particular those that have fallen on their backs.

East London. *City and port, southeastern South Africa*. The city, in Eastern Cape province, was founded in 1847 as an early settlement of British Kaffraria and was originally known as *Port Rex*, probably for one John *Rex* who took surveys here, although popularly said to refer to George *Rex*, an illegitimate son of *George* III, as if punning on his Latin title, *George Rex* ("King George"). It then settled to its present name, apparently referring to its (longitudinal) location to the *east* of [1]**London**, England. The city also lies on South Africa's south*east* coast. The indigenous name of East London is *Igaabab*, "place of buffaloes," reflected in the city's location at the mouth of the *Buffalo* River.

Eau Claire. *City, northern United States.* The Wisconsin city takes its name from the *Eau Claire* River on which it lies, at its confluence with the Chippewa. The river's own name, meaning "clear water," was given it in the 18th century by French trappers and traders.

Ebbw Vale. *Town, southeastern Wales.* The town has a half Welsh, half English name relating to the valley of the *Ebbw* River in which it lies. The river name may mean "horse river," from a Celtic word related to modern Welsh *ebol*, "colt." Horses probably worked or were watered here, or had a regular crossing place at this point.

Eberswalde-Finow. *City, northeastern Germany.* The city was formed in 1970 on the amalgamation of the two towns *Eberswalde*, from *Eber*, a short form of the personal name *Eberhard*, and *wald*, "forest," and *Finow*, a river name, now that of the canal here, from Middle Low German *ven*, "marshland" (English *fen*).

Ebro. *River, northeastern Spain.* The name probably goes back to a basic root word meaning simply "river," as Indoeuropean *var* or Celtic *iber*. The Romans knew the river as *Hiberus* or *Iberus* (*see* **Iberia**).

Ecbatana *see* **Hamadan**

Ech-Cheliff. *Town, northern Algeria.* The town has had several incarnations. It was founded by the French in 1843 as *Orléansville* (for **Orléans**) on the site of the Roman settlement of *Castellum Tingitanum*, itself named for the *Tingitani*, the people of *Tingis* (*see* **Tangier**). It was then renamed *Al-Asnam*, but was struck by an earthquake in 1954 and another in 1980, after which it was renamed as now, for the *Chelif* River here, to avoid a name that had become associated with earthquakes.

Echmiadzin. *City, western Armenia.* The city, capital of the ancient kingdom of Armenia and seat of the Armenian patriarch, dates from the 6th century B.C. In the 2d century B.C. it was known as *Vardkesavan*. It then became *Vagarshapat*, for the Armenian king *Vagarsh* (reigned A.D. 117–140), with Iranian *-abad*, "inhabited place," "town." In 1945 it took its present name, that of its famous monastery, when the latter was enclosed within the territory of the town. Its own name means "settlement of the only begotten (Son of God)" (literally "the only begotten came down"). Its Tatar name is *Uch-Kilissa*, "three churches," i.e. "Trinity church" (Turkish *üç*, "three," and *kilise*, "church").

Echternach. *Town, eastern Luxembourg.* The town was known to the Romans as *Epternacum*, presumably from a Celtic personal name and the Gallo-Roman suffix *-acum*.

Eckernförde. *City and resort, northern Germany.* The name was earlier that of a castle here, built on the isthmus at the end of what is now Eckenförde Bay. The name is thus that of the spit of land, meaning literally "squirrel passage," from Middle Low German *ēkeren*, "squirrel," and *vōrt*, "ford," "passage." But the castle was also called *Eckernburg*, so that the present name could be taken to mean "ford by squirrel castle."

Ecuador. *Republic, northwestern South America.* The country's name is the Spanish word for "equator," referring to its location. The equator traverses Ecuador just to the north of its capital, **Quito**, which until 1830 was the name of the country as a whole.

Edam. *Town, western Netherlands.* The town arose by a *dam* on the *Ye* River, which flows into the IJsselmeer here. The river name itself means simply "river." *Cp.* **Amsterdam**, **Rotterdam**, **Schiedam**.

Eden. *Historic region, eastern Mesopotamia.* The geographic region, where God planted a garden and where Adam and Eve were placed (and from where they were expelled), is traditionally thought to derive its name either from Akkadian *edinu*, "plain," or from a related West Semitic root meaning "delight," "abundance." In the Old Testament, the Greek loanword *paradeisos* (English *paradise*) is used for the garden of Eden (Genesis 2:8).

Edessa *see* **Urfa**

Edinburg. *City, southern United States.* The Texas city was founded near Hidalgo by the Scotsman John Young, who named it *Edinburgh* for his native city. It became the Hidalgo county seat in 1852, and when the seat was moved to Chapin in 1908, this latter town was renamed commemoratively (in 1911) for the earlier one, with the final *h* dropped for distinctiveness.

Edinburgh. *Capital of Scotland.* The city's name is traditionally interpreted as meaning "castle of *Edwin*," as if from Old English *Eadwinesburh*, referring to the 7th-century king of Northumbria who is said to have built the original fort here on the site of the present medieval Edinburgh Castle. But the name was recorded before his time, so cannot relate to him. A document of c.600 names the fortress as *Eidyn*, which may mean "fort on a slope," the *-dyn* corresponding to Gaelic *dùn*, "fort." The name then appeared in the form *Din Eidyn*, with the actual Gaelic word prefixing this, so that the modern Gaelic name of Edinburgh is *Dùn Eideann*. The present form of the name came when Old English *burh*, "fort," was suffixed to *Eidyn* in place of the Gaelic prefixed *dùn*. A simplified form of the Gaelic name gave that of **Dunedin**, New Zealand.

Edirne. *City, western Turkey.* The name has evolved as a smoothed and reduced form of Greek *Adrianopolis*, "*Hadrian*'s city," for the Roman emperor who in C.A.D. 125 rebuilt and renamed the original settlement of *Uskudama*, its own name from Thracian *usku*, "high," and *dama*, "dwelling." The city was regularly known as *Adrianople* down to 1922, when it was restored to the Turks following its possession by Bulgaria.

Edmonton. *City, west central Canada.* The capital of Alberta was so named in 1877 for *Fort Edmonton*, originally built some 20 miles (32 km) from the present town in 1795. The fort was destroyed by Native Americans in 1807 and rebuilt on its present site the following year. The name itself was given by William Tomison for the village of *Edmonton*, near (now in) London, England, as a compliment to his secretary, John Peter Prudens, a Hudson's Bay Company clerk, who was born there.

Edo *see* **Tokyo**

Edom. *Historic region, southwestern Jordan.* The region bordering ancient Israel, mentioned several times in the Bible (Numbers 20:14, etc.), derives its name from a root word meaning "red," referring to the color of its rock and soil formations. The name is also that of the elder of the twins born to Isaac and Rebekah, initially called Esau, who at his birth "came out red" (Genesis 25:25) and later requested "that same red pottage" that his brother Jacob had, "therefore was his name called Edom" (25:30).

Edward, Lake. *Lake, east central Africa.* The lake, divided between Uganda and the Democratic Republic of Congo, was discovered in 1888 by the Welsh-born U.S. explorer Henry Morton Stanley, and originally named by him *Albert Edward Nyanza*, for the Prince of Wales, *Albert Edward* (1841–1910), the future Edward VII. *Nyanza* is the Bantu word for "lake." In 1908 the king himself approved the alteration of the name to *Lake Edward*. For five years from 1973 the lake was renamed *Lake Idi Amin Dada*, for the Ugandan head of state (1925–2003). After his overthrow in 1979, however, it reverted to its earlier name.

Egedesminde. *Town, western Greenland.* The town was founded in 1759 and named for the Norwegian missionary Hans *Egede* (1686–1758), first missionary to the Inuit of Greenland. It was originally sited 75 miles (120 km) south of its present location on the island of *Aasiaat*, to which it moved in 1763. It is now usually known by the Greenlandic name of the island (properly *Asiaat*), meaning "the spiders." *See also* **Nuuk**.

Eger. *Town, northern Hungary.* The town takes its name from the *Eger* River on which it lies, the river's own name deriving from Hungarian *eger*, a dialect form of *égerfa*, "alder tree." The German name of the town is *Erlau*.

Egmont, Mt. *Mountain, northern New Zealand.* The mountain, in west central North Island, was so named by Captain Cook in 1770 in honor of John Perceval, 2d Earl of *Egmont* (1711–1770), first lord of the Admiralty. The peak's Maori name is *Taranaki*, said to mean "barren mountain." *See also* **Taranaki**.

Egypt. *Republic, northeastern Africa.* The region here was known to the Romans as *Ægyptus* and to the Greeks as *Aguptos*. Both these came from Egyptian *ḥūt-kā-ptaḥ*, "temple of the soul of Ptah," for the creative god who was chiefly associated with the ancient city of **Memphis**. (The Greek form of the name was popularly derived from *aia gupos*, "land of the vulture.") This original name was at first that of Memphis itself, but was adopted by the Greeks for the country as a whole. The Egyptian name of Egypt was *Kemet*, "black country," probably referring to the dark skins of the ancient Egyptians. This was adopted from the biblical name of *Ham*, son of Noah. The Arabic name of Egypt is *miṣr*, itself from that of *Mizraim*, a son (descendant) of Ham, whose name in turn came from Assyrian *miṣir*, "fort." Hence also *Mısır* as the Turkish name of Egypt and *Mistri* as the modern Greek name of Cairo.

Ehime. *Prefecture, southwestern Japan.* The prefecture, in the island of Shikoku, derives its name from Japanese *ai*, "to love," and *hime*, "young lady," "princess."

Ehingen. *City, southwestern Germany.* The name of the city, formally known as *Ehingen an der Donau*, from its location on the **Danube**, means "(settlement of) *Aho*'s people."

Eichsfeld. *Hill district, eastern Germany.* The district, northwest of Thuringia, is generally said to derive its name from German *Eich*, "oak," and *Feld*, "field," describing its prominent natural features. But the name may actually be based on a former river name *Eichisa*, that of the upper reaches of the Unstrut here.

Eichstätt. *City, southern Germany.* The name means "place of oaks," from Old High German *eih*, "oak," and *stat*, "place," describing the site where the city first emerged in the 8th century.

Eifel. *Plateau region, western Germany.* The name is of uncertain origin. Proposed derivations include: (1) An alteration of German *Hoch-*

feld, from *hoch*, "high," and *Feld*, "field"; (2) From Old High German *eiver*, "eagerness" (modern German *Eifer*); (3) An alteration of *Euphalia*, "good *Phalia*," from Greek *eu*, "well," and the basis of **Westphalia**. But these all seem very contrived, and a derivation from Old High German *aik*, "oak," and *fil*, a derivative of Indoeuropean *pel*, "broad and flat," seems more plausible, giving a meaning "plateau covered with oak trees."

Eilat. *City and port, southern Israel*. The city, Israel's only outlet to the Red Sea, at the head of the Gulf of Aqaba, derives its name from Hebrew *elōn*, "oak." It is mentioned several times in the Bible, and King Solomon, for example, "made a navy of ships in Ezion-Geber, which is beside Eloth, on the shore of the Red Sea" (1 Kings 9:26). The name is also spelled *Elat*.

Eilenburg. *City, eastern Germany*. The city's name was recorded in 961 as *Ilburg*, suggesting an origin in Slavic *il*, "mud," "silt," referring to land by the Mulde River here, and Germanic *burg*, "fortress," "town." The first part of the name has apparently been influenced by German *Eule*, "owl."

Eindhoven. *Town, southern Netherlands*. The name has evolved from Old Dutch *eind*, "end," and *hoven*, "property." The town arose as a "property at the end" of Woensel, now a district of Eindhoven itself.

Einsiedeln. *Town, east central Switzerland*. In 904 St. Benno entered the hermitage (German *Einsiedelei*) of St. Meinrad (martyred 861) here and added a chapel. In 934 Provost Eberhard of Strasbourg founded an abbey on the site, and the present town, now the most famous pilgrim center in Switzerland, arose around it. Its French name is *Notre-Dame-des-Ermites*, "Our Lady of the Hermits."

Eire *see* **Ireland**

Eisenach. *City, central Germany*. The city, founded in the mid–12th century by a crossing over the Hörsel River, may derive its name from Old High German *īsan*, "iron," and *aha*, "water," referring to a stream containing ferric oxide.

Eisenerz. *Town, central Austria*. The town has been noted for its iron mining since Roman times. Hence its name, from German *Eisenerz*, "iron ore."

Eisenhüttenstadt. *City, eastern Germany*. The city arose in 1961 on the amalgamation of two old towns, *Fürstenberg an der Oder* and *Schönfließ*, with *Stalinstadt*, "*Stalin*'s town," a planned residential community set up in 1950–53 for workers at a metallurgical complex founded in 1950. The name thus derives from a combination of German *Eisenhütte*, "ironworks," and the *-stadt* of *Stalinstadt*.

Eisenstadt. *City, eastern Austria*. The city has a name meaning "iron town," from Germanic words that gave modern German *Eisen*, "iron," and *Stadt*, "town." The reference is to the iron-ore deposits here. The town is first mentioned in 1264. *Cp.* **Eisenach**.

Eisleben. *City, central Germany*. The name of the city, first mentioned in the 10th century, means "*Iso*'s estate," with a Germanic personal name. The city is formally named *Lutherstadt Eisleben*, as the religious reformer Martin *Luther* (1483–1546) was born and died here.

Ekaterinburg *see* **Yekaterinburg**

Ekibastuz. *City, northeastern Kazakhstan*. The city takes its name from a nearby "two-headed" (i.e. L-shaped) lake, its own name comprising Kazakh *yeki*, "two," *bas*, "head," and *tuz*, "salt lake."

El Aaiún. *Town, western Morocco*. The former capital of Spanish Sahara (1940–76) (now Western Sahara) has a name representing Arabic *al-'ayūn*, "the springs."

Elam. *Historic region, southwestern Iran*. The name of the ancient country, approximating to modern Khuzestan, is a shortened form of Akkadian *Elamtu*, itself from Elamite *Halamti*. The name is traditionally associated with *Elam*, the son of Shem (Genesis 10:22), regarded as progenitor of the Elamites.

El Ashmunein *see* **Hermopolis**

Elat *see* **Eilat**

Elazığ. *City, eastern Turkey*. The city evolved in the 19th century from an Ottoman military garrison and is said to have been at first called *Mamure-tul-Aziz*, "built by *Aziz*," from Turkish *mamul*, "made," "manufactured," and the personal name. This was shortened to *Elaziz* and then modified to *Elazığ*.

Elba. *Island, northwestern Mediterranean Sea*. The Italian island takes its name from the *Ilates*, a Ligurian people who at one time inhabited it. Their own name is of uncertain origin. The Greek name of Elba is *Aithalia*, from *aithalos*, "soot," alluding to the pollution (even then) from local metalworks.

El Banco. *City, northern Colombia*. When the Spanish conquistador Gonzalo Jiménez de Quezada arrived at a Native American village here in 1537 he called it *Barbudo*, "bearded one," for its bearded chief. In 1544 it was renamed *Tamalameque* (now a town a few miles southeast) by Alonzo de San Martín. In 1749 José Domingo Ortiz, a freed black slave carrying a statue of the Virgin Mary, arrived at the site, and settlers called it *Nuestra Señora de la Candelaria de El Banco*, "Our Lady of Candlemas of the riverbank," referring to the Magdalena River here. The name was subsequently reduced to its present form.

Elbe. *River, central Europe.* The river, flowing through the Czech Republic and Germany, has a name meaning "white," from the Indoeuropean root *albh* that also gave Latin *albus*, as perhaps for **Albion**. This same root soon acquired the generic meaning "river." Hence Norwegian *elv*, "river."

Elberfeld. *Historic town, western Germany.* The former town, which in 1929 combined with others to form the city of **Wuppertal**, has a name meaning "*Albiro*'s open land," with a West Frankish personal name.

Elbląg. *City and port, northern Poland.* The city, near the eastern mouth of the Vistula, derives its name from Old Norse *elfr*, "river," referring to this location. The German form of the name is *Elbing*.

Elbrus. *Mountain, southwestern Russia.* The highest peak in the Caucasus has a name variously derived from Iranian, Arabic, Turkic, and other languages, with meanings such as "high mountain," "snowy ridge," and the like. It seems probable that it ultimately goes back to the Indoeuropean root word *alp*, "mountain," that gave the name of the **Alps**. *Cp.* **Elburz**.

Elburz. *Mountain range, northern Iran.* The range's name almost certainly has the same origin, whatever that may be, as Russia's **Elbrus**.

El Cantara. *Town, northeastern Egypt.* The town, on the east bank of the Suez Canal, has a name meaning "the bridge," from Arabic *el*, "the," and *ḳanṭara*, "bridge" (*cp.* **Alcántara**), referring to the crossing point of the canal here for traffic from northern Sinai and Israel. In the 1970s a new town built on the west bank of the canal was called *El Cantara el Gharbiya*, from Arabic *ğarbi*, "western" (*cp.* **Algarve**), which meant that the original town became *El Cantara esh Sharkiya*, from Arabic *sharki*, "eastern" (*cp.* **Sharjah**).

Elche. *City, southeastern Spain.* The city was known to the Romans as *Illici*, a name of Iberian origin perhaps going back to the root word *al*, "salt." The Catalan name of the city is *Elx*.

Elea. *Historic city, southern Italy.* The ancient city, known to the Roman as *Velia*, derives its name from Greek *elaia*, "olive tree."

Elephantine. *Island, southeastern Egypt.* The island, in the Nile River, derives its name from Greek *elephantinos*, "of ivory," from *elephas*, "elephant," "ivory," translating its Egyptian name

of *Abu*, "elephant." The reason for the name is uncertain. According to one account, Egyptians saw elephants here for the first time. According to another, the rocks in the Nile here, worn smooth by the water, were thought to resemble the backs of a herd of elphants. The island's Arabic name is *Jazirat Aswan*, "**Aswan** island."

El Escorial. *Village, central Spain.* The name of the village represents Spanish *escorias*, "slag," "dross" (English *scoria*), referring to former mining refuse here.

Eleusis. *Historic city, southeastern Greece.* The ancient city, famous as the site of the Eleusinian Mysteries, appears to derive its name either from Greek *eleusis*, "arrival," or possibly from *hals*, "salt."

Eleuthera. *Island, northeastern Bahamas.* The Caribbean island was granted in 1649 to the English governor of Bermuda, William Sayle (died 1671), who gave it a Greek name meaning "(place of) freedom" (Greek *eleutheros*, "free") in the hope that, as the center of a puritan colony, it would be a place "where every one might enjoy his own opinion on religion without control or question."

El Faiyum. *Province, northern Egypt.* The province takes its name from the region here, a great depression in the Western Desert known in Arabic as *al-fayyūm*, from Coptic *Fiom*, itself from *f-*, a form of *p-*, "the," and *iom*, "sea," "lake," referring to the ancient Lake Moeris (now Lake Qarun). The name is also that of the province's capital city.

El Ferrol. *City and port, northwestern Spain.* The city takes its name from Old Spanish *farol* (modern *faro*), "lighthouse," referring to the one that formerly marked the entrance to its harbor. From 1939 to the early 1980s it was known as *El Ferrol del Caudillo*, since it was the birthplace of General Franco (1892–1975), the *caudillo* (leader) of Spain.

El Fustat *see* **Cairo**

El Gezira. *State, central Sudan.* The name is Arabic for "the island," "the peninsula," referring to the territory here, between the White and Blue Nile rivers south of their convergence at Khartoum.

[1]**Elgin.** *Town, northeastern Scotland.* The town's name means "little Ireland," from *Ealg*, one of the early Gaelic names for Ireland, and the diminutive suffix *-in*. The name would have denoted a colony of Scots who had emigrated here from Ireland and set up a "home from home."

[2]**Elgin.** *City, east central United States.* The Illinois city was founded in 1835 and is said to

take its name from the Scottish hymn "The Song of *Elgin*," referring to ¹**Elgin**, Scotland.

Elis. *Historic region, south central Greece*. The name of the region, an ancient city-state, is of uncertain origin. It may relate to Greek *helos*, "marsh."

Elisabethville *see* **Lubumbashi**

Elista. *City, western Russia*. The city, founded in 1865, is the Kalmyk capital and has a Kalmyk name meaning "sandy," from *ilis*, "sand." In 1944, when the Kalmyks were exiled to Central Asia for their alleged collaboration with the Germans, the city was renamed *Stepnoj*, "(town) of the steppes." The former name and status were restored in 1957.

Elizabeth. *City, eastern United States*. The New Jersey city was settled in 1664 and named *Elizabethtown* for Lady *Elizabeth* Carteret, wife of Sir George Carteret (c.1610–1680), one of the colony's first proprietors. The present form of the name was adopted in 1740.

El Jadida. *City and port, western Morocco*. The settlement developed after 1502 around a Portuguese fort and was originally known as *Mazagan*, for the *Mazg'anna* people who inhabited the region in medieval times. It was resettled by Moroccan Jews in 1821 and then given its present Arabic name, from *el-brija el-jadīda*, "the new little port." All that is now left is "the new."

El-Kelaâ des Srarhna. *Town, western Morocco*. The town's Arabic name means "citadel of the *Srarhna*," referring to its former status as capital of the local Berber-Arab *Srarhna* people. (The *des* of the name is French.)

Ellesmere Island. *Island, northern Canada*. The island, in Nunavut, was discovered in 1616 by William Baffin (*see* **Baffin Island**) but remained unnamed until 1852, when the expedition of Sir Edward A. Inglefield named it for Francis Egerton, 1st Earl of *Ellesmere* (1800–1857), whose title came from *Ellesmere*, Shropshire, England.

El Lisan. *Peninsula, south central Jordan*. The Dead Sea peninsula derives its name from Arabic *al-lisān*, "the tongue."

Ellis Island. *Island, eastern United States*. The island, in Upper New York Bay, famous as a point of entry for immigrants, is named for Samuel *Ellis*, who acquired it in 1785. It was purchased from his heirs in 1808 by the State of New York and turned over to the federal government.

Ellsworth Land. *Region, Antarctica*. The region, a plateau at the base of the Antarctic Peninsula, was discovered in 1935 by the American explorer Lincoln Ellsworth (1880–1951), who named it for his father, James William *Ellsworth* (1849–1925).

Ellwangen. *City, southern Germany*. The name means "elk meadow," from Old High German *elaho*, "elk," and *wang*, "meadow." Local legend has reinterpreted the name as *Elchfang*, recorded in the 9th century as *Elehenfanc*, supposedly referring to a hunt in which an elk was caught (*fangen*, "to catch"). But an "elk meadow" would anyway be grassland in which this animal came to be hunted for sport.

El-Mansura *see* **Mansura**

Elmina. *Town, southern Ghana*. The town, one of the oldest European settlements in Africa, was founded by the Portuguese in 1471 and given a name meaning "the mine."

Elmshorn. *City, northwestern Germany*. The name probably means "corner of land where elms grow," from Middle Low German *elm*, "elm," and *hōrn*, "horn," "projecting piece of land."

El-Oued. *Town, northeastern Algeria*. The town's name represents Arabic *al-wādī*, "the river." There is no river here now, but there once was, before it was swallowed up by the encroaching sands.

El Paso. *City, southern United States*. The Texas city lies at the foot of Mt. Franklin below a pass where the Rio Grande emerges from the Rockies. The original site was in 1598 thus given the Spanish name of *El Paso del Norte*, "the pass of the north," and this was later shortened to simply *El Paso*. The town was not actually laid out until 1859.

El Puente del Arzobispo. *Town, central Spain*. The name means "the archbishop's bridge," for the *archbishop* who had a *bridge* built across the Tagus River here in 1390.

El Salvador. *Republic, northwestern Central America*. The country's Spanish name means "the Savior," as a title of Christ. It was originally given by Spanish colonists in 1524 to the fort located where the country's capital, **San Salvador**, is now, and spread from this to the whole territory.

Elsinore *see* **Helsingør**

El Taiybe. *Village, central West Bank*. The large Arab village, mostly populated by Christians, has an Arabic name meaning "the goodness," from Arabic *el*, "the," and *ṭaiyib*, "good."

Eltville am Rhein. *Town, western Germany*. The name of the town, on the **Rhine**, is a form of Latin *Alta Villa*, "high estate," recorded thus in the 11th century. But this cannot be the original name, as Latin *villa* would have given modern German *-weil*, and it is thus likely that the Latin name translated an earlier German one such as *Hohstat*, itself perhaps an alteration of *Hohstad*, "high bank," referring to the riverside location. The latinized form of the name may have been introduced to distinguish the place from nearby **Höchst**, whose own name was also similarly *Hostat*, with the same meaning.

Ely. *Town, eastern England.* The Cambridgeshire town has an Old English name meaning "eel district," from *āl*, "eel," and *gē*, "district" (*cp.* **Surrey**). This would have been an administrative district in Anglo-Saxon times. The name was later associated with Old English *īeg*, "island," appropriately enough for the town's location on an "island" of rock rising above the fens in the northeastern part of the district known as *Isle of Ely*, a former county.

Emden. *City and port, northwestern Germany.* The name of the city was recorded in the 10th century as *Emutha*, referring to its location at the *mouth* of the *Ehe* River. The river's own name (earlier *Ee*) derives from an Old Frisian form of Old High German *aha*, "water." (Emden is near the **Ems** River estuary but does not thus actually take its name from it.)

Emilia-Romagna. *Region, north central Italy.* The first part of the name derives from the *Via Aemilia*, the Roman road across the region laid out in 187 B.C. under the consulate of Marcus *Aemilius* Lepidus. The second part relates to the fact that in the 8th century five cities here, formerly under Lombard rule, passed to the pope of *Rome*. Until 1948 the region was known simply as *Emilia*.

Emmaus. *Historic town, east central Israel.* The biblical town (Luke 24:13) has a name of Aramaic origin, from *hammat*, "hot spring."

Emmendingen. *Town, southwestern Germany.* The name means "(settlement of) *Anemuot*'s people," with a personal name unrecorded elsewhere.

Emmerich. *City, western Germany.* The name was recorded in 828 as *in villa Embrici*, with the personal name probably a latinized genitive form of the Frankish name *Embriko*, that of the original landowner here.

Ems. *River, northwestern Germany.* The river was known to the Roman as *Amisia* and to the Greeks as *Amasios*, both names ultimately deriving from the Indoeuropean root *am*, "river bed."

Enderby Land. *Region, Antarctica.* The region, in the Australian Antarctic Territory, was discovered in 1831 by the English explorer John Briscoe. He named it for the whaling firm of Samuel *Enderby* & Sons who had financed his expedition and who owned the *Tula*, the ship on which he undertook it.

Endor. *Historic town, northern Israel.* The biblical town, famous for the "witch of Endor" visited by Saul (1 Samuel 28:7–14), has a name of uncertain origin. It may represent Hebrew *'ēn-dōr*, "spring of time," from *'ēn*, "spring of," construct state (*see* **Ramat Gan**) of *'ayin*, "spring," and *dōr*, "time." Or it may relate to the Greek people known as the *Dorians*.

Enfield. *Borough of London, southeastern England.* The town has a name meaning "*Ēana*'s open land," with the Anglo-Saxon personal name followed by Old English *feld*, "open land" (modern *field*). The "open land" would have been a clearing in the former woodland here.

En Gedi. *Village, southwestern Israel.* The biblical village and oasis (Joshua 15:62), now a kibbutz, on the western shore of the Dead Sea, derives its name from Hebrew *'ēn-gedī*, "spring of the kid," from *'ēn*, "spring of" (as for **Endor**), and *gedī*, "kid."

Engelberg. *Town, central Switzerland.* The town and resort has a name popularly interpreted as "mount of angels." According to local legend, on the death of the founder of the Benedictine abbey here in 1120, the singing of angels was heard from the mountain above, so that in 1142 Pope Calixtus II named the abbey thus. The name then passed to the town that grew up around it. A more prosaic origin derives the name from Latin *angulus*, "corner," referring to the abbey's site in the narrow valley.

Engels. *City, western Russia.* The city, on the Volga south of Saratov, was founded in 1747 and was originally known as *Pokrovka*, for its church, which was dedicated to the Protection of the Virgin (Russian *Pokrov*, literally "covering"). In 1914 the name was modified to *Pokrovsk*, then in 1931 the city was renamed as now in honor of Friedrich *Engels* (1820–1895), the German socialist leader and colleague of Karl *Marx*, who gave the name of **Marks**, north of Saratov.

England. *Kingdom, western Europe.* The largest country of the British Isles takes its name from the *Angles*, the people who in the 5th and 6th centuries A.D. came here from the region known as *Angeln* ("angle of land") in what is now Schleswig-Holstein, northwestern Germany.

English Bazar. *City, northeastern India.* The West Bengal city was chosen in 1676 as the site of the British East India Company's silk factories. Hence its name, which has an alternate vernacular form *Angrezabad*, with the final *-abad* the Iranian suffix meaning "inhabited place," "town."

En Harod. *Kibbutz, northern Israel.* Israel's first large kibbutz was founded in 1921 and named for the nearby biblical "well of *Harod*" (Judges 7:1) where Gideon and his men camped. The well's own name means "trembling." (The first group of men dismissed by Gideon here before the battle against the Midianites were those who were "fearful and afraid," i.e. "trembled.")

En Hashofet. *Settlement, northwestern Israel.* The name of the settlement means "spring of the judge," from Hebrew '*ēn*, "spring of" (as for **Endor**), and *shōpēṭ*, "judge," in honor of U.S. judge Louis D. Brandeis (1856–1941), leader of the American Zionist movement.

Enna. *City, southern Italy.* The city, in central Sicily, has a pre–Greek name of uncertain origin. In medieval times it came to be known as *Castrogiovanni*, as if "St. John's castle," but this was really a corruption of its Arabic name, *Kasr-Yani*, itself a form of its Roman name, *Castrum Hennae*. It resumed its original name in 1927.

En Sarid. *Village, central Israel.* The village was founded in 1950 by survivors of the Holocaust. Hence its name, meaning "spring of the survivors," from Hebrew '*ēn*, "spring of" (as for **Endor**), and *sārid*, "survivor."

Enschede. *City, eastern Netherlands.* The city's Old Dutch name was *Aneschedhe*, from *ane*, "at," "on," and *schedhe* (modern German *Scheide*), "boundary," "border." Enschede is close to the border with Germany.

Ensenada. *City and port, northwestern Mexico.* The city takes its name from Spanish *ensenada*, "inlet," referring to its location on a bay of the Pacific.

En Shemer. *Kibbutz, central Israel.* The kibbutz was founded in 1927 and has a name meaning "spring of *Shemer*," from Hebrew '*ēn*, "spring of" (as for **Endor**), and the biblical *Shemer* who gave the name of **Samaria**.

Entebbe. *City, south central Uganda.* The former British administrative center of Uganda was founded as a garrison post in 1893 and is said to take its name from the local phrase *entebe za mugula*, "headquarters of *Mugula*," referring to a local chief who held authority here.

Entre Ríos. *Province, eastern Argentina.* The province's Spanish name means "between the rivers," describing its location between the Paraná, to the west, and the Uruguay, to the east, the latter forming the Uruguayan border.

Enugu. *City, southern Nigeria.* The city derives its name from local words *enu ugwu*, "at the top of the hill," itself a borrowing of the name of the village of *Enugu* Ngwo, just west of the city. Enugu actually lies at the foot of a plateau, while Enugu Ngwo is on it, as its name indicates.

En Vered. *Settlement, western Israel.* The cooperative settlement, on the Plain of Sharon, was founded in 1930 on the site of an ancient settlement with a Hebrew name meaning "spring of the rose."

Eolie Islands. *Island group, southeastern Tyrrhenian Sea.* The volcanic islands, belonging to Italy and also known as the *Aeolian Islands*, derive their name from the *Aeolians*, the people who once inhabited them. Their own name is traditionally traced to their mythical ancestor, *Aeolus*, regarded by some as identical with the *Aeolus* who was god of the winds. The islands are also known as the *Lipari Islands*, for the largest of their number, its own name said to derive either from *Liparus*, an early ruler, or from Greek *liparos*, "fat," "rich."

Épernay. *Town, northeastern France.* The town's present name has evolved from its Roman name of *Sparnacum*, from Gaulish *sparno*, "thorn," with the Gallo-Roman suffix *-acum*.

Ephesus. *Historic city, western Turkey.* The name of the long-ruined biblical city is generally said to derive from Greek *ephoros*, "overseer," "ruler," referring to its importance as a religious center and to the fact that it was specifically "a worshiper of the great goddess Diana" (Acts 19:35).

Epidaurus. *Historic town and port, east central Greece.* The town, in the northeastern Peloponnese, has a name that may represent Greek *epidasus*, "rather bushy," referring to the dense vegetation here.

Épinal. *Town, northeastern France.* The name of the town derives ultimately from Latin *spina*, "thorn," referring to thorn bushes formerly here. *Cp.* **Épinay-sur-Seine**.

Épinay-sur-Seine. *Town, northern France.* The town, now a suburb of Paris, derives its basic name from Latin *spina*, "thorn," referring to thorn bushes once here. *Cp.* **Épinal**. The addition locates the town on the **Seine** River and distinguishes it from similarly named places.

Epirus. *Region, northwestern Greece.* The region takes its name from Greek *ēpeiros*, "mainland," so distinguishing it from Greece's large island territory.

Epping. *Town, southeastern England.* The Essex town has a name meaning "(settlement of the) upland people," from Old English *yppe*, "raised place" and *-ingas*, "dwellers at," referring to the high ground at the northern end of Epping Forest. The original settlement was at the village now known as *Epping Upland*, northwest of the present town.

Epsom. *Town, southern England.* The Surrey

town has an Old English name meaning "*Ebbi*'s homestead," with the final *-om* representing *hām*, "homestead."

Equatorial Guinea. *Republic, western Africa.* The name indicates the country's location near (but not quite on) the *equator* in the extensive region long known as **Guinea**. Until 1968 the republic had the colonial name of *Spanish Guinea.*

Ercolano. *Town, southern Italy.* The town derives its name from the former ancient city of *Herculaneum* here, its own name paying tribute to *Hercules* (Greek *Heracles*), the great hero of classical mythology. *Cp.* **Ereğli.**

Erebus, Mt. *Volcano, Antarctica.* The active volcano, on Ross Island, was so named by the British explorer Sir James Ross for one of his ships in his expedition here in 1841. The name, that of the darkness of the underworld in classical mythology, is appropriate for a volcano, with its hidden "darkness." A second ship, the *Terror*, gave the equally apt name for a nearby (now extinct) volcano.

Erechim. *City, southern Brazil.* The city was founded in 1909 as *Boa Vista do Erechim*, from Portuguese *boa vista*, "good view," and the existing name, from a Tupí-Guaraní word meaning "small field." From 1939 through 1944 Erechim was known as *José Bonifácio.*

Ereğli. *City, south central Turkey.* The city's name is a corruption of its original classical name *Heraclea Cybistra*, so called for its dedication to *Heracles* (Roman *Hercules*), the great hero of classical mythology. The city of the same name in northern Turkey was similarly known as *Heraclea Pontica*. *Cp.* **Ercolano.**

Erevan *see* **Yerevan**

Erfurt. *City, east central Germany.* The city, first mentioned in 742 as *Erphesfurt*, has a name meaning "ford over the *Erphesa*," from a former name of the Gera River here, itself based on Old High German *erph*, "dark-colored," "brownish."

Eridu. *Historic city, southern Iraq.* The ancient Sumerian city has a name meaning "beautiful city."

Erie, Lake. *Lake, central North America.* The lake, between the United States and Canada, takes its name from that of a Native American people here. Their own name means "long tail," probably referring to the panther or puma, their totemic animal.

Eritrea. *State, northeastern Africa.* The state, a former province of Ethiopia, was created as an Italian colony in 1890 and named by the Italians for the *Mare Erythreum*, the Roman name (from Greek *eruthros*, "red") of the **Red Sea,** by which it lies.

Erkelenz. *City, western Germany.* The name evolved from a form *Herculencia*, a shortening of *Herculentiacum*, "place named after *Hercules.*" The Latin name is recorded in Rhenish inscriptions.

Erkrath. *City, western Germany.* The name represents the Old German personal name *Everik* or *Everrik*, an early form of modern *Eberich*.

Erlangen. *City, south central Germany.* The city derives its name from Old High German *erila*, "alder," and *wang*, "field," "meadow." The meaning is thus "fields overgrown with alder trees."

Ermine Street. *Roman road, England.* The ancient road, from London to York, takes its name from the *Earningas*, the Anglo-Saxon people through whose territory it passed. Their own name, meaning "*Earna*'s people," is also preserved in the village of *Arrington*, Cambridgeshire, on Ermine Street.

Erne, Lough. *Lake, southern Northern Ireland.* The lake, in Co. Fermanagh, takes its name from a people known as the *Erni* or *Ernai*, said to have inhabited the region before the lake existed. The meaning of their own name is unknown.

Erode. *City, southeastern India.* The city, in Tamil Nadu state, has a Tamil name meaning "wet skull," referring to a Hindu temple here from the 10th century.

Er Rif. *Hill region, northern Morocco.* The name represents Arabic *ar-rīf*, "the coastland." The coast here was thus obviously regarded as the region's dominant feature, rather than its hills.

Erzgebirge. *Mountain range, central Europe.* The range, in Germany and the Czech Republic, has a German name meaning "ore mountains," referring to its natural wealth. Metals and minerals found naturally here include gold, silver, lead, copper, tungsten, and pitchblende. Some languages translate the name into the vernacular, such as Czech *Krušné Hory* and Russian *Rudnyye gory*, and the French sometimes refer to the mountains as *Monts Métallifères*. English *Ore Mountains* is also found.

Erzincan. *City, eastern Turkey.* The city has frequently been damaged by earthquakes, most recently in 1939. Its name is accordingly said to derive from Turkish *ezmek*, "to crush," and *can*, "life." But this is simply folk etymology.

Erzurum. *City, eastern Turkey.* The city's name represents Arabic *arḍ ar-rūm*, "land of *Rome*," meaning that the territory here belonged to the Byzantine Christians. The city arose around a Byzantine fortress named *Theodosiopolis* ("town of *Theodosius*," for the 5th-century

A.D. Eastern Roman emperor *Theodosius* II) that fell to the Arabs in 653.

Esbjerg. *Town and port, southwestern Denmark.* The name is said to have evolved from earlier *Eskebjerg*, meaning "ash-tree hill," or "ash-tree rock," from Old Norse *eski*, "ash-tree place," and *berg*, "hill," or *bjarg*, "rock."

Eschweiler. *City, western Germany.* The name, first recorded in the 10th century, means "estate where ash trees grow," from Old High German *ask*, "ash," and the *-weiler* element (from Medieval Latin *villare*) commonly found in western Germany and eastern France.

Escondido. *City, southwestern United States.* The California city was laid out in 1885 and named with the Spanish word meaning "hidden," referring to its secluded site in a valley.

Esdraelon, Plain of. *Plain, northern Israel.* The plain's name is the Greek form of its original Hebrew name *yisre'el*, "God will sow," "may God make fruitful," referring to the fertility of the region. The biblical form of the name is *Jezreel* (Judges 6:33, etc.).

Esfahan *see* **Isfahan**

Eskilstuna. *Town, southeastern Sweden.* The town, a trade center in the 12th century (although not chartered until 1659), is named for the English missionary bishop *Eskil*, martyred in c.1080.

Eskişehir. *City, west central Turkey.* The city's name means "ancient city," from Turkish *eski*, "old," "ancient," and *şehir*, "town." The reference is to the nearby ruined Phrygian city of *Dorylaeum*.

Espelkamp. *Town, northern Germany.* The town arose in 1949 as a settlement for World War II refugees on the site of a munitions factory built in 1939 in a wood of this name, itself that of a nearby village, meaning "enclosed land by the aspen copse," from Old High German *asp*, "aspen," Middle Low German *lō*, "copse," and Middle Low German *kamp*, from Latin *campus*, "field."

Espírito Santo. *State, eastern Brazil.* The coastal state has a name meaning "Holy Spirit," from the dedication given to the spot where the Portuguese explorer Vasco Fernandes Coutinho landed (the site of the future state capital, Vitória) on May 23, 1535.

Essaouira. *City and port, western Morocco.* The name of the city, founded in 1760, is a French-influenced form of Arabic *as-sawira*, "the little wall," referring to the original defensive structure here on a peninsula overlooking the Atlantic. Under French colonial rule the city was known as *Mogador*, a Berber corruption of *Mag-*

doul, the name of a Muslim holy man buried here.

Essen. *City, western Germany.* The city's name was recorded in the 9th century as *Astnide*, "place of smelting," from Middle Low German *ast*, "forge," and the Old Saxon collective suffix *-ithi*. Essen's famous steelworks and ironworks evolved in the 19th century from an early metal-processing industry.

Essex. *County, southeastern England.* The county takes its name from the *East Saxons*, whose kingdom here in the 7th century included not only the present county but also that of Middlesex and much of Hertfordshire.

Esslingen. *City, southwestern Germany.* The city, near Stuttgart, is mentioned in 777 as the site of a daughter house of the abbey of St. Denis at Paris, France. The name means "(settlement of) *Azzilo*'s people." The formal name of the city is *Esslingen am Neckar*, for its location on the **Neckar.**

Essonne. *Department, northern France.* The department is named for the river here, its own name having the Medieval Latin form of *Exona*. This represents a pre–Latin root element *ax* with the *-ona* suffix found in a number of western European river names. The root word probably goes back to proto-Indoeuropean *apsa*, "river."

Estaimpuis. *Town, southwestern Belgium.* The town, on the French border, has a part-Flemish, part-French name meaning "stone well."

Estância. *City, northeastern Brazil.* The coastal city has a Portuguese name meaning "stopping place," "resort."

Este. *Town, northern Italy.* The original name of the town was *Ateste*, from *Atesis*, the Roman name of the **Adige** River, on which it lay until the 6th century, when the river changed its course.

Estinnes. *Town, southern Belgium.* An earlier form of the name was *Lestines*, apparently based on a Celtic word meaning "court," "hall" (Welsh *llys*). The full form of the current name is *Estinnes-au-Mont*, for the town's proximity to **Mons.**

Estonia. *Republic, northeastern Europe.* The Baltic country takes its name from its indigenous people, the *Estonians*. Their own name may mean "waterside dwellers," from a Baltic word *aueist*. The name does not relate to a form of German *Est*, "east," despite the appropriateness of this for the region.

Estremadura. *Region, west central Spain.* The region is so named as it is the "extremity of the **Douro**," otherwise the territory farthest from this river. An alternate spelling of the name is

Extremadura. The identically named historic region of western Portugal is so called for the same reason.

Esztergom. *Town and river port, northern Hungary*. The town, known to the Romans as *Strigonium*, derives its name from a Slavic personal name meaning "shaven-headed" (Russian *strigu*, "I cut"). Its German name is *Gran*, from the river known to the Hungarians as *Garam* ("pine water"), a tributary of the Danube.

Étampes. *Town, northern France*. The town's name derives from its Low Latin form, *Stampae*, of unknown origin and meaning.

Ethiopia. *State, northeastern Africa*. The country's name represents the Greek word for its indigenous people. This was *aithiops*, "burnt appearance," from *aithō*, "I burn," and *ōps*, "aspect," "appearance," referring to their dark skins. The local name for the country is *Abyssinia*, said to derive from an Amharic root *ḥbsh*, "mixed," referring to the mixed black and white races who at one time inhabited the region, although this derivation is disputed by some Amharic scholars. Hence *Habeşistan* as the Turkish name of the country, with *-istan* as for **Afghanistan**. Ethiopia is mentioned several times in the Bible (Genesis 2:13, etc.) and Cush (Genesis 10:6) is identified as the father of Ethiopians (*see* **Cush**).

Etna. *Volcano, southern Italy*. The active volcano, in northeastern Sicily, probably derives its name from Phoenician *attūnā*, "furnace," rather than Greek *aithō*, "I burn," despite the similarity of sense. The Sicilian name of Etna is *Mongibello*, probably representing Italian *monte bello*, "beautiful mountain," influenced by Arabic *jabal*, "mountain."

Etobicoke. *City, southern Canada*. The Ontario city has a name of Native American origin meaning "place where alders grow."

Eton. *Town, south central England*. The former Berkshire town lies by the Thames River, and its name refers to this location. It means "river settlement," from Old English *ēa*, "river," and *tūn*, "farm," "settlement."

Etruria. *Historic region, central Italy*. The ancient country has a name of uncertain origin, although its adjectival form, *Etruscan*, reveals an element *-sc-* that links it with the names of **Tuscany** and the **Basque Country** and that itself probably means "water." In the case of Etruria, this could refer to the Arno and Tiber rivers, between which it lies.

Et-Tih. *Desert, northeastern Egypt*. The desert, in the central Sinai Peninsula, has the full Arabic name *et-tīh-banī-isrā'īl*, "the wanderings of the children of **Israel**," referring to the journey of the Israelites through the wilderness to Mt. Sinai, as described in Exodus.

Ettlingen. *City, southwestern Germany*. The city, which arose on the site of a Roman camp, has a name meaning "(settlement of) *Etini's* people."

Euboea. *Island, east central Greece*. The Aegean island, the largest in the Greek archipelago after Crete, has a Greek name meaning "rich in cattle," from *eu*, "good," "well," and *bous*, "ox," "cow." The mountains of Euboea still have good pastures for sheep and cattle.

Euclid. *City, northern United States*. The Ohio city was settled in 1798 and named for the 3d-century B.C. Greek mathematician by the surveyors who came here with Moses Cleaveland (*see* ²**Cleveland**), an agent of the Connecticut Land Company.

Eugene. *City, western United States*. The Oregon city takes its name from *Eugene* Skinner, who founded it in 1846. The personal name, meaning "well born," is propitious for a new town.

Euphrates. *River, southwestern Asia*. The river, mentioned in the Bible (Genesis 2:14, etc.), flows southeast through Syria and Iraq to join with the Tigris as the Shatt al-Arab and enter the Persian Gulf. It has a Greek-looking name that may actually derive from Akkadian *ur*, "river," and *at*, "father," so that it is the "father of rivers," so called for its size, or similarly from *u*, "very," and *pratu*, "wide." Its Arabic name is *nahr al-furāt*, from *nahr*, "river," and a form of the original name.

Eurasia. *Continental landmass*. The name combines those of the continents of **Europe** and **Asia**, and sems to have first appeared in a German textbook, H. Reusche's *Handbuch der Geographie*, published in 1858. (The adjective *Eurasian* predates this, however.)

Eureka. *City and port, western United States*. The California city was laid out in 1850 and named with the state motto, adopted the previous year. It was taken from the exclamation (Greek *heurēka*, "I have found it") made by Archimedes on realizing, when bathing, that the volume of a solid could be calculated by measuring the water displaced when it was immersed. American pioneers used the word to name places where they struck gold (as particularly in California) or where a favorable site was found for a settlement, such as one with a good supply of fresh water.

Europe. *Continent west of Asia*. The continent's name remains of uncertain origin. It has been traditionally linked with *Europa*, the Phoenician princess of Greek mythology, and also with Greek *euros*, "breadth," as if a "broad" region. But it is almost certainly pre–Greek, and may derive from Phoenician *'ereb*, "evening," "west," as distinct from **Asia**, "land of the rising sun."

Euskirchen. *City, western Germany.* The first part of the city's name probably represents the genitive form of a Frankish personal name based on *Awi*. The second part, from Old High German *kiricha*, "church," denotes that the place arose around a church built by the named person on his land.

Eutin. *Town, northeastern Germany.* The town was founded by Count Adolf II of Schaumburg with Dutch settlers as a border post during the war between the Germans and the Wends. Its name, recorded in the late 12th century as *pagus Utinensis*, "*Uta*'s district," with an Old Polabian personal name, was originally that of a Slav stockade on an island in a lake opposite the Dutch settlement mentioned.

Evansville. *City, east central United States.* The Indiana city was founded in 1812 and named for Robert M. *Evans*, a colonel of the militia and member of the territorial legislature.

Even Shmu'el. *Village, southern Israel.* The Jewish village, founded in 1957, was originally named *Oman*. This was then changed as now to mean "stone of *Shmu'el*," honoring the Canadian Jewish industrialist *Samuel* Bronfman (1890–1971), a major financial contributor to developments in Israel.

Everest, Mt. *Mountain, southern Asia.* The world's highest mountain, on the border of Tibet and Nepal in the central Himalayas, was so named in 1865 for Sir George *Everest* (1790–1866), British surveyor general of India. He really had more to do with maps than mountains, but the name is coincidentally appropriate for an abiding peak, which will "ever rest." The mountain's Tibetan name is *Chomolangma*, "mother goddess of the world," from *chomo*, "goddess" (literally "highest one"), *lang*, "world" (literally "elephant," which symbolizes the world), and *ma*, "mother."

Everett. *City and port, northwestern United States.* The Washington city was settled in 1862 and named for *Everett* Colby, the son of Charles L. Colby, a local land investor.

Everglades. *Marshland, southeastern United States.* The expanse of swampy land and rivers in southern Florida has a name that is less obvious than it seems. *Glade* here has its Southern sense of "marshy area." *Ever* appears to have a spatial sense, instead of its usual temporal one, denoting a region that is extensive or even figuratively "endless." The overall meaning is thus something like "extensive area of marshland."

Evesham. *Town, west central England.* The Worcestershire town has an Old English name meaning "*Ēof*'s riverside land," with the Anglo-Saxon personal name followed by *hamm*, literally "hemmed-in land." The reference is to the town's location in a bend of the Avon River.

Évian-les-Bains. *Town and resort, eastern France.* The town, on the southern shore of Lake Geneva, has a name recorded in the 8th century as *Laquatico*. This derives from Latin *aquianum*, based on *aqua*, "water." The reference is to the mineral springs here, as confirmed by the second part of the name, meaning literally "the baths."

Évreux. *Town, northwestern France.* The town takes its name from the *Eburovices*, the Gaulish people who at one time inhabited the region. Their own name means "conquering with the yew," presumably referring to the yew wood from which they made their spears or bows.

Exeter. *City, southwestern England.* The Devon city takes its name from the *Exe* River on which it lies. The second part of the name is a reduced form of Old English *ceaster*, "Roman station," a borrowing from Latin *castrum*, "camp." The Roman name of the settlement here was *Isca Dumnoniorum*, the first word representing the Celtic river name (itself based on an Indoeuropean root *eis*, "moving quickly"), the second being the name of the *Dumnonii*, the Celtic people who gave the name of **Devon**.

Extertal. *Town, northwestern Germany.* The town, a municipality formed in 1969 out of 12 villages, takes its name from the valley (German *Tal*) of the *Exter* River, its own name meaning "magpie."

Extremadura *see* **Estremadura**

Eyre, Lake. *Lake, south central Australia.* The lake, in South Australia, is named for the British colonial administrator Edward John *Eyre* (1815–1901), who discovered it in 1840. He may have been aware that his own name originally meant "heir," so that the lake would be his "heritage."

Faenza. *City, northern Italy.* The city derives its name from Latin *faventia*, "silence," "meditation," presumably describing its tranquil location.

Faeroes. *Island group, North Atlantic.* The Danish islands, north of the British Isles, derive their name from Faeroese *Føroyar*, "sheep islands," from *før*, "sheep," and *oy*, "island," plural *oyar*. Sheep are still plentiful on the islands. *Cp.* **Fair Isle.**

Faial. *Island, North Atlantic.* The westernmost island of the central Azores derives its name from Portuguese *faia,* "beech tree." The reference is to the wax myrtle, formerly abundant here, which early Portuguese explorers took to be beech trees.

Fairbanks. *City, northwestern United States.* The Alaska city was founded in 1902 during a gold strike and takes its name from Charles W. *Fairbanks* (1852–1918), a senator from Indiana who led a commission to settle the Alaska boundary dispute.

Fairfield. *City, southwestern United States.* The California city was founded in 1859 by Robert H. Waterman, a ship's captain, who named it for his home town in Connecticut. That town was settled in 1639 and named either for one of the many English villages *Fairfield* or in a generally propitious sense for an attractive site that was a "fair field" for settlement.

Fair Isle. *Island, northern Scotland.* The first word of the Shetland island name represents Old Norse *faar,* "sheep." Sheep still graze freely here and Fair Isle knitwear is well known. *Cp.* **Faeroes.**

Fairweather, Mt. *Mountain, western Canada.* British Columbia's highest peak was so named in 1778 by Captain Cook who sighted it from the sea while sailing in "fair weather."

Faisalabad. *City, northeastern Pakistan.* The city's name means "*Faisal*'s town," with Iranian *ābād,* "town," following the personal name, that of King *Faisal* of Saudi Arabia (1905–1975), who was widely respected in Pakistan. The city acquired the name in 1979. Its earlier name was *Lyallpur,* "*Lyall*'s town," with Hindi *pur,* "town," added to the name of Sir Charles James *Lyall* (1845–1920), lieutenant governor of the Punjab, who laid it out in 1890.

Faizabad. *City, northern India.* The city, in Uttar Pradesh state, was founded in 1730 by Sadat 'Ali Khan, first nawab of Oudh, who gave it a propitious name meaning "town of riches." The Iranian name is found elsewhere, often in the spelling *Fayzabad,* as in Afghanistan and Tajikistan.

Falkensee. *Town, eastern Germany.* The residential town was formed in 1923 on the amalgamation of the villages of *Falkenhagen* and *Seegefeld,* and takes its name from the first parts of these names, respectively meaning "hedged enclosure with falcons" and "marshy open land."

Falkirk. *Town, central Scotland.* The name translates as "speckled church," from Old English *fāg,* "variegated," and *cirice,* "church." The original church here must have been built of mottled stone.

Falkland Islands. *Island group, South Atlantic.* The islands were so named in 1690 by Captain John Strong for Anthony Cary, 5th Viscount *Falkland* (1656–1694), who as treasurer of the navy had financed Strong's expedition here. Strong had originally given the name just to Falkland Sound, between the two main islands, and the name *Falkland's Islands* is first recorded only in 1765, when the British admiral John Byron took possession of the group. The islands' original name was *Davis Land,* for their discoverer in 1592, John *Davis* (*see* **Davis Strait**). In 1594 they were recorded as *Hawkins Maidenland,* so named by Sir Richard *Hawkins* in honor of Elizabeth I, the Virgin ("Maiden") Queen. The Spanish name for the islands is *Islas Malvinas,* from the *Malouins,* the French name of the inhabitants of **St. Malo,** France, who attempted to colonize them in 1764 under the French navigator Louis-Antoine de Bougainville (*see* **Bougainville**). Viscount Falkland's title comes from *Falkland,* southeastern Scotland, where it means "folkland," referring to land held by folkright, or common law.

Fall River. *City, northeastern United States.* The Massachusetts city has a name translating its original Native American (Quequechan) name which literally meant "falling water." The reference is to the Taunton River here, a source of abundant waterpower.

Falmouth. *Town and port, southwestern England.* The Cornish town takes its name from the *Fal* River, at the mouth of which it lies. The meaning of the river's name is unknown. Names beginning with *F-* are rare in Celtic languages, so it either originally began with another letter or is not Cornish. It may well be pre-Celtic.

False Bay. *Bay, southwestern South Africa.* The bay, southeast of Cape Town in Western Cape province, has a name translated from the Portuguese *Cabo Falso.* Early navigators frequently mistook this bay for Table Bay, their intended destination to the north, the other side of the Cape of Good Hope.

Falun. *City, central Sweden.* The city's name represents Swedish *falun,* "treeless plain," "wasteland," alluding to the former topography here.

Famagusta. *Town and port, eastern Cyprus.* The name ultimately goes back to Phoenician *khamat,* "fort." Under the Romans this became *Fama Augusta,* as if "fame of *Augustus.*" That gave the present name. The Greeks adapted the same original name differently, as *Ammokhostos,* as if from *ammos,* "sand," and *khōstos,* "heaped up," giving an apparent sense of "(port by the) sand dune."

Fano. *Town, central Italy.* The town was

founded on the site of the ancient Roman *Fanum Fortunae*, "temple of fortune," i.e. of the goddess *Fortuna*, bringer of luck, said to have been built here in the 3d or 2d century B.C., and takes its name from the first word of this.

Fareham. *Town, southern England*. The Hampshire town has an Old English name meaning literally "fern homestead," referring to a settlement among the ferns here.

Farewell, Cape. *Headland, southern Greenland*. The cape, in Danish *Kap Farvel*, is so named as it was the point of departure in 1586 of the English explorer John Davis (*see* **Davis Strait**) when he set sail on a voyage to Canada. The name is found elsewhere, as for the northern extremity of South Island, New Zealand, where it was the point of departure in 1770 of Captain Cook when he set sail for the east coast of Australia. "Farewell" means not only "goodbye" but also literally "journey well."

Fargo. *City, northern United States*. North Dakota's largest city was founded in 1871 and named for William George *Fargo* (1818–1881), a pioneer in the shipment of express goods.

Faridabad. *City, northwestern India*. The city, in Haryana state, was founded in 1607 by Shaikh *Farid*, treasurer of Emperor Jahangir, and is named for him. The *-abad* is the Iranian suffix meaning "inhabited place," "town."

Faridpur. *City, central Bangladesh*. The city is named for the Muslim holy man *Farid* ud-Din Mas'ud, whose shrine is here. The second part of the name is Hindi *pur*, "town."

Farnborough. *Town, southern England*. The Hampshire town has an Old English name meaning "fern hill," from *fearn*, "fern," and *beorg*, "hill." There is no obvious hill here now, but the reference is probably to the lowish rise that has Farnborough Park at its southern end, north of the town center.

Faroe Islands *see* **Faeroes**

Farrukhabad. *City, north central India*. The city, in Uttar Pradesh state, was founded in 1714 by the local Mughal governor Muhammad Khan Bangash and named for the Mughal emperor *Farrukh*-siyar (ruled 1713–19). *Farrukhnagar*, in Haryana state, is also named for him, with Hindi *nagar*, "town." Farrukhabad forms a joint municipality with **Fatehgarh**.

Fars *see* **Iran**

Fatehgarh. *City, north central India*. The city, in Uttar Pradesh state, was founded in 1714 when a fort was built on the site of **Farrukhabad**, with which it now forms a joint municipality. The name means "fort of victory," from Hindi *fateh*, "victory," and *garh*, "fort."

Fatehpur. *Town, northern India*. The town, in Uttar Pradesh state, was founded in the 15th century and has a name meaning "town of victory," from Hindi *fateh*, "victory," and *pur*, "town."

Fatehpur Sikri. *Town, northern India*. The town, in Uttar Pradesh state, was founded as his capital in 1569 by the Mughal emperor Akbar on the site of the village of *Sikri* and named by him "town of victory," as for **Fatehpur**, to commemorate his conquest of Gujarat in 1573.

Fátima. *Town, central Portugal*. The town is named for *Fatima*, a 12th-century Moorish princess, bearer of the same name as the daughter of Muhammad, the founder of Islam. Despite this Muslim connection, the town is a place of Christian pilgrimage, to the shrine of Our Lady of Fatima, where three young peasant children are said to have seen a vision of the Virgin Mary in 1917.

Favara. *Town, southern Italy*. The town, in south central Sicily, is believed to be of Arabic origin and to derive its name from Arabic *al-fawwarah*, "the gurgling one," for a fast-flowing stream here.

Faya. *Town, northern Chad*. The town, with a name of uncertain origin, was renamed *Largeau* following the capture in 1913 of the local district of Borkou by the French army officer Colonel Étienne *Largeau*. It reverted to its original indigenous name in the 1970s.

Fayetteville. *City, eastern United States*. The North Carolina city was founded in 1783 when the two settlements of Cambelltown and Cross Creek were united and renamed for Marie-Joseph Paul Yves Roch Gilbert du Motier, marquis de *Lafayette* (1757–1834), the French soldier and statesman who aided the colonists in America from 1777. *Cp.* ¹**Lafayette**.

Fécamp. *Town and port, northern France*. The town's present name has evolved from its Roman name of *Fiscannum*. This itself derives from Old German *fisk*, "fish," and *hafn*, "port," so that the name is similar to that of **Fishguard**, Wales. Fécamp lies on the English Channel.

Feira de Santana. *City, northeastern Brazil*. The city's Portuguese name originally had the form *Feira de Sant'Anna*, "St. Anne's fair," referring to the regular cattle fairs formerly held here.

Feldberg. *Mountain, southwestern Germany*. The highest peak in the Black Forest derives its name from the equivalent of modern German *Feld*, "field," and *Berg*, "mountain," implying a mountain whose slopes are covered with grass rather than trees.

Felixstowe. *Town and port, eastern England*. The Suffolk town has a name that appears to mean "*Felix*'s holy place," with the personal name followed by Old English *stōw*, "assembly place." This is the traditional origin of the name, which is said to commemorate St. *Felix*, first bishop of East Anglia. However, a 13th-century record of the name has it as *Filchestou*, which derives from another personal name, *Filica*. This man's name was thus assimilated to that of the bishop.

Fellbach. *Town, southwestern Germany*. The town has a river name, recorded in 1121 as *Velbach*, probably a short form of *Velwinbach*, from Old High German *felwa*, "willow," and *bah*, "stream."

Feodosiya. *Town, southern Ukraine*. The town, on the southeastern Crimea coast, was founded by Greek colonists in the 6th century B.C. with the name of *Theodosia*, "god-given (place)." In the 13th century a Genoese trading station called *Kaffa* was established here, its name of unknown meaning. In 1783, when the Crimea passed to Russia, the old Greek name was restored in its Russian form.

Fergana. *City, eastern Uzbekistan*. The city takes its name from the *Fergana* valley in which it lies, its own name representing Pamir *pargana*, a term for a semicircular mountain valley. The town was founded in 1876 and was originally known as *Novyj Margelan*, "new *Margelan*," for what is now the town of *Margelan*, 13½ miles (22 km) to the northwest. In 1910 it was renamed *Skobelev*, in memory of the Russian general Mikhail Dmitrievich *Skobelev* (1843–1882), who served much of his military career in central Asia and commanded forces in this region. The city received its present name in 1924.

Fermanagh. *County, southwestern Northern Ireland*. The name is that of the *Fear Manach*, "men of *Monach*," the latter being the name of these people's leader. They came to settle here from their native Leinster after assassinating the son of its king.

Fernando de Noronha. *Island, South Atlantic*. The island, belonging to Brazil, derives its name from *Fernando de Noronha*, the Portuguese ship's captain who discovered it in 1503.

Fernando Po *see* **Bioko**

Ferrara. *City, northern Italy*. The city is said to derive its name from Latin *ferrarius*, "blacksmith," itself from *ferrum*, "iron." However, the name has not been recorded earlier than the 8th century, and evidence for the Roman original is lacking.

Fez. *City, north central Morocco*. The name is of uncertain origin. It may represent Arabic *fas*, "ax," although the sense of this is not clear.

Fezzan. *Desert region, southwestern Libya*. The region of deserts and oases was formerly known as *Phazania*, deriving this name from the *Phazani*, the people who inhabited this part of the Sahara. The meaning of their own name is uncertain.

Fianarantsoa. *Town, southeastern Madagascar*. The town derives its name from Malagasy *fianàrana*, "study," "school," and *sòa*, "good," implying a place where one learns what is good.

Fichtelgebirge. *Mountain region, southeastern Germany*. The mountains, on the Czech-German border, have a name first applied only in the 19th century and first recorded in the 16th century. It is based on German *Fichte*, "spruce," and thus denotes a mountainous area where this tree is found.

Fidenza. *Town, northern Italy*. The town was long known as *Borgo San Donnino*, "fortress of St. *Domninus*," for the saint said to have been martyred here in the early 4th century. In 1927 it adopted its present name, a form of its original Latin name *Fidentia*, "confidence."

Fiesole. *Town, north central Italy*. The Tuscan town dates from the 9th or 8th century B.C. and was recorded with the Roman name of *Faesulae* in the 3rd century B.C. This itself derives from Etruscan *vipsul* or *visul*, a word of unknown meaning.

Fife. *Region, eastern Scotland*. The ancient kingdom, later a county and now an administrative region, traditionally takes its name from one *Fib*, a legendary ancestor of the Picts. The exact source of the name remains uncertain.

Fiji. *Island state, South Pacific*. The name is of uncertain origin. In its present form, it probably represents that of *Viti*, the main island in the group.

Filderstadt. *Town, southwestern Germany*. The town, now a suburb of Stuttgart, was formed in 1975 on the amalgamation of five villages. Its original name was *Filderlinden*, from an old nominative plural of Old High German *feld*, "open land," and modern German *Linden*, "lime trees." German *Stadt*, "town," was substituted for the latter soon after.

Finistère. *Department, northwestern France*. The tip of the western end of Brittany has a name that derives from Latin *finis terrae*, "end of the earth," denoting a region's westernmost region. The name thus equates to that of its counterpart in England, **Land's End**. The cape's Breton name, *Penn-ar-Bed*, literally "head of the world," is similar. *Cp.* **Finisterre, Cape**.

Finisterre, Cape. *Cape, northwestern Spain*. The name of the cape goes back to Latin *finis ter-*

rae, "end of the earth," denoting Spain's westernmost point. The local form of the name is *Cabo Fisterra*. **Cp**. **Finistère**.

Finland. *Republic, northern Europe*. The name obviously means "land of the *Finns*," referring to the country's indigenous people. Their own name comes from a Germanic word *finna* or *fenna*, "(fish) scale," to which English *fin* is directly related. This is a translation of Finnish *suomus* in the same sense, from which comes *Suomi*, the Finnish name of Finland. The reference is said to be to the garments of fish skin worn in early times. However, some authorities claim another origin for the indigenous name in Finnish *suo*, "marsh," and *maa*, "land," referring to Finland's many lakes. The corollary of this would then be a Germanic word related to English *fen*, so that Finland is "fenland."

Finnmark. *County, northern Norway*. The large county has a name meaning "borderland of the *Finns*," from Norwegian *finne*, "Finn," and *mark*, "field," "ground." The county borders **Finland**.

Finschhafen. *Town and port, eastern Papua New Guinea*. The town, claimed by Germany in 1894, has a name meaning "*Finsch*'s harbor," for the German explorer Otto *Finsch* (1839–1917).

Finsteraarhorn. *Mountain, southern Switzerland*. The highest peak in the Bernese Alps has a German name meaning "peak of the dark *Aar*," from the name of the *Aar* River, which flows from the glaciers here, and which is known in its upper reaches as the *Finsteraar*, "dark *Aar*," and *Horn*, "peak." The river is "dark" because its stream is hidden in the sheets of ice.

Firozpur. *City, northwestern India*. The city, in Punjab state, was founded by *Firuz* Shah Tughluq (reigned 1351–88), sultan of Delhi, and is named for him, with Hindi *pur*, "town," added.

Firth of Forth *see* **Forth**

Firuzabad. *Town, southern Iran*. The town, said to have been founded in the 3d century A.D., was originally known as *Gur*, from Iranian *gūr*, "grave." This was changed as now in the mid–10th century when it was felt to have undesirable connotations. The present name thus means "town of victory," from Iranian *firuz*, "victorious," and *abad*, "town."

Fishguard. *Town and port, southwestern Wales*. The Pembrokeshire town has a Scandinavian name, from Old Norse *fiskr*, "fish," and *garthr*, "yard." The original "fish yard" here would have been for trapping fish or for keeping them in when trapped. The Welsh name of Fishguard is *Abergwaun*, "mouth of the *Gwaun* (River)," for

its location. The river's own name represents Welsh *gwaun*, "marsh," "moor."

¹Fitzroy. *River, northwestern Australia*. The river, in Western Australia, was explored by Lieutenant John Stokes of HMS *Beagle* in 1838 and named by him for the British naval officer Robert *Fitzroy* (1805–1865), a former captain of the ship (which sailed around the world with Charles Darwin aboard as naturalist).

²Fitzroy. *River, eastern Australia*. The river, in Queensland, is named for Sir Charles *Fitz Roy*, governor of New South Wales (which then extended to here) from 1845 to 1855.

Fiume *see* **Rijeka**

Flagstaff. *City, southwestern United States*. The Arizona city gained its name in 1876, when lumberjacks celebrating the 4th of July nailed an American flag to the top of a tall ponderosa pine here and called the as yet unnamed settlement *Flagstaff*.

Flaminian Way. *Roman road, central Italy*. The ancient road, running between Rome and Rimini, is named for the Roman general Gaius *Flaminius*, who built it in 220 B.C. Its Roman name was *Via Flaminia*.

Flanders. *Historic region, northwestern Belgium*. The region has a Flemish name that probably represents *vlakte*, "plain," and *wanderen*, "to wander," implying a flat and extensive region. The name is still in use today for the two Belgian provinces of *East Flanders* and *West Flanders*. The current Flemish form of the name is *Vlaanderen*, and the French form *Flandre*.

Fleetwood. *Town and port, northwestern England*. The Lancashire town has a modern name by British standards. It derives from that of its founder in the 1830s, Sir Peter Hesketh *Fleetwood* (1801–1866). The name is coincidentally appropriate for a maritime town, which could have arisen by a *fleet* or stream flowing out of a *wood*.

Flensburg. *City and port, northern Germany*. The city derives its name from Old Danish *flen*, "fork prong," and *burg*, "fort," probably referring to the pointed head of Flensburger Fjord where it arose in the 12th century.

Flinders Ranges. *Mountain region, southern Australia*. The mountains, in South Australia, take their name from the English explorer Matthew *Flinders* (1774–1814), who sighted them in 1802 from Spencer Gulf on the south coast.

Flin Flon. *City, south central Canada*. The Manitoba city, on the border with Saskatchewan, derived its name from a fictional prospector, Professor Josiah *Flin*abbatey *Flon*atin, in J.E. Preston-Muddock's dime novel *The Sunless City*

(1905), a copy of which is said to have been found on the site in 1913.

Flint. *Town, northeastern Wales.* The town and its county have a name that means what it says, referring to the hard rock here on which Flint Castle was built in the 13th century.

¹Florence. *City, central Italy.* The city had the Roman name of *Colonia Florentia,* "flowering colony," referring either literally to its abundance of flowers or figuratively to its "flourishing" growth and expansion. This is the generally accepted origin of the name, although the 16th-century Italian sculptor and writer Benvenuto Cellini claimed a source in Latin *Fluentia,* "flowing," referring to the location of Florence on the Arno River. The modern Italian form of the name is *Firenze,* evolving from Old Italian *Fiorenza.*

²Florence. *City, southeastern United States.* The Alabama city was founded in 1818 and named for ¹Florence, Italy, by its Italian surveyor, Ferdinand Sanona.

³Florence. *City, eastern United States.* The South Carolina city was founded in the 1850s and was originally called *Wilds,* for a local judge. In c.1859 it was renamed as now for *Florence* Harllee, daughter of William W. Harllee, a local railroad official.

Flores Sea. *Sea, southern Indonesia.* The sea, between the eastern end of the Java Sea and western end of the Banda Sea, takes its name from the island of *Flores* here. The island's own name is Portuguese for "flowers," alluding to its rich flora.

Florianópolis. *City and port, southern Brazil.* The city was founded by the Spanish in 1542 but in 1675 passed to the Portuguese, who in 1700 established a convict settlement here called *Desterro,* "exile," "banishment." The town retained this name until 1893, when it was renamed as now in honor of the Brazilian president *Floriano* Peixoto (1842–1895).

Florida. *State, southeastern United States.* The state, occupying a prominent peninsula, derives its name from Spanish *florida,* "flowering," perhaps originally with reference to the region's fertile vegetation, but more likely representing *Pascua florida,* literally "flowering Easter," as the Spanish name of Palm Sunday. This would then historically refer to March 20, 1513, the day when the expedition of the Spanish explorer Ponce de León discovered the peninsula.

¹Flushing. *Town and port, southwestern Netherlands.* This form of the name is an English corruption of the town's Dutch name, *Vlissingen.* It has a basic sense "flowing," "current" (modern Dutch *fluissen,* "to flow strongly," related to English *flush*), referring to the town's location at the mouth of the West Scheldt estuary.

²Flushing. *Historic village, eastern United States.* The original settlement in what is now the Queens district of New York City was established in 1645 by English Puritans who had been living in ¹**Flushing** (Vlissingen) in the Netherlands.

Foça *see* **Phocaea**

Foggia. *City, southeastern Italy.* The name is said to come from a local dialect word for a type of grain store, itself going back to Latin *fovea,* "pit," and so related to *fovere,* "to keep warm."

Föhr. *Island, northern Germany.* The North Sea island, in the North Frisian Islands, derives its name from Old High German *faran,* "to travel," giving a sense on the lines of "passage," "way through," perhaps because it had to be passed by boats sailing to islands further from the shore.

Foligno. *Town, central Italy.* The town was known to the Romans as *Fulginium,* from its legendary founder, one *Fulginius.*

Folkestone. *Town and port, southeastern England.* The Kent town has a name of Old English origin meaning "*Folca's* stone," from an Anglo-Saxon personal name, rather than "people's stone," as sometimes explained, as if the first part of the name represented *folc,* "people" (modern *folk*). The stone itself would probably have been a meeting point, and Folkestone is known to have been the center of its hundred (county subdivision).

Fond du Lac. *City, northern United States.* The city arose in 1785 as a French trading post at the southern end of Lake Winnebago. Hence its name, French for "bottom of the lake."

Fontainebleau. *Town, northern France.* The town's name was recorded in the 12th century as *fontem Blahaud,* from Latin *fons, fontis,* "spring," and a personal name of Germanic origin. The spring here would have been owned by this man, or associated with him in some way.

Fontenay-le-Comte. *Town, western France.* The main part of the town's name goes back to Latin *fontanum,* a derivative of *fons, fontis,* "spring." The second part, meaning "the count," relates to the count whom Louis IX of France appointed here in the 13th century when he made the town the capital of Bas-Poitou. There are several places in France with similar names, such as *Fontenai, Fontenoy, Fontenelle,* etc., all from the same source, and many with distinguishing additions, as here.

Foochow *see* **Fu-chou**

Forbach. *Town, northeastern France.* The town has a name of Old German origin, from *forha*, "Scots pine," and *bach*, "stream."

Forchheim. *City, southeastern Germany.* The city derives its name from Old High German *forha*, "Scots pine," and *heim*, "house," "abode," denoting a settlement among the named trees.

Forest of Dean *see* **Dean, Forest of**

Forez. *Historic region, central France.* The region takes its name from Latin *Forensis pagus*, "land of *Feurs*," from the town of *Feurs*, Loire, its former capital. Its own name, from Latin *forum*, "public square," "market," was recorded in the 4th century as *Forum Segusiavorum*, from the *Segusiavi* tribe, whose capital it was. Their name in turn is based on Gaulish *sego-*, "victory," "strength."

Forfar. *Town, eastern Scotland.* The town has a Gaelic name which probably means "ridge wood," from Old Gaelic *fothir fàire*, although it is possible the second word was originally *faire*, "watching," referring to a lookout site here. If so, it would not have been the town itself, which is on level ground, but on a nearby hill. The name is also that of a former county here.

Forlì. *City, northern Italy.* The city was known to the Romans as *Forum Livii*, "*Livius*'s market," said to refer to its founder in the 2d century B.C., *Livius* Salinator. The present name evolved as a reduced form of the Latin name.

Formentera. *Island, western Mediterranean Sea.* The fourth largest island of the Balearic group derives its name from Catalan *forment*, "wheat" (Latin *frumentum*, "corn"), so that it is the "island of wheat."

Formosa *see* **Taiwan**

Forst. *City, eastern Germany.* The city, by the Polish border, derives its name from Old High German *forst*, "nobleman's woodland" (English *forest*).

Fortaleza. *City and port, northeastern Brazil.* The city arose in the early 17th century from a small village by a Portuguese fort built to provide defense against attack from Native Americans. Its name is thus simply the Portuguese word for "fortress."

Fort Collins. *City, west central United States.* The Colorado city arose after 1864 around a fort named for its commander, Lieutenant William O. *Collins* (1809–1880) of Fort Laramie.

Fort-de-France. *Capital of Martinique.* The city was founded in 1640 at a time when Martinique, in the West Indies, had not long been settled by the French, and it was thus given a name, meaning "fort of France," that related to its status as an "outpost."

Forth. *River, south central Scotland.* The river has a Celtic name deriving from a root word meaning "silent one," referring to its slow current. In the name of its estuary, *Firth of Forth*, *firth* is a word of Scandinavian origin related to Norwegian *fjord* and so to English *ford*. The estuary name has a Celtic word order, as in *Mull of Kintyre*, where the generic Celtic word would originally have been followed by the specific name in the genitive case. The Gaelic name of the Forth is *Abhainn dubh*, "black river."

Fort-Lamy *see* **N'djamena**

Fort Lauderdale. *City, southeastern United States.* The Florida city was founded in 1895 and arose around the fort that was apparently named for Major William *Lauderdale*, leader of an expedition against the Seminole in 1838.

Fort Myers. *City, southeastern United States.* The Florida city arose around a fort built for defense against the Seminole in 1839 and named for General Abraham C. *Myers* (1811–1889).

Fort Portal. *Town, western Uganda.* The town is named for the British diplomat Sir Gerald *Portal* (1858–1894), sent here by the government in 1893 to report whether the British should retain this region of Africa or leave it. The town was founded that year and was initially known as *Fort Gerry*.

Fort Smith. *Region, northern Canada.* The southwestern district of the Northwest Territories is named for the town that was the former territorial capital. Its own name comes from Donald A. *Smith*, governor of the Hudson's Bay Company, which set up a post on the Slave River here in 1874. The district was formed in the early 1970s by the territorial government from a large part of the former district of *Mackenzie*, itself named for its chief river. *See* **Mackenzie**.

Fort Wayne. *City, east central United States.* The Indiana city takes its name from General "Mad" Anthony *Wayne* (1745–1796), who constructed a log stockade here in 1794 after the Battle of Fallen Timbers. There had earlier been a French trading post here.

Fort William. *Town, northwestern Scotland.* The town takes its name from the fort here, originally built in 1655 but rebuilt in 1690 and named for the reigning monarch, *William* III (1650–1702).

Fort Worth. *City, southern United States.* The Texas city takes its name from General William J. *Worth* (1794–1849), hero of the Mexican War (1846–48) and commander of the troops in Texas at the time of its foundation as a frontier outpost in 1849.

Fo-shan. *City, southeastern China.* The city,

in Kwangtung province, has a name meaning "mountain of the Buddha," from Chinese *fó*, "Buddha," and *shān*, "mountain." Its original name was *Nan-hai*, from Chinese *nán*, "south," and *hǎi*, "sea."

Fosse Way. *Roman road, England*. The ancient route between Lincoln and Exeter is so named because it had a *fosse* or ditch on either side.

Fossombrone. *Town, central Italy*. The town was known to the Romans as *forum Sempronii*, "market of *Sempronius*," and this gave the present name.

Fougères. *Town, northwestern France*. The town had the Medieval Latin name of *Fulgerii*, from *filicaria*, "fern" (modern French *fougère*).

Foulness. *Island, southeastern England*. The Essex island is noted for its wildfowl and has a name directly relating to this. It comes from Old English *fugol*, "bird" (modern German *Vogel*, English *fowl*), and *næss*, "promontory." The latter word implies that the island was at one time part of the mainland.

Fouta Djallon. *Mountainous region, western Guinea*. The region takes its name from Mande *fouta*, "plain," and the *Dialonke* people who formerly inhabited it. Their own name derives from Mande *dyalon*, "slope."

Framingham. *Town, northeastern United States*. The Massachusetts town was settled in 1650 and named for the English town of *Framlingham*, Suffolk, with which one or more of the settlers presumably had links.

France. *Republic, western Europe*. The country takes its name from the *Franks,* the Germanic people who spread from the east into Gaul in the 4th century A.D. The origin of their name is disputed. It may derive from an Old German word *franka*, "brave" (modern English *frank*), or come from a personal name *Francio* or *Francus*. A recent theory suggests a source in the Germanic word *wrang*, from *wringen*, "to wring," "to wrench," so that the meaning is "the wrenched ones," referring to people uprooted from their original homeland. The German name of France is *Frankreich*, "kingdom of the Franks." *See also* **Franconia**, **Frankfurt**.

Franceville. *Town, southeastern Gabon*. The town was founded in 1880 by the French explorer Pierre Savorgnan de Brazza (*see* **Brazzaville**) and named by him for his native land.

Franche-Comté. *Historic region, east central France*. The name translates literally as "free county." The reference is to the *county* of Burgundy, as distinct from the *duchy* of Burgundy further west (the Burgundy of today). In 1361 the duchy escheated (reverted) to the French crown, to which it had previously belonged, but the county remained a domain of Margaret I, widow of the count of Flanders. It was thus a "free county," since it had not passed to the crown.

Francistown. *Town, eastern Botswana*. The town is named for the British goldminer and prospector Daniel *Francis* (1840–1920), who visited the site in 1869 and was subsequently granted land here by the Matabele chief Lobengula.

Franconia. *Historic region, south central Germany*. The former duchy has a Medieval Latin name derived from that of the *Franks*, who inhabited it from the 7th century. For the origin of their own name, *see* **France**.

Frankenthal. *City, southwestern Germany*. The city arose from a Frankish village recorded in 772 as *Franconadal*. Hence its name, meaning "valley (settlement) of the *Franks*." The original village lay right by the Rhine, but the river later changed its course here.

Frankfort. *City, east central United States*. The state capital of Kentucky was founded in 1786 and originally named *Frank's Ford*, for Stephen *Frank*, a frontiersman killed in 1780 at a ford here over the Kentucky River. The present form of the name was probably influenced by Germany's **Frankfurt**.

Frankfurt. *City, west central Germany*. The city's name means "ford of the *Franks*," referring to the point where it arose, by a crossing on the Main River used by the Frankish army. It is distinguished from its namesake in eastern Germany by the addition of the river name as *Frankfurt am Main*. The eastern Frankfurt, with a name of identical origin, is similarly specified as *Frankfurt an der Oder*. For the origin of the name of the Franks, *see* **France**.

Franklin. *Historic region, northern Canada*. The former district, in the northern Northwest Territories, was established in 1895 and named for the British explorer Sir John *Franklin* (1786–1847), who disappeared in the Arctic here in a search for the Northwest Passage.

Františkovy Lázně. *Town and resort, western Czech Republic*. The resort, with its mineral springs, was founded in 1791 under the German name of *Franzensbad*, "*Francis*'s spring," so called in honor of the Holy Roman Emperor *Francis* II (1768–1835), later *Francis* I of Austria. The present name is the Czech equivalent of this. *Cp.* **Mariánské Lázně**.

Franz Josef Land. *Island group, northwestern Russia*. The islands, in the Arctic Ocean, were discovered in 1873 by the Austrian expedition of Julius von Payer and Carl Weyprecht and named by them for the Austrian emperor *Franz Josef* I (1830–1916). For some time the archipelago was also known as *Fridtjof Nansen Land*, for the Norwegian explorer, who visited the islands in 1896.

Frascati. *Town, central Italy*. The town arose around the 9th-century church of St Mary and St. Sebastian *in frascata* (Italian, "in the bushes"), and takes its name from this locational description.

Fraser. *River, southwestern Canada*. The river, in British Columbia, is so named for the American-Canadian fur trader Simon *Fraser* (1776–1862), who explored the Rocky Mountains in 1806–08 and who journeyed down the river, mistakenly supposing it to be the Columbia.

Frauenfeld. *Town, northeastern Switzerland*. The name amounts to "Our Lady's field," as the land here belonged to the abbot of Reichenau, where the Benedictine abbey is dedicated to the Virgin Mary. (The German equivalent of "Our Lady" is *Unsere Liebe Frau*, literally "our dear woman.")

Fray Bentos. *City, western Uruguay*. The city was founded in 1859 and has a Spanish name meaning "Brother Benedict," that of an 18th-century religious hermit of the region.

Frechen. *City, western Germany*. The name was originally that of a stream here now known as the *Frechener Bach*. Its own name derives from the Germanic adjective *freka*, "greedy" (English dialect *freck*), and the river-name suffix *-ana*, denoting a stream with a rapid current.

Fredericia. *City and port, central Denmark*. The city, in eastern Jutland, is named for *Frederick* III of Denmark (1609–1670), who founded it in 1650 as a fortress to defend Jutland.

Fredericksburg. *City, eastern United States*. The Virginia city was laid out in 1727 and named for Prince *Frederick* Louis (1707–1751), son of George II and father of George III.

Fredericton. *City, eastern Canada*. The capital of New Brunswick was laid out in 1785 and named for Prince *Frederick* Augustus (1763–1827), second son of George III. The original form of the name was *Frederick Town*, but it subsequently coalesced as now.

Frederiksberg. *City, eastern Denmark*. The city, now a district of Copenhagen, was settled by *Frederick* III of Denmark (1609–1670) in 1651 and named for him. *Cp.* **Frederiksborg**.

Frederiksborg. *County, eastern Denmark*. The county takes its name from *Frederiksborg* Castle, Hillerød, built in 1602–20 by Christian IV of Denmark and named for his son, the fu-

ture *Frederick* III (1609–1670). *Cp.* **Frederiksberg**.

Frederikshavn. *City and port, northern Denmark*. The city was originally a fishing village called *Fladstrand*, "flat beach." It gained its present name in 1818 when it was chartered. The name, meaning "*Frederick*'s harbor," honors *Frederick* VI of Denmark (1768–1839).

Fredrikstad. *Town and port, southeastern Norway*. The town is named for *Frederick* II of Norway (1534–1588) who founded it as a fortress town in 1567.

Freeport. *Town and port, northern Bahamas*. The town, on the south coast of Grand Bahama, was founded by the Bahamian government in 1955 as a "free port" in which businesses and industries were to be licensed by a new port authority in return for tax exemptions and other privileges for 99 years.

Free State. *See* **Orange Free State**.

Freetown. *Capital of Sierra Leone*. The city was founded in 1787 as a haven for freed or rescued African slaves sent from England by British abolitionists. Hence the name.

Freiberg. *City, eastern Germany*. The city was founded in the late 12th century as a silver-mining community and its name refers to the extensive mining rights that were subsequently granted to the "free miner" (German *Freiberger*).

Freiberg am Neckar. *Town, southwestern Germany*. The town, now a suburb of Stuttgart on the **Neckar** River, was formed in 1972 on the unification of the three small villages *Beihingen*, *Geisingen*, and *Heutingsheim*. It took the name of a historic estate at Beihingen, itself named after the lords of *Freyberg*, who came from the castle so called ("free fort") near Biberach, but with *y* changed to *i*.

Freiburg. *City, southwestern Germany*. The city was founded in 1120 by the dukes of Zähringen as a free market town. Hence its name, from the equivalent of modern German *frei*, "free," and *Burg*, "fort," "town." The same dukes founded **Fribourg**, named similarly. The city is sometimes called *Freiburg im Breisgau*, for distinction from *Freiburg in Schlesien*, now *Świebodzice*, southwestern Poland, which translates the name. *Breisgau*, a district between the Rhine and the Black Forest, has a name meaning "*Brisios*' district," with a Gaulish personal name.

Freising. *City, southern Germany*. The town, growing from the site of a castle in the 8th century, has a name meaning "(settlement of) *Frigis*'s people," with an Old Bavarian personal name.

Freital. *City, eastern Germany*. The town arose

in a broad valley (*Tal*) in 1921 on the amalgamation of three villages. (Nine more were added between 1922 and 1974.) The name was based on that of **Freiberg**, since both towns had coal mining as their main industry.

Fréjus. *Town, southeastern France.* The town was founded by *Julius* Caesar in 49 B.C. and originally bore the Latin name *Forum Julii*, "*Julius's* market." Its present name is a conflation of these two words. *Cp.* **Friuli**.

Fremantle. *City and port, southwestern Australia.* The city, in Western Australia, was founded in 1829 and named for Captain Charles *Fremantle* (1800–1869), the British naval officer who brought the first settlers here.

Fremont. *City, southwestern United States.* The California city was formed in 1956 through the amalgamation of five communities and named for John C. *Frémont* (1813–1890), the American mapmaker and explorer of the Far West.

French Guiana. *State, northeastern South America.* The country, an overseas department of France, derives its main name from that of the extensive region here. *See* **Guyana**. It has been a *French* overseas region since 1637. *See also* **Cayenne**.

Fresno. *City, southwestern United States.* The California city was settled in 1872 with its name the Spanish word for "ash tree," these being native to the area.

Freudenberg. *Town, western Germany.* The town takes its name from the frontier fortress of the counts of Nassau around which it arose in the late 14th century. The fort has a name found elsewhere meaning "castle of joy," implying a happy outcome in any attack or defense.

Freudenstadt. *City, southwestern Germany.* The city was founded in 1599 by Duke Frederick I of Württemberg as a model town, designed by his architect Heinrich Schickhardt in the Renaissance style. Its first inhabitants were miners from the nearby silver mines, then manual workers in general. Its main occupants, however, were Protestant refugees from Carinthia and Styria, and it was they who inspired the expressive name, German for "town of joy," adopted in 1601.

Fribourg. *City, western Switzerland.* The city has a name meaning "free fort." It was founded in 1157 by the dukes of Zähringen as a military post to control a ford over the Saane River here. *Cp.* **Freiburg**.

Friedberg. *Town, central Germany.* The town arose in the late 12th century on the site of a Roman fort known as *castellum in monte Tauno*, "castle on Mt. Taunus." The German name

means "castle of defense," from Old High German *fridu*, "protection," "safety." A smaller town of the same name in southern Germany has a similar origin but with the name implying "royal protection," since the castle was built to defend a ducal customs post by a bridge over the Leck River.

Friedrichroda. *Town, central Germany.* The town and resort, first mentioned in the 11th century, has a name meaning "*Friedrich's* clearing," for its founder, one *Friedrich* (Frederick).

Friedrichsdorf. *Town, western Germany.* The town was founded in 1687 by 27 Huguenot families, who had been granted land here by Landgrave *Frederick* II of Hesse-Homburg (1633–1681).

Friedrichshafen. *City, southwestern Germany.* The city, on Lake Constance, was founded in 1811 on the amalgamation of the free city of *Buchhorn* with the secular monastery and village of *Klosten* and named "*Frederick's* harbor" for *Frederick* I of Württemberg (1754–1816), who had established a number of trading and industrial centers between the two places.

Friedrichstadt. *Town, northwestern Germany.* The name means "*Frederick's* town," for Duke *Frederick* III of Schleswig-Holstein-Gottorp (1597–1659), who founded a settlement here for Dutch Arminians in 1621.

Friendly Islands *see* **Tonga**

Friesland. *Province, northern Netherlands.* The province is named for its original inhabitants, the *Frisians*, who also gave the name of the **Frisian Islands**.

Frisian Islands. *Island chain, southeastern North Sea.* The islands, off the coast of the Netherlands, Germany, and Denmark, take their name from their indigenous people, known to the Romans as the *Frisii*. Their name is generally said to derive either from Old High German *fri*, "free," or from Old Frisian *frisiaz*, "frizzy," referring to their curly hair. A source in Indoeuropean *fers* or *fars*, "coast," has also been proposed, and seems more likely.

Fritzlar. *Town, western Germany.* The town arose around a Benedictine abbey founded by St. Boniface in 724. Its name derives from Old High German *fridu*, "protection," "safety," and -*lar*, "enclosure" (as for **Goslar** and **Wetzlar**). There may have been an earlier pagan place of worship here.

Friuli. *Historic region, northeastern Italy.* The present name is a much eroded form of the region's Roman name *Forum Julii*, "market place of *Julius*," i.e. of *Julius* Caesar. *Cp.* **Fréjus**.

Frobisher Bay. *Bay, northern Canada.* The

bay, in southeastern Baffin Island, Nunavut, is named for the English navigator Sir Martin *Frobisher* (c.1535–1594), who discovered it in 1576.

Frunze *see* **Bishkek**

Fu-chou. *City and river port, southeastern China.* The capital of Fukien province derives its name from Chinese *fú*, "happiness," and *zhōu*, "region." *Cp.* **Fukien**. The conventional English form of the name is *Foochow*.

Fuego. *Volcano, southern Guatemala.* The volcano's name is the Spanish word for "fire."

Fuente Obejuna. *City, southern Spain.* The city's name means "sheep spring," from Spanish *fuente*, "fountain," "spring," and the adjective *ovejuna*, "sheep." The name was formerly a single word, *Fuenteovejuna*.

Fuenterrabía. *City, northwestern Spain.* The city, known to the French as *Fontarabie*, is popularly said to derive its name either from Latin *fons rapidus*, "rapid spring," or Spanish *fuente*, "spring," and the invading *Arabs* against whom the original fortress here was built. But the city is in the Basque Country and its Basque name, by which it is now often known, is *Hondarribia*, meaning "sandy river."

Fuji, Mt. *Mountain, central Japan.* The extinct volcano has a name of uncertain meaning. The two Japanese ideographs that phonetically make up the basic name can be understood as "prosperous man," but this is hardly the actual sense. A meaning "fire spitter" or "incomparable" has been suggested. The Japanese toponymist Kagami has interpreted the name as "beauty of the long slope hanging in the sky," but this seems unduly elaborate, even allowing for poetic license. The mountain is also known as *Fujiyama*, with *yama* simply the Japanese for "mountain."

Fujinomiya. *City, central Japan.* The city, in the island of Honshu at the foot of Mt. **Fuji**, arose around the Sengen Shrine, the main shrine for the worship of Mt. Fuji since the 9th century. Hence its name, meaning "shrine of *Fuji*," with the mountain's name followed by Japanese *no*, "of," and *miya*, "Shinto shrine."

Fujisawa. *City, eastern Japan.* The city, in the island of Honshu, derives its name from Japanese *fuji*, "wistaria," and *sawa*, "marsh."

Fujiyama *see* **Fuji, Mt.**

Fukien. *Province, southeastern China.* The province has a name meaning "happy colony," from Chinese *fú*, "happiness," and *jiàn*, "to found," "to establish." *Cp.* **Fu-chou**.

Fukui. *Prefecture, western Japan.* The prefecture, in the island of Honshu, with its capital city of the same name, derives its name from

Japanese *fuku*, "fortune," "blessing," and *i*, "well."

Fukuoka. *City and port, southern Japan.* The city, in the island of Kyushu, has a name meaning "hill of happiness," from Japanese *fuku*, "fortune," "happiness," and *oka*, "hill." *Cp.* **Fukushima, Fukuyama**.

Fukushima. *City, central Japan.* The city, in the island of Honshu, has a name meaning "island of happinesss," from Japanese *fuku*, "fortune," "happiness," and *shima*, "island." *Cp.* **Fukuoka, Fukuyama**. The region here is not literally an island, but is mountainous, with many lakes and swamps.

Fukuyama. *City, southern Japan.* The city, in the island of Honshu, has a name meaning "mountain of happiness," from Japanese *fuku*, "fortune," "happiness," and *yama*, "mountain." *Cp.* **Fukuoka, Fukushima**.

Fulda. *City, central Germany.* The city takes its name from the *Fulda* River here. The river's name derives from Old High German *fulta*, "land" (related to German *Feld*, "field"), and *aha*, "water."

Funabashi. *City, eastern Japan.* The city, in the island of Honshu on the inner coast of Tokyo Bay, has a name meaning "floating bridge," from Japanese *fune*, "ship," "boat," and *hashi*, "bridge."

Funafuti. *Capital of Tuvalu.* The town has the same name as its island, whose own name may represent a Polynesian word *futi*, "banana," or else *Futi*, the name of one of the wives of a local ruler, with *funa-* added as a feminine prefix.

Funchal. *Capital of Madeira.* The city and port, on the south coast of the Ilha da Madeira, was founded in 1421 by the Portuguese explorer João Gonçalves Zarco, who named it for the abundance of fennel (Portuguese *fenolh*) growing on the nearby cliffs.

Fundy, Bay of. *Bay, eastern Canada.* The bay, between New Brunswick and Nova Scotia, has a name of uncertain origin. Portuguese *fondo*, "deep," and French *fendu*, "split," have been suggested. If the latter, the reference could be to the way in which the bay "splits" Nova Scotia from the mainland.

Funen *see* **Fyn**

Furneaux Islands. *Island group, southeastern Australia.* The islands, off the northeast coast of Tasmania, are named for the English ship's captain Tobias *Furneaux* (1735–1781), who discovered them in 1773 as a member of James Cook's expedition.

Fürstenfeldbruck. *City, southern Germany.* The town has a name first recorded in 1678 and officially adopted in 1908. The original name of the settlement was *Bruck*, "bridge," referring to the saltway over the Amper River laid out by Henry the Lion in the 12th century. In 1258 Duke Ludwig the Strict founded a Cistercian abbey here but in 1263 moved it to a nearby estate of his called *Fürstenfeld*, "field of the prince" (meaning "field of the duke"). Hence the name.

Fürstenwalde. *City, eastern Germany.* The city was founded on the Spree River in c.1254 by the margraves of Brandenburg. Its name, meaning "princely woodland clearing," denotes its noble origin.

Fürth. *City, southern Germany.* The city arose in the 8th century at the point where the road from Frankfurt am Main to Regensburg crossed the Rednitz River. Hence its name, meaning "ford."

Furtwangen. *City, southwestern Germany.* The city arose by a crossing of the Breg River at a site recorded in 805 as *Wangen*, "(place) by the meadows." *Furt* ("ford") was added by the 12th century.

Fu-shun. *City, northeastern China.* The city, in Liaoning province, derives its name from Chinese *fǔ*, "to comfort," "to console," and *shùn*, "along," "to obey."

Fu-sin. *City, northeastern China.* The city, in Liaoning province, derives its name from Chinese *fù*, "mound," "abundant," and *xīn*, "new."

Füssen. *City, southern Germany.* The city arose on the site of a Roman frontier station mentioned in a Latin inscription of the 3rd to 5th century A.D. referring to a *praepositus militum Fotensium*, "officer of the soldiers of *Fotensium*." Excavations later revealed a 5th-century Roman fort named (in the locative plural) as *Foetibus*. Both these names have latinized forms of Germanic *fōt*, "foot," describing the site of the original settlement here at the foot of the Allgäu Alps. *Cp.* **Piedmont.**

Fyn. *Island, central Denmark.* The island, between mainland Jutland, to the west, and Sjælland, to the east, has a name that may mean "pasture" or "abounding in cattle." An alternate form is *Funen*.

Gabès. *Town and port, southeastern Tunisia.* The town's name ultimately goes back to its Punic form *Takape*. The meaning of this is uncertain, but it could relate to a damp or irrigated place.

Gabon. *Republic, western Africa.* The country takes its name from that of the river here. When the Portuguese discovered its estuary in the late 15th century, they named it *Gabão*, the Por-

tuguese word for "hood," presumably on account of its shape or for the "hood" of jungle foliage from which the river debouched.

Gaborone. *Capital of Botswana.* The city was founded in the late 1950s and named for a local Tswana king (chieftain), who reigned here from 1880 to 1931.

Gabrovo. *Town, central Bulgaria.* The town takes its name from Bulgarian *gabar*, "hornbeam," a tree that formerly flourished here.

Gadsden. *City, southeastern United States.* The Alabama city was founded in 1846 and was at first known as *Double Springs*. It was soon renamed for James *Gadsden* (1788–1858), the American soldier and diplomat who negotiated the *Gadsden* Purchase of Mexican territory in 1853.

Gaeta. *Town and port, western Italy.* The town had the Roman name of *Caieta*, itself deriving from Greek *kaiata*, "lowland," describing the terrain here northwest of Naples.

Gaggenau. *City, southwestern Germany.* The city, on the Murg River, has a name meaning "*Gacko*'s riverside (settlement)," from Old High German *auwa*, "island," "land by water." The name has been popularly explained as "cackling meadow," from German *gackern*, "to cackle," and *Au*, "meadow," and this has given rise to a local legend about a gosling.

Gaillard Cut. *Section of Panama Canal, central Panama.* The southeastern section of the Panama Canal, *cut* through Culebra Mountain, is named for the American engineer who planned its construction, David du Bose *Gaillard* (1859–1913).

Gainesville. *City, southeastern United States.* The Florida city developed around a trading post known as *Hog Town*, founded in 1830. In 1854 it was renamed for General Edmund P. *Gaines* (1777–1845), a commander during the War of 1812.

Galápagos Islands. *Island group, eastern Pacific.* The islands, off the west coast of Ecuador, South America, are so named for the giant land tortoises (*galápagos*) that the Spanish found here on landing in 1535. The discoverer was Tomás de Berlanga, bishop of Panama, who originally called the islands *Las Encantadas* ("the enchanted ones"). The names of the five largest islands encapsulate much of Spain's royal and religious heritage: *Fernandina, Isabela, Santa Cruz, San Salvador, San Cristóbal.*

Galata. *District of Istanbul, northwestern Turkey.* The area where the Golden Horn meets the Bosporus is said to derive its name from Greek *gala*, "milk," referring to the many dairies here. But there is no historical evidence to support this, any more than there is for a derivation from Italian *calata*, "invasion."

Galaţi. *City and river port, southeastern Romania*. The city probably takes its name from Latin *Galatia*, although evidence for a Roman settlement here remains uncertain. If there was such a settlement, its name could be related to that of **Galatia**. A Gaulish chief named Brennos has been mentioned in this connection.

Galatia. *Historic region, central Turkey*. The region was conquered by the Gauls in the 3d century B.C. and has a name that is directly related to, and based on, that of **Gaul** itself.

¹**Galicia**. *Historic region, central Europe*. The region may have a name that ultimately derives from Lithuanian *galas*, "end," "peak," referring to the mountains here. Some authorities, however, prefer to relate the name to that of **Gaul**.

²**Galicia**. *Historic region, northwestern Spain*. The region may take its name from a Celtic root word *cala*, "watercourse," alluding to the local people, who lived near the sea. Some authorities, however, prefer to relate the name to that of **Gaul**.

Galilee. *Region, northern Israel*. The region takes its name from Hebrew *gālil*, "district," "circle," a noun which, in the construct state, requires a genitival noun. Hence the biblical "Galilee of the nations," Hebrew *gālil goyim* (Isaiah 9:1). The "nations" would have been the foreigners who came to settle here, or who had been forcibly deported here. The region in turn gave the name of the *Sea of Galilee*. The lake (as it properly is) is also known as *Sea of Chinnereth* (Numbers 34:11, etc.), from Hebrew *kinnor*, "harp," describing its shape, *Lake of Gennesaret* (Luke 5:1, etc.), from Hebrew *ge*, "valley," and either *netser*, "branch," or *natsor*, "to guard," "to watch" (the name may have given that of **Nazareth**), and *Sea of Tiberias* (John 6:1, etc.), from the town of *Tiberias* at its southwestern end, named for the 1st-century A.D. Roman emperor *Tiberius*.

Galle. *City and port, southern Sri Lanka*. The city, on the Indian Ocean, takes its name from Sanskrit *galla*, "stone," "rock," referring to its location on a rocky promontory. Hence its earlier name of *Point de Galle*. The Portuguese, here in the 17th century, associated the name with *galo*, "cock," "rooster," which explains the depiction of this bird in the city's coat of arms.

Gallipoli. *Town and port, northwestern Turkey*. The town's name has evolved from Greek *Kallipolis*, "beautiful town," from *kalos*, "beautiful," and *polis*, "town." This also gave the mod-

ern Turkish name of the town, which is *Gelibolu*. (Popular etymology renders this as "full of roses," from Turkish *gül*, "rose," and *bol*, "abundant.") An identically named town and port in southern Italy has the same origin.

Galloway. *Region, southwestern Scotland*. The region takes its name from the people who formerly inhabited this peninsula. They were known in Gaelic as the *Gall-Ghóidil*, "stranger Gaels," as a race of mixed Irish and Norse descent who settled here from the 9th century. For a name of partly similar origin, *see* **Argyll**.

Galveston. *City and port, southern United States*. The Texas city, on the island of the same name, was so named in 1777 by troops of Bernardo de *Gálvez* (1746–1786), Spanish governor of Louisiana (and later viceroy of Mexico).

Galway. *County, western Ireland*. The county takes its name from the town here. Its own name means "stony," from the Gaelic word that is modern Irish *gall*, "stone." The reference is both to the town's rocky location and to the stony bed of the Corrib River at the mouth of which it stands.

Gamala. *Historic city, central Palestine*. The ancient city, on the Golan Heights, derives its name from Aramaic *gamal*, "camel," referring to its site, on a dip between two hills, like a camel's humped back. In the Bible, Judas of Galilee (Acts 5:37), a more important figure than might be supposed, is also known as Judas of Gamala, or Judas the Gaulonite.

Gambia. *Republic, western Africa*. The country takes its name from its main river, which came to be so called by Portuguese explorers in the 15th century as a corruption of its indigenous name, *Ba-Dimma*. This means simply "the river."

Gambier Islands. *Island group, South Pacific*. The islands, in French Polynesia, were discovered in 1797 and named for the British naval commander James *Gambier*, 1st Baron Gambier (1756–1833).

Gampola. *Town, central Sri Lanka*. The name of the former capital is a smoothed form of the full name *Gangasiripura*, "royal city on the river," referring to the early kingdom set up here on the Mahaweli (Sanskrit *gaṅgā*, "river").

Gand *see* **Ghent**

Gander. *Town, eastern Canada*. The Newfoundland town takes its name from the lake here, itself so called for the many wild geese found in the area.

Gandhara. *Region, northwestern Pakistan*. The region, which extends into part of eastern Afghanistan, derives its name from its former inhabitants, whose own name is preserved in that of **Kandahar**.

Gandhinagar. *City, west central India*. Construction of the new capital of Gujarat state began in 1966, with the first government offices transferred here from nearby Ahmadabad in 1970. The city was named in honor of the Indian leader Mahatma *Gandhi* (1869–1948), with Hindi *nagar* meaning "city."

Gandzha *see* **Gyandzha**

Ganges. *River, northern India*. The most sacred river of the Hindus takes its name from Sanskrit *gaṅgā*, meaning simply "current," "river."

Gangtok. *City, northeastern India*. The capital of Sikkim state derives its name from Tibetan *gang*, "hill," and *tok*, "summit," describing its location above terraced slopes. It lies at an altitude of 5,600 feet (1,700 m).

Gan Shomron. *Settlement, western Israel*. The settlement, founded in 1934 in the Plain of Sharon, has a Hebrew name meaning "garden of **Samaria**."

Gao. *Town, eastern Mali*. The town derives its name from Fulani (Peul) *kunku*, "island," referring to its location on the Niger River. The Arabs corrupted this to *kawkaw*, which became *Gaogao*, and finally *Gao*.

Gap. *Town, southeastern France*. The town was known to the Roman as *Vapincum*, a name of obscure, possibly Ligurian, origin. Under French influence, the initial *V-* was regarded as a Germanic *W-*, so became *G-* (just as French *guerre*, "war," came from Frankish *werra*). The Provençal poet Frédéric Mistral claimed that the name came from *gavot*, "Gavot," a Provençal nickname, meaning "goitrous," for a local people who inhabited this region of the Alps.

Garda, Lake. *Lake, northern Italy*. The lake takes its name from that of the town here, its own name meaning "guard," "watchtower." The Roman name of the town was *Benacus*, "two waters," as Garda stands at the point where the lake divides into two bays.

Garland. *City, southern United States*. The Texas city was established in 1887 on the consolidation of the two communities of *Duck Creek* and *Embree*. It was named for Augustus H. *Garland* (1832–1899), governor of Arkansas and attorney general.

Garmisch-Partenkirchen. *Town, southern Germany*. The present town was formed in 1935 on the amalgamation of the two communities *Garmisch* and *Partenkirchen*. The former name means "*Germar*'s district," the latter "(settlement of the) *Parthians* by the church."

Garonne. *River, southwestern France*. The river's name goes back to a pre–Indoeuropean root word *kar* or *gar*, meaning "stone," "rock." *Cp*. **Caria**.

Gary. *City, east central United States*. The Indiana city, noted for its steel production, was founded in 1906 by the United States Steel Corporation and named for its chairman, Judge Elbert H. *Gary* (1846–1927).

Gascony. *Historic region, southwestern France*. The former province was known to the Romans as *Vasconia*, and the present name evolved from this. The Roman name itself refers to the *Basques* (see **Basque Country**), whose region this is.

Gastonia. *City, eastern United States*. The North Carolina city was settled in the late 18th century and named for the congressman and judge William *Gaston* (1778–1844).

Gatchina. *City, western Russia*. The city is said to take its name from the local word *gat*, used for a wooden causeway laid over marshland. From 1923 through 1929 it was renamed *Trotsk*, for the revolutionary leader Leon *Trotsky* (1879–1940), and from 1929 through 1944 *Krasnogvardeysk*, from Russian *Krasnaya Gvardiya*, "Red Guards," the title of the units of armed factory workers employed by the Bolsheviks to seize power at the time of the 1917 Revolution.

Gateshead. *Town, northeastern England*. The town, near Newcastle upon Tyne, has a name meaning "goat's head," from Old English *gāt*, "goat," and *hēafod*, "head," "headland." The reference is to the headland overlooking the Tyne River where goats were kept.

Gath. *Historic city, Israel*. The exact location of the ancient city, mentioned several times in the Bible (2 Samuel 1:20, etc.), is uncertain. Its name is usually translated "winepress" (*cp*. **Gethsemane**), although in Ugaritic texts the word *gat* refers to a processing center for agricultural products.

Gatineau. *City, southeastern Canada*. The Quebec city takes its name from the *Gatineau* River on which it lies. The river was itself named for the French fur trader Nicolas *Gatineau*, said to have drowned in its waters in c.1683.

Gaul. *Historic region, western Europe*. The region, corresponding approximately to modern France (although originally of much wider extent), was so named for its indigenous people, the *Gauls*. Their own name may represent a Gaulish word *gal* or *gala*, meaning "brave," or else be a form of a Celtic word meaning "white." Some authorities associate the name with a Germanic word *walho*, "stranger" (*cp*. **Wales**). France's national symbol, the cockerel, came into being through a similarity between Latin *Gal-*

lia, "Gaul" (or *Gallus,* "a Gaul"), and *gallus,* "cockerel," with a common link in the fighting spirit of both man and bird.

The Romans extended the name of the original Gaul to include northern Italy, where the region was known as *Gallia Cisalpina,* "Gaul this side of the **Alps**," as against Gaul proper, *Gallia Transalpina,* "Gaul across the Alps" (*see* **Provence**). The original Gaul was conquered by Caesar in the Gallic Wars of 58–50 B.C., his account of which famously mentioned its ethnic divisions: "*Gallia est omnis divisa in partes tres*" ("Gaul as a whole is divided into three parts"). These were: *Aquitania* (*see* **Aquitaine**), *Celtica* (modern central France), and *Belgica* (*see* **Belgium**). The three were jointly known as *Tres Galliae* ("three Gauls") or, disparagingly, *Gallia Comata* ("long-haired Gaul"). (The Romans at first saw the Gauls as barbarians.) *Gallia Celtica* was also known as *Gallia Lugdunensis,* for its capital, *Lugdunum* (*see* **Lyons**). These three provinces were later joined by *Narbonensis* (*see* **Narbonne**).

Gauri Shankar. *Mountain, south central Asia.* The mountain, in the Himalayas on the border between Nepal and Tibet, derives its name from Sanskrit *gaurī,* "white," "fair," a nickname of the goddess Parvati, wife of the Hindu god Shiva, and *shaṃkara,* "conferring happiness" (from *sham,* "auspicious," and *kara,* "making"), a nickname of Shiva himself. The mountain is traditionally regarded as the abode of both these gods. (Parvati's own name means "daughter of the mountains," and she is the daughter of Himavat, king of the mountains, himself a personification of the **Himalayas**.)

Gauteng. *Province, northeastern South Africa.* The smallest of the provinces created in South Africa in 1994 derives its name from Sotho *gauta,* itself ultimately from Afrikaans *goud,* "gold," and *teng,* "there," "inside," corresponding to the English nickname *Golden City* for **Johannesburg**. The Zulu name of Johannesburg is *eGoli* (or *Egoli*), with the same meaning. For a few months in 1994 Gauteng was originally known as the *PWV,* standing for *Pretoria-Witwatersrand-Vaal* (*Triangle*), denoting its geographic location around the cities of Pretoria and Johannesburg.

Gawler Ranges. *Mountain ranges, southern Australia.* The hill and mountain ranges in South Australia were first sighted in 1839 by the British explorer Edward John Eyre (*see* **Eyre, Lake**) and named by him for George *Gawler* (1795–1869), second governor of South Australia.

Gaza. *City and port, southwestern Palestine.* The name of the largest city of the Gaza Strip is an Arabic form of Hebrew *'az,* "force," "strength," referring to the original fortress here. The *Gaza Strip* itself, in what was formerly southwestern Palestine, is so called for its elongated shape by the Mediterranean, between Egypt and Israel. It came into being in 1949, after the first Arab-Israeli War.

Gaziantep. *City, south central Turkey.* The original medieval name of the city was *Hamtap,* of uncertain origin and meaning. Under the Ottoman Empire this name was reinterpreted as *Ayintab,* from Arabic *'ayn ṭab,* "good spring." Following occupation by the British and French the city was returned to Turkey in 1922 when it was renamed as now, from Turkish *gazi,* "war veteran," and a further form of the original name. The new name was given by Mustafa Kemal (later Atatürk), founder of the Turkish republic, and was meant to denote the city's heroic resistance to European occupation.

Gdańsk. *City and port, northern Poland.* The city has a Gothic name, from *Gutisk-anja,* "end of the *Goths,*" as these people's territory extended to here. The city's former German name, *Danzig,* misleadingly suggests an association with the *Danes.* Cp. **Gdynia**.

Gdynia. *City and port, northern Poland.* The Baltic port has a name of the same basic origin as that of **Gdańsk**, and the two cities are only 10 miles (16 km) apart. The German form of the name is *Gdingen*.

Geelong. *Town and port, southeastern Australia.* The town, in Victoria, has an Aboriginal name probably meaning "marshy place." According to some sources, however, the name represents Aboriginal *jillong,* said to mean "place of the companion," referring to a long-legged water bird that frequented the area.

Geislingen an der Steige. *City, southwestern Germany.* The city, on the Fils River, was founded in the 13th century and has a name meaning "(settlement of) *Gisilo*'s people." The second part of the name was added in 1903 to distinguish this town from two others identically named. It comes from a field name, itself from a mill, recorded in 1415 as *mulin vnder der Staig,* "mill below the steep road."

Gelderland. *Province, eastern Netherlands.* The province takes its name from the dukes whose castle, built in the 10th century, was at what is now the city of *Geldern* in western Germany. The origin of the name is uncertain. It is possible that *Geldara* was the name of a stretch of the Niers River here.

Gelsenkirchen. *City, western Germany.* The

present city was created in 1928 on the amalgamation of the three towns of *Gelsenkirchen*, *Buer*, and *Horst*, and until 1930 was known as *Gelsenkirchen-Buer*. The name apparently means "(place with a) church of yellow stone."

Gemlik. *Town and port, northwestern Turkey*. The port, on the Sea of Marmara, is said to derive its name from Turkish *gemlık*, "place of ships."

General San Martín. *City, eastern Argentina*. The city, a suburb of Buenos Aires, and originally known as *San Martín*, is named for the Argentine liberator José de *San Martín* (1778–1850).

General Santos. *City and port, southern Philippines*. The city, in southern Mindanao, was originally called *Buayan* but in 1954 was renamed for Paulino *Santos*, the Spanish army officer who directed the settlement of the Koronadal Valley here in the late 1930s.

General Sarmiento. *City, eastern Argentina*. The city, northwest of Buenos Aires, is named for Domingo Faustino *Sarmiento* (1811–1888), president of Argentina from 1868 to 1874.

Geneva. *City, southwestern Switzerland*. The city's name is probably of proto-Indoeuropean origin, from *gan*, "estuary," refering to Geneva's location at the point where the Rhône flows out of Lake Geneva. Some authorities, however, derive the name from an Indoeuropean root word *gen*, "bend" (modern French *genou*, "knee"), describing the curve of Lake Geneva at its southern end, where the city lies. The French name of Geneva is *Genève* and the German *Genf*. Cp. **Genoa**.

Gennesaret *see* **Galilee**

Genoa. *City and port, northwestern Italy*. The city lies at the head of the Gulf of Genoa and its name relates to this location, either from the Indoeuropean root word *gen*, "curve," "bend," or from proto-Indoeuropean *gan*, "mouth." The Italian form of the name is *Genova*. Cp. **Geneva**.

Gent *see* **Ghent**

George. *Town, southwestern South Africa*. The town, in Western Cape province, was originally named *Georgetown*, for *George* III of England (1738–1820), who presented a Bible to the church here. The present name was adopted in 1811.

¹George, Lake. *Lake, eastern United States*. The New York lake was visited by the French Jesuit missionary Father Isaac Jogues in 1646 and christened by him *Lac du Saint-Sacrament*, "lake of the Holy Sacrament." In 1755 the British army officer Sir William Johnson renamed it as now for *George* II of England (1683–1760). Its

Native American name is *Andiatarocte*, said to mean "place where the lake contracts."

²George, Lake. *Lake, southeastern Australia*. The lake, in New South Wales, was discovered by the British explorer Joseph Wild in 1820 and named for *George* IV of England (1762–1830).

Georgetown. *Capital of Guyana*. The city was founded by the English in 1781 and named by them in honor of *George* III (1738–1820). It was then occupied by the Dutch, who called it *Stabroek*, "stagnant pool," for its location at the mouth of the Demerara River. The English recaptured the town in 1812 (in the same king's reign) and restored the original name.

George Town. *City and port, western Malaysia*. The city, on the island of Penang, was founded in 1786 and was originally known as *Fort Cornwallis*, for Charles *Cornwallis*, 1st Marquis Cornwallis (1738–1805), governor general of India. It was subsequently renamed for *George* IV of England (1762–1830).

¹Georgia. *Republic, southwestern Asia*. The former Soviet republic takes its name from its historic indigenous people, the *Gurz*. Their own name is of uncertain origin (it has been related to the *Kura* River here), but came to be associated with St.*George*, the country's patron saint. The Georgians call themselves *Kartveli* and their country *Sakartvelo*. The Russian name of Georgia is *Gruziya*.

²Georgia. *State, southern United States*. The state was colonized by the British in 1732 and named by them in honor of *George* II (1683–1760).

Georgsmarienhütte. *City, northwestern Germany*. The city arose by an iron and steel works (*Hütte*) which in 1856 moved to a nearby farming community and was renamed as the *Georgsmarienhütte Bergwerks- und Hüttenverein*, for King *George* V (1819–1878) of Hanover and his wife, Queen *Mary*.

Gera. *City, east central Germany*. The city, dating from the late 10th century, derives its name from that of a now lost stream. Its own name may go back to the Indoeuropean root *gher*, "to gurgle."

Geraldton. *Town, southwestern Australia*. The town, in Western Australia, was founded in 1850, originally as *Gerald Town*, and named for Governor Charles *FitzGerald*.

Gerizim, Mt. *Mountain, central Palestine*. According to Samaritan tradition the oldest, most central, and highest mountain in the world, mentioned four times in the Old Testament (Deuteronomy 11:29, etc.), has the Hebrew name *garīzīm*, from the verb *garoz*, "to be cut out."

Germany. *Republic, central Europe.* The precise origin of the country's name remains uncertain. It is generally held to lie either in Celtic words meaning "neighboring people" (Old Irish *gair*, "neighbor," and *maon*, "people") or else to be of Germanic origin, from *gari*, "spear," and *man*, "man." A source in Germanic *ger-man*, "greedy hand," or *ger-man*, "head man," has also been suggested. The names of Germany vary in different languages. The French call it *Allemagne*, from the *Alemanni*, the people who once inhabited the region, their own name meaning literally "all men," implying a single group or totality of people. The Germans themselves call their country *Deutschland*, literally "land of the *Dutch*." The reference is not to the modern Dutch but to a wider group who spoke a common vernacular, as distinct from the learned Latin of the church. (Their name derives from Old High German *diutisc*, "national." Modern Italian *tedesco*, "German," is directly related.) The Finns know Germany as *Saksa*, "land of the Saxons" (*see* **Saxony**), while to the Hungarians the country is *Németország*, from *német*, "German," a word itself related to *néma*, "dumb," "mute," as their speech is unintelligible. (Russians call Germans *nemtsy* for the same reason, from *nemoj*, "dumb.")

Germiston. *City, northeastern South Africa.* The Gauteng city was founded in 1887. In 1904 it was named for a farmstead near Glasgow, Scotland, that was the birthplace of John Jack, a gold-mining pioneer here.

Gerona. *City, northeastern Spain.* The city was known to the Romans as *Oppidum Gerunda* or simply *Gerunda*. The origin and meaning of this are unknown.

Gethsemane. *Estate, western Jordan.* The exact location of the place where Jesus prayed in anguish just before his arrest (Matthew 26:34, etc.) is unknown, but it was probably somewhere near the Mount of Olives. Its name agrees with such a site, as it represents Aramaic *gaṯ-šĕmānê*, "oilpress."

Gettysburg. *Town, eastern United States.* The Pennsylvania town derives its name from that of its founder in the 1780s, General James *Gettys*. It was originally known as *Gettys-town*, but adopted the present form of its name in 1800.

Geysir. *Geyser, southwestern Iceland.* The spouting hot spring, which gave the English word *geyser*, has a name meaning "gusher," from Icelandic *geysa*, "to gush."

Ghana. *Republic, western Africa.* The country takes its name from that of a former tribal chieftain here, his own name being a form of royal title equating to "king." The original territory of the name was much larger than present Ghana. Until 1957 the country was known as *Gold Coast*, from the gold discovered here by Portuguese explorers in the late 15th century.

Ghardaïa. *City, north central Algeria.* The city was founded in the 11th century and takes its name from the cave (Arabic *ghar*) traditionally said to have been inhabited by the female saint *Daïa*.

Ghats. *Mountain range, southern India.* The range, divided into the Eastern Ghats and Western Ghats, takes its basic name from Hindi *ghāṭ*, "pass," "mountain."

Ghazipur. *Town, northern India.* The town, in Uttar Pradesh state, was originally known as *Gadhipur* but this was changed to *Ghazipur* in about 1330, supposedly in honor of the Muslim ruler *Ghazi* Malik. The name ends with Hindi *pur*, "town."

Ghent. *City, northwestern Belgium.* The city may derive its name from Celtic *condate*, "confluence," referring to its site at the confluence of the Lys and Scheldt rivers, although some authorities see a source in non–Indoeuropean *gand*, "gravel," as possibly for Germany's *Gande* River (*see* **Bad Gandersheim**). The Flemish form of the name is properly *Gent*, and the French form *Gand*.

Giant Mountains *see* **Riesengebirge**

Gibeon. *Historic city, central West Bank.* The biblical city (Joshua 9:3, etc.) has a name of Hebrew origin, possibly from *giv'a*, "hill," or *gev*, "ditch," "water tank," and *'ayin*, "spring."

Gibraltar. *British colony, southern Spain.* The name represents Arabic *jabal ṭāriq*, "mountain of *Tariq*," from *jabal*, "mountain" (the Rock of Gibraltar on the peninsula here), and the name of *Tariq* ibn Ziyad, the Berber chief who captured the peninsula in A.D. 711.

Gibson Desert. *Desert, western Australia.* The desert, in central and eastern Western Australia, was discovered in 1873 by the Anglo-Australian explorer Ernest Giles, who crossed it in 1876. He named it for his traveling companion, Alfred *Gibson*, whom he had sent to pick up a supply of water from a previous camp but who never returned.

Giessen. *City, west central Germany.* The city, on the Lahn River, takes its name from the castle by which it arose in the 12th century. The name means literally "by the streams," from an early German word related to English *gush* and *geyser*, referring to the castle's location by the former streams at the mouth of the Wieseck, a tributary of the Lahn. The administrative district of

Giessen was created in 1980 and took its name from its second largest city.

Gifhorn. *City, northern Germany.* The first part of the name is of obscure origin and meaning. The second part refers to the *horn* (spur) of land between the Aller and Ise rivers on which the city arose.

Gifu. *City, central Japan.* The city, in the island of Honshu, derives its name from Japanese *ki*, a simple phonetic sign, and *fu*, "hill."

Gilan. *Province, northwestern Iran.* The name derives from Arabic *jīl*, the name of a herb growing locally.

Gilbert Islands *see* **Kiribati**

Gilead. *Historic region, northwestern Jordan.* The biblical name (Genesis 31:21, etc.) is traditionally derived from *Gilead*, grandson of Manasseh, as the progenitor of the Gilead tribe. His own name, and possibly in reality the placename itself, is probably based on the Aramaic root word *gal*, "heap of stones." *Cp.* **Gilgal.**

Gilgal. *Historic village, western Jordan.* The biblical name is Aramaic in origin and means "circle of stones," from *gil*, "circle," and *gal*, "heap of stones." The precise location of the village is uncertain, but its stones almost certainly formed a sacred circle of some kind: "And those twelve stones, which they took out of Jordan, did Joshua pitch in Gilgal" (Joshua 4:20). According to the Old Testament, the name had a symbolic origin. The generation of Israelites born in the wilderness was circumcised at the place where the stones were raised, "And the Lord said to Joshua, This day have I rolled away the reproach of Egypt from off you. Wherefore the name of the place is called Gilgal unto this day" (Joshua 5:9). This interpretation would involve a pun on Hebrew *gll*, "to roll (away)."

Gillingham. *Town, southeastern England.* The Kent town has an Old English name meaning "homestead of *Gylla*'s people." The *G* is pronounced soft in this name (as in *gin*) but hard (as in *gig*) for the smaller town of *Gillingham*, Dorset, although its origin and meaning are exactly the same. It is unlikely that they are named for the same man, however, as they are too far apart.

Gippsland. *Region, southeastern Australia.* The region, in Victoria, was so named in 1840 by the Polish explorer Count Strzelecki in honor of Sir George *Gipps* (1791–1847), the British governor of New South Wales (which then extended this far south).

Girardot. *City and river port, central Colombia.* The city is named for the Colombian patriot Atanasio *Girardot* (1791–1813), hero of the Battle of Bárbula (1813), in which he lost his life.

Giresun. *City and port, northeastern Turkey.* The city was known to the Greeks as *Kerasos* and to the Romans as *Cerasus*, representing the respective words for "cherry tree." (French *cerise* and English *cherry* are related.). Giresun is now better known for its hazelnuts than its cherries, however.

Gironde. *Department, southwestern France.* The department takes its name from that of the *Gironde*, the estuary here of the **Garonne** and Dordogne rivers. It is an alternate form of the name of the former river, so shares its origin.

Gisborne. *City and port, northeastern New Zealand.* The city, in eastern North Island, was surveyed in 1870 and named for Sir William *Gisborne*, British colonial secretary of the day.

Gisors. *Town, northwestern France.* The town had the Medieval Latin name of *Gisortis* or *Gisortium*, perhaps deriving from a Gaulish personal name *Gisus*, with Gaulish *ritu*, "ford," added. The river here is the Epte.

Giurgiu. *City, southern Romania.* The city is said to derive its name from *San Giorgio*, "St. George," that of a medieval fort built on an island in the Danube here by Genoese navigators.

Giv'at Brenner. *Kibbutz, western Israel.* The kibbutz, founded in 1928, has a Hebrew name meaning "hill of *Brenner*," for the Socialist-Zionist writer Yosef Hayyim (Joseph Chaim) *Brenner* (1881–1921).

Giza. *City, northern Egypt.* The city has a name of Arabic origin, representing Egyptian *Er-ges-her*, "beside the high," referring to its location next to the Great Pyramid, the largest of the three, known as *Cheops*. (The Greek name is a form of that of its builder, *Khufu*, second king of the 4th dynasty of pharoahs, whose ancestral home was at *Menat Khufu*, near al-Minya.)

Gjirokastër. *City, southern Albania.* The city's name represents its Greek name of *Argyrokastron* (Italian *Argirocastro*), "silver castle," describing the white stone of a fortress here.

Gladbeck. *City, western Germany.* The name, first recorded in c.900, means "shining stream," from Old High German *glat*, "shining," and *bah*, "stream." *Cp.* **München-Gladbach.**

Gladstone. *City and port, eastern Australia.* The Queensland city was settled in 1847 and named for the British statesman and future prime minister, William Ewart *Gladstone* (1809–1898).

Glamorgan. *Historic county, southern Wales.* The name, preserved in the modern unitary authority *Vale of Glamorgan*, means "*Morgan*'s shore," from Welsh *glan*, "bank," "shore," followed by the personal name *Morgan*, said to be that of a 7th-century prince of Gwent. The Welsh name of Glamorgan is *Morgannwg*, "Morgan's territory."

Glarus. *Town, east central Switzerland*. The name of the valley here was recorded in the 9th century as *Clarona*. This probably derives from Latin *clarus*, "clear," denoting an area cleared of trees. However, some authorities trace it back to St. *Hilarius*, to whom the monastery here was dedicated. The French form of the name is *Glaris*.

Glasgow. *City and port, south central Scotland*. Scotland's largest city has a Gaelic name meaning "green hollow," from *glas*, "green," and *cau*, "hollow." This would have been a natural feature by the Clyde River here at the time when the present town arose, possibly in the 6th century A.D.

Glastonbury. *Town, southwestern England*. The Somerset town has a name meaning "fortified place of the people of *Glastonia*," from the Roman name of the place, popularly explained as meaning "city of glass" but in fact probably based on a Celtic word meaning "woad." Old English *burh*, "fort," was then added to this.

Glauchau. *Town, east central Germany*. The town, dating from the 13th century, has a Slavic forest name, from Old Sorbian *Gluchov*, from *gluch*, "quiet place," "dense forest."

¹Glendale. *City, southwestern United States*. The Arizona city was founded in 1892 in the Salt River Valley and given a name that was both descriptive of the location and generally promotional. (In fact a *glen* and a *dale* are both valleys, but the combination of the words is attractive.)

²Glendale. *City, southwestern United States*. The California city was laid out in 1886 at the southern end of the San Fernando Valley and given a name that was both descriptive and generally favorable.

Glen Ellyn. *Village, north central United States*. The Illinois village, now a Chicago suburb, has had seven different names: *Babcock's Grove* (1833) (for its original settlers, Ralph and Morgan *Babcock*), *DuPage Center* (1834), *Stacy's Corners* (1835), *Newton's Station* (1849), *Danby* (1851), *Prospect Park* (1882), and *Glen Ellyn* (1889), this last for *Ellyn*, wife of the village president, Thomas E. Hill.

Glenrothes. *Town, southeastern Scotland*. The Fife town was designated a New Town in 1948 and named for the *glen* that forms part of many Scottish placenames (although there is no actual

valley here) and the earls of *Rothes*, who have long been connected with the region.

Gliwice. *Town, southern Poland*. The town takes its name from a Slavic word meaning "stall," "stable," related to modern Polish *chlew*, "pigpen," referring to a stage or relay post where horses were exchanged on the road between Opole and Kraków. The German name of the town is *Gleiwitz*.

Gloucester. *City, west central England*. The city, in the county of the same name, was a Roman settlement, as indicated by its final *-cester*, representing Old English *ceaster*, a borrowing from Latin *castrum*, "camp." The first part of the name represents the town's Roman name of *Glevum*, itself deriving from a Celtic root word meaning "bright," either literally, referring to the sparkling waters of the Severn River here, or metaphorically, in the sense "famous."

Glückstadt. *City, northern Germany*. The city, on the Elbe River estuary, was founded in 1616 by King Christian IV of Denmark as a trading port. The name, meaning "town of good fortune," was given propitiously for future rivalry with Hamburg.

Gmunden. *Town, north central Austria*. The name derives from Old High German *gimundi*, "river mouth." The town lies at the point where the Traun River flows out of the Traunsee, a mountain lake.

Gniezno. *Town, west central Poland*. The origin of the town's name has been the subject of much speculation and no small fantasy. According to tradition, Lech, the mythological founder of Poland, founded it as his capital or "nest" (Polish *gniazdo*). But it may have been a "nest" in some other sense, either because it was well fortified or because it was naturally sheltered by the surrounding hills. The city's coat of arms shows the white eagle (the occupant of the nest) that is Poland's national emblem.

Goa. *State, southwestern India*. The state, a former Portuguese possession, derives its name from local words *goe mat*, "fertile land."

Gobi. *Desert, central Asia*. The desert, extending across territory shared by Mongolia and China, has a name of Mongolian origin, from *gov'*, "steppe," "desert." The Chinese know the desert as *shāmò*, meaning simply "desert," from *shā*, "sand," and *mò*, "wasteland."

Goch. *City, western Germany*. The city, chartered in 1229, derives its name from a Frankish personal name *Gōk*, itself meaning "cuckoo" (English dialect *gowk*).

Godavari. *River, central India*. The river, sacred to Hindus, has a name traditionally derived from Sanskrit *go*, "cow," and *davari*, "giving," referring to a river that waters cattle. A more likely origin is in Telugu *gode*, "border," and Sanskrit *vāri*, "water," denoting a river that serves as a frontier.

Godthåb *see* **Nuuk**

Godwin-Austen, Mt. *see* **K2**

Goiânia. *City, south central Brazil.* The city was founded in 1933 to replace the former state capital of *Goiás*, itself named for the state here, formerly *Goyaz*, in turn named for the local *Goya* people.

Golan Heights. *Hill region, southwestern Syria.* The region takes its name from the biblical city of *Golan* (Deuteronomy 4:43). Its own name is of uncertain origin. Some authorities relate it to Hebrew *galgal*, "circle," "circuit," as for **Galilee** and **Gilgal**. The 1st-century A.D. Jewish historian Flavius Josephus refers to the area as *Gaulanitis*.

Golconda. *Historic city, southern India.* The ancient fort and ruined city, near Hyderabad in Andhra Pradesh state, derives its name from Telugu *golla*, "shepherd," and *konḍa*, "hill."

Gold Coast. *City, eastern Australia.* The city, which is basically a chain of seaside resorts along the Queensland coast, is so named for its golden sands. The name was created for promotional purposes, as were those of some of the individual resorts, such as *Mermaid Beach* and *Surfers Paradise*.

Gold Coast *see* **Ghana**

Golden Gate. *Strait, western United States.* The strait between the Pacific and San Francisco Bay, California, was so named in 1846 by the American general and explorer Charles Frémont (1813–1890), who based it on that of the **Golden Horn**. The name gained added significance with the 1848 California gold rush.

Golden Horn. *Inlet, northwestern Turkey.* The Bosporus inlet, forming the harbor of Istanbul, was so named for its abundance of fish, especially tunny, which are trapped here on entering from the Black Sea. The second word of the name describes the curving shape of the inlet, but the overall name also suggests a cornucopia, or "horn of plenty." The Turkish name of the inlet is simply *Haliç*, "gulf," "channel."

Golgotha. *Hill, central Israel.* The hill that was the place of Jesus' crucifixion, near Jerusalem, derives its name from Aramaic *gûlgaltā*, "skull," as explained in the Vulgate (Latin version of the Bible): "*Golgotha, quod est Calvariae locus*," "A place called Golgotha, that is to say, a place of a skull" (Matthew 27:33). The hill was a place of execution, hence the suggestion made by St. Jerome, writing in the 4th century, that it was so called because skulls of executed prisoners littered the ground here. But the reference is almost certainly to the shape of the hill. It was also known as *Calvary*, from Latin *calva*, "bald head," "skull," as mentioned in another Gospel passage: "The place, which is called Calvary" (Luke 23:33).

Goliad. *Historic city, southern United States.* The former Texas city, the scene of conflict between American and Mexican forces, is said to be named anagrammatically for the Mexican patriot and priest Miguel *Hidalgo* y Costilla (1753–1811) (*cp.* **Hidalgo**). But the name could also derive from the biblical giant *Goliath*.

Gomel. *City, southeastern Belarus.* The city's name is recorded as *Gom* in a document of 1142, which suggests an origin in Slavic *gom*, "hill," related to English *holm*. The location of Gomel on the raised right bank of the Sozh River appears to confirm this.

Gómez Palacio. *City, north central Mexico.* The city, now a suburb of Torreón in the state of Durango, was founded in 1886 and named for Francisco *Gómez Palacio*, then state governor.

Gomorrah. *Historic city, south central Israel.* The biblical city (Genesis 10:19, etc.) derives its name from Hebrew *'omer*, "sheaf," referring to its corn. Archaeological research has shown that the plain where Gomorrah and its associated city, **Sodom**, stood was probably unusually fertile. Its precise location is uncertain, but it was somewhere near the southern end of the Dead Sea.

Gondwana. *Region, central India.* The region, regarded as part of an ancient supercontinent, takes its name from *Gond*, the people who ruled here from the 12th to the 18th century, and Hindi *van*, "forest."

González. *Town, northeastern Mexico.* The town is named for Manuel *González* (1833–1893), president of Mexico from 1880 to 1884.

Good Hope, Cape of. *Cape, southern South Africa.* The southern extremity of the African continent was so named optimistically by King John II of Portugal after it was rounded by Vasco da Gama in 1497. The specific "good hope" was that of reaching India and its riches by this route. The cape was first rounded in 1488 by Bartolomeu Dias, who more realistically called it *Cabo Tormentoso*, "cape of storms," for the rough seas here, where the waters of the Atlantic meet those of the Indian Ocean.

Goodwin Sands. *Shoals, eastern English Channel.* The name of the notorious shoals in the Strait of Dover may derive from the Old English personal name that gave modern *Godwin*. This means "good friend," and may have been deliberately given to the shoals with the aim of placating any evil spirit that lurked in the waters. But the reference could also be historic, to Earl *Godwine* of Kent, who held the island here that later sank to become the treacherous sands, an event traditionally dated 1097.

Göppingen. *City, southwestern Germany*. The city, founded in the mid–12th century, has a name meaning "(settlement of) *Geppo*'s people," with an Old German personal name.

Gorakhpur. *City, northeastern India*. The city, in Uttar Pradesh state, derives its name from the *Gurkhas*, the mainly Nepalese people, with Hindi *pur* meaning "town." The Gurkhas' own name comes from Sanskrit *gauh*, "cow," and *rakṣā*, "guard," "protection." The Gurkhas are Hindus, for whom the cow is a sacred animal.

Gordium. *Historic city, northwestern Turkey*. According to legend, the ancient Anatolian city was founded by the Phrygian king *Gordius*, who contrived the convoluted knot ("Gordian knot") that was later cut by Alexander the Great.

Gorgan. *City, northern Iran*. The city is said to take its name from Iranian *gorgan*, the plural of *gorg*, "wolf," referring to the wickedness of its original inhabitants. But this is simply a folk etymology advanced to explain an otherwise obscure name. Its original name was *Asterabad*, "star city," but in the 1930s it was renamed as now following its destruction by an earthquake.

Gorizia. *City, northeastern Italy*. The city, on the Slovenian border, derives its name from Slavic *gora*, "mountain," referring to the hills to the east. Its earlier German name was *Görz*. Just across the border is the new Slovenian town of *Nova Gorica*, formed after the Italo-Yugoslav border settlement of 1947, which divided the city between the two countries.

Gorky *see* **Nizhny Novgorod**

Görlitz. *City, southeastern Germany*. The city has a Slavic name related to modern Russian *goret'*, "to burn," denoting woodland cleared by burning. The town lies mainly on the west bank of the Neisse River. The part of the town on the east bank passed in 1945 to Poland and is called *Zgorzelec*, a name of identical origin (and closer to the Slavic source).

Gorlovka. *City, eastern Ukraine*. The coal-mining city takes its name from the Russian mining engineer Pyotr Nikolayevich *Gorlov*, who sank the first mineshaft here in 1867. The Ukrainian form of the name is *Horlivka*.

Gorzów Wielkopolski. *City, northwestern Poland*. The city, founded in 1257 by John I, margrave of Brandenburg, has a Polish name mean-

ing "stronghold in Great Poland." It was known to the Germans as *Landsberg an der Warthe*, "fortress of the rulers on the *Warthe*," for the *Warta* River here. *Cp.* **Landsberg am Lech**.

Gosainthan. *Mountain, southern Tibet*. The Himalayan peak has a name meaning "place of God," from Hindi and Nepalese *gosāïn*, "god," "ascetic," and *thān*, "place," "temple."

Gosford. *City, southeastern Australia*. The city, in New South Wales, was founded in 1839 and named for Archibald A. *Gosford*, 2d Earl of Gosford (1776–1849), governor in chief of British North America.

Goshen. *Historic region, northern Egypt*. The biblical name (Genesis 45:10, etc.) may be Semitic in origin. Its meaning is unknown.

Goslar. *City, north central Germany*. The city, at the foot of the Harz Mountains, has a name meaning "enclosure by the *Gose*," the latter being the name of a tumbling mountain stream. Its own name means "bubbling one," from an Indoeuropean root word that also gave English *gush* and *geyser*.

Göteborg. *City and port, southwestern Sweden*. The city's name means "fort of the Goths," from Swedish *Got*, "Goth," and *borg*, "fort." The name is also spelled *Gothenburg*. The Goths also gave the names of the Polish cities of **Gdańsk** and **Gdynia**. *See also* **Gotland**.

Gotha. *City, central Germany*. The city, first mentioned as *Gothaha* in 775, derives its name from Old Saxon *gota*, "water channel," perhaps originally suffixed with Old High German *aha*, "water." The city was the capital of the duchy of *Saxe-Coburg-Gotha*, which was the name of the royal house of Albert, consort of Queen Victoria, and (1901–17) that of the present British royal family. *See also* **Coburg, Saxony**.

Gothenburg *see* **Göteborg**

Gotland. *Island, southern Baltic Sea*. The island's name relates directly to that of the *Goths*, and it is possibly these people actually originated here. For other names relating to them, *see* **Gdańsk, Gdynia, Göteborg**.

Göttingen. *City, central Germany*. The city's name is not likely to be based on Germanic *got*, "god," as sometimes stated, but rather derives from Old Saxon *gota*, "water channel." The name as a whole thus probably means "(place of the) people by the water channel," referring to the Leine River here.

Gottwaldov *see* **Zlín**

Governador Island. *Island, southeastern Brazil*. The largest island in Guanabara Bay, linked to Rio de Janeiro by bridge, is named for Correio de Sá, first *governor* of Rio.

Gozo. *Island, Mediterranean Sea.* The second largest of the Maltese islands, known to the Romans as *Gaulus*, has a name said to mean "island of fish." Its Maltese name is *Ghaudesh.*

Graaff-Reinet. *Town, southern South Africa.* The town, in Eastern Cape province, was founded in 1786 and named for Cornelis Jacob van de *Graaff*, governor of the Cape from 1795 to 1791, and his wife Cornelia, née *Reinet.*

Graham Land. *Region, Antarctic.* The peninsula that contains the region of this name, south of the Falkland Islands, was claimed for Britain in 1832 by the English explorer John Biscoe, who called it after Sir James *Graham* (1792–1861), then first lord of the Admiralty. The American name for the peninsula, on the other hand, was *Palmer Peninsula*, for the American explorer Nathaniel *Palmer* (1799–1877), who had led an expedition here in 1820. In 1964 placename committees in both the USA and Britain agreed to "partition" the peninsula, so that the northern half is now *Graham Land*, and the southern **Palmer Land**. The overall name for the peninsula is now simply *Antarctic Peninsula.*

Grahamstown. *City, southern South Africa.* The city, in Eastern Cape province, was founded in 1812 by Colonel John *Graham* as a frontier garrison post against the Xhosa (known then as Kaffirs) and is named for him.

Grain Coast. *Historic region, western Africa.* The former name of a part of the Atlantic coast, corresponding approximately to the coast of modern Liberia, derives from the region's early export of the spice known as "grains of paradise," otherwise seeds of the melegueta pepper.

Grampians. *Mountain system, central Scotland.* The mountains have a name of uncertain origin. Attempts have been made to derive it from a *Mons Graupius* here mentioned by the 2d-century A.D. Roman writer Tacitus: "*Agricola ad montem Graupium pervenit*" ("Agricola reached Mt. Graupius"). It has been established, however, that Tacitus' mountain was actually Bennachie, an upland region not even in the Grampians. The name was thus probably introduced by 16th-century antiquaries, who based it on *Graupius* (and apparently misread the *u* as *n*, this later becoming *m*), to replace the earlier name of *The Mounth* for the region here. This itself comes from Gaelic *monadh*, "hilly district."

Granada. *City, southern Spain.* The city was founded in the 8th century by Arabs on the site of an Iberian settlement known to the Romans as *Illiberis*, from words related to Basque *hiri*, "town," and *berri*, "new." Its present name is said to derive from Latin *granatum*, "pomegranate,"

referring either to local cultivation of this fruit, or to the city's location on four hills, like the fourfold sections of a pomegranate, with the Alhambra at its center. Another theory takes the name from Moorish *Karnattah*, perhaps meaning "hill of strangers." The Iberian name is preserved in the *Sierra Elvira* range of mountains above the city.

Granby. *City, southeastern Canada.* The city, in Quebec, was founded in 1851 and named for the British soldier John Manners, marquess of *Granby* (1721–1770).

Gran Chaco. *Region, south central South America.* The vast plain derives the first word of its name from Spanish *gran*, "big," and the second from a Quechua word meaning "hunting land."

Grand Canal. *Inland waterway, northeastern China.* The series of waterways links Hangchou, in Chekiang province, with Beijing, a distance of c.1,085 miles (1,747 km). Its English name translates Chinese *dà yùnhé*, "great canal," from *dà*, "great," and *yùnhé*, "canal."

Grand Canyon. *Gorge, western United States.* The ravine in the Colorado River, Arizona, was at first known in English as the *Big Canyon*, the latter word being an anglicization of Spanish *cañón*. American Civil War veteran Major John Wesley Powell explored the canyon in 1871 and in his subsequent report changed the name from the factual *Big Canyon* to the more resonant *Grand Canyon*. The actual Spanish name for the gorge is simply *el Cañón del Colorado*, "the Colorado Canyon."

Grand Forks. *City, northern United States.* The North Dakota city stands at the confluence of the Red River of the North and the Red Lake River. Hence its name, a translation of *Les Grandes Fourches*, a description applied to the site by French fur traders encamped here in the late 18th century.

Grand Island. *City, north central United States.* The Nebraska city takes its name from an island in the Platte River here, called by early French-Canadian trappers *La Grande Île*, "the big island."

Grand-Mère. *City, southeastern Canada.* The Quebec city's French name means "grandmother," referring to a rock in the St.-Maurice River here that, according to Native Americans, suggested the profile of an old woman. The rock was later moved ashore when a hydroelectric dam was built.

Grand Rapids. *City, northern United States.* The Michigan city was founded in 1826 by rapids on the *Grand* River. Its own name was adopted from that of *La Grande Rivière*, "the big river," given it by French explorers in the early 18th century.

Grangemouth. *Town and port, central Scotland*. The town lies on the Firth of Forth at the *mouth* of a small river called the *Grange* Burn, itself so named for the *grange* of Newbattle Abbey nearby.

Granite City. *City, east central United States*. The Illinois city takes its name from the *graniteware* (enameled ironware) factory set up here in 1891.

Granollers. *City, northeastern Spain*. The city was known to the Romans as *Granullaria* for its agricultural importance, from Latin *granum*, "grain," and the present name evolved from this.

Grantham. *Town, eastern England*. The Lincolnshire town has an Old English name meaning "gravel village," from conjectural *grand*, "gravel" (modern English *grind*), and *hām*, "village." The soil here is mostly clay and sand.

Grasse. *Town, southeastern France*. The town takes its name from the Roman personal name *Crassus*, meaning "fat."

Graubünden. *Canton, eastern Switzerland*. The name derives from German *Grauerbund*, "Gray League." This was a league founded here in 1395 to combat the rising power of the Habsburgs, and itself so called for the homespun gray cloth worn by its members. The French name of the canton is *Grisons*, the Italian *Grigioni*, and the Romansh *Grishun*, all implying "gray."

Gravesend. *Town, southeastern England*. The Kent town, on the Thames estuary, has a name meaning "end of the grove," from Old English *grāf*, "grove," and *ende*, "end." The original grove here was probably at the east end of the town, where the Riverside Leisure Area is today.

Graz. *City, southeastern Austria*. The city has a name of Slavic origin, from *gradets*, "small fort." In the 9th century there was probably a fort on the rocky cone called the Schlossberg ("castle mount") that dominates the city.

Great Alföld. *Plain, central Hungary*. The name represents Hungarian *al*, "below," and *föld*, "land," describing the great plain's natural characteristic. Its Hungarian name is *Nagyalföld*, where *nagy* means "big," "great."

Great Australian Bight. *Bay, southern Australia*. The great embayment, officially defined as extending from West Cape, Western Australia, to South West Cape, Tasmania, has a self-descriptive name referring to its size, geographical location, and nature, a *bight* being a wide bay.

Great Barrier Reef. *Coral reef, Coral Sea*. The reef, off the northwest coast of Australia, is so named for the lengthy barrier it forms here, requiring careful negotiation by ships approaching the shore.

Great Bear Lake. *Lake, northwestern Canada*. The lake, in the Northwest Territories, was discovered some time before 1800 by North West Company traders and later named for the *bears* that are found on its shores. It is *Great* simply on account of its size, and although Canada has a *Little Bear Lake*, it is much further south, in Saskatchewan, and the two names are not geographically associated.

Great Britain *see* (1) **Britain**; (2) **Brittany**

Great Dividing Range. *Series of mountain ranges, eastern Australia*. The ranges, running north to south through Queensland, New South Wales, and Victoria, are so named because they divide the east coast territory from the outback.

Great Falls. *City, northwestern United States*. The Montana city stands on the Missouri River and is named for the 96 ft (29 m) *falls* here.

Great Fish. *River, southern South Africa*. The river, in Eastern Cape province, is named for its abundance of *fish*. The English name translates Khoi (Hottentot) *Oub*. The Portuguese called it the *Rio de Infante*, "river of the prince."

Great Grimsby *see* **Grimsby**

Great Khingan Mountains. *Mountain range, northeastern China*. The range derives its name from Chinese *xīng*, "to prosper," and *ān*, "peaceful," "calm."

Great Lakes. *Lakes, central North America*. The five lakes, beween the United States and Canada, form the largest group of lakes in the world. Hence their accurately descriptive name.

Great Salt Lake. *Lake, western United States*. The lake, in northern Utah, is the largest inland body of *salt* water in the Western Hemisphere. Hence its name. *See also* **Salt Lake City**.

Great Slave Lake. *Lake, northwestern Canada*. The lake, in the Northwest Territories, is so named for the *Slave*, the Native American people who formerly lived on its shore. Their name translates their own name for themselves, *Awokanak*. This was given them by the Cree, who plundered and *enslaved* them. The **Slave** River flows into the lake on its southern shore.

Great Smoky Mountains. *Mountain range, eastern United States*. The mountains, a range of the Appalachians along the border between North Carolina and Tennesssee, are so named for their characteristic smokelike haze.

Great Yarmouth *see* **Yarmouth**

Greece. *Republic, southern Europe*. The country is named for its indigenous people, the

Greeks. Their own name may derive from an Indoeuropean root element *gra*, "venerable." The name originally applied to the inhabitants of a much smaller region, corresponding to just a part of Epirus, in northwestern modern Greece. It then spead to a wider territory. The Greeks' own name for their country is *Hellas*, traditionally derived from *Hellen*, the mythical son of Deucalion. The historical origin of the name is unknown. The Turkish name of Greece is *Yunanistan*, "land of the Ionians," while the Arabic and Hindi name is *yūnān*. See **Ionian Islands.**

Greeley. *City, west central United States.* The Colorado city was founded in 1870 as a cooperative agricultural enterprise and was accordingly originally known as *Union Colony*. It was subsequently renamed as now for the newspaper editor Horace *Greeley* (1811–1872), who had supported the venture.

Green Bay. *City, northern United States.* The Wisconsin city is named for its location on the bay of the same name, an inlet of northwestern Lake Michigan. The bay is so named for the forests that lie along its northern shores.

Greenland. *Island, northeastern North America.* The name of the world's largest island means what it says, "green land," and was given the mainly cold and icy country in 982 by the Norse navigator Erik the Red with the aim of attracting settlers. The name was actually not inappropriate for the point where Erik landed, a smooth grassy plain on the southwest coast, near the modern settlement of Qaqortoq, where the climate is relatively mild through the influence of the Gulf Stream. The indigenous Greenlandic name of Greenland is *Kalaallit Nunaat*, "land of the people."

Green Mountains. *Mountain range, northeastern United States.* The mountains, in Vermont, to the east of Lake Champlaign, are so named for their coniferous forests, which keep them green all the year round. It was these mountains that gave the name of **Vermont** itself.

Green River. *River, western United States.* The river, which flows generally south from Wyoming to enter the Colorado in Utah, is probably so named for the green soapstone banks along its course rather than for the color of its waters.

Greensboro. *City, eastern United States.* The North Carolina city was founded in 1808 and named for General Nathanael *Greene* (1742–1786), commander of the American Revolutionary forces at the Battle of Guilford Courthouse near here in 1781.

Greenville. *City, southeastern United States.* The South Carolina city was originally known as *Pleasantburg* when the area here was settled in the 1760s. It was renamed as now in 1821, probably for Isaac *Green* (1762–1831), an early pioneer settler.

Greenwich. *Borough of London, southeastern England.* The borough and former Kent village has an Old English name meaning "green trading place," from *grēne*, "green," and *wīc*, "port," "trading place." The name implies that the site by the Thames River here was unusually grassy.

Greenwich Village. *District of New York City, eastern United States.* The residential district took its name from **Greenwich**, England, with *green* additionally an attractive term for a new settlement. The second word of the name indicates that the place originated as a *village* settlement in colonial times.

Greifswald. *City, northeastern Germany.* The original town here passed in 1249 to the princes of Pomerania, who named it "griffin forest," from the equivalent of modern German *Greif*, "griffin," and *Wald*, "wood." The griffin was the fabulous creature represented in the princes' coat of arms (they also themselves took the name *Greif*), while the forest was the wooded country surrounding the town.

Greiz. *City, central eastern Germany.* The city arose in the 12th century at the foot of a Slav hillside refuge with a fort. The name thus derives from Old Sorbian *grodishche*, "fortified settlement."

Grenada. *Island state, southern West Indies.* The island was discovered by Columbus on August 15, 1498, and originally named by him *Concepción*, for the Immaculate *Conception*. At some later stage it was apparently renamed for the Spanish kingdom (or city) of **Granada.**

Grenadines. *Island group, southern West Indies.* The islands, at the eastern end of the Caribbean Sea, extend between St. Vincent and **Grenada**, and are named for the latter. The name itself is a Spanish diminutive form, as if "Little Grenadas." (Administratively, the northern islands form part of St. Vincent and the Grenadines, and the southern islands are a dependency of Grenada.)

Grenoble. *City, southeastern France.* The city's present name has evolved from its Roman name of *Gratianopolis*, "city of *Gratian*," referring to the 4th-century Roman emperor Flavius *Gratianus*, who founded an episcopal see here. For a brief period in 1793, at the time of the French Revolution, the city was renamed *Grelibre*, its *-noble* being taken as an aristocratic epithet, and so discarded in favor of a democratic -*libre*, "free."

Grevenbroich. *City, western Germany*. The city, on the Erft River, has a name first recorded in 962 as *Brouche*, from Old High German *bruoh*, "swamp," "morass." The first part of the name, a genitive form of Middle Low German *grēve*, "count," was added in the 14th century to show the town's affiliation (from 1307) to the countship of Jülich.

Grijalva. *River, southeastern Mexico*. The river is named for the Spanish explorer Juan de *Grijalva* (1480?–1527), who discovered it in 1518.

Grimsby. *Town and port, eastern England*. The Lincolnshire town has a Scandinavian name meaning "*Grim*'s village." *Grim*, meaning "masked person" (who looked *grim*), was one of the names of the Norse god Odin, and the Danes who gave the name seem to have held that he actually founded it. In 1979 the town was officially named *Great Grimsby* for purposes of distinction from the village of *Little Grimsby* to the south.

Grindelwald. *Village and resort, south central Switzerland*. The Alpine village derives its name from the wood (German *Wald*) that is shut off from the Haslithal valley by a *grindel*, "railfence."

Grisons *see* **Graubünden**

Grodno. *City, western Belarus*. The name means literally "city," and is based on the Slavic *grad* found in such well-known names as **Belgrade**. Grodno is first recorded in a document of 1183.

Gronau. *City, northwestern Germany*. The city, first mentioned in 1365, arose around a fort built amid marshy meadows. Hence its name, meaning "green island."

Groningen. *City, northeastern Netherlands*. The city, first mentioned in the 11th century, has a name based on Old German *groni*, "green," presumably referring to its grassy, fertile location.

Gross-Gerau. *City, central Germany*. The city, built on the site of a Roman camp, derives its name from that of a now lost stream or river, itself related to **Gera**. The city is *Gross* ("great") by comparison with the nearby village of *Klein-Gerau* (*klein*, "little").

Grottaglie. *Town, southern Italy*. The town is so named for the *grottoes* (Italian *grotta*, "cave") in the local rocks.

Grozny. *City, southwestern Russia*. The city, capital of Chechnya, arose from a Russian fortress of this name erected in 1818. The name, Russian for "fearful," "awesome," was given to a fort that was regarded as a threat to the enemy in the ongoing Russo-Turkish wars. In 1997, following fighting between Chechen nationalists and Russian troops, Grozny was locally renamed *Dzhokhar-Ghala*, "city of *Dzhokhar*," for the Chechen president *Dzhokhar* Dudayev (1944–1996), killed in the combat.

Grudziądz. *City, north central Poland*. The city, founded in the 10th century as a stronghold against Prussian attack, has a name based on Slavic *grad*, "fortress." Its German name is *Graudenz*.

Gruyères. *Town, western Switzerland*. The town and its surrounding district of *La Gruyère* are said to derive their name from Low Latin *gruaria*, "region frequented by cranes," from Latin *grus*, "crane." The counts of Gruyère have a coat of arms depicting a crane.

Gstaad. *Village and resort, west central Switzerland*. The Alpine village derives its name from a word related to German *Gestade*, "bank," referring to its location in the valley of the Saane River.

Guadalajara. *City, central Spain*. The name represents Arabic *wādī al-ḥajāra*, "river of the stones," referring to the Henares River on which the city stands. The city's Roman name was *Arriaca* or *Carraca*, based on an earlier name of the river, itself deriving from Iberian *caruca*, "stony." The Arabic name was thus a translation of this. The city of *Guadalajara* in west central Mexico was given the name of the Spanish town when it was founded in 1531.

Guadalcanal. *Island, South Pacific*. The largest of the Solomon Islands was discovered in 1568 by the Spanish navigator Álvaro de Mendaña de Neira, who named it for his home town in Spain, *Guadalcanal*. Its own name is based on Arabic *wādī*, "river," as for **Guadalquivir**.

Guadalquivir. *River, southern Spain*. The longest river in southern Spain derives its name from Arabic *al-wādī al-kabīr*, "the big river" (literally "the river the big").

Guadalupe. *Town, southwestern Spain*. The town takes its name from the Sierra de *Guadalupe*, the mountain on the slopes of which it lies. The mountain's own name comes from that of the river here, which itself comes from Arabic *wādī*, "river," and *Lupus*, the former name of the river, meaning "wolf." The town's famous 12th-century monastery, dedicated to the Virgin Mary, prompted the transfer of the name to many Spanish colonial settlements, especially in Mexico. *Cp.* **Guadeloupe**.

Guadeloupe. *Island group, eastern West Indies*. The island now known as *Basse-Terre* ("low land"), or *Guadeloupe* proper, was named by

Columbus in 1493 in honor of Santa María de **Guadalupe** in Spain. The other island in the group here is *Grande Terre* ("great land").

Guadix. *Town, southern Spain*. The town was known to the Romans as *Acci*. Its present name is a corruption of its Arabic name, *wādī-ash*, "river of life," that of the small river here.

Guam. *Island, western Pacific*. The indigenous Chamorro form of the island's name is *Guahan*, literally "we have," referring to the island's possessions. Following a local legend, names of areas on Guam correspond to parts of the human body, with **Agana**, the capital, at the center.

Guanabacoa. *City, western Cuba*. The city's Native American name means "place of waters," referring to the many mineral springs locally.

Guangdong *see* **Kwangtung**

Guangxi *see* **Kwangsi**

Guangzhou *see* **¹Canton**

Guarda. *City, north central Portugal*. The city was founded in 1197 as a defensive post against the Moorish invaders. Hence its name, from Portuguese *guarda*, "guard," "defense."

Guardafui *see* **Ras Asir**

Guatemala. *Republic, northwestern Central America*. The country takes its name from Native American *Quauhtemellan*, "land of the eagle," this presumably being a totemic bird. An alternate origin could be in *Uhatzmalha*, "mountain where water gushes," referring to the volcano of Agua, near Guatemala City.

Guayaquil. *City and river port, western Ecuador*. The city was founded in 1537 by the Spanish explorer Francisco de Orellana and named by him *Santiago de Guayaquil*, in honor of *Santo Iago*, "St. James," on whose feastday (July 25) it was founded, and of the local chief *Guaya* and his wife *Quila*.

Guban. *Region, northwestern Somalia*. The coastal region derives its name from a local word meaning "burned," referring to the plain here, which was cleared by burning.

Guben. *City, eastern Germany*. The city arose in 1200 on the right bank of the Neisse River near an old Slav settlement. The name thus relates to the latter, from Old Sorbian *guba*, "mouth," referring to its site at the junction of the Lubst River with the Neisse. In 1945 a small part of the city on the right bank passed to Poland and became the town of *Gubin*, while the section on the left bank, originally a monastic settlement, grew into an independent industrial city. From 1961 through 1990 Guben was renamed *Wilhelm-Pieck-Stadt*, for the German Communist leader *Wilhelm Pieck* (1876–1960).

Guelph. *City, southeastern Canada*. The Ontario city was founded in 1827 and named for the *Guelphs*, a Hanoverian branch of the British royal family. (The name itself is related to English *whelp*.)

Guernsey. *Island, Channel Islands, western English Channel*. The second largest of the Channel Islands has a Scandinavian name that probably means "*Grani*'s island." This is preferable for linguistic reasons to the traditional interpretation of "green island," as if referring to the fertile soil here. The final -*ey* is Old Norse *ey*, "island." *See also* **Sarnia**.

Guerrero. *State, southwestern Mexico*. The state is named for Vicente *Guerrero* (1782–1831), a hero of Mexico's wars for independence. (His name happens to mean "conquering warrior.")

Guiana *see* **Guyana**

Guienne. *Historic region, southwestern France*. The name of the former province evolved from Latin *Aquitania* (*see* **Aquitaine**), the earlier name of this region. The name is also spelled *Guyenne*.

Guildford. *City, southern England*. The Surrey city has an Old English name meaning literally "golden ford," referring to the golden sandy soil by the Wey River here.

Guinea. *Republic, western Africa*. The name originally applied to a much larger coastal region that extended from present Senegal to as far south as Gabon. It derives from Tuareg *aginaw*, "black people." *See also* **Guinea-Bissau**.

Guinea-Bissau. *State, western Africa*. The state has the same basic name as that of **Guinea**. The second part is the name of its capital, itself from the name of the indigenous people here, the *Bijuga*. The meaning of their own name is uncertain.

Gujarat. *State, western India*. The name is that of an ancient dynasty, the *Gujars*, who ruled the region in the 8th and 9th centuries. They also gave the name of the cities of *Gujranwala* and *Gujrat* in Pakistan. The origin of their name is uncertain.

Gulfport. *City and port, southern United States*. The Misssissippi city was founded in 1887 as a site for the terminus of the *Gulf* and Ship Island Railroad. Its name basically indicates its status as a *port* on the *Gulf* of Mexico.

Gulf Stream. *Ocean current, North Atlantic*. The relatively warm current is so named for its location in the eastern part of the *Gulf* of Mexico. The name was proposed (or promoted) in 1772 by Benjamin Franklin. It had earlier been known as the *Florida Stream*.

Gulistan. *City, central Uzbekistan*. The city arose in the late 19th century as the village of *Golodnaya Step'*, Russian for "hungry steppe," taking this name from the former barren region where it is located. In 1922 it was renamed *Mirzachul*, from Uzbek *mirza*, "edge," and *chul*, "desert," "waterless steppe," with reference to the same region. In 1961 it was raised to town status and given its present name, meaning (by contrast) "place of roses," from a Turkic word related to modern Turkish *gül*, "rose," and the Iranian suffix *-stan*, "inhabited place," "town."

Gullfoss. *Waterfall, southwestern Iceland.* The waterfall on the Hvítá ("white") River, also known in English as the *Gull Falls*, has an Icelandic name meaning "golden falls," with reference to the bright rainbows frequently seen here.

Gulmarg. *Town and resort, northern India.* The town, in Jammu and Kashmir state, has a Hindi name meaning "meadow of flowers," from *gul*, "flower," "rose," and *marg*, "meadow" (literally "death," from Sanskrit *marga*, "path," i.e., in Hinduism, the path to salvation through death).

Gumma. *Prefecture, central Japan.* The prefecture, in the island of Honshu, derives its name from Japanese *gun*, "group," "herd," and *ma*, "horse."

Gummersbach. *City, western Germany.* The city, dating from the 12th century, has a name recorded in 1109 as *Gumeresbraht*, "*Gummar*'s claim," denoting a delimited area of forest allotted to the named man through his clearing and use of it. The second part of the name has altered under the influence of German *Bach*, "stream."

Gümüşhane. *City, northeastern Turkey.* The city's origins are obscure, but its name derives from Turkish *gümüş*, "silver," referring to the *silver* mines here that were mentioned by Marco Polo in the 14th century.

Gunnbjørn Mountain. *Mountain, southeastern Greenland.* The mountain was named for a 9th-century Icelandic voyager.

Gusev. *City, western Russia.* The city was so named after World War II for the Soviet Army officer S.I. *Gusev*, killed defending the town the previous year. Its earlier German name was *Gumbinnen*, apparently from Lithuanian *gumbis*, "fish trap," referring to the town's location at the point where the Rominte River flows into the Pissa.

Gustavo Díaz Odraz. *Town, eastern Mexico.* The town is named for *Gustavo Díaz Ordaz* (1911–1979), president of Mexico from 1964 to 1970.

Güstrow. *City, northern Germany.* The city was founded in 1226 on the site of a Slav village and adopted its name, from Old Polabian *guscer*, "lizard," denoting a place frequented by these reptiles.

Gütersloh. *City, west central Germany.* The city's name, first recorded in 1184, means "*Guther*'s grove," from Old High German *lōh*, "copse," "grove."

Guyana. *Republic, northern South America.* The country's name is probably of Native American origin with a meaning something like "respectable." Some authorities have derived it, however, from Guarani *guai*, "born," and *ana*, "kin," implying a united and interrelated people, while others have traced it back to a Native American word *guiana*, "land of water," referring to the many rivers here. The variant name *Guiana* or *Guayana* was generally used for the whole region of northeastern South America here, between the Orinoco, Negro, and Amazon rivers and the Atlantic. Until it gained independence in 1966, Guyana was known as *British Guiana*. *See also* **French Guiana**.

Guyenne *see* **Guienne**

Güzelbahçe. *Town, western Turkey.* The small town is famed for its fine gardens. Hence its name, from Turkish *güzel*, "beautiful," and *bahçe*, "garden."

Gwalior. *City, central India.* The city, in Madhya Pradesh state, takes its name from an ancient rock fortress here, first mentioned in the 6th century. Its name is said to derive from a small shrine inside it dedicated to the hermit *Gwali*. The name *Gwaliawar* then became *Gwaliar* or *Gwalior*.

Gwandu. *Town, northwestern Nigeria.* The town is named for the surrounding *gandu*, "royal farmlands," which belonged to the Songhai captain Muhammadu Kanta, founder in 1516 of the Kebbi kingdom.

Gwent. *Historic county, southwestern Wales.* The former county (1974–96) adopted a historic name for the region that is probably of pre-Celtic origin, meaning something like "place." The name implies a region that was favorable for some purpose, such as trading. The conjectural word that gave the name is also seen in the first syllable of the name of **Winchester**.

Gweru. *City, central Zimbabwe.* The city takes its name from the river here, its own name representing Bantu *iKwelo*, "steep place," referring to its high banks.

Gwynedd. *County, northwestern Wales.* The county was formed in 1974 and given a historic regional name said to derive from that of *Cunedda*, a 5th-century ruler who had a kingdom here. One of his sons, Ceredig, is said to have given the name of **Cardigan**.

Gyandzha. *City, western Azerbaijan.* The city takes its name from the river here. Its own name is of obscure origin, despite attempts to associate it with the **Ganges**. Gyandzha was founded in the 5th century. In 1804 it was renamed *Yelizavetpol*, as if "Elizabethopolis," for the German princess Louise Maria Augusta (1779–1826), daughter of the margrave of Baden-Anspach, who took the name *Yelizaveta* Alekseyevna (*Elizabeth* Alexeevna) on marrying the Russian czar Alexander I in 1793. In 1918 the city reverted to its original name, but in 1935 was further renamed *Kirovabad*, for the Soviet Communist leader Sergei *Kirov* (1886–1934). (*Cp.* **Vyatka**.) The final *-abad* means "inhabited place," "town," as for ¹**Hyderabad** and other Asian towns. In 1989 it again reverted to its original name.

Gympie. *City, eastern Australia*. The Queensland city was originally known as *Nashville*, for John *Nash*, who found gold here in 1867. Its present name represents *gimpi-gimpi*, the Aboriginal (Gabi) word for the stinging tree (*Laportea gigas*), commonly found in the scrub here.

Gyomaendrőd. *City, southeastern Hungary*. The first part of the name is of obscure origin. The second part is a form of the Hungarian personal name *Endre*, "Andrew."

Gyöngyös. *City, northern Hungary*. The name is that of the river here, itself meaning "sparkling," "bubbling," from Hungarian *gyöngy*, "pearl."

Győr. *City, northwestern Hungary*. The city's name appears to derive from the personal name *Jewr*. Its Roman name was *Arrabona*, from the *Rába* River here and Celtic *bona*, "foundation," "fort," as for **Bonn**. This gave the city's current German name of *Raab*.

Gyula. *City, southeastern Hungary*. The city derives its name from the personal name *Gyula*, "Julius."

Gyumri *see* **Kumayri**

Haardt Mountains. *Mountain range, southwestern Germany*. The mountains, noted for their densely forested slopes, derive their name from Old High German *hard*, "wooded upland." *Cp.* **Harz**.

Haarlem. *City, western Netherlands*. The city's name probably derives from Dutch *haar*, "height," and *lem*, "silt," referring to the location here beside the Spaarne River, which is slightly elevated by comparison with the surrounding low-lying plain. *Cp.* **Harlem**.

Habsburg. *Castle, northern Switzerland*. The castle, built in the first part of the 11th century, gave the name of the counts of *Habsburg* or *Hapsburg*, later that of various royal houses, and

notably of Austria-Hungary. The name itself represents an original *Habichtsburg*, "hawk's castle."

Hachioji. *City, central Japan*. The city, in the island of Honshu, derives its name from Japanese *hachi*, "eight," *ō*, "king," and *shi*, a borrowing of Chinese *zǐ*, "son."

Hacıbektaş. *Town, central Turkey*. The name is that of the Persian mystic *Hajji Bektash Wali* (1308–1370), who developed the Bektashi religious order in this town. (*Hajji* is a term for a Muslim who has made a pilgrimage to Mecca, while *Wali* amounts to "Saint.")

Hackensack. *City, eastern United States*. The New Jersey city was settled by the Dutch and originally called *New Barbadoes*. In 1921 it was renamed as now, allegedly for the *Ackinchesacky*, a Native American people. The meaning of their name is uncertain.

Hackney. *Borough of London, southeastern England*. The borough has an Old English name meaning "*Haca*'s island," the "island" here being dry land among marshes.

Hadera. *City, western Israel*. The city, founded in 1890, derives its name from Arabic *khaḍra*, "green," alluding to the well-watered terrain here.

Hadhramaut. *Region, east central Yemen*. The name of the coastal region may be identical to that of the Arabian tribal group who trace their origin back to the biblical *Hazarmaveth* (Genesis 10:26), a descendant of Shem. A source has also been proposed in Arabic *khaḍra*, "green," and *maut*, "death." But this seems unlikely, if only because in Arabic the adjective always follows the noun. And what could a "green death" be?

Haeju. *City and port, southwestern North Korea*. The name derives from Korean *hae*, "sea," and *chu*, "region," from Chinese *hǎi* and *zhōu* in the same sense.

Hafnarfjördhur. *Town and port, southwestern Iceland*. The town's name means simply "port fjord," from Old Icelandic *hafnar*, "port" (English *haven*), and *fjördhur*, "fjord."

Hagen. *City, western Germany*. The city's name derives from Old High German *hagan*, "thornbush," so means "hedged-in place," referring to its original site, in a corner of land between the Ennepe and Volme rivers around an old church and a residence of the archbishop of Cologne.

Hagerstown. *City, eastern United States*. The Maryland city was laid out in 1762 by the land developer Jonathan *Hager* (1714–1775) and originally named *Elizabeth Town*, for his wife. In

1814 it was incorporated as *Hager's Town*, and soon after settled to the present form of the name.

Hague, The. *City, southwestern Netherlands.* The English name of the Dutch seat of government (but not capital) is a form of its indigenous name, *Den Haag*, itself a short form of its full name, *'s Gravenhage*. This means "the count's hedge," referring to the hedge that originally enclosed the hunting lodge of the counts of Holland here. (Grammatically, the name analyzes as *'s*, a remnant of the genitive form of the old definite article, *graven*, the old genitive form of *graaf*, "count," and *hage*, from Germanic *haga*, "hedge.") The French know the city as *La Haye*.

Haguenau. *Town, northeastern France.* The town takes its name from the Germanic personal name *Hagino*, itself from *hago*, "forest," and *auwa*, "water." The German form of the name is *Hagenau*.

Hai. *River, northern China.* The river, in Hopeh province, derives its name from Chinese *hǎi*, "sea." Together with its many tributary streams, it flows into the Po Hai (Po Gulf) to the east.

Haifa. *City and port, northwestern Israel.* The city derives its name from Hebrew *kef*, "rock," "cliff," referring to its location on the heights of Mt. Carmel. The Aramaic form of the same word lay behind the surname *Cephas* ("rock") given by Jesus (John 1:42) to the disciple Peter ("rock").

Hai-k'ou. *City and port, southern China.* The city, in Hainan province, derives its name from Chinese *hǎi*, "sea," and *kǒu*, "mouth," referring to its role as the chief port on the island of **Hainan**.

Hailar. *City, northeastern China.* The city, in Inner Mongolia, derives its name from Chinese *hǎi*, "sea," and *kǒu*, "mouth." It is not actually near the sea, but on the Hai-la-erh River, which flows west into the Argun.

Hainan. *Island and province, southern China.* China's largest island (after Taiwan), in the South China Sea, has a name meaning "southern sea," from Chinese *hǎi*, "sea," and *nán*, "south."

Hainaut. *Province, southwestern Belgium.* The province bases its name on that of the *Haine* River that flows through it as a tributary of the Scheldt. The final part of the name represents the Germanic element *gawja* (modern German *Gau*), "district." The river's own name is also of Germanic origin, from *hago*, "forest." The Flemish form of the province name is *Henegouwen*.

Haiphong. *City and port, northern Vietnam.* The city's name means "sea room," from Vietnamese *hái*, "sea," and *phòng*, "room." The reference is to the natural harbor here.

Haiti. *Island republic, central West Indies.* The republic, occupying the western part of the island of Hispaniola, has a name that would have originally applied to the island as a whole. It probably represents Arawak *haiti*, "land of mountains." The French form of the name is *Haïti*.

Hajar. *Mountain chain, northern Oman.* The chain, a series of limestone ridges and tablelands, derives its name from Arabic *hajar*, "stone."

Hajdúböszörmény. *Town, northeastern Hungary.* The former capital of the **Hajdúság** region takes the first part of its name from the *haiduks* here at one time and the second part from the *böszörmény*, literally "ferocious Armenians," the Hungarian name for the Muslim Ismailites who settled here.

Hajdúdorog *see* **Hajdúság**
Hajdúhadház *see* **Hajdúság**
Hajdúnánás *see* **Hajdúság**
Hajdúság. *Region, northeastern Hungary.* The region is inhabited by descendants of the *haiduks*, or foot soldiers, who were granted lands here, their own title coming from Hungarian *hajdúk*, the plural of *hajdú*, "robber." (The second half of the name is Hungarian *ság*, "wooded mountain.") There are many towns here with *Hajdú-* names, as *Hajdúhadház* (with *had*, "war," and *ház*, "house"), *Hajdúdorog* (with personal name *Dorog*), *Hajdúnánás* (with personal name *Nánás*), *Hajdúszoboszló* (with personal name *Szoboszló*), and the more important **Hajdúböszörmény**, the region's former capital.

Hajdúszoboszló *see* **Hajdúság**
Hakirya. *District, Tel Aviv, western Israel.* The quarter of government offices and public services in the center of Tel Aviv was formerly the German colony of *Sarona*, founded in 1871, with a name of Arabic origin meaning "crusader." The present name, adopted in 1948 when the district became the provisional seat of most government offices of Israel, is Hebrew for "the city."

Hakodate. *City and port, northern Japan.* The city, in the island of Hokkaido, derives its name from Japanese *hako*, "box," and *tate*, "house," "fort." The reference is to the fort of *Goryokaku*, the only Western-style fort in Japan, begun in 1855 as the seat of the Hakodate magistracy, which lies in the city center. (It has now been converted to a park.) The fort's own name means "government square."

Halberstadt. *City, central Germany.* The second part of the name is Old High German *stat*, "place." The first part is probably the old river name *Halvara*, perhaps that of the present Holtemme.

Halden. *Town, southeastern Norway.* The town was founded in 1661 and from 1665 to 1928 was known as *Fredrikshald*, "Frederick's stronghold," for the fortress here, itself named for *Frederick* III (1609–1670), king of Denmark and Norway. The present name means simply "the stronghold."

Haldensleben. *Town and canal port, central Germany.* The town, formed in 1938 through the union of *Neuhaldensleben* ("new") and *Altheldensleben* ("old"), has a name meaning "*Hahald*'s inherited estate," with a Germanic personal name. *Cp.* **Aschersleben.**

Haleakala. *Mountain, central Hawaii, United States.* The dormant volcano, in eastern Maui Island, has a Hawaiian name meaning "house of the sun." The allusion is to a local legend which tells how the demigod Maui imprisoned the sun here in order to lengthen the day.

Halesowen. *Town, west central England.* The former West Midlands town has a name meaning "*Owen*'s corners of land." The Welsh prince *Owain* ap Dafydd, nephew of King Henry II by his sister Emma, became Lord of *Hales* in 1204. The "corners of land" (Old English *halas*) were probably small valleys.

Halicarnassus. *Historic city, southwestern Turkey.* The ancient city has a name of pre–Greek origin and unknown meaning. Its present site is the town of **Bodrum.**

¹Halifax. *Town, northern England.* The former West Yorkshire town has an Old English name meaning "area of coarse grass in the corner of land," from *halh*, "secluded spot," and *feax*, "rough grass." The latter word literally means "hair," giving a popular interpretation "holy hair," as if the first word were Old English *hālig*, "holy," supposedly referring to the hair on the head of a virgin killed by a lustful priest when she spurned his advances.

²Halifax. *City, eastern Canada.* The capital of Nova Scotia was founded by the British in 1749 and named for George Montagu Dunk, 2d Earl of *Halifax* (1716–1771), president of the Board of Trade.

Halle. *City, east central Germany.* The city has long been famous for its salt manufacture, and this is probably the basic sense of its name, from Middle High German *hal*, "saltworks." But an alternate origin in Old Saxon *halla*, "hall," is also possible, meaning a pillared, semi-enclosed building, perhaps here itself a saltworks. Any link between the neuter noun *hal* and feminine noun *halla* is uncertain.

Hallein. *Town, north central Austria.* The town, founded in the 12th century, benefited early from the saltworks at nearby Dürrnberg. Hence its name, meaning "little saltworks." *Cp.* **Halle.**

Hallstatt. *Archaeological site, west central Austria.* The name is now associated with the Bronze and Iron Age graves here, excavated in the 19th century. But the name means "place of salt" (*cp.* **Halle**), referring to the prehistoric salt mine here, in which bodies of the original miners were preserved.

Halmahera. *Island, central Indonesia.* The largest island of the Moluccas has an indigenous name meaning "motherland."

Halq al-Wadi. *Town and port, northern Tunisia.* The town, an outpost for Tunis, has an Arabic name meaning "river's throat," from *ḥalk*, "gullet," and *wādi*, "river," referring to the harbor narrows here, now linked to Tunis by a canal. Hence the town's alternate French name of *La Goulette*, "the gully," "the narrows."

Hälsingborg. *City and port, southwestern Sweden.* The city lies opposite the Danish town of **Helsingør** (English *Elsinore*), and is named for it, with Swedish *borg*, "fort," added. The name is also spelled *Helsingborg*.

Hama. *City, western Syria.* The city ultimately derives its name from Phoenician *khamat*, "fort." Hama was a noted Hittite settlement.

Hamadan. *City, western Iran.* The city derives its name from Old Persian *Hangmatana*, itself from Greek *Hagbatana*. This represents the name of *Ecbatana*, the ancient Medean capital from which the modern city evolved. Its own name ultimately goes back to the personal name *Agbatas*. This is of uncertain origin, but may be related to the Arabic name *Ahmed*.

Hamakita. *City, central Japan.* The city, on the island of Honshu, lies northeast of **Hamamatsu.** Hence its name, from that of the coastal city and Japanese *kita*, "north."

Hamamatsu. *City, southern Japan.* The city, on the south coast of the island of Honshu, derives its name from Japanese *hama*, "shore," and *matsu*, "pine."

Hamburg. *City and river port, northern Germany.* The second part of the name relates to modern German *Burg*, "fort," referring to the moated castle built in c.825 on a promontory between the Alster and Elbe rivers. The first part is more problematical. It could represent Old High German *hamma*, "ham," "back of the knee," in the transferred sense "bend," "angle," denoting the location of the castle by a river bend, or else an early form of Middle High German *hamme*, "enclosed area of pastureland."

Hamden. *Town, eastern United States.* The Connecticut town, immediately north of New Haven, was settled in 1664 and named for the English Puritan patriot John *Hampden* (1594–1643).

Hämeenlinna. *City, southwestern Finland.* The city is named for the nearby medieval castle of *Häme*, from *Hämeen*, the genitive of this name, and Finnish *linna*, "castle." The Swedish name of the city is *Tavastehus*, from the *Tavastians*, a Finnish people here, and Swedish *hus*, "house," "castle."

Hameln. *City, north central Germany.* The city takes its name from the river on which it stands, which here flows into the Weser. The river's own name probably derives from Old High German *hamel*, "broken," "maimed," Middle High German *hamel*, "steep hill," "cliff," referring to the rugged terrain. The conventional English form of the name is *Hamelin*.

Hamersley Range. *Mountain range, northwestern Australia.* The range, in Western Australia, was discovered in 1861 by the explorer and mineral surveyor Francis T. Gregory and named by him for Edward *Hamersley*, a financial backer of his expedition.

Hamhung. *City, east central North Korea.* The city derives its name from Korean *ham*, "salt taste," and *hŭng*, "happiness."

[1]Hamilton. *Town, southwestern Scotland.* Until 1445 the former Lanarkshire town was known as *Cadzow*, a name of uncertain origin and meaning. Its present name is said to come from an English family called *Hamilton* who came to settle here. Their own name would come from a placename, itself from Old English *hamel*, "broken," and *tūn*, "farm," referring to a farm in rugged country.

[2]Hamilton. *Capital of Bermuda.* The seaport town was founded in 1790 and named for Henry *Hamilton* (died 1796), governor of Bermuda at the time.

[3]Hamilton. *City and port, southern Canada.* The original site here at the western end of Lake Ontario was initially named *Burlington Bay.* When the present city was first settled in 1813 it was renamed for George *Hamilton* (1787–1835), son of the Hon. Robert Hamilton, of Niagara, who had bought a farm here the previous year and divided it into building lots. *See also* **St. Catharines.**

[4]Hamilton. *City, east central United States.*

The Ohio city arose on the site of *Fort Hamilton*, built in 1791. It was itself named for the American federalist politician Alexander *Hamilton* (1755–1804).

[5]Hamilton. *City, northern New Zealand.* The city, in central North Island, originated in 1864 as a military settlement on the site of a deserted Maori village. It was named for Captain John *Hamilton*, a British naval officer killed fighting Maoris.

Hamm. *City, northwestern Germany.* The city, founded in 1226 by Count Adolf I on a crossing of the Lippe River, derives its name from a local form of Middle Low Dutch *ham*, "bay," "outer curve of a river bend."

Hammamat. *Town and port, northeastern Tunisia.* The town, a popular resort, takes its name from Arabic *al-ḥammāmat*, "the bathing places."

Hammerfest. *Town and port, northern Norway.* Europe's northernmost town was chartered in 1789 and derives its name from Norwegian *hammer*, "cliff," "crag" (English *hammer* is related), and *feste*, "to fortify" (English *fastness*).

Hammond. *City, north central United States.* The Indiana city was founded in 1869 and is named for George H. *Hammond* (1838–1886), who set up a meatpacking house here together with Marcus M. Towle. It is said they tossed a coin to see whose name would be given.

Hampshire. *County, southern England.* The county takes its name from **Southampton**, on which it has long been historically based. That city was originally known as *Hampton*, so that *Hampshire* is a reduced form of *Hamptonshire*. The county's abbreviated name is *Hants*, from the Domesday Book spelling of the name as *Hantescire*, itself a reduced form of Norman French *Hantunescire*, in which original *-mt-* has become *-nt-*.

Hampstead. *District of London, southeastern England.* The name of the former borough is of Old English origin and corresponds to modern *homestead*. In Anglo-Saxon times this would have meant a small settlement or even sometimes just a single dwelling, such as a farm.

Hampton. *City and port, eastern United States.* The Virginia city dates from 1610 and is named for Henry Wriothesley, 3d Earl of *Southampton* (1573–1624), a leader in the formation of the Virginia Company of London and a councillor for the Plantation of New England. The earl, a patron of Shakespeare, took his title from **Southampton**, itself originally called *Hampton*.

Han. *River, southeastern China.* The river, a tributary of the Yangtze, derives its name from Chinese *hàn*, "Han," "Chinese," itself from the name of the *Han* dynasty (206 B.C.–A.D.221). The river is also known as the *Han Shui*, the latter word representing Chinese *shuĭ*, "water."

Hanau. *City and port, central Germany.* The city, known formally as *Hanau am Main*, arose around a castle between the Kinzig and **Main** rivers. Hence its name, referring to this insular site, from Middle High German *hagen*, "hedged enclosure," and Old High German *ouwa*, "island," "land by water."

Hang-chou. *City, eastern China.* The city, in Chekiang province, derives its name from Chinese *háng*, with no actual meaning, and *zhōu*, "region." The conventional form of the name is *Hangchow*.

Han-k'ou. *City and river port, east central China.* The city, in Hupeh province, derives its name from Chinese *hàn*, for the *Han* dynasty that ruled China from 206 B.C. through A.D.221, and *kŏu*, "mouth." *See also* **Wu-han**.

Hanoi. *Capital of Vietnam.* The city's name means "inside the river," from Vietnamese *hà*, "river," and *nôi*, "inside." Hanoi was founded in the 5th (or possibly 8th) century within a bend of the Red River, and from 1428 through 1787 was known as *Dông Kinh*, "eastern capital," a name corrupted by Europeans to *Tonquin*. In the French colonial period (1883–1945), this name, in the form *Tonkin*, was used to refer to the entire region.

Hanover. *City, northern Germany.* The name of the city means "on the high bank," from Middle Low German *hôch*, "high," and *over*, "bank," referring to its location on the Leine River and the Mittelland Canal, at the point where the spurs of the Harz and Mittelgebirge mountains join to form the North German Plain. The name corresponds exactly to that of the English town of *Heanor*, Derbyshire, from Old English (*æt thǣm*) *hēan ofre*. The German form of the name is *Hannover*.

Han-tan. *City, eastern China.* The city, in Hopeh province, derives its name from Chinese *hándān*, with no actual meaning known.

Hanumangarh. *City, northwestern India.* The city, in Rajasthan state, has a name meaning "*Hanuman*'s fort," from *Hanuman*, the divine monkey chief in Hindu mythology, and Hindi *garh*, "fort." Before 1805 the city was known as *Bhatner*, for the *Bhatti* Rajputs. *Cp.* **Andaman Islands**.

Han-yang. *City, east central China.* The city, in Hupeh province, derives its name from Chinese *hàn*, for the *Han* dynasty that ruled China from 206 B.C. through A.D.221, and *yáng*, "sun," "male." *See also* **Wu-han**.

Haparanda. *Town and port, northeastern Sweden.* The town has a Finnish name meaning "aspen shore," "coast where aspens grow," from *haapa*, "aspen," and *ranta*, "shore."

Harare. *Capital of Zimbabwe.* The city takes its name from that of a former village or district here, itself named for *Neharawa*, an African chief, whose own name means "he who does not sleep." Until 1982 the city was named *Salisbury*, for Robert Gascoyne Cecil, 3d Marquess of *Salisbury* (1830–1903), British prime minister at the time of the town's foundation (as *Fort Salisbury*) in 1890.

Harbin. *City, northeastern China.* The capital of Heilungkiang province, on the Sungari River, has a Chinese name of Manchu origin meaning "place where fish are dried." It was a fishing village until as recently as 1896, when it became the Russian construction center of the Chinese Eastern Railway.

Harer. *City, eastern Ethiopia.* The city's name, also spelled *Harar*, is said to be an Amharic corruption of a word meaning "trading post."

Haridwar. *Town, northern India.* The town, one of the most sacred places of Hindu pilgrimage in India, in Uttaranchal state, has a name meaning "gate of *Hari*," this being a name of Vishnu, one of the principal deities of Hinduism. (*Hari* literally means "reddish-brown," but is traditionally understood to mean "deliverer.") *Cp.* **Haryana**.

Hari Rud. *River, central Asia.* The river rises in central Afghanistan and flows generally west and north into Turkmenistan to lose itself in the sands of the Kara Kum. Its name derives from Old Persian *harawaia*, "river rich in water," to which Iranian *rūd*, "river," has been tautologically added. *See also* **Herat**.

Harlech. *Town, northwestern Wales.* The town, famous for its 13th-century castle, has a name that refers specifically to the castle site on a craggy hilltop. It means "beautiful rock," from words corresponding to modern Welsh *hardd*, "beautiful," "handsome," and *llech*, "slab," "smooth rock."

Harlem. *District of New York City, eastern United States.* The district of Manhattan arose from the village created here in 1658. It was named *Nieuw Haarlem* for **Haarlem** in the Netherlands by Peter Stuyvesant, governor of the Dutch colony of New Netherland in this region of eastern America.

Harlingen. *City, southern United States.* The Texas city was founded in the early 1900s and named for *Harlingen*, in the Netherlands, which like the Texas town is located on a barge canal.

Harlow. *Town, southeastern England.* The Essex town has a name meaning "army mound," from Old English *here*, "army," and *hlāw*, "mound." The reference is to an administrative center and meeting place, the latter being for the local hundred (county subdivision). The actual site of the "army mound," that of a Romano-Celtic temple, is just northwest of Harlow Mill railroad station.

Harper. *Town and port, southeastern Liberia.* The town was founded in 1834 by a group of freed black American slaves sponsored by the Maryland Colonization Society and was originally called *Cape Palmas*, for the headland here. In 1857 the town passed to Liberia, and the port was renamed for Robert Goodloe *Harper* (1766–1825) of the American Colonization Society. It was Harper who named both **Liberia** itself and **Monrovia**, its capital.

Harpers Ferry. *Village, eastern United States.* The West Virginia village was settled in 1734 by Robert *Harper*, who set up a *ferry* across the Potomac here and a grist mill on the Shenandoah.

Harran. *Historic city, southeastern Turkey.* The ancient city, mentioned in the Bible as *Haran* (Genesis 11:31, etc.), derives its name from Assyrian *harranu*, "way," "road," referring to its location on the road from Nineveh to Carchemish.

Harris. *Island region, northwestern Scotland.* The southern section of the island of Lewis with Harris, in the Outer Hebrides, derives its name from Gaelic *na-h-earaidh*, "that which is higher," referring to its topography, by comparison with lower Lewis, to the north. The form of the name may have been influenced by Old Norse *hár*, "high."

Harrisburg. *City, eastern United States.* The state capital of Pennsylvania was founded as a trading post on the Susquehanna River in *c.*1718 and known as *Harris' Ferry* until 1785, when it became a town. The name is that of John *Harris* (1727–1791), eldest son of the English settler John Harris who had established (and given his name to) the original settlement.

Harrogate. *Town, northern England.* The North Yorkshire town has a Scandinavian name that probably means "road to the cairn," from Old Norse *hǫrgr*, "heap of stones," "cairn," and *gata*, "way," "road." However, *gata* had a later sense "pasture," evolving when a particular road became a right of way for leading cattle to pastureland, and this could also make sense. Harrogate arose following the discovery of medicinal springs in c.1571 and for a time was known as *Spaws*, from **Spa**.

Harrow. *Borough of London, southeastern England.* The name represents Old English *hearg*, the word for a heathen temple. There must have been a Saxon shrine of this kind here, presumably on the summit of the hill where St. Mary's Church stands today. There has long been a Christian church on the site, and Pope Gregory the Great, in the late 6th century, specifically urged missionaries to convert heathen temples into places of Christian worship wherever they could. Harrow has the alternate name of *Harrow-on-the-Hill*, pointing up the historic sense.

Hartford. *City, eastern United States.* The state capital of Connecticut, founded in 1635 by English settlers, was named for **Hertford**, England, the birthplace of one of their number, William Stone. The spelling has preserved that of the English town's name in the 17th century. It also represents its pronunciation, which has remained unchanged despite the vowel alteration.

Hartlepool. *Town and port, northeastern England.* The east coast town, on the bay of the same name, has a name meaning "pool by the island where stags are seen," the pool being the present town's harbor and the "island" the peninsula on which it stands. The headland was probably so named for the stags grazing there, rather than for its curving contour, like a stag's antlers. The middle *-le-* of the name evolved from Old English *ēg*, "island."

Harwich. *Town and port, southeastern England.* The Essex town's name means "military settlement," from Old English *here-wīc*. There was a sizeable Danish military camp here in the 9th century.

Haryana. *State, north central India.* The name of the state probably means "abode of Vishnu," from *Hari*, a name of the Hindu god Vishnu (*cp.* **Haridwar**), and Sanskrit *ayana*, "home," since the region was the birthplace of the Hindu religion. However, a derivation in *hari*, "green," may also be possible, referring to the fertility of the countryside.

Harz. *Mountain range, central Germany.* The mountains derive their name from Old High German *hard*, "forest," "wooded upland." Much of the region is still heavily wooded. *Cp.* **Haardt Mountains**.

Harzgerode. *City, central Germany.* The city lies in the Lower Harz Mountains but is not named for them, as shown by historic forms of the name (*Hazekerode* in 1326). The actual meaning is "*Hazako*'s clearing." The present form of the name, indeed influenced by **Harz**, first appeared in the 17th century.

Hasan Abdal. *Town, northern Pakistan.* The town takes its name from the Buddhist site of *Hasan Abdal*, dating from the 2d century B.C. In British colonial times it was known as *Campbellpore*, from the Scottish army officer Sir Colin Campbell, Lord Clyde (1792–1863), who effected the relief of Lucknow (1857). The *-pore* in this name is Hindi *pur*, "town."

¹**Hastings.** *Town and resort, southern England.* The East Sussex town has a name meaning "(place of) *Hæsta*'s people." It is not known who Hæsta was, but his name probably arose as a nickname meaning "violent" (modern *hasty*). The territory of his family or followers would have been much more extensive than that occupied by the present town.

²**Hastings.** *City, northeastern New Zealand.* The city, in eastern North Island, was settled in 1864 and named for Warren *Hastings* (1732–1818), first governor general of India.

Hatfield. *Town, southeastern England.* The Hertfordshire town derives its name from Old English *hæth*, "heather," and *feld*, "open land," so that the sense is "open land where heather grows."

Hatteras, Cape. *Cape, eastern United States.* The North Carolina cape, and the island here, are both named for a Native American people. Their own name is of unknown origin and meaning.

Hattiesburg. *City, southern United States.* The Mississippi city was settled in 1881 by the Confederate soldier and statesman William Harris Hardy, who named it for his wife *Hattie*.

Hattingen. *City, northwestern Germany.* This is not an *-ingen* name like **Hechingen**, as is evident from its first recorded form of *Hatneghen* in 1019. The second part of this is Middle Low German *egge*, "edge," "corner" (modern German *Ecke*, English *edge*). The first part is of uncertain origin.

Hatuey. *Town, eastern Cuba.* The name is that of an indigenous warrior, the last chief of the Taino, who fought the Spaniards. He was burned at the stake in 1512.

Hatvan. *City, northern Hungary.* The city derives its name from the identical Hungarian personal name meaning "sixty."

Haugesund. *Town and port, southwestern Norway.* The town's name derives from Norwegian *haug*, "hill," and *sund*, "sound," "strait." The hill in question is Harald's Hill, to the north of the town. The strait is the Karmsund, running south from the town between the mainland and the island of Karmøy.

Hauraki Gulf. *Gulf, northeastern New Zealand.* The large north-facing gulf, in eastern North Island, has a Maori name meaning "north wind."

Hauran. *Region, southwestern Syria.* The region, east of the Jordan River, has a Hebrew name meaning "hollow land," referring to the many caverns in the mountainous northeast.

Havana. *Capital of Cuba.* The city was founded in 1514 by the Spanish soldier and administrator Diego Velázquez, who named it *San Cristóbal de la Habana*, "St. Christopher of the *Habana*." The final word of this probably represents the name of a local Native American people. Its meaning is unknown.

Havant. *Town, southern England.* The Hampshire town has an Old English name meaning "*Hama*'s spring," with the Anglo-Saxon personal name followed by *funta*, "spring" (modern *fountain*). The reference is perhaps to a Roman spring nearby. The *m* of the personal name has blended with the *f* of *funta* to produce the *v*.

Haverhill. *City, northeastern United States.* The Massachusetts city was founded in 1640 by the Reverend John Ward, who named it for his birthplace, the English town of *Haverhill*, Suffolk.

Havlíčkův Brod. *City, central Czech Republic.* The city was earlier named *Německý Brod* (in World War II, German *Deutsch-Brod*), "German ford," referring to the crossing of the Sazava River here. In 1945 the present name was adopted, in honor of the Czech political poet and publicist Karel *Havlíček*-Borovsky (1821–1856).

Hawaii. *Island state of United States, central Pacific.* The name is a corruption of the original Polynesian *Owhyii*, "place of the gods," referring to the two volcanoes Mauna Kea and Mauna Loa, regarded as the abode of the gods on Hawaii itself, as the largest island of the group. When Captain Cook discovered the islands in 1778 (although they were already known to Spanish sailors in the 16th century) he named them *Sandwich Islands* in honor of John Montagu, 4th Earl of *Sandwich* (1718–1792), then first lord of the Admiralty, and this name was in regular use, as well as the indigenous one, down to the late 19th century. *Cp.* **South Sandwich Islands.**

Hawera. *Town, northwestern New Zealand.* The town, in western North Island, has a Maori name meaning "burnt place," said to refer to an intertribal battle.

Hawke Bay. *Bay, northeastern New Zealand.* The bay, an inlet of the Pacific on the east coast of North Island, was so named in 1769 by Captain Cook in honor of Edward *Hawke*, 1st Baron

Hawke (1705–1781), then first lord of the Admiralty. The local government region here is *Hawke's Bay*.

Haydarpaşa. *District of Istanbul, northwestern Turkey*. The eastern district of Istanbul, on the Asian side of the Bosporus, takes its name from *Haydar*, vizier of Sultan Selim III (1761–1808), who built the barracks here. *Paşa* (English *pasha*) is the title of a Turkish officer of rank.

Hayward. *City, southwestern United States*. The California city was founded in 1851 by William *Hayward*, who opened a hotel here after failing to find gold.

Hazarajat. *Region, central Afghanistan*. The name of the mountainous region represents Afghan *hezārajāt*, from *hezār*, a tribal name meaning "thousand," *jā*, "place," and *t*, a plural indicator.

Hazorea. *Kibbutz, northern Israel*. The kibbutz, founded in 1934, has a Hebrew name meaning "the sower."

Heathrow. *Airport, southeastern England*. London's major airport derives its name from a former *row* of cottages here by Hounslow *Heath*. The place was merely a hamlet down to the early 20th century, and the airport itself dates from 1946.

Hebrides. *Island group, northwestern Scotland*. The name is of uncertain origin. The Roman name of the islands was *Ebudae* or *Hæbudes*, and the present form of the name is apparently due to a miscopying at some stage of the *u* as *ri*. The Norse name for the islands was *Sudhreyar*, "southern islands," referring to their location with regard to the Orkneys. *Cp.* **Sutherland**.

Hebron. *City, southern West Bank*. The city derives its name from Hebrew *khavor*, "to join," "to unite," referring to its importance as a religious center. Its Arabic name is *al-khalīl*, "the bosom friend," or in full, *al-khalīl ar-rahman*, "the bosom friend of the merciful" (implying "bosom friend of God"), the Muslim name for Abraham, said to be buried here. The ancient name of Hebron was *Kirjath-arba* (Genesis 23:2), from Hebrew *qiryat arba'*, "city of the four," otherwise Greek *Tetrapolis*, referring either to the four united settlements here in biblical times, or to the city's location on four hills, or to four famous persons. (According to St. Jerome, they were Adam, Abraham, Isaac, and Jacob.) But Joshua 14:15 has a different origin: "And the name of Hebron before was Kirjath-arba; which Arba was a great man from the Anakims."

Hechingen. *City, southwestern Germany*. The city, first recorded in 786 as *Hahhingum*, derives its name from a personal name based on Germanic *hanha*, "strong," "swift," and the *-ingen* suffix meaning "people of."

Heerenveen. *Town, northern Netherlands*. The town was founded in 1551 and has a name meaning "peat bog of the lords," from Dutch *heer*, plural *heeren*, "lords," and *veen*, "bog," "marsh" (English *fen*).

Heerlen. *City, southeastern Netherlands*. The city's name has evolved from *Coriovallum*, that of the Roman settlement here. Its own name derives from Gaulish *corios*, "army," and Latin *vallum*, "fortification," as originally for **Cherbourg**, France.

Hegyalja. *Region, northeastern Hungary*. The mountainous region has a name amounting to "foothills," from Hungarian *hegy*, "mountain," and *alj*, "bottom," "lower part."

Heidelberg. *City, southwestern Germany*. The city probably derives its name from an early form of modern German *Heidelbeere*, "bilberry," referring to the presence of this shrub on the wooded slopes of the Odenwald. The *-beere* became *-berg*, as if meaning "mountain," by association with the hills.

Heidenheim. *City, southwestern Germany*. The city arose in the 13th century around a castle on the site of a Roman settlement by the Brenz River. Its name refers to the location, from Middle High German *hæle*, "slippery," "smooth," and *heim*, "house," "dwelling place." The full name of the city is *Heidenheim an der Brenz*, the river name itself deriving from Germanic *brandi*, "spring," "source."

Heilbronn. *City, southwestern Germany*. The city, on the Neckar River, has a name meaning "holy spring," from words equating to modern German *heilig*, "holy," and *Brunnen*, "spring." The spring in question was a stream in a wooded ravine on the present Kirchbrunnenstraße ("Church Spring Street").

Heiligenblut. *Village, southern Austria*. The name is German for "holy blood," referring to a church here preserving a vial traditionally said to contain some of Christ's blood.

Heiligendamm. *Town and resort, northeastern Germany*. The town, on the Baltic Sea, takes its name from a shingle bank almost 2 miles (3 km) long thrown up along the coast here in c.1430 following a severe storm. This was named the *Heilige Damm*, "holy dam," for its apparently miraculous formation.

Heiligenstadt. *Town and resort, southeastern Germany*. The noted health resort has a name meaning "city of the saints," from German *Heiligen*, "saints," and *Stadt*, "town," "city." The Martinskirche here formerly housed the relics of St. Aureus, bishop of Mainz, and St. Justina, his sister, transferred here from Mainz in the 9th century. The relics are now in the Ägidienkirche. Since 1950 the town's official name has been *Heilbad Heiligenstadt*, "Heiligenstadt spa." (The *Heil-* in the first word of this equates to English *heal*, while the *Heilig-* in the second word corresponds to *holy*.)

Heilungkiang. *Province, northeastern China.* The province derives its name from the Chinese name of the **Amur** River that forms its northern border with Russia. The river name means "river of the black dragon," from *hēi*, "black," *lóng*, "dragon," and *jiāng*, "river." *See also* **Sakhalin**.

Heimaey *see* **Vestmannaeyjar**

Heinsberg. *City, western Germany.* The city, near the Dutch border, arose around a castle of the same name, meaning "*Hein*'s castle," with the personal name a short form of *Heinrich*.

Hejaz. *Province, western Saudi Arabia.* The name represents Arabic *ḥijāz*, "obstacle," from *ḥajāza*, "to divide." The reference is to the physical location of the province, between the high plains that border the Red Sea.

Hekla. *Volcano, southwestern Iceland.* The volcano derives its name from Icelandic *hekla*, "hood," "cowl," referring to the mantle of mist that covers its summit.

Helena. *City, northwestern United States.* The state capital of Montana, founded in 1864, was probably given the name of *Helena*, Minnesota, from where an early settler must have come.

Helensburgh. *Town and port, western Scotland.* The name means "*Helen*'s town," for Lady *Helen* Sunderland, wife of Sir James Colquhoun of Luss, who founded the town in 1776.

Helicon, Mt. *Mountain, east central Greece.* The mountain has a descriptive name, from Greek *helix, helikos*, "spiral," "twisted," "winding," alluding to its shape.

Heligoland. *Island, eastern North Sea.* The German island, also known as *Helgoland*, derives its name from an early equivalent of modern German *heilig*, "holy," and *Land*, "land," referring to an ancient shrine here.

Heliopolis. *Historic city, northern Egypt.* The city, near the apex of the Nile delta, was a center of sun worship, as its name implies, from Greek *hēlios*, "sun," and *polis*, "city," and the sun god worshipped here was Re (Ra). The city's biblical name was *On* (Genesis 41:45, etc.), and it is also referred to as *Beth-shemesh* (Jeremiah 43:13). The latter Hebrew name, meaning "house of the sun," is rendered in the Septuagint (Greek version of the Old Testament) as *Heliop-*

olis, while the name *On* itself means "pillar (city)," referring to the stone obelisks set up to the sun god. (Two of these obelisks are the "Cleopatra's Needles" on London's Victoria Embankment and in New York's Central Park.)

Heliopolis *see* **Baalbek**

Hellespont *see* **Dardanelles**

Hellweg. *Plateau, western Germany.* The plateau, between the Ruhr and Lippe rivers, is an ancient migration route or "corridor." The second part of the name is almost certainly German *Weg*, "way," "route," while the first part has been popularly derived from Middle High German *helle*, "hell," giving a supposed sense "road to hell." But early forms of the name preclude this on phonetic grounds.

Helmand. *River, southwestern Afghanistan.* The name of the river goes back to Sanskrit *setumant*, "having a bridge," from *setu*, "bridge," and *mant*, "having." In its lower reaches the river flows under the desert sands without surfacing, so there are many points where it can be "bridged" or crossed.

Helmstedt. *City, north central Germany.* The city, founded in the 9th century, has a name meaning "*Helmo*'s place," with the personal name followed by Old High German *stat*, "place," "site."

Helsingør. *Town and port, eastern Denmark.* The town, the *Elsinore* of Shakespeare's *Hamlet*, has a name probably combining that of a local people with Norwegian *ör*, "tongue of land," referring to its coastal location on the Øresund. *See also* **Helsinki**.

Helsinki. *Capital of Finland.* The city was founded in 1550 by King Gustav Vasa of Sweden with the name of *Helsingfors*, from *Helsing*, the Old Norwegian name of a local people (as probably for **Helsingør**), and *fors*, "waterfall." The present name is the Finnish form of this. The city was originally on the estuary of the Vantaa River, where the waterfall was, but in 1640 moved down to its present location on a promontory in the Gulf of Finland in order to gain more open access to the sea.

Helvetia *see* **Switzerland**

Hemel Hempstead. *Town, southeastern England.* The Hertfordshire town has an Old English name that overall means "homestead in broken country." The first word represents *hamol*, a term used for "broken" land, otherwise a terrain with a mixture of steep hills and deep valleys, as in the country surrounding the town. The second word is the same as the name of **Hampstead**. Recorded as *Hamelamestede* in the Domesday Book, the name was reduced to just

Hemsted by the 16th century, when the lost first element was restored.

Hempstead. *Town, eastern United States.* The New York town was founded in 1640 by John Carman and the Reverend Robert Fordham and named for their native English town of **Hemel Hempstead**, Hertfordshire.

Henderson. *City, eastern United States.* The North Carolina city was settled in 1713 and when the town was laid out in 1840 it was named for Chief Justice Leonard *Henderson* (1772–1833), of the state's Supreme Court.

Heng-yang. *City, southeastern China.* The city, in Hunan province, derives its name from Chinese *héng*, "to weigh," "scales," and *yáng*, "light," "sun."

Henley. *Town, central England.* The Oxfordshire town, often known as *Henley-on-Thames*, has a name meaning "(settlement by the) high wood," from a form of Old English *hēah*, "high," and *lēah*, "wood." Henley lies at the foot of the Chiltern Hills.

Hennef. *Town, western Germany.* The town takes its name from the *Hanfbach*, the stream by which it arose in the 10th century. The stream's name probably derives from conjectural Germanic *hanan*, "to sing," "to purl," with Indogermanic *ap*, "water," added.

Henry, Cape. *Cape, eastern United States.* The Virginia cape, south of the entrance to Chesapeake Bay, is the site of the landing in 1607 of the first English settlers in America. They named it for *Henry* Frederick (1594–1612), 13-year-old son of James I and future Prince of Wales. *Cp.* **Charles, Cape.**

Henry Mountains. *Mountain range, western United States.* The range, in southern Utah, is named for the American scientist Joseph *Henry* (1797–1878).

Henzada. *Town, southwestern Myanmar.* The town's name is said to derive from Myanmar (Burmese) words meaning "lamentation of the goose," from a local legend about the death of a goose.

Heraklion. *City and port, southern Greece.* The city, on the north coast of Crete, has a name that derives from the Roman port of *Heracleum* formerly here, its own name associated with *Heracles* (*Hercules*), the hero of classical mythology. As the capital of Saracen Crete in the 9th century it took the Arabic name *khandak*, meaning "moat." This was corrupted to *Candia* by the Venetians, to whom Crete passed in the early 13th century. This name then came to denote the island as a whole. The current Greek form of the city's name is *Iráklion*. *Cp.* **Herculaneum.**

Herat. *City, western Afghanistan.* The city takes its name, also spelled *Harat*, from the **Hari Rud** River on which it lies.

Hérault. *Department, southern France.* The department is named for the river here. Its own name ultimately goes back to the Indoeuropean root element *ar*, "water," "river."

Hercegovina *see* **Bosnia-Hercegovina**

Herculaneum. *Historic city, southwestern Italy.* The ancient city, at the foot of Mt. Vesuvius, has a name traditionally linked with that of *Hercules*, the hero of classical mythology. *Cp.* **Heraklion.**

Heredia. *City, central Costa Rica.* The city was founded in the 1570s and originally called *Cubujuquí*, then *Villavieja* (Spanish, "old town"). In 1763 it was named as now for the Spanish president of the high tribunal, whose surname was *Heredia*.

Hereford. *Town, western England.* The town, in the county of the same name, has a name meaning "army ford," from Old English *here*, "army," and *ford*, "ford." An "army ford" was probably one where an army could march across a river without breaking formation. A Roman road crosses the Wye River at Hereford, so the ford would have been there. The Welsh name of Hereford is *Henffordd*, as if meaning "old ford" (Welsh *hen*, "old," and *ffordd*, "ford").

Hereroland. *Region, eastern Namibia.* The region is named for the *Herero* people, who inhabit it. Their own name is said to represent the sound of a spear in flight.

Herford. *City, northwestern Germany.* The city arose around a Benedictine nunnery founded in 823 at the point where the Aa River joins the Werre. Its name means "army ford," from Old High German *heri*, "army," and *furt*, "ford," denoting a place where Frankish armies crossed the Aa. *Cp.* **Hereford.**

Hermon, Mt. *Mountain ridge, southern Lebanon.* The ridge, on the border between southeastern Lebanon and southwestern Syria, derives its name from Hebrew *hrm*, "sacred," referring to its long-established sacred connections. Its current Arabic name is *Jabal ash-Shaikh*, "mountain of the chief." According to the Bible, the Sidonians called the ridge *Sirion* and the Amorites *Shenir* (Deuteronomy 3:9), and the three different names may actually be those of the ridge's three peaks. Another Arabic name for the snowcapped heights is *Jabal et-Talj*, "mountain of snow."

Hermopolis. *Historic town, east central Egypt.* The ancient town on the Nile River has a Greek name meaning "city of *Hermes*," not for the

Greek god identified with the Roman Mercury, but for *Hermes* Trismegistus, identified with Thoth, the Egyptian god of learning, whose temple was here. The site was also known as *Khmunu*, from Egyptian *khemen*, "eight," translating Greek *ogdoas, ogdoados*, "ogdoad," "group of eight," for the eight gods who created the universe, also venerated here. The Coptic form of this name, *Shmun*, gave the present Arabic one, *El Ashmunein*.

Herne. *City, western Germany*. The name, first recorded in 891 as *Haranni*, probably derives from Middle Low German *hare*, "hill," describing the site of the original abbey here.

Herrnhut. *Town, southeastern Germany*. The town arose in 1722 on the estate of Count Nikolaus Ludwig von Zinzendorf as a colony of Moravian Brethren. Its name translates as "protection of the Lord," meaning a place in God's keeping.

Herstal. *Town, eastern Belgium*. The town, now an industrial suburb of Liège, derives its name from Old High German *hari*, "army," and *stal*, "place," implying that there was a permanent military encampment here, at the point where Roman roads intersect and cross the Meuse River. The French form of the name is *Héristal*.

Herten. *City, western Germany*. The city arose as a farming community by a castle of this name, itself adopted by the lords who owned it from an 11th-century monastery. Its meaning is unknown.

Hertford. *Town, southeastern England*. The town, in the county of the same name, has an Old English name meaning what it says, "hart ford," denoting a site on the Lea River here where stags regularly crossed. *See also* **Hartford**.

Herzegovina *see* **Bosnia-Hercegovina**

Herzliyya. *City, west central Israel*. The city was founded in 1924 with the financial backing of American Zionists and named for Dr. Theodor *Herzl* (1860–1904), founder of modern Zionism.

Herzogenrath. *City, western Germany*. The city arose around an 11th-century castle and was original known as *Rode* (the *-rath* of the present name), meaning "clearing." From the 12th through the 18th century the town belonged to the duchy of Limburg, giving the first part of the name, from German *Herzog*, "duke." The city is still known locally as simply *Rode*.

Hesse. *State, central Germany*. The name goes back to *Hassi* or *Hatti*, the Roman name of a people who originally inhabited this region. The meaning of their own name is uncertain. The German form of the name is *Hessen*.

Hestmona. *Island, north central Norway*. The island, in the Norwegian Sea, has a name meaning "horseman island," referring to the outline of its rocky summit, which resembles a horseman wearing a cloak.

Hhohho. *District, northwestern Swaziland*. The name, pronounced as a guttural "*hwo-hwo*," is said to derive from the barking cry of baboons.

Hialeah. *City, southeastern United States*. The Florida city was settled in 1910 and is said to take its name from a Seminole word meaning "pretty prairie" or "high prairie."

Hibernia *see* **Ireland**

Hidalgo. *State, east central Mexico*. The state was established in 1869 and named for Miguel *Hidalgo* y Costilla (1753–1811), the revolutionary Mexican patriot. *Cp.* **Goliad**.

Hidrovia *see* **Hydrovia**

Higashiosaka. *City, southern Japan*. The city, in the island of Honshu, was formed in 1967 by the merger of three other towns and is named for its location, east of **Osaka**, from Japanese *higashi*, "east," and that city's name.

Highgate. *District of London, southeastern England*. The name means what it says, and refers to a "high gate," that is, a former tollgate here on a high section of the old Great North Road as it ran uphill on its way out of London.

Highlands. *Mountainous region, northwestern Scotland*. The region is so named by contrast with the *Lowlands* to the south. The Highlands are traditionally regarded as the "real" Scotland, with its Celtic speech and distinctive customs. Although the *High* is meant literally, it also suggests a superiority of some kind over the Lowlands.

High Point. *City, eastern United States*. The North Carolina city was laid out in 1853 at the "highest point" of the North Carolina Railroad between Goldsboro and Charlotte. Hence the name.

High Wycombe. *Town, southeastern England*. The Buckinghamshire town is *High* by contrast with the less important (rather than lower-lying) *West Wycombe*, a nearby village that is now part of High Wycombe itself. The main part of the name probably represents Old English *wīcum*, the dative plural of *wīc*, "dwelling," giving a meaning "(place) at the dwellings," but it could also derive from the *Wye* River here and Old English *cumbum*, dative plural of *cumb*, "valley," referring to the two Wycombes, High and West.

Hildburghausen. *Town, central Germany*. The name means "*Hildburg's* houses," denoting a settlement founded by a woman of this name.

Hilden. *City, northwestern Germany*. The city

derives its name from the raised site by the Itter River where it arose, from a word related to modern German *Halde*, "mound."

Hildesheim. *City, north central Germany*. The city's name is a shortening of original *Hildinesheim*, from the Old German personal name *Hildin* and Old High German *heim*, "house," "abode."

Himachal Pradesh. *State, northern India*. The name is Hindi in origin, with *Himachal* another name for the **Himalayas**, from Sanskrit *hima*, "snow," "winter," and *chal*, "to be stormy," and *Pradesh* meaning "country." The state is actually in the Himalayas northwest of Uttar Pradesh.

Himalayas. *Mountain system, southern Asia*. The great mountain system has a Hindi name meaning "abode of snow," from Sanskrit *hima*, "snow," "winter," "cold," and *ālaya*, "abode," "house," itself from *ā-*, a prefix denoting a slight increase, and *laya*, "place of rest." *See also* **Kanchenjunga**.

Himeji. *City, south central Japan*. The city, on the island of Honshu, derives its name from Japanese *hime*, "young lady," "princess," and *-ji*, "route," "distance."

Hindu Kush. *Mountain range, central Asia*. The name is Iranian in origin and represents *hendu kosh*, "killer of Indians," from *hendū*, "Indian," "Hindu," and *koshtan*, "killer." The name was given by the Persians to a mountain pass here where Indian slaves had perished in the bitter winter.

Hindustan. *Historic region, northern India*. The name means "Hindu land," from Iranian *hēndu*, "Hindu," and *ostān*, "country."

Hippo (Regius) *see* **Annaba**

Hippo (Zarytus) *see* **Bizerta**

Hirosaki. *City, northern Japan*. The city, in the island of Honshu, derives its name from Japanese *hiro*, "broad," "wide," and *sakini*, "before," "recently."

Hiroshima. *City, southern Japan*. The city's name relates to its location on the delta of the Ota River in the southwest of the island of Honshu, and means "broad island," from Japanese *hiro*, "broad," "wide," and *shima*, "island."

Hispaniola. *Island, central West Indies*. The island, divided politically into Haiti and the Dominican Republic, derives its name from the original Spanish title for it, *la isla española*, "the Spanish island," said to have been given by Columbus in 1492. The name is thus not a diminutive meaning "little Spain," as sometimes proposed.

Hitachi. *City, eastern Japan*. The coastal city, in the island of Honshu northeast of Tokyo,

derives its name from Japanese *hi*, "sun," "daytime," and *-ta* or *-tachi*, "ended."

Hobart. *City and port, southeastern Australia*. The capital of Tasmania was founded in 1804 and named for Robert *Hobart*, 4th Earl of Buckinghamshire (1760–1816), the British colonial secretary.

Hoboken. *City, eastern United States*. The site of the New Jersey city was purchased by the Dutch in c.1640 from the Lenni Lenape (Delaware) Indians, who smoked stone pipes. The name is thus said to derive from Algonquian words meaning "land of the tobacco pipe." But it is really a transference of the name of *Hoboken*, now a suburb of Antwerp, Belgium, not far from the Dutch border.

Ho Chi Minh City. *City and port, southern Vietnam*. The city's present name, adopted in 1976 when it ceased to be the capital of South Vietnam, honors *Ho Chi Minh* (1890–1969), president of North Vietnam. Its earlier name, still locally in use, was *Saigon*, that of the river on which the city lies. Its own origin is disputed. According to some authorities, it is a corruption of *Ta Ngon*, "end of the dam," although this would be more suitable for a settlement than a river. The city has had other names over the years, including *Rung Gon*, "wood of kapok trees," and *Ben Nghe*, "landing place of buffaloes."

Höchst. *District of Frankfurt, western Germany*. The present industrial district evolved from the main residence of the archbishops of Mainz by the Nidda River here, near the point where it joins the Main. Its name, recorded in 790 as *Hostat*, refers to the raised site, from early equivalents of modern German *hoch*, "high," and *Stadt*, "town."

Hódmezővásárhely. *City, southeastern Hungary*. The city's name analyzes as Hungarian *hód*, "beaver," *mező*, "field," *vásár*, "fair," and *hely*, "place," i.e. "place of the fair by the field of beavers." The fair would have been a market.

Hof. *City, east central Germany*. The city arose around a royal residence (*Hof*) in the 13th century in the region of Regnitzland, so called from the *Regnitz* River, and was at first itself called *Regnitz*. Since the river name designated the whole region, the new settlement was distinguished from it by adding *Hof* (*Raegentzhof* in 1323, *Hofregnitz* in 1553), and eventually became simply *Hof*.

Ho-fei. *City, eastern China*. The city, in Anhwei province, derives its name from Chinese *hé*, "to close," "to unite," "together," and *féi*, "rich," "fertile."

Hohe Acht. *Mountain, western Germany*. The

highest peak of the Eifel derives its name from Gaulish *acaunum*, "rock," "cliff," now prefixed by German *hohe*, "high."

Hohenstaufen. *Mountain, southwestern Germany*. The peak, in the Swabian Jura, bears the ruins of the ancestral castle of the same name, destroyed in 1525. It was built in 1079 by the founder of the Hohenstaufen dynasty, Count Frederick, who named it *Staufen* after the mountain, which itself derived its name from Old High German *stouf*, "cup," from its appearance as an upturned cup. A settlement *Staufen* arose below the castle, which thus in 1360 added *Hohen*, "high," for distinction from it.

Hohenzollern. *Mountain, southwestern Germany*. The mountain, in the Swabian Alps, takes its name from the original castle of the noted princely dynasty, whose origins have been traced back to Count Burchard I of *Zollern* in the early 11th century. This was itself named after the mountain, recorded in 1099 as *Zolro*. The name is of uncertain origin, although a source in Old High German *zolra*, "sugarloaf peak" has been suggested. The counts added *Hohen* ("high") to their title in the 14th century, and the mountain also took the prefix. The present 19th-century castle is the third on the site.

Hohhot. *City, northern China*. The capital of Inner Mongolia has a name of Mongolian origin, from *hoh*, "blue," and *hot*, "city." The reference is probably to the dark, blue-tinged stone of its original Buddhist temples. The name is also found in the form *Huhehot*. *Cp.* **Ulanhot**.

Ho-kang. *City, northeastern China*. The city, in Heilungkiang province, derives its name from Chinese *hè*, "crane," and *găng*, "hillock," "mound."

Hokkaido. *Island, northern Japan*. The name of Japan's second largest island means "northern sea province," from Japanese *hoku*, "north," *kai*, "sea," and *dō*, "way," "province," encapsulating its geographical and administrative status. Serious settlement on the island began only in 1869, before which it was known as *Yezo*, a name written with two pictograms: *ebi*, meaning "lobster," "shrimp," and *ebisu*, meaning "wild," "savage," "Ainu."

Holland *see* **Netherlands**

Hollywood. *District of Los Angeles, western United States*. The California site that would become the film center of the world was named by a Mrs. Deida Wilcox, the wife of Horace H. Wilcox, a Kansas City real estate man, who in 1886 retired with her husband to a large ranch that stood here. They began parceling their land in 1891 and in 1903 the growing community was incorporated as a village, retaining the original name of the ranch, *Hollywood*. In most places of the name in the United States the meaning is literal, "holly wood," whereas in the British Isles it is often "holy wood."

Holstein *see* **Schleswig-Holstein**

Holsteinsborg *see* **Sisimiut**

Holyhead. *Town and port, northwestern Wales*. The name, meaning "holy headland," relates to the town's site on the island of Anglesey. Holyhead has long been a Christian center. The headland in question is Holyhead Mountain, to the west of the town. (*Cp.* **Penzance**.) The Welsh name of the town is *Caergybi*, "*Cybi*'s fort," for the Celtic saint to whom the parish church is dedicated.

Holy Island *see* **Lindisfarne**

Homburg. *City, southwestern Germany*. The city is named for the *Hohenberg* family of Lotharingian counts, who took their own name in the 12th century from the fort built here two centuries earlier on a raised site with a name meaning simply "high hill."

Home Counties. *Region of southeastern England*. The counties are those closest to London, i.e. Surrey, Kent, Essex, and (formerly) Middlesex, although the term may also encompass more remote counties, such as Berkshire, Buckinghamshire, and Hertfordshire. These are the rural counties where the gentry had their homes, conveniently close to the capital for business or pleasure there. The name is rarely found on maps.

Homs. *City, west central Syria*. The name is an Arabic form of the city's earlier Latin name *Emesus* or *Emesa* (Greek *Emesos* or *Emesa*), of uncertain meaning.

Honan. *Province, north central China*. The province has a name meaning "south of the river," from Chinese *hé*, "river," and *nān*, "south," describing its location to the south of the Yellow River. *Cp.* **Hopeh**.

Hondarribia *see* **Fuenterrabía**

Honduras. *Republic, northern Central America*. The country's name is the Spanish word meaning "depths." The story goes that when Columbus reached this land in 1524, he and his crew noticed the unusual depth of the sea and gave thanks to God for their safe passage over such dangerous waters. Whether this is so or not, the name does accurately describe the coastal waters here. *See also* **Belize**.

Honfleur. *Town and port, northern France*. The town's name means "*Hun*'s inlet," from the Germanic personal name *Hun* or *Hunn*, and Old English *flēot*, "inlet," "creek."

Hong. *River, northern Vietnam.* The river, rising in southern China and flowing southeast through northern Vietnam to enter the Gulf of Tonkin, has a Vietnamese name meaning "red," referring to the silt rich in iron oxide that it carries. It is also known in English as *Red River*.

Hong Kong. *Administrative region, southeastern China.* The name of the special administrative region of China, from 1841 through 1997 a British crown colony, represents the Cantonese pronunciation of Chinese *xiānggǎng,* "fragrant port," from *xiāng,* "perfume," "scent," and *gǎng,* "port," "harbor," in romanized form *Hsiangkang* or *Xianggang.* The reference is probably to the currents of Hong Kong Harbour, between mainland Kowloon and Hong Kong Island, which are sweetened by the fresh water carried down from the estuary of the Xi Jiang River to the west. However, the "perfume" could also have emanated from ships carrying opium, or from the incense factories formerly lining the coast here.

Honiara. *Capital of Solomon Islands.* The town's name represents the fuller form *Naghoniara,* "place of the east wind," or "(place) facing the trade winds," with *ara* the local word for such winds. Honiara is on the north coast of the island of Guadalcanal.

Honolulu. *City and port, northwestern Hawaii, United States.* The state capital of Hawaii, on southeastern Oahu Island, has an indigenous name meaning "calm harbor," from Hawaiian *hono,* "port," "harbor," and *lulu,* "calm." The harbor is naturally sheltered.

Honshu. *Island, central Japan.* Japan's largest island derives its name from Japanese *hon,* "main," "principal," and *shū,* "region." The island is thus Japan's "mainland."

Hooghly. *River, northeastern India.* The river, in West Bengal state, is said to take its name from Bengali *hoglā,* "elephant grass" (*Typha elephantum*). The name is also spelled *Hugli.*

Hook of Holland. *Cape, southwestern Netherlands.* The name translates the cape's Dutch name, *Hoek van Holland,* "corner of Holland." It is a "hook" in the sense of being an angle of land. The name is also that of a port here.

Hoorn. *Town, northwestern Netherlands.* The town and former port derives its name from Dutch *hoorn,* "horn," referring to its original horn-shaped harbor. *See also* **Horn, Cape**.

Hopeh. *Province, northeastern China.* The province has a name meaning "north of the river," from Chinese *hé,* "river," and *běi,* "north," describing its location to the north of the Yellow River. *Cp.* **Honan**.

Horeb *see* **Sinai, Mt**.

Hormuz. *Island, southern Persian Gulf.* The Iranian island, in the strait of the same name, has a name representing Greek *Harmoson* or *Harmosa,* itself probably the name of the Zoroastrian god *Ormuzd,* in turn a form of the name of *Ahura Mazda,* the god of goodness and light.

Horn, Cape. *Cape, southern South America.* The southernmost point of South America was rounded in 1616 by the Dutch navigators Willem Schouten and Jakob le Maire, who named it for the former's birthtown of **Hoorn**. Its own name means "horn," so was further appropriate for a headland or peninsula. *Cp.* **Horne Islands**.

Horne Islands. *Island group, southwestern Pacific.* The two volcanic islands, in the southwestern part of Wallis and Futuna, were sighted in 1616 by the Dutch navigators Willem Schouten and Jakob le Maire and named by them for the former's birthtown of **Hoorn** in Holland. *Cp.* **Horn, Cape**.

Horsham. *Town, southern England.* The West Sussex town has a name meaning "horse enclosure," from Old English *hors,* "horse," and *hamm,* "river meadow," or *hām,* "homestead." The implication is that horses would have been bred here.

Hortobágy. *Region, eastern Hungary.* The name is that of the river here, a tributary of the Tisza. Its own origin and meaning are unknown.

Hoshangabad. *Town, central India.* The town, in Madhya Pradesh state, was founded in 1406 by Sultan *Hoshang* Shah of Malwa, and is named for him, with Iranian *ābād* meaning "inhabited place," "town."

Hospitalet. *City, northeastern Spain.* The satellite city of Barcelona took its name in the 16th century from the small *hospital* that sheltered travelers and pilgrims here. The full form of the name is *L'Hospitalet de Llobregat,* for the *Llobregat* River here.

Hot Springs. *City and resort, south central United States.* The Arkansas city, settled in 1807, has a self-explanatory name referring to its 47 thermal springs.

Houma. *City, southern United States.* The Louisiana city was founded in c.1810 and named for the local Native Americans, the *Houma.* Their own name is said to derive from Choctaw *humma,* "red," although the precise sense is uncertain.

Hounslow. *Borough of London, southeastern England.* The name means either "*Hund*'s mound," with the Anglo-Saxon personal name followed by Old English *hlāw,* "mound," "barrow," or "hound's mound." If the former, the mound could have been the burial place of the man named.

Houston. *City and port, southern United States*. The Texas city was founded in 1836 and named for the first president of Texas, Sam *Houston* (1793–1863).

Hövsgöl. *Province, northwestern Mongolia*. The name is that of the lake here, itself meaning "lake of many waters."

Howe, Cape. *Cape, southeastern Australia*. The southeasternmost point of mainland Australia was sighted in 1776 by Captain Cook, who named it for Richard *Howe*, Earl Howe (1726–1799), then treasurer of the Royal Navy.

Höxter. *Town, central Germany*. The name, first recorded in 822 as *villa Huxori* (with *villa* meaning "village"), is of uncertain origin. The second part is the collective suffix *-eri*. The first part may represent Middle Dutch *hoec*, "corner" (English *hook*), referring to a bend in the Weser River here.

Hoyerswerda. *City, eastern Germany*. The city is said to have been founded in 1268 by Count *Hoyer* of Friedeburg, and this gave the first part of the name. The second part is from Middle Low German *werd*, "island," "promontory," referring to the site of the original settlement on the Schwarze Elster River.

Hradec Králové. *Town, northwestern Czech Republic*. The town's name derives from words corresponding to modern Czech *hrad*, "castle," "fort," and *králova*, "queen," giving an overall sense "royal fortress." The town was fortified in the 14th century and was associated with Elizabeth of Poland, queen of Hungary (died 1381). The German name of the town is *Königgrätz*, a part translation, part corruption of the Czech.

Hrubieszów. *Town, southeastern Poland*. The town, dating from at least the 15th century, bases its name on the personal name *Hrubiesz*.

Hsi. *River, southern China*. The longest river in southern China derives its name from Chinese *xī*, "west." The name is more narrowly applied to its lower course, before it enters the South China Sea to the west of Macau.

Hsia-kuan *see* ²**Ta-li**

Hsia-men *see* **Amoy**

Hsiang. *River, east central China*. The river, a tributary of the Yangtze, derives its name from Chinese *xīang*, the old name of **Hunan** province, in which it runs.

Hsiang-fan. *City, east central China*. The city, in Hubei province, derives its name from Chinese *xīang*, "to assist," "to help," and *fán*, "cage."

Hsiang-kang *see* **Hong Kong**

Hsiang-t'an. *City, east central China*. The city, in Hunan province, derives its name from Chinese *xīang*, the old name of the province, and *tán*, "deep pool."

Hsin-hsiang. *City, eastern China*. The city, in Honan province, derives its name from Chinese *xīn*, "new," and *xīang*, "native place."

Hsi-ning. *City, central China*. The capital of Tsinghai province derives its name from Chinese *xī*, "west," and *níng*, "peaceful," "tranquil." The city has long been a strategic point on the western frontier with Tibet.

Hsüan-hua. *City, northeastern China*. The city, in Hopeh province, derives its name from Chinese *xuān*, "to declare," "to proclaim," and *huà*, "to change," "to dissolve."

Huai-nan. *City, eastern China*. The city, in Anhwei province, is not far south of the *Huai* River. Hence its name, from Chinese *huái*, the river name, and *nán*, "south."

Huambo. *City, west central Angola*. The city's name is a Portuguese corruption of the indigenous name *Ouimbundu*, the meaning of which is uncertain. The town was founded in 1912 by Portuguese settlers and in 1928 was renamed *Nova Lisboa*, "new **Lisbon**," the aim being to emphasize colonial ties. (It was intended to be the new Angolan capital.) The city reverted to the earlier name in 1975.

Huancavelica. *City, central Peru*. The town was founded in 1572 following the discovery of mercury here and was given the Spanish name *Villa Rica de Oropesa*, "rich town of *Oropesa*," for the Spanish town of this name. It became known as *Huancavelica*, however, a Spanish corruption of the Quechua name of the site, meaning "stone idol," and was officially declared a city with this name in 1581.

Huancayo. *City, central Peru*. The city's name derives from the Quechua word meaning "*Huanca* people," referring to the local Native Americans of this name.

Huang Hai. *Sea, western Pacific*. The sea, between Korea and northeastern China, is still widely known by its English name of *Yellow Sea*, translating Chinese *huáng*, "yellow," and *hăi*, "sea." The reference is to the color of the silt-laden water discharged into it from many rivers. One of them was the **Huang Ho**.

Huang Ho. *River, north central and eastern China*. China's second longest river is still widely known by its English name of *Yellow River*, translating Chinese *huáng*, "yellow," and *hé*, "river." The reference is to the yellow silt suspended in its waters. It formerly flowed into the **Huang Hai**, named for it, but its course was diverted in 1852 and it now enters the Gulf of Chihli to the north.

Huang-shih. *City, eastern China.* The city, in Hupeh province, derives its name from Chinese *huáng*, "yellow," and *shí*, "stone," "rock." The name was originally that of the landing on the Yangtze River here serving the original small town of Shih-tan-yao.

Huánuco. *City, central Peru.* The city derives its name from a Native American word meaning "arid."

Huascarán. *Mountain, west central Peru.* The mountain, in the Andes, is named for *Huascar* (died 1532), the Inca chieftain who was the heir to the Inca Empire.

Hubli-Dharwad. *City, southwestern India.* The city, in Karnataka state, was formed in 1961 on the amalgamation of the two towns *Hubli* and *Dharwad. Hubli*, also known as *Hubballi* or *Pubballi*, has a name meaning "old village"; *Dharwad*, earlier *Daravada*, means "gateway town."

Huddersfield. *Town, northern England.* The former West Yorkshire town has an Old English name meaning either "*Hudrǣd*'s open land," with the rare Anglo-Saxon personal name followed by *feld*, "open land" (modern *field*), or "open land of the shelter," from *hūder* and *feld*.

Hudson. *River, eastern United States.* New York's main river was explored in 1809 by the English navigator Henry *Hudson* (died 1611) and is named for him. *See also* **Hudson Bay.**

Hudson Bay. *Inland sea, northeastern Canada.* The sea, in the Northwest Territories, where it is joined to the Atlantic by Hudson Strait, is named for the English navigator Henry *Hudson* (died 1611), who explored it in 1610. His crew mutinied in the bay, and cast him adrift there to die. He also gave the name of New York's **Hudson** River.

Hue. *City, central Vietnam.* The former capital of Annam has a name that ultimately derives from Chinese *huá*, "China" (literally "brilliant," "prosperous"), used as an abbreviation for *huáqiáo*, "overseas China," a term for a Chinese living outside China.

Huelva. *City and port, southwestern Spain.* The city's name was recorded by Pliny in the 1st century A.D. as *Onuba*. This is probably of Punic origin, but its meaning is unknown.

Huesca. *City, northeastern Spain.* The city was known to the Romans as *Osca*. This may derive from the *Oscans*, the people who mostly inhabited southern Italy, but who may have had a settlement here.

Hugli *see* **Hooghly**

Huhehot *see* **Hohhot**

Hull. *City and port, northeastern England.* The east coast city takes its name from the small *Hull* River which here enters the much larger Humber. The river's own name may come from a Celtic root word meaning "muddy." The city's official name is *Kingston-upon-Hull.* The first part of this refers to *King* Edward I, who exchanged lands elsewhere for the port in 1292. Another name of Hull in the 12th and 13th centuries was *Wyke.* This represents either Old English *wīc*, "dairy farm," "trading place," or Old Norse *vík*, "creek," "inlet," as for **Wick,** Scotland. The former seems more likely.

Humber. *River, northeastern England.* The estuarial river, flowing into the North Sea, has a name of uncertain origin. It may have a Celtic base meaning "good river," the final *-ber* meaning "river." A "good river" would have been one favorable for fishing and trading, although the name may have been a "placatory" one, designed to appease a destructive river god. The Humber has dangerous currents.

Humboldt. *River, western United States.* The Nevada river was named in 1843 by the U.S. explorer John C. Frémont for the German naturalist Alexander von *Humboldt* (1769–1859), explorer of uncharted territory in South America.

Hunan. *Province, central China.* The province has a name meaning "south of the lake," from Chinese *hú*, "lake," and *nán*, "south," describing its location with regard to Lake Dongting. *Cp.* **Hupeh.**

Hunedoara. *Town, western Romania.* The town bases its name on a personal name, presumably that of an early landowner or even of its founder. The final *-ara* represents Hungarian *vár*, "fortress," "castle."

Hungary. *Republic, central Europe.* The country does not derive its name from its indigenous inhabitants, as is often the case, since these are the *Magyar*, itself probably meaning simply "people." The Hungarian name of Hungary is accordingly *Magyarország*, "*Magyar* land." The English name is traditionally said to derive from that of the *Huns*, who who built up a vast empire in this part of Europe in the 5th century. Related equivalent names are French *Hongrie*, German *Ungarn*, Russian *Vengriya*, and Ukrainian *Ugorshchina*, but Turkish *Macaristan*, like the Hungarian, means "land of the *Magyar*."

Hungnam. *City and port, eastern North Korea.* The city derives its name from Korean *hŭng*, "happiness," and *nam*, "south."

Hunsrück. *Mountain region, western Ger-*

many. The southernmost region of the Rhenish Uplands has a name meaning literally "dog's back," from Old High German *hunt*, "dog" (English *hound*) and *rukke*, "back" (English *ridge*), originally referring just to the area around Simmern and Kirchberg. Alternate derivations in Old High German *hūn*, a dative form of *hōh*, "high," or Old High German *hunto*, "head of a hundred," or Germanic *hun*, "brown," "dark," are mere conjectures.

Hunter. *River, southeastern Australia.* The river, in New South Wales, was named *Coal River* in 1791 by convicts, with reference to the *coal* outcrops along its course. In 1797 it was renamed as now for John *Hunter*, colonial governor from 1795 to 1800.

Huntingdon. *Town, east central England.* The Cambridgeshire town, formerly in Huntingdonshire, has an Old English name meaning "hunter's hill," meaning a hill favored by huntsmen. The hill referred to is probably the low broad one on which the town lies overlooking the Ouse River.

¹Huntington. *Town, eastern United States.* The New York town was so named in 1653 for Oliver Cromwell's English birthplace, **Huntingdon.**

²Huntington. *City, eastern United States.* The West Virginia city was laid out in 1870 when Collis P. *Huntington* (1821–1900) built the western terminal of the Chesapeake and Ohio Railway.

Huntington Beach. *City, southwestern United States.* The California coastal city, originally known as *Shell Beach*, then *Pacific City*, was renamed as now in 1903 for the railroad executive Henry E. *Huntington* (1850–1927), nephew of Collis P. *Huntington* (see ²**Huntington**).

Huntsville. *City, southeastern United States.* The Alabama city was originally called *Twickenham* by Leroy Pope, for the village near London, England, that was the home of his kinsman, the poet Alexander Pope. In 1811 it was renamed as now for the Revolutionary war veteran John *Hunt* of Virginia, who first settled the area in 1805.

Hupeh. *Province, central China.* The province has a name meaning "north of the lake," from Chinese *hú*, "lake," and *běi*, "north," describing its location with regard to Lake Dongting. *Cp.* **Hunan.**

Huron, Lake. *Lake, east central North America.* The lake, in the northeastern United States and southeastern Canada, takes its name from the *Huron*, the Native American people who lived on its shores. Their own name was given

by French colonists in the 16th century, and derives from obsolete French *huron*, "bristle-haired." The reference was probably to the people's headdress rather than to their natural hair.

Húsavík. *Town, northern Iceland.* Iceland's oldest settlement has a name meaning "bay of houses." Legend tells how a Swedish voyager, Gardar, blown off course, built a house and wintered here in 864.

Hussein Dey. *Suburb of Algiers, northern Algeria.* The industrial suburb takes its name from *Hussein* III, last *dey* (governor) of Algiers (1818 to 1830).

Husum. *City and port, northwestern Germany.* The city, first mentioned in the 13th century, has a name meaning "by the houses," from the dative plural form (ending -*um*) of Old Danish *hus*, "house." The original settlement here consisted of three separate villages.

Huy. *Town, south central Belgium.* The town takes its name from the *Hoyoux* River, which joins the Meuse here. Its own name derives from Old High German *ouwa*, "island," "raised land by water."

Hvar. *Island, eastern Adriatic Sea.* The Croatian island, off the coast of Dalmatia, was settled by Greeks in the 1st century B.C. and was known to them as *Pharos*, a name adopted from that of the former island (now a peninsula) off Alexandria, Egypt. Its own name is of unknown origin. The Italian name of Hvar is *Lesina*, from Slavic *les*, "forest."

Hwange. *City, western Zimbabwe.* The city bears the name of a local chief, *Hwange* Rusumbami, head of a section of the Rozvi tribe. Until 1982 the name was spelled *Wankie*.

Hwang Hai *see* **Huang Hai**

Hwang Ho *see* **Huang Ho**

¹Hyderabad. *City, south central India.* The capital of Andhra Pradesh state was founded in 1589 with the name *Bhagyanagar*, "city of good fortune." In 1591 it was renamed as now by Muhammad Quli Qutb Shah, sultan of Golconda, for his son *Haidar*, "lion," with Iranian *ābād*, "town." The former princely state of Hyderabad took its name from the city, as its former capital.

²Hyderabad. *City, southern Pakistan.* The city was founded in 1768 by Ghulam Shah Kalhora, ruler of Sind, and named for Ali, self-titled *Haidar*, "lion," son-in-law of Muhammad, the founder of Islam. *Cp.*¹**Hyderabad.**

Hydrovia. *Waterway, South America.* The proposed waterway, involving the straightening and deepening of the Paraná River system, has a name meaning simply "waterway," from Spanish *hidro-*, "water," and *vía*, "way" (or Portuguese *hidro-* and *via*). Hence the alternate spelling *Hidrovia*. (The name could also be seen as Greek *hydro-* and Latin *via*.) The project was implemented in 1994.

Hyères. *City, southeastern France*. The name of the city ultimately goes back to Latin *area*, "open space."

Hyogo. *Prefecture, south central Japan*. The prefecture, in the island of Honshu, derives its name from Japanese *hyō*, "army," and *ko*, "store."

Hyrcania. *Historic region, northern Iran*. The name probably comes from the Greek personal name *Hyrkanos*, the meaning of which is unknown. The Old Persian name of the region, based on this, was *Varkana*, interpreted as "wolf's land."

Hythe. *Town, southeastern England*. The Kent town and former port derives its name from Old English *hȳth*, "landing place." Although the modern town is on the coast, the original reference would have been to a landing place inland on the Lympne River.

Iaşi. *City, northeastern Romania*. The city's present name is a Romanian form of its German name, *Jassy*, itself said to derive from German *Jäger*, "hunter," denoting a former people here who were noted as bowmen. But this looks like an attempt to explain an otherwise obscure name.

Ibadan. *City, southwestern Nigeria*. The city's name is of Arabic origin, from *'ibāda*, "worship," itself from *'ibād*, the plural of *'abd*, "servant." The actual beginnings of Ibadan are shrouded in mystery, although the city has long been a center of Islam.

¹Ibaraki. *Prefecture, east central Japan*. The prefecture, in the island of Honshu, derives its name from Japanese *ibara*, "thorn," and *ki*, "castle."

²Ibaraki. *City, west central Japan*. The city, in the island of Honshu, derives its name from Japanese *ibara*, "thorn," and *ki*, "tree."

Ibbenbüren. *City, northwestern Germany*. The city's name means "(settlement) by the houses of *Ibbo*," with an Old German personal name.

Iberia. *Peninsula, southwestern Europe*. The peninsula occupied by Spain and Portugal derives its name from that of its indigenous people, the *Iberians*. Their own name comes from that of the **Ebro**, the river that flows east across the peninsula into the Mediterranean.

Ibiza. *Island, western Mediterranean Sea*. The Spanish island, in the Balearic Islands, has a name of Punic origin, representing *ī busim*, "island of perfumes," from *ī*, "island," and *busim*,

"perfumes." The reference is to the aromatic shrubs and trees found widely across the island's mostly hilly terrain. The local Catalan name of Ibiza (and of its capital of the same name) is *Eivissa*.

Icaria. *Island, eastern Greece*. The Aegean island is traditionally said to take its name from *Icarus*, the son of Daedalus in Greek mythology who fell into the sea here when the wax on his wings melted after he flew too close to the sun. Its more likely origin is in Pelasgian *īkar*, "timber," referring to the island's formerly plentiful forestland.

Iceland. *Island republic, North Atlantic*. The name means what it says, "ice land," from Icelandic *ís*, "ice," and *land*, "land." The name was given to the island by the Viking settler Floki, who came here in 960. Today the name is something of a misnomer, since Iceland's climate is comparatively mild, with an average January temperature ranging from 0°C on the coast to -10°C in the mountains, and a corresponding July temperature from 11°C to 0°C. But when the name was given, over a millennium ago, the climate may well have been different. The Icelandic name of Iceland is thus *Ísland*.

I-ch'ang. *City, east central China*. The city, in Hupeh province, derives its name from Chinese *yí*, "suitable," "appropriate," and *chāng*, "prosperous," "flourishing."

Ichikawa. *City, east central Japan*. The city, on the Edo river in the island of Honshu, derives its name from Japanese *ichi*, "market," and *kawa*, "river."

Ichinomiya. *City, central Japan*. The city, in the island of Honshu, has a name meaning "shrine of the one," from Japanese *ichi*, "one," *no*, indicating possession, and *miya*, "shrine." The reference is to the Shinto temple (the Masumida Shrine) around which the town developed in the 7th century.

I-ch'un. *City, northeastern China*. The city, in Heilungkian province, derives its name from Chinese *yī*, "he," "she," and *chūn*, "springtime."

Ida, Mt. *see* **Idi**

Idaho. *State, northwestern United States*. The name is said to be of Native American origin, but its language and meaning are obscure and it could be a pseudo–Indian creation. An interpretation "fish eaters" has been suggested, although most authorities favor "gem of the mountains," referring to the region's natural deposits of gold and silver.

Idar-Oberstein. *City, southwestern Germany*. The city was formed in 1933 on the amalgamation of the towns of *Idar*, named after the *Idar*

River, its own name of unknown origin, and *Oberstein*, named after a 14th-century castle, its own name indicating its site above (*ober*) an earlier fort of stone (*Stein*).

Idealtepe. *District of Istanbul, northwestern Turkey.* The resort district of Istanbul, on the Sea of Marmara, was originally called *Süreyyaplaji*, "*Süreyya's* beach," from a female personal name. The current name means "ideal hill," denoting a suitable place for a new settlement, from Turkish *ideal*, "ideal," and *tepe*, "hill."

Idi. *Mountain, central Crete, southern Greece.* The mountain, the Mt. *Ida* of classical mythology, has a name that is said to represent Doric Greek *ide*, "thick wood," "timber."

Idi Amin Dada, Lake *see* **Edward, Lake**

Idrija. *Town, western Slovenia.* The town takes its name from the river on which it stands. The origin of the river's own name has been the subject of much speculation. Some authorities link it with Greek *hudrarguros*, "quicksilver," "mercury," referring to the mercury mines for which Idrija is famous. But it probably comes from a basic Indoeuropean root element *dhr-* meaning simply "water," "river."

Ife. *Town, west central Nigeria.* The town may be so called for the identically named Yoruba god of divination. The fact that it was a holy place and that it has gold mines has led some to associate it with the biblical region of *Ophir* (1 Kings 9:28), but its own location remains uncertain.

Ifni. *Historic region, southwestern Morocco.* The former Spanish province derives its name from Tuareg *isafen*, the plural of *asif*, "water," "river." The region is mostly arid semidesert, and the name refers to its location on the Atlantic coast.

Iglesias. *Town, southern Sardinia.* The Italian town derives its name from a Sardinian form of Latin *ecclesia*, "church." Iglesias is noted for its 13th-century cathedral, probably built on the site of an earlier church.

Iguaçu. *River, southern Brazil.* The river, a tributary of the Paraná, has a Guaraní name meaning "great water."

IJsselmeer. *Lake, northwestern Netherlands.* The lake is named for the *IJssel* River that flows into it, with Dutch *meer* meaning "lake." The river's own name derives from a root word meaning simply "water," "river." (In Dutch, the digraph *ij*, pronounced like English "eye," is regarded as a single letter, so that when it begins a proper name it is written as a double capital.) The lake was formed in 1932 from the southern part of the former *Zuider Zee*, its own name

meaning "southern sea," by contrast with the **North Sea**, and perhaps also the *Ostsee*, "eastern sea," the German name of the Baltic Sea.

Île-de-France. *Historic region, north central France.* The region around Paris came to be known as the "island of France" in the 15th century with reference to the rivers that bound it, the name *France* having a much more local application than today.

Ilhéus. *City and port, northeastern Brazil.* The city originated in 1532 as a Portuguese colonial settlement named *São Jorge dos Ilhéos*, "St. George of the islands," referring to the four islands off the coast here that provide shelter for the harbor.

Ilium *see* **Troy**

Illawarra. *Region, southeastern Australia.* The coastal region in New South Wales, extending south of Sydney, derives its name from Aboriginal *alowrie*, "high pleasant place by the sea."

Illiers-Combray. *Town, northwestern France.* The town was originally just *Illiers*, perhaps from a Germanic personal name *Illhari*. *Combray* was the fictional name used for Illiers in the novels of Marcel Proust, who often spent his childhood holidays here, and was officially added to the original name in 1970. The real *Combray* is further north, near Caen, and it is possible that Proust actually based the name on that of *Combres*, near Illiers.

Illimani. *Mountain, eastern Bolivia.* The snow-capped peak of the Bolivian Andes has a Quechua name meaning "snow mountain."

Illinois. *State, north central United States.* The state ultimately takes its name from the Algonquian people known as the *Illini*, itself probably meaning simply "men," "warriors." The final *-ois* was added by French settlers to name the river that flows through the state.

Illyria. *Historic region, southeastern Europe.* The region, in extent approximating to the former Yugoslavia and Albania, has a name of obscure origin. It may come from a conjectural root word *is-lo* meaning "living," although the precise sense of this is uncertain.

Ilmenau. *City, east central Germany.* The city takes its name from the *Ilm* River on which it lies. The river's own name, a shortened form of *Ilmenau*, probably derives from an Indoeuropean base *el-*, "to flow," rather than Old High German *elm*, "elm," as sometimes stated. (The Ilm, a tributary of the Saale, should not be confused with the identically named *Ilmenau*, a tributary of the Elbe.)

Iloilo. *City, western Philippines.* The city, on the island of Panay, has a name that was corrupted by the Spanish from an original *Ilong-Ilong*, "nose-shaped," referring to the winding course of the Jaro River as it enters the sea here.

Ilulíssat. *Town, western Greenland.* The town was founded by the Danes in 1741 and originally named *Jakobshavn*, "*Jakob*'s harbor," for *Jakob* Severin, who in a 1739 naval battle defeated four Dutch ships in Disko Bay. In 1985 it received its present Greenlandic name, meaning "icebergs." Hundreds of icebergs are formed each year off the west coast of Greenland.

Imeretia. *Historic region, western Georgia.* The name derives from Georgian *imer*, "beyond," and the suffix *-eti*, "land," giving an overall sense amounting to "back country." The region is separated from eastern Georgia by the Likh range of mountains.

Imperatriz. *City, north central Brazil.* The city was founded by Portuguese Jesuit missionaries in 1852 on the site of a Native American village on the Tocantins River. They originally named it *Santa Teresa*, primarily for *St. Teresa* of Ávila, but also for the Brazilian empress *Teresa Cristina*, wife of Dom Pedro II (*see* **Teresópolis**). In 1856 the settlement was raised to town status and in 1862 renamed *Vila Nova da Imperatriz*, "new town of the empress," as Teresa Cristina had offered the city her royal patronage. The name was later shortened as now.

Imperia. *Town and port, northern Italy.* The town was formed in 1923 by the union of two other towns and several villages, and takes its name from the river known as the *Torrente Impero* that crosses it. The river's own name has become associated with Latin *imperium*, "empire," but its actual origin is disputed.

Ince, Cape. *Cape, northern Turkey.* The cape derives its name from Turkish *ince*, "narrow," "thin," referring to its shape. It is also known by its full Turkish name of *Inceburun*, where *burun* means "cape."

Inchon. *City and port, northwestern South Korea.* The city, near the mouth of the Han River, derives its name from Korean *in*, "virtue," and *ch'ŏn*, "river."

Independence. *City, central United States.* The Missouri city was settled in 1837 and named for President Andrew Jackson (1767–1845), celebrating his love of *independence*.

India. *Republic, southern Asia.* The country takes its name from the **Indus**, the river that flows through it (and also Pakistan). The indigenous Hindi name of India is *Bhārat*, from Sanskrit *bhārata*, the name of an ancient hero, whose own name is based on the root *bhṛ*, "carrying," "supporting," itself related to English *bear*.

(When India gained independence in 1947 it was thought by many that the new republic would adopt this name, but Nehru, the state's first prime minister, demanded that his country retain its long-familiar name.)

Indiana. *State, north central United States.* The future state was given its Latin-style name in the mid–18th century by French settlers or developers, with reference to the *Indian* (Native American) peoples whose territory it was.

Indianapolis. *City, north central United States.* The state capital of **Indiana** was founded in 1821 and given a name based on that of the territory itself, with Greek *polis*, "city," added. *Indianapolis* and **Oklahoma City** are the only two U.S. state capitals to be named for their states.

Indian Ocean. *Ocean between India and Antarctica.* The world's third-largest ocean was so named by Europeans for **India**, a land that promised exotic riches, with the eastward route across the ocean being the route to India. The name first appears on Johannes Schöner's terrestrial globe of 1515 as *Oceanus Orientalis Indicus*, "Eastern Indian Ocean," so called by contrast with the *Western Ocean*, as the Atlantic was then known.

Indochina. *Peninsula, southeastern Asia.* The name for the extensive peninsula between **India** and **China** was proposed in the early 19th century by the Scottish poet and orientalist John Leyden, who lived and worked in India from 1803 until his premature death in 1811 at the age of 35.

Indonesia. *Island republic, southeastern Asia.* The name, meaning "Indian islands," was based on that of **Polynesia**, and relates to the *Indian Ocean*, to the west of the group, with Greek *nēsos*, "island," giving the rest of the name. The name itself was already in use in the first half of the 19th century, and was soon adopted by geographers. The alternate name *East Indies* has long been applied primarily to Indonesia (*cp.* **West Indies**).

Indore. *City, central India.* The largest city in Madhya Pradesh state takes its name from the *Indreshwar* Hindu temple erected here in 1741.

Indus. *River, Asia.* The river, rising in Tibet and flowing generally southwest through **India** (named for it) and Pakistan to the Arabian Sea, has a name representing Sanskrit *sindhu*, "river." *Cp.* **Sind**.

Inglewood. *City, southwestern United States.* The California city was settled in 1873 and laid out by the Centinela-*Inglewood* Land Company in 1887, where *Inglewood* is said to come from a place in Canada that was the home of the sister-in-law of N.R. Vail, one of the directors.

Ingolstadt. *City, southern Germany.* The city, first recorded in the 8th century as a Frankish crown estate, has a name meaning "*Ingold's* place," the personal name followed by Old High German *stat*.

Ingushetia. *Republic, southwestern Russia.* The republic takes its name from its indigenous inhabitants, the *Ingush*, their own name deriving from the mountain village of *Angush*. Their name for themselves is *Khamur*, "mountain dwellers."

I-ning. *City, northwestern China.* The city, in the Uighur Autonomous Region of Sinkiang, derives its name from Chinese *yī*, "he," "she," and *níng*, "rather."

Inkerman. *Town, southern Ukraine.* The town, in the southwestern Crimea, has a name said to be of Turkish origin meaning "new fortress," from *yeni*, "new," and *kerman*, "fort."

Inland Sea. *Sea, southwestern Japan.* The sea, between the islands of Honshu to the north and Shikoku and Kyushu to the south, is so named because it is closed at its eastern end by the island of Awaji and is connected with the outer sea by four separate straits. Its Japanese name is *Setonaikai*, from *seto*, "strait" (from *se*, "stream," and *to*, "gate"), and *naikai*, "inland sea" (from *nai*, "inside," and *kai*, "sea").

Inner Mongolia *see* **Mongolia**

Innsbruck. *City, western Austria.* The city is named for the *Inn* River on which it stands, with the second part of the name meaning "bridge" (modern German *Brücke*). The river itself has a name of Celtic origin, from a root word *enos*, "water."

Inowrocław. *City, north central Poland.* The city's name is recorded in a Latin document of 1158 as *Junior Vladislavia*, rendering Old Polish *juny Wlodislaw*, "young *Vladislav*," with "young" meaning "new," and added to differentiate this place from older **Wrocław**. This earlier bipart name gradually evolved to the present one. (In 1583 it was already a single word, as *Junevladislavia*, and by 1905 it had become *Inowrazław*.) The original name of the settlement here was *Siedlce*, a name found elsewhere in Poland meaning "village" (*see* **Siedlce**). Hence the city's German name of *Hohensalza*, "upper *Siedlce*," distinguishing it from some "lower" place.

Interlaken. *Town, west central Switzerland.* The town, between Lakes Brienz and Thun, has a name relating to this location, from Latin *inter lacus*, "between the lakes." The town grew up in the 12th century around an Augustinian convent. Hence the name's Latin origin.

Inuvik. *Town, northwestern Canada.* The town, in the Northwest Territories on a channel of the Mackenzie River, was built by the Canadian government in the 1950s as a model community and given an Inuit (Eskimo) name meaning "place of man." The town gave its name to the region created here in the early 1970s.

Invercargill. *City, southern New Zealand.* The southernmost city of South Island was settled in 1855 as *Kelly's Point*. In 1857 it adopted its present name, in honor of the Scottish colonist William *Cargill* (1784–1860), with *Inver-* denoting its location on the Waihopai River near its confluence with the New River Estuary. The name was thus created on the basis of Scottish *Inver-* names such as **Inverness**, although in this case the second element is a personal name, not a river name.

Inverness. *Town, northwestern Scotland.* The town has a name beginning with the *Inver-* found for many other coastal places. It represents Gaelic *inbhir*, "river mouth," "confluence," and corresponds to the *Aber-* in Scottish and Welsh names such as **Aberdeen** and **Aberystwyth**. *Inver-* is usually followed by the name of the river at the mouth of which the town lies. In the case of Inverness this is thus the *Ness* (*see* **Ness, Loch**). *See also* **Invercargill**.

Investigator Strait. *Strait, southern Australia.* The strait, between the Australian mainland and Kangaroo Island, South Australia, takes its name from the ship in which the English explorer Matthew Flinders navigated it in 1802.

Iona. *Island, northwestern Scotland.* The Hebridean island was originally known simply as *I*, probably representing a Celtic word meaning "yew tree." This was incorporated into various forms of the name, and in an early 8th-century Latin text the island is named as *Ioua insula*, "island of yews." The first word of this was subsequently miscopied as *Iona*, possibly through a spurious association with the biblical prophet *Jonah*. Hence the island's present name.

Ionia. *Historic region, western Turkey.* The region derives its name from the *Ionians*, the settlers from mainland Greece who crossed the Aegean Sea to set up colonies here in around 1000 B.C. Their own name has been popularly linked with *Ion*, son of Creusa and Apollo in Greek mythology, although it is almost certainly pre–Greek. Some authorities relate it to Sanskrit *yoni*, "womb," "vulva," from a "female," moonworshiping people.

Ionian Islands. *Islands, western Greece.* The islands, off the west coast of Greece in the sea of the same name, take their name from the *Ionian* Greeks who settled in **Ionia**. In some languages a form of "Ionian" gave the word for "Greek," as Turkish *Yunan*. The Turkish name of Greece is thus *Yunanistan*, "land of the Ionians," and the Arabic and Hindi name simply *yūnān*.

Iowa. *State, north central United States.* The state is named for the river that flows through it. Its own name derives from that of a Native American people, itself said to mean either "sleepy ones" or "palefaces." The name has been recorded in a variety of spellings over the years, and a French map of 1673 has it as *Ouaouia-tonon*.

I-pin. *City, south central China.* The city, in Szechwan province, derives its name from Chinese *yí*, "suitable," "appropriate," and *bīn*, "guest."

Ipoh. *City, western Malaysia.* The city, on the Malay Peninsula, takes its name from a local tree whose poisonous resin was formerly used by local people for hunting.

Ipswich. *Town and port, eastern England.* The Suffolk town has an Old English name meaning "*Gip*'s trading place," with the Anglo-Saxon personal name followed by *wīc*, "trading place," "port."

Iqaluit. *Town, northern Canada.* The capital of Nunavut, on Baffin Island, has an Inuktitut name meaning "place of many fish." It was earlier called *Frobisher Bay*, for the English explorer Martin *Frobisher* (c.1535–1594), who discovered the bay here in 1576. It adopted its native name in 1987.

Iráklion *see* **Heraklion**

Iran. *Republic, southwestern Asia.* The country's name ultimately goes back to Sanskrit *arya*, "Aryan," referring to people living in a mountainous land, from the root element *ar*, "mountain." Iran is essentially a region of plateaux and mountains, the former rendering the latter prominent. *Cp.* **Ararat.** The earlier name of Iran (until 1935) was *Persia.* This is traditionally derived from *Perses*, son of the Greek mythological hero Perseus. Its actual origin is in *Fars*, the indigenous name of Persia, now that of a province in southwestern Iran. (It was originally *Pars*, or *Persis*, but the initial *P* changed to *F* under Arab influence.) It in turn took its name from the *Farsi* or *Parsi*, the Iranian people who settled here in the 7th century B.C., their own name representing Old Persian *parsi*, "pure." Their descendants, the *Parsees*, fled to India to escape Muslim persecution.

Iraq. *Republic, southwestern Asia.* The country's name represents Arabic *al-ʻirāq*, perhaps meaning "the bank," with reference to its location in the basin of the Tigris and Euphrates rivers.

Ireland. *Republic, western Europe.* The original indigenous name of Ireland was *Ériu*, from a conjectural Old Celtic *Iveriu*, perhaps meaning "good land." This later became *Éire*, the official name of the country from 1937 through 1949. The Roman name of Ireland, *Hibernia*, influenced by Latin *hibernus*, "wintry," evolved as a corruption of *Ivernia*, itself from the Old Celtic original. The present name *Ireland* was generally adopted during the 12th-century Anglo-Norman conquest, with English *land* added to the indigenous name. Later, the Irish name *Éirinn*, grammatically the dative form of *Éire*, was anglicized as *Erin* by the 19th-century romantic movement, which adopted it from such writers as the poet Thomas Moore, whose *Irish Melodies* (1807) has the lines: "Let Erin remember the days of Old, / Ere her faithless sons betrayed her." The name of Ireland was long traditionally derived from Irish *iar-*, "west," describing the land's geographical position in the British Isles.

Irian Jaya. *Province, eastern Indonesia.* The province, as the western half of the island of New Guinea, has a name of Malay origin. *Irian* is the Indonesian name for the island of New Guinea as a whole, meaning "cloud-covered." *Jaya* means "victory," "glory," and replaced *Barat*, "west," as the second word of the name in 1969, when the province gained independent recognition, with its capital at **Jayapura.**

Irkutsk. *City, east central Russia.* The Siberian city takes its name from the *Irkut* River on which it lies. The river's own name is said to be of Ainu origin, meaning "big bend."

Irrawaddy. *River, central Myanmar.* The river's name is of Sanskrit origin, ultimately from *airāvata* ("risen from the waters"), the name of a sun god. He is the prototype of the elephant, produced at the churning of the ocean, and is regarded as Indra's beast of burden.

Irtysh. *River, northeastern Kazakhstan/central Russia.* The name of the Siberian river probably has its origin in a Turkic root element *ir*, "to flow." The current in the river's upper reaches is rapid and turbulent.

Irvington. *Town, eastern United States.* The New Jersey town, now an industrial suburb of Newark, was settled in 1666 as *Camptown*. In 1852 it was renamed as now in honor of U.S. author Washington *Irving* (1783–1859).

Isabela. *Province, northern Philippines.* The province, in northeastern Luzon, was created in 1856 and named for Queen *Isabella* II of Spain (1830–1904).

Ischia. *Island, southern Italy.* The island, at

the entrance to the Bay of Naples, is said to derive its name from Etruscan *iscla*, meaning simply "island."

Isère. *River, southeastern France*. The river's name may mean "holy river," from a pre–Celtic root *is*, "holy," "sacred," and the common Indo-european element *ar*, "river." The Romans knew the river as the *Isara*.

Iserlohn. *City, western Germany*. The city, founded around a mint in the 11th century, was refounded on a higher site by Count Engelbert I in the 13th century. The name means "(place in the) woods where iron is mined," from Middle Low German *īser*, "iron," and the dative plural of *lō*, "wood," "copse." Iron has long been mined in the wooded region around the town, and laid the foundation of its flourishing metal industry.

Isfahan. *City, west central Iran*. The city's name has been variously explained. The traditional origin is in Avestan *espahan*, the plural of *sepah*, "army." It has also been derived from *esb*, "horse," with the Iranian plural ending, or from a word *han*, "country," "land." The first of these is perhaps the likeliest.

Ishikari. *River, northern Japan*. The river, in the island of Hokkaido, derives its name from Ainu *ishikaribetsu*, "greatly meandering river," describing the course of its lower reaches.

Ishikawa. *Prefecture, west central Japan*. The prefecture, in the island of Honshu, derives its name from Japanese *ishi*, "stone," "rock," and *kawa*, "river."

Isis *see* **Thames**

İskenderun. *City and port, southern Turkey*. The city, formerly familiar as *Alexandretta*, derives its name from Turkish *İskender*, "Alexander." It lies at or near the site of the ancient city of *Alexandria ad Issum*, founded to commemorate the victory of *Alexander* the Great over Darius III at *Issus* in 333 B.C. The name was also known in the English corrupt form *Scanderoon*.

Islamabad. *Capital of Pakistan*. Construction of Pakistan's capital city (since 1967) began in 1961, when Karachi was found unsuitable as a capital. Its name means "city of Islam," from Arabic *islām*, "Islam," and Iranian *ābād*, "inhabited place," "city."

Ismailia. *City, northeastern Egypt*. The city was founded in 1863 as a halfway station on the Suez Canal, then being built, and takes its name from *Ismail* Pasha (1830–1895), viceroy of Egypt, who had encouraged the canal's construction.

Ispahan *see* **Isfahan**

Israel. *Republic, southwestern Asia*. The republic, established in 1948 in the former British mandate of Palestine, takes its name from the biblical land of the Hebrews, itself from the name given to Jacob when he wrestled with God. His own Hebrew name is traditionally interpreted as "He who fights with God," as in the account of his encounter: "Thy name shall be called no more Jacob, but Israel: for as a prince thou hast power with God and with men, and hast prevailed" (Genesis 32:28). Although thus originally a personal name, its future as the name of a people and a nation is announced immmediately after this name change, which God reiterates: "Thy name shall not be called any more Jacob, but Israel shall be thy name... Be fruitful and multiply; a nation and a company of nations shall be of thee, and kings shall come out of thy loins" (Genesis 35:10–11). *See also* **Palestine**.

Issyk-Kul. *Lake, northeastern Kyrgyzstan*. The lake has a Kyrgyz name meaning "warm lake," from *ysyk*, "warm," and *köl*, "lake." The lake never freezes over in winter.

Issy-les-Moulineaux. *Town, northern France*. The town, now a suburb of Paris, was known by the Medieval Latin name of *Issiacum*, from the Gaulish personal name *Iccius* or *Icisius*, and the Gallo-Roman suffix *-acum*. The rest of the name means "the little mills," from a diminutive of French *moulin*, "mill."

Istanbul. *City, northwestern Turkey*. The former Turkish capital is traditionally said to derive its name from Byzantine Greek *eis tēn polin*, "into the city," implying that its people are city dwellers. (Because of its size and importance, local inhabitants would have simply referred to "the city" rather than giving it a distinctive name, much as London businessfolk talk of "the City" today.) A popular account traces the name back to a form *Islambul*, "city of Islam," with the final *-bul* from Greek *polis*, "city." This would seem plausible if the name had not existed long before the city became a Muslim capital in 1453. Its earlier name was *Constantinople*, "city of *Constantine*," referring to the Roman emperor *Constantine* the Great, who made the city of Byzantium his capital and renamed it for himself in A.D.330. It is thus evident that *Constantinople* has evolved (losing *Con-* and *-tin-*) into present-day *Istanbul*, so that the names are one and the same. The original city of *Byzantium* is said to derive its name from its Greek founder in the 7th century B.C., *Buzas* of Megara. The Russian name of Constantinople was *Tsargrad*, "city of the emperor." Constantinople was officially renamed Istanbul in 1930, an event recalled in Jimmy Kennedy and Nat Simon's 1953 hit, "Istanbul (Not Constantinople)."

Istria. *Peninsula, southeastern Europe.* The peninsula, in modern Croatia and Slovenia, extends into the Adriatic Sea and is named for the *Istaevones*, a Germanic people who formerly inhabited it. The meaning of their own name is uncertain. The Romans knew the region as *Histria* or *Istria*.

Italy. *Republic, southern Europe.* The country is traditionally said to take its name from the *Vitali*, a northern people who settled in the southern part of the region that is now Calabria, the toe of the Italian "boot." Their own name, which later spread to the rest of the peninsula, is believed to be linked in some way with Latin *vitulus*, "calf." But the actual origin may be in an Illyrian word, or in the name of a legendary or even historical ruler known to the Romans as *Italus*. The Polish name of Italy, *Włochy*, and the Hungarian name, *Olaszország*, derive ultimately from the tribal name.

Itasca, Lake. *Lake, northern United States.* The Minnesota lake was stated to be the true source of the Mississippi by the U.S. superintendent of Native American affairs, Henry R. Schoolcraft, when he visited it in 1832, and he is said to have devised its name, from elements of Latin *veritas*, "truth," and *caput*, "head," "source." Local legend, however, derives it from *Iteska*, Hiawatha's daughter, the river (or its source) representing her tears of anguish at being spirited away to the underworld. If Schoolcraft's creation is the true origin, he presumably devised it to suggest a Native American name.

Ithaca. *Island, western Greece.* The island, in the Ionian Sea, almost certainly derives the first part of its name from Phoenician *ī*, "island," as for **Ibiza**. The rest is of unknown origin.

Itsuku. *Island, southern Japan.* The island, in the Inland Sea, takes its name from the 6th-century Shinto shrine here, itself named for one of the daughters of Susanowo, the Shinto storm god.

Itzehoe. *City, north central Germany.* The city, founded in 810 around a Carolingian castle, has a name first recorded in the 12th century as *Ekeho*, perhaps meaning "oak wood."

Ivano-Frankovsk. *City, western Ukraine.* The city was founded in 1662 as the Polish town of *Stanisławów*, for *Stanisław* Potocki, a member of a landed Polish family who owned estates here. In 1945 it was ceded to the Soviet Union (as *Stanislav*) and 1962 was renamed as now for the Ukrainian writer *Ivan* Yakovlevich *Franko* (1856–1916), who was born in western Ukraine

and who spent most of his life there. The Ukrainian form of the name is *Ivano-Frankivs'k*.

Ivanovo. *City, western Russia.* The city is traditionally said to be named for *Ivan* the Terrible (1530–1584), but there is little to support this and the identification of the eponymous *Ivan* remains uncertain. In 1871 the original village merged with the neighboring one of *Vosnesenskaya* to become the town of *Ivanovo-Voznesensk*, a name it retained until 1932 when it dropped the addition. The name of the second village comes from its Church of the Ascension (Russian *Vozneseniye*).

Ivory Coast *see* **Côte d'Ivoire**

Ivrea. *Town, northwestern Italy.* The town was known to the Romans as *Eporedia*, and this gave the present name. The Roman name appears to represent Gaulish *epos*, "horse," and *redo*, "to ride." The allusion would be to a racecourse here at some time.

Ivry-sur-Seine. *Town, northern France.* The town, now a suburb of Paris, had the Medieval Latin name of *Ivriacum*, from Gaulish *iuos*, "yew," and the Gallo-Roman suffix *-acum*. This gave the main part of the present name. The rest of the name, indicating its location on the **Seine**, distinguishes it from *Ivry-la-Bataille*, a village west of Paris (so named for a *battle* of 1590).

Iwate. *Prefecture, north central Japan.* The prefecture, in the island of Honshu, derives its name from Japanese *iwa*, "rock," and *te*, "hand."

Izhevsk. *City, western Russia.* The city arose as an iron works in 1760 and is named for its location on the *Izh* River. The meaning of the river name is unknown. From 1984 through 1987 Izhevsk was renamed *Ustinov*, for the Soviet defense minister, Dmitry Fyodorovich *Ustinov* (1908–1984).

İzmir. *City and port, western Turkey.* The city is said to derive its name from Byzantine Greek *eis Smurnē*, "to Smyrna," but it is more likely to be a corruption of *Smyrna* itself. This comes from Greek *smurna*, "myrrh." The gum resin is obtained locally and exported for the manufacture of perfume and incense, as well as for medicinal use.

İzmit. *City, northwestern Turkey.* The city's name represents Byzantine Greek *eis Mēdian*, "to Nicomedia," this being its historic name. The ancient name derives from that of *Nicomedes* I (died c.250 B.C.), king of Bithynia, who rebuilt the city as his new capital in 264 B.C.

İznik *see* **Nicaea**

Iztaccíhuatl. *Mountain, central Mexico.* The dormant volcano has a name meaning "white woman," from Nahuatl *iztac*, "white," and *cíhu-*

atl, "woman," referring to its snow-covered peaks. It is also known as "sleeping woman," since from New Mexico its three peaks resemble the head, breast, and feet of a recumbent female figure.

Jabalpur. *City, central India.* The city, in Madhya Pradesh state, derives its name from the Hindi personal name *Jabal* and *pur*, "town."

Jablonec nad Nisou. *City, northern Czech Republic.* The first and main word of the city's name remains the subject of dispute among toponymists. Some see a source in Italian *gabella*, "tax," referring to a customs post, while others claim a (more likely) origin in Slavic *yablonya*, "apple tree." The rest of the name means "above the *Nisa*," referring to the river here. The German form of the name is *Gablonz*. Cp. **Neugablonz**.

Jabneh. *Historic city, western Israel.* The ancient city of Palestine, mentioned in the Bible (2 Chronicles 26:6), has a Hebrew name meaning "God builds." An alternate form of the name is *Jabneel* (Joshua 15:11). The modern name of the site is *Yibna*.

Jáchymov. *Town and resort, northwestern Czech Republic.* The town arose from a silver mine opened here in the early 16th century. The mine was named for *St. Joachim* (father of the Virgin Mary), and this name passed to both the valley here, *Sankt Joachimsthal*, and to the town itself. The present Czech name is the equivalent, with the saint's name alone and the possessive ending *-ov*. The silver coins first minted here in 1519 ultimately gave the name of the *dollar* (German *Taler*, shortened from *Joachimsthaler*).

¹**Jackson**. *City, southern United States.* The state capital of Mississippi was originally a trading station known as *Fleur's Bluff*. The town that grew from it was selected as capital in 1821 and renamed in honor of Andrew *Jackson* (1767–1845), 7th president of the United States.

²**Jackson**. *City and river port, east central United States.* The Tennessee city was settled in the early 1920s and was originally known as *Alexandria*. It was renamed in 1922 in honor of Andrew *Jackson* (1767–1845), 7th president of the United States.

Jacksonville. *City, southeastern United States.* The Florida city was settled by the French in 1564 on a Native American site known as *Wacca Pilatka*, "cows' ford," for its location on the St. Johns River. During the English period (1763–83) this name was anglicized as *Cowford*. In 1822 it was renamed as now in honor of Andrew *Jackson* (1767–1845), first governor of Florida and 7th president of the United States.

Jacobabad. *City, south central Pakistan.* The city was founded in 1847 by the district's first commissioner, General John *Jacob* (1812–1858), and is named for him, with Iranian *ābād* meaning "inhabited place," "town."

Jade Bay. *Bay, northwestern Germany.* The North Sea inlet, known in German as *Jadebusen*, takes its name from the *Jade* River that flows into it. The river's own name is of uncertain origin. Old Frisian *jat*, "passage," "breach," has been suggested, referring to an area of land submerged by storm tides.

Jaffa. *City and port, western Israel.* The ancient city, now part of Tel Aviv-*Jaffa* (Tel Aviv-*Jafo*), has a name representing Hebrew *yafe*, "beautiful." The reference is to the town's attractive site on a promontory overlooking the Mediterranean. The city is the biblical *Joppa* (2 Chronicles 2:16, etc.).

Jaffna. *City and port, northern Sri Lanka.* The city was originally the capital of a Tamil kingdom, and its name is a Portuguese corruption of the Tamil for "port of the lyre." The reference is to the shape of the harbor.

Jahanabad. *Town, eastern India.* The town, in Bihar state, has a name meaning "town of *Jahan*," from the Mughal emperor Shah *Jahan* (1592–1666) and Iranian *ābād*, "peopled," "inhabited place."

Jahangirabad. *Town, north central India.* The town, in Uttar Pradesh state, has a name meaning "*Jahangir*'s town," from the Mughal emperor *Jahangir* (1569–1627) (whose name means "conqueror of the world") and Iranian *ābād*, "peopled," "inhabited place."

Jahazgarh. *Town, north central India.* The small town, in Haryana state, owes its origin to a fort built here in the 1790s by George Thomas (c.1756–1802), an Irish adventurer, who set himself up as rajah of Hansi. He called his garrison *Georgegarh*, from his own first name and Hindi *garh*, "fort," but Indians understood this as *Jahazgarh*, as if from Hindi *jahāz*, "ship," and *garh*.

Jaipur. *City, northwestern India.* The capital of Rajasthan state has a Hindi name meaning "*Jai*'s town," with the personal name followed by *pur*, "town." The name is that of Maharaja Sawai *Jai* Singh II, who founded the city in 1727 to replace Amber as the capital of the princely state of Jaipur.

Jaisalmer. *City, northwestern India.* The city, in Rajasthan state, was founded in 1156 by Rawal *Jaisal*, a chief of the Rajputs, and is named for him.

Jakarta. *Capital of Indonesia.* The city has a

Malay name that is a form of its historic name *Jayakarta*. This means "victory (and) prosperity," and was the name given the former city of *Sunda Kelapa* in 1527 by Prince Fatillah, sultan of Bantam, after he had conquered it. In 1619 Dutch colonists built a fortress here and called it **Batavia**, for the historic region of this name in the Netherlands. The name then passed to the city that grew up around it. The earlier name was readopted in 1949, following the declaration of independence by Indonesia in 1945. (Until 1972 the spelling was usually *Djakarta*.)

Jakobshavn *see* **Ilulíssat**

Jalalabad. *City, eastern Afghanistan*. The city is named for the Mughal emperor *Jalal* ud-Din Muhammad Akbar (1542–1605), who founded it in c.1560, with the last part of the name representing Iranian *ābād*, "peopled," "inhabited place."

Jamaica. *Island state, southern West Indies*. The name represents the island's Arawak name *Xaymaca*, meaning "rich in springs" or "land of springs." Many short streams flow from Jamaica's mountains. When Columbus first sighted the island in 1494 he named it *Santiago* (*cp.* **Santiago**), but the original Amerindian name prevailed.

Jamalpur. *City, north central Bangladesh*. The city has a name meaning "town of glory," from Hindi *jamāl*, "glory," and Iranian *ābād*, "peopled," "inhabited place."

James Bay. *Bay, east central Canada*. The bay, a southern extension of Hudson Bay, is named for the English Arctic navigator Captain Thomas *James* (c.1593–c.1635), who explored it in 1631.

¹Jamestown. *Capital of St. Helena*. The town and port was founded in 1659 and named for the Duke of York, the future *James* II of England (1633–1701).

²Jamestown. *City, eastern United States*. The New York city was founded in 1811 and named for *James* Prendergast, who purchased a large packet of land here and built a mill.

Jamshedpur. *City, northeastern India*. The city, in Jharkhand state, was founded in 1907 by the industralist Dorabji *Jamsetji* Tata (1859–1932), and is named for him, with Hindi *pur*, "town," added. An alternate name for the city is *Tatanagar*, "*Tata*'s city."

Janesville. *City, northern United States*. The Wisconsin city was settled in 1835 by the pioneer Henry F. *Janes*, and is named for him. (He later moved west to found *Janesville*, Minnesota, and *Janesville*, Iowa.)

Jan Mayen. *Island, Arctic Ocean*. The Norwegian volcanic island, east of Greenland, is named

for the Dutch navigator *Jan May*, who rediscovered it in 1611 after Henry Hudson had visited it in 1607.

Japan. *Island state, western Pacific*. The Japanese name for the country is *Nippon*, from *nichi*, "sun," and *hon*, "origin." The western form of the name represents the Chinese pronunciation of the two Japanese pictograms, which is *rìběn*, pronounced approximately "Jipen." This has the same meaning, from Chinese *rì*, "sun," and *běn*, "origin." Hence the English form of the name. The reference is to Japan's eastern location with regard to China. Hence also "Land of the Rising Sun" as a byname for Japan, whose national flag is white with a central red "sun disk."

Jarosław. *Town, southeastern Poland*. The town takes its name from *Yaroslav* the Wise (978–1054), grand prince of Kiev, who founded it in the 11th century. *Cp.* **Yaroslavl**.

Jarres, Plain of. *Region, north central Laos*. The plain derives its name from the many stone funerary *jars* that were discovered here by the French in the 19th century. The present form of the name is half English, half French. It has alternate forms that are either one or the other, respectively *Plain of Jars* and *Plaine des Jarres*.

Jarrow. *Town, northeastern England*. The Tyneside town derives its name from the people known as the *Gyrwe*, who at one time inhabited the region. Their own name means "fen people."

Jastrzębie-Zdrój. *City, southwestern Poland*. The city's name means "hawks' spring," from Polish *jastrząb*, "hawk," and *zdrój*, "spring," "source." The city was formerly a thermal spa.

Jászberény. *City, central Hungary*. The city is one of several prefixed *Jász*- to the east of Budapest. The prefix represents the name of the people known as *Jazygians*. The rest of the name is also probably tribal. Other towns are *Jászapáti*, from Hungarian *apát*, "abbot," and *Jászárokszállás*, with *árok*, "ditch," "trench," and *szállás*, "(living) quarters."

Java. *Island, southern Indonesia*. The island's name represents Sanskrit *yavadvīpa*, "island of barley," from *yava*, "barley," and *dvīpa*, "island." Java has long been noted for its varied agricultural produce.

Jayapura. *Town and port, northeastern Indonesia*. The capital of Irian Jaya has a name meaning "victory city," from *jaya*, "victory" (which also gave the name of **Jakarta** and of **Irian Jaya** itself, as well as being the Indonesian name of New Guinea), and Sanskrit *pur*, "house," "town." Under Dutch colonial administration the town was known as *Hollandia*, and from

1963 through 1969 *Sukarnapura*, for *Sukarno* (1901–1970), Indonesia's first president.

Jedda *see* **Jiddah**

Jefferson City. *City, east central United States.* The state capital of Missouri was founded in 1821 and named in honor of Thomas *Jefferson* (1743–1826), 3d president of the United States. The name of the popular president is found for a large number of counties, cities, towns, and villages in the USA.

Jelenia Góra. *City, southwestern Poland.* The city is located in the Sudeten Mountains and takes its name from one of them. Its meaning is "deer mountain," from Polish *jeleń*, "deer," and *góra*, "mountain." German speakers know the city by its equivalent name of *Hirschberg*.

Jelgava. *City, central Latvia.* The city was founded in 1266 when the Livonian knights built a castle here. It came to be called *Mitava*, from Latvian *mit*, "to exchange," as it was a trading place. (Hence its German name of *Mitau*.) This name then passed to the town that grew up around it. The present name, from Liv *jalgab*, "town," gradually superseded it. *See also* **Livonia.**

Jemaa. *Town, central Nigeria.* The town originated in *c.*1810 when Malam Usman, a Muslim preacher, founded the settlement of *Jema'an-Darroro*, "followers of a learned man from *Darroro*." He subsequently became emir of the region (until 1833).

Jena. *City, eastern Germany.* The city is first recorded in the 9th century as *Jani*, a name apparently from Old High German *jāni*, "strip of mown grass," "swathe of cut corn." The word properly refers to the passage of the mower or scythe over the grass or corn and the long strip so produced, as a Germanic development of the Indoeuropean root element *ei*, "to go." This name *Jani* was then probably adopted for the vineyards planted on the local Muschelkalk (shelly limestone). Later, in the 18th century, the word *Jahne* came to be used for the rows of vines tended on the mountainside.

Jerez. *City, southwestern Spain.* The city takes its name from *Ceres*, the Old Spanish name for a Tuscan town that was famous for its wines, as Jerez itself is. (The name gave English *sherry*.) The full name of the town is *Jerez de la Frontera*, "Jerez of the frontier," alluding to the historic limit of Moorish territories in this part of Spain. The addition distinguishes it from **Jerez de los Caballeros.**

Jerez de los Caballeros. *Town, western Spain.* The town, founded in 1229, has a name of the same origin as **Jerez.** It was earlier known as *Jerez de Badajoz*, for its proximity to **Badajoz,** but was then renamed for the Knights Templars (Spanish *caballeros*, "knights"), to whom the city had been given.

Jericho. *Historic city, western Jordan.* The biblical city (Numbers 22:1, etc.) has a Hebrew name that may ultimately derive from *yarēakh*, "moon," "month," and so relate to an ancient moon cult practiced here.

Jersey. *Island, Channel Islands, western English Channel.* The chief of the Channel Islands has a name that is traditionally explained as a corruption of its Roman name, *Caesarea*. But this was actually the name of **Sark,** and Jersey probably has a Scandinavian name meaning "*Geirr's* island," with the final *-ey* representing Old Norse *ey*, "island." The personal name means "spear."

Jersey City. *City, eastern United States.* The New Jersey city was settled by Dutch trappers in 1618 and was originally known as *Paulus Hook*. It was renamed as now in 1820 for its state of **New Jersey.**

Jerusalem. *Capital of Israel.* The city has a name of uncertain origin. Cuneiform texts give it in the form *Urusalimmi*, and Egyptian hieroglyphs as *Shalam*. It is possible that *uru* means "house," "town," while *salim* means "peace." The name overall could thus mean "town of peace." Some authorities, however, hold that the second part of the name is that of the Canaanite god *Shalim*, regarded as the city's "patron," and that the first part represents the Hebrew root *yrh*, usually meaning "to throw" or "to shoot" but here having the sense "to lay a foundation." The name would then mean "(place) founded by Shalim." The regular Arabic name of Jerusalem is *al-ḳuds*, "the holy one." Hence its Turkish name of *Kudüs*. The mysterious Hebrew name *Ariel* found for Jerusalem in the Old Testament (Isaiah 29:1, Ezekiel 43:15, etc.) is said to mean "altar hearth," denoting a future sacrifice. *See also* **Salem.**

Jeseník Mountains. *Mountain range, northern Czech Republic.* The range, forming the eastern section of the Sudeten mountains, derives its name from Czech *jesen*, "ash tree." The mountains are extensively forested.

Jesselton *see* **Kota Kinabalu**

Jessore. *City, southwestern Bangladesh.* The city's name is said to be a corruption of *yasohara*, "glory-depriving," since Jessore eclipsed Gaur, the former capital of Bengal, in importance.

Jezreel. *Historic city, central Palestine.* The biblical city (1 Samuel 29:1, etc.), capital of the northern kingdom of Israel under Ahab, has a

Hebrew name meaning "God will sow," from *yizra'*, "he will sow," and *el*, "God." (The name is directly associated with that of Hosea's first son.) The Jezreel referred to in the Apocrypha as *Esdraelon* (Judith 3:9, etc.), the Greek form of the name, is the valley of Jezreel (Joshua 17:16), separating Galilee from Samaria.

Jharkhand. *State, eastern India*. The state, created in 2000, has a name meaning "forest region."

Jiddah. *City and port, western Saudi Arabia*. The name derives from Arabic *judda*, "sign," "landmark." The city arose in the 7th century as the Red Sea port for Mecca and came to serve as an important staging point for Muslims making a pilgrimage to that city. The name is also spelled *Jedda*.

Jihlava. *City, western Czech Republic*. The city takes its name from the river on which it lies, its own name deriving from Old Czech *jihla* (modern Czech *jehla*), "needle." This is traditionally said to refer to the needles of the pine forest through which it passes, but is more likely to allude to a feature of its course, such as a narrowing of its banks or a "threading" of its stream through rocks. German speakers know the city as *Iglau*, a form of its Czech name. (The name may have been influenced by German *Igel*, "hedgehog," an animal that coincidentally has spines or "needles.")

Jirja. *Town, eastern Egypt*. The town, also known as *Girga*, derives its name from the ancient Coptic monastery here of *Mar Girgis*, dedicated to St. *George*.

Joachimsthal. *Town, northeastern Germany*. The town, with a name meaning "*Joachim*'s valley," was founded in 1604 by *Joachim* Frederick (1546–1608), elector of Brandenburg, and is named for him.

João Pessoa. *City, northeastern Brazil*. The city was founded in 1585 by Portuguese colonists with the name of *Filipea de Nossa Senhora das Neves*, "Filipea of Our Lady of the Snows," for *Philip* I of Portugal (Philip II of Spain) and the dedication of its church. Following further renamings (*Frederikstad* and *Paraíba*) it finally gained its present name in 1930, for *João Pessoa*, the Brazilian state president who was assassinated in Recife that year in the Vargas revolution.

Jodhpur *City, northwestern India*. The city, in Rajasthan state, was founded in 1459 by Rao *Jodha*, the local ruler, and is named for him, with *pur* the Sanskrit word for "house," "town."

Jogjakarta *see* **Yogyakarta**

Johannesburg. *City, northeastern South Africa*. The city was founded in 1886 after the discovery of gold and has an Afrikaans name meaning "*Johannes*' town." The identity of the named person is uncertain. The main contenders are *Johann* Rissik (1857–1925), principal clerk of the office of the surveyor general of Transvaal at the time, and Christian *Johannes* Joubert (1834–1911), chief of mining and local politician. *See also* **Gauteng**.

Johanngeorgenstadt. *Town, east central Germany*. The town was founded in 1654 as a silver-mining settlement by Bohemian Protestants. In 1656 it was chartered by *John George* (*Johann Georg*) I (1585–1656), elector of Saxony, and named for him.

John o'Groats. *Locality, northeastern Scotland*. The traditional northeastern point of mainland Britain may take its name from a Dutchman, *Jan de Groot*, said to have been a bailie (municipal officer) to the earls of Caithness here in the 15th century. The name would have been that of his house.

Johnson City. *City, east central United States*. The Tennessee city arose in 1857 around a railroad water tank and was originally called *Johnson's Depot*, for Henry *Johnson* (1809–1874), the first postmaster. In 1859 it was renamed *Haynesville*, for Landon C. *Haynes*, later a Confederate senator, but was again renamed for *Johnson* in 1861, the name taking the present form.

Johor. *State, western Malaysia*. The state, on the southwestern Malay Peninsula, is said to take its name from a local word meaning "to tie." The reference would be to Johor Strait here, which "ties" Malaya to the island of Singapore.

Johor Baharu. *City, western Malaysia*. The city, at the southern end of the Malay Peninsula, was originally known as *Tanjung Putri*, for Ibrahim *Temenggong*, ruler of **Johor** from 1825 to 1862. It was renamed *Johor Bahru*, "new *Johor*," in 1866, when it replaced *Johor Lama*, "old *Johor*," 18 miles (29 km) east, as state capital.

Joinville. *City, southeastern Brazil*. The city was founded by German immigrants in 1851 on the site of land given as a dowry by Dom Pedro, emperor of Brazil, to his sister, who had married François d'Orléans, prince de *Joinville* (1818–1900), son of Louis-Philippe of France.

Joliet. *City, north central United States*. The Illinois city was settled in 1833 and named *Juliet* in honor of *Juliet* Campbell, daughter of a settler. In 1845 it was renamed as now for Louis *Jolliet* (1645–1700), the French-Canadian explorer who visited the site in 1673.

Jonesboro. *City, east central United States*. The Arkansas city was founded in 1859 and named for state senator William A. *Jones*.

Jönköping. *City, southern Sweden.* The second part of the city's name derives from Swedish *köping*, "trading settlement," as for **Norrköping** and **Nyköping**. The first part is of uncertain origin. It may be a river name.

Jonquière. *City, eastern Canada.* The Quebec city arose as an agricultural settlement in the mid–19th century and was named for Jacques-Pierre de Taffanel, marquis de la *Jonquière*, governor of New France from 1749 to 1752.

Joplin. *City, east central United States.* The Missouri city was founded in 1871 by John Cox, who named it for his friend, the Reverend Harris G. *Joplin*, a Methodist minister who had come here with Cox in c.1840.

Joppa *see* **Jaffa**

Jordan. *Kingdom, southwestern Asia.* The country is named for the river that flows through it. Its own name is of Semitic origin but disputed meaning. It may represent *yārod*, "to go down," referring to its strong current. However, all rivers "go down," and it is not clear why the Jordan should have been singled out for this common characteristic. Most biblical mentions of the river refer to it with the definite article (*hayyardēn*), suggesting that the name is a common noun meaning simply "river." This theory is supported by the fact that biblical writers never refer to the "Jordan River" but simply "Jordan," e.g. "When it [the ark of the covenant] passed over Jordan, the waters of Jordan were cut off" (Joshua 4:7). The Bible mentions the Jordan more often than any other river. From 1921 through 1946 Jordan was known as *Transjordan*, "across the *Jordan*," meaning the territory across the river from Israel. (This name was retained until 1949 for the short-lived kingdom formed on the territory that became East Jordan.)

Jotunheimen. *Mountain range, south central Norway.* The mountains have a Norwegian name meaning "giant's home." Their earlier name, still also sometimes used, was *Jotunfjell*, "giant's mountains." Both names go back to the early Norse sagas.

Juan de Fuca Strait. *Strait, western North America.* The strait, between Washington state, USA, and Vancouver Island, Canada, is said to be named for *Juan de Fuca*, real name possibly Apostolos Valerianos, a Greek navigator in the service of Spain who sailed through it in 1592.

Juan Fernández Islands. *Island group, South Pacific.* The group of three islands, west of (and belonging to) Chile, are named for the Spanish navigator *Juan Fernández*, who discovered them in c.1593. Their individual names are *Más a Tierra* ("nearer the land"), *Más Afuera* ("farther

out"), and *Santa Clara* ("St. Clare"). In 1704 the Scottish seaman Alexander Selkirk, after a quarrel with his captain, was put ashore on Más a Tierra and remained there alone until 1709. His adventures are said to have inspired Daniel Defoe's novel *Robinson Crusoe* (1720), so that Más a Tierra now appears on many maps as *Isla Róbinson Crusoe* and Más Afuera as *Isla Alejandro Selkirk*.

Juan-les-Pins. *Resort, southeastern France.* The Mediterranean resort derives the first part of its name from the bay here, the *golfe Juan*. Its original name was *Gourjan* or *Gourjean*, the meaning of which is uncertain. *Gour* may mean "river." The rest of the resort name means "the pines."

Juárez. *City, northern Mexico.* The city, also known as *Ciudad Juárez*, was originally known as *El Paso del Norte*, "the pass of the north," for a major ford formerly here over the Río Grande. (The river forms the border between Mexico and the United States, and *El Paso*, Texas, lies across it.) It was renamed as now in 1888 for the Mexican president Benito *Juárez* (1806–1872), who had made his headquarters here in 1865 when fighting against the French.

Judaea. *Historic region, southern Palestine.* The region, in the modern West Bank, derives its Graeco-Roman name from the ancient kingdom of *Judah*, with Jerusalem as its center, that was itself named for the people whose eponymous ancestor was the fourth son of Jacob (Genesis 29:35, etc.).

Judah *see* **Judaea**

Judenburg. *Town, south central Austria.* The name means "town of the *Jews*" (German *Juden*), referring to the Jewish merchants and moneylenders who founded the town in the 11th century. The municipal coat of arms shows a head wearing a Jewish hat.

Jugoslavia *see* **Yugoslavia**

Jujuy. *Province, northwestern Argentina.* The province derives its name from the *xuxuyoc* (type of Inca provincial governor) encountered here by the Spanish in the late 16th century.

Julianehåb *see* **Qaqortoq**

Jülich. *Town, western Germany.* The town arose around the 3d-century Roman fort of *Juliacum*, "settlement of *Julius*," and this gave its present name (not referring to *Julius* Caesar).

Jumilla. *City, southeastern Spain.* The Roman name of the settlement here was *Juncellus*, apparently for a local type of reed (Latin *juncus*, "reed," "rush"). By medieval times the name had become *Jumilla* or *Jumyella*, as now. Arabs construed this as *jemina amlet* or *jeminalet*, "country of the sons of *Amlet*."

Junagadh. *City, western India.* The city, in Gujarat state, has a name popularly interpreted as "old fort," but although the second part of the name is certainly Hindi *gadh*, "fort," the first part may actually represent *Yavan*, the Hindi name of the Greeks, from a form of "Ionian," testifying to a Greek presence in India. *See also* **Ionian Islands.**

Juneau. *City and port, northwestern United States.* The state capital of Alaska was settled in 1881 when gold was discovered here and takes its name from one of the prospectors, Joe *Juneau*.

Jungfrau. *Mountain, south central Switzerland.* The mountain's German name means "maiden," or literally "young woman," and relates to the peak's appearance, which resembles a nun in a white habit. It may also have a secondary allusion to its pure white ("virgin") snows. The name was probably meant to "pair" (or contrast) with that of the nearby mountain called *Mönch* ("monk") for its dark cliffs.

¹Jura. *Mountain range, eastern France/western Switzerland.* The name is said to derive from Gaulish *iuris* or *iuri*, meaning "wooded mountain."

²Jura. *Island, western Scotland.* The name of the island, in the Inner Hebrides, is a reduced form of its original name, recorded in a document of 678 as *Doirad Eilinn*, "*Doirad*'s island." The final *-a* of the present name probably evolved under the influence of Old Norse *ey*, "island."

Jüterbog. *Town, northeastern Germany.* Despite the animal on the town's coat of arms, the name does not come from German *Bock*, "buck," "ram," nor does it derive from Slavic words meaning "*Utro* (the) god," or "god of the morning," from Slavic *utro*, "morning," and *bog*, "god." But the town's site on an eastern slope does suggest a Slavic sense "(place on the) morning side," from *bok*, "side."

Jutland. *Peninsula, northern Europe.* The peninsula, comprising continental Denmark and the northernmost part of Germany, is named for its indigenous people, the *Jutes*, their own name probably meaning "men," "people." (A popular account says that Jutland is so called because it "juts out.")

Juventud, Isla de la. *Island, western Cuba.* The island, in the Caribbean Sea south of western Cuba, was originally known as *Isla de Pinos*, Spanish for "island of pines." It took its present name, meaning "island of youth," in 1978, when the 11th World Youth and Student Festival was held here, in recognition of the contribution made by the young people of Cuba to its agricultural development. The name appears on some maps in the English form *Isle of Youth*.

Jyväskylä. *City, south central Finland.* The name represents Finnish *jyvä*, "grain," "corn," and *kylä*, "village." The city lies in a fertile region at the northern end of Lake Päijänne.

K2. *Mountain, northeastern Pakistan.* The mountain is so designated as it is the second in the **Karakoram** Range and is the second highest (after Everest) in the world. It was also the second to be surveyed in the range (in 1856, by Colonel T.G. Montgomerie of the Survey of India). The mountain's name is *Mt. Godwin-Austen*, given in 1888 for the British explorer and geographer, Colonel Henry Haversham *Godwin-Austen* (1834–1923), who made the first maps and descriptions of this region. Its local name is either *Dapsang*, supposedly from Tibetan words meaning "clear sign," i.e. "wonderful appearance," or *Chogori*, from Tibetan *cho*, "highest," *go*, "head," and *ri*, "mountain."

Kabataş. *District of Istanbul, northwestern Turkey.* The name derives from Turkish *kaba*, "coarse," "rough," and *taş*, "stone," "rock," said to refer to a huge rock formerly here.

Kabul. *Capital of Afghanistan.* The city takes its name from the river on which it lies, a tributary of the Indus. The meaning of its own name is uncertain.

Kabwe. *Town, central Zambia.* The town has a Lala name meaning "small stone," "pebble." Its original name was *Broken Hill*, given in 1904 by an Australian mining engineer, Thomas G. Davey, who discovered the site with its precious minerals and who adopted the name of **Broken Hill** from his home country. The current name was given in 1965.

Kabylia. *Region, northern Algeria.* The mountainous coastal region takes its name from the *Kabyle*, the Berber people who inhabit it. Their own name derives from Arabic *kabīle*, "tribe."

Kadıköy *see* **Chalcedon**

Kadoma. *Town, central Zimbabwe.* The town was founded in 1906 and named for a local Tonka chief. Until 1980 the name was spelled *Gatooma*.

Kaduna. *Town, north central Nigeria.* The town takes its name from the river on which it lies. The river's own name represents the Hausa word for "crocodiles."

Kaesong. *City, southwestern North Korea.* The fortified city, one of the oldest in Korea, derives its name from Korean *kae*, "to open," and *sŏng*, "castle," "fortress." Its earlier name was *Songdo*, "city of pines," referring to the pine-covered mountains that surround it.

Kaffeklubben Island. *Island, Arctic Ocean.* The island, east of Greenland, was discovered by the American explorer Robert E. Peary in 1900. In 1921 it was visited by the Danish explorer Lauge Koch and he named it as now, from Danish *kaffeklub*, "coffee club," for the *Kaffeklub* at the Mineralogical Museum in Copenhagen.

Kaffraria. *Historic region, southeastern Africa.* The name was used for the region of present South Africa that was colonized by the Portuguese and British. It derives from the *Kaffirs*, a name formerly used for all black peoples of southern Africa other than the Khoikhoin (Hottentots) and San (Bushmen). It represents Arabic *kāfir*, "infidel," and is now a derogatory term for such people.

Kafr esh-Shaykh. *Governorate, northern Egypt.* The governorate, in the Nile Delta, was created in 1949 and originally named *Fu'adiyah*, for *Fu'ad* I (1868–1936), first king of Egypt. Following the overthrow of the Egyptian monarchy in 1952, the area took its present Arabic name (in 1955) from its capital city, meaning "village of the chief."

Kafr Kanna *see* **Cana**

Kafr Misr. *Village, northern Israel.* The Arab village was founded in the 19th century by immigrants from Egypt. Hence its name, "village of Egypt," from Arabic *kafr*, "village," and *Misr*, "Egypt" (*see* **Egypt**).

Kafr Yasif. *Township, northwestern Israel.* The Arab township arose on the site of a Jewish settlement perhaps named for the 1st-century A.D. Jewish historian *Josephus* Flavius, from Arabic *kafr*, "village," and *Yasif*, "Joseph(us)."

Kagawa. *Prefecture, southern Japan.* The prefecture, in the island of Shikoku, has a name meaning "river of perfume," from Japanese *ka*, "perfume," and *kawa*, "river." It is uncertain to which of the many rivers here the epithet applies.

Kagoshima. *City and port, southwestern Japan.* The city, in the island of Kyushu, has a name that means "fawn island," from Japanese *ka*, "deer," *ko*, "child," "young," and *shima*, "island."

K'ai-feng. *City, northeastern China.* The former capital of Honan province derives its name from Chinese *kai*, "to open," and *feng*, "to seal."

Kaikoura Range. *Mountain range, southern New Zealand.* The range, in northeastern South Island, has a Maori name said to mean "to eat crawfish," alluding to a legend from Maori mythology.

Kaiserslautern. *City, western Germany.* The city takes its name from the emperor (German *Kaiser*) Frederick I Barbarossa (c.1122–1190), who built a fortress by the *Lauter* River here in 1152. The river's own name, recorded in the 7th century as *Hlutraha*, means "bright water," from Old High German *hlūttar*, "pure," "clear," "bright" (related English *loud*), and *aha*, "water."

Kaiserstuhl. *Massif, southwestern Germany.* The volcanic massif has a name meaning "emperor's chair," referring to its impressive size. The name is first recorded in 1304 as *Keiserstuol*.

Kalahari. *Desert, southern Africa.* The great desert, in Botswana, Namibia, and South Africa, is said to derive its name from a Tswana word *kgaligadi* for a region that lacks surface water, as applies here.

Kalamazoo. *City, northern United States.* The Michigan city, first settled in 1829, has a name of Algonquian origin said to mean "he who smokes" or "boiling water," presumably alluding to the rapids on the identically named river here.

Kalat. *Town, west central Pakistan.* The town derives its name from Arabic *kal'a*, "fortress." The Arabic word has a final *-t* only when the first part of a compound name, as **Calatayud**, so that *Kalat* here presumably means "fort of—," the second part of the name having been dropped.

Kalaupapa. *Peninsula, central Hawaii, United States.* The peninsula, on northern Molokai Island, has a Hawaiian name meaning "flat plain."

Kalevala. *Town, northwestern Russia.* The town, in Karelia, was originally known by the Finnish name *Uhtua*, from a root element *uht* which may mean "stream," "river." In 1963 it adopted its present name, from the *Kalevala*, the Finnish national epic whose own name is a poetic name for Finland meaning "land of heroes." The epic consists of ballads and folk tales collected by Elias Lönnrot in this part of Karelia and elsewhere and published by him in 1849.

Kalgan. *City, northeastern China.* The city, in Hopeh province, derives its name from Mongolian *khaalga*, "gateway," "frontier," referring to its location at the point where the main caravan route from Peking to Inner Mongolia passed through the Great Wall of China. The city is also known by the Chinese name *Chiang-chia-k'ou*, from *zhāng*, "leaf," *jiā*, "house," "home," and *kǒu*, "mouth."

Kalgoorlie. *City, southwestern Australia.* The city, in Western Australia, has an Aboriginal name variously interpreted as "pear-shaped seed pod," "climbing plant," or "three parallel tracks." The reference is probably to a type of shrub here.

Kaliakra, Cape. *Cape, northeastern Bulgaria.*

The cape, on the Black Sea, has a Greek name meaning "beautiful point," from *kalos*, "beautiful," and *akra*, "point," "summit," "promontory."

Kalimantan. *Region, southern Borneo*. The Indonesian name for the island of Borneo as a whole, now applied to the Indonesian part only, represents the Malay name for Borneo's indigenous inhabitants, the *Kalimantan*. Their own name derives from Sanskrit *kāliman*, "blackness," to which Malay *tanah*, "country," has been added. The reference is to the people's very dark skins.

Kalinin *see* **Tver**

¹Kaliningrad. *City and port, western Russia*. The city, founded in 1255 as a fortress of the Teutonic Knights, originally bore the German name of *Königsberg*, "royal mount," honoring the German emperor Ottokar II (c.1223–1278). (The "mount" was the oak-covered rise by the Pregolya River where the fort was built.) In 1946, after World War II, the city was transferred from Prussia to the USSR and was renamed as now for the Soviet statesman Mikhail *Kalinin* (1875–1946).

²Kaliningrad. *City, western Russia*. The city, on the northeastern outkirts of Moscow, arose in the 1930s as an industrial satellite and dormitory town of the capital with a Soviet name as **¹Kaliningrad**.

Kalisz. *City, west central Poland*. The name was recorded by Ptolemy in the 2d century A.D. as *Calicia*. This may be related to the Slavic root element *kal*, "mud," with the rest of the name representing a placename suffix. The overall meaning would thus be "muddy place," "marsh." Kalisz is on the Prosna River. The German form of the name is *Kalisch*.

Kalmykia. *Republic, southwestern Russia*. The republic is named for its indigenous people, the *Kalmyks*, a Mongoloid people. Their name is a corrupt form of *Khalmg*, their own name for themselves, from a Mongolian word meaning "mixed." The reference is to the mixed races of Mongol nomads who settled in this region from the 17th century.

Kalocsa. *City, south central Hungary*. The origin of the city's name is uncertain. The first part may represent Turkic *kal*, "to remain."

Kaluga. *City, western Russia*. The city is said to take its name from an identical Slavic term for a raised area in marshland. This certainly describes the town's original site on land by the Yachenka River. The fort here, built in the 14th century, was moved in the 16th century to the site of the present town, almost 2 miles (3 km) to the south, on the banks of the Oka River.

Kalutara. *Town and port, southwestern Sri Lanka*. The town stands at the mouth of the *Kalu* River and is named for it, from Sinhalese *kalu*, "black," and *tara*, "port."

Kama. *River, western Russia*. The longest tributary of the Volga has a name that may derive from Votyak *kam*, meaning simply "river."

Kamaran. *Island, southern Red Sea*. The island, off the coast of Yemen, to which it belongs, has a name of Arabic origin meaning "two moons," said to refer to a double reflection of the moon that can be seen here.

Kamchatka. *Peninsula, northeastern Russia*. The Siberian peninsula takes its name from the *Kamchadal*, the people who inhabit this region. Their own name is said to represent Koriak *konchachal*, "men of the far end."

Kamenets-Podolsky. *City, western Ukraine*. The first word of the city's name derives from Russian *kamen'*, "rock," "stone," referring to the stony terrain here. There are other places of the name, so that the second word was added for purposes of distinction. It locates this Kamenets in the region known as **Podolia**. *Cp.* **Podolsk**. The Ukrainian form of the name is *Kam'yanets'-Podil's'kyy*.

Kamienna Góra. *Town, southwestern Poland*. The town has a name meaning "rocky mountain," referring to its location at the foot of the Riesengebirge. Its German name is *Landeshut*, "protection of the district" (*cp.* **Landshut**), referring to this same strategic site, by a key route over these mountains.

Kamloops. *City, southwestern Canada*. The city, in British Columbia, arose in 1810 on a site originally recorded as *Cumloups*. This represents a Native American word meaning "meeting of the waters." Kamloops lies astride the confluence of the North and South Thompson rivers.

Kampala. *Capital of Uganda*. The city is said to take its name from the African antelope known as the *impala*. If so, the reason for the name is unclear.

Kamptee. *City, central India*. The city, in Maharashtra state, is said to have derived its name from the British army designation "Camp T."

Kampuchea *see* **Cambodia**

Kanagawa. *Prefecture, east central Japan*. The prefecture derives its name from Japanese *kan*, "god," *na*, "what?," and *kawa*, "river."

Kanazawa. *City and port, west central Japan*. The city, in the island of Honshu, derives its name from Japanese *kana*, "metal," and *sawa*, "marsh."

Kanchenjunga. *Mountain, southern Asia*. The

world's third highest mountain, in the Himalayas on the Nepal-Sikkim border, has a Tibetan name meaning "five treasures of the snows," from *kang*, "snow," *chen*, "having," *dzod*, "treasure," and *nga*, "five." The reference is to the mountain's five snowy peaks.

Kanchipuram. *City, southern India.* The sacred Hindu city, in Tamil Nadu state, formerly known as *Conjeeveram*, is said to have a name of Sanskrit origin meaning "golden city." But the first part of the name may actually represent *cutchy*, a local name for the heart-leaved moonseed plant.

Kan-chou. *City, southeastern China.* The city, in Kiangsi province, derives its name from Chinese *gàn*, the *Kan* River, which flows through the city (and gave the old name of **Kiangsi** itself), and *zhōu*, "region."

Kandahar. *City, south central Afghanistan.* The city takes its name from that of the region's former people, the *Ghandara*, whose own name comes from Sanskrit *gandha*, "odor," "perfume," referring to the spices and aromatic herbs which they traded and with which they anointed themselves.

Kandy. *City, central Sri Lanka.* The former capital of the Sinhalese kings derives its name from Sinhalese *kandha*, "mountain." Kandy is sited at a height of 1,600 feet (488 m) amidst noted mountain scenery. The city's local Sinhalese name is *Mahanuwara*, "great city."

Kaneohe. *Town, northern Hawaii, United States.* The town, on eastern Oahu Island, has a Hawaiian name meaning "bamboo husband," referring to some local legend or even actual event.

Kangaroo Island. *Island, southern Australia.* The island, south of mainland South Australia, is fairly obviously named for its abundance of *kangaroos*. The name was given by Matthew Flinders (*see* **Flinders Ranges**), who landing here in 1802 found a welcome source of food "after four months' deprivation from almost any fresh provisions."

KaNgwane. *Historic homeland, eastern South Africa.* The former black homeland, created in 1977 in eastern Transvaal for those Swazis not living in Swaziland, has a Swazi name meaning "land of the *Ngwane*," from the placename prefix *ka-* and *Ngwane*, the Nguni clan from whom the Swazis came. Their own name comes from that of their chief, *Ngwane* III, who in c.1750 led a group of Nguni to settle in this region.

Kanniyakumari. *Town, southeastern India.* According to legend, the town, in Tamil Nadu state, takes its name from the goddess *Kanya*

Kumari, who killed a demon on this site. *See* **Comorin, Cape**.

Kano. *City, northern Nigeria.* The city was founded some time before the 9th century and is said to be named for *Kano*, a blacksmith of the Gaya tribe who came here in search of iron. The city gave the name of the historic kingdom here, said to have been founded in 999.

Kanpur. *City, northern India.* The city in Uttar Pradesh state, long familiar as *Cawnpore*, was a mere village when it was acquired in 1801 by the British and made into a frontier station. Its name is said to mean '*Kanha*'s town," from the name of a local zemindar (tax farmer), with Hindi *pur*, "town," added, but *Kanha* is also a name of the Hindu god Krishna, and this is more likely to be the real origin.

Kansas. *State, central United States.* The state takes its name from the river that flows through it. Its own name comes from the *Kansa*, the Native American people who formerly inhabited the region. Their name in turn is said to means "people of the south wind."

[1]Kansas City. *City, central United States.* The Kansas city, contiguous with **[2]Kansas City**, was formed as a consolidation of eight separate towns, the earliest of which was *Wyandotte*, laid out in 1857 and named for the *Kansa* Native Americans (*see* **Kansas**). One of the towns, *Kansas City*, arose in the 1870s, and all of the communities combined under the present name in 1886.

[2]Kansas City. *City, central United States.* The Missouri city, contiguous with **[1]Kansas City**, was chartered as the town of *Kansas* in 1850, after the *Kansa* Native Americans (*see* **Kansas**), and acquired its present name in 1889.

Kansu. *Province, northern China.* The province derives its name from Chinese *gān*, "gentle," "benevolent," and *sù*, "respectful," "grave."

Kanto. *Region, central Japan.* The plain and the mountain range to the west of it, in the island of Honshu, derive their name from Japanese *kan*, "gateway," "barrier," and *tō*, "east," from Chinese *guān* and *dōng*, in the same sense.

Kao-hsiung. *City and port, southwestern Taiwan.* The city derives its name from Chinese *gāo*, "high," and *xióng*, "grand," "mighty." From 1920 through 1945, while under Japanese administration, the city was known as *Takao*, the Japanese pronunciation of the Chinese characters for *Kao-hsiung*.

Kapfenberg. *Town, east central Austria.* The town takes its name from the fortress by which it arose in the late 12th century. The name means "lookout point," from an early form of modern German *gaffen*, "to gape," and *berg*, "fort."

Kapilavastu. *District, southern Nepal.* The birthplace of the Buddha, and the region of his boyhood, derives its name from Sanskrit *kapila,* "brown," *kapi,* "monkey," and *vastu,* "reality."

Kaposvár. *City, southwestern Hungary.* The city takes its name from the *Kapos* River on which it lies, with Hungarian *vár,* "castle," added to the river name, itself from Hungarian *kapu,* "gate," "entrance," relating to its passage through marshes to the country beyond.

Kapuvár. *City, western Hungary.* The name means literally "gate castle," from Hungarian *kapu,* "gate," and *vár,* "castle," referring to the entrance to a medieval defensive site here.

Kara-Bogaz Gol. *Lake, northwestern Turkmenistan.* The lake, a former inlet of the Caspian Sea, has a Turkmen name meaning "lake of the black strait," from *kara,* "black," *bogaz,* "strait" (literally "throat"), and *köl,* "lake." The "strait" is the former narrow entrance to the inlet. The black color is that of dried salt deposits here.

Karacadağ. *Mountain, southeastern Turkey.* The name means "blackish mountain," from Turkish *karaca,* "blackish" (from *kara,* "black"), and *dağ,* "mountain."

Karachi. *City and port, southern Pakistan.* Pakistan's former capital takes its name from the *Kulachi,* the Baluchi people who at one time occupied the region. The meaning of their own name is uncertain.

Karaganda. *City, east central Kazakhstan.* The city derives its name from Kazakh *karagan,* "black acacia," a tree that grows (or grew) in this region.

Karakalpakstan. *Republic, western Uzbekistan.* The republic takes its name from its indigenous inhabitants, the *Karakalpak,* their own name being of Turkic origin and meaning "black cap," apparently referring to their traditional headdress. The final Iranian *-stan* is "land."

Karakol. *City, eastern Kyrgyzstan.* The city has a Turkic name meaning "black lake," from *kara,* "black," and *kol,* "lake." From 1889 through 1921 and again from 1939 through 1991 it was renamed *Przhevalsk,* for the Russian explorer Nikolay Mikhaylovich *Przhevalsky* (1839–1888), who died here.

Karakoram. *Mountain range, northern India and Pakistan.* The range has a Turkic name meaning "black mountains," from *kara,* "black," and *koram,* "mountain."

Kara Kum. *Desert, Turkmenistan.* The desert has a Turkic name meaning "black sands," from *kara,* "black," and *kum,* "sand." The reference is to sands overgrown with vegetation, as distinct from the clear white sands found in other deserts.

Karaman. *Town, south central Turkey.* The town, originally called *Laranda,* was renamed as now for the chieftain of a Turkic tribe who conquered it in c.1250 and set up the independent Muslim state of *Karamania.*

Kara Sea. *Sea, northern Russia.* The sea, an arm of the Arctic Ocean, takes its name from the *Kara* River that flows into it. The river's own name derives from Mongolian *khar,* "black."

Karatau. *Mountain range, southern Kazakhstan.* The range has a Turkic name meaning "black mountain," alluding to mountains that lose their snow cover in summer, as distinct from those that retain it all the year round.

Karatsu. *Town and port, southern Japan.* The town, in the island of Kyushu, has a name meaning "China port," from *kara,* a Japanese name for China, and *tsu,* "harbor," "port." The name reflects the town's history as a port trading with China and Korea.

Karawanken. *Mountain range, south central Europe.* The range, forming much of the border between northern Slovenia and southern Austria, derives its name from a Celtic word related to Gaulish *caruos* and Latin *cervus,* "stag." The meaning is thus "mountain of stags."

Karelia. *Republic, northwestern Russia.* The name is that of the *Karelians,* the region's indigenous people, whose own name may derive from Finnish *karja,* "herd," referring to their main occupation as herdsmen or shepherds.

Kariba. *Town, northern Zimbabwe.* The town derives its name from a Tonka word meaning "little trap," alluding to the gorge here, where the Kariba River narrows between hills of hard rock, seen as a trap for birds, mice, and other small creatures.

Karimnagar. *City, southern India.* The city, in Andhra Pradesh state, is said to take its name from its garrison commander, Syed *Karim* ud-Din. Hence its name, with Hindi *nagar,* "city."

Karl-Marx-Stadt *see* **Chemnitz**

Karlovac. *City, northwestern Croatia.* The city takes its name from the fort built here in 1579 as a defense against the Turks. It was named for the Habsburg Archduke *Charles* (1540–1590). The German name of the city is *Karlstadt.*

Karlovo. *Town, central Bulgaria.* The town is named for *Karl* Ali-bey, to whom it was granted in the 15th century by the Turkish sultan Bayazid II. From 1953 through 1962 it was known as *Levskigrad,* for Vasil *Levski* (1837–1873), original name Vasil Ivanov Kunchev, the Bulgarian revolutionary leader who fought to free his country from Turkish rule, and who was born here. (Kunchev's assumed name means "lion-like," a nickname given him for his courage. He was executed by the Turks.)

Karlovy Vary. *City, northwestern Czech Republic.* The Czech name means "*Charles*'s hot springs," seen also in its historic German name of *Karlsbad.* The city was founded between 1347 and 1358 by the Holy Roman Emperor *Charles* (Karl) IV (1316–1378). Karlovy Vary is a noted health resort with warm thermal springs.

Karlskrona. *Town and port, southern Sweden.* The town's name means "*Charles*'s crown," given in honor of its founder in 1679, *Charles* XI of Sweden (1655–1697).

Karlsruhe. *City, southwestern Germany.* The name means "*Charles*'s rest," from German *Karl,* "Charles," and *Ruhe,* "rest," commemorating the margrave *Karl* Wilhelm von Baden-Durlach (1679–1738), who in 1715 built a hunting lodge here on the edge of the Black Forest as a place of retreat.

Karlstad. *City, southwestern Sweden.* The city was originally known as *Tingvalla,* for the *ting,* or meetings of the legislature, held here. In 1584 it was renamed "*Charles*'s town," in honor of *Charles* IX of Sweden (1550–1611), who chartered it.

Karlstadt. *Town, central Germany.* The town was founded in 1200 by Conrad of Querfurt, bishop of Würzburg, and named for *Charlemagne* (German *Karl der Große*), depicted in the civic coat of arms.

Karme Yosef. *Village, central Israel.* The village, now a commuter suburb of Tel Aviv, was founded in 1938 and given a name meaning "*Joseph*'s vineyard," for *Joseph* Sappir, a leading member of the Israeli Liberal Party.

Karmi'el. *Town, northern Israel.* The town was founded in 1964 and has a Hebrew name meaning "God's vineyard."

Karnak. *Village, northern Egypt.* The village, on the Nile, is the site of the ancient city of Thebes. Its name is said to derive from the pre–Indoeuropean root word *kar,* "stone." If so, it is strangely similar to that of the village of **Carnac,** northwestern France, with its many megalithic monuments.

Karnal. *City, northwestern India.* The city, in Haryana state, is said to derive its name from that of *Karna,* its legendary founder, and a warrior in the ancient epic poem the *Mahabharata.*

Karnataka. *State, southwestern India.* The name is of Tamil origin, from *kaṟuppu,* "black," and *nāṭu,* "country," "land." Until 1973 the state was known as *Mysore,* from Sanskrit *mahiṣūru,* "town of buffaloes." The allusion is said to be to the destruction of the buffalo demon Mahisas-

ura by the Hindu goddess Camunda. The town of *Mysore* kept the old name.

Karnei Shomron. *Settlement, central West Bank.* The settlement, in the Samarian highlands, was founded in 1977 by Orthodox Jewish settlers and given a Hebrew name meaning "horns of Samaria." The "horns" are the hills in this part of **Samaria,** whose Hebrew name is *shōmron.*

Kärnten *see* **Carinthia**

Karroo. *Tableland, southern South Africa.* The extensive plateau has a name representing Khoi (Hottentot) *garo,* "desert."

Kars. *City, northeastern Turkey.* The city is ancient, dating from the 4th century A.D. Its name is thus equally old, and the subject of etymological speculation, including an origin in Georgian *kari,* "gate," or Armenian *khars,* "bride." The latter gave rise to a legend about an Armenian king's bride who liked the location so much that her frequent visits to it caused it to be named for her. Both explanations lack factual support.

Karshi. *City, southern Uzbekistan.* The city arose on the caravan route from Samarkand and Bukhara to Afghanistan and was originally known as *Nakhsheb* or *Nesef.* It received its present name in the 14th century when a fort was built here, from Turkic *karshi,* "fortress" (literally "against").

Kasanje. *Historic kingdom, northern Angola.* The kingdom was founded in c.1620 and named for its warrior leader, *Kasanje.*

Kashgar. *City, western China.* The city, in the Sinkiang Uighur autonomous region, has a name of Turkic origin, from *kash,* "jade," and *gar,* "stone," "rock," giving an overall sense "mountain of jade."

Kashmir. *Historic region, northern India.* The name evolved from Sanskrit *kāshyapamara,* "land of *Kashyap,*" the latter being the name of a famous sage.

Kassel. *City, central Germany.* The city, founded in the 10th century, takes its name from Frankish *casella,* "fortification," from Latin *castellum,* referring to the Romano-Franconian stronghold here.

Kastelanska Rivijera. *Resort area, southern Croatia.* The resort region, on the Dalmatian coast, has a name meaning "castle riviera." It is also known as simply *Castela* (or Italian *Castelli*), and consists of seven small villages each named after a Venetian castle. Hence its other alternate name *Sedam Kastela,* "seven castles."

Kastellorizon. *Island, southeastern Aegean Sea.* The easternmost of the Dodecanese group of islands was originally named *Château Roux* ("red castle") by the medieval Knights of Rhodes, describing its red rocks. (*Cp.* **Châteauroux.**) The present name is a corruption of this.

Kastoría. *Town, northwestern Greece.* The town appears to derive its name from Greek *kastor*, "beaver," an animal that became the basis of the local fur trade (which is now mink).

Kasur. *City, eastern Pakistan.* The city is traditionally said to have been founded by *Kusa*, son of Rama, the hero of Hindu mythology.

Katahdin, Mt. *Mountain, northeastern United States.* Maine's highest point, consisting of a number of peaks, derives its name from an Algonquian (Abnaki) word meaning "main mountain."

Katanga. *Province, southern Democratic Republic of Congo.* The name of the province is a Hausa word meaning "ramparts," "fortifications," with reference to its former capital, Yoruba. From 1972 through 1997, when in **Zaire**, the province was known as *Shaba*, the Swahili word for "copper," referring to the rich deposits of this metal here.

Katherina, Gebel. *Mountain, northeastern Egypt.* The highest peak in the Sinai Peninsula (and in Egypt as a whole) takes its name from St *Catherine* of Alexandria, whose relics are preserved here. (Her body is said to have been transported here by angels.) But it is unlikely that the 4th-century saint ever existed, and her cult dates only from the 9th century. The peak is also known as *Mt. Catherine.*

Kathiawar. *Peninsula, west central India.* The peninsula, in Gujarat state, has a name meaning "land of the *Kathi*," i.e. the people of *Cachchh* (formerly spelled *Kutch* or *Cutch*), its own name meaning "marshland." The *Rann of Cachchh*, a region of saline mudflats here, between the peninsula and the mainland, derives the first word of its name from Sanskrit *īrina*, "salt swamp."

Kathmandu. *Capital of Nepal.* The city has a Nepalese name meaning "wooden temples," from *kaṭh*, "wooden," and *māṇḍū*, "temple." Most of the temples here are still timber-built. Until the 16th century, the city was known as *Kantipur*, "town of beauty," from Nepalese *kāṅti*, "beauty," "charm," and *pur*, "town."

Katoomba. *Town, southeastern Australia.* The town, in New South Wales, derives its name from an Aboriginal word meaning "waterfalls." The reference is to the nearby falls, 800 ft (245 m) high.

Katowice. *City, southern Poland.* The city's name is based on the Slavic root word *kot*, "cat,"

itself probably the basis of a personal name. From 1953 through 1956 the town was known as *Stalinogród*, "*Stalin*'s town." The German form of the name is *Kattowitz.*

Katsina. *Town, northern Nigeria.* The town was founded in c.1100 and named for *Katsina*, wife of the local king Janzama and a princess of Daura, the legendary home of the Hausa people, to the east.

Kattakurgan. *City, east central Uzbekistan.* The city derives its name from Iranian *kanta*, "walled place," and *kurgan*, "burial place," "tumulus."

Kattegat. *Strait, eastern North Sea.* The name of the strait between Denmark and Sweden derives from Old Norse *kati*, "boat," and *gata*, "way," "strait," denoting a navigable channel. The name is popularly explained as meaning "cat's throat," as if from Danish *kat* or Swedish *katt*, "cat," and the former French name for the strait was *Trou de Chat* ("cat's hole") as a mistranslation of the original.

Kaufbeuren. *City, southern Germany.* The city, founded in the 9th century around a Carolingian castle, derives its name from Old High German *kouf*, "trade," "business," and *būr*, "house," referring to its salt and cereal trade. (The "trade" part of the name first appeared in the 15th century.)

Kaunas. *City, central Lithuania.* The former provisional capital of Lithuania, at one time known as *Kovno*, has a name of uncertain origin. It has been tentatively linked to Slavic *kovati*, "to forge" (steel).

Kaura Namoda. *Town, northern Nigeria.* The town takes its name from a Fulani warrior, *Kaura Namoda*, who was installed as king of the local state of Zamfara in the early 19th century. *Kaura* is a title amounting to "warlord."

Kavarna. *Town, northeastern Bulgaria.* The town, on the Black Sea coast, is said to have a name meaning "good water," thus aligning it with **Varna**, farther south on the same coast. But this origin lacks linguistic support.

Kawagoe. *City, east central Japan.* The city, on the Shingashi River in Honshu island, derives its name from Japanese *kawa*, "river," and *ko*, "crossing."

Kawaguchi. *City, east central Japan.* The city, now effectively a suburb of Tokyo in the island of Honshu, has a name meaning "river mouth," from Japanese *kawa*, "river," and *kuchi*, "mouth." The reference is to the city's location at the mouth of a small tributary of the Ara River.

Kawaihae. *Town and port, southern Hawaii, United States.* The town, in northwestern Hawaii

Island, has a Hawaiian name meaning "water of wrath." The allusion is to an incident in which local people fought for water from a pool in an arid area.

Kawasaki. *City and port, east central Japan.* The city, a suburb of Tokyo in Honshu island, has a name meaning "river cape," from Japanese *kawa*, "river," and *saki*, "cape," "promontory." This describes its location on Tokyo Bay at the mouth of the Tama River.

Kawm Umbu. *Town, southeastern Egypt.* The town has an Arabic name meaning "hill of *Umbu*," from *kom*, "hill," and the name of the historic city of *Ombos*, just to the southwest.

Kayseri. *City, central Turkey.* The city's name is a Turkish alteration of **Caesarea**, as which it was named in the 1st century B.C. Its full Roman name was *Caesarea Cappadociae*, "Caesarea of **Cappadocia**," to distinguish it from other cities of the same name.

Kazakhstan. *Republic, west central Asia.* The country takes its name from its indigenous people, the *Kazakhs*, whose own name comes from the Turkic root word *kazak*, "nomad." The second half of the name is Iranian *ostān*, "country," "land." The Kazakhs gave the name of the Cossacks.

Kazan. *City, western Russia.* The capital of Tatarstan has a name representing Tatar *kazan*, "cauldron." This refers to the strong current of the Kazanka River on which the town stands, now at its confluence with the Volga, but originally some 28 miles (45 km) upstream.

Kazanluk. *Town, central Bulgaria.* The town, in the Kazanluk Basin, has a name alluding to its geographical location, from Turkish *kazan*, literally "cauldron," "boiler."

Kazbek. *Mountain, southwestern Russia.* The mountain, an extinct volcano in the central Caucasus, takes its name from the village of *Kazbegi* that lies at its eastern foot in northern Georgia. It was itself named for the Georgian prince and poet Aleksandr *Kazbegi* (1848–1893), a wealthy local landowner, who was born here. (It was then known as *Stepantsminda*, "St. Stephen.") The peak's other Georgian name is *Mkinvartsveri*, "glacier mountain," from *mkinvari*, "glacier," and *tsveri*, "mountain." Its Ossetic name is *Urskhokh*, "white mountain," alluding to its permanent snow cover. Yet another name is *Khrestts'upp*, "cross peak," for the ruined church of *Tsminda Sameba* ("Holy Trinity") on its slopes.

Kebnekaise. *Mountain range, northern Sweden.* The range has a Lapp name meaning "kettle top," referring to the appearance of one of its peaks.

Kecskemét. *City, central Hungary.* The name of the city, which dates from the 10th century, remains of obscure origin.

Keeling Islands *see* **Cocos Islands**

Keetmanshoop. *Town, southeastern Namibia.* The town was founded in 1866 as a German Lutheran mission station and named for Johann *Keetman*, a noted member of the missionary society. The second part of the name is Afrikaans *hoop*, "hope."

Keewatin. *Region, northern Canada.* The region, in the Northwest Territories, has a name of Cree origin meaning "people of the north wind." Hence the lines in Longfellow's *Hiawatha*:

"Ruler shall you be thenceforward
Of the Northwest-Wind, Keewaydin,
Of the home-wind, the Keewaydin."

Keflavík. *Town and port, southwestern Iceland.* The town takes its name from the small bay on which it lies. The meaning is "bay of sticks," from Icelandic *kefla*, genitive plural of *kefli*, "stick," "piece of wood," and *vík*, "bay." The reference is to the flotsam often encountered by fishermen here.

Kehl. *Town, southwestern Germany.* The town, founded as a French fortress in 1680, has a much older name than this first recorded in 1326 as *Kenle*. It probably derives from Middle High German *kanel*, "channel," a loanword from Latin *canalis*, referring to an old channel of the Rhine River here.

Keighley. *Town, northern England.* The former West Yorkshire town has a name of Old English origin meaning "*Cyhha*'s woodland clearing." The name is pronounced "Keethly," in which the *th* sound is an attempt to preserve that of Old English *h*, which was something like the *ch* in Scottish *loch*.

Kelantan. *State, northwestern Malaysia.* The state, in West Malaysia, on the Malay Peninsula, has a name meaning "land of the jujube tree," from Malay *koli*, "jujube," and *tanah*, "country," "land."

Kelowna. *City, southwestern Canada.* The city, in British Columbia, has a name that is a corruption of a Native American word meaning "grizzly bear."

Kemerovo. *City, southern Russia.* The city probably derives its name from that of one *Kemerov*, owner of coal workings here. Its name before 1932 was *Shcheglovsk*, from *Shcheglovo*, a former village that combined with it to form the present town.

Kempen. *City, western Germany.* The name literally means "fields," referring to the enclosed plots of land laid out by various local lords in or before the 9th century to form a huge woodland region.

Kempten. *City, southern Germany.* The city arose around a Benedictine abbey founded in 752 by the Iller River on the site of a Roman settlement called *Cambodunum*, a name of Celtic origin meaning "fort on the (river) bend," and its present name evolved from this. **Hamburg** probably has a name of identical meaning.

Kendal. *Town, northwestern England.* The Cumbria town lies on the *Kent* River and takes its name from it, with *-dal* representing modern *dale*, "valley." The original name of the town was *Kirkby*, "village with a church," from Old Norse *kirkja*, "church," and *bý*, "village." *Kendal* was then added to this to distinguish this village from others identically named. The first word of *Kirkby Kendal* finally dropped to leave the second alone.

Kenilworth. *Town, central England.* The Warwickshire town has an Old English name meaning "*Cynehild*'s enclosure," with the female personal name followed by *worth*, "enclosure."

Kenitra. *City and port, northwestern Morocco.* The town was founded in 1913 and was originally named *Port-Lyautey*, for the French army officer Louis Hubert *Lyautey* (1854–1934), who ordered it to be built. There was already a fort here already named *Kenitra*, however, and this name was adopted for the town in 1958. It represents a diminutive of Arabic *al-kantara*, "the bridge."

Kennedy, Cape *see* **Canaveral, Cape**

Kennewick. *City, northwestern United States.* The Washington city was laid out in 1892 and has a name of Native American origin believed to mean "grassy place."

Kenora. *Town, southern Canada.* The Ontario town was founded in 1879 as *Rat Portage*, with reference to migration of muskrats here between Lake of the Woods and the Winnipeg River. In 1904 this was changed to the present *Kenora*, an artificial name created from the first two letters of *Keewatin*, its sister town, of nearby *Norman*, and of its own former name *Rat Portage*.

Kenosha. *City, northern United States.* The Wisconsin city, at the Pike River estuary on Lake Michigan, was founded in 1835 and was at first known as *Pike Creek* and *Southport* before adopting its present name in 1850. It represents an Algonquian (Potawatomi) word meaning "pike" or "pickerel."

Kensington. *Borough of London, southeastern England.* The borough's Old English name means "estate associated with *Cynsige*." The fact that Kensington is a royal borough, with aristo-

cratic associations, has led to a popular (but erroneous) association with the name *Kingston*, as for **Kingston upon Thames**.

Kent. *County, southeastern England.* The county and historic kingdom has a name dating back to at least the 1st century B.C., when it was recorded by the Greek geographer Strabo as *Kantion*. It may derive from a Celtic root element *cant*, "border," "edge," referring to a part of the coast here, although probably a much smaller region than that of the present county. Another possibility is the Celtic source of Breton *gant* and Welsh *gan*, "with," denoting a place of assembly, such as that of an army.

Kentau. *City, south central Kazakhstan.* The city, on the slopes of the Karatau Mountains, has a Kazakh name meaning "broad mountain."

Kentucky. *State, east central United States.* The state takes its name from the river that rises in it and that flows north to the Ohio. The river's own name is said to represent Iroquois *kentake*, "meadowland," although more colorful meanings have also been suggested, such as "land of tomorrow," "land dark with blood" (alluding to intertribal wars), and "land of green reeds."

Kenya. *Republic, eastern Africa.* The country takes its name from Mt. *Kenya*, the dormant volcano that is its highest peak. The mountain's own name is probably a shortening of its Kikuyu name, *Kirinyaga*, representing *kere nyaga*, "white mountain," referring to its permanent snows and glaciers.

Kerala. *State, southwestern India.* The state probably derives its name from Tamil *keralam*, "mountain range," referring to the Western Ghats here.

Kerch. *City and port, southern Ukraine.* The city, in eastern Crimea, was founded in the 6th century B.C. by Greek colonists under the name *Panticapaeum*. The origin of this is uncertain, although the initial *Pan-* may mean "all." The present name, first recorded in the 11th century, may derive from the Slavic root *krch*, "metalworker." The city is noted for its iron and steel mills.

Kerguelen Islands. *Island group, southern Indian Ocean.* The subantarctic islands are named for the French sailor who discovered them in 1772, Yves-Joseph de *Kerguelen* de Trémarec (1734–1797). When Captain Cook came here in 1776 he named the largest island *Desolation Island*, describing it as the most desolate and barren he had ever seen. It is now itself *Kerguelen*.

Kerkyra *see* **Corfu**

Kermadec Islands. *Island group, southwestern*

Pacific. The islands, northwest of (and belonging to) New Zealand, were discovered in 1793 by the French navigator Joseph d'Entrecasteaux (*see* **D'Entrecasteaux Islands**), who named them for his first officer, Jean Michel Huon de *Kermadec* (1748–1793).

Kerman. *City, southeastern Iran.* The city takes its name from the *Carmani*, the people who formerly inhabited the region. Their own name is of obscure origin.

Kermanshah. *City, western Iran.* The name represents Sanskrit *karmansha*, "destroying a good work," the name of a tributary of the Ganges, from *karman*, "work," and *sha*, "destroying."

Kerpen. *City, western Germany.* The city, which arose by a Carolingian castle on the Roman road from Cologne to Aachen, probably derives its name from Latin *carpinus*, "hornbeam."

Kerry. *County, southwestern Ireland.* The county takes its name from the former people in this region. They were led by *Ciar*, who in early legend appears as the son of King Fergus and Queen Maeve.

Kerulen. *River, eastern Mongolia.* The name ultimately derives from Evenki *herelgen*, "plain," "valley."

Keski-Suomi. *Province, south central Finland.* The name of the province means "middle Finland," from Finnish *keski*, "middle," "center," and *Suomi*, "Finland."

Ketchikan. *City and port, northwestern United States.* The Alaska city, on Revillagigedo Island, has a Native American (Tlingit) name meaning "spread wings of prostrate eagle," referring to the appearance of part of the course of a nearby creek.

Kętrzyn. *City, northern Poland.* The city adopted its name in 1946, on the suggestion of the Polish linguist and toponymist Kazimierz Nitsch, in honor of the Polish historian and toponymist Władysław *Kętrzynski* (1838–1918). Its earlier German name was *Rastenburg*, from German *Rast*, "rest," "repose," and *Burg*, "fort," "town."

[1]Kettering. *Town, central England.* The Northamptonshire town has an Old English name meaning "(settlement of) *Cytra's* people." The Anglo-Saxon personal name is conjectural.

[2]Kettering. *City, east central United States.* The Ohio city was founded in 1841 and was originally known as *Van Buren Township*, for Martin *Van Buren* (1782–1862), 8th president of the United States. In 1952 it was renamed as now for the industrial scientist Charles F. *Kettering* (1876–1958).

Key West. *City, southeastern United States.* The city, in southwestern Florida, lies on a sand and coral island about 100 miles (160 km) from the mainland. Its name is traditionally said to represent an English corruption of Spanish *cayo hueso*, "bone reef," referring to human bones found by Spanish explorers here. But it is more likely to come from *cayo oeste*, "western reef," since the cay or island is one of the most westerly in the Florida Keys. *Cp.* **Turks and Caicos Islands**.

Kežmarok. *City, northern Slovakia.* The city, of mixed Slavic and German origin, is known by the German name of *Kaisersmarkt*, suggesting a meaning "*Caesar's* market." It is likely, however, that this is a corruption of *Käsemarkt*, "cheese market." The city has long been a noted trading center.

Kfar Azza. *Settlement, western Israel.* The cooperative settlement was founded in 1951 and named for nearby **Gaza**. The first word is Hebrew for "village."

Kfar Blum. *Kibbutz, northern Israel.* The kibbutz was founded in 1943 and named for the French Jewish socialist and premier Léon *Blum* (1872–1950). The first word is Hebrew for "village."

Kfar Etzion. *Kibbutz, south central West Bank.* The kibbutz was founded in 1943 and named for Shmuel *Holzmann* who purchased land here in 1932 (Hebrew *etz* is German *Holz*, "wood"). The first word is Hebrew for "village."

Kfar Habad. *Township, central Israel.* The township was founded in 1949 by Russian immigrants who were members of the *Habad* tendency in Hasidism. The first word is Hebrew for "village."

Kfar Hanasi. *Kibbutz, northern Israel.* The kibbutz was founded in 1948 and named for the Russian chemist and Zionist leader Chaim Weizmann (1874–1952), Israel's first president (Hebrew *nasi*, "president"). The first word is Hebrew for "village."

Kfar Hasidim. *Settlement, northern Israel.* The coooperative settlement was founded in 1924 by *Hasidic* Jews from Poland. Hence the name. The first word is Hebrew for "village."

Kfar Ruppin. *Kibbutz, northeastern Israel.* The kibbutz was founded in 1938 and named for the director of Palestine settlement Arthur *Ruppin* (1876–1943). The first word is Hebrew for "village."

Kfar Syrkin. *Settlement, central Israel.* The cooperative settlement, founded in 1936, is named for Nachman *Syrkin* (1868–1924), a founder of Zionist socialism. The first word is Hebrew for "village."

Kfar Szold. *Kibbutz, northern Israel.* The kibbutz was founded in 1942 and named for the U.S.-born Zionist and philanthropist Henrietta *Szold* (1860–1945). The first word is Hebrew for "village."

Kfar Vitkin. *Village, west central Israel.* The village was founded in 1930 and named for the Russian-born Zionist labor pioneer Joseph *Vitkin* (1876–1912). The first word is Hebrew for "village."

Kfar Warburg. *Settlement, central Israel.* The cooperative settlement was founded in 1939 and named for the Zionist leader Otto *Warburg* (1859–1938). The first word is Hebrew for "village."

Kfar Yehoshua. *Settlement, northern Israel.* The agricultural settlement takes its name from the Ukrainian-born Yishuv pioneer *Yehoshua* (Joshua) Hankin (1864–1945), who developed tracts of land in the Plain of Jezreel for development. The first word is Hebrew for "village."

Khabarovsk. *City, southeastern Russia.* The city was founded in 1658 by Russian Cossacks and named by them for the peasant explorer Yerofei *Khabarov* (c.1610–after 1667) who reached the Amur River here in 1649.

Khabur. *River, southwestern Asia.* The river, a tributary of the Euphrates in southeastern Turkey and northeastern Syria, has an Iranian name meaning "source of fertility." The Khabur has long been important for irrigating the fertile region of northeastern Syria.

Khairpur. *City, south central Pakistan.* The city, founded in 1783, has a name meaning "town of well-being," from Hindi *khair*, "well-being," and *pur*, "town."

Khakassia. *Republic, central Russia.* The republic is named for its indigenous inhabitants, the *Khakass*, a Turkic people who were originally nomadic herdsmen. Their own name derives from the word *khas*, "person," "man."

Khamis Mushayt. *City, southwestern Saudi Arabia.* The city, a traditional trading center, derives its name from Arabic *khamīs*, "Thursday," and the name of the *Mushayt* people, who held a weekly market here on that day.

Khan Tengry. *Mountain, eastern Kyrgyzstan.* The peak, in the Tien Shan range, has a name meaning "lord of the sky," from Mongolian *tengri*, "sky," "heaven," and *khan*, "lord," "master."

Khanty-Mansiysk. *City, central Russia.* The city, in western Siberia, derives its name from the two indigenous peoples of the region, the *Khant*, formerly known as the *Ostyak*, and the *Mansi*, formerly known as the *Vogul*. The two earlier names gave the town's original name of *Ostyako-Vogulsk* on its founding in 1931. The present name was adopted in 1940.

Kharbata. *Village, central West Bank.* The Arab village, in the Samarian Highlands, has an Arabic name meaning "ruined place," from Arabic *kharbaṭ*, "to spoil."

Kharkov. *City, northeastern Ukraine.* The former Ukrainian capital is traditionally said to take its name from *Kharko*, the Cossack who founded it in 1656. The Ukrainian form of the name is *Kharkiv*.

Khartoum. *Capital of Sudan.* Founded in 1821 as an Egyptian army camp, the city has an Arabic name, from *al-khurṭūm*, a short form of *ras al-khurṭūm*, "end of an elephant's trunk," from *ra's*, "head," "end," *al*, "the," and *khurṭūm*, "trunk." The reference is to the narrow stretch of land here between the White Nile and Blue Nile.

Khaskovo. *Town, southern Bulgaria.* The town arose in the late 14th century with the Turkic name *Has-koy*, meaning "sultan's village." The *-ovo* of the present name evolved through Slavic influence.

Kherson. *City and port, southern Ukraine.* The name ultimately derives from Greek *khersos*, "dry land," and *nēsos*, "island," a term used for an "island" or peninsula that was attached to dry land. This exactly describes the Crimea, where Kherson is located. The Greeks used the name for various peninsulas in Europe. This particular ancient region is also known as the *Tauric Chersonese*, for the native *Tauri*, as distinct from the *Thracian Chersonese*, on the modern Gallipoli peninsula, so called for the *Thracians*.

Khiva. *City, western Uzbekistan.* The city takes its name from an ancient well here known as *Khejvak*. The meaning of this is unknown.

Khmelnitsky. *City, west central Ukraine.* The city arose as a fortified post in the 15th century with the name of *Ploskurov*, for its location in the valley of the *Ploskaya* River. This name was subsequently modified to *Proskurov*, and remained as such until 1954, when the present name was adopted. It marked the tricentennial of the union of Ukraine and Russia, and was given in honor of the Ukrainian leader and patriot, Bogdan *Khmelnitsky* (c.1595–1657), who favored such a union. The Ukrainian form of the name is *Khmel'nyts'kyy*.

Khmunu *see* **Hermopolis**

Khodzhent. *City, northwestern Tajikistan.* The city is of ancient origin. In the 6th and 5th centuries B.C. the settlement here was known as *Cyropolis*, for *Cyrus* the Great (c.600–529), founder of the Persian empire. In the 4th century B.C. it was captured by Alexander the Great and renamed for him as *Alexandria Eskhata*, "outer Alexandria." The second word is Greek *eskhatos*, "furthermost," and implies that the city was the outermost of the places called *Alexandria* in the king's empire. By the 7th century A.D. the name had become *Khudzhand* or *Khodzhent*, a highly corrupt form of this. In 1936 the city was renamed *Leninabad* for *Lenin*, with *-abad* the Iranian element meaning "inhabited place," "town." In 1990 it reverted to its earlier name, the indigenous form of which is *Khudzhand*.

Khorasan. *Historic region, central Asia.* The region, in northeastern Iran, southern Turkmenistan, and northern Afghanistan, was originally a territory organized by the Sasanian people into four quarters, each named for its cardinal point. Hence the name of this eastern quarter, meaning "land of the sun," from Iranian *khawr*, "sun," and *āsān*, "to become," "to materialize."

Khorramabad. *City, western Iran.* The city's Iranian name means "joyous town," from *khorram*, "glad," "joyous," and *ābād*, "inhabited place," "town."

Khorramshahr. *City and port, southwestern Iran.* The city's Iranian name means "joyous city," from *khorram*, "glad," "joyous," and *shahr*, "city." The sense is a religious Islamic one. Its earlier name, originally that of the port here, was *Mohammerah*, for *Muhammad*, the founder of Islam.

Khubsugul. *Province, northern Mongolia.* The province takes its name from the *Hövsgöl* lake here, its own Mongolian name meaning "full lake."

Khudzhand *see* **Khodzhent**

Khuzestan. *Region, southwestern Iran.* The name of the region means "land of the *Khuz*," the latter being its indigenous inhabitants, known to the Romans as the *Hussi*, with *-stan* meaning "country." The region's former name was *Arabestan*, "land of the *Arabs*."

Khwarezm. *Historic region, central Asia.* The region, along the Amu Darya in the territory of present-day Turkmenistan and Uzbekistan, has a name representing Iranian *khwārazm*, from *khawr*, "sun." This name gave that of the 9th-century Muslim mathematician *al-Khwarismi*, whose own name (influenced by Greek *arithmos*, "number") gave the English term *algorithm*.

Kiangsi. *Province, southeastern China.* The province has a name meaning "west of the river," from Chinese *jiāng*, "river," and *xī*, "west," referring to its original location to the west of the Yangtze. (Following changes in administra-tive divisions, the province is now south of the river.)

Kiangsu. *Province, eastern China.* The name of the province means "river of revival," from Chinese *jiāng*, "river," and *sū*, "to revive," "to recover consciousness."

Kicking Horse Pass. *Mountain pass, western Canada.* The pass, in the Canadian Rockies on the border between Alberta and British Columbia, is so named from an incident in 1858, when James Hector (1834–1907), of Captain John Palliser's expedition, was kicked in the chest by his horse while crossing the river here.

Kidderminster. *Town, west central England.* The Worcestershire town has an Old English name meaning "*Cydder*'s monastery." The monastery in question was founded here in the 8th century on the site now occupied by All Saints church.

Kidron. *Stream, central Israel.* The sporadic stream to the east of Jerusalem, mentioned in the Bible (2 Samuel 15:23, etc.), has a name representing Hebrew *qidrōn*, from *qador*, "to be dark," referring to the color of its water, which is thick with sediment. The Arabic name of the brook is *Wadi en-Nar*, "river of fire," from *wādi*, "river," *en*, "the," and *nar*, "fire."

Kiel. *City and port, northern Germany.* The city was founded in 1240 by Count Adolf IV of Holstein and takes its name from Old Norse *kill*, "bay," "gulf," referring to the Kiel Fjord, an inlet of the Baltic Sea, on which it stands. *Cp.* **Catskill Mountains**.

Kielce. *City, southeastern Poland.* The city, first mentioned in the late 11th century, derives its name from the personal name *Kielec*, itself representing Polish *kiel*, "fang," "tusk," with a diminutive suffix.

Kiev. *Capital of Ukraine.* The city is said to take its name from a prince *Kiy* who supposedly founded it in the 9th century. But this is probably an attempt to explain an otherwise obscure name. The Ukrainian form of the name is *Kyyiv*.

Kigali. *Capital of Rwanda.* The city takes its name from Mt. *Kigali*, near which it arose in the 19th century when this territory became part of German East Africa. The mountain's name comprises the Bantu prefix *ki-* and Rwanda *gali*, "broad," "wide."

Kilauea. *Volcano, southern Hawaii, United States.* The world's largest volcanic crater, in southeastern Hawaii Island, has a Hawaiian name meaning "much spewing," referring to its repeated eruptions of lava.

Kildare. *County, eastern Ireland.* The county is named for its town, itself with a name meaning "church of the oak," from Irish *cill*, "church," and *doire*, "oak." St. Brigid is said to have founded a nunnery here in the 5th or 6th century in a pagan oak grove.

Kilimanjaro. *Mountain, northeastern Tanzania.* Africa's highest point, a recently extinct volcano, has a Swahili name meaning "mountain of the god of cold," from *kilima*, "mountain," and *njaro*, "god of cold." Kilimanjaro is famous for its glaciers.

Kilkenny. *County, southeastern Ireland.* The county takes its name from its town. Its own name represents Irish *Cill Chainnigh*, "church of (St.) *Kenneth*."

Killarney. *Town, southwestern Ireland.* The town, in Co. Kerry, has a name representing Irish *Cill Airne*, "church of the sloes."

Killeen. *City, southern United States.* The Texas city was laid out in 1882 by the Santa Fe Railway and named for Frank P. *Killeen*, a civil engineer with the line.

Kilmarnock. *Town, southwestern Scotland.* The town's name means "St. *Ernan*'s church," from Gaelic *cill*, "church," and the saint's name prefixed by *mo-* and suffixed by *-oc*. Gaelic *mo* means "my," and the suffix *-oc* denotes a diminutive. Overall the name thus effectively means "church of my little Ernan," implying a personal dedication to this saint, a 6th-century disciple of St. Columba.

¹Kimberley. *City, central South Africa.* The city was founded in 1871 following the discovery of diamonds here and was named for John Wodehouse, 1st Earl of *Kimberley* (1826–1902), then British secretary of state for the colonies. The earl's title came from his birthplace, *Kimberley*, Norfolk.

²Kimberley. *Region, northwestern Australia.* The plateau region of northern Western Australia was surveyed, and some gold found, in the 1880s, and named for John Wodehouse, 1st Earl of *Kimberley* (1826–1902), then British secretary of state for the colonies. The region is also referred to as *The Kimberleys*.

Kimch'aek. *City and port, eastern North Korea.* The city began to develop in the late 19th century from a fishing village cvalled *Songjin*. In 1952 its name was changed as now in memory of *Kim Ch'aek*, commander of the North Korean army, killed in the Korean War.

Kinabalu, Mt. *see* **Kota Kinabalu**

King Country. *Region, northern New Zealand.* The geographical region, in west central North Island, was so called by Europeans because it was here that the Maori *king* Tawhiao sought refuge in 1865 following the Maori Wars.

King George Sound. *Inlet, southwestern Australia.* The natural harbor, in Western Australia, was charted by George Vancouver in 1791 and named by him for *George* III of England (1738–1820), then reigning. The earlier form of the name was *King George III Sound*.

King Leopold Ranges. *Mountain chain, northwestern Australia.* The mountains, in northern Western Australia, were sighted in 1879 by the explorer Alexander Forrest who named them for *Leopold* II (1835–1909), king of the Belgians.

King's Lynn. *Town and port, eastern England.* The name of the Norfolk town essentially means "king's (manor on the) *Lynn*," the latter being the Celtic name, meaning "pool," of the mouth of the Ouse River where the town stands. The *king* in question is Henry VIII, who granted the town two charters in 1524 and 1537, the latter changing its name from *Lynn* to *King's Lynn*, as now. Locally the town is still called just *Lynn*.

King Sound. *Inlet, northwestern Australia.* The inlet, in northern Western Australia, was explored in 1838 by John Stokes and John Wickham, captains of the *Beagle*, who named it for the surveyor Phillip Parker *King* (1793–1856).

Kingsport. *City, east central United States.* The Tennessee city arose as a settlement on the Holston River in c.1750 and was variously known as *Island Flats*, *Boat Yard*, and *Christiansville* until 1774, when Colonel James *King* established a mill here. The name then became *King's Mill Station*, *King's Port*, and finally *Kingsport*, as now. The *port* indicates that the town was a shipping point.

¹Kingston. *Capital of Jamaica.* The city and port, founded in 1692 after the former capital, Port Royal, was destroyed in an earthquake, is named in honor of *King* William III (1650–1702), who had come to the English throne three years earlier.

²Kingston. *City, southern Canada.* The Ontario city was founded by the French in 1673 on the site of the Native American village of *Cataraqui*. It received its present name from the British in 1783, in honor of *King* George III (1738–1820), then reigning.

Kingston upon Hull *see* **Hull**

Kingston upon Thames. *Borough of London, southeastern England.* The former Surrey town, on the **Thames** River, was a royal possession as early as the 9th century, when it was already a "king's estate," as its name states. It is not certain for which king it was originally named, but several Anglo-Saxon kings were crowned here.

King William Island. *Island, northern Canada.* The island, in Nunavut, southwest of the Boothia Peninsula, was discovered by the British explorer James Ross in 1830 and named for the reigning monarch, *William* IV (1765–1837).

Kinki. *Region, south central Japan.* The region, in the island of Honshu, derives its name from Japanese *kin*, "proximity," and *ki*, "imperial capital," referring to its situation near the former imperial capital of Kyoto.

Kinshasa. *Capital of Democratic Republic of Congo.* The city has a Bantu name of unknown meaning. It was founded in 1881 and until 1965, as capital of the Belgian Congo, was known as *Léopoldville*, for the Belgian king *Léopold* II (1835–1909). This name was given by the explorer H.M. Stanley in honor of his royal patron.

Kirchheim unter Teck. *City, southern Germany.* The city, below (*unter*) the *Teck*, has a name meaning "church settlement," referring to its original missionary church. The mountain peak, which gave the name of the ducal *Teck* family (George V of England married Mary of Teck), may derive its own name from an Indoeuropean root word meaning "to burn."

Kirgizia *see* **Kyrgyzstan**

Kiribati. *Island republic, western Pacific.* The islands were discovered in 1765 by the British commodore John Byron. In 1788 Captain Thomas *Gilbert* arrived here after helping to convey the first shipload of convicts to Australia, and in the 1820s the main group of islands was named for him as the *Gilbert Islands*. The present name, adopted in 1979 when the islands gained their independence, represents a local (Gilbertese) pronunciation of his name. *See also* **Kiritimati.**

Kırıkkale. *Town, central Turkey.* The town's name means "broken fort," from Turkish *kırık*, "broken," and *kale*, "fort." The reference is to a ruined fort where the original village stood here.

Kirin. *Province, northeastern China.* The province derives its name from Chinese *jí*, "luck," "favor," and *lín*, "forest." The forests in the western part of the province are noted for their valuable wild animals, such as the Manchurian hare, prized for its fur, and certain snakes, used to destroy harmful rodents in gardens and orchards.

Kiritimati. *Island, central Pacific.* The world's largest atoll, in the Line Islands (part of Kiribati), was discovered by Captain Cook on December 24, 1977, Christmas Eve, and he accordingly named it *Christmas Island*. The present name is a local (Gilbertese) pronunciation of the first word of this.

Kirkcaldy. *Town and port, eastern Scotland.* The name of the Fife town does not begin with

the *Kirk-*, meaning "church," found in many Scottish placenames, such as **Kirkwall**. It represents Celtic *caer*, "fort," with the rest of the name that of the hill known as *Caledin*, from Celtic *caled*, "hard," and *din*, "fort," denoting a rocky eminence. Apparently the meaning of the latter word was lost on those who added *caer* to a name already incorporating "fort." For a similar name, *see* **Kirkintilloch.**

Kirkcudbright. *Town, southern Scotland.* The town's name means "(St.) *Cuthbert*'s church," the saint in question being the 7th-century Northumbrian monk who made many missionary journeys to this part of Scotland. The *Kirk-* of the name represents Old Norse *kirkja*, "church," and the fact that it precedes the name suggests that it is a translation of Gaelic *cill*, "church," since in Gaelic placenames the generic term precedes the personal name, rather than following it, as in Old Norse and Old English.

Kirkintilloch. *Town, west central Scotland.* As with **Kirkcaldy**, the first part of the former Dunbartonshire town's name does not mean "church" but represents Celtic *caer*, "fort." The name overall thus means "fort at the head of the hillock," the rest of the name representing Gaelic *ceann*, "head," and *tulaich*, the genitive of *tulach*, "hillock." The fort referred to is a Roman one on the Antonine Wall.

Kırklareli. *City, northwestern Turkey.* The city originally bore the Byzantine Greek name of *Saranta Ekklesies*, "forty churches." This later became the Turkish equivalent, *Kırkkilise*, from *kırk*, "forty," and *kilise*, "church." In 1924 the name was modified as now.

Kirkwall. *Town and port, northeastern Scotland.* The chief town of the Orkney Islands has a Scandinavian name meaning "church bay," from Old Norse *kirkja*, "church," and *vágr*, "bay." The church is the 12th-century cathedral of St. Magnus, while the bay is the Bay of Kirkwall, on which the town lies.

Kirov *see* **Vyatka**

Kirovograd. *City, south central Ukraine.* The city was founded in 1764 near the Fort of St. *Elizabeth* that had been built in 1754 by the Russian empress *Yelizaveta* (Elizabeth) Petrovna (1709–1762) in order to defend the southern borders of Russian from invasion by the Turks and Tatars. In 1775 it was named for her as *Yelizavetgrad*, "*Elizabeth*'s town." In 1924 it was renamed *Zinovievsk*, for the Soviet politician and Comintern chairman, Grigory *Zinoviev* (1883–1936), who was born here. In 1934 it was further renamed *Kirovo* for the Communist leader Sergei *Kirov* (*see* **Vyatka**), assassinated that year.

In 1936, on the execution of Zinoviev for alleged complicity in Kirov's murder, it was again renamed *Kirovograd*. This means "city of *Kirovo*," but also implies "*Kirov*'s city," which would strictly be *Kirovgrad*, but that name was already assigned elsewhere (to former *Kalata* in western Russia). The Ukrainian form of the name is *Kirovohrad*.

Kiryat. For names in Israel beginning thus, *see* **Qiryat.**

Kiryu. *City, central Japan.* The city, in the island of Honshu, derives its name from Japanese *kiri*, "paulownia" (a tree of the figwort family), and *u*, "birth."

Kisalföld. *Region, northwestern Hungary.* The name means "little plain," from Hungarian *kis*, "little," and *alföld*, "plain." The region is "little" by comparison with the central **Great Alföld.**

Kisangani. *City, northeastern Democratic Republic of Congo.* The city has a Swahili name meaning "in the sand," with reference to the fine, sandy soil here on the Congo River. It was founded by Europeans in 1883 and was originally known as *Falls Station*, for the nearby Stanley *Falls*. It then became *Stanleyville*, for the Welsh-born U.S. explorer Sir Henry Morton *Stanley* (1841–1904), who opened up the Congo region in the early 1880s. In 1966 it was renamed as now, the name already being in local use.

Kishangarh. *City, northwestern India.* The city, in Rajasthan state, has a name meaning "*Kishan*'s fort," alluding to its founder in 1611, *Kishan* Singh, a Rajput. Hindi *garh* is "fort."

Kishinev. *Capital of Moldova.* The city, first mentioned in 1466, probably derives its name from Old Moldovan *kishineu*, "spring," "artesian well," a word ultimately related to Low Latin *pissiare*, "to urinate." The Moldovan form of the name is *Chişinău*.

Kishiwada. *City, south central Japan.* The city, facing Osaka Bay in the island of Honshu, derives its name from Japanese *kishi*, "bank," "shore," *wa*, "harmony," and *ta*, "rice field."

Kiskőrös. *City, central Hungary.* The name means "little (place of) ash trees," from Hungarian *kis*, "little," and a dialect form of *kőrisfa*, "ash tree." The name contrasts with that of **Nagykőrös**, further north.

Kiskunfélegyháza. *City, central Hungary.* The name means "church of the little *Cuman* district," from Hungarian *kis*, "little," *Kun*, "Cuman," the people settled here by King Béla IV in the early 13th century, *fél*, "district" (literally "half"), and *egyház*, "church" (from *egy*, "one," and *ház*, "house").

Kiskunhalas. *City, south central Hungary.* The name means "(place of) fish of the little *Cuman* settlement," from Hungarian *kís*, "little," "*Cuman*" (as for **Kiskunfélegyháza**), and *hal*, "fish." The fish in question would have been in the nearby small Halas Lake.

Kiskunmajsa. *City, south central Hungary.* The name means "(place of) *Majsa* of the little *Cuman* settlement," from Hungarian *kís*, "little," "*Cuman*" (as for **Kiskunfélegyháza**), and the personal name *Majsa*, a pet form of *Mojzes* (Moses).

Kislovodsk. *City, southwestern Russia.* The town was founded in 1803 as a spa. Hence its name, from Russian *kislaya voda*, literally "sour water," as a popular form of *uglekislaya voda*, "carbonic water," referring to the water of its springs.

Kissidougou. *Town, southeastern Guinea.* The name means "town of the *Kissi*," with the ethnic name followed by Dyula *dugu*, "village," "town," as for **Ouagadougou.**

Kistelek. *Town, southern Hungary.* The name means "*Kis*'s patch of ground," with the Hungarian personal name followed by *telek*, "piece of ground."

Kisújszállás. *Town, east central Hungary.* The name means "*Kis*'s new living quarters," with the Hungarian personal name followed by *új*, "new," and *szállás*, "quarters."

Kisvárda. *Town, northeastern Hungary.* The name means "little castle," from Hungarian *kis*, "little," and *vár*, "castle."

Kitakami. *River, northern Japan.* The river, in the island of Honshu, takes its name from the mountain range here. Its own name means "northern summit," from Japanese *kita*, "north," and *kami*, "summit," "head."

Kitakyushu. *City, southern Japan.* The city, in the island of **Kyushu**, was formed in 1963 from the amalgamation of five towns and has a name describing its location, from Japanese *kita*, "north," and the name of the island.

Kitchener. *City, southern Canada.* The Ontario city was founded in c.1807 by Bishop Benjamin Eby and settled by German immigrants. It was at first known as *Sand Hill*, *Ebytown*, and *Berlin*. In 1916, when this last name became unacceptable in World War I, it was renamed as now, to commemorate Horatio *Kitchener*, 1st Earl Kitchener (Kitchener of Khartoum) (1850–1916), British field marshal and secretary of state for war, drowned when the ship taking him to Russia was sunk by a German mine.

Kitikmeot. *Region, northern Canada.* The Nunavut region was originally called *Central Arctic*. In 1982 it received its present (Inuinnaqtun) name, meaning "from the center." It refers to the fact that the Inuit were originally an inland rather than a coastal people.

Kitzingen. *City, central Germany.* The city, which arose in the early 11th century by a major crossing of the Main River, has a name meaning "(settlement of) *Chitzo*'s people."

Kiviōli. *Town, northeastern Estonia.* The town has a name meaning "shale oil," referring to its function as an oil-shale mining center.

Kızıl Adalar. *Island group, Sea of Marmara.* The Turkish islands, southeast of Istanbul, have a name meaning "red islands," from Turkish *kızıl*, "red," and *ada*, "island," plural *adalar*. The color refers to the copper for which one of the main islands, Heybeli, was noted in ancient times. (Hence its Greek name of *Chalcitis*, from Greek *khalkos*, "copper.")

Kızıl Dağ. *Mountain, north central Turkey.* The mountain, near the source of the **Kızıl Irmak**, has a name meaning "red mountain," from Turkish *kızıl*, "red," and *dağ*, "mountain."

Kızıl Irmak. *River, central Turkey.* The name of Turkey's longest river means "red river," from Turkish *kızıl*, "red," and *ırmak*, "river." The reference is to the red clay washed down from its source in the **Kızıl Dağ.** *Cp.* **Yeşilırmak.**

Kladno. *City, western Czech Republic.* The city probably derives its name from Slavic *klada*, "log," "beam," alluding to a place where trees had been felled. The name itself has an adjectival form. *Cp.* **Kłodzko.**

Klagenfurt. *City, southern Austria.* Local legend derives the city's name from a mythical woman known as the *Klagefrau*, "weeping woman," who supposedly kept the ford (*Furt*) over the Glan River here. The true origin of the name remains uncertain, although a tradition traces it to Latin *Claudii Forum*, "*Claudius*'s market," for a Roman emperor.

Klaipeda. *City and port, eastern Lithuania.* The city's name is of uncertain origin. The second part appears to represent Lithuanian *peda*, "territory." The German name of the town is *Memel*, a corruption of **Neman**, the name of the river on which it stands.

Klerksdorp. *City, north central South Africa.* The Gauteng city was founded in 1837 by Afrikaner farmers (Boers) and given a name meaning "*Klerk*'s village," for Jacob de *Clerq* (popularly De *Klerk*) (1791–1888), the first landdrost (district magistrate).

Kleve. *City, western Germany.* The city arose below a hill on which a 10th-century castle stood. Hence its name, from Middle Low German *klif*, "cliff," "steep drop." The name, spelled *Cleve* until 1935, gave the title of the counts of *Cleve*, and so the name of Anne of *Cleves*, wife of Henry VIII.

Kłodzko. *City, southwestern Poland.* The city takes its name from the Nysa *Kłodzka* River here, its own name probably deriving from Slavic *klada* (Russian *koloda*), "log," "beam," denoting an area cleared of trees. *Cp.* **Kladno.** The German form of the city's name is *Glatz*.

Klondike. *River, northwestern Canada.* The river, a tributary of the Yukon, has a name that is said to derive from a Native American word *throndik*, meaning "river of fish."

Klosterneuburg. *Town, northeastern Austria.* The town arose in the 12th century around a castle and was originally called *Neuburg*, "new fortified place." An Augustinian abbey was founded at about the same time as the castle and the area around it became known as *Klosterneuburg*, from German *Kloster*, "monastery" (English *cloister*). This name then spread to the town as a whole.

Knoxville. *City, eastern United States.* The Tennessee city and original state capital was settled in 1786 and named for General Henry *Knox* (1750–1806), the Revolutionary hero.

Kobe. *City and port, central Japan.* The city, in the island of Honshu, has a name meaning "house of the god," from Japanese *kō*, "god," and *he*, "house."

Koblenz. *City, western Germany.* The present form of the city's name has evolved from its Roman name of *Confluentes*, from Latin *confluens*, "confluence." Koblenz stands at the confluence of the Rhine and the Moselle.

Kochi. *Prefecture, southern Japan.* The prefecture, in the island of Shikoku, derives its name from Japanese *kō*, "high," and *chi*, "knowledge."

Ko-chiu. *City, southern China.* The city, in Yunnan province, derives its name from Chinese *ge*, "one," and *jiù*, "old," "former."

Kodiak Island. *Island, northwestern United States.* The island, in southern Alaska, was originally known as *Kikhtak*, from the Inuit (Eskimo) word meaning "island." This gradually altered to the present form of the name.

Kofu. *City, east central Japan.* The city, in Honshu island, derives its name from Japanese *kō*, "first rank," and *fu*, "prefecture."

Kohat. *Town, northwestern Pakistan.* The town is traditionally said to take its name from its founder in the 14th century, the Buddist rajah *Kohat*.

Koh-i-Baba. *Mountain range, central Afghanistan.* The Iranian name means "grandfather mountain," as the country's main mountain ridge.

Kohistan. *Region, south central Asia.* The mountainous region, in Pakistan and Afghanistan, has a name meaning "land of mountains," "highland country," from Iranian *kūh*, "mountain," and *ostān*, "country."

Kohtla-Järve. *City, northeastern Estonia.* The city, founded in 1900, derives its name from Estonian *koht*, "place," and *järv*, "lake," relating to its location near the Gulf of Finland.

Kokand. *City, eastern Uzbekistan.* The city's name appears to be based on Iranian *kan* or *kent*, "town," but the initial *Ko-* is unexplained.

Kokchetav. *City, northern Kazakhstan.* The city was founded in 1824 as a Cossack village and has a Turkic name meaning "green mountain." The reference is to the hills with pine-covered slopes which stand out here among the steppes.

Kokomo. *City, east central United States.* The Indiana city was laid out in 1844 and named for the Miami chief *Kokomo*. His own name means "black walnut."

Koko Nor. *Lake, northwestern China.* China's largest lake has a name meaning "blue lake," referring to the color of its waters, from Mongolian *hoh*, "blue," and *nuur*, "lake." Its Chinese name, *Tsinghai*, also that of the province here, means the same, from *qīng*, "blue," and *hǎi*, "lake."

Kola Peninsula. *Peninsula, northwestern Russia.* The peninsula is named for the *Kola* River here. Its own name represents a Finno-Ugric root word *kol* or *kul* meaning "fish."

Kolarovgrad *see* **Shumen**

Kołobrzeg. *City and port, northwestern Poland.* The city was founded as a Slav stronghold in the 8th century and appears to have a name meaning "by the coast," from words related to Russian *okolo*, "near," "by," and *bereg*, "coast." The city's German name is *Kolberg*, in which Slavic *breg*, "coast," has become Germanic *berg*, "hill," "fort."

Kolomna. *City, western Russia.* The name may derive either from Finno-Ugrian *kolm*, "grave," "cemetery," or from Russian dialect *kolomen*, "neighborhood." A traditional origin in Russian *kolonna*, "column," must be ruled out on linguistic grounds.

Kolomyya. *City, western Ukraine.* The name probably means "(place) by the *Myya*," from a Slavic word related to Russian *okolo*, "by," and the name of a small river that joins the Prut here.

Komandorsky Islands. *Island group, northeastern Russia.* The islands, in the southwestern Bering Sea, were discovered in 1741 by the Russian navigator *Commander* Vitus Bering (*see*

Bering Sea), who died on one of them, and are named for him. The islands are sometimes known in English as the *Commander Islands*.

Komárno. *City, southwestern Slovakia.* The city's name probably derives from Slovak *komár*, "mosquito," referring to the unwelcome presence of these insects here at the confluence of two rivers with the Danube.

Komárom. *City, northern Hungary.* The city's name has the same origin as that of **Komárno**, across the Danube, which here forms the border between Hungary and Slovakia. The two cities were long united.

Kommunarsk *see* **Alchevsk**

Kommunizma, Pik *see* **Communism, Peak**

Komsomolsk. *City, eastern Russia.* The city was built in 1932 on the Amur River by members of the *Komsomol*, the Young Communist League. Hence the name, which in its full form is *Komsomolsk-na-Amure*, "Komsomolsk-on-Amur," so named to be distinguished from other places called *Komsomolsk*.

Kondopoga. *City, northwestern Russia.* The city, in Karelia, has a name of uncertain origin. The second part almost certainly derives from a Balto-Finnic word related to Finnish *pohja*, "foundation." The first could also be of Finnish origin, from *honka*, "pine," *kontio*, "bear," or *kontu*, "peasant plot."

Königsberg *see* ¹**Kaliningrad**

Königsee. *Town, central Germany.* The town, founded in 1200 by the counts of Schwarzburg, appears to have a name meaning "(place by the) king's lake," from Old High German *kuning*, "king," and *sēo*, "lake." There was presumably an early royal estate here.

Königssee. *Lake, southern Germany.* The lake takes its name from the settlement at its northern end of the same name, recorded in 1133 as *Chunigesse*, "(place by the) king's lake," as for **Königsee**. The lake is also known as *Bartholomäussee*, for the church dedicated to St. *Bartholomew* built on its western shore in 1697.

Königstein. *Town, central Germany.* The town, known in full as *Königstein im Taunus*, lies in the **Taunus** below the ruins of a 13th-century fortress. Its name, meaning "king's rock," dates from this time and refers to the German king who held sovereignty over the castle. There is another town of the same name in east central Germany, in Saxonian Switzerland, where the name applies similarly to a nearby flat-topped mountain on which the kings of Bohemia built a castle in the early 13th century.

Königstuhl. *Mountain, southwestern Germany.* The massif, near Heidelberg, has a name meaning "king's seat," referring to a sandstone block here with "*kongst*" inscribed on the front surface. It must originally have resembled something like a throne, and gave rise to a tale about a seat where a pagan king used to sit in olden times.

Königswinter. *City, western Germany*. The city, on the Rhine, probably derives the second part of its name from Late Latin *vinitorium*, "vineyard" (from Latin *vinitor*, "wine grower"). The first part of the name, recorded from the 13th century, means "king," perhaps referring to an early royal estate here.

Konotop. *City, northern Ukraine*. The name is said to derive from Slavic *kon*, "horse," and *topit'*, "to sink," denoting a difficult passage by horse-drawn transport over muddy or miry ground.

Konstantinovka. *City, eastern Ukraine*. The city arose in 1869 as a railroad station on the line from Kharkov. It was presumably named for Grand-Duke *Konstantin* (1827–1892), son of Czar Nicholas I and brother of Alexander II. The Ukrainain form of the name is *Kostyantynivka*.

Konstanz *see* **Constance, Lake**

Kontagora. *Town, western Nigeria*. The town, founded in 1864, has a name said to represent the local words *kwanta gora*, "lay down your gourds." But this is probably an anecdotal attempt to explain an otherwise obscure name.

Konya. *City, southwestern Turkey*. The city's name is a corruption of its original Greek name *Ikonion* (Latin *Iconium*). This is popularly derived from Greek *eikōn, eikonos*, "image," "icon." The reference is to the classical story telling how Prometheus made men out of mud here to replace those drowned during the Flood. The city was thus the first to emerge when the waters receded. (According to another legend, the image was the gorgon's head with which Perseus conquered the native population before founding the Greek city.) The actual source of the name is unknown.

Kópavogur. *Town, southwestern Iceland*. The coastal suburb of Reykyavík has a name meaning "bay of baby seals," from Icelandic *kópa*, genitive plural of *kópur*, "young seal," and *vogur*, "bay."

Koper. *Town and port, southwestern Slovenia*. The town, on the Istrian peninsula, was known to the Romans as *Capris*, giving its present Slavic name. Its Italian name, partly influenced by the Latin, is *Capodistria*, "headland of **Istria**." However, from 1278 through 1797, under Venetian rule, the town was capital of Istria, and the Italian name is popularly said to refer to this status.

Kopet-Dag. *Mountain range, southwestern Asia*. The range, on the border between Iran and Turkmenistan, has a name representing Turkic *kop*, "many," and *dağ*, "mountain."

Kopparberg. *Town, south central Sweden*. The town, a former copper-mining center, has a name meaning "copper mountain."

Kopřivnice. *Town, eastern Czech Republic*. The name derives from Czech *kopřiva*, "nettle," denoting the former agricultural use of this plant. The town's German name is similar, as *Nesseldorf*, "nettle village." The name is found elsewhere in Slavic countries, as *Koprivnica*, Croatia, and *Koprivshtitsa*, Bulgaria.

Kordestan. *Region, northwestern Iran*. The geographical region has a name meaning "land of the *Kurds*," referring to its principal inhabitants. The people's own name may derive from Iranian *kard*, "active." *Cp.* **Kurdistan**.

Kordofan. *Region, central Sudan*. The region was formerly inhabited by Nubian-speaking peoples, and the name may thus be based on Nubian *kurta*, "men."

Korea. *Country, eastern Asia*. The name is now borne by the contiguous countries of *North Korea* (formally the Democratic Republic of Korea) and *South Korea* (the Republic of Korea), proclaimed in 1948. The basic name derives from Chinese *gāolì*, that of a dynasty founded in 918, and itself meaning "high serenity." The Japanese name of Korea is *chosen*, from Korean *chosŏn*, meaning "land of morning calm," from *cho*, "morning," and *sŏn*, "calm."

Körös *see* **Nagykőrös**

Korsakov. *City and port, eastern Russia*. The city, at the southern end of Sakhalin Island, was named in 1946 for the Russian hydrographer Voin Andreyevich Rimsky-*Korsakov* (1822–1871), who charted the Tatar Strait between Sakhalin and mainland Russia. Under Japanese rule (1905–45) the town was known as *Otomari*.

Kortrijk *see* **Courtrai**

Kosciusko, Mt. *Mountain, southeastern Australia*. The mountain, in New South Wales, was discovered in 1839 by the Polish explorer Paul Strzelecki and named by him for the Polish patriot Tadeusz *Kościuszko* (1746–1817). The present name is a slightly simplified form of this.

Kosice. *City, southeastern Slovakia*. The city may derive its name from a personal name *Kosa*, or else possibly from Old Slovak *kosa*, "clearing," related to modern Slovak *kosit'*, "to reap."

Kosovo. *Province, western Serbia*. The province may derive its name from Serbian *kos*, "blackbird," or more likely from a personal name.

Kosovska Mitrovica. *Town, south central Ser-*

bia. The first word of the name denotes the town's location in the province of **Kosovo**, at the same time distinguishing it from **Sremska Mitrovica**, to the north. The second word comes from the dedication of its church to St. *Dimitri*. This dedication is typically found in non–Catholic regions of Slav countries.

Kostroma. *City, western Russia*. The city takes its name from the river on which it stands. The river's own name has been the subject of some speculation, since the final *-ma* suggests a Finno-Turkic origin. Those favoring a Slavic source derive it from *kostra*, "bast," "fiber." The folk etymology is in Russian *kostyor*, "bonfire," as if timber were transported over the river by being floated on huge "bonfires."

Kostrzyn. *Town, western Poland*. The town derives its name from the personal name *Kostrz*, the final *-yn* being a possessional suffix. The German form of the name is *Küstrin*. (This town must not be confused with the identically named Kostrzyn east of Poznań, known in German as *Kostschin*.)

Koszalin. *City, northwestern Poland*. The city, known to the Germans as *Köslin*, apparently derives its name from Slavic *koza*, "goat," or *kozien*, "stag," denoting a place where these animals were kept, in the latter case in a hunting preserve.

Kőszeg. *Town, western Hungary*. The name represents Hungarian *köves szeglet*, "rocky corner," describing the town's geographical location.

Kota Baharu. *City, western Malaysia*. The city, on the Malay Peninsula near the Thai border, has a Malay name meaning "new fort." The earlier form of the name was *Kota Bahru*.

Kota Kinabalu. *City and port, northeastern Malaysia*. The capital of Sabah was founded in the late 19th century and originally named *Jesselton*, for Sir Charles *Jessel*, a director of the British North Borneo Company. In 1968 it acquired its present name, meaning "fort of *Kinabalu*," from Malay *kota*, "fort," and the name of nearby Mt. *Kinabalu*. The mountain is regarded as the spiritual home of the indigenous Dusan, and its name is a form of their term for it, *Akinabalu*, "revered place of the dead."

Kotelny Island. *Island, northeastern Russia*. The largest of the New Siberian Islands, in the Arctic Ocean, has a name meaning "kettle" (Russian *kotyol*). The story goes that when the Russian merchant Ivan Lyakhov discovered the island in 1773, one of his party left a copper kettle behind. On returning two years later to chart the island, Lyakhov found the kettle, a symbol

of habitation, and named the uninhabited island accordingly.

Köthen. *City, east central Germany*. The city, recorded in the 11th century as *Cothin*, probably has a name of Slavic origin (possibly from *kot*, "plashing") that came to be taken as Middle Low German *kōte*, "cottage."

Kotor. *City and port, western Montenegro*. The name of the city was recorded in 680 as *Catarum*. It is pre–Slavic in origin, and of uncertain meaning. The Serbian toponymist and folklorist Vuk Karajić tells how the Romans had a *tor*, "cattle pen," here, and how the place subsequently became known as *kod tora*, "by the pen" (from Serbo-Croat *kod*, "by," "near").

Kozhikode *see* **Calicut**

Kragujevac. *Town, central Serbia*. The town probably derives its name from a personal name that is itself based on Serbo-Croat *kraguj*, "gerfalcon," although it is possible the name originated from the bird itself, if it was common here.

Krakatoa. *Volcanic island, western Indonesia*. The volcano, in Sunda Strait between Sumatra and Java, has a name relating to its fissile nature, from the Malay prefix *ke-* and Javanese *rekatak*, "to split."

Kraków. *City, southern Poland*. The city is said to take its name from *Krak*, its supposed founder in the 10th century or earlier. The meaning of his name is unknown.

Kraljevo. *City, central Serbia*. The city dates from the 12th century and the nearby Zica monastery is the site of the crowning of Serbian kings in early medieval times. Hence the name, from Serbo-Croat *kralʼ*, "king." From 1945 through 1961 the city was known as *Rankovichevo*, for the leading Serbian Communist Aleksandar *Rankovich* (died 1983). The earlier royalist name was readopted, however, when he fell from favor.

Kramatorsk. *City, eastern Ukraine*. The city arose in the 19th century and gained importance with the opening of the ironworks here in 1887. For this reason its name has been popularly derived from French *crématoire*, "crematory," supposedly referring to its furnaces. But the factory was built in a village already named *Krematorka*, so the name thus derives from that. Its origin may be in Slavic dialect *kroma*, "edge," and *Tor*, the latter being the name of the river here, now the *Kazyonnyj Torets*. The overall sense would thus be "(place by the) edge of the *Tor*."

Kranj. *Town, northern Slovenia*. The town had the Roman name of *Carnium*, probably based ultimately on pre–Indoeuropean *kar*, "stone," "rock."

Krapkowice. *Town, southwestern Poland.* The town was earlier known by the German name *Krappitz*, from the Roman settlement *Carodunum* here, a Gaulish name meaning "fort of the chariots."

Krasnodar. *City, southwestern Russia.* The city was originally named *Yekaterinodar* when founded in 1793. This means "*Catherine*'s gift," from Russian *Yekaterina*, "*Catherine*," and *dar*, "gift." The reference is to the Russian empress *Catherine* the Great (1729–1796), who gave land to Cossacks here as her "gift." When the town was taken by the Red Army in 1920 during the Civil War, its name was changed to *Krasnodar*, from Russian *krasnyj*, "red," and the same *dar*.

Krasnodon. *City, eastern Ukraine.* The city arose in 1912 as a coal-mining settlement in the *Donbass* and the latter part of its name relates to this. Its original name was *Sorokino*, for settlers named *Sorokin*. The present name was adopted in 1938, with Russian *krasno-*, "red," denoting the revolutionary color.

Krasnokamsk. *City, western Russia.* The city, founded in 1929 around a cellulose plant on the *Kama* River, has a name meaning literally "red *Kama*," from Russian *krasnyj*, "red" (in the revolutionary sense, though earlier meaning "beautiful"), and the river name. The city is now a satellite of Perm.

Krasnoturinsk. *City, west central Russia.* The city arose in 1758 from a copper mine by the *Turya* River. The mining settlement that developed was at first known as *Turinskiye Rudniki*, "*Turya* mines." It was called as now in 1944, with the first part of the name representing Russian *krasnyj*, "red," both in the revolutionary sense and with reference to the color of the copper. The river's own name is said to derive from Mansi *tur*, "river," and *ya*, "lake." "River of lakes" thus describes its upper reaches.

Krasnovodsk *see* **Turkmenbashy**

Krasnoyarsk. *City, south central Russia.* The city, founded in 1628, has a name that means either "red bank" or "beautiful bank," from Russian *krasnyj*, which now means "red" but earlier meant "beautiful," and *yar*, "bank." If "red," the reference would be to the color of the soil here. The bank is that of the Yenisey River where the original fort was built around which the town arose.

Krasny Luch. *City, eastern Ukraine.* The city was founded in the 1890s as *Krindachyovka*, presumably from some personal name. In 1926 it took its present name, meaning "red ray," both symbolic, for a future-focused Soviet town, and descriptive, for a coal-mining center.

Krefeld. *City and river port, western Germany.* The medieval city's name means literally "crow field," denoting an area of open land where crows regularly flocked.

Kremenchug. *City, east central Ukraine.* The city's name may derive either from a Slavic word related to Russian *kremen'*, "flint," or else from a Turkic source akin to modern Turkish *kerman*, "fort." Either way the reference seems to be to a stronghold, and the town was actually founded as a fortress in 1571. The Ukrainian form of the name is *Kremenchuk*.

Kremlin-Bicêtre. *District of Paris, northern France.* The name is something of a curiosity. The first part derives from an inn here, *Au sergent du Kremlin*, "at the (sign of the) Kremlin sergeant," referring to Napoleon's 1812 invasion of Russia. The second part was long held to be a corruption of **Winchester**, referring to the bishop of that English city who represented the sovereign of England during the Hundred Years War with France (1338–1453). However, a recent authority suggests that the name is actually a corruption of Old French *bissexte*, "bissextile," the term for the extra day in a leap year (February 29). This day was regarded as unlucky, so that the word came to be used for anything ill-omened. It later developed a special sense to refer to a ruined castle, or to ruins believed to be haunted, and this was possibly the original meaning here.

Krems. *City, northeastern Austria.* The city takes its name from the *Krems* River here, its own name probably from a Slavic word meaning "pebble," referring to its stony bed.

Kreuzlingen. *Town, northeastern Switzerland.* The town is said to derive its name from a monastery which claimed to hold a relic of the True Cross (German *Kreuz*, "cross"). The reference could also be to a small cross (*Kreuzlein*) marking the boundary between the town and nearby Konstanz, Germany.

Krishnanagar. *City, northeastern India.* The West Bengal city has a name meaning "*Krishna*'s town," from *Krishna*, the Hindu god who is an avatar (incarnation) of Vishnu, and Hindi *nagar*, "town." The name also occurs in the form *Krishnagar*.

Kristiansand. *City and port, southwestern Norway.* The city is named for its founder, King *Christian* (Danish *Kristian*) IV of Denmark and Norway (1577–1648), who built a fort here in 1641. The second part of the name is Norwegian *sand*, "sand." *Cp.* **Kristiansund**.

Kristianstad. *City and port, southern Sweden.* The city was founded in 1614 as a Danish fortress and is named for its founder, King *Christian* (Danish *Kristian*) IV of Denmark and Norway (1577–1648). The latter part of the name is Norwegian *stad*, "town."

Kristiansund. *City and port, western Norway.* The city was incorporated in 1842 and named for King *Christian* (Danish *Kristian*) IV of Denmark and Norway (1577–1648). The latter part of the name represents Norwegian *sund*, "strait," "inlet" (English *sound*). Because of the similarity between this town's name and that of **Kristiansand**, it is postally known as *Kristiansund N.* (for *nord*, "north"), while its near namesake is *Kristiansand S.* (for *sør*, "south").

Kristinehamn. *Town and lake port, west central Sweden.* The town was originally a trading center known as *Bro*, "spring," "stream." It received its present name, meaning "*Christina's* port," when it received a new charter in 1642. The name honored 16-year-old Queen *Christina* of Sweden (1626–1689), who succeeded to the throne at the age of eight.

Krivoy Rog. *City, south central Ukraine.* The city is located in a broad bend of the Dnieper, and it is to this that the name refers, as the Russian for "curved horn," with the latter word (*rog*) here more in the sense "headland." The Ukrainian form of the name is *Kryvyy Rih*.

Krk. *Island, northwestern Croatia.* The island, at the head of the Adriatic Sea, was known to the Romans as *Curicum*, and this produced the present name. The origin of the name is unknown, although some have linked it with *Kerkyra*, the Greek name of **Corfu**. The Italian name of Krk is *Veglia*, as if meaning "old," perhaps comparing the island with the town of *Krk* at its southern end.

Kronach. *Town, south central Germany.* The town takes its name from the river on which it lies. The river's own name is probably a blend of Old High German *krano*, "crane," and *aha*, "flowing water," denoting a river where these birds were regularly seen.

Kronshtadt. *Town and port, western Russia.* The town, on Kotlin Island in the Gulf of Finland, was founded by Peter the Great in 1704 as a fortified post to guard the sea approaches to St. Petersburg. The original fort was named *Kronshlot*, representing Swedish *Kronslott*, "crown castle." In 1723 it received its present name, from German *Krone*, "crown," and *Stadt*, "town." Unusually, this patently royalist, non–Russian name never underwent an ideological Soviet name change.

Kroonstad. *City, east central South Africa.* The name of the Free State city, founded in 1855, appears to mean "crown town," as for **Kronshtadt**. Local lore claims that it derives from a ford known as *Kroondrift*, so called because a horse called *Kroon* broke its leg there.

Kropotkin. *City, southwestern Russia.* The city arose in the late 19th century as the village of *Romanovsky Khutor*, "*Romanov's* village." In 1921 it was renamed as now to commemorate the Russian revolutionary and geographer, Pyotr Alekseyevich *Kropotkin* (1842–1921).

Krugersdorp. *City, northeastern South Africa.* The city, in Gauteng province, was founded after the discovery of gold here in 1887 and named for Paul *Kruger* (1825–1904), then president of the South African Republic (Transvaal). Afrikaans *dorp* is "village" (German *Dorf*, English *thorp*).

Kruševac. *Town, eastern Serbia.* The town's name derives from Serbo-Croat *kruška*, "pear," either directly from the tree bearing this fruit or from a personal name based on the word.

Ksar el-Kebir. *City, northern Morocco.* The city was founded in the 8th century and has a name representing Arabic *al-ḳaṣr al-kebīr*, "the great palace." The name is also found in the form *Alcazarquivir*, a Spanish corruption of the original.

Kuala Lumpur. *Capital of Malaysia.* The city, in west central West Malaysia, has a name meaning "muddy confluence," from Malay *kuala*, "mouth," "estuary," and *lumpur*, "mud." The reference is to the confluence of the Kelang and Gombak rivers here.

Kuban. *River, southwestern Russia.* The origin of the name is uncertain, although some link it with the *Kabul* River, a tributary of the Indus, which gave the name of **Kabul**, capital of Afghanistan.

Kuei-lin. *City, southern China.* The city, in Kwangsi Chuang region, has a name meaning "forest of sweet osmanthus," from Chinese *guì*, "sweet osmanthus" (an evergreen shrub with fragrant flowers, as its Greek name indicates), and *lín*, "forest."

Kuei-yang. *City, southern China.* The capital of Kweichow province derives its name from Chinese *guì*, "precious," "noble," and *yáng*, "light," "sun."

Kufstein. *Town, western Austria.* The name is said to derive from German *Kuppe*, "rounded hilltop," and *Stein*, "stone," "rock," referring to the rock on which the medieval fortress here was built.

Kuito. *Town, central Angola.* The town has a local name meaning "place of meat," from *ko*, "place," and *osito*, "meat." The reference is to the large number of animals here. Before 1975 the town had the colonial name *Silva Porto*, for the Portuguese explorer António Francisco Ferreira da *Silva Porto*, who died here in 1890.

Kukawa. *Town, northeastern Nigeria*. The town is said to derive its name from *kuka*, the local name of the baobab (*Adansonia digitata*), a tree rare in this region.

Kültepe. *Archaeological site, central Turkey*. The ancient mound, covering the Bronze Age city of Kanesh, has a name meaning "ash hill," from Turkish *kül*, "ash," and *tepe*, "hill."

Kulyab. *City, southwestern Tajikistan*. The city is said to take its name from Turkic *kul*, "lake," and Iranian *ab*, "water." Kulyab is in the valley of the Yakhsu River, but there is no obvious lake here.

Kumamoto. *Prefecture, southern Japan*. The prefecture and its capital, in the island of Kyushu, derive their name from Japanese *kuma*, "bear" (the animal), and *moto*, "basis," "foundation."

Kumasi. *City, south central Ghana*. The city was founded in the late 17th century by Osei Tutu, the first great Ashanti chief, on the advice of a fetish priest. The priest planted the seeds of two *kum* trees in different places, and one sprouted to show where the Ashanti capital was to be. Hence the name, representing *kum asi*, "under the *kum*."

Kumayri. *City, northwestern Armenia*. The city arose in medieval or earlier times with a name of obscure origin. In 1837 a fort was built by the settlement that had developed and in 1840 it was raised to the status of a town under the name *Aleksandropol*, "*Alexandra's* town," for the wife of Nicholas I, born Princess Charlotte of Prussia, who became *Alexandra* after adopting the Orthodox faith. (The final *-pol* is Greek *polis*, "town.") In 1924, on the death of *Lenin*, the town was renamed *Leninakan*, with *-akan* the Turkic element meaning "town." In 1990 the city reverted to its original name (in its indigenous form, *Gyumri*).

Kunhegyes. *Town, east central Hungary*. The first part of the name refers to the *Cuman* people, as for **Kiskunfélegyháza**. The second part is Hungarian *hegyes*, "hilly country."

Kunlun Mountains. *Mountain ranges, western China*. The name of the mountain system comprises two Chinese syllables, *kūn* and *lún*, that have no meaning aside from this word.

K'un-ming. *City, southern China*. The capital of Yunnan province derives its name from Chinese *kūn*, "elder brother," and *míng*, "light," "brightness," the latter giving the name of the *Ming* dynasty (1368–1644).

Kunszentmárton. *City, east central Hungary*. The first part of the name refers to the *Cuman* people, as for **Kiskunfélegyháza**. The second part denotes the dedication of the church to St. *Martin* (Hungarian *szent*, "saint," and *Márton*, "Martin").

Kunszentmiklós. *City, central Hungary*. The first part of the name refers to the *Cuman* people, as for **Kiskunfélegyháza**. The second part denotes the dedication of the church to St. *Nicholas* (Hungarian *szent*, "saint," and *Miklós*, "Nicholas").

Kuopio. *City, south central Finland*. The city's name is a Finnish alteration of Swedish *köping*, "market town." Cp. **Jönköping**, **Linköping**, **Norrköping**, **Nyköping**.

Kurashiki. *City, southwestern Japan*. The city, in the island of Honshu, derives its name from Japanese *kura*, "store," "warehouse," and *shiki*, "stall," "stand." The city was a noted trading center in the 17th through 19th centuries, with many storage houses.

Kurdistan. *Region, southeastern Turkey*. The name means "land of the *Kurds*," this nomadic people's own name perhaps representing Iranian *kard*, "active."

Kure. *City and port, southwestern Japan*. The city, in the island of Honshu, derives its name from Japanese *kureru*, "to give."

Kurgan. *City, southwestern Russia*. The city arose in 1662 on the site of a fortified settlement known as *Tsaryovo Gorodishche*, "royal fort." Nearby was a burial mound called *Tsaryov Kurgan*, "royal tumulus." The settlement was destroyed in 1738 when a road was built, but was re-established and on gaining town status in 1782 adopted the second word of the mound's name as its own name. There are many other burial mounds in the area.

Kuril Islands. *Island chain, eastern Russia*. The islands, extending between the Kamchatka Peninsula and Japan, are all of volcanic origin and for this reason their name has been said to derive from Russian *kurit'*, "to smoke." But the actual origin is more likely to be from a local word meaning simply "men," "people." The Japanese know the Kurils as *chishima*, "thousand islands," from *chi*, "thousand," and *shima*, "island."

Kuroshio. *Ocean current, western Pacific*. The strong surface current, between the northeastern Philippines and the east coast of Japan, derives its name from Japanese *kuro*, "black," and *shio*, "tide," "current." The current appears as a deeper blue than the water through which it flows. Hence its name. Its Chinese name, *hēichǎo*, has the same sense, from *hēi*, "black," and *chǎo*, "tide."

Kursk. *City, western Russia.* The city takes its name from the small *Kur* River here. Its own name may derive from Finnish *kuru*, "deep valley."

Kurukshetra. *City, northwestern India.* The city, an important Hindu pilgrimage center in Haryana state, has a large water reservoir that is said to have been founded by Rajah *Kuru*, ancestor of the Kauravas and Pandavas of the Hindu epic poem *Mahabharata*. The name thus means "*Kuru*'s field," with Hindi *kshetra*, "field," "area," "place of pilgrimage."

Kurume. *City, southern Japan.* The city, in the island of Kyushu, derives its name from the Japanese syllables *ku*, *ru*, and *mai*, which have no meaning aside from their combination in this name.

Kuşadası. *Town, western Turkey.* The town's name means "island of birds," from Turkish *kuş*, "bird," and *adası*, "island of" (from *ada*, "island," and the suffix *-ı*, which becomes *sı* after a vowel).

Kushiro. *City and port, eastern Japan.* The city, in the island of Hokkaido, takes its name from the river at the mouth of which it lies. The river's own name represents Japanese *kushi*, "bracelet," and *ro*, "route," "way," alluding to its course.

Kustanay. *City, northern Kazakhstan.* The city was founded in 1883 on a site of the same name. The original form of the name appears to have been *Kostana*, possibly from Kazakh *kos*, "two," and the name of the *Tara* people who formerly inhabited this region. But it is not clear what there were two of.

Kutaisi. *City, western Georgia.* The city is said to derive its name from Kazakh *kuan*, "parched," "scorched," referring to hot, arid terrain. But the town is actually surrounded by picturesque woodland and meadows, so that another source seems likely. This may be in Kazakh *kuanu* or Bashkir *kyanyu*, "to rejoice," either from a personal name or for the pleasantness of the location, a "place of joy."

Kutná Hora. *City, central Czech Republic.* The town, a silver-mining center in medieval times, with a famous mint, has a name of Germanic origin meaning "mountain of the pit," from Middle High German *kutte*, "pit," and Slavic *gora*, "mountain," the latter referring to its location on high tableland. The German name of the town is *Kuttenberg*.

Kuwait. *Independent state, southwestern Asia.* The state, on the northwest coast of the Persian Gulf, takes its name from its capital, which is known in Arabic as *al-kuwayt*. This represents a diminutive of *kūt*, a word that in the dialect of the inhabitants of southern Iraq and the eastern part of the Arabian Peninsula denotes a kind of fortress-like house surrounded by smaller houses and encircled with water, something like a medieval English manor with its outbuildings and moat.

Kuybyshev *see* **Samara**

Kuznetsk. *City, western Russia.* The city's name refers to the blacksmiths (Russian *kuznetsy*) who set up here in the 18th century to work the local iron-ore deposits.

KwaNdebele. *Historic homeland, northeastern South Africa.* The former Bantu homeland, in what is now Mpumalanga province, was established in 1979 when many *Ndebele* were expelled from their nearby homeland of Bophuthatswana. The name means "place of the *Ndebele*," the people formerly known as the *Matabele* (*see* **Matabeleland**). The homeland was reintegrated into South Africa in 1994.

Kwangju. *City, southwestern South Korea.* The city's name derives from Korean *kwang*, "light," "brightness," and *chu*, "province," from Chinese *guāng* and *zhōu*, in the same sense.

Kwangsi. *Region, southern China.* The autonomous region has a name meaning "vastness of the west," from Chinese *guǎng*, "huge," "vast," and *xī*, "west." The name is also spelled *Guangxi*. The region lies west of **Kwangtung**.

Kwangtung. *Province, southeastern China.* The name of the province means "vastness of the east," from Chinese *guǎng*, "huge," "vast," and *dōng*, "east." The name is also spelled *Guangdong*. The province lies east of **Kwangsi**. *See also* **Canton**.

KwaZulu. *Historic homeland, eastern South Africa.* The name is that of the former Bantu homeland set up for *Zulus* in 1972 in place of the former English-named territory of *Zululand*. The indigenous name has basically the same meaning as the old, "land of the Zulus," with *Kwa-* the Nguni locative formative (meaning "at the place of") usually prefixed to the name of a person or people. The Zulus derive their name from their ancestor *uZulu* (died probably 1709), the founding leader of the dominant amaZulu clan. His own name came from *izulu*, "sky," a word which later came to mean "heaven." In 1994 KwaZulu united with **Natal** to form the new province of *KwaZulu Natal*. *Cp.* **KwaNdebele**.

Kweichow. *Province, southwestern China.* The name of the province means "precious region," from Chinese *guī*, "precious," and *zhōu*, "region."

Kwekwe. *City, central Zimbabwe.* The town was founded in 1902 and named for the river here. Its own onomatopoeic name means "croak-croak," referring to the sound of frogs in its waters at night.

Kwidzyn. *Town, northern Poland.* The town arose from a castle founded by the Teutonic Knights in 1233 on the island of *Quiridin* in the Vistula River nearby. The origin of the island name is uncertain. The knights named the island *Marieninsel*, "Mary's island," for the Virgin *Mary*, patron saint of their order, and the town that arose nearby on the Liebe River was similarly *Marienwerder*, "Mary's river island," with Middle Low German *werde*, "river island" (as for **Bischofswerda**).

Kwinana. *Town and port, southwestern Australia.* The town, in Western Australia, is named for a ship wrecked offshore here in 1922. Its own name came from an Aboriginal word meaning "young woman."

Kyakhta. *City, eastern Russia.* The Siberian city, on the frontier with Mongolia, derives its name from the Mongolian word for the cereal grass *Triticum repens*, a good fodder for transport animals. The name was originally that of a village here, near which the fortress of *Troitskosavsk*, dedicated to the Holy Trinity (Russian *Troitsa*) and St. *Sava*, was built in 1728. The fortress name was that of the town that grew up until 1934, when the original village name was adopted.

Kyaukpyu. *Town and port, western Myanmar.* The coastal town has a Myanmar (Burmese) name meaning "white stones," describing the white pebbles on the beach here.

Kyeryong. *Mountain, western South Korea.* The mountain has a Korean name meaning "cock dragon," referring to its outline, which resembles a dragon with a rooster's comb.

Kyoto. *City, central Japan.* The city, in the island of Honshu, derives its name from Japanese *kyō*, "capital," and *to*, also "capital." It was founded in 794 as the capital of Japan under the name *Heionkyo*, "capital of calm and peace," from *hei*, "calm," *on*, "peace," and *kyō*, "capital." Other past names have been *Miyako*, "capital," "metropolis," and *Saikyo*, "western capital," the latter being its name after the Meiji Restoration in 1868 when the imperial household moved to Tokyo.

Kyrgyzstan. *Republic, central Asia.* The republic is named for its indigenous people, the *Kyrgyz*. Their own name is said to derive from a Turkic root word *kir*, "steppe," and *gizmek*, "to wander," implying a nomadic existence. Popu-lar etymology derives the name from a legend about forty girls and a dog (Turkic *kyrk*, "forty," and *kyz*, "girl"), or from a tale about the tents of one horde being forty in number while those of the other were a hundred (Turkic *kyrk*, "forty," and *is*, "hundred."). The *-stan* is Iranian *ostān*, "country," "land."

Kyushu. *Island, southern Japan.* The southernmost of Japan's four main islands has a name meaning "nine provinces," from *kyū*, "nine," and *shū*, "province," respectively from Chinese *jiǔ* and *zhōu*, in the same sense. This describes its former administrative division. It is now divided into seven prefectures.

Kyustendil. *City, southwestern Bulgaria.* The city's name means "*Constantine*'s land," referring to *Constantine* Dragash, the local feudal lord to whom it belonged in the 14th century. Its name from 1018 to this time was *Velbuzhd*, from an Old Slavonic word meaning "camel." This may itself have derived from a personal name, although it could equally have referred to a hill shaped like a camel's hump. The town's name in Roman times was *Pautalia*, from a Thracian word meaning "source," "spring." It is not known what its name was from the 6th through 10th century.

Kyzyl Kum. *Desert, west central Asia.* The desert, in Kazakhstan and Uzbekistan, has a Turkic name meaning "red sands." It is not noticeably red, and differs little in color from the **Kara Kum** ("black sands") to the west. However, some areas have reddish or brick-colored sands, so that the name may have originally applied to these, then spread to the whole desert.

Kyzyl-Kyya. *City, southwestern Kyrgyzstan.* The city, a coal-mining centre, has a Kazakh name name meaning "red rock."

Kzyl-Orda. *City, south central Kazakhstan.* The city has a Kazakh name meaning "red fort," the color having the revolutionary sense, with possibly an additional allusion to the *Red* Army. (*Orda* literally means "horde," and like that word goes back to a Turkic original meaning "camp," "army.") The city was founded in 1820 and was originally known as *Ak Mechet*, from the Turkish words for "white mosque." In 1853 it was renamed *Perovsk*, for the Russian general Vasily *Perovsky* (1795–1857), commander of the forces who captured the fortified settlement here that year. It adopted its present name in 1925.

Laayoune *see* **El Aaiún**

La Baule-Escoublac. *Town and resort, northwestern France.* The Brittany town is a joint municipality formed from *La Baule* and *Escoublac*. *La Baule* may derive its name from Latin *betulla*, "birch," or else French *bauler*, "to howl" (of wind). *Escoublac* represents the Gaulish personal name *Scopilus* with the Gallo-Roman suffix *-acum*.

Labé. *Town, west central Guinea*. The city was founded in the 1720s by the Dialonke people and named for their chief, Manga *Labé*.

Labrador. *Region, eastern Canada*. The name of the peninsular region almost certainly derives from Portuguese *lavrador*, "laborer," although the precise application of this remains uncertain. One theory claims that when the Italian-born navigator John Cabot came here in 1498 he named the land for a Portuguese sailor, João Fernandez, who had already visited the region and described it, and who was known as *o lavrador*, "the farmer," as he had a smallholding in the Azores. Another account attributes the name to the Portuguese navigator Gaspar Côrte-Real, who reached the peninsula in 1501 and named it *Terra de lavradores*, "land of laborers," for the workers he saw everywhere tilling the soil.

Labuan. *Island, East Malaysia*. The island, off northwestern Borneo, is said to have a name meaning "anchorage island," from Malay *labuh*, "to anchor."

La Carolina. *Town, southern Spain*. The town was founded in 1781 in the reign of *Charles* III of Spain (1716–1788) as a settlement for German immigrants. Hence the name, from the adjectival form of *Carolus*, the king's Latin name (Spanish *Carlo*).

Laccadive Islands *see* **Lakshadweep**

Lacedaemonia *see* **Sparta**

La Chaux-de-Fonds. *Town, western Switzerland*. The first main word of the town's name possibly derives from a pre–Indoeuropean root word *calma* meaning "bare height" (*cp.* **Caria**). The name as a whole is sometimes explained as referring to two former springs here, one of which froze in winter while the other did not. The first was known as *Font Froide*, "cold spring," while the second was *Chaude Font*, "warm spring." But this smacks strongly of a traveler's tale.

Lachine. *City, southeastern Canada*. The Quebec city was first settled in 1667 by the French explorer René-Robert Cavelier, sieur de La Salle (1643–1687), while he was searching for a westward route to China. Its name comes from the mocking phrase describing his stated destination, *la petite Chine*, "little China." The second word of this was later dropped and the other two combined as now. *See also* **La Salle**.

Lackawanna. *City, eastern United States*. The New York city was settled in 1850 as part of West

Seneca and was at first known as *Limestone Hill*. In 1899 it was chosen as the site of the *Lackawanna* Steel Company (now the Bethlehem Steel Corporation), and adopted its name. The company's name came from the *Lackawanna* River, Pennsylvania, with its own name from a Delaware word meaning "the stream that forks."

Laconia. *Historic region, southern Greece*. The region was named for its inhabitants, but the origin and meaning of their own name is unknown. *See also* **Sparta**.

La Coruña. *City and port, northwestern Spain*. The city is said to derive its name from Latin *columna*, "column," referring to the Tower of Hercules, the Roman lighthouse still in use off the coast here, although an alternate origin could be in a Celtic word related to Irish *cluain*, "meadow." The name is sometimes found in the traditional English form *Corunna*, while in the mouths of English sailors the port was long called the *Groyne*, as if referring to a prominent breakwater here. ("CORUNNA, or GROYNE, a port-town of Gallicia in Spain." *Encyclopædia Britannica*, 1771.)

La Crosse. *City, northern United States*. The Wisconsin city arose in 1841 around a trading post that French explorers called *Prairie La Crosse*, for the game of *lacrosse* played by Native Americans here.

Ladakh. *Region, northern India and Pakistan*. The region, in Kashmir, contains the western Himalayas and Karakoram Range. Hence its name, which represents Tibetan *ladag*, "land of passes," from *la*, "pass," and *dag*, "pleasant," "open." It is also known locally as *maryul*, "land of butter," from *mar*, "butter," and *yul*, "land," "country."

Ladenburg. *Town, west central Germany*. The town arose on the site of a Roman settlement called *Lopodunum*, apparently from a Romano-Celtic personal name *Lopos* (although this has not been attested elsewhere) and Celtic *dunum*, "hill," "fort." This eventually gave the present form of the name, but with Old High German *burg*, "fort," replacing the Celtic *dunum*.

Ladoga, Lake. *Lake, northwestern Russia*. Europe's largest lake takes its name from the ancient town of *Ladoga* (now *Staraya Ladoga*, "old Ladoga") 7½ miles (12 km) south of it on the Volkhov River. The town took its name from a tributary of the Volkhov, and that river's name in turn represents its Finnish name of *Alodejoki*, "low-place river," from *alode*, "low place," and *joki*, "river," denoting its location with regard to the Volkhov.

Ladysmith. *City, eastern South Africa*. The

city, in KwaZulu Natal, was founded in 1847 and originally named *Windsor*, for a local trader. It was renamed for *Lady Smith*, born Juana Maria de los Dolores de León, wife of Sir Harry Smith (1787–1860), governor of the Cape Colony.

[1]Lafayette. *City, east central United States*. The Indiana city was laid out in 1825 and named for the Marquis de *Lafayette* (1757–1834), the French aristocrat who fought with the French colonists against the British, and who was then making his last visit to America. *Cp.* **Fayetteville**.

[2]Lafayette. *City, southern United States*. The Louisiana city arose in 1824 as the village of *Vermilionville*, presumably for some place already named *Vermilion* (for the color of the soil). In 1884 it was renamed as now for the Marquis de *Lafayette* (1757–1834), the French aristocrat who fought with the French colonists against the British. *Cp.* **Fayetteville**.

Lafia. *City, central Nigeria*. The city's name is from local words said to mean "comfortably settled."

Lagos. *City and port, southwestern Nigeria*. Nigeria's former capital was given its name by Portuguese colonists, who arrived here in 1472. The coast has many lagoons, and this suggested the name *Lagos*, "lakes," partly descriptively but also with reference to the city and harbor of *Lagos* in southern Portugal.

La Gruyère *see* **Gruyères**

Laguna. *City and port, southeastern Brazil*. The city takes its name from its location near the entrance to a shallow inlet or *lagoon*.

Laguna District. *Region, north central Mexico*. The agricultural area is named for the shallow lakes (Spanish *lagunas*) formed on the plain here.

La Habra. *City, southwestern United States*. The name of the California city apparently derives from Spanish *abra*, "pass," with reference to a gap in the hills here.

Lahaina. *City and port, central Hawaii, United States*. The city, in northwestern Maui Island, has a Hawaiian name meaning "cruel sun," presumably alluding to some local legend.

Lahore. *City, northeastern Pakistan*. The original name of the city is said to have been *Lohawar*, from its legendary founder *Loh*, or *Lava*, a son of Rama, an incarnation of Vishnu, and his wife Sita.

Lahti. *City, southern Finland*. The city was founded in 1905 on a bay of Lake Vesijärvi and has a name that is simply the Finnish word for "bay."

Lake Charles. *City, southern United States*. The Louisiana city was settled in c.1781 and named for *Charles* Sallier, an early settler who built his home by the *lake* here.

Lake District. *Region, northwestern England*. The Cumbria district is named for the *lakes* that are its prime natural feature, among them *Bassenthwaite, Buttermere, Coniston Water, Derwentwater, Ennerdale Water, Grasmere, Haweswater, Rydal Water, Thirlmere, Ullswater, Wast Water*, and **Windermere**. The region is also known as *Lakeland*.

> I always say there is no such thing as bad weather in Lakeland, only bad clothing [Hunter Davies, "A fine time in Lakeland," *The Sunday Times*, September 19, 2004].

Lakeland. *City, southeastern United States*. The Florida city was founded in 1883 and named for the many *lakes* in the area.

Lakeland *see* **Lake District**

Lakewood. *City, northern United States*. The Ohio city, on Lake Erie, was surveyed in 1806 and at first known as *Rockport*, then *East Rockport*, before taking its present name in 1889, with reference to its *wood*ed *lake*shore.

Lakhdaria. *Town, north central Algeria*. The town, originally called *Palestro*, is named for Commandant Si *Lakhdar*, a War of Independence hero.

Lakhdenpokhya. *Town, northwestern Russia*. The Karelian town, on Lake Ladoga, has a Finnish name meaning "bottom of the bay," from *lahden*, genitive of *lahti*, "bay," and *pohja*, "bottom." The reference is to the town's location at the far end of a long, narrow inlet.

Lakshadweep. *Island group, Arabian Sea*. The islands, off the southwest coast of (and belonging to) India, derive their name from Sanskrit *laksha dvīpa*, "hundred thousand islands," from *laksha*, "hundred thousand," and *dvīpa*, "island." This number is an extreme exaggeration, and there are actually only 36 islands. The group was formerly familiar as the *Laccadive Islands*.

Lalibela. *Town, northeastern Ethiopia*. The religious and pilgrimage center is named for *Lalibela* (late 13th-early 14th century), the best-known monarch of the region, who is said to have built the 11 monolithic churches for which it is famous.

La Línea. *City, southwestern Spain*. The city, on the frontier with Gibraltar, has a name that is Spanish for "the line," referring to this border. The full name is *La Línea de la Concepción*, for the Immaculate *Conception* of the Virgin Mary.

[1]Lalitpur. *Town, northern India*. The town, in Uttar Pradesh state, is said to have been founded by a southern Indian king who named it after his wife, *Lalita*. But the name may really be as for ²**Lalitpur**.

²**Lalitpur**. *Town, east central Nepal.* The town has a Nepalese name meaning "pleasant town," from *lalit*, "agreeable," "pleasant," and *pur*, "town." Its alternate name is *Patan*, from Nepalese *pat*, "linen," "silk."

La Mancha. *Region, central Spain.* Spain's central plateau has a name of Arabic origin, from *mansha*, "dry land," from *nashsha*, "to be dry." In its present form, the name misleadingly suggests an origin in Spanish *la mancha*, "the spot," "the patch" (e.g. of vegetation). The French name of the Spanish region is *La Manche*, identical to that of the English Channel (*see* **Manche**).

Lambeth. *Borough of London, southeastern England.* The borough borders the Thames, and its name relates to this river. Its meaning is "landing place for lambs," from Old English *lamb*, "lamb," and *hȳth*, "landing place."

Lampedusa. *Island, central Mediterranean Sea.* The Italian island, midway between Malta and Tunisia, is said to derive its name from Italian *lampada*, "lamp," referring to its lighthouse. But it was known to the Greeks in the 1st century A.D. as *Lopadusa* and its name thus predates this. The origin of the Greek name itself is uncertain.

Lampertheim. *Town, central Germany.* The town was recorded in 832 as *Langobardonheim*, from a genitive plural form of the name of the Germanic *Langobardi* tribe (*see* **Lombardy**) and Old High German *heim*, "house," "abode." The implication is that the original settlement here was founded by these people, just as **Bad Dürkheim** probably was by the Thuringians.

Lanai. *Island, central Hawaii, United States.* The island, west of Maui Island, has a Hawaiian name meaning "conquest day," alluding to some local event. Apart from Hawaii itself, Lanai is the only inhabited Hawaiian island to have a name with a known etymology.

Lanark. *Town, south central Scotland.* The town has a Celtic name that in modern terms can be seen in Welsh *llannerch*, "glade." This is therefore the original sense.

Lancashire. *County, northwestern England.* The county takes its name from that of its county town, ¹**Lancaster**, i.e. it is effectively *Lancastershire*.

¹**Lancaster**. *Town, northwestern England.* The county town of **Lancashire**, to which it gave its name, is on the *Lune* River, and this forms the first part of the name. The second part is Old English *ceaster*, "Roman station," a borrowing

from Latin *castrum*, "camp." The Roman name of the encampment here is unknown, although presumably it began with *L*. The river's name is probably Celtic in origin, with a possible meaning "health-giving one."

²**Lancaster**. *City, northern United States.* The Ohio city was founded in 1800 and named for *Lancaster*, Pennsylvania, from where many of the first settlers had come. That city, originally known as *Gibson's Pasture* or *Hickory Town*, was so named in 1729 when it became the county seat of *Lancaster* County, itself named for ¹**Lancaster**, England.

Lan-chou. *City, north central China.* The capital of Kansu province derives its name from Chinese *lán*, "orchid," implying sophistication, and *zhōu*, "region," "city."

Landau. *City, southwestern Germany.* The city, known formally as *Landau in der Pfalz*, from its location in the **Palatinate**, has a regional name, with *Land*, "district," either followed by the second element of *Fröschaue*, "frog meadow," a now drained area of nearby marshland, or from a short form of *Landtagsau*, denoting a region of waterside land belonging to the *Landtag*, or local state assembly.

Landes. *Region, southwestern France.* The name goes back to Gaulish *landa*, "enclosure," "land," implying a delimited region of some kind here.

Landsberg am Lech. *City, southwestern Germany.* The city arose around a 12th-century castle built by Henry the Lion at a crossing of the *Lech* River. Its name refers to this origin, denoting a fortress (*burg*) belonging to the local ruler (*Landesherr*). The river name is of Celtic origin, related to Welsh *llech*, "flagstone," and Breton *lec'h*, "tombstone," describing its stony bed.

Land's End. *Peninsula, southwestern England.* England's westernmost point, in Cornwall, has a self-descriptive name, although *land* here has more the sense of "mainland." The Cornish name of the entire Land's End peninsula is *Penwith*, with the same meaning, from *pen*, "head," "end," and *weth*, "district." The name has parallels in those of **Finistère** in France and **Pembroke** in Wales.

Landshut. *City, southeastern Germany.* The city evolved from the fortress built in 1204 by Duke Ludwig I of Bavaria to guard a new bridge over the Isar River here. Its name thus derives from the equivalent of modern German *Land*, "district," and *Hut*, "protection."

Landskrona. *Town and port, southern Sweden.* The town was founded in c.1412 by Eric of Pomerania, king of Sweden, Denmark, and Norway, and has a Swedish name meaning "crown land," "royal region," from *land*, "district," and *krona*, "crown."

Langenfeld. *City, western Germany.* The city was founded in 1910 on the amalgamation of two former villages, *Richrath* and *Reusrath*, and was thus known as *Richrath-Reusrath* until 1936, when it took its present name, adopted from a place called *Altlangenfeld*, "old long field."

Langenhagen. *City, western Germany.* The city was laid out some time before 1248 as a so-called *Hagenhufendorf* (enclosed village with strips of farmland behind each house), and was at first called *Nigenhagen*, "new enclosure." The present name, first recorded in 1312, replaced *Nigen-* by *Langen-*, "long," referring to the straggling shape of the settlement, by then combined with two other villages.

Langjökull. *Ice field, west central Iceland.* The large ice field has an Icelandic name meaning "long glacier."

Langres. *Town, northeastern France.* The town takes its name from the *Lingones*, a Gaulish people whose own name is of uncertain origin. (It may derive from Gaulish *ling*, "to jump," referring to a war dance.) The Roman name of the town was *Andematunnum*, also presumably of ethnic origin.

Languedoc. *Historic region, south central France.* The name of the ancient province represents French *langue d'oc*, "language of *oc*," *oc* being the word for "yes" in the south of France, as distinct from *oïl*, in the north, where they spoke the *langue d'oïl*. *Oc* itself comes from Latin *hoc*, "this," and *oïl* from *hoc ille* (*fecit*), "this he (did)." (It was the latter word that gave modern French *oui*, "yes.")

Lansdowne. *Town, northeastern India.* The town, in Uttaranchal state, was founded as a hill station in 1887 and named for the British diplomat Henry Petty-Fitzmaurice, 5th marquess of *Lansdowne* (1845–1927), viceroy of India from 1888 to 1894.

Lansing. *City, northern United States.* The state capital of Michigan was founded in 1847 and named by settlers from the village of *Lansing*, New York, itself named for the politician and lawyer John *Lansing* (1754–1829).

Lanús. *City, eastern Argentina.* The city, now a suburb of Buenos Aires, was originally a region known as *Cuatro de Junio*, Spanish for "fourth of June," referring to the military coup d'état of the Group of United Officers that took place on June 4, 1943. In 1955 it was renamed as now for its railroad station, itself named for Juan and Anacarsis *Lanús*, who donated land here.

Lan Xang *see* **Laos**

Lanzarote. *Island, Canary Islands, North Atlantic.* The easternmost of the Canary Islands is named for *Lanciloto* Malocello, an Italian navigator in Portuguese service, who built a castle here in the 14th century. His first name, the Italian form of *Lancelot*, was later altered to the Spanish equivalent, in order to conform to other Spanish names in the islands.

Laodicea. *Historic town, southwestern Turkey.* The name goes back to that of *Laodice*, the 3d-century B.C. Syrian queen who was the wife of Antiochus II. There are other places of the name. The city and port of *Latakia*, western Syria, has a name that is a modern form of *Laodicea*.

Laois. *County, central Ireland.* The county is named for a people known as the *Laeighis*, whose leader, *Lughaidh Laeighseach*, was granted lands here in the kingdom of Leinster as a reward for expelling invaders from Munster. The name is also anglicized as *Leix*. From 1557 through 1920 the county was known as *Queen's County*, for Mary I (1516–1558), *queen* of England and Ireland, whose name was also given to the county town of *Maryborough*, now Port Laoise. *Cp.* **Offaly**.

Laon. *Town, northern France.* The town was known to the Romans as *Laodunum* or *Lugdunum*. The latter was also the Roman name of **Lyons**, so that both places appear to have names of identical origin.

Laos. *Republic, southeastern Asia.* The country derives its name from that of its legendary founder, *Lao*, whose own name may have the same origin as that of *Lo* (*see* **Lahore**). The Laotians' own name for their land is *Pathet Lao*, "country of Lao." The first word of this is from Pali *pradesa*, itself from Sanskrit *pradesha*, as for **Andhra Pradesh**, India. The traditional name of the kingdom of Laos, founded in 1353, is *Lan Chang*, Thai *lanchang*, "a million elephants," from *lan*, "million," and *chang*, "elephant." This name contrasted with that of *Lan Na*, Thai *lanna*, "a million rice fields," the name of the historic kingdom of **Chiang Mai**.

La Paz. *Capital of Bolivia.* The administrative capital of Bolivia has a Spanish name meaning "the peace." The city was founded in 1548 by the Spanish conquistador Captain Alonso de Mendoza, who originally named it *Pueblo Nuevo de Nuestra Señora de la Paz*, "new town of Our Lady of Peace." When it became part of independent Bolivia in 1825, this name was changed to *La Paz de Ayacucho*, "the peace of *Ayacucho*," to commemorate the 1824 battle of *Ayacucho*, Peru, in which the Spanish viceroy La Serna was defeated by General Sucre (*see* **Sucre**), so gaining Peru's independence. The name was later shortened as now.

La Pérouse Strait. *Strait, northwestern Pacific.* The strait, between Sakhalin island, Russia, and Hokkaido, Japan, is named for the French explorer Jean-François de Galaup, comte de *La Pérouse* (1741–c.1788), who passed through it in 1787.

Lapland. *Region, northern Europe.* The region, in northern Scandinavia and northwestern Russia, is named for its inhabitants, the *Lapps*, whose name may ultimately come from a root word meaning "frontier," referring to a remote people. The Lapps' own name for themselves is *Sami*, "marsh folk."

La Plata. *City and port, eastern Argentina.* The city was founded in 1882 on the *Río de la Plata* and is named for it. The *Río de la Plata*, known in English as the *River Plate*, is actually the estuary of the Paraná and Uruguay rivers. It was discovered in 1516 by the Spanish explorer Diaz de Solís, who named it *Mar Dolce*, "sweet sea," for its currents of apparently fresh water. It was then named for him as *Río de Solís*, "river of *Solís*," although it is not properly a river at all. It was explored by Sebastian Cabot in 1526 and he gave it its present name, "silver river," in the hope that the silver ornaments he saw local people wearing were a portent of rich silver mines in the area. In fact they had stolen them from the expedition led by the Portuguese explorer Alejo García. (*Cp.* **Argentina**.) In 1946 the city was renamed *Eva Perón* in honor of the social reformer *Eva Perón* (1919–1952), second wife (married 1945) of president Juan Perón, but the original name was restored following his overthrow in 1955.

La Possession. *Town, northwestern Réunion.* The town arose on the coastal site where the French took *possession* of the island of **Réunion** in 1642.

Lappeenranta. *City, southeastern Finland.* The city, at the southern end of Lake Saimaa, has a name meaning "shore of the *Lapps*," with Finnish *ranta*, "shore." In 1649 the town's governor persuaded the Swedish government to grant privileges to the important trading place of *Lapvesi*, as it was then known (Finnish *vesi*, "water"). That year Queen Christina of Sweden duly signed an instrument of foundation, incorporating the emblem of a savage for the new town. This gave the Swedish name of the city, *Villmanstrand*, from *villman*, "savage" (literally "wild man"), and *strand*, "shore."

Laptev Sea. *Sea, northern Russia.* The arm of the Arctic Ocean on the north coast of Russia takes its name from the Russian explorer cousins Dmitri and Khariton *Laptev*, who led a lengthy Arctic expedition over the period 1739–42. The sea has borne the name only since 1913. An earlier name was *Nordenskjöld Sea*, for the Swedish Arctic explorer Nils *Nordenskjöld*, who discovered it in 1878.

Lapu-Lapu. *City, central Philippines.* The city, on Mactan Island, was originally known as *Opon*. It was subsequently renamed as now in honor of Chief *Lapulapu*, who on April 27, 1521, killed the Portuguese navigator Ferdinand Magellan on the island and was thus the first Filipino to defeat a Western conqueror.

L'Aquila. *City, central Italy.* The present city was founded in c.1240 by the Holy Roman Emperor Frederick II. Its name is thus popularly derived from Italian (and Latin) *aquila*, "eagle," referring to this imperial foundation, and the city's canting coat of arms accordingly displays a fine crowned eagle. But the Roman settlement here was known as *Aquilae*, from *aquae*, "waters," "springs," and this is the actual origin of the name.

Larache. *City and port, northern Morocco.* The city's name is a Spanish corruption of Arabic *al-'arā'ish*, "the huts," from *al*, "the," and the plural of *'arīsh*, "hut."

Laramie. *City, west central United States.* The Wyoming city was founded in 1868 on the river of the same name. The river was named for Jacques *La Ramie*, a French-Canadian fur trapper killed near it by Native Americans in c.1819.

Larderello. *Village, central Italy.* The Tuscan village, whose volcanic steam-holes formerly produced boric acid (but now only electricity), takes its name from the French-born Italian industrialist Francesco *Lardarel* (1789–1858), who in 1818 initiated the extraction of boric acid from thermal mists.

Laredo. *City, southern United States.* The Texas city was founded in 1755 by a Spaniard as a ferry crossing on the Rio Grande and named for *Laredo*, Spain.

¹La Rioja. *Region, northern Spain.* The autonomous region, superseding in 1980 the province of *Logroño*, derives its name from Spanish *río Oja*, "river *Oja*," a tributary of the Ebro. (The district gave the name of the well-known Spanish red wine, misassociated by some with Spanish *roja*, "red.")

²La Rioja. *City, northwestern Argentina.* The city was founded in 1591 by Spaniards exploring for gold and silver, who named it after the historic region of **¹La Rioja** in their home country.

Larissa. *City, east central Greece*. The city, the chief town of Thessaly, has a pre–Greek, Pelasgian name meaning "citadel." There were other cities of the name in ancient Greece. The name is also spelled *Larisa*.

Laristan. *Region, southern Iran*. The Iranian name means "land of the *Lurs*," the people who formerly inhabited the region. *Cp.* **Lorestan**. The name is also spelled *Luristan*.

Larkana. *Town, southern Pakistan*. The town is named for the *Larak*, a neighboring people.

Larnaca. *Town and port, southeastern Cyprus*. The town derives its name from Greek *larnax*, *larnakos*, "chest," "funerary urn," referring to the many tombs beneath the ground here.

Larne. *Town, northeastern Northern Ireland*. The town, in Co. Antrim, has the Irish name *Latharna*, "(territory of) the people of *Lathair*." Legend tells how Lathair, a pre–Christian monarch of Ireland, was granted a share of the country equal to that given to each of his 24 siblings. Only Lathair's portion survived, however, with the name of its possessor. Whatever the case, the name originally designated a much larger area than that of the present town.

La Rochelle. *City and port, western France*. The port had the Latin name *Rupella* in the 10th century, from *rupes*, "cave." By the 12th century this had become *Rochella*, by association with French *roche*, "rock." The name is not inappropriate for the site of the present city on the Bay of Biscay.

La Roche-sur-Yon. *Town, western France*. The Medieval Latin name of the town was *Roca super Eon*, from pre–Latin *rocca*, "rock," and the name of the *Yon* River, itself from a basic pre–Latin root element meaning simply "river."

La Salle. *City, southeastern Canada*. The Quebec city was settled in 1685, when the French explorer René-Robert Cavelier, sieur de *La Salle* (1643–1687), set up a fortified site at first named *Saint-Sulpice*, "St. *Sulpicius*," and then *La Petite Chine* or *Lachine* (*see* **Lachine**). It received its present name in 1912, when a group of people moved to the site of the present Lachine, taking the name with them, so that the old Lachine was incorporated under the name of its founder.

Las Cruces. *City, southern United States*. The New Mexico city was founded in 1848. Local legend tells how a Spanish caravan of oxcarts was ambushed by the Apaches and the corpses left where the town now stands. Another caravan, following behind, buried the bodies and placed crosses over the graves. Hence the name, Spanish for "the crosses."

La Serena. *City, northern Chile*. The city was founded by Spanish colonists in c.1543 and named for the birthplace in Spain of the Spanish conquistador Pedro de Valdivia (c.1498–1553).

Lashkargah. *Town, southern Afghanistan*. The town, said to date from the 11th century, has an Iranian name meaning "place of the army."

Las Palmas. *City and port, Canary Islands*. The port, on Grand Canary Island, has a straightforward descriptive name, from Spanish *las palmas*, "the palm trees," which are plentiful here.

La Spezia. *City and port, northern Italy*. The origins of the city, formerly known simply as *Spezia*, are obscure. The site is known to have been inhabited in Roman times, and for that reason the name has been associated with Latin *species*, "splendor," "beauty," referring to the city's imposing location at the head of the gulf of the same name. But the actual meaning is uncertain.

Las Piedras. *City, southern Uruguay*. The city has a Spanish name meaning "the stones," "the rocks."

Lassen Peak. *Mountain, southwestern United States*. The California volcano, at the southern end of the Cascade Range, is named for the early (and long-lived) settler Peter *Lassen* (1793–1895).

Las Tunas. *Province, south central Cuba*. The Spanish name of the province means "the prickly pears."

Las Vegas. *City, western United States*. The Nevada city's Spanish name translates as "the meadows." Mormon settlers were attracted here in 1855 by the artesian wells in the dry valleys along the Old Spanish Trail, and named the location descriptively.

Latakia *see* **Laodicea**

Latina. *City, south central Italy*. The city, capital of the province of the same name, was founded in 1932 by Mussolini in the reclaimed Pontine Marshes and takes its name from its region of **Lazio**, known in classical times as *Latium*. Until 1947 both city and province were known as *Littoria*.

Latin America. *Region, Central and South America*. The name is used for those countries and regions of Central and South America, including the West Indies, where Spanish, Portuguese, and French are spoken. These are Romance languages, derived from Latin. (Most of the countries are Spanish-speaking. The main exceptions are Brazil, where the language is Portuguese; Belize and Guyana, where it is English; Surinam, where it is Dutch; and French Guiana, where it is French.)

Latium *see* **Lazio**

Latvia. *Republic, northeastern Europe.* The country is named for its native inhabitants, the *Letts,* whose own name is of uncertain origin. There may be a link between their name and that of adjacent **Lithuania**.

Lauenburg. *Historic region, northern Germany.* The former duchy took its name from the town of *Lauenburg* on the Elbe here. Its own name, recorded in 1182 as *Lavenborch,* derives from Middle Low German *lauwe,* "lion," referring to the depiction of this heraldic beast in the coat of arms of the local lord who built the medieval castle here. The Polish town of *Lębork,* German *Lauenburg,* founded in 1341 by the Teutonic Knights, who built a castle, has a name of identical origin.

Lauf an der Pegnitz. *City, southern Germany.* The city arose around a mill by a waterfall on the *Pegnitz* River. Hence its name, from Middle High German *louf,* "race," referring to this watercourse. The river's own name derives from an Indoeuropean root word meaning simply "current."

Launceston. *City and port, southeastern Australia.* The city, in northern Tasmania, was surveyed in 1826 and named for the native town in Cornwall, England, of Philip G. King, third governor of New South Wales.

Lauro Müller. *City, southeastern Brazil.* The city takes its name from the first governor of its state, Santa Catarina, following the establishment of the republic of Peru in 1889.

Lausanne. *City, western Switzerland.* The city, on the northern shore of Lake Geneva, is said to derive its name from Gaulish *leusa,* "flat rock," and *onna,* "river," but a more likely origin is in a corruption of its Roman name, *Lausodunum,* meaning "fort on the *Laus* (River)," with the river name itself meaning "stony." There has never been a river of any size here.

Lauterbrunnen. *Town, south central Switzerland.* The town is famous for its many springs and waterfalls. Hence the name, from German *lauter,* "pure," and *Brunnen,* "spring."

¹**Laval**. *Town, northwestern France.* The name means simply "the valley," and Laval stands on a hill overlooking the Mayenne River.

²**Laval**. *City, southeastern Canada.* The Quebec city, occupying the whole of Jesus Island in the St. Lawrence River, takes its name from a former name of the island, which in 1699 was granted to the Society of Jesus and named for François de Montmorency *Laval* (1623–1708), the first Roman Catholic bishop of Canada. The present city was created in 1965 when all of the island's 14 towns and cities were merged into a single agglomeration. (Four of these already had *Laval* in their names.)

Lavalleja. *Department, southeastern Uruguay.* The department is named for Juan Antonio *Lavalleja* (1784–1853), a hero of Uruguay's struggle for independence.

Lavi. *Kibbutz, northern Israel.* The kibbutz, founded by orthodox Jews in 1948, has a Hebrew name meaning "lion."

¹**Lawrence**. *City, central United States.* The Kansas city was founded in 1854 and named for Amos A. *Lawrence,* a New England textile manufacturer.

²**Lawrence**. *City, northeastern United States.* The Massachusetts city was founded in 1845 as an industrial promotion formed by a group of Boston financiers, one of whom was Abbot *Lawrence* (1792–1855).

Lawton. *City, south central United States.* The Oklahoma city was organized in 1901 and named for General Henry W. *Lawton* (1843–1899), killed in action in the Philippines.

Lazarevac. *Town, north central Serbia.* The town is named for *Lazar* (*Lazarus*) (c.1329–1389), king of Serbia, killed fighting the Turks in the battle of Kosovo (Kosovo Polje).

Lazio. *Region, western Italy.* The region, originally a small area southwest of Rome known as *Latium,* may have derived its name from Latin *latus,* "broad," "wide," with reference to the plain of the lower Tiber here. Whatever the origin, it was this region that gave the name of the *Latin* language.

Leamington. *Town, central England.* The Warwickshire town derives its name from the *Leam* River on which it lies, with the river's own Celtic name meaning "elm river." The final *-ton* is Old English *tūn,* "farm." The town's full formal name is *Royal Leamington Spa.* In 1830 11-year-old Princess Victoria visited the town with her mother, the Duchess of Kent, and granted the honorific title in 1838, the year of her coronation as Queen Victoria. The last word of the full name refers to the town's medicinal springs, the object of the royal visit.

Leatherhead. *Town, southern England.* The Surrey town, on the Mole River, has a name of Old English origin probably meaning "public ford," from *lēode,* "people" (related modern German *Leute*), and *rida,* "riding path," "ford that can be ridden." A recent interpretation of the name as "gray ford," from words of Celtic origin, is now generally refuted.

Lebanon. *Republic, southwestern Asia.* The country derives its name from the Semitic root *lbn*, "white," referring either to the snowy peaks of its many mountains or, according to some, to its white chalk and limestone cliffs. The Bible seems to support the former origin: "Will a man leave the snow of Lebanon?" (Jeremiah 18:14).

Lebombo Mountains. *Mountain range, southeastern Africa.* The range, on the border between South Africa and Mozambique, derives its name from Zulu *ubombo*, "big ridge." The southernmost section of the range, in eastern South Africa, is actually known as the *Ubombo*.

Lębork *see* **Lauenburg**

Lebowa. *Historic homeland, northeastern South Africa.* The former black Bantu homeland, in what is now Limpopo province, was established in 1972 for the Northern Soto people. Its name indicates this, and means simply "northern." In 1994 it was reintegrated into South African territory.

Lecce. *City, southeastern Italy.* The name, popularly derived from Italian *leccio*, "holm oak," is said to have evolved from the Roman town of *Lupiae*, on the site of which the city may have been built.

Leeds. *City, northern England.* The name of the former West Yorkshire city was originally that of the region here, itself deriving from a people who lived by what is now the Aire River. They were so called from an earlier name of the river, which must have begun with something like *Lat-*, itself of Celtic origin and meaning "boiling," referring to its current.

Leer. *City and river port, western Germany.* The city arose by the Ems River around a missionary church built in 783 and takes its name from Old Friesian *hlēri*, "(cattle) pen."

Leeuwarden. *City, northern Netherlands.* The city's name represents a Frisian original *Ljouwert*. The first part of this is probably a personal name. The second part may mean "hill of refuge."

Leeuwin, Cape. *Cape, southwestern Australia.* The cape, in Western Australia, was so named in 1801 by Matthew Flinders (*see* **Flinders Ranges**) for the Dutch ship *Leeuwin* ("lioness") that discovered it in 1622.

Leeward Islands. *Island group, eastern West Indies.* The name implies that the islands are sheltered from the prevailing winds. Here, these are the northeasterly trade winds, from which the Leewards are more sheltered than the **Windward Islands**. The name occurs similarly for other island groups, such as the *Leeward Islands* northwest of Hawaii in the North Pacific, and those in the Society Islands, French Polynesia, in the South Pacific. The latter are also known

by their French name of *Îles sous-le-Vent* (literally, "islands below the wind").

Legaspi. *City and port, central Philippines.* The city, in southern Luzon, was founded in c.1639 and originally named *Albay*. In 1925 it was renamed as now for the Spanish conquistador Miguel López de *Legazpi* (c.1510–1572), first Spanish governor general of the Philippines.

Leghorn *see* **Livorno**

Legnica. *City, southwestern Poland.* The city, known to the Germans as *Liegnitz*, derives its name from Slavic *leg*, "meadow," "marsh." Legnica lies by the Kaczawa River in the lowlands of Silesia.

Lehavot Havivah. *Kibbutz, western Israel.* The name means "flames of *Havivah*," in memory of Slovakian-born *Havivah* Reik (1914–1944), parachuted into Nazi-occupied Slovakia in World War II on an intelligence and sabotage mission but captured and executed by the Germans.

Le Havre. *City and port, northern France.* The port was founded in 1517 by Francis I of France as *Le Havre-de-Grâce*, "the harbor of grace," taking this name from the chapel already here called *Notre Dame de Grâce*, "Our Lady of Grace." The name was later shortened as now. *See also* **Newhaven**.

Leicester. *City, central England.* The city, in the county of the same name, was a Roman station, as indicated by the *-cester*, which represents Old English *ceaster*, "Roman fort," a borrowing from Latin *castrum*, "camp." The first part of a name with this element is usually the name of the local river. In the case of Leicester, this is the Soar, which does not fit. The reference must therefore be to the small stream called the *Leire*, a tributary of the Soar. Its own name is of unknown origin, but it gave the name of the *Ligore*, a local people, and it was their name, rather than that of the stream, that ultimately gave the city's name. The overall sense is thus "Roman station of the people who lived by the Leire."

Leiden. *City, western Netherlands.* The city's name is of Germanic origin, from *leitha*, "canal," a word ultimately related to English *lead* (in the sense "conduct"). Leiden is on a canal that leads to the North Sea. The name has an alternate spelling *Leyden*.

Leinster. *Historic region, eastern Ireland.* The name of the former province means "place of the *Lagin*," these being a Celtic people who probably came to Ireland in the 3d century B.C. Their own name may relate to modern Irish *laighean*, "spear," so that they were the "spear folk." The final part of the name represents Irish *tír*, "land," as for **Munster** and **Ulster**.

Leipzig. *City, eastern Germany*. The city has a name of Slavic origin, from Old Sorbian *lipa*, "lime," showing that the Slavs had territory this far west and that lime trees were a special feature here. *Cp.* **Liepaja**, **Lipetsk**.

Leitrim. *County, northwestern Ireland*. The county takes its name from the village of *Leitrim*, its own name representing Irish *Liatroim*, "gray ridge."

Leix *see* **Laois**

Lelystad. *City, north central Netherlands*. The city was founded in 1957 on recently drained land by the IJsselmeer and named for Cornelis *Lely* (died 1929), the Dutch engineer and statesman who designed the Zuider Zee reclamation project.

Le Mans. *City, northwestern France*. The city's original name was *Celmans*, a reduced form of *Cenomanis*. As such, it was the capital of the people known as the *Cenomani*, whose own name may derive from Gaulish *ceno*, "far," and a root meaning "to go." The initial *Cel-* of *Celmans* was subsequently taken to represent French *cel*, "which," and as this made little sense it was replaced by *le*, "the." Hence the present form of the name.

Lemnos. *Island, northeastern Greece*. The Aegean island has a name of Phoenician origin meaning "white" (*cp.* **Lebanon**). Phoenician sailors must have been impressed by the pale-colored volcanic rock here.

Lena. *River, east central Russia*. The Siberian river has a name that may represent Evenki *yelyuyon*, meaning simply "river."

Leninabad *see* **Khodzhent**

Leninakan *see* **Kumayri**

Leningrad *see* ¹**St. Petersburg**

Leninogorsk. *City, eastern Kazakhstan*. The city was originally named *Ridder*, for an Englishman, Philip *Ridder*, who in 1786 discovered a mine here containing gold, silver, copper, and lead. In 1941 the town was renamed as now for *Lenin*, with the second half of the name implying both Russian *gorod*, "town," and *gornyj*, "mining (settlement)." A Kazakh news report of June 27, 2002, announced the city's intention to revert to the earlier name.

Lenin Peak. *Mountain, south central Asia*. The mountain, in the Transalay Range on the border of southwestern Kyrgyzstan and northwestern Tajikistan, was discovered in 1871 by the Russian naturalist A. P. Fedchenko and named by him *Kaufman Peak*, for Konstantin Petrovich *Kaufman* (1818–1882), then governor general of Turkestan. On the death of *Lenin* in 1924 it was proposed that the mountain be renamed for him, in the belief that this was the Soviet Union's highest peak. (It was later discovered that Communism Peak and Victory Peak were higher.) The new name was actually given in 1928, when the Academy of Sciences of the USSR was actively exploring the Pamirs here.

Leninsk-Kuznetsky. *City, southern Russia*. The original name of the town was *Kolchugino*, presumably from a family name. In 1925 it was renamed as now for *Lenin*, who had died the previous year, with the second part of the name added to distinguish this *Leninsk* from others and to denote its location in the **Kuznetsk** Coal Basin.

Lenínváros *see* **Tiszaújváros**

Lennox Hills. *Hills, south central Scotland*. The name probably derives from a form of Gaelic *leamhan*, "elm tree." *Cp.* **Leven, Loch**.

Lens. *Town, northern France*. The name goes back to a Roman female personal name *Lenna*.

Lenti. *Town, western Hungary*. The name is an altered form of *Németi*, from Hungarian *Német*, "German," describing the former inhabitants of this region of western Hungary.

Lentini. *Town, southern Italy*. The town, in eastern Sicily, is one of the oldest Greek settlements in Italy and derives its name from Greek *leōn, leontos*, "lion."

Leominster. *City, northeastern United States*. The Massachusetts city was incorporated as a town in 1740 and named for the English town of *Leominster*, Herefordshire.

León. *Historic region, northwestern Spain*. The region is said to derive its name from the first word of Latin *legionis septimae*, "of the seventh legion," referring to the military force that occupied its capital when it was a Roman station. The city of *León* here has a name of the same origin. Not surprisingly, its canting coat of arms depicts a red, gold-crowned lion (Spanish *león*).

Leonberg. *Town, southern Germany*. The town arose around a castle of the counts of Calw here, who named it *Löwenberg*, "lion castle," after the lion on their coat of arms.

Léopoldville *see* **Kinshasa**

Lepanto. *Town and port, western Greece*. The port's name is an Italian form of its original Greek name of *Epakhtos*, itself an alteration of *Naupaktos*, from Greek *naus*, "ship," and *pegnunai*, "to fix," "to fasten," denoting a safe anchorage. The modern Greek form of the name is *Návpaktos*.

Lepontine Alps. *Section of Central Alps, central Europe*. The mountains, on the border between Switzerland and Italy, are named for the *Lepontii*, a Celto-Ligurian people of northern Italy. The meaning of their name is unknown. Their name also gave that of the *Leventina* valley in southern Switzerland.

Leptis. *Historic city, northwestern Libya.* The coastal city, known as *Leptis Magna* ("great") to be distinguished from *Leptis Minor* in eastern Tunisia, has a name that is probably of Punic origin with a meaning "anchorage," "harbor." The site of Leptis Magna is now known as *Labdah* or *Lebda*, and that of Leptis Minor as *Lamta*.

Le Puy. *City, south central France.* The city's Medieval Latin name was *Podium*, from classical Latin *podium*, "height," and this gave the present name. The reference is to the distinctive volcanic peaks in the locality, notably the Rocher Corneille ("crow rock") and Mont Aiguilhe ("needle mount").

Lérida. *City, northeastern Spain.* The city has a name of Iberian origin, originally *Ilduro* or *Ildirda*, but unknown meaning.

Lerwick. *Town and port, northern Scotland.* The capital of the Shetland Islands has a Scandinavian name meaning "mud bay," from Old Norse *leirr*, "mud," and *vík*, "inlet," "bay." The bay in question is Bressay Sound.

Lesbos. *Island, eastern Greece.* The name of the Aegean island probably had the original sense "wooded."

Leskovac. *Town, southeastern Serbia.* The town derives its name from Serbo-Croat *lieska*, "hazel nut," implying that hazel trees grew here.

Lesotho. *Kingdom, southern Africa.* The name comes from the *Sotho* who are the country's indigenous people. Their own name means "black," "dark-skinned." The initial *Le-* is a singular noun prefix. The plural noun prefix is *Ba-*, which gave *Basutoland* as the former colonial name of Lesotho.

Leszno. *Town, west central Poland.* The town, founded in the 15th century, derives its name from Slavic *les*, "wood," "forest." Its German name is *Lissa*.

Letchworth. *Town, southeastern England.* The Hertfordshire town has an Old English name probably meaning "lockable enclosure," from *lycce*, "locked place" (related to modern *lock*), and *worth*, "enclosure." The reference is presumably to a place that was secure or protected in some way.

Lethbridge. *City, southwestern Canada.* The Alberta city was founded in the 1880s as a mining town called *Coalbanks*. It was renamed as now in 1885, on the arrival of the Canadian Pacific Railway, for William *Lethbridge* (1824–

1901), president of the Northwest Coal and Navigation Company.

Leucas. *Island, eastern Ionian Sea.* The Greek island derives its name from Greek *leukos*, "white," specifically referring to the white cliffs at its southwestern tip. Its modern Greek name is *Levkás*.

Leuze. *Town, western Belgium.* The name probably means "marsh," from the same Gaulish root that gave *Lutetia* as the Roman name of **Paris**, France. Leuze is on a branch of the Dender River. Its full name is *Leuze-en-Hainaut*, for its location in the province of **Hainaut**.

Levallois-Perret. *District of Paris, northern France.* The present district was originally a town formed in 1867 through the amalgamation of four hamlets: *Levallois*, Courcelles, *Champerret*, and Villiers. The first of these represents the name of its founder in 1846, Nicolas-Eugène *Levallois* (1816–1879). *Champerret* derives its name from Latin *campus petrosus*, "stony ground." However, it so happened that a former landowner here was one Jean-Jacques *Perret*. His (shorter) name was therefore chosen for the second part of the new town's name.

Leven, Loch. *Lake, western Scotland.* The lake takes its name from the river that flows into it. The river's own name derives from Gaelic *leamhan*, "elm-tree." *Cp.* **Lennox Hills.**

Leverkusen. *City, west central Germany.* The city was formed in 1930 on the amalgamation of a number of villages with the town of Wiesdorf, where the chemist Karl *Leverkus* (1805–1889) had set up an ultramarine factory, naming it *Leverkusen* in 1862 for his ancestral seat near Wermelskirchen.

Levittown. *City, eastern United States.* The unincorporated residential city on Long Island, New York, was developed between 1946 and 1951 by *Levitt* & Sons, Inc. Hence the name, which subsequently became generic for similar housing developments elsewhere in the country. (The second such development was at *Levittown*, Pennsylvania, built between 1951 and 1955.)

Levskigrad *see* **Karlovo**

Lewes. *Town, southern England.* The name of the East Sussex town was long thought to derive from Old English *hlǣwas*, "hills," "mounds," referring to the many tumuli nearby. A recent theory proposes a different origin, however, in Old English *lǣw*, "injury," "gash," referring to the great gap in the South Downs here through which the Ouse River flows to the sea.

Lewisham. *Borough of London, southeastern England.* The name means "*Lēofsa's* homestead," with an Anglo-Saxon personal name.

Lewis Range. *Mountain range, northwestern United States.* The range, a section of the Rockies in Montana, is named for the American explorer Meriwether *Lewis* (1774–1809), who with William Clark led the first overland expedition to the Pacific Northwest (1804–06).

Lewiston. *City, northeastern United States.* The Maine city was settled in 1770 on the Androscoggin River and is said to be named for a drunken Native American called *Lewis* who drowned there.

Lexington. *City, east central United States.* The Kentucky city was settled in 1779 and named for the 1775 Battle of *Lexington*, Massachusetts. That Lexington, settled in 1640, became an independent township in 1713 and was named for the village of *Lexington* (now *Laxton*), Northamptonshire, England, the home of its original settlers. In 1974 the Kentucky city merged with Fayette county to create an urban county government *Lexington-Fayette* (*see* **Fayetteville**, ¹**Lafayette**).

Leyden *see* **Leiden**

Lhasa. *Capital of Tibet.* The name is Tibetan and means "city of the gods," from *lha*, "god," and *sa*, "city," "land." Lhasa was long the center of Lamaism.

L'Haÿ-les-Roses. *Town, northern France.* The first part of the town's name derives from the Roman personal name *Laius*. The latter part refers to the town's famous *rose* gardens. The original French form of the first part was *Lay*, but the initial *L* became detached as if to denote the definite article ("the"), suggesting *la haie*, "the hedge." (*Cp. La Haye* as the French name of The **Hague**.)

Lhotse. *Mountain, eastern Nepal.* The mountain, just south of Mt. Everest on the Nepal-Tibet border, has a Tibetan name meaning "southern summit," from *lho*, "south," and *tse*, "summit," "peak." There are actually two peaks of the name, *Lhotse I* and *Lhotse II.* The former, which is the higher, is also known as *E1*, a designation given by the Survey of India in 1931. It is an abbreviation of *Everest 1*, as the mountain is sometimes regarded as part of the Everest massif.

Liaoning. *Province, northeastern China.* The province derives its name from Chinese *liáo*, the *Liao* River here, and *níng*, "peace," "calm."

Liao-yang. *City, northeastern China.* The city, in Liaoning province, derives its name from Chinese *liáo*, the *Liao* River, and *yáng*, "light," "sun."

Liao-yüan. *City, northeastern China.* The city, in Kirin province, derives its name from Chinese *liáo*, the *Liao* River, and *yuán*, "spring," "source." It is near here that the named river rises.

Liberec. *City, northern Czech Republic.* The city, founded in c.1350, originally had the German name of *Reichenberg*, apparently meaning "rich mountain," perhaps referring to the richness of the river valley amid the Riesengebirge in which it lies. In local speech the name was slurred as *Riberg*, and this in turn gradually evolved to the present *Liberec*, with the initial *R* becoming *L*.

Liberia. *Republic, western Africa.* The present country arose from the project for the settlement of black slaves begun in 1816 by the American Colonization Society (ACS). Land for the purpose was acquired in 1821 on the site of present-day Monrovia (the capital) and the first emigrants arrived in 1822. In 1824 the American ACS member Robert Goodloe Harper (*see* **Harper**) named the colony *Liberia*, from Latin *liber*, "free."

Libourne. *Town, southwestern France.* The town was founded in 1270 and takes its name from Roger de *Leybourne*, English seneschal of Gascony. His own name comes from *Leybourne*, Kent.

Libreville. *Capital of Gabon.* The city was founded in 1849 by a group of liberated black slaves in what was then French Equatorial Africa. Hence the French name, which with an English history would have exactly equated to that of **Freetown**, capital of Sierra Leone.

Libya. *Republic, northern Africa.* The country is very old and is recorded in Egyptian hieroglyphics of 2000 B.C. The meaning of the name is obscure. Some biblical scholars regard the name of *Lehabim* (Genesis 10:13), a descendant of Noah, as a reference to the Libyan people, who are elsewhere in the Old Testament referred to as "the Lubims" (2 Chronicles 12:3). The Greeks used the name Libya to denote most of North Africa west of the Nile and even, in some contexts, the whole of Africa.

Licata. *Town and port, southern Italy.* The town, in southern Sicily, is said to derive its name from Arabic *al-kal'at*, "the fortress." The original name may have included its possessor. *See* **Kalat**.

Lichfield. *Town, west central England.* The Staffordshire town has a part Celtic, part Old English name meaning "open land by the gray wood." The *Lich-* represents Celtic words related to modern Welsh *llwyd*, "gray," and *coed*, "wood." The *-field* is Old English *feld*, "open land." The "gray wood" in question gave the name of the Roman town of *Letocetum* at nearby Wall.

Lichtenburg. *Town, north central South Africa.* The town, in North West province, was founded in 1866 and proclaimed in 1873, when President T.F. Burgers allegedly declared that the town would be a shining beacon in the Western Transvaal. Hence perhaps the name, meaning "town of light."

Lida. *City, western Belarus.* The city, founded in 1326 as a castle of the Lithuanian duke Gedymin, derives its name from a Lithuanian word denoting a forest clearing.

Lido. *Island reef, northeastern Italy.* The name of the island bathing beach near Venice is simply the Italian word for "beach," ultimately from Latin *litus*, "shore." The name was adopted generically for fashionable beaches or bathing places elsewhere, especially in British English.

Liechtenstein. *Principality, central Europe.* The small state between Switzerland and Austria takes its name from members of the princely house of *Liechtenstein*, who created it in 1719 when they united the barony of Schellenberg, already held by them here, with the county of Vaduz. The house originated in the 12th century in the Austrian castle of *Liechtenstein* (German, "light stone") near Vienna.

Liège. *City, eastern Belgium.* The city ultimately derives its name from that of the Frankish people formerly here known simply as *leudi*, "people" (modern German *Leute*). The Late Latin name of the town developed from this as *Leodium*, and eventually gave the present name. This is the French form, formerly familiar as *Liége*. (The grave accent in *Liège* was officially approved over the acute in 1946.) The Flemish form of the name is *Luik*, while German speakers know the city as *Lüttich*.

Lien-yün-kang. *City and port, eastern China.* The city, in Kiangsu province, derives its name from Chinese *lián*, "to join," *yún*, "cloud," and *găng*, "port."

Lienz. *Town, southern Austria.* The town has come to be known by a former river name, itself ultimately from Indoeuropean *leu*, "mud," "morass," denoting a stream flowing through a marsh.

Liepaja. *City and port, western Latvia.* The city may derive its name either from Latvian *liepa*, "lime tree," or from Estonian *liva*, "sand," referring to the sandy shore here by the Baltic Sea. *Cp.* **Leipzig**, **Lipetsk**. The German form of the name is *Libau*, and the Russian *Libava*.

Liguria. *Historic region, northwestern Italy.* The region is said to take its name from the Celtic god *Lugus* (who also gave the name of

Carlisle and **Lyons**). The *Ligurian Sea* is named for the region.

Likasi. *City, southeastern Democratic Republic of Congo.* The origin of the city's name is uncertain. Before 1966 it was known as *Jadotville*, for the Belgian mining engineer Jean *Jadot* (1862–1932), president of the Union Minière du Haut-Katanga, established here in 1910.

Lille. *City, northern France.* The city probably derives its name from Old French *l'isle*, "the island," denoting its location between arms of the Deûle River. The Flemish form of the city's name is *Rijssel*, a short form of *ter ijsel*, "the island." However, another theory derives the name from a Germanic personal name *Rizili*, altered to *Rizle* or *Lizle*, itself taken to represent the Old French form.

Lillebonne. *Town, northwestern France.* The name is a corrupt form of the town's Roman name, *Juliobona*, itself from *Julius*, complimenting *Julius* Caesar, and Gaulish *bona*, "foundation," "village."

Lilongwe. *Capital of Malawi.* The city takes its name from the river on which it arose in 1902. The river's own name is of obscure origin. It probably has a basic sense "river," "water."

Lima. *Capital of Peru.* The name is a Spanish corruption of Quechua *Rimak*, which itself represents the name of a god and his temple, from *rima*, "to speak." The reference is to the priests of old who addressed the faithful from a place of concealment inside the statues of the gods they worshiped, rather like a Catholic priest in a confessional (if one regards this as a sort of "god box"). The city was founded on January 6, 1535, by Francisco Pizarro, the Spanish conqueror of Peru, and he initially named it *Ciudad de los Reyes*, "city of the kings," for the feast of the Epiphany that day, celebrating the manifestation of Christ to the Three Wise Men (Three Kings of the East).

Limavady. *Town, northern Northern Ireland.* The town, in Co. Londonderry, has the Irish name *Léim an Mhaidadh*, "leap of the dog." This originally related to the site of a former castle here overhanging a deep glen (valley) of the Roe River. A local legend tells how a dog leaped the gorge bearing a message of impending danger.

Limburg. *Historic region, western Europe.* The former duchy, in a region now divided into the adjacent provinces of *Limburg*, respectively in northeastern Belgium and the southeastern Netherlands, takes its name from Germanic *lindo*, "lime tree," and *burg*, "fortress." This originally applied to the settlement that is now the

Belgian town of *Limbourg*, east of Liège. The name thus spread from this to the whole region.

Limerick. *Town and river port, southwestern Ireland*. The town, in the county of the same name, has a name meaning "bare ground," as represented by its Irish name, *Luimneach*, from the root word *lom*, "bare," "thin." The land so described would have originally been on the lower reaches of the Shannon River, on which the town stands. The name could also have applied figuratively to a place that was exposed and difficult to defend.

Lim Fjord. *Fjord, northern Denmark*. The fjord, extending across northern Jutland from the North Sea to the Kattegat, is said to derive its name from Old Norse *limr*, "limb," "branch," alluding to its appearance as an elongated inlet.

Limoges. *City, west central France*. The city's name derives from that of the original people here, the *Lemovices*, whose own name means "conquering with the elm," presumably because they made their spears or bows from elm wood. The Latin adjectival form of their name, *Lemovicinus*, gave that of the historic province of *Limousin*.

Limousin *see* **Limoges**

Limpopo. *River, southeastern Africa*. The river's name is a Portuguese (or possibly English) corruption of its local African name, *Lebepe* or *Lebempe*, said to mean either "dark river," "crocodile river," or "river of waterfalls." Some authorities relate it to local words *uku popozi*, "to rush." The Boer name for the Limpopo was *Krokodil Rivier*. In 2002 South Africa's former Northern province was renamed for the river, which forms the country's northern border with Zimbabwe.

Linares. *City, northern Mexico*. The city was founded in 1716 during the viceroyalty of the duke of *Linares*, who took his title from *Linares*, southern Spain.

¹Lincoln. *City, eastern England*. The city, in the county of the same name, has a name recorded by Ptolemy in the 2d century A.D. as *Lindon*. This represents the Celtic word for "pool," corresponding to modern Welsh *llyn*. The reference was to a widening of the Witham River today represented by Brayford Pool. The Romans established a station for retired veterans of the Ninth Legion on the high ground overlooking the pool, and to the latinized name of the place, *Lindum*, added *colonia*, "colony." The name and word subsequently coalesced to give the present name. Unusually, the name never acquired the *-chester* or *-caster* found in the modern names of towns that were Roman stations.

(It is possible that Anglo-Saxons understood the meaning of *colonia* and so felt no need to add their usual *ceaster*.)

²Lincoln. *City, central United States*. The state capital of Nebraska was laid out in 1859 as *Lancaster*. When the town was selected as capital in 1867, it was renamed commemoratively for Abraham *Lincoln* (1809–1865), 16th president of the United States. The president's family name ultimately derives from the English city of ¹**Lincoln**.

Lindau. *City, southern Germany*. The city takes its name from the island in Lake Constance on which it arose, namely "lime-tree island," from Old High German *linta*, "lime," and *ouwa*, "island."

Lindisfarne. *Island, northeastern England*. The island, in the North Sea off the Northumberland coast, has a name traditionally explained as meaning "island of the travelers to and from *Lindsey*," for the historic northern region of Lincolnshire that was itself named from an early form of the name of ¹**Lincoln** with Old English *ēg*, "island," added. The second part of the name, according to this theory, would thus derive from Old English *faran*, "to journey," referring to the pilgrims who at one time must have made regular journeys from Lindsey to Lindisfarne by virtue of the island's repute as an ancient monastic site. (Hence its alternate name of *Holy Island*.) But the distance between the places is considerable, and the name probably has some other origin. One recent theory interprets it as "domain of *Lindis*," from *Lindis*, the name of a river estuary on the island, and a Celtic word related to Irish *fearann*, "domain." The name is first recorded in 635, when the Irish monk St. Aidan established a Christian missionary center on Lindisfarne. A purely Celtic origin is thus a real possibility.

Line Islands. *Island group, central Pacific*. The islands extend north and south of the equator (the "Line"). Hence their name.

Lingen. *City, northwestern Germany*. The city arose as a trading center on the Ems River and takes its name from Dutch dialect *linge*, "canal."

Lingga Archipelago. *Island group, southwestern Indonesia*. The islands, southeast of Singapore, derive their name from Sanskrit *liṅga*, "linga," "phallus." The reference is to a mountain here, which resembles a huge phallus.

Linköping. *City, southern Sweden*. The city's name means "flax market," from Swedish *lin*, "flax" (related English *linen*), and *köping*, "market" "trading place."

Lintgen. *Town, south central Luxembourg*. The

town, on the Alzette River, derives its name from the Roman settlement of *Lindiacum* here. Its own name is based on a Celtic word meaning "pool" related to Welsh *llyn*, "lake." *Cp.* ¹**Lincoln**.

Linz. *City and river port, northern Austria.* The city's name probably goes back ultimately to Germanic *lindo*, "lime tree," as for **Limburg**.

Lion, Gulf of. *Inlet, southern France.* The French name of the Mediterranean bay is *Golfe du Lion*, apparently meaning "lion gulf." It seems unlikely that real lions were involved, and according to one account the name may refer to stone statues of lions on the coast here at some time. Another theory relates the name to the mistral, the strong, cold wind that in winter blow down the Rhône River and makes the sea roar like a lion. Both explanations seem equally fanciful, but nobody has yet come up with anything better. (The name was formerly often spelled *Gulf of Lyons*, as if for the city of **Lyons**. Presumably the Rhône, which flows south from Lyons to the gulf, was regarded as providing the link.)

Lipari Islands *see* **Eolie Islands**

Lipetsk. *City, western Russia.* The city takes its name from the small *Lipovka* River here. Its own name comes from Russian *lipa*, "lime tree." *Cp.* **Leipzig**, **Liepaja**.

Lippe. *Historic region, north central Germany.* The former state took its name from the medieval lords (later, counts) of *Lippe*, their title coming from their lands on the *Lippe* River (*see* **Lippstadt**).

Lippstadt. *City, northwestern Germany.* The city was founded in 1185 on the *Lippe* River, known in Roman times as the *Lupia*, with a name of uncertain origin.

Lisbon. *Capital of Portugal.* The city's name is popularly traced back to that of its supposed founder, the legendary Greek hero *Ulysses*. The actual origin is uncertain, although some claim a derivation in Phoenician *alis-ubbo*, "joyful bay."

Lisburn. *Town, eastern Northern Ireland.* The town, in Co. Antrim, has the Irish name *Lios na gCearrbhach*, "fort of the gamblers," referring to a site nearby where "outlaws" used to gamble with cards and dice. The English form of this name was *Lisnagarvey*. At some point in the 17th century the name became *Lisburn*. The origin of this is uncertain, although the -*burn* is popularly associated with a fire in the town. The *Lis*- is presumably Irish, as before.

Lisianski. *Island, northwestern Hawaii, United States.* The island, one of the Leeward Islands, was discovered in 1805 by the Russian navigator Yury *Lisyansky* (1773–1837), and is named for him.

Lisichansk. *City, eastern Ukraine.* The city arose in 1710 as a Cossack defensive post on a wooded riverside slope known as *Lis'ya Balka* or *Lisichij Bajrak*, "fox gully." The latter gave the present name. The Ukrainian form of the name is *Lysychans'k*.

Lisieux. *City, northwestern France.* The city derives its name from the *Lexovii*, a Gaulish people formerly here. Their own name is said to mean "leaning," perhaps referring to men who limp through battle injuries, and so implying "warriors" or "veterans."

Liski. *City, western Russia.* The city takes its name from the small *Lyska* River here. The meaning of its own name is unknown. In 1928 the growing settlement was renamed *Svoboda*, "freedom." In 1943 it reverted to *Liski* but in 1965 was again renamed as *Georgiu-Dezh*, for the Romanian Communist leader Gheorge *Gheorghiu-Dej* (1901–1965). In 1991 it finally settled on its original name.

Lithuania. *Republic, northeastern Europe.* The country may take its name from an earlier name of the Neman River that runs through it. The meaning of the name is obscure. It has been associated by some with Latin *litus*, "shore," referring to the Baltic here. Others link it with neighboring **Latvia**, although that country's own name is also of uncertain origin.

Litoměřice. *Town, northern Czech Republic.* The original name of the town, recorded in 993, was *Lyutomirichi*, "*Lyutomir's* people," from a personal name found elsewhere in western Slavic lands. The German form of the town's name is *Leitmeritz*.

Littlehampton. *Town and resort, southern England.* The West Sussex town was originally simply *Hampton*, from the Old English word meaning "homestead." It later added *Little*-, perhaps to be distinguished from **Southampton**, further west along the English Channel coast in the neighboring county of Hampshire, and itself also originally *Hampton*. But the distance between the two places (some 40 miles, or 64 km), makes this particular link rather unlikely.

Little Rock. *City, south central United States.* The state capital of Arkansas was given its name in 1722 by the French explorer Bernard de la Harpe, who finding two distinctive rock formations on the Arkansas River here, called the larger one *Grande Roche* and the smaller *Petite Roche*. The "little rock" subsequently became the base for a railroad bridge, while the "big rock," 2 miles (3.2 km) away, was the site of an army post. In 1812 a trapper named William Lewis built his home at the "little rock," and this was the basis for the present city. *See also* **North Little Rock.**

Liu-chou. *City, southern China.* The city, in Kwangsi Chuang autonomous region, derives its name from Chinese *liŭ,* "willow," "osier," and *zhōu,* "department," "state."

Livadiya. *Town and resort, southern Ukraine.* The health resort, now a suburb of Yalta, in the southern Crimea, is said to derive its name from Greek *libas, libados,* "spring," "stream."

Liverpool. *City and port, northwestern England.* The name of the Merseyside city literally means "livered pool," i.e. one clotted with weeds. The pool in question was a tidal creek, now filled in, into which two streams drained. A mythical creature called the *Liver bird* (rhyming with "diver") was invented to explain the name, and was adopted as the city's emblem, supporting its coat of arms, while the *Royal Liver Building,* a large office block here, has twin towers surmounted by statues of the birds.

Livingstone. *Town, southern Zambia.* The town, on the Zambezi Falls, was founded in 1905 and named in honor of the Scottish explorer David *Livingstone* (1813–1873), who discovered the falls in 1855. Its alternate name is *Maramba,* a local word for the plantain, a type of banana tree.

Livonia. *Historic region, northwestern Europe.* The former Russian province on the Baltic Sea is said to derive its name from a word related to Estonian *liiv,* "sand." This certainly suits its location.

Livorno. *City and port, northwestern Italy.* The city takes its name from the *Liburni,* the people who at one time inhabited the region. Their own name is of uncertain origin. The name was long familiar in the English form *Leghorn,* a corruption presumably created by English sailors.

Lizard, The. *Peninsula, southwestern England.* The Cornwall peninsula, the southernmost point of the English mainland, has a Cornish name meaning "court (on a) height," from *lys,* "court," and *ardh,* "height." The "court" would have been a local administrative center on the lines of a modern town hall.

Ljubljana. *Capital of Slovenia.* The city's name has been popularly associated with the Slavic root word *ljub,* "dear," as if it were a "beloved" or favorite place. But the true origin is probably pre–Slavic, and remains obscure. The city's German name is *Laibach,* from the Roman name *Labacum.*

Llandudno. *Town and resort, northwestern Wales.* The town, in Gwynedd, has a name meaning "St. *Tudno*'s church" from Welsh *llan,* "church" (originally "enclosure," and ultimately related to English *land*), and the saint's name. Little is known about St. Tudno, as is the case with many Welsh saints whose names are preserved in placenames.

Llanelli. *Town and port, southern Wales.* The town, in Dyfed, has a name meaning "St. *Elli*'s church," from Welsh *llan,* "church" (*see* **Llandudno**), and the name of the female saint, said to have been a daughter of the legendary prince Brychan (*see* **Brecon Beacons**).

Llano Estacado. *Plateau, southern United States.* The extensive plateau, along the border between Texas and New Mexico, has a Spanish name meaning "staked plain" (as which it is equally known in English). The name is said to refer to the lines of *stakes* that were set up here to guide travelers, or according to another account, to the stalks of a yucca plant here resembling stakes.

Llantrisant. *Town, southern Wales.* The Monmouthshire town has a name meaning "church of the three saints," from Welsh *llan,* "church" (*see* **Llandudno**), *tri,* "three," and *sant,* "saint." The three saints in question, to whom the town's parish church is dedicated, are Illtud, Dyfodwg, and Gwynno.

Lobos Islands. *Island group, northwestern Peru.* The Pacific islands derive their name from Spanish *lobo,* "wolf," here meaning "sea wolf" (*lobo marino*), i.e. "seal," an animal regularly found here. The largest and northernmost island is *Isla Lobos de Tierra,* "landward seal island," while to the south are the *Islas Lobos de Afuera,* "seaward seal islands."

Locarno. *Town, southern Switzerland.* The name is of uncertain origin, despite attempts to derive it from (false) Latin *lacuna vara,* "(settlement on the) crooked bay," for the town's location at the northern end of Lake Maggiore, or (genuine) Latin *lucerna,* "lamp" (*cp.* **Lucerne**), referring to a light tower here, serving as a guide to fishing boats on the lake. The true source may be in a personal name.

Loch Ness *see* **Ness, Loch** (similarly for other Scottish lake names, also Irish ones with *Lough*)

Łódź. *City, central Poland.* The name is identical with the standard Polish word meaning "boat," as represented in the city's coat of arms, which shows a simple dugout boat and paddle. The meaning is appropriate for the town's location in a region of rivers, but the actual origin of the name may be in a quite different word. In World War II, under German occupation, the city was renamed *Litzmannstadt* for the German World War I general Karl *Litzmann* (1850–1936).

Lofoten Islands. *Island group, Norwegian Sea.* The islands, off the northwest coast of Norway, have a name of obscure origin. It has been popularly interpreted as "fox foot," from Norwegian *lo*, "fox," and *fot*, "foot."

Logan, Mt. *Mountain, northwestern Canada.* Canada's highest mountain, in southwestern Yukon Territory, is named for Sir William *Logan* (1798–1875), founder of the Geological Survey of Canada.

Lohamei ha-Getaot. *Kibbutz, northwestern Israel.* The kibbutz was founded in 1949 by survivors of the Warsaw ghetto. Hence its Hebrew name, meaning "fighters of the ghetto."

Löhne. *City, northwestern Germany.* The city, on the Werre River, ultimately derives its name from the Indoeuropean root element *leu*, "mire."

Loire. *River, central and western France.* The river was known to the Romans as *Liger*, which can perhaps be traced back to an Indoeuropean source *leg* or *lig*, meaning "mud." The *-er* of the Roman name may represent the Indoeuropean *ar*, "water," found also in **Aragon** and other river names.

Lomas de Zamora. *City, eastern Argentina.* The city, now a suburb of Buenos Aires, dates from the 16th century. Its name commemorates Juan *de Zamora*, one of the founders of Buenos Aires, who was granted a landholding here on the slopes (Spanish *lomas*).

Lombardy. *Region, north central Italy.* The region had the Latin name of *Langobardus*. This relates to its former inhabitants, the *Langobardi* or *Lombards*, a Germanic people who invaded Italy in the 6th century. Their own name may mean "longbeards," from Germanic *lang*, "long," and *bart*, "beard," although some authorities prefer an interpretation "long axes," from *lang* and *barta*, "ax." The Italian form of the name is *Lombardia*.

Lomé. *Capital of Togo.* The city derives its name from a local word meaning "little market."

Lomond, Loch. *Lake, south central Scotland.* The lake takes its name from the nearby mountain of Ben *Lomond*. Its own name derives from a Celtic word meaning "beacon hill."

Lompoc. *City, southwestern United States.* The California city was founded in 1874 as a farming community and has a Native American (Chumash) name meaning "shell mound."

Łomża. *City, northeastern Poland.* The city arose in the late 10th or early 11th century, when the region here was settled by Baltic-speaking peoples. Its name is thus thought to represent Lithuanian *lamza*, "deer." The city's coat of arms depicts a leaping deer, but this in itself is no guarantee of the actual meaning.

[1]**London.** *Capital of United Kingdom.* Despite its familiarity, the city's name remains of obscure, probably pre–Celtic origin. A recent theory derives it from two Indoeuropean roots that combine to mean "boat river," referring to the Thames, on which London stands, as a river that needed a boat to be crossed, as against one that could be forded. Whatever the origin, the name would have applied to what is now the City of London, the capital's historical center.

The wealth of suppositions regarding the source of the name has included the following, in reverse order of probability: (1) From a Celtic personal name *Londinos*, "wild one"; (2) From Celtic *llwyn dinas*, "forest town"; (3) From Celtic *lon dun*, "hill fort"; (4) From Celtic *llyn dun*, "fort by the pool"; (5) From Celtic *llong dinas*, "ship harbor"; (5) From a king *Lud* and Old English *tūn*, "town," so that *London* is "*Lud's* town" just as *Ludgate* Hill, leading to St. Paul's Cathedral, is "*Lud's* gate"; (6) From Latin *Luna*, "Moon," and Celtic *dun*, "hill," "fort," as St. Paul's Cathedral was built on a hill where there was anciently a temple of Diana, the goddess of the Moon. Shakespeare refers to London as "Lud's town" in *Cymbeline* (1610).

[2]**London.** *City, southeastern Canada.* The name and site of the Ontario city were chosen in 1792, although the city itself was not founded until 1826. It was named for [1]**London**, England, and like the British capital is on the Thames River. Its streets and bridges are also named for those of its English eponym.

Londonderry. *City and port, northern Northern Ireland.* The city, in the county of the same name, was originally an ecclesiastical settlement known simply as *Derry*, representing its Irish name *Doire*, "oak wood." It gained its addition in the early 17th century, when James I granted a charter authorizing merchants from [1]**London** to make a settlement here. The name is now often shortened as *Derry*.

Londrina. *City, southeastern Brazil.* The city was founded in 1930 by a group of Japanese and German settlers with the backing of the Companhia de Terras Norte do Paraná, a Portuguese subsidiary of the English firm Paraná Plantations Ltd. A director of the subsidiary, Dr. João Domingues Sampaio, proposed that the development be named for [1]**London**, the English firm's city of origin.

Long Beach. *City, western United States.* The California city, on San Pedro Bay, was laid out in 1881 and originally named *Willmore City,* for its founder, W.E. *Willmore.* It was subsequently promoted as a seaside resort and in 1888 renamed as now for its *beach,* 8½ miles (15.5 km) *long.*

Longford. *Town, east central Ireland.* The town, in the county of the same name, has a seemingly English name which is actually Irish. It represents *An Longfort,* "the fortress," from *longfort,* "fort," "camp." Longford was the site of a fortress of the O'Farrells, although no trace of it remains today.

Long Island. *Island, eastern United States.* The island, as the southeasternmost part of New York state, has a self-descriptive name. The island extends 118 miles (190 km) from the mouth of the Hudson River and has a width of from 12 to 23 miles (19 to 37 km).

Longjumeau. *Town, northern France.* The name is a corruption of the town's Medieval Latin name, *Nongemellum,* itself an altered form of *Noviomagus,* meaning "new market," from Gaulish *novio,* "new," and *magos,* "field," "market," "town." The present form of the name has been influenced by French *long,* "long," and *jumeau,* "twin." *Noviomagus* was a fairly common Roman name, as also for **Chichester** in England and **Nijmegen** in the Netherlands.

Longmont. *City, west central United States.* The Colorado city was founded in 1871 as a farming community and named for Major Stephen H. *Long* (1784–1864), discoverer of *Longs* Peak (the *mont*), to the west.

Longueuil. *City, southeastern Canada.* The Quebec city was founded in 1657 by the French colonist Charles le Moyne de *Longueuil* (1626–1685) and is named for him.

Longview. *City, southern United States.* The Texas city was so named in 1870 by surveyors for the Texas and Pacific Railroad, who were impressed by the *long*-distance *view* here.

Longwy. *Town, northeastern France.* The town has a name of Germanic origin, from words corresponding to Old English *lang,* "long," and *wīc,* "village." A "long village" is a straggling one on a single road.

Lons-le-Saunier. *Town, eastern France.* The town had the Medieval Latin name of *Ledo Salnerius* or *Ledo Salinarius.* The first word of this probably comes from Gaulish *ledone,* "neap tide," "stagnant water," referring to some standing pool here. The second word is French *saunier,* "salt worker," referring to a worker in the local salt mines. The town has been a saltwater spa since Roman times.

Lop Nor. *Lake bed, northwestern China.* The former saline lake, in the Uighur Autonomous Region of Sinkiang, derives the first part of its name from an altered form of Tibetan *dap,* "mud," "silt," and the second from Mongolian *nuur,* "lake."

Lorain. *City, northern United States.* The Ohio city arose in 1807 as a trading post called *Black River.* In 1836 it was incorporated as the village of *Charlestown* and in 1874 was renamed as now for its county, itself named for **Lorraine,** France.

Lorch. *Town, southern Germany.* The name represents an alteration of the city's Roman name, quoted in a text of 1139 which refers to "*locus qui dicitur Laureacus*" ("a place called *Laureacus*"), from a Romano-Celtic personal name followed by the Gallo-Roman suffix *-acum.* The town of *Lorch* in central Germany, as a Roman settlement called *Lauriacum,* has a name of the same origin.

Lorelei. *Cliff, western Germany.* The cliff, on the right bank of the Rhine River, associated with the legend of a siren who tempts sailors to destruction, derives the second part of its name from Rhenish dialect *Lei,* "cliff," "rock." The first part is perhaps from Middle High German *lüren,* "to lie in wait," "to peek," denoting a cliff from which a lookout could be kept. In later versions of the legend, the name became that of the seductive maiden herself, probably influenced by the female name *Lore.*

Lorestan. *Province, western Iran.* The province, also known as *Luristan,* has a name meaning "land of the Lurs," referring to the people who formerly lived here. *Cp.* **Laristan.**

Loreto. *Town, central Italy.* The town and place of pilgrimage is famous for the *Santa Casa* ("Holy House"), supposedly the house of the Virgin Mary, which according to legend was transported through the air by angels in 1291 from Nazareth to a hill in Dalmatia, from there in 1294 across the Adriatic to a laurel grove (Latin *lauretum*) near Recanati, and thence in 1295 to its present site. Hence the name.

Lorient. *City and port, western France.* The city was founded as a port on the Bay of Biscay in 1664 by the French East India Company (*Compagnie de l'Orient*) and was named for them. The incongruity of a west-coast town having a name meaning "the east" does not seem to have concerned the namers.

Lörrach. *City, southwestern Germany.* The city's name, first recorded in the early 12th century as *Lorracho,* is probably that of a river, perhaps from Alemannic dialect *Lore,* "larch," and the -*ach* suffix found elsewhere in river names that derives from Old High German *aha*, "water."

Lorraine. *Historic region, eastern France.* The name of the former province evolved from its Medieval Latin name of *Lotharingia.* This represents *Lotharii regnum*, "kingdom of *Lothair*," referring to *Lothair* II (835–869), for whom the kingdom was created. It was bequeathed to him by his father, the emperor Lothair I, grandson of Charlemagne.

Los Angeles. *City, western United States.* The California city was founded in 1781 on a Spanish grant and was originally named *El Pueblo de Nuestra Señora de los Ángeles*, "the town of Our Lady of the Angels" (or according to another account, *El Pueblo de la Reyna de los Ángeles*, "the town of the Queen of the Angels"). The name was gradually shortened to its present form, and is now colloquially abbreviated even further as simply *L.A.*

Los Baños. *Town and resort, north central Philippines.* The town, in southwestern Luzon, has a Spanish name meaning "the baths," referring to the thermal springs that flow from the base of Mt. Makiling nearby.

Los Islands. *Island group, Guinea.* The Atlantic islets, off Conakry, Guinea, are said to be named for the idols (*los idolos*) found here by early Portuguese navigators. The French name of the islands is *Îles de Los.*

Los Lagos. *Region, southern Chile.* The region's Spanish name means "the lagoons," referring to the many lakes here, especially in the north.

Los Ríos. *Province, west central Ecuador.* The Spanish name of the province means "the rivers," referring to the Río Guayas and its many headwaters that cross the lowland here.

Los Teques. *City, north central Venezuela.* The city's Spanish name derives from the local Native Americans, whose chief, Guaicaipuro (died c.1560), was born here.

Lot. *River, southwestern France.* The river was known to the Roman as *Oltis*, which may go back to a pre–Celtic root element *ol*, "to flow," or come from Gaulish *ollow*, "all," "big." The initial *L-* of the present name arose as the definite article, i.e. as if *L'Ot.*

Lothian. *Region, southern Scotland.* The region has a name of obscure origin. It may be an ethnic name, derived from an individual called *Leudonus*, although nothing is known about him. *See also* **Midlothian.**

Louangphrabang *see* **Luang Prabang**

Loughborough. *Town, central England.* The name of the Leicestershire town means "*Luhhede's* fortified place," with the Anglo-Saxon personal name followed by Old English *burh*, "fort."

Louisbourg. *Town, southeastern Canada.* The Nova Scotia town, on Cape Breton Island, was founded in 1713 by French settlers from Newfoundland and named for *Louis* XIV of France (1638–1715). The name was formerly spelled *Louisburg.*

Louisiana. *State, southern United States.* The state was named in 1682 by the French explorer René- Robert Cavelier, sieur de la Salle, for *Louis* XIV of France (1638–1715). The name originally applied to the whole of the Mississippi basin as French colonial territory.

Louisville. *City and river port, east central United States.* The Kentucky city was founded by the French in 1778 and given its name in 1780 in honor of *Louis* XVI of France (1638–1715) in recognition of his aid during the American Revolution.

Louny. *Town, northwestern Czech Republic.* The town, first mentioned in 1115, derives its name from a personal name *Loun* or *Lun.* The final -*y* of the name is the plural ending, denoting the people or descendants of the named individual. The German form of the name is *Laun.*

Lourdes. *Town, southwestern France.* The pilgrimage town takes its name from one *Luridus* or *Lordus*, here in the time of Charlemagne (late 8th and early 9th centuries).

Lourenço Marques *see* **Maputo**

Louth. *County, northeastern Ireland.* The county's name is that of a small village here, its own original Irish name being *Lughmhaigh.* The latter half of this represents Irish *magh*, "plain," but the first part is of uncertain origin. It does not appear to be a personal name.

Louvain. *City, central Belgium.* The city derives its name from the personal name *Lubianos*, meaning "loved one." The town's Flemish name of *Leuven* and its German name of *Löwen* wrongly suggest a meaning "lions," although this heraldic beast does not appear on the city's coat of arms.

Low Countries *see* **Netherlands**

Lowell. *City, northeastern United States.* The Massachusetts city was originally settled in 1653 as a farming community named *East Chelmsford.* It was incorporated as a town in 1826 and renamed as now for Francis C. *Lowell* (1775–1817), the American pioneer textile industrialist, born farther down the Merrimack River at Newburyport.

Lower Egypt. *Region, northern Egypt.* The region is so named because it centers on the *lower* reaches and delta of the Nile River, as against *Upper Egypt*, nearer its source.

Lowestoft. *Town and port, eastern England*. The Suffolk town has a Scandinavian name meaning "*Hlothvér*'s dwelling place," with the personal name followed by Old Danish *toft*, originally with the sense "building site."

Loyalty Islands. *Island group, southwestern Pacific*. The islands, in New Caledonia, were discovered in 1827 by the French explorer Jules Sébastien César Dumont d'Urville and named by him for the trust and goodwill shown him by the islanders. The French name is *îles Loyauté*.

Lo-yang. *City, eastern China*. The city, in Honan province, derives its name from Chinese *luò*, the *Luo* River here, and *yáng*, "light," "sun."

Loznica. *Town, western Serbia*. The town derives its name from Serbo-Croat *loza*, "wild vine."

Luanda. *Capital of Angola*. The city's name comes from a local word meaning "tax," "duty." The reference is to the cowrie shells on the Atlantic coast here, which were at one time used by local people to pay their dues to the king of the Congo.

Luang Prabang. *City, northern Laos*. The city was the residence of the monarch of Laos from 1353 and was originally named *Muong Luong*, "royal town," from Laotian *muong*, "town," "city," and *luong*, "great," "royal." In c.1563 the royal court moved to Vientiane, and the town was renamed as now for *Pra Bang*, a Sinhalese gold Buddha that had been brought to the town when it first became a royal residence. The name is now often spelled *Louangphrabang*.

Lubbock. *City, southern United States*. The Texas city was founded in 1890 and named for Colonel Tom S. *Lubbock*, a signer of the Texas Declaration of Independence (1836).

Lübeck. *City and port, northern Germany*. The city, founded in 1143 by Count Adolf II of Schauenburg and Holstein as a trading town on the site of an abandoned Slav fort, takes its name from the former principality of the *Liubichi*, the descendants of a prince *Liub* ("beloved"). The second part of their name was influenced by Lower Middle German *beke* (modern German *Bach*), "stream."

Lublin. *City, eastern Poland*. The origin of the city's name remains uncertain. On phonetic grounds it is unlikely to derive from Slavic *lub*, "bark," "baste." As early as 1555 a folk etymology was current that it was so called because its founder liked (*lub*) to eat the tench (*lin*) in the Bystrzyca River here.

Lubumbashi. *City, southeastern Democratic Republic of Congo*. The city was founded by the

Belgians in 1910 and originally named *Élisabethville*, for Queen *Élisabeth* (1876–1965), wife (from 1900) of Albert I, king of the Belgians. In 1966 the city adopted its present name, that of the small stream on which it stands. Its meaning is uncertain.

Lucca. *City, north central Italy*. The city's name ultimately goes back to Celtic *luc*, "marshland." Lucca is low-lying in the valley of the Serchio River.

Lucerne. *City, central Switzerland*. The name of the city is of uncertain origin, although various theories have been proposed to account for it. The three traditional contenders, which all relate to the lake of the same name on which Lucerne lies, propose derivations from different Latin words: (1) *lucerna*, "lamp," referring to the phosphorescent fish in the lake; (2) *lucius*, "pike," from the abundance of these fish here; (3) *lutum*, "mud," for the shore here. A fourth, more likely explanation, is that the name comes from that of the monastery founded in the 8th century here by St. *Leodegar*. The German name of Lake Lucerne is *Vierwaldstätter See*, "lake of the four forest cantons," referring to the four cantons that surround it: Lucerne, Nidwalden, Uri, and Unterwalden. The French and Italian names, respectively *lac des Quatre Cantons* and *lago dei Quattro Cantoni*, are similar.

Lu-chou. *City, south central China*. The city, in Szechwan province, derives its name from Chinese *lú*, the *Lu* River, and *zhōu*, "region," "department."

Lucknow. *City, northern India*. The city, in Uttar Pradesh state, takes its name from Hindi *lakhnaū*, a short form of Sanskrit *lakshmaṇavati*, from *lakshmaṇa*, "sign," "mark," referring to the goddess *Lakshmi*, whose own name symbolizes prosperity and happiness.

Lüdenscheid. *City, west central Germany*. The city, originally a Frankish settlement, has a name meaning "*Ludolf*'s territory," with the second part of the name related to modern German *scheiden*, "to divide," "to separate."

Lüderitz. *Town and port, southern Namibia*. The town takes its name from the German merchant Franz Adolf *Lüderitz* (1834–1886), who acquired the site in 1883 and persuaded his government to place this part of Africa under its protection. It did so in 1884, as *German Southwest Africa*.

Ludhiana. *City, northwestern India*. The city, in Punjab state, was founded in 1480 by members of Delhi's ruling *Lodi* dynasty, and is named for them.

Ludlow. *Town, western England*. The Shropshire town has an Old English name meaning "mound by the loud one." The mound in question is a large tumulus that was demolished in 1199 when the parish church was enlarged. The "loud one" is the current of a crossing over the Teme River below.

Ludwigsburg. *City, southwestern Germany.* The city was founded in the early 18th century by Duke Eberhard *Ludwig* of Württemberg (1676–1733) around his castle, and is named for him.

Ludwigsfelde. *Town, eastern Germany.* The town was founded in 1750 by the Prussian statesman Ernst *Ludwig* von der Gröben on the site of the former village of Damsdorf and was named "*Ludwig*'s fields" after him.

Ludwigshafen. *City and river port, southwestern Germany.* The city was founded in 1607 as a bridgehead on the Rhine and was originally known as *Rheinschanze*, literally "Rhine entrenchment." In 1843 it was renamed as now, "*Ludwig*'s harbor," for King *Ludwig* (Louis) of Bavaria (1786–1868).

Ludwigslust. *Town, northern Germany.* The town arose around a hunting lodge built in 1724 by Duke Christian *Ludwig* of Mecklenburg and was named "*Ludwig*'s pleasure" after him.

Lugano. *Town and resort, southern Switzerland.* The town, on the lake of the same name, has a name that ultimately goes back to Gaulish *lacvanno*, "lake dweller," these being the people who at one time inhabited this region.

Lugansk. *City, eastern Ukraine.* The city takes its name from the *Lugan* River on which it arose around an iron foundry in 1795. The river's own name is of uncertain origin. In 1935 the town was renamed *Voroshilovgrad*, for the Soviet military leader and statesman, Marshal Kliment *Voroshilov* (1881–1969), who engaged in revolutionary activities here. It retained this name until 1958, when it reverted to *Lugansk* following Voroshilov's involvement in the plot to oust Khrushchev. In 1970, after the death of the now rehabilitated Voroshilov, it again became *Voroshilovgrad*, and kept this name until 1989, when it once more reverted to the original. The Ukrainian form of the name is *Luhans'k*.

Lugo. *Town, northwestern Spain.* The town's name represents the first word of its Roman name, *Lucus Augusti*, "sacred wood of *Augustus*," referring to one or other of the Roman emperors so named.

Luján. *City, eastern Argentina.* The city, near Buenos Aires, is named for the Spanish conquistador Pedro *Luján*, who died here in 1536 in a battle with the Native Americans.

Luleå. *City and port, northern Sweden.* The city takes its name from that of the *Lule* River that enters the Gulf of Bothnia here, with Swedish *å*, "river," added.

Lund. *City, southwestern Sweden.* The city was founded in c.1020 by the Danish king Cnut (Canute), who is said to have named it for [1]*London*, England. But this is folk etymology, based on a spurious interpretation of its Medieval Latin name, *Londinum Gothorum*, "*Londinum* of the Goths." The first part of this is actually of Celtic origin and probably means "forest."

Lundy. *Island, southwestern England.* The Devonshire island, in the Bristol Channel, is famous for its puffins. Its name actually means "puffin island," from Old Norse *lundi*, "puffin," and *ey*, "island." Puffins still nest on the island.

Lüneburg. *City, northwestern Germany.* The city's name derives from that of a castle recorded in 956 as *Luniburc*, from Old High German *burg*, "fort," added to conjectural Old Saxon *hli-uni*, related to Old English *hlēo*, "refuge," "defense" (modern English *lee*).

Lünen. *City, western Germany.* The city, on the Lippe River, derives its name from conjectural Old Saxon *hliuni*, related to Old English *hlēo*, "defense." *Cp.* **Lüneburg.**

Lunéville. *City, northeastern France.* The city had the Medieval Latin name of *Lienatis villa* or *Lunivilla*, and this gave the present name. The first part of the original name is of uncertain origin. It hardly represents French *lune*, "moon." The second evolved into the common French *ville*, "town."

Luni. *River, western India.* The river's name is a shortening of its Sanskrit name, *lāvaṇāvāri*, "salt river," referring to its excessive salinity.

Lurgan. *Town, east central Northern Ireland.* The town, in Co. Armagh, has a name representing Irish *An Lorgain*, "the strip of land." The name is found fairly commonly elsewhere in Ireland.

Lusaka. *Capital of Zambia.* The city was founded by Europeans in 1905 and named for *Lusaakas*, headman of a nearby village.

Lusatia. *Historic region, eastern Germany.* The region, centered on the Neisse and upper Spree rivers, is named for a Slav people, the *Lusizi*, their own name based on Old Sorbian *lug*, "meadow." They were thus the "meadow dwellers." The German name of the region is *Lausitz*.

Lü-shun. *City and port, northeastern China.* The city, in Liaoning province, and now part of the conurbation of *Lü-ta* (*see* **Dairen**), derives its name from Chinese *lü*, "to travel," and *shùn*, "along." Its was formerly familiar as *Port Arthur*, so named for one Lieutenant *Arthur*, an English naval officer who reconnoitered the site at the time of its founding as a British naval base in 1857 during the Anglo-French war against China. This name was actually given in 1860 by Arthur's commanding officer, Rear Admiral Sir Michael Seymour.

Lusitania. *Historic region, southwestern Europe*. The region, corresponding approximately to modern Portugal and western Spain, is named for the *Lusitani*, the people who once lived here. Their own name is of uncertain origin, but has been linked with the Celtic personal name *Luso* or with the Ligurian god *Lugus* whose name also lies behind those of **Carlisle** and **Lyons** (and **Liguria** itself).

Lü-ta *see* **Dairen**

Luton. *Town, southeastern England*. The Bedfordshire town has an Old English name meaning "settlement on the *Lea*," this being the river on which Luton stands.

Lutsk. *City, northwestern Ukraine*. The city takes its name from Slavic *luka*, "river bend," referring to its location on a bend of the Styr River.

Luxembourg. *Grand duchy, western Europe*. The small country, bounded by Belgium, France, and Germany, derives its name from Germanic *luttila*, "little," and *burg*, "fort," "castle," originally that of its capital city, which grew up from the 10th century around the castle on the rocky promontory here. The present form of the name evolved through Medieval Latin *Luciliburgum*. The name is also that of the adjacent province of *Luxembourg*, Belgium, while the German form of the grand duchy's name is *Luxemburg* and the Luxemburgian *Letzebuerg*.

Luxor. *Town, northern Egypt*. The name of the ancient town, on the Nile, is a corruption of Arabic *al-ḳuṣūr*, "the palaces," from the plural of *ḳaṣr*, itself from Latin *castrum*, "camp," for the various temples here. There are also remains of Roman camps.

Luzon. *Island, northern Philippines*. The chief and largest island of the Philippines is said to derive its name from *losong*, a local word for a pestle for pounding rice. But this may be simply an attempt to find a meaning for an otherwise obscure name.

Lvov. *City, western Ukraine*. The city was founded in the mid–13th century by Prince Daniil Romanovich of Galicia, who is said to have named it for his son, *Lev* (Leo). The German name of the city is *Lemberg*, and the Ukrainian *L'viv*. The city's canting coat of arms

depicts a lion (Slavic *lev*) and a castle, the latter alluding to the second half of the German name.

Lyallpur *see* **Faisalabad**

Lycaonia. *Historic region, southern Turkey*. The ancient region of Anatolia traditionally derives its name from *Lycaon*, the legendary king of Arcadia in Greek mythology.

Lycia. *Historic region, southwestern Turkey*. The name of the region is that of its indigenous people, the *Lycians* or *Luka*, whose own name may have derived from an ancestor, himself called "wolf" (Greek *lukos*.)

Lydia. *Historic region, western Turkey*. The name is said to derive from one *Ludos*, the supposed ancestor of the *Lydian* people. In the Bible, the people known as *Ludim* (Genesis 10:13), the Hebrew name for the Lydians, are said to be the descendants of Mizraim (Egypt), and thus of Ham, second son of Noah, although *Lud* (Genesis 10:22) is said to be the son of Shem, Noah's first son. There also appears to be some cross-identity between the *Ludim* and the *Lubim*, or Libyans (*see* **Libya**), and the Libyans and Lydians are mentioned together (Jeremiah 46:9), as Libya and Lydia are (Ezekiel 30:5).

Lynchburg. *City, eastern United States*. The Virginia city arose from a ferry landing on the James River, settled in 1757. It was named for John *Lynch*, the ferry owner and operator of the original site.

Lynn. *City, northeastern United States*. The Massachusetts city was settled in 1629 and originally known as *Saugus*. It was reorganized as a town in 1631 and in 1637 renamed for *Lynn Regis*, now **King's Lynn**, England, where the Revd. Samuel Whiting, first minister of Lynn, had been a curate.

Lyonnais. *Historic region, southeastern France*. The former province took its name from its capital, **Lyons**, of which *Lyonnais* is the adjectival form.

Lyons. *City, southeastern France*. The Roman name of the city was *Lugdunum*, representing its Gaulish name *Lugdunu*. The last part of this means "fort." The first part may derive from the god *Lugus* who also gave the name of **Carlisle**, England. The French form of the name has no final *s*. In 1793, at the time of the French Revolution, Lyons was renamed *Ville-Affranchie*, "enfranchized town," as it was "freed" that year by revolutionary troops after an uprising by the citizenry.

Lytham St. Anne's. *Town and resort, northwestern England*. The compound name is the result of the amalgamation in 1922 of the two Lancashire towns of *Lytham* and *St. Anne's*. The first name represents Old English or Old Norse *hlithum*, the dative plural of *hlith* or *hlith*, "slope," probably referring to the coastal sand dunes here. The second name is that of the town's parish church, which was the first building to be erected when it began to develop in the late 19th century.

Lyttelton. *Town and port, southeastern New Zealand.* The town, in eastern South Island, was laid out in 1849 and originally known as *Port Cooper*. In 1858 it was renamed as now for Lord George William *Lyttelton* (1817–1876), a founder of the Canterbury Association, the English pastoral company formed to settle land in New Zealand. *Lyttelton* was originally planned as a name for **Christchurch**. It is a coincidentally appropriate name for a new settlement that begins as a "little town."

Lyubertsy. *City, western Russia.* The city is said to take its name from a personal name *Libor* or *Lyubor*, presumably that of its founder or an early landowner here, southeast of Moscow.

Ma'ale Adumim. *City, south central West Bank.* The city arose as an Israeli settlement founded in 1975 in the Judaean Wilderness, east of Jerusalem. Its Hebrew name means "red ascent," referring to the route from the Jordan valley to Jerusalem, where the rocks are of a reddish color. The border area between the tribes of Judah and Benjamin is described in Joshua 15.

Ma'ale Hahamisha. *Kibbutz, eastern Israel.* The kibbutz, in the Judaean Highlands, has a Hebrew name meaning "ascent of the five," referring to its five founders, murdered by Arabs in 1938, the year of its foundation.

Maarianhamina. *Town and port, southwestern Finland.* The town, known in Swedish as *Mariehamn*, on the island of Ahvenanmaa (Åland), was founded in 1861 by Alexander II, czar of Russia, and named "*Maria*'s harbor" for his wife, *Maria* Alexandrovna (died 1880).

Maas *see* **Meuse**

Maassluis. *Town, southwestern Netherlands.* The town, on the New Waterway, the canal running from the New *Maas* River, derives its name from the latter (*see* **Meuse**) and Dutch *sluis*, "sluice."

Maastricht. *Town, southeastern Netherlands.* The first part of the town's name refers to its location on the *Maas* River (*see* **Meuse**). The second part evolved from Latin *trajectus*, "crossing," referring to the ford here in Roman times.

McAllen. *City, southern United States.* The Texas city was founded in 1905 and named for John *McAllen*, a Scottish settler who had built a ranch here.

Macao *see* **Macau**

McArthur. *River, northern Australia.* The river, in Northern Territory, was discovered in 1845 by the explorer Ludwig Leichhardt who named it for the sheep ranchers James and William *McArthur*.

Macau. *Administrative region, southern China.* The name of the former Portuguese overseas territory is a Portuguese corruption of South Chinese *ama*, the name of a patron goddess of sailors, and *ngao*, "bay," "port." The official Chinese name of Macau is *Aomin*, from *ào* (pronounced *ngao* in the south), "bay," and *mén*, "door," "gate," describing its location at the head of the Pearl River estuary. The name is also spelled *Macao* in the West.

MacCarthy Island. *Island, central Gambia.* The island, on the Gambia River, was originally known as *Lemain Island*. It was renamed as now for Sir Charles *MacCarthy* (1770–1824), British colonial governor of Sierra Leone.

Macclesfield. *Town, northwestern England.* The name of the Cheshire town means "*Maccel*'s open land," with the Anglo-Saxon personal name followed by Old English *feld*, "open land" (modern *field*). The land in question was probably at one time part of the forest that existed here in the Peak District.

M'Clure Strait. *Strait, northern Canada.* The strait, in the Northwest Territories between Banks Island and Queen Elizabeth Islands, is named for Robert *M'Clure* (1807–1873), the British explorer who led a search here for the missing members of Franklin's expedition (*see* **Franklin**) in 1850–54.

MacDonnell Ranges. *Mountain system, central Australia.* The mountains, in Northern Territory, were visited in 1860 by the Scottish explorer John McDouall Stuart and named for Sir Richard *MacDonnell* (1814–1881), governor of South Australia (which formerly included Northern Territory).

Macedonia. *Republic, southern Europe.* The name of the ancient region of the Balkan Peninsula is popularly linked with the mythological *Macedon*, son of the Greek god Zeus. Its actual origin may be in Greek *makednos*, literally "tail," referring to the raised terrain here. Some authorities, however, derive the name from Illyrian *maketia*, "cattle," with reference to the pastures here. *Macedonia* is also the name of the neighboring region of northern Greece, divided into the prefectures of *Eastern Macedonia and Thrace* (*see* **Thrace**), *Central Macedonia*, and *Western Macedonia*.

Macerata. *City, central Italy.* The city derives

its name from Medieval Latin *Vicus Maceratae*, "settlement of the ruins," from Latin *maceria*, "wall," referring to the ruins of the Roman town of *Helvia Recina*, by which it arose in the 10th and 11th centuries.

Macgillycuddy's Reeks. *Mountain range, southwestern Ireland.* The range, in Co. Kerry, was a place of refuge for the powerful sept (tribal division) of the *Mac Gillycuddys*, whose descendant still bears the title *Mac Gillicuddy of the Reeks*. *Reeks* is a variant of English *ricks*, meaning "ridges."

Machilipatnam. *City and port, southeastern India.* The city, in Andhra Pradesh state, and the first British settlement (1611) on the Bay of Bengal, has a Sanskrit name meaning "town of fish."

Machu Picchu. *Historic city, south central Peru.* The ruined city of the Incas has a name of Quechua origin, from *machu*, "old man," and *pikchu*, "peak." The city stands on high cliffs in the Andes.

Macías Nguema Bijogo *see* **Bioko**

Mackay. *City and port, northeastern Australia.* The Queensland city was founded in 1862 and named for Captain John *MacKay* (1838–1914), who had explored the region in 1860.

McKeesport. *City, eastern United States.* The Pennsylvania city, at the junction of the Monongahela and Youghiogheny rivers, was settled in c.1775 by David *McKee*, a ferry operator, and laid out in 1795 by his son John.

Mackenzie. *River, northwestern Canada.* Canada's longest river, in the Northwest Territories, is named for the Scottish fur trader and explorer Sir Alexander *Mackenzie* (1764–1820), who discovered it and led an expedition down it in 1789. He also gave the name of the *Mackenzie Mountains*, a northern extension of the Rocky Mountains to the west of the river.

McKinley, Mt. *Mountain, northwestern United States.* The Alaska mountain, North America's highest peak, was so named in 1896 by the prospector William A. Dickey in honor of William *McKinley* (1843–1901), elected 25th president of the United States that year. Its Native American name is *Denali* ("the great one"), and the Russians knew it simply as *Bolshaya Gora* ("big mountain"). There was a strong lobby in the mid–1970s to restore the indigenous name.

McMurdo Sound. *Bay, Antarctica.* The bay, a western extension of Ross Sea, was discovered in 1841 by the Scottish explorer James Clark Ross, who named it for one of his officers, Archibald *McMurdo*, Scottish captain of the research ship *Terror*.

Macon. *City, southeastern United States.* The

Georgia city was laid out in 1823 and named for Nathaniel *Macon* (1757–1837), North Carolina senator and Revolutionary patriot.

Mâcon. *City, east central France.* The city's name ultimately goes back to the Ligurian root word *mat*, "mountain," with the Ligurian suffix *-asco*. The current form of the name evolved from the city's Roman name of *Matisco*, genitive *Matisconis*. Mâcon lies in the Saône valley on the eastern edge of the Massif Central.

Macquarie, Lake. *Lake, southeastern Australia.* The lake, in New South Wales, is named for Lachlan *Macquarie* (1761–1824), Scottishborn governor of New South Wales from 1809 to 1821.

Ma'daba. *Town, west central Jordan.* The ancient city, mentioned in the Bible as *Medeba* (Joshua 13:16, etc.), has a name of uncertain origin. A meaning "flowing water" has been suggested.

Madagascar. *Island republic, western Indian Ocean.* The island, off the east coast of Africa, takes its name from the Somali capital **Mogadishu.** The name was first recorded in the 13th century by Marco Polo, who instead of applying it to the eastern Somali coast, where it properly belonged, took it to be the name of the island. He did so because, when noting the name in its original Arabic, he translated the word *jazīra* as "island," whereas it can actually mean either "island" or "peninsula." When the Portuguese explorer Diego Dias discovered Madagascar on August 10, 1500, St. *Laurence*'s Day, he named it accordingly *São Lourenço*. The island now had two names: one given by Dias, the other recorded by Marco. When the duplication was discovered in 1531 it was Marco's name that was preferred. There has never been an indigenous Malagasy name for Madagascar, but only local names for different parts of the island. From 1960 through 1975 the official name of Madagascar was *Malagasy Republic*, from an early (corrupt) form of the island name.

Madeira. *Island group, eastern Atlantic.* The group, west of northwestern Africa, forms an administrative district of Portugal and takes its name from Portuguese *madeiro*, "log," "wood" (related to English *material*), since the largest island here is (or was) covered in trees.

Madhubani. *Town, northeastern India.* The town, in Bihar state, derives its name from Sanskrit *madhu*, "honey," and *banī*, "forest," referring to the wild honey found in nearby forests.

Madhya Pradesh. *State, central India.* The state's name describes its geographical location in India, from Sanskrit *madhya*, "center," "middle," and *pradesh*, "state."

Madinah 'Isa. *Town, north central Bahrain.* The town was laid out in the early 1960s and named for Sheikh '*Isa* ibn Salman al-Khalifah, then ruler of Bahrain. (His forebear, Ahmad al-Khalifah, ousted the Persians in 1783, and he himself was succeeded on his death in 1999 by his son, Sheikh Hamad ibn '*Isa* al-Khalifah, who assumed the title of king in 2002.) *Madīna* is the Arabic word for "city."

Madinat ash-Sha'b. *Town, southern Yemen.* The suburb of Aden was founded in 1959 as the capital of the Federation of South Arabia and was originally named *al-Ittihad*, from Arabic *ittiḥād*, "unity." It was given its present name, meaning "city of the people," after Yemen (Aden) was founded in 1967.

Madinat as-Sadat. *City, northern Egypt.* The industrial city began to be built in the early 1980s and has a name meaning "city of *Sadat*," from Arabic *madīna*, "city," and the name of Anwar el-*Sadat* (1918–1981), president of Egypt from 1970 to his assassination.

Madison. *City, northern United States.* The state capital of Wisconsin was founded in 1836 and named commemoratively in the year of his death for James *Madison* (1751–1836), 4th president of the United States.

Madras *see* **Chennai**

Madre de Dios. *River, southeastern Peru.* The river, a tributary of the Amazon, was named by Spanish explorers *Río Madre de Dios*, "Mother of God river," in honor of the Virgin Mary.

Madrid. *Capital of Spain.* The city's name is of uncertain origin. Some authorities derive it from Latin *materia*, "materials," in allusion to the timber originally used for building here. Others prefer a source in Latin *matrix, matricis*, "river bed," with the present spelling evolving under Arabic influence. However, Madrid is not on a major river, but on the small Manzanares, and the town originated from a small Moorish fort on a bluff above this river, rather than by its bed. The fort's earliest mention, dated A.D. 932, names it as *Majerit*.

Madura. *Island, southern Indonesia.* The island, off the northeast coast of Java, derives its name from Sanskrit *madhura*, "gentle," "calm" (literally "honeyed"). The reference is presumably to the mild climate. *Cp.* **Madurai**.

Madurai. *City, southern India.* The city, in Tamil Nadu state, derives its name from Sanskrit *madhura*, "gentle," "calm," presumably in the same sense as for **Madura**. The name was spelled identically to that of the island until 1949.

Maebashi. *City, central Japan.* The city, in the island of Honshu, has a name meaning "before the bridge," from Japanese *mae*, "before," and *hashi*, "bridge."

Mafeking *see* **Mafikeng**

Mafeteng. *Town, southwestern Lesotho.* The name is said to mean either "place of crossing," referring to the original town site by a crossing of the Caledon River, or, when the town was transferred to its present site in 1874, "place of single women," referring to the unmarried daughters of a local chief.

Mafikeng. *Town, northern South Africa.* The town, in North-West province, has a name of Tswana origin meaning "place of rocks," from *mafika*, the plural of *lefika*, "rock," "cliff," and *-eng*, "place of." The name was long familiar in the corrupt form *Mafeking*, introduced by British colonists (perhaps by association with *king*). In 1994 Mafikeng combined with the new town of **Mmabatho** as capital of the new North-West province.

Magadan. *City and port, northeastern Russia.* The city, on the Sea of Okhotsk, arose in the 1930s. Despite its recent history, the origin of its name remains obscure. A source in Evenki *mongodan*, "alluvium," has been proposed. It could also be based on an Evenki personal name, such as *Magda*.

Magdala. *Historic town, northwestern Israel.* The biblical town (Matthew 15:39, etc.), which gave the name of Mary *Magdalene*, has a name of Aramaic origin, from *magdala'*, "tower." The present Hebrew name of Magdala is *Migdal*.

Magdalena. *River, north central Colombia.* The river was discovered by the Spanish explorer Rodrigo Galbán de Bastidas on July 22, 1502, the feastday of St. Mary *Magdalene*, and is named for it.

Magdeburg. *City, east central Germany.* The city, first mentioned in 805 as *Magathaburg*, is apparently named for a woman called *Magda*, although her identity is uncertain. She may have been a local landowner. Her name, meaning "maid," could alternately allude to an unnamed pagan goddess. The city's coat of arms has displayed a maid (*Magd*) above a fortress (*Burg*) since the 13th century.

Magellan, Strait of. *Strait, southern South America.* The strait between the mainland of South America and the archipelago of Tierra del Fuego was discovered in 1520 by the Portuguese navigator Fernão de Magalhães (Ferdinand *Magellan*) (c.1480–1521) and is named for him.

Magenta. *Town, northern Italy.* The town takes its name from the Roman general and emperor Marcus Aurelius Valerius *Maxentius* (died 312), who had his headquarters here.

Maggiore, Lake. *Lake, central Europe.* Italy's second largest lake, its northern end in Switzerland, has an Italian name meaning "greatest." The reference is to its size by comparison with the nearby Como and Lugano lakes (or according to some, Orta and Varese lakes). Lake Maggiore's Roman name was *Verbanus Lacus*, based on an original name of uncertain origin. (It does not derive from Latin *verbenae*, "sacred boughs.") Hence its alternate Italian name *Verbano*. *Cp.* **Verbania**.

Maghnia. *Town, northwestern Algeria.* The town is named for Lalla *Maghnia*, a local (female) Muslim saint, whose mausoleum is here.

Maghreb. *Region, northwestern Africa.* The name of the region that includes Morocco, Algeria, and Tunisia, as well as the *Maghreb* Desert, represents Arabic *maġrib*, from *ġarb*, "west," describing its general location.

Magnesia. *Historic region, eastern Greece.* The name comes from the *Magnetes*, a people who formerly inhabited the region. Their own name is of uncertain origin.

Magnitogorsk. *City, western Russia.* The city arose in 1930 by Mt. *Magnitnaya* (Russian, *Magnitnaya gora*, "magnetic mountain"), and is named for it. The mountain has a rich stock of magnetite (magnetic iron ore), and the city is Russia's largest iron and steel plant.

Mahabaleshwar. *Town, west central India.* The town, a health resort in Maharashtra state, has a name meaning "(place of the) god of great power," from Sanskrit *mahā*, "big," "great," *bal*, "strength," "power," and *īshvar*, "god," a name of the Hindu god Shiva. The town was also known as *Malcompeth*, for the Scottish administrator in India, Sir John *Malcolm* (1769–1833), who founded it in 1829.

Mahajanga. *Town and port, northwestern Madagascar.* The town's Malagasy name may mean "healing one," referring to the curative waters of the Betsiboka River here. The name was formerly familiar in the form *Majunga*.

Mahanadi. *River, central India.* The river's name means simply "great river," from Sanskrit *mahā*, "big," "great," and *nadī*, "river."

Maharashtra. *State, west central India.* India's third largest state has a Sanskrit name, apparently from *mahā*, "big," "great," and *rāṣṭra*, "kingdom," "empire." However, the meaning could also be "*Mahar* kingdom," from the name of the largest scheduled caste ("untouchables") here before the arrival of the Maratha (Mahratta)

in the 17th century. The name is first recorded in the 7th century.

Mahaweli Ganga. *River, Sri Lanka.* Sri Lanka's longest river has a Sinhalese name meaning "great sandy river," from *maha*, "great," *weli*, "sand," and *ganga*, "river" (*cp.* **Ganges**).

Mahe. *Town, southwestern India.* When the coastal town, in Pondicherry Union Territory, was captured by the French in 1726, they altered its indigenous name of *Mayyali* to *Mahé* in honor of Bertrand François *Mahé*, comte de la Bourdonnais, who also gave the name of **Mahé**.

Mahé. *Island, western Indian Ocean.* The main island of the Seychelles was so named in 1742 by the French ship's captain Lazare Picault in honor of Bertrand François *Mahé*, comte de la Bourdonnais (1699–1753), commander of the French royal navy. *See also* **Seychelles**.

Mahébourg. *Town and port, southeastern Mauritius.* The former capital of Mauritius is named for Bertrand François *Mahé*, comte de la Bourdonnais (1699–1753), governor of Mauritius from 1735 to 1740. *Cp.* **Mahé**.

Mahón. *Town and port, Balearic Islands.* The capital of Minorca had the Roman name *Portus Magonis*, "port of *Mago*," for the Carthaginian general *Mago* (died c.203 B.C.), brother of Hannibal. The name was long familiar in its English form of *Port Mahon* and French form of *Port-Mahon* before finally dropping the *Port*. The Catalan form of the name is *Maó*.

Maidenhead. *Town, southern England.* The former Berkshire town is on the Thames River and has a name traditionally interpreted as "maidens' landing place," the *-head* representing Old English *hȳth*. The name does not necessarily imply that young women landed their boats here. It was probably simply the place where they regularly met.

Maidstone. *Town, southeastern England.* The Kent town has a name that probably means what it says, "maidens' stone," implying a stone of some kind, such as a boundary marker, where young women and girls regularly met. However, the first part of the name may represent Old English *mǣgth*, "folk," "people," not *mægth*, "maid," in which case the stone would have been a general assembly point. Support for this origin lies in the historic status of Maidstone as the capital of western Kent.

Main. *River, western Germany.* The river, a tributary of the Rhine, had the Roman name of *Moenis* or *Moenus*, probably from an Old European root word *moin*, meaning simply "water."

[1]**Maine.** *Historic region, northwestern France.* The former province takes its name from the

river that flows through it. The river's own name may be of Gaulish origin, from *magio*, "big," although it could equally have come from the people here, the *Cenomani* (who gave the name of **Le Mans**).

²**Maine**. *State, northeastern United States.* The state is usually said to be so called because it was originally referred to as "the *main land*" for distinction from the many offshore islands here. However, it is more likely to have been named for the French province of ²**Maine**. The precise reasons for the adoption of this name are uncertain, but it is known that early French explorers referred to the region west of the Kennebec River here as *Maine*, while the region to the east was *Acadie* (*see* **Acadia**).

Mainz. *City and river port, western Germany.* The city had the Roman name of *Mogontiacum* or (according to Tacitus) *Moguntiacum*. This is thought to derive from the personal name *Mogontios*, that of either a local landowner or a Gaulish god. The present name is a much reduced form of the original. French speakers know the city as *Mayence*.

Maitland. *City, southeastern Australia.* The city, in New South Wales, was founded as a convict settlement in 1818 and was at first named successively as *The Camp*, *Molly Morgan Plains*, and *Wallis Plains*. A second town was surveyed in 1829 to the east of Wallis Plains and was called *Maitland*, later *East Maitland*. Wallis Plains was renamed *West Maitland* in 1835. The present name was adopted in 1944 when these and other towns here were united as a single city. The name appears to honor Lieutenant General Sir Peregrine *Maitland* (1777–1854), British colonial governor in Upper Canada.

Majorca. *Island, western Mediterranean Sea.* The largest of the Balearic Islands derives its name from Latin *major*, "greater." The Spanish form of the name is *Mallorca*. *Cp.* **Minorca**.

Makarska. *Town, southern Croatia.* The town, on the Dalmatian coast, has a name that may derive from a Slavic word meaning "damp," "wet" (Serbo-Croat *mokar*).

Makeyevka. *City, southeastern Ukraine.* The city takes its name from a coalmine here in the 18th century owned by one *Makeyev* (or according to some sources a Scot named *Mackay*). The original name of the town, from 1898 through 1931, was *Dmitriyevsk*. The Ukrainian form of the name is *Makiyivka*.

Makhachkala. *City and port, southwestern Russia.* The capital of Dagestan, on the Caspian Sea, takes its name from *Makhach*, the nickname (a pet form of *Mahomet*) of the Dagestani revolutionary leader *Mahomet*-Ali Dakhadayev (1882–1918), with -*kala* the Armenian word for "fort," "settlement." Before 1922 the town was known as *Petrovsk-Port*, for the fort said to have been built here by *Peter* the Great. Dakhadayev set up the local Soviet government here, but was killed in the Civil War.

Makkah *see* **Mecca**

Makó. *City, southeastern Hungary.* The city is named for the soldier to whom the original village here was granted by King Endre II in the 13th century.

Makran. *Region, southeastern Iran.* The coastal region, a former province, has a name of uncertain origin. According to one theory, it derives from Iranian *māhī*, "fish," and *khvārān*, "eater," the "fish eaters" perhaps being identified with the *Ichthyophagoi* mentioned in 2d-century A.D. Greek texts. According to another, it represents Iranian *māh kerān*, from *māh*, "capital," "chief town," and *kerān*, "shore," "coast."

Malabar Coast. *Region, southwestern India.* The region derives its name from a combination of Tamil *malay*, "mountain" (*cp.* **Malaya**), and Iranian *barr*, "continent."

Malabo. *Capital of Equatorial Guinea.* The town and port derives its name from that of *Malabo* (died 1937), king of the Bubi. He was one of the two sons of Moka, whose other son, *Bioko*, gave the name of **Bioko**, the island on which Malabo is located. The town was founded in 1827 by the English vice admiral William F. Owen, who named it *Port Clarence*, for the Duke of *Clarence* (1765–1837), the future king William IV. In 1843 the island, then known as *Fernando Po*, passed to the Spanish, who renamed the town *Santa Isabel*, "St. Elizabeth," for Queen *Isabella* II of Spain (1830–1904). The town was given its present name in 1973.

Malacca, Strait of. *Strait, Southeast Asia.* The channel between the Malay Peninsula and the Indonesian island of Sumatra takes its name from a region of southwestern peninsular Malaysia. Its own name may derive either from Sanskrit *mahā*, "great," and *laṅkā*, "island" (*cp.* **Sri Lanka**), or from Malay *melaka*, "emblic," a tree of the spurge family, found widely here. The city of *Melaka* (formerly *Malacca*), West Malaysia, on the Strait of Malacca, was founded in 1400.

Maladeta. *Mountain, northeastern Spain.* The mountain, in the Pyrenees near the French border, derives its name from the pre–Indoeuropean root elements *mala* and *dikta*, both meaning "mountain" (*cp.* **Malaya**). The present form of the name has been influenced by Latin *maledictus*, "cursed," as if referring to hostile mountain terrain. The Spanish name of the massif here is accordingly *Montes Malditos* and the French *Monts Maudits*, conveying this very meaning.

Málaga. *City and port, southern Spain.* The city, a leading resort, has a name of Phoenician origin, from *malaka*, "queen," referring to its prime location, today in the center of the Costa del Sol.

Malakoff. *Town, northern France.* The town, now a suburb of Paris, takes its name from the Russian village of *Malakhov*, in the Crimea, which was captured by the French in 1855 during the Crimean War. The direct source of the name was an inn called *À la tour de Malakoff*, "at (the sign of) the Malakoff Tower," referring to a tower that was destroyed in 1870 during the siege of Paris. The Russian *Malakhov* bears the surname of some noted (or notorious) local person, perhaps a sailor who set up a tavern there.

Malatya. *City, east central Turkey.* The name evolved from the city's Roman name of *Melitene*, itself from a Hittite original *Milid*, of unknown origin.

Malawi. *Republic, southeastern Africa.* The country takes its name from its indigenous people, who are known to have inhabited the region since the 14th century. Their own name means "flames," perhaps referring to the reflection of the rays of the rising sun in the waters of Lake Malawi here. From 1893 through 1907 the country was known as the *British Central Africa Protectorate*, and from 1907 through 1964 *Nyasaland*, for Lake *Nyasa*, the alternate name of Lake Malawi, as the Swahili word simply meaning "lake."

Malaya. *Peninsula, Southeast Asia.* The western and continental part of Malaysia has a name that probably derives from Tamil *malay*, "mountain," referring to one of the region's most distinctive natural features. *See also* **Malaysia**.

Malaysia. *Federation, Southeast Asia.* The name was devised in the early 19th century by British geographers for the Malayan archipelago as a whole, with *-sia* added to *Malay* to form a classical-style name (like **Andalusia**) that happened to suggest the archipelago's location in Asia. The name now properly applies to the federation that comprises territory in the southern half of the Malay Peninsula (*West Malaysia*) and the northwestern part of the island of Borneo (*East Malaysia*).

Malbork. *City, northern Poland.* The medieval town arose on the site of a Prussian estate named for its castle of *Marienburg*, "Mary's fortress," itself founded in 1274 by the Teutonic Knights,

whose patron saint was the Virgin *Mary* (*cp.* **Kwidzyn**). This remains the city's German name today.

Malchen. *Mountain, western Germany.* The highest peak in the Bergstrasse, near Bensheim, derives its name from Old High German *malsc*, "proud," "towering." It is also known as the *Melibocus*, a Latin name misapplied by the Alsatian humanist Beatus Rhenanus (1485–1547) from Ptolemy's name *Melibokon oros* for the Harz mountains. This Greek-looking name probably derives from Germanic *melith*, "honey," and Old High German *buoh*, "wood," i.e. "wood where bees swarm."

Malden. *City, northeastern United States.* The Massachusetts city was settled in 1640 and was originally known as *Mystic Side*, for the *Mystic* River here. In 1649 it was incorporated and named in honor of Joseph Hills, speaker of the Massachusetts House of Deputies, who was a native of the English town of **Maldon**, Essex.

Maldives. *Island republic, northern Indian Ocean.* The islands probably take their name from Sanskrit *mālādvīpa*, "garland of islands," from *mālā*, "garland," and *dvīpa*, "island." Some authorities, however, derive the first part of the name from Tamil *malay*, "mountain," as for **Malaya**. The islands themselves are not mountainous, but were formed from a submerged volcanic mountain range.

Maldon. *Town, southeastern England.* The Essex town has a name meaning "hill with a cross," from Old English *mǣl*, "cross," and *dūn*, "hill." The Anglo-Saxons probably erected a cross or crucifix for religious services on the commanding site where All Saints church now stands.

Mali. *Republic, western Africa.* The name was originally that of a larger empire here, itself extinct from the 17th century. It may derive from the *Malinke*, an indigenous people here, or else come from a Mande (Malinke) word meaning "hippopotamus." The Malinke themselves derive their name from Mande *ma*, "mother," and *dink*, "child," i.e. "child of the mother," alluding to the matrilinear descent of Malinke families.

Malines *see* **Mechelen**

Malmédy. *Town, eastern Belgium.* The town's name was recorded in 648 as *Malmundarium*. The origin of this is disputed, but it probably derives from a Germanic personal name *Malamund*, that of the original landowner here.

Malmö. *City and port, southeastern Sweden.* As it stands, the name derives from Swedish *malm*, "ore," and *ö*, "island," although the latter word is really an alteration of earlier *haug*, "mound." The reference is to the sandpiles originally here when the town arose in the 12th century or earlier.

Malta. *Island republic, central Mediterranean Sea.* The island's name goes back to what was probably a pre–Indoeuropean root element *mel*, "high," referring to its rocks. The classical Greek name of Malta was *Melitē*, represented by the biblical *Melita*, where St. Paul landed (Acts 28:1). Hence an alternate proposed origin in Greek *melitta*, a form of *melissa*, "bee," "honey." Malta was formerly well known for its production of honey.

Malvern Hills. *Hills, west central England.* The hills, between southwestern Worcestershire and eastern Herefordshire, are near enough to the border with Wales to have a Welsh name. It means "bare hill," from *moel*, "bare," and *bryn*, "hill." The name has passed to the town of *Great Malvern*, village of *Little Malvern*, and district of Great Malvern known as *Malvern Link*. The second word of this last represents Old English *hlinc*, "ridge."

Malvinas *see* **Falkland Islands**

Malwa Plains. *Plains, northern India.* The plains are named for the *Malloi* peoples, who ruled the Punjab in the 4th century B.C.

Malwa Plateau. *Plateau, central India.* The plateau's name is a form of Sanskrit *mālav*, a term meaning "part of the abode of Lakshmi," referring to the Hindu goddess of wealth.

Man, Isle of. *Island, Irish Sea.* The island, midway between England and Ireland, is traditionally said to derive its name from the Irish sea god *Manannán mac Lir*, but it is likely his name came from that of the island, not the other way around. The name is properly of Gaelic origin and means "mountain," referring to the mountainous mass that culminates in Snaefell in the center of the island. (*Cp. Môn*, as the Welsh name of **Anglesey**, the island that lies due south of Man.) The Manx name of Man is *Ellan Vannan*, where *ellan* is "island" and *Vannan* the mutated form of *Mannan*. The Romans knew Man as *Mona*, a name that they may have unconsciously but correctly associated with Latin *mons*, "mountain." Man is a dependency of the British Crown but is not part of the United Kingdom.

Manabí. *Province, western Ecuador.* The name is said to derive from Guaraní *panambi*, "butterfly."

Manado. *City and port, central Indonesia.* The city, in northeastern Sulawesi, is so called for the indigenous people of this name who came to settle here from the Sangihe Islands, to the north. The meaning of their own name is uncertain.

The name also has the form *Menado*, especially locally.

Managua. *Capital of Nicaragua.* The city takes its name from Lake *Managua*, its own name coming from Guaraní *ama*, "rain," and *nagua*, "spirit," "ghost," alluding to its tutelary deity.

Manama. *Capital of Bahrain.* The name is Arabic in origin, from *al-manāma*, "the place of rest," "the place of dreams," from *al*, "the," and *manāma*, "dream."

Manapouri, Lake. *Lake, southern New Zealand.* New Zealand's deepest lake, in southeastern South Island, derives its name from a Maori word meaning "lake of the sorrowing heart." According to legend, its waters are the tears of dying sisters.

Manatí. *Town, north central Puerto Rico.* The town, on the coastal lowlands, takes its name from the *manatee*, the aquatic animal frequently found in Caribbean coastal waters.

Manaus. *City and river port, northwestern Brazil.* The city, on the Rio Negro, takes its name from the *Manáos*, a Native American people formerly here. The meaning of their name is uncertain.

Manche. *Department, northwestern France.* The department has a coastline on the English Channel, known to the French as *La Manche*, "the sleeve," for its narrowing profile, and is named for it.

[1]**Manchester.** *City, northwestern England.* The city was originally a Roman station, as is indicated by the *-chester*, from Old English *ceaster*, a borrowing from Latin *castrum*, "camp." The actual Roman name of the station was *Mamucium*, itself probably from Celtic *mamma*, "breast," alluding to the rounded hill on which the Roman fort was built. This gave the initial *Man-* of the name. The adjective *Mancunian*, meaning "of Manchester," seems to have arisen from a miscopying of the Roman name as *Mancunium*.

[2]**Manchester.** *City, northeastern United States.* The New Hampshire city was settled in 1722 and at first known as *Old Harry's Town*. After 1735 it became *Tyngstown*, when it was granted to Captain William *Tyng* by the Massachusetts Bay Colony. In 1751 it was incorporated as the town of *Derryfield*. It developed when one of America's first textile mills was built here in 1805, and was renamed as now in 1810, apparently at the suggestion of local merchant Samuel Blodget, who had admired the barge canals at [1]**Manchester**, England, and who constructed the first canal around the Amoskeag Falls here.

Manchuria. *Region, northeastern China.* The name derives from that of the region's indigenous people, the *Manchu.* Their own name is the Manchu word for "pure." When under Japanese domination, from 1932 through 1945, Manchuria was known as *Manchukuo,* "Manchu land," from Chinese *mǎnzhōu,* "Manchu," and *guó,* "land."

Mandalay. *City, central Myanmar.* The former Burmese capital derives its name from Sanskrit *maṇḍala,* "circle," "disk," "mandala." Mandalay is an important center of Buddhism, a religion in which the mandala is a circular symbol representing the evolution and involution of the universe.

Manfredonia. *Town, east central Italy.* The town was founded in c.1260 by *Manfred* (c.1232–1266), king of Naples and Sicily, and is named for him.

Mangalore. *City and port, southwestern India.* The city, in Karnataka state, derives its name from Sanskrit *maṅgala,* "happiness," "good fortune," and *pur,* "town." The form of the name appears to have been influenced by the name of **Bangalore,** due east of it.

Mangochi. *Town, south central Malawi.* The town arose in 1891 as a military post on Lake Malawi named *Fort Johnston,* for Sir Harry Hamilton *Johnston* (1858–1927), commissioner of Nyasaland (present Malawi). The present name, adopted in 1964, is that of the chief who held authority here at the time when the town was founded.

Manhattan. *Island, eastern United States.* The island, administratively a borough of New York City, derives its name from that of the Native American people who once inhabited it. Their own name has been variously explained. Two possibly anecdotal interpretations are "place of drunkenness" or "place where we were cheated," referring to alleged incidents here. In the former, Henry Hudson, of the **Hudson** River, held a reception in 1609 on board ship for a delegation of Native Americans. In the latter, land was purchased in 1610 from the Native Americans here for an absurdly low sum.

Manila. *Capital of the Philippines.* The city's name is said to represent Tagalog *may,* "there is," and *nila,* the indigenous name of a shrub of the indigo family.

Manipur. *State, northeastern India.* The name derives from that of the state's indigenous people. Their own name is of uncertain origin.

Manisa. *City, western Turkey.* The city's present name derives from its classical Greek name of *Magnesia,* from the *Magnetes,* the people who are thought to have been its first inhabitants. *See also* **Magnesia.**

Manitoba. *Province, central Canada.* The province takes its name from the lake here, itself named for one of its islands. The island's name in turn derives from Algonquian *manitou,* "great spirit."

Mannheim. *City, southwestern Germany.* The city, first mentioned in 764 as *Manninheim,* takes its name from the Old German personal name *Manno* and Old High German *heim,* "house," "abode." The name as a whole thus means "abode of *Manno.*"

¹Mansfield. *Town, north central England.* The Nottinghamshire town takes the first part of its name from the *Maun* River, on which it lies, and the second part from Old English *feld,* "open land." The name of the source of the river was recorded in 1232 as *Mammesheved,* "headland of *Mamme.*" The first part of this probably refers to one of the rounded sandstone hills nearby, from the same Celtic word *mamma,* "breast," that gave the name of ¹**Manchester.** The hill thus gave the name of the river.

²Mansfield. *City, northern United States.* The Ohio city was laid out in 1808 and named for Jared *Mansfield,* surveyor general of the United States, who had been directed by President Jefferson to inspect this territory.

Mansura. *City, northeastern Egypt.* The city has an Arabic name, from *al-manṣūra,* "the victory," commemorating the battle of 1250 in which the Crusaders were defeated by the Mamelukes, with the capture of Louis IX of France (St. Louis). The name is also found as *El-Mansura.*

Mantiqueira Mountains. *Mountain range, eastern Brazil.* The mountains take their name from a Native American word meaning "place where the clouds lie."

Mantua. *City, northern Italy.* The city probably derives its name from that of *Mantus,* the Etruscan god of the underworld, mentioned by Dante in the *Divine Comedy* (*Inferno,* 20). The Italian form of the name is *Mantova.*

Manukau. *City, northern New Zealand.* New Zealand's third-largest city, in northern North Island, derives its name from Maori *manu,* "bird," and *kau,* "single."

Manzanares. *City, south central Spain.* The city derives its name from Spanish *manzanar,* "apple orchard."

Manzanillo. *City and port, eastern Cuba.* The name represents Spanish *manzanillo,* "manchineel," the tree *Hippomane mancinella,* native to the West Indies. Its milky sap is poisonous, giving rise to a belief that to sleep in its shade is to risk one's life. There is a town and port of the same name in southwestern Mexico.

Manzil Bu Ruqaybah. *Town, north central Tunisia.* The town was founded by the French in the 1880s and originally named *Ferryville*, for the French premier Jules François Camille *Ferry* (1832–1893), who actively encouraged French colonial expansion in Africa. In 1963 it was renamed as now for Habib ben Ali *Bourguiba* (1903–2000), Tunisia's first president. The first word of the name is Arabic *manzil*, "halting place." The name is also found in the form *Menzel Bourguiba.*

Manzini. *Town, central Swaziland.* The town was founded in 1890 with the Afrikaans name of *Bremersdorp*, "*Bremer*'s village," for Albert *Bremer*, a trader who had set up a store here in 1887. The present name was adopted in 1960 from *Manzini* Motsa, the local chief who held authority here.

Maputo. *Capital of Mozambique.* The city and port takes its name from that of the river which flows into the bay on which it lies. This was in turn named for one of the sons of the local chief Muagobe, here in the 18th century. Maputo developed around a Portuguese fortress built in 1787 and until 1976 was known as *Lourenço Marques*, for the Portuguese trader who first explored the region in 1544.

Mar, Serro do. *Mountain range, southern Brazil.* The range has a Portuguese name meaning "mountain range of the sea." The mountains descend abruptly to the Atlantic here.

Maracaibo. *City and port, northwestern Venezuela.* The city takes its name from the lake here, itself so named by the Spanish conquistador Alonso de Hojeda for the cacique (Native American chief) whom he met here in 1499. The city's original Spanish name, when founded in 1571, was *Nueva Zamora*, "new *Zamora*," for **Zamora**, Spain.

Marajó. *Island, northeastern Brazil.* The island has a name that refers to its location in the Amazon delta, from Guaraní *para*, "river," and *jho*, "to go out." *Cp.* **Maranhão.**

Maranhão. *State, northeastern Brazil.* The state is named for the island off its north coast on which its capital of **São Luís** lies. The island is now also called *São Luís*, but earlier had a name of Guaraní origin, from *para*, "river," *na*, "parent," and *jho*, "to go out," which evolved to the current form. *Cp.* **Marajó.**

Marathon. *Historic town, southeastern Greece.* The town was named for the nearby plain, with its own name coming from Greek *marathron*, "fennel," a plant that grew abundantly here.

Marburg. *City, central Germany.* The city arose in the 12th century around a fortress (*burg*) belonging to the margraves of Thuringia. Its name is a shortened form of *Marbachburg*, from the *Marbach*, a stream here whose own name means "border stream," from Old High German *marca*, "border," and *bach*, "stream," the border itself being that of the margraves' territory.

Marches, The. *Region, central Italy.* The Italian name of the region is *le Marche*, "the borders," referring to the three provinces at the border of the Holy Roman Empire into which it was divided in the 10th century. The same basic word is found elsewhere for a border territory, such as the historic region of *Marche* in central France, bordering Aquitaine, and the so-called *Welsh Marches*, the border country between England and Wales. The word itself derives from an Indoeuropean base *marg*, "border," found also in modern English *margin* and *mark*. *Cp.* **Denmark.**

Mar del Plata. *City, eastern Argentina.* The coastal city had its beginnings in 1746 as the Spanish mission station of *Nuestra Señora del Pilar*, "Our Lady of the Pillar," for the cathedral of this dedication in Saragossa, Spain, where the Virgin Mary is said to have appeared in A.D. 40 standing on a pillar erected in honor of St. James. The mission station was abandoned in 1751 and in 1856 a fishing village arose here with the name *La Peregrina*, "the pilgrim." The town that developed took the name of the region, Spanish for "sea of the *Plata*," i.e. the River *Plate* (*see* **La Plata**), further up the coast.

Marechal Deodoro. *Town, northeastern Brazil.* The town, originally called **Alagoas**, for the state of which it was formerly the capital, was renamed as now in 1939 for *Marshal* Manuel *Deodoro* da Fonseca (1827–1892), Brazil's first president.

Margarita Island. *Island, northern Venezuela.* The island, in the Caribbean north of (and belonging to) Venezuela, is famous for its pearls. Hence its name, from Spanish *margarita*, "pearl."

Margate. *Town and resort, southeastern England.* The name of the coastal town in Kent means literally "gate by the pool," from Old English *mere*, "sea," "pool," and *geat*, "gate," "gap." The reference is to a gap in the cliffs here by a pool that today no longer exists.

Margherita, Mt. *Mountain, central Africa.* The highest summit of the Ruwenzori Range, on the border between Uganda and the Democratic Republic of Congo, was first climbed in 1906 by an expedition of the Italian mountaineer

Luigi Amedeo, duca d'Abruzzi, and was named for Queen *Margherita* of Italy (1851–1926), wife of Umberto I.

Margilan. *City, eastern Uzbekistan*. The city is one of the oldest in the Fergana Valley, dating back to at least the 8th century. The origin of its name is unknown.

Margit Island. *Island, north central Hungary*. The island, in the Danube River at Budapest, is named for St. *Margaret* of Hungary (1242–1270), daughter of King Béla IV, who had lived in a convent here. Her short life was due to her self-imposed duties and disciplines.

Mariana. *City, eastern Brazil*. The city, at first known as *Vila de Albuquerque* (*see* **Albuquerque**) and *Vila de Carmo*, received its present name (initially in the spelling *Marianna*) in 1745 in honor of the archduchess *Marianna* of Austria, wife of John V of Portugal.

Mariana Islands. *Island group, western Pacific*. The islands were so named in 1668 by the Spanish (as *Islas Marianas*) in honor of Queen *Mariana* of Austria (1634–1696), widow of Philip IV of Spain. The name was given by Jesuits in place of the earlier Portuguese name *Islas dos Ladrões*, "islands of thieves," given by Magellan (from personal experience) on his discovery of the archipelago in 1521.

Mariánské Lázně. *Town and resort, western Czech Republic*. The town was a fashionable spa in the 18th and 19th centuries, when it was known by the German name of *Marienbad*. Both names have the same meaning, "*Mary*'s springs." The thermal springs had an image of the Virgin *Mary* at their entrance, but local people associated the name more readily with that of *Maria* Theresa (1717–1780), archduchess of Austria and queen of Hungary and Bohemia. *Cp.* **Františkovy Lázně**.

Mariazell. *Town, east central Austria*. The name of Austria's prime place of pilgrimage means "*Mary*'s cell," referring to the 12th-century wood carving of the Virgin *Mary* in the Gnaden Church.

Maribor. *City, northern Slovenia*. The city had the Old German name of *Marbachburg*, "fortress of the boundary stream," exactly as for **Marburg**. It arose in the 12th century around a fortress built by the margraves of Pettau on a stream marking the border of their territory. The present form of the name has been influenced by Slavic *bor*, "pine forest."

Marie Byrd Land. *Region, Antarctica*. The region, between the Ross Ice Shelf and Ellsworth Land, was discovered in 1929 by the U.S. explorer Richard E. Byrd (1888–1957) and named by him for his wife, *Marie Byrd*, née Ames. The region is also known simply as *Byrd Land*.

Marie-Galante. *Island, Caribbean Sea*. The island, a dependency of Guadeloupe in the Lesser Antilles, was discovered in 1493 by Christopher Columbus, who named it for his flagship, the *Santa María*, nicknamed *Mariagalante* ("Gallant Mary").

Mari El. *Republic, western Russia*. The republic takes its name from the *Mari*, its indigenous Finno-Ugric people. Their own name, in their own language, means "person," "man." The second word of the name is Mari *el*, "territory."

Marienberg. *Town, east central Germany*. The town was founded in 1521 by Duke Henry the Good of Saxony as a mining (*berg*) settlement and placed under the protection of the Virgin *Mary*.

Mariental. *Town, south central Namibia*. The town was founded in 1912 by local German Lutheran missionaries, one of whom, Herman Brandt, named it "*Maria*'s valley," for his wife.

Marietta. *City, northern United States*. The Ohio city was founded in 1788 and named by General Rufus Putnam in honor of Queen *Marie Antoinette* of France (1755–1793), wife of Louis XVI, in token of her assistance in the American Revolution. (She would soon be executed in the French Revolution.)

Marijampolė. *City, southern Lithuania*. The city arose around a monastery in the 18th century and was originally called *Starapole*, "old field." This name was later modified to the present one, meaning "*Mary*'s field," for the dedication of the monastery to the Virgin *Mary*. From 1955 through 1989 the city was renamed *Kapsukas*, for the Lithuanian revolutionary leader Vincas Simanovič Mickēvičius-*Kapsukas* (1880–1935).

Mariscal Estigarribia. *Town, northwestern Paraguay*. The town was originally a military outpost called *López de Filippis*. In 1945 it was renamed as now for the Paraguayan general (Spanish *mariscal*, literally "marshal") José Félix *Estigarribia* (1888–1940), whose tactics in the Chaco war of 1932–35 established Paraguayan control over the region. He was president of Paraguay from 1930 to his death in an airplane crash.

Maritsa. *River, southeastern Europe*. The river, rising in Bulgaria and flowing south between Turkey and Greece into the Aegean Sea, derives its name from Thracian *mari*, "sea," "swamp."

Mariupol. *City and port, southeastern Ukraine*. The city was founded by Greek colonists in 1779 on the Sea of Azov and given a Greek name (as if *Mariopolis*) meaning "*Mary's* town," for the German princess *Maria* Fyodorovna (originally Sophia Dorothea of Württemberg), wife of the future (from 1796) emperor of Russia, Paul I. From 1948 through 1989 the city was known as *Zhdanov*, for the Soviet politician and Communist leader Andrei *Zhdanov* (1896–1948), who was born here.

Marj 'Uyun. *Town, southern Lebanon*. The town, on a fertile plain, has a name meaning "meadow of the springs," from Arabic *marj*, "meadow," and *'uyūn*, plural of *'ain*, "spring."

Marken. *Island, west central Netherlands*. The island, in the IJsselmeer, has a name meaning "borderland" (*cp*. **Marches**). It was separated from the mainland in the 13th century during the formation of the Zuider Zee but is now connected to it again by a breakwater.

Marks. *City, western Russia*. The city, on the Volga north of Saratov, was founded in 1767 as a settlement for German and Swiss immigrants by *Catherine* the Great (1729–1796) and was accordingly named *Yekaterinenshtadt* (German *Katharinenstadt*), "Catherine's town." (The Russian empress was herself of German origin.) It was also known as *Baronsk*, for the Dutch *Baron* de Beauregard who initiated the colony. In 1920 the city was renamed *Marksshtadt* (as if *Marxstadt*) for the German founder of Communism, Karl *Marx* (1818–1883). a name that "paired" with **Engels** south of Saratov. The German "town" suffix was dropped in 1941.

Marl. *City, western Germany*. The city was formed in 1900 through the amalgamation of a number mining communities on the site of a village recorded in 890 as *Meronhlara*, "mares' fold," from Old Saxon *meriha*, "mare," and Old High German *lār*, "pen," "fold." The present name is a contraction of this.

¹Marlborough. *Town, southern England*. The Wiltshire town has a name of disputed origin. Its second part is Old English *beorg*, "mound," "hill," not *burh*, "fort." The first part may be either the personal name *Mǣrla* or Old English *meargealla*, "gentian," the plant being grown for medicinal purposes. The mound in question is the one on which the castle was built.

²Marlborough. *Region, central New Zealand*. The former province, in northeastern South Island, takes its name from the English general John Churchill, 1st Duke of *Marlborough* (1650–1722), whose title came from **¹Marlborough**. The region's capital is **Blenheim**, named for the duke's great victory.

Marmara, Sea of. *Sea, northwestern Turkey*. The sea between the Bosporus and the Dard-

anelles takes its name from its island of *Marmara*. The island derives its own name from Greek *marmaros*, "marble," a stone which is still quarried here, together with granite and slate.

Marne. *River, northeastern France*. The river derives its name from Gaulish *matir*, "mother." The reference is probably to a "mother goddess" believed to dwell in its waters in ancient times.

Marondera. *Town, eastern Zimbabwe*. The town arose in 1890 and took its name from *Marondera*, a local chief of the Barozwi people. Until 1982 the name had the corrupt form *Marandellas*.

Maroua. *Town, northern Cameroon*. The town is named for a 19th-century Fulani chief.

Marquesas Islands. *Island group, South Pacific*. The islands, in French Polynesia, were discovered by the Spanish explorer Álvaro de Mendaña de Neira in 1595 and named by him *Islas Marquesas*, in honor of his uncle, the *Marquis* Antonio de Mendoza (c.1490–1552), viceroy of New Spain, who had financed his expedition.

Marrakesh. *City, west central Morocco*. The former Moroccan capital, founded in 1062, derives its name from a Berber word meaning "fortified." The name came to give that of **Morocco** itself.

Marsala. *Town and port, southern Italy*. The town, in western Sicily, has a name that is probably of Arabic origin, from *marsā-allah*, "port of *Allah*" (i.e. of God), or possibly *marsā-'ali*, "port of *Ali*." The town was founded by the Arabs in the 9th century on the ruins of the ancient city of *Lilybaeum*, itself founded by the Carthaginians in 397 B.C.

Marseilles. *City and port, southern France*. The city's present name has evolved from its original Greek name of *Massilia*. This is probably pre–Latin in origin, and may be based on the Ligurian root word *mas*, "spring." In 1793, at the time of the French Revolution, Marseilles was punished for its royalist allegiance by being renamed *Ville-sans-Nom*, "Town Without a Name" (which is even so a name). The *r* in the name may have come about through an association with *Mars*, the Roman god of war. The French form of the name has no final *s*.

Marshall. *City, southern United States*. The Texas city was founded in 1841 and named for John *Marshall* (1755–1835), fourth chief justice of the United States.

Marshall Islands. *Island group, western Pacific*. The islands were explored in 1788 by the British naval captains John *Marshall* and Thomas Gilbert (*see* **Kiribati**) and are named for the former. The group had already been sighted in 1529 by the Spanish navigator Álvaro Saavedra.

Martha's Vineyard. *Island, northeastern United States.* The island off Cape Cod, Massachusetts, was discovered by Gabriel Archer in 1602 and apparently named by him for a woman called *Martha* and for the *vines* he saw growing there. An alternate origin sees the name as a corruption of *Martin Wyngaard*, the name of a Dutch seaman.

Martin. *City, northwestern Slovakia.* The city is named for St. *Martin*, to whom its 13th-century church is dedicated.

Martinique. *Island, eastern West Indies.* The Caribbean island, an overseas department of France, has a name of uncertain origin. According to one account, when Columbus approached the island in 1493 he saw a group of women on the shore calling *"madinina!"* The meaning of this was not known, but it was taken to be the name of the island and as such was recorded on early charts, only to be subsequently corrupted to its present form under the influence of the name of St. *Martin*. Another account claims that Columbus visited the island on June 15, 1502, the feastday of St. *Martin*, and that he named the island from the saint. The indigenous name of the island is *Madiana*, said to mean "island of flowers," or (as the women called) *Madinina*, "fertile island with luxuriant vegetation."

Marusthali. *Desert region, northwestern India.* The region of the Great Indian Desert has a Sanskrit name meaning "land of the dead," referring both to its barrenness and to those who have perished here.

Mary. *City, southeastern Turkmenistan.* The city's name goes back to the 3rd century B.C., when *Antiochus* the Great, king of the Seleucid kingdom of Syria, founded here the fortified settlement of *Antiochia Margiana*, "boundary *Antioch*," so called to distinguish it from the biblical *Antioch*, now the Syrian city **Antakya**. This lengthy name was gradually smoothed to *Merv*. In 1884 the present town was built some 19 miles (30 km) away, adopting the old name, which in 1937 assumed its Turkic form.

Maryborough. *City, eastern Australia.* The Queensland city was founded in 1843 and named for the *Mary* River here, itself named for Lady *Mary* Fitzroy, née Lennox (died 1847), first wife of Sir Charles Fitzroy (1796–1858), governor of New South Wales (which then extended here) from 1846 to 1855.

Maryland. *State, eastern United States.* The original territory of the state was granted in 1632 by Charles I to George Calvert, Lord Baltimore, as a proprietary colony, and was named for Queen Henrietta *Maria* (1609–1669), Charles's wife.

Masan. *City, southeastern South Korea.* The name derives from Chinese *mǎ*, "horse," and *shān*, "mountain."

Mascara. *Town, northwestern Algeria.* The town was founded as a military garrison in 1701 and has an Arabic name meaning "mother of soldiers," from *umm*, "mother," and *'asker*, "army," "soldiers." The name is now often spelled *Mouaskar*.

Mascarene Islands. *Island group, western Indian Ocean.* The name is collective for the islands of Mauritius, Réunion, and Rodriguez. It derives from the Portuguese explorer Pedro de *Mascarenhas*, who discovered **Réunion** in c.1513.

Maseru. *Capital of Lesotho.* The city has a name representing Sesotho *maseru*, the plural of *leseru*, "red sandstone." The reference is to the rocky height where Commandant J.H. Bowker, high commissioner for South Africa, built his headquarters in 1869 when the former Basutoland (present Lesotho) was placed under his authority.

Mashhad. *City, northeastern Iran.* The city's name is a conflation of Iranian *mahal*, "place," and *shahādat*, "martyr." It was the place of martyrdom in 818 of Ali Reza, eighth Shi'ite imam, and is now a holy city and place of pilgrimage of Shi'ite Muslims. An alternate form of the name is *Meshed*.

Mashonaland. *Region, northeastern Zimbabwe.* The region, now divided into three provinces, takes its name from its indigenous *Mashona* or *Shona* people. Their own name is of uncertain origin, but according to one theory represents Zulu *tshona langa*, "sunset," i.e. "people of the east."

Massachusetts. *State, northeastern United States.* The state takes its name from the Algonquian people who originally inhabited this region, with their own name deriving from *mass-adchu-seuck*, "people of the big hill." The hill in question was actually the group of hills now known as the Blue Hills. The Pilgrim Fathers founded the Plymouth Colony here in 1620 and gave the indigenous name to the bay, from which it subsequently passed to the territory and state. The name is first recorded (without its final *s*) in 1614.

Massif Central. *Plateau, south central France.* The mountainous plateau has a name that refers both to its geographical location and to the masses of crystalline rocks that underlie it.

Masuria. *Region, northeastern Poland.* The

region derives its name from the personal name *Mazew*, presumably that of a landowner here. *See also* **Mazovia.**

Masvingo. *Town, south central Zimbabwe.* The town was founded in 1890 as a military post named *Fort Victoria*, for Queen *Victoria* (1819–1901). When Zimbabwe gained independence in 1980, it was renamed *Nyanda*, said to be the name of the wife of the legendary African leader Monomotapa. In 1982 the town adopted its present name, meaning "caves."

Matabeleland. *Region, western Zimbabwe.* The region takes its name from the *Matabele*, the people who inhabit it. Their name derives from *matebele*, a term applied by the Sotho-Tswana people to the invading Zulus, either because they sank down (*teba*) behind their large shields when fighting or from *thebe*, "shield," itself. (*Ma-* is a Sotho or Tswana plural noun prefix.) *See also* **KwaNdebele.**

Matadi. *City and river port, western Democratic Republic of Congo.* The city takes its name from a Kikongo word meaning "stone." The name has been associated with the Bantu nickname, *Bula Matari*, "breaker of stones," given the explorer H.M. Stanley for his orders to Africans to crush rocks on the banks of the Congo here when setting up a trading station in 1879.

Matamoros. *City, northeastern Mexico.* The city, near the mouth of the Rio Grande, was founded in 1700 as *San Juan de los Esteros*. "St. John of the estuary." It was renamed as now in 1851 in honor of the Mexican priest and patriot Mariano *Matamoros* (1770–1814), captured in battle and executed in Spain. The placename is formally prefixed with *Heroica*, "heroic (city)."

Matapan, Cape *see* **Taínaron, Cape**

Matapédia. *River, southeastern Canada.* The Quebec river has a Native American name meaning "joining of two rivers." The reference is to its confluence with the Restigouche.

Mátészalka. *Town, northeastern Hungary.* The name is of obscure origin.

Mathura. *City, north central India.* The city, in Uttar Pradesh state, where it is the reputed birthplace of the god Krishna, is said to have been originally called *Madhupura*, from *Madhu*, a demon who reigned here, and Hindi *purā*, "town." According to Hindu mythology, Lavan, Madhu's son and successor, was killed here by Shatrughna, son of king Dashrath of Ayodhya.

Mato Grosso. *Plateau, southwestern Brazil.* The name of the forested plateau, also that of a state, is Portuguese for "dense forest," from *mato*, "forest," "bush," and *grosso*, "thick," "dense."

Matopo Hills. *Hills, southwestern Zimbabwe.* The hills are associated with folklore and tradition, and are said to have been so named by the Ndebele king Mzilikazi with reference to their granite domes, which resembled the bald heads of the elders of his tribe. Hence their Ndebele name, *amaTobo*, "the bald heads."

Matsu. *Island group, East China Sea.* The islands, off the east coast of China (but belonging to Taiwan), derive their name from Chinese *mā*, "mother," and *zǔ*, "ancestor." The name refers to a legend about a girl who drowned in the ocean when looking for her father and who later appeared as a goddess to bless the fishermen.

Matsue. *City, southwestern Japan.* The city, near the Sea of Japan in the island of Honshu, has a name meaning "bay of pines," from Japanese *matsu*, "pine," and *e*, "bay."

Matsumoto. *City, central Japan.* The city, in the island of Honshu, derives its name from Japanese *matsu*, "pine," and *moto*, "origin," "source."

Matsusaka. *City, south central Japan.* The city, in the island of Honshu, derives its name from Japanese *matsu*, "pine," and *saka*, "slope."

Matsuyama. *City and port, southwestern Japan.* The city, in the island of Shikoku, derives its name from Japanese *matsu*, "pine," and *yama*, "mountain."

Matterhorn. *Mountain, central Europe.* The mountain, on the Swiss-Italian border, derives its name from German *Matte*, "meadow," "pastureland," and *Horn*, "horn," the latter referring to the curved outline of the mountain's peak, which is actually the end of a ridge. The French and Italian names of the mountain, respectively *Mont Cervin* and *Monte Cervino*, derive from Italian *cervino*, "cervine," "deer-like," comparing the peak similarly to a deer's curved antlers.

Maubeuge. *Town, northern France.* The town had the Medieval Latin name *Malbodium*, from the Germanic personal name *Malbold*.

Maui. *Island, Hawaii, United States.* Hawaii's second largest island is said to take its name from a Polynesian demigod.

Mauna Kea. *Volcano, southeastern Hawaii, United States.* The extinct volcano, in north central Hawaii Island, has a Hawaiian name meaning "white mountain," from *mauna*, "mountain," and *kea*, "white." Mauna Kea is often snow-capped. *Cp.* **Mauna Loa.**

Mauna Loa. *Volcano, southeastern Hawaii, United States.* The active volcano, in south central Hawaii Island, has a Hawaiian name meaning "long mountain," from *mauna*, "mountain," and *loa*, "long." *Cp.* **Mauna Kea.**

Mauretania *see* **Mauritania**

Mauritania. *Republic, northwestern Africa.* The country takes its name from the ancient region of *Mauretania*, its own name coming from the *Moors* who inhabited it. The Moors themselves derive their name either from Greek *mauros*, "dark," referring to the color of their skin, or from Punic *mahurim* or *mauharin*, "western," denoting the geographical region here. *Cp.* **Maghreb**.

Mauritius. *Island state, eastern Indian Ocean.* The island was discovered by the Portuguese in 1505 but settled by the Dutch in 1598, when they named it in honor of the future Prince of Orange, *Maurice* of Nassau (1567–1625), stadholder (governor) of the United Provinces of the Netherlands from 1584.

Mayenne. *Town, northwestern France.* The town takes its name from the river here. Its own name is probably either pre–Indoeuropean in origin, from a root element *med* found in river names, or from Gaulish *medios*, "middle," denoting the river's location between two others (the Sarthe and the Vilaine).

Maykop. *City, southwestern Russia.* The city, capital of the Adygei Republic, was founded in 1857 as a Russian fortress. Its name is said to represent an earlier Adygei form *Myekuape*, representing *miye*, "apple tree," *ko*, "valley," and *pe*, "river mouth," giving an overall sense "mouth of the apple tree valley." But some authorities prefer a less contrived origin in Turkic *may*, "oil," and *kopa*, "marsh," referring to a site where crude oil seeps up to the surface from below ground.

Maymyo. *Town, central Myanmar.* The town takes its name from a British army officer, Colonel (later Major General) James *May* (1837–1903), of the 5th Bengal Infantry, stationed here in 1886.

Mayo. *County, northwestern Ireland.* The county takes its name from the identically named village here. Its own name means "plain of the yew tree," as represented in its current Irish name of *Maigh Eo*. The village became important through its nearby abbey, which was founded in the 7th century and became a center of learning.

Mazandaran. *Province, northern Iran.* The province, bordering the Caspian Sea, has an Iranian name meaning "gate of *Mazan*," from the personal name *māzan* and *dar*, "gate."

Mazar-e Sharif. *City, northern Afghanistan.* The city's name means "tomb of the sharif," from Afghani *mazār*, "tomb," and *sharīf*, "sharif," the term for a descendant of Muhammad through his daughter Fatima. (The word itself is Arabic in origin, meaning "noble," "illustrious.") The

reference is to the reputed discovery here of the tomb of the caliph Ali, Muhammad's son-in-law.

Mazatlán. *City and port, western Mexico.* The city and resort has a Nahuatl name meaning "place of the deer."

Mazkeret Batya. *Village, western Israel.* The Jewish village was founded in 1883 and sponsored by the French philanthropist Baron Edmond de Rothschild, who gave it a Hebrew name meaning "in memory of *Batya*," for his Viennese mother, *Betty* (1805–1886), who married his father (her uncle), James Rothschild, when she was 17.

Mazovia. *Historic region, eastern Poland.* The region derives its name from the personal name *Mazew*, presumably that of a landowner here at some time. **Masuria** has the same origin.

Mazra'a el-Qabaliya. *Village, central West Bank.* The Arab village has an Arabic name meaning "southern hamlet," from *mazra'a*, "hamlet," and *kibli*, "southern."

Mazra'a el-Sharqiya. *Village, central West Bank.* The Arab village has an Arabic name meaning "eastern hamlet," from *mazra'a*, "hamlet," and *sharki*, "eastern."

Mbabane. *Capital of Swaziland.* The city takes its name from the river on which it lies. The river's own name is said to represent *lubabe*, the local word for a type of shrub used for animal fodder.

Mbandaka. *City, northwestern Democratic Republic of Congo.* The city probably takes its name from a local chief who held authority here before it became a colonial administrative center in 1886. Its earlier name, until 1966, was *Coquilhatville*, for Camille-Aimé *Coquilhat* (1853–1892), Belgian governor of Congo Free State from 1891 to 1892.

Mbanza Congo. *Town, northwestern Angola.* The town, capital of the Congo kingdom from the 16th through 18th centuries, has a name that relates to this status, meaning "city of the Congo." The name was recorded as *Ambassa Congo* in 1490 by Portuguese missionaries, who in c.1530 renamed their settlement here *São Salvador do Congo*, "St. Savior of the Congo." The present name dates from 1980.

Mbuji-Mayi. *City, south central Democratic Republic of Congo.* The city has a Swahili name meaning "water goat," alluding to some local legend. Until 1966 it was known as *Bakwanga*, an ethnic name derived from that of the *Kwango* River in the southwest of the country.

McAllen. Names in *Mc*- (or *M'*-) are entered as if spelled *Mac*-.

Mdina. *Town, west central Malta.* The ancient town derives its name from Arabic *madīna,* "town," "city." *Cp.* **Medina.**

Mead, Lake. *Reservoir, southwestern United States.* The reservoir, formed by the Hoover Dam on the Arizona-Nevada border, is named for Elwood *Mead* (1858–1936), reclamation commissioner from 1924 to his death.

Meath. *County, eastern Ireland.* The name represents the county's Irish name of *An Mhí,* "the middle." Meath was the fifth and final province of Ireland to be established, and the name refers to its historic location between the provinces of Ulster to the north, Connacht to the west, and Leinster to the south. (The other province was Munster, in the south of the country.) Its territory was more extensive than today, and included what is now the county of **Westmeath.**

Meaux. *Town, northern France.* The town takes its name from the *Meldi,* the Celtic people who formerly inhabited the region. Their own name has been related to the Greek roots *mel,* "sweet," "pleasing," and *dol,* "valley," "winding river," presumably alluding to the Marne River, which forms a wide loop here.

Mecca. *City, western Saudi Arabia.* The city's name has been traced back to a Phoenician word *maqaq,* "ruined," although some authorities favor an origin in Arabic *maḥrāb,* "sanctuary," referring to an ancient place of worship which with the rise of Islam in the 7th century became a Muslim shrine. Mecca was the birthplace of Muhammad, and is the holiest city of Islam. The name is now spelled *Makkah* on many maps.

Mechelen. *City, northern Belgium.* The city derives its name from Old High German *mahal,* "meeting place," "place of judgement," referring to its former status as a center for the dispensation of justice, rather like an Anglo-Saxon moot in England. The alternate English form of the name is *Mechlin,* and its French form is *Malines.*

Mecklenburg. *Historic region, northeastern Germany.* The region derives its name from that of a castle here, its own name comprising Old High German *michil,* "great," and *burg,* "fortress." There was a fortified Germanic territory here by the Baltic coast before the 7th century, at which time it was occupied by Slav peoples who had themselves replaced earlier Germanic peoples. The castle name is first recorded in 995 as *Michelenburg,* translating the earlier Slavic name *Wiligrad,* from Old Slavonic *velij,* "great," and *grad,* "fort."

Medan. *City, western Indonesia.* The name of the city, in northeastern Sumatra, is an abbreviated form of Malay *medan perang,* "field of bat-

tle." The reference is to a conflict here between the Muslim kingdom of Aceh and the neighboring kingdom of Deli.

Médéa. *Town, north central Algeria.* The town had the Roman name of *Lamida,* of uncertain origin, and the present name evolved from this, as if from Latin *medius,* "middle," referring to a supposed location between two other places.

Medellín. *City, northwestern Colombia.* The city was founded in 1675 and named for the village of *Medellín* in southwestern Spain.

¹Medford. *City, northwestern United States.* The Massachusetts city was founded in 1630 along the Mystic River and given a name implying "middle ford."

²Medford. *City, western United States.* The Oregon city was founded in 1883 on Bear Creek, in the Rogue River valley, and named for **¹Medford,** Massachusetts, the meaning being equally appropriate.

Media. *Historic region, northwestern Iran.* The region is named for its indigenous people, the *Medes.* Their own name is said to come from that of *Medos,* their first king.

Medicine Hat. *City, southwestern Canada.* The Alberta city arose as a police post in 1882 and is said to take its name from an incident in which a cowardly Cree *medicine* man lost his *hat* after fleeing from Blackfoot warriors. But the actual origin may more prosaic, albeit involving a medicine man and his headdress.

Medina. *City, western Saudi Arabia.* The second holiest city in Islam (after Mecca) derives its name from Arabic *al-madīna,* meaning "the city." This is a short form of one of its formal names, *madīnat an-nabi,* "city of the Prophet," or *madīnat rasūl allāh,* "city of the messenger of Allah," in each case referring to Muhammad, whose tomb is here. The city's pre–Islamic name was *Yathrib,* mentioned in the Koran (33:14).

Medinat as-Sadat. *City, northern Egypt.* The new town, between Cairo and Alexandria, has an Arabic name meaning "city of *Sadat,*" for the Egyptian president Anwar el-*Sadat* (1918–1981).

Medinat Sitta Uktuber. *City, northern Egypt.* The new town, near the Giza pyramids, has an Arabic name meaning "city of the 6th of October," commemorating the assassination of Egyptian president Anwar el-Sadat on *October 6,* 1981.

Mediterranean Sea. *Sea between Europe, Asia, and Africa.* The name derives from Latin *Mediterraneum mare,* "sea in the middle of the land," referring to its geographical location, where it is virtually enclosed by the three continents mentioned. The Romans also knew it as *Mare inter-*

num, "inner sea," and *Mare nostrum*, "our sea,"
as it lay at the heart of the Roman empire. Many
languages translate the Latin name into the vernacular, such as German *Mittelmeer*, but the
Turkish name for the Mediterranean is *Akdeniz*,
"white sea," as opposed to *Karadeniz*, the **Black
Sea**. Arabic names for the sea include *al-bahr al-
mutawassiṭ*, "the middle sea," *al-bahr ar-rūm*,
"the sea of Rome," and, as for the Turks, *al-bahr
al-abyaḍ*, "the white sea."

Medvednica. *Mountain region, central Croatia*. The name means "bear mountain," from
Serbian *medved*, "bear."

Medvezhyegorsk. *Town and port, northwestern Russia*. The Karelian town arose on the site
of a village called *Medvezhya Gora*, "bear mountain," presumably alluding to the bears formerly
here. The Finnish name of the town is
Karhumäki, from *karhu*, "bear," and *mäki*, "hill."

Medway. *River, southeastern England*. The
river, in the county of Kent, has a pre–English
name probably meaning "middle water" (rather
than "middle way"). It divides the county as it
flows through a broad gap in the North Downs,
so that those who live east of it are traditionally
known as *Men of Kent*, while those to the west
are *Kentishmen*.

Megalopolis. *City, central Greece*. The now
relatively small town, in the central Pelopon-
nesus, bears the name of what was once a a huge
city founded in the 4th century B.C. and populated by the wholesale plantation of the inhabitants of over 40 villages. Hence its name, Greek
for "big city."

Meghalaya. *State, northeastern India*. The
state derives its name from Sanskrit *megha*,
"cloud," and *ālaya*, "stay." The region is notorious for its lengthy rain season.

Meilen. *Town, northern Switzerland*. The
name evolved from *Mediolanum*, that of the
Roman settlement here, itself of Gaulish origin
and meaning "middle of the plain," exactly as
for **Milan**.

Meiningen. *City, central Germany*. The city,
first mentioned in 982, has a name meaning
"(settlement of) *Megino*'s people."

Meissen. *City, southeastern Germany*. The city,
on the Elbe River, was founded in 929 by Henry
of Saxony as a defensive settlement and apparently takes its name from a nearby stream now
known as the *Meisabach*. Its own name is probably of pre–Slavic origin but unknown meaning.

Meknès. *City, north central Morocco*. The city
takes its name from the *Miknassa* Berbers, who
founded it in the 10th century as *Meknassa ez-
Zeitoun*, "Meknès of the olives." Their own

name represents Arabic *miknās*, from the verb
kanasa, "to sweep," "to carry off."

Mekong. *River, Indochina*. The river, rising in
southern China, then flowing south through
Laos, Cambodia, and Vietnam to enter the
South China Sea, has a name of Thai origin,
representing *menam*, "river" (from *me*, "mother,"
and *nam*, "water"), and *khong*, "water," in other
words simply "river."

Melaka *see* **Malacca, Strait of**

Melanesia. *Island group, southwestern Pacific*.
The islands, north of Australia, have a name
meaning "black islands," created from Greek
melas, "black," and *nēsoi*, "islands." The reference is either to the dark landscapes or, more
likely, to the dark skins of most of the inhabitants. The name, of 19th-century origin, was
based on that of **Polynesia**.

[1]Melbourne. *City and port, southeastern Australia*. The capital of Victoria was so named in
1837 in honor of William Lamb, 2d Viscount
Melbourne (1779–1848), the British prime minister of the day. The statesman's aristocratic title
comes from the family seat at *Melbourne* Hall,
Derbyshire, England.

[2]Melbourne. *City, southeastern United States*.
The Florida city was settled in 1878 and is said
to have been named by its first postmaster, C.J.
Hector, for his native city of **[1]Melbourne**, Australia.

Melibocus *see* **Malchen**

Melilla. *Town, northeastern Morocco*. The
town, a Spanish possession, has a name based on
Berber *mell*, "white," presumably referring to the
color of the rocks here.

Melitopol. *City, southern Ukraine*. The city
arose in the early 19th century on the site of the
village of *Novo-Aleksandrovsk*. It was raised to
town status in 1841 and given a Greek-style name
meaning "honey town," from Greek *meli*,
"honey," and *polis*, "town." The name had been
intended for a new town here in the second half
of the 18th century, when such names were in
vogue, but it was never built. Melitopol is on
the *Molochnaya* ("milky") River, and it is possible the names were meant to interrelate, as if the
region were a sort of biblical "land flowing with
milk and honey."

Melo. *City, eastern Uruguay*. The city was
founded in 1795 as a Spanish military post and
was named for Pedro de *Melo* de Portugal y Vil-
lena (1733–1798), viceroy of the Río de la Plata
territory from 1795 to 1797.

Melos. *Island, southeastern Greece*. The most
southwesterly of the major islands in the
Cyclades is said to derive its name from Greek

mēlon, "apple." It was this island that gave the name of the famous statue of Aphrodite known as the Venus de *Milo.* The name is also spelled *Milos.*

Melun. *Town, northern France.* The present name of the town is a reduced and smoothed form of its Roman name, *Melodunum,* itself deriving from Gaulish *metelo,* "harvester," and *dunon,* "fort." *Cp.* **Meudon.** The town arose on an island between two branches of the Seine River.

¹**Melville Island.** *Island, northern Australia.* The island, in the Timor Sea north of Northern Territory, was sighted by Abel Tasman (*see* **Tasmania**) in 1644 and named in 1814 by Captain Phillip Parker King (*see* **King Sound**) in honor of Robert Saunders Dundas, 2d Viscount *Melville* (1771–1851), first lord of the Admiralty.

²**Melville Island.** *Island, northern Canada.* The island, one of the largest of the Parry Islands, divided between the Northwest Territories and Nunavut, was discovered in 1819 by Sir William Parry (*see* **Parry Islands**) and named for Robert Saunders Dundas, 2d Viscount *Melville* (1771–1851), first lord of the Admiralty.

Memmingen. *City, southern Germany.* The city, first mentioned in 1128, has a name meaning "(settlement of) *Mamo*'s people," with an Old German personal name.

¹**Memphis.** *Historic city, northern Egypt.* The name of the ruined city, capital of ancient Egypt, is a Greek form of its Egyptian name *Mennefer.* This means "his beauty," from *men,* "his," and *nefer,* "beauty." The reference is to the comeliness of the pharaoh Pepi I, reigning in the 24th century B.C. (The name of the 14th-century B.C. Egyptian queen *Nefertiti* similarly means "beauty has come.") Memphis appears once in the Bible under its familiar name (Hosea 9:6) but more often under its Hebrew name of *Noph* (Isaiah 19:13, etc.).

²**Memphis.** *City, east central United States.* The Tennessee city was so named in 1826 for the ancient Egyptian city of ¹**Memphis,** either to suggest a place of grandeur or because its location by the Mississippi River evoked that of its historic namesake on the Nile. The city has a coliseum shaped like an Egyptian pyramid as a tribute to its eponym.

Menai Strait. *Strait, northwestern Wales.* The sea channel between mainland Wales and the island of Anglesey has a Celtic name meaning "carrying," referring to its strong current. The original word has its equivalent in modern Welsh *men,* "wagon," "cart."

Menderes. *River, southwestern Turkey.* The

river, the Roman *Maeander* (from Greek *Maiandros*), has a name of obscure origin. The river's winding course gave the English verb *meander.*

Mendip Hills. *Hill range, southwestern England.* The first part of the name of the Somerset hills is apparently of Celtic origin and related to modern Welsh *mynydd,* "mountain," "hill." The second half may represent Old English *yppe,* "raised place," "hill."

Mendoza. *City, western Argentina.* The city was founded by Spanish colonists in c.1560 and named for Antonio de *Mendoza* (c.1490–1552), first viceroy of New Spain.

Menongue. *Town, southeastern Angola.* The name is that of a former chief here. The town was earlier known as *Serpa Pinto,* for the Portuguese explorer Alexandre Alberto da Rocha de *Serpa Pinto* (1846–1900). The original name was readopted in 1980.

Menton. *Town and resort, southeastern France.* The town has an ancient name deriving ultimately from a pre–Celtic root element *men,* meaning "rock." The present name happens to coincide with the French word for "chin," and it is popularly said to originate from this, as if referring to the promontory to the east of the town. (The actual reference is to the rocky amphitheater below which the town lies.)

Menzel Bourguiba *see* **Manzil Bu Ruqaybah**

Merano. *Town, northern Italy.* The town, first mentioned in 857 as *Mairania,* has a Germanic name, from *maran,* "moraine," referring to the landslide that buried the original Roman settlement here.

Merapi, Mt. *Mountain, southern Indonesia.* Indonesia's most active volcano, in the center of the island of Java, has a name meaning "mountain of fire."

Merced. *City, southwestern United States.* The California city was founded in 1872 and named for the *Nuestra Señora de la Merced* ("Our Lady of Mercy") River here.

Mercedes. *City, west central Argentina.* The city, founded in 1856 as *Fuerte Constitucional,* was renamed as now in 1861 in honor of its patroness, the *Virgen de la Merced* ("Virgin of Mercy").

Mercia. *Historic region, central England.* The Anglo-Saxon kingdom occupied territory between Wales to the west, Wessex to the south, and East Anglia to the east. It was thus peripheral from the point of view of the latter two. Hence its name, as a latinized form of Old English *Mierce,* "people of the border country," from *mearc,* "border." *Cp.* **Marches.**

¹**Mérida.** *Town, southwestern Spain.* The town's name represents the second part of its Roman name of *Augusta Emerita.* This means "completed by *Augustus,*" and commemorates the town's foundation in 25 B.C. by the emperor *Augustus.*

²**Mérida.** *City, southeastern Mexico.* The city was founded in 1542 and named for ¹**Mérida,** Spain.

³**Mérida.** *City, western Venezuela.* The city was founded in 1558 and named for ¹**Mérida,** Spain.

Meriden. *City, eastern United States.* The Connecticut city was settled in 1661 by Jonathan Gilbert, who named it for his English birthplace, *Meriden* Farm near Dorking, Surrey.

Meridian. *City, southern United States.* The Mississippi city was settled in 1854 at the junction of the Vickburg-Montgomery and the Mobile and Ohio railway lines and named by a settler who thought that *meridian* meant "junction." (He was probably thinking of *median,* as a junction is an intermediate point where two lines meet.)

Merioneth. *Historic county, western Wales.* The old county's name is more accurately represented by that of the corresponding present administrative district of *Meirionnydd.* This is based on the personal name *Meirion,* that of the son (or possibly grandson) of the 5th-century ruler Cunedda. The latter's name gave that of the present unitary authority of **Gwynedd,** in which the district lies. The name as a whole thus means "seat of *Meirion.*"

Merlo. *Town, eastern Argentina.* The town, west of Buenos Aires, was founded soon after the settlement of that city in 1580 and named for the local landowner, Francisco de *Merlo.*

Merrimack. *River, northeastern United States.* The river, in New Hampshire and Massachusetts, has an Algonquian name of uncertain meaning. Suggestions include "sturgeon," "catfish," "deep place," and "swift water."

Merseburg. *City, east central Germany.* The city's name is probably based on Old High German *meri,* "lake" (English *mere*), with Old High German *burg,* "fort," added. The name originally applied to a 9th-century frontier fortress by the Saale River, in which the "lake" was a pool or loop.

Mers el-Kébir. *Town and port, northwestern Algeria.* The town's name represents Arabic *al-marsā al-kabīr,* "the big port," from *al,* "the," *marsā,* "port" (*cp.* **Marsala**), and *kabīr,* "big."

Mersey. *River, northwestern England.* The name means "boundary river," from Old English *mǣre,* "boundary," and *ēa,* "river." The Mersey originally formed the boundary between the Anglo-Saxon kingdoms of Mercia and Northumbria, and later that between the counties of Cheshire and Lancashire. When the new county of Merseyside was formed in 1974, this historic link was broken overnight.

Merthyr Tydfil. *Town, southern Wales.* The town, south of the Brecon Beacons, has a name meaning "*Tydfil*'s burial place," from Welsh *merthyr,* "martyr," and the personal name *Tydfil,* that of a female saint, said to be the daughter of Brychan (who may have given the name of the **Brecon Beacons**). According to tradition Tydfil was murdered by pagans in the 5th century and buried here. The town's parish church is dedicated to her.

Merv *see* **Mary**

Merzig. *City, western Germany.* The city arose on the site of a Roman settlement recorded in 369 as *praedium Martiaticum,* "estate of *Martius,*" and the present name evolved from this.

Mesa. *City, southwestern United States.* The Arizona city has a Spanish name meaning "table," referring to the "tableland" site where it was founded in 1878.

Mesabi Range. *Range, northern United States.* The Minnesota iron range, the largest of three, has an Ojibwa name meaning "giant."

Meseta Central. *Plateau, southwestern Europe.* The plateau, in the Iberian Peninsula, derives its name from the diminutive form of Spanish and Portuguese *mesa,* "table."

Meshed *see* **Mashhad**

Mesopotamia. *Historic region, southwestern Asia.* The region, corresponding to the greater part of modern Iraq, has a name of Greek origin meaning "between the rivers," from *mesos,* "middle," and *potamos,* "river," referring to its location between the Tigris and the Euphrates. The name occurs in the Bible (Genesis 24:10), where the Hebrew original has *ʾăram nahărayim,* "land within the river," meaning the area within the bend of the Euphrates itself. *Mesopotamia* is also a region of northeastern Argentina between the Paraná and Uruguay rivers, while classical scholars at Oxford, England, dubbed a strip of land between the Cherwell and a branch of this river with the name.

Mesquite. *City, southern United States.* The Texas city was established in 1873 and named for the *mesquite* shrubs formerly here.

Messene. *Town, southwestern Greece.* The ancient town, in the southwestern Peloponnese, derives its name from Greek *mesos,* "middle," referring to its location in *Messenia,* of which it became the capital. It was Messene that gave the name of **Messina.**

Messina. *City and port, southern Italy.* The Sicilian port was so named in the 4th century A.D. by immigrants from the Greek city of **Messene** in the southwestern Peloponnese.

Metroland. *Region, southeastern England.* The name, with its connotations of middle-class respectability, was devised in 1915 by the *Metropolitan* Railway Company for the districts of its operation northwest of London in the counties of Middlesex, Hertfordshire, and Buckinghamshire.

Metz. *City, northeastern France.* The city's Roman name was *Mediomatricum*, from the *Mediomatrici*, the Gaulish people whose capital it was in Roman times. Their own name is usually said to mean "those living between the rivers," from Gaulish *medios*, "middle," and *matir*, "mother," the latter referring to the mother goddess who personified a Gaulish river, but a more plausible sense is "those of the median mothers," as if *Mediomateres*, referring to the mothers of the "world in the middle," i.e. between heaven and hell. The present name is essentially based on the first syllable of the long Roman name, which had already been shortened to *Mettis* in Medieval Latin.

Meudon. *City, northern France.* The city, now a suburb of Paris, was known to the Romans as *Meclodunum*, from Gaulish *metelo*, "harvester," and *dunon*, "fort." *Cp.* **Melun.**

Meuse. *River, western Europe.* The river, rising in France and flowing through Belgium and the Netherlands to the North Sea, probably derives its name from a Germanic word *mos*, "marsh" (modern English *moss*), referring to the low-lying terrain through which it runs. Its Dutch name is *Maas*, as for **Maastricht.** *See also* **Moselle.**

Mexicali. *City, northwestern Mexico.* The city is close to the border with California, USA. Hence its name, from *Mexi*co and *Cali*fornia, devised as a symbol of international friendship. *Cp.* **Calexico.**

Mexico. *Republic, southern North America.* The country's name is a smoothed-down Spanish rendering of the earlier Nahuatl name of its capital, now **Mexico City.** This was *Metztlixihtlico*, meaning either "in the middle of the moon," or "in the middle of the magueys" (a type of agave plant). The city was founded by the Aztecs in 1325 on an island in a lake that was itself called *Metztliatl*, from *metztli*, "moon," to whom the lake was dedicated as a goddess, and *atl*, "water." *See also* **New Mexico.**

Mexico City. *Capital of Mexico.* The city's name passed early to the country of which it has always been the capital (*see* **Mexico.**) Its Nahuatl name was *Tenochtitlán*, "(place of the) nopal rock," from *tetl*, "rock," and *nuchtli*, "nopal," a species of cactus that symbolized the heart of a human sacrifice to the sun god. According to legend, when the Aztecs arrived here they found a rock with a crevice out of which a nopal was growing. On the rock sat an eagle with a snake in its beak. The device of the rock and the nopal, with the eagle holding the snake, became the tribal totem of the Aztecs, and is today represented on the Mexican national flag. The city's present name dates from Spanish colonial times (16th century), with English *City* added to distinguish it from the country. The Spanish form of the name is *Méjico* or *México*.

Mezhdurechensk. *City, southern Russia.* The city is located at the point where the Usa River enters the Tom. Hence its name, meaning "between the rivers," from Russian *mezhdu*, "between," and a derivative of *reka*, "river." In classical terms the name equates exactly to **Mesopotamia.** (Russian *mezhdu* is actually related to Greek *mesos*.)

Mezőberény. *Town, southeastern Hungary.* The name derives from Hungarian *mező*, "field," and *Berény*, a tribal name.

Mezőcsát. *Town, northeastern Hungary.* The name derives from Hungarian *mező*, "field," and the personal name *Csát*.

Mezőhegyes. *Town, southeastern Hungary.* The name derives from Hungarian *mező*, "field," and *hegyes*, "hilly district."

Mezőkeresztes. *Village, northeastern Hungary.* The name derives from Hungarian *mező*, "field," and the personal name *Keresztes* (a former equivalent of the Latin name *Crucis*).

Mezőkovácsháza. *Town, southeastern Hungary.* The name derives from Hungarian *mező*, "field," and *Kovácsháza*, "Kovács' house," from the personal name *Kovács* ("smith") and *ház*, "house."

Mezőkövesd. *Town, northeastern Hungary.* The name derives from Hungarian *mező*, "field," and *kövesd*, "gravelly soil."

Mezőtúr. *Town, east central Hungary.* The name derives from Hungarian *mező*, "field," and *túr*, "aurochs" (a kind of wild ox, now extinct).

Mezzogiorno. *Region, southern Italy.* The region, roughly corresponding to the historic kingdom of Naples, has a name that is the Italian for "midday." Southern Italy generally is known as the *Mezzogiorno* because the sun is at its hottest there at midday. *Cp.* **Midi.**

Mhlambanyatsi. *Town, western Swaziland.* The name is that of the river here, itself meaning "place where buffaloes wallow."

Miami. *City, southeastern United States.* The Florida city and resort takes its name from that of a Native American people whose own name is of uncertain origin. It may derive from Ojibwa *oumaumeg*, "people of the peninsula."

Michigan. *State, northern United States.* The state takes its name from that of the lake here. Its own name is Algonquian, from *michaw*, "big," and *guma*, "lake." The name reflects that of the Great Lakes, of which Lake Michigan is the third largest.

Michoacán. *State, west central Mexico.* The state has an indigenous name meaning "land of fisheries." The name relates to the state's two large lakes, Chapala and Pátzcuaro, where fishermen use special lightweight nets known as butterfly nets.

Michurin. *City, eastern Bulgaria.* The city derives its present name from the Russian biologist and horticulturist Ivan *Michurin* (1855–1936). Prior to 1950 it was known as *Tsarevo*, apparently translating the Byzantine name *Vasiliko*, from Greek *basileus*, "king," although the Bulgarian form of this, *Bosilkovo*, could actually represent a Slavic word meaning "cornflower."

Michurinsk. *City, western Russia.* The city, founded in 1636, was originally known as *Kozlov*. It adopted its present name in 1932 in honor of the Russian horticulturist Ivan Vladimirovich *Michurin* (1855–1935), who lived, worked, and died here.

Micronesia. *Island group, western Pacific.* The name, based on that of **Polynesia**, was created in the early 19th century from Greek *mikros*, "small," and *nēsoi*, "islands." The islands are relatively small when compared to those of Melanesia to the south.

Middelburg. *Town, southwestern Netherlands.* The town's Dutch name meaning "middle town," referring to its central location on the former Walcheren Island.

Middlesbrough. *Town and port, northeastern England.* The town, on the Tees River, has an Old English name meaning "middle fortified place," from *midleste*, "middlemost," and *burh*, "fort." It is not certain in what way the fort was "middlemost." It is possible that "Middle" was originally the name of a region here, with the Tees as its northern boundary.

Middlesex. *Historic county, southeastern England.* The name of the county means "(land of the) Middle Saxons," meaning the ones between the East Saxons of **Essex** and the West Saxons of **Wessex**. The original territory was much larger than the county, and included the whole of London. *Cp.* **Sussex**.

[1]**Middletown**. *City, eastern United States.* The Connecticut city was settled in 1650 and so named for its location on the Connecticut River, *mid*way between the upstream towns and the river mouth.

[2]**Middletown**. *City, northern United States.* The Ohio city was founded in 1802 and named for its location *mid*way between Dayton and Cincinnati.

Middle West. *Region, north central United States.* The extensive region, also known as the *Midwest*, is so called because it lies *mid*way between the Appalachian and Rocky mountains in the *west*ern part of the United States.

Midi. *Region, southern France.* The region, usually known in English as "the south of France," has a French name meaning "midday," the time when the sun is at its hottest. *Cp.* **Mezzogiorno**.

[1]**Midland**. *City, northern United States.* The Michigan city arose in the 1830s and is named for its county, itself so called as it is approximately in the *middle* of the state.

[2]**Midland**. *City, southern United States.* The Texas city was founded in 1844 and named for its location *mid*way between El Paso and Fort Worth.

Midlands. *Region, central England.* The blanket name for the central counties of England has been in use since at least the 17th century, and refers to those regions that are geographically in the *middle* of the country. It is usually divided into *East Midlands* and *West Midlands*, the latter being the name of a former metropolitan county centered on Birmingham.

Midlothian. *Historic county, southeastern Scotland.* The county was so named as it lay between the counties of *East Lothian* and *West Lothian*. In many ways Midlothian is synonymous with Edinburgh, where Walter Scott's novel *The Heart of Midlothian* is set. *See also* **Lothian**.

Midway Islands. *Island group, central Pacific.* The two small islands are so named as they are located approximately *mid*way between America and Asia.

Midwest *see* **Middle West**

Mie. *District, south central Japan.* The name of the prefecture, in the island of Honshu, means "triple," from Japanese *mi*, "three," and *-e*, "-fold." The reference is to its three administrative divisions.

Miercurea-Ciuc. *City, east central Romania.* The city, formerly part of Hungary, derives its name from Romanian *mercuri*, "Wednesday," and the Hungarian personal name *Csík*, denoting a town with a weekly Wednesday market.

The identical Hungarian name is *Csíkszereda*, from *szerda*, "Wednesday."

Mikhaylovgrad *see* ¹**Montana**

Mikkeli. *Town, southeastern Finland*. The town, known in Swedish as *Sankt Michel*, is named for the dedication of its main church to St. *Michael*.

Milan. *City, northern Italy*. The city had the Roman name of *Mediolanum*, from Gaulish *medios*, "middle," and *lanu*, "plain," referring to its location in the broad plain of the Po River. The present name (in Italian, *Milano*) evolved as a worn-down form of this. *Cp.* **Meilen**.

Mildura. *City, southeastern Australia*. The city, in Victoria, derives its name from an Aboriginal word meaning "red earth."

Milford. *City, eastern United States*. The Connecticut city was settled in 1639 and is said to be named for the Welsh town of **Milford Haven** or the English town of *Milford*, Hampshire.

Milford Haven. *Town and port, southwestern Wales*. The Pembrokeshire town is named for the large natural harbor (haven), an inlet of St. George's Channel, on which it stands. The first word of the name represents Old Norse *melr*, "sandy bank," and *fjǫrthr*, "inlet," "fjord."

Milford Sound. *Inlet, southern New Zealand*. The inlet, in southwestern South Island, was named by a whaler in the 1820s for its resemblance to the natural harbor of **Milford Haven**, Wales.

Millau. *Town, southern France*. The town was known in the 11th century by the Old Provençal name of *Amigliauvo*. This represents the Roman personal name *Æmilius*.

Millville. *City, eastern United States*. The New Jersey city was first settled in the 1700s along the Maurice River and after being known as *Shingle Landing*, *Maurice River Bridge*, and *The Bridge*, finally gained its present name, referring to the many local *mills*.

Milos *see* **Melos**

Milton Keynes. *Town, south central England*. The former Buckinghamshire town, designated a New Town in 1967, takes its name from the original village here. The first word of the name means "middle farm." The second names Hugh de *Cahaignes*, who held land here in the 12th century. His name derives from *Cahaignes* or *Cahagnes*, in northern France.

Milwaukee. *City and lake port, northern United States*. The Wisconsin city, on Lake Michigan, takes its name from the river at the mouth of which it lies. The river's name is Algonquian in origin, perhaps meaning "good country," referring to the pastures here.

Minas. *City, southeastern Uruguay*. The city was founded in 1783 and has a Spanish name referring to the surrounding *mines*.

Minas Gerais. *State, eastern Brazil*. The name of the state is Portuguese for "general mines," referring to its important gold, diamond, and iron mines, the largest in the country.

Minatitlán. *City and river port, south central Mexico*. The city, founded in 1822, has a hybrid Spanish-Nahuatl name meaning "*Mina's* place," for Don Francisco Javier *Mina* (1789–1817), a Spanish guerrilla chief in Mexico.

Min Chiang. *River, eastern China*. The river, in Fukien province, derives its name from Chinese *mín*, an old name of Fukien, and *jiāng*, "river." An alternate English name is *Min River*. There is another river of the name in Szechuan province, central China, but there *Min* represents a different Chinese *mín*, the name of a mountain.

Mindanao. *Island, southern Philippines*. The name of the second-largest island of the Philippines is a Spanish contraction of its Malay name *Magindanau*, probably meaning "place by a lake" or "main lake."

Mindelo. *City and port, northwestern Cape Verde*. The city, Cape Verde's main port, is named for the Portuguese port of *Mindelo*. A former alternate name for the city is *Porto Grande*, "big harbor."

Minden. *City, northwestern Germany*. The city, on the Weser River, grew from a military bishopric founded by Charlemagne in 800. It derives its name from *Mime*, that of a water sprite.

Mindoro. *Island, west central Philippines*. The name of the mountainous island is said to be a contraction of Spanish *mina de oro*, "gold mine." But the island is not known for its gold, and the name may be a Spanish attempt to make a Malay name meaningful.

Mindszent. *Village, southern Hungary*. The name means "All Saints," from Hungarian *mind*, "all," and *szent*, "saint," describing the dedication of the village church.

Mineralnye Vody. *City, southwestern Russia*. The city is a spa on the northern edge of the Caucasus Mountains. Hence its name, Russian for "mineral waters."

Mingechaur. *City, central Azerbaijan*. The city, on the (now dammed) Kura River, has a name with various popular interpretations, such as "no way through" or "turn back," referring to the formerly impassable ravine of the Kura through the mountains here. A more likely origin is in the name of the Arab military commander *Minkojavar*, who invaded Transcaucasia in the 9th century.

Mingrelia. *Region, western Georgia*. The lowland region derives its name from Turkic *ming-reul*, "thousand springs."

Minneapolis. *City and river port, central United States*. The **Minnesota** city, incorporated in 1867, takes the first part of its name from its state and the second part from Greek *polis*, "city."

Minnesota. *State, northern United States*. The state takes its name from the river that flows through its southern part. The river's name itself derives from Sioux *minne*, "water," and *sota*, perhaps "cloudy," with reference to the drab color of the water from its reflection of gray skies.

Minorca. *Island, western Mediterranean*. The second largest of the Balearic Islands was known to the Romans as *Minorica*, a name based on Latin *minor*, "lesser," "smaller," the comparison being with larger **Majorca**. The Spanish form of the name is *Menorca*.

Minsk. *Capital of Belarus*. The city is probably so called from the river name *Men*, this being an earlier name of the Svisloch (or a section of it), on which Minsk stands. The origin of the river name itself is uncertain.

Miquelon *see* **St. Pierre and Miquelon**

Miqve Yisrael. *Settlement, western Israel*. Israel's oldest agricultural school for Jews was founded in 1870 with a Hebrew name meaning "hope of Israel." As for the names of many other settlements and towns, the reference is biblical, symbolizing the bond of early Jewish settlers: "O the hope of Israel, the saviour thereof in time of trouble, why shouldest thou be as a stranger in the land?" (Jeremiah 14:8).

Miraflores. *City, western Peru*. The coastal city, just south of Lima, has a name said to represent Spanish *mira flores*, "look at the flowers." But this is probably a meaningful alteration of an earlier otherwise obscure Native American name.

Miranda de Ebro. *City, northern Spain*. The name of the ancient city has been derived from Latin *miranda*, "(place) to be admired," but it is probably pre–Latin in origin. The second part of the name derives from the **Ebro** River here.

Mirande. *Town, southwestern France*. The town derives its name from Provençal *miranda*, "watchtower," from the verb *mirar*, "to look," "to watch."

Mirpur Khas. *Town, southeastern Pakistan*. The town was founded in 1806 by *Mir 'Ali Murad Talpur* and is named for him, with Sanskrit *pur*, "town," added. Hindi *khās* is "special."

Mirzapur. *City, northern India*. The city, in Uttar Pradesh state, derives its name from Hindi *mirza*, "prince" (a word of Iranian origin), and Sanskrit *pur*, "town."

Mishawaka. *City, east central United States*. The name of the Indiana city, laid out in 1833, is said to derive from the Potawatomi word for "country of dead trees."

Mishmar Ha'emek. *Kibbutz, northwestern Israel*. The kibbutz, founded in 1926 at the foot of the Samarian Highlands, has a Hebrew name meaning "guardian of the valley."

Mishmar Hayarden. *Settlement, northeastern Israel*. The cooperative settlement, founded in 1890, has a Hebrew name meaning "guardian of the **Jordan**," referring to its location near this river.

Misiones. *Province, northeastern Argentina*. The province takes its name from the Jesuit *missions* set up by the Spanish among the Guaraní people here in the 17th and 18th centuries.

Miskolc. *City, northeastern Hungary*. The city derives its name from the Hungarian personal name *Miscu* or *Misca*, a form of *Mihály*, "Michael."

Mississauga. *City, southeastern Canada*. The Ontario city was first settled in the early 19th century on land purchased from the *Mississauga* Native Americans, and is named for them. Their own name comes from the *Mississauga* River that flows into Lake Huron, itself representing *missi*, "great," "many," and *saki*, "outlet," referring to a river that has many channels at its mouth.

Mississippi. *State, southeastern United States*. The state takes its name from the river that forms its western border with Arkansas and Louisiana. The river's name derives from words common to many Native American languages and means "great water." One of the earliest records of the river name, in 1666, is *Messipi*.

Missouri. *State, central United States*. The state is named for the river that flows east across it to join the Mississippi on its eastern border. Its own name is is believed to derive from Illinois *weemihsoorita*, meaning "one who has a wood boat," referring to the dugout canoes of the Missouri Indians. The river's earlier name was *Pekitanoul*, said to mean "muddy waters."

Mistassini Lake. *Lake, eastern Canada*. Quebec province's largest lake has a Native American name meaning "great stone," referring to a large rock in it.

Mitaka. *City, eastern Japan*. The city, just west of Tokyo in the island of Honshu, has a name meaning "three hawks," from Japanese *mi*, "three," and *taka*, "hawk." The reference is to the former use of the locality as a hawking field.

Mitla. *Archaeological site, southwestern Mexico.* The religious center of the Zapotec, near Oaxaca, has a Nahuatl name meaning "abode of the dead."

Mito. *City, eastern Japan.* The city, on the Naka River in the island of Honshu, has a name meaning "water gate," from Japanese *mizu,* "water," and *to,* "gate."

Miyagi. *Prefecture, north central Japan.* The prefecture, in the island of Honshu, derives its name from Japanese *miya,* "Shinto temple," and *ki,* "castle," "citadel."

Miyazaki. *City and port, southwestern Japan.* The capital of the prefecture of the same name, in the island of Kyushu, derives its name from Japanese *miya,* "Shinto temple," and *saki,* "cape." The city has a Shinto shrine dedicated to the first emperor of Japan.

Mizoram. *State, northeastern India.* The state's name means "land of the *Mizo,*" referring to the Tibeto-Burman-speaking people who had long been in opposition to India and for whom the union territory was set up in 1972 in recognition of their national aspirations. The present state was established in 1987. The people's name derives from a local word meaning "highlander."

Mizpah. *Historic city, southern Palestine.* There are five places of this name in the Bible, of which the best known is the former capital of the Babylonian province of Judah (1 Kings 15:22, etc.). The name represents Hebrew *mişpâ,* "lookout post," "watch tower." Hence its repeated occurrence, sometimes in the spelling *Mizpeh.*

Mizpe Ramon. *Township, southern Israel.* The Jewish township, founded in 1954, has a Hebrew name meaning "overlooking *Ramon,*" referring to the famous *Ramon* erosional crater.

Mlet. *Island, eastern Adriatic Sea.* The island off the Dalmatian coast, belonging to Bosnia-Hercegovina, has a name that is probably of pre–Indoeuropean origin and related to that of **Malta.** Its meaning is uncertain.

Mmabatho. *City, northern South Africa.* The former capital of Bophuthatswana has a name meaning "mother of the people," referring to the dominance of the Tswana here. In 1994 it merged with **Mafikeng** as the capital of the new North-West province and the combined conurbation adopted that town's name.

Moab. *Historic region, southwestern Jordan.* The ancient kingdom derives its name from its historic inhabitants, the *Moabites,* themselves named for their ancestor, the biblical *Moab* who was the son of Lot (Genesis 19:37). His own name is popularly said to mean "of the father," from Hebrew *me,* a form of *min,* "of," "from," and *ab,* "father."

Mobile. *City and port, southeastern United States.* The name of the Alabama city, former capital of French Louisiana, is a gallicized form of a Native American name of uncertain origin. It is probably a tribal name.

Mobutu Sese Seko, Lake *see* **Albert, Lake**

Moca. *City, north central Dominican Republic.* The city was founded in 1780 and has a Native American name referring to the *moca,* or partridgewood, an indigenous cabbage-palm tree.

Moçambique. *Town and port, northeastern Mozambique.* The town's name is the Portuguese form of **Mozambique,** of which it was formerly the capital.

Mochudi. *Town, southeastern Botswana.* The town was settled by the Tswana people in 1871 and took its name from *Motshodi,* the man who pioneered the site. His own Setswana name means "one who dishes out food from a pot," referring to the traditional hospitality of the Tswana toward visitors.

Modena. *Town, western Italy.* The name has been taken from Latin *Mutina,* an epithet of Lara, a nymph of classical mythology, whose tongue was cut out so that she was dumb (Latin *mutus*), but the city dates from pre–Roman times and a pre–Latin source is likely.

Modesto. *City, southwestern United States.* The California city was founded in 1870 by the Central Pacific Railway and acquired its name, Spanish for "modest," when W.C. Ralston, a railway director, "modestly" declined to have the settlement named in his honor.

Modlin. *Town, east central Poland.* The town appears to derive its name from a base word *modl,* "damp (place)," referring to its location on the Vistula at the mouth of the Narew River. In the 19th century it was known by the Russian name *Novogeorgiyevsk,* "new *Georgiyevsk.*"

Mödling. *Town, northeastern Austria.* The town has a name of Slavic origin meaning "boundary" (Polish *miedza*), probably referring to a boundary stream here.

Moeris, Lake. *Historic lake, northern Egypt.* The once large lake, now represented by the smaller Lake Qarun, derives its name from Egyptian *mer-ur,* "big lake," from *mer,* "lake," and *ur,* "big." The present form of the name is due to Greek influence.

Moers. *City, western Germany.* The city arose on the site of a Roman camp known as *Asciburgium,* "fort where ash trees grow." Its name derives from that of a stream here, itself earlier called *Moerse*, perhaps from a Germanic word meaning "moor," "marsh."

Mogadishu. *Capital of Somalia*. The city and port, dating from the 10th century, derives its name from Arabic *mukaddas*, "holy." The name is also found in the italianized form *Mogadiscio*. *See also* **Madagascar**.

Mogilyov. *City, east central Belarus*. The name of the city suggests Russian *mogila*, "grave," and for this reason is said to refer to the ancient burial mound on which it arose. But it may actually derive from a personal name.

Mohács. *Town, southern Hungary*. The town, on the Danube, derives its name from a Slavic form of Hungarian *moha*, "moss."

Mohaka. *River, northern New Zealand*. The river, in east central North Island, derives its name from a Maori term meaning "place for dancing."

Mohammedia. *City and port, northwestern Morocco*. The city, originally named *Fedala*, was renamed as now in 1959 in honor of *Mohammed V* (1909–1961), king (earlier sultan) of Morocco, who ruled from 1927 to his death.

Mohenjo-Daro. *Archaeological site, southeastern Pakistan*. The famous ruined city site, a relic of Harappan (Indus valley) civilization, has a Sind name meaning "mound of the dead."

Mold. *Town, northeastern Wales*. The Flintshire town has a name of Norman-French origin, representing a coalescing of *mont hault*, "high hill." The hill in question is the one to the northwest of the town known as Bailey Hill, where there was a Celtic and possibly a Roman fort, and later a medieval castle. The town's Welsh name is *Yr Wyddgrug*, "the burial mound."

Moldavia *see* **Moldova**

Moldova. *Republic, southeastern Europe*. The country borders on Romania and takes its name from the river now territorially in that country. The river's own name probably goes back to an Indoeuropean root element *mel*, "dark," "black." The republic was long known as *Moldavia*.

Molenbeek-Saint-Jean. *Town, central Belgium*. The town, now a suburb of Brussels, arose as a village overlooking a stream. Hence the first word of its name, from Flemish *molenbeek*, "mill stream." The rest of the name refers to the dedication of its church to *St. John*.

Moléson. *Mountain, western Switzerland*. The Alpine peak, in the Bernese Alps, derives its name from a local word related to French *mélèze*, "larch," denoting the presence of these trees here.

Moline. *City, east central United States*. The Illinois city was laid out in 1843 by a milling firm, and its name apparently represents Spanish *molino* or French *moulin*, "mill."

Mölln. *City, northern Germany*. First mentioned in 1188, the city arose around two small lakes, and its name refers to one or both of them, from Slavic *mul*, "mud," "cloudy water."

Molotov *see* **Perm**

Moluccas. *Island group, eastern Indonesia*. The islands, in the Malay Archipelago, have a Malay name meaning "main (islands)," from *molok*, "main," "chief." The reference may be to their central location, between New Guinea and Sulawesi, rather than their size or importance. The indigenous form of the name is *Maluku*. (The Moluccas should not be confused with the Strait of **Malacca**.)

Mombasa. *City and port, southern Kenya*. The city was founded in the 11th century by Arabs, who named it after a town in Oman, itself from Arabic *mumbaṣa*, of uncertain meaning.

Monaco. *Principality, western Europe*. The name of the state, an enclave in southeastern France, is popularly derived from Greek *Monoikos*, "solitary," a byname of the god Hercules, said to refer to a statue of Hercules Monoecus that stood here in the 7th or 6th century B.C. However, the name is more likely to be of Ligurian origin, from *monegu*, "rock," a word reflected in the ethnic adjective *Monegasque*. Another theory proposes a source in Basque *muno*, "mountain." Monaco is some distance from the Basque Country, but it is known that the influence of the Basques and their language was quite widely felt in France as a whole. The mountain in question would be the one that gave the name of **Monte Carlo**, the principality's capital.

Monaghan. *County, northeastern Ireland*. The county's name is that of its chief town, which itself represents Irish *muineach*, "little thickets."

Monashee Mountains. *Mountain range, southwestern Canada*. The mountains, in British Columbia, were originally known as the *Gold Range*, for the *gold* found in their southern foothills. They were renamed as now by an early Scottish prospector, David McIntyre, from a Gaelic phrase meaning "mountain of peace," from *monadh*, "mountain," and *sìth*, "peace."

Monastir. *Town and port, northeastern Tunisia*. The town has the Arabic name of *al-munastīr*, said to be from Latin *monasterium*, "monastery." It is possible that a Christian monastery existed here before the coming of Islam. But this is by no means certain, since texts of the 17th and 18th centuries record the name as *Munasir* and *Manasir*. Moreover, local people regularly pronounce the name "Mistir." The town's historic name was *Ruspina*, of Phoenician origin and uncertain meaning.

Mönchengladbach. *City, western Germany.* The city arose around a monastery founded in the 10th century. Its name thus means "monks' *Gladbach*," the latter name being that of the river here, meaning "shining stream," from words corresponding to modern German *glatt*, "smooth," "clear," and *Bach*, "stream." Until 1951 the official form of the name was *München-Gladbach*, then to 1960 *Mönchen-Gladbach*. (The first of these names led to postal confusion with *München*, i.e. **Munich**.)

Moncton. *City and port, southeastern Canada.* The city, in New Brunswick, was settled by French colonists on the site of a Native American village some time after 1698, and at first was known as *Big Bend*, for its site at the head of the estuary of the Petitcodiac River. In 1855 it was renamed as now for Lieutenant Colonel Robert *Monckton* (1726–1782), leader of a British military expedition against the French at Fort Beauséjour in 1755.

Monemvasía. *Town, southern Greece.* The town lies on the southeast coast of the Peloponnese at the foot of a rock that is just offshore. It is joined to the mainland by a causeway. Hence the name, meaning "(town of the) one approach." (It was from here that *malmsey* wine was first exported.)

Mongolia. *Republic, east central Asia.* The country takes its name from its indigenous people, the *Mongols*, whose own name derives from the Mongolian root word *mengu* or *mongu*, "brave," "unconquered." It should be noted that *Inner Mongolia* is an autonomous region of northern China, from Chinese *nèi*, "inner," and *ménggŭ*, "Mongolia," so called by contrast with *Outer Mongolia*, i.e. Mongolia proper. The two have been separate entities since the 17th century.

Monmouth. *Town, southeastern Wales.* The town, in the county of the same name, takes its name from the *Monnow* River, at the mouth of which it stands, at its confluence with the larger Wye. The river's own name may mean "fastflowing." The town's Welsh name is *Trefynwy*, "homestead on the *Mynwy*," the latter being the more accurate form of the river name.

Monreale. *Town, southern Italy.* The town, in southwestern Sicily, had the Medieval Latin name *Mons Regalis*, "royal mountain," referring to *Monte Caputo*, on the slope of which King William II of Sicily founded a Benedictine monastery in the 12th century.

Monroe. *City, southern United States.* The Louisiana city, on the Ouachita River, was founded in 1785 by French colonists under a Frenchman in Spanish service, and was at first called *Fort Miro*. It received its present name in 1819 to mark the arrival of the *James Monroe*, the first steamboat to ascend the river. The vessel itself was named for *James Monroe* (1758–1831), 5th president of the United States.

Monrovia. *Capital of Liberia.* The city and Atlantic port was founded in 1822 by the American Colonization Society as a haven for freed black slaves. It was named by Robert Goodloe Harper (*see* **Harper**), a founder member of the Society, for James *Monroe* (1758–1831), 5th president of the United States. Harper also named **Liberia** itself.

Mons. *Town, southwestern Belgium.* The town derives its name from Latin *mons*, "mountain," a meaning seen in its alternate Flemish name of *Bergen*. The name is a virtual misnomer, since there is hardly a hill here, let alone a mountain. The town is set on a knoll between two rivers, however, so that must be the reference.

¹Montana. *Town, northwestern Bulgaria.* The town was originally a Roman settlement called *Montanensia*. It was later known as *Golyama Kutlovitsa*, "great hollow," and from 1891 *Ferdinand*, for *Ferdinand* I (1861–1948), king of Bulgaria. After World War II it was renamed *Mikhaylovgrad*, for Khristo *Mikhaylov* (1893–1944), a prominent Communist official. In 1993, after Communist rule had ended, it took its present name, based on the Roman original.

²Montana. *State, northwestern United States.* The name of the state is a latinized form of Spanish *montaña*, "mountainous area." It was proposed by Representative James M. Ashley of Ohio when the Montana Territory was organized in 1864 from a portion of the former Nebraska Territory. The reference is to the Rocky Mountains, which occupy much of the western part of the state.

Montargis. *Town, north central France.* The town derives its name from Latin *mons, montis*, "hill," and the Gaulish personal name *Argio*.

Montauban. *Town, southwestern France.* The town had the Medieval Latin name of *Mons Albanus*, apparently meaning "white hill" from *mons, montis*, "hill," and *albanus*, "white."

Montbéliard. *Town, eastern France.* The town dates from the 8th century and derives its name from Latin *mons, montis*, "hill," and a personal name of Germanic origin, *Pelicardis* or *Biligardis*.

Mont Blanc. *Mountain, eastern France.* France's highest peak, on the French-Italian and French-Swiss border, has a French name meaning "white mountain," referring to its permanent snow cover. The Italian name is similar, as *Monte Bianco*.

Mont-de-Marsan. *Town, southwestern France.* The town was founded in 1141 by Pierre, vicomte de *Marsan*, who took his title from the small region of *Marsan* here. Its own name probably represents the Roman personal name *Marcianus*, that of a local landowner. The first word of the name, literally "mount," denotes the medieval fortification here.

Monte Carlo. *Capital of Monaco.* The town, founded in 1866, has a name of Italian origin meaning "*Charles*'s mountain." The compliment was to the prince then reigning, *Charles* III of Monaco (1818–1889). The mountain is the escarpment at the foot of the Maritime Alps on which the town stands.

Montecristo. *Island, northern Tyrrhenian Sea.* The Italian island, between Corsica and Italy, has a name evidently meaning "mount of *Christ*." The name became familiar from the novel *The Count of Monte Cristo* (1844) by Alexandre Dumas *père*, whose grandfather, the Marquis de La Pailleterie, owned a sugar plantation at a place called *Montechristo* in Santo Domingo. This presumably influenced the writer's choice of name. He himself spelled it *Monte-Cristo*, with a hyphen.

Montego Bay. *City and port, northwestern Jamaica.* The city's name is a part translation, part corruption of its earlier Spanish name, *Bahía de Manteca*, "bay of butter." This probably refers to its role as a lard ("hog's butter") center.

Montélimar. *Town, southeastern France.* The Medieval Latin name of the town was *Montellum Aymardi*, "little hill of *Aymard*," the latter being a Germanic personal name.

Montenegro. *State, southeastern Europe.* The state has an Italian name meaning "black mountain," this being a translation of the Serbo-Croat name *Crna Gora*. The allusion is to the predominantly somber color of the region, which is mountainous and heavily forested. In 2003, together with **Serbia**, Montenegro formed the new republic of *Serbia and Montenegro* from the former **Yugoslavia**.

Monterey. *City, southwestern United States.* The California city, capital of Spain's Pacific empire from 1774 to 1825, takes its name from the bay here, itself named in 1603 for the Spanish colonist Gaspar de Aceveda y Zúñiga, conde de *Monterrey* (c.1560–1606), founder of **Monterrey**, Mexico.

Montería. *City and river port, northwestern Colombia.* The present city originated as a meeting place for hunters. Hence its name, from Spanish *montería*, "hunting."

Monte Rosa. *Mountain, south central Europe.* The snow-covered mountain mass, on the border between Switzerland and Italy, derives the second word of its name from Italian dialect *roëse*, "glacier." This has been assimilated to Italian *rosa*, "rose," as if referring to its rose-colored peaks in the rays of the setting sun. The mountain's French name is similarly *Mont Rose*, in turn possibly influenced by the Scottish name **Montrose**.

Monterrey. *City, northern Mexico.* The city was founded in 1579 by the Spanish colonist Gaspar de Aceveda y Zúñiga, conde de *Monterrey* (c.1560–1606), later viceroy of New Spain.

Montevideo. *Capital of Uruguay.* The city and port has an intriguing name that has so far defied definitive interpretation. Traditional accounts include the following: (1) The Portuguese explorer Magellan exclaimed "*Monte vidi eo*," "It was I who saw the mountain," referring to a mountain with a fine view here; (2) A Portuguese chart inscription read *monte VI de O*, "sixth mountain from the west," to designate this same mountain; (3) Spanish *monte*, "mountain," combined with Latin *video*, "I see." These all seem equally fanciful. The name does appear to refer to a hill or mountain, however, and the reference must be to the hill called the *Cerro* (also meaning "hill") that rises at the entrance to the bay on which the city stands, and that serves as a landmark when viewed from the sea. The city itself was founded in 1726 by Bruno Mauricio de Zabala, governor of Buenos Aires.

[1]**Montgomery**. *Town, eastern Wales.* The town, in Powys, takes its name from Roger de *Montgomery*, the Norman owner of the manor here. He himself came from *Montgommery* near Caen in northern France. The Welsh name of the town is quite different, as *Trefaldwyn*, "homestead of *Baldwin*," for the Norman who later recaptured the castle here after it had been taken by the Welsh.

[2]**Montgomery**. *City, southeastern United States.* The state capital of Alabama was so named in 1819 in commemoration of Richard *Montgomery* (1738–1775), the Revolutionary officer and hero who was killed leading an assault on Quebec.

Montluçon. *City, central France.* The city takes its name from Latin *mons, montis*, "hill," and the Roman personal name *Luccius*.

Montmartre. *District of Paris, northern France.* The district had the Roman name of *Mons Martyrum*, "martyrs' mount." The reference was to St. Denis, first bishop of Paris, beheaded in 258 together with two companions, a priest named Rusticus and a deacon Eleutherius. This Christian name replaced the earlier pagan one of *Mons Mercurii*, "Mercury's mount." *See also* **St.-Denis**.

Montmorency. *Town, northern France*. The town, now a northern suburb of Paris, derives its name from Latin *mons, montis*, "hill," and the Roman personal name *Maurentius*. From 1689 until the French Revolution (1789) it was known as *Enghien*, a name transferred here from the town in Belgium by the aristocratic Condé family, whose ducal title it was, when they inherited the estates of the equally distinguished Montmorency family here. The earlier name was resurrected for the modern residential settlement and spa of *Enghien-les-Bains*, "*Enghien*-the-springs," just south of Montmorency.

Montparnasse. *District of Paris, northern France*. The name represents French *Mont Parnasse*, "Mt. *Parnassus*," the Greek mountain that was sacred to the gods (*see* **Parnassus**). The former hill here was leveled during construction of the Boulevard Montparnasse.

Montpelier. *City, northeastern United States*. The state capital of Vermont was founded in 1780 and named for **Montpellier**, France, with a slight modification of spelling, in token of gratitude for French support during the American Revolution.

Montpellier. *City, southern France*. The city's present name evolved from its Medieval Latin name of *Mons pislerius*, a variant of *Mons pestellarius*, from Latin *mons*, "mountain," and *pestellum*, a form of *pastellum*, "woad," used locally for dyeing. There is hardly a mountain here in the accepted sense, and the city lies in a fertile plain.

Montreal. *City, southeastern Canada*. The Quebec city takes its name from the *Mont Réal*, "royal mount," the hill around and upon which it was first settled by the French in 1642. The hill itself, near the Native American town of *Hochelaga*, was so named in 1534 by the French sailor and colonist Jacques Cartier in honor of Francis I of France, who had financed his expedition here. The original name of the city was *Ville Marie de Montréal*, "*Mary's* town of Royal Mount." This was shortened as now in 1724. The name is today often found in the French form *Montréal*.

Montreuil. *Town, northern France*. The town, now a suburb of Paris, takes its name from Latin *monasteriolum*, "little monastery," a diminutive form of *monasterium*, "monastery." The town is also known as *Montreuil-sous-Bois*, "Montreuil-by-the-wood," to distinguish it from other places

of the same name. The wood in question is the Bois de Vincennes.

Montreux. *Town and resort, western Switzerland*. The town arose in the 9th century by a monastery on an island at the eastern end of Lake Geneva. Hence its name, which has evolved from Latin *monasterium*, "monastery." *Cp.* **Münster**.

Montrose. *Town and port, eastern Scotland*. The town has a Gaelic name meaning "moor of the promontory," from *moine*, "moor," and *ros*, "promontory." Montrose is on a low peninsula.

Montrouge. *Town, northern France*. The town, now a suburb of Paris, had the Medieval Latin name *Mons Rubicus*, "red mountain," referring to the reddish soil in the locality. The present name is the French equivalent of this.

Montserrat. *Island, eastern West Indies*. The island was discovered by Columbus in 1493 and named for the monastery of *Santa María de Montserrat* near Barcelona in Spain. The monastery itself was named for the mountain on which it stands, its own name representing Catalan *mont*, "mountain," and *serrat*, "serrated." The reference is to the mountain's jagged pinnacles. This literal sense is also appropriate for the island, which has a range of sharply angled mountain peaks.

Monza. *City, northern Italy*. The city was known in Roman times as *Modicia*, a name of uncertain origin.

Moose Jaw. *City, southern Canada*. The Saskatchewan city was founded in 1882 and takes its name from the river here. Its own name probably translates a Native American original describing the contours of the river, or of some part of it, as resembling the jaw of a moose.

Moravia. *Historic region, eastern Czech Republic*. The region takes its name from the *Morava* River here. The river's own name derives from Germanic words *mar*, "marsh," and *ahwa*, "water."

Moray. *Historic region, northeastern Scotland*. The name means "sea settlement," from Old Celtic words related to modern Welsh *môr*, "sea," and *tref*, "homestead," "town." The historic province gave the name of the *Moray Firth*, the arm of the North Sea that extends inland here as far as Inverness.

Morbihan. *Department, northwestern France*. The department, in Brittany, takes its name from *Morbihan* Bay off its west coast. The bay is almost landlocked. Hence its name, from Breton *mor bihan*, "little sea."

Mordvinia. *Republic, western Russia*. The republic, formerly familiar as *Mordovia*, is named for its indigenous Finno-Ugric *Mordvin* people. Their own name probably comes from a root word *mordyo*, "person," "man."

Morecambe. *Town and resort, northwestern England*. The Lancashire town takes its name from the bay on which it lies. Its own name derives from Celtic elements *mori*, "sea," and *cambi*, "curved," describing its rounded coastline. The town's name dates only from the 19th century, when the resort arose, and its former name was *Poulton-le-Sands*, the first word of this meaning "farm by a pool."

Morelos. *State, central Mexico*. The state is named for José María *Morelos* y Pavón (1765–1815), a hero of Mexico's war for independence from Spain (1811–15), in which he was captured and executed.

Moreno. *City, eastern Argentina*. The city, now an extension of Buenos Aires, was founded in 1860 and named for Mariano *Moreno* (1778–1811), the Spanish patriot who was a leader in Argentina's bid for independence.

Morioka. *City, north central Japan*. The city, in the island of Honshu, derives its name from Japanese *mori*, "to give good measure," and *oka*, "hill."

Morocco. *Kingdom, northwestern Africa*. The name derives from *marūkus*, the old Arabic form of the name of **Marrakesh**, the country's former capital. The first recorded occurrence of the name in the Western world is as *Marroch* in the medieval *Nibelungenlied*. Many languages spell the name with the first vowel as *a*, as French *Maroc*, German *Marokko*, and the English spelling with *o* probably arose from an association with the *Moors*, who settled in northwestern Africa generally. The Arabic name of Morocco is *al-maġrib al-akṣa*, "the far west." (*cp.* **Maghreb**), while the Turkish name is *Fas*, from **Fez**, the oldest of Morocco's four imperial cities.

Morón. *City, eastern Argentina*. The city, just west of Buenos Aires, derives its name from **Morón de la Frontera**, Spain. From 1930 through 1943 it was known as *Seis de Septiembre*, "sixth of September," for a military uprising that took place on this date in the former of these years.

Morón de la Frontera. *City, southwestern Spain*. The city derives the first word of its name from Hebrew *moram*, "raised site," given by Arabs to describe its location near the foothills of the Penibético Mountains. The rest of the name, Spanish for "of the frontier," alludes to the city's situation at the edge of the historic Muslim kingdom of Granada.

Morvan. *Mountain range, east central France*. The name of the range is said to derive from Celtic words meaning "black mountain," although a source in a personal name is more likely.

Moscow. *Capital of Russia*. The immediate source of the name is the *Moskva* River on which the city stands. Its own name is of uncertain origin, but it probably goes back to a word or element meaning simply "river," whatever its language may have been.

Moselle. *River, western Europe*. The river, flowing through France, Luxembourg, and Germany into the Rhine, has a name meaning simply "little **Meuse**," from Latin *Mosella*, the diminutive of *Mosa*, the Roman name of the Meuse. Both rivers rise in northeastern France, but the Moselle is only a quarter the length of the Meuse.

Mosonmagyaróvár. *City, northwestern Hungary*. The city was formed in 1939 by the union of *Moson* (German name *Wieselburg*) with *Magyaróvár* (German name *Ungarisch-Altenburg*). *Moson* derives its name from Old German *mussum*, "swamp" (English *moss*). *Magyaróvár* means "Hungarian old castle." The meanings generally correspond in the respective German names, although *Wieselburg* is more exactly "castle in the meadow."

Mosquito Coast. *Region, eastern Nicaragua*. The Caribbean coastal region, with its swamps and tropical rain forests, is said to be named for the biting insect, which thrives in such conditions. The name was then given by European explorers to the Native American people who inhabited this region, so that they are known as the *Mosquito* or the *Miskito*, among other spellings. But it is equally possible that the people gave the name of the region, as is often the case, and that it was corrupted by Europeans to the name of the insect.

Most. *City, northwestern Czech Republic*. The city, on the Bílina River, has a Slavic name meaning "bridge." Its German name of *Brüx* has the same sense. *Cp.* **Bruges**.

Mostar. *Town, southern Bosnia-Hercegovina*. The town, on the Neretva River, has a name apparently representing Serbo-Croat *stari most*, "old bridge," although it is uncertain why the word order is inverted. The stone bridge, built in 1566 to replace an earlier wooden suspension bridge, was destroyed in 1993 during the Balkans War, but was rebuilt with international aid in 2004.

Mosul. *City, northern Iraq*. The city name represents Arabic *al-mawṣūl*, "the joined," from *waṣal*, "to join," referring to the city's settlement at a point where the Tigris River was crossed by both a bridge and a ford.

Motherwell. *Town, south central Scotland.* The name of the town is usually said to mean what it says, referring to a old *well* here dedicated to the Virgin Mary (the *Mother* of God), although Maggie Scott, writing in *Scottish Place-Name News* (No. 17, Autumn 2004), suggests that the first part of the name is actually Middle Scots *moder*, "source (of a stream)," a word related to English *mud*.

Moulay Idriss. *Town, north central Morocco.* The town takes its name from *Moulay Idriss* I (died 791), founder of the first Arab dynasty in Morocco, whose shrine is here. (His son, Idriss II, founded Fez.) *Moulay* is more familiar in the English spelling *mullah*, the title of a learned Muslim teacher.

Moulins. *Town, central France.* The town derives its name from Medieval Latin *molina*, "mill," referring to a water mill on the Allier River here.

Mount Abu. *Town, northwestern India.* The town, in Rajasthan state, takes its name from the mountain here, itself originally called *Arbuda*, "wisdom," and mentioned in the *Mahabharata*, the great Indian epic.

Mount Gambier. *City, southern Australia.* The city, in South Australia, lies at the foot of the mountain for which it is named. The mountain itself was sighted in 1800 by the English naval officer James Grant and named by him for the British admiral James *Gambier* (*see* **Gambier Islands**).

Mount Isa. *City, northern Australia.* The city, in western Queensland, is said to have been named by John Campbell Miles, who discovered silver-lead ore deposits here in 1923 and called one of his leases after his sister, *Isa*belle.

Mount Vernon. *City, eastern United States.* The New York city was settled in 1664 and was at first a village considered part of Eastchester Township. It was subsequently named for George Washington's home in Virginia. This is on an estate that was originally known as *Hunting Creek Plantation* but that was renamed in 1740 by Lawrence Washington, George's elder half-brother, for Admiral Edward *Vernon* (1684–1757), under whom he had served in the Caribbean.

Mourne Mountains. *Mountain range, southeastern Northern Ireland.* The mountains take their name from that of the *Mughdorna* people who formerly inhabited the region, with their own name coming from that of their leader, *Mughdorn*.

Moyobamba. *City, north central Peru.* The city, founded in 1539, derives its name from Quechua *mayupampa*, "circular plain."

Mozambique. *Republic, southeastern Africa.* The name is a Portuguese corruption of Arabic *mūsā malik*, "Musa king," from *mūsā*, "Musa," the name of an early African ruler here, and *malik*, "king."

Mpumalanga. *Province, northeastern South Africa.* The province, part of **Transvaal** until 1994, has a Zulu name meaning "sunrise," "the sun comes out."

Mühldorf am Inn. *City, southeastern Germany.* The city arose by a Roman crossing of the *Inn* River (*see* **Innsbruck**) and has a name meaning "mill village," from Old High German *mūli*, "mill," and *dorf*, "village."

Mühlhausen. *City, central Germany.* The city, first recorded in 775 as *Mulinhuso, ubi Franci homines commanent*, "Mühlhausen, where the Franks live," derives its name from early forms of German *Mühle*, "mill," and *Haus*, "house," referring to the mills on the Unstrut River here. The full name is *Mühlhausen in Thüringen*, the addition serving to distinguish it (by its location in **Thuringia**) from **Mulhouse**, its French namesake.

Mühlheim. *City, western Germany.* The city, on the Main River, has a name first recorded in 758 as *Mulinheim*, from early forms of modern German *Mühle*, "mill," and *Heim*, "settlement."

Mukden *see* **Shen-yang**

Mülheim an der Ruhr. *City, western Germany.* The city, first mentioned in 1000, arose by the **Ruhr** River as a "mill settlement." *Cp.* **Mühlheim**.

Mulhouse. *City, northeastern France.* The city is close enough to the German border to have a German name. It is the French form of *Mülhausen*, "mill houses," from *Mühle*, "mill," and *Haus*, "house." The town arose as a settlement by a mill on the Ill River. *Cp.* **Mühlhausen**, **Mühlheim**.

Mull. *Island, western Scotland.* The island, in the Inner Hebrides, has a name of uncertain origin. Some authorities derive it from Old Norse *múli*, "snout," "headland," which would suit its topography, but others prefer a source in Gaelic *meuileach*, "dear one," implying that the island was "favored" in some way.

Mumbai *see* **Bombay**

Muncie. *City, east central United States.* The name of the Indiana city was originally *Munseetown*, given for the *Munsee*, a Delaware people who formerly lived here but who sold their land to the government and moved west.

Munich. *City, southern Germany.* The city was founded in 1158 by Henry the Lion, Duke of Bavaria and Saxony, who granted the Benedictine monks here the right to set up a market by the Isar River. Hence its name, from a Germanic root word that gave modern German *Mönch*, "monk." The city's German name is *München*. Its Italian name, rather confusingly, is *Monaco*.

Munster. *Historic region, southern Ireland.* The ancient kingdom has a name that means "land of the *Mumu*," with the ethnic name followed by the Old Norse genitive ending *s* and Irish *tír*, "land."

Münster. *City, northwestern Germany.* The city's name is first recorded in 1086 as *Monasterium*, for the monastery founded here by St. Liudger, appointed first bishop of Münster in 804. *Cp.* **Montreux**.

Murcia. *Region, southeastern Spain.* The former kingdom takes its name from its capital city, its own name from Arabic *mursakh*, "fortified."

Murfreesboro. *City, east central United States.* The Tennessee city was established in 1811 on land donated by a Revolutionary soldier, Colonel William Lytle, and named for a friend of his, Colonel Hardy *Murfree* (1752–1809).

Murmansk. *City and port, northwestern Russia.* The city takes its name from the coastal region of *Murman* here. This itself probably comes from a combination of Finno-Ugric *mur*, "sea," and *ma*, "land," although some authorities prefer an origin in the ethnic name *Norman*, "northerner," as a general name in medieval times for a Scandinavian. The town arose in 1915 as the northern terminus of the railroad to the Arctic coast. As such, it was originally named *Romanov-na-Murmane*, "*Romanov*-in-Murman," for the Russian royal family. It was renamed two years later.

Murom. *City, western Russia.* The city, first mentioned in 862, takes its name from the *Muroma*, a local people. Their name is of Finno-Ugrian origin but uncertain meaning.

Muroran. *City and port, northern Japan.* The city, in Hokkaido island, derives its name from Japanese *muro*, "cellar," and *ran*, "orchid," symbolic of sophistication.

Murray. *River, southeastern Australia.* Australia's principal river was discovered in 1824 by the English emigrant explorer W.H. Hovell and Australian bushman Andrew Hume, and the former originally named it for his companion as the *Hume*. In 1830 it was renamed by the British explorer Captain Charles Sturt in honor of Sir George *Murray* (1772–1846), colonial secretary at that time.

Murrumbidgee. *River, southeastern Australia.* The river, in southern New South Wales, has an Aboriginal name said to mean "big water."

Murshidabad. *City, northeastern India.* The West Bengal city is said to have been founded by the Mogul emperor Akbar in the 16th century and was originally named *Makhsudabad*. In 1704 the nawab *Murshid* Kuli Khan founded the Muslim capital of Bengal here and renamed it for himself.

Muscat. *Capital of Oman.* The city and port has the Arabic name of *Masqat*, said to mean "hidden." The reference is to the port's location, isolated from the interior of the country by a range of hills.

Muskegon. *City, northern United States.* The Michigan city takes its name from the river that enters Lake Michigan here. Its own name comes from an Ojibwa word meaning "swampy."

Muskogee. *City, south central United States.* The Oklahoma city was founded in 1872 and named for the *Muskogee* (Creek) people. Their own name is probably of Algonquian origin but uncertain meaning.

Mu-tan-chiang. *City, northeastern China.* The city, in Heilungkiang province, derives its name from the *Mu-tan* River on which it lies, from Chinese *mǔ*, "male," *dān*, "red," and *jiāng*, "river."

Mutare. *Town, eastern Zimbabwe.* The town was founded in 1891 and takes its name from the Nyika form of the name of the river on which it lies. The river's own name means "river of ore." Until 1982 the town was known as *Umtali*, the Shangaan form of the name.

Muzaffarnagar. *Town, northern India.* The town, in Uttar Pradesh state, was founded in c.1633 by Khan-e Jahan, who named it for his father, *Muzaffar* Khan, with Hindi *nagar*, "town," added. *Cp.* **Muzaffarpur**.

Muzaffarpur. *Town, northeastern India.* The town, in Bihar state, was founded in the 18th century by *Muzaffar* Khan and is named for him, with Hindi *pur*, "town," added. *Cp.* **Muzaffarnagar**.

Mweru, Lake. *Lake, central Africa.* The lake, divided between the Democratic Republic of Congo and Zambia, has a Bantu name meaning "white," referring to the color of its waters.

Myanmar. *Republic, southeastern Asia.* The country long familiar as *Burma* adopted the more accurate form of its name in 1989. It represents Myanmar (Burmese) *myanma*, "the strong," the indigenous people's name for themselves.

Mycenae. *Historic city, southern Greece.* The long ruined city is traditionally said to have been founded by Perseus and named for the nymph *Mycene*. The actual origin of the name is uncertain.

Myitkyina. *Town, northeastern Myanmar.* The town, on the Irrawaddy River, has a Myanmar (Burmese) name meaning "close to the big river."

Mysia. *Historic region, northwestern Turkey.* The region takes its name from its indigenous people, the *Mysians*. Their own name is of unknown origin.

Mysore *see* **Karnataka**

Mytilene. *Town and port, eastern Greece.* The chief town of Lesbos, in the east of the island, has a name of pre–Greek origin and unknown meaning. A proposed derivation from Greek *mutilos*, "mussel," is thus simply an attempt to explain an obscure name.

Mytishchi. *City, western Russia.* The city, near Moscow, is on the site of a medieval portage where a levy (*myt*) was raised from travelers and their goods. Hence the name.

Myvatn. *Lake, northern Iceland.* The shallow lake has a name meaning "mosquito lake," from Icelandic *my*, "mosquito," and *vatn*, "lake." The insects are attracted by the lake's hot springs.

Naberezhnyye Chelny. *City, western Russia.* The city, on the Kama River in Tatarstan, was originally a fishing village known as *Chelny*, from the plural form of Russian *chelno*, "boat." When it was raised to town status in 1930, the first word was added, meaning "quayside," "embankment." From 1982 through 1988 the city was renamed *Brezhnev*, for the Soviet head of state Leonid *Brezhnev* (1906–1982). (The choice of name would naturally have been politically and topically apposite, but may have been further prompted by the echo of *Naberezhnyye* in *Brezhnev*.)

Nablus. *City, north central West Bank.* The name of Samaria's chief city is an Arabic corruption of its original Greek name *Neapolis*, "new city" (*cp.* **Naples**), as which it was founded in the 1st century A.D. near the site of the ancient biblical town of *Shechem* (Genesis 12:6, etc.), with which it is commonly identified. The name of the biblical city probably derives from the Hebrew word for "shoulder," describing its site on the slope of Mt. Ebal.

Nabul. *Town, northeastern Tunisia.* The name evolved from the 1st-century A.D. Roman colony of *Neapolis*, its own (Greek) name meaning "new town" (*cp.* **Naples**). It was "new" by comparison with the original Phoenician settlement here.

Nádudvar. *Town, eastern Hungary.* The name derives from Hungarian *nád*, "reed," "rush," and *udvar*, "court," "yard," describing an original country house surrounding by a reed fence.

Naft Safid. *Town, southwestern Iran.* The oil town has an Iranian name meaning "white oil." An oil field was opened here in 1945.

Nagaland. *State, northeastern India.* The state was established in 1964 at the request of its indigenous people, the *Naga*. The origin of their name is disputed. Some derive it from Sanskrit *nāga*, "snake," used as the name of a mythical creature with the body of a man as its upper half and that of a snake as its lower. Others see the origin in Hindi *naṅgā*, "naked," or *naga*, "hill," as the people are hill dwellers. It may really be based on a word *nok* meaning "people."

Nagano. *City, central Japan.* The city, in the island of Honshu, derives its name from Japanese *naga*, "long," and *no*, "field," "plain."

Nagaoka. *City, central Japan.* The city, in the island of Honshu, derives its name from Japanese *naga*, "long," and *oka*, "hill."

Nagapattinam. *City and port, southern India.* The city, in Tamil Nadu state, is said to have a name meaning "snake town," from Hindi *nāga*, "snake," and *pattan*, "town," "city."

Nagasaki. *City and port, southwestern Japan.* The city, in the island of Kyushu, has a name that describes its location, from Japanese *naga*, "long," and *saki*, "headland," "promontory."

Nagaur. *Town, western India.* The town, in Rajasthan state, is said to take its name from its traditional founders, the *Naga* Rajputs (warrior rulers of Rajputana). *See* **Nagaland**.

Nagercoil. *City, southern India.* The city, in Tamil Nadu state, has a name meaning "snake temple," referring to the long established Saiva temple here.

Nagorno-Karabakh. *Region, southwestern Azerbaijan.* The administrative region derives the first part of its name from Russian *nagornyj*, "mountainous." The second part has been explained as deriving from Turkic words meaning "black garden," referring to the black grapes of the vineyards here. But this is probably an attempt to explain a name whose actual meaning is unknown.

Nagoya. *City, central Japan.* The city, in the island of Honshu, derives its name from Japanese *na*, "name," *ko*, "old," and *ya*, "house." The "old house" is the great castle built by a shogun here in 1610 for his son as the *daimyo* (local lord).

Nagpur. *City, central India.* The city, in Maharashtra state, derives its Hindi name from that of the *Nag* River, itself named for the *Naga* people (*see* **Nagaland**), with *pur*, "fort," "town," added.

Nagyatád. *Town, southwestern Hungary.* The name derives from Hungarian *nagy*, "big (place)," and the personal name *Átad*.

Nagykálló. *Town, northeastern Hungary.* The name derives from Hungarian *nagy,* "big," and either a Hungarian term for a fulling mill or a word of Slavic origin meaning "mire" (Polish *kał*).

Nagykanisza. *City, southwestern Hungary.* The name means "big (place of the) magistrate," from Hungarian *nagy,* "big," and the possessive form of *kenéz,* the term for a village magistrate.

Nagykáta. *Town, north central Hungary.* The name derives from *nagy,* "big," and *káta,* a word of Pecheneg origin meaning "earthwork."

Nagykőrös. *City, central Hungary.* The name means "big (place of) ash trees," from Hungarian *nagy,* "big," and a dialect form of *kőrisfa,* "ash tree." The name contrasts with that of **Kiskőrös,** further south. Neither name is related to that of the *Körös* River in southeastern Hungary, whose meaning is unknown.

Nagyvárad *see* **Oradea**

Nahalal. *Settlement, north central Israel.* Israel's first cooperative settlement, founded in 1921 by the Russian-born agriculturist Eliezer Lipa Joffe, took the Hebrew name of a biblical city in northern Palestine, itself meaning "pasture."

Nahariyya. *City, northwestern Israel.* The city was founded in 1934 as an agricultural settlement and derives its name from Hebrew *nahar,* "river," alluding to the Nahal Ga'aton watercourse, which flows through it.

Nahuel Huapí, Lake. *Lake, southwestern Argentina.* The lake has an Araucanian name meaning "island of the jaguars," alluding to the presence of these animals here. The lake is dotted with islands, so that "island" in the name effectively designates the lake itself.

Nairn. *Town and resort, northeastern Scotland.* The town takes its name from the river at the mouth of which it stands. The river's own name is of Celtic origin and may mean "penetrating one." Early records of the town's name show that it was originally *Invernairn,* the *Inver-* denoting the river mouth, as for **Inverness.** This element was later dropped.

Nairobi. *Capital of Kenya.* The city's name represents the Swahili word for "marsh," referring to the waterhole of the pastoral Maasai where the town was founded as a railhead camp in 1899.

Najibabad. *Town, north central India.* The town, in Uttar Pradesh state, arose around the fort built in 1775 by the Afghan leader *Najib* ud-Daula, whose tomb is here. The name thus means "city of *Najib.*"

Nakhichevan. *City, southwestern Azerbaijan.* The city has an ancient name recorded by Ptolemy in the 2d century A.D. as *Naxouana.* It has been popularly derived from Armenian *nakh,* "first," and *idzhevan,* "landing," supposedly referring to the mountain here where Noah's Ark came to rest after the Flood. More realistically, it probably represents the personal name *Nahich* or *Nahuch,* with the Armenian suffix *-avan,* "settlement."

Nakhodka. *City and port, southeastern Russia.* The city, on the Sea of Japan, derives its name from that of the bay here. The bay was discovered in 1859 and named from Russian *nakhodka,* "find," "discovery," referring to its suitability for ships in this far region. The bay is calm and sheltered, and would be a welcome "godsend" for a ship seeking refuge from stormy seas.

Nakhon Pathom. *Town, central Thailand.* The town has a name meaning "first town," from Thai *nakhon,* "town," and *pathom,* "first." The implication is that the town was the first to be founded in Thailand.

Nakhon Ratchasima. *Town, east central Thailand.* The town's name means "border town of the king," from Thai *nakhon,* "town," *racha,* "king" (from Sanskrit *rāja*), and *sima,* "border."

Nakhon Sawan. *Town, west central Thailand.* The name means "paradise town," from Thai *nakhon,* "town," and *sawankh,* "paradise."

Nakhon Si Thammarat. *Town and port, southern Thailand.* The name of the town means "town of the good and just king," from Thai *nakhon,* "town," *si,* "good," *thamm,* "justice," "dharma," and *rat,* "king," "royal."

Nalchik. *City, southwestern Russia.* The name of the Kabardino-Balkar capital is said to represent Cherkess *nalshych,* "tearing off the horseshoe," supposedly referring to the sticky soil here. But this looks like a popular etymology devised to explain a name of unknown meaning.

Namaqualand. *Region, southwestern Africa.* The coast region, partly in Namibia and partly in South Africa, takes its name from the Khoikhoin (Hottentot) *Nama* people who formerly lived here. The origin of their own name is uncertain. *Namaqua* is the plural of *Nama.* Cp. **Namibia.**

Namibe. *City and port, southwestern Angola.* The city takes its name from the *Namib* desert, which gave the name of **Namibia.** Until 1982 the town was known as *Moçâmedes,* for the Barão de *Moçâmedes* (Baron of *Mossâmedes*), governor of Portuguese West Africa from 1784 through 1790. The baron took his title from *Mossâmedes,* in central Brazil.

Namibia. *Republic, southwestern Africa.* The

country derives its name from the *Nama*, the indigenous people whose land it is. The origin of their own name is uncertain. *Cp.* **Namaqualand.** Namibia was formerly known simply as *South West Africa* (internationally until 1968).

Nam Tso. *Lake, western China.* The salt lake, in eastern Tibet, has a Tibetan name meaning "heavenly lake." Its Mongolian name, *Tengri Nor*, means the same, and is a translation.

Namur. *City, south central Belgium.* The city has a name of Gaulish origin, although the meaning is disputed. The source may be in *nemeto*, "holy wood," in *nanto*, "valley" (*cp.* **Nantes**), or possibly in *nam*, "to wind," with the suffix *-uco*, referring to a bend in the Sambre or Meuse river here.

Nanaimo. *City, southwestern Canada.* The city, on Vancouver Island, British Columbia, was originally known as *Colvilletown*, for Andrew *Colville*, governor of the Hudson's Bay Company from 1852 to 1856. In 1860 the Native American name began to take over, from *sne-ny-mo*, "big strong people." There were many small tribes here and they formed a confederation under this name.

Nan-ch'ang. *City, southeastern China.* The capital of Kiangsi province derives its name from Chinese *nán*, "south," and *chāng*, "prosperous," "flourishing."

Nan-ch'ung. *City, south central China.* The city, in Szechwan province, has a name meaning "filling the south," from Chinese *nán*, "south," and *chōng*, "to fill," "to replenish." The reference is to the extremely fertile and productive plain here.

Nancy. *City, northeastern France.* The city's Medieval Latin name was *Nanceiacum* or *Nantiacum*. This derives from the Gaulish personal name *Nantio*, with the Gallo-Roman suffix *-acum*.

Nanda Devi. *Mountain, northern India.* The mountain, in the Himalayas, is believed by Hindus to be the abode of the goddess *Nanda*, wife of the god Shiva. Hence its name. (Her own name represents Hindi *nandā*, "riches," "happiness," while *devī* is "goddess.") The nearby peak *Nanda Kot* is said to be "Nanda's castle" (Hindi *kot*, "fort," "castle").

Nanded. *City, western India.* The city, in Maharashtra state, derives its name from *Nanda tat*, "*Nanda* border," referring to the boundary of the historic Magadha kingdom here, ruled by the *Nanda*.

Nanga Parbat. *Mountain, northern Pakistan.* The mountain, in the western Himalayas, has a name meaning "bare mountain," from Hindi *nangā*, "naked," "bare," and *parvat* (Punjabi *parbat*), "mountain."

Nanking. *City, east central China.* The capital of Kiangsu province was so named in 1421, when it became a subsidiary capital of China after a period (from 1368) as the overall capital. It was the "southern capital" (Chinese *nán*, "south," and *jīng*, "capital"), as against **Beijing** (Peking), the "northern capital." It was again capital of China from 1928 through 1937, but retained its name.

Nan Ling. *Mountain ranges, southern China.* The series of mountain ranges, dividing Hunan and Kiangsi provinces, derives its name from Chinese *nán*, "south," and *lǐng*, "range." The ranges are also known in English as the *Nan Mountains* (confusingly, in view of the **Nan Shang**).

Nan-ning. *City and port, southern China.* The capital of Kwangsi province derives its name from Chinese *nán*, "south," and *níng*, "peace," "calm."

Nan Shang. *Mountain ranges, northwestern China.* Despite its location, the complex of mountain ranges derives its name from Chinese *nán*, "south," and *shān*, "mountain." The ranges are thus "southern" in relation to some more northern territory. They are also known in English as the *Nan Mountains* (confusingly, in view of the **Nan Ling**).

Nanterre. *Town, northern France.* The town, now a suburb of Paris, had the Roman name *Nemptum Dorum*, deriving from Gaulish *nemeto*, "sacred wood," and *duron*, "gate," "house," "village."

Nantes. *City and port, northwestern France.* The city's name comes from the *Namnetes* or *Nannetes*, the Gaulish people who formerly inhabited the region, with their own name probably from Gaulish *nanto*, "valley." Nantes is at the head of the Loire estuary. The Breton name of Nantes is *Naoned*.

Nantucket. *Island, northeastern United States.* The island off the Massachusetts mainland has a Native American name of uncertain origin. An early map marks the island as *Natocko*.

Nan-t'ung. *City and port, eastern China.* The city, on the Yangtze estuary in Kiangsu province, has a name meaning "southern communication," from Chinese *nán*, "south," and *tōng*, "to penetrate," "to communicate." The city has long been a commercial and communications center.

Nantwich. *Town, northwestern England.* The Cheshire town was formerly a center of salt production, and this is indicated by its name, which means "famous saltworks." The first half of the name represents Middle English *named*, "renowned" (literally "named"), and the second half Old English *wīc*, "settlement," "special place," with specific reference to the saltworks.

Napa. *City and river port, southwestern United States.* The California city, on the river of the same name, is probably named for a Native American people here at the time of settlement in the 19th century. The meaning of their own name is uncertain.

Naperville. *City, east central United States.* The Illinois city was laid out in 1832 by Captain Joseph *Naper*, who built a sawmill here on the Du Page River, and is thus named for him.

Napier. *City and port, northeastern New Zealand.* The city, in eastern North Island, was laid out in 1856 and named for Sir Charles *Napier* (1782–1853), British military commander in India.

Naples. *City and port, southwestern Italy.* The city's name is of Greek origin, from *Neapolis*, "new city," representing *neos*, "new," and *polis*, "city." Naples was laid out by Greek colonists in the 5th century B.C. on a checkered plan, an innovation for its day. The adjective *Neapolitan*, meaning "of Naples," more clearly preserves the Greek original. The Italian name of Naples is *Napoli*.

Nara. *City, southern Japan.* The city, in Honshu island, derives its name from Japanese *na*, "what?," and *ryō*, "good."

Narayanganj. *City and river port, east central Bangladesh.* The city is named for its 12th-century temple of *Lakshmi-Narayana*, dedicated to *Lakshmi*, the Hindu goddess of fortune and beauty, wife of Vishnu, also known as *Narayan*. Hindi *ganj* is "market."

Narbada *see* **Narmada**

Narbonne. *City, southern France.* The ancient town had the Roman name of *Narbona*. This was probably based on an Iberian or Aquitanian root element *nar*, "river," found in various river names. Narbonne was originally on the Mediterranean coast but is now some way inland.

Narmada. *River, central India.* The river has a name meaning "giving pleasure," from Sanskrit *narma*, "pleasure," and *da*, "to give." Hindus believe the Narmada sprang from the body of the god Shiva. The name is also spelled *Narbada*.

Narni. *Town, central Italy.* The town arose on the site of the Roman settlement of *Narnia*, itself named after the *Nera* River here, its own name probably meaning basically "river," as for **Narbonne**.

Narodnaya, Mt. *Mountain, northwestern Russia.* The highest peak in the Urals was discovered in 1927, on the eve of the 10th anniversary of the Russian Revolution, and given a name meaning "of the people," from the adjectival form of Russian *narod*, "people." But this was based on the mountain's existing local name of *Narodaiz*, where the final *-iz*, meaning "rock," "mountain," is added to a word of unknown origin or meaning. The name was thus adopted and adapted for ideological purposes.

Narsimhapur. *Town, central India.* The town, in Madhya Pradesh state, takes its name from the *Narasimha* temple here, itself named for the "man lion" (Hindi *nar*, "male," and *siñh*, "lion") that is an incarnation of the Hindu god Vishnu, with Hindi *pur*, "town," added.

Narvik. *Town and port, northern Norway.* The town's name relates to the inlet at the head of which it lies. The meaning is "narrow bay," from Old German *narwa*, "narrow," and Old Norse *vík*, "bay."

Nashua. *City, northeastern United States.* The New Hampshire city was settled in c.1655 and was originally in Massachusetts, where it was chartered in 1673 as *Dunstable*. It passed to New Hampshire in 1741 and took its present name in 1837 from the river here, its own name said to mean "beautiful river with pebbly bed."

Nashville. *City, east central United States.* The state capital of Tennessee was founded in 1779 and named for the Revolutionary general Francis *Nash* (1742–1777), killed in battle. The official name of the city is now *Nashville-Davidson*, the latter being the county that merged with Nashville in 1963. Its own name also honors a Revolutionary general killed in battle, William L. *Davidson* (1746–1781).

Nassau. *Capital of the Bahamas.* The city, on the northeast coast of New Providence Island, was laid out in 1729 on a site that had borne the name from the 1690s. It was given in honor of King William III of England (1650–1702), of the house of Orange-*Nassau*, who succeeded to the throne in 1689. The royal Dutch title comes from the former duchy of *Nassau* in western Germany. This took its name from what is now the village of *Nassau* in Lahn River valley, the name itself deriving from Old High German *nass*, "wet," perhaps as the original name of the stream now known as the *Kaltbach*, "cold stream," a tributary of the Lahn.

Nasser, Lake. *Lake, northeastern Africa.* The lake, in southern Egypt and northern Sudan, was formed in the 1960s following construction of the Aswan High Dam. It is named for Gamal Abdel *Nasser* (1918–1970), Egyptian president from 1956 to his death. The Sudanese know their portion of the lake as *Lake Nubia* (*see* **Nubia**).

¹Natal. *Historic province, eastern South Africa.* The province was named for the port of the same name here. This has its origin in Portuguese *Costa do Natal*, "Christmas coast," the name given to the maritime region here by the Portuguese navigator Vasco da Gama when he first sighted it on or around December 25, *Christmas* Day, 1497. In 1994 Natal combined with **Kwa-Zulu** to form the new province of *KwaZulu Natal*.

²Natal. *City and port, northeastern Brazil.* The city was founded by the Portuguese in 1597 by a fort known as *Treis Reis Magos*, "three Wise Men." It was raised to town status in 1611 and took its present name, similarly seasonable, from Portuguese *Natal*, "Christmas."

Natchez. *City, southern United States.* The Mississippi city was founded in 1716 and was originally known as *Ft. Rosalie*. In 1729 it survived a massacre by the *Natchez* Native Americans and was subsequently renamed for them. Their own name is believed to mean "woods," "timber."

Natron, Lake. *Lake, northeastern Tanzania.* The lake, named for its *natron* deposits, has an alternate name *Lake Soda*.

Naumburg. *City, east central Germany.* The city, founded in the early 11th century by the margraves of Meissen, has a name meaning "new fort," referring to the defensive post they built over the Saale River here.

Nauplia. *City and port, south central Greece.* The city, in the Peloponnese, probably arose as a port for Argos. Hence its name, from Greek *naus*, "ship," and *pleō*, "I sail," i.e. "naval station." (In Greek mythology, *Nauplius* was the son of the sea god Poseidon.)

Nauru. *Island republic, southwestern Pacific.* The name of the island is of obscure origin. The same goes for its capital, *Makwa*. The island was named *Pleasant Island* by the British navigator John Frean, who was accorded a friendly welcome by the islanders when he landed here in 1798.

Navarino *see* **Pylos**

Navarre. *Historic region, southwestern Europe.* The ancient kingdom in northern Spain and southern France has a name of pre–Latin origin probably based on *nava*, "plain." This despite the Pyrenees that divide the region. The Spanish form of the name is *Navarra*.

Navoi. *City, eastern Uzbekistan.* The city was originally a settlement called *Kermine*. In 1958 it was raised to town status and renamed as now

for the Uzbek poet and philosopher Alisher *Navoi* (1441–1501).

Návpaktos *see* **Lepanto**

Nawabganj. *Town, north central India.* The town, in Uttar Pradesh state, was founded in the late 18th century by Shuja ud-Daula, a *nawab* of Oudh. Hence the name, with Hindi *ganj*, "market."

Naxos. *Island, southeastern Greece.* The Aegean island, in the Cyclades, is said to derive its name from that of an ancestor of the people who originally inhabited it. The meaning of his own name is uncertain.

Nazaré. *Town and port, western Portugal.* The town is named for **Nazareth**, Christ's childhood home.

Nazareth. *City, northern Israel.* The biblical town has a name of uncertain origin. Although mentioned several times in the New Testament (Matthew 2:23, etc.), it is not found in the Old Testament or in any contemporary rabbinical texts. Some scholars see the name as a corruption of that of *Gennesaret*, the lake also known as the *Sea of Galilee* (*see* **Galilee**). At the time of Jesus, Nazareth was an obscure village, and the present city dates from some time after the dawn of the Christian era.

N'djamena. *Capital of Chad.* The city has a name said to mean "resting place," from a local word used for a place where travelers can find refuge from the heat. Until 1973 it was known as *Fort-Lamy*, for the French army officer and explorer François *Lamy* (1858–1900), killed during the battle in which French colonial troops defeated and killed the Sudanese adventurer Rabih az-Zubayr.

Ndola. *Town, northern Zambia.* The town, on the border with the Democratic Republic of Congo, takes its name from a local word meaning "clear spring."

Neagh, Lough. *Lake, east central Northern Ireland.* The largest lake in the British Isles has the Irish name *Loch nEachach*, meaning "*Eochaid*'s lake." The named man is a legendary king of Munster said to have drowned in the lake when it suddenly flooded in the 1st century A.D.

Neanderthal. *Valley, western Germany.* The valley east of Düsseldorf, now a conservation area, has a name meaning "*Neander*'s valley," for Joachim *Neander*, the graecized name (meaning "new man") of the German pastor and poet Joachim *Neumann* (1650–1680), who liked to roam here in the 1670s. The name gave that of "*Neanderthal* Man," whose fossilized remains were found here in 1856.

Neath. *Town, southern Wales.* The town, near

Swansea, is named for the river on which it lies. The river's name is Celtic in origin and probably means "shining one."

Nebitdag. *City, western Turkmenistan.* The city takes its name from a nearby mountain, its own name representing Turkmen *nebit*, "oil," "petroleum" (English *naphtha*), and *dag*, "mountain." The city is the headquarters of the Turkmen oil industry.

Nebo, Mt. *Mountain, north central Jordan.* The biblical mountain (Deuteronomy 34:1, etc.) derives its name from that of *Nabu*, the Mesopotamian god of learning and writing. His own name means "speaker," "announcer."

Nebraska. *State, central United States.* The state is named for the river which flows through it, with the river's own name deriving from a Sioux word meaning "flat," "shallow." The river is actually known by its French colonial name of **Platte**, with the same meaning.

Neckar. *River, southwestern Germany.* The tributary of the Rhine had the Medieval Latin name of *Nicar*, from an Indoeuropean root element *neik*, "violent," "turbulent," referring to its fast current

Neenah. *City, northern United States.* The Wisconsin city was settled in 1835 and at first known as *Winnebago Rapids*, for its location on Lake *Winnebago*. In 1856 it was renamed as now, from the Native American (Winnebago) word meaning "water," "current."

Negev. *Region, southern Israel.* The name of the semidesert region is the Hebrew word for "south," "dry land."

Negro, Rio *see* **Rio Negro**

Negros. *Island, central Philippines.* The island was so named by the Spanish in 1780, from (plural) *negros*, "black," alluding to the dark skins of the islanders.

Neisse. *River, southwestern Poland.* The river, forming part of the border with Germany, has a name that probably derives from the Indoeuropean root element *neid-*, "to flow," "to stream." The Polish form of the name is *Nysa*.

Neiva. *City, south central Colombia.* The city, on the Magdalena River, was founded in 1512 by the Spanish military officer Diego de Ospina and named by him for the *Neiva* River in Haiti.

Nejd. *Region, central Saudi Arabia.* The name of the flat desert region represents Arabic *najd*, "plateau."

Nellore. *City, southern India.* The city, in Andhra Pradesh state, is said to have a Tamil name meaning "good town." However, its local Sanskrit name is *Dhanyapuram*, "rice town"

(Hindi *dhānya*, "crop," and *purā*, "town"), suggesting that *Nell-* is Malayalam *nel*, "rice."

Nelson. *City and port, central New Zealand.* The city, in northern South Island, was settled in 1842 and named for the British admiral Horatio *Nelson*, Lord Nelson (1758–1805), hero of the battles of the Nile (1798) and Trafalgar (1805).

Neman. *River, western Europe.* The river, rising in Belarus and flowing generally west to enter the Baltic Sea in Lithuania, has the Lithuanian name *Nemunas*, meaning "river," "current." Its German name is *Memel*, a corrupt form of this. *See also* **Klaipeda.**

Nemi, Lake. *Lake, central Italy.* The lake was known to the Romans as *Nemorensis lacus*, as well as *Speculum Dianae*, "mirror of *Diana*," with reference to the temple and *nemus* ("grove") here that was sacred to that goddess. A description of Turner's painting of the lake opens Sir James Frazer's famous anthropological study *The Golden Bough* (1890–1915): "Who does not know Turner's picture of the Golden Bough? The scene ... is a dream-like vision of the little woodland lake of Nemi —'Diana's Mirror', as it was called by the ancients."

Nemours. *Town, northern France.* The Roman name of the town was *Nemausus*, as for **Nîmes.** It is therefore probably of identical origin and meaning.

Nepal. *Kingdom, southern Asia.* The name represents Sanskrit *nepāla*, said to be from *nipat*, "to fly down" (itself from *ni*, "down," and *pat* "to fly"), and *ālaya*, "abode," "house." The reference would be to the villages that lie below the many mountains here.

Nepalganj. *Town, southwestern Nepal.* Nepal's largest town, close to the border with India, has a name meaning "market of **Nepal.**" The town is a noted trading center.

Nesebŭr. *Town and resort, eastern Bulgaria.* The town's present name is a corruption of its original name, *Mesembria*, which is of Thracian origin and represents *messa*, "cape," "promontory," and *bria*, "town." This describes the location of Nesebŭr on an island that is connected to the mainland by a narrow strip of land.

Nesher. *Township, northwestern Israel.* The township, founded in 1926, has a Hebrew name meaning "eagle."

Ness, Loch. *Lake, northwestern Scotland.* The lake takes its name from the river that flows out of it to **Inverness.** The river's own name probably represents an Old Celtic word meaning "roaring one."

Netanya. *City, west central Israel.* The city was

founded in 1928 and named for the American-Jewish merchant and philanthopist *Nathan* Straus (1848–1931). The name is also spelled *Natanya*.

Netherlands. *Kingdom, northwestern Europe.* The English name translates the country's Dutch name of *Nederland,* "lower land." The name was originally given to this region of Europe by the Austrians, who saw it as low-lying by comparison with the mountainous terrain of their own country, while today *Low Countries* is sometimes used as a composite name for the three countries Belgium, the Netherlands, and Luxembourg (*see* **Benelux**). An alternate name for the Netherlands, especially among the British, is *Holland.* The origin of this is disputed. It may represent Old Dutch *Holtland,* "forest land," or else *Holland,* "hollow land." This part of continental Europe was certainly well wooded at one time. But the latter etymology seems more likely, referring to the flat terrain, of which a good proportion is below sea level and thus "hollow." The name is used administratively for the two western provinces of *Noord-Holland* (North Holland) and *Zuid-Holland* (South Holland).

Netivot. *Town, southern Israel.* The town, founded in 1956 to house Jewish immigrants, has a Hebrew name meaning "roads."

Netzer Sereni. *Kibbutz, central Israel.* The kibbutz was founded by Holocaust survivors in 1948 and named for the Italian-born Jewish war hero Enzo *Sereni* (1905–1944), who parachuted into Europe in World War II and was captured and executed by the Nazis. *Netzer* is Hebrew for "branch," "sprout."

Neubrandenburg. *City, northeastern Germany.* The city was founded in 1248 by the margraves of **Brandenburg** as a fortified outpost. Hence its name, meaning "new *Brandenburg.*"

Neuburg an der Donau. *City, southern Germany.* A Bavarian ducal palace was originally built here by the **Danube** on the site of a Celtic and Roman settlement. In the 10th century a fort was added nearby, and was later named *Novum Burgum,* "new fort." (A document of c.1015 states that *burg* here should be understood as "town" rather than "fort.")

Neuchâtel. *Town, western Switzerland.* The town's name corresponds exactly to that of England's ¹**Newcastle**, from French *neuf,* "new," and *châtel,* an older form of *château,* "castle." The Medieval Latin name of the town, recorded in the 11th century, was *Novum Castellum,* and the "new castle" dates from this time.

Neugablonz. *Town, southern Germany.* The town's name means "new *Gablonz,*" distinguish-

ing it from *Gablonz,* the German name of **Jablonec nad Nisou**, in the Czech Republic. As (probably) for that town, the origin here is Slavic, with *Gablonz* representing *Jablonec* and meaning "apple tree."

Neuilly. *District of Paris, northern France.* The name derives from the male personal name *Nobilis* or *Novellius,* itself probably formed from Latin *novellus,* a diminutive of *novus,* "new," and referring to the owner of newly-cleared land. The name is found elsewhere in France, and the different places are usually distinguished by a suffix naming their rivers. This one is thus *Neuilly-sur-Seine,* while another district of Paris is *Neuilly-sur-Marne.*

Neumünster. *City, north central Germany.* The city arose by an Augustinian monastery recorded in 1136 with the Latin name *Novum Monasterium,* "new monastery," and this gave the present name.

Neunkirchen. *City, southwestern Germany.* The city has a name first recorded in 1281 as *Nonkirke,* meaning "(settlement by the) new church."

Neusiedl. *Town, eastern Austria.* The town's name means "new settlement." It lies on the northern shore of the *Neusiedler See,* named after it. The southern part of the lake is in Hungary, where it is known as the *Fertő-tó,* "swamp lake."

Neuss. *City, western Germany.* The city arose on the site of a Roman settlement recorded by Tacitus as *Novaesium.* The origin and meaning of this are unknown.

Neustadt an der Weinstrasse. *City, southwestern Germany.* The city's name is the German equivalent of its Medieval Latin name, recorded in 1235 as *Nova Civitas,* "new town." The rest of the name is not only for distinguishing purposes but locates this particular "new town," founded in 1200, in the *Weinstraße,* "wine route," the center of the Rhineland-Palatinate wine trade. The addition is recent, and was adopted by the city from 1936 through 1945 and again from 1950. Its earlier name was *Neustadt an der Haardt,* from the slope of the **Haardt Mountains** on which it arose.

Neustrelitz. *City, northeastern Germany.* The city was founded by Duke Adolf Friedrich III in 1733 after the earlier ducal residence at nearby *Strelitz* had burned down. The basic name is of Slavic origin and means "(settlement of the) archers," from Old Slavic *strela,* "arrow."

Neustria *see* **Austria**

Neu-Ulm. *City, southern Germany.* The city grew up from 1810 on the right bank of the Danube opposite **Ulm**. It officially adopted its present name, meaning "new *Ulm*," on April 1, 1814.

Neuwied. *City, western Germany.* The city was founded in 1653 as a settlement for religious refugees by a castle built in 1648 belonging to Count Frederick III of *Wied*. Hence the name, "new *Wied*," by contrast with an earlier castle *Wied*, later *Altwied*, some 5 miles (8 km) away.

Neva. *River, western Russia.* The river has a name of Finnish origin, from *neva*, "marsh," "peat bog." The name is a historic one for Lake **Ladoga**, which drains through the Neva into the Gulf of Finland. The river's name therefore probably relates directly to the lake rather than to its marshy delta.

Nevada. *State, western United States.* The state's name is a shortening of that of the [2]**Sierra Nevada**, the mountain range in eastern California that forms Nevada's western boundary.

Nevers. *Town, central France.* The town takes its name from the *Nièvre* River on which it stands. The river's own name probably represents a basic root element *nev* meaning "water," "river." The historic province of *Nivernais* took its name from Nevers. The Roman name of the town was *Noviodunum*, from Gaulish *novio*, "new," and *dunon*, "fort."

Nevis. *Island, eastern West Indies.* The island, in the Leeward Islands, is said to have been so named by Christopher Columbus in 1493 for the resemblance of its cloud-topped mountain to *las nieves*, "the snows." Nevis forms an independent state together with **St. Kitts**.

[1]**Newark**. *Town, north central England.* The Nottinghamshire town has an Old English name meaning "new work," referring to the Anglo-Saxon fort that was built over the former Roman one. The full formal name of the town is *Newark-on-Trent*, for its location on the **Trent** River.

[2]**Newark**. *City and port, eastern United States.* The New Jersey city was settled by Puritans from Connecticut in 1666 and is said to have been given its name by the Rev. Abraham Pierson for his home town of [1]**Newark**, England. However, other sources claim that the name had a biblical interpretation, as *New Ark*, or that the newly-built settlement was a *New Work*, like its English namesake. It may well have been a blend of two or all of these.

New Bedford. *City and port, northeastern United States.* The Massachusetts city, in Bristol County, was settled in 1652, originally as part of Dartmouth. In 1787 it was incorporated as *Bedford*, for **Bedford**, England, but was later called *New Bedford* for distinction from *Bedford* in Middlesex County.

New Britain. *Island, South Pacific.* The largest island of the Bismarck Archipelago, Papua New Guinea, was so named in 1699 by the British navigator William Dampier. The archipelago passed into German hands (as its name still implies) in 1884, when New Britain became *Neu-Pommern*, "New **Pomerania**." The original name was readopted after World War I, when the territory was mandated to Australia.

New Brunswick. *Province, eastern Canada.* The province was created in 1784, when it was separated off from Nova Scotia, and it was then given its present name, in honor of George III (1738–1820). He was of the house of Hanover, which had the alternate name of **Brunswick**.

Newbury. *Town, southern England.* The West Berkshire town has a name meaning "new town," or more exactly "new market town." In many English placenames a final *-bury* (from Old English *burh*) means "fortified settlement." But Newbury arose only in the 12th century, later than most other places with this element, so its name requires a more specific interpretation.

New Caledonia. *Island territory, southwestern Pacific.* The main island of the group, annexed by France in 1853, was discovered by Captain Cook on September 4, 1774, and named by him *Caledonia*, the Latin name of Scotland. He chose the name to complement that of the neighboring *New Hebrides* (now **Vanuatu**), which he had named shortly before. Moreover New Caledonia is to the south of Vanuatu and is larger in area, just as mainland Scotland is in relation to the Hebrides.

[1]**Newcastle**. *City and river port, northeastern England.* The city, formally known as *Newcastle upon Tyne*, has a name that means what it says, referring to the "new castle" that was built in 1080 by Robert Curthose, son of William the Conqueror, on the site of a former Roman fort. The name is found elsewhere in England with the same meaning, as for *Newcastle*-under-Lyme, Staffordshire, where the "new castle" was built in the 12th century. *Cp.* **Neuchâtel, Nyborg**.

[2]**Newcastle**. *City and port, southeastern Australia.* The city, in New South Wales, arose as a penal settlement in 1801 and developed as a coal port, taking its name from the *Newcastle* coalfield nearby, itself appropriately named for [1]**Newcastle**, England, whose principal export was formerly coal.

New Delhi *see* **Delhi**

New England. *Territory, northeastern United States.* The territory that now comprises America's six northeastern states was given its name in 1614 by the English captain John Smith. The name turned out to be appropriate, since the first English settlement was established six years later at Plymouth, Massachusetts, by Puritans from Plymouth, England. Smith had actually given the name in a generally commemorative way for his homeland, rather than with an eye to future colonial development by his fellow countrymen.

New Forest. *Forest region, southern England.* The woodland region, mainly in Hampshire, was "new" when it was created as a hunting preserve by William the Conqueror in the 11th century. Its name is recorded in the Domesday Book (1086) as *Nova Foresta*.

Newfoundland. *Province, eastern Canada.* The name means what it says, denoting newly discovered land. It evolved from the *new founde isle* recorded by its discoverer John Cabot in 1497, with *New founde launde* appearing in official documents as early as 1502. The French name of the province is *Terre-Neuve*, with the "found" element omitted.

New Guinea. *Island, western Pacific.* The island, to the north of Australia, was sighted in 1526 by the Portuguese navigator Jorge de Meneses but not named until 1546, when the Spanish explorer I. Ortiz de Retes so called it from the resemblance (as it seemed to him) of the indigenous people here to those of **Guinea** in West Africa. The name is now used geographically for the island and administratively for part of the territory of the independent state of *Papua New Guinea* (*see* **Papua**).

New Hampshire. *State, northeastern United States.* The state was given its name in 1629 by the English settler Captain John Mason, of Portsmouth, **Hampshire**, who had been granted territory here.

Newhaven. *Town and port, southern England.* The East Sussex port has a name meaning "new harbor," referring to the harbor that was built in the 16th century when the lower section of the Ouse River was diverted from nearby Seaford to enter the sea here. The French port of **Le Havre**, due south of Newhaven across the English Channel, was itself known by the English name of *Newhaven* for some time after its foundation in 1517.

New Haven. *City and port, eastern United States.* The Connecticut city was settled in 1638 and was originally called *Quinnipiac*, for the river at the mouth of which it lies. It was renamed as now in 1640, the name describing its status as a "new harbor."

New Hebrides *see* **Vanuatu**

New Ireland. *Island, South Pacific.* The island,

in the Bismarck Archipelago, Papua New Guinea, was discovered by the Dutch in 1616 but not named until 1767, when the English navigator Philip Carteret arrived here. He discovered that the island named **New Britain** was not one island, as had been thought, but two, so he named the smaller one, to the northeast, to compliment (and complement) the larger.

New Jersey. *State, eastern United States.* The state was so named in 1664 by one of the proprietors of the territory, Sir George Carteret, for his native island of **Jersey** in the Channel Islands.

Newmarket. *Town, eastern England.* The name of the Suffolk town dates from the 13th century, when the settlement gained the right to hold a "new market."

New Mexico. *State, southwestern United States.* The state's name is an English translation of its original Spanish name, *Nuevo México*. This was given the territory in 1562 by the Spanish explorer Francesco de Ibarra in the hope that it would become as rich as neighboring **Mexico**.

New Orleans. *City and port, southern United States.* The Louisiana city was founded by the French in 1718 and named *Nouvelle Orléans* in honor of the French regent, Philippe, duc d'**Orléans** (1674–1723). The name was anglicized when the city passed from the French to the United States with the Louisiana Purchase (1803). The French still know the city as *La Nouvelle-Orléans*.

¹Newport. *City and port, southeastern Wales.* The former Monmouthshire city was chartered in the 14th century and has a self-explanatory name describing it as a "new port," that is, a new town with a harbor here at the mouth of the Usk River. The name is found elsewhere in England and Wales, in some cases for an inland town. This is because Old English *port* could mean both "town with a harbor" and "town with a market."

²Newport. *City and port, northeastern United States.* The Rhode Island city was founded in 1639 by a group of Puritans from Massachusetts who had earlier founded *Portsmouth* in the north of the island. The name may have sprung as much from this as from a *Newport* in England (*see* **¹Newport**).

Newport News. *City and port, eastern United States.* The Virginia city is believed to have derived its original name from two of its founders in c.1621, Christopher *Newport* and William *Newce*, with the latter's name subsequently altered through popular association with the word *news*. But it was a "new port" in any case from the start.

New Providence. *Island, central Bahamas.*
The name of the principal island of the Bahamas
is said to derive from a 16th-century governor's
thanks to "Divine Providence" for surviving a
shipwreck here. *New* was added later to avoid
confusion with a small island off British Honduras (now **Belize**).

Newquay. *Town and resort, southwestern England.* The Cornish town has a name dating from
1349, when Bishop Lacy of Exeter granted an
indulgence for a *new quay* to be built here. The
Cornish name of the town is *Towan Blistra.* The
first word means "sand dune," but the second is
of obscure origin.

New Rochelle. *City, eastern United States.* The
New York city was founded by a group of
Huguenot refugees in 1688 and named for **La
Rochelle**, France.

Newry. *Town, southeastern Northern Ireland.*
The name of the town in Co. Down represents
its Irish name *An tIúr,* "the yew tree." According to tradition, St. Patrick planted a yew tree
at the head of the lough (lake) here when he
founded a monastery in the 6th century.

New Siberian Islands. *Island group, northeastern Russia.* The Arctic archipelago takes its
name from the single island of *New Siberia* here,
itself so named in 1920 by the Russian polar
explorer M. M. Gedenshtrem, who saw it as an
extension of **Siberia** (though not at that stage as
an island). The Russian name of the group is
Novosibirskiye ostrova.

New South Wales. *State, southeastern Australia.* The name was originally that chosen for
the whole of the east coast of Australia in 1770
by Captain Cook, who fancied a resemblance
between this coastline and that of southern
Wales. (There is some evidence that he planned
to call the territory *New Wales,* but added *South*
to denote its location in the southern hemisphere.) The territory named *New South Wales*
then came to include the whole of the Australian
continent except Western Australia. The establishment of new colonies gradually reduced its
size, until it was finally delimited as now in 1915.

Newton. *City, northeastern United States.* The
Massachusetts city was settled in 1639 as part of
Cambridge. It was separated from it in 1688 as
New Town and adopted the present form of this
name in 1691. The city has since extended its
bounds to include 14 residential "villages," eight
of which have *Newton* in their names.

Newton Abbot. *Town, southwestern England.*
The Devon town has a basic Old English name,
meaning "new farm," "new village," that is the
most common in England. Many places of the

name thus need distinguishing, and here the
added word indicates that this *Newton* was given
to the *abbot* of Torre Abbey (*see* **Torquay**), to
the south.

New York. *City and state, eastern United
States.* The Dutch founded the settlement of
New Amsterdam on Manhattan Island in 1625
and the Dutch colony of *New Netherlands* developed from it. When the English defeated the
Dutch in 1664, they renamed it *New York* in
honor of the duke of **York** and Albany (1633–
1701), the future James II, to whom it had been
entrusted by his brother, Charles II. *See also*
[1]**Albany**. New York state was an original state of
the Union, admitted in 1788.

New Zealand. *Island state, southwestern
Pacific.* The name of the independent state is a
partly anglicized form of the original Dutch
name, *Nieuw Zeeland,* "new sea land," given to
some extent descriptively but chiefly with reference to the Dutch province of **Zeeland**. The
islands were discovered in 1642 by the Dutch
explorer Abel Tasman (*see* **Tasmania**), and he
originally named them *Staaten Landt,* "land of
the States," with reference to the original name
of the Netherlands as the *United Provinces.* The
Dutch authorities changed the name the following year. The Maori name for New Zealand,
Aotearoa, "land of the long white cloud," was
introduced relatively recently.

Neyshabur. *Town, northeastern Iran.* The
town is named for its supposed founder, King
Shapur I (died A.D. 272). The name is also
spelled *Nishapur.*

Nezahualcóyotl. *City, central Mexico.* The
city, one of Mexico City's largest (and poorest)
suburban municipalities, created in 1963, takes
its name from the Aztec philosopher and poet
Nezahualcóyotl ("Hungry Coyote") (1402–1472),
king of Texcoco.

Niagara. *River, eastern United States.* The
river, on the border between the United States
and Canada, has a name that may represent
Native American (Huron or Iroquois) *nee-agg-
arah,* "thundering water," referring to the famous
falls. A more likely origin, however, is in an Iroquois word meaning "neck of land," or more precisely "land cut in two," referring not to the falls
themselves but describing the point where the
Niagara River flows into Lake Ontario.

[1]**Niagara Falls**. *City, northeastern United
States.* The New York city, at the great falls of
the **Niagara** River, has its origins in *Fort
Schlosser,* a British fort built here in 1761. In 1805
a grist mill and settlement were founded under
the name of *Manchester,* and the village subse-

quently combined with others under the present name. The city lies opposite ²**Niagara Falls**, Canada.

²**Niagara Falls.** *City, southeastern Canada.* The Ontario city, on the left bank of the **Niagara** River, opposite ¹**Niagara Falls**, USA, was originally named *Elgin* when it began to develop in 1853. It was renamed *Clifton* in 1856 and received its present name in 1881.

Niamey. *Capital of Niger.* According to one account, the city derives its name from the orders of an African chief here to his seven slaves, *Wa niammane*, "stay here." This then became *Niamma* and finally *Niamey*. But this is just one of a number of stories purporting to explain the name, and its actual origin remains uncertain.

Nicaea. *Historic city, northwestern Turkey.* The city is said to have been given its name in honor of *Nikaia*, wife of the 3d-century B.C. Macedonian general Lysimachus, who captured it. Its present Turkish name is *İznik*, from Greek *eis Nikian*, "to Nicaea."

Nicaragua. *Republic, central Central America.* The region of the country that is now Nicaragua was visited in 1522 by the Spanish conquistador Gil González Dávila, who is said to have named it for *Nicarao*, a local Native American chieftain.

Nice. *City and port, southern France.* The city was founded in the 3d or 2d century B.C. by Greek colonists from Massilia (now **Marseilles**). They dedicated it to *Nike*, the Greek goddess of victory, in gratitude for their defeat of the Ligurians (or Etruscans). *Cp.* **Nicosia.** The Italians know Nice as *Nizza*.

Nicobar Islands. *Island group, Bay of Bengal.* The islands, belonging to India, have a name that is said to represent an original form *Nakkavaram*, "land of the naked," from Hindi *nagñā*, "naked," and *varam*, "country." The reference is presumably to the nudity of the people. (An Arab historian, writing in c.1300, relates that the men were entirely unclothed while the women wore only a girdle of coconut leaves.) An alternate theory sees the name as an alteration of *Narikeladvipa*, "coconut islands," from Hindi *nārikel*, "coconut (tree)," and *dvīp*, "island." *Cp.* **Cocos Islands.**

Nicomedia *see* **İzmit**

Nicosia. *Capital of Cyprus.* The city was founded before the 7th century B.C. and either dedicated to *Nike*, the Greek goddess of victory (whose name actually means "victory"), or named for some particular victory in battle. The Greek name of Nicosia is *Levkosía*, from Greek *leukos*, "white," "shining," and this gave the city's Turkish name of *Lefkoşa*. (The Greek and Turk-ish names are now more usual than *Nicosia* in official literature and media reports.)

Nidwalden *see* **Unterwalden**

Nienburg. *City, western Germany.* The city arose in the early 11th century as a defensive post by a crossing of the Weser River with a name meaning simply "new fort."

Nieuwpoort. *Town and port, western Belgium.* The name means what it says, and the town was established in the 12th century as a *new port* on the North Sea at the mouth of the Yser River.

Niger. *Republic, western Africa.* The country takes its name from the river that flows through its western part. The first Arab explorers called the river *nahr al-anhur*, "river of rivers," translating the local Tuareg name for it, *egereou n-igereouen*, from *egereou*, "big river," "sea," and this word's plural, *igereouen*. It was the second part of the latter name that probably gave the modern *Niger*. The present form of the name is first recorded in the writings of the Arab explorer Leo Africanus, who noted it in 1526 as *Niger*, probably under the influence of Latin *niger*, "black," as if the river name meant "river of the blacks."

Nigeria. *Republic, western Africa.* The country takes its name from the **Niger** River, which flows south through it to the Gulf of Guinea from neighboring Niger.

Niigata. *City and port, northwestern Japan.* The city, at the mouth of the Shinano River in the island of Honshu, derives its name from Japanese *nii-*, "new," and *kata*, "inlet," "lagoon."

Niihama. *City and port, southern Japan.* The city, in the island of Shikoko on the Inland Sea coast, derives its name from Japanese *nii-*, "new," and *hama*, "beach." It was originally a fishing village.

Nijmegen. *City, eastern Netherlands.* The city has derived its name from that of the Roman settlement of *Noviomagus*, from Gaulish *novio*, "new," and *magos*, "place," "market." There were many other places of the name in Europe. *Cp.* **Chichester, Longjumeau, Noyon.**

Nikko. *City and resort, central Japan.* The city, a mountain resort in central Honshu, has a name meaning "sunlight," alluding to its splendor. There is a Japanese proverb: "Do not say *kekkō* ("excellent") until you have seen *Nikko*."

Nikolayev. *City and port, southern Ukraine.* The city is so named either because it was founded on December 6, 1788, the feastday of St. *Nicholas* (Russian *Nikolai*), or because the first ship to be launched here (in 1790) was the 44-gun frigate *St. Nicholas*, named for the patron saint of sailors. The Ukrainian form of the name is *Mykolayiv*.

Nikolayevsk. *Town and port, eastern Russia.* The town, at the mouth of the Amur River, was founded in 1852 as a trading post in the reign of *Nicholas* I (1796–1855), and is named for him. Its full name is *Nikolayevsk-na-Amure,* "Niko-layevsk-on-**Amur**," with the addition given in 1926 to distinguish this town from others identically named, such as *Nikolayevsk* in western Russia (now *Pugachyov*).

¹Nikopol. *Town, east central Ukraine.* The town, on the Dnieper River, was founded in 1781 on the site of a village called *Nikitin Rog,* "*Ni-kita*'s horn," referring to the promontory here. Its original name was *Slavyansk,* "Slav town," but this did not become permanent because at that time there was a fashion for Greek-style names in this part of Russia (as it then was). Doubtless under the influence of the village name it was thus renamed *Nikopol,* as if *Nicopolis,* "victory town."

²Nikopol. *Town, northern Bulgaria.* The town, on the Danube, was founded in the 7th century during the period of Byzantine supremacy in Bulgaria, and was originally known by the Greek name of *Nicopolis,* "town of victory." The name does not appear to mark any special victory, and may have been adopted from another *Nicopolis* further south, on the Rositsa River. This was founded by the Romans in the time of Trajan and was so named to mark their victory over the Dacians in A.D. 102.

Nikšić. *Town, west central Montenegro.* The town was originally a Roman encampment called *Anagastum.* The meaning of this is not known, but it is probably based on an ethnic name. By the 12th century this name had become *Onogost,* and the present form of it is a further Montenegrin corruption.

Nile. *River, eastern and northeastern Africa.* The river name is one of the oldest in the world, going back to the Semitic root word *nahal,* meaning "river." The Nile is mentioned more than once in the Bible, but never by name. It is always referred to as "the river" (Hebrew *yĕ'ōr*), as: "Pharaoh dreamed: and, behold, he stood by the river" (Genesis 41:1). *See also* **Jordan.** The *Blue Nile,* rising in Ethiopia and flowing southeast then northwest to join the White Nile at Khartoum, has a name translating Arabic *al-baḥr al-azraḳ,* said to refer to the reflection of the blue of the sky in the waters of the river when it is running low. The *White Nile,* from Arabic *al-baḥr al-abyaḍ,* is the Nile proper as it flows northward through Sudan to join the Blue Nile at Khartoum. The reference here is said to be to the color of the water when the river is in flood

and carrying materials in suspension. But another theory sees the colors as symbolic, "blue" denoting east, and "white" west. *Cp.* **White Sea.**

Nilgiri Hills. *Mountains, southeastern India.* The mountains, in Tamil Nadu state, have a name meaning "blue hills," from Hindi *nīl,* "blue," and *giri,* "hill," "mountain." The reference, in part, is to their many eucalyptus trees. *Cp.* **Blue Mountains.**

Nîmes. *City, southern France.* The city was known to the Roman as *Nemausus,* a name ultimately going back to Gaulish *nemo,* "sanctuary." **Nemours,** in the north of France, has a name of identical origin.

Nineveh. *Historic city, northern Iraq.* The ancient capital of Assyria is said to derive its name from that of *Ninus,* the mythological first king of Assyria and husband of Semiramis. According to the Bible, however, Nineveh was founded in Assyria by Nimrod, grandson of Noah (Genesis 10:11), and "the land of Assyria" is equated with "the land of Nimrod" (Micah 5:6). This suggests there may be some sort of connection between the names *Nineveh* and *Nimrod,* especially since the latter is said to have given the name of the historic city of *Nimrud,* only 23 miles (37 km) from Nineveh.

Ning-po. *City and river port, eastern China.* The city, in Chekiang province at the confluence of the Yung River and its tributary, the Yu-yao, has a name meaning "calm waves," from Chinese *níng,* "calm," and *bō,* "wave."

Ningsia. *Region, northern China.* The autonomous region derives its name from Chinese *níng,* "peaceful," "calm," and *xià,* for *Hsia,* the first known (but possibly legendary) Chinese dynasty, traditionally dated from 2205 B.C. to 1766 B.C.

Niort. *City, western France.* The city was known in the 6th century as *Noiordo,* a name that represents *Novioritu,* from Gaulish *novio,* "new," and *ritu,* "ford." Its later Latin name was *Nyrax, Nyractis.* The ford would have been over the Sèvre Niortaise River here.

Nipigon, Lake. *Lake, southeastern Canada.* The lake, in west central Ontario, has a Native American name meaning "deep, clear water."

Nipissing, Lake. *Lake, southeastern Canada.* The lake, in southeastern Ontario, has a Native American name meaning "little water."

Niš. *City, southern Serbia.* The city takes its name from the *Nisava* River on which it lies. The river's own name is probably based on a Slav word related to Serbo-Croat *niz,* "down," "below," describing a river at the bottom of a valley. *Cp.* **Neisse.**

Nishinomiya. *City, central Japan.* The city, in the island of Honshu, derives its name from Japanese *nishi*, "west," and *miya*, "temple," "palace," with the middle *-no-* the sign of the genitive. The overall meaning is thus "temple of the west." There are temples here dating from the 7th and 8th centuries.

Niterói. *City, southeastern Brazil.* The coastal city, a suburb of Rio de Janeiro, was founded in 1671 and became a village in 1819 with the Portuguese name of *Villa Real do Praia Grande*, "royal town of the big beach." It was made a city in 1836 when it took its present name, from a Native American term meaning "hidden water."

Nitsanim. *Kibbutz, western Israel.* The kibbutz, near the Mediterranean, was founded in 1943 with a Hebrew name meaning "buds."

Nivernais *see* **Nevers**

Nizamabad. *City, southern India.* The city, in Andhra Pradesh state, has a name meaning "city of the nizam," from the title (meaning "governor") of the hereditary ruler of the former state of Hyderabad, which in 1956 was divided between Andhra Pradesh, Mysore (Karnataka), and Maharashtra.

Nizhny Novgorod. *City, western Russia.* The name of the city means literally "lower **Novgorod**," relating it to the older town northwest of Moscow. The latter became the center of a principality in the 9th century, an event regarded as the founding of the Russian state, and for this reason was often known as *Novgorod Velikij*, "Novgorod the great." The later Novgorod, which originally shared its name (meaning "new town") when founded in the 13th century, was therefore "lower" or less important by comparison, and was subsequently designated as such. The name thus only coincidentally refers to the city's more southerly location than its eponym. From 1932 through 1990 Nizhny Novgorod was known as *Gorky*, for the Russian writer Maxim Gorky (1868–1936), who was born here. (He is said to have opposed the renaming.)

Nizhny Tagil. *City, west central Russia.* The city's name means "lower *Tagil*," indicating its location further down the river of this name than *Verkhny Tagil*, "upper *Tagil*." The river's own name is said to be of Ugric origin, meaning simply "stream," "river."

Nkongsamba. *City, western Cameroon.* The city's name is said to derive from a local word meaning "seven hills," describing its location.

Nobeoka. *City and port, southern Japan.* The city, in the island of Kyushu, derives its name from Japanese *nobe*, "all," "total," and *oka*, "hill." Kyushu is a mountainous island.

Nogent-sur-Marne. *Town, northern France.* The town, now a suburb of Paris, has a basic name deriving from Gaulish *novio*, "new," and the Latin suffix *-entum*. The name thus originally denoted a new Gaulish settlement, and places so designated often became Roman towns named *Novientum* or *Novigentum*. In modern times they have come to be differentiated by distinguishing suffixes, as here with the name of the **Marne** River on which the town stands.

Nógrád. *County, northern Hungary.* The county takes its name from the village of the same (Slavic) name, meaning "new fortress," for what is now an old and ruined fortress. *Cp.* **Novgorod.**

Noirmoutier. *Island, western France.* The island, in the Bay of Biscay off the west coast of France, is noted for its monastery. It was this that gave its name, from Latin *Nigrum Monasterium*, a corruption (suggesting a meaning "black monastery") of *Nerium Monasterium*, from the phrase *in Herio monasterio*, "in the monastery of *Herus*." The original name of the island was thus *Herus*. The meaning of this is unknown. French *Noir-* in the present name translates the misleading Latin *Nigrum*.

Noisy-le-Grand. *Town, northern France.* The name ultimately derives from Latin *nux, nucis*, "nut." This *Noisy*, distinguished from others as "the great," was at one time noted for its nut trees.

Nola. *Town, southern Italy.* The town has a long history and was known as *Novla*, "new town," even before it passed to the Romans in 313 B.C. Its present name is a form of this early name.

Nome. *City and port, northwestern United States.* The city, in western Alaska, arose in c.1898 when gold was discovered here and was at first named *Anvil City*, for nearby *Anvil* Creek. When the mining stampede had died down it was renamed as now for the cape to the east, itself said to have been named for a British cartographer's query on a chart of 1849, "? Name." An alternate origin is quoted below.

Cape Nome derives its name from the Indian word "*No-me*," which signifies in English, "I don't know." In former days, when whalers anchored here to trade, the invariable answer given by the natives to all questions put by the white men was "*No-me*," meaning that they did not understand, and the name of the place was thus derived [Harry de Windt, *From Paris to New York by Land*, 1904].

Nord. *Department, northern France.* The department's name, meaning "north," describes its location along the Belgian frontier and by the Strait of Dover. All four French cardinal points, *nord, sud, est, ouest*, were adopted from Old English.

Norden *see* **Scandinavia**

Nordhausen. *City, north central Germany.* The city, first mentioned in 929, derives its name from Old High German *nord*, "north," and *husen*, "houses," "settlement." Just 3 miles (5 km) to the south is the smaller contrasting *Sundhausen*, "southern houses" (Old High German *sund*, "south").

Nordiya. *Settlement, west central Israel.* The settlement was founded in 1948 and named for the Zionist leader Max *Nordau* (original name Simon Maximilian Südfeld) (1849–1923).

Nördlingen. *City, southern Germany.* The city, on the Eger River, has a name meaning "(settlement of) *Nordilo*'s people," with an Old German personal name.

¹**Norfolk.** *County, eastern England.* The county is so named as it was settled in Anglo-Saxon times by the "northern folk," i.e. by the northern group of East Anglian peoples, as distinct from the southern group, who inhabited what is now ¹**Suffolk.**

²**Norfolk.** *City and port, eastern United States.* The Virginia city was founded in 1682 and named for the English county of ¹**Norfolk.**

Norfolk Island. *Island, South Pacific.* The island, between New Caledonia and New Zealand, was discovered by Captain Cook in 1774 and named by him for Edward Howard, 9th Duke of *Norfolk* (1686–1777).

Norilsk. *City, northern Russia.* The city, founded in 1935, derives its name from the local root word *nor* or *nar*, "water," found in the names of many lakes and rivers here, north of the Arctic Circle.

Normal. *Town, east central United States.* The Illinois town adjoins Bloomington and was itself called *North Bloomington* until 1857. That year the Illinois State *Normal* University was founded. The town grew up around the school and took its title, a *normal* school being a teachers' training college.

Norman. *City, south central United States.* The Oklahoma city arose in 1889 and was named for Abner *Norman*, a Santa Fe Railway engineer.

Normandy. *Historic region, northern France.* The region was named for its inhabitants, the *Normans*, themselves so called as they were descendants of the Vikings or *Norsemen* ("northmen"), the 10th-century Scandinavian conquerors of the region and of its indigenous French. *Cp.* **Norway.**

Norrbotten. *County, northern Sweden.* The county's name represents its Old Swedish name of *Nurra butn*, from *Nurra*, "north," and *butn*, "bottom," "end." To the south of it lies **Västerbotten.**

Norrköping. *Town and port, southeastern Sweden.* Despite its location, the town has a name meaning "northern trading place," from Swedish *norr*, "north," and *köping*, "trading place," "village." It is "north" by comparison with the much smaller *Söderköping*, "southern village," just south of it.

Norrland. *Region, northern Sweden.* The region's self-descriptive name means simply "northern land," from Swedish *norr*, "north," and *land*, "land."

Northampton. *City, central England.* The city, in the county of the same name, was originally *Hampton* (or its Anglo-Saxon equivalent), meaning "home farm." It then added *north* to be distinguished from its southern namesake, now **Southampton**, although that town's earlier name of *Hampton* had a different meaning. The two cities are some distance apart but were linked by a north-south route in medieval times.

North Carolina *see* ¹**Carolina**

North Dakota *see* **Dakota**

Northeim. *Town, north central Germany.* The town arose in the 10th century on the site of a Frankish settlement of this name, called "northern abode," by contrast with nearby *Sudheim*, "southern abode." The village of *Medenheim*, "middle abode," lies between them.

Northern Ireland. *Territory, western United Kingdom.* Geographically, the name represents the *northern* part of the island of **Ireland.** Politically, the name became official in 1920, when British prime minister David Lloyd George introduced the Government of Ireland Act, which provided for the establishment of two self-governing units, one comprising six of Ulster's (mainly Protestant) nine counties ("Northern Ireland") and the other comprising the remaining (mainly Catholic) 23 counties of Ireland ("Southern Ireland"). Northern Ireland is now often unofficially called **Ulster** in consequence.

Northern Land *see* **Severnaya Zemlya**

Northern Territory. *Territory, north central Australia.* The territory, with its self-explanatory name, nearly had a more original name. It was annexed to South Australia in 1863, having earlier been part of New South Wales. The following year the name *Alexandra Land* was proposed for it, in honor of Princess *Alexandra* (1844–1925), the future wife of Edward VII, and this was officially adopted for a time. In World War

II the name *Churchill Land* was put forward, in honor of Sir Winston *Churchill* (1874–1965), and when Queen *Elizabeth* II (born 1926) visited Australia in 1954, in the course of her first Commonwealth tour, *Elizabeth Land* was similarly suggested. But the prosaic name prevailed.

North Korea *see* **Korea**

North Land *see* **Severnaya Zemlya**

North Little Rock. *City, south central United States.* The Arkansas city was settled in 1812 and was at first known as *Cantillon*. In 1853 it became *Huntersville*, and then *Argenta Town*, for the Hotel *Argenta*, built here in the late 1850s. It was annexed by the city of **Little Rock** in 1891, then incorporated as a town in 1901 and renamed as now.

North Sea. *Sea, northwestern Europe.* The sea, between continental Europe and the British Isles, was so named by the Dutch by contrast with the *Zuider Zee*, "southern sea" (*see* **IJsselmeer**). The Romans knew it as the *Oceanus Germanicus*, "German sea," and the Danes have sometimes referred to it as the *Vesterhavet*, "western sea." The name *German Sea* was in general English use down to at least the 18th century: "NOR-FOLK, a county of England, bounded by the German sea on the north and east" (*Encyclopædia Britannica*, 1771).

Northumberland. *County, northeastern England.* The name is effectively "North Humber Land," and refers to the Anglo-Saxon people who occupied land to the north of the **Humber** River. Their kingdom here from the 7th to 9th century had the Medieval Latin name of *Northumbria*. Its territory was much larger than the present county and included land north of the Tweed in what is now southeastern Scotland.

Northumbria *see* **Northumberland**

North-West Frontier Province. *Province, northwestern Pakistan.* The province, created in 1901, is bounded to the north and west by Afghanistan, and the "frontier" of the name is the border so formed. The name should not be confused with that of the former *North-West Provinces* of India, now part of Uttar Pradesh state.

Northwest Territories. *Region, northern Canada.* The extensive region, generally more in the north of Canada than the *northwest* (which geographically includes the Yukon Territory), originally embraced the five administrative regions (*territories*) of Baffin, Fort Smith, Inuvik, Keewatin, and Kitikmeot. In 1999 the new territory of **Nunavut** was created out of the eastern portion of the Northwest Territories, reducing the region to less than half its original area.

Norton. *Town, north central Zimbabwe.* The town took its name from that of a farm family murdered in 1896 during the Shona uprisings.

Norway. *Kingdom, northwestern Europe.* The country derives its name from Old Norse *Norrevegr*, "northern way." The Vikings or Norsemen sailed on three main routes between Scan-dinavia and the rest of Europe: the "eastern way" through the Baltic, the "western way" across the North Sea, and the "northern way" along the coast of what is now *Norway*.

Norwich. *City, eastern England.* The Norfolk city has an Old English name meaning "northern trading settlement." The name originally applied to the northernmost of at least four separate settlements, and because it was the most important (on a Roman road as well as the Wensum River) its name was gradually extended to include the others. It is possible the predominance of this name over the others may also have been influenced by that of ¹**Norfolk**, of which Norwich has long been the administrative center.

Nosy-Be. *Island, northwestern Madagascar.* The island's name means "big island," from Malagasy *nòsy*, "island," and *be*, "big." The island is the largest of those off the northwest coast here. The name is also spelled *Nossi-Bé*.

Notre Dame Mountains. *Mountain range, southeastern Canada.* The mountains, a continuation of the Green Mountains of Vermont, USA, to the Gaspé Peninsula, Quebec province, Canada, have a name meaning "Our Lady" (the Virgin Mary) given by the French explorer Samuel de Champlain.

Nottingham. *City, north central England.* The city, in the county of the same name, has an Old English name meaning "homestead of *Snot*'s people," with the initial *S-* of the personal name dropped by the Normans, who found it difficult to pronounce *sn*. It has been retained, however, for the nearby village of *Sneinton*, now an eastern district of the city, where the reference is to the same man. This name is a reduced form of what might otherwise have been *Snottington*, "farm of *Snot*'s people."

Nouadhibou. *Town and port, northwestern Mauritania.* The town was founded by the French in 1905 as *Port-Étienne*, named for the French colonial official Eugène *Étienne* (1844–1921). In the 1960s it adopted an existing indigenous name meaning "well of jackals."

Nouakshott. *Capital of Mauritania.* The city is said to derive its name from a Berber (Zenaga) dialect phrase *in wakchodh*, "having no ears," from *akchud*, "ear." This was presumably the name or nickname of a local chief here at one time.

Nouméa. *Capital of New Caledonia.* The name is a French spelling of the indigenous name *Numea*, of disputed origin. The town and port was founded in 1854 as a French penal colony under the name *Port-de-France.*

Nova Friburgo. *City, southeastern Brazil.* The city was founded in 1818 by 100 Swiss immigrant families who had been transferred here by royal decree from **Fribourg**. Hence the "new" name.

Nova Gorica *see* **Gorizia**

Novara. *City, northwestern Italy.* The city originated as the Roman colony of *Novaria*, perhaps a form of Latin *novalia*, a term for newly cleared woodland or a field plowed for the first time.

Nova Scotia. *Province, eastern Canada.* The name of the province is Latin for "new **Scotland**." The territory was granted in 1621 by James I to the Scotsman Sir William Alexander, Earl of Stirling, with the royal conveyance including words referring to lands "to be known as Nova Scotia, or New Scotland." Unusually, the Latin form of the name prevailed. The territory of Nova Scotia was earlier part of **Acadia**.

Novaya Zemlya. *Island group, northwestern Russia.* The Arctic archipelago has a Russian name meaning "new land." The name was given to a land (rather than specifically island) that promised new trade from fishing, hunting, and the like, as distinct from existing trading settlements on the mainland. The name appears on older maps and charts as *Nova Zembla*, and in modern French is still *Nouvelle-Zemble*. This form of the name was actually due to the French, who found it difficult to pronounce the combination *ml* without an intermediary *b*. Something similar happened in the name of **Wimbledon**.

Novgorod. *City, western Russia.* The city has a Russian name meaning "new town," from *novyj*, "new," and *gorod*, "town." The city was founded in the 9th century, and is one of the oldest in Russia, but was obviously regarded as "new" by comparison with existing towns. The Varangians (Scandinavians who settled in Russia from the 8th century) knew it as *Holmgard*, "island town," referring to its location on raised land by the Volkhov River. *See also* **Nizhny Novgorod**.

Novi Pazar. *City, southern Serbia.* The medieval capital of Serbia has a Croatian name meaning "new market." Its former Turkish name was *Yenibazar*, with the same meaning.

Novi Sad. *City and river port, western Serbia.* The city has a Croatian name meaning "new garden," and its Hungarian name of *Újvidék* ("new region") and German name of *Neusatz* ("new set-

tlement") have a similar sense. Novi Sad was founded in the 17th century as the seat of the Serbian patriarch.

Novocherkassk. *City, southwestern Russia.* The city was founded in 1805 when *Cherkasskaya*, the capital of the Don Cossacks, on the Don River, was moved here because of frequent flooding. Hence the present name, meaning "new *Cherkassk*." The original town, now *Starocherkassk*, "old *Cherkassk*," was named for the *Cherkess* or *Circassians*, who had gone to settle there from the Caucasus. *See also* **Cherkassy**, **Circassia**.

Novo Hamburgo. *City, southern Brazil.* The city was founded by Germans in 1927 and has a Portuguese name meaning "new **Hamburg**."

Novokuznetsk. *City, southern Russia.* The name of the Siberian city means "new *Kuznetsk*." It arose in 1617 as the village of *Kuznetsk*, so called for its iron mines, from Russian *kuznets*, "blacksmith." When a steelworks was set up here on the Ob River in 1929 its name was modified to *Novokuznetsk* in order to distinguish it from **Kuznetsk** in central Russia. From 1932 through 1961 it was known as *Stalinsk*, as one of the many places renamed for *Stalin*.

Novo Mesto. *City, southern Slovenia.* The city, founded in 1365, has a Slavic name meaning "new town."

Novorossiysk. *City and port, southwestern Russia.* The Black Sea port has a name meaning "new **Russia**," from Russian *novo-*, "new," and *Rossiya*, "Russia." This was the name given to territory here that had passed from Turkey to Russia at the end of the 18th century. The town itself arose as a fortified post in 1838.

Novosibirsk. *City, south central Russia.* The largest city in Siberia arose in 1894 at a crossing of the Ob River during construction of the Trans-Siberian Railroad. The original name of the site here was *Gusevka*. In 1903 it became *Novonikolayevsk*, "new *Nicholas* town," for the reigning czar, *Nicholas* II (1868–1918), with "new" distinguishing it from the existing **Nikolayevsk**. In 1926 it adopted its present name, meaning "new **Siberia**." The name was chosen by local people from a shortlist offered by a regional newspaper.

Nowa Huta. *City, southern Poland.* The industrial city, now a suburb of Kraków, has a name meaning "new ironworks," from Polish *nowa*, the feminine of *nowy*, "new," and *huta*, "ironworks," a word borrowed from German *Hütte*, "foundry."

Nowa Sól. *Town, west central Poland.* The town was founded in 1609 beside a newly opened saltworks. Hence its name, Polish for "new salt." Its equivalent German name is *Neusalz*.

Noyon. *Town, northern France*. The town has a smoothed form of its original Roman name of *Noviomagus*, "new market." *Cp.* **Chichester, Longjumeau, Nijmegen**.

Nsanje. *Town, southern Malawi*. The town takes its name from the local word for a type of grass found growing along the Shire River here. Its earlier colonial name was *Port Herald*, perhaps given propitiously for a town located at the southern approach to the country from Mozambique.

Nubia. *Region, northeastern Africa*. The region, in Sudan and Egypt, is named for its indigenous people, the *Nubians*. Their own name is said to be related to Coptic *noubti*, "to weave," referring to the important local craft of basket-making, although another theory links it with Nubian *nub*, "gold," alluding to the craft of making of gold-based jewelry and ornaments.

Nueva Casas Grandes. *City, northern Mexico*. The city was established in 1886 4 miles (7 km) from the extensive, multistoried, ancient ruins known as *Casas Grandes*, Spanish for "big houses." Hence its name, "new *Casas Grandes*."

Nueva Gerona. *City, southwestern Cuba*. The capital of the island of Isla de la Juventud was founded in 1830 by Don Francisco Dionisio Vives, governor and captain-general of Cuba, and named "new **Gerona**," for the Spanish city.

Nueva San Salvador. *City, west central El Salvador*. The city was founded in 1854 as *Nueva Ciudad de San Salvador*, "new city of **San Salvador**," after the named capital city had been destroyed in an earthquake. It later adopted the shorter form of this name.

Nuevo Laredo. *City and port, northeastern Mexico*. The city, founded in 1755, has a name meaning "new **Laredo**," as it lies on the Rio Grande opposite this Texas, USA, town.

Nuevo León. *State, northern Mexico*. The state was founded in 1824 in a region already named by Spanish explorers and settlers as a "new **León**."

Nuku'alofa. *Capital of Tonga*. The indigenous name, sometimes said to mean "abode of love" or "loving home," as if relating to the *Friendly Islands*, Cook's name for **Tonga**, more properly means "the south," describing Tonga's location with respect to most other islands in Polynesia.

Nullarbor Plain. *Plain, southern Australia*. The low plateau, in South Australia, has no water or trees. Its pseudoclassical name refers to the latter lack, and was devised from Latin *nullus*, "no," and *arbor*, "tree," by the explorer Alfred Delissier.

Numazu. *City, central Japan*. The city, at the mouth of the Kano River on the island of Honshu, derives its name from Japanese *numa*, "marsh," and *tsu*, "port."

Numidia. *Historic region, northern Africa*. The region, approximating to modern Algeria, is named for its indigenous inhabitants, the *Numidians*. Their own name is a form of the word *nomad*, referring to their roving existence. The word itself literally means "go from one pasture to another," and ultimately derives from Greek *nomē*, "pasture."

Nunavik. *Region, northeastern Canada*. The region of northern Quebec has an Inuit name meaning "great land." The region is not a political unit, unlike **Nunavut**.

Nunavut. *Territory, northeastern Canada*. The region covers the traditional lands of the Inuit (Eskimo) people. Hence its name, meaning "our land" in the Inuit language Inuktitut. The territory was created from the eastern portion of the **Northwest Territories** in 1999.

Nunivak. *Island, northwestern United States*. The island, in the Bering Sea off western Alaska, has an Inuit name meaning "big land," referring to its size. *Cp.* **Nunavik**.

Nuremberg. *City, south central Germany*. The second part of the name is certainly German *Berg*, "mountain." The meaning of the first part is uncertain. It has been derived from Middle High German *knorre*, "projecting bones," or *knür*, "cliff," or Middle German dialect *Nörr* or *Nürn*, "cliff." The Medieval Latin name of the city was *Norinberga*, and the German form of the name is *Nürnberg*.

Nuristan. *Region, eastern Afghanistan*. The region derives its name from Afghani or Iranian *nūrestān*, "land of light" (i.e. "land of the enlightened"), from *nūr*, "light," and *ostān*, "land," "country." The name was introduced at the turn of the 20th century, when the indigenous population, who practiced animism, was forcibly converted to Islam. The region's earlier name was *Kafiristan*, "land of the *Kaffir*," i.e. of non–Muslims. *Cp.* **Kaffraria**.

Nürnberg *see* **Nuremberg**

Nusa Tenggara Barat. *Province, southern Indonesia*. The province, comprising the western Lesser Sunda Islands, has an Indonesian name meaning "western southeast islands." The adjoining province of *Nusa Tenggara Timur*, which includes the eastern Lesser Sunda Islands, has a corresponding name meaning "eastern southeast islands." The Lesser Sunda Islands are generally southeast of Borneo.

Nuuk. *Capital of Greenland*. The town and

port, on Greenland's southwest coast, has a Greenlandic name meaning "summit," denoting its supremacy. Its earlier name (until 1979) was *Godthåb*, "good hope," from Danish *godt*, the neuter form of *god*, "good," and *håb*, "hope." The town was founded in 1721 by the Norwegian missionary Hans Egede (*see* **Egedesminde**), who is said to have so named it for his "good hope" of converting the indigenous population. But the name may have actually been suggested by the *Cape of Good Hope* in southern Africa, also on the southwest coast.

Nyanza. *Province, southwestern Kenya.* The province has a Bantu name meaning "lake," referring to its location on the eastern shore of Lake *Victoria*, whose alternate name is *Victoria-Nyanza* (*see* **Victoria, Lake**).

Nyasa, Lake *see* **Malawi**

Nyasaland *see* **Malawi**

Nyborg. *City and port, central Denmark.* The city, on eastern Fyn Island, has a Danish name meaning "new castle," referring to the *new castle* built here in 1170. *Cp.* ¹**Newcastle.**

Nyergesújfalu. *Town, northern Hungary.* The first part of the town's name is the surname *Nyerges* ("saddler"). The second part means "new village" (Hungarian *új*, "new," and *falu*, "village").

Nyíregyháza. *City, northeastern Hungary.* The name of the city means "church of *Nyír*," from the name of a village *Nyír* ("birch") and *egyház*, "church." The name implies that the original village was destroyed, leaving only the church, around which the present city arose.

Nyköping. *Town and port, southeastern Sweden.* The town, dating from before 1250, has a name meaning "new trading place," from Swedish *ny*, "new," and *köping*, "trading place," "village." The port of *Nykøbing* in southern Denmark has a name of identical meaning.

Nymburk. *Town, west central Czech Republic.* The town, first mentioned in the 13th century, has a name of Old High German origin meaning "new town," corresponding to modern German *Neuburg*. (The actual German name of the town is *Nimburg*.)

Oahu. *Island, northwestern Hawaii, United States.* The third largest of the Hawaii islands is said to have a Hawaiian name meaning "place of assembly." But this etymology lacks academic support.

Oakham. *Town, east central England.* The name of the Rutland town does not relate to oaks but means "*Oca*'s riverside meadow," with the Anglo-Saxon personal name followed by Old English *hamm*, "meadow," "riverside pasture."

Oakham is on a tongue of land between two streams.

Oakland. *City and port, western United States.* The California city was founded in 1852 and named for the *oak* trees on the coast*land* here.

Oakville. *Town, southeastern Canada.* The Ontario town, incorporated in 1857, is so named because it was originally the center of an *oak*-stave industry.

Oamaru. *Town and port, southeastern New Zealand.* The town, in southeastern South Island, has a Maori name meaning "place of sheltered fire," presumably referring to a location where fires could burn without being extinguished.

Oaxaca. *City, southern Mexico.* The city's name is said to represent a Nahuatl original *Huaxaca*, meaning "at the point of the acacia."

Ob. *River, central Russia.* The name of the Siberian river probably derives from the Indoeuropean root element *ab*, "water."

Oban. *Town and port, western Scotland.* The town has a Gaelic name meaning "little bay," referring to the small bay on which it stands.

Oberammergau. *Village, southwestern Germany.* Famous for its decennial Passion Play (from 1634), the village has a name meaning "district over the *Ammer* River," from German *ober*, "over," *Ammer*, and *Gau*, "district." The river name ultimately derives from Indoeuropean *ab*, "water." Oberammergau is in the foothills of the Alps.

Oberhausen. *City, western Germany.* The city was created in 1862 by combining seven hamlets into a single industrial estate around *Oberhausen* railroad station, itself named in 1847 after a nearby castle. The castle was so called because it was the "higher house" on a key crossing of the Emscher River.

Obwalden *see* **Unterwalden**

Ocala. *City, southwestern United States.* The Florida city arose around Ft. King, established in 1827. Its Native American (Timucua) name is of uncertain origin and meaning, but presumably denoted a territory here.

Ocaña. *City, northern Colombia.* The city was founded by the Spanish in c.1570 and was originally called *Nueva Madrid*, "new **Madrid**." It was subsequently renamed for the Spanish town of *Ocaña*, southeast of Madrid.

Oceania. *Region, Pacific Ocean.* The collective name for the seas and islands of the Pacific, sometimes equated specifically with the South Sea Islands, was created in 1812 by the Danish geographer Conrad Malte-Brun, who appears to have based it on *Oceanus*, the name of the Greek

Titan god of the stream believed to flow around the earth. His own name gave the word *ocean*.

Oceanside. *City, southwestern United States.* The California city developed as a beach resort following the arrival of the Southern Pacific Railroad in 1883 and has a descriptive name denoting its location be*side* the Pacific *Ocean*.

Ochsenfurt. *Town, south central Germany.* The town, on the Main River, has a name meaning "oxen ford," from earlier forms of modern German *Ochse*, "ox," and *Furt*, "ford." The reference is to a regular crossing of oxen here, as at **Oxford.** *Cp.* **Schweinfurt.**

Odawara. *City, south central Japan.* The city, in the island of Honshu, derives its name from Japanese *o*, "little," *ta*, "rice field," and *hara*, "field," "plain."

Odense. *City and port, southern Denmark.* The city takes its name from that of the Norse god *Odin*, to whom the site here was sacred at the time of its foundation in the 10th century.

Odenwald. *Mountain region, southwestern Germany.* The wooded upland region has a name of uncertain origin, although the second part corresponds to modern German *Wald*, "forest."

¹Odessa. *City and port, southern Ukraine.* The city was founded in 1795 by order of Catherine the Great at a time when Greek-style placenames were in vogue in this part of Russia (as it then was). Its name was based on that of *Odessos*, an ancient Greek colony said to have been near here. The name has been erroneously linked with that of the mythical *Odysseus*.

²Odessa. *City, southern United States.* The Texas city arose on a location said to have been named in 1881 by Russian railroad construction workers, who fancied a resemblance between the prairie region here and the plains around their native **¹Odessa.**

Offaly. *County, east central Ireland.* The county's name is an English form of its Irish name, *Uíbh Fhailí*, "(place of the) descendants of *Failghe*," referring to the legendary ancestor of the people who inhabited the region. From 1577 through 1920 the county was known as *King's County*, so named by Mary I, queen of England and Ireland, in honor of her husband, *King* Philip II of Spain (1527–1598), whose name was also given to the former county town of *Philipstown*, now Daingean. *Cp.* **Laois.**

Offenbach. *City and river port, west central Germany.* The city, formally known as *Offenbach am Main* for its location on the **Main** River, has a name first recorded in 977 as *Ovenbach*, "Ovo's stream," with an Old German personal name.

Offenburg. *City, southwestern Germany.* The city took its name from a medieval castle belonging to the margraves of Zähringen. Its own name, first recorded in 1101, means "*Offo's* fort."

Ogden. *City, western United States.* The Utah city was laid out in 1850 and at first named *Brownsville*. It was subsequently renamed for the fur trader Peter S. *Ogden* (1794–1854), who explored this region in the 1820s.

O'Higgins. *Region, central Chile.* The former province is named for Chile's first president, Bernardo *O'Higgins* (c.1776–1842), commander of the forces that won his country's independence from Spain. (He was the son of a Spanish officer of Irish origin.)

Ohio. *State, north central United States.* The state takes its name from the river that forms its southern and eastern border with Kentucky and West Virginia. Its own name derives from an Iroquois or other Native American word meaning "beautiful." French colonists here named the river similarly as *La Belle Rivière*.

Ohrid. *Town, southwestern Macedonia.* The town, on the lake of the same name, takes its own name from Serbo-Croat *hrid*, "crag," denoting the rock on which it originally stood. This despite the account offered by the 12th-century Byzantine writer Anna Comnena: "Lake Lychnidos is now called Achrida after the Bulgarian king Mochri, who is now called Samuel."

Oise. *River, northern France.* The river had the Roman name *Isara* or *Esara*, from the pre–Celtic root element *is*, "holy," "sacred," and *ar*, "water," "river."

Oita. *City and port, southern Japan.* The city and prefecture of the same name, in the island of Kyushu, derive their name from Japanese *ō*, "big," and *wa*, "to be divided," "to comprehend."

Oka. *River, western Russia.* The river, a tributary of the Volga, has a name of uncertain origin. It has been variously derived from Gothic *aka*, "water," "river," Finnish *joki*, "river," and Slavic *oko*, "eye," this last in the sense of an open expanse of water. Whatever the actual origin, the meaning is likely to be simply "water," "river."

Okavango. *River, southern Africa.* The river, rising in Angola then flowing south and east to enter marshland in Botswana, is so called for the people of northern Namibia of this name, itself from that of one of their first chiefs, *Kavango*.

Okayama. *City, central Japan.* The city, in the island of Honshu, derives its name from Japanese *oka*, "hill," and *yama*, "mountain."

Okazaki. *City, central Japan.* The city, near the coast in the island of Honshu, derives its name from Japanese *oka*, "hill," and *saki*, "cape," "promontory."

Okeechobee, Lake. *Lake, southeastern United States.* The Florida lake has a Native American (Seminole) name meaning "big water."

Okefenokee Swamp. *Swamp, southeastern United States.* The swamp, in southeastern Georgia and northern Florida, has a name that probably derives from a Seminole word meaning "trembling water," referring to its famous floating islands.

Okhotsk, Sea of. *Sea, eastern Russia.* The sea between the east coast of Siberia and the Kamchatka peninsula takes its name from the *Okhota* River that flows into it. Its own name has been popularly linked with Russian *okhota*, "hunt," but actually comes from Evenki *okat*, "river."

Okinawa. *Island, southwestern Japan.* The name derives from Japanese *oki*, "open sea," and *nawa*, "cord," "chain." The reference is to the string of islands that extend into the East China Sea here.

Oklahoma. *State, southwestern United States.* The state has a Native American name proposed in 1866 by the Revd. Allen Wright, chief of the Choctaws, to designate land in what was then known simply as *Indian Territory*. It means "red people," from Choctaw *okla*, "people," and *humma*, "red." The name relates to the copper color of the Choctaw people's skins. Hence terms for Native Americans such as *redskins* and *Red Indians* (now marked "offensive" in many dictionaries).

Oklahoma City. *City, southwestern United States.* The state capital of Oklahoma was founded in 1889 when around 10,000 homesteaders gathered to stake out land claims in central **Oklahoma**. Although in use from the first, the city's name was not adopted by the U.S. Post Office until 1923. *Oklahoma City* and **Indianapolis** are the only two U.S. state capitals to be named for their states.

Oktemberyan. *City, western Armenia.* The city was originally called *Sardarabad*, from *sardar*, more usually spelled *sirdar*, a former term for a commander-in-chief in Persia and Turkey, and Iranian *ābād*, "town." In 1947 it was given its present name, Armenian for "October," marking the 30th anniversary of the *October Revolution* in Russia.

Öland. *Island, western Baltic Sea.* The island, off the southeast coast of Sweden, has a name that merely means "island," from Swedish *ö*, "island," and *land*, "land."

Olathe. *City, central United States.* The Kansas city was founded in 1857 and derives its name from the Shawnee word for "beautiful." The town's organizer, John Barton, said that the

name he wanted was Shawnee *wessee*, "meadow beautiful," but whenever he asked the Shawnee for such a word, they always told him *olathe*.

Oldenburg. *City, northwestern Germany.* The city, first mentioned in 1108, has a Germanic name meaning "old fortress," referring to the 11th-century castle built to protect the road from Bremen to Jever in the border territory between Saxony and Friesland. Medieval Latin documents record the name as both German *Aldenburg* and Slavic *Starigrad*, with the same meaning. The castle also gave the name of the former state of *Oldenburg*, originally a countship.

Old Faithful. *Geyser, western United States.* The well-known geyser, in Yellowstone National Park, Wyoming, is so named because it spouts regularly ("faithfully") every 65–70 minutes. The name was given in 1870 by the explorer General H. D. Washburn.

Oldham. *Town, northwestern England.* The town, near Manchester, has a name meaning "old promontory," with the latter half not the usual Old English *-ham* ("village") but Old Norse *holm*, "island" "promontory." The reference is to the spur on which the town is situated. It may have been called "old" simply because it was a place where people had long lived.

Oléron, Île d'. *Island, western France.* The island, in the Bay of Biscay, was known to the Romans as *Uliarus*. This is a name of Venetian origin but uncertain meaning.

Oleśnica. *Town, southwestern Poland.* The name means "place where alders grow," from an early form of Polish *olsza*, "alder." The German form of the name is *Oels* or *Öls*.

Olinda. *City, northeastern Brazil.* The city was founded in 1537 by the Portuguese colonial official Duarte Coelho Pereira, who is said to have exclaimed: "*Oh, linda situação para uma vila!*" ("Oh, what a beautiful spot for a town!"). But this is a purely romantic origin devised to explain an obscure name.

Olives, Mount of. *Ridge, western Jordan.* The ridge just east of Jerusalem, familiar from the Bible (Matthew 6:26, etc.), takes its name from its southern summit, where *olive* groves were long cultivated. An alternate form of the name is *Olivet* (Acts 1:12), from Latin *olivetum*, "olive grove."

Olomouc. *City, eastern Czech Republic.* The city, on the Morava River, has a name representing Old Czech *holy mauc*, from *holy*, "bald," and *mauc*, "rock." The German form of the name is *Olmütz*.

Olsztyn. *City, northeastern Poland.* The city's name is a Polish alteration of German *Allenstein*, "castle on the *Alle* River," this being the river also known as the *Lava* or (in its Polish form) *Łyna*. The river's own name is of Baltic origin with a meaning "animal," for its fierce current.

¹Olympia. *Historic plain, southern Greece*. The plain and sanctuary in the western Peloponnese, site of the original Olympic Games, is named for Zeus, greatest of the Greek gods, whose throne was on Mt. **Olympus**. The sanctuary here was dedicated to him, as were the Olympic Games themselves.

²Olympia. *City, northwestern United States*. The state capital of Washington was founded in 1851 under the name of *Smithfield*. It was subsequently renamed for the nearby *Olympic Mountains*, whose highest peak was named in 1788 by the English traveler John Meares for Mt. **Olympus**.

Olympic Mountains *see* **²Olympia**

Olympus, Mt. *Mountain, northeastern Greece*. The mountain is said to base its name on an Indoeuropean root word *ulu*, "to turn," describing its rounded summit.

Omagh. *Town, west central Northern Ireland*. The town, in Co. Tyrone, has a name based on Irish *magh*, "plain." The initial *O-* is unexplained.

Omaha. *City and river port, central United States*. The Nebraska city is named for the Sioux *Omaha* people formerly here. Their own name is said to mean "those living upstream on the river." The river in question would be the Missouri.

Oman. *Sultanate, southeastern Arabia*. The name was recorded by Pliny in the 1st century A.D. as *Omana*. It is said to derive from the founder of the state, *Oman* ben Ibrahim al-Khalil (named in some sources as *Oman* ben Kahtan).

Omdurman. *City, central Sudan*. Sudan's largest city is said to derive its name from the Muslim holy man *Um-Mariyam* (1646–1730), who is buried here. The Arabic form of the name is *Umm Durman*.

Omiya. *City, south central Japan*. The city, in the island of Honshu, where it is now a suburb of Tokyo, derives its name from Japanese *ō*, "big," and *miya*, "shrine." Omiya is the site of the Shinto Hikawa Shrine, said to have been set up here in the 5th century B.C.

Ömnögovĭ. *Province, southern Mongolia*. The name is Mongolian for "southern **Gobi**," for the desert in which the province lies.

Omsk. *City, south central Russia*. The Siberian city lies at the confluence of the Irtysh and *Om* rivers, and is named for the latter. Its own

name is said to derive from Tatar *om*, "calm," "smooth," describing its slow current.

Omuta. *City, southern Japan*. The city, in the island of Kyushu, derives its name from Japanese *ō*, "big," *mu*, "pupil of the eye," and *ta*, "rice field."

Onega, Lake. *Lake, northwestern Russia*. The name of Europe's second-largest lake may be linked with that of the *Onega* River northeast of it, although the distance between the two is considerable The river's own name is said to represent Finnish *Enojoki*, "main river," from *enin*, "most," and *joki*, "river." The Finnish name of the lake is *Äänisjärvi*, from *ääni*, "sound," "voice," and *järvi*, "lake," and similarly that of the river *Äänisjoki*, but it is unlikely that the Finnish and Russian names are related. It is quite possible that the names of lake and river are of entirely different origin.

Oneida, Lake. *Lake, eastern United States*. The lake, in New York State, takes its name from the Native American people who formerly lived here but who then moved west to settle by Lake Ontario. Their name represents Iroquois *oneyote*, "people of the standing stone."

Oneşti. *City, eastern Romania*. The original 15th-century settlement of this name was developed as a new town in 1953 and named *Gheorge Gheorgiu-Dej*, for the Romanian patriot and Communist leader (1901–1965). In 1990 it reverted to its original name.

¹Ontario. *Province, southeastern Canada*. The province takes its name from the lake here, its own name said to represent Iroquois *oniatariio*, "beautiful lake."

²Ontario. *City, southwestern United States*. The California city, now a suburb of downtown Los Angeles, was settled in 1882 by George and William Chaffey, who named it for their native Canadian province.

Opatija. *Town and resort, northwestern Croatia*. The town derives its name from Croatian *opatija*, "abbey," referring to the old Benedictine monastery of San Giacomo al Palo in its main park. The Italian form of the name is *Abbazia*.

Opatów. *Town, southeastern Poland*. The town derives its name from a Polish derivative of Latin *abbas, abbatis*, "abbot," with the Slavic possessive suffix *-ow*. Land here was owned by the *abbot*.

Opava. *City, eastern Czech Republic*. The city takes its name from the *Opava* River, here forming the border with Poland. The precise meaning of the river's name is disputed, although it is almost certainly based on Indoeuropean *ar*, "water." The German form of the city's name is

Troppau. The initial *Tr-* of this probably represents a form of *der*, "the," meaning "(settlement on) the Opava."

Opelika. *City, southeastern United States.* The Alabama city derives its name from a Native American (Creek) word meaning "swamp." There is no obvious swamp here today.

Opole. *City, southern Poland.* The city derives its name from Slavic *opaliti*, "to light," "to burn," referring to a site originally cleared by burning. The German form of the name is *Oppeln*.

Oporto. *City and port, western Portugal.* The name of the city is simply Portuguese *o porto*, "the port." It was this port that gave the name of **Portugal** itself. The Portuguese name of the city is *Porto*.

Oradea. *City, northwestern Romania.* The city's name is a romanianized form of the second part of its Hungarian name, *Nagyvárad*, from *nagy*, "big," and *vár*, "castle." Its German name, *Großwardein*, is a part translation of the Hungarian. Oradea was ceded to Romania by Hungary in 1919, and for some time afterward its name was *Oradea Mare*, the second word being Romanian *mare*, "big."

Oran. *City and port, northwestern Algeria.* The city, founded in the 10th century by Andalusian merchants, derives its name from Arabic *wahrān*, the name of a medieval Berber chief, from Berber *iren*, "lions." The Romans knew the site as *Portus divinus*, "divine harbor," or *Portus magnus*, "great harbor."

¹Orange. *Town, southeastern France.* The town was known to the Roman as *Arausio*, from a pre–Indoeuropean root element *ar*, "mountain" with the suffix *-aus*. This was subsequently corrupted to the present name. It was this town, or more precisely the principality based on it, that gave the title of William of *Orange* (1650–1702), otherwise William III, king of Great Britain and Ireland, as well as that of the Dutch royal house. *See also* **Orange Free State.**

²Orange. *City, southeastern Australia.* The city, in New South Wales, takes its name from a region here that was itself so called in 1828 by Sir Thomas Mitchell in memory of William, Prince of *Orange* (1772–1843), the future William I, king of the Netherlands, his commander during the Peninsular War.

³Orange. *City, southwestern United States.* The California city was founded as *Richland* in 1868 and renamed as now in 1875 for its *orange* groves.

Orange Free State. *Historic province, east central South Africa.* The province was situated between the *Orange* and Vaal rivers and took its name from the former. The river was given its

name in 1777 by the Dutch explorer R.J. Gordon in honor of the Dutch royal house of *Orange*, itself named for **¹Orange**, France. After the abolition of apartheid and the reorganization of provincial governments in 1994, the Orange Free State became simply *Free State*, a name previously in use from 1854 to 1901 for the original Boer republic. (The name translates Afrikaans *frijstaat*, "free state," "republic.") This name was long used in a derogatory sense for a region regarded as backward or primitive by those living elsewhere in South Africa, so that "Free State coal," for example, was dried dung used as fuel.

Ord. *River, northwestern Australia.* The river, in Western Australia, was discovered in 1879 by Alexander Forrest and named for Sir Harry *Ord* (1819–1885), then governor of Western Australia.

Ordzhonikidze *see* (1) **Vladikavkaz,** (2) **Yenakiyevo**

Oregon. *State, northwestern United States.* The state's name is of disputed origin. It may derive from Shoshonean *ogwa*, "river," and *pe-on*, "west," as a former Native American name of the present Columbia River that forms its northern border with Washington. Another account attributes the name to a French cartographer's error, when on a map of 1715 he transcribed the name of the *Wisconsin* River as *Ouariconsint* but wrote *Ouaricon* on one line and *sint* on the next. *Ouaricon* was then anglicized as *Oregon*. The difficulty here is that Oregon and Wisconsin are not neighboring states.

Orem. *City, western United States.* The Utah city is named for Walter C. *Orem* (1873–1951), president of the Salt Lake and Utah Electric interurban railroad, although he never lived here.

Orenburg. *City, southwestern Russia.* The city, on the Ural River, takes its name from the *Or* River on which it originally stood, with German *Burg*, "fort," denoting the stronghold that was built on that river in 1735. The fort was subsequently moved almost 200 miles (300 km) westward from the Or, but kept its name. (The city of *Orsk* stands on the original site, so has a name of identical origin.) From 1938 through 1957 Orenburg was known as *Chkalov*, for the Soviet pilot Valery *Chkalov* (1904–1938), killed when testing a new type of fighter aircraft.

Orense. *Town, northwestern Spain.* The town's name evolved from its Roman name of *Originis Aquae*, "waters of the source," referring to its hot springs.

Orestias. *Town, northeastern Greece.* The town takes its name from *Orestia*, the Byzantine name of *Adrianople* (now **Edirne**), 12 miles (19 km) to the north.

Orillia. *City, southeastern Canada.* The Ontario city, surveyed in 1839, was so named by Sir Peregrine Maitland, governor of Upper Canada from 1818 to 1828, who had served in Spain. Hence the name's origin in Spanish *orilla*, "border," "shore," referring to the town's location between Lakes Couchiching and Simcoe.

Orinoco. *River, Venezuela.* The river's name derives from Guaraní *ori-noko*, "place of paddling (a canoe)." The long river is readily navigable in many of its sections.

Orissa. *State, eastern India.* The name represents Sanskrit *oḍradesha*, *oḍra* being the name of a local people, and *desha* meaning "country."

Orizaba. *City, east central Mexico.* The city was founded by the Spanish in the 16th century on the site of an Aztec military post called *Ahuaializapan*, "pleasant waters," referring to the fertile valley here. The present name is thus an altered form of this. The name was also given by the Spanish to a volcano here, Mexico's highest point. Its more fitting Nahuatl name is *Citlaltépetl*, "star mountain."

Orkney Islands. *Island group, northern Scotland.* The final *-ey* of the name is Old Norse *ey*, "island," but the first part is of uncertain origin. It may derive from a word meaning "whale," "sea monster," related to English *orc* in this sense.

Orlando. *City, southeastern United States.* The Florida city was first settled in c.1844 and was initially known as *Jernigan*. It was renamed as now in 1857 to honor *Orlando* Reeves, an army sentry killed in 1835 during the Seminole Wars.

Orléans. *City, north central France.* The city was given the Roman name *Aurelianum* when it was rebuilt in the 3d century A.D., in honor of the emperor *Aurelius*, and this evolved to its present name. Its earlier Roman name was *Genabum*, from proto-Indoeuropean *gen*, "bend" (in a river), and pre–Indoeuropean *apa*, "water." The city is on the Loire. *See also* **New Orleans**.

Ormskirk. *Town, northwestern England.* The Lancashire town has a name meaning "*Orm*'s church," with the Scandinavian personal name *Ormr*, followed by Old Norse *kirkja*, "church," replacing an earlier Old English *cirice*. It is not known who Ormr was, but his name means "serpent" (modern English *worm*).

Orne. *River, northern France.* The river's Roman name was *Olina*, perhaps from Celtic *olno*, "ash tree."

Orontes. *River, southwestern Asia.* The river, rising in Lebanon and flowing generally north then west to enter the Mediterranean in Turkey,

derives its name from Old Persian *Elwend*, "flowing one." Its Arabic name is *nahr al-'āṣī*, "the rebellious river," for its poor navigability.

Orosháza. *Town, southeastern Hungary.* The town has a name meaning "*Oros*'s house," with the personal name followed by Hungarian *ház*, "house."

Oroszlány. *Town, northwestern Hungary.* The name derives from the personal name *Oroszlán* ("lion").

Orsk *see* **Orenburg**

Orumiyeh. *City, northwestern Iran.* The name of the city, formerly familiar as *Urmia*, is ancient and of uncertain origin and meaning. From 1926 through 1980 the city was known as *Reza'iyeh*, so named for *Reza* Shah (1878–1944), founder of the Pahlavi dynasty, which reigned from 1925 through 1979.

Oruro. *City, west central Bolivia.* The city has a Native American name meaning "black and white," referring to animal paintings on rocks here. Its colonial name when founded by Spanish settlers in 1606 was *Real Villa de San Felipe de Austria*, "royal town of St. Philip of Austria."

Orvieto. *Town, central Italy.* The present form of the town's name evolved from its Roman name of *Urbs Vetus*, "old town." The Roman town arose on the site of an earlier Etruscan one.

Oryakhovo. *City, northwestern Bulgaria.* The city derives its name from the island of *Orekhov* here, itself named for its hazel trees (Bulgarian *orekh*, "hazel nut").

Oryol. *City, western Russia.* The city's name happens to be the Russian word for "eagle." Hence the figure of this bird on its civic coat of arms. Its actual origin, however, is in that of the small *Orel* (now *Orlik*) River that flows into the Oka here. Its own name is believed to be of Turkic origin, meaning "bend," "angle."

Osaka. *City and port, southern Japan.* The city, in the island of Honshu, derives its name from Japanese *ō*, "big," and *saka*, "slope," "hill." Osaka lies on a river delta between mountain ranges to east and west.

Osh. *City, southern Kyrgyzstan.* The city's name dates from at least the 9th century and is believed to derive from the *Ush*, an Iranian people who formerly inhabited the region. The meaning of their own name is unknown.

Oshawa. *City, southeastern Canada.* The Ontario city, on Lake Ontario, was founded in 1795 as *Skea's Corners*. In 1842 it was renamed as now, from a Native American term for a stream crossing.

Oshkosh. *City, northern United States.* The Wisconsin city was settled in 1836 and was at first called *Athens*. In 1840 it received its present name, that of a long-lived Menominee chief (1759–1858).

Osijek. *City and river port, eastern Croatia.* The city, on the Drava River, has a name based on Slavic *sech'*, "to cut," denoting an area of cleared woodland, either to mark a boundary or for agricultural purposes. The German form of the name is *Esseg*, and the Hungarian *Eszék*.

Oslo. *Capital of Norway.* The city's name is probably based on Old Norwegian *os*, "estuary," "river mouth," referring to its location at the northern end of Oslo Fjord (an inlet of the Skagerrak), although some authorities derive it from *As*, a Scandinavian god, and *Lo*, the river near which the old city arose. Its Medieval Latin name was *Ansloga*. After a disastrous fire in 1624 the city was rebuilt under the new name of *Christiana*, for King *Christian* IV (1577–1648) of Denmark and Norway. In 1877 this became *Kristiania*. The old name was readopted in 1924 to mark the tercentennial of the city's restoration.

Osma. *Town, north central Spain.* The name comes from the Roman settlement of *Oxoma* here, from the superlative form of Gaulish *uxellos*, "high," as for the French island of *Ouessant* (*see* **Ushant**).

Osnabrück. *City, northwestern Germany.* The city may derive its name from *Osna*, as a former name of the *Hase* River here, and Old Saxon *bruggia*, "bridge," although historic records of the river name lack the *n* of *Osna*. The name itself probably derives from Old High German *hasan*, "gray."

Ossetia. *Region, southeastern Europe/southwestern Asia.* The region, divided by the Caucasus as *North Ossetia* (in Russia) and *South Ossetia* (in Georgia), derives its basic name from its indigenous inhabitants, the *Ossetians*. Their own name is probably of Iranian origin and may represent a root element *os* meaning "speedy."

Ossining. *Village, eastern United States.* The New York village arose in 1680 on a site known as *Philipsburg Manor*. Two hamlets, *Sparta* and *Hunters Landing*, developed, and in 1813 these were incorporated as the village of *Sing Sing*, so named for the *Sin Sinck* Native Americans. The name was changed to *Ossining* in 1901 to avoid associations with *Sing Sing* State Prison, established here in 1824. (In 1969 this was itself renamed *Ossining* Correctional Facility.)

Ostend. *City and port, northwestern Belgium.* The city's name means "east end," from Flemish *oosten*, "east," and *einde*, "end." Ostend (in Flemish *Oostende*) is at the eastern end of a long beach, at the other end of which is the less well known *Westende*.

Osterode. *City, central Germany.* The city, formally known as *Osterode am Harz*, for its location at the foot of the **Harz** Mountains, has a name meaning "eastern clearing," probably for its location in relation to *Suterode*, "southern clearing." The name was probably transferred to the former town of *Osterode* in East Prussia, now *Ostróda*, northeastern Poland.

Ostia. *Historic town, west central Italy.* The former Roman town, at the mouth of the Tiber, has a name indicating this location, from Latin *ostium*, "estuary." There is now a village of the name near the site of the original town, whose own excavated ruins are known as *Ostia Antica*, "ancient Ostia."

Ostrava. *City, eastern Czech Republic.* The city, above the confluence of the Oder and *Ostravice* rivers, takes its name from the latter. The river's own name derives from Czech *ostrov*, "island."

Ostróda *see* **Osterode**

Ostrołęka. *City, northeastern Poland.* The city, on the Narew River, has a name that means "sharp bend," referring to the alteration in the river's course here, from Slavic words related to Polish *ostry*, "sharp," and *łęk*, "bow."

Ostrowiec Świętokrzyski. *City, southeastern Poland.* The first word of the city's name is the Polish for "little island," denoting a slightly raised site in lowland. The second word is the name of the nearby **Świętokrzyskie Mountains**.

Ostrów Wielkopolski. *City, west central Poland.* The first word of the city's name is the Polish for "island," here meaning a relatively elevated site in low-lying terrain. The second word distinguishes this "island" from others, and is the adjectival form of the Polish for "Great Poland," denoting the central Polish plain here.

Oswego. *City and port, eastern United States.* The New York city lies along Lake Ontario at the mouth of the *Oswego* River, and takes its name from the latter, itself representing Iroquois *oshwe-geh*, "great pouring-out place."

Oswestry. *Town, western England.* The Shropshire town has an Old English name meaning "*Oswald*'s tree," with the personal name followed by *trēow*, "tree." The name is traditionally linked with King *Oswald* of Northumbria, but he was killed in battle in 642, long before the name is first recorded (in c.1180), and the long time gap between the names makes any historical link unlikely.

Otaru. *City and port, northern Japan.* The city, in the island of Hokkaido, derives its name either from Japanese *o-*, "little," and *taru*, "barrel," or according to some from Ainu *otarunai*, "sandy beach."

Otjiwarongo. *Town, northern Namibia*. The town has a name meaning "place of fat cattle." It was given by the cattle-grazing Herero when they moved into the area in the early 19th century, displacing the Bergdama (Damara) and San (Bushmen) who inhabited it.

Otranto, Strait of. *Strait, southern Europe*. The strait, between southern Italy and Albania, is named for the Italian port of *Otranto*, the country's easternmost town. Its own name comes from the Roman name *Hydruntum*, itself from Late Greek *Hudranton*, "water town," based on *hudōr*, "water."

Otsu. *City and port, southern Japan*. The city, on Lake Biwa in the island of Honshu, derives its name from Japanese *ō*, "big," and *tsu*, "port."

Ottawa. *Capital of Canada*. The Ontario city takes its name from that of the river on which it stands. The river's own name derives from Algonquian *adawe*, perhaps meaning "big river," or according to another account, "merchant," from the name of a people who lived by it and controlled local trade. The city took the name when it became capital in 1854. It was founded in 1827 as *Bytown*, so named for the English army officer John *By* (1781–1836) of the Royal Engineers, who had been entrusted with the construction of the Rideau Canal here.

Ouachita. *River, southern United States*. The river, rising in Arkansas and flowing generally southeast into the Red River in Louisiana, derives its name from that of a Native American people. The meaning of their own name is uncertain. Proposed interpretations include "big hunt," "sparkling water," and "country of large buffaloes."

Ouagadougou. *Capital of Burkina Faso*. The city is said to take its name from two different local African languages, with *ouaga* meaning "come" in one, and *dougou* meaning "village" in the other. But this is almost certainly an attempt to make an obscure name meaningful. The spelling of the name is due to French influence, and its English equivalent would be *Wagadugu*.

Oudenaarde. *Town, western Belgium*. The town's name, recorded in 1148 as *Aldenarda*, means "old plowland," from Dutch *oud*, "old," and *ard*, "plowland," "arable district." The French form of the name is *Audenarde*.

Oudh *see* **Ayodhya**

Ouessant *see* **Ushant**

Ouezzane. *City, northern Morocco*. The city was founded in 1727 as a Muslim religious community on the site of a village called *Dechra Jebel er-Rihan*, "village of the mount of myrtles." Its present name ultimately derives from Arabic *wa'z*, "preaching."

Ouidah. *Town and port, southern Benin*. The town was a center for European traders from the early 17th century, and they are said to have based the name on that of a nearby Portuguese fort called *São João de Ajuda*, "St. John of Aid." The name is also sometimes spelled *Whydah*.

Oulu. *City and port, western Finland*. The name basically means "water," "river," with reference to the *Oulu* River at the mouth of which the city stands. Its Swedish name is *Uleåborg*, which is the same name with *borg*, "fort," added.

Oum er-Rbia. *River, western Morocco*. The name is Arabic for "mother of springtime," from *umm*, "mother," *er*, "the," and *rabī'*, "spring."

Ouro Prêto. *City, eastern Brazil*. The city was founded in 1698 as a gold-mining settlement named *Vila Rica de Ouro Prêto*, Portuguese for "rich town of black gold," referring to the black color of the gold mixed with iron ore panned in the streams here. The first half of the name was then dropped.

Ouse. *River, central and eastern England*. The river, rising in Northamptonshire, has a name meaning simply "water," from a Celtic root word with counterparts in Greek *hudōr*, Gaelic *uisce*, English *wash*, and ultimately *water* itself. There are other rivers of the name elsewhere in England. This one is the longest, and as such is often distinguished as the *Great Ouse*.

Outremont. *City, southeastern Canada*. The Quebec city, on Montreal island adjoining Montreal, was originally called *Côte-Sainte-Catherine*, "St. Catherine's coast." In 1875 it was renamed as now for its relation to Montreal, i.e. on the far side of *Mont-Royal*, from French *outre*, "across" (in compound words), and *Mont*.

Overijssel. *Province, eastern Netherlands*. The province lies to the north of the IJssel River (*see* **IJsselmeer**). Hence its name, meaning "over the IJssel," as viewed from the south or center of the country. The name thus equates to those beginning *Trans-*, such as **Transvaal**.

Overland Park. *City, central United States*. The Kansas city, now a residential suburb of Kansas City, was settled in 1906 on the old Santa Fe Trail, the famed *overland* wagon trail and commercial route from Independence, Missouri, to Santa Fe, New Mexico. Hence the name.

Oviedo. *City, northern Spain*. The Roman name of the city was *Ovetum*, popularly derived from Latin *vetus*, "old." The actual origin remains obscure.

Owensboro. *City, east central United States.* The Kentucky city was laid out in 1816 and at first named *Rossborough*. It was subsequently renamed as now in honor of Colonel Abraham *Owen*, a veteran of early Kentucky wars.

Owen Stanley Range. *Mountain range, central Papua New Guinea.* The range, in southeastern New Guinea, is named for the British naval officer and hydrographer *Owen Stanley* (1811–1850), who explored the New Guinea coast from 1845 to 1850.

Oxford. *City, south central England.* The city, in the county of the same name, has a name that means what it says, denoting the *ford* for *oxen* originally here across the Thames River. The ford in question is thought to have been just below Folly Bridge. Oxford's civic coat of arms thus correctly depicts a stylized ox over a ford.

Oxnard. *City, southwestern United States.* The California city was founded in 1898 and grew up around a sugar-beet factory founded by Henry *Oxnard*.

Oxus *see* **Amu Darya**

Ozarks. *Upland region, south central United States.* The forested highland region, mainly in southern Missouri and northern Arkansas, is said to derive its name from a form of French *aux Arks*, denoting country belonging to the **Arkansas** Native Americans.

Ózd. *City, northeastern Hungary.* The city takes its name from the *Uz* people who formerly inhabited the region.

Paarl. *Town, southwestern South Africa.* The town, in Western Cape province, derives its name from the rock granite domes that crown the nearby ridge. These were called the *Diamandt ende Peerlberg*, "diamond and pearl mountains," by Abraham Gabbema when he saw them glistening with dew in the morning sun one day in 1657. The valley was colonized and called *De Paarl* in 1687, and the present town was founded with this name in 1690.

Pacific Ocean. *Ocean between Arctic and Antarctic.* The world's largest and deepest ocean was given its name by the Portuguese navigator Ferdinand Magellan in 1520, originally as *Mar Pacifico*, "calm sea," to mark the fact that he had encountered no storms on his voyage of exploration from Tierra del Fuego to the Philippines. In some languages, the Pacific is known by a name meaning "great ocean," as Turkish *Büyük Okyanus*.

Padang. *City and port, western Indonesia.* The city, in Sumatra, takes its name from the nearby *Padang* Mountains, whose own name represents Malay *padang*, "plain," "field."

Paderborn. *City, northwestern Germany.* The first part of the city's name is that of the small *Pader* River on which it stands. The second part represents Old High German *brunno*, "well," "spring," referring to the springs in which the river emerges from below the cathedral. The meaning of the river name is uncertain.

Padma. *River, Bangladesh.* The river, a channel in the Ganges Delta, has a Sanskrit name meaning "lotus."

Padua. *City, northeastern Italy.* The city, known to the Romans as *Patavium*, probably derives its name from Gaulish *padi*, "pine," referring to the pine forests that are found here in the valley of the **Po**. The Italian name of the city is *Padova*.

Pagalu *see* **Annobón**

Pai-ch'eng. *City, northeastern China.* The city, in Kirin province, derives its name from Chinese *bái*, "white," and *chéng*, "city," thus equating to **Belgrade**, among other places.

Painted Desert. *Plateau, southwestern United States.* The section of high plateau in Arizona was so named in 1858 by Lieutenant Joseph C. Ives, a government explorer, to describe the region's brilliantly colored shales, marls, and sandstones. These are banded with bright red, yellow, blue, and white, and look as if they have been *painted*.

Paisley. *Town, southwestern Scotland.* The town's name has the basic meaning "church," from a Celtic word, Middle Irish *baslec*, that itself came from Latin *basilica* (in turn from Greek *basilikos*, "royal"). The town was given its name by the "Scots" who came from Ireland to settle in western Scotland from the late 6th century.

Pakistan. *Republic, southern Asia.* The republic was formed in 1947 from the predominantly Muslim parts of India and given a name that was apparently proposed in the early 1930s by a group of Muslim students at Cambridge University, England. (One Chandhari Rahmat Ali is sometimes said to have been the name's actual creator.) It represents the initials of *P*unjab, *A*fghanistan, and *K*ashmir with the common Iranian placename suffix *-stan* meaning "country." At the same time the name puns on Iranian *pāk*, "pure," so that Pakistan is the "land of the pure."

Paks. *Town, west central Hungary.* The town has a name of uncertain origin.

Palatinate. *Historic region, western Germany.* The region is so named because it was under the jurisdiction of a count *palatine*, a leading secular prince of the Holy Roman Empire. He took his title from that of the official who originally guarded the *palace* (Latin *palatium*) of the Roman emperor. The German name of the region is *Pfalz*, a corruption of Latin *palatinus*, "of the palace." Hence German *Pfalzgraf*, "count palatine."

Palau. *Island group, western Pacific.* The islands, generally considered a part of the Carolines, and administered by the United States, have a name that is a corruption of *Panloq*, the name of the main island. The meaning of this is unknown.

Palawan. *Island, western Philippines.* The westernmost island of the Philippines has a local (Buginese) name meaning "gate of combat." The island in effect serves as a barrier against the violence of the South China Sea.

Palayankottai. *City, southern India.* The city, in Tamil Nadu state, is also known as *Palamkotta*, a name meaning "camp fort."

Paldiski. *Town and port, northwestern Estonia.* The town, founded in 1718 by order of Peter the Great, was first named *Rogervik* in 1723, then *Baltiysky port* (Russian for "Baltic port") in 1783. Its present name, adopted in 1917, is an Estonian form of this. Germans know Paldiski as *Baltischport*.

Palembang. *City and river port, southwestern Indonesia.* The city, in southern Sumatra, has a name of disputed origin, partly because of the proliferation of languages on the island. The name may relate to the Musi River on which the city stands. According to one account, it thus means "river of tides," referring to the varying level of its waters. A more realistic proposal is an origin in Malayan *lembang*, "lowland," with the initial *Pa-* a placename prefix.

Palencia. *City, north central Spain.* The city was known to the Romans as *Palantia*. This is a river name that probably comes from the Indoeuropean root element *pel*, "to flow."

Palermo. *City and port, southern Italy.* The city, in northwestern Sicily, arose between the 8th and 6th centuries B.C. as a Phoenician settlement named *Machanat*, "fortress," "stronghold," from *machanat choshbin*, literally "camp of weavers." It was subsequently known to the Greeks as *Panormos* and to the Romans as *Panormus*, from Greek *pan*, "all," and *ormos*, "roadstead," implying a safe anchorage for all ships. At least 17 places of this name have been recorded on the Mediterranean seaboard, so that the name became virtually generic. The present name evolved from the earlier one.

Palestine. *Historic region, southwestern Asia.* The region, a former British mandate approximately coextensive with Israel and that part of

Jordan west of the Jordan River (the modern West Bank), has a name meaning "land of the *Philistines*," these being the non–Semitic people who inhabited it in biblical times. Their own name is Hebrew in origin, perhaps deriving from a root word *palosh* meaning "to invade." In Assyrian inscriptions their land is named as *Palastu* or *Pilistu*. Parts of historic Palestine began to regain their autonomy in the 1990s but negotiations with Israel stalled under the premiership of Benjamin Netanyahu and collapsed in 2001. Despite continuing conflict, a "road map" peace plan was launched in 2003 by the European Union, Russia, the United Nations, and the United States with the aim of establishing an autonomous Palestinian state by 2005.

Palestrina. *Town, central Italy.* The town's name evolved from its Roman name *Praeneste*, Greek *Praineston*, apparently from Latin *prae-*, earlier *prai-*, "before," and a non–Indoeuropean root said to denote a town on a river. The present name has been influenced by Italian *palestra*, "gymnasium."

Palisades. *Cliffs, eastern United States.* The sandstone bluffs along the west bank of the Hudson River, in southeastern New York and northeastern New Jersey, are so called from a special use of *palisade* in its original sense to mean a line of stakes or pales serving to form an enclosure or defense. The name, now generic to describe any such columnar formation, first became familiar in the early 19th century.

> The Palisades — Hudson River... This singular precipice varies in height from fifty to two hundred feet, and presents a naked front of columnar strata, which give it its descriptive name [Nathaniel P. Willis, *American Scenery*, 1838].

Palk Strait. *Strait, Bay of Bengal.* The strait between India and Sri Lanka is sometimes said to be so called from a Sinhalese word meaning "whirlpool." It is actually named for Sir Robert *Palk* (1717–1798), governor of Madras.

Pallavaram. *Town, southern India.* The name of the town, in Tamil Nadu state, is said to be an alteration of *Pallapuram*, from the *Pallas*, a caste claiming descent from the *Pallava* dynasty of rulers, and Hindi *purā*, "town." Pallavaram is now a suburb of Chennai.

Palma. *Town and port, Majorca, western Mediterranean Sea.* The chief town of the Balearic Islands derives its name from the Spanish word for "palm." It is a translation of Phoenician *tamar*, the original name of Majorca.

Palm Beach. *Town and resort, southeastern United States.* The town, in southeastern Florida, was settled in 1873 as *Palm City*. It was given its present name in 1887 when it was developed as a resort.

Palmer Land. *Section of Antarctic Peninsula, Antarctic*. The southern part of the Antarctic Peninsula is named for its discoverer, the American explorer Nathaniel *Palmer* (1799–1877), who led an expedition here in 1820. *See also* **Graham Land**.

Palmerston North. *City, central New Zealand*. The city, in southern North Island, was founded in 1866 and named for the British prime minister Henry John Temple, 3d Viscount *Palmerston* (1784–1865). The second word of the name was added to distinguish the city, in *North* Island, from the smaller town of *Palmerston* in South Island. The viscount's own title comes from *Palmerston*, Co. Dublin, Ireland. *See also* **Darwin**.

Palm Springs. *City, southwestern United States*. The California city was originally known by the Spanish name of *Agua Caliente*, "hot water," for its hot springs. The present resort was established in 1884 and adopted its English name, referring to its native *palms* and the aforementioned *springs*.

¹Palmyra. *Historic city, south central Syria*. The name of the long ruined city is said to derive from its abundance of *palm* trees and its production of dates. However, it is mentioned in the Bible under its earlier name of *Tadmor* (1 Kings 9:18, etc.), and it is possible that *Palmyra* evolved as a form of this.

²Palmyra. *Island, central Pacific*. The uninhabited island, in the Northern Line Islands, was discovered in 1802 by Captain Sawle of the American ship *Palmyra* and named by him for it. Presumably the ship itself was named for ¹*Palmyra*.

Palo Alto. *City, western United States*. The California city has a Spanish name meaning "tall tree," referring to the lofty redwood by which Gaspar de Portolá's expedition of 1769 is said to have camped. The site was developed in 1891.

Palomar, Mt. *Mountain, southwestern United States*. The mountain, in southern California, was formerly called *Smith Mountain* but in 1901 reverted to its original Spanish name, meaning "place of pigeons."

Pamiers. *Town, southern France*. The town derives its name from the historic Syrian city of *Apameia ad Orontem*, built in the 4th century B.C. by the Macedonian general Seleucus Nicator and named for his wife *Apama*. The name was probably brought to France in the 13th century by Roger-Bernard II, comte de Foix, who gave it to the fort he built here as a memorial to the First Crusade.

Pamirs. *Mountain region, central Asia*. The complex of mountain ranges, mainly in Tajikistan, Kyrgyzstan, and China, has a name for which various explanations have been proposed: (1) From Sanskrit *upa-meru*, "near (Mt.) Meru"; (2) From Iranian *pāye-mihr*, "foot of Mithra" (i.e. at the feet of the sun god); (3) From Iranian *pā morğ*, "foot of the bird": (4) From Iranian *pāye marg*, "foot of death." The general sense appears to be "valley at the foot of a mountain."

Pampas. *Plain, central Argentina*. The plain is named from the Spanish plural form of a Quechua word meaning simply "plain," "flat region."

Pamphylia. *Historic region, southern Turkey*. The coastal region, mentioned in the Bible (Acts 13:13, etc.), has a Greek name meaning "(region of) all races," from *pan*, "all," and *phulon*, "race." The name implies a territory inhabited by a mixture of peoples.

Pamplona. *City, northern Spain*. The name is a corrupt form of the city's Roman name, *Pompeiopolis*, "*Pompey*'s city," referring to the Roman emperor *Pompey*, who founded it in 68 B.C.

Panagyurishte. *Town, west central Bulgaria*. The town derives its name from Greek *panaguris*, the Doric form of *paneguris*, "general assembly," denoting a place of gathering for games, religious ceremonies, fairs, and other public festivals. The final *-ishte* is a Slavic suffix meaning "place." The name would not originally have applied to the town but to the site on which it arose, apparently no earlier than the 15th century.

Panama. *Republic, southern Central America*. The name is probably of Guaraní origin and has been traditionally interpreted as meaning "place of many fish." Its actual origin is uncertain. The name was originally that of the city founded on the Pacific coast in 1519 but destroyed in 1671. It was later rebuilt on a slightly different site and became the present *Panama City* (Spanish *Panamá*) and the country's capital.

Panama City. *City and port, southeastern United States*. The Florida city was founded in c.1765 and originally known as *Old Town*. Later, it developed into a fishing village called *St. Andrew*, presumably for the biblical personage, who was a fisherman. It was subsequently renamed as now for the Canal Zone city (*see* **Panama**). Its namer, developer George W. West, noticed that it was on a straight line between that city and Chicago.

Panevėžys. *City, north central Lithuania*. The

city takes its name from the *Nevėžys* River on which it lies. In Lithuanian names, *Pa-* means "along," like Russian *Po-* in names such as **Podolia**.

Panjshir. *Valley, north central Afghanistan.* The name is that of the river here, itself meaning "five lions" (Iranian *panj*, "five," and *shir*, "lion"), supposedly for the five men who labored for Sultan Mahmud in building the so-called "Sultan Dam" here.

Panmunjom. *Village, northwestern South Korea.* The village, the scene of peace talks in 1951–53, derives its name from Korean *p'an*, "floor," "flat," *mun*, "door," "gate," and *chŏm*, "shop."

Pannonia. *Historic region, western Hungary.* The former province of the Roman Empire has a name of uncertain origin, despite attempts to derive it from Ligurian *pannus*, "rag," or the Greek god *Pan*.

Pantelleria. *Island, eastern Mediterranean Sea.* The Italian island, between Sicily and Tunisia, may derive its name from Low Latin *pantaleria*, "roof," "canopy," referring to some natural feature.

Pao-chi. *City, eastern China.* The city, in Shensi province, derives its name from Chinese *bǎo*, "treasure," "jewel," and *jī*, "chicken," "rooster."

Paola. *Town, eastern Malta.* The town was founded in 1626 by Antoine de *Paule*, grand master of the Hospitalers (Knights of St. John of Jerusalem), and is named for him.

Pao-ting. *City, eastern China.* The city, in Hopeh province, derives its name from Chinese *bǎo*, "to protect," "to defend," and *dìng*, "to decide," "to fix."

Pao-t'ou. *City, east central China.* The city, in Inner Mongolia, derives its name from Chinese *bāo*, "to wrap," "to envelop," and *tóu*, "head," "top."

Papeete. *Capital of French Polynesia.* The town and port, on Tahiti, is said to derive its name from Tahitian *pape*, "water," and *ete*, "basket," referring to a place where people came with baskets to get water.

Papenburg. *Town, northwestern Germany.* The town arose in 1630 as Germany's first fen colony, taking the name of an existing place, a town on the northern border of the diocese of Münster. Its own name, first recorded in 1379, apparently means "*Papen*'s fort," with an East Frisian family name.

Paphlagonia. *Historic region, northern Turkey.* The region's name is traditionally derived from that of *Paphlagon*, the son of Phineus in Greek mythology.

Paphos. *Town, southwestern Cyprus.* The town takes its name from an ancient Greek settlement nearby, mentioned in the Bible (Acts 13:6, etc.). Its own name is of obscure origin.

Papua. *Region, New Guinea Island, western Pacific.* The region, now part of the independent state of Papua New Guinea, takes its name from the *Papuans* who are its indigenous people. Their own name represents Malay *pua-pua*, "frizzled," referring to their tightly curled hair.

Pará. *State, northern Brazil.* The state derives its name from Guaraní *para*, "river," referring to the Amazon and many other rivers here that wind their way over the floodplain. The name particularly applies to the navigable eastern mouth of the Amazon.

Paraguay. *Republic, central South America.* The country takes its name from the river that flows through it and that forms its northeastern border with Brazil and southwestern border with Argentina. Its own name derives from Guaraní *para*, "water," "river," and *guay*, "born." This was in turn the name of a local chieftain who agreed to a treaty with the first Spanish explorers.

Paraíba. *State, northeastern Brazil.* The state takes its name from the river here, its own name representing Guaraní *para*, "water," "river," and *hiba*, "arm." There are actually two rivers of the name: *Paraíba do Norte*, "northern Paraíba," and *Paraíba do Sul*, "southern Paraíba."

Paramaribo. *Capital of Surinam.* The city and port, at the mouth of the Surinam River, derives its name from Guaraní *para*, "water," "river," and *maribo*, "inhabitants."

Paraná. *State, southern Brazil.* The state takes its name from the river that flows through it. Its own name represents Guaraní *para*, "water," "river," and *aná*, "parent," "union," describing its formation by the confluence of the Rio Grande and the Paranaíba.

Paranaíba. *River, southern Brazil.* The river, a headstream of the Paraná, has a Guaraní name meaning "bad water," denoting water unsuitable for fishing or navigation. There is an additional implied contrast with a river named *Paracuta*, "good water."

Parbhani. *City, west central India.* The city, in Maharashtra state, derives its name from the *Prabhavati* ("house of light") Temple here.

Pardesiya. *Village, central Israel.* The Jewish settlement, founded in 1942, derives its name from Hebrew *pardes*, "citrus orchard," describing the orchards that surround the village.

¹Paris. *Capital of France.* The city takes its name from the *Parisii*, the Celtic people whose capital of *Lutetia* was here. Their own name is of uncertain origin. Proposed etymologies include: (1) Celtic *par*, "boat," and *gwys*, "men"; (2) Greek *baris*, "boat"; (3) Latin *Bar Isis*, "son of Isis," *bar* being a word of Aramaic origin. All these look equally contrived, and a more likely source is in the name of a Celtic god, meaning "shaper," "maker." Even so, "boat" is the traditional choice, and is reflected in the city's coat of arms, which depicts a galley sailing over the waves together with the Latin motto, *Fluctuat nec mergitur*, "It is buffeted but does not sink." (The Île de la Cité actually looks like a boat making its stately way down the Seine River.) The earlier name *Lutetia* probably derives from Gaulish *luto*, "mud," "marsh," referring to the low-lying ground by the Seine.

²**Paris**. *City, southern United States.* The Texas city was laid out in 1845 and named for ¹**Paris**, France, in recognition of French aid during the Revolutionary War.

¹**Parma**. *City, northern Italy.* The city takes its name from that of the river on which it lies. This itself represents the name of the Etruscan people who inhabited the region. The meaning of their own name is uncertain, but it has been associated with Arabic *barma*, "circle." The Roman colony founded here in 183 B.C. came to be known under the Emperor Augustus as *Julia Augusta*, while the Greeks knew the city in Byzantine times as *Chrysopolis*, "golden city."

²**Parma**. *City, northern United States.* The Ohio city, a suburb of Cleveland, was settled in 1816 and at first known as *Greenbriar*. In 1826 it was renamed as now, for ¹**Parma**, Italy.

Parnassus. *Mountain, central Greece.* The mountain is said to derive its name from a Hittite word *parna*, "abode." This may relate to the fact that it was later sacred to Apollo and the Muses of Greek mythology.

Pärnu. *City, southwestern Estonia.* The city, first mentioned in 1251, is named for the river here, its own name deriving from Estonian *pärn*, "lime tree." The German form of the name is *Pernau*.

Paropamisus. *Mountain range, northwestern Afghanistan.* The name is of uncertain meaning. The initial *Par-* may be of Sogdian origin with a sense "side," "foot," referring to the location of the range with regard to the Pamirs, to the north. Even the application of the name varies. It is generally used of the range at the western end of the Hindu Kush, but is applied by some historical geographers to the Hindu Kush itself. The name also appears in the Greek-influenced form *Parapanisus*.

Parramatta. *City, southeastern Australia.* Aus-

tralia's second-oldest settlement, now a suburb of Sydney, New South Wales, was founded in 1788 and originally called *Rose Hill*. In 1791 it was given its present Aboriginal name, said to mean "head of the river." The river here is the *Parramatta* itself.

Parry Islands. *Island group, northern Canada.* The islands, in Nunavut, are named for the English explorer Sir William Edward *Parry* (1790–1855), who visited them in 1819.

Parthia. *Historic region, western Asia.* The region, roughly coextensive with modern Khorasan province in northeastern Iran, has a name of Scythian origin meaning "banished," "exiled," referring to its original inhabitants.

¹**Pasadena**. *City, southwestern United States.* The California city, now a suburb of Los Angeles, has a name of artificial origin. When it was founded by Thomas B. Elliott in 1874 as *Indiana Colony*, a Native American name was sought. Since there were no such people locally, a missionary working among the Chippewa (Ojibwa) was entrusted with the task of providing a name that meant "crown of the valley," an apt description of the location. He accordingly sent back four long Native American names, ending respectively -*pa*, -*sa*, -*de*, -*na*. The founder quietly dropped the rest of the names and joined these four elements together to make the new name.

²**Pasadena**. *City, southern United States.* The Texas city, now a suburb of Houston, was founded in 1895 and named for ¹**Pasadena**, California, apparently in the belief that the name was a Spanish word meaning "land of flowers." (The namer may have been thinking of *Pascua florida* as an origin for the name of **Florida**.) The reference was to the flowering fields along Vince's Bayou here.

Pascoal, Mt. *Mountain, eastern Brazil.* The mountain was the first land sighted by the Portuguese navigator Pedro Álvarez Cabral on April 22, 1500, Easter Day. Hence its name, from Portuguese *Pascoa*, "Easter."

Pasewalk. *Town, northeastern Germany.* The town arose around a Pomeranian castle in the 12th century and has a name explained in a document of 1150 as "wolf town" (*"Posduwlc, id est urbs Wolfi"*). The precise origin of the name is uncertain. The second part could indeed represent Old Polabian *volk*, "wolf," but the same word also meant "portage" (where boats are hauled overland), and this could be the true sense.

Pashupati. *Town, central Nepal.* Nepal's holiest town takes its name from the temple of

Pashupatinath here, dedicated to the Hindu god Shiva, one of whose names, in his aspect of god of fertility, is *Pashupati*, "lord of cattle," from Hindi *pashu*, "beast," "cattle," and *pāti*, "lord."

Paso de los Libres. *Town and river port, northeastern Argentina*. The original settlement by the Uruguay River here arose in the 18th century as a Jesuit mission. The present town, with a Spanish name meaning "pass of the free," was founded in 1843 by General Joaquín Madariaga as leader of a group of 103 survivors in the ongoing war against Brazil.

Passaic. *City, eastern United States*. The New Jersey city is named for the river on which it lies. The river's own name is said to come from a Delaware word meaning either "peace" or "valley."

Passau. *City, southeastern Germany*. The city, at the confluence of the Danube, Inn, and Ilz rivers, arose on the site of a Celtic settlement called *Boiodurum*, "fortified place of the *Boii*" (*see* **Bavaria**). A later Roman frontier post here was named *Castra Batava*, "camp of the *Batavi*" (*see* **Batavia**). The present name evolved from this last, recorded as *Batavis* in 511, *Pazauge* in 786, and *Pazzau* in 1329.

Pásztó. *Town, northern Hungary*. The town derives its name from the identical personal name of Slavic origin, itself meaning "stallion."

Patagonia. *Region, southern South America*. The region, in Argentina and Chile, has a name that was originally applied by European explorers to the local Tehuelche (Chonan) people who inhabited the Atlantic coast here. One account derives it from Spanish or Portuguese *pata*, "paw," "animal's foot," referring to the llama-skin shoes that they wore, while another attributes it to the Portuguese explorer Ferdinand Magellan, who was struck by the resemblance of the Tehuelche to *Patagon*, a dog-headed monster in the prose romance *Amadís de Gaula* (1508) by the Spanish writer Garci Ordóñez de Montalvo, and named them accordingly. *Cp*. **California**.

Patan *see* ²**Lalitpur**

Paterson. *City, eastern United States*. The New Jersey city was founded in 1791 and named for William *Paterson* (1745–1806), then governor of New Jersey.

Patmos. *Island, Aegean Sea*. The Greek island, the smallest of the Dodecanese, mentioned in the Bible (Revelation 1:9), was known in medieval times as *Palmosa*, supposedly for its *palm* trees. But this was almost certainly a corruption of a much older name of obscure origin.

Patna. *City, northeastern India*. The capital of Bihar state, founded in the 5th century B.C., has

a name that is an abbreviated form of its original name *Pataliputra*, from Hindi *pāṭala*, literally "pale red," the name of a flower of the begonia family, and *putra*, "son."

Patras. *City and port, western Greece*. The city, in the northwestern Peloponnese, is traditionally said to take its name from the Achaean leader *Patreus*.

Pau. *City, southwestern France*. The city's name may represent the pre–Indoeuropean root word *pal*, "mountain." This would have originally been the name of the *Gave de Pau*, the river that flows down to and through the town from the Pyrenees nearby.

Pavia. *Town, northern Italy*. The town had the Late Latin name of *Papia*, from the local *Papiria* people. Its Roman name was *Ticinum*, from the **Ticino** River here.

Pavlodar. *City, northeastern Kazakhstan*. The city was founded in 1720 as a military outpost called *Koryakovsky forpost*. It gained its present name in 1861, modeled on that of *Yekaterinodar* (*see* **Krasnodar**). The meaning is "*Paul*'s gift," from Russian *Pavel*, "*Paul*," and *dar*, "gift." The reference is presumably to *Paul* (1754–1801), emperor of Russia from 1796 to his death. Just as *Yekaterinodar* was "*Catherine*'s gift," named for *Catherine* the Great, so *Pavlodar* was named similarly for her son.

Pavlograd. *City, southeastern Ukraine*. The city was founded in 1779 as the village of *Luganskoye*. The following year a fort was built nearby and named for *Paul* (1754–1801), the future emperor of Russia. The name then passed to the town (*-grad*). The Ukrainian form of the name is *Pavlohrad*.

Pawtucket. *City, northeastern United States*. The Rhode Island city, first settled in 1671, has an Algonquian name meaning "at the falls," these being on the Blackstone River here (locally itself known as the *Pawtucket*).

Paysandú. *City, western Uruguay*. The city's hybrid name means "Father *Sandú*," from Guaraní *pay*, translating Spanish *padre*, "father," and the name of its founder in 1772, the priest Policarpo *Sandú*.

Pazardzhik. *Town, west central Bulgaria*. The town arose in the 14th century with the fuller name *Tatar Pazardzhik*, "(place of the) Tatar market." The first word was dropped from the name in 1934. *Cp*. **Dobrich**.

Peace. *River, western Canada*. The river, in British Columbia and Alberta, is named for *Peace* Point, Alberta, where the Cree and Beaver Native Americans settled their territorial dispute.

Peak District. *Upland region, north central*

England. The plateau region, one of Britain's original National Parks, takes its name from the *Peak* or *High Peak*, an area of millstone grit hills in northern Derbyshire. The name is thus general, and does not refer to a specific peak.

Pearl Coast. *Coastal region, northern Venezuela*. The seaboard between Cumaná and Trinidad was so named by Spanish mariners for the extensive pearl fisheries here, while the islands off the coast were similarly known as the *Pearl Islands*. *See* **Margarita Island**.

Pearl Harbor. *Inlet, northwestern Hawaii, United States*. The inlet, in southern Oahu Island, is so named for the pearl oysters that formerly grew here. The English name translates the Hawaiian name *Wai Momi*, "pearl waters."

Pearl Islands. *Island group, Gulf of Panama*. The Panama-owned islands, as their name implies, are noted for their *pearl* fishing industry. *Cp.* **Pearl Coast**.

Peary Land. *Region, northern Greenland*. The Arctic region is named for the U.S. Arctic explorer Robert E. *Peary* (1856–1920), who partially explored it in 1892, 1895, and 1900.

Peć. *Town, southwestern Serbia*. The city's name apparently means "cave," from a Slavic word related to Russian *pech'*, "oven," and ultimately to Latin *specus*, "cavity," "hollow." *Cp.* **Pécs**.

Pechora. *River, northwestern Russia*. The river's ancient name has long baffled toponymists, who are inclined to derive it from that of a Nenets or Komi people called *Pechera* or *Pechora*. It is almost certainly unrelated to Russian *peshchera*, "cave," as sometimes suggested.

Pécs. *City, southwestern Hungary*. The city's name seems to mean "cave," from a word ultimately related to Latin *specus*, "cavity," "hollow." However, the former German name of Pécs was *Fünfkirchen*, "five churches," translating its earlier Medieval Latin name *Quinque Ecclesiae*, and this suggests that *Pécs* may actually derives from a Slavic word for "five" (as Polish *pięć*).

Peebles. *Town, southeastern Scotland*. The town, in the former county of the same name, has a name meaning "shelters," from a word of Celtic origin related to modern Welsh *pebyll*, the plural of *pabell*, "tent," itself related to English *pavilion*. The reference is to shepherds' huts or shielings used in summer pastures here. The Celtic plural has gained an extra English plural *-s*.

Peel. *Town and port, Isle of Man, Irish Sea*. The town, on the island's southwest coast, takes its name from its historic (now ruined) castle, from Middle English *pel*, literally "enclosure"

(modern *pale*, as in "beyond the pale"). Before the 16th century, Peel was known as *Holmetown*, "island town," and this is reflected in its Manx name of *Port-na-Hinsey*, "port of the island."

Pegu. *City and port, southern Myanmar*. The city's name derives from Burmese *pekhu*, of uncertain meaning, but traditionally interpreted as "conquered by stratagem."

Pehowa. *City, northwestern India*. The name of the city, in Haryana state, evolved from its Sanskrit name *Prthudaka*, "pool of *Prthu*," son of the legendary king Vena.

Peiping *see* **Beijing**

Peipus, Lake. *Lake, western Europe*. The lake, in eastern Estonia and western Russia, is said to derive its name from Finnish *peipponen*, "finch," or more exactly from the genitive plural of this, *peipposen*. It is thus apparently "(lake) of finches." The Estonian form of the name is *Peipsi*. Its Russian name is *Chudskoye*, from an Old Russian ethnic name, *Chud*, applied to various Finno-Ugrian peoples, including those of Estonia. The name itself probably means "stranger," and is related to Russian *chuzhdyj*, "alien," denoting a non–Slav people.

Peking *see* **Beijing**

Pelée, Mt. *Mountain, Martinique, French West Indies*. The active volcanic mountain has a French name meaning "bald," referring to the appearance of its slopes. Its actual French name is thus *Montagne Pelée*, "bald mountain."

Pelhřimov. *Town, south central Czech Republic*. The town is first mentioned in 1289 as *Piligrimov*, showing its origin to be in a word related to English *pilgrim* (from Latin *peregrinus*). The reference is not to actual pilgrims but to a person so nicknamed, presumably the founder of the original settlement or a landowner here. The final *-ov* is the Slavic possessive suffix.

Pelion. *Mountain, northeastern Greece*. The name probably goes back ultimately to the pre–Indoeuropean root element *pala*, "rock."

Peloponnese. *Peninsula, southern Greece*. The name means "island of *Pelops*," from Greek *Pelopos*, genitive of *Pelops*, the name of the son of Tantalus in Greek mythology, and *nēsos*, "island." A former name was *Morea*, said to be from Latin *morus*, "mulberry tree," referring either to the peninsula's shape, like that of a mulberry leaf, or to the growing of mulberries here. A Slavic origin in a word meaning "sea" (Russian *more*) has also been proposed.

Pemba. *Island, western Indian Ocean*. The island, in the Indian Ocean off the coast of East Africa, has a name that is Bantu in origin but of uncertain meaning. Its Arabic name is *al-jazīra* *al-khaḍrā'*, "the green island," implying that it is more fertile than neighboring Zanzibar.

Pembroke. *Town and port, southwestern Wales.* The town, in the county of the same name, lies on a peninsula somewhat similar to **Land's End** in Cornwall, England. Its name indicates this natural feature and is an exact Celtic equivalent, from words corresponding to modern Welsh *pen*, "head," "end," and *bro*, "region," "land." There seems to have been a general westward drive that gave identical names to west-coast headlands. Others are **Finistère** in France and Cape **Finisterre** in Spain.

Penang. *Island, western Malaysia.* The island, to the west of the Malay Peninsula, has a name representing Malay *pinang*, "areca" (a genus of palm tree with egg-shaped nuts).

Pend Oreille, Lake. *Lake, northwestern United States.* The lake, in northwestern Idaho, is named for the French name, *Pend d'Oreille*, of the Kalispel Native Americans, themselves so called because they wore ear pendants (modern French *pendant d'oreille*).

Penedo. *City, northeastern Brazil.* The city was founded in the 16th century by the Portuguese. Hence its name, from Portuguese *penedo*, "rock," for its site on a cliff above the São Francisco River.

Penghu Islands *see* **Pescadores**

Pen-hsi. *City, northeastern China.* The city, in Liaoning province, derives its name from Chinese *běn*, "root," "origin," and *xī*, "stream."

Pennines. *Mountain chain, England.* England's main mountain chain, extending south from the Scottish border to central England, has a name probably based on Celtic *penno*, "hill." The name is not found before the 18th century, however, and it is now known to have been invented by the literary forger Charles Bertram (1723–1765) in a work attributed to the 14th-century chronicler Richard of Cirencester. The source of his invention is a passage in William Camden's *Britannica* (1586) referring to the *Pennine Alps* (Italian *Alpi Pennine*) on the Italo-Swiss border and to the **Apennines** in Italy.

Pennsylvania. *State, eastern United States.* The state is not named for its founder in 1682, the English Quaker William Penn (1644–1718), but for his father, Admiral Sir William *Penn* (1621–1670). Moreover, the name was not given by Penn himself, who actually opposed it, but by Charles II, who had granted him territory here the previous year. The following extract from a letter of March 14, 1681, by Penn to his friend Robert Turner charts the actual naming process:

After many waitings, watchings, solicitings, and disputes in Council, this day my country was confirmed to me under the great seal of England, with large powers and privileges, by the name of *Pennsylvania*; a name the new king would give it in honor of my father. I chose New Wales, [that] being, as this is, a pretty hilly country; but Penn being Welsh for *a head* (as Penmanmoire [Penmaenmawr] in Wales, and Penrith in Cumberland, and Penn in Buckinghamshire), [they] called this Pennsylvania, which is the high or head woodlands; for I proposed, when the secretary, a Welshman, refused to have it called New Wales, *Sylvania*, and they added *Penn* to it; and though I much opposed it, and went to the king to have it struck out and altered, he said it was past, and would take it upon him; nor could twenty guineas move the under-secretary to vary the name; for I feared lest it should be looked on as a vanity in me, and not as a respect to the king, as it truly was, to my father, whom he often mentions with praise [Quoted in A. Howry Espenshade, *Pennsylvania Place Names*, 1925].

Penobscot. *River, northeastern United States.* Maine's longest river has a Native American name said to mean "river of rocks." It gave the name of the *Penobscot* Native Americans.

Penrith. *City, southeastern Australia.* The New South Wales city, now a suburb of Sydney, was founded in 1815 and was originally known as *Evan* and *Castlereagh*, before being renamed as now in 1818 for the English town of *Penrith*, Cumberland (now Cumbria).

Pensacola. *City and port, southeastern United States.* The Florida city was founded by the Spanish in the mid–16th century and has a name said to mean "long-haired people," referring to a group of Native Americans here, from Choctaw *panshi*, "hair," and *okla*, "people."

Pentland Firth. *Strait, northern Scotland.* The strait, between mainland Scotland and the Orkney Islands, has a name meaning "Pictland," i.e. "land of the Picts," a description used generally by the Vikings for the northern region of Scotland. *Firth* is also of Scandinavian origin, meaning "narrow inlet," "strait."

Pentland Hills. *Hills, southeastern Scotland.* The name has a Celtic base, from *penn*, "hill," "head," to which English *land* has been added. The name overall thus denotes a hilly region.

Penza. *City, western Russia.* The city was founded in 1663 and takes its name from the river here. Its own name may derive from a word related to Nenets *penzya* or Komi *pendzey*, both terms for a dried-up river.

Penzance. *Town and port, southwestern England.* The Cornwall town has a Cornish name meaning "holy headland," from *pen*, "hill," "head," and *sans*, "holy" (related to English *saint*). The reference is to the old chapel of St. Mary, now represented by St. Mary's church, which formerly stood on the headland here. *Cp.* **Holyhead.**

Peoria. *City, north central United States.* The Illinois city takes its name from the *Peoria*, one of the five Native American peoples in the Illinois Confederacy. Their own name is said to mean "carriers."

Peraea. *Historic region, eastern Jordan.* The region of ancient Palestine derives its name from Greek *peran*, "beyond," denoting a land *beyond* or east of the Jordan River. The name is mentioned by the 1st century A.D. Jewish historian Josephus, but does not occur in the Bible, where the Septuagint (Greek version of the Old Testament) simply has *peran tou Iordanou*, "beyond the Jordan" (Genesis 50:10, etc.). *Cp. Transjordan* as a former name of **Jordan.**

Perak. *Region, northwestern Malaysia.* The region, in northwestern West Malaysia, on the Malay Peninsula, has a Malay name meaning "tin," referring to its plentiful deposits of this metal, the object of many foreign and local incursions.

Perche. *Historic region, northern France.* The region had the Medieval Latin name of *Saltus Perticus,* the first word from Latin *saltus,* "woodland pasture," the second from *pertica,* "pole," "rod" (English *perch*). The reference is to a well-wooded region.

Pereira. *City, west central Colombia.* The city was founded by the Spanish in 1863 and named for Francisco *Pereira* Gamba, who donated land for the purpose.

Pergamino. *City, eastern Argentina.* According to a text of 1626, the city is said to take its name from Spanish *pergamino,* "parchment," referring to an incident in which a group of Spanish lost some parchment documents here.

Pergamum. *Historic city, western Turkey.* The city, a former Greek capital, has a name that may derive from Greek *purgos,* "tower," "fortress." The name is now represented by the town of *Bergama* on the site.

Périgord. *Region, southwestern France.* The region takes its name from the *Petrucorii,* the Gaulish people who once inhabited it. They also gave the name of **Périgueux.**

Périgueux. *City, southwestern France.* The city, in the Dordogne, takes its name from the *Petrucorii,* the Gaulish people who at one time inhabited this region. Their own name means "four armies," from Gaulish *petru,* "four," and *corios,* "army," referring to the combined military resources of the four administrative regions here. *Cp.* **Périgord.**

Perm. *City and river port, central Russia.* The city, on the Kama River, has a name that may derive from Finnish *perämaa,* "rear land," from *perä,* "rear," "back," and *maa,* "land," "country." The reference would be to a town that lay further inland (to the north) on the Kama than some other place nearer its confluence with the Volga. The town was founded in 1780. From 1940 through 1957 it was known as *Molotov,* for the Soviet foreign minister Vyacheslav *Molotov* (1890–1986).

Pernambuco. *State, northeastern Brazil.* The state derives its name from Guaraní *paraná,* "big river," and either *puku,* "wide," or perhaps more likely *mbuku,* "arm." The name was also formerly that of its capital, **Recife.**

Pernik. *Town, west central Bulgaria.* The town is mentioned in 10th-century texts as *Perunik* and *Peringrad,* which suggests an origin in the name of *Perun,* the Slav pagan god of thunder. From 1949 through 1963 the town was known as *Dimitrovo,* for the Bulgarian Communist leader Georgi *Dimitrov* (1882–1949), postwar prime minister of Bulgaria. (*Cp.* **¹Dimitrovgrad.**)

Perpignan. *City, southern France.* The name of the city ultimately derives from the Gaulish personal name *Perpennio.*

Persepolis. *Historic city, southwestern Iran.* The ancient capital of Persia, founded in the 6th century B.C. under Darius the Great, has a name meaning simply "town of the *Persians,*" from Greek *Persēs,* "a Persian," and *polis,* "town." The Iranian name of the site is *takht-e jamshīd,* "throne of *Jamshid,*" a legendary king whose name was substituted for that of Darius when the latter was forgotten.

Persia *see* **Iran**

¹Perth. *Town, central Scotland.* The town, in the former county of the same name, has a name of Pictish origin probably meaning "bush," "thicket," from a word related to modern Welsh *perth* in the same sense.

²Perth. *City, western Australia.* The capital of Western Australia was settled in 1829 and named for *Perth*shire, Scotland, native county of Sir George Murray (1772–1846), then British colonial secretary. He also gave the name of the **Murray** River.

Perth Amboy. *City and port, eastern United States.* The New Jersey city was settled in the late

17th century and was originally known simply as *Amboy*, from an Algonquian word perhaps meaning "level piece of ground." The first word of the name was subsequently added in honor of James Drummond, 4th Earl of *Perth* (1648–1716), who in 1685 permitted the immigration of many oppressed Scots to Middlesex County, New Jersey.

Peru. *Republic, western South America.* The country takes its name from the *Birú* or *Perú* River here, itself deriving from Guaraní *biru* or *piru*, meaning simply "water," "river."

Perugia. *City, central Italy.* The name of the city may be Etruscan in origin, and perhaps represents *phaersu*, the name of a devil that led the souls of the dead to the underworld, with this name itself indirectly related to Latin *persona*, "mask." The Roman name of Perugia was *Perusia*.

Perushtitsa. *Town, southern Bulgaria.* The town's name is of disputed origin. It has been derived by some from the Slav pagan god *Perun*, who may have had a cult here. *Cp.* **Pernik**, **Pirna**.

Pervouralsk. *City, western Russia.* The city, in the Central Urals, arose in 1732 when an ironworks was built, the original name of the site being *Shaytanka*, for the small river here. In 1933 the town was given its present name, meaning "first (in the) **Urals**," from Russian *pervo-*, "first," and *Ural*. The city's ironworks were the *first* to be built in these mountains.

Pesaro. *City, central Italy.* The city, on the Adriatic Sea, was known to the Romans as *Pisaurum*, perhaps from an Etruscan word *pisa*, "mouth," referring to the site at the mouth of the Foglia River.

Pescadores. *Island group, southwestern Taiwan.* The islands, between Taiwan and the Chinese mainland, have a name given in the 16th century by the Portuguese to mean "(islands of) fishermen." The fishing industry is still important here. The are also known as the *Penghu* Islands, after the Chinese name of the largest island in the group, meaning "flooding lakes."

Pescara. *City and port, eastern Italy.* The city, on the Adriatic Sea, takes its name from the river at the mouth of which it stands. The river's own name derives ultimately from Latin *piscis*, "fish."

Peshawar. *City, northern Pakistan.* The city, at the eastern end of the Khyber Pass, has a name that was officially given it in the 16th century by the Mughal emperor Akbar. It is a corruption of its earlier Hindi name *purashāpura* or *parashāvara*, meaning "frontier town." Peshawar is one of the oldest cities in Pakistan and was capital of the ancient kingdom of Gandhara.

Petah Tiqwa. *City, west central Israel.* The city, northeast of Tel Aviv-Jaffa, was founded in 1878 as the first modern Jewish agricultural settlement in Palestine, and as such is generally known as '*Em ha-Moshavot*, "mother of villages." Its name represents Hebrew *peṭah-tiqwâ*, "door of hope," from *peṭah*, "door," "gate," and *tiqwâ*, "hope." The reference is biblical: "And I will give her ... the valley of Achor for a door of hope" (Hosea 2:15).

Petaluma. *City, southwestern United States.* The California city was founded in 1852 and named for the rancho here, its own name representing Miwok *pe'ta*, "flat," and *lu'ma*, "back."

¹Peterborough. *City, east central England.* The former Cambridgeshire (earlier Northamptonshire) city arose in the 7th century around a monastery called *Medeshamstede*, probably meaning "*Medi*'s homestead." The monastery was ravaged by the Danes in the 9th century, but restored in the 10th century as a Benedictine abbey, and by the time of Domesday Book (1086) the settlement was a fortified town called simply *Burg*, "town." *Peter* was then added to this from the dedication of the abbey. The dedication is now that of the cathedral, built on the abbey site in the 12th century.

²Peterborough. *City, southeastern Canada.* The Ontario city arose from a sawmill founded in 1821 by Adam *Scott*, with the site subsequently known as *Scott's Plains*. In 1825 a large group of Irish immigrants settled here, and the community was renamed for their director, Colonel *Peter* Robinson (1785–1838).

Peterhead. *Town and port, northeastern Scotland.* The town's name relates to the former 12th-century St. *Peter*'s Kirk (Church) that stood on a headland here. More precisely, the headland was named for the church, and then the town for the headland, on which it was founded in the late 16th century.

Petersburg. *City, eastern United States.* The Virginia city arose around a fort built in 1645 and is allegedly named for its commander, Major *Peter* Jones. However, there are other individuals named *Peter* or *Peters* who could equally have given the name.

Pétionville. *Town, southern Haiti.* The town, now a suburb of Port-au-Prince, is named for Alexandre Sabès *Pétion* (1770–1818), the Haitian liberator and president who was born and died in Port-au-Prince.

Petra. *Historic city, southwestern Jordan.* The long-ruined rock city has a name that derives directly from Greek *petra*, "rock."

Petrodvorets. *Town, western Russia.* The

town, on the Gulf of Finland west of St. Petersburg, arose from the residence built by *Peter* the Great in 1704 for him to stay at during his frequent journeys from St. Petersburg to the fortress then being built at Kronstadt. Hence its name, meaning "*Peter's* palace," from Russian *Pyotr*, "Peter," and *dvorets*, "palace." Until 1944 it was known as *Petergof*, representing German *Peterhof*, with the same sense.

Petrograd *see* ¹**St. Petersburg**

Petrokrepost *see* **Shlisselburg**

Petrolina. *City, northeastern Brazil.* The name has nothing to do with oil or gas. The city was founded in 1840 on the left bank of the São Francisco River opposite the town of Juàzeiro and was accordingly first named *Passagem de Juàzeiro*, "Juàzeiro crossing." In 1862 it was renamed as now in memory of Dom *Pedro* I (1798–1834), first emperor of Brazil, and his wife, Dona Maria *Leopoldina* (1797–1826), daughter of Francis II, emperor of Austria. The name thus combines their own names. *Cp.* **Petrópolis.**

Petropavlovsk. *City, northern Kazakhstan.* The city was founded in 1752 as the fort of *St. Peter* (Russian *Pyotr*) and *St. Paul* (Russian *Pavel*), so named from the dedication of the church within its precincts.

Petropavlovsk-Kamchatsky. *City and port, eastern Russia.* The city takes the latter part of its name from the **Kamchatka** Peninsula, where it was founded in 1740 by the Danish navigator Vitus Bering (*see* **Bering Sea**). The first part of the name represents those of two of his ships, the *St. Peter* (Russian *Pyotr*) and *St. Paul* (Russian *Pavel*). This was the original name, and the second part was added in 1924 to distinguish this town from **Petropavlovsk.**

Petrópolis. *City, southeastern Brazil.* The city, north of Rio de Janeiro, was founded in 1845 by Bavarian immigrants with the backing of Dom *Pedro* II (1825–1891), second and last emperor of Brazil, and is named for him, the Greek-style name meaning "*Peter's* town." *See also* **Teresópolis.**

Petrovaradin. *Town, northern Serbia.* The suburb of Novi Sad has a name meaning "*Peter's* fort" (Hungarian *Pétervárad*, German *Peterwardein*), supposedly for *Peter* the Hermit, who is said to have assembled an army here for the First Crusade in 1096.

Petrozavodsk. *City, northwestern Russia.* The capital of Karelia has a name meaning "*Peter's* factory," from Russian *Pyotr*, "Peter," and *zavod*, "works," "factory." It arose from the ironworks founded here by *Peter* the Great in 1703 to exploit the natural ore deposits.

Pfalz *see* **Palatinate**

Pforzheim. *City, southwestern Germany.* The city, which arose on the site of a Roman settlement by a crossing of the Enz River, probably derives the first part of its name from a dialect form of Latin *portus*, "harbor," a word that in Medieval Latin also meant "landing place," "crossing point," "customs post," as probably applied here. The second part is Old High German *heim*, "house," "abode."

Pharos *see* **Hvar**

Philadelphia. *City and port, eastern United States.* The Pennsylvania city was founded in 1682 by the English Quaker William Penn. He gave it the name of the ancient city in what is now western Turkey, the seat of one of the "Seven Churches" mentioned in the Bible (Revelation 1:11), apparently interpreting this as "brotherly love," from Greek *philo-* "loving," and *adelphos*, "brother." However, the biblical city was actually named for its founder, Attalus II *Philadelphus*, 2d-century B.C. king of Pergamum, whose title or byname meant "loving the brethren," which is not quite the same.

Philae. *Island, southeastern Egypt.* The name of the island, in the Nile River, has become popularly associated with Greek *philos*, "loved," "pleasing." It actually represents Coptic *pilak*, "corner," "end," probably referring to its location on the border with Nubia. Its local Arabic name is *jazīrat anas al-wujūd*, "island of *Anas el-Wujud*." The latter, with a name conventionally translated as "delight of the world," is a character in the *Arabian Nights*. His tale tells how he traces his beloved to the island, where she has been locked up by her father, only to find that she has escaped.

Philippi. *Historic town, northern Greece.* The town takes its name from *Philip* II, king of Macedonia, who developed and fortified it in 356 B.C. in order to control its gold mines.

Philippines. *Island republic, southeastern Asia.* The islands were discovered in 1521 by the Portuguese navigator Ferdinand Magellan, and he named them *St. Lazarus Islands*, because he had made his discovery on December 17, the feast-day of St. *Lazarus*. Their present name was given by the Spanish explorer Ruy López de Villalobos, who landed on the island that is now Mindanao in 1543 and called it *Filipina* in honor of the future king *Philip* II of Spain (1527–1598).

Phnom Penh. *Capital of Cambodia.* The city's name means "mountain of plenty," from Cambodian *phnŏm*, "mountain," "hill," and *penh*, "full." A Cambodian tradition derives the name from an elderly rich lady called *Don Penh*, who is said to have built a shrine at this spot, so that the meaning is supposedly "*Penh*'s hill." But this is simply local legend at work.

Phocaea. *Historic city and port, western Turkey.* The port derives its name from Greek *phōkē*, "seal," probably referring to the monk seals that were at one time abundant in the Mediterranean. (Turkish *fok*, "seal," derives from the Greek word, as does French *phoque*.) The modern town and seaside resort of *Foça* stands on the site of the original city.

Phocis. *Historic region, central Greece.* The district of ancient Greece is said to derive its name from Greek *phōkē*, "seal," as for **Phocaea**, presumably referring to seals in the Gulf of Corinth, to the south. The name is represented by the modern department of *Fokís*.

Phoenicia. *Historic region, western Syria.* The ancient country takes its name from its indigenous people, the *Phoenicians*. Their own name is traditionally derived from that of *Phoenix*, son of Agenor, king of Tyre, their legendary ancestor. Its actual origin is uncertain. It has been linked with Greek *phoinix*, "purple," since it was the Phoenicians who invented the purple dye. But this word probably derives from their ethnic name, not the other way around. The relationship, if any, between the mythical bird *phoenix* and the Phoenicians is similarly obscure.

Phoenix. *City, southwestern United States.* The state capital of Arizona was founded in 1867 on the ruins of an ancient Native American city. As a new town built on the site of an earlier one, it was thus like the *phoenix*, the legendary bird that periodically burned itself and then arose from its own ashes.

Phrygia. *Historic region, west central Turkey.* The name of the ancient country may derive either from Greek *phrugō*, "I burn," or from Pelasgian *bher*, "to move rapidly." The Phrygians were noted for their impetuosity.

Piacenza. *City, northern Italy.* The city was founded in the 3d century B.C. with the Roman name of *Placentia*. This means "caring," "pleasing," and refers to the way in which the remnants of Scipio's army were cared for here after the Battle of Trebia in 218 B.C.

Pianosa. *Island, Tyrrhenian Sea.* The Italian island, in the Tuscan Archipelago, was known to the Romans as *Planasia*, from Latin *planus*, "flat," referring to its level terrain.

Piatra-Neamṭ. *City, northeastern Romania.* The city's name means "stronghold of the Germans," from Romanian *piatra*, "rock," and *neamṭ*, "German." This translates the town's 13th-century Latin name, *Castrum Teutonicum*, "Teutonic camp," referring to a fortification of the Teutonic Knights.

Picardy. *Historic region, northern France.* The region takes its name from Old French *pic* (modern *pique*), "pike," this being the weapon for which the people of Picardy were noted in former times. The French form of the name is *Picardie*.

Pico. *Island, North Atlantic.* The island of the Azores takes its name from its volcanic mountain, *Alto Pico*, "high peak."

Piedmont. *Region, northwestern Italy.* The region derives its name from Old Italian *pie di monte*, "foot of the mountain," referring to its location at the foot of the Alps.

Piedras Negras. *City, northeastern Mexico.* The city was founded in 1849 and given a Spanish name meaning "black rocks," referring to its locality. In 1888 it was renamed *Ciudad Porfirio Díaz*, for the Mexican president *Porfirio Díaz* (1830–1915), but reverted to its original name following his downfall in 1911.

Pierre. *City, northwestern United States.* The state capital of South Dakota takes its name from the French fur trader *Pierre* Chouteau (1789–1865), who set up a market here in 1837 to trade with the Native Americans.

Pietermaritzburg. *City, southeastern South Africa.* The former capital of Natal and (briefly) co-capital of KwaZulu Natal province was founded in 1839 and named commemoratively for the Voortrekker (Afrikaner settler) leaders *Pieter* Retief (1780–1838) and Gerrit *Maritz* (1798–1839), who both lost their lives to the Zulus. The lengthy name is abbreviated locally to *Maritzburg*.

Pietersburg *see* **Polokwane**

Pikes Peak. *Mountain, west central United States.* The mountain, in the Front Range of the Rocky Mountains, Colorado, is named for the American army officer and explorer Zebulon M. *Pike* (1779–1813), who discovered it (and unsuccessfully attempted to scale it) in 1806.

Piła. *City, west central Poland.* The city, first recorded in the 15th century, derives its name from Polish *piła*, "saw," referring to the original sawmill here. Hence its German name of *Schneidemühl*, "sawmill." The city still has important lumber mills.

Pilatus. *Mountain, central Switzerland.* The mountain is said to derive its name from Latin *pileatus*, "wearing a *pileus*" (a type of felt cap), referring to its cloud cover. According to legend, the mountain is named for Pontius *Pilate*, either because he committed suicide here by drowning himself in a lake, or because rocks here resemble his appearance in profile. (No known portrait of Pilate actually exists.)

Pilcomayo. *River, Bolivia*. The river, rising in the eastern Andes and flowing generally southeast to join the Paraguay near Asunción, Paraguay, has a Guaraní name said to mean "river of the birds."

Pilsen *see* **Plzeň**

Pindus Mountains. *Mountain range, central Greece*. The chief range of mainland Greece is said to derive its name from Greek *pidax*, "spring," referring to the streams that feed the region's many rivers.

Pine Bluff. *City, south central United States*. The Arkansas city was settled in 1819 as the trading post of *Mount Marie*. It was renamed as now in 1832 for its forest of giant *pines* on a high *bluff* overlooking the Arkansas River.

P'ing-hsiang. *City, eastern China*. The city, in Kiangsi province, derives its name from Chinese *píng*, "duckweed," and *xiāng*, "country," "native place."

Pinsk. *City, southern Belarus*. The city, first mentioned in 1097, takes its name from the *Pina* River which joins the Pripyat here. The origin of the river name is uncertain. It is not likely to derive from Russian *pena*, "foam."

Piotrków Trybunalski. *City, central Poland*. The city, first mentioned in 1217, was originally just *Piotrków*, from the Polish personal name *Piotr*, "Peter." The second word of the name, the adjectival form of Polish *trybuna*, "tribunal," was added when in 1578 the city became one of the two seats of crown tribunal, the highest court of justice in Poland. The status was held until the late 18th century.

Piraeus. *City and port, southwestern Greece*. The city was founded in the 5th century B.C. as a port for Athens. Its name is based on Greek *peran*, "beyond," referring to its original location, across marshes from the mainland. *Cp.* **Peraea**.

Pirate Coast *see* **United Arab Emirates**

Pirdop. *Town, west central Bulgaria*. Many etymologies have been offered to explain the town's name, from Slavic *pri dub*, "by the oak," or *pir doba*, "feast in good time," to Greek *purgopolis*, "town of towers," or *puropolis*, "town of fires," the latter for the frequent peatbog fires in time of drought. The actual source may be in a Thracian name *Burdana*, believed to mean "ford (over) water," referring to a crossing of the river here. A more recent theory traces the name back to an original form *Protopopintsi*, based on Greek *protopapas*, "protopope," a priest of high rank in the Greek Church. Under Turkish influence this name would have been shortened to *Protop* and then corrupted to *Pirdop*.

Pirenópolis. *City, central Brazil*. The city, founded in 1727, takes its name from the nearby mountain range *Serra dos Pireneus*, itself named for its resemblance to the **Pyrenees**.

Pirmasens. *City, southwestern Germany*. The first part of the city's name evolved from that of St. *Pirmin*, who founded a Benedictine abbey here in 740. The second part derives from conjectural Old High German *einsna*, "solitary place," referring to the abbey, where each monk had his cell.

Pirna. *Town, eastern Germany*. The town probably has a name of Slavic origin. A source in the name of the pagan god *Perun* has been suggested, referring to a rock here that was a center of his cult. The name has nothing to do with the pears (German *Birne*) appearing in the town's coat of arms.

Pisa. *City, northwestern Italy*. The city has an Etruscan name of uncertain meaning. A possible sense "estuary" has been suggested, which would describe Pisa's situation at the mouth of the Arno River.

Pisco. *City and port, southwestern Peru*. The city was founded in 1640 at the mouth of the *Pisco* River and is named for it. The river's own name is Quechua for "bird."

Pisgah. *Mountain, north central Jordan*. The name of the biblical mountain, from where Moses was shown the Promised Land and where he died (Deuteronomy 3:27, 34:1), is usually rendered from the Hebrew as "peak" or "slope." The name is also borne by several peaks and places in the United States.

Pisidia. *Historic region, southern Turkey*. The ancient region of Asia Minor derives its name from its inhabitants, the *Pisidians*. Their own name is of unknown origin.

Pissevache. *Waterfall, southwestern Switzerland*. The cascade, on the Salanfe River, has a descriptive name meaning literally "cow piss."

Pistoia. *City, north central Italy*. The city is said to derive its name from Latin *pistor*, "pounder," meaning a person who pounds or mills grain, i.e. a baker. But this may simply be an attempt to make sense of an otherwise obscure name. The original settlement here passed to the Romans in *c.*561 B.C.

Pitcairn Island. *Island, South Pacific*. The island was discovered in 1767 by the English colonist Philip Carteret, and is named for Robert *Pitcairn* (1747–1770), the midshipman who first sighted it from HMS *Swallow*. The name is suitably apt for the rugged island, with its many "pits" and "cairns."

Pittsburgh. *City and port, eastern United States.* The Pennsylvania city was founded in 1754 by French colonists and originally named *Fort Duquesne*, for the French governor of New France (future Canada), Michel-Ange *Duquesne* (1702–1778). In 1758 it was captured by the English and renamed in honor of the British statesman William *Pitt* the Elder (1708–1778), then virtual prime minister.

Pittsfield. *City, northeastern United States.* The Massachusetts city was incorporated as a town in 1761 and named, like **Pittsburgh**, for the British statesman William *Pitt* the Elder.

Plano. *City, southern United States.* The Texas city was first settled in 1845 and originally called *Fillmore*. In 1851 it received its present name, from the Spanish word for "flat," "plain," describing its location in a prairie region.

Plasencia. *City, western Spain.* The city arose as a Moorish town named *Ambroz*. When Alfonso VIII of Castile retook it from the Moors in the 12th century, he renamed it as now, "*ut Deo placeat et hominibus*," "that it may be pleasing to God and men," the Latin text explicating the choice of name

Plassey. *Village, northeastern India.* The West Bengal village, famous as the scene of the British victory over the forces of the nawab of Bengal in 1847, probably derives its name from Hindi *palāsh*, "dhak" (the forest tree *Butea frondosa*).

Plata, Río de la *see* **La Plata**

Plataea. *Historic city, east central Greece.* The ancient city of Boeotia derives its name from Greek *platus*, "flat," referring to the level ledge on which it lay on the northern side of Mt. Cithaeron.

Plate, River *see* **La Plata**

Platte. *River, central United States.* The Nebraska river is a mile wide in places, and consequently very shallow. Hence its name, from French *plat*, "shallow." *See also* **Nebraska**.

Plauen. *City, east central Germany.* The city, on the Weisse Elster River, arose in the 12th century on the site of a Slav village. Its name goes back to Old Sorbian *plav*, "watering place," or *plaviti*, "to water," "to take by boat."

Pleven. *City, northern Bulgaria.* The city takes its name from the small *Pleva* River on which it lies. The river's own name derives from a Slavic root word meaning "to swim," "to float," indirectly related to English *flow*.

Ploieşti. *City, southeastern Romania.* The city has a name based on the personal name *Ploaie*,

itself identical to the standard Romanian word meaning "rain."

Plovdiv. *City, southern Bulgaria.* The city's name is a Slavic adaptation of its earlier Thracian name *Pulpudava*, "*Philip's* town," from *Pulp*, "Philip," and *dava*, "town," referring to *Philip* II, king of Macedonia, who conquered it in 341 B.C. The Greeks translated this name as *Philippopolis*. When the Romans captured the city in 46 B.C., however, they renamed it *Trimontium*, "three hills," for the hills on which it lies by the Maritsa River.

[1]Plymouth. *City and port, southwestern England.* The name of the Devon city means "(place at the) mouth of the *Plym* (River)." The river derives its own name from *Plympton* ("plum-tree farm"), now a district of Plymouth itself, although not actually on the river. The earlier name of Plymouth was *Sutton Prior*, "prior's southern village," from the Anglo-Saxon settlement here in which the manor was held by the priory of Plympton. The name survives in *Sutton* Pool, one of Plymouth's three main harbors.

[2]Plymouth. *Town, northeastern United States.* The Massachusetts town is the site of the first permanent European settlement in New England, the *Colony of New Plymouth*. It was founded in 1620 by the Pilgrims who had sailed in the *Mayflower* from **[1]Plymouth**, England, for which they named it.

Plzeň. *City, western Czech Republic.* The city derives its name from Old Czech *plz*, "damp," "moist." It was founded in 1292 5½ miles (9 km) southeast of a settlement and castle of the same name (now *Plzenec*) that had itself been built on a damp and slippery site where several small rivers meet to form the Berounka. The German name of the city is *Pilsen*.

Po. *River, northern Italy.* The river has a name of Romano-Gaulish origin, representing *padi*, "pines." At one time there was an extensive region of pine forest around the river's mouth. *Cp.* **Padua**.

Pobedy, Pik *see* **Victory Peak**

Pocatello. *City, western United States.* The Idaho city was settled in 1882 and named for a Native American (Bannock) chief who granted rights of way here to the railroads. His own name means "the wayward."

Poços de Caldas. *City, southeastern Brazil.* The name is Portuguese for "wells of hot springs," referring to the city's hot sulfur springs.

Podgorica. *Capital of Montenegro.* The city has a Slavic name meaning "under the mountain," from *pod*, "under," and *gora*, "mountain," referring to its situation in a depression sur-rounded on three sides by mountains. From 1946 through 1992 it was known as *Titograd*, "*Tito's* town," for the Yugoslav head of state, Josip Broz Tito (1892–1980).

Podolia. *Region, western Ukraine.* The region, between the Dniester and Southern Bug rivers, derives its name from Russian dialect *podol*, a term for a plain below higher ground, from *po-*, "along," and Slavic *dol*, "lowland" (Russian *dolina*, "valley"). Podolia lies below the Car-pathians.

Podolsk. *City, western Russia.* The city arose around the village of *Podol*, its own name mean-ing "lower land," from Russian *po*, "along" (as for **Podolia**), and Slavic *dol*, "lowland" (Russian *dolina*, "valley"). The terrain here is lower and flatter than the hill country to the south and west.

Pohjanmaa. *Plain, western Finland.* The low-land plain lies along the Gulf of Bothnia. Hence its name, from Finnish *Pohjanlahti*, "Gulf of Bothnia" (*see* **Bothnia, Gulf of**), and *maa*, "country."

Pohjois-Karjala. *Province, east central Fin-land.* The province, bordering Russia to the east, has a name meaning "North Karelia," from Finnish *pohjois-*, "northern," and *Karjala*, "**Kare-lia.**"

Pohnpei. *Island, western Pacific.* The island, in the eastern Caroline Islands, derives its name from local words *poh*, "on," *n*, "of," and *pei*, "rockwork," so that the general sense is "rocky island." The island is high, coral-capped, and volcanic. The name is also found in the form *Ponape*.

Pointe-à-Pitre. *City and port, Guadeloupe, West Indies.* The city, on Grande-Terre island, has a name meaning "*Peter's* point," after a fisher-man who had a wharf here in the 17th century at the entrance to the Rivière Salée, the ocean channel separating Basse-Terre island from Grande-Terre.

Pointe-Noire. *City and port, southwestern Congo.* The city takes its French name from the Atlantic coastal site ("black point") on which it was founded in 1883.

Poissy. *Town, northern France.* The town's name evolved from its Roman name of *Pinci-acum*. This represents the Latin personal name *Pincius*, with the Gallo-Roman suffix *-acum*.

Poitiers. *City, south central France.* The city takes its name from the *Pictones*, the Gaulish people who at one time inhabited the region. Their own name is probably related to that of the *Picts*. The former Roman name of the set-tlement here was *Lemonum* or *Limonum*, from Gaulish *lemo*, "elm." Poitiers was the capital of **Poitou.**

Poitou. *Historic region, west central France.* The ancient province has a name of the same origin as that of its capital, **Poitiers**, i.e. from the Gaulish people known as the *Pictones*.

Pokrovsk *see* **Engels**

Poland. *Republic, central Europe.* The coun-try takes its name from its indigenous people, the *Poles*, whose own name represents Polish *pole*, "field," "plain," as they are primarily plain dwellers. Poland is almost entirely a lowland country, with many lakes and rivers. The Polish name of Poland is *Polska*. The English name is either effectively "Pole-land" or else perhaps evolved from the German name *Polen*, with the *-en* assimilated to *-land*. In some languages the name is quite different, as Turkish *Lehistan*, "*Lech's* country," from the personal name of the legendary founder of the Polish people.

Polokwane. *City, northeastern South Africa.* The capital of Limpopo province was founded in 1884 and originally named *Pietersburg*, for General *Pieter* Joubert (1834–1900), commander of the Boer forces in the war of 1880–81. It received its present indigenous name, meaning "place of safety," when the former Northern province was renamed **Limpopo**.

Polotsk. *City, northern Belarus.* The city takes its name from the *Polota* River, which joins the Western Dvina here. The river's own name prob-ably derives from the Slavic root *pal*, "marsh."

Poltava. *Town, central Ukraine.* The town takes its name from that of a river here. Its own name appears to mean "along the *Ltava*," from Slavic *po*, "along," and *Ltava*, the earlier name of the river, perhaps itself based on Indoeuro-pean *ap*, "water," "river." Poltava itself is now on the Vorskla.

Polynesia. *Island group, central Pacific.* The name means "many islands," from Greek *polus*, "many," and *nēsoi*, "islands." It is the oldest of the Greek-based island group names and was invented for the archipelago by the French his-torian and archaeologist Charles de Brosses, who introduced it in his *Histoire des navigations aux terres australes* (1756), detailing the different regions of Australasia and Polynesia. It so hap-pens that *pulo* is the Malaysian word for "island," and a theory exists that the name actually refers to the original settlers here, who had migrated from other islands.

Pomerania. *Region, north central Europe.* The region, bordering on the Baltic, has a name of Medieval Latin origin based on Polish *pomorze*, "coastland," literally "(land) along the sea," from *po*, "along," and *morze*, "sea." The German name for the region is *Pommern*. *Cp.* **Pomorie**.

Pomona. *City, southwestern United States.* The California city was promoted in 1875 as an agricultural center and named for *Pomona*, the Roman goddess of fruit.

Pomorie. *Town and resort, eastern Bulgaria.* The Black Sea resort has a name meaning "by the sea," from the Slavic prefix *po*, "by," "along," and Bulgarian *more*, "sea." *Cp.* **Pomerania**. Until 1934 it was known as *Ankhialo*, from its Roman name *Anchialus*, itself from Thracian *akhelo*, "water."

Pompano Beach. *City, southeastern United States.* The Florida city was first settled by fishermen around 1900 and named for the *pompano*, the choice food fish *Trachinotus carolinus*, found off the Atlantic coast here. The word *Beach* was added when the resort was incorporated as a town in 1945.

Pompeii. *Historic city and port, southern Italy.* The city probably derives its name from Oscan *pompe*, "five," referring to its five districts.

Ponape *see* **Pohnpei**

Ponce. *City and port, southern Puerto Rico.* The city was founded in the 17th century and named for the Spanish explorer Juan *Ponce* de León (1460–1521), who founded Puerto Rico's oldest settlement, Caparra, in 1509 and who subsequently discovered Florida.

Pondicherry. *City and port, southeastern India.* The city, originating in 1674 as a French trading post, has a name of Tamil origin meaning "new town," from *putu*, "new," and *chēri*, "village," "town." The English form of the name evolved from *Pondichéry*, the French form of the original.

Pontchartrain, Lake. *Lake, southern United States.* The Louisiana lake was discovered in 1699 by Pierre Le Moyne, sieur d'Iberville, and named for the French politician and explorer Louis, comte de *Pontchartrain* (1643–1727).

Pontefract. *Town, northern England.* The former West Yorkshire town has a pure Latin name meaning "broken bridge," from *ponte fracto*, the ablative (locative) case of *pontus fractus*. It is now thought that the original "broken bridge" was over a small stream here, and that it must have given access to a main route northward. It is not known when or how the bridge was broken. The earliest record of the name dates from the 12th century. The Anglo-Saxon name of the settlement here was *Tanshelf*, "*Tædden's* shelf of land," preserved in the name of *Pontefract Tanshelf* railroad station.

Pontevedra. *City, northwestern Spain.* The Medieval Latin name of the city was *Pons Vetus*, "old bridge," referring to the Roman bridge that (with later additions) still spans the Lérez River here.

Pontiac. *City, northern United States.* The Michigan city was settled in 1818 and named for the Ottawa chief and intertribal leader *Pontiac* (c.1720–1769), said to be buried nearby.

Pontine Islands. *Island group, Tyrrhenian Sea.* The volcanic islands, off the coast of central Italy, are said to derive their name from Greek *pontos*, "sea." The main island of the group is *Ponza*.

Pontine Marshes. *Historic marshland, south central Italy.* The marshland, reclaimed only in the 1930s under Mussolini, derives its name from the former Roman town of *Pometia* here. Its own name is dubiously derived from Latin *pomum*, "fruit," as if giving a meaning "orchard." *See also* **Latina**.

Pontivy. *Town, northwestern France.* The town, in Brittany, derives its name from Breton *pont*, "bridge," and *Ivy*, the name of a local saint who founded a monastery here in the 7th century. In 1805 *Napoleon* built a new town to the south of the medieval town center, so that the combined town was renamed *Napoléonville* until 1814 and again, for his nephew, *Napoleon* III, from 1848 through 1871.

Pontoise. *Town, northern France.* The town has a name meaning "bridge on the **Oise**," from French *pont*, "bridge," and the river name. The original bridge here dates back to at least the 4th century A.D.

Pontus. *Historic region, northeastern Turkey.* The ancient district of Anatolia derives its name from Greek *pontos*, "sea," referring to its location by the Black Sea.

Pontypool. *Town, southern Wales.* The town, north of Newport, has a half Welsh, half English name meaning "bridge by the pool," from Welsh *pont*, "bridge," *y*, "the," and English *pool*. The "pool" was probably a stretch of the Llwyd River on which the town stands.

Pontypridd. *Town, southern Wales.* The name of the town, near Cardiff, represents its original Welsh name of *Pont y Tŷ Pridd*, from *pont*, "bridge," *y*, "the," *tŷ*, "house," and *pridd*, "earth." There must have been a "bridge by the earthen house" over the Rhondda or Taff River here at some time. The word for "house" disappeared from the name, since the two letters that comprise it are already present in the initial *pont y*, and were thus regarded as redundant.

Ponza *see* **Pontine Islands**

Poole. *Town and port, southern England.* The

former Dorset town has a name that means what it says, and that refers to the "pool" or harbor here.

Popocatépetl. *Volcano, southeastern Mexico.* The name is Nahuatl in origin and means "smoking mountain," from *popokani,* "to smoke," and *tepetl,* "mountain," implying an active volcano.

Porcupine. *River, northwestern North America.* The river, in Yukon Territory, Canada, and Alaska, United States, is so named for the animal, found in the forests here.

Pordenone. *City, northeastern Italy.* The city derives its name from that of the Roman river port *Portus Naonis,* "port of the *Naone* (River)."

Pori. *City, southwestern Finland.* The city's present name is an eroded form of its original Swedish name *Björneborg,* "bear castle," given it by Duke John of Finland, later King John III of Sweden, who founded it in 1558. The city's coat of arms shows a crowned bear's head.

Porirua. *City, central New Zealand.* The city, in southern North Island, has a Maori name meaning "two tribes," from *pori,* "people," "tribe," and *rua,* "two."

Portadown. *Town, eastern Northern Ireland.* The town, in Co. Armagh, has a name representing Irish *Port an Dúnáin,* "landing place of the little fort," from *port,* "landing place," *an,* "the," and *dúnán,* the diminutive of *dún,* "fort." The "little fort" would have guarded a strategic crossing of the Bann River here.

Portalegre. *Town, central Portugal.* The name evolved from an earlier Latin form *Portus Alacer,* literally "lively port," implying a busy market or brisk trading place. *Cp.* **Pôrto Alegre.** The Roman name of the town was *Ammaia.*

Port Arthur. *City and lake port, southern United States.* The Texas city is named for *Arthur* C. Stilwell, who in 1895 organized the town as a *port* and railroad terminus.

Port Arthur *see* **Lü-shun**

Port-au-Prince. *Capital of Haiti.* The city and port is probably named for a French or English ship called the *Prince* that had taken shelter in the bay here some time in the early 18th century. The name originally applied to the bay, as *Le Port du Prince,* then passed to the town, founded in 1749 (originally under the name *L'Hôpital,* "the hospital").

Porta Westfalica. *Town, northeastern Germany.* The town was formed in 1973 on the amalgamation of the town of Hausberge with 13 villages. It takes its name from the *Westphalian Gap,* the point where the Weser River passes through the ranges of the Weserbergland, known

in German as the *Westfälische Pforte* and in Latin as the *Porta Westfalica. See also* **Westphalia.**

Port Blair. *Town and port, Andaman Islands, Indian Ocean.* The town, founded as a British penal colony in 1789, is named for a Lieutenant *Blair* of the Indian Navy, who first surveyed the islands.

Port Elizabeth. *City and port, southern South Africa.* The city, in Eastern Cape province, arose as a military station in 1799 and was originally named *Port Frederick,* for *Frederick* Augustus, Duke of York and Albany (1763–1827), second son of George III. In 1820 it was renamed as now by the acting governor of the Cape, Sir Rufane Donkin, in memory of his wife *Elizabeth,* who had died two years previously, aged 28.

Port-Gentil. *City and port, western Gabon.* The city arose from a number of French commercial houses here in the late 19th century and is named for the French colonial administrator Émile *Gentil* (1866–1914), governor of the French Congo from 1904 to 1908.

Port Glasgow. *Town, western Scotland.* The town, on the Firth of Clyde, was founded in 1668 as a *port* for **Glasgow.** The deepening of the Clyde prevented this, however, and instead the town concentrated on shipbuilding, with Glasgow being its own port.

Port Harcourt. *City and port, southern Nigeria.* The city was founded in 1912 and named for the British colonial secretary of the day, Lewis *Harcourt,* 1st Viscount Harcourt (1863–1922).

Port Hueneme. *City and port, southwestern United States.* The California city was founded in 1874 with the Chumash name *Wene me,* "place where one rests," so called because it was halfway between two existing Chumash villages.

Port Jackson. *Sea inlet, southeastern Australia.* The natural harbor that serves Sydney, New South Wales, was sighted in 1770 by Captain Cook, who named it for Sir George *Jackson* (1725–1822), a secretary to the Admiralty. It is possible that Cook did not actually enter the harbor, for if he had, he would have instantly appreciated its natural advantages and given it a grander name.

Port Kelang. *City and port, western Malaysia.* The city, at the mouth of the *Kelang* River, is the port of Kuala Lumpur, the Malaysian capital. The port opened in 1901 and was originally named *Port Swettenham* for the British colonial administrator Sir Frank *Swettenham* (1850–1946), who built a railroad from Kuala Lumpur to here.

[1]**Portland.** *City and port, northeastern United States.* The Maine city was settled by the English

in 1632 and originally known by a series of names: *Machigonne, Indigreat, Elbow, The Neck, Casco,* and *Falmouth.* Following its double destruction, first by the Native Americans, then by the British, it was rebuilt in 1786 and renamed as now for the Isle of *Portland,* England (*see* **Portland, Isle of**).

²Portland. *City and river port, western United States.* The Oregon city was laid out in 1844 and, so the story goes, named on the toss of a coin for **¹Portland,** Maine, rather than Boston, Massachusetts.

Portland, Isle of. *Peninsula, southern England.* The Dorset peninsula (rather than actual island) has a name meaning "land by the port," the latter being Portland Harbour, between the Isle of Portland itself and the mainland coastal town of Weymouth.

Port Louis. *Capital of Mauritius.* The city and port was founded in 1735 by Bertrand François Mahé, comte de la Bourdonnais, governor of the French colony on Mauritius, and named for *Louis* XV of France (1710–1774).

Port Moresby. *Capital of Papua New Guinea.* The city and port had its harbor explored in 1873 by Captain John Moresby, and he named it for his father, Admiral Sir Fairfax *Moresby* (1786–1877). Locally the city is known as simply *Moresby.*

Port Nicholson. *Inlet, central New Zealand.* The inlet of Cook Strait, indenting southern North Island, New Zealand, is named for Captain John *Nicholson,* harbormaster at Sydney, Australia, in 1826. It is also known as *Wellington Harbour,* for **³Wellington,** which lies on it.

Pôrto Alegre. *City and port, southern Brazil.* The city has a Portuguese name meaning "joyful port," from *porto,* "port," and *alegre,* "joyful" *Cp.* **Portalegre.** The town was founded in c.1742 by about 60 married couples from the Azores, and was originally known as *Pôrto dos Casais,* "port of the couples."

Portobelo. *Village and port, northern Panama.* The settlement on the Caribbean coast was founded in 1597 by the Spanish and took the name of the bay here, itself named in 1502 by Columbus as "beautiful harbor." Its strategic and commercial importance led to its being attacked several times by British buccaneers, as a result of which its name was adopted (in the spelling *Portobello*) for various places in Britain and other English-speaking countries.

Porto Carras. *Resort complex, northeastern Greece.* The private resort, on the Sithonian coast, was built up from the late 1960s on land owned by the Greek shipping and wine magnate John *Carras.*

Port of Spain. *Capital of Trinidad and Tobago.* The name of the city and port, in northwestern Trinidad, is an English translation of its original name, *Puerto de España.* This was given by Spanish colonists to their new capital in 1595 after their original settlement had been destroyed by the British.

Porto Koufo. *Bay and harbor, northeastern Greece.* The bay is enclosed by rocky headlands that muffle the sound of the sea. Hence its name, "deaf harbor," from modern Greek *koufos,* "deaf."

Porto-Novo. *Capital of Benin.* The city and port was settled by the Portuguese in the 16th century as a center of the slave trade and was given a name meaning "new port." It was "new" through the merging of two existing coastal villages.

Porto Seguro. *City and port, southeastern Brazil.* The town, founded in 1526, has a Portuguese name meaning "safe harbor." It was here, on April 22, 1500, that the explorer Pedro Cabral first set foot on Brazilian soil and claimed the land for the king of Portugal.

Pôrto Velho. *City, western Brazil.* The city, on the Madeira River, has a name meaning "old port."

Portoviejo. *City, western Ecuador.* The city, founded by Spanish colonists in c.1535 near the coast, moved to its present inland site in 1628. Its name, meaning "old port," thus relates to the original site.

Port Pirie. *City and port, southern Australia.* The city, in South Australia, was founded in 1848 and named for the schooner *John Pirie,* which had brought English settlers here in 1845. It was itself named for the Scottish merchant *John Pirie* (1781–1851), a director of the South Australia Company.

Port Said. *City and port, northeastern Egypt.* The city was founded in 1859 when work on the Suez Canal began. It was named in honor of *Sa'id* Pasha (1822–1863), viceroy of Egypt, who had granted a concession to the French diplomat Ferdinand de Lesseps for the construction of the canal.

¹Portsmouth. *City and port, southern England.* The Hampshire city's name means "(place at the) mouth of the port," the "port" being its own harbor. The names of most English towns in *-mouth* begin with that of the river which enters the sea at the point where the town stands. This one is different.

²Portsmouth. *City and port, northeastern United States.* The New Hampshire city arose as a fishing settlement in 1623 at the mouth of the

Piscataqua River and was originally named for it. (The river's Abnaki name means "place where the river divides.") It was then named *Strawbery Banke* and grew to become a busy port. In 1653 it was named for [1]**Portsmouth**, England, as a *port* at the *mouth* of a river.

[3]**Portsmouth**. *City and port, eastern United States.* The Virginia city was founded in 1752 and named for [1]**Portsmouth**, England. It is actually a *port* at the *mouth* of the Elizabeth River.

Port Sudan. *City and port, northeastern Sudan.* Sudan's major seaport, on the Red Sea, was founded in 1905 and named for the country that it was designed to serve.

Port Talbot. *Town and port, southeastern Wales.* The town, near Swansea, arose in 1836 and was named for the *Talbot* family of nearby Margam Abbey, local landowners and financial backers of the new port.

Portugal. *Republic, southwestern Europe.* The maritime country to the west of Spain derives its name from Latin *Portus Cale*, "port of *Cale*," itself the original name of **Oporto**, *Cale* being a former port near the mouth of the Douro River. Its own name is said to derive from the base of Latin *calere*, "to be warm," since the harbor here never iced up.

Portugalete. *Town and port, northern Spain.* The town, now a suburb of Bilbao, was founded in 1322 and named for its function as a *portus galorum*, Latin for "galley-slave port."

Portuguesa. *State, northwestern Venezuela.* The state is named for the *Portuguesa* River here, a tributary of the Orinoco. Its own name means "Portuguese."

Port-Vila. *Capital of Vanuatu.* The meaning of *Vila*, an indigenous name often used alone for the town and port, has long been lost.

Porvoo. *City, south central Finland.* The city, an early medieval trading post on the Gulf of Finland, gained its name as a Finnish form of its Swedish name *Borgå*, from *borg*, "castle," and *å*, "water."

Posadas. *City and river port, northeastern Argentina.* The city arose as a Paraguayan trading post called *Trinchera de los Paraguayos*, "trench of the *Paraguayans*." In 1869 this name was modified to *Trinchera de San José*, "*St. Joseph*'s trench." In 1879 the city received its present name, in honor of the Argentine politician and national hero Gervasio Antonio de *Posadas* (1757–1833).

Postojna. *Town, western Slovenia.* The strategically sited town apparently derives its name from Slovenian *postoj*, "halt," "rest," presumably because it is located approximately midway between Ljubljana and Trieste. Its German name was *Adelsberg*, "eagle's castle," for a nearby (now ruined) fortress. Hence the eagle on the town's coat of arms. The Italian form of the name is *Postumia*.

Potchefstroom. *Town, east central South Africa.* The town, in North-West province, was founded in 1838 by the Boer leader Andries Hendrik *Potgieter* (1792–1852) and apparently named for him. The last part of the name is presumably Afrikaans *stroom*, "stream," alluding to the Mooi River on which the town lies. It is not clear why Potgieter's name should have been distorted in this way, unless it was influenced by Afrikaans *potscherf*, "potsherd." The second element of the name could actually be *chef*, as Potgieter was the chief of the Voortrekkers, the Dutch farmers who traveled north from Cape Colony in the second half of the 1830s to evade British rule.

Potenza. *City, southern Italy.* The Roman settlement of *Potentia* ("power") was founded in the 2nd century B.C. on a site not far from the present city and and this gave its current name.

Potgietersrus. *Town, northern South Africa.* The town, in Limpopo province, was founded in 1852 and at first given the Afrikaans name *Vriedenburg*, "town of peace," symbolizing a reconciliation between the Voortrekker leaders Andries Pretorius (who gave the name of **Pretoria**) and Andries Potgieter (founder of **Potchefstroom**). In 1858 it was renamed *Pietpotgietersrust*, "*Piet Potgieter*'s rest," for *Pieter Potgieter*, son of Andries. This awkward name was later shortened to *Potgietersrust* and in 1939 the final *t* was dropped.

Potomac. *River, east central United States.* The river, in West Virginia, Virginia, and Maryland, has a name first recorded in 1608 by the English explorer John Smith as *Patawomeck*, which he took to be the name of a local people. It was later established that the name actually means "where goods are brought in," referring to a stretch of riverside land where Native Americans had set up a trading post.

Potosí. *City, southern Bolivia.* The city takes its name from nearby *Potosí* Mountain, a mountain of ore containing hundreds of mines. The mountain's own name is popularly derived from Quechua *potojchi*, "to explode," referring to the rumblings in its interior.

Potsdam. *City, east central Germany.* The city's name is apparently of Slavic origin, representing *po*, "by," "near," and a word related to English *stamp*, "to stamp," "to pound," denoting a settlement that arose by some kind of stamping device. The earliest record of the name is *Poztupimi* in 993. The second part of the name was probably influenced by Dutch names ending *-dam*, such as **Amsterdam**.

Poughkeepsie. *City, eastern United States.* The New York city was settled in 1683 on the Hudson River and derives its name from an Algonquian term said to mean "waterfall."

Powys. *County, east central Wales.* The county, established in 1974, bears the name of a former kingdom in this part of Wales. Its own name means "provincial," and evolved from Latin *paganensis*, the adjectival form of *pagus*, "province," "district" (the source of English *pagan*). The name implies that the people who lived here were "country folk," inhabiting open and unprotected land, unlike those who lived in regions to the north and south, where hills and valleys provided shelter.

P'o-yang. *Lake, eastern China.* The large lake, in Kiangsi province, derives its name from Chinese *pó*, a proper name, and *yáng*, "light," "sun."

Požarevac. *Town, eastern Serbia.* The town probably derives its name from Serbo-Croat *pozharevats*, "forestland cleared by burning," from *pozhar*, "(forest) fire." *Cp.* **Slavonska Požega.** The German form of the name is *Passarowitz*.

Poznań. *City, western Poland.* The city had the Medieval Latin name of *Poznani civitas*, deriving from the original name of the landowner here, itself apparently based on *pan*, "lord." The city is ancient, and already existed as a small settlement in the early 9th century. The German form of the name is *Posen*.

Pozzuoli. *City and port, southwestern Italy.* The port was founded by the Greeks in c.529 B.C. as *Dicaearchia*, "city of justice." It was then captured by the Romans and renamed *Puteoli*, as which it is mentioned in the Bible (Acts 28:13). The name derives from either Latin *puteus*, "pit," or *putere*, "to stink," or even a blend of both, referring to the disagreeable odor from the sulfur springs here. The present name then evolved from this.

Prachuap Khiri Khan. *Province, central Thailand.* The province has a Thai name said to mean "mountainous and fertile land."

Prague. *Capital of Czech Republic.* The city's name is usually interpreted as "threshold," from a Slavic word related to Czech *práh* in this sense. But although the origin is almost certainly Slavic, it is likely to be not in this word but in one related to modern Czech *pražiti*, a term for woodland cleared by burning. The Czech form of the name is *Praha*.

Praia. *Capital of Cape Verde.* The city and port has a Portuguese name meaning simply "beach," "shore." Praia is on the southern shore of São Tiago (Santiago) Island.

Praslin Island. *Island, western Indian Ocean.* The second largest island of the Seychelles takes its name from César Gabriel de Choiseul, duc de *Praslin* (1712–1785), French minister of the marine.

Prato. *Town, central Italy.* The name ultimately derives from Latin *pratum* (modern Italian *prato*), "meadow," describing the site by the Bisenzio River by which the town arose in early medieval times.

Přerov. *City, eastern Czech Republic.* The city, dating from the 11th century, has a Slavic name meaning "before the plain," meaning that of the Morava River.

Presidente Hayes. *Department, central and western Paraguay.* The department, set up in 1944, is named for the U.S. *President* Rutherford B. *Hayes* (1822–1893), who acted as arbiter in the border dispute between Paraguay and Argentina following the War of the Triple Alliance (1865–70).

Presov. *City, eastern Slovakia.* The name is a Slovak form of the Hungarian personal name *Eperjes* (itself from *eper*, "strawberry," "mulberry").

Preston. *City, northwestern England.* The Lancashire town has an Old English name found elsewhere in Britain meaning "priests' village." The name does not necessarily imply that priests lived here, but that the place was an endowment for priests who served a church somewhere else.

Prestwick. *Town and port, southwestern Scotland.* The town is close enough to the English border to have an Old English name. It means "priests' outlying farm," with the farm itself probably an endowment to support a religious house elsewhere.

Pretoria. *City, northeastern South Africa.* The administrative capital of South Africa and former capital of Transvaal was founded in 1855 and named commemoratively for the Boer statesman Andries *Pretorius* (1798–1853). The indigenous name of Pretoria is **Tshwane.**

Preveza. *City and port, western Greece.* The city's name is a corruption of its 3d-century B.C. classical name, *Berenicia*, presumably given for one of the wives (queens) or daughters (princesses) of the Ptolemies of Egypt, or for some other *Berenice*.

Pribilof Islands. *Island group, northwestern United States.* The islands, west of (and part of) Alaska, were discovered in 1788 by the Russian navigator Gavril *Pribylov* (died 1796), and are named for him.

Prilep. *City, south central Macedonia*. The city has a name found elsewhere in Slavic countries apparently representing a word related to Russian *prilepit'*, "to adhere to," referring to a settlement close to a natural feature such as a mountain, forest, or river. There is no mountain in this case.

Primosten. *Resort village, southern Croatia*. The name is a dialect form of *Premosten*, "beyond the bridge," from Serbo-Croat *pre-*, "beyond," and *most*, "bridge." The seaside resort is on an island that was joined to the mainland by a causeway in 1564.

Prince Albert. *City, south central Canada*. The Saskatchewan city was founded in 1866 and named commemoratively for *Prince Albert* (1819–1861), consort of Queen Victoria. Cp. **Alberta**.

Prince Edward Island. *Island province, eastern Canada*. The island was discovered by the French in 1534 and originally named *Île Saint-Jean*, "St. John's island." This name continued in use (in its English form from 1763) until 1799, when the island was renamed in honor of *Prince Edward* Augustus (1767–1820), Duke of Kent, the father of Queen Victoria.

Prince George. *City, western Canada*. The city, in British Columbia, originated in 1807 as the fur-trading post of *Fort George*, so named for *George* III of England (1738–1820). The present name was taken in 1915 when the town was incorporated as a city, presumably in honor of the future *George* VI (1895–1952).

Prince of Wales, Cape. *Cape, northwestern United States*. The Alaskan cape, the most westerly point in mainland North America, was so named in 1778 by Captain Cook in honor of the *Prince of Wales*, the future George IV of England (1762–1830). The name has been opposed by Russian geographers and historians, who claim the honor should have gone to Mikhail Gvozdev, the Russian navigator who discovered and plotted the cape in 1732, almost half a century before Cook.

Prince Rupert. *City and port, western Canada*. The city, in British Columbia, was so named in 1906 as the result of a competition. It honors *Prince Rupert* (1619–1682), first governor of the Hudson's Bay Company.

Princess Astrid Coast. *Region, Antarctic*. The coastal region, a possession of Norway, was named for *Princess Astrid* (1905–1935), daughter of Prince Charles of Sweden and wife of Leopold III, king of the Belgians.

Princess Charlotte Bay. *Inlet, northeastern*

Australia. The bay, indenting northeastern Queensland, was sighted in 1815 by the British naval officer Charles Jeffreys and named by him for *Princess Charlotte* (1796–1817), daughter of the Prince Regent, the future George IV of England.

Princeton. *Town, eastern United States*. The New Jersey town was settled in 1696 and at first called *Stony Brook*, for the Long Island home of one of the settlers. It was renamed as now in 1724 in honor of *Prince* George (1683–1760), the future George II of England.

Príncipe. *Island, Gulf of Guinea, western Africa*. The island, which with **São Tomé** forms a republic, was named by the Portuguese *Ilha do Príncipe*, "island of the prince," in honor of *Prince* Alphonso, the future Alphonso V (1432–1481), king of Portugal.

Pripet Marshes. *Marshland, eastern Europe*. The vast area of marshland, in southern Belarus and northern Ukraine, takes its name from the *Pripyat* River that flows through it. The river's own name is of uncertain origin and meaning. It may derive from a local word *pripech'* used for a sandy river bank.

Priština. *City, southern Serbia*. The town takes its name from the river here, its own name probably deriving from Serbo-Croat *prišt*, "ulcer," "tumor," referring to its "boiling."

Prome *see* **Pyè**

Provence. *Historic region, southeastern France*. The former province has a name that means simply "province." This seemingly unoriginal name came about because it was the first Roman *provincia* to be founded beyond the Alps (in the 2d century B.C.). The Latin word itself, popularly derived from *pro*, "before," and *vincere*, "to conquer," but really of uncertain origin, designated a territory outside of Italy brought under Roman domination. The actual name of the province was *Gallia Transalpina*, "transalpine **Gaul**."

Providence. *City and port, eastern United States*. The state capital of Rhode Island was founded in 1636 by the English-born American clergyman Roger Williams, who so named it for "God's merciful providence to me in my distress." Williams had been banned from Plymouth Colony for his unorthodox religious beliefs, and the settlement became a refuge for dissenters. (The official name of Rhode Island state itself is *Rhode Island and Providence Plantations*.)

Provins. *Town, eastern France*. The town derives its name from the Latin personal name *Probus*, meaning "excellent," "upright."

Provo. *City, western United States*. The Utah city was settled in 1849 as *Fort Utah*. The following year its name was changed as now to honor Étienne *Provost*, a French-Canadian trapper and explorer.

Prudentópolis. *City, southeastern Brazil*. The city was founded in 1892 and at first named *São João de Capanema*, "St. John of Capanema." In 1894 it was renamed as now for *Prudente* de Morais (1841–1902), elected Brazil's first civilian president that year.

Prussia. *Historic state, northern and central Germany*. The state took its name from the *Borussi*, a Slav people who originally inhabited it. The source of their name is uncertain. (Their territorial name *Borussia* survives in the German football teams *Borussia* Dortmund and *Borussia* Mönchengladbach.) The German form of the name is *Preussen*.

Przemyśl. *City, southeastern Poland*. The city arose in about the 8th century and is said to take its name from its founder. His own name means "plan," "stratagem."

Pskov. *City, western Russia*. The city may derive its name from that of a river, in turn perhaps based on Old Russian *ples*, "reach," "stretch of river from one bend to the next." Pskov is actually on the Velikaya River.

Puebla. *City, southern Mexico*. The city was founded in 1532 and originally named by the Spanish Franciscan friar Toribio de Motolinía as *Puebla de los Ángeles*, "city of the angels," since he believed angels aided its construction. Its full formal name is now *Heróica Puebla de Zaragoza*, for General Ignacio *Zaragoza* (1829–1862), who defeated French forces here in 1862.

Pueblo. *City, west central United States*. The Colorado city was laid out in 1860 and has a Spanish name meaning simply "town."

Puente-Genil. *Town, southern Spain*. The town takes its name from the bridge (Spanish *puente*) over the *Genil* River here.

Puerto Barrios. *Town and port, northeastern Guatemala*. The town, built in the early 20th century, is named for the Guatemalan general and politician Justo Rufino *Barrios* (1835–1885).

Puerto Bertoni. *Town, southeastern Paraguay*. The town, on the Paraná River, is named for the Swiss naturalist and ethnologist Moises *Bertoni*, who settled here in 1890 and lived here until his death in 1929.

Puerto Cabello. *City and port, northern Venezuela*. In colonial times, the waters of the city's harbor were said to be so smooth that ships could be moored to the dock by a single hair (Spanish *cabello*). That, at least, is the popular explanation of the name, which must actually have a less fanciful origin. Spanish *caballo*, "horse," "knight," may have been the original word behind the name.

Puerto Deseado. *Town and port, southeastern Argentina*. The name of the Patagonian port is a Spanish equivalent of its original English name *Port Desire*, given by the English circumnavigator Thomas Cavendish in 1586 on anchoring his ship *Desire* in the fine harbor here.

Puerto Madryn. *Town and port, southeastern Argentina*. The town was founded in 1865 by a group of Welshmen who named the new settlement in honor of Sir Loves Jones Parry, baron of *Madryn* Castle in Wales.

Puerto Maldonado. *Town and river port, southeastern Peru*. The town is said to be named for the Ecuadorian explorer Dom Pedro *Maldonado* (1704–1748), although it is not mentioned in official documents until 1902.

Puerto Montt. *City and port, southern Chile*. The city was founded in 1853 and named for Manuel *Montt* (1809–1880), president of Chile from 1850 to 1861.

Puerto Real. *Town and port, southern Spain*. The port here was known to the Romans as *Portus Gaditanus*, "port of **Cádiz**," this city being just 7 miles (11 km) to the west. In 1488 it was renamed as now, "royal port," when it was rebuilt by the Spanish monarchs Ferdinand and Isabella.

Puerto Rico. *Island state, central West Indies*. The Caribbean island has a Spanish name meaning "rich harbor." It was given by Columbus to the large bay on the north side of the island when he came here in 1493. He named the island itself *San Juan*, "St. John," either because he arrived on June 24, *St. John*'s Day, or, according to another account, as a tribute to the Spanish heir apparent, Don *Juan*, son of Ferdinand II and Queen Isabella. The bay's name subsequently passed to the whole island, while that of the island was adopted for the capital, *San Juan*, on the bay itself.

Puget Sound. *Inlet, northwestern United States*. The deep inlet, indenting northwestern Washington state, derives its name from Peter *Puget*, an officer in the expedition led by George Vancouver in 1792.

Pula. *City and port, western Croatia*. The original settlement here was captured by the Romans in the 2nd century B.C. but then destroyed by Augustus, who rebuilt it and named it *Pietas Julia*, "piety of *Julius*," for *Julius* Caesar. ("Piety" here denotes dutiful respect.) The present name evolved from this.

Pulicat. *Town, southern India*. The town, in

Tamil Nadu state, is traditionally said to have gained its name as a corruption of earlier *Paliyaverkadu*, meaning "jungle of old mimosas," but another theory derives it from *Pazhaverkadu*, "old acacia forest."

Punjab. *Province, eastern Pakistan.* The province derives its name from Iranian *panjāb*, "five rivers," from *panj*, "five," and *āb*, "water," "river." The five rivers in question, as tributaries of the Indus, are the Jhelum, Chenab, Ravi, Beas, and **Sutlej**, the latter being the longest.

Punta Arenas. *City and port, southern Chile.* Chile's southernmost city, founded in 1849, has a Spanish name meaning "sandy point," alluding to the Brunswick Peninsula where it is located.

Punta del Este. *City and resort, southeastern Uruguay.* The modern beach resort has a Spanish name meaning "east point," describing its location on a peninsula jutting into the Atlantic.

Puntarenas. *City, western Costa Rica.* The city has a Spanish name meaning "sandy point," referring to its location on a long spit of land protruding into the Gulf of Nicoya. *Cp.* **Punta Arenas**.

Purus. *River, north central South America.* The river, rising in Peru and flowing generally northeast across Brazil into the Amazon, derives its name from that of a Native American people. Their own name is said to mean "cannibal."

Purvachal. *Mountain ranges, eastern India.* The ranges, also known in English as *Eastern Highlands*, have a name meaning "eastern mountains," from Hindi *pūrv*, "east," and *achal*, "mountain."

Pusan. *City and port, southeastern South Korea.* The city's name means "pot mountain," from Korean *pu*, "pot," "caldron," and *san*, "mountain." The allusion is to the shape of the mountain at the foot of which the city lies.

Pushkin. *City, western Russia.* The city near St. Petersburg was originally a Finnish village taken by the Russians under Peter the Great in 1708 and presented to his wife Catherine as a summer residence. The name of the locality was *Saari*, Finnish for "island," implying in this case a site raised above the surrounding terrain. This was russified as *Sarskoye selo*, "Saari village," but as the place was the residence of the czar, the name was reinterpreted as *tsarskoye selo*, "czar's village," and the growing village was officially named as such (*Tsarskoye Selo*) in 1808. In 1918, following the Russian Revolution, the royal residence and its grounds were commandeered as a holiday resort for children from worker and peasant families and was accordingly renamed

Detskoye Selo, "children's village." (The czarist name would almost certainly have been changed anyway.) In 1937 the town was given its present name, marking the centenary of the death of the Russian national poet Aleksandr Sergeyevich *Pushkin* (1799–1837), who had penned his earliest works as a student here.

Pusht-i-Kuh. *Mountain range, western Iran.* The range has an Iranian name meaning "back of the mountain," from *pusht*, "back," and *kūh*, "mountain."

Püspökladány. *Town, eastern Hungary.* The name derives from Hungarian *püspök*, "bishop," denoting the holder of the original settlement, and (apparently) the tribal name *Ladány*.

Putney. *District of London, southeastern England.* The district, just south of the Thames River, has a Old English name meaning "*Putta's* landing place," with the Anglo-Saxon personal name followed by a now well disguised *hȳth*, "landing place."

Putnok. *Town, northeastern Hungary.* The name is of Slavic origin, meaning "wayside (place)," denoting a settlement by a road or river (here the Sajó).

Putrajaya. *City, western Malaysia.* Construction of Malaysia's capital designate began in 1995, with 2020 as its planned completion year. Its name means "glory of *Putra*," with Malay *putra*, "victory," "glory," added to the name of Malaysia's first prime minister, Tunku Abdul Rahman *Putra* al-Haj (1903–1990).

Puttalam. *Town, northwestern Sri Lanka.* The name derives from Tamil *puda*, "new," and *alam*, "salt pans," referring to the major salterns here.

Puu Kukui. *Mountain, central Hawaii, United States.* The volcanic peak, in western Maui Island, has a Hawaiian name meaning "candlenut hill," alluding to its shape.

Puy-de-Dôme. *Mountain, south central France.* The mountain, an extinct volcano, derives the first word of its name from Latin *podium*, "height." The second part represents the Gaulish personal name *Duma*, popularly reinterpreted as French *dôme*, "dome."

Pyatigorsk. *City, southwestern Russia.* The city was founded in 1830 and named with the Russian equivalent of *Beshtau*, the Turkic name of a nearby mountain. This means "five mountains," referring to its five main peaks. The elements of the name are thus Russian *pyat'*, "five," and *gora*, "mountain."

Pyè. *Town, southern Myanmar.* The town's name is Burmese for "capital," referring to its former status as capital of the Pyu people. An alternate name for the town is *Prome*, representing a mispronunciation of the Burmese name by non–Burmese people (and especially the British).

Pylos. *Historic harbor, southwestern Greece.* The name, found for places elsewhere in Greece, derives from Greek *pulos*, a form of *pulē*, "gate," "entrance." This Pylos is also known as *Navarino*, said to be a corruption of Greek *tōn Avarinon*, "to *Avarinos*," a location named for the *Avars* who settled here during the 6th to 8th centuries A.D.

Pyongyang. *Capital of North Korea.* The city, in the west of the country on the Taedon River, derives its name from Korean *p'yŏng*, "flat," and *yang*, "land," describing the terrain here.

Pyrenees. *Mountain range, southwestern Europe.* The range between France and Spain is traditionally said to derive its name from the Greek nymph *Pyrene*, daughter of Bebryx, king of the Narbonne region. She was raped by a drunken Hercules, gave birth to a snake, and fled in horror to the mountains, where she was torn apart by wild animals. Hercules later found her body and buried her here, naming the mountains in her memory. (Her own name appears to derive from Greek *pur*, "fire," and *eneos*, "dumb," "speechless," and may have itself translated the name of some Celtic goddess. The suggestion of Celtic *ber* or *per*, "peak," "summit," in the name may have inspired her colorful story.) In medieval times there was no overall name for the range and local people would have known only the names of individual mountains and valleys.

Qaqortoq. *Town and port, southwestern Greenland.* The town was founded by the Norwegian merchant Anders Olsen in 1755 as *Julianehåb*, "*Juliana*'s harbor," for Queen *Juliana* Maria, second wife of Frederick V of Denmark (1723–1766). In 1985 it received its present Greenlandic name, meaning "white." The reference is said to be to the flocks of white seagulls here, or to the rocks whitened by their excrement.

Qatar. *Emirate, eastern Arabia.* The state probably derives its name from a form of Arabic *ḳaṭrān*, "tar," "resin," relating to the country's rich resources of petroleum and natural gas.

Qena. *City, eastern Egypt.* The city's name is a corruption of its original Greek name of *Caene*. This represents Greek *kainē*, "new," referring to the town's later foundation than that of Coptos (now Qift), 14 miles (23 km) to the south.

Qeqertarsuaq. *Island, western Greenland.* The island is the largest on the Greenland coast. Hence its name, Greenlandic for "large island." The name is also that of the island's largest settlement, founded by the Danes in 1773 and originally named *Godhavn*, "good harbor."

Qeshm. *Island, southern Iran.* The largest island in the Persian Gulf has an Iranian name meaning "beautiful." Its Arabic name is *Jazirat at-Tawilah*, "the long island," from *jazīra*, "island," and *ṭawīl*, "long."

Qift *see* **Coptos**

Qinghai *see* **Koko Nor**

Qiryat 'Anavim. *Kibbutz, eastern Israel.* The kibbutz was founded in 1919 by the Russian-born agronomist Akiva Jacob Ettinger (1872–1945) who turned it into a model settlement for growing fruit and grapes. Hence its Hebrew name, "town of grapes." The first component of this name and those below is also spelled *Kiryat*.

Qiryat Arba' *see* **Hebron**

Qiryat Bialik. *City, northwestern Israel.* The city was founded in 1934 with a Hebrew name meaning "*Bialik*'s town," for the Hebrew poet Chaim Nachman *Bialik* (1873–1934).

Qiryat Ekron. *Settlement, central Israel.* The Jewish urban settlement derives its name from the biblical city of *Ekron*, which may have been nearby. Its own Hebrew name has been said to mean "eradication," "emigration," but probably means simply "the city," from a word related to *qiryat*.

Qiryat Gat. *City, central Israel.* The city was founded in 1952 with the Hebrew name "town of *Gat*," for the Philistine city of **Gath**, believed by some to have been nearby.

Qiryat Haim. *Town, northwestern Israel.* The town, now a suburb of Haifa, has a Hebrew name meaning "*Haim*'s town," for the Labor Zionist leader *Chaim* Arlosoroff (1899–1933).

Qiryat Haroshet. *Settlement, northwestern Israel.* The settlement was founded as a workers' village in 1935 near the site of the biblical *Harosheth* (Judges 4:2), its own name meaning "workmanship." In 1979 it became part of Qiryat Tivon.

Qiryat Mal'akhi. *Town, central Israel.* The town has a Hebrew name meaning "town of angels," for the Jewish community in **Los Angeles** who lent their support to the immigrant camp set up in 1951.

Qiryat Motzkin. *City, northwestern Israel.* The city, founded in 1934, has a Hebrew name meaning "*Motzkin*'s town," for the Russian Zionist leader Leo *Motzkin* (1867–1933).

Qiryat Shemona. *Town, northern Israel.* The town, founded in 1949, has a Hebrew name meaning "town of the eight," referring to the eight Jewish defenders of the nearby settlement of **Tel Hay** who were killed by Arabs in 1920, including their leader, Josef Trumpeldor (*see* **Tel Yosef**).

Qiryat Tivon. *Township, northwestern Israel.* The township was founded as a garden suburb in 1947. Its Hebrew name means "town of nature," for its emphasis on ecology and the environment.

Qiryat Yam. *City, northern Israel.* The city, founded after World War II as a settlement for demobilized soldiers, has a Hebrew name meaning "town by the sea," for its location near the Mediterranean.

Qiryat Ye'arim. *Settlement, central Israel.* The settlement arose as a youth village in 1952. In 1975 a religious settlement was founded nearby and both were named for the biblical city of *Kiriath-Jearim*, located in this region. Its name means "town of woodlands."

Qom. *City, north central Iran.* The city's name is an Arabic abbreviation of *komendān*, the name of one of the seven villages that combined to form the present town in A.D. 730. This itself may have been the name of one of the city's original Shi'ite founders.

Qu'Appelle. *River, southern Canada.* The river, in Saskatchewan and Manitoba, has a French name meaning "who calls," translating its Cree name *kah-tep-was*, "river that calls." The allusion is to the cries of a spirit said to haunt its waters.

Quatre Bornes. *Town, western Mauritius.* The town's French name means "four boundaries," referring to the boundary stones that formerly marked the limits of four extensive sugar estates here.

Queanbeyan. *City, southeastern Australia.* The city, in New South Wales, originated in 1828 as an estate called *Queen Bean,* an approximate phonetic rendering of an Aboriginal word meaning "clear water." The name was later corrected as now.

Quebec. *City, eastern Canada.* The city, capital of the province of the same name, derives its name from Algonquian *quilibek,* "place where waters narrow," referring to the gradually narrowing channel of the St. Lawrence River here, or more specifically to the narrows at Cape Diamond. The city arose around the stockhouse built in 1608 by the French explorer Samuel de Champlain and was long in French hands, so that the name is now often found with the French spelling *Québec.* (Its present-day inhabitants are largely French-speaking, and the city stands at the ideological heart of French Canada.)

Quedlinburg. *Town, central Germany.* The town, which arose around a fort built by Henry I (Henry the Fowler) in 922, has a name meaning "fort of the *Quitlinge,*" these being "*Quitilo's* people." (The personal name derives from Old Saxon *quethan,* "to say," archaic English *quoth,* "said.")

Queen Alexandra Range. *Mountain range, Antarctica.* The range, in Ross Dependency, was discovered in 1908 by the British explorer Ernest H. Shackleton and named for *Queen Alexandra* (1844–1925), consort of Edward VII of England.

Queen Charlotte Islands. *Island group, western Canada.* The islands, off British Columbia, were so named in 1787 by the Englishman George Dixon for his trading vessel the *Queen Charlotte,* itself named for *Queen Charlotte* (1744–1818), wife of George III.

Queen Elizabeth Islands. *Island group, northern Canada.* The large group, including the Parry and Sverdrup groups, as well as Ellesmere, Melville, and Devon islands, among others, was named in 1953 for *Queen Elizabeth* II of England (born 1926), the year of her coronation.

Queen Maud Land. *Region, Antarctica.* The major region of Antarctica south of South Africa was claimed by Norway in 1939 and named commemoratively for *Queen Maud* (1869–1938), daughter of Edward VII of England and wife of Haakon VII of Norway. The name also appears on maps in its Norwegian form of *Dronning Maud Land.*

Queens. *Borough of New York City, eastern United States.* The borough, on western Long Island, takes its name from the county established in 1683 and itself named for Catherine of Braganza (1638–1705), *queen* consort of Charles II of England.

Queensland. *State, northeastern Australia.* The state was founded in 1859 when it was formed from the northern portion of the colony of New South Wales, which originally extended the length of the eastern Australian coast. The name *Cooksland* was at first proposed for it, for the English explorer who had visited the coast in 1770. But it was the compliment to *Queen* Victoria (1819–1901) that prevailed, especially as the name complemented that of **Victoria,** the state that had already been set off from the southern portion of New South Wales in 1851.

Quelimane. *City and port, eastern Mozambique.* The city was founded by the Portuguese as a trading station in 1544 and probably derives its name from Swahili *kilima,* "mountain." There is no obvious mountain here, so the name may have originally applied to a mountain people who came to settle in this region.

Quemoy. *Island, western Pacific.* The name of the island, a military outpost of Taiwan in Formosa Strait, off the southeast coast of China, is a corrupt form of Chinese *jīnmén*, "golden gate."

Quercy. *Historic region, southwestern France.* The region derives its name from that of the Celtic *Cadurci* people who at one time inhabited it. They also gave the name of **Cahors**.

Querfurt. *Town, central Germany.* The name, first recorded in the 9th century, means "ford by the mill," from Old High German *quirna*, "mill" (English *quern*, "hand mill"), and *furt*, "ford," "passage." The ford would have been over the small Querne River here, named for the town.

Quetta. *City, west central Pakistan.* The name of the strategically sited city is a corruption of Pashto *kwatkot*, "fort."

Quetzaltenango. *City, southwestern Guatemala.* The city, founded in 1524, has a Nahuatl name meaning "place of the quetzal," the latter being the rare bird of the rain forests that was worshiped by the Maya. (Its name was adopted for Guatemala's basic unit of currency.)

Quezon City. *City, northern Philippines.* The city, a virtual suburb of the capital, Manila, in Luzon island, is named for the Philippine (but not Filipino) statesman Manuel Luis *Quezón* y Molín (1878–1944), the country's first president, who in 1937 selected this site for the new capital of the free Philippines. It duly replaced Manila as capital in 1948, but in 1976 the capital returned to Manila.

Quiberon. *Peninsula, northwestern France.* The peninsula and the town on it, in Brittany, have a name that is probably Breton in origin but of disputed meaning. Proposals for one or other (or both) include: (1) *kêr broenn*, "town of reeds," referring to the marshes here; (2) *gwez brein*, "rotten trees," similarly; (3) *kebrienn*, "chevron," referring to the shape of the long peninsula; (4) *kêr brec'hagn*, "infertile town," alluding to the unsalubrious site. But the name may actually be Old Welsh, from *co*, "big," and *peroen*, "owner," with reference to the settlers who took possession of the territory here when they were driven out of Britain by the Anglo-Saxons in the 5th century A.D. *Cp.* **Brittany**.

Quilmes. *City, eastern Argentina.* The city, southeast of Buenos Aires, takes its name from the *Kilmes*, a Native American people who settled on the site in 1666 under the direction of José Martínez de Salazar, governor of Río de la Plata province.

Quilon. *Town and port, southwestern India.* The town, in Kerala state, has a name recorded by Marco Polo in the 13th century as *Coilum*, said to derive from a Tamil word meaning "palace."

Quimper. *City, northwestern France.* The city, in Brittany, has the Breton name *Kemper*, from *kember*, "confluence," itself from Gaulish *comboro*, in the same sense. Quimper stands at the confluence of the Odet and Steir rivers. In 1793, when some places in France were renamed at the time of the Revolution, Quimper was temporarily known as *Montagne-sur-Odet*, for the Montagnes Noires ("black mountains") to the northeast of the town.

¹Quincy. *City, northeastern United States.* The Massachusetts city, now a suburb of Boston, was settled in 1625 and was originally known as *Mount Wollaston*. It was later renamed *Merry Mount*, then *Braintree*, and in 1792, when incorporated as a town, took its present name, honoring Colonel John *Quincy* (1689–1767), a local resident and member of the Massachusetts House of Representatives. Presidents John Adams and his son, John *Quincy* Adams (*see* ²**Quincy**), were both born in Quincy.

²Quincy. *City, east central United States.* The Illinois city was settled in 1822 and was at first known as *Bluffs*. It became the county seat on March 4, 1825, the day of the inauguration of President John *Quincy* Adams (1735–1826), and was renamed in his honor.

Quintana Roo. *State, southeastern Mexico.* The region from which the present state was formed in 1974 is named for the Mexican writer and patriot Andrés *Quintana Roo* (1787–1851).

Quito. *Capital of Ecuador.* The city takes its name from the *Quitu*, a now extinct Native American people. The meaning of their own name is uncertain. Quito was founded in 1533 and until 1830 its name was also that of the country as a whole.

Qum *see* **Qom**

Qumran. *Historic site, southern Israel.* The site known as *Khirbet Qumran*, on the northwestern shore of the Dead Sea, noted for the discovery of the Dead Sea Scrolls in 1947, derives its name from Arabic *khirbi*, "ruin," and *Qumran*, the name of a river nearby.

Qwaqwa. *Historic homeland, eastern South Africa.* The former black state, in what is now Free State province, was the territory of the southern Sotho (Basuto) people. Its name (ironically) means "whiter than white," referring to the white sandstone hill that dominates the area. The earlier Afrikaans name of the region was *Witsieshoek*, "*Witsie's* corner," for a chief who was defeated here in c.1857. (His own name may have been associated with Afrikaans *wit*, "white," and so linked to the modern name.)

Rabat. *Capital of Morocco.* The city's name

represents Arabic *ar-ribāṭ*, from *al*, "the," and *ribāṭ*, the word for a fortified monastery, in this case one to guard the frontier. Rabat arose from a camp set up here in the 12th century.

Racibórz. *City, south central Poland*. The city is traditionally said to be named for its 9th-century Slav founder, Prince *Racibor*, whose own name means "army conqueror." The equivalent German name is *Ratibor*.

Racine. *City and port, northern United States*. The Wisconsin city, on Lake Michigan, has a name of disputed origin. Some authorities derive it from Algonquian *pakwasewin*, "place where wild rice is gathered." Others see a source in French *racine*, "root," itself translated from some Native American language.

Ráckeve. *Town, north central Hungary*. The name derives from Hungarian *rác*, "Serbian," and the personal name *Keve*.

Radebeul. *Town, east central Germany*. The name is that of the Slav village from which the town arose in early medieval times. It means "*Radobyl*'s settlement," with an Old Sorbian personal name.

Radnorshire. *Historic county, eastern Wales*. The former county has a name of English origin meaning "red bank," from Old English *rēad*, "red," and *ōfer*, "bank," "slope." The reference is to the red loamy soil found on the hill slopes here.

Radolfzell. *Town, southwestern Germany*. The name means "*Radolf's* cell," referring to St. *Radolf* (died 947), bishop of Verona, whose tomb is here. The town is formally known as *Radolfzell am Bodensee*, for its location on Lake Constance (*see* **Constance, Lake**).

Radom. *City, east central Poland*. The city, first mentioned in 1154, probably derives its name from the Slavic personal name *Radomir*.

Rae Bareli. *Town, northern India*. The town, in Uttar Pradesh state, derives its name from the *Bhar* people who were the original inhabitants of the region. The first word is Hindi *rāe*, "prince."

Raetia. *Historic region, western Europe*. The ancient Roman province, in Alpine parts of present Austria, Switzerland, and Germany, was named for its indigenous people, the *Raeti*, themselves named for *Raetus*, an Etruscan ruler defeated by the Gauls in northern Italy. The name is also spelled *Rhaetia*.

Ragusa *see* **Dubrovnik**

Rainier, Mt. *Mountain, northwestern United States*. The highest mountain in the state of Washington and in the Cascade Range is named for the British admiral Peter *Rainier* (1742–

1808). The name was given in 1792 by Rainier's friend, Captain George Vancouver (*see* **Vancouver**). The mountain's Native American name is *Tacoma*, said to be either an Algonquian word meaning "near to heaven" or else a generic term meaning simply "mountain." *See also* **Tacoma**.

Raipur. *City, east central India*. The capital of Chhattisgarh state was founded in the 14th century by *Rai* Brahma Deo of the Ratnapur dynasty and is named for him, with Hindi *pur*, "town," added.

Rajasthan. *State, northwestern India*. The state has a Hindi name meaning "land of kings," from Sanskrit *rāja*, "king," "prince," and *sthāna*, "stay," related to Iranian *ostān*, "land," "country." *See also* **Rajputana**.

Rajgir Hills. *Hill region, central India*. The hills, consisting of two parallel ridges, take their name from the village of *Rajgir* between them. This in turn is named for the locality *Rajagriha*, "royal residence," referring to the residency here of the legendary Magadha emperor Jarasandra of the Hindu epic *Mahabharata*.

Rajputana. *Historic region, northwestern India*. The former group of princely states, now roughly coextensive with **Rajasthan**, derives its name from the *Rajput*, the Hindu military caste who claim descent from the Kshatriya, the original warrior caste. Their own name means "sons of the king," from Sanskrit *rāja*, "king," "prince," and *putra*, "son."

Raleigh. *City, eastern United States*. The state capital of North Carolina was founded in 1792, soon after the American Revolution, and named for the English writer and explorer Sir Walter *Raleigh* (1552–1618), who had attempted to colonize America.

Ramah. *Historic town, central Israel*. The biblical town (Joshua 18:25) on the borders of Ephraim derives its name from Hebrew *rama*, "height," "hill." There are other places of the name, which is also spelled *Ramath* (Joshua 19:8), *Ramaah* (Ezekiel 27:22), and *Rama* (Matthew 2:18).

Ram Allah. *Town, West Bank*. The town, on the crest of the Judaean Hills north of Jerusalem, has an Arabic name meaning "height of God."

Ramanathapuram. *Town, southeastern India*. The town, in Tamil Nadu state, has a name meaning "town of the lord *Rama*," from the name of the Hindu god *Rama*, an incarnation of Vishnu, with Hindi *nath*, "master," "lord," and *pur*, "town."

Rama's Bridge *see* **Adam's Peak**

Ramat David. *Kibbutz, northwestern Israel*. The kibbutz was founded in 1926 with a Hebrew name meaning meaning "hill of *David*," with *ramat* as for **Ramat Gan** and the personal name that of the British prime minister *David* Lloyd George (1863–1945), a lifelong supporter of Zionism.

Ramat Gan. *City, central Israel.* The city, founded in 1921 as a satellite city for Tel Aviv-Jaffa, has a Hebrew name meaning "hill of (the) garden," from *ramat*, construct state of *rama*, "hill," and *gan*, "garden," "orchard." (In Semitic languages, the construct state is the state in which one noun depends on another, where in Indoeuropean languages the second noun would be in the genitive case.)

Ramat ha Sharon. *Town, western Israel.* The town, founded in 1923, has a name meaning "hill of *Sharon*," with *ramat* as for **Ramat Gan** and the town's location in the Plain of **Sharon**.

Ramat Yohanan. *Kibbutz, northern Israel.* The kibbutz was founded in 1931 with a Hebrew name meaning "hill of *Yohanan*," with *ramat* as for **Ramat Gan** and the personal name (English *John*) that of the South African statesman *Jan* Smuts (1870–1950), who felt an affinity with the ancient Hebrews.

Rambouillet. *Town, northern France.* The town derives its name from a personal name that is a diminutive of the Germanic name *Rambo*. The final part of the name represents Gaulish *ialon*, "clearing," "village."

Rameswaram. *Island, southeastern India.* The island, between mainland India and Sri Lanka, derives its name from *Rama*, an incarnation of the god Vishnu. His temple here was built on the site supposedly sanctified by his footprints as he crossed to rescue his wife, Sita, from the demon Ravana.

Ramla. *City, central Israel.* The city, southeast of Tel Aviv-Jaffa, is the only one founded by Arabs in Palestine. Hence its Arabic name, from *raml*, "sand," referring to its location on the coastal plain.

Rampur. *City, north central India.* The city, in Uttar Pradesh state, has a name meaning "city of *Rama*," for the god who is an incarnation of Vishnu. The name is found elsewhere in India.

Ramsey. *Town and resort, Isle of Man, Irish Sea.* The town, on the island's northeast coast, takes its name from the stream at the mouth of which it stands. The stream has a Scandinavian name meaning "river of wild garlic," from Old Norse *hramsa*, "wild garlic," and *á*, "river."

Ramsgate. *Town and resort, southeastern England.* The Kent town has a name meaning "raven's gate," from Old English *hræfn*, "raven," and *geat*, "gate." It is not certain who or what the "raven" was. It may have been the name of a raven-shaped rock or a personal name. It may even have applied to the actual birds, as regular visitors here. The "gate" is the gap in the cliffs at this point.

Randstad. *Conurbation, west central Netherlands.* The industrial and metropolitan conurbation, comprising many major industrial cities extending in a crescent, has a name meaning "ring city," from Dutch *rand*, "border," "ring," and *stad*, "town," "city."

Rangoon *see* **Yangon**

Rangpur. *City, northwestern Bangladesh.* The city's name means "abode of bliss," from Sanskrit *rang*, "brightness," "bliss," and *pur*, "stronghold," "town."

Rapallo. *City, northwestern Italy.* The city, on the Italian Riviera, is said to derive its name from a dialect word meaning "marsh."

Rapid City. *City, north central United States.* The South Dakota city, settled in 1876, derives its name from its location on *Rapid* Creek, itself so called for its swift current.

Raritan. *River, eastern United States.* The New Jersey river is said to derive its name from an Algonquian word meaning "stream overflows."

Ras al-Khaimah. *Emirate, United Arab Emirates.* The member state of the United Arab Emirates has an Arabic name that literally means "head of the tent," from *ra's*, "head," *al*, "the," and *khaimi*, "tent." The name is properly that of the peninsula here on which the present town of the same name stands as the emirate's capital, and is said to refer to a large tent set up as a landmark by an early chief.

Ras Asir. *Cape, northeastern Somalia.* The name means "*Asir* headland," from Arabic *ra's*, "headland," and *Asir*, an Arabic name for southern Arabia (and now for a province in southwestern Saudi Arabia), opposite which it lies, itself meaning "difficult country" (literally "captive"). The former name of the cape was *Guardafui*, from Arabic *gard*, "desert," and *Hafun*, the name of the district here, in turn meaning "border headland," from *ra's*, "headland," and *haffi*, "edge," "border." (*Guardafui* is popularly explained as representing a Portuguese equivalent of French *gardez-vous*, "look out," as navigation off the cape is potentially dangerous.)

Rashid. *Town, northeastern Egypt.* The town was founded in c.A.D. 800 by the caliph Harun ar-*Rashid*, and is named for him. It is more familiar as *Rosetta*, the European form of this name, made famous by the *Rosetta* Stone, discovered in 1799 by the French scholar Jean-François Champollion.

Rasht. *City, northwestern Iran.* The city derives its name from Iranian *reshte*, "thread." Rasht was formerly famous for its spinning mills. The name is also spelled *Resht*.

Rastatt. *City, southwestern Germany.* The city, on the Murg River, derives its name from Middle High German *rast*, "rest," "repose," and *stete*, "place," "settlement," referring to a place conveniently sited for travelers on the old Rhine valley road here.

Ratisbon *see* **Regensburg**

Ratnagiri. *Town, western India.* The town, in Maharashtra state, has a name meaning "jewel mountain," from Hindi *ratna*, "jewel," and *giri*, "hill," "mountain."

Ratnapura. *Town, southwestern Sri Lanka.* The town has a Hindi name meaning "jewel town," from *ratna*, "jewel," and *pur*, "town." The description is literal rather than metaphorical, since Ratnapura is the center of the country's jewel industry.

Raub. *Town, western Malaysia.* The town, in central West Malaysia (Malay Peninsula), arose in the 1880s as a gold-mining settlement and has a Malay name meaning "to scoop with the hands." The reference is to the way in which at one time it was possible to work the abundant ore here.

Ravenna. *City and port, northeastern Italy.* There are contradictory accounts regarding the founding of the city. It is certainly very old, and became part of Roman Gallia Cisalpina in the late 2d century B.C. Its name may be of Etruscan origin, but its meaning is unknown.

Ravensburg. *City, southwestern Germany.* The city takes its name, meaning "*Hraban's* fort," from the castle by which it arose in the 11th century.

Rawalpindi. *City, northern Pakistan.* The city, in Punjab state, has a name representing Hindi *rāvalpiṅḍi*, "village of the *Ravals*," these being a tribe of yogis (ascetics).

Rawson. *Town and river port, southern Argentina.* The town was founded in 1865 by Welsh settlers and named for Guillermo *Rawson* (1821–1890), Argentine minister of the interior.

Razgrad. *Town, northeastern Bulgaria.* The town's name is said to be a corruption of *Davusdava*, "Dacian town" or "wolf town," the name of the settlement here in the 1st century A.D. The name was recorded in 16th-century documents as *Khrazgrad* or *Arazgrad*. However, Slavicists prefer a sense "ruined fortress," from *raz-*, a prefix denoting undoing or destruction, and *grad*, "fort," "town."

Ré, Île de. *Island, western France.* The island,

in the Bay of Biscay west of La Rochelle, was known to the Romans as *Radis*. Whatever this meant, it subsequently became *Rhea*, by asssociation with the Greek goddess of fertility or the Roman vestal virgin *Rhea* Silvia (the mother of Romulus and Remus).

¹Reading. *Town, southern England.* The former Berkshire town has an Old English name meaning "(place of) *Rēada's* people," with the Anglo-Saxon personal name meaning "red-haired one."

²Reading. *City, eastern United States.* The Pennsylvania city was laid out in 1748 on land owned by Thomas and Richard Penn, sons of William Penn, founder of Pennsylvania, and named for ¹**Reading**, England, the Penn family's English home town.

Recife. *City and port, eastern Brazil.* The city was originally named *Cidade de Recife* by the Portuguese in *c.*1535. This means "reef town," and alludes to the reef that lies off the coast here. Recife was formerly known as **Pernambuco**, now the name of the state of which it is the capital.

Recklinghausen. *City, western Germany.* The city, originally a Saxon settlement, has a name meaning "houses of *Rikold's* people."

Redcliffe. *City and resort, eastern Australia.* The Queensland city, now a suburb of Brisbane, takes its name from the peninsula on which it stands. Its own name was originally *Humpybong*, from Aboriginal *umpi bong*, "dead houses," referring to the cluster of deserted dwellings here. In 1799 the English navigator Matthew Flinders renamed the peninsula as now for its *red cliffs*.

Red Deer. *City, southwestern Canada.* The Alberta city takes its name from the *Red Deer* River on which it stands. The river was so misnamed by Scottish settlers, who confused the elk they saw here with the *red deer* of Scotland.

Redding. *City, southwestern United States.* The California city was founded in 1872, on land owned by the California and Oregon railroad, and named for B.B. *Redding*, a railroad land agent.

Redditch. *Town, west central England.* The Worcestershire town has an Old English name meaning "red ditch," referring to the color of the soil here, rather than of the water in some ditch.

Redlands. *City, southwestern United States.* The California city, in the southwestern corner of the San Bernardino Valley, was founded in 1881 and takes its name from the *red* soil of the region.

Redondo Beach. *City and resort, southwestern United States.* The California city developed as a *beach* resort near the site of the Rancho *Sausal Redondo,* "round willow grove," and is named for it.

Red River. *River, south central United States.* The river, a tributary of the Mississippi, has a name describing the color of the water at various points on its course, caused by silt washed down from the red soil or rocks through which it flows. Other rivers of the name are so called for the same reason.

Red River *see* **Hong**

Redruth. *Town, southwestern England.* The Cornish town has a name meaning "red ford," with the second part of the name being "red," not the first. The two elements represent Cornish *rid,* "ford," and *ruth,* "red," with the adjective following the noun as normally in Celtic languages. There is no river at Redruth, so the ford must have been over the small stream on which the parish church stands to the southwest of the town, where the water would have been reddened by mining waste.

Red Sea. *Sea between Arabia and Africa.* The sea's name is translated literally into many languages. The reason for the particular color is disputed. Theories to account for it include: (1) It is that of the algae in its waters and along its shores; (2) It is that of the sandstone along its coasts; (3) It refers to the Himyarites, a local tribe whose name is said to mean "red" (but really comes from *Himyar,* a legendary king of Yemen); (4) "Red" means "south," just as "black" can mean "north" (*see* **Black Sea**). This last explanation is favored by some modern scholars, but the first is the one generally held. The sea's Hebrew name is *yam sûp,* "reed sea," but this may refer to a different body of water, and the "Red Sea" that the Israelites crossed in the Bible (Exodus 14) may actually have been the marshes of Lake Timsah, now part of the Suez Canal. The Greeks knew the Red Sea as *thalassa eruthra* (*see* **Eritrea**).

Regensburg. *City, southeastern Germany.* The city has a name meaning "fortified town on the *Regen* (River)." It originated in A.D. 179 as a Roman stronghold called *Castra Regina* on the site of a Celtic settlement probably known as *Radaspona.* This gave *Ratisbon* as its alternate name, while the Roman name gave the more familiar *Regensburg,* with Germanic *burg,* "fortress." The first half of the Celtic name is of uncertain origin, but the second appears to be *bona,* "foundation," as for **Bonn.** The river's own name derives from an Indoeuropean root *reg,* "damp," related to modern German *Regen,* "rain."

Reggio di Calabria. *City and port, southern Italy.* The city derives the first and main word of its name from Latin *regius,* "royal." Its original Roman name was *Regium Julium,* "royal (town of) *Julius* (Caesar)." The rest of the name indicates its location in **Calabria** and distinguishes it from **Reggio nell'Emilia.**

Reggio nell'Emilia. *City, northern Italy.* The city derives the first and main word of its name from Latin *regius,* "royal." Its Roman name was *Regium Lepidum,* "royal (town of) Marcus Aemilius *Lepidus,*" this being the Roman statesman who supported Julius Caesar and who after Caesar's death formed a triumvirate with Mark Antony and Octavian. The rest of the name indicates the city's location in *Emilia* (now **Emilia-Romagna**) and distinguishes it from **Reggio di Calabria.** (Italian *nell'* means "in the" before a feminine noun beginning with a vowel.)

Regina. *City, southern Canada.* The capital of Saskatchewan was given its name in 1882 by the governor general of Canada, the Marquess of Lorne, in honor of his wife's mother-in-law, Queen Victoria, whose Latin title was *Victoria Regina,* "Victoria, Queen."

Registan *see* **Rigestan**

Rehoboth. *Town, central Namibia.* The town was founded in 1844 and given the biblical name of *Rehoboth* (Genesis 10:11, etc.) by a missionary who built a mission station here for the Rhenish (German Lutheran) Missionary Society. Presumably the founder was aware of the appropriate meaning of the name, "broad places." *Cp.* **Rehovot.**

Rehovot. *City, central Israel.* The city was founded in 1890 by Jewish immigrants from Russia and named for the biblical town of *Rehoboth,* with reference to the allusion in Genesis 26:22: "And he called the name of the place Rehoboth; and he said, For now the Lord hath made room for us, and we shall be fruitful in the land." The name itself is Hebrew for "roominess." The original Rehoboth was in what is now southern Israel, southwest of Beersheba, while the present city is in central Israel, some 12 miles (20 km) south of Tel Aviv. *Cp.* **Rehoboth.**

Reichenau. *Island, southern Germany.* The island, in western Lake Constance, has a name meaning "rich pastures," from early forms of German *reich,* "rich," and *Au,* "meadow," "pasture." These were cultivated by the monks of the medieval monastery for which the island is famous.

Reims. *City, northeastern France.* The city takes its name from the *Remi,* a Gaulish people whose own name means "dominant ones." The name gave that of *Remigius*, or *Rémi*, the 6th-century bishop of Reims whose name in turn gave that of **Domrémy-la-Pucelle**. The city's name is still sometimes found in the English spelling *Rheims*, at one time also the former French spelling.

Reindeer Lake. *Lake, northern Canada*. The lake, one of the largest in Canada, in northeastern Saskatchewan and northwestern Manitoba, is named for the local *reindeer*. The name itself is a translation of an original Native American name.

Remagen. *City, western Germany*. The city grew up around the Roman fort known as *Rigomagus*, its name apparently from Gaulish *rix*, "king," and *magos*, "field," "market." The name implies that there was a Celtic royal settlement here. *Cp.* **Riom**.

Remiremont. *Town, eastern France*. The town had the Medieval Latin name of *Romarici mons*, "hill of *Romaric*." The named person is St. *Romaric*, who founded a monastery on the hills above the town in 620.

Remscheid. *City, northwestern Germany*. The city, first mentioned in the 12th century, arose beside the Wupper River around a church on a rounded hill and an estate of the counts of Berg. The name probably refers to the latter, meaning "*Remi*'s territory," although the personal name is uncertain.

Rendsburg. *City, northwestern Germany*. The city, on the Schleswig and Holstein border, has a name recorded in 1199 as *Reinoldesburch*, referring to an early fortress here built by one *Reinhold*.

Renfrew. *Town, west central Scotland*. The town has a name of Celtic origin meaning literally "current point," from words related to modern Welsh *rhyn*, "point," and *ffrwyd*, "current." Renfrew stands at the confluence of the small Gryfe River with the Clyde.

Rennell Island. *Island, southwestern Pacific*. The southernmost of the Solomon Islands is named for the English geographer James *Rennell* (1742–1830).

Rennes. *City, northwestern France*. The city takes its name from the *Redones*, the Gaulish people whose capital it was. Their own name derives from Gaulish *redo*, "to ride," "to travel." The Roman name of Rennes was *Condate*, "confluence," referring to the Ille and Vilaine rivers, which meet here.

Reno. *City, western United States*. The Nevada city was settled in c.1860 and ar first named *Lake's Crossing*, for M.C. *Lake*, who acquired a crossing over the Truckee River here. It was sub-

sequently named for the Virginia-born Union general Jesse Lee *Reno* (1823–1862), killed in the Civil War.

Repton *see* **Ripon**

Resht *see* **Rasht**

Resistencia. *City, northeastern Argentina*. The city was founded in the mid–18th century as a Jesuit work mission named *San Fernando del Río Negro*. This was abandoned in 1773, and the city was refounded in 1878 as a frontier colony. Its name means "resistance," referring to its role as a military outpost during the wars against Indians.

Reşiţa. *City, southwestern Romania*. The city's name is a German-influenced form of Slavic *Rechitsa*, based on *reka*, "river."

Réunion. *Island, western Indian Ocean*. The island, east of Madagascar, and a French possession since 1642, was discovered by the Portuguese explorer Pedro de *Mascarenhas* in c.1513. When the French first occupied it they accordingly called it *île Mascareigne*. (*Cp.* **Mascarene Islands**.) In 1649 it was renamed *île Bourbon*, for the French royal house, but in 1793, at the time of the Revolution, it was further renamed *Réunion* to commemorate the *reunion* of the revolutionaries from Marseilles with the National Guard in Paris on August 10, 1792. Under Napoleon it was for a while known as *île Bonaparte*, then with the restoration of the monarchy in 1815 it reverted to *île Bourbon*. Finally, with the 1848 Revolution, it regained its former name *Réunion* and has retained it since.

Reutlingen. *City, southwestern Germany*. The city, arising in the 11th century from the union of five villages at a crossing of the Echaz River, has a name meaning "(settlement of) *Riutilo*'s people."

Revere. *City, northeastern United States*. The Massachusetts city was settled in 1626 and initially known as *Rumney Marsh*. It was then successively part of Boston and Chelsea until 1846, when it was separately incorporated as *North Chelsea*. It was renamed as now in 1871 in honor of Paul *Revere* (1735–1818), the folk hero of the American Revolution who was born and died in Boston.

Revillagigedo Islands. *Island group, eastern Pacific*. The islands, west of (and administered by) Mexico, take their name from Count *Revilla Gigedo*, viceroy of Mexico from 1789 to 1794.

Rewari. *City, northwestern india*. The city, in Haryana state, is said to have been founded by Rajah Rao (or Rewat) and named by him after his daughter, *Rewari*.

Reykjavík. *Capital of Iceland*. The city, on the

island's southwest coast, has a name meaning "bay of smoke," from Icelandic *reykja*, "to smoke," and *vík*, "bay." The allusion is to the steam or vapor given off by the natural hot springs here, which are utilized for the city's heating system.

Reza'iyeh *see* **Orumiyeh**

Rhaetia *see* **Raetia**

Rheims *see* **Reims**

Rheine. *City, northwestern Germany.* The city, on the Ems River, has a name of uncertain origin.

Rhine. *River, central and western Europe.* The river's name goes back ultimately to Indoeuropean *rei*, "to flow," related to Old English *rīth*, "stream." The spelling with *h* has been influenced by *Rhēnos*, the Greek form of the name. The German form is *Rhein*, the French *Rhin*.

Rhode Island. *State, northeastern United States.* The islands here were visited in 1524 by the Italian navigator Giovanni da Verrazzano, who is said to have observed (or imagined) a similarity between Block Island and the Greek island of **Rhodes** in the Aegean Sea. But the Dutch explorer Adriaen Block (who gave the name of Block Island) named the island *Roodt Eylandt*, "red island," for the color of the soil, and it was probably this name that was rendered in an English form by 17th-century settlers, with the spelling influenced by that of the Greek island. There is evidence, moreover, that the same settlers thought that the original name applied to the largest island in the group, known to Native Americans as *Aquidneck*, and so used it for the present Rhode Island. The territory of today's state, extending far beyond this island, is officially known as *Rhode Island and Providence Plantations*. (*See* **Providence**.)

Rhodes. *Island, southeastern Greece.* The island, in the southeastern Aegean Sea, off the southwest coast of Turkey, has a name that could represent Greek *rhodon*, "rose," or *rhoia*, "pomegranate." Either is possible, since the island's ancient inhabitants adopted the rose as the emblem of their sun god, and many pomegranate trees grow here. But the name is more likely to be pre–Greek, and derive from Phoenician *erod*, "snake." The island, mentioned in the Bible (Acts 21:1), is known to have been full of snakes in olden times.

Rhodesia *see* **Zimbabwe**

Rhodope. *Mountain range, southeastern Europe.* The range, on the border between Bulgaria and Greece, is said to take its name from *Rhodope*, the wife of Haemus in Greek mythology, who was changed into a mountain here as

a punishment for fancying herself more beautiful than Juno. In fact *Haemus* is another name for the *Balkan Mountains* (*see* **Balkans**), running across Bulgaria. If this range represents Rhodope's husband, then he presumably suffered a like fate for a similar reason. However, the Greeks derived the name from Greek *haima*, "blood," explaining that the monster Typhon lost a great deal of blood here when Zeus pelted him with thunderbolts. But the characters were almost certainly inspired by the mountains, which must have originally had some pre–Greek name.

Rhondda. *Town, southern Wales.* The town takes its name from that of the river on which it lies. The river's own name means "noisy one," from Welsh *rhoddni* (with the *dd* and the *n* transposed).

Rhône. *River, western Europe.* The river of Switzerland and France has an ancient name perhaps deriving from a pre–Indoeuropean root element *rod*, "to flow." Whatever the actual origin, the meaning is likely to be simply "river."

Rhum *see* **Rum**

Rhyl. *Town and port, northern Wales.* The town has a name of mixed Welsh and English origin, with Welsh *yr*, "the," prefixed to Old English *hyll*, "hill." There is hardly a hill here now in the normal sense, but the ground does rise to the south of the town.

Rialto. *Island, Venice, northeastern Italy.* The island, on the Grand Canal, derives its name from *Rivoalto*, a former name of **Venice** itself, meaning "high bank" (modern Italian *ripa alta*).

Ribatejo. *Historic region, central Portugal.* The former province derives its name from Portuguese *riba*, "bank," and *Tejo*, the Portuguese name of the **Tagus**, denoting its location along this river.

Ribeirão Prêto. *City, southeastern Brazil.* The city's Portuguese name means "black river," alluding to the *Prêto* River on which it stands. The city was originally known as *Entre Rios*, "between rivers," and *São Sebastião do Ribeirão Prêto*, "*St. Sebastian* of the black river," before settling to the present name.

Richland. *City, northwestern United States.* The Washington city originated in the early 20th century as a farming village named for Nelson *Rich*, a local *land*owner and state legislator.

¹Richmond. *Town, southeastern England.* The former Surrey town was originally known as *Sheen*, from an Old English word meaning "shelters." When Henry VII built a palace here in 1501, to replace the former one that had been destroyed by fire, he renamed it *Richmond*, for his former title of Earl of *Richmond*, from the town of this name in North Yorkshire. Its own name is of Norman (French) origin and means "strong hill," either for its lofty location, or simply as a name "imported" from a place called *Richemont* in France.

²**Richmond.** *City and river port, eastern United States.* The state capital of Virginia was laid out in 1737 on what is now Church Hill by the English colonial official William Byrd, who named it for his home town of ¹*Richmond*, Surrey, probably because he fancied a similarity between the site of the settlement, on the James River, and that of the English town, on the Thames.

³**Richmond.** *City and port, southwestern United States.* The California city was settled in 1823 and named for ²*Richmond*, Virginia.

Ried. *Town, northern Austria.* The town derives its name from Old High German *reoda*, "clearing," denoting a settlement in land cleared of trees and bushes.

Riesa. *City, eastern Germany.* The city, on the Elbe River, arose around a Benedictine monastery referred to in a document of 1119 as *monasterium in Reszowa*. The latter name derives from Old Sorbian *rez*, "cleft," referring to the runnels and channels in the river terrace here.

Riesengebirge. *Mountain range, central Europe.* The range, on the border between Poland and the Czech Republic, has a German name meaning "giant mountains." Its Czech name is *Krkonoše*, said to be from *krk*, "nape," "neck," and *noše*, "litter," "stretcher," while its Polish name is *Karkonosze*, from corresponding *kark* and *nosze*. The reference would presumably be to a col or cleft in the mountains. The range is sometimes known as *Giant Mountains* in English.

Rif *see* **Er Rif**

Riga. *Capital of Latvia.* The city and port probably derives its name either from Old Lithuanian *rīnga*, "bend," "curve," referring to that of the Western Dvina River on which it lies, or Latvian *rīdziņa*, "stream," with reference to one of that river's tributaries.

Rigestan. *Region, southwestern Afghanistan.* The region has an Iranian name meaning "land of sand." The arid plateau here is mostly a sandy desert. The name is also spelled *Registan*.

Rigi. *Mountain mass, central Switzerland.* The mountains derive their name from Old High German *righe*, "abyss," "precipice." The highest peaks are known as the *Rigi-Kulm*, the second part of which represents Latin *culmen*, "summit." The name is also spelled *Righi*.

Riihimäki. *City, southern Finland.* The city

derives its name from Finnish *riihi*, "granary," "loft," and *mäki*, "hill," "slope."

Rijeka. *City and port, northwestern Croatia.* The city has changed hands several times in its long history, passing back and forth in the 20th century between Italy and Yugoslavia. Its present name is simply the Croat word for "river," corresponding to its Italian name of *Fiume* (Latin *flumen*, "river"). The river in question is the one known in Serbo-Croat as *Rječina* and in Italian as *Fiumara*. The German name of Rijeka is *Sankt Veit am Flaum* (or *am Pflaum*), rendering the city's Roman name of *fanum Sancti Viti ad flumen*, "temple of St. Vitus on the river" (earlier *Vitopolis*).

Rila. *Mountain range, southwestern Bulgaria.* Bulgaria's highest mountain range is named for the river that flows through it. Its own name ultimately derives from the Indoeuropean root *rei*, "to flow."

Rimavská Sobota. *Town, southern Slovakia.* The first word of the name is that of the *Rima* River here (now the *Rimava*). The second is Slovak *sobota*, "Saturday," denoting a weekly market on this day. The Hungarian name, *Rimászombat*, is similar (with *szombat*, "Saturday").

Rimini. *City and port, northern Italy.* The city had the Roman name of *Ariminum*, from *Ariminus*, the former name of the Marecchia River here. The origin of this is unknown.

Rimouski. *City and river port, southeastern Canada.* The Quebec city has a Micmac name said to mean "land of the moose."

Rimske Toplice. *Village, central Slovenia.* The name is Slovenian for "Roman hot baths," referring to the warm springs here, known since Roman times.

Rio Branco. *City, western Brazil.* The city is named for the river which enters the Acre River here. Its own Portuguese name means "white river," contrasting its relatively clear water with that of the **Rio Negro**, of which it is a tributary.

Rio Claro. *City, southeastern Brazil.* The city has a Portuguese name meaning "clear river," referring to the Corumbataí River along which it lies. Its original name was *São João Batista do Ribeirão Claro*, "St. John the Baptist of the clear river," and it was also known as *São João Batista do Morro Azul*, "St. John the Baptist of the blue hill." The first of these, and therefore the present name, alludes to the Jordan, the "clear river" in which John baptized Jesus.

Rio de Janeiro. *City and port, southeastern Brazil.* The former capital of Brazil has a Portuguese name meaning "January river." The expedition led by Amerigo Vespucci discovered the bay here on January 1, 1502, and named it for the auspicious day believing they had entered the estuary of a large river. But there is no river here at all, so the name is one of the world's major misnomers. The city was founded on the bay in 1565 and originally named *São Sebastião do Rio de Janeiro*, after *St. Sebastian*, name saint of the young king *Sebastian* of Portugal (1554–1578). The city is now often known as *Rio*.

Río de Oro. *Region, southern Western Sahara.* The region has a Spanish name meaning "river of gold." This translates the original name given by members of a Portuguese expedition of 1436 to the sea inlet at what is now the region's principal town of Dakhla (formerly Villa Cisneros), where they had found local people trading gold dust.

Rio Gallegos. *City, southern Argentina.* The city was founded in 1885 and takes its name from the *Gallegos* River on which it lies. The river itself is named for Blasco *Gallegos*, one of Ferdinand Magellan's pilots, who discovered it in 1520.

[1]Rio Grande. *River, southern North America.* The river, forming much of the boundary between the United States and Mexico, has a name of Spanish origin meaning simply "big river." In Mexico itself it is known as the *Río Bravo*, "wild river." The name is found elsewhere in the Americas, noticeably in Brazil (in the Portuguese form *Rio Grande*).

[2]Rio Grande. *City and port, southern Brazil.* The city, on the river of the same name ("big river"), arose near the site of a Portuguese fort called *Estreito* ("strait"), built in 1737. Its garrison was moved to the present site in 1745, and the settlement became a town in 1751 with the name *São Pedro do Rio Grande do Sul* ("St. Peter of the Rio Grande of the south"), the latter word contrasting this "big river" with one further north. The river in turn gave the name of the state **Rio Grande do Sul**.

Rio Grande do Norte. *State, northeastern Brazil.* The state takes its name from the *Rio Grande* ("big river") here, now usually known as the Potengi. The second part of the name ("of the north") contrasts the state and its river with **Rio Grande do Sul**.

Rio Grande do Sul. *State, southern Brazil.* The state takes its name from the (relatively minor) *Rio Grande* ("big river") here, which enters the Atlantic at [2]**Rio Grande**. The second part of the name ("of the south") contrasts the state and its river with **Rio Grande do Norte**.

Riom. *Town, central France.* The town's present name evolved from its Medieval Latin name

of *Ricomagensis vicus*, from Gaulish *rix*, "king," and *magos*, "field," "market." *Cp.* **Remagen**.

Río Muni. *Province, eastern Equatorial Guinea.* The mainland province derives its name from Spanish *río*, "river," and a corrupt form of a local African word meaning "silence." It is thus the "silent river," referring to the estuary of the Utamboni, in the southwest of the province.

Rio Negro. *River, northern Brazil.* The river, a tributary of the Amazon, has a Portuguese name meaning "black river," referring to its vegetal debris, not its sediment. *Cp.* **Rio Branco**.

Río Tinto. *River, southwestern Spain.* The name is Spanish for "tainted river," for the yellow color of its waters, long polluted by the working of the copper mines here.

Ripon. *Town, northern England.* The North Yorkshire town takes its name from the Anglian people known as the *Hrype* who formerly inhabited this region. Nothing is known about them except their name, which also lies behind the name of the town of *Repton* in Derbyshire, presumably because some of them went to settle there.

Rishon le Ziyyon. *City, west central Israel.* The second oldest Jewish village of Palestine, now the largest satellite city of Tel Aviv, was founded in 1882 by Russian Jews and has a Hebrew name meaning "first to Zion." The allusion is biblical: "The first shall say to Zion, Behold, behold them: and I will give to Jerusalem one that bringeth good tidings" (Isaiah 41:27).

Rishpon. *Settlement, western Israel.* The cooperative settlement, near the Mediterranean coast, was founded in 1936 near the site of the ancient city of *Arshaf*, its own name representing that of *Reshef*, the Canaanite-Phoenician god of lightning and plagues.

Riverina. *Region, southeastern Australia.* The mainly rural region in south central New South Wales has a name based on English *riverine*, referring to the many rivers, major and minor, that form its borders and flow across it.

Rivers. *State, southern Nigeria.* The state is named for the many channels, known locally as *rivers*, that form the delta of the Niger here. *Cp.* **Delta**.

Riverside. *City, southwestern United States.* The California city was laid out in 1870 be*side* the Santa Ana *River* and is named descriptively for its location.

Riviera. *Coastal region, southeastern France.* The name, from Italian *riviera*, "coast," generally applies to the length of Mediterranean coast between Cannes in France and La Spezia in Italy.

In France, what English speakers call the *French Riviera* mostly corresponds to what the French call the **Côte d'Azur**. The *Italian Riviera* is divided into the *Riviera di Ponente*, "west coast," to the west of Genoa, and *Riviera di Levante*, "east coast," east of Genoa. England has both the *Cornish Riviera*, as the south coast of Cornwall, and the *English Riviera*, as the south coast of Devon and Dorset.

Rivoli. *Town, northwestern Italy.* The town had the Roman name of *Ripulae*, from Latin *ripulae*, "little banks," referring to the *Dora Riparia* River to the west, noted for its steep banks.

Rivoli Veronese. *Town, northeastern Italy.* The town, called *Veronese* ("of **Verona**") for distinction from **Rivoli** near Turin, derives its name, like its namesake, from Latin *ripulae*, "little banks," from the steep banks of the Adige River here. Napoleon's victory over the Austrians here in 1797 gave the name of the *rue de Rivoli* in Paris, France.

Riyadh. *Capital of Saudi Arabia.* The city, also known (with greater accuracy) as *Er Riad*, derives its name from Arabic *ar-riyāḍ*, "the gardens," from *al*, "the," and *riyāḍ*, the plural of *rawḍa*, "garden." The city, originally walled, arose around a small oasis.

Road Town. *Capital of British Virgin Islands.* The town and port, in southern Tortola Island, is named for the *roads* off the coast here, as a place where ships may lie at anchor.

Roanne. *Town, east central France.* The town had the Roman name of *Rodumna*, probably deriving from the Celtic (or pre–Celtic) root element *rod*, "water," "river," as for the **Rhône**. Roanne is on the Loire River.

Roanoke Island. *Island, eastern United States.* The island, near the entrance to Albemarle Sound, North Carolina, has a name of Native American origin said to mean either "place where white shells were found" or "shells used for money."

Robson, Mt. *Mountain, western Canada.* The highest peak in the Canadian Rockies, in eastern British Columbia, is probably named for Colin *Robertson* (sic) (1793–1842), an official of the Hudson's Bay Company.

Roca, Cape. *Cape, western Portugal.* The westernmost cape in continental Europe, also known by its Portuguese name of *Cabo da Roca*, derives its name from Portuguese *roca*, "rock."

Rochdale. *Town, northwestern England.* The town, near Manchester, has an Old English name that was recorded in the Domesday Book (1086) as *Racedham*, apparently meaning "homestead with a hall," from *reced*, "building," "hall,"

and *hām*, "homestead." This name then passed to the river here, as the *Rached*. Later, the river valley became known as the *Rached-dale*, which eventually gave *Rochdale* as the name of the town. Finally, the *-dale* was dropped to give the modern river name of *Roch*. But it is equally possible that the river gave the name in the first place, not the other way around. In that case, the original meaning would have been "homestead by the *Roch* (River)."

Rochefort. *City and river port, western France.* The town's name represents pre–Latin *rocca*, "rock," and Latin *fortis*, "strong." In its most basic sense the reference is to a natural defense provided by a rock. Here the name refers to the stronghold built by the Charente River to repel Norman invaders.

[1]**Rochester**. *City and port, southeastern England.* The former Kent city has the distinctive *-chester* element which shows it to have been a Roman station, from Old English *ceaster*, a borrowing from Latin *castrum*, "camp." The initial *Ro-* is all that remains, as the stressed second syllable, of the name of the Roman station itself, which was *Durobrivae*. This comprises the two Celtic elements *duro*, "fort," and *briva*, "bridge." Remains of the Roman bridge over the Medway River here have been discovered.

[2]**Rochester**. *City, northeastern United States.* The New Hampshire city was incorporated as a town in 1722 and named for Lawrence Hyde, 1st Earl of *Rochester* (1642–1711), the namer being his friend, Governor Samuel Shute.

[3]**Rochester**. *City and canal port, eastern United States.* The New York city was founded in 1811 and originally named *Rochesterville*, for its founder, the pioneer Colonel Nathaniel *Rochester* (1752–1831). In 1822 the name was shortened as now.

[4]**Rochester**. *City, northern United States.* The Minnesota city was settled in 1854 and named for [3]**Rochester**, New York.

Rockford. *City, north central United States.* The second-largest city in Illinois was founded in 1834 and at first named *Midway*, as the site of a coach stop halfway between Chicago and Galena. It was renamed for its site by a *ford* across the *Rock* River here, itself named for its *rocks*. Cp. **Rock Island**.

Rockhampton. *City and river port, eastern Australia.* The Queensland city was laid out on the Fitzroy River in 1858 and named for the *rock* formations here and for *Hampton*, England, the birthplace of land commissioner W.H. Wiseman.

Rock Island. *City, north central United States.*

The Illinois city takes its name from the *island* in the Mississippi River, near the mouth of the *Rock* River, opposite which it was founded in 1835, originally under the name *Stephenson. Cp.* **Rockford.**

Rocky Mount. *City, eastern United States.* The North Carolina city, founded in 1816, is named for the nearby *rocky mounds* and ridges.

Rocky Mountains. *Mountain system, western North America.* The name is not directly self-descriptive but is an approximate translation of the name of the former Native American people here known as the *Assiniboin* (*see* **Assiniboine**). The mountains are in fact not noticeably rocky.

Rodez. *Town, southern France.* The town takes its name from the *Ruteni,* the people who formerly inhabited the region. Their name may mean "swift ones." Rodez had the Roman name of *Segodunum,* from Gaulish *sego,* "strength," and *dunon,* "fort." *Cp.* **Wallsend.**

Rodriguez. *Island, western Indian Ocean.* The island, northeast of (and a dependency of) Mauritius, was sighted in 1645 by the Portuguese in 1645, who named it for one of their number.

Roermond. *City, southeastern Netherlands.* The city takes its name from its location at the mouth (Dutch *mond*) of the *Roer* River, at its confluence with the Meuse.

Rohilkhand. *Region, northern India.* The region, in Uttar Pradesh state, takes its name from the *Rohilla,* a people of Afghan origin who settled here. Their name means "inhabitants of *Roh,*" a district of Afghanistan. The second part of the name is Hindi *khand,* "portion," "division."

Rohtak. *City, northwestern India.* The name of the city, in Haryana state, is a shortened form of its original name of *Rohtasgarh,* "*Rohtas*' fort," said to refer to Rajah *Rohtas,* the Rajput who founded it.

Rolândia. *City, southern Brazil.* The city arose in the 1930s when German Jews fleeing the Nazi regime settled here and named their new home for the medieval statue of *Roland* in the city of Bremen, symbolizing imperial jurisdiction. The city's indigenous name, which it officially adopted for a time after World War II, is *Caviúna.*

Romagna *see* **Emilia-Romagna**

Roman. *City, northeastern Romania.* The city is named for its founder, *Roman* I, voevode (ruling prince) of Romania from 1391 to 1394, who in a letter of 1392 referred to it as "our town of Roman."

Romania. *Republic, southeastern Europe.* The country arose as an outpost of the Roman Empire in the early 2d century A.D. when the Dacians crossed the Danube and settled here, intermingling and interbreeding with the local people. The resulting meld came to be known by the Latin name of *Romani,* "people from ¹Rome," and this gave the present name, adopted officially in 1861 when the principalities of Moldavia and Wallachia united.

Romans-sur-Isère. *Town, southeastern France.* The town had the Medieval Latin name *villa Romanis,* from the personal name *Romanus,* "Roman." The rest of the name distinguishes this town from others similarly named by adding its location on the **Isère** River.

¹Rome. *Capital of Italy.* The city is popularly said to take its name from *Romulus,* its legendary founder in 753 B.C. But his own name almost certainly comes from that of the city, so another source must be sought. It may lie in *Roma* or *Ruma* as an earlier name for the **Tiber** River on which Rome stands, with this itself likely to be of Etruscan origin but possibly related to Greek *rhein,* "to flow." The Italian name of Rome is *Roma.* Slav languages name the city with *i* or *y* instead of *o,* as Russian *Rim.* This is because the name came to them via the South Slavs, with whom an original *o* altered into an *i.*

²Rome. *City, eastern United States.* The New York city was fortified by the British as early as 1725 and was at first called *Fort Stanwix,* for Major General John *Stanwix* (c.1690–1766), who built the fort named for him in 1758. The community that developed here after the Battle of Oriskany (1777) was mapped by Dominick *Lynch* in 1782 and called *Lynchville.* In 1819 the settlement was incorporated as a village and renamed *Rome* "for the heroic defense of the Republic made there," i.e. at Oriskany.

Romny. *City, northern Ukraine.* The city has a name of Baltic origin, possibly from Lithuanian *romus,* "quiet." This could have been an earlier name for the Sula River here.

Roncesvalles. *Village, northern Spain.* The traditional site of the Battle of Roncesvalles (August 15, 778), in which Basque mountain warriors massacred the rearguard of Charlemagne's forces, derives its name from Old French *Rences vals,* "valleys of brambles." The present French form of the name is *Roncevaux.* The Basque name is *Orreaga,* from *orre,* "juniper," and the suffix *-aga,* "abounding in."

Rondônia. *State, west central Brazil.* The state was established in 1943 as the territory of *Guaporé.* In 1956 it was renamed as now for the Brazilian explorer and protector of Native Americans, Marshal Cândido Mariano da Silva *Rondon* (1865–1958).

Rondonópolis. *City, central Brazil.* The city is named for the explorer Cândido Mariano da Silva *Rondon* (*see* **Rondônia**).

Ronne Ice Shelf. *Ice shelf, Antarctica.* The body of floating ice in the Weddell Sea is named for the Norwegian-born American explorer Finn *Ronne* (1899–1980), who visited Antarctica nine times and who discovered areas in the Weddell Sea never visited by earlier explorers.

Roodepoort. *City, northeastern South Africa.* The Gauteng city, just west of Johannesburg, derives its name from that of the farm on which it originated in 1888 as a gold mining camp. The name is Afrikaans for "red gate," referring to the red soil on the farm.

Roosendal. *Town, southern Netherlands.* The town's Dutch name means "valley of roses," and is that of the site on which it arose around a church built in 1268.

Rorschach. *Town and port, northeastern Switzerland.* The town and resort, on Lake Constance, derives its name from an early form of German *Röhr*, "reeds," and *Schachen*, "lakeside," denoting a marshy place by water.

Rosario. *City and river port, east central Argentina.* The city, on the Paraná River, was at first a community with the Spanish name *Pago de los Arroyos*, "region of the rivers." In 1725 the site of a villa at the center of the community was named *Rosario*, "rosary," and a church built here in 1735 was named *Nuestra Señora del Rosario*, "Our Lady of the Rosary." The name thus has a religious origin.

Roscoff. *Town and port, northwestern France.* The town, in Brittany, has a name meaning "hill of the blacksmith," from Breton *roz*, "mound," "hill," and *gov*, "smithy."

Roscommon. *County, north central Ireland.* The county takes its name from its town, whose own name is an English form of its Irish name, *Ros Comáin*, "*Comán*'s wood." St. *Comán* founded a monastery here in the 8th century.

Rosenheim. *City, southeastern Germany.* The city takes its name from a medieval castle here. Its own name is of heraldic origin and refers to the three roses in a bend on the shield of the counts of Wasserburg.

Rosetta *see* **Rashid**

Rosh Ha'ayin. *Town, central Israel.* The Jewish town, founded in 1950 on the site of a deserted British army base, itself laid out on the site of the biblical city of Aphek, has a Hebrew name meaning "head of the spring," referring to the nearby abundant springs which give rise to the Yarkon River.

Rosh Pina. *Village, northeastern Israel.* The Jewish village was founded in 1882 by the French philanthropist Baron Edmond de Rothschild and given a Hebrew name meaning "headstone," as it was to be the cornerstone of Jewish settlement throughout Galilee. The reference is specifically biblical: "The stone which the builders refused is become the head stone of the corner" (Psalm 118:22).

Roskilde. *City, eastern Denmark.* The former Danish capital (from the 10th century to 1443) had the Old Danish name *Hroarskilde*, from *Hroar*, the king who is its legendary founder, and *kilde*, "spring."

Ross and Cromarty. *Historic county, northern Scotland.* The former county derives the first part of its name from Gaelic *ros*, "moorland," "promontory," referring to the general nature of the country, and the second from the town of *Cromarty*. Its own name means "crooked place," based on an Old Gaelic word that gave modern Gaelic *crom*, "crooked." The reference is to the irregular coastline here, northeast of Inverness.

Ross Dependency. *Region, Antarctica.* The Antarctic region south of (and administered by) New Zealand is named for the Scottish polar explorer Sir James *Ross* (1800–1862), who carried out magnetic surveys here in his expedition of 1839–43. Also named for him here are the *Ross* Sea, *Ross* Island, and *Ross* Ice Shelf.

Rostock. *City and port, northeastern Germany.* The city had the Medieval Latin name of *Rostochium*, popularly interpreted as representing either *Rosenstadt*, "city of roses," or *roter Stock*, "red stick." The true origin is not Germanic but Slavic, from Old Polabian *rostok*, "diffluence" (the opposite of a confluence, i.e. the point where a river's current flows in different directions). Rostock is at the head of the estuary of the Warnow River at the point where it divides into two.

Rostov. *City and river port, southwestern Russia.* The city arose in 1761 as a fortress with a church dedicated to St. Dmitry of *Rostov*, this being the ancient city northeast of Moscow. Its own name is of uncertain origin but may represent a personal name. The southern city is often known as *Rostov-on-Don* (Russian *Rostov-na-Donu*), for the **Don** River, to be distinguished from its northern eponym.

Rosyth. *Town and port, eastern Scotland.* The town has a name that seems to comprise Gaelic *ros*, "headland," and Old English *hȳth*, "landing place." But although both words suit the topography, their combination is unlikely, so that the actual origin of the name remains uncertain.

Rothaar Hills. *Mountain range, western Ger-*

many. The southernmost mountain region of the Sauerland has a name meaning "red hills," the color being that of the soil on the southwestern slope, where iron ore has long been mined. The German name of the range is *Rothaargebirge.*

Rothenburg ob der Tauber. *City, south central Germany.* The city, above the deep valley of the *Tauber* River, has a name meaning "red fort," referring to the color of the walls of a former fortress here. The river name derives ultimately from a Celtic word meaning simply "water," as for the **Douro.** The preposition *ob* means "upon," referring to the site of the city some 200 feet (60m) above the river.

Rotherham. *Town, northern England.* The former South Yorkshire town takes its name from the *Rother* River here, with the final *-ham* meaning "homestead." The river's own name is probably Celtic in origin with a meaning "chief river."

Rotherhithe. *District of London, southeastern England.* The district, by the Thames River, has an Old English name meaning "landing place for cattle." A former alternate form of the name was *Redriff,* as in Jonathan Swift's *Gulliver's Travels* (1726) ("I left fifteen Hundred Pounds with my Wife, and fixed her in a good House at *Redriff*").

Rotorua. *City, northern New Zealand.* The city, in central North Island, arose in the 1870s and takes its name from the lake by which it lies. Its own name is Maori in origin, meaning literally "hole lake," from *roto,* "lake," and *rua,* "hole." The lake fills a deep crater that was probably created by a volcanic explosion, and this is the "hole."

Rotterdam. *City and port, southwestern Netherlands.* The city's name means "(place by a) dam on the *Rotte* (River)," this being a minor tributary of the Nieuwe Maas. *Cp.* **Amsterdam.**

Rottnest Island. *Island, Indian Ocean.* The Australian island, northwest of Fremantle, was discovered by the Dutch in 1658 but named in 1696 by a Dutch sea captain, Willem de Vlamingh. The name means "rat nest," as the island appeared to be infested with large rats. They were actually quokkas, a type of small-tailed wallaby, now protected by the island's status as a wildlife preserve.

Roubaix. *City, northern France.* The city has a name meaning "horse stream," from Old German *hros,* "horse," and *baki,* "stream." A "horse stream" is one where horses were watered or with a place where they regularly crossed. For a name of identical meaning, in another language, *see* **Ebbw Vale.**

Rouen. *City and river port, northern France.* The city's present name is a reduced form of its Roman name, *Rotomagus.* The latter part of this is Gaulish *magos,* "field," "market." The first half may either represent Gaulish *roto,* "wheel," or be the personal name *Roto.* If the former, the reference could be to the Gaulish love of chariot racing.

Roussillon. *Historic region, southern France.* The former province takes its name from the town that was its original capital (before Perpignan). The town had the Roman name of *Ruscino,* the origin of which is uncertain.

Rovereto. *Town, northern Italy.* The town's name derives from Medieval Latin *roboretum,* "oak grove," from Latin *robor* or *robur,* "oak."

Rovno. *City, northwestern Ukraine.* The city probably derives its name from a Slavic word related to Russian *rovnyj,* "level," and *ravnina,* "plain," referring to the flat terrain here. The Ukrainian form of the name is *Rivne.*

Roxas. *City, central Philippines.* The city, on the island of Panay, was originally called *Capiz,* and is still sometimes so known. It was later renamed as now for Manuel *Roxas* (1892–1948), first president of the Philippines.

Roxburgh. *Historic county, southeastern Scotland.* The former county takes its name from the village here so called. Its own name is Old English in origin and means "*Hrōc*'s fort," with the Anglo-Saxon personal name meaning "rook." *Cp.* **Rugby.**

Royal Oak. *City, northern United States.* The Michigan city was settled in 1819 and is said to be named for the *royal oak* in Shropshire, England, in which Charles II hid after his defeat in the Battle of Worcester (1651).

Rub' al-Khali. *Desert, southern Arabian Peninsula.* The desert, extending south from Saudi Arabia into Yemen and Oman, has an Arabic name meaning "quarter of the desert," from *rub',* "quarter," *al,* "the," and *khālī,* "desert." "Quarter" here describes an area of the desert that is shaped like a crescent moon, in its first quarter. The English name of the region is *Empty Quarter.*

Rubicon. *Stream, northern Italy.* The stream, historically the boundary between Italy and Cisalpine Gaul, has a name deriving from Latin *rubicundus,* "ruddy," referring to the color of its soil.

Ruda Śląska. *Town, south central Poland.* The town, in former Upper Silesia, was founded in medieval times as a mining settlement. Hence its name, Polish for "Silesian ore."

Rüdesheim. *Town, western Germany.* The

town, known formally as *Rüdesheim am Rhein*, for its location by the **Rhine**, where it arose in Frankish times, has a name meaning "*Ruodin*'s abode," with the short form of an Old German personal name such as *Rudolf* or *Rupert*.

Rudolf, Lake. *Lake, eastern Africa*. The lake, mostly in northern Kenya but with a small section in southern Ethiopia, was discovered in 1888 by the Hungarian explorer Count Samuel Teleki and the Austrian explorer Ludwig von Höhnel, who named it for the Austrian crown prince *Rudolf* (1858–1889), son of Franz Joseph I, emperor of Austria. (They named the smaller Lake *Stefanie* in southern Ethiopia for Rudolf's wife, Princess *Stephanie* of Belgium.) Lake Rudolf is now often known as *Lake Turkana*, for the *Turkana*, a local people of Hamitic origin. The meaning of their name is uncertain.

Rudolstadt. *City, east central Germany*. The city, founded in the 9th century on the site of a Frankish fortress, has a name meaning "*Rudolf*'s settlement."

Rueil-Malmaison. *City, northern France*. The city, now a suburb of Paris, had the Medieval Latin name of *Rodolium*, representing the first part of the present name. This goes back to Gaulish *roto*, "wheel," "race,"and *ialon*, "clearing," denoting a site of chariot racing. The second part of the name relates to the château of *Malmaison* built here in 1622. The name literally means "bad house," alluding to a house built on an unpromising site, such as broken terrain or marshland.

Rufisque. *Town and port, western Senegal*. The name is said to be a local corruption of the town's original Portuguese name *Rio Fresco*, "fresh river."

Rugby. *Town, central England*. The Warwickshire town originally had an Old English name meaning "*Hrōca*'s fortified place" which could have produced a modern form *Rocksbury*. (*Cp.* **Roxburgh**.) The Danes then substituted *bý*, "village," for Old English *burh* to give the present name.

Rügen. *Island, northeastern Germany*. Germany's largest island, in the Baltic Sea, was inhabited in the 2d and 3d centuries by Slav peoples, so may have a name of Slavic origin. Alternately, the name could derive from the Germanic people known as the *Rugii*, who came from Norway to settle on the Pomeranian coast in the 2d century B.C. The meaning of their own name is unknown.

Ruhr. *Industrial region, western Germany*. The region takes its name from its river, in the valley of which many important industrial cities lie.

The river's own name has been derived from Old High German *ruora*, "violent motion," but a more likely origin is in the Indoeuropean root element *reu*, "to rend," "to hollow," describing its natural channel. The German name of the region is *Ruhrgebiet*, "Ruhr region."

Rum. *Island, western Scotland*. The island, in the Inner Hebrides, has a name representing Gaelic *rùim*, "room," referring to its relative area by comparison with neighboring Eigg and Muck. The quasi–Gaelic spelling *Rhum* was current from 1888 to 1957 and was introduced by the island's English owners, the Bullough family.

Rumelia. *Historic region, southern Bulgaria*. The name of the former Ottoman possessions in the Balkans derives from Turkish *Rum*, "Rome," and *il*, "land," "district," the "land of the Romans" referring to the Byzantine Christians.

Runcorn. *Town, northeastern England*. The former Cheshire town stands on the southern bank of the Mersey River. Its Old English name refers to this location and means "spacious bay," or nearer to the original, "roomy cove," from *rūm*, "roomy," "spacious," and *cofa*, "cove," "bay." The bay in question is Runcorn Gap, where the Mersey broadens out to the west of the Runcorn-Widnes Bridge.

Runnymede. *Meadow, southern England*. The meadow by the Thames River near Egham, Surrey, has a name meaning "council island meadow," from Old English *rūn*, "secret," "council." *ēg*, "island," and *mæd*, "meadow." King John drew up the Magna Carta here in 1215, and the name implies that the site was already a meeting place for royal or other assemblies then.

Ruse. *City and river port, northern Bulgaria*. The city, on the Danube, was founded by the Romans in the 1st century B.C. and was known as *Sexantaprista*, "harbor of the sixty (ships)." The Turks built a new town on the site with the name of *Rusçuk*. The origin of this is uncertain, but it was adopted by later Christian inhabitants in the form *Ruse*, as if deriving from Bulgarian *rus*, "fair-haired," "blond." This alternated with *Chervena*, a name of similar sense, meaning "red-haired" (Bulgarian *cherven*, "red"). Eventually *Ruse* became official.

Rüsselsheim. *City, west central Germany*. The city's name, meaning "*Rucilo*'s abode," derives from that of the Frankish prince who founded it in the 9th century.

Russia. *Republic, eastern Europe/northern and western Asia*. The name is probably Scandinavian in origin, from the Old Finnish name *Rus* given to the Varangians who entered the country from the north in the 9th century. Their own name probably means "followers." Many modern toponymists, however, link the name with that of the *Ruotsi* ("rowers"), the Swedish people who served as oarsmen on Viking ships. The latter also gave *Ruotsi* as the Finnish name of **Sweden**. The medieval name of Russia, in use down to the 17th century, was *Muscovy*, from the source of the name of **Moscow**, while for much of the 20th century the name Russia was used for the country officially known as the **Soviet Union**. The Russian name of Russia is *Rossiya*.

Rustavi. *City, southeastern Georgia*. The city arose in 1948 when an ironworks began operating. It took the name of of a former nearby town, itself meaning "(place at the) source of the stream," from Georgian *ru*, "stream," "canal," and *tavi*, "beginning," "source." The reference is to the irrigation canal that leads from the Kura River here.

Ruthenia. *Historic region, central Europe*. The region, represented today by the Transcarpathian (Zakarpatska) province, western Ukraine, takes its name from the *Rutheni*, the Slavic people who at one time inhabited it. Their name is related to that of *Rus*, the old name of **Russia**.

Rutland. *Historic county, east central England*. England's former smallest county, now a unitary authority, has an Old English name meaning "*Rōta*'s estate," with the Anglo-Saxon personal name followed by *land*, used both for a small-ish, well-defined estate, as here, or more commonly for a much larger region, as in **Northumberland**.

Ruwenzori. *Mountain range, central Africa*. The mountain group, between Lake Albert and Lake Edward, has a local name said to mean "lord of the clouds," referring to its frequent cloud cover. The mountains are generally believed to be Ptolemy's "Mountains of the Moon," so called from the appearance of their peaks. *See also* **Comoros**.

Rwanda. *Republic, central Africa*. The country is named for its indigenous people, but the meaning of their own name is obscure.

Ryazan. *City, western Russia*. The city probably derives its name from the *Erzian*, a Mordvinian people who inhabited the region. The meaning of their own name is uncertain.

Rybinsk. *City and river port, western Russia*. The city, on the Volga, is first mentioned in the 12th century, having arisen as a fishing village. Hence its name, based on Russian *ryba*, "fish." *Cp.* **Rybnik**. It became a town in 1777. From 1946 through 1957 it was known as *Shcherbakov*, for the Soviet Communist leader Aleksandr

Shcherbakov (1901–1945). It then reverted to its original name, but was again renamed, as *Andropov*, from 1984 through 1989, this time for the Soviet president Yuri *Andropov* (1914–1984), who had worked as a Volga boatman and studied here.

Rybnik. *Town, southern Poland*. The town arose in the 10th century as a fishing village on the Nacyna River. Its name alludes to its commercial role, from Slavic *rybnik*, "fish pool," denoting a location on the river where fish were trapped or kept after being caught. *Cp.* **Rybinsk**.

Ryukyu Islands. *Island chain, western Pacific*. The islands, south of (and belonging to) Japan, have a name meaning "ball of jewels," from Japanese *ryū*, "jewel," and *kyū*, "ball." The "ball" is the arc that the chain of islands describes between Taiwan and Japan. The islands were also known in English as the *Lew-Chew* or *Loo-Choo* Islands, from Chinese *liúqiú* in the same sense.

Rzeszów. *City, southeastern Poland*. The city, founded in the 14th century, has a name derived by some from Polish *rzesza*, "crowd," "group of settlers," referring to its original inhabitants. But a more likely origin is an Old Polish personal name such as *Rzech*, with the final -*ow* denoting possession.

Rzhev. *City, northwestern Russia*. The city probably takes its name from that of a local stream or river, from Russian *rzha*, "rust," denoting the color of its water. The main river here is the Volga.

Saalfeld. *City, east central Germany*. The city, founded on the site of a 9th-century Frankish palace, has a name meaning "open land on the Saale," after the river by which it stands. The river name, first recorded in the 2d century B.C. in the Greek form *Salas potamos*, derives from Indoeuropean *sal*, "stream," "current."

Saar. *River, western Europe*. The river in France and Germany ultimately derives its name from the Indoeuropean root element *ser*, "to flow." *See also* **Saarbrücken**.

Saarbrücken. *City, western Germany*. The city arose in the 10th century by a Frankish royal castle near a Roman *bridge* (German *Brücke*) over the **Saar** River. Hence the name.

Saaremaa. *Island, western Estonia*. The island, in the Baltic Sea, has a name meaning simply "island land," from Estonian *saare*, "island," and *maa*, "land." The island's German name is *Ösel*, based on Danish *ø*, Swedish *ö*, "island."

Saarlouis. *City, southwestern Germany*. The city, on the **Saar** River, was founded in 1680 by *Louis* XVI of France and named by him. The French city passed to Prussia in 1815 and from

1936 through 1945 was known for political reasons as *Saarlautern*, after the incorporated district of *Fraulautern*, itself named after the Augustinian nunnery (German *Frau*, "woman") founded in the 12th century by Adalbert of *Lautern*. Earlier, at the time of the French Revolution (1793), the town was renamed *Saarlibre*, substituting egalitarian *libre* ("free") for royal *Louis*. It reverted to *Saarlouis* in 1804.

Saba. *Historic kingdon, southwestern Arabia.* The ancient kingdom, mentioned several times in the Bible, notably in the story of King Solomon and the Queen of *Sheba* (1 Kings 10:1–13), derives its name from Hebrew *shéva'*, "seven," "oath," as in the name of **Beersheba**.

Sabah. *State, eastern Malaysia.* The state, formerly *North Borneo*, is said to derive its name from a local word meaning "downstream" or "downwind," presumably referring to its location with regard to the current of some river, such as the Limbang, to the south.

Sable, Cape. *Cape, southeastern United States.* The southernmost point of the continental United States, at the southwestern tip of Florida, derives its name from French *sable*, "sand."

Sable Island. *Island, eastern Canada.* The Nova Scotia island, the exposed part of a lengthy sand shoal in the Atlantic, derives its name from French *sable*, "sand."

Sabrina Coast. *Region, Antarctica.* The region of coastland, part of Wilkes Land south of New Zealand, was sighted in 1839 by John Balleny in the cutter *Sabrina* and named for it. The ship's own name is the Roman name of the **Severn** River, England.

Sachsenheim. *Town, southwestern Germany.* The town was formed in 1971 on the amalgamation of the existing town *Gross-Sachsenheim* ("great") with the village *Klein-Sachsenheim* ("little"). A meaning "abode of the *Saxons*" is more likely than a derivation from an original founder called *Sahso*.

Sacramento. *City, western United States.* The state capital of California takes its name from the river on which it was first settled in 1839. The river's own Spanish name was given in 1808 in honor of the Holy *Sacrament*.

Sado. *Island, west central Japan.* The fifth largest Japanese island derives its name from Japanese *sa*, "to help," and *to*, "ford."

Safed Koh. *Mountain range, southern Asia.* The range, between Afghanistan and Pakistan, derives its name from Iranian *sefid kūh*, "white mountain."

Saffron Walden. *Town, southeastern England.* The Essex town was originally known simply as

Walden, an Old English name meaning "valley of the Britons," from *walh*, "foreigner," "Briton," and *denu*, "valley." Later, *Saffron* was added to distinguish this Walden from others. The prefix refers to the fields of *saffron* grown locally from the 15th century for medicinal use.

Saga. *City, southern Japan.* The city, in the island of Kyushu, derives its name from Japanese *sa*, "to help," and *ga*, "compliments."

Sagar. *City, central India.* The city, in Madhya Pradesh state, is situated around a lake. Hence its name, from Hindi *sagar*, "lake."

Saginaw. *City, northern United States.* The Michigan city takes its name from the *Saginaw* River on which it lies. The river's own name represents an Ojibwa word meaning "land of the *Sauks*," this being the name of a Native American people meaning "outlet."

Sagunto. *Town, eastern Spain.* The town had the Roman name of *Saguntum*, said to refer to its founders, Greek colonists from the island of Zante (Greek *Zakinthos*).

Sahara. *Desert, northern Africa.* The name represents Arabic *ṣaḥrā'*, "desert," the feminine of *aṣhar*, "fawn-colored."

Saharanpur. *City, northern India.* The city, in Uttar Pradesh state, was founded in c.1340 and is named for the Muslim saint *Shah Haran* Chishti, with Hindi *pur*, "town," added.

Sahel. *Region, western and north central Africa.* The semiarid region derives its name from Arabic *sāḥil*, "sea coast," "shore," referring to its Atlantic seaboard. The coastal plain of *as-Sahil*, eastern Tunisia, on the Mediterranean seaboard, has a name of the same origin.

Saida *see* **Sidon**

Saigon *see* **Ho Chi Minh City**

St.-Affrique. *Town, southern France.* The town arose around the tomb of *St. Africanus*, 6th-century bishop of Comminges.

St. Albans. *City, southeastern England.* The Hertfordshire city takes its name from the 3d-century martyr *St. Alban*, to whom the abbey here is dedicated. (It stands on the site where he was executed.) The Roman name of St. Albans was *Verulamium*, of uncertain origin and meaning.

St.-Amand-des-Eaux. *Town and spa, northern France.* The first part of the town's name represents Latin *Sanctus Amandus*, "St. Amandus," a 7th-century bishop of Tongeren, Belgium, who founded a Benedictine abbey here. The second part refers to the mineral waters (French *eaux*, "waters") for which the town is noted. *Cp.* **St.-Amand-Montrond.**

St.-Amand-Montrond. *Town, central France.*

The first part of the town's name represents Latin *Sanctus Amandus*, "St. *Amandus*," a 7th-century bishop of Tongeren, Belgium. The second part refers to the nearby hill of *Mont-Rond*, "round hill." *Cp*. **St.-Amand-des-Eaux.**

St. Andrews. *Town and port, eastern Scotland.* The town takes its name from Scotland's patron saint, *St. Andrew*, whose relics are said to have been been brought here in the 8th century. They were "lost," however, in the 16th century, on the destruction of the cathedral dedicated to him here.

St. Augustine. *City, southeastern United States.* The oldest continuously settled city in the United States was founded in 1565 by the Spanish admiral Pedro Menéndez de Avilés. He named it for *St. Augustine* of Hippo, on whose feastday, August 28, he had sighted the coast.

St. Bernard Pass. *Mountain pass, south central Europe.* There are two passes of the name in the Alps: the *Great St. Bernard Pass*, between Italy and Switzerland, and the *Little St. Bernard Pass*, between Italy and France. They are both named for the hospice for travelers founded in the 10th century near the Great St. Bernard Pass by *St. Bernard* of Menthon (923–1008).

St.-Brieuc. *City and port, northwestern France.* The city, in Brittany, is named for the 5th-century Breton saint *Brieg*. In 1793, at the time of the French Revolution, the town was temporarily renamed *Port-Brieuc*.

St. Catharines. *City, southern Canada.* The Ontario city was established in 1790 and named in 1809 for *Catharine* Askin Hamilton, first wife of Robert Hamilton, member of the first legislative council of Upper Canada. (He was the father of George Hamilton, who gave the name of ³**Hamilton**, along the coast of Lake Ontario to the west.)

St. Charles. *City, east central United States.* The Missouri city was founded by the French in 1769 and originally named *Les Petites Côtes*, "the little hills." The site was transferred to the Spanish in 1770 and in 1771 was renamed for the dedication of the church to the Italian cardinal *San Carlos Borromeo*, "St. Charles Borromeo" (1538–1584). The name was shortened and anglicized as now in 1896.

St. Clair, Lake. *Lake, eastern North America.* The lake, on the border between Michigan, USA, and Ontario, Canada, was named in 1679 for *St. Clare* by the French explorer Robert Cavelier, sieur de La Salle. The name became subsequently associated with that of the American general Arthur *St. Clair* (1736–1818), who took part in the Quebec campaign during the French

and Indian Wars and saw action in the American Revolution.

St.-Claude. *Town, eastern France.* The town is named for *St. Claudius*, 7th-century bishop of Besançon. Its earlier Roman name was *Condate*, "confluence," referring to its location on the Bienne River, here joined by a lesser stream.

¹**St.-Cloud.** *City, northern France.* The city, now a suburb of Paris, derives its name from *Clodoald*, son of the Merovingian king Clodomir, who founded a monastery here in the 6th century.

²**St. Cloud.** *City, northern United States.* The Minnesota city was laid out in 1854 and named for the French city of ¹**St.-Cloud.** The name was given by the city's founder, John L. Wilson, after reading a biography of Napoleon, in which he noted that "the Empress Josephine spent much of her time at the magnificent palace at St. Cloud."

St. Croix. *Island, eastern West Indies.* The largest of the United States Virgin Islands was discovered in 1493 by Columbus and named by him *Santa Cruz*, "holy cross." The present name is the French form of this, introduced by French colonists in the 17th century.

St.-Cyr. *Town, northern France.* The town's name honors *St. Cyriacus*, an early 4th-century martyr. The name is found for several places in France, and this one, west of Versailles, is formally known as *St.-Cyr-l'École*. The suffix refers to the school (*école*) for the daughters of impoverished noblemen founded here in 1685. The building later housed the military academy founded by Napoleon in 1808.

St.-Denis. *Town, northern France.* The town, now a suburb of Paris, takes its name from *St. Denis*, 3d-century bishop of Paris and now its patron saint. He was beheaded on **Montmartre** with two companions in 258 and is said to have afterwards carried his head to this site, a distance of about 3 miles (5 km).

St.-Dié. *Town, northeastern France.* The town had the Medieval Latin name of *Sanctus Deodatus*, for an 8th-century bishop of Nevers. His own name means "gift of God," from Latin *datus*, "given," and *Deo*, "by God."

St.-Dizier. *Town, northeastern France.* The town had the Roman name of *Fanum Desiderii*, "temple of *Desiderius*." This later became associated with one or other of the French saints *Didier* (the French form of the Latin name).

Ste.-Foy. *City, southeastern Canada.* The Quebec city was founded in 1698 and named for a village in France, itself named for the 3d-century virgin martyr *St. Faith*. It is uncertain which particular village is involved.

Saintes. *City, western France.* The city was known to the Romans as *Mediolanum Santonum,* "middle plain of the *Santones,*" from the name of a Gaulish people. (*Cp.* **Milan.**) Later the name became popularly associated with the French *Saint,* "saint," that begins many French place-names. *See also* **Saintonge.**

Stes-Maries-de-la-Mer. *Town, southern France.* The town, on the coast of the Camargue, takes its name from the dedication of its church to the three *Marys* of the Gospels: *Mary* Magdalene, *Mary* the mother of James and Joses (also called Salome), and *Mary* the wife of Cleopas (and sister of the Virgin Mary). According to local legend, the three Marys escaped here by sea with their black servant, Sarah.

Ste.-Thérèse. *City, southeastern Canada.* The Quebec city dates from 1789 and is named for *Thérèse* de Blainville, granddaughter of the seignior who made the first land grants for it in c.1730

St.-Étienne. *City, east central France.* The city was founded in the 11th century and dedicated to *St. Stephen* (French *Saint-Étienne*), the first Christian martyr.

St.-Eustache. *Town, southeastern Canada.* The Quebec town was settled by the French in 1768 and named for a former local seignior, *Eustache* Lambert, or more exactly for his patron saint, *St. Eustace.*

St.-Flour. *Town, south central France.* The town is named for *St. Florus,* apostle of the Auvergne in the 4th and 5th centuries.

St.-Gall. *Town, northeastern Switzerland.* The town and its canton are named for *St. Gall,* a 7th-century Irish monk and hermit who was a pioneer of Christianity in Switzerland. The German form of the name is *Sankt Gallen.*

St.-Gaudens. *Town, southern France.* The name is that of *St. Gaudentius,* martyred in 475 in the region of Toulouse.

St. George. *City, western United States.* The Utah city was settled in 1861 by Mormons and named for *George* A. Smith, a counselor to Brigham Young.

St. George's Channel. *Strait, British Isles.* The strait, between Wales and Ireland, takes its name from a late legend that *St. George,* patron saint of England, came to Britain by this sea route. The name appears to date from not much earlier than the 16th century.

St.-Germain. *District of Paris, northern France.* The district's full name is *Saint-Germain-en-Laye.* This represents its Medieval Latin name of *Sanctus Germanus in Laya.* The personal name is that of *St. Germanus,* 5th-century bishop of

Auxerre. The last part of the name alludes to the former forest here, from Old French *l'aye* (now *la haie*), "the hedge." (*Cp. La Haye* as the French name of The **Hague.**)

St.-Ghislain. *Town, southwestern Belgium.* The town takes its name from the 7th-century hermit *St. Gislenus,* who founded the Benedictine abbey here and whose tomb is here.

St. Gotthard Pass. *Mountain pass, south central Switzerland.* The Alpine pass is named for the travelers' hospice built here in the 11th century by *St. Gotthard* (960–1038), bishop of Hildesheim.

St. Helena. *Island, southeastern Atlantic.* The island, a British colony off the southwest coast of Africa, was discovered by the Spanish navigator in Portuguese service João da Nova on May 22, 1502, the feastday of *St. Helen,* and was named accordingly.

St. Helens. *Town, northwestern England.* The Merseyside town takes its name from a medieval chapel-of-ease dedicated to *St. Helen* that stood on the site of the present St. Helen's church. The town arose only in the 17th century.

St. Helens, Mt. *Mountain, northwestern United States.* The volcanic peak, in the Cascade Range, Washington, was named by Captain George Vancouver for Alleyne Fitzherbert, Baron *St. Helens* (1753–1839), British ambassador to Spain from 1790 to 1794.

St. Helier. *Town and resort, Channel Islands, western English Channel.* The chief town of Jersey is named for *St. Helier,* a Frankish missionary who is said to have been martyred here in 555.

St.-Hubert. *City, southeastern Canada.* The Quebec city was instituted as a parish in 1862 and named for *St. Hubert,* 8th-century bishop of Maastricht and Liège, Belgium, and patron of hunters. He also gave the name of the town in southeastern Belgium where his tomb is in the abbey church.

St.-Hyacinthe. *City, southeastern Canada.* The Quebec city was founded in 1760 and named for *Hyacinthe* Delorme, who had purchased the seigniory in 1753.

St. Ives. *Town and resort, southwestern England.* The Cornish town is named for *St. Ia,* a female saint, who according to legend was wafted across the sea from Ireland on a leaf to land here some time in the 6th or 7th century.

St.-Jean-de-Luz. *Town, southwestern France.* The town had the Medieval Latin name of *Sanctus Johannes de Luis,* "*St. John* of *Luis,*" the latter word representing either the personal name *Lucius* or the name of the pagan god *Lug* (cp.

Lyons). The town's Basque name is *Donibane-Lohizun*, from *done*, "saint," *Iban*, "John," and *lohizun*, "muddy," from *lohi*, "mud," suggesting that *Luz* may actually mean "muddy place." (*Cp. Lutetia* as the Roman name of ¹**Paris**.)

St. John. *City and port, southeastern Canada.* The New Brunswick city takes its name from the river here. This was discovered by the French explorer Samuel de Champlain on June 24, 1604, the feastday of *St. John*, so was named accordingly. The town was founded in 1783 and originally named *Parr Town*, for Colonel John *Parr* (1725–1791), governor of Nova Scotia. It was renamed as now in 1785.

St. John's. *City and port, eastern Canada.* The capital of Newfoundland stands on the site of a natural harbor said to have been discovered by *John* Cabot on June 24, 1497, the feastday of *St. John*. If so, the name both commemorates the explorer and honors his personal saint.

St. Joseph. *City, central United States.* The Missouri city was laid out in 1843 by *Joseph* Robidoux, a French-Canadian trapper, who named it for his patron saint. The city's colloquial name is *St. Joe*.

St. Kilda. *Island, western Scotland.* The westernmost island of the Outer Hebrides is popularly said to bear the name of *St. Kilda*, a "virtually unknown saint who has given his (or her) name to the remote island" (*Oxford Dictionary of Saints*, 1978). But there was no such saint, and the name arose from a misreading on charts of its Old Norse name, *Skildar*. This probably means "shields," and may have been intended to describe the outline of the island and its surrounding islets as seen from sea level. (The dictionary's misinformation was corrected in later editions.)

St. Kitts. *Island, eastern West Indies.* The island, in the Leeward Islands, was visited by *Christopher* Columbus in 1493 and named by him for his own patron saint. The name was later colloquially shortened as now by English settlers who arrived in 1623. St. Kitts forms an independent state with **Nevis**.

St.-Lambert. *City, southeastern Canada.* The Quebec city was founded by Jesuits in 1647 and named for Raphael *Lambert* Closse (1618–1692), merchant and sergeant major of the garrison here.

St.-Laurent. *City, southeastern Canada.* The Quebec city, now a suburb of Montreal, is named for its location in the center of Montreal Island in the *St. Lawrence* River, whose French name is *St. Laurent*.

St. Lawrence. *River, eastern Canada.* The

river, forming the boundary between Canada and the USA for part of its course, was explored by the French navigator Jacques Cartier in 1534 and was so named by him because he arrived here on August 10, the feastday of *St. Lawrence*. The river gave its name to the *Gulf of St. Lawrence* and to the modern *St. Lawrence Seaway*.

St.-Lô. *Town, northwestern France.* The town takes its name from *Lauto*, a 6th-century bishop of Coutances. His name is Germanic in origin.

¹**St. Louis**. *City and port, western Senegal.* The former capital of Senegal was founded in 1659 at the mouth of the Senegal River and named notionally for *Louis* XIV of France (1638–1715) but actually for his patron saint, *St. Louis* (1215–1270), otherwise Louis IX of France.

²**St. Louis**. *City and river port, central United States.* The Missouri city was founded in 1764 by the French and named for *St. Louis* (1215–1270), otherwise Louis IX of France, canonized in 1297. *Cp.* **Louisiana**.

St. Lucia. *Island, southeastern West Indies.* The island, in the Windward Islands, is said to have been discovered by Columbus on December 13, 1502, the feastday of *St. Lucy*, Sicilian virgin martyr, and named for her accordingly.

St.-Malo. *Town and port, northwestern France.* The town is named for *St. Maclovius*, 6th-century bishop of Aleth (now St.-Servan), who founded a monastery here. *See also* **Falkland Islands**.

St. Martin. *Island, eastern West Indies.* The island, in the Leeward Islands, was visited by Columbus on November 11, 1493, the feastday of *St. Martin*. Hence its name.

¹**St.-Maurice**. *Town, southwestern Switzerland.* The town has Switzerland's oldest abbey, founded in 515 over the tomb of *St. Maurice*, leader of the Theban Legion, said to have been martyred with his fellow legionnaires in the late 3d century. He also gave the name of **St. Moritz**.

²**St.-Maurice**. *River, southeastern Canada.* The river, in southern Quebec, was discovered by the French navigator Jacques Cartier in 1535 and subsequently named for *Maurice* Poulin, who was granted a seigniory at its mouth in 1668. The river was earlier known as *Trois Rivières*, "three rivers," referring to its three branches at this point.

St.-Maur-les-Fossés. *City, northern France.* The city, now a suburb of Paris, is named for the monastery built here in the 7th century by Benedictine monks from *St.-Maur*-sur-le-Loir, itself named for *St. Maurus*, a 6th-century monk. The final word of the city's name represents Latin *fossa*, "trench," "ditch," referring to those of the early fortification here.

St. Moritz. *Town and resort, southeastern Switzerland.* The famous winter-sports center is named for the martyred *St. Maurice* (see [1]**St.-Maurice**), to whom an abbey was dedicated here in the 6th century.

St.-Nazaire. *Town and port, northwestern France.* The town takes its name from *St. Nazarius*, 5th-century abbot of Lérins.

St.-Omer. *Town, northeastern France.* The town takes its name from a monastery founded in the 7th century here by *St. Omer*, bishop of Thérouanne.

Saintonge. *Historic region, western France.* The region was named for its chief city, **Saintes**.

St.-Ouen. *Town, northern France.* The town, now a suburb of Paris, takes its name from *Audowin*, a 7th-century bishop of Rouen. His name is Germanic in origin.

St. Paul. *City, northern United States.* The state capital of Minnesota is named for the log chapel built here on the Mississippi in 1841 by the Canadian missionary Lucien Galtier and dedicated to *St. Paul*.

St.-Paul-Trois-Châteaux. *Town, southeastern France.* The town's name seems to mean "*St. Paul* (of the) three castles." But this is misleading. *St. Paul* is not the apostle but a local 4th-century bishop. And "three castles" is a popular mistranslation of the name of the *Tricastini*, a Gaulish people who gave the earlier name of the place, recorded in 6th-century Latin as *Civitas Trecastininsis*. Their own name has the same origin as that of the *Tricasses* who gave the name of **Troyes**.

St. Peter Port. *Town and port, Channel Islands, western English Channel.* The main town of Guernsey is named for the dedication of its church to *St. Peter*, the patron of fishermen, with *Port* emphasizing the town's role as a port of call and center of commerce.

[1]**St. Petersburg.** *City and port, western Russia.* The former Russian capital (1712–1914), on the Gulf of Finland, was founded by *Peter* the Great in 1703 and is named both for him and for his personal saint. In 1914, following Germany's declaration of war on Russia, the Germanic name was slavicized to *Petrograd*, "*Peter's* town." In 1924, the year of the death of *Lenin*, it was renamed for the founder of Communism and the Soviet Union as *Leningrad*. It reverted to its original name in 1991.

[2]**St. Petersburg.** *City and resort, southeastern United States.* The Florida city was settled in 1876 by John C. Williams and *Peter* A. Demens, and was named for the latter's birthplace, [1]**St. Petersburg**, Russia, as well as for himself.

St. Pierre and Miquelon. *Island group, western Atlantic.* The two small islands, French territory just south of Newfoundland, have names that apparently derive respectively from a navigator called *Peter* in some language (perhaps Portuguese rather than French) and one called *Michael* (in a diminutive form if this name). In 1520 St. Pierre was named (the equivalent of) *Island of the Eleven Thousand Virgins* by the Portuguese navigator João Alvarez Faguendez, who arrived here on October 21, feastday of St. Ursula and her virgin companions. *See* **Virgin Islands**.

St.-Quentin. *Town, northeastern France.* The town is named for *St. Quintinus*, said to have been martyred here in the 3d century.

St. Thomas. *City, southeastern Canada.* The Ontario city was founded in 1817 and was originally known as *Sterling*. It was renamed for Colonel *Thomas* Talbot (1771–1853), who made it the capital of the settlement that he had founded in 1803.

St. Vincent. *Island, southeastern West Indies.* The island, in the Windward Islands, was discovered by Columbus on January 22, 1498, the feastday of *St. Vincent* of Saragossa, 4th-century Spanish deacon and martyr. Hence its name.

Saipan. *Island, western Pacific.* The main island of the Marianas has a name of Micronesian (Caroline) origin meaning "deserted," "uninhabited." The original islanders were deported by the Spanish, and Caroline settlers so named the island when they came here in the 17th century.

Saitama. *Prefecture, east central Japan.* The prefecture, bordering on Tokyo in the island of Honshu, derives its name from Japanese *saki*, "cape," "promontory," and *tama*, "ball," "bowl."

Sajószentpéter. *Town, northern Hungary.* The river name *Sajó* is followed by Hungarian *szent*, "saint," and *Péter*, "Peter," denoting the dedication of the town's church.

Sakai. *City, south central Japan.* The city, in the island of Honshu, derives its name from Japanese *sakai*, "frontier," apparently referring to a former border or boundary here.

Sakha. *Republic, northeastern Russia.* Russia's second largest republic, formerly familiar as *Yakutia* (see **Yakutsk**), has a name meaning effectively "river dwellers," as the people's own name for themselves derives from Siberian (Samoyed) *sakha*, "river." Sakha occupies the basins of four great rivers, Lena, Yana, Indigirka, and Kolyma, which flow to the Arctic Ocean here.

Sakhalin. *Island, eastern Russia.* The island, north of Japan, has a name that resulted from an error. On a map made by French missionaries in the early 18th century, the lower part of the Amur River, which flows into the Tatar Strait opposite the northern end of Sakhalin, was named as *Saghalien anga hata*. This was a corrupt form of a Manchurian phrase meaning "course of the black river." The French geographer Jean-Baptiste d'Anville used their map to compile an atlas of China and the Far East, published in 1737, and because the name extended from the river mouth across to the island, took it as applying to the latter rather than the former. In the course of time the name became established for the island, instead of the river, but was shortened to *Saghalien*, the first word noted by the missionaries.

Salaberry-de-Valleyfield. *City and port, southeastern Canada.* The city arose on a group of islands in the St. Lawrence River when a paper mill was built here in 1870. This gave the second part of the name, from that of the *Valleyfield* Paper Mills, Edinburgh, Scotland. The first part honors Charles Michel d'Irumberry de *Salaberry* (1778–1829), French commander of the Canadian forces at the Battle of Châteauguay in 1813.

Salamanca. *City, western Spain.* The city's name is of obscure origin. Its Latin form was *Salmantica* or *Salamantica*, and it is thus almost certainly pre–Roman. The city of *Salamanca* in central Mexico is named for the Spanish original.

Salamis. *Historic city, eastern Cyprus.* The name of the long-abandoned city derives from Phoenician *salam*, "peace." Under the Romans it was known as *Constantia*, for the emperor *Constantius* II who rebuilt it in the 3d century A.D. It was destroyed by the Arabs in 648. The Greek island of *Salamis* has a name of the same origin.

Salavat. *City, western Russia.* The city, in Bashkortostan, was founded in 1948 as a major oil center and named for the Bashkir national hero *Salavat* Yulayev (1752–1800).

Sala y Gómez. *Island, South Pacific.* The island, northeast of Easter Island, is named for *Sala y Gómez*, the Spanish navigator who discovered it in 1793. The island belongs to Chile.

Saldanha Bay. *Bay, southwestern South Africa.* The landlocked harbor is named for the early 16th-century Portuguese navigator António de *Saldanha*, who anchored in Table Bay, to the south, in 1503.

Salé. *City and port, northwestern Morocco.* The old walled city, at the mouth of the Wadi Bou Regreg opposite Rabat, has a Berber name meaning "rock."

Salekhard. *City, northern Russia.* The city was founded in 1595 and originally named *Obdorsk*,

from the **Ob** River and Komi *dor*, "nearby (place)." In 1933 it was renamed as now, from Nenets *salya*, "headland," and *khard*, "house," "settlement," referring to its location on a bend of the Ob.

¹Salem. *City, southeastern India.* The city, in Tamil Nadu state, derives its name from Tamil *sēla nād*, a form of *cēra nād*, denoting the visit of an early *Cera* king.

²Salem. *City, western United States.* The state capital of Oregon was founded in 1840 and originally had the Native American name of *Chemeketa*, "place of rest." This was translated into the name of the biblical town of *Salem* (Genesis 14:18), traditionally identified with **Jerusalem**.

³Salem. *City, northeastern United States.* The Massachusetts city was founded in 1626 and took its name from the biblical city of *Salem* (Genesis 14:18), itself identified with **Zion** (Psalm 76:2) and so with **Jerusalem**. *See also* **Winston-Salem**.

Salerno. *City and port, southwestern Italy.* The city, near the mouth of the Irno River, has a name of pre–Indoeuropean origin, deriving from the root word *sala*, "current" (of water).

Salford. *Town, northwestern England.* The town, near Manchester, has an Old English name meaning "willow-tree ford," from *salh*, "willow" (modern *sallow*), and *ford*, "ford." The river here is the Irwell.

Salgótarján. *Town, north central Hungary.* The town lies in the valley of the *Tarján* River near *Salgó* Castle. The latter name means "bright," "shining."

Salinas. *City, southwestern United States.* The California city takes its name from the *Salinas* River, in the valley of which it lies. The river's name represents Spanish *salinas*, "salt marshes."

Salisbury. *City, southern England.* The Wiltshire city was known to the Romans as *Sorviodunum*, their encampment being not where the town is now but on higher ground to the north on the site of the Iron Age hill fort known as Old Sarum. The name is Celtic in origin, with *-dunum* meaning "fort." The meaning of *Sorvio-* is obscure. The Anglo-Saxons apparently associated it with their word *searu*, "trick," "armor," supposedly describing the hill fort, and substituted equivalent *burh* for Celtic *-dunum*. This gave the Domesday Book (1086) record of the name as *Sarisberie*. The first *r* of this then became *l* under Norman influence. The present city arose in the 13th century, when the dry, bleak heights of Old Sarum were abandoned for the lush, fertile meadows below. *Sarum* apparently represents *Sar*, an abbreviation of the early spelling *Saresbury*, with the Latin ending *-um*. The present city is now officially *New Sarum*, by contrast with the historic *Old Sarum*.

Salisbury *see* **Harare**

Sal Island. *Island, northeastern Cape Verde.* The northeasternmost island of Cape Verde derives its name from Portuguese *sal*, "salt," referring to the saltworks for which it is noted.

Salon-de-Provence. *Town, southeastern France.* The first word of the town's name represents Old German *seli*, "room," "hall," "castle," with the Latin suffix *-onem*, denoting the hilltop fortification here. The second part of the name distinguishes this place from others by its location in **Provence**.

Salonika. *City and port, northeastern Greece.* The name is a shortened European form of the city's Roman name, *Thessalonica*, itself representing the Greek personal name *Thessalonikē*, that of the wife of its founder in 316 B.C., the Macedonian king Cassander. (She was the sister of Alexander the Great, and her own name means "victory of **Thessaly**.")

Salop *see* **Shropshire**

Salt Lake City. *City, west central United States.* The state capital of Utah was founded by Brigham Young and members of the Church of Jesus Christ of Latter-day Saints (Mormons) in 1847 as a refuge from persecution, and took its name from the **Great Salt Lake** near which it is located. (It was actually known as *Great Salt Lake City* until 1868.) The city is now the world capital of the Mormons.

Saltsjöbaden. *Town and resort, eastern Sweden.* The seaside resort has a name meaning "salt-sea bathing place," the "salt sea" being the inlet of the Baltic here, so named for distinction from the fresh-water lakes found further inland in this part of Sweden.

Salvador. *City and port, eastern Brazil.* The city was founded by the Portuguese in 1549 and originally called *Cidade do Salvador*, "city of the Savior," a name which in due course evolved into the lengthy formal title *Cidade do São Salvador da Bahia de Todos os Santos* (*see* **Bahia**).

Salween. *River, southeastern Asia.* The river, flowing through China and Myanmar, has a name representing Burmese *thanlwin*, of uncertain origin. Its Tibetan name is *nagchu*, "black water," from *nag*, "black," and *chu*, "water."

Salzburg. *City, western Austria.* The city derives its name from early forms of German *Salz*, "salt," and *Burg*, "fort," "castle." The region here is rich in salt mines. The Roman name of the city was *Salisburgum*.

Salzgitter. *City, north central Germany.* The city was formed in 1942 under the name *Watenstedt-Salzgitter* on the amalgamation of 28 villages with the *Reichswerke AG für Erzbergbau und Eisenhütten* ("State Mining and Smelting Works") founded in 1937. The present name, dating from 1951, was originally that of the village of *Gitter*, "(place of) goats," with added *Salz*, "salt," referring to the long-exploited brine springs here. The name *Watenstedt* means "*Wado*'s settlement."

Salzkammergut. *Region, north central Austria.* The region's German name means literally "salt chamber goods." The reference is to the salt deposits here, which have been mined since the Iron Age.

Samara. *City and river port, southwestern Russia.* The city was founded in 1586 as a military defensive post and was named for the river that joins the Volga here. Its own name is of Kyrgyz origin, probably meaning "hollow one." In 1935 Samara was renamed *Kuybyshev*, for the Communist leader Valerian *Kuybyshev* (1888–1935), who escaped here in 1916 from exile in Siberia and became a Bolshevik activist while working at a local steelworks. The original name was re-adopted in 1991.

Samaria. *Historic region, Palestine.* The region and its capital, in the modern West Bank, derive their name from the Hebrew personal name *Shemer*, that of the owner of the hill here which King Omri bought as a site to build a city (1 Kings 16:24) in the 9th century B.C.

Samarkand. *City, southeastern Uzbekistan.* The city derives its name from that of the former Greek city here of *Marakanda*, captured by Alexander the Great in 329 B.C. Its own name derives from Old Persian *asmara*, "stone," "rock," and Sogdian *kand*, "fort," "town." *Cp.* **Tashkent**.

Samoa. *Island group, South Pacific.* The Polynesian islands are said to derive their name either from that of a local chieftain or from an indigenous word meaning "place of the moa." The latter is a large bird, now extinct, that may have been the islanders' totem. The islands are politically divided into the independent nation of *Samoa* (until 1997 *Western Samoa*), west of the 171° meridian, and *American Samoa*, east of the meridian.

Samos. *Island, eastern Greece.* The island, in the Aegean Sea west of Turkey, has a name representing Greek *samos*, "dune," "seaside hill." The reference is to the hills in the south of the island, which contrast with the otherwise broad plains. *See also* **Samothrace**.

Samothrace. *Island, northeastern Greece.* The

island, in the northeastern Aegean Sea, has a name meaning "(people from) **Samos** (of) **Thrace**." The island was first populated by Carians and Thracians, then, in the 8th century B.C., by settlers from Samos, some 200 miles (320 km) to the south.

Samsun. *City and port, northern Turkey.* The city derives its name from Greek *eis Amison,* "to *Amisus,*" this being the name, of uncertain origin, of the original city that was founded here in the 7th century B.C.

Sana. *Capital of Yemen.* The name represents Arabic *ṣan'ā',* of unknown meaning.

San Angelo. *City, southern United States.* The Texas city, on the Concho River, was founded in 1869 and originally known as *Over-the-River.* It was renamed *Santa Angela* for a sister-in-law of Bart J. De Witt, one of the founders. The name was later masculinized as being easier to pronounce.

San Antonio. *City, southern United States.* The Texas city takes its name from the river on which it was founded in 1718. The river was so named because it was discovered by Spanish explorers on May 19, 1691, the feastday of *St. Anthony.*

San Bernardino. *City, southwestern United States.* The California city takes its name from the original site here, itself named by Spanish missionaries for the Franciscan friar *St. Bernardino* of Siena (1380–1444). The site was sold to Mormons, who laid out the present town in 1852.

San Cristóbal de Las Casas. *City, southeastern Mexico.* The city was founded by the Spanish in 1527 and was originally known as *Villa Real,* "royal town." It was then renamed five times before finally gaining its present name, honoring the missionary and bishop Bartolomé de Las Casas (1474–1566), known as "Apostle of the Indians" for his protection of Native American interests.

San Diego. *City and port, southwestern United States.* The California city was originally named *San Miguel* ("St. Michael") when the bay here was first sighted by Spanish explorers in 1542. In 1602 the explorer Sebastián Vizcaíno anchored in the port and renamed it for *San Diego* de Alcalá de Henares (St. Didacus), a 15th-century Franciscan friar, whose name had also been given to Vizcaíno's ship

Sandomierz. *Town, southeastern Poland.* The town derives its name from the Slavic personal name *Sudomir.* The *-an-* of the name represents the Polish nasal *u.*

Sandusky. *City, northern United States.* The

Ohio city, on the shore of Lake Erie, has a Native American name said to mean "cold stream" or "pure water."

Sandwich. *Town, southeastern England.* The Kent town has an Old English name meaning "sandy trading place," from *sand,* "sand," and *wīc,* "trading place," "port." The sand is not that of the seashore but of the local soil, favorable for agriculture. Owing to changes in the coastline, Sandwich is now 2 miles (3 km) from the sea.

Sandwich Islands *see* **Hawaii**

San Felipe. *City, central Chile.* The city was founded by the Spanish in 1740 as *San Felipe el Real,* "St. *Philip* the royal," honoring the reigning monarch, *Philip* V of Spain (1683–1746).

¹**San Fernando.** *City and port, southwestern Spain.* The city, on an island south of Cádiz, was founded in 1776 and originally known by the island's own name, *Isla de Léon,* "lion island." It was renamed as now in 1813 in honor of *Ferdinand* VII of Spain (1784–1833) during the Spanish War of Independence (Peninsular War).

²**San Fernando.** *City and port, Trinidad and Tobago.* The city, in southwestern Trinidad, was founded in 1786 and named for *Ferdinand* II the Catholic (1452–1516), king of Aragon and Sicily.

San Francisco. *City and port, western United States.* The California city is named for *St. Francis* of Assisi (Spanish *San Francisco*). The name was originally given in 1595 to a bay somewhere here and vaguely to the mainland by a Spanish *Franciscan* friar, Junipero Serra. A Spanish overland expedition then arrived here in 1769 and gave the name specifically to the present bay. A Franciscan mission was subsequently founded by the bay in October 1776, perhaps on the feastday of St. *Francis* itself (October 4). However, Sir *Francis* Drake had already been here in 1578 and is said to have named the bay *Port St. Francis,* partly for himself, partly for his personal saint. It is uncertain whether he actually entered the bay. The city could hardly have any other name with all these Franciscan associations.

San Francisco Gotera. *City, eastern El Salvador.* The city, originally known as *Gotera,* was renamed as now in 1887 in memory of *Francisco* Morazán (1792–1842), Honduran president of the Central American Federation from 1830 to 1840.

San Giovanni Rotondo. *Town, southeastern Italy.* The main part of the town's name honors *St. John.* The final word refers to an ancient circular (Latin *rotundus*) baptistery here.

Sangre de Cristo Mountains. *Mountain range, west central United States.* The mountains, a section of the southern Rockies in Colorado and New Mexico, were so named in 1719 by the Spanish explorer Antonio Valverde y Cosio, who is said to have cried "*Sangre de Cristo!*" ("blood of Christ!") on seeing their red-tinted, snowy peaks at sunrise.

San Isidro. *City, eastern Argentina*. The city, north of Buenos Aires, arose around the chapel of *San Isidro* Labrador, built here in 1706 and dedicated to *St. Isidore* the Farmer (c.1080–1130), patron of Madrid.

San Jose. *City, southwestern United States*. The California city was founded in 1777 as a Spanish military supply base by *José* Joaquin Moraga and was named for him, initially in the form *Pueblo de San José de Guadalupe*, "town of *St. Joseph* of **Guadalupe**."

San José. *Capital of Costa Rica*. The city was settled by the Spanish in 1736 and originally named simply *Villa Nueva*, "new town." It was subsequently renamed for *St. Joseph*, although the reason for the choice of this particular saint is uncertain.

¹San Juan. *Capital of Puerto Rico*. The city was founded in 1511 by the Spanish explorer *Juan* Ponce de León, who named it both for himself and for his name saint (*St. John*).

²San Juan. *City, west central Argentina*. The city was founded in 1562 by *Juan* Jufré y Montesa, governor of the captaincy general of Cuyo, and is named for him and his name saint (*St. John*).

San Justo. *City, eastern Argentina*. The city, now a suburb of Buenos Aires, was founded in 1856 on land donated on behalf of the *Justo* Villegas family, and is named for them.

Sankt Augustin. *Town, western Germany*. The town arose in 1969 on the amalgamation of eight villages. Its name comes from the parish church of *St. Augustine* at Menden, one of the eight.

Sankt Gallen *see* **St.-Gall**

Sankt Goar. *Town, western Germany*. The name is a dedication to *St. Goar*, a secular priest from Aquitaine, who became a hermit here. A stone figure of him in the town church bears the inscription "*St. Goar manachus obiit 611*" ("St. Goar died 611") (*manachus* is Latin *monachus*, "monk").

Sankt Ingbert. *City, western Germany*. The city, originally named *Lendelfingen*, "(settlement of) *Landolf*'s people," takes its name from a hermitage dedicated to the Frankish missionary *St. Ingobert*.

Sankt Pölten. *City, northeastern Austria*. The city arose in the 8th century around an abbey dedicated to *St. Hippolytus*. Its present name represents a germanicized form of the saint's name.

Sankt Wendel. *Town, western Germany*. The name is that of *St. Wendolin*, said to be a Scottish king's son, who was a hermit here in the 7th century. The town arose around a pilgrimage church built over his grave. An earlier name was recorded in c.800 as *Basonis villam*, from the *Bosenbach* River here, which rises in the nearby *Bosenberg*, itself apparently named for a Frankish settler called *Baso*.

Şanlıurfa. *City, southeastern Turkey*. The city, formerly known as *Urfa*, derives its name from Turkish *şanlı*, "famous," and Arabic *ar-ruhā*, itself an alteration of its Syriac name of *urhoy*, that of the Arab people who founded it in 130 B.C. It was also long known as *Edessa*, from the city of this name in northern Greece. The origin of its own name is uncertain.

Sanlúcar de Barrameda. *City and port, southwestern Spain*. The first word of the medieval town's name represents Old Spanish *sant lugar*, "holy place," with reference to a nearby pagan temple dedicated to the morning star Venus. The last word is of Arabic origin and means "sandy gateway," referring to the sandbank that formerly obstructed navigation up the Guadalquivir River here.

San Luis Obispo. *City, southwestern United States*. The California city arose from the Spanish mission of *San Luis Obispo de Tolosa*, "St. Louis, bishop of Toulouse," that was itself founded in 1772. The named saint is the French Franciscan friar and bishop *Louis* of Toulouse (1274–1297), born *Louis* d'Angio.

San Marino. *Republic, southern Europe*. Europe's smallest republic, an enclave in central Italy, takes its name from *St. Marinus*, a deacon of Dalmatian origin who established a hermitage on Monte Titano here in the early 4th century.

San Martín. *Department, northeastern Peru*. The department was formed in 1906 and named for the Argentine soldier and liberator José de *San Martín* (1778–1850).

San Mateo. *City, southwestern United States*. The California city arose around a creek named by Spanish explorers in 1776 after *St. Matthew*.

San Miguel de Allende. *City, north central Mexico*. The city was founded in 1542 by the Franciscan monk Juan de *San Miguel* and is named for him and, subsequently, for Ignacio *Allende* (1779–1811), a Mexican hero of the revolution against Spain.

San Miguel de Tucumán. *City, northwestern Argentina*. The city was founded in 1565 by Spanish colonists and named for *St. Michael*.

The second part of the name refers to a local Native American people, with their own name based on *tukum*, the word for a type of palm tree.

San Pédro. *Town and port, southwestern Côte d'Ivoire*. The name is that of one *Pedro*, a companion of the Portuguese navigators João de Santarém and Pero de Escobar, who came ashore here in 1497.

San Remo. *Town and port, northwestern Italy*. The town was originally known as *San Romulo*, "*St. Romulus*," for the bishop who founded it in the 6th century. In the 15th century the name became *San Remo*, either through confusion with the French saint's name *Rémi* (Italian *Remigio*) or more likely as a contraction of the Latin name *Sancti Romuli in Eremo*, "(church of) St. Romulus in the Hermitage."

San Salvador. *Capital of El Salvador*. The city was founded by Spanish colonists on August 6, 1526, the feastday of the Transfiguration of the *Savior*. Hence the name, Spanish for "Holy Savior." *Cp*. **El Salvador**, **Salvador**.

San Sebastián. *City and port, northern Spain*. The city, first mentioned in 1014, is named for *St. Sebastian*. The reason for the choice of this particular saint is uncertain. It may be because he was supposed to afford protection against the plague, an affliction feared in many parts of southern Europe in medieval times. *Cp*. **São Sebastião**.

Sans Souci *see* **Bogor**

Santa Ana. *City, western United States*. The California city, a suburb of Los Angeles, is named for *St. Anne*, mother of the Virgin Mary. The name was given to the river here on July 28, 1769, two days after St. Anne's day, by the soldiers of the expedition led by Gaspar de Portolá, Spanish governor of the Californias. The padres had actually bestowed on the stream "*el dulcísimo nombre de Jesús de los Temblores*" ("the most sweet name of Jesus of the Earthquakes"), because of the earthquakes felt at that time, but the soldiers' name prevailed.

Santa Barbara. *City and resort, southwestern United States*. The coastal site of the California city was so named by the Spanish in 1602 for *St. Barbara*, patron saint of sailors.

Santa Catarina. *State, southern Brazil*. The region here was given various names by early Spanish and Portuguese mapmakers. Its present name is said to have been given by the 16th-century Italian navigator Sebastian Cabot, when in Spanish service, in honor of *St. Catherine* of Alexandria.

Santa Clara. *City, southwestern United States*.

The California city arose around the Spanish mission of *Santa Clara de Asís*, "*St. Clare* of Assisi," itself founded in 1777. St. Clare (1194–1253) was the founder of the Poor Clares, the women's religious order based on that founded by her contemporary, St. Francis.

¹Santa Cruz. *City, eastern Bolivia*. The city was founded by Spanish missionaries on September 14, 1560, the feastday of the Exaltation of the *Cross*. Hence its name, Spanish for "Holy Cross."

²Santa Cruz. *City, southwestern United States*. The California city arose on the site of the Spanish mission *Santa Cruz*, "Holy Cross," itself founded in 1791.

Santa Cruz de Tenerife. *City and port, Canary Islands*. The city, on the island of **Tenerife**, was so named by the Portuguese explorer Ferdinand Magellan, who landed here on September 14, 1520, the feastday of the *Holy Cross*.

¹Santa Fe. *City, southwestern United States*. The state capital of New Mexico was founded in 1610 by Spanish missionaries and originally named *Villa Real de la Santa Fé de San Francisco de Asís*, "royal town of the holy faith of St. Francis of Assisi." The name was later shortened as now.

²Santa Fe. *City, northeastern Argentina*. The city was founded by Spanish missionaries in 1573 as *Santa Fé de Vera Cruz*, "holy faith of the True Cross." The name was subsequently shortened as now.

Santa Isabel *see* **Malabo**

Santa Maria. *City, western United States*. The California city was founded in 1874 and originally named *Central City*. In 1882 it was renamed as now, for *St. Mary*, so adding to the dozens of places already bearing this popular saint's name (not always bestowed in honor of the Virgin Mary).

Santa Monica. *City and resort, southwestern United States*. The California city was laid out in 1875 and named for a nearby spring known by the Spanish name *Las Lágrimas de Santa Monica*, "the tears of *St. Monica*." St. Monica was the mother of St. Augustine of Hippo, and her tears were her expression of sorrow that for many years (until he was 33) her son was not a Christian.

¹Santander. *City and port, northern Spain*. The city is said to derive its name from *St. Hemiterius* (Spanish *Santo Emiterio*), martyred at Calahorra, northern Spain, in the 4th century.

²Santander. *Department, north central Colombia*. The department was established in 1886 and named commemoratively for General Francisco de Paula *Santander* (1792–1840), president of New Granada (Colombia) from 1833 to 1837.

¹**Santarém**. *Town, west central Portugal.* The town's name is an alteration of Portuguese *Santa Irena*, "*St. Irene*," the saint to whom it was dedicated. *Cp.* **Thera**.

²**Santarém**. *City, northern Brazil.* The city was founded in 1661 as a Jesuit mission and named for ¹**Santarém**, Portugal.

Santa Rosa. *City, southwestern United States.* The California city was founded in 1833 and probably named for *St. Rosa* of Lima (1586–1617), the first American saint.

Santiago. *Capital of Chile.* The city was founded in 1541 by the Spanish conquistador Pedro de Valdivia and named by him in honor of *St. James* (Spanish *Santo Iago*), a saint widely venerated in Spain. *See also* **Santiago de Compostela**.

Santiago de Compostela. *City, northwestern Spain.* The city has been a popular place of pilgrimage since the 9th century, for it is here that the shrine of the apostle *St. James* the Great is to be found. Hence the first part of the name, from Spanish *Santo Iago*, "*St. James.*" The second part is traditionally explained as representing Latin *Campus Stellae*, "field of the star," referring to the legend that the tomb containing the saint's relics was revealed by the appearance of a bright star over it, something in the manner of the birth of Jesus. But a more likely origin is in Latin *compos stellae*, "possessing the star," indicating that the city holds the shrine.

Santiago de Cuba. *City, eastern Cuba.* The city was founded in 1514 by Diego Velázquez, first governor of **Cuba**, and named for *St. James* (Spanish *Santo Iago*), Spain's most popular saint.

Santiago de los Caballeros. *City, northern Dominican Republic.* The city was founded in 1494 by Christopher Columbus (or in 1495 by his brother Bartolomeo) and named for *St. James* (Spanish *Santo Iago*), the most widely venerated saint in Spain. The second part of the name was added in 1504 when 30 *caballeros* ("knights") of the Order of St. James moved here from nearby La Isabela.

Santo Domingo. *Capital of Dominican Republic.* The city's name is Spanish for "Holy Sunday." It was originally the name of the island itself, given in 1697 in commemoration of the fact that the Spanish had established a colony here on a *Sunday* in 1496. The island had actually been discovered four years earlier by Columbus, who named it simply *la isla española*, "the Spanish island." This was later corrupted to **Hispaniola**, as if meaning "little Spain." From 1936 through 1961 Santo Domingo was known as *Ciudad Trujillo*, "*Trujillo* city," commemorating

the Dominican army officer and statesman Rafael *Trujillo* de Molina (1891–1961). The city reverted to its original name when his oppressive rule led to his assassination. *See also* **Dominican Republic**.

Santorin *see* **Thera**

Santos. *City and port, southeastern Brazil.* The city was founded by the Portuguese in 1543 on the site of the Native American village of *Enguaga-çe* ("big pestle") and named for the Hospital of *Todos os Santos* ("All Saints") in Lisbon.

Santos Dumont. *Town, southeastern Brazil.* The town, originally called *Palmyra* (*see* ¹**Palmyra**), was renamed as now in the 1930s for the Brazilian aviation pioneer Alberto *Santos-Dumont* (1873–1932), who was born here.

São Caetano do Sul. *City, southeastern Brazil.* The city, now an industrial suburb of São Paolo, was founded by Benedictine monks in 1631 and named for *St. Cajetan* (1480–1547), Italian founder of the Theatine order, a congregation of clergy bound by vows. The addition to the name means "southern," by contrast with *São Caetano de Odivelas* in the north of the country.

São Leopoldo. *City, southern Brazil.* The city, the first German colony in southern Brazil, was founded in 1824 and named for Dona Maria *Leopoldina* (1797–1826), wife of the Brazilian emperor Dom Pedro I (1798–1834). The name was subsequently masculinized. *Cp.* **Petrolina**.

São Luís. *City and port, northeastern Brazil.* The city, on the island of **Maranhão**, and thus formerly known as *São Luíz do Maranhão*, was founded in 1612 by the French naval officer Daniel de la Touche de la Ravardière and named nominally for *Louis* XIII of France (1601–1643) but actually for *St. Louis*, otherwise *Louis* IX of France (1214–1270). The city was thus originally known as *St.-Louis*, and the Portuguese adopted the name in their own language when they captured it in 1615.

Saône. *River, eastern France.* The river's name probably derives from that of a primitive Celtic or pre–Celtic river god, perhaps originally called something like *Sauc*, to which was added the Gaulish suffix -*onna*, "river." Its historical name is *Arar*, from the Indoeuropean root word *ar*, "river."

São Paolo. *City, western Brazil.* South America's most populous city was founded by two Portuguese priests as a Jesuit mission station on January 25, 1554, the feastday of the Conversion of *St. Paul* (Portuguese *São Paolo*).

São Sebastião. *Island, southeastern Brazil.* The island is said to have been discovered by Amerigo

Vespucci on January 20, 1502, feastday of *St. Sebastian*. The saint was often invoked against the plague in potentially insalubrious spots, as here, and this could explain the particular choice of name.

São Tomé. *Island, Gulf of Guinea, western Africa*. The island, which with **Príncipe** forms a republic, was discovered by the Portuguese on December 21, 1471, the feastday of *St. Thomas* (Portuguese *São Tomé*).

São Vicente. *Island, Cape Verde*. The name of the Portuguese island dedicates it to *St. Vincent* (*see* **St. Vincent**).

Sapporo. *City, northern Japan*. The city, in the island of Hokkaido, has a name meaning "pavilion of banknotes," from Japanese *satsu*, "paper money," and *horo*, "tent," "pavilion." It was founded in 1871 by the Japanese government as a center for the commercial development of the island.

Saragossa. *City, northeastern Spain*. The city's name is an English form of its Spanish name *Zaragoza*. This is itself a corruption, through Arabic, of its Roman name *Caesarea Augusta*, referring to the emperor *Caesar Augustus*, under whom it became a Roman colony in 27 B.C.

Sarajevo. *Capital of Bosnia-Hercegovina*. The present city was effectively founded by the Turks in the 15th century and originally named *Bosna-Saray*, the first part of this for the *Bosna* River here (*see* **Bosnia-Hercegovina**), the second part as the Turkish word for "palace." The present name is the Slavic adjectival form of this, i.e. "(town) of the palace."

Sarangpur. *City, central India*. The city, in Madhya Pradesh state, rose to importance in the 13th century under *Sarang* Singh Khichi, and is named for him.

Saransk. *City, western Russia*. The city was founded in 1641 on the *Insar* River and is named for it. The river's own name means "big marsh." The added *-an-* of the placename is unexplained.

Sarasota. *City and resort, southeastern United States*. The Florida city's name appears on maps of the 1700s in such forms as *Sara Zota* and *Sarasote*. This is said to represent the name of a nearby Seminole village, meaning "point of rocks."

Saratoga Springs. *City and resort, eastern United States*. The New York city, with its many natural mineral *springs*, arose in the late 18th century on the site of an old Indian camping ground named *Sa-ragh-to-ga*, "place of swift water."

Saratov. *City, southwestern Russia*. The city has a name of Tatar origin, from *sary*, "yellow," and *tau*, "mountain." It was founded in 1590 on the high right bank of the Volga River, where the

country is mountainous, and where one of the mountains, now called *Sokolovaya*, has yellowish slopes.

Sarawak. *State, central Malaysia*. The name of the state, in northwestern Borneo, is said to be a corruption of the Malay name *Sarakaw*, meaning "the cove."

Sárbogárd. *Town, west central Hungary*. The first part of the town's name is from the *Sárvíz* River here, itself from Hungarian *sár*, "mud," and *víz*, "water." The second part is the personal name *Bogárd* (from *bogár*, "beetle").

Sardinia. *Island, western Mediterranean Sea*. The island, west of (and belonging to) Italy, has a name that may have originated as that of a local deity or have derived from an Iberian people, the *Sards*, who emigrated here from northern Africa. The original form of the name is uncertain. The Phoenicians knew the island as *Shardan*, and this name was found on a Punic stele dating from the 7th century B.C. *Sardinia* is properly the Roman form of the name.

Sargasso Sea. *Ocean area, North Atlantic*. The relatively calm expanse of ocean is so named for the seaweed of the *Sargassum* genus found floating here in huge masses. The seaweed gets its own name from Portuguese *sargaço*, itself perhaps from *sargo*, a type of grape, referring to its berrylike air sacs.

Sarh. *City, southern Chad*. Chad's second largest town is named for its dominant ethnic group, the *Sara*. It was earlier known as *Fort-Archambault*, for the French colonial officer, Lieutenant Gustave *Archambault* (1872–1899).

Sark. *Island, Channel Islands, western English Channel*. The fourth largest of the five main Channel Islands has a name of uncertain origin. Recent research has shown that the island's Roman name was probably *Caesarea*, a name formerly assigned to Jersey, the largest island. This is popularly connected with Julius *Caesar*, but probably evolved from some earlier name. The French name of Sark is *Sercq*.

Sarmiento, Mt. *Mountain, southern Chile*. The peak, in Tierra del Fuego, takes its name from the Spanish explorer Pedro *Sarmiento* de Gamboa (1532–?1592), author of a history of the Incas.

Sarnia. *City and lake port, southeastern Canada*. The Ontario city, on Lake Huron, was founded in 1833 and named in 1836 for what was then popularly regarded as the Roman name of **Guernsey**, in the Channel Islands. (It was actually that of Herm.) The name was proposed by Sir John Colborne, who had been governor of Guernsey before his appointment as lieutenant governor of Upper Canada.

Sarthe. *River, northwestern France.* The river derives its name from the Indoeuropean root element *ser* or *sar*, "to flow."

Sárvár. *Town, western Hungary.* The town's original name was *Sársziget*, "muddy island," from Hungarian *sár*, "mud," and *sziget*, "island," referring to its location by the Gyöngös River. The second part of the name became *vár*, "fortress," when a castle was built here in the 14th century.

Sasebo. *City, southwestern Japan.* The city, in the island of Kyushu, derives its name from Japanese *sa*, "to help," *se*, "generation," "world," and *ho*, "guarantee."

Saskatchewan. *Province, western Canada.* The province takes its name from the river that runs across it from the Rocky Mountains to Lake Winnipeg. Its own name has evolved from its Cree name, *kis-is-ska-tches-wani-sipi*, "rapid-flowing river."

Saskatoon. *City, western Canada.* The Saskatchewan city derives its name from Cree *mis-sask-guah-too-min*, "fruit of the tree of many branches," the name of a kind of serviceberry. The name was chosen in 1882 for the town, a proposed temperance colony, by its founder, John H. Lake of Toronto.

Sassandra. *Town and port, southern Côte d'Ivoire.* The name is said to be a contraction of *Santo Andrea*, "St. Andrew," given by the Portuguese explorers João de Santarém and Pero de Escobar when they landed here on November 30, 1497, St. *Andrew*'s Day.

Satara. *Town, western India.* The town, in Maharashtra state, was named for the 17 gates and towers of its fort, from Marathi *satarā*, "seventeen."

Satpura Range. *Hill range, western India.* The range, part of the Deccan plateau, has a name meaning "seven folds," from Hindi *sat*, "seven," and *purā*, "apartment," "fold."

Satu Mare. *City, northwestern Romania.* The name of the city, near the Hungarian border, is usually explained as meaning "large village," from Romanian *sat*, "village," and *mare*, "big." But it is actually a modified form of the original Hungarian name *Szatmár*, a personal name of Turkic origin (probably originally *Szákmar*), perhaps that of the first governor of the medieval castle here.

Saudi Arabia. *Kingdom, southwestern Asia.* The country was founded in 1932 by the Muslim leader Ibn Sa'ud (1880–1953), and is named for him. His name derives from Arabic *sa'd*, "good fortune," "happiness," but it is purely a coincidence that the main part of the Arabian peninsula was known to the Romans as *Arabia Felix*, "Arabia the fortunate." (*See* **Yemen**.)

Sauerland. *Region, northwestern Germany.* The region's name means "bitter land," alluding to the relatively poor soil and rugged terrain. Folk etymology, however, relates the name to the fierce ("bitter") resistance of its indigenous Saxon people to Charlemagne and the Franks.

Sault Sainte Marie. *City, southeastern Canada.* The city is named for its location at the *falls* (obsolete French *sault*) on St. *Mary*'s River between Lake Huron and Lake Superior. The falls themselves were named (for St. *Mary*) by French missionaries in 1668. The Canadian city lies opposite the identically named city in Michigan, USA.

Saumur. *Town, western France.* The town had the Medieval Latin name *Salmurus*. This represents pre–Celtic *sala*, "marshland," and a second element of unknown meaning.

Savannah. *City and port, southeastern United States.* The Georgia city was founded in 1733 and named for the river at the mouth of which it lies. The river was probably named for a local Native American people, who were themselves named by the Spanish for the *savanna*-like grassy plain here.

Savonlinna. *Town, southeastern Finland.* The name derives from *Savonia*, a historic region of this part of Finland, and Finnish *linna*, "fortress." The Swedish name of the town is *Nyslott*, "new castle." The town arose around the 15th-century *Olavinlinna* (Swedish *Olofsborg*, "Olaf's fortress").

Savoy. *Historic region, southeastern France.* The region had the Roman name of *Sapaudia*, but the origin and meaning of this are unknown. The French form of the name is *Savoie*.

Savyon. *Settlement, western Israel.* The Jewish urban settlement, now a suburb of Tel Aviv, was founded in 1954 by South African immigrants and given a Hebrew name meaning "dandelion," a plant that grew in profusion here.

Sawatch Mountains. *Mountain range, west central United States.* The range of the Rocky Mountains in Colorado is named from a Native American (Ute) word meaning "spring of blue earth."

Saxony. *Region, southeastern Germany.* The region takes its name from its indigenous people, the *Saxons*, whose own name derives from Old High German *sahs* (Old English *seax*), "single-bladed sword," the weapon they favored. The word originally applied to a stone dagger, and is an altered form of Latin *saxum*, "stone," "rock." The root word also gave *Saksa* as the

Finnish name of Germany, while the German name of Saxony itself is *Sachsen* and the French *Saxe*.

Scafell. *Mountain, northwestern England*. The bare mountain, in the Lake District, Cumbria, has a name of Scandinavian origin meaning "bald-head hill," from Old Norse *skalli*, "bald head" (English *skull*) and *fjall*, "hill" (English *fell*). Scafell gave the name of nearby *Scafell Pike*, England's highest mountain. *Pike* means "pointed summit."

Scandinavia. *Region, northwestern Europe*. The composite name for Norway and Sweden, with the addition of Denmark (and often also Finland and Iceland), evolved from *Scania*, the Roman name for the region, with the addition of a Germanic element *aujo* (the *-avia*) meaning "island." The meaning of *Scania* is uncertain. It may also be "island." It is represented today by *Skåne*, the name of a historic province of southern Sweden (now also a county). An alternate name for the region is *Norden*, "the north," used to avoid the physiographic and cultural limitations of the regular name and to distinguish the countries from the rest of continental Europe.

Scapa Flow. *Sea basin, northern Scotland*. The large natural anchorage in the Orkney Islands has a Scandinavian name meaning "sea bay of the boat isthmus," from Old Norse *skalpr*, "boat" (related to English *scalp*), *eith*, "isthmus," and *flóa*, "flood," "bay." The "isthmus" is the stretch of land south of Kirkwall, forming the bay's eastern shore.

[1]**Scarborough**. *Town and port, northeastern England*. The North Yorkshire resort is said to take its name from its 10th-century Viking founder, Thorgils *Skarthi* (Thorgils Harelip). If so, the name means "*Skarthi*'s fortified place." An alternate origin derives the name from Old Norse *skarth*, "gap," and *berg*, "hill." A "hill by a gap" well describes the topography, with the "gap" being the valley through which the town is approached from the south. But early forms of the name point to the first etymology.

[2]**Scarborough**. *City, southeastern Canada*. The Ontario city, originally known as *Glasgow*, was renamed in 1793 at the suggestion of the wife of John G. Simcoe, lieutenant governor of Upper Canada, since the bluffs here by Lake Ontario reminded her of the cliffs at [1]*Scarborough*, England.

Schaffhausen. *Town, north central Switzerland*. The town has a German name meaning "sheephouse," from early forms of *Schaf*, "sheep," and *Haus*, "house." The town is first mentioned

in 1045 and there must have been a sheepshed here some time before that. The name does thus not mean "ship house," as sometimes popularly explained, with supposed reference to the warehouses in which ships coming up the Rhine here stored their cargoes. The French form of the name is *Schaffhouse*.

Scheldt. *River, western Europe*. The river, rising in France and flowing through Belgium to enter the North Sea in the Netherlands, had the Roman name of *Scaldis*. This appears to derive from a pre–Latin root element meaning "shallow." The French know the river as the *Escaut*, the Belgians as the *Schelde*.

Schenectady. *City, eastern United States*. The New York city was founded as a Dutch settlement in 1661 and named for the nearby Mohawk village of *Schaunactada*, its own name said to mean "other side of the pinelands."

Schiedam. *Town, southwestern Netherlands*. The town, chartered in 1273, is named for an early *dam* on the *Schie* River here. *Cp.* **Amsterdam, Edam, Rotterdam**.

Schlangenbad. *Village, western Germany*. The village, a resort with warm springs, arose in 1700 around two bathhouses. Its name means "snake bath," referring to the Aesculapian snake (*Elaphe longissima*), a type of harmless climbing snake, found locally. In classical times the snake was sacred to Aesculapius, the god of medicine, and it was deliberately introduced to health resorts by the Romans. (In art, Aesculapius is shown carrying a staff with a snake coiled around it.)

Schleswig-Holstein. *State, northwestern Germany*. The present state evolved from the 15th-century union of the two duchies of *Schleswig* and *Holstein*. The former takes its name from the town and port here, itself with a name meaning "trading place on the *Schlei*," for the inlet of the Baltic here, its own name meaning "muddy one." The latter has a name meaning "woodland settlers," from early forms of German *Holz*, "wood," and *siedeln*, "to settle." The second half of the historic dative form *Holtsaten* later became associated with German *Stein*, "stone," to give the present form of the name.

Schmalkalden. *Town, central Germany*. The town takes its name from the small river here, its own name meaning "little cold one," from Old High German *smal*, "small," "little," and *kalt*, "cold."

Schouten Islands. *Island group, southwestern Pacific*. The islands, north of (and belonging to) Papua New Guinea, are named for the Dutch explorer Willem *Schouten* (?1567–1625), the first European to visit them in 1616. They should not be confused with the Indonesian islands of the same name off the north coast of Irian Jaya, now usually known as *Supiori*, from their main island.

Schwabach. *City, southern Germany.* The city arose on the site of a Frankish royal palace by the small river of the same name, meaning "river of the *Swabians*" (*cp.* **Swabia**).

Schwäbisch Gmünd. *City, southwestern Germany.* The first word of the name refers to the town's location at the foot of the *Schwäbische Alb* (Swabian Alps). The second relates to the many river and stream confluences locally (German *Mündung*, "mouth," "confluence.").

Schwäbisch Hall. *City, southern Germany.* The name translates as "Swabian *Hall*," the first word denoting the city's location in the historic region of **Swabia**, the second referring to its saline springs and salt trade, from Middle High German *hal*, "saltworks." *Cp.* **Halle**, **Solbad Hall**.

Schwalmstadt. *Town, central Germany.* The town derives its name from the *Schwalm* River on which it lies, with German *Stadt*, "town." The river's name derives from Old High German *swellan*, "to rise," "to bubble up" (English *swell*).

Schwechat. *Town, northeastern Austria.* The town takes its name from the river on which it lies. The river's name goes back to Old High German *swehhan*, "to stink," presumably referring to a sewer here.

Schwedt. *City, eastern Germany.* The city, formally known as *Schwedt an der Oder*, for its location by the West *Oder* River, is first mentioned as a town in 1265. Its name is of Slavic origin, from a word related to Russian *svet*, "light," perhaps referring to a forest clearing here.

Schweinfurt. *City, central Germany.* The city, on the Main River, derives its name from Old High German *swīn*, "swine," "pig," and *furt*, "ford." The reference is to a ford where pigs regularly crossed the river, as oxen did at **Ochsenfurt**, further south on the same river.

Schwerin. *City, northern Germany.* The city derives its name, first recorded in the 11th century, from Old Polabian *zverin*, "game enclosure," from *zver*, "wild animal," "beast."

Schwyz. *Town, central Switzerland.* The town, in the canton of the same name, was originally a village called *Suittes*, perhaps from Old High German *suedan*, "to burn," referring to a region of forest cleared by burning. It was *Schwyz* that gave the name of **Switzerland** as a whole.

Scilly, Isles of. *Island group, southwestern England.* The islands, southwest of Land's End, Cornwall, have a name of uncertain origin. It may be connected with that of the Roman god

Sulis, who gave *Aquae Sulis* as the Roman name of **Bath**. The final *-y* may represent Old Norse *ey*, "island," although it is not clear whether the name originally applied to a single island or to the group as a whole. The *c* was added in the 16th or 17th century for distinction from the word *silly*, which originally meant "blissful" (aptly for these British "islands of the blessed"), but which later meant "foolish."

Scotia Sea. *Region of South Atlantic.* The sea, southeast of the Falkland Islands and South America, is named for the ship *Scotia* in which members of the Scottish National Antarctic Expedition visited this region in 1902–04. *See also* **Scotland**.

Scotland. *Country, northern Great Britain.* The former kingdom takes its name from its indigenous people, the *Scots*. They originated as Celtic raiders from northern Ireland who crossed to settle in what was then known as *Caledonia* in the 5th and 6th centuries. By about the 9th century, *Caledonia* was being called *Scotia* in Latin texts. (*Cp.* **Nova Scotia**.) The ultimate meaning of their name is uncertain, although some authorities link it with Old Welsh *ysgthru*, "to cut," referring to the people's custom of tattooing themselves. *Caledonia* took its name from another people, the *Caledons*. Their name is similarly obscure, but a source in Celtic *kal*, "hard," has been suggested, as a figurative description for people who were hardy. The name is familiar from the *Caledonian Canal*, which extends across Scotland from the North Sea to the Atlantic.

Scotts Bluff. *Promontory, central United States.* The promontory, or *bluff*, on the North Plate River in western Nebraska, is named for the fur trader Hiram *Scott*, who died here. He was a member of the Bonneville expedition of 1832.

Scottsdale. *City, southwestern United States.* The Arizona city, now a suburb of Phoenix, is named for Winfield *Scott* (1837–1910), who settled the site in 1895. There is no obvious *dale* or valley here, although several canals run across the city.

Scranton. *City, eastern United States.* The Pennsylvania city was originally settled in 1788 under the name *Deep Hollow*. It was then known as *Unionville*, *Slocum Hollow*, and *Harrison* before it was finally named as now in 1851, for the *Scranton* family who established the Lackawanna Iron and Coal Company here in 1840.

Scunthorpe. *Town, eastern England.* The Lincolnshire town has a Scandinavian name meaning "*Skúma's* outlying settlement," with the Danish personal name followed by Old Norse *thorp*, a term for an outlying farm dependent on a larger one. Most English places named *thorp* have remained small villages, but Scunthorpe grew rapidly in the 19th century when iron-ore deposits were discovered here.

Scutari *see* (1) **Shkodër**, (2) **Üsküdar**

Scythia. *Historic region, eastern Europe/western Asia*. The precise boundaries of the historic region are uncertain, but it lay generally north of the Black Sea in what is now Ukraine, with a central point in the Crimea. The name is that of the people formerly here. Their own name goes back to an Indoeuropean root word *sku*, "shepherd," describing their nomadic way of life.

Sde Eliyahu. *Kibbutz, northern Israel*. The kibbutz was founded in 1939 with a Hebrew name meaning "*Eliyahu*'s field," for *Eliyahu* Gutmacher (1796–1875), one of the first rabbis to represent religious Zionism. "Field" here means cultivated land.

Sde Nahum. *Kibbutz, northeastern Israel*. The kibbutz was founded in 1937 with a Hebrew name meaning "*Nahum*'s field," for the Zionist leader *Nahum* Sokolov (1859–1936).

Sde Warburg. *Settlement, western Israel*. The cooperative settlement, in the Plain of Sharon, was founded in 1938 and given a Hebrew name meaning "*Warburg*'s field," for Otto *Warburg* (1859–1938), third president of the World Zionist Organization.

Sde Yaakov. *Settlement, northwestern Israel*. The cooperative settlement was founded in 1923 with a Hebrew name meaning "*Jacob*'s field," for Rabbi Isaac *Jacob* Reines (1839–1915), founder of the Mizrachi movement.

Sdot Yam. *Kibbutz, western Israel*. The kibbutz, founded in 1940 as a fishing settlement on the Mediterranean coast, has a Hebrew name meaning "fields of the sea."

Seattle. *City and port, northwestern United States*. The Washington city was founded in 1853 and named for *Seatlh* (c.1790–1866), a Native American chief who befriended white settlers here. It is said that Seatlh objected to the adoption of his name for the growing town, since his eternal sleep would be interrupted every time a mortal mentioned it. (Hence the title of the 1993 movie, *Sleepless in Seattle*.)

Sebastopol *see* **Sevastopol**

Sebeş. *Town, central Romania*. The town is one of the original seven founded by Saxon colonists in Transylvania in the 12th and 13th centuries. Hence its Hungarian name *Szászsebes*, from *szász*, "Saxon," and the river name *Sebes* ("swift"), now alone remaining. The town's German name is *Mühlbach*, "millstream."

Sebnitz. *City, eastern Germany*. The city, near the border with the Czech Republic, has a name representing Slavic *zhabnitsa*, "pond," a word itself based on *zhaba*, "toad." The name was recorded in 1223 as *Sabniza*.

Secunderabad. *City, south central India*. The town, in Andhra Pradesh state, was founded in 1806 in the name of *Sikander* Jah (Asaf Jah III) of the Nizam dynasty of Hyderabad, with Iranian *ābād*, "inhabited place," "town," added.

Sedan. *Town, northeastern France*. The town's name may derive from Gaulish *setu*, "long," although the precise sense of this is uncertain.

Segovia. *City, central Spain*. The city, founded in the 8th century B.C., derives its name from Celtic *sego*, "strong," "powerful," implying a fortified settlement.

Seinäjoki. *Town, western Finland*. The name derives from Finnish *seinä*, "wall," and *joki*, "river."

Seine. *River, northern France*. The river had the Roman name of *Sequana*, perhaps itself deriving from Celtic *soghan*, "calm," or from a pre–Celtic root *sec*, meaning "to spring," "to gush," as a general term for flowing water. *See also* **Sologne**.

Selenga. *River, north central Asia*. The river, rising in Mongolia and flowing generally north then west into Lake Baikal, Russia, derives its name from Evenki *sele*, "yellow," referring to the yellowish iron-ore deposits found in its valley.

Sélestat. *Town, northwestern France*. The Medieval Latin name of the town was *Scalistatus*. This represents Old High German *sclade*, "marshland," and *state*, "place." These words gave the town's modern German name of *Schlettstadt*.

Seleucia. *Historic city, southern Turkey*. There are several ancient cities of the name in what are now Turkey and Syria, and in each case they derive from one or other of the dynasty of kings known as the *Seleucids*, whose founder in the 4th century B.C. was *Seleucus* Nicator, the Macedonian general of Alexander the Great. Their name is popularly derived from Greek *selas*, "brightness."

Selinus. *Historic city, southern Italy*. The ancient Greek city in southern Sicily derives its name from Greek *selinon*, "parsley," "wild celery," a plant that still grows locally.

Selkirk. *Town, southeastern Scotland*. The name of the town means "church by the hall," from Old English *sele*, "dwelling," "house," "hall," and either Old English *cirice* or Old Norse *kirkja*, "church."

Selkirk Mountains. *Mountain range, south-*

western Canada. The range, a section of the Columbia Mountains in British Columbia, is named for Thomas Douglas, 5th Earl of *Selkirk* (1771–1820), a philanthropic backer of settlements in Canada.

Semarang. *City and port, southern Indonesia.* The city, in northern Java, has a local name meaning "nest," perhaps referring to the abundance of fish here.

Semey. *City and river port, northeastern Kazakhstan.* The city, founded in 1718, was originally known as *Kamennyye mecheti,* "stone mosques." It then took its familiar Russian name *Semipalatinsk,* meaning "seven chambers," from the nearby ruins of a Buddhist monastery with seven buildings. The name was modified as now in 1994 following Kazakhstan's independence in 1991.

Semipalatinsk *see* **Semey**

Semmering Pass. *Mountain pass, eastern Austria.* The pass, through the Eastern Alps, is said to derive its name from a Germanic corruption of an earlier Slavic name *Smrnik,* itself based on *smrk* (the *r* serving as a vowel), "pine forest."

Sendai. *City, north central Japan.* The city, in the island of Honshu, derives its name from Japanese *sen,* "hermit," and *dai,* "stand," "pedestal."

Senegal. *Republic, western Africa.* The country takes its name from its main river, which forms the northern border with Mauritania. Its own name may derive from a local word meaning "navigable."

Senegambia. *Coastal region, western Africa.* The name, officially adopted for the confederation of **Senegal** and **Gambia** (1982–89), was already in use in the late 19th century.

Senglea. *Town, eastern Malta.* The town was founded in 1554 by Claude de la *Sengle,* grand master of the Knights of Malta, and is named for him.

Senigallia. *Town, central Italy.* The town takes its name from the *Senonian Gauls* who founded it in the 6th century B.C. In 289 B.C. it accordingly became the Roman colony of *Sena Gallica.* Cp. **Sens.**

Senlis. *Town, northern France.* The Roman name of the town was *Civitas Silvanectum,* from the *Silvanectes,* the Gaulish people who inhabited the region, and their name (based on Gaulish *selua,* "possession") gave the present name.

Sens. *Town, north central France.* The town was known to the Romans as *Senones,* and was the capital of the Gaulish people of this name. Their name itself may be based on Gaulish *senos,* "old."

Seoul. *Capital of South Korea.* The city's name represents Korean *soul,* meaning simply "capital." Seoul was the capital of (unified) Korea from 1392 to 1910, when the country was annexed to Japan.

Sept-Îles. *City and port, eastern Canada.* The Quebec city, on the St. Laurence estuary, has a French name meaning "seven islands." There are actually only six true islands here, the seventh being a part of the mainland that resembles one. The city is also known by the English name *Seven Islands.*

Septimania. *Historic region, southern France.* The region, between the Pyrenees and the Rhône River, derives its name from Latin *septimanus,* "of the seventh." The reference is probably to a colony of veteran Roman soldiers of the *Seventh Legion* based here, although in early medieval times the region also comprised *seven* cities or dioceses.

Serampur. *Town, eastern India.* The West Bengal town was founded in 1799 as a Danish settlement named *Fredriksnagar,* "Frederick's town," for *Frederick* VI of Denmark (1768–1839). Its present name is a corruption of *Sriramapur,* "city of holy *Rama,*" for *Rama,* an incarnation of the god Vishnu.

Serbia. *Republic, southeastern Europe.* The country takes its name from its indigenous inhabitants, the *Serbs.* Their own name may have evolved from a Caucasian root word *ser* simply meaning "man." In 2003 Serbia joined neighboring **Montenegro** to form the new republic *Serbia and Montenegro* from the former **Yugoslavia.**

Serendip *see* **Sri Lanka**

Sergiyev Posad. *City, western Russia.* The city's name means "*Sergius*'s trading quarter," referring to the monastery of the Holy Trinity and St. *Sergius* here, founded in 1337–40 by St. *Sergius* of Radonezh. In 1919 the name was abbreviated to *Sergiyev.* In 1930 it was changed altogether to *Zagorsk,* for the Russian revolutionary Vladimir *Zagorsky* (1883–1919), killed in the Civil War. The town reverted to its original name in 1991.

Seringapatam. *Town, southern India.* The town, in Karnataka state, is named for its 12th-century temple, dedicated to *Sri Ranga,* an epithet, meaning "holy pleasure," of the Hindu god Vishnu. The town's name is thus a corruption of *Srirangapatnam,* "town of *Sri Ranga.*"

Serov. *City, west central Russia.* The city arose in 1894 around an ironworks producing rails for the Trans-Siberian Railroad and was originally called *Nadezhdinsk,* for *Nadezhda* Polovtseva, the works owner. In the 1930s the city was briefly renamed *Kabakovsk*, for the Soviet Communist official Ivan Dmitriyevich *Kabakov* (1891–1937), a victim of the Great Purge, but in 1939 was named as now for Anatoly *Serov* (1910–1939), a Soviet pilot who was born near here and who was killed in an air crash.

Serpukhov. *City, western Russia.* The city, dating from at least the 14th century, is said to take its name from a Russian dialect word *serpukh* meaning "sickle." But it may actually represent a river name. The city itself is on the Ob.

Sesto San Giovanni. *City, northern Italy.* The city, now an industrial suburb of Milan, derives the first word of its name from Italian *sesto*, "sixth," in turn from Latin *sextus*, denoting a location by a *sixth* Roman milestone. The rest of the name is a dedication to *St. John*. Similar names are found elsewhere in Italy, as *Sesto Fiorentino*, near **Florence**.

Sète. *Town, southern France.* The town derives its name from the pre–Indoeuropean root element *set*, "mountain," referring to nearby Mont St.-Clair. The name was spelled *Cette* from the 17th century down to 1936, and a whale (Latin *cetus*) appears in the town's canting coat of arms.

Sete Lagoas. *City, eastern Brazil.* The city has a Portuguese name meaning "seven lakes."

Setonaikai *see* **Inland Sea**

Setúbal. *City and port, southwestern Portugal.* The city's name evolved from its Roman name of *Cetobriga*, from Celtic words meaning "wooded hill." English sailors at one time corrupted the name to *St. Ubes*.

Sevagram. *Town, west central India.* The town, in Maharashtra state, was originally known as *Segoam*. It was given its present name by Mahatma Gandhi, who settled here in 1936 to create a model community. The name means "village of service," from Hindi *sevā*, "service," and *grām*, "village."

Sevan, Lake. *Lake, eastern Armenia.* The lake derives its name from Armenian *sev*, "black," "dark," referring to the color of the water.

Sevastopol. *City and port, southern Ukraine.* The city, in the southwestern Crimea, was founded in 1784 and in the manner of the day given a name of Greek origin, in this case meaning "great city," from *sebastos*, "reverenced," "august," and *polis*, "city." Sevastopol was awarded the title of "Hero City" for its resistance against German forces in World War II, a title coincidentally close to its actual name, given the definition of a hero as a man of bravery who is revered for his noble achievement.

Sevenoaks. *Town, southeastern England.* The Kent town has a name that means what it says, referring to *seven oaks* here at one time. There was probably a medieval legend connected with the name, and the number itself may simply have indicated a plurality. Various groups of seven oaks have been planted over the years as a visible evocation of the name, the most recently in 1955. (Six of these were blown down in the 1987 storms, but were replaced within weeks.)

> The White Hart Hotel on the Tonbridge Road is 700 feet above sea level ... and about a mile from the centre of the town. Near this Hotel are the SEVEN OAKS, from which the town is assumed to have taken its name. But if this is so, these cannot be the original trees, as Sevenoaks is first mentioned in a Pre-Conquest document. So one must assume the trees standing to-day were planted on the same spot as the original ones. Other oaks have since been planted — seven at the North end of the Vine Cricket Ground to commemorate the Coronation of King Edward VII [in 1902], and seven saplings of scarlet American Oak planted in 1946 to commemorate the Second World War and as a tribute to our American allies [*The Guide and Handbook to Sevenoaks & District*, 1948].

Severn. *River, eastern Wales/western England.* Britain's longest river has an ancient name of uncertain origin. Tacitus, writing in the 2d century A.D., recorded the name as *Sabrina*. This appears to be of Celtic origin, although no word is known which makes it meaningful. It may be the name of the goddess of the river, as in Milton's "Sabrina fair, / Listen where thou art sitting / Under the glassy, cool, translucent wave" (*Comus*, 1637). The Welsh name of the Severn, of the same origin, is *Hafren*.

Severnaya Zemlya. *Island group, northern Russia.* The islands, in the Arctic Sea, have a generally descriptive Russian name meaning "northern land," and on some English maps actually appear as *Northern Land* or *North Land*. They were discovered in 1913 and were originally named *Emperor Nicholas II Land* (Russian *Zemlya imperatora Nikolaya II*), for the reigning czar. In 1926 they were given their present non-royalist name. There are four main islands with Soviet names, in order of size (and in translation): *October Revolution, Bolshevik, Komsomolets*, and *Pioneer*. (The order grades down from Soviet mainspring to members of adult, youth, and child Communist organizations.)

Severodvinsk. *City and port, northwestern Russia.* The town's name means "Northern

Dvina," from the river near which it lies. From 1938 through 1957 it was known as *Molotovsk*, for the Soviet statesman Vyacheslav *Molotov* (1890–1986), who also gave the former name of **Perm**, among others.

Sevilla. *City, western Colombia.* The city was founded in 1903 with the name *San Luis*, "*St. Louis.*" It was renamed as now, for **Seville** (Spanish *Sevilla*), Spain, when it became a municipality in 1914.

Seville. *City and river port, southwestern Spain.* The city's name is ultimately of Phoenician origin, from *sefela*, "plain," "valley." Seville is an inland port on the Guadalquivir estuary, where the terrain is low-lying. The Spanish form of the name is *Sevilla*.

Sèvre. *River, western France.* There are two rivers of the name that both rise in the department of **Deux-Sèvres**, named for them. One, the *Sèvre Nantaise*, "*Nantes* Sèvre," flows northwest to enter the Loire at **Nantes**. The other, the *Sèvre Niortaise*, "*Niort* Sèvre," flows west through **Niort** to enter the Bay of Biscay. The basic name represents pre–Indoeuropean *sav*, "hollow," with the root element *ar*, "water."

Sèvres. *Town, northern France.* The town, now a suburb of Paris, takes its name from that of a former river here, presumably a tributary of the Seine. It is itself of pre–Indoeuropean origin, and identical to the **Sèvre** of western France.

Seychelles. *Island republic, western Indian Ocean.* The islands were discovered by the Portuguese in 1502 and originally called (the equivalent of) *The Seven Sisters*. In 1742 they were explored by the French naval officer Lazare Picault for the governor of Mauritius, Bertrand François Mahé, comte de la Bourdonnais (*see* **Mahé**), and named by him *La Bourdonnais*. In 1756 the islands were formally annexed by France and were renamed for the French finance minister, Jean Moreau de *Séchelles*. The spelling of the name was later altered by the English, who took the islands from the French in 1794.

Seydhisfjördhur. *Town and port, eastern Iceland.* The town's name derives from Icelandic *seydhis*, "ptisan," "barley water," and *fjördhur*, "fjord," "inlet." The allusion is to the cloudy appearance of the water here.

Sfîntu Gheorghe. *City, central Romania.* The city, named for *St. George*, has the similar Hungarian name *Sepsiszentgyörgy*.

Shaba *see* **Katanga**

Shahjahanpur. *City, northern India.* The city, in Uttar Pradesh state, was founded in 1647 in the reign of the Mogul emperor *Shah Jahan*

(1592–1666) and was named in his honor, with Sanskrit *pur*, "town," added. His own name, really a title, means "king of the world," from Persian *shah*, "king," and *jahan*, "world," and some of this exalted meaning may have rubbed off on the city itself. *Cp.* **Shahpura, Shajapur**.

Shahpura. *Town, northwestern India.* The town, in Rajasthan state, was founded in c.1629 in the reign of the Mughal emperor *Shah Jahan* (1592–1666) and was named for him, with Sanskrit *pur*, "town," added. *Cp.* **Shahjahanpur, Shajapur**.

Shajapur. *Town, central India.* The town, in Madhya Pradesh state, was founded in c.1640 by the Mughal emperor *Shah Jahan* (1592–1666) and was named for him, with Sanskrit *pur*, "town," added. The name is a corruption of *Shahjahanpur*. *Cp.* **Shahjahanpur, Shahpura**.

Shakardarah. *Town, eastern Afghanistan.* The name of the town is Farsi for "sugar valley."

Shaker Heights. *City, northern United States.* The Ohio city, now a residential suburb of Cleveland, was founded in 1905 on the site of *North Union*, a former *Shaker* colony. The second word of the name alludes to the rising terrain here.

Shakhty. *City, western Russia.* The city dates from the early 19th century and developed into a coal-mining center. Hence its name, Russian for "pits." Until 1920 it was known as *Aleksandrovsk-Grushevsky*, for the Russian czar *Alexander* II (1818–1881) and the *Grushevka* River here.

Shamva. *Town, northeastern Zimbabwe.* The town takes its name from the *tsamvi*, a species of wild fig that grows here. It was originally known as *Abercorn*, for James Hamilton, 2d Duke of *Abercorn* (1838–1913), first president of the British South Africa Company.

Shang-ch'iu. *City, eastern China.* The city, in Honan province, derives its name from Chinese *shāng*, "trade," "commerce," and *qiū*, "hill." It arose as a market town at the meeting point of three trading routes.

Shang-chou. *City, eastern China.* The city, in Shensi province, derives its name from Chinese *shāng*, "trade," "commerce," and *zhōu*, "county," referring to the longstanding reputation of its inhabitants as traders.

Shanghai. *City and port, eastern China.* The name of the city essentially means "by the sea," from Chinese *shàng*, "on," "above," and *hǎi*, "sea." Shanghai is on the East China Sea coast near the mouth of the Yangtze.

Shan-hai-kuan. *Town, northeastern China.* The town, in Hopeh province on the coast of the Gulf of Chihli, takes its name from the formerly strategic defile here on the route from Peking to Manchuria. Hence the name, Chinese for "pass between the mountains and the sea," from *shān*, "mountain," *hǎi*, "sea," and *guàn*, "pass."

Shannon. *River, Ireland*. Ireland's longest river has a name meaning something like "old man river," from a Celtic root word related to modern Irish *sean*, "old." The Shannon was probably believed to personify an ancient water god.

Shansi. *Province, northeastern China*. The name of the province means "west of the mountain," from Chinese *shān*, "mountain," and *xī*, "west," referring to its location to the west of the sacred mountain **Tai Shan**. *Cp.* **Shantung**.

Shantung. *Province, northeastern China*. The coastal province has a name meaning "east of the mountain," from Chinese *shān*, "mountain," and *dōng*, "east." The reference is to its location with regard to the sacred mountain **Tai Shan**. *Cp.* **Shansi**.

Shao-hsing. *City, eastern China*. The city, in Chekiang province, derives its name from Chinese *shào*, "to join," and *xīng*, "to prosper."

Shao-kuan. *City, southeastern China*. The city, in Kwangtung province, derives its name from Chinese *sháo*, "harmony," and *guān*, "barrier," "customs post," referring to the city's importance in medieval times as a trading center.

Shao-yang. *City, southeastern China*. The city, in Hunan province, derives its name from Chinese *shào*, "family name," and *yáng*, "sun," "male."

Sharjah. *Emirate, United Arab Emirates*. The name represents Arabic *ash-shārikah*, "the eastern," referring to the emirate's location on the Oman promontory, east of the Persian Gulf.

¹Sharon. *Plain, western Israel*. The coastal plain, extending from Mt. Carmel to Tel Aviv, and mentioned several times in the Bible (1 Chronicles 27:29, etc.), has a name traditionally derived from Hebrew *yashar*, "straight," "flat," in other words "plain," although some derive it from Hebrew *shar*, "singer." The latter sense would presumably relate to its famed fertility: "[The desert] shall blossom abundantly, and rejoice even with joy and singing: the glory of Lebanon shall be given unto it, the excellency of Carmel and Sharon, they shall see the glory of the Lord" (Isaiah 35:2).

²Sharon. *City, eastern United States*. The Pennsylvania city was laid out in 1815 and named for the biblical plain of **¹Sharon** that was rich and fertile.

Sha-shih. *City, eastern China*. The city, in Hupeh province on the Yangtze River, derives its name from Chinese *shā*, "sand," and *shì*, "town," "market."

Shatt al-Arab. *River, southeastern Iraq*. The tidal river, formed by the confluence of the Tigris and the Euphrates, has an Arabic name meaning "river of the Arabs," from *shaṭṭ*, "edge," "bank," "salt lake," *al*, "the," and *'arab*, "Arabs."

Shawinigan. *City, eastern Canada*. The Quebec city, on the St.-Maurice River, takes its name from the nearby *Shawinigan Falls*, themselves named from an Algonquian word meaning "crest," referring to a rocky crest near the falls over which a portage formerly led.

Sheba *see* **Saba**

Sheboygan. *City, northern United States*. The Wisconsin city, on Lake Michigan, takes its name from the river at the mouth of which it lies. The river's own name is Algonquian in origin but of uncertain meaning. An interpretation "reed-like" has been suggested, referring to a tubular object.

Shechem *see* **Nablus**

Sheerness. *Town and port, southeastern England*. The Kent town has a name meaning "bright headland," from Old English *scīr*, "bright," "clear," and *næss*, "headland." The headland on which the town lies was probably "bright" by virtue of its low-lying terrain, overlooking the estuaries of the Thames and Medway.

Shefar'am. *City, northern Israel*. The Arab city was founded on the site of a former Jewish settlement in 1761 by the Bedouin ruler Dahar el-Umar, who named it *Shafa Umar*, "health of Umar," and the present name derives from this.

Sheffield. *City, northern England*. The former South Yorkshire city has a name that means "open land by the *Sheaf*," this being a small river that flows through the middle of the town to enter the larger Don. The river's own name means "dividing one," from Old English *scēath*, "sheath," and it formed the boundary between Derbyshire and the former West Riding of Yorkshire. The second part of the name is Old English *feld*, "open land" (modern *field*).

Shelikhov, Gulf of. *Gulf, eastern Russia*. The gulf, a northern extension of the Sea of Okhotsk, is named for Grigory *Shelikhov* (1747–1795), the Russian merchant who explored this region from 1775. He also made many visits to Russian America (Alaska), where *Shelikov* Strait, between the mainland and Kodiak Island, is similarly named for him.

Shelikov Strait *see* **Shelikhov, Gulf of**

Shenandoah. *River, eastern United States*. The Virginia river has an Algonquian name usually translated as "spruce stream." However, other renderings include "great plains" and even "beautiful daughter of the stars."

Shensi. *Province, eastern China.* The province derives its name from Chinese *shăn*, a proper name with no known meaning, and *xī*, "west." *See also* **China.** The first syllables of the names of the neighboring provinces **Shansi** and Shensi sound identical in Chinese except in tone. Hence the arbitrary alteration in European transliteration of *a* to *e* for the latter. (In the Pinyin transliteration, Shansi is *Shanxi* and Shensi is *Shaanxi*, the latter doubling the *a* for similar differentiation.)

Shen-yang. *City, northeastern China.* The capital of Liaoning province derives its name from Chinese *shĕn*, a river name, and *yáng*, "sun," "male." Its former name as the capital of the Manchu dynasty was *Mukden*, a Manchurian name said to mean "divine wind."

Shepparton. *City, southeastern Australia.* The city, in Victoria, arose in the 1850s and is named for an early settler, Sherbourne *Sheppard*, who took up a sheep run on the site in 1843, when he was 23.

Sheppey, Isle of. *Island, southeastern England.* The island off the north coast of Kent has an Old English name meaning "sheep island," from *scēap*, "sheep," and *īeg*, "island." The island would have been a suitable place for sheep to be kept with its good grazing and its coasts as a natural "pen" to prevent straying.

Sherbrooke. *City, southeastern Canada.* The Quebec city arose as a fur-trading post east of Montreal and in 1818 was named for Sir John *Sherbrooke* (1764–1830), governor general of Canada.

Sherman. *City, southern United States.* The Texas city was founded in the 1840s and named for General Sidney *Sherman* (1805–1873), a cavalry officer during the Texas Revolution.

's Hertogenbosch. *City, southern Netherlands.* The city's Dutch name means "duke's forest," from Old Dutch *des Hertogen Bosch*, comprising *des*, "of the," *hertogen*, genitive of *hertog*, "duke," and *bosch*, "forest." The duke in question is Henry I of Brabant, who founded the city in 1185 and who had a hunting lodge nearby. The French name of the city is *Bois-le-Duc*, with the same meaning.

Sherwood Forest. *Historic forest, central England.* The ancient forest, chiefly in Nottinghamshire, has an Old English name meaning "shire wood." This denotes its special status, as a wood owned by the shire (county), either as a hunting ground or as common pastureland.

Shetland Islands. *Island group, northern Scot-*

land. The name of the northernmost group of Scottish islands probably derives from Old Norse *hjalt*, "hilt," and *land*, "land." The "hiltland" would have been the sword-shaped outline of the islands, or of the group's largest island, Mainland.

Shiga. *Prefecture, south central Japan.* The prefecture, in the island of Honshu, derives its name from Japanese *ji*, "more and more," and *ga*, "compliment."

Shih-chia-chuang. *City, northeastern China.* The capital of Hopeh province derives its name from Chinese *shí*, "stone," "rock," *jiā*, "family," "house," and *zhuāng*, "village."

Shikarpur. *City, southern Pakistan.* The city has a name meaning "town of the hunter," from Hindi *shikārī*, "hunter," and *pur*, "town."

Shikoku. *Island, southern Japan.* The smallest of Japan's main islands has a name meaning "four provinces," from Japanese *shi*, "four," and *koku*, "province." The island is divided into the four prefectures Ehime, Kagawa, Kochi, and Tokushima.

Shiloh. *Historic village, central West Bank.* The ancient holy site, mentioned in the Bible (Joshua 18:1, etc.), may derive its name from an altered form of Hebrew *shalo*, "to be peaceful."

Shimane. *Prefecture, southwestern Japan.* The prefecture, facing the Sea of Japan in the island of Honshu, derives its name from Japanese *shima*, "island," and *ne*, "root," "base."

Shimizu. *City and port, central Japan.* The city, on the south coast of the island of Honshu, derives its name from Japanese *shin*, "China," "Manchuria," and *mizu*, "water." It was long an important post town on the Eastern Sea Highway.

Shimonoseki. *City and port, southern Japan.* The city, in the island of Honshu, has a name meaning "lower barrier," from Japanese *shimo*, "lower," "bottom," *no*, the sign of the genitive case, and *seki*, "barrier," "tollgate."

Shinano. *River, central Japan.* Japan's longest river, in the island of Honshu, derives its name from Japanese *shin*, "faith," and *nō*, "dark," "dense."

Shiraz. *City, southwestern Iran.* The city, famous for its wine, derives its name from Elamite *sher*, "good," and *raz*, "grape." There are said to be 170 different kinds of grapes grown locally.

Shire. *River, southern Africa.* The river, in Malawi and Mozambique, has a name of uncertain origin. It may represents a Nyanja word meaning "woodland," "undergrowth," implying that the river's source is far inland.

Shizuoka. *City, central Japan.* The city, in the

island of Honshu, derives its name from Japanese *shizu*, "still," "calm," and *oka*, "hill."

Shkodër. *City, northwestern Albania*. The city's name ultimately goes back to an Illyrian root word of uncertain form and meaning. The Italian form of the name is *Scutari*, which potentially confuses it with **Üsküdar** in Turkey.

Shlisselburg. *Town, western Russia*. The town on the River Neva east of St. Petersburg arose around the fort that was founded on *Orekhovyj* ("Nut") Island in 1323 and that was originally named for it as *Oreshek*. In 1612 the fort fell to the Swedes and was renamed *Nöteborg*, from Swedish *nöt*, "nut," translating Russian *orekh*, and *borg*, "fort." In 1702 it was recaptured by Russian forces under *Peter* the Great ("This nut was very tough," he wrote, "but, thank God, we cracked it"), and, in his westernizing way, he gave it the German name of *Schlüsselburg*, "key fort," for its strategic position in a line of defense to the Baltic Sea. The following year he founded St. Petersburg. The town that grew up retained the name of the fort until 1944, when it was renamed *Petrokrepost*, "*Peter*'s fortress," from Russian *Pyotr*, "Peter," and *krepost'*, "fortress," commemorating Peter's victory. The timing of the renaming, in the final months of World War II, was intended to imply the Soviet Union's coming victory over the Germans. In 1991 it reverted to the earlier name *Schlüsselburg*, but in the Russian transliterated form *Shlisselburg*.

Sholapur. *City, southwestern India*. The city, in Maharashtra state, has a Hindi name representing *sholā*, "flame," and *pur*, "town."

Shreveport. *City and river port, southern United States*. The Louisiana city derives its name from Henry M. *Shreve* (1785–1851), a river captain and steamboat builder, who in 1835 opened the Red River here for navigation by clearing log jams and who in 1837 helped found the city that bears his name.

Shrewsbury. *Town, western England*. The county town of **Shropshire**, to which it gave its name, derives its own name from conjectural Old English *scrobb*, "scrubland," and *burh*, "fortified place." The origin can be better seen in early records of the name, such as 12th-century *Scrobbesbyrig*. The present spelling of the name may have come about by association with *shrew*, which was formerly pronounced to rhyme with *show*. The name is still usually pronounced "Shrowsbury," although some local people (and those unfamiliar with it) say "Shroosbury." The Welsh name of Shrewsbury is *Amwythig*, "(place) around the trees," a rough translation of the English name.

Shropshire. *County, western England*. The county takes its name from that of its chief town, **Shrewsbury**. It is thus essentially *Shrewsbury-shire*, although the *-bury* of the town name has disappeared and the initial *Scrobbes-* has become *Shrop-*. The conventional abbreviated form of the county name is *Salop*, from a late 11th-century Norman spelling of it as *Salopescira*, with *l* for *r*, as for **Salisbury**. This short form was officially adopted for the county name from 1974 through 1980. The name was unpopular with local people, and especially with the European Member of Parliament for what was then Salop and Staffordshire, who discovered when attending debates in continental Europe that French *salope* means "slut."

Shumen. *City, northeastern Bulgaria*. The city takes its name from the *Shumka* River on which it stands. The river's own name derives from Bulgarian *shuma*, "forest." From 1950 through 1965 Shumen was renamed *Kolarovgrad*, in commemoration of the Bulgarian Communist leader Vasil *Kolarov* (1877–1950), who was born here.

Shurugwi. *Town, central Zimbabwe*. The town was founded in 1899 and took its name from a nearby bare oval granite hill that resembled the shape of a pigpen (*shurugwi*) of the local Venda people. The name was formerly spelled *Selukwe*.

Shwebo. *Town, north central Myanmar*. The town is the birthplace of Alaungpaya, founder of the dynasty that bears his name. It was originally known as *Moksobomyo*, "(town of the) hunter chief," but in c.1753 was renamed as now by Alaungpaya himself, with a meaning "(town of the) golden leader."

Si *see* **Xi Jiang**

Sialkot. *City, eastern Pakistan*. The name ultimately derives from Sanskrit *śṛgālā*, "jackal," so implies "place of jackals."

Siam *see* **Thailand**

Sian. *City, east central China*. The capital of Shensi province has a name meaning "western peace," from Chinese *xī*, "west," and *ān*, "peace," "calm."

Šiauliai. *City, northern Lithuania*. The origin of the city's name is uncertain. It probably comes from a personal name such as *Saul*. The German form of the name is *Schaulen*.

Šibenik. *City and port, southwestern Croatia*. The city's name is found in similar forms for various hill sites in the northern Czech Republic and southeastern Germany. It has been derived from a common Slavic word meaning "gallows" (Russian *shibenitsa*), allegedly because the bodies of hanged criminals were left displayed on such hills by way of a deterrent. In the case of Šibenik, the hill would be the one behind the town on which St. Anne's fortress stands. The name has also been less convincingly derived from the phrase *vetar šiba*, "the wind whips," referring either to the strong winds here or else to the old Slav custom of building huts from wind-strewn withies and branches.

Siberia. *Region, eastern Russia*. The broad region, extending from the Ural Mountains to the Pacific, has a name of disputed origin. The following are contenders: (1) From *Sibir*, the name of a Tatar people; (2) From Mongolian *shiver*, "marsh"; (3) From *Siber*, the name of a legendary hound said to have emerged from the depths of Lake Baikal (a sort of "Beast of Baikal"); (4) From a form of Russian *sever*, "north." The name is certainly an ancient one, and the etymologies proposed here are in descending order of probability, with even the first dubious. The Russian name of Siberia is *Sibir*.

Sibiu. *City, west central Romania*. The city had the Roman name of *Cibinium*, based on that of the *Cibin* River here. Its own name is of uncertain origin, but has been associated with a root word *siba*, "cornel" (a type of dogwood). The Hungarian name of the city is *Nagyszeben*, "big *Cibin*." The German name is quite different, as *Hermannstadt*, "*Hermann*'s town," for one of the colonists from Saxony who refounded it in the 12th century.

Sichuan *see* **Szechwan**

Sicily. *Island, southern Italy*. The island takes its name from its former indigenous inhabitants, the *Siceli* or *Sicani*, with the former, according to ancient writings, driving the latter (who arrived later) to the west. The origin of their name is uncertain, although a meaning "corn reapers" has been suggested,

Sidi Bel Abbès. *City, northwestern Algeria*. The city's name is the equivalent of "Sir Bel Abbes," from Arabic *saydī* or *sīdī*, a title approximating to "Sir," "Saint," and a personal name, that of the marabout (Muslim saint) *bāl-ʿabbās*, whose tomb is here. There are many names of this type in North Africa, with *Sidi* followed by the name of the Muslim saint whose tomb is at the place in question.

Sidi Okba. *Town, central Algeria*. The town takes its name from the Arab warrior and Muslim saint *Okba* ben Nafi, who was killed by Berbers in 684 and whose tomb is here. *Cp*. **Sidi Bel Abbès**.

Sidirokastron. *Town, northeastern Greece*. The name means "iron castle," from modern Greek *sidero*, "iron," and *kastro*, "castle." When under Turkish rule, the town was known similarly as *Demir-Hissar*, from Turkish *demir*, "iron," and *hisar*, "fortress." The meaning is not literal, and denotes a fort built of dark-colored stone while also implying a stronghold. *Cp*. **Vasvár**.

Sidon. *City and port, southwestern Lebanon*. The ancient city, formerly important in Phoenicia, was founded in the 3d millenium B.C. and is mentioned several times in the Bible, mainly in the New Testament (Matthew 11:21, etc.). Its Canaanite name was *Sidunu*, derived from the root *ṣwd*, "hunting," "fishing." The name now often appears on maps as *Saida*.

Siebengebirge. *Hill group, western Germany*. The hills, southeast of Bonn, have a name that means "seven hills." "Seven" should not be taken literally, but simply denotes a plurality, and there are actually around 40 wooded hills in the group. Even so, the seven hills are traditionally named as **Drachenfels**, *Wolkenburg*, *Lohrberg*, *Grosser Ölberg*, *Nonnenstromberg*, *Petersberg*, and *Löwenburg*. (The name should not be confused with *Siebenbürgen*, the German name of **Transylvania**.)

Siedlce. *City, east central Poland*. The city, first recorded in 1448, has a basic Slavic name meaning "settlement" (Russian *seleniye*). *See also* **Inowrocław**.

Siegburg. *Town, western Germany*. The name does not mean "victory castle" (from German *Sieg*, "victory") but "castle on the *Sieg*," for the river here, itself so named from a conjectural pre–Celtic form *Segina*, of uncertain meaning. The original castle here was converted into a Benedictine abbey in 1064 and the town grew up around it.

Siegen. *City, western Germany*. The city, first mentioned in 1089, takes its name from the *Sieg* River here, as for **Siegburg**.

Siena. *City, central Italy*. The city is popularly said to have been named for *Senus*, son of Remus, its supposed founder. It is more likely, however, to have come from the *Senones*, the Gaulish people who settled here in ancient times. Their own name may derive from Gaulish *senos*, "old." *Cp*. **Sens**.

Sierra Leone. *Republic, western Africa*. The name literally means "lion mountains," from Spanish *sierra*, "mountain chain," and *león* (or Italian *leone*), "lion." The name was recorded in 1462 as *Serra da Leão* by the Portuguese navigator Pedro de Sintra. An earlier record of 1457, however, made by the Venetian explorer Alvise Ca' da Mosto, includes the following gloss (in translation): "...and [they] named this mountain Serre-Lionne, because of the great noise that is made here by the fearful sound and bursting of the thunderbolts that always resound over it, continually surrounded by stormclouds." If this is the true origin, the name refers to the rumbling of thunder over the mountains, not the roaring of lions, which are anyway not found in this part of Africa.

Sierra Madre. *Mountain range, southeastern Mexico.* Mexico's main mountain system, as an extension of the Rockies, has a Spanish name meaning "mother range."

Sierra Nevada. *Mountain range, southeastern Spain.* The Spanish name means simply "snowy mountains," from *sierra*, "mountain chain" (implying one with jagged peaks), and *nevada*, feminine of *nevado*, "snowy." The description is equally apt for the range of the same name in eastern California. *See also* **Nevada**.

Sighetu-Marmaţiei. *City, northern Romania.* The city, on the Tisza River, derives the first word of its name from Hungarian *sziget*, "island." (It was actually part of Hungary in World War II.) The second word identifies it as being in the county of *Maramureş*. The name also occurs in the form *Sighetul Marmaţiei*, where the suffix *-ul* is the Romanian definite article ("the"). The equivalent Hungarian name is *Máramarossziget*.

Sighişoara. *Town, central Romania.* The town arose in the 12th century on the site of a Roman fort with a name recorded in a document of 1280 as *Castrum Sex*, "six-sided camp," referring to the shape of the fort as an irregular hexagon. This formed the basis of the name, which was later influenced by the *Saxon* Germans who colonized the town in the 13th century. The Romanian name thus represents Hungarian *Segesvár*, where *vár* is "fort." The German form of the name is *Schässburg*.

Sigirya. *Village, central Sri Lanka.* The ancient remains of the royal place of King Kasapya, built here in the 5th century B.C., attract many tourists, who climb to the lofty site through the open jaws and throat of a huge lion. Hence the name, from Sinhalese *sinha*, "lion," and *giriya*, "throat."

Sigmaringen. *Town, southwestern Germany.* The name was originally that of the 11th-century castle around which the town arose. It means "(place of) *Sigimar*'s people" and was apparently transferred to the castle from the nearby village of *Sigmaringendorf*, "village of *Sigimar*'s people."

Sigüenza. *Town, central Spain.* The town derives its name from the Roman settlement of *Seguntia* here, its own name from Celtic *sego*, "strong," "powerful," as for **Segovia**.

Sikkim. *State, northeastern India.* The name may represent Sanskrit *shikhin*, "summit," referring to the Himalayas here, or even specifically to Mt. Kanchenjunga, on the state's western border. According to another theory, the name derives from the Limbu words *su him*, "new house."

Silesia. *Region, east central Europe.* The region, mostly in southwestern Poland, derives its name either from the *Ślęza* River here, a tributary of the Oder, or from the mountain called *Ślęz*, itself named for the *Silingi* or *Silingae*, a Vandalic people whose religious center the mountain was. The Polish name of the region is *Śląsk* and the German *Schlesien*. *See also* **Freiburg**.

Silhouette Island. *Island, western Indian Ocean.* The third largest island of the Seychelles is not named for its outline but for the French finance minister Étienne de *Silhouette* (1709–1767), successor to Jean Moreau de Séchelles (who gave the name of the **Seychelles**).

Silistra. *City, northeastern Bulgaria.* The city's name is a corruption, under Romanian influence, of its Roman name *Durostorum*. This means "strong fort," and may in turn be a translation of an earlier Phoenician name.

Siloam. *Pool, south central West Bank.* The pool near old Jerusalem has its name interpreted in the Bible: "Go, wash in the pool of Siloam (which is by interpretation, Sent)" (John 9:7). The sense is of water sent through a conduit, here the ancient tunnel which diverted water underneath Jerusalem to the pool inside the city wall. The name also occurs as *Shiloah* (Isaiah 8:6) and *Siloah* (Nehemiah 3:15).

Simbirsk. *City, western Russia.* The city was founded in 1648, originally as *Sinbirsk*, probably from a Tatar personal name. From 1924 through 1991 it was known as *Ulyanovsk*, for V.I. *Ulyanov*, better known as Lenin, who was born here.

Simcoe, Lake. *Lake, southeastern Canada.* The Ontario lake was discovered by Samuel de Champlain in 1650 and originally known as *Lac aux Claies*, "hurdle lake." It was subsequently renamed as now by John G. Simcoe (1752–1806), British governor general of Upper Canada from 1792 to 1796, for his naval officer father, Captain John *Simcoe*.

Simferopol. *City, southern Ukraine.* The city, in the southern Crimea, was founded in the 17th century under the Tatars and was originally known by the Turkish name of *Ak-Mechet*, "white mosque." The present name dates from 1783, when the Crimea became part of Russia. It is Greek in origin, as for several other towns in this part of Russia founded or named at that time, and means "expedient city," from *sumpherōn*, "useful," "profitable," and *polis*, "city." The town was essentially planned as a trading center, and its coat of arms depicts a beehive surrounded by bees.

Simonstown. *Town, southwestern South Africa*. The town, in Western Cape province, was founded by the Dutch in 1741 as a naval depot and named for *Simon* van der Stel (1639–1712), commander of Cape Colony from 1679 to 1691 and governor from 1691 to 1699. *Cp.* **Stellenbosch**.

Simplon. *Mountain pass, south central Europe*. The Alpine pass between Switzerland and Italy takes its name from the Swiss village of *Simpelen*, itself said to mean "soft heights." The Romans recorded the name in various ways, including *Sempronius* and *Scipionis*, assimilated to the names of Roman leaders.

Simpson Desert. *Desert, central Australia*. The arid region, largely in southeastern Northern Territory, was named in 1929 by Dr. Cecil Thomas Madigan, who crossed it by air that year. He gave the name in honor of Alfred Allen *Simpson* (1875–1939), president of the Royal Geographical Society of Australasia, which had sponsored Madigan's exploration. The desert had been entered earlier by the English explorer Charles Sturt, but remained nameless until Madigan's time.

Sinai, Mt. *Mountain, northeastern Egypt*. The mountain, at the southern end of the peninsula named for it, is believed to take its name from *Sin*, a moon god worshiped by the Sumerians, Akkadians, and ancient Arabs. The mountain has several peaks, and the one mentioned in the Bible (Exodus 19:1, etc.) is probably the present-day *Jebel Musa*, "mountain of Moses." Mt. Sinai is also referred to in the Bible as *Horeb* (Exodus 3:1, etc.), its name from Hebrew *horev*, "aridness."

Sinaia. *Town, east central Romania*. The town arose around a monastery built here in 1695 and itself named allusively for St. Catherine's monastery on Mt. *Sinai* (*see* **Sinai, Mt.**).

Sind. *Province, southeastern Pakistan*. The province takes its name from Sanskrit *sindhu*, "river," referring to the **Indus** (a name of the same origin), in the valley of which it lies. *See also* **Ayodhya**.

Sindelfingen. *Town, southwestern Germany*. The town, first mentioned in 1133, has a name meaning "(place of) *Sindolf*'s people."

Singapore. *Republic, southeastern Asia*. The name derives from Sanskrit *simhapura*, "lion town," from *simha*, "lion," and *pur*, "house," "town." The sense is hard to explain, since lions have never been found here. There may have been some sort of metaphorical reference, to a "lion-like" person or people, as there could have been for *Ceylon* (*see* **Sri Lanka**), or possibly there was some link with Ceylon itself. Both Singapore and Ceylon are Asian islands with names of similar "lion" origin and they share an identical geographical location south of a mainland peninsula. Physically, too, it would have been relatively easy to cross the Bay of Bengal from one to the other. By way of folk etymology, a Malayan legend tells how an Indian prince came to Singapore in the 7th century and took the first animal he saw to be a lion. Today the royal beast is represented by two lions supporting the coat of arms of its identically named capital.

Sinjil. *Village, western West Bank*. The Arab village was built on the site of a Crusader settlement and its name is an arabicized form of that of the famous French crusader Raymond de *Saint-Gilles*, comte de Toulouse (c.1052–1105).

Sinkiang. *Region, northwestern China*. The region, formally known as the *Uighur Autonomous Region of Sinkiang*, has a name meaning "new frontier," from Chinese *xīn*, "new," and *jiāng*, "frontier."

Sinop. *City and port, northern Turkey*. The city is traditionally said to have been named either for the mythological *Sinope*, Asopus's daughter, carried here by Apollo, or for the equally legendary Amazon queen *Sinova*. The real origin of the name is uncertain.

Sint-Niklaas. *Town, northern Belgium*. The town is named for *St. Nicholas*, to whom its 15th-century church is dedicated. (The Dutch dialect name of St. Nicholas, *Sante Klaas*, gave that of *Santa Claus*.)

Sinuiju. *City, northwestern North Korea*. The city developed during the Japanese occupation of Korea (1910–45) and took its name, prefixed by Korean *sin*, "new," from the old city of *Uiju*, 7 miles (11 km) to the west. Its own name derives from Korean *ŭi*, "justice," and *chu*, "province."

Siófok. *Town, west central Hungary*. The town, a resort on Lake Balaton, derives the first part of its name from the *Sió* River, the lake's only outlet, and Hungarian *fok*, "drainage channel."

Sion. *Town, southwestern Switzerland*. The Roman name of the town was *Sedunum*, apparently from Celtic *dunum*, "hill," referring to the twin hillocks here, each topped by the remains of a medieval castle. The German form of the name is *Sitten*.

Sion *see* **Zion**

Sioux City. *City, north central United States.* The Iowa city was laid out in 1848 by William Thompson of Illinois and at first known as *Thompsonville*. In 1849 it was settled by Theophile Bruguier, a French-Canadian trader, who came here with his *Sioux* wives and their father, Chief War Eagle, and received its present name accordingly. The Sioux' own name is an abbreviation of *Nadouessioux*, "adders" (i.e. "enemies"), a name given them by the Ojibwa. *Cp.* **Sioux Falls**.

Sioux Falls. *City, northern United States.* The South Dakota city was founded on *Big Sioux* River in 1857 and named for the river and its *falls. See also* **Sioux City**.

Sirsa. *City, northwestern India.* The city, in Haryana state, is said to take its name from the Rajah *Saras*, who founded it in c.A.D. 250.

Sisak. *Town, northern Croatia.* The town, on the Sava River, has a name of Celtic origin meaning "marsh," "swamp." Its Roman name was *Siscia*.

Sisimiut. *Town and port, western Greenland.* The town has a Greenlandic name meaning "place of fox earths." Its earlier Danish name was *Holsteinsborg*, "Holstein castle," for the historic Danish region of *Holstein* and Danish *borg*, "castle," "fort." *See* **Schleswig-Holstein**.

Sitamarhi. *City, northwestern India.* The city, in Bihar state, is sacred in Hindu mythology because it is dedicated to *Sita*, the wife of Vishnu. Hence the name. *Cp.* **Sitapur**.

Sitapur. *City, northern India.* The city, in Uttar Pradesh state, has a name meaning "town of *Sita*," for the wife of the Hindu god Vishnu in his incarnation as Rama.

Sitka. *City and port, northwestern United States.* The Alaska city and former capital, on Baranof Island, arose from the fort founded by A. A. Baranov in 1799. The city proper dates from 1804, when it was known by the Russian name of *Novoarkhangelsk*, "new **Arkhangelsk**," for its location, similar to that of the Russian city and port (though not so far north). After 1867 it was known by its present name, probably from a Tlingit word meaning "by the sea."

Sivas. *City, east central Turkey.* The city's present name evolved from its Roman name of *Sebastia*, from Greek *sebastos*, "great," "magnificent," perhaps in turn linking it with the Roman emperor Caesar *Augustus*, the Greek word translating his title. Other classical names of Sivas were *Diospolis* ("city of Zeus") and *Megalopolis* ("city of the great one," i.e. of the emperor Pompey).

Siwalik Hills. *Hill range, southern Asia.* The

hills, running parallel with the Himalayas in northern India and Nepal, derive their name from Sanskrit *shiva*, "Shiva," the Hindu god, and *alika*, "brow."

Siwan. *Town, northeastern India.* The town, in Bihar state, derives its name from Sanskrit *savayāna*, "bier." According to legend, the Buddha's bier rested here for a time on its journey to Kusinara for cremation.

Sjælland. *Island, eastern Denmark.* Denmark's largest island has a name meaning "sea land," from Old Norse *sjá*, "sea," and *land*, "land." The name is sometimes anglicized as *Zealand*. *Cp.* **New Zealand, Zeeland**.

Skagerrak. *Strait, east central North Sea.* The arm of the North Sea between Norway and Denmark takes its name from *Skagen*, a Danish port that stands on it, and Norwegian *rak*, "race" (in the sense "current of water"). *Skagen* derives its name from the headland (Old Norse *skagi*) on which it lies.

Skåne *see* **Scandinavia**

Skegness. *Town and resort, eastern England.* The Lincolnshire town has a Scandinavian name said to mean "*Skeggi*'s promontory," with the personal name (meaning "bearded one") followed by Old Norse *nes*, "headland." Alternately, the name could directly mean "beard headland," referring to a headland that juts out like a beard. Either way, there is no obvious promontory here, but at one time the North Sea came right up to the southern side of the town.

Skeleton Coast. *Coastal region, northwestern Namibia.* The Atlantic seaboard extending south from Cape Fria to Cape Cross derives its name from the animal detritus strewn along its shore.

It was only here [at Cape Fria] that we realised how aptly named the Skeleton Coast is, since it is littered with the bleached bones of whales and seals and men. The ocean off Namibia was once full of whales, but the men who hunted them were lured to their deaths by the treacherous Atlantic fogs. One hundred years later, the wooden ribs of their ships now mingle with the ribs of the whales they pursued [Isabel Wolff, "Seasoned by the Sun," *The Times Magazine*, June 5, 1993].

Skiddaw. *Mountain, northwestern England.* The mountain, in Cumbria, has a name that could mean either "ski height" or "crag height," from Old Norse *skith*, "ski," "snowshoe," or *skyti*, "crag," and *haugr*, "height," "hill." "Ski height" would have described the mountain's outline, like that of a snowshoe. But the second origin seems more likely, referring to its craggy summit.

Skikda. *City and port, northeastern Algeria.* The present city was founded by the French in 1838 and was originally named *Philippeville,* for Louis-*Philippe* of France (1773–1850). The current name was adopted in 1962, as a reversion to the local form of the original name *Rusicade,* that of the port from which the town arose. Its meaning is uncertain. (The initial *Rus-* may represent Arabic *ra's,* "headland," referring to some nearby cape.)

Skokie. *Village, east central United States.* The Illinois village (of city size), now a suburb of Chicago, was settled in 1834 and originally known as *Niles Center.* In 1940 it received its present name, from the Potawatomi word meaning "swamp."

Skopje. *Capital of Macedonia.* The city has an ancient name of Illyrian or Macedonian origin and uncertain meaning. Its earliest record, in Roman times, is as *Scupi.* The city was the home town of the Roman emperor Justinian I, who rebuilt it in A.D. 535 after an earthquake and renamed it for himself as *Prima Justiniana,* "first (town) of *Justinian.*" The name is also spelled *Skoplje,* while the Turks know it as *Üsküb.*

Skwierzyna. *Town, western Poland.* The name has been said to derive from Polish *świerk,* "spruce," meaning a settlement among such trees, but a source in Slavic *zver,* "wild animal" (Polish *zwierzyna,* "game"), is more likely, denoting a game enclosure that was later turned into pastureland. The German form of the name is *Schwerin.*

Skye. *Island, western Scotland.* The largest and northernmost island of the Inner Hebrides is said to derive its name from Gaelic *sgiath,* "wing." The reference is allegedly to the "divided" appearance of the island from the mainland, with its two mountain masses in the north and south rising as "wings" either side of the central lower land. The actual origin may be in some other as yet unidentified word.

Slave. *River, west central Canada.* The river was explored by Samuel Hearne in 1771 and named for the *Slave* people who lived on its banks. For the origin of their name, *see* **Great Slave Lake.**

Slave Coast. *Coastal region, western Africa.* The region around the Bight of Benin is so named because it was from here that most African *slaves* were deported to other countries from the 16th through 19th century.

Slavonia. *Region, northern Croatia.* The region is so named for its predominantly *Slav* population. *Cp.* **Slovakia, Slovenia.**

Slavonska Požega. *Town, east central Croatia.* The second (and originally only) word of the town's name represents Slavic *pozhega,* a term used for an area of woodland cleared by burning. *Cp.* **Požarevac.** The first word locates this particular place in **Slavonia.**

Slavonski Brod. *City and river port, eastern Croatia.* The name locates the city in **Slavonia** by a ford (*brod*) or crossing of the Sava River, which here forms the border with Bosnia-Hercegovina.

Slavyansk. *City, eastern Ukraine.* The city was founded in 1676 as a fortress named *Tor,* after the river by which it lay. In 1784 the growing settlement was raised to town status as *Slovensk,* denoting its *Slav* population. In 1794 it assumed the Russian form of its name, now Ukrainian *Slov'yansk.*

Slieve Donard. *Mountain, eastern Northern Ireland.* The highest peak in the Mourne Mountains, Co. Down, has a name meaning "*Donart's* mountain," from Irish *sliabh,* "mountain," "upland," and the personal name, said to be that of a disciple of St. Patrick who built a church on the mountain's summit.

Sligo. *County, northwestern Ireland.* The county takes its name from the town here. Its own name means "shelly place," from Irish *slige,* "shell." The reference is to the stony bed of the Garavogue River that flows through the town.

Sliven. *Town, east central Bulgaria.* The town probably derives its name from Slavic *sliva,* "plum tree," formerly abundant here.

Slonim. *City, western Belarus.* The city's name is based on Slavic *slon,* "protected" (related Russian *zaslon,* "hiding place"). The town arose in the 10th century as a fortified point in a low-lying valley.

Slough. *Town, southern England.* The former Berkshire town has a name that means what it says, referring to the marshy terrain formerly here. Despite the unpromising site and name, the latter evoking John Bunyan's Slough of Despond, the town has enjoyed rapid industrial and residential development thanks to its proximity to London on a major road and rail (and formerly canal) route.

Slovakia. *Republic, central Europe.* The country takes its name from its predominantly *Slav* population. The Czechs and Slovaks united in 1918 to form the new state of *Czechoslovakia,* in which the territorial name appears as the second part. *See also* **Czech Republic.**

Slovenia. *Republic, southeastern Europe.* The country is named for its indigenous population, the *Slovenes,* who arrived here in the 6th century and who speak a *Slav* language closely related to Serbo-Croat.

Slŭnchev Bryag. *Town and resort, eastern Bulgaria*. Bulgaria's prime seaside resort, on the Black Sea, has a descriptively promotional name meaning "sunny shore." It is no misnomer, as the resort has an average 2,300 hours of sunshine a year, and up to 11 hours daily in July and August. The names of both this resort and **Zlatni Pyasŭtsi** often appear in English translation in tourist literature: "Resorts such as Sunny Beach and Golden Sands are experiencing a new lease of life" (*The Times*, July 17, 2004). An equivalent name is Spain's **Costa del Sol**.

Słupsk. *City, northern Poland*. The city takes its name from the *Słupia* river on which it lies. Its own name is based on Slavic *stolp*, "pillar," "post," denoting a form of fish trap here. The origin is better seen in *Stolp*, the German name of the city (and *Stolpe*, that of the river).

Slutsk. *City, central Belarus*. The city takes its name from the *Sluch* River on which it lies. The river name probably derives from Slavic *luk*, "bend," "bow," denoting its winding course.

Småland. *Historic province, southern Sweden*. The name of the province means literally "small land," referring to the many small provinces from which this larger one grew.

Smith Sound. *Sea passage, Arctic Ocean*. The passage, between Ellesmere Island, Canada, and northwestern Greenland, was discovered in 1616 by William Baffin (*see* **Baffin Island**) and named for Sir Thomas *Smith* (c.1558–1625), promoter of voyages to search for a Northwest Passage.

Smolensk. *City, western Russia*. The city's name is based on Russian *smola*, "resin," "tar," "pitch," probably alluding to the dark, resinous soil here.

Smyrna *see* **İzmir**

Snaefell. *Mountain, Isle of Man, Irish Sea*. The highest mountain on the Isle of Man has a Scandinavian name meaning "snow mountain," from Old Norse *snær*, "snow," and *fjall*, "mountain." Snaefell is often snow-capped. There are two mountains of the same name in Iceland, from Icelandic *snjór*, "snow," and *fell*, "hill." *Cp.* **Snowdon**.

Snake. *River, northwestern United States*. The river, which forms part of the border between Idaho and Oregon, is not named for its winding course but for the *Snake* people who formerly lived along its banks in Idaho. The Snake are a Shoshone people, and their name is still sometimes used loosely for the Shoshone in general. Its own origin is uncertain.

Śniardwy. *Lake, southeastern Poland*. The lake's name has been linked with Slavic *smrad*, "stench," referring to the foul exhalations from its waters. An early record of the name has it as *Smarden*. German speakers know the lake as the *Spirding*.

Śnieżka. *Mountain, eastern Europe*. The highest peak in the Riesengebirge, on the Czech-Polish border, derives its name from Polish *śnieżka*, "snowball."

Snowdon. *Mountain, northern Wales*. The highest mountain in Wales has an Old English name meaning "snow hill," from *snāw*, "snow," and *dūn*, "hill." Snowdon is not permanently snow-capped, but its heights have a snow covering for much of the year. The English name would have translated the original Welsh, although the modern Welsh name is *Yr Wyddfa*, "the cairn place," from *gwyddfa*, "tumulus," "grave." Like mountains elsewhere, Snowdon formerly served as a burial place. The general English name for the mountainous region is *Snowdonia*, while the equivalent Welsh is *Eryri*. This is said to mean "place of eagles" (Welsh *eryr*, "eagle"), and the eagles of Snowdonia were traditionally regarded as oracles of peace and war. (When they flew high, victory was in the air, and when they flew low, a defeat was presaged.) But the name really means "snow" (modern Welsh *eira*) or "snowy" (*eiraog*). The 9th-century *Historia Brittonum* thus names the mountains as *montes Heriri*, while the medieval *Annales Cambriae* refers to them as *Montes Ereri*.

Snowy Mountains. *Mountain range, southeastern Australia*. The mountains, in New South Wales, are fairly obviously named for their snow-covered peaks. The snow covering is not permanent, however, but for only three to six months of the year. *See also* **Snowy River**.

Snowy River. *River, southeastern Australia*. The river, in New South Wales, is named for its source on the eastern slopes of the **Snowy Mountains**, where it is fed by melting snows.

Sochi. *City and resort, southwestern Russia*. The Black Sea resort derives its name from that of a Cherkess (Circassian) people. The origin of their own name is uncertain.

Society Islands. *Island group, South Pacific*. The islands, at the heart of French Polynesia, were first discovered by the Portuguese in 1607. In 1767 they were rediscovered by the English navigator Samuel Wallis (*see* **Wallis and Futuna Islands**), and in 1769 were visited by Cook, who named them for the Royal *Society*, the commissioners and backers of his expedition to observe the transit of Venus.

Socotra. *Island, northwestern Indian Ocean.* The island, belonging to Yemen, derives its name from Sanskrit *dvīpa sukhatara*, "happy island," from *dvīpa*, "island," and *sukhatara*, the comparative of *sukha*, "pleasant," "agreeable." Similar propitious names were given to other islands or island groups, such as *Fortunate Islands* for the Canaries, or the *Islands of the Blessed* of classical mythology. (**Sri Lanka** has a modern-day equivalent.)

Södermanland. *County, east central Sweden.* The county's name means "land of the southern people," as distinct from neighboring **Västmanland**. *Cp.* **Norrland**, **Uppland**.

Sodom. *Industrial location, southeastern Israel.* The important potash works lie near the southwest shore of the Dead Sea, a possible site of the biblical city destroyed for its wickedness (Genesis 19:24). Its name is of uncertain origin. Both "field" and "burning" have been proposed. Of the 44 references to Sodom in the Bible, 23 include a reference to **Gomorrah**.

Soest. *City, northwest Germany.* The name, first recorded in 836 as *Sozat*, is of uncertain origin.

Sofala. *Province, central Mozambique.* The province derives its name from Arabic *sufalah*, "lowland," a term applied by the Arabs to the whole region between the Limpopo and Zambezi rivers.

Sofia. *Capital of Bulgaria.* The city was given its name by the Turks in the 14th century when they converted its 6th-century church of St. *Sophia* into a Muslim mosque, as they had done at Constantinople (Istanbul). The city was originally known as *Serdica*, for the *Serdi*, a Thracian people. In the 1st century A.D. it was known as *Ulpia Serdica*, in honor of the Roman emperor Marcus *Ulpius* Trajanus. In the early 9th century it was seized by the Bulgarians, who renamed it *Sredets*, "center," "middle" (probably also influenced by the earlier name). St. Sophia is not the name of a saint but represents the "holy wisdom" (Greek *sophos*, "wise") which the Eastern Church regards as being incarnate in Christ and present in the Holy Spirit.

Sogdiana. *Historic region, central Asia.* The ancient region, centering on the valley of the Zeravshan River, in modern Uzbekistan, was originally known by the Old Persian name of *Sughda* or *Sughuda*, meaning "pure," "clean."

Sogne Fjord. *Inlet, western Norway.* The inlet of the Norwegian Sea derives its name from the small town of *Sogndal* on its northern shore. Its own name represents Norwegian *sogne*, "parish," and *dal*, "valley."

Soissons. *City, northern France.* The city is named for the *Suessiones*, the Gaulish people who inhabited the region and whose capital it was. Their own name may be based on Gaulish *suexs*, "six."

Sokoto. *City, northwestern Nigeria.* The city, long a trade center for a wide region, bases its name on Arabic *sūk*, "market."

Sol, Isla del. *Island, western Bolivia.* The island, in Lake Titicaca, has a Spanish name meaning "island of the sun," referring to the Temple of the Sun here, traditionally the place where the two founders of the Inca dynasty, Manco Capac and Mama Ocllo, were sent to earth by the sun god. The island is also known as *Isla de Titicaca* (see **Titicaca, Lake**).

Solbad Hall. *Town and spa, western Austria.* The town arose in the mid–13th century around salt mines, and its salt deposits are still worked today. Hence its name, which effectively has "salt" twice, from an early form of German *Salz*, "salt," and *Bad*, "spring," referring to its mineral springs, and Middle High German *hal*, "saltworks." *Cp.* **Salzburg**, **Schwäbisch Hall**.

Soledar. *Town, eastern Ukraine.* The town, a noted salt-mining center, arose in the 19th century with the name *Bryantsovsky rudnik*, "Bryantsov's mine," presumable for its original owner. In the 1920s it became simply *Rudnik*, then in 1938 *imeni Karla Libknekhta*, "named for *Karl Liebknecht*," for the German revolutionary *Karl Liebknecht* (1818–1883), a founder member of the German Communist Party. In 1965 the town was raised to city status and this name was modified to *Karlo-Libknekhtovsk*. In 1991 it was given its present name, meaning "gift of salt" (Russian *sol'*, "salt," and *dar*, "gift").

Solent. *Sea channel, southern England.* The channel between the Isle of Wight and mainland England has a name of uncertain origin. A meaning "place of cliffs," from Phoenician or Punic, has been proposed. The Roman name for the whole sea tract here, including the Solent and Southampton Water, was *Magnus Portus*, "great harbor."

Soli. *Historic city, northwestern Cyprus.* The ancient Greek city is traditionally said to have been named for the Athenian lawgiver *Solon*, who supposedly visited Cyprus.

Soligorsk. *City, south central Belarus.* The city arose in 1958 as a potassium-mining center. Hence its name, from Russian *sol'*, "salt," referring to the potassium salts found here, and *gorod*, "town."

Solihull. *Town, central England.* The town, now a residential suburb of Birmingham, has a name meaning "(place by the) muddy hill," from Old English *solig*, "muddy," and *hyll*, "hill."

Solikamsk. *City, northwestern Russia.* The city derives the first part of its name from Russian *sol'*, "salt," referring to its salt (and potassium) mines, and the second part from the **Kama** River, on which it lies.

Solingen. *City, western Germany.* The city's name, recorded in 965 as *Solagon*, represents the dative plural of Old High German *solag*, "wallowing place (of pigs)." The name does not contain the *-ingen* suffix meaning "people of" as in **Meiningen** and **Tübingen**.

Sologne. *Region, north central France.* The region was originally named something like *Secalonia*, from the pre–Celtic root element *sek*, "river," as in *Sequana*, the Roman name of the **Seine** River, an unknown element *al*, and a Latin suffix *-onia*.

Solomon Islands. *Island state, southwestern Pacific.* The islands were so named in 1568 by the Spanish explorer Álvaro de Mendaña de Neira. The story goes that on landing he saw islanders wearing gold ornaments and believed he had discovered the legendary land of Ophir from which gold was brought to King *Solomon* (1 Kings 9:29).

Solothurn. *Town, northwestern Switzerland.* The town, in the canton of the same name, was known to the Romans as *Solodurum* or *Salodurum*, apparently from Celtic *sal*, "salt," and Gaulish *duron*, "fort." The French form of the name is *Soleure*.

Solway Firth. *Inlet, northeastern Irish Sea.* The arm of the Irish Sea between Scotland and England has a Scandinavian name meaning "inlet of the pillar ford," from Old Norse *súla*, "pillar," *vath*, "ford," and *fjorthr*, "firth," "inlet." The "pillar" is almost certainly the Lochmaben Stone, a granite boulder that marks the end of the ford on the Scottish side and that was a regular meeting place for the settling of border disputes.

Somalia. *Republic, northeastern Africa.* The country takes its name from the *Somalis* who are its indigenous people. The origin of their own name is uncertain, but the following have been proposed: (1) From a Cushitic word meaning "dark," "black," referring to the color of their skin (*cp.* **Ethiopia**, **Sudan**); (2) From a local phrase *soo mal*, meaning "go and milk," implying a hospitable people, who offered milk to their guests; (3) From the name of a local chief; (4) From Arabic *zāmla*, "cattle," referring to the many herds here.

Somerset. *County, southwestern England.* The

Old English name means "*Somerton* settlers," i.e. "people who have come to live at *Somerton*," this being a town near the middle of the county. Its own name means "summer settlement," referring to a dwelling place by pastures that can be used only in summer, because they are too damp or marshy for the purpose in winter. The *-set* is as for **Dorset**.

Somerville. *City, northeastern United States.* The Massachusetts city, now a suburb of Boston, was settled in 1630 and originally known as *Cow Commons*. Its present name is said to honor Captain Richard *Somers* (1778–1804), a naval hero killed in the war with Tripoli.

Somme. *River, northern France.* The river derives its name from a Gaulish root element *su*, "good," and an element perhaps meaning "gentle."

Somnath. *Historic city, west central India.* The ancient ruined city in Gujarat state, site of the temple of Shiva, derives its name from Sanskrit *somanātha*, "lord of the *soma*" (the intoxicating juice of a plant used in ancient religious ceremonies and personified as a god).

Somogy. *County, southwestern Hungary.* The county derives its name from the town of *Somogy* (now in the neighboring county of Baranya), its own named based on Hungarian *som*, "cornel."

Sondershausen. *Town, central Germany.* Early forms of the town's name, such as *Sundershusen* in 1125, suggest an origin in Old High German *suntar*, "apart" (related English *sunder*), and *husen*, "houses," denoting a detached or isolated settlement.

Sonora. *State, northwestern Mexico.* The state has a Spanish name meaning "sonorous," referring to the local marble deposits, which when struck emit a ringing sound.

Soochow *see* **Su-chou**

¹Sopot. *Town and port, northern Poland.* The town derives its name from a Slavic root meaning "spring," "stream," as for **²Sopot**. The German form of the name is *Zoppot*.

²Sopot. *Town, central Bulgaria.* The town derives its name from a Slavic root meaning "spring," "stream." From 1950 through 1965 it was renamed *Vazovgrad*, to commemorate the birth centenary of the Bulgarian writer and patriot Ivan *Vazov* (1850–1921), who was born here.

Sopron. *Town, western Hungary.* The town, earlier known by the German name *Ödenburg*, derives its present name from a form of the personal name *Sophronius*.

Soroca. *City, northern Moldova.* The name,

formerly spelled *Soroki*, derives from Moldovan *saraki*, "poverty," denoting the impoverished state of the original settlement. (It is now a flourishing town in an orchard area.) The present form of the name has been influenced by Russian *soroka*, "magpie."

Sortavala. *City and lake port, northwestern Russia.* Known formerly as *Serdobol*, and in Finland until 1940, the city has a name of uncertain origin. According to one theory, it may derive from Finnish *sortaa*, "to oppress," or *sortua*, "to fall," "to collapse," referring to an early battle in which local warriors suffered defeat. But placenames formed from verbs are not common in Finnish territory, and the origin may actually be in a Karelian (Finnish) personal name *Sortava*. Another theory takes the name from Finnish *sorttawa*, "cleaving," as the settlement arose by a deep inlet on Lake Ladoga. It is generally held that *Serdobol*, the Russian form of the name, evolved from the Finnish, although it could be the other way around, so that the origin is Slavic. The town was founded in 1632.

Sosnowiec. *City, southern Poland.* The city's name means "gathering of pines," from *sosna*, "pine tree," and *wiec*, "meeting," "gathering." The German form of the name is *Sosnowitz*.

Soufrière. *Town, southwestern St. Lucia.* The town takes its name from a nearby volcanic crater. Its own name is French for "sulfur mine," referring to its sulfur springs and strong sulfurous smell. There are volcanoes of the same name on Basse-Terre island, Guadeloupe, and on St. Vincent.

Sousse. *Town and port, northeastern Tunisia.* The town was founded by the Phoenicians in the 11th century B.C. and was originally known as *Hadrumetum*. When the Vandals conquered it in the 5th century A.D. it became *Hunericopolis*, for *Huneric*, son of the Vandal king Genseric. Following the Byzantine invasion of the 6th century it was further renamed *Justinianopolis*, for the Byzantine emperor *Justinian* I (483–565). The meaning of the present name is uncertain. It may be of Berber origin and relate to *Marsa Susa* in Libya, also on the coast, or even the plain of *Sous* in southern Morocco. There is unlikely to be any link with **Susa**, although an alternate form of the name is *Susah*.

South Africa. *Republic, southern Africa.* The purely geographical name for the southern part of Africa was well established by the 19th century, as it was for *North Africa*, *East Africa*, and *West Africa*. It became official for the present country when the *Union of South Africa* came into being in 1910. The indigenous African name for South Africa is *Azania*, adopted from classical geography, where it was probably based on Arabic *zanj*, "dark-skinned African." *Cp.* **Zanzibar**.

Southampton. *City and port, southern England.* The name distinguishes the city as a "southern *Hampton*," by contrast with a "northern *Hampton*." The latter came to be **Northampton**, and the two towns were linked by a north-south route in medieval times. Unlike it, however, the *Hampton* that is now *Southampton* has a different meaning. It is "promontory settlement," not "home farm," since the first part of the name is Old English *hamm*, "hemmed-in land," not *hām*, "homestead." Southampton arose on a broad promontory between the Itchen and Test rivers. *See also* **Hampshire**.

Southampton Island. *Island, northern Canada.* The island, in Nunavut at the entrance to Hudson Bay, was discovered in 1613 by Thomas Button and named for Henry Wriothesley, 3d Earl of *Southampton* (1573–1624), an active member of the Virginia Company.

South Australia. *State, south central Australia.* The state (not actually the southernmost, which is Victoria), was formed as a province under its self-descriptive name in 1836. Other names considered for it at the time included *Williamsland*, for King *William* IV of England (1765–1837), and, more realistically, *Central State*. *See also* **Northern Territory**.

South Bend. *City, east central United States.* The Indiana city, founded in 1820, takes its name from the most *southerly bend* in the St. Joseph River here.

South Carolina *see* **¹Carolina**

South China Sea. *Sea, western Pacific.* The sea is so named for its location off the *south* coast of *China*, as distinct from the *East China Sea*, off the east coast. The sea is also known simply as the *China Sea*. The Chinese name for it is *nán hăi*, "southern sea."

South Dakota *see* **Dakota**

Southend. *Town and resort, southeastern England.* The Essex town, more fully known as *Southend-on-Sea*, gained its name from its original location at the *southern end* of the parish of Prittlewell, now a district of Southend itself. The present town developed only in the early 19th century.

South Georgia. *Island, South Atlantic.* The island, one of the Falkland Islands dependencies, was first charted by Captain Cook in 1775 during his circumnavigation of the Antarctic continent. He named it *Isle of Georgia* for King *George* III of England (1738–1820), patron of his voyage. It is *south* purely geographically, not by contrast with a "North Georgia" (although Cook may possibly have had the American **Georgia** in mind, named for George III's grandfather).

South Korea *see* **Korea**

Southland. *Region, southern New Zealand.* The local government region, in southwestern South Island, is obviously named for its geographical location. At the same time, its name may have been intended to mirror that of *South Holland*, given that region's location in the southwestern Netherlands, and the Dutch origin of the name of **New Zealand** itself.

South Orkney Islands. *Island group, South Atlantic.* The Antarctic islands, between the Scotia Sea and the Weddell Sea, were sighted and partially charted in 1821 by the English sealer George Powell and at first named *Powell's Group.* They then received their present name, after the **Orkney Islands**, since they lay in a slightly lower latitude than the **South Shetland Islands**, just as the Orkneys lie in a slightly lower latitude than the **Shetland Islands**.

Southport. *Town and resort, northwestern England.* The Merseyside town arose around a seaside hotel in the late 18th century. It was presumably called *south* for its location on the southern shore of the Ribble River estuary, and there is no corresponding "Northport."

South Sandwich Islands. *Island group, South Atlantic.* The islands, north of the Weddell Sea, were discovered in 1775 by Captain Cook and originally named by him *Sandwich Land*, in honor of John Montagu, 4th Earl of *Sandwich* (1718–1792), then first lord of the Admiralty. The present form of the name was given in 1819 by the Russian explorer F.F. Bellingshausen (*see* **Bellingshausen Sea**), in order to distinguish the islands from the *Sandwich Islands*, now **Hawaii**.

South Shetland Islands. *Island group, South Atlantic.* The islands, part of the British Antarctic Territory, were first sighted in 1819 by the English sealer William Smith, who originally called them *New South Britain.* He then renamed them *South Shetland*, because they lay in about the same latitude in the southern hemisphere (62° 0') as the **Shetland Islands** in the northern hemisphere (60° 30').

South Shields. *City and port, northeastern England.* The city lies on the southern side of the Tyne River estuary, opposite *North Shields.* The name common to both towns represents Middle English *shele*, "shieling," "shed," referring to the fishermen's huts that formed the original settlements from which the towns grew.

Southwark. *Borough of London, southeastern England.* The name means "southern work," describing a defensive post on the southern side of the Thames at the southern end of London Bridge, where it was founded in Roman times as an outpost of the City of London.

Sovetsk. *City and river port, western Russia.* The city's original name was *Tilsit*, for the *Tilse* River here, its own name deriving from a Lithuanian word meaning "marshy." In 1946 the town was given its present name, from Russian *sovetskij*, "Soviet."

Sovetskaya Gavan. *City and port, eastern Russia.* The city's Russian name means "Soviet harbor." It is properly that of the bay here that was discovered in 1853 by the Russian naval officer Nikolai Boshnyak and that was originally named *Imperatorskaya gavan'*, "imperial harbor," in honor of the reigning czar and emperor of Russia, Nicholas I. The bay was renamed as now in 1926.

Soviet Union. *Historic empire, eastern Europe/ northern and western Asia.* The country familiarly known as **Russia** was formally titled the *Union of Soviet Socialist Republics* (*USSR*), less formally *Soviet Union*, from 1922 through 1991. The 15 constituent republics were **Armenia, Azerbaijan**, *Belorussia* (now **Belarus**), **Estonia, Georgia, Kazakhstan**, *Kirgizia* (now **Kyrgyzstan**), **Latvia, Lithuania**, *Moldavia* (now **Moldova**), **Russia, Tajikistan, Turkmenistan, Ukraine**, and **Uzbekistan**. *Soviet* represents Russian *sovet*, "council," meaning the elected governmental and administrative council in each of the republics. Each republic's official title comprised the adjectival form of its national name followed by the words *Soviet Socialist Republic*, e.g. *Armenian Soviet Socialist Republic*. (The name of Russia was slightly different, as *Russian Soviet Federated Socialist Republic*.)

Soweto. *Urban complex, northeastern South Africa.* The complex consists of several townships to the southwest of Johannesburg set aside for blacks in 1963 by the South African white government. Hence the name, an acronym of *South-Western Townships.* The name was originally proposed in August 1961 by one Concita Stanissis of Sunnyside, Pretoria.

Sozopol. *Town and resort, eastern Bulgaria.* The Black Sea resort was originally the Thracian town of *Apollonia*, so named for the Greek god *Apollo*, whose cult was observed in several Greek colonies on the Black Sea coast. With the coming of Christianity in the 3d century, the present name was adopted, meaning "city of salvation," from Greek *sōzein*, "to save," and *polis*, "town."

Spa. *Town and resort, eastern Belgium.* The town, whose mineral springs caused the word *spa* to be used for similar resorts elsewhere in Europe, derives its name from Walloon *espa*, "spring," "fountain."

Spain. *Kingdom, southwestern Europe.* The country has a name of uncertain origin. It has been tentatively derived from Basque *ezpain* or *ezpañ*, "lip," "edge," perhaps in the sense "bank," "shore." Others see a source in Punic *span*, "rabbit," alluding to the multitude of these animals here at one time, while classicists favor a link with *Hesperus*, in that it is a western land, a "land of the setting sun." (By coincidence, its latitude is identical to that of Japan, its oriental opposite, the "land of the rising sun.") The Spanish name of Spain is *España*.

Spanish Main. *Historic region, northern South America.* The coastal region between the mouth of the Orinoco River and Panama, famous (or infamous) for its buccaneers and raiders, was so called from the *Spanish* possessions on the *main*-land. English *main* may have originally translated Spanish *tierra firme* ("mainland"), although the term later came to apply to the sea area off the coast here, or to the sea routes followed by Spanish ships. The name as a whole dates from the 17th century.

Sparta. *Historic city, southern Greece.* The ancient city-state derives its name from Greek *spartē*, a term for a cord made from the shrub *spartos*, a type of broom. The name seems to imply that the cord was used for marking out the lines along which the city's foundations were laid. Its alternate name was *Lacedaemon*, related to that of **Laconia**, of which it was the capital. The second part of this name is obscure, and there are no grounds for basing it on Greek *daimōn*, "demon."

Spartanburg. *City, southeastern United States.* The South Carolina city was established in 1785 and named for the *Spartan* Rifles, a regiment of the local militia that fought in the American Revolution.

Spencer Gulf. *Inlet, southern Australia.* The inlet of the Indian Ocean, in South Australia, was explored by Matthew Flinders in 1802 and named by him for George John *Spencer*, 2d Earl Spencer (1758–1834), who was first lord of the Admiralty at the time when Flinders's ship was commissioned.

Spessart. *Mountain range, western Germany.* The mountains, with their wooded slopes, have a name meaning "woodpecker woods," from Old High German *speht*, "woodpecker," and *hard*, "forest," "wooded upland" (*cp.* **Haardt Mountains**).

Speyer. *City and river port, southwestern Germany.* The city derives its name from the *Speyer* River, which enters the Rhine here. The original Roman settlement here was *Noviomagus*, "new market," as for **Nijmegen** and elsewhere. In the 3d century A.D. it became known as *Nemetum civitas*, "state of the *Nemeti*," for the tribe of this name. Finally, in the 6th century, it took its present name. The river may derive its name from Old High German *spīwan*, "to spout." The city was long known in English as *Spires*, as if referring to its many churches. Hence the historical Diet of *Spires* (1529).

Spitsbergen. *Island, Arctic Ocean.* The main island of Svalbard, north of (and belonging to) Norway, has a Dutch name, from *spits*, "points," and *bergen*, "mountains." The name was given by the Dutch explorer Willem Barents who came here in 1596. A 15th-century name for the island was *Grumant*, from Swedish *Grönland*, "green land," adopted from **Greenland**, of which Spitsbergen was then believed to be an eastern extension. It is hardly a "green land" in the literal sense.

Spittal. *Town, southern Austria.* The town is named for a *hospital* (as a charitable institution for the destitute) founded in 1191 on the site where it subsequently arose.

Split. *City and port, western Croatia.* The name is a reduced form of the city's Roman name, *Spalatum*. This itself comes from Latin *palatium*, "palace." The emperor Diocletian built a grand palace here in the early 4th century A.D. in what was then the port of *Salona*. In the 7th century, following the sacking of Salona by the Avars, the inhabitants built a new town over the palace ruins, using its remaining walls and pillars as foundations. The Italian name of Split is *Spalato*.

Spokane. *City, northwestern United States.* The Washington city has a name of Native American (Salish) origin, said to derive from *spo-kan-ee*, "sun." This may have originally been the name of a chief, passing from him to the people, then to the river where they lived, and finally to the present city, incorporated in 1881.

Sporades. *Island groups, Aegean Sea.* The Greek islands are widely scattered, as their name implies, from Greek *sporas*, *sporados*, "disseminated." There may be an intentional contrast with the **Cyclades**.

Spratly Islands. *Island group, South China Sea.* The islands, midway between Vietnam and the Philippines, are said to be named for the English mariner who sighted them in 1791. Their Chinese name is *Nansha*, from *nán*, "south," and *shā*, "sand," "grit," referring to the reefs here.

Spree. *River, northeastern Germany.* The river derives its name either from Middle High German *sprāwen*, "to spray," or directly from this verb's Indoeuropean root *spreu*, "to scatter," "to spread," referring to the way it divides into a network of channels in the marshy region known as the *Spreewald* ("Spree Forest").

¹Springfield. *City, north central United States.* The state capital of Illinois arose around a log cabin erected here in 1818 and took its name from nearby *Spring* Creek. The name is found elsewhere, and has favorable associations for a new settlement, with its implication of fresh water and rich pastures.

²Springfield. *City, northeastern United States.* The Massachusetts city was founded in 1635 by the English settler William Pynchon (1590–1662) and named for his birthplace, the Essex village of *Springfield*, now a suburb of the city of Chelmsford.

³Springfield. *City, east central United States.* The Missouri city was settled in 1829 near the James River and named for the local *springs*.

⁴Springfield. *City, northern United States.* The Ohio city was laid out in 1801 and named by the wife of Simon Kenton, an early settler, for the *springs* in nearby cliffs.

Srebrenica. *Town, eastern Bosnia-Hercegovina.* The name derives from Serbo-Croat *srebro*, "silver," referring to the rich deposits of silver (and lead) that led to the founding of the town in 1387 as a mining center.

Sredna Gora. *Mountain range, central Bulgaria.* The name of the range means "middle mountain," describing not only its location across the center of the country but also its situation between the Balkan Mountains to the north and the Rhodope to the south.

Sremska Mitrovica. *Town, northern Serbia.* The first word of the town's name relates to the region here known as *Srem* (Roman *Syrmia*), its own name of uncertain origin. It was added to distinguish this town from **Kosovska Mitrovica**. The second word derives from the dedication of the town's church to St. *Dimitri*.

Sri Jayewardenepura Kotte. *Legislative capital of Sri Lanka.* The city, in the suburb of *Kotte* near the executive capital **Colombo**, derives the first part of its name from Sanskrit *shrī*, a title of respect used generally as the equivalent of *Mr.*, and the name of J.R. *Jayewardene* (1906–1996), Sri Lanka's president from 1978 to 1989, with Hindi *pura*, "town," added.

Sri Lanka. *Island republic, northern Indian Ocean.* The island, just south of India, has a name that represents Sanskrit *shrī*, "happiness," "holiness," and *laṅkā*, "island." It is thus effectively "island of the blessed." It gained its independence in 1972, and before this was familiar as *Ceylon*, from Sanskrit *simha*, "lion," either applied metaphorically, to a "lion-like" people, the *Sinhalese*, or implying that there were actual lions here. There may have been once, but there are none now. A former English literary name for Ceylon was *Serendip* or *Serendib* (the source of English *serendipity*). This is an Arabic corruption of Sanskrit *simhaladvīpa*, "island of the place of lions." *See also* **Singapore**, **Socotra**, **Tamluk**.

Srinagar. *City, northern India.* The city, in Jammu and Kashmir state, has a name meaning "town of happiness," from Hindi *shrī*, "fortune," "happiness," and *nagar*, "town." Srinagar enjoys a favorable location in the fertile Vale of Kashmir.

Srirangam. *Town, southeastern India.* The town, in Tamil Nadu state, derives its name from Hindi *shrī*, "fortune," "happiness." and the *Ranganatha* temple here dedicated to the god Vishnu. *Cp.* **Seringapatam**.

Stade. *Town and river port, northwestern Germany.* The town arose in c.800 as a trading settlement on the Schwinge River. Its name, from Old High German *stad*, "bank," denotes the original site.

Stafford. *Town, west central England.* The town, in the county of the same name, has an Old English name meaning "ford at the landing place," from *stæth*, "landing place," and *ford*, "ford." Stafford is on the Sow River, and the ford must have been at its limit of navigation, which was thus a landing place.

Stakhanov. *City, eastern Ukraine.* The city arose in the mid–19th century as the coal-mining settlement of *Kadiyevka*, presumably named for its founder. It was renamed *Sergo* in 1937 but reverted to its original name in 1940. It received its present name in 1978, honoring Aleksei *Stakhanov* (1906–1977), the legendary Soviet coal miner, whose heroic efforts at the coalface here in the 1930s inspired the Stakhanovite movement.

Stalingrad *see* **Volgograd**

Stamford. *City, eastern United States.* The Connecticut city, now a suburb of New York, was founded in 1641 by settlers from Wethersfield, near Hartford, and named for the English town of *Stamford*, Lincolnshire, from where some of their number had originally emigrated. Its own name, meaning "stone ford" (over the Welland River), is not exactly appropriate for the stateside city, which is located at the mouth of the Rippowam River on Long Island Sound.

Stanley. *Capital of Falkland Islands.* The town was so named in 1844 for the English colonial secretary Edward *Stanley*, 14th Earl of Derby (1799–1869), styled "Lord Stanley" until 1851. It was Stanley himself who ordered the transfer of the main settlement in the Falklands from Port Louis to the site of Stanley, although the name was given not by him but by Major-General Richard Moody, lieutenant governor and vice admiral of the islands. The name is sometimes alternately *Port Stanley*.

Stanovoy Range. *Mountain range, eastern Russia.* The range, extending east from the Olekma River, derives its name from the standard Russian word meaning "main," "chief," distinguishing this range from the many smaller ones in this part of Siberia.

Stans. *Town, central Switzerland.* The name is said to derive from Latin *in stagnis*, "in the marshes."

Stara Planina *see* **Balkans**

Stara Zagora. *City, central Bulgaria.* The city, or its location, has had many names over the centuries. There was originally a Thracian settlement here named *Beroea*. This became the Roman town of *Augusta Trajana*, named for the 2d-century A.D. emperor *Trajan*. The Turks knew the town as *Eski-Hisar*, "old fortress," and this name gave the present one, with Turkish *eski* replaced by Slavic *stara*, "old," and *Hisar* corrupted to *Zagra* and then to *Zagora*, as if meaning "beyond the mountain."

Starbuck Island. *Atoll, southwestern Pacific.* The uninhabited island, in the Line Islands, part of Kiribati, is named for Vincent *Starbuck*, the British master of a whaling ship, who sighted it in 1823.

Stargard Szczeciński. *City, northwestern Poland.* The city's main name means "old town," while the addition locates it in the province of **Szczecin**. Its German name is *Stargard in Pommern*, locating it in **Pomerania**.

Stary Oskol. *City, western Russia.* The city was founded in 1593 as *Oskol*, so named for the river here, its own name of uncertain origin. In 1655 another town downstream on the same river, then known as *Tsarev Alekseyev*, for the Russian *czar Aleksei* Mikhailovich, was renamed *Novy Oskol*, "new *Oskol*." *Oskol* then became *Stary Oskol*, "old *Oskol*," for purposes of differentiation.

Staten Island. *Island, eastern United States.* The New York City island was settled by the Dutch from 1630 and they named it for the *Staten-Generaal*, "states general," of the Dutch Republic.

Stavropol. *City, southwestern Russia.* The city

was founded as a fortress in 1777 and given a Greek-style name in the fashion of the day. It means "city of the cross," from *stauros*, "cross," and *polis*, "city." The name was probably adopted from the *Stavropol* that is now **Tolyatti**. From 1935 through 1943 the present Stavropol was renamed *Voroshilovsk*, for the Soviet statesman Kliment *Voroshilov* (1881–1969).

Steiermark *see* **Styria**

Steinfurt. *Town, western Germany.* The present town was formed in 1975 from the amalgamation of *Burgsteinfurt* and *Borghorst*. *Burgsteinfurt* was originally just *Steinfurt*, "stone ford" (*cp.* **Stamford**), for its location by a crossing of the river now known as the Steinfurter Aa. *Burg* ("fort") was added later to distinguish it from *Drensteinfurt*. *Borghorst* derives its name from Old High German *horst*, "wooded hill," added to a first element of uncertain origin. There is no record of a fort (*burg*) here.

Stellenbosch. *Town, southwestern South Africa.* The oldest European town in South Africa after Cape Town, in Western Cape province, was founded in 1679 and named after himself by Simon van der *Stel* (1639–1712), first governor of the Cape, with Dutch *bosch*, "bush," "forest," added. *Cp.* **Simonstown**.

Stendal. *City, central Germany.* The name means "rocky valley," from Old Saxon *stēn*, "stone," "rock," and *dal*, "valley," denoting the site of an early Saxon village here by a crossing of the Uchte River.

Stepanakert *see* **Xankändi**

Sterlitamak. *City, western Russia.* The city, in Bashkortostan (former Bashkiria), was founded in 1766 at the point where the *Sterlya* River enters the Belaya, and is named for it, with Bashkir *tamak*, "mouth," added. The meaning of the river name is unknown.

Stevenage. *Town, southeastern England.* The Hertfordshire town has a name meaning "(place at the) strong oak," from Old English *stīth*, "stiff," "strong," and *āc*, "oak." There must have been a specially stout oak tree here at one time.

Stewart Island. *Island, southern New Zealand.* New Zealand's third largest island (after North Island and South Island) is named for the English whaler Captain William *Stewart*, who visited it in 1809 and proved that it was an island, not a peninsula of South Island, as Captain Cook had earlier supposed. Its Maori name is *Rakiura*, "sky glow."

Steyr. *City, central Austria.* The city is named for the river on which it lies, the river's own name having a Slavic origin and meaning "stream" (Russian *struya*). *Cp.* **Stry**.

Stip. *Town, east central Macedonia*. The ancient town, on the Bregalnica River, was known in classical times as *Antibos*, a form of Greek *Antipolis*, "opposite the town," referring to its location with regard to some facing settlement or natural object. (*Cp.* **Antibes**.) The present name evolved from this, an intermediary form being *Ostib*.

Stirling. *Town, south central Scotland*. The town, in the former county of the same name, has a name that has never been satisfactorily explained. It may have derived from an earlier name of the Forth River on which it lies. Gaelic *sruth*, "river," has been proposed in this connection.

Stirling Range. *Mountain range, southwestern Australia*. The mountains, in Western Australia, were sighted in 1802 by Matthew Flinders and named for Sir James *Stirling* (1791–1865), first governor of the state.

Stockholm. *Capital of Sweden*. Sweden's largest city, on an arm of the Baltic Sea, arose in the mid–13th century on the site of a fishing village. Its name combines Swedish *stäk*, "bay," or *stock*, "stake," "pole," and *holm* "island." The overall sense is thus either "island in the bay" or "island on poles," the latter implying a settlement built by a landmark or over the remains of some earlier foundation.

Stockport. *Town, northwestern England*. The town, near Manchester, has a name found elsewhere in England meaning "market place at a dependent hamlet," from Old English *stoc*, "dependent hamlet," and *port*, "market place."

Stockton. *City, southwestern United States*. The California city was founded in 1847 and was at first known as *Tuleburg*. It was laid out and incorporated in 1850 and renamed as now for Commodore Robert F. *Stockton* (1795–1866), who had claimed California for the United States in 1846.

Stockton-on-Tees. *Town, northeastern England*. The town, on the **Tees** River, has an Old English name meaning "farm at a dependent hamlet," from *stoc*, "secondary settlement," "dependent hamlet," and *tūn*, "farm." The river name distinguishes this *Stockton* from the many others.

Stoke-on-Trent. *City, west central England*. The former Staffordshire city, often referred to simply as *Stoke*, has a name representing Old English *stoc*. The basic meaning of this was "place," but it often implied, as here, a place that was dependent on another. The name of the **Trent** River was added to distinguish this *Stoke* from others.

Stolberg. *City, western Germany*. The city takes its name from the fortress of the noble *Stalberg* family built in the 12th century atop the steep chalk cliff here. The name probably means "steel fort," denoting the strength of the castle.

Stonehenge. *Ancient monument, southern England*. The prehistoric stone circle in Wiltshire has a name essentially meaning "stone gallows," from Old English *stān*, "stone," and *hengen*, "(instrument for) hanging." The reference is to the gallows-like appearance of the trilithons, with two upright stones and a third across the top as a lintel.

Stornoway. *Town and port, northwestern Scotland*. The town, on Lewis with Harris Island, in the Western Hebrides, has a name that probably means "steerage bay," from Old Norse *stjórn*, "steerage," "rudder," and *vágr*, "bay." The implication is that the original harbor here required special maneuvering in order to dock.

Strabane. *Town, western Northern Ireland*. The town, in Co. Tyrone, has the Irish name *An Srath Bán*, "the white riverside land," referring to the light color of the soil here by the Mourne River.

Stralsund. *City and port, northeastern Germany*. The city arose in the 13th century on the site of a Slav settlement by the *Strelasund*, an inlet of the Baltic Sea. The inlet name derives from a combination of Old Polabian *strela*, "river arm" and Middle Low German *sunt*, "strait" (English *sound*), denoting the channel between the mainland and the island of Rügen. The city's coat of arms shows an upward-pointing arrow, as if the name came from Middle Low German *strāl*, "arrow" (modern German *Strahl*, "ray"). The small town of *Strehla*, on the Elbe River in eastern Germany, has a name of identical origin, and also a coat of arms with an arrow.

Strasbourg. *City, northeastern France*. The city is near enough to Germany to have a Germanic name. It means "fortress on the street," from Old German *straza*, "street," and *burg*, "fort." The town arose by an important route leading westward from the Rhine over the Vosges Mountains. The Roman name of the town was *Argentoratum*, associated (perhaps symbolically) with Latin *argentum*, "silver."

[1]**Stratford**. *City, northeastern United States*. The Connecticut city was settled in 1639 and probably named for **Stratford-upon-Avon**, England.

[2]**Stratford**. *City, southern Canada*. The Ontario city was founded in 1831 on the Avon River and originally named *Little Thames*, as was the river. The present name was adopted soon

after, for **Stratford-upon-Avon**, England, in honor of William Shakespeare, whose plays are regularly performed at the Festival Theatre here.

³**Stratford**. *Town, north central New Zealand.* The town, in west central North Island, was constituted in 1882 and originally named *Stratford-on-Patea*, for its location on the *Patea* River. The name as a whole, later shortened as now, was given for **Stratford-upon-Avon**, England, in honor of William Shakespeare, and many of the town's streets are named for characters from his plays.

Stratford-upon-Avon. *Town, central England.* The Warwickshire town has a name that occurs in many parts of England and that almost always has the same meaning. This is "ford on a Roman road," from Old English *strǣt*, "Roman road" (a word borrowed from Latin *via strata*, "paved way," and giving modern *street*), and *ford*, "ford." The Roman road here ran over the **Avon** River, as the full name indicates.

Strathclyde. *Region, western Scotland.* The name is much older than the former administrative region (1975–96). It means "valley of the **Clyde**," from Gaelic *srath*, "valley," usually implying a broad one, and the river name.

Straubing. *City, southeastern Germany.* The city arose in the 6th century on the site of a Roman camp called *Sorviodurum*, "*Sorvius's* fort." The present name, first recorded in the 9th century, means "(settlement of) *Strupo's* people," with an Old Bavarian personal name.

Strehla *see* **Stralsund**

Stromboli. *Island, southeastern Tyrrhenian Sea.* The volcanic island, one of the Lipari Islands, derives its name from Greek *strongulos*, "round," describing its shape. Hence its former name of *Strongyle*.

Strømø. *Island, Faeroe Islands, North Atlantic.* The largest of the Faeroe Islands has a Danish name meaning "island of the current," from *strøm*, "stream," "current," and *ø*, "island."

Stroud. *Town, southwestern England.* The Gloucestershire town derives its name from Old English *strōd*, a term used for marshland overgrown with brushwood.

Stry. *City, western Ukraine.* The city takes its name from the *Stry* River here, its own name meaning simply "stream" (Russian *struya*). *Cp.* **Steyr**. The Ukrainian form of the name is *Stryy*.

Stuttgart. *City, western Germany.* The city derives its name from Middle High German *stuotgarte*, from *stuot*, in its original collective sense "herd of breeding mares," and *garte*, "garden." The reference is to the horse-breeding establishment (stud farm) set up here in 950 by Duke Hermann I of Swabia.

Styria. *Province, southeastern Austria.* The province has the German name of *Steiermark*, deriving from the **Steyr** River here and Old High German *marcha*, "border territory" (as for the **Marches**).

Subarnarekha. *River, northeastern India.* The river, rising in Jharkhand state and flowing east to enter the Bay of Bengal, has a name meaning "streak of gold," from Hindi *subaran*, "gold," and *rekhā*, "line." The reference is to the copper-mining region through which it passes.

Subiaco. *Town, central Italy.* The town, known in Roman times as *Sublaqueum*, has a name meaning "below the lake," referring to its location below three small lakes where the emperor Nero built a villa.

Subotica. *City, northern Serbia.* The city derives its name from Slavic *subbota*, "Saturday" (literally "sabbath"), referring to a regular weekly market on this day. *Cp.* **Szombathely**. When part of Austria-Hungary the city was renamed *Maria-Theresiopel*, "city of *Maria Theresa*," referring to *Maria Theresa* (1717–1780), queen of Hungary and Bohemia and archduchess of Austria. The Hungarian form of the name is *Szabadka*.

Suceava. *City, northeastern Romania.* The city takes its name from the river on which it stands. The river's own name is based on Romanian *suci*, "to wind," "to turn," describing its course.

Su-chou. *City, northeastern China.* The city, in Kiangsu province, derives its name from Chinese *sū*, "thyme," and *zhōu*, "region."

Süchow. *City, eastern China.* The city, in Kiangsu province, derives its name from Chinese *xú*, "slowly," and *zhōu*, "region."

Sucre. *Capital of Bolivia.* The judicial capital of Bolivia (the administrative capital is **La Paz**) was founded in 1539 by the Spanish conquistador Pedro de Anzúrez on the site of the Native American village of *Chuquisaca* (said to mean either "golden bridge" or "headquarters of the Chacas"), and was at first known as *La Plata*, "the silver" (*cp.* **La Plata**). It became the capital in 1839 and in 1840 was renamed as now to commemorate the liberator of Ecuador, Antonio José de *Sucre* (1795–1830), Bolivia's first president, assassinated while returning home from talks in Bogotá on a proposed union between Ecuador, Colombia, and his native Venezuela. The name is also that of a department in northern Colombia and a state in northeastern Venezuela.

Sudan. *Republic, northeastern Africa.* The country has a name of Arabic origin, from *balad* *as-sūdān,* "land of the blacks," comprising *balad,* "land," "country," *al,* "the" (here *as* before *s*), and *sūdān,* the plural of *aswad,* "black." The name was originally given by Arab travelers to what is now Nubia. *Cp.* **Ethiopia, Somalia.**

Sudbury. *City, southern Canada.* The Ontario city, in Canada's largest mining region, is named for *Sudbury,* Suffolk, England, birthplace of the wife of James Worthington, superintendent of the construction of the Canadian Pacific Railway main line, which passes through here.

Sudest. *Island, southwestern Pacific.* The island, in the Louisiade Archipelago, Papua New Guinea, has a French name meaning "southeast," describing its location southeast of New Guinea.

Sudetenland. *Mountain region, northern Czech Republic.* The region, bordering Poland, takes its name from the *Sudeten* Mountains here. Their name is an ancient one, mentioned by Ptolemy in the 2d century A.D., but its meaning is obscure. It may be Illyrian in origin.

Suez. *City and port, northeastern Egypt.* The name represents Arabic *as-suways,* from Egyptian *suan,* "beginning," referring to the port's location at the northern end of the Red Sea and now also of the canal that bears the city's name.

¹Suffolk. *County, eastern England.* The county is named for the "south folk," the southern group of East Anglian peoples, whose name, as for their neighbors, the "north folk" of **¹Norfolk,** was adopted for their region without the addition of a territorial word such as *land.*

²Suffolk. *City, eastern United States.* The Virginia city was settled in 1720 and was at first known as *Constant's Warehouse,* for John *Constant,* who set up a tobacco business here. In 1742 it was renamed as now for the county of **¹Suffolk,** England.

Sühbaatar. *Town, northern Mongolia.* The town was founded in 1940 and named in honor of the Mongolian revolutionary leader Damdiny *Sühbaatar (Sukhe-Bator)* (1893–1923). (He was originally surnamed *Sukhe,* "ax," but was granted the honorific *Bator,* "hero," for combating pro-Japanese forces and adopted it as part of his name.) He also gave the name of **Ulan Bator.**

Suhl. *City, central Germany.* The city, on the Lauter River, derives its name from that of a stream or river here, itself from Old High German *sul,* "marshy place."

Sukarnapura *see* **Jayapura**

Sukhe Bator *see* **Sühbaatar**

Sukhumi. *City and port, western Georgia.* The Black Sea port has a name given by the Turks when they captured the town in 1455. They called it *Suhumkale,* with *kale* meaning "fort"

but the first part of the name of disputed origin. It may represent Turkish *su,* "water," and *kum,* "sand," but is more likely to be an alteration of its earlier Georgian name. This was *Tskhumi,* meaning "hot." Sukhumi was founded in the 7th century B.C. as the Greek colony of *Dioscurias,* said to be so named for the *Dioscuri,* the twins Castor and Pollux of classical mythology.

Sulaimaniya. *Town, northeastern Iraq.* The town was founded in 1781 and named for *Suleyman* Abu Layla, then pasha of Baghdad.

Sulawesi. *Island, eastern Indonesia.* There are various theories claiming to explain the name. One of the more convincing is that it is an ethnic name, from Malay *sula,* "spear," "lance," and *besi,* "iron," alluding to the weapon favored by its indigenous people. However, it is possible that the present name is simply a corruption of *Celebes,* its formerly familiar name. This is said to have been given by the Portuguese explorers who discovered the island in 1512. They allegedly applied the name *Os Célebres,* "the famous ones," "the celebrated ones," to the dangerous capes on the island's northeast coast. This name then spread to the whole island.

Sulina. *Town and port, eastern Romania.* The town, on the Black Sea coast at the mouth of the Danube, has a name that probably derives from Slavic *sol',* "salt," referring to the river channel here.

Sultan Kudarat. *Province, southern Philippines.* The province, in southwestern Mindanao, was created in 1973 and named for *Qudarat* Nasir ud-Din, the first and most powerful *sultan* of Maguindanao, from c.1645 to c.1671.

Sultanpur. *Town, northern India.* The ancient town, in Uttar Pradesh state, has a name meaning "town of the sultan," for the Muslim sultans who ruled here. The name is found elsewhere in India.

Sumatra. *Island, western Indonesia.* The name of the mountainous island is said to derive from Sanskrit *samudradvīpa,* "ocean island," from *samudra,* "ocean," and *dvīpa,* "island." The reference would presumably be to the Indian Ocean. The island's Indonesian name is *Sumatera.*

Sumgait. *City, eastern Azerbaijan.* The city, founded in 1944 as a suburb of Baku, takes its name from the river that enters the Caspian Sea here. The river's own name is of probably of pre–Turkic origin but unknown meaning. Folk etymology derives it from Azerbaijani *su jum gajyt,* "return, my water."

Šumperk. *City, eastern Czech Republic.* The name is a Czech form of German *Schönberg,* "beautiful mountain," describing the location of the town in the foothills of the Jeseniks. The full German name of the city is *Mährisch Schönberg*, the first word meaning "*Moravian*," for the region of **Moravia** here.

Sumy. *City, northern Ukraine*. The city grew from the fortress built in 1652 on the *Sumka* River, for which it is named. Legend tells how three bags (Russian *suma*, "bag") were found buried when the foundations of the fortress were being dug. This is merely a folk etymology, though it does account for the three moneybags displayed in the city's coat of arms.

Sunda Islands. *Island group, Indonesia*. The islands, between the South China Sea and the Indian Ocean, are named for the *Sunda* people of western Java. The meaning of their own name is uncertain.

Sunderland. *City and port, northeastern England*. The name of the city, near Newcastle, represents Old English *sundor-land*, literally "sundered land," referring to land detached from a main estate. The term was probably used in a specific sense for private land set off from common land.

Sungari. *River, northeastern China*. The river, in Heilungkiang and Kirin provinces, has a Manchurian name representing *sungari ula*, "river of milk," based on *sun*, "milk," referring to its clouded waters. Its Chinese name is *Sunghua* or *Sunghuajiang*, from *sōng*, "pine," *huā*, "flower," and *jiāng*, "river."

Sunnyvale. *City, southwestern United States*. The California city was settled in 1850 and originally known as *Murphy's Station*, then *Encinal*, Spanish for "oak grove." It was given its present part-descriptive, part-promotional name on its incorporation in 1912.

Suomenlinna. *Island fortress, southern Finland*. The fortress, in Helsinki harbor, derives its name from *Suomi*, the Finnish name of Finland (*see* **Finland**), and *linna*, "fort." The fortress was actually built by the Swedes in 1749, and its Swedish name is thus *Sveaborg*, "Swedish fort." *Cp*. **Svealand**.

Superior, Lake. *Lake, central North America*. The name of the largest and deepest of the five Great Lakes, on the border of the USA and Canada, is an English adoption (without being a full translation) of its French name, *Lac Supérieur*, "upper lake." It is "upper" because its mean surface elevation above sea level is slightly higher, at 600 ft (180 m), than that of Lake Huron or Lake Michigan, at 579 ft (176 m). It is also the furthest north.

Surabaya. *City and port, southern Indonesia*.

The city, on the north coast of Java, has a Malay name representing *sura*, "hero," and *baya*, "danger." The reference is to the resistance offered by its inhabitants to invading or attacking forces, not least during Indonesia's struggle for independence in 1945–49. *Cp*. **Surakarta**.

Surakarta. *City, southern Indonesia*. The city, in central Java, has a Malay name representing *sura*, "hero," "heroic," and *karta*, "prosperous," "flourishing." *Cp*. **Surabaya**.

Surat. *City, west central India*. The city, in Gujarat state, is said to have been founded in the early 16th century with the name *Surajpur*, "city of *Surya*," for the Hindu sun god. The present name either evolved from this or, according to one account, represents *Surashtra*, perhaps meaning "good region."

Suresnes. *Town, northern France*. The town, now a suburb of Paris, had the Medieval Latin name of *Soresnae* or *Surisnae*. The origin of this is unknown. The final -*na* and the fact that these names are plural suggests that the source may be in a river name. Suresnes itself is on the Seine, and a number of streams rise in nearby Mont Valérien.

Surinam. *Republic, northeastern South America*. The country is named for the river that flows north through it to the Atlantic. Its own name (also spelled *Suriname*) is of obscure origin.

Surrey. *County, southeastern England*. The county's name means "southern district," from Old English *sūther*, "southerly," and *gē*, "district." The name was given to the district inhabited by the Saxons of the middle Thames valley. The Middle Saxons of **Middlesex** were north of the river, between the East Saxons of **Essex** and the West Saxons of **Wessex**, and a distinctive name was thus needed for the Saxons here, south of the river. South again were the South Saxons of **Sussex**.

Surtsey. *Island, southern Iceland*. The volcanic island, off the south coast of Iceland, emerged from the Atlantic in a fiery eruption in November 1963. In 1965 it was named by the Icelandic government as "*Surt's* island," from *Surt*, the fire demon of Norse mythology, and Icelandic *ey*, "island."

Susa. *Historic city, southwestern Iran*. The former capital of the Persian Empire probably derives its name from an Old Persian root element identical to that in Hebrew *shoshanna*, "lily." The city appears in the Bible as *Shushan* (Esther 1:2, etc.). Its ruins are now found at the village of *Shush*.

Susah *see* **Sousse**

Susquehanna. *River, eastern United States*.

The river, in New York, Pennsylvania, and Maryland, has a Native American name meaning "winding water," describing its meandering course.

Sussex. *County, southern England.* The county, administratively divided into *East Sussex* and *West Sussex*, has a name meaning "southern Saxons," denoting the southernmost Anglo-Saxon kingdom. *Cp.* **Essex**, **Middlesex**, **Wessex**. *See also* **Surrey**.

Sutherland. *Historic region, northern Scotland.* The former county has a Scandinavian name meaning (apparently illogically) "southern territory," from Old Norse *súthr*, "south," and *land*, "land." To the Norsemen who settled in Orkney and Shetland, this mainland territory actually was "southern."

Sutlej. *River, eastern Pakistan.* The river has a Sanskrit name meaning "hundred channels," since it channels the collected waters of all five rivers of the **Punjab** into the Indus.

Sutton. *Town, southeastern England.* The former Surrey town has an Old English name found widely in England. It means "southern farm," from *sūth*, "south," and *tūn*, "farm." The name usually implies that there was a corresponding "northern farm," although not necessarily named as such. In the case of this town, the northern equivalent was *Acton* ("oak-tree farm").

Suwałki. *City, northeastern Poland.* The precise origin of the city's name is uncertain. The initial *Su-* corresponds to Latin *co-*, denoting combination, and the name as a whole could mean "place of military forces," "encampment." But this interpretation lacks documentary support.

Suwannee. *River, southeastern United States.* The river, in Georgia and Florida, was named *Guasaca Esqui*, "river of reeds," by early Native Americans. Its present name is said to be an English corruption of Spanish *San Juan*, "St. John." It is the *Swanee* River of Stephen Foster's song "Old Folks at Home."

Svalbard. *Island group, Arctic Ocean.* The islands, north of Norway, with Spitsbergen as the largest, derive their name from Norwegian *sval*, "cool," "chill," and *bård*, "shore."

Svealand. *Region, central Sweden.* The region is named for the *Svear* (known to the Romans as *Suiones*) who were its original inhabitants, and who gave the name of **Sweden** itself.

Svendborg. *Town and port, southern Denmark.* The town, in southern Fyn Island, was recorded in 1229 as *Swineburgh*. The derivation is in Old Norse *svín*, "swine," "wild boar," and *borg*, "fortified place," "castle." The first part of

the name was later associated with the Danish personal name *Svend*.

Sverdlovsk *see* **Yekaterinburg**

Sveti Konstantin. *Resort, northeastern Bulgaria.* The Black Sea resort was first developed in 1956, at a time when the virtues of socialism were being promoted internationally by eastern bloc countries, and was accordingly at first named *Druzhba*, Bulgarian (and also Russian) for "friendship." Its present name means "St. Constantine," for the saint to whom the ancient monastery here is dedicated.

Svetlovodsk. *City, east central Ukraine.* The name translates as "bright water" (Russian *svetlyj*, "light," "bright," and *voda*, "water"), referring to the nearby Kremenchug Reservoir, built in 1954–60. The Ukrainian form of the name is *Svitlovods'k*.

Svilengrad. *Town, southeastern Bulgaria.* The town derives its name from Bulgarian *svila*, "silk," and *grad*, "town," referring to the local manufacture of silk.

Swabia. *Historic region, southwestern Germany.* The region takes its name from the *Suebi*, the Germanic people who were its original inhabitants. Their own name comes from Old German *sweba*, "free," "independent," related to Latin *suus* and Russian *svoj*, "one's own." The German form of the name is *Schwaben*. *Cp.* **Sweden**.

Swakopmund. *Town, northwestern Namibia.* The town, laid out as a German military base in 1897, has a name meaning "mouth of the *Swakop*," from the *Swakop* River and German *Mund*, "mouth." The river derives its name from Khoikhoin *tsoa-xoub*, from *tsoa*, "hole," and *xoub*, "excrement," describing the deposits of mud and sewage that it leaves on its banks after flooding.

Swansea. *Town and port, southern Wales.* The town has a Scandinavian name meaning "*Sveinn*'s island," with the personal name followed by Old Norse *ey*, "island." The town lies at the mouth of the Tawe River, as denoted by its Welsh name of *Abertawe*.

Swartberg. *Mountain range, southern South Africa.* The Afrikaans name means "black mountain," referring to the dark appearance of the mountains.

Swatow. *City, southern China.* The city, in Kwangtung province, derives its name from Chinese *shàn*, "to net a fish," and *tóu*, "head," "chief."

Swaziland. *Kingdom, southeastern Africa.* The country, bordered by Mozambique to the north and South Africa to the south, takes its name from that used by the Zulus to denote its indigenous people, the *Swazi*. Their own name for themselves is *Swati*, from King *Mswati* (reigned

1836–68), who consolidated the Swazi in the 1840s.

Sweden. *Kingdom, northwestern Europe*. The country takes its name from its original inhabitants, the *Svea*, known to the Romans as *Suiones*, whose own name probably derives from Old German *sweba*, "free," "independent," although a source in *geswion*, "kinsman," has also been suggested. The former English name of Sweden was *Swedeland*, but from the 17th century the present name prevailed, probably from the country's German name of *Schweden*, itself a plural form of the ethnic name. The Swedish name of Sweden is *Sverige*, "kingdom of the *Svea*." See *also* **Svealand**.

Swellendam. *Town, southern South Africa*. The town, in Western Cape province, was founded in 1747 and named for Hendrik *Swellengrebel* (1700–1760), the local Dutch governor, and his wife Helena, née ten *Damme*. The name happens to suggest a Dutch name in *-dam*, such as **Amsterdam**.

Świdnica. *Town, southwestern Poland*. The town has a name of Slavic origin meaning "privet," denoting a presence of this plant here. The German form of the name is *Schweidnitz*.

Świętokrzyskie Mountains. *Mountain range, south central Poland*. The name of the mountains translates as "Holy Cross," referring to a former Benedictine abbey situated on one of them.

Swindon. *Town, southern England*. The Wiltshire town has an Old English name that literally means "swine down," "hog hill." The hill on which Old Swindon stands was at one time a pasture for pigs.

Świnoujście. *City and port, northwestern Poland*. The city is named for its location at the *mouth* (Polish *ujście*) of the *Świna* River. The name is a part-translation of the town's former German name, *Swinemünde*. The river's own name is based on Germanic *svin*, "wild boar" (English *swine*).

Switzerland. *Republic, west central Europe*. The country takes its name from **Schwyz**, one of its cantons, which in 1291 united with the cantons of Uri and Unterwalden to form the nucleus of the Swiss Confederation. The names for Switzerland in its four official languages are respectively French *Suisse*, German *Schweiz*, Italian *Svizzera*, and Romansh *Svizra*. To avoid partiality, it uses none of these in its official documents, such as its postage stamps, but instead calls itself *Helvetia*, its Roman name, from the *Helvetii*, the former people here. The origin of their own name is unknown.

Sydney. *City and port, southeastern Australia*.

The capital of New South Wales, Australia's largest city and its first British settlement, was founded in 1788 and named for the British home secretary, Thomas Townshend, 1st Viscount *Sydney* (1733–1800).

Syktyvkar. *City, northwestern Russia*. The capital of the Komi Republic was founded in 1586 with the name of *Ust-Sysolsk*, "mouth of the *Sysola*," from the river here. In 1930 it received its present name, from *Syktyv*, the Komi name of the Sysola, and *kar*, "town."

Sylhet. *City, eastern Bangladesh*. The city's name is a slurred form of *Srihatta*, from Hindi *shrī*, "fortune," and *haṭṭ*, "market."

Sylt. *Island, northern Germany*. The northernmost and largest of the North Frisian islands derives its name from an Old North Frisian alteration of Low German *Süll*, "threshold" (English *sill*), referring to its elongated shape and its role as a wave breaker. A traditional derivation takes the name from Danish *sild*, "herring," as a bird's-eye view of the island's shape.

[1]**Syracuse**. *City and port, southern Italy*. The city, in southeastern Sicily, was founded by Corinthian colonists in the 8th century B.C. and has a name of pre–Hellenic origin, possibly representing Phoenician *serah*, "to feel ill," referring to the original settlement's unhealthy location by a swamp.

[2]**Syracuse**. *City, eastern United States*. The New York city was so named in 1825 by its first postmaster, who had learned of the Sicilian [1]**Syracuse** and who felt that its location was similar to that of the New York settlement, which was also near a marsh. He was probably also attracted by the classical prestige that the name might carry.

Syr Darya. *River, central Asia*. The river, in Kazakhstan, Kyrgyzstan, and Uzbekistan, has a name meaning "secret river," from Uzbek *sir*, "secret," "mystery," and *dario*, "river." The name implies respect for the power of the river as a "living thing" that, godlike, "moves in a mysterious way."

Syria. *Republic, western Asia*. The country's name is often said to be a shortened form of **Assyria**. There are no grounds for such an origin, although the true source of the name remains uncertain. It appears as *Suri* in Babylonian cuneiform writings dating from c.4000 B.C.

Syv Systre. *Waterfall, west central Norway*. The waterfall, plunging several hundred feet into the Geiranger Fjord, has a Norwegian name meaning "seven sisters." The reference is to the seven separate streams that unite at the summit of the falls.

Szarvas. *Town, southeastern Hungary.* The name was recorded in the 13th century as *Szorvosholm*, from Hungarian *szarvas*, "deer," and *halom*, "hill." The present name is a shortened form of this.

Százhalombátta. *Town, north central Hungary.* The "socialist town" built in the 1960s to accommodate Hungary's largest oil refinery has a name meaning "place of a hundred mounds," from Hungarian *száz*, "hundred," and *halom*, "mound," referring to a former cemetery here.

Szczecin. *City and port, northwestern Poland.* The city derives its name from Polish *szczotka*, "brush," presumably in allusion to the thick grass that formerly grew here, although the word could originally have been a personal nickname. German speakers know the city as *Stettin*.

Szechwan. *Province, southwestern China.* The name means "four rivers," from Chinese *sì*, "four," and *chuān*, "river." The reference is to the four main tributaries of the Yangtze, which flows through the province.

Szeged. *City, southeastern Hungary.* The city derives its name from Hungarian *szeg*, "corner," describing its original location at the confluence of the Tisza and Maros rivers.

Szeghalom. *Town, southeastern Hungary.* The town derives its name from Hungarian *szeg*, "corner," and *halom*, "hill," describing the site of the original settlement, on a rise at the junction of two rivers.

Székesfehérvár. *City, west central Hungary.* The city's name analyzes as Hungarian *székes*, "royal seat," *fehér*, "white," and *vár*, "fort." This translates its Medieval Latin name of *Alba regalis*, and is in turn reflected in the city's German name of *Stuhlweißenburg*. The town was chosen in the 10th century by Stephen I, king of Hungary, to be the Hungarian capital, and kings were crowned here from 1027 through 1527.

Szekszárd. *Town, south central Hungary.* The town is said to derive its name from a personal name or nickname meaning "topknot," from Hungarian *szeg*, a form of *szög*, "angle," and *szár*, "baldhead," describing a person who had shaved his head so as to leave a single lock atop.

Szentendre. *Town, north central Hungary.* The name means "*St. Andrew*," from the patron saint of the town's main church.

Szentes. *City, southern Hungary.* The city derives its name from a personal name meaning "pious one" (Hungarian *szent*, "saint").

Szigetszentmiklós. *City and river port, north central Hungary.* The name means "*St. Nicholas*'s island," from Hungarian *sziget*, "island," *szent*, "saint," and *Miklós*, "Nicholas," referring to the city's location on Csepel Island in the Danube.

Szigetvár. *City, southwestern Hungary.* The name means "island castle," from Hungarian *sziget*, "island," and *vár*, "castle," referring to the medieval fortress here by the Fekete River.

Szikszó. *City, northeastern Hungary.* The name means "marshy valley," from Hungarian *szék*, "marsh," and *aszó*, "valley."

Szolnok. *City, east central Hungary.* The city, dating from at least the 9th century, derives its name from a personal name.

Szombathely. *City, western Hungary.* The city's name means "Saturday place," from Hungarian *szombat*, "Saturday" (literally "sabbath"), and *hely*, "place." A Saturday fair and market were at one time regularly held here. The city's German name is *Steinamanger*, said to mean "stone in the meadow" (*Stein am Anger*), referring to a disastrous earthquake in A.D. 455 that left the town in ruins. *Cp.* **Subotica**.

Tabasco. *State, southeastern Mexico.* The state's name represents a Native American word meaning "damp earth," referring to the terrain here, which is low-lying and flat, and to a large extent covered with lagoons and swamps.

Tabigha. *Locality, northeastern Israel.* The locality on the northern shore of the Sea of Galilee, the reputed scene of the biblical Feeding of the Five Thousand, derives its name from an altered form of Greek *Heptapegon*, "seven springs."

Table Mountain. *Mountain, southwestern South Africa.* The mountain, overlooking Cape Town, was originally named *A Meza*, "the table," by Portuguese navigators of the 15th century. The name refers to the almost horizontal layers of sandstone that give the mountain its flat-topped appearance. It also has a "tablecloth," a flat white cloud cover that forms in a southeasterly wind to hang down over its steep sides. The mountain in turn gave the name of *Table Bay* here. *Cp.* **Trabzon**.

Tábor. *Town, south central Czech Republic.* The name has been the subject of much etymological debate. Some authorities link it with the biblical Mt. *Tabor* (*see* **Tabor, Mt.**), while others derive it from Hungarian *tábor*, "camp." The former origin is supported by the fact that the town was founded by the Hussites in the 15th century, and they could have imported the biblical name.

Tabor, Mt. *Mountain, northern Israel.* The mountain probably derives its name from Hebrew *ṭabbūr*, "navel," implying that it was formerly regarded as the "middle of the world." It is mentioned several times in the Old Testament

(Hosea 5:1, etc.), and although not referred to by name in the New Testament is regarded in Christian tradition as the site of the transfiguration of Jesus, described as occurring on a "high mountain" (Matthew 17:1, etc.). Many races regarded their local mountain as a "navel" or "middle of the world," and there are two places in the Old Testament where Hebrew *ṭabbūr haarets* (Greek *omphalos tēs gēs*, Latin *umbilicus terrae*) is translated "middle of the land" (Judges 9:37) or "midst of the land" (Ezekiel 38:12).

Tabriz. *City, northwestern Iran.* The city's name is popularly derived from Greek *tauros*, "bull," but is more likely to originate in Iranian *taprīz*, "causing heat," referring to the local thermal springs.

Tabuaeran. *Atoll, west central Pacific.* The atoll, one of the Line Islands, and part of Kiribati, was formerly known as *Fanning* Island, for the American mariner Edmund *Fanning*, who discovered it in 1798. (It is still owned by Fanning Island Plantations, Ltd., a copra-processing company.) In 1979, when Kiribati gained independence, it took its indigenous name, meaning "heavenly footprint."

Tacoma. *City, northwestern United States.* The Washington city was settled in 1864 and originally named *Commencement City*, with reference to the bay here, which was the starting point in 1841 of a surveying party. It was soon after named as now with the Native American name for Mt. Rainier, to the southeast. *See* **Rainier, Mt.**

Taconic Mountains. *Mountain range, northeastern United States.* The range of the Appalachian Mountains is said to derive its name from an Algonquian word meaning "tree," "forest."

Tacuarembó. *City, north central Uruguay.* The city takes its name from a Guaraní word for a type of firm, slender reed that grows locally. The city was founded in 1831 and was originally given the Spanish name *Villa de San Fructuoso*, "town of *St. Fructuosus*," for a 3d-century bishop of Tarragona who was martyred with two of his deacons.

Taegu. *City, southern South Korea.* The city has a name meaning "big hill," from Korean *tae*, "big," and *ku*, "hill."

Taejon. *City, western South Korea.* The city's name means "big field," from Korean *tae*, "big," and *chon*, "field."

Taganrog. *City and port, southwestern Russia.* The city is said to derive its name from Tatar *tagan*, "trivet," and Russian *rog*, "horn," the latter in the sense "promontory." Taganrog is on a raised rocky cape, overlooking the Sea of Azov,

and the name seems to imply that a signal fire or beacon was set up on a large iron tripod here at some time.

Tagawa. *City, southern Japan.* The city, in the island of Kyushu, derives its name from Japanese *ta*, "rice field," and *kawa*, "river."

Tagus. *River, southwestern Europe.* The river of Spain and Portugal has a name that may ultimately derive from Phoenician *dag*, "fish." Some authorities, however, associate the name with that of the Philistine god *Dagon*, whose own name is of Hebrew origin and said to mean "little fish" (although this could be a folk etymology).

Tahiti. *Island, South Pacific.* The Tahitian name of the island, in the east of the Society Islands, is *Otaheiti*, perhaps from Polynesian *iti*, "little," and *nui*, "island," referring not to the island itself, which is the largest in French Polynesia, but to one of its extinct volcanoes. It was discovered in 1606 by the Portuguese explorer Fernandez de Queiros and originally name *Sagittaria*, for the arrows (Latin *sagitta*) carried by the islanders. In 1767 the English navigator Samuel Wallis (*see* **Wallis and Futuna Islands**) claimed it as *King George III Island*, but the following year the French navigator Louis Antoine de Bougainville (*see* **Bougainville**) made a rival claim under the name of *Nouvelle-Cythère*, "new Cythera," for the Greek island where Aphrodite was worshiped. The local name prevailed.

Tahoe, Lake. *Lake, western United States.* The lake, on the California-Nevada border, derives its name from a Washo word meaning simply "big lake."

Ta-hsüeh Mountains. *Mountain chain, south central China.* The mountains, in Szechwan province, have a descriptive name meaning "great snowy (ones)," from Chinese *dà*, "big," "great," and *xuě*, "snow."

T'ai-chung. *City, west central Taiwan.* The name of the city means "middle Taiwan," from Chinese *tái*, a short form of **Taiwan**, and *zhōng*, "middle." This describes its location both generally in Taiwan and with respective regard to **T'ai-pei** and **T'ai-nan**.

T'ai-hang Mountains. *Mountain range, northeastern China.* The range, forming the boundary between Shansi and Hopeh provinces, derives its name from Chinese *tài*, "highest," "too," and *háng*, "line," "row."

T'ai Lake. *Lake, eastern China.* The large lake, between Chekiang and Kiangsu provinces, derives its name from Chinese *tài*, "highest," "too."

T'ai-nan. *City, southwestern Taiwan.* The former capital of Taiwan has a name meaning "southern Taiwan," from Chinese *tái*, a short form of **Taiwan**, and *nán*, "south." *Cp.* **T'ai-chung**, **T'ai-pei**.

Taínaron, Cape. *Cape, southern Greece*. The southernmost point of mainland Greece has a name of Phoenician origin, from *tanar*, a term for a place where iron or glass was made. Its former name was *Cape Matapan*, from Greek *metopon*, "forehead," "front," alluding to its shape.

T'ai-pei. *Capital of Taiwan*. The city's name means "northern Taiwan," describing its location in the island, from Chinese *tái*, a short form of **Taiwan**, and *běi*, "north." The name is now often spelled *Taibei*. *Cp.* **T'ai-chung**, **T'ai-nan**.

T'ai Shan. *Mountain, eastern China*. China's most sacred mountain, the principal peak of the T'ai Mountains, in Shantung province, derives its name from Chinese *tài*, "peaceful," and *shān*, "mountain." It is also known as *Dongyue*, from Chinese *dōng*, "east," and *yuè*, "peak," as one of the five holy peaks of China. *See also* **Shansi**, **Shantung**.

Taiwan. *Island state, western Pacific*. The island, off the southeast coast of China, has a name that means "terrace bay," from Chinese *tái*, "terrace," and *wān*, "bay." The reference is to the island's terrain, which slopes down to the sea in a series of "terraces" of alternating plateaux and hills. It was formerly known as *Formosa*, "beautiful," a name given for its striking scenery by Portuguese explorers here in 1590.

Taiyba. *Village, central West Bank*. The large village, said to have been visited by Jesus, has a name meaning "goodness," from Arabic *ṭaiyib*, "good."

T'ai-yüan. *City, northeastern China*. The capital of Shansi province derives its name from Chinese *tái*, "highest," "too," and *yuán*, "open country," "plain." This describes its geographical location, as the last plain before the mountains, working from east to west.

Tajikistan. *Republic, south central Asia*. The country takes its name from its indigenous people, the *Tajiks*, with Iranian *ostān*, "country," "land," added. The people take their name from Sanskrit *tājika*, "Persian," as a word originally used to distinguish Arabs from Turks, and that itself represents the name of the *Tay*, an Arab people.

Takamatsu. *City and port, southern Japan*. The city, in the island of Shikoku, derives its name from Japanese *taka*, "high," "tall," and *matsu*, "pine tree."

Takaoka. *City, central Japan*. The city, in the island of Honshu, derives its name from Japanese *taka*, "high," and *oka*, "hill."

Takasaki. *City, central Japan*. The city, in the island of Honshu, derives its name from Japanese *taka*, "high," and *saki*, "cape," "promontory."

Takla Makan. *Desert, western China*. The first part of the name represents Turkish *takla*, "to level," "to flatten." The second part is of uncertain origin.

Talavera de la Reina. *City, central Spain*. The city, known to the Roman as *Caesarobriga*, "*Caesar*'s fort," probably derives the first word of its name from a pre–Roman personal name *Talavus*. The second part of the name, Spanish for "of the queen," dates from the 11th century, when King Alfonso VI presented the town to his *queen*, Maria of Portugal, as a wedding present.

Taldy-Kurgan. *City, southeastern Kazakhstan*. The city arose in the 19th century as the village of *Gavrilovka*, presumably so called from a personal name. In 1920 it was renamed as now, referring to the local topography. Kazakh *taldy* is a term for an area of willow trees, and *kurgan* means "hill."

¹**Ta-li**. *City, southern China*. The city, in Yunnan province, derives its name from Chinese *dà*, "big," "great," and *lǐ*, "reason," "truth." This (original) Ta-li should not be confused with the identically named ²**Ta-li** only 10 miles (16 km) to the southeast.

²**Ta-li**. *City, southern China*. The city, in Yunnan province, shares the name of ¹**Ta-li**, 10 miles (16 km) to the northwest, which it adopted in the mid–1980s on gaining increased importance over its original namesake. Its name prior to this was *Hsia-kuan*, from Chinese *xià*, "down," "below," and *guān*, "to close," "to pass."

Tallahassee. *City, southeastern United States*. The state capital of Florida has a Native American name meaning "old town," from Creek *talwa*, "town," and *hasi*, "old." The present city dates from the 16th century, when it was established under Spanish colonial rule. *Cp.* **Tulsa**.

Tallinn. *Capital of Estonia*. The city and port derives its name from Old Estonian *tan-linn*, "Danish fort," from *dan*, "Danish" (modern Estonian *taani*), and *linn*, "fort," "castle." Tallinn was founded in 1219 by the Danish king Valdemar II. Its former name until 1917 was *Reval* or *Revel*, from Old Danish *rev*, "sandbank" (English *reef*), alluding to its location on the Gulf of Finland.

Tamaulipas. *State, northeastern Mexico*. The name is said to mean "place of rubber," from Nahuatl *tam*, "place," and *ulli*, "rubber," although the production of natural rubber is not a major activity here.

Tambov. *City, western Russia.* The city takes its name from the small river on which it stands. Its own name is said to represent Mordvinian *tombaks*, "marshy."

Tamil Nadu. *State, southeastern India.* The state has a Tamil name meaning "*Tamil* land," from *tamil*, "Tamil," and *nātu*, "land," "country." The Tamil themselves take their name from the *Damila*, a warrior people mentioned in ancient Buddhist texts. Their own name is ultimately of obscure origin.

Tamluk. *City, northeastern India.* The West Bengal city derives its name from Sanskrit *tāmra*, "copper," a metal formerly exported from here when the town was a port for trade with Southeast Asia. (The original form of the name was *Tamralipta*, with the second part of this an ethnic name.) A Sanskrit name for the island of Ceylon was *tāmradvīpa*, "copper island."

Tammisaari. *Town and port, southwestern Finland.* The town derives its name from Finnish *tammi*, "oak," and *saari*, "island." Its Swedish name is *Ekenäs*, with the same meaning.

Tampa. *City and port, southeastern United States.* The city's name is said to represent Cree *itimpi*, "near it," although the precise reference here is obscure. Another proposed interpretation is "split wood for fires."

Tampere. *City, southwestern Finland.* The name is a Finnish form of Swedish *Tammerfors*, itself a translation of Finnish *Tammerkoski*, from the name of the rapids on which the town was founded in 1779. Finnish *koski* and Swedish *fors* both mean "waterfall," "rapids." The first part of the name is of uncertain origin. It may represent a personal name or derive from Finnish *tammi*, "oak."

Tampico. *City and port, eastern Mexico.* The city's name is of Nahuatl origin and said to mean "hilly place." But the terrain is low-lying and swampy, so some other interpretation is more likely.

¹**Tamworth.** *Town, west central England.* The Staffordshire town takes its name from the *Tame* River on which it lies, with the second part of the name representing Old English *worthig*, "enclosure." The river name is almost certainly related to that of the **Thames.**

²**Tamworth.** *City, southeastern Australia.* The city, in New South Wales, was founded in 1848 by a British land development company and named for ¹**Tamworth**, Staffordshire, then the parliamentary constituency of the British prime minister, Sir Robert Peel.

Tananarive *see* **Antananarivo**

Tanezrouft. *Desert region, northern Africa.* The region of the Sahara, in southern Algeria and northern Mali, derives its name from Tuareg *tanezruft*, "waterless desert." The region lacks not only water but also vegetation, and was long avoided by travelers.

Tanganyika *see* **Tanzania**

Tangier. *City and port, northern Morocco.* The city is said to be named for the goddess *Tingis*, daughter of the giant Atlas. But an origin in a Semitic word *tigisis*, "harbor," is more likely. The name was long familiar in English as *Tangiers*, presumably by association with **Algiers**.

T'ang-shan. *City, northeastern China.* The city, in Hopeh province, derives its name from Chinese *táng*, "*Tang*" (the dynasty that reigned from 618 through 907), and *shān*, "mountain."

Tanzania. *Republic, eastern Africa.* The present country was formed in 1964 on the union of *Tanganyika* and **Zanzibar**. Its name thus symbolically combines equal elements from those two names (*Tan-* and *Zan-*) with the Latin-style placename suffix -*ia*. *Tanganyika* took its name from the lake here, Africa's second largest, now divided between Tanzania and the Democratic Republic of Congo. Its own name was explained by the English explorer Sir Richard Burton, who discovered it in 1858, as representing local words *kou tanganyika*, "to join," in the sense that it was a place where waters met or tribes gathered, while H.M. Stanley, in Africa in 1871, took it from *tonga*, "island" (*cp.* **Tonga**), and *hika*, "flat." Another theory derives the name from the *nyika* nut (*Trapa natans*), a type of water chestnut, whose plants float on the lake in great masses.

Taolanaro. *Town and port, southeastern Madagascar.* The town derives its name from Malagasy *taola*, "bones," and *gnaro*, "many," "numerous." There are said to be many human remains here. The French built a fort here in 1643 under the name *Fort-Dauphin*, for the *Dauphin* of France (*see* **Dauphiné**), and this name continued some time under the Malagasy form *Faradofay*.

Taormina. *Town, southern Italy.* The town, in eastern Sicily, was known to the Romans as *Tauromenium*, from *Monte Tauro*, "bull mountain," below which it arose, and perhaps Greek *monē*, "a stay."

T'ao-yüan. *City, northern Taiwan.* The city's name means "garden of peach trees," from Chinese *táo*, "peach tree," and *yuán*, "garden."

Tápiószentmárton. *Village, north central Hungary.* The first part of the name is that of the *Tápió* River here. The second part means "*St. Martin*" (Hungarian *szent*, "saint," and *Márton*,

"Martin"), for the patron saint of the village church.

Tarai. *Region, northern India.* The region of northern India and southern Nepal, parallel to the Himalayas, has a name meaning "moist land," describing its marshy terrain, caused by its many springs and streams.

Taranaki. *Region, northwestern New Zealand.* The local government region, in western North Island, derives its name from the Maori name of Mt. **Egmont,** the large volcano that dominates it.

Tarangambadi. *Town and port, southern India.* The town, on the Bay of Bengal in Tamil Nadu state, has a name meaning literally "wave town," based on Hindi *tarang,* "wave." The town was under Danish rule from 1620 through 1845, and Danish missionary publications carried the name *Trangambaria* on their front page. The regular European form of the name was *Tranquebar.*

Taranto. *City and port, southern Italy.* The city may derive its name from Illyrian *darandos,* "oak," referring to the abundance of these trees here at some time, although some authorities see an origin in an Indoeuropean root element *ter* or *tor,* "current."

Tarascon. *Town, southeastern France.* The Roman name of the town was *Tarasco, Tarasconis,* perhaps from a pre–Indoeuropean root element *tar,* "rock," "stone," with *-asc* and *-on* as suffixes. The town is associated with a legendary monster called *La Tarasque,* said to have ravaged the region until it was tamed by St. Martha. This suggests that the name may actually be ethnic in origin, and even related to the name of the *Etruscans* (*see* **Etruria**).

Tarawa. *Island, north central Kiribati.* The island, an atoll that is the country's capital, has a name said to derive from I-Kiribati (Gilbertese) *te,* "the," and *rawa,* "run," referring to a channel through a reef here.

Taraz. *City, southeastern Kazakhstan.* The city, one of the oldest in Kazakhstan, derives its name from the *Talas* River here. In 1856 it was renamed *Auliye-Ata,* Uzbek for "holy father," referring to Karakhan, founder of the medieval Turkic Karakhanid dynasty. In 1936 it was further renamed *Mirzoyan,* and in 1938 became *Dzhambul,* for the Kazakh folk poet *Dzhambul* Dzhabayev (1846–1945), himself named after a local mountain. Finally, in 1997, it reverted to its original name. (It should not be confused with *Talas,* Kyrgyzstan, a town on the same river.)

Tarbes. *Town, southwestern France.* The name of the town is related to that of the *Tarbelles,* a people who inhabited this region of Aquitaine. The meaning of their own name is uncertain.

Târgovişte *see* **Tîrgovişte**

Tarifa. *Town and port, southern Spain.* The town takes its name from *Tarif* ibn Malik, the first Berber chief to sail cross the narrowest part of the Strait of Gibraltar and land in Spain.

Tarim. *River, northwestern China.* The chief river of the Uighur Autonomous Region of Sinkiang has a name of Uighur origin meaning "river flowing into the sand."

Tarn. *River, southern France.* The river may ultimately derive its name from Indoeuropean *tar,* "swift water," or else Gaulish *taran,* "thunder," referring to the same tumultuous current. The Tarn is renowned for its many gorges.

Tarnów. *City, southern Poland.* The city's name has its origin in the personal name *Tarn,* with the final *-ów* a possessive suffix. The name was recorded in 1119 as *Thurnow.*

Tarragona. *City and port, northeastern Spain.* The city was known to the Romans as *Tarraco.* This may have related to the *Taruscans,* a people whose own name may be linked to that of the *Etruscans* (*see* **Etruria**).

Tarrytown. *Village, eastern United States.* The village, now a suburb of New York City, was settled by the Dutch in the 17th century. Its name may thus derive from Dutch *tarwe,* "wheat," referring to the wheat grown locally, although an origin in a personal name *Tarry* or *Terry* is also possible. It is hardly likely that the reference is to the farmers who used to *tarry* at the taverns here, as sometimes said.

Tarsus. *Town, southeastern Turkey.* The ancient town, birthplace of St. Paul (Acts 9:11, etc.), is first mentioned in the 7th century B.C. Its name is almost certainly of Phoenician origin but its meaning is obscure. It is not related to the biblical port of *Tarshish* (1 Kings 10:22), on the Mediterranean coast. (Its own name may represent Hebrew *tarshīsh,* "chrysolite," or else derive from Akkadian *rashashu,* "to be smelted.")

Tartu. *City, eastern Estonia.* The city is said to derive its name from *Tar,* an ancient local god. The original settlement here dates from the 5th century and until 1918 the town that developed was known as *Dorpat.* The origin of this is uncertain, but the following have been proposed: (1) An Estonian name meaning "fortress of *Tar,*" for the god mentioned; (2) A Finnish name from *tarpatto,* "(place of) aurochs," this being a now extinct species of ox; (3) An eastern name from root elements meaning "bull idol," from a word related to Hebrew *tor,* Greek *tauros*, etc., "bull," and a Turkic word related to modern Turkish *put*, "idol." The city proper dates from 1030, when the fort of *Yuryev* was built here and named for Yaroslav the Wise, Grand Prince of Kiev (c.978–1054), baptized *Yury* ("George").

Tarvisio *see* **Treviso**

Tashauz *see* **Dashhowuz**

Tashkent. *Capital of Uzbekistan*. The ancient city has a name representing Sogdian *tash*, "stone," and *kand*, "fort," "town." The date of its foundation is unknown. It is first mentioned in the 5th or 4th century B.C. by the name of *Chach* or *Shash*, and first under its present name in the 11th century.

Tasmania. *Island state, southern Australia*. The island, south of the state of Victoria, was so named in 1853 for the Dutch navigator Abel Janszoon *Tasman* (1603–1659), who discovered it in 1642. He himself named it *Van Diemen's Land*, for Anthony *van Diemen* (1593–1645), Dutch governor general of the Dutch East Indies. *See also* **Van Diemen Gulf**.

Tata. *Town, northern Hungary*. The town, dating from the 9th century, derives its name from a personal name of Germanic origin.

Tatabánya. *City, northern Hungary*. The original village of *Tata* here, with a personal name of Germanic origin, had Hungarian *bánya*, "mine," added when the present town arose as a "socialist city" in the 1950s to exploit lignite deposits.

Tatarstan. *Republic, western Russia*. The republic, in east central European Russia, has a name meaning "land of the *Tatars*," for the Turkic people whose own name is of uncertain origin. A source in a Mongolian word meaning "lurer," "trapper," has been proposed. (Their name is also spelled *Tartar*, apparently by association with *Tartarus* as a name of hell.)

Tatra Mountains. *Mountain group, central Europe*. The mountains, the chief group of the Carpathians, between Poland and the Czech Republic, have a name that ultimately goes back to Greek *tethron*, "end," "extremity."

Ta-t'ung. *City, northeastern China*. The city, in Shansi province, derives its name from Chinese *dà*, "big," "great," and *tóng*, "alike," "similar."

Tauberbischofsheim. *Town, southwestern Germany*. The town was originally named *Bischofsheim*, "bishop's abode," for St. Boniface, archbishop of Mainz, to whom it was given in c.725 by the Frankish king Charles Martel. The name of the *Tauber* River, ultimately from Celtic *dubro*, "water" (as for **Dover**), was added later

to distinguish the town from *Neckarbischofsheim*, on the **Neckar**.

Tauern. *Mountain chain, western Austria*. The chain, divided into the *Hohe Tauern* and *Niedere Tauern*, respectively "high and "lower," derives its basic name from Indoeuropean *taur* or *tier*, "great."

¹Taunton. *Town, southwestern England*. The Somerset town takes its name from the *Tone* River on which it lies. The river's own name means "flowing one," from an Indoeuropean root element *ta* that also gave the name of the **Thames**. The *-ton* is Old English *tūn*, "farm," "settlement."

²Taunton. *City, eastern United States*. The Massachusetts city was organized as a town in 1639 and named for **¹Taunton**, England, the home town of one of the early proprietors, Elizabeth Poole.

Taunus. *Mountain range, west central Germany*. The wooded highland probably derives its name from a Germanic form of Celtic *dunu*, "height" (related English *down*). Despite its etymological antiquity, the name was first current only in the 19th century, and the range's earlier name was simply *die Höhe*, "the height," for its extended elevation above the plains of the Rhine and Main rivers. Historically, the name *Taunus* properly belongs to **Friedberg**.

Taupo, Lake. *Lake, northern New Zealand*. New Zealand's largest lake, in central North Island, derives its name from Maori *taupo nui a Tia*, "great cloak of *Tia*," referring to a local legend.

Tauranga. *City and port, northern New Zealand*. The city, in central North Island, derives its name from a Maori word meaning either "resting place" or "safe anchorage."

Taurus. *Mountain range, southern Turkey*. The range probably derives its name from the Celtic root element *tauro*, related to English *tor* and meaning simply "hill," "mountain." The Greeks understandably took the name to represent *tauros*, "bull." *Cp.* **Turin**.

Taxila. *Historic city, northwestern Pakistan*. The archaeological site of three successive cities came by its name as a Greek corruption of its original name *Taksasila*, meaning "rock of *Taksa*," referring to *Taksa*, in Hindu mythology the son of Bharata, younger brother of Rama, an incarnation of Vishnu.

Tay. *River, central Scotland*. The name of Scotland's longest river may mean "strong one" or "silent one," from a conjectural Celtic name *Tausos*.

Ta-yeh. *City, east central China*. The city, in

Hupeh province, has a name meaning "great smelting (place)," from Chinese *dà*, "big," "great," and *yě*, "to smelt." The reference is to the nearby hills containing iron deposits. In the 10th and 11th centuries the area also produced copper.

Taygetus. *Mountain range, southern Greece.* The name is traditionally derived from *Taygete*, the daughter of Atlas in Greek mythology, the range's resident nymph.

Taymyr Peninsula. *Peninsula, northern Russia.* The peninsula is named for the *Taymyra* River that flows north through it into the Kara Sea. Its own name is said to be Evenki in origin with a meaning "copious," "rich," referring not to its waters but to its abundance of fish.

Tbilisi. *Capital of Georgia.* The city derives its name from Georgian *tbili*, "warm," alluding to the hot sulfur springs here. The name was long familiar as *Tiflis*, a Turkish corrupt form.

Tczew. *Town and river port, north central Poland.* The town, on the Vistula, has a Slavic name meaning "place of reeds." The German form of the name is *Dirschau*.

Te Anau, Lake. *Lake, southern New Zealand.* The name of the lake, in southwestern South Island, is probably a shortened form of the Maori name *Te Ana-au*, "cave of the swirling water."

Te Aroha. *Town, northern New Zealand.* The town takes its name from a nearby extinct volcano. Its own Maori name means "the loved one," referring to a local legend.

Tees. *River, northern England.* The river's name is probably Celtic in origin and possibly means "boiling one," "seething one," alluding to its many waterfalls and rapids and its strong current.

Tegelen. *Town, southeastern Netherlands.* The town derives its name from Dutch *tegel*, "tile," referring to the local tileworks and potteries.

Tegernsee. *Lake, southeastern Germany.* The lofty lake is believed to derive its name from a conjectural Old High German adjective *tegar*, "great," "extensive." It is nearly 4 miles (6.5 km) long and almost a mile (1.6 km) wide.

Tegucigalpa. *Capital of Honduras.* The city has a Native American name meaning "silver mountain," referring to the silver mines nearby.

Tehran. *Capital of Iran.* The city's Iranian name probably means "flat," "level," "lower," referring to its location in the foothills of the Elburz Mountains, although some authorities derive it from Old Persian *teh*, "warm," and *ran*, "place." The name has the alternate spelling *Teheran*.

Tehuantepec, Isthmus of. *Isthmus, southern Mexico.* The narrowest part of southern Mexico

derives its name from Nahuatl *tecuani*, "beast (of prey)," probably denoting some totemic animal, and *tepetl*, "mountain."

Tekirdağ. *City and port, northwestern Turkey.* The city was founded in the 7th century B.C. as a Greek settlement named *Bisanthe*. It then became the capital of Thrace in the 1st century B.C. and was renamed *Rhaedestus*, a name later modified as *Rodosto*. In 1923 it took its present name from a nearby mountain, its own name meaning "mottled mountain," from Turkish *tekir*, "spotted," and *dağ*, "mountain."

Tel Aviv. *City and port, western Israel.* The city was founded in 1909 and given the name of a Babylonian city mentioned in the Bible: "Then I came to them of the captivity at Tel-abib, that dwelt by the river of Chebar, and I sat where they sat, and remained there astonished among them seven days" (Ezekiel 3:15). The text refers to a colony of deported Jews, one of whom is Ezekiel himself. The biblical town originally had an Akkadian name meaning "hill of the flood." The like-sounding Hebrew name substituted for this meant "hill of the ear (of corn)" or "hill of springtime." The direct source of the current name is the novel *Altneuland* ("Old New Land") (1902), by Theodor Herzl, the founder of modern Zionism, which was translated into Hebrew as *Tel Aviv*, in the sense "spring hill." The city has been officially known as *Tel Aviv-Yafo* since it incorporated the latter city (**Jaffa**) in 1950.

Teleorman. *County, southern Romania.* The name is of Turkish origin and probably means "dense forest" (*teli orman*), although some authorities interpret it as "forest of foxes."

Telford. *Town, western England.* The Shropshire town, designated a New Town in 1963, is one of the few British new towns to have a new name. It is that of the Scottish civil engineer Thomas *Telford* (1757–1834), who was appointed surveyor of Shropshire in 1786, a post that involved the construction of buildings and bridges and that led to many famous engineering feats elsewhere in Britain.

Tel Hay. *Historic settlement, northern Israel.* The former settlement, now the memorial site of a battle in 1920 between Arab rebels and Jewish fighters (*see* **Qiryat Shemona**), has a Hebrew name meaning "hill of life," as an onomatopoeic derivation of its former Arabic name, *Talha*.

Tell el-Amarna. *Historic site, north central Egypt.* The site of the tombs and ruins of the city of Akhetaton, dating from the 14th century B.C., takes its name from the Bedouin tribe of the *Bani Amran*, "sons of *Amran*," with initial Arabic *tall*, "hill."

Tel Yosef. *Kibbutz, northeastern Israel.* The kibbutz, founded in 1921, has a name meaning "hill of *Yosef*," for the Zionist military hero *Josef* Trumpeldor (1880–1920), killed with other Jewish settlers at **Tel Hay**, where he is buried. *See also* **Qiryat Shemona.**

Temirtau. *City, east central Kazakhstan.* The city's name means "iron mountain," from Kazakh *temir*, "iron," and *tau*, "mountain," referring to the abundance of iron ore locally.

Tempe. *City, southwestern United States.* The Arizona city, now a suburb of Phoenix, was first settled in 1877 by Charles T. *Hayden*, father of Arizona's first representative and later senator, Carl T. Hayden (1877–1972), and initially known as *Hayden's Ferry*, for its location on the Salt River. In 1880 it was renamed as now for the Vale of *Tempe* in northern Greece, dedicated to the god Apollo.

Tempelhof. *District of Berlin, western Germany.* The former town, first mentioned in 1241, derives its name from the Knights *Templars*, who held an estate here (modern German *Hof*, "farm," "court").

Temple. *City, southern United States.* The Texas city was founded by the Gulf, Colorado, and Santa Fe Railroad in 1880 and named for Major B.M. *Temple*, chief railroad engineer.

Tenerife. *Island, east central Atlantic.* The largest of the Canary Islands, off the northwest coast of Africa, takes its name from its volcano, now known as *Pico de Tenerife*. This represents a former local name *Chinerfe*. The meaning of this is uncertain, but "white mountain" has been proposed. The volcano's Roman name was *Nivaria*, "snowy."

Tennessee. *State, east central United States.* The state takes its name from the river that rises in it and that loops down into Alabama before crossing it northward to flow into the Ohio. Its own name represents Cherokee *tanasi* (or some similar spelling), probably meaning simply "river."

Tenochtitlán *see* **Mexico City**

Tenos. *Island, eastern Greece.* The island, one of the Cyclades, derives its name from Phoenician *tenok*, "snake," referring to the abundance of these reptiles here. Its former Greek name, with identical meaning, was *Ophiousa*, from *ophis*, "snake." The modern Greek form of the name is *Tínos*.

Ten Thousand Smokes, Valley of. *Region, northwestern United States.* The volcanic region, in southern Alaska, is named for the thousands of fumaroles (steam, smoke, and gas jets) in the valley floor here. The valley itself was created in 1912 by the eruption of two volcanoes.

Teotihuacán. *Historic city, central Mexico.* The pre–Columbian city, with its famous Pyramid of the Sun, has a Nahuatl name meaning "place of the gods."

Tepe Gawra. *Archaeological site, northern Iraq.* The site of ancient settlements, on a sequence of 24 levels and sublevels, has a Kurdish name meaning "great mound."

Tepic. *City, west central Mexico.* The city takes its name from the river here, its own name representing a Nahuatl word meaning "hard stone," referring to its bed.

Teplice. *City, northwestern Czech Republic.* The city is a health resort with warm springs in the Erzgebirge (Ore Mountains). Hence its name, from Czech *teplý*, "warm," "hot." The German form of the name is *Teplitz*.

Teplodar. *Town, southern Ukraine.* The town, founded in 1981, has a name meaning "gift of warmth" (Russian *teplo-*, "warm," and *dar*, "gift"), for its thermal (*teplovaya*) electric power station.

Teramo. *City, central Italy.* The city's name evolved from its Roman name of *Interamnium*, from Latin *inter*, "between," and *amnis*, "river," describing its location at the confluence of the Tordino and Vezzola rivers. *Cp.* **Terni.**

Terceira. *Island, North Atlantic.* The island, in the central Azores, has a Portuguese name meaning "third," as it was the *third* island in the Azores to be discovered by the Portuguese.

Teresina. *City, northeastern Brazil.* The city was founded in 1852, originally as *Therezina*, and was named for the Brazilian empress *Teresa* Cristina, wife of Dom Pedro II (*see* **Teresópolis**)

Teresópolis. *City, southeastern Brazil.* The city and mountain resort was founded in 1890, originally as *Therezópolis*, and named for the Brazilian empress *Teresa* Cristina Maria (1822–1889), wife of Dom Pedro II (1825–1891), second and last emperor of Brazil. (She was the daughter of Francis I, king of the Two Sicilies, and his second wife, Marie-Élisabeth of Bourbon.) The city is not far from **Petrópolis**, named for her husband, where the remains of the royal couple were placed in a chapel in 1920 following their death in exile in Europe.

Terezín. *Town, northern Czech Republic.* The town was founded in 1780 as a fortified post dedicated to the Holy Roman empress *Maria Theresa* (1717–1780). Its German name, notorious from the ghetto and concentration camp for Jews set up here by Nazi Germany in World War II, is *Theresienstadt*.

Termini Imerese. *Town and port, southern*

Italy. The town, in northern Sicily, had the Roman name *Thermae Himerenses,* "springs of *Himera,*" the latter being a town nearby that was destroyed by the Carthaginians in 409 B.C. The town is noted for its thermal saline springs.

Terni. *City, central Italy.* The city's name evolved from its Roman name of *Interamnium,* from Latin *inter,* "between," and *amnis,* "river," referring to its location between two branches of the Nera river. *Cp.* **Teramo.**

Ternopol. *City, western Ukraine.* Despite appearances, the city does not have a Greek-style name, like that of **Mariupol** or **Stavropol,** but a Slavic one, from a combination of Russian *tyorn,* "thorn," and *pole,* "field," referring to a tract of grassland overrun by blackthorn. The name was formerly spelled *Tarnopol,* and the Ukrainian form is *Ternopil'.*

Terre Haute. *City, east central United States.* The Indiana city was laid out in 1811 on a plateau above the Wabash River. Hence its French name, meaning "high land."

Terror, Mt. *see* **Erebus, Mt.**

Teschen *see* **Cieszyn**

Teshik Tash. *Archaeological site, southern Uzbekistan.* The prehistoric cave site, noted for its Neanderthal child burial, derives its name from Uzbek *teshik,* "hole," and *tosh,* "stone."

Tete. *City and river port, western Mozambique.* The city's name derives from a Chisema word meaning "reed," "canebrake," referring to its location on the Amazon River.

Teton Range. *Mountain range, northwestern United States.* The section of the northern Rockies, in northwestern Wyoming, was visited in the early 19th century by French fur trappers, who referred to the *High, Middle* and *Grand* peaks as *les trois tétons,* "the three teats." Hence the name.

Tétouan. *City, north central Morocco.* The city has a name of Berber origin meaning "springs."

Teutoburg Forest. *Hill range, northeastern Germany.* The name of the range of wooded hills is first recorded by Tacitus in the 1st century A.D. as *Teutoburgiensis saltus,* referring to the famous battle of A.D. 9 in which the Germans under Arminius defeated the Roman legions under Varus. The Latin adjective *Teutoburgiensis* derives from an assumed placename *Teutoburgium,* "people's fort," with the first syllable from Old High German *thiota,* "people." The hills are thus named for a Germanic fortress.

Texarkana. *Twin cities, southern United States.* The dual municipality, astride the Texas-Arkansas boundary and also near the Louisiana border, was settled in 1874 and derives its name from a blend of *Tex*as, *Ark*ansas, and Louisi*ana.*

Texas. *State, southern United States.* The state is said to derive its name from a Native American word *techas,* meaning "friends," "allies." The story goes that in 1690 the Spanish monk Damian was greeted on his arrival at the coast here with cries of "*techas! techas!*" as a form of greeting.

Teyateyaneng. *Town, northwestern Morocco.* The town takes its name from the nearby *Teja-Tejane* River, its own name meaning "quicksands," referring to its bed. The name is often abbreviated as *TY.*

Thailand. *Kingdom, southeastern Asia.* The country takes its name from its indigenous population, the *Thais.* Their own name means "free people," from Thai *tha,* "to be free." The Thais' own name for their country is *prathesthay,* "land of the free," with *prathes* meaning "land," "country." Until 1939, and again briefly from 1945 to 1948, the country was known as *Siam,* from Thai *sayam,* from Sanskrit *syāma,* "dark," referring to the skin color of the native Thais.

Thame. *Town, south central England.* The Oxfordshire town takes its name from the river on which it lies, the river name itself having the same origin as that of the **Thames,** of which it is a tributary.

Thames. *River, southern England.* The river, rising in Gloucestershire and flowing east through Oxford to enter the North Sea beyond London, has a name that ultimately derives from the Indoeuropean root element *ta,* "to flow." There are other rivers in Britain with names of like origin, such as the *Taff* in Wales (*see* **Cardiff**), *Tamar* in Cornwall, *Tame* (*see* ¹**Tamworth**), *Thame* (*see* **Thame**), *Tone* (*see* **Taunton**), and *Teviot* in Scotland. The Thames at Oxford is known as the *Isis,* an artificial name produced from the latter half of *Tamesis,* the Roman name of the Thames. (Classical scholars at Oxford would prefer to associate the name with the Egyptian goddess *Isis.*)

Thanet, Isle of. *Peninsula, southeastern England.* The Kent peninsula has an ancient name, known to the Romans as *Tanatis* or *Tanatus.* The origin is uncertain but may lie in a Celtic root word *tan,* "fire," referring to a lighthouse or beacon here. Thanet was actually an island at one time.

Thar Desert. *Desert region, northwestern India/southeastern Pakistan.* The region derives its name from Hindi *thul,* "rising ground," "ridge," referring to its sand ridges.

Tharrawaddy. *Town, southern Myanmar.* The town is named for the Myanmar (Burmese) king *Tharrawaddy* (died 1846).

Thebes. *Historic city, northeastern Egypt.* The name of the long-ruined city is a Greek form of Semitic *ta-ope*, "the capital," denoting its status as the religious and administrative center of ancient Egypt. Its Egyptian name was *Waset*, from the sacred *was* or scepter. It was also *Nīt* or *Nīut*, "abode," "city," or *No-Ammon*, "abode of Ammon." The latter gave its biblical name of *No* (Nahum 3:8). The Greeks also knew it as *Diospolis*, "town of Zeus." The Egyptian city probably gave the name of *Thebes* in east central Greece, an equally ancient town.

Thera. *Island, southern Greece.* The volcanic island, one of the Cyclades, is said to derive its name from *Theras*, the Spartan chief who colonized it. Its earlier name was *Kalliste* (*Callista*), "beautiful." It later became known as *Santorin*, from Italian *Santa Irini*, "*St. Irene*," an early 4th-century martyr together with her companions Agape and Chione.

Thermopylae. *Historic pass, eastern Greece.* The pass has a name meaning literally "hot gates," from Greek *thermos*, "hot," and *pulai*, the plural of *pulē*, "gate," "door." The reference is to the hot sulfur springs here. The former narrow pass along the coast is now a rocky plain about 6 miles (10 km) from the sea.

Thessalonika *see* **Salonika**

Thessaly. *Region, east central Greece.* The region has a name of Illyrian origin but unknown meaning.

Thiès. *Town, west central Senegal.* The town's name represents a local pronunciation of French *caisse*, "case," "chest," alluding to a depot here where crates of materials were stored from c.1885 during construction of the Dakar to St. Louis railroad. The present town grew from the depot.

Thingvellir. *Plain, southwestern Iceland.* The level plain with lava floor takes its name from the *Thingvellir*, the historic meeting place of the *Althing* (parliament) from 930 through 1798. The name comprises Icelandic *thing*, "assembly" (English *thing*), and *vella*, "to spurt" (English *well*), referring to the geysers here. Iceland's largest lake, *Thingvallavatn*, is also here, with *vatn*, "water," "lake," added.

Thionville. *Town, northeastern France.* The first part of the town's name represents the Germanic personal name *Theudo*. The second part is Latin *villa*, "farm," the source of French *ville*, "town." When under German control from 1870 through 1919 the town was known as *Diedenhofen*. This is essentially the same name, with *Dieden* a possessive form of the personal name, and German *Hof*, "farm," corresponding to Latin *villa*.

Thompson. *River, southwestern Canada.* The river, in southern British Columbia, was explored by Simor Fraser (*see* **Fraser**) in 1808 and named for David *Thompson* (1770–1857), the English explorer mistakenly credited with having reached its upper course.

Thonon-les-Bains. *Town and resort, southeastern France.* The town has a name of uncertain origin. It could derive from a Celtic word meaning something like "town on water," referring to its location on Lake Geneva. On the other hand, it may simply represent a Germanic word related to English *town*. The second part of the name, meaning "the baths," refers to the mineral springs here.

Thorshavn. *Capital of Faeroe Islands.* The town and port has a name meaning "*Thor*'s port," from *Thor*, the Norse god of thunder, and Faeroese *havn*, "harbor," "port." The name is also spelled *Tórshavn*.

Thousand Islands. *Island group, eastern North America.* The name is a conservative misnomer for the more than 1,800 small islands that lie in the St. Lawrence River. The isles on the western side are mostly in Canada, while those on the east are in New York, USA.

Thrace. *Historic region, southeastern Europe.* The region, in the eastern part of the Balkan Peninsula, varied its limits at different periods. Its name comes from its indigenous people, the *Thracians*, whose own name may represent Semitic *raqiwa*, "firmament."

Three Kings Islands. *Island group, northern New Zealand.* The three small islands, north of the northern extremity of North Island, were so named by Abel Tasman (*see* **Tasmania**) when he sighted them on January 6, 1643, the feast of the Epiphany, the day when the three wise men (three kings) brought gifts to the infant Jesus.

Thule. *Settlement, northwestern Greenland.* In 1910 the Danish Arctic explorer Knud Rasmussen set up a trading post for the *Thule* Inuit (Eskimos) here and named it for them. Their own name related to the *Thule* prehistoric culture, itself named for *Thule*, an island six days' sailing north of Orkney, Scotland, discovered in the 4th century B.C. by the Greek navigator Pytheas. (It gave the Latin phrase *ultima Thule*, "farthest *Thule*," for any remote place.) The name itself is of uncertain origin. Proposed etymologies include: (1) From Greek *tholos*, "mud," "silt"; (2) From Greek *tēle*, "far"; (3) From Celtic *thual*, "north"; (4) From *Thulus*, its (probably legendary) king; (5) From Sanskrit *tula*, "Libra" (the constellation). In World War II the name of the trading post was adopted for the U.S. air base here, and in 1953 the Thule Inuit were obliged to move their settlement, together with its name, to *Qaanaaq*, a new site 62 miles (100 km) north. The air base meanwhile became known as *Dundas*, but subsequently, to avoid ambiguity over the Thule name, was officially renamed *Pituffik*.

Thun. *City, central Switzerland*. The city, founded in the 12th century, takes its name from Gaulish *dunon*, "hill fort." The French form of the name is *Thoune*.

Thunder Bay. *City and lake port, southern Canada*. The city, on the western shore of Lake Superior, derives its name from the bay here. Its own name translates a Native American phrase alluding to some occasion on which thunder was heard.

Thurgau. *Canton, northeastern Switzerland*. The canton derives its name from the *Thur* River here, its own name from Indoeuropean *dur*, "current," and German *Gau*, "district." The French name of the canton is *Thurgovie*.

Thuringia. *Region, southern Germany*. The region takes its name from the *Thoringi* or *Thuringi* who formerly lived here. Their own name may derive from Old Scandinavian *thori*, "people," "crowd." The German form of the name is *Thüringen*.

Tiaret. *City, northern Algeria*. The city, formerly known as *Tagdempt*, arose from the 8th-century Muslim town of *Tiharet*, its own name said to be Berber for "the lioness."

Tiber. *River, central Italy*. The river is traditionally said to derive its name from *Tiberinus*, a king of Alba Longa who was drowned in it. But its true origin is likely to be in Celtic *dubro*, "water," as for **Dover**.

Tiberias *see* **Galilee**

Tibesti. *Mountain range, northwestern Chad*. The mountains are named for the *Tibu*, a Berber tribe of the Sahara. Their own name is said to mean "bird," either because they communicate by "whistling" or because they run rapidly, but a better origin is in Berber *tu*, "mountain," and *bu*, "dweller."

Tibet. *Region, southwestern China*. The autonomous region is known to Tibetans as *bod* or *bodyul*, literally "*Bod* land," from their own name for themselves, of uncertain meaning. This was eventually corrupted, under Chinese and Arabic influence, to *Tibet*. The Chinese name of Tibet is *xīzàng*, "storehouse of the west."

Tibidabo, Mt. *Mountain, northeastern Spain*. The mountain, just outside Barcelona, has a name popularly derived from the (Latin) biblical words of Satan when tempting Christ in the wilderness and taking him up "into an exceeding high mountain": "*Haec omnia tibi dabo si cadens adoraberis me*" ("All these things will I give thee, if thou wilt fall down and worship me") (Matthew 4:9). The actual origin of the name is uncertain.

Ticino. *Canton, southern Switzerland*. The canton derives its name from that of the *Ticino* River, which rises here and flows generally south into Italy to join the Po. Its own name, recorded by the Romans as *Ticinus*, probably means simply "river." The German name of the canton is *Tessin*.

Ticonderoga. *Village, eastern United States*. The New York village arose on a neck of land between Lake George and Lake Champlain and is named for its location, from an Iroquois phrase meaning "between two waters."

Tidewater. *Region, eastern United States*. The low-lying plain in eastern Virginia, on the shore of Chesapeake Bay, is named for the tidal estuaries of the Potomac, Rappahannock, James, and York rivers that cross it.

Tien Shan. *Mountain range, central Asia*. The range, crossing the border between Russia and China, has a Chinese name meaning "heavenly mountain," from *tiān*, "heaven," "day," and *shān*, "mountain."

Tientsin. *City, northeastern China*. China's third largest city, at the confluence of several streams, has a name meaning "ford of heaven," from Chinese *tiān*, "heaven," "day," and *jīn*, "ford."

Tiergarten. *District of Berlin, western Germany*. The residential district takes its name from the deer park that existed here down to the 18th century. (German *Tiergarten* now means "zoo" but literally means "animal garden," while English *deer* itself originally meant "animal" generally.)

Tierra del Fuego. *Island group, southern South America*. The archipelago has a Spanish name meaning "land of fire." The Portuguese navigator Ferdinand Magellan discovered the islands in 1520 and named them for the many fires he saw here, either as camp fires on land or as navigational lights on boats at sea. The indigenous Indians are said to have kept fires burning constantly because the high moisture level of the air made it hard to set light to any wood.

Tiflis *see* **Tbilisi**

Tighina. *City, southeastern Moldova*. The city, on the Dniester River, has a name of uncertain origin and meaning. It was formerly called *Bendery*, from a Turkic word meaning "harbor."

Tigray. *Historic region, northern Ethiopia*. The

region is named for the *Tigre* people, its indigenous inhabitants. The origin of their own name is uncertain. The name is also spelled *Tigrai* and *Tigre*.

Tigris. *River, southwestern Asia*. The river, in Turkey and Iraq, derives its name from Old Persian *tigra*, "arrow," referring to its rapid current. Its Sumerian name, *Tigrushu*, was similar, from *tig*, "spear," *ru*, "to conquer," "to overthrow," and *shu*, "to capture," "to catch." It was thus the "river running with a conquering spear." In Turkey the Tigris is a typical mountain stream, flowing swiftly in a narrow valley.

Tilburg. *City, southern Netherlands*. The first part of the city's name, *Til*, is a pet form of the personal name *Theodulus*. The second part is Dutch *burg*, "castle." The overall sense is thus "fortified place dedicated to St. *Theodulus*." The city was a small village until 1860, after which it grew rapidly.

Tilbury. *Town and port, southeastern England*. The former Essex town has a name meaning "*Tila*'s fortified place," with the Anglo-Saxon personal name followed by Old English *burh*, "fort."

Timaru. *City and port, southeastern New Zealand*. The city, in eastern South Island, has a Maori name said to mean "cabbage-tree shelter."

Timbuktu. *City, central Mali*. The city derives its name from a Songhai word meaning "hollow," referring to the depression in which it lies on the edge of the Sahara. The name was at one time often spelled *Timbuctoo*, especially as a byname for a very remote place.

Timişoara. *City, western Romania*. The name of the town, meaning "fort on the *Timiş* (River)," is a Romanian form of Hungarian *Temesvár*, with the river name followed by Hungarian *vár*, "fort." The river's name is probably related to that of the **Thames**.

Timmins. *City, eastern Canada*. The Ontario city was settled when gold was discovered in 1905. It was named for Noah A. *Timmins* (1867–1936), president of the company that developed the mine here.

Timor. *Island, southern Malay Archipelago*. The island's name represents Malay *timur*, "east," referring to its geographical location to the east of Java and Sumatra. The former Portuguese province of *East Timor*, annexed by Indonesia in 1975, thus had the apparently tautological indigenous name of *Timor Timur*.

Timsah, Lake. *Lake, northeastern Egypt*. The full Arabic name of the lake, near Ismailia, is *baḥr et-timsāh*, "crocodile lake."

Tinos. *Island, southwestern Greece*. The island, one of the Cyclades, derives its name from Phoenician *tenok*, "snake," referring to the presence of these reptiles here.

Tipperary. *Town, southern Ireland*. The town, in the county of the same name, derives its name from Irish *Tiobraid Árann*, "well of the *Ara*," the latter being the river on which the town stands. The river's own name is that of the region here, and means "ridged place," or literally "kidney," Irish *ára*, as for the **Aran Islands**.

Tiranë. *Capital of Albania*. The city was founded in c.1600 by the Turkish general Barkinzade Suleyman Pasha, who is said to have named it for **Tehran**, the Persian (now Iranian) capital, in order to commemorate a Turkish victory in Persia. But the name is already recorded as *il borgo di Tirana* in a Venetian document dated 1572, so that this explanation is unlikely. Its origin is thus uncertain, but it may relate in some way to the name of the **Tyrrhenian Sea**. Its alternate form is *Tirana*.

Tiraspol. *City, eastern Moldova*. The city, on the **Dniester** River, was founded in 1792 and given a Greek-style name representing *Tyras*, the ancient Greek name of this river, and Greek *polis*, "town."

Tîrgovişte. *City, south central Romania*. The city derives its name from Slavic *torg*, "market," and the location suffix -*işte*, giving a meaning "market place." *Cp.* **Turgovishte**.

Tîrgu Mureş. *City, north central Romania*. The city derives its name from Romanian *tîrgu*, "market," and the name of the *Mureş* River on which it lies. The Hungarian name of the city is similar, as *Marosvásárhely*, from the river name and *vásárhely*, "market place."

Tîrnava Mare. *River, central Romania*. The first word of the name represents Slavic *torn*, "blackthorn." The second word is Romanian *mare*, "great." Almost parallel to the north is the *Tîrnava Mica*, "little *Tîrnava*."

Tirol *see* **Tyrol**

Tiruchchirappalli. *City, southern India*. The city, in Tamil Nadu state, has a name formerly familiar as *Trichinopoly*. It is of Malayalam origin and means "town of the sacred rock," from *tiru*, "holy," *sita*, "rock," and *palli*, "town." *Trichinopoly* may have arisen through Greek influence, as if originally *Trichinopolis*, which would mean "city of hair." (This is not as surreal as it seems: *see* ¹**Halifax**.)

Tirunelveli. *Town, southeastern India*. The town, in Tamil Nadu state, derives its name from Tamil *tiru*, "holy," *nel*, "rice field," "paddy," and *veli*, "fence." The allusion is to a legend that the

Hindu god Shiva protected a devotee's rice crop here. The name is also spelled in the corrupt form *Tinnevelly*.

Tiruppur. *Town, south central India*. The town, in Tamil Nadu state, derives its name from Tamil *tiru*, "holy," and Hindi *pur*, "town," "city." The town has a famous Hindu temple.

Tiryns. *Historic city, southeastern Greece*. The ancient city, noted for its architectural remains, may derive the first part of its name from Greek *tursis*, "tower." The ending is the non–Indo-european -*inthos* found in names such as **Zakinthos**.

Tiszaföldvár. *Town, east central Hungary*. The town, on the *Tisza* River (*see* **Tiszafüred**), derives the second part of its name from Hungarian *föld*, "earth," and *vár*, "castle," denoting the material with which the original defensive post here was built. *Cp.* **Tiszavasvár**.

Tiszafüred. *City, northern Hungary*. The city lies on the *Tisza* River, a tributary of the Danube, its own name a reduced form of its Roman name *Pathissus*, perhaps from Sanskrit *pathas*, "water." The second part of the city's name derives from *für*, a dialect form of Hungarian *fürj*, "quail."

Tiszaújváros. *City, northeastern Hungary*. The city arose on the site of a village called *Tisza-szederkény*, from *Tisza*, the river on which it lies (*see* **Tiszafüred**), and another river name based on *szeder*, "bramble." It was a "socialist town" at first called *Lenínváros*, "Lenin's town," a name complemented by that of *Sztálinváros*, now **Dunaújváros**. In 1990 the city was renamed as now, with Hungarian *új*, "new," and *város*, "city," added to the river name.

Tiszavasvár. *City, eastern Hungary*. The city, on the *Tisza* River (*see* **Tiszafüred**), derives the second part of its name from Hungarian *vas*, "iron," and *vár*, "castle." An "iron castle" is a strong or dark-colored one, as if made of iron. *Cp.* **Vasvár**.

Titicaca, Lake. *Lake, western South America*. South America's second-largest lake, between Peru and Bolivia, may derive its name from Quechua *titi*, "lead" (the metal), and *kaka*, "mountain chain," although some authorities see a source in an Aymara word meaning "rock of the jaguar." When seen from above (or on a map) the lake resembles the outline of this animal, its head in Bolivia and its tail in Peru. *See also* **Sol, Isla del**.

Titograd *see* **Podgorica**

Tivoli. *Town, central Italy*. The town has a name of Illyrian origin but uncertain meaning. It may be related to Albanian *timbi*, "rock." The

gardens of the town's Villa d'Este, with their fine fountains, gave the name of the famed *Tivoli* pleasure gardens in Copenhagen, Denmark, opened in 1843.

Tizi Ouzu. *Town, northern Algeria*. The town has a Berber name, from *tizi*, "pass," referring to the pass here into the mountains of Kabylia, and *ouzou*, "broom," referring to the plant that grew in it.

Tlaxcala. *Town, east central Mexico*. The town has a Nahuatl name said to mean "house of bread."

Tlemcen. *City, northwestern Algeria*. The city derives its name from Berber *tilimsane*, "springs." The earliest settlement on the site was the Roman *Pomaria*, "orchards." The town that arose was at first known as *Agadir*, "embankment" (*see* **Agadir**), before gaining its present name in the 13th century. The name is now also spelled *Tilimsen*.

Toamasina. *City and port, eastern Madagascar*. The city's name is said to derive from Malagasy *tòa*, "how," and *màsina*, "salt." The story goes that King Radama I, reigning in the early 19th century, saw the sea for the first time here and, tasting the water, exclaimed, "How salty it is!" This unlikely tale may in fact mask an actual reference to salt. The city was formerly known as *Tamatave*, a French corruption of its present name, which the Portuguese, here in the 17th century, corrupted rather more imaginatively to *São Tomé*, "St. Thomas."

Tobago. *Island, southeastern West Indies*. The island, part of the republic of Trinidad and Tobago, was so named by Columbus when he discovered it in 1498. He took it from Haitian *tambaku*, "pipe," alluding to the islanders' strange habit of lighting the dried cut leaves of the tobacco plant in a pipe and inhaling the toxic fumes, which they believed had medicinal properties.

Tobolsk. *City, northwestern Russia*. The city takes its name from the *Tobol* River on which it lies. The river's own name is of uncertain origin. It may be related to Russian *tavolga*, "meadowsweet."

Tobruk. *City and port, northern Libya*. The city's name is a corruption of its original Greek name *Antipyrgos*, "opposite the tower," from *anti*, "opposite," and *purgos*, "tower." The bay here was sheltered from the wind by an island with a tower on it.

Tocantins. *River, north central Brazil*. The river, named for a Native American people, gave the identical name of the state through which it flows as well as the names of various towns and cities on it, among them *Tocantínia, Tocanti-nópolis*, and *Tocantópolis*.

Tochigi. *Prefecture, central Japan.* The prefecture, in the island of Honshu, derives its name from Japanese *tochi*, "horse chestnut," and *ki*, "tree."

Togo. *Republic, western Africa.* The country was named *Togoland* in 1884 by the German explorer Gustav Nachtigall, who based it on that of a small coastal village where he signed a treaty with the local people. The original name of the village, now called *Togoville*, is said to have been *Miayi To Godo*, "we shall go beyond the hill," although it is more likely to have come from nearby Lake *Togo*, whose own name represents *to*, "water," and *go*, "edge," "shore."

Tohoku. *Region, northern Japan.* The region, in northern Honshu, derives its name from Japanese *tō*, "east," and *hoku*, "north," describing its geographical location.

Tokaj. *Town, northeastern Hungary.* The town may derive its name from Slavic *tok*, "current," referring to its location at the confluence of the Bodrog and Tisza rivers. The region here was populated by Slavs before the arrival of the Magyar in the 9th century. But *Tokay* could also represent a personal name of Turkic origin.

Tokushima. *City, southern Japan.* The city, in the prefecture of the same name, in the island of Shikoku, derives its name from Japanese *toku*, "virtue," "goodness," and *shima*, "island."

Tokyo. *Capital of Japan.* The city's name means "eastern capital," from Japanese *tō*, "east," and *kyō*, "capital." It was so named by contrast with **Kyoto**, the capital until 1868, to the west of it. Before that date Tokyo was known as *Edo*, "estuary," for its location at the head of Tokyo Bay.

Tolbukhin *see* **Dobrich**

[1]**Toledo.** *City, central Spain.* The name of the city ultimately derives from Celtic *tol*, "hill," "rise." Toledo is on a rugged promontory overlooking the Tagus River.

[2]**Toledo.** *City and lake port, northern United States.* The Ohio city was established in 1833 when the two villages of Port Lawrence and Vistula were consolidated and named for [1]**Toledo**, Spain.

Toliara. *Town and port, southwestern Madagascar.* The town's name is traditionally explained as follows. A foreign traveler in Madagascar asked a local canoeist where he was about to land. The man thought he was being asked where there was a mooring place, so replied *tòly eròa*, "the moorage there." This then became the name of the place. But folk etymology is patently at work here.

Tolmin. *Town, western Slovenia.* The town, in a region that formerly belonged to Italy, has a name that probably derives from Celtic *tol*, "hill," "mountain." The Italian form of the name is *Tolmino*.

Tolna. *Town, west central Hungary.* The name derives from Latin *teloneum*, "tollhouse," referring to the ferry dues exacted when crossing the river here, now a cut-off arm of the Danube.

To-lun. *Town, northern China.* The town, in Inner Mongolia, has a name representing Mongolian *dolon nor*, "seven lakes."

Tolyatti. *City, western Russia.* The city was founded in 1738 as a fortified post on the Volga with the Greek name of *Stavropol*, "city of the cross," from *stauros*, "cross," and *polis*, "city." This was given to mark the "christening" (conversion to Christianity) of the Buddhist Kalmuck prince, Peter Taisha, together with some of his compatriots. In the mid–1950s the town was flooded during construction of the huge V.I. Lenin dam and hydroelectric station, and was moved to a higher location. In 1964 it was renamed *Tolyatti*, for the Italian Communist leader Palmiro *Togliatti* (1893–1964), who paid several visits to the Soviet Union and who died there during one of them.

Tombstone. *City, southwestern United States.* The Arizona city was ironically named by a prospector, Ed Schieffelin, who discovered silver here in 1877 after being told that all he would find would be his *tombstone*. He founded the city two years later.

Tomsk. *City, central Russia.* The city takes its name from the *Tom* River on which it lies. The river's own name is of uncertain origin. It may mean simply "river," and so be related to that of the **Thames**.

Tonbridge. *Town, southeastern England.* The Kent town, on the Medway River, has an Old English name meaning "bridge by the village," from *tūn*, "village," and *brycg*, "bridge." The reference is to a bridge that led to the original village here from some other part of the manor. *See also* **Tunbridge Wells**.

Tonga. *Island kingdom, southwestern Pacific.* The island group has a name of local origin said to mean simply "island." It was discovered in 1616 by the Dutch. When Captain Cook came here in 1773 he named the group *Friendly Islands*, from the welcome accorded him by the islanders, and this name is still sometimes found on modern maps as an alternant.

Tongatapu. *Island group, southern Tonga.* The islands have a local name meaning "sacred **Tonga**," from the main name of the group and

Tongan *tabu*, "holy" (the source of English *taboo*).

Tongeren. *City, eastern Belgium*. The Roman name of Belgium's oldest city was *Aduatuca Tungrorum*, for the Germanic *Tungri* tribe. The origin of their own name is uncertain. The French form of the name is *Tongres*.

Tonkin. *Historic region, northern Vietnam*. The former French protectorate has a Vietnamese name meaning "eastern capital," from *dông*, "east," and *kinh*, "capital." The name properly applied to the protectorate's capital, now that of Vietnam overall, **Hanoi**.

Tonle Sap. *Lake, west central Cambodia*. The name of the lake means "big freshwater lake," from Cambodian *tonle*, "big lake," and *sap*, "fresh," "not salt."

Toowoomba. *City, eastern Australia*. The name of the Queensland city probably derives from Aboriginal *toowoom*, the word for a local type of melon.

Topeka. *City, central United States*. The state capital of Kansas derives its name from a Sioux word said to mean either "smoky hill" or "good place to grow potatoes."

Torbat-e Haydariyeh. *Town, northeastern Iran*. The name means "tomb of *Haidar*," for a 12th-century mystic buried here.

Torbat-e Jam. *Town, northeastern Iran*. The name means "tomb of *Jam*," for an 11th-century mystic poet buried nearby.

Torez. *City, southeastern Ukraine*. The city was founded in the 1770s as *Alekseyevka*. It was then renamed *Alekseyevo-Leonovo* in 1840 and *Chistyakovo* in the 1870s before receiving its present name in 1964 in memory of the French politician and Communist leader Maurice *Thorez* (1900–1964), who died at sea en route to Yalta.

Torgau. *City, eastern Germany*. The city's name was recorded in 973 as *Turguo*, representing an adjectival form of Old Sorbian *torg*, "market."

Törökszentmiklós. *Town, east central Hungary*. The first part of the name is the personal name (or nickname) *Török* ("Turkish"). The rest represents the dedication of the town church to *St. Nicholas* (Hungarian *szent*, "saint," and *Miklós*, "Nicholas").

Toronto. *City, southern Canada*. The capital of Ontario takes its name from that of a Native American village recorded as *Tarantou* on a map of 1656. This is said to derive either from Iroquois *taron-to-hen*, "wood in the water," or Huron *deondo*, "meeting place." The present city was founded in 1793 when Governor John Graves Simcoe moved the capital from Newark (now Niagara) to Toronto Bay and renamed it *York*, in honor of Frederick Augustus, Duke of York (1763–1827), son of George III. It reverted to its original name in 1834.

Torquay. *Town and resort, southwestern England*. The Devonshire town has a name meaning "*Torre* quay." The quay here was built in medieval times by monks from nearby *Torre* Abbey, with the abbey itself named for the hill (Old English *torr*, modern *tor*) below which it lay.

Torrance. *City, southwestern United States*. The California city was founded in 1911 by Jared S. *Torrance*, owner of the townsite, and named for him.

Torre Annunziata. *City and resort, southern Italy*. The city, now a suburb of Naples, has a name meaning "tower of the Annunciation," from Italian *torre*, "tower," and *Annunziata*, "feast of Our Lady of the Annunciation." The reference is to a chapel and hospital here with this dedication, built in 1319.

Torrelavega. *City, northern Spain*. The city was founded in the 14th century and owes its name to the Garcilago *de la Vega* family, prominent here in medieval times. The initial *torre* is Spanish "tower."

Torrens, Lake. *Lake, southern Australia*. The lake, in eastern South Australia, was discovered in 1839 and named for the English economist, Colonel Robert *Torrens* (1780–1864), a founder of the colony of South Australia in 1834.

Torres Strait. *Strait, southwestern Pacific*. The strait, between Australia and New Guinea, was so named in 1769 in memory of the Spanish navigator Luis Váez de *Torres* (1560–?1614), who discovered it in 1606 during his circumnavigation of New Guinea. At the time he did not realize it was a strait, as he was unaware of the existence of Australia.

Torres Vedras. *Town, western Portugal*. The town's Medieval Latin name *Turres Veteres*, "old towers," gave its present name.

Tórshavn *see* **Thorshavn**

Tortola. *Island, eastern West Indies*. The largest of the British Virgin Islands derives its name from Spanish *tórtola*, "turtledove," alluding to the birds noticed here by early Spanish explorers.

Tortuga Island. *Island, southeastern Caribbean Sea*. The uninhabited island, a dependency of Venezuela, has a Spanish name meaning "turtle," referring to the many turtles on its coast. There is another island of the name in the Gulf of California, northwestern Mexico, and yet another off northern Haiti, the latter known locally by its French name *île de la Tortue*.

Toruń. *City, northern Poland*. The city was founded by the Teutonic Knights in 1231 and named for *Toron*, the name given by the Crusaders to the Palestinian town of *Tibnin*, one of the principal fiefs of the kingdom of Jerusalem. German speakers know the city as *Thorn*.

Torzhok. *City, western Russia*. The city, first recorded in 1139, has a name meaning "trading place," from Russian *torg*, "market."

Tottori. *City and port, southwestern Japan*. The city, in the prefecture of the same name, in the island of Honshu, derives its name from Japanese *tori*, "bird," and *toru*, "to catch," "to capture."

Toul. *Town, northeastern France*. The town had the Roman name of *Tullum*, deriving from Celtic *tol*, "height," "hill."

Toulon. *City and port, southeastern France*. The city ultimately derives its name from either Celtic *tol*, "height," or Ligurian *tol* or *tel*, "spring." *Cp.* **Toulouse**. In 1793, at the time of the French Revolution, Toulon was temporarily renamed *Port-de-la-Montagne*, "mountain harbor," referring to the nearby Faron Mountains.

Toulouse. *City, southern France*. The city had the Roman name of *Tolosa*, probably deriving from Celtic *tol*, "height," "hill." The reference would be to the Pyrenean foothills nearby. *Cp.* **Toulon**.

Touraine. *Historic region, west central France*. The region takes its name from the *Turoni*, the Gaulish people who inhabited it. Their own name may derive from a Celtic word meaning "powerful." *See also* **Tours**.

Tourcoing. *City, northern France*. The city had the Medieval Latin name of *Thorcunium*, based on the Germanic personal name *Thorkun*.

Tournai. *City, western Belgium*. The city is traditionally said to derive its name from the Roman personal name *Turnus*, that of a legendary king or leader. The Roman name of the settlement was *Turnacum*, while the modern Flemish name is *Doornik*.

Tours. *City, west central France*. The city was the capital of the ancient province of **Touraine**, and like it derives its name from the *Turoni*, the Gaulish people who formerly inhabited the region. Their own name may derive from a Celtic word meaning "powerful."

Töv. *Province, central Mongolia*. The name is simply Mongolian for "central."

Townsville. *City and port, northeastern Australia*. The Queensland city was founded in 1864 and named for Captain Robert *Towns*

(1794–1873), a Sydney merchant who financially promoted settlement in the area.

Toyama. *City and port, central Japan*. The city, in the island of Honshu, derives its name from Japanese *to*, "to thrive," and *yama*, "mountain."

Toyohashi. *City, south central Japan*. The city, in the island of Honshu, derives its name from Japanese *toyo*, "excellent," "rich," and *hashi*, "bridge."

Toyonaka. *City, southern Japan*. The city, in the island of Honshu, derives its name from Japanese *toyo*, "excellent," "rich," and *naka*, "inside," "interior."

Trabzon. *City and port, northeastern Turkey*. The city is said to derive its name from Greek *trapeza*, "table," referring to the flat tableland between two deep ravines on which it was founded. *Cp.* **Table Mountain**. The name was formerly familiar as *Trebizond* for the medieval Greek empire that at its greatest extent included Georgia, the Crimea, and the entire southern Black Sea coast east of the Sakarya River.

Trafalgar, Cape. *Cape, southwestern Spain*. The cape has an Arabic name, representing either *ṭaraf al-ḡarb*, "end of the west" (*cp.* **Maghrib**), or *ṭaraf al-aḡarr*, "end of the column." If the latter, the reference would be to the so-called Pillars of Hercules, the two promontories at the eastern end of the Strait of Gibraltar, which legend says were built by Hercules.

Tralee. *Town, southwestern Ireland*. The name of the town, in Co. Kerry, represents Irish *Trá Lí*, "strand of the *Lee*," from *trá*, "strand," "beach," and the name of the *Lee* River, which enters Tralee Bay here.

Trani. *Town and port, southeastern Italy*. The town has a much reduced form of its original Roman name, *Trajanopolis*, "city of *Trajan*," for the Roman emperor *Trajan*, who founded it in the 1st century A.D.

Transcaucasia. *Region, central Asia*. The region now represented by Armenia, Azerbaijan, and Georgia, south of the **Caucasus** Mountains, has a name meaning "across the Caucasus," from Latin *trans*, "that side of," "over," and the name of the mountains. *Cp.* **Transkei**, **Transvaal**, **Transylvania**.

Transjordan *see* **Jordan**

Transkei. *Historic homeland, southern South Africa*. The former Bantu homeland has a name that means "across the *Kei* (River)," from Latin *trans*, "over," across," and the name of the river across which it lies from **Ciskei**. The name was probably patterned on that of **Transvaal**. In 1994 Transkei was reintegrated with South Africa.

Transvaal. *Historic province, northeastern South Africa.* The name of the province means "across the **Vaal** (River)," from Latin *trans*, "across," and the river name. The province lay to the north of the river, as distinct from the Orange Free State, to the south. In 1994 Transvaal was reorganized into four provinces: **Gauteng, Mpumalanga** (at first *Eastern Transvaal*), *Northern*, and part of *North-West*.

Transylvania. *Historic region, central and northwestern Romania.* The region's name means "beyond the forest," from Medieval Latin *trans*, "across," "over," and *sylva*, "wood." "forest." Transylvania is shut in by the Carpathian Mountains to the north and east, the Transylvanian Alps to the south, and the Bihor Mountains to the west, the latter being thickly wooded. The Hungarian name of the region, *Erdély*, means the same, from *erdő*, "forest," and *elve*, "beyond," but the German name, *Siebenbürgen*, is different. Folk etymology interprets this as "seven forts," as if from the seven fortified towns of Hermannstadt (**Sibiu**), Klausenburg (**Cluj**), Kronstadt (**Braşov**), Bistritz (**Bistriţa**), Mediasch (*Mediaş*), Mühlbach (**Sebeş**), and Schässburg (**Sighişoara**), but it apparently derives from *Cibinium*, the Roman name of Hermannstadt.

Trapani. *City, southern Italy.* The city, in northwestern Sicily, was known in Roman times as *Drepanum*, from Greek *drepanē*, "sickle," referring to the curving promontory on which it lies.

Trás-os-Montes. *Historic province, northeastern Portugal.* The name of the former province means "across the mountains," referring to the three sierras that formed its western boundary. (Its northern and eastern boundary was the border with Spain, while the southern boundary was the Douro River.)

Traunstein. *City, southeastern Germany.* The city was originally simply *Traun*, from its location on the river of this name, itself from the Indoeuropean root *dru*, "to run," "to race," referring to its current. The *-stein* of the city name, meaning "stone," first recorded in 1245, relates to a stronghold here.

Travancore. *Region, southwestern India.* The former princely state, in the kingdom of Kerala, is said to derive its name from Malayalam *tiru*, "holy," *varán*, "prosperous," and *kodu*, "kingdom."

Travemünde. *Town and resort, northern Germany.* The town, now a district of Lübeck, has a name meaning "mouth of the *Trave*," from its location on the estuary of this river. The river's name has been derived from Slavic *trava*, "grass," but probably goes back to Indoeuropean *drouos*, "(river) course."

Trebizond *see* **Trabzon**

Trece Martires. *City, north central Philippines.* The city, in southern Luzon, has a Spanish name meaning "thirteen martyrs," referring to the 13 Filipino revolutionaries executed by the Spanish at Cavite in 1896.

Treinta y Tres. *City, east central Uruguay.* The name, Spanish for "thirty-three," alludes to the 33 Uruguyan patriots who in 1825, under General Juan Antonio Lavalleja, successfully invaded from Argentina what was then Brazilian-held territory during Uruguay's war of independence (1811–30).

Trelew. *City, southeastern Argentina.* The city was founded in 1865 by immigrants from Wales, who named it from Welsh *tre*, "village," and the Welsh pioneer *Lewis* Jones (1836–1904), who had obtained a concession to build a railroad here.

Trent. *River, central England.* The river's name may mean "great wanderer," from the Celtic intensive ("great") prefix *tri-* and a word *santon* related to modern Welsh *hynt*, "way," Latin *semita*, "footpath," and French *sentier*, "path." (This could also be *Sentona*, the name of a "goddess of the way.") The allusion is to a river liable to flooding, so that it "wanders" from its normal course. The Trent is famous for its spring tides ("neaps") and its tidal bore ("eagre"), and at one time could have flooded regularly when these occurred. It rarely floods today because it has been contained by embankments.

Trento. *City, northern Italy.* The city's present name has evolved from its Roman name of *Tridentum*, from Latin *tres*, "three," and *dens, dentis*, "tooth," referring to a triple-peaked mountain nearby. Hence the adjective *Tridentine* to refer to the city or an event connected with it The city was long known in English as *Trent*. Hence the Council of *Trent* (1543–63), an ecumenical council of the Roman Catholic church, convoked in Trento (but by some wrongly referred to the English **Trent**).

Trenton. *City, eastern United States.* The state capital of New Jersey has a name representing *Trent's town*, for William *Trent*, the Philadelphia merchant who laid it out in 1714. The name was actually given in 1721.

Tres de Febrero. *City, eastern Argentina.* The city, now a suburb of Buenos Aires, has a Spanish name meaning "third of February," alluding to the Battle of Caseros on February 3, 1852, in which the Argentine military ruler Juan Manuel de Rosas was defeated.

Tres Marías. *Island group, eastern Pacific.* The uninhabited islands, off the coast of west central Mexico, have a name meaning "three Marys," referring to the three Marys of the Bible, as represented by the Spanish names of the main islands: *María Madre* ("Mary Mother," or Virgin Mary, mother of God), *María Magdalena* (Mary Magdalene), and *María Cleofas* (Mary, wife of Cleopas).

Trèves *see* **Trier**

Treviso. *City, northeastern Italy.* The city was known to the Roman as *Tarvisium,* from a Celtic word meaning "bull" (Gaulish *taruos,* Welsh *tarw*), denoting a stronghold. The town of *Tarvisio,* to the northeast near the Austrian border, has a name of the same origin.

Triberg. *Town, southwestern Germany.* The town, a Black Forest resort, has a name meaning "three mountains," for its location between the three mountains Kapellenberg, Kroneck, and Sterenberg.

Trichinopoly *see* **Tiruchchirappalli**

Trichur. *Town, southwestern India.* The town, in Kerala state, has a Hindi name meaning "small holy place." The town has a Hindu temple that is the object of an annual pilgrimage.

Trier. *City, western Germany.* The city, founded by the Roman emperor Augustus in c.15 B.C., was the capital of the Gaulish people known as the *Treveri,* and is named for them. Their own name may represent Celtic *tre,* "across," and *wer,* "crossing," referring to a crossing place on the Moselle River here. French speakers know the city as *Trèves.*

Trieste. *City and port, northeastern Italy.* The city has a Venetian name meaning "trade," "market," from Illyrian *terga,* a word related to Swedish and Russian *torg,* "trading place." *Cp.* **Tîrgoviște, Torzhok, Turku.** Trieste has long been a major trading city and transit port.

Triglav. *Mountain, northwestern Slovenia.* The mountain has a Slavic name meaning "triple-peaked," referring to the three peaks of its summit. Its Italian name, similarly, is *Tricorno.*

Trincomalee. *Town and port, northeastern Sri Lanka.* The town is said to derive its name from Tamil *tri,* "three," *kona,* "peak," and *malai,* "hill," referring to the peninsula on which it lies.

¹Trinidad. *Island, southeastern West Indies.* The island, part of the republic of Trinidad and Tobago, has a Spanish name meaning "Trinity." It was discovered by Columbus in 1498 and was so named by him either because he arrived on June 10, *Trinity* Sunday, or more likely because three mountain peaks here suggested the Holy *Trinity.*

²Trinidad. *City, northeastern Bolivia.* The city was founded in 1686 as a Jesuit mission station and given a Spanish name meaning "Trinity," for the feast of the Holy *Trinity.*

¹Tripoli. *Capital of Libya.* The name represents Greek *tri-,* the combining form of *treis,* "three," and *polis,* "town." As *Tripolis,* this was originally the name of a Phoenician colony here in northern Africa, itself so called from its three chief cities of Oea (which became the present Tripoli), Leptis Magna, and Sabratha. The entire western part of Libya was known as *Tripolitania* when an Italian colony from 1912 through 1919, and this name is still in use for the northwestern part. The Arabic name of the city is *ṭarābulus al-ǧarb,* "Western Tripoli," for distinction from ²**Tripoli.**

²Tripoli. *City and port, northwestern Lebanon.* The name represents Greek *tri-,* "three," and *polis,* "town," referring to the Phoenician triple federation of Sidon, Tyre, and Aradus. The Arabic name of the city is *ṭarābulus ash-shām,* "Syrian Tripoli," for distinction from ¹**Tripoli.**

Tripolis. *Town, central Greece.* The town, in the central Peloponnese, has a name meaning "three cities," from Greek *tri-,* "three," and *polis,* "city." It was founded in the 14th century to replace the three ancient cities of Pallantium, Tegea, and Mantineia.

Tripolitania *see* ¹**Tripoli**

Tripura. *State, northeastern India.* The state has a Hindi name meaning "three towns," from *tri,* "three," and *pur,* "town."

Tristan da Cunha. *Island group, South Atlantic.* The name, properly that of the largest island of the five, commemorates the group's discoverer in 1506, the Portuguese admiral *Tristan da Cunha* (1460–1540).

Trivandrum. *City and port, southwestern India.* The capital of Kerala state has a name that is a contracted alteration of its Malayalam name, *Tiruvanantapuram,* "town sacred to *Ananta,*" from *tiru,* "sacred," *Ananta,* a name of the god Vishnu, and *pur,* "town."

Trnava. *City, western Slovakia.* The city takes its name from the river on which it lies. Its Hungarian name is *Nagyszombat,* literally "great Saturday," referring to a weekly market.

Troisdorf. *Town, western Germany.* The industrial town has a name first recorded in 1076 as *Truhtesdorf,* from a personal name based on Old High German *truht,* "crowd," and *dorf,* "village."

Trois-Rivières. *City, southeastern Canada.* The Quebec city, on the St. Lawrence River, has a French name meaning "three rivers," referring to the three channels at the mouth of the St. Maurice River here. The city's English name *Three Rivers* is still in alternate use.

Trollhätten. *Town, southwestern Sweden.* Despite appearances, the first part of the name may not represent *troll*, the cave-dwelling giant (or dwarf) of Scandinavian folklore. The second part of the name may be a Saami word meaning "waterfall," referring to the falls on the Göta River here.

Tromsø. *City and port, northern Norway.* The city takes its name from *Troms*, the department of which it is the capital, and Danish *ø*, "island." The meaning of the department name is uncertain. It originally applied to the sea current between the island where the city lies and the Norwegian mainland.

Trondheim. *City and port, central Norway.* Norway's third-largest city takes its name from *Throndr*, that of the fjord (now *Trondheim Fjord*) on which it lies, and Old Norwegian *heimr*, "house," "town." The former fjord name may be related to that of *Thor*, the Norse god of thunder, or to Old Norwegian *thörr*, "thunder" itself. The city has undergone a number of name changes. Founded in 997 as the village of *Kaupangr*, it was renamed *Nidaros* ("estuary of the *Nid* River") in 1016 and *Trondhjem* in the 16th century. The name *Nidaros* was readopted in 1930, but after objections by the inhabitants was abandoned a year later in favor of the previous name, this time in the reformed spelling *Trondheim*.

Trossachs. *Region, central Scotland.* The scenic region between Loch Katrine and Loch Achray has a Gaelic name meaning "transverse hills," referring to the hills that divide the lochs. According to some sources the name is a borrowing of the Welsh placename *Trawsfynydd*, "across the mountain."

Trouville. *Town and resort, northwestern France.* The town, on the English Channel, derives its name from the Scandinavian personal name *Thorulfr* and Latin *villa*, "residence." The resort's full name is *Trouville-sur-Mer*, "*Trouville*-on-Sea."

¹Troy. *Historic city, western Turkey.* The ancient city site, just south of the Dardanelles, has a name traditionally derived from *Tros*, the legendary king of Phrygia who founded it. There were actually nine cities of the name, each built on the ruins of its predecessor. The alternate name of Troy was *Ilium*, a Latin form of Greek *Ilion*, itself similarly associated with *Ilus*, another legendary founder.

²Troy. *City, eastern United States.* The New York city was laid out in 1786 and at first called *Vanderheyden's Ferry*, for the Dutch family of this name who owned land here by the Hudson River. In 1789 the town was renamed as now for the ancient Greek city of ¹**Troy**.

Troyan. *Town, north central Bulgaria.* The name of the town, on the Osum River, has been associated with the *Trajan Way*, the campaign route followed by the Roman emperor *Trajan* in the early 2d century A.D.

Troyes. *City, northeastern France.* The city had the Roman name of *Civitas Tricassium*, indicating that it was the capital of the Celtic people known as the *Tricasses*. Their own name is said to mean "those with three tresses." The present form of the name evolved from this, with a spelling perhaps influenced by the name of ¹**Troy**.

Trucial States *see* **United Arab Emirates**

¹Trujillo. *Town, western Spain.* The town's modern name evolved from its Roman name of *Turris Julia*, "tower of *Julius*," meaning *Julius Caesar*.

²Trujillo. *City and port, northwestern Peru.* The original settlement was founded in 1534 and the following year raised to city status by the Spanish conquistador Francisco Pizarro, who named it for his birthplace of ¹**Trujillo**. The same Spanish town gave the names of *Trujillo*, Honduras, and *Trujillo*, Venezuela (but not, except indirectly, the *Trujillo* that is now **Santo Domingo**, Dominican Republic).

Truro. *Town, southwestern England.* The Cornish town has a name apparently deriving from Cornish *try*, "three" or "very" (as an intensive prefix), and *berow*, "a boiling," perhaps referring to the floods that occur in winter when the two fast rivers Allen and Kenwyn meet to form the Truro River.

Truth or Consequences. *Town, southwestern United States.* The New Mexico town was settled in the mid–19th century and at first called *Hot Springs*, for its thermal mineral waters. The present name was adopted in 1950 when the radio and television personality, Ralph Edwards, agreed to hold his game show *Truth or Consequences* here annually as a promotional event.

Trutnov. *Town, northern Czech Republic.* The town probably derives its name from a personal name or nickname, with the final -*ov* the Slavic possessive suffix. Czech folklore associates the name with the giant *Trut* who killed a dragon in the Riesengebirge (Giant Mountains) here. The German form of the name is *Trautenau*.

Tsaidam. *Swamp region, west central China.* The region of salt lakes and saline swamps, in

Tsinghai province, derives its name from Tibetan *tshai*, "salt," and *dam*, "marsh."

Tsarskoye Selo *see* **Pushkin**

Tselinograd *see* **Astana**

Tshwane. *Municipal area, northeastern South Africa.* The indigenous (Sotho) name of **Pretoria** is properly that of the Apies River here, so called after his son, *Tshwane*, by the African chief Mushi, who settled here in the early 17th century. The name itself significantly means "we are the same," or "we are one because we live together," and formally applies to the "megacity" or metropolitan municipality created in 2000 from 13 municipal councils, among them Pretoria itself.

Tsinghai *see* **Koko Nor**

Tsingtao. *City and port, eastern China.* The city, in Shantung province, derives its name from Chinese *qīng*, "green," "blue," and *dǎo*, "island," originally referring to the island in the natural harbor here.

Tsinling Mountains. *Mountain range, northern China.* The range derives its name from Chinese *qín*, the old name of Shensi province, toward its eastern end, and *líng*, "mountain range."

Tsitsihar. *City, northeastern China.* The city, in Heilungkiang province, derives its name from Chinese *qí*, "neat," "complete," *hā*, a phonetic symbol, and *ěr*, the formant used to denote a populated place of medium size.

Tsu. *City and port, southern Japan.* The city, in the island of Honshu, has a name that is simply the Japanese word for "port."

Tsun-i. *City, southern China.* The city, in Kweichow province, derives its name from Chinese *zūn*, "respect," "esteem," and *yì*, "justice."

Tsushima. *Island group, southwestern Japan.* The group of five small islands, in the Korea Strait, between Japan and South Korea, derives its name from Japanese *tsui*, "pair," "couple," and *ma*, "horse," from the supposed resemblance of two of the islands to a pair of horses.

Tuamotu. *Island group, South Pacific.* The group of about 80 small islands in French Polynesia has an indigenous name meaning "far islands," from a root word related to Tahitian *motu*, "island." An alternate name is *Paumotu*, "cloud of islands."

Tübingen. *City, southwestern Germany.* The city, dating from the 11th century, has a name meaning "(settlement of) *Tuwo*'s people," from an Old German personal name, itself a short form of a name such as *Dunmin* or *Dunwald*.

Tucson. *City, southwestern United States.* The Arizona city was founded in 1700 as a Jesuit mission station and adopted the Native American name of Sentinel Mountain here, *Chuk Shon*, meaning "black base." The present name is a Spanish-influenced form of this.

Tucumán. *Province, northwestern Argentina.* The province is named for its chief city of **San Miguel de Tucumán**.

Tudela. *Town, northern Spain.* The name of the town was recorded in 959 as *Villa Teudela*, and a derivation has been suggested in Gothic *theuda*, "people." But this seems unlikely, as also does an origin in the name of a Roman god.

Tula. *City, western Russia.* The name of the city south of Moscow is said to derive from an identical Baltic word meaning simply "settlement," "colony." Tula is first mentioned in 1146.

Tulcea. *City, southeastern Romania.* The name of the city may be of Turkish origin and relate to *tilki*, "fox." The documentary evidence for this interpretation is lacking, however.

Tulle. *Town, central France.* The town had the Medieval Latin name of *Tutelae*, from *Tutela*, the name of a pagan god.

Tulsa. *City, south central United States.* The Oklahoma city arose in 1836 as a Creek settlement, the immigrants naming it for their former town in Alabama. The name itself is said to represent Creek *talwa*, "town," and *hasi*, "old." *Cp.* **Tallahassee.**

Tumaco. *City, southwestern Colombia.* The city is named for *Tumas*, the Native American chief who founded it in 1570.

Tumkur. *City, southern India.* The city, in Karnataka state, is said to have a name meaning "tabret" (a small tabor), from the instrument traditionally used by the herald of a rajah.

Tunbridge Wells. *Town, southeastern England.* The Kent town arose around the *wells* (springs) discovered here in 1606, and takes its name from **Tonbridge**, 5 miles (8 km) away. The name thus means "(place of) wells near Tonbridge." The vowel difference now distinguishes the two towns. Tonbridge was *Tunbridge* at the time of the discovery, reflecting the pronunciation of the name, but with the rise of Tunbridge Wells it reverted to the earlier spelling. The formal name of the town is *Royal Tunbridge Wells*, the prefix being granted by Edward VII in 1909 for the many royal visitors.

T'ung-hua. *City, northeastern China.* The city, in Kirin province, derives its name from Chinese *tōng*, "open," "through," and *huà*, "to change," "to dissolve."

T'ung-ting. *Lake, central China.* The large lake, in Hunan province, derives its name from Chinese *dòng*, "hole," "cave," and *tíng*, "court," "yard."

Tunis. *Capital of Tunisia.* The city has an ancient name that has been related by some to that of the Phoenician goddess *Tanith.* *See also* **Tunisia.**

Tunisia. *Republic, northern Africa.* The country takes its name from that of its capital, **Tunis,** which itself was also used for the former Berber state to the south and west of Carthage. The present form of the name, with its Latinate placename suffix *-ia,* evolved from French *Tunisie,* adopted for the territory here when it became a French protectorate in 1881. The new name was slow to catch on in English, so that as recently as the early 20th century the same name was used for both country and city, as it still is in some languages, e.g. Spanish *Túnez.*

Turgovishte. *City, eastern Bulgaria.* The city derives its name from Slavic *torg,* "market," and the locational suffix *-ishte,* giving a meaning "market place." Its name until 1934 was *Eski-Dzhumaia,* "old market," from Turkish *eski,* "old," and *cuma,* "Friday," the regular market day. *Cp.* **Tîrgovişte.**

Turin. *City, northwestern Italy.* The Roman name of the city was *Augusta Taurinorum,* referring to the *Taurini,* the Ligurian people whose capital it was. Their own name may derive from Celtic *tauro,* "mountain," or else *tur,* "water." The civic authorities have popularly interpreted it as "bull" (Latin *taurus*), and the city's canting coat of arms depicts a splendidly belligerent bull. The Italian form of the name is *Torino.*

Turkana, Lake *see* **Rudolf, Lake**

Turkestan *see* **Turkistan**

Turkey. *Republic, southeastern Europe/southwestern Asia.* The country takes its name from that of its indigenous people, the *Turks.* Their own name may mean "strong," "powerful." The Turkish name of Turkey is *Türkiye.*

Turkistan. *Region, central Asia.* The region, comprising the former Soviet Asian republics with names ending in *-stan* (Kazakh*stan,* Kyrgyz*stan,* Tajiki*stan,* Turkmeni*stan,* Uzbeki*stan*), has a name that means "land of the *Turks,*" from Iranian *tork,* "Turk," and *ostān,* "land," "country." All five countries speak a Turkic language. The name is also spelled *Turkestan.* *See also* **Turkmenistan.**

Turkmenbashy. *City and port, northwestern Turkmenistan.* The city, a port on the Caspian Sea, was founded as the military post of *Krasnovodsk* in 1869. The name translates as "red water," from Russian *krasno-,* "red," and *voda,* "water." This was "red" not in the revolutionary sense but literally, since the bay here was earlier known as *Krasnyye Vody,* "red waters." The rea-

son for the particular color is uncertain. The water may have had a reddish hue, or the rocks on the shore been tinged with red. In 1994 the city was renamed as now, the name meaning "*Turkmen* headland," for the peninsula here.

Turkmenistan. *Republic, south central Asia.* The country's name means "land of the *Turkmen,*" with the people's own name means "Turk-like," from Iranian *tork,* "Turk," and the root of *mandan,* "to be like," "to resemble." The people were formerly nomadic, unlike the genuine "settled" Turks of Turkey to whom they were otherwise akin. They are or were also known in English as *Turcoman* or *Turkoman,* with the latter part of the name popularly associated with *man* (as *Chinaman,* etc.)

Turks and Caicos Islands. *Island groups, northern West Indies.* The two groups of islands, a British dependency north of Hispaniola, take their respective names from the *turk's cap* or *turk's head* cactus (*Cactus intortus*), found in the West Indies, so named for its cap of whitish hairs like a fez, and the plural of Spanish *cayo,* "rock," "reef" (English *cay* or *key,* related to *quay*). *Cp.* **Key West.**

Turku. *City and port, southwestern Finland.* The name of the former capital of Finland (to 1812) derives from Swedish *torg,* "market place." *Cp.* **Tîrgovişte, Torzhok, Trieste, Turgovishte.** The Swedish name of the city is *Åbo,* from *å,* "river," and *bo,* "to inhabit." The river here is the Aura.

Turnu-Măgurele. *City, southern Romania.* The first word of the name is probably Romanian *turn,* "tower." The second part is Romanian *măgura,* "hill."

Tuscaloosa. *City, southern United States.* The Alabama city was founded in 1816 and named for the Choctaw chief *Tuscaloosa* ("black warrior") who fought the Spanish explorer Hernando de Soto in southern Alabama in 1540. The *Black Warrior* River here is also named for him.

Tuscany. *Region, central Italy.* The region takes its name from the *Etruscans* (*see* **Etruria**), its original indigenous inhabitants. The Italian name of Tuscany is *Toscana.*

Tutrakan. *Town, northeastern Bulgaria.* The town, on the Danube, was known in Roman times as the fortified settlement of *Transmarisca,* "across the *Maritsa,*" the latter being the river that flows east across southern Bulgaria. The present name is probably of the same origin as that of the historic town of *Tmutarakan* in southwestern Russia, and Russian immigrants may have transported it here. The Russian name derives from Turkic *tamantarkan,* "title of rank."

Tuva. *Republic, southern Russia*. The Siberian republic derives its name from its indigenous people, the *Tuvans*. The origin of their own name is uncertain. The republic was formerly known as *Tannu-Tuva*, the first part of this representing the name of the *Tannu-Ola* mountain range. Before 1921 the region was in Outer Mongolia and was known as *Uriankhai*, from a Mongolian name for these same people meaning "previous ones," i.e. those who were here before the Mongols.

Tuvalu. *Island republic, southwestern Pacific*. The archipelago consists of nine islands, although its name means "eight standing together," from Tuvaluan *tu*, "to stand up," and *valu*, "eight." This is because on one of the islands, Nui, the local language is not Tuvaluan but I-Kiribati (Gilbertese). The group originally formed part of the *Gilbert and Ellice Islands*, named for Thomas *Gilbert*, who gave the modern name of **Kiribati**, and Alexander *Ellice*, head of a Canadian shipping company and owner of the ship *Rebecca* on which the American soldier Arent de Peyster visited the islands in 1819. Tuvalu officially adopted its present name in 1978 on gaining independence.

Tuz, Lake. *Lake, central Turkey*. The shallow saline lake has a self-descriptive name, from Turkish *tuz*, "salt." Salt is mined here.

Tuzla. *Town, eastern Bosnia-Hercegovina*. The town's name represents Turkish *tuzla*, "saline," from *tuz*, "salt." Tuzla has long been known for its deposits of rock salt, and similarly had the Medieval Latin name of *Soli*, "salts."

Tver. *City and river port, western Russia*. The city, on the Volga, is of ancient origin and probably has a name meaning "fortress," from a word related to modern Russian *tvyordyj*, "firm," "solid." From 1931 through 1991 it was known as *Kalinin*, for the Soviet titular head of state, Mikhail *Kalinin* (1875–1946), who was born near here. *Cp.* **¹Kaliningrad**.

Tweed. *River, northern England*. The river, forming the border between England and Scotland, has a name that has never been satisfactorily explained. It may be pre–Celtic and non–Indoeuropean.

Tychy. *Town, southern Poland*. The town arose around a 17th-century brewery and has a name representing modern Polish *cichy*, "quiet." This hardly describes the present industrial town, which has grown considerably since the early 1950s.

Tyler. *City, southern United States*. The Texas city was laid out in 1846 and named for John *Tyler* (1790–1862), 10th president of the United States.

Tyne. *River, northeastern England*. The river derives its name from the pre–English element *tei*, "to melt," "to flow."

Tyre. *Town and port, southern Lebanon*. The ancient port and kingdom, mentioned several times in the Bible (Joshua 19:29, etc.), derives its name from Phoenician *tsor*, "stone," "rock." Its current name is *Sur*, representing Arabic *ṣūr*, of the same origin.

Tyrol. *Region, western Austria*. The mountainous region is so called for the castle of the same name near Merano. Its own name, that of its location, probably comes ultimately from Celtic *tir*, "land." *Cp.* **Tyrone**.

Tyrone. *County, west central Northern Ireland*. The county's name represents Irish *Tír Eoghain*, "*Eoghan*'s land," referring to *Eoghan* (Owen), the semilegendary ruler whose descendants (the O'Neills) are said to have owned the territory. The *Tír* of the Irish name is also represented by the final *-ter* of **Leinster**, **Munster**, and **Ulster**.

Tyrrhenian Sea. *Sea, southern Europe*. The part of the Mediterranean Sea between Sardinia and Italy had the Greek name of *Tyrrhenos*. This may be a Greek form of the name of the *Etruscans* (*see* **Etruria**) or else derive from *turris*, "tower," a word also of Etruscan origin.

Tyumen. *City, central Russia*. The city has a name of Tatar origin meaning "ten thousand," from *tyu*, "ten," and *men*, "thousand." The reference may be to the 10,000 soldiers that the khan had in his army, or to the number of his subjects. Tyumen is one of the oldest cities in Siberia, and was founded in 1586 on the site of the Tatar settlement of *Chingi-Tura*, "town of *Chingis*," i.e. *Chingis* Khan (Genghis Khan) (c.1155–1227), itself dating from the 14th century.

Tzu-kung. *City, southern China*. The city, in Szechwan province, derives its name from Chinese *zì*, "oneself," "since," and *gòng*, "tribute."

Ubangi. *River, central Africa*. The river, forming part of the boundary between the Democratic Republic of Congo and the Central African Republic, derives its name from Bantu *u*, "land," "country," and *bangi*, "rapid," referring to the swiftness of its current and the territory through which it flows. The name is also spelled *Oubangi*.

Ube. *City and port, southwestern Japan*. The city, in the island of Honshu, derives its name from Japanese *u*, "roof," "house," "sky," and *be*, "part," "section."

Udaipur. *City, northwestern India*. The city, in Rajasthan state, was founded in c.1560 with a name from Hindi *uday*, "rising," "birth," "growth," and *pur*, "town," giving a sense "city of good fortune" or "city of sunrise." In 1568 it was made the capital of the princely state of the same name by Maharana *Udai* Singh, so came to be associated with his name.

Udhampur. *Town, northern India.* The city is named for *Udham* Singh, eldest son of Gulab Singh, founder and ruler (1846–57) of the Jammu and Kashmir state in which it is located. His name is followed by Hindi *pur*, "town."

Udmurtia. *Republic, western Russia.* The republic is named for its indigenous people, the *Udmurts*. Their own name is based on an Iranian word *murt*, "person," indirectly related to English *mortal*. The Udmurts were formerly known as the *Votyaks*, and this name is represented by the initial *Ud-* of their present name. *See also* **Vyatka**.

Ufa. *City, western Russia.* The capital of Bashkortostan takes its name from the river on which it lies. The river's own name may derive from an Indoeuropean root element *ap* meaning "water," "river."

Uganda. *Republic, eastern Africa.* The country derives its name from Swahili *u*, "land," "country," and *Ganda*, the name of its indigenous people. Their own name is of uncertain origin.

Uijongbu. *City, northwestern South Korea.* The city, on the outskirts of Seoul, has a name meaning "the cabinet," as it was the site of the Cabinet office during the Choson dynasty (1392–1910).

Uitenhage. *Town, southern South Africa.* The town, in Eastern province, was founded in 1804 by J.A. *Uitenhage* de Mist (1749–1823), a Dutch government official, and is named for him.

Ukraine. *Republic, central Europe.* The name represents Old Russian *oukraina*, "border country," from *ou*, "by," "at," and *kraj*, "region." The territory was so called becase it was the borderland or "frontier zone" of medieval Russia at the time of the Tatar invasion in the 13th century. The name is thus the Slavic equivalent of the **Marches**. Ukraine was formerly also known as *Little Russia*, so called by contrast with *Great Russia*, when the medieval principality here became separated from "mainstream" czarist Russia as a result of the Mongol invasion.

Ulan Bator. *Capital of Mongolia.* The more accurate name of the city is *Ulaanbaatar*, "(town of the) red hero," from Mongolian *ulaan*, "red," and *baatar*, "hero." It was so named in 1924 in honor of the Mongolian revolutionary hero Damdiny *Sühbataar* (*see* **Sühbaatar**), who was born near here and who died here. The town was founded in 1639 as the migratory (from 1778

settled) capital of the Lamaist church in Mongolia under the name of *Urga*, from a Mongolian word meaning "palace." In 1706 it was renamed *Ikh-khureheh*, "great monastery," and in 1911 *Niislel-khureheh*, "capital monastery."

Ulanhot. *Town, northeastern China.* The town, in Inner Mongolia, derives its name from Mongolian *ulaan*, "red" (not necessarily in the revolutionary sense), and *hot*, "city." *Cp.* **Hohhot**. The Chinese form of the name, of the same origin, is *Wu-lan-hao-te* (represented as *wūlán-hàotè*).

Ulan-Ude. *City, southeastern Russia.* The capital of Buryatia has a name that represents Mongolian *Ulaan-Ude* or *Ulaan-üd*, from *ulaan*, "red," in the revolutionary sense, and *üüd*, the name of the river *Uda* on which it stands. Until 1934 it was known as *Verkhneudinsk*, "upper *Uda*," not because it stands on the upper reaches of the river (it is actually at its mouth) but for distinction from the town of *Nizhneudinsk*, "lower *Uda*," on another river of this name more than 400 miles (660 km) to the northwest. The river name itself probably represents an ethnic name of unknown meaning.

Uliastay. *Town, west central Mongolia.* The town, which arose in 1773 as a Chinese fortress, has a Mongolian name meaning "poplar grove." It is also known as *Jibhalanta*, "magnificent city."

Üllő. *Village, north central Hungary.* The village derives its name from a personal name of Turkic origin meaning "prince," "chief" (Turkish *ulu*, "great man").

Ulm. *City, southwestern Germany.* The city does not derive its name from German *Ulme*, "elm," but either from the Indoeuropean root element *uel*, "to turn," "to wind," referring to the course of the Blau River as it enters the Danube here, or else from the root *el*, "to flow." Either way, the reference would be to the confluence of the Blau with the Danube.

Ulster. *Historic region, northern Ireland.* The name of the former province and kingdom, now often used for Northern Ireland itself, means "land of the *Ulaidh*," these being the people who originally inhabited the region, their name associated with Irish *ula*, "sepulcher," "tomb." The second part of the name is the Old Norse genitive (possessive) ending *-s* followed by Irish *tír*, "district." *Cp.* **Leinster**, **Munster**.

Ulu Dağ. *Mountain, northwestern Turkey.* The mountain's name means simply "big mountain," from Turkish *ulu*, "big," and *dağ*, "mountain."

Ulundi. *Town, eastern South Africa.* The capital of KwaZulu Natal has a Zulu name meaning "high place."

Umbria. *Region, central Italy.* The region takes its name from its original inhabitants, the *Umbri*, whose own name comes from that of the *Umbro* River here. The river's name probably derives from Greek *ombros*, "shower," "rain," or more generally, "water." This origin has created a legend tracing the people back to the days of the biblical Flood.

Umeå. *Town, northeastern Sweden.* The town takes its name from the river on which it lies. The river's own name comprises *Ume*, its name proper, of uncertain meaning, and *å*, "river."

Umtata. *Town, southeastern South Africa.* The former capital of Transkei, in Eastern Cape province, is named for the river on which it stands. The river's own name means something like "the taker," referring to its destructive flooding.

Unaka Mountains. *Mountain range, southeastern United States.* The section of the Blue Ridge and Appalachian mountain system, extending from Virginia to Georgia, has a Cherokee name meaning "white," referring either to a frequent white haze over the mountains or to white rocks at some point.

Ungava. *Region, eastern Canada.* The region, a broad peninsula in northern Quebec province, has a name of Inuit (Eskimo) origin meaning either "unknown land" or "far land."

United Arab Emirates. *Federation, southwestern Asia.* The federation of Arab states, formed in 1971, consists of seven emirates: **Abu Dhabi**, **Ajman**, **Dubai**, Fujairah, **Ras al-Khaimah**, **Sharjah**, and Umm al-Qaiwain. The emirates were formerly known as the *Trucial States*, denoting the maritime *truce* that was originally agreed in 1820 between the British government and the Arab sheikhdoms making up the present country. (The adjective *trucial* as applied to a truce is used only in this name or in related names such as *Trucial Coast* or *Trucial Oman*.) All of the states except Fujairah are located on the Persian Gulf coast, a region formerly notorious for its pirates and known as the *Pirate Coast*.

United Kingdom. *Island nation, northwestern Europe.* The British nation, comprising the four countries **England**, **Scotland**, **Wales**, and **Northern Ireland**, became formally known as the *United Kingdom* in 1801. The first three countries are known collectively as *Great Britain* (*see* **Britain**).

United States of America. *Federal republic, southern North America.* The full official name of the country often known simply as **America** came into being during the discusssions that led to the Declaration of Independence (1776), in which it appears in the subtitle: "The Unani-mous Declaration of the Thirteen United States of America." Since the name *America* can have several applications, depending on a qualifying word, such as *North America*, *South America*, *Central America*, **Latin America**, etc., various proposals have been made over the years for a more concise name for the United States and its people(s). One of the best known is *Usona*, an acronym of *United States of North America*, apparently suggested by the English writer Samuel Butler (1835–1902). However, this name has been adopted only in Esperanto, in which the country is called *Usono* and an inhabitant *Usonano*. The familiar abbreviation *USA* could serve as an acronym readily enough, but has never been adopted.

Unterwalden. *Historic canton, central Switzerland.* The German name, meaning "under the forest," describes the location of the region below the forest slopes of the Bernese Oberland. The canton is divided into the two semicantons of *Nidwalden* and *Obwalden*, respectively "lower forest" and "upper forest." Nidwalden borders Lake Lucerne below Obwalden, to the south.

Upper Egypt *see* **Lower Egypt**

Uppland. *Province, east central Sweden.* The name means literally "upper land," denoting the region's location by comparison with **Södermanland** and **Västmanland** to the south and west. The name also relates to that its town of **Uppsala**.

Uppsala. *City, eastern Sweden.* The city's name means "up from *Sala*," from Swedish *upp*, "up," "above," and *Sala*, denoting its location at the head of navigation on the Fyrisån River, further up from *Sala* ("shepherds' huts"), a village now known as *Gamla Uppsala*, "old Uppsala." Until the 13th century the settlement was known as *Östra Aros*, "eastern *Aros*," the latter from *ar*, "river," and *os*, "mouth." Cp. **Västerås**. Uppsala's name has been popularly explained as "upper houses," from *upp*, "up," and *säla*, "house," "hall," as if denoting houses on the upper west bank of this river.

Ur. *Historic city, southern Iraq.* The name of the city of ancient Mesopotamia derives from Sumerian *uru*, meaning simply "city." In the Bible, Ur is always referred to as "Ur of the Chaldees" (Genesis 11:28, etc.) (*see* **Chaldea**). The Arabic name of the locality is *Tell al-Muqayyar*, "hill of the tar."

Urals. *Mountain range, western Russia.* The mountains, forming the natural boundary between Europe and Asia, have a name said to represent Vogul *urala*, "mountain peak," from *ur*, "mountain," and *ala*, "summit," "roof." This would have originally applied to a single peak, presumably the highest, Mt. Narodnaya. Some authorities, however, take the name from Tatar *ural*, "boundary," "frontier." The range gave the name of the *Ural* River that rises in its southern part.

Urartu *see* **Ararat**

Urbana. *City, east central United States.* The Illinois city was settled in 1822 and named for *Urbana*, Ohio, itself laid out in 1805 and given a name intended to evoke both *urban* (as a city) and *urbane* (describing its civilized inhabitants).

Urbino. *Town, central Italy.* The town, founded by the Umbrians, had the Roman name of *Urbinum Hortense* or *Urvinum Metaurense*, from a diminutive form of Latin *urbs, urbis*, "town." The latter name refers to the town's location on the *Metauro* River.

Urfa *see* **Şanlıurfa**

Uri. *Canton, central Switzerland.* The name of the canton is traditionally associated with Latin *urus*, "aurochs" (a type of wild ox, now extinct), and this animal appears on its coat of arms. There may actually be some obscure reference to a totemic animal.

Urmia *see* **Orumiyeh**

Uruapan. *City, west central Mexico.* The city was founded in 1533 and derives its name from a Native American (Tarascan) phrase meaning "(place where) flowers abound."

Uruguaiana. *City and river port, southwestern Brazil.* The city takes its name from the **Uruguay** River, which here forms the border between Brazil and Argentina.

Uruguay. *Republic, southeastern America.* The country takes its name from that of the river which forms its western boundary with Argentina. The river's name is said to derive from that of a Native American people who lived along its banks, their own name perhaps representing *uru*, "bird," and *guay*, "tail," referring to some long-tailed bird that was their totemic creature.

Urumchi. *City, northwestern China.* The city, in the Uighur Autonomous Region of Sinkiang, has a Mongolian name meaning "fine pasture."

USA *see* **United States of America**

Uşak. *City, western Turkey.* The city arose around the 1st-century A.D. Roman settlement of *Flaviopolis*, "*Flavius*'s town," presumably so called for one of the Flavian emperors. It took its present name after the arrival of Turkmen settlers in the 11th century, supposedly either from Turkish *aşık*, "lover," or Turkish *uşak*, "boy," "servant." The first of these is said to refer to a place where an annual "talent show" was held for young people to select a future spouse.

Ushant. *Island, northwestern France.* The island off the tip of Brittany was known to the Romans as *Uxantis* or *Uxisama*, from Gaulish *ux*, "high," and the superlative suffix *-isamo*. The overall sense is thus "very high." The island is rocky, but not noticeably elevated. Its still current English name is a corruption of its French name *Ouessant*, itself influenced in spelling by *ouest*, "west."

Üsküdar. *Town, northwestern Turkey.* The town, across the Bosporus from Istanbul, is now a residential suburb of that city. Its historic name was *Chrysopolis*, "golden city," for its proximity to the **Golden Horn**. Its current name derives from Latin *scutarii*, literally "shieldmakers," referring to a Roman legion created by Constantine, whose headquarters were here. This gave the town's formerly familiar name *Scutari*, of which the present name is a Turkish form. *See also* **Shkodër**.

USSR *see* **Soviet Union**

Ussuriysk. *City, eastern Russia.* The city is named for the *Ussuri* River on which it lies. The river in turn is named for the Nanay people who lived on its banks. Their own name is of unknown origin.

Ústí nad Labem. *City and river port, northwestern Czech Republic.* The city takes its name from Czech *ústí*, "estuary," *nad*, "on," and *Labe*, the Czech name of the **Elbe**, the river on which it lies. The "estuary" is that of the smaller Bílina, which enters the Elbe here. The city's German name is *Aussig*, a corruption of the first word, perhaps influenced by *Aussicht*, "view," as if referring to the outlook from the medieval Střekov Castle here, on a precipitous crag across the river.

Ust-Kamenogorsk. *City, eastern Kazakhstan.* The city was founded as a fort in 1720 and takes its name from its location at the mouth (Russian *ust'ye*) of the *Kamennaya* River, which here enters the Irtysh. The finals *-gorsk* represents Russian *gorod*, "town." The river's name means "stony," "rocky."

Usulután. *City, southeastern El Salvador.* The city has a Native American name said to mean "city of ocelots."

Utah. *State, west central United States.* The state has a name of Native American origin, variously explained as meaning "high up," "tall men," "mountain dwellers," or at any rate someone or something "lofty." Utah is in the Rocky Mountains. The state of *Deseret*, organized by the Mormons in 1849, would have included present-day Utah, but was refused recognition by Congress. Its name, according to the Book of Mormon meaning "land of the honeybee," survives for some Utah placenames, such as *Deseret Peak*.

Uthagamandalam. *Town, southeastern India.* The town, in Tamil Nadu state, was founded by the British in 1821 and given an indigenous name said to mean "stone house," for the first European bungalow built in the hills here. The formerly familiar European form of the name was *Ootacamund*.

¹Utica. *Historic city, northern Tunisia.* The city has a name of Phoenician origin probably meaning "old." Utica was founded in the 8th or 7th century B.C. and was one of the chief Phoenician colonies in northern Africa.

²Utica. *City, eastern United States.* The New York city was incorporated as a village in 1798 and named for the historic city of ¹Utica in Tunisia. The name is said to have been drawn from a hat.

Utrecht. *City, central Netherlands.* The city's name comes from Old German *ut*, "out," "outside," and the name of the Roman settlement here. This was *Trajectum castrum*, "fort by the ford," from Latin *trajectus*, "river crossing" (*cp.* **Maastricht**), and *castrum*, "fortified camp." The present name originally applied to the town that arose below this settlement. The river here is the Oude Rijn (Old Rhine), a tributary of the Lek.

Utsunomiya. *City, central Japan.* The city, in the island of Honshu, derives its name from Japanese *u*, "roof," "house," "sky," *tsu*, "capital," *no*, the genitive (possessive) particle, and *miya*, "Shinto temple." The overall description is thus of an administrative capital that arose around a Shinto temple.

Uttaranchal. *State, northeastern India.* The state, created in 2000, has a name meaning "northern border," referring to its location adjacent to Nepal and China. The name was imposed over the locally preferred name *Uttarakhand*, "northern portion."

Uttar Pradesh. *State, northern India.* The state has a Hindi name meaning simply "northern state," from *uttar*, "north," and *pradesh*, "state." *Cp.* **Andhra Pradesh**.

Uusikaupunki. *Town and port, southwestern Finland.* The town, founded in 1617, has a name meaning "new town," from Finnish *uusi*, "new," and *kaupunki*, "town." Its Swedish name of *Nystad* has the same meaning.

Uusimaa. *Province, southern Finland.* The name means "new land," from Finnish *uusi*, "new," and *maa*, "land." The Swedish name of the province is *Nyland*, with the same meaning.

Uzbekistan. *Republic, southeastern Asia.* The country takes its name from its indigenous people, the *Uzbeks*, together with Iranian *ostān*, "country." The people are said to derive their name from the Mongol leader Ghiyath ad-Din Muhammad *Uzbek* (*Öz Beg*), a khan of the Golden Horde (reigned 1313–42). If so, the Uzbeks were formed relatively late as a race.

Uzhgorod. *City, western Ukraine.* The city takes its name from the *Uzh* River on which it lies and Russian *gorod*, "town" (here more in the sense "fortified place"). The meaning of the river's own name is uncertain. When previously in Austria-Hungary, the town was known as *Ungvar*, where *Ung-* is the river name and *-var* is Hungarian *vár*, "fort," "town." The Ukrainian form of the name is *Uzhhorod*.

Uzlovaya. *City, western Russia.* The industrial city, near Tula, arose by a major railroad junction. Hence its name, from Russian *uzel*, "junction" (literally "knot").

Vaal. *River, north central South Africa.* The river, which formerly marked the border between the Orange Free State and **Transvaal**, derives its name from Afrikaans *vaal*, "pale," referring to its muddy waters when it is in flood and carrying silt.

Vaasa. *City and port, southwestern Finland.* The city takes its name from that of the *Vasa* dynasty of Swedish kings who ruled over Sweden and Poland from 1523 through 1818. The town was granted the privilege of bearing their name by Charles IX of Sweden on its foundation in 1606. The dynasty's own name comes from that of their estate near Uppsala, Sweden. The name was officially changed in 1917 to *Nikolainkaupunki*, "Nicholas's town," for *Nicholas* II of Russia (1868–1918), of which Finland was then part. But Finland declared its independence later that year when the Russian empire collapsed and the name never caught on.

Vadodara. *City, western India.* The city, in Gujarat state, derives its name from Sanskrit *vaṭodar*, from *vaṭa*, "banyan" (a type of large fig tree). Vadodara was formerly the capital of the princely state of *Baroda*, and was itself known by this name, a form of the original.

Vaduz. *Capital of Liechtenstein.* The city is traditionally said to derive its name from Latin *vallis dulcis*, "sweet valley," denoting its agreeable situation in the valley of the Rhine. But it is more likely to represent Old German *Valdutsch*, from Latin *vallis* and Old German *dutsch*, "German." The reference would also be to the Rhine, but in its capacity as a predominantly German river.

Valaam. *Island, northwestern Russia.* The island, in the northwestern part of Lake Ladoga, is famous for its medieval monastery. Hence the popular derivation of the name either from the biblical prophet *Balaam* (Numbers 22–24) or, because this personage was regarded unfavorably by Orthodox Christians, from the pagan god *Baal* (1 Kings 16:31, etc.), the principal object of Canaanite worship. But the Finnish name of the island is *Valamo*, said to mean "height," and the Russian name is simply a form of this.

Valais. *Canton, southern Switzerland.* The canton, known as *Wallis* in German, *Vallese* in Italian, and *Vallais* in Romansh, derives its name from Latin *vallis*, "valley." The valley in question is that of the upper Rhône River.

Valdai Hills. *Hill region, western Russia.* The hills have a name of Finno-Ugric origin, from a root element *vara-* or *varye*, "hills," and *valda*, "region." The overall sense is thus simply "hilly district."

Valdivia. *City and river port, south central Chile.* The city was founded in 1552 by the Spanish conquistador Pedro de *Valdivia* (c.1498–1554), who also founded Santiago and Concepción. It is thus named for him.

Val-d'Or. *Town, eastern Canada.* The Quebec town was founded by miners in 1934 and has a French name meaning "golden valley." There is gold here but no actual valley, and the name may have been suggested by some existing *Golden Valley.* (There are counties of the name in Montana and South Dakota, USA, various river valleys in western England, and a *Golden Vale* in western Ireland.)

Valence. *Town, southeastern France.* The town ultimately takes its name from the Roman personal name *Valentius*, itself from Latin *valens*, "strong," "healthy."

¹Valencia. *City and port, eastern Spain.* The city was known to the Romans as *Valentia Edetanorum*, "fort of the *Edetani*," the first word representing Low Latin *valentia*, "strength," a derivative of Latin *valere*, "to be strong," "to be healthy." The *Edetani* were a Tarraconese people from northern Spain.

²Valencia. *City, northwestern Venezuela.* The city was founded in 1555 as *Nueva Valencia del Rey*, "new *Valencia* of the king," by Alonso Díaz Moreno, a Spanish soldier from ¹**Valencia.**

Valenciennes. *Town, northern France.* The town is said to take its name from that of the Roman emperor *Valentinian* I (321–375), ruling at the time of its foundation. The town's canting coat of arms features swans, as if the name came from French *val de cygnes*, "valley of swans."

Valentia. *Island, southwestern Ireland.* The island, off the southwest coast, has a name representing Irish *Béal Inse*, "estuary of the island," referring to the sound that separates the island from the mainland. The present form of the name appears to have been influenced by that of ¹**Valencia**, and the two names are pronounced alike (as "Valensha") by many English speakers

Valetta. *Capital of Malta.* The city is named for Jean Parizot de la *Valette* (1494–1568), the French general and grand master of the Order of Malta who founded it in 1566. The name is also spelled *Valletta.*

Valladolid. *City, northwestern Spain.* The city's name is probably of Arabic origin, from *balad ūlīd*, "town of *Ulid*," although it is not known who Ulid was. Some authorities prefer a derivation from Spanish *valle*, "valley," and *Olid*, said to be the name of the city's founder. Others again propose an origin in Medieval Latin *Vallisoletum*, "valley of olive trees," from Latin *vallis*, "valley," and *olea*, "olive tree."

Vallejo. *City, southwestern United States.* The California city is named for General Mariano G. *Vallejo* (1808–1890), who in 1850 offered land here for the new state capital of California (as which it served briefly in 1852 and 1853).

Valletta *see* **Valetta**

Valois. *Historic region, northern France.* The former duchy had the Medieval Latin name of *pagus Vadensis*, from Latin *pagus*, "district," and a word perhaps from *vadus*, "ford," presumably referring to a crossing of the Oise River here. The *d* of the name became *l* by association with Latin *vallis*, "valley," also that of the Oise.

Valparaíso. *City and port, central Chile.* The name means "valley of paradise," from Spanish *valle*, "valley," and *paraíso*, "paradise." The reference is to the city's scenically striking site, on mountain slopes above a broad bay, which was discovered in 1536 by the Spanish conquistador Juan de Saavedra.

Valtellina. *Valley, northern Italy.* The Alpine valley of the upper Adda River has a name that can be understood as *val di Teglio*, "valley of *Teglio*," from the small town of *Teglio* here. Its own name comes from Italian *tiglio*, "lime tree." The German form of the name is *Veltlin.*

Van, Lake. *Lake, eastern Turkey.* The lake is named for the nearby city of *Van*, its own name recorded by Ptolemy in the 2d century A.D. as *Bouana*. It ultimately represents Iranian *hane*, "settlement."

Vanadzor. *City, northern Armenia.* The city was originally known as *Karaklis*, a Turkic name meaning "black church" (Turkish *kara*, "black," and *kilise*, "church"). In 1935 it was renamed

Kirovakan, for the Communist party leader Sergey Mironovich *Kirov* (1886–1934), who established Soviet power in the Caucasus, with Turkic *-kan*, "town," added. It adopted its present name in 1993 from the *Vanadzoriget* River here.

Vancouver. *City and port, southwestern Canada.* The British Columbia city was first settled in 1865 and named for *Vancouver* Island, itself so called for the English navigator George *Vancouver* (1757–1798), who sailed with Captain Cook on his second and third voyages and who surveyed the Pacific coast here in 1792.

Vanderbijlpark. *Town, northeastern South Africa.* The town, in Gauteng province, was laid out in 1944 on the recommendation of Dr. Hendrik Johannes *van der Bijl* (1887–1948), founder of the South African Iron and Steel Corporation (Iscor), as a dormitory town for his workers. The *park* denotes its "garden city" plan.

Van Diemen Gulf. *Inlet, northern Australia.* The inlet of the Arafura Sea, in Northern Territory, was reached in 1644 by the Dutch navigator Abel Tasman (*see* **Tasmania**) and named by him for Anthony *Van Diemen* (1595–1645), then governor general of the Dutch East Indies.

Vannes. *Town, northwestern France.* The town, in Brittany, was the capital of the Gaulish people known as the *Veneti*, and is named for them. Their own name may derive from Gaulish *vindo*, "white," although some sources prefer an origin in Indoeuropean *venis*, "friend." The Breton name of the town is *Guened*.

Vanua Levu. *Island, Fiji, southwestern Pacific.* The second largest island of Fiji, northeast of Viti Levu, has a local name meaning "great land." It was discovered by the Dutch navigator Abel Tasman (*see* **Tasmania**) in 1643 and was formerly known as *Sandalwood Island.*

Vanuatu. *Island republic, southwestern Pacific.* The islands, west of Fiji, have a local (Bislama) name meaning "our land," based on Polynesian *vanua*, "land," "country." Until 1980, when they gained independence, the islands were known as the *New Hebrides*, a name given by Captain Cook in 1774 for their supposed resemblance to the **Hebrides**, off the northwest coast of Scotland.

Varanasi. *City, northeastern India.* The city, one of the seven sacred cities of the Hindus, in Uttar Pradesh state, derives its name from the *Varana* and *Asi* rivers, tributaries of the Ganges, on which it lies. The name was formerly familiar in the corrupt form *Benares.*

Varanger Fjord. *Inlet, northeastern Norway.* The inlet derives its name from Old Norse *varp*,

"casting," referring to the casting of fishing nets, and *angr*, "fjord," "inlet." The latter component is found in the names of many Norwegian fjords, such as *Hardanger* and *Stavanger.*

Varna. *City and port, northeastern Bulgaria.* The city is said to derive its name from the Slavic root word *vran* or *vrana*, "black" (literally "crow-colored"), presumably with reference to its location on the Black Sea. Bulgarian toponymists favor a different origin, from Indoeuropean *vara*, "water." The town was founded in the 6th century B.C. under the name of *Odessos.* From 1949 through 1956 it was known as *Stalin*, for the Soviet Communist dictator.

Vásárosnamény. *Town, northeastern Hungary.* The first part of the town's name is Hungarian *vásár*, "market." The second part is of uncertain origin and meaning.

Västerås. *City and river port, central Sweden.* The city's name means "western river mouth," from Swedish *väster*, "western," *å*, "river," and *os*, "mouth." It stands at the mouth of the Svart River on Lake Mälar. The town was originally *Aros*, "river mouth" (*cp.* **Uppsala**), then *Västra Aros*, "western *Aros*," these two words finally coalescing as now.

Västerbotten. *County, north central Sweden.* The county's name means "western (valley) bottom," representing a historic name for this region that also gave the name of *Bothnia* (*see* **Bothnia, Gulf of**). To the north of it lies **Norrbotten**.

Västermanland. *County, central Sweden.* The name means "land of the western people," as distinct from neighboring **Södermanland**. *Cp.* **Norrland, Uppland.**

Vasvár. *Town, western Hungary.* The name means "iron castle," from Hungarian *vas*, "iron," and *vár*, "castle." The German name of the town is identical, as *Eisenburg.* The sense is not literal, but describes a fortress built of dark-colored stone while also implying a stronghold. *Cp.* **Tiszavasvár.**

Vatican. *Papal state, western Italy.* The city and state, an enclave in Rome, takes its name from the hill on which it stands. The hill's own name represents Latin *mons vaticinia*, "hill of prophecies," from *vates*, "prophet." The Vatican as a papal residence dates from the 5th century.

Vatnajökull. *Glacier, southeastern Iceland.* The extensive snowfield has a name meaning literally "water glacier," from Icelandic *vatn*, "water," and *jökull*, "glacier."

Vättern. *Lake, southern Sweden.* The lake has a basic name deriving from Swedish *vatten*, "water."

Vaucluse. *Department, southeastern France.*

The department's name derives from the region's Roman name of *Vallis Clausa*, "closed valley." The valley in question is that of the Rhône (to the north) and the Durance (to the south), which is bounded to the east by steeply rising mountains.

Vaud. *Canton, southwestern Switzerland.* The canton derives its Germanic name from its original inhabitants, referred to as *walho*, "strangers," by their neighbors (*cp.* **Wales**). The German form of the name is *Waadt*.

Vauxhall. *District of London, southeastern England.* The district, south of the Thames River, has a name that means "*Vaux*'s hall," referring to the manor that was held here in the 13th century by the Norman *Falkes* de Bréauté.

Vazovgrad *see* ²**Sopot**

Velikiye Luki. *City, western Russia.* The city's Russian name means literally "big bends," referring to its location in a bend of the Lovat River. Although grammatically plural, the name is better rendered in a singular sense, "big bend," as only one bend is involved.

Veliko Tŭrnovo. *Town, central Bulgaria.* The name, of uncertain origin, may be based on Bulgarian *tŭrn*, "thorn." *Veliko* is "Great."

Velingrad. *Town, southwestern Bulgaria.* The town was formed in 1948 on the union of three villages and named for the revolutionary activist *Vela* Peeva (1922–1944), who was born here. She was killed on May 3, 1944, at Byalata-Skala in the Rhodope Mountains when repelling German occupying forces.

Venda. *Historic homeland, northeastern South Africa.* The former Bantu homeland, in what is now Limpopo province, is named for the *Venda* people who came from the north to settle here in the 18th century. Their own name is said to mean either "world" or "land." In 1994 the homeland was reincorporated into South Africa.

Vendée. *Department, western France.* The region is named for the river here, its own name perhaps deriving from Gaulish *vindos*, "white."

Vendôme. *Town, north central France.* The town had the Roman name of *Vindocinum*, from Gaulish *vindos*, "white," and an element of unknown meaning.

Veneto. *Region, northern Italy.* The region, also known as *Venetia*, takes its name from the *Veneti*, the people who gave the name of **Venice**, its capital.

Venezuela. *Republic, northern South America.* The country's name is a Spanish diminutive of *Venecia*, "Venice." The region was so named by Spanish seamen who came here in 1499 and saw by Lake Maracaibo a Native American village built on piles or stakes. This reminded them of the Italian city, so they named it the equivalent of "Little Venice."

Venice. *City and port, northeastern Italy.* The city takes its name from the *Veneti*, the original inhabitants of the region. Their own name may mean "white" (*cp.* **Vannes**). The Italian name of Venice is *Venezia*, while the Germans know it as *Venedig. See also* **Veneto, Venezuela.**

Venlo. *City, southeastern Netherlands.* The city, on the Maas (Meuse) River, derives its from Middle Dutch *venne*, "marsh" (English *fen*), and *lōh*, "wood."

Ventimiglia. *City and port, northwestern Italy.* The name outwardly suggests an origin in Italian *venti miglia*, "twenty miles." It is actually a corruption of the city's Roman name, *Album Intimelium* or *Albintimilium*, from the name of a Ligurian people. The original meaning is unknown.

Ventnor. *Town and resort, southern England.* The town, on the south coast of the Isle of Wight, is believed to derive its name from a local family called *Vintner*, who owned a farm here in or before the early 17th century.

Ventspils. *City and port, western Latvia.* The city takes its name from the *Venta* River that enters the Baltic here, with Latvian *pils*, "town," added. It was earlier known as *Vindava*, from its former German name of *Windau*. This also represents the river's name, which itself is of unknown origin.

Ventura. *City, western United States.* The California city, on the Pacific coast, arose on the site of the *San Buenaventura* ("St. Bonaventure") mission founded in 1782 by the Spanish Franciscan missionary Junípero Serra, and the present name is a shortened form of this.

Veracruz. *City and port, east central Mexico.* The city has a Spanish name meaning "True Cross," referring to the original cross of the Crucifixion. The town was founded in Holy Week 1519 by the Spanish conquistador Hernán Cortés and named propitiously by him *Villa Rica de la Vera Cruz*, "rich town of the True Cross." The original site was then abandoned as unsuitable and the present city arose on a new site, but with the same name, in 1599. Its official full name is now *Veracruz Llave*, the latter word commemorating General Ignacio de la *Llave*, governor of Veracruz state from 1857 to 1860.

Verbania. *Town, northern Italy.* The town, a resort on Lake Maggiore, takes its name from the Roman name of the lake, *Verbanus Lacus. See* **Maggiore, Lake.**

Vercelli. *City, northern Italy.* The city is said

to derive its name from a Gaulish god called *Vercellius*, his name meaning "great striker," literally "(he with the) great hammer," from *ver-*, "above," "super-," and *cellos*, "hammer."

Verde, Cape *see* **Cape Verde**

Verden. *Town, northwestern Germany.* The town, dating from the 10th century, has a name meaning "(place) at the ford," from Old Saxon *ferdi*, the dative form of *fard*, "way," "ford," referring to a crossing of the Aller River here.

¹Verdun. *Town, northeastern France.* The town had the Roman name *Virodunum*, meaning "*Vero*'s fort," with the Gaulish personal name followed by *dunon*, "fort."

²Verdun. *City, southeastern Canada.* The Quebec city was granted in 1672 to Zacharie Dupuis, a French military pioneer, and named for his birthplace, the town of *Saverdun*, southwestern France.

Vereeniging. *City, east central South Africa.* The city, in Gauteng province, arose in 1882 on the discovery of coal here and takes its name from the final word of the Afrikaans title of the mining company, *De Zuid-Afrikaansche en Oranje Vrijstaatsche Kolen- en Mineralen-Mijn Vereeniging*, "The South African and Orange Free State Coal and Mineral Mines Association."

Veresegyház. *Village, north central Hungary.* The name of the village means "red church," from Hungarian *vörös*, "red," and *egyház*, "church," presumably referring to the color of the stone.

Vergina. *Village, northeastern Greece.* The village, a noted archaeological site, is named for a legendary queen of ancient Beroea (present Veroia).

Verkhoyansk. *City, eastern Russia.* The Siberian city has a name meaning "(town on the) upper *Yana*," from Russian *verkh*, "height," and a river name of uncertain origin. The city is at the confluence of two rivers that here form the *Yana*.

Vermont. *State, northeastern United States.* The state has a French name that fairly obviously means "green mountain." However, the standard French form of the name would be *Mont Vert*, suggesting that the present name was given by an English settler who deliberately or ignorantly reversed the order of the words in the French original. The mountains in question are the **Green Mountains**, to the east of Lake Champlain.

Verona. *City, northeastern Italy.* The city's original Celtic name was *Vernomago*, from *verno*, "elder tree," and *mago*, "field," "place."

Versailles. *City, northern France.* The city's

name is of disputed origin. Proposed derivations include: (1) From Latin *versus*, "slope," with a suffix *-alia*; (2) From Latin *versum*, "turned," and *alae*, "wings," referring to a former windmill here; (3) From Medieval Latin *versagium*, a legal term for a type of tax on forests; (4) From Old French *val de Gallie*, "valley of *Gaul*." Only the first of these can be regarded as anything like plausible.

Vert, Cape *see* **Cape Verde**

Vesoul. *Town, eastern France.* The town had the Medieval Latin name of *Vesulium*, from Celtic *ves*, "mountain," and the suffix *-ulum*. The "mountain" is the nearby isolated conical hill known as *La Motte* (from Low Latin *motta*, "height," a word of pre–Celtic origin).

Vestmannaeyjar. *Island group, southern Iceland.* The name means "islands of the westmen," from Icelandic *vestmann*, "westman," and *eyjar*, the plural of *ey*, "island." The "westmen" were Irishmen slain here by the Norwegians. (Ireland is the western island of the British Isles, and its name has been popularly derived from Irish *iar*, "west.") The name is also that of the group's chief town, on the island of *Heimaey* ("home island").

Vesuvius. *Volcano, southwestern Italy.* The name may ultimately derive from a pre–Celtic root element *ves* meaning simply "mountain," although some authorities prefer an origin in Oscan *fesf*, "smoke," "steam," referring to the actual volcano rather than the mountain. As a "steamer" ("smoke without fire") Vesuvius thus essentially contrasts with **Etna**, a "flamer" ("fire without smoke").

Veszprém. *City, western Hungary.* The city was founded in the 11th century and is said to take its name from the Polish prince *Bezprím*, son of Bolesław I the Brave (967–1025), king of Poland.

Vevey. *Town, western Switzerland.* The town, on Lake Geneva, had the Roman name of *Vibiscum*, from the *Vibisci*, a Celtic people. The name is popularly derived from Latin *bivium*, "place where two ways meet," as if referring to the town's location at the junction of roads leading respectively to Lausanne and Moudon. The German form of the name is *Vivis*.

Viborg. *City, north central Denmark.* The city's Scandinavian name means "holy hill," from *vi*, "holy," and *borg*, "hill" (*cp.* **Vyborg**). The town's original site was a center of pagan worship.

Vicente López. *City, eastern Argentina.* The city, now a suburb of Buenos Aires, is named for the Argentine historian *Vicente López* (1815–

1903), author of the country's national anthem.

Vicenza. *City, northeastern Italy.* The city had the Roman name of *Vicetia* or *Vicentia*. The meaning of this is uncertain.

Vich. *City, northeastern Spain.* The city had the Roman name *Vicus Ausonensis*, for the *Ausetanos*, an Iberian people. The first word of this name, Latin *vicus*, "settlement," gave the present name.

Vichy. *Town and spa, central France.* The name of the town may derive from Latin *vicus calidus*, "warm settlement," referring to the warm alkaline springs for which it is famous. Equally, it could represent the Roman personal name *Vippius*, with the Gallo-Roman suffix *-acum*.

[1]**Victoria.** *State, southeastern Australia.* The state was set off from New South Wales as a separate territory in 1851 and named for Queen *Victoria* (1819–1901).

[2]**Victoria.** *City, southwestern Canada.* The capital of British Columbia was founded in 1843 and named for Queen *Victoria* (1819–1901).

[3]**Victoria.** *Historic capital of Hong Kong.* The city and port was founded in 1842 and named for Queen *Victoria* (1819–1901). There has been no actual capital since the reversion of Hong Kong to China in 1997, and the government offices are now in Central & Western District, enclosing the historic Victoria.

[4]**Victoria.** *Capital of Seychelles.* The city and port, on Mahé, the largest island, was founded in 1841, originally as *Port Victoria*, and named for Queen *Victoria* (1819–1901).

[5]**Victoria.** *City, southern United States.* The Texas city was founded in 1824 by Spanish settlers and named to honor both *Nuestra Señora de Guadalupe de Jesus Victoria* (Our Lady of Guadalupe) and Guadalupe *Victoria* (original name Manuel Félix Fernández) (1786–1843), the first Mexican president, who changed his name to mark his commitment to the cause of Mexican independence. (The patriots had adopted the image of Our Lady of **Guadalupe**, the patron saint of Mexico, as their symbol.)

[6]**Victoria.** *River, northern Australia.* The longest river in Northern Territory was discovered in 1839 by Captain J.C. Wickham of HMS *Beagle* and named for Queen *Victoria* (1819–1901), who had come to the throne two years previously.

Victoria, Lake. *Lake, east central Africa.* The lake, its northern half in Uganda and southern half in Tanzania, was discovered by the English explorer John Hanning Speke in 1858 and named by him for Queen *Victoria* (1819–1901).

Its alternate name is *Victoria Nyanza*, the second word of which is Bantu for "lake."

Victoria Falls. *Waterfall, southern Africa.* The falls, on the Zambezi River between Zimbabwe and Zambia, were discovered by the British explorer David Livingstone in 1855 and named by him for Queen *Victoria* (1819–1901). The indigenous (Kalolo-Lozi) name for the falls is *Mosi-oa-tunya*, "the smoke that thunders."

Victoria Island. *Island, northern Canada.* Canada's third-largest island, divided between the Northwest Territories and Nunavut, was discovered by Thomas Simpson in 1838 and named for Queen *Victoria* (1819–1901), who had come to the throne the previous year.

Victoria Land. *Region, eastern Antarctica.* The region, between the Ross Sea and Wilkes Land, was discovered in 1841 by a British expedition led by Sir James Clark Ross and named for Queen *Victoria* (1819–1901).

Victory Peak. *Mountain, central Asia.* The mountain, in the Tien Shan range, on the border between Kyrgyzstan and China, was first climbed by Soviet mountaineers in 1938 and originally named *Komsomol 20th Anniversary Peak*, commemorating the founding of the Communist youth organization in 1918. Its height was first calculated in 1943 by a team of Soviet topographers and it was given its present name then, marking the *victories* won, and to be won, by Soviet forces in World War II. The mountain's Russian name is *pik Pobedy*, "peak of victory." *Cp.* **Communism, Peak**.

Viedma. *City, south central Argentina.* The city is named for the Spanish explorer Francisco de *Viedma*, who in 1779 built a fort here called *Mercedes de Patagones*, "mercies of the Patagonians" (meaning the indigenous Tehuelche people).

Vienna. *Capital of Austria.* The city's present name evolved from its Roman name of *Vindobona*, representing Celtic *vindo*, "white," and *bona*, "foundation," "fort." The first part of this probably refers not to the fort but to the waters of the small *Wien* River which joins the Danube here.

Vienne. *City, southeastern France.* The Roman name of the city was *Vienna*, from a Gaulish name of unknown meaning. It may be based on Indoeuropean *vindo*, "whiteness," referring to the waters of the Rhône River on which it stands. To that extent it may share a common origin with **Vienna**.

Vientiane. *Capital of Laos.* The city has a Laotian name meaning "town of sandalwood," from *vieng*, "fortification," "town," and *chăn*, "sandalwood." The present spelling evolved through French influence.

Viersen. *City, western Germany.* The city, arising in Frankish times on an old Roman road, probably derives its name from that of a stream *Versina*, itself from Old High German *frisc*, "fresh," "cool."

Vietnam. *Republic, southeastern Asia.* The country, formerly divided (1954–76) as North Vietnam and South Vietnam, has the Vietnamese name *Viêt-Nam*, from *Viêt*, the name of a former principality of southern China, and *nam*, "south." *See also* **Annam**.

Vigo. *City and port, northwestern Spain.* The city ultimately derives its name from Latin *vicus*, "settlement," "village." *Cp.* **Vich**, **Vichy**.

Vijayanagar. *Historic kingdom, southern India.* The former kingdom took its name from its capital. Its own name means "town of victory," from Sanskrit *vijaya*, "victory," and *nagara*, "town." The city was the center of Hindu resistance against Muslim invaders until it was destroyed in 1565.

Vila Real. *Town, northern Portugal.* The town was founded in the 13th century and was originally known as *Panoias*. It was renamed "royal town," from Portuguese *vila*, "town," and *real*, "royal," when its inhabitants presented it to Isabella of Portugal (died 1496).

Vila Velha. *City, eastern Brazil.* The coastal city, settled in 1535, has a Portuguese name meaning "old town."

Villach. *City, southern Austria.* The city's name is believed to have evolved from an earlier form *Biliacon*, from a Celtic word meaning "tree" (Old Irish *bile*), although some sources prefer an origin in a Slavic word meaning "white" (Russian *belyj*), perhaps referring to the water of the springs here.

Villa Hayes. *Town, central Paraguay.* The town, founded in 1855 by Paraguayan president Carlos Antonio López, was renamed in honor of Rutherford B. *Hayes* (1822–1893), 19th president of the United States, who acted as arbiter in the border dispute between Paraguay and Argentina after the War of the Triple Alliance (1865–70).

Villahermosa. *City, southeastern Mexico.* The city was founded by the Spanish in 1596 and was originally named *Villa Felipe II*, "*Philip II* town," for *Philip II* of Spain (1527–1598). It was given its present name, meaning "beautiful city," in 1915.

Villa Obregón. *City, central Mexico.* The city, just outside Mexico City, is named for General Álvaro *Obregón* (1880–1928), president of Mexico from 1920 to 1924, who was assassinated here.

Villavicencio. *City, central Colombia.* The city was founded by the Spanish in 1840 and named for the Ecuadorian soldier Antonio *Villavicencio* (1775–1816), a fighter for independence from Spain.

Villaviciosa. *Town and port, northwestern Spain.* The town was originally known as *Tierra de Maliayo*, "bad land," alluding to its unfavorable site for building. *Villa*, "town," was substituted for *Tierra*, "land," and the "badness" was reinterpreted in moral terms, giving *viciosa*, "depraved," "addicted to vice."

Villefranche-sur-Saône. *Town, east central France.* The town's name means "free town," in the sense of a town founded by a lord and granted special tax exemptions with the aim of attracting residents. There are several places so named. This is the largest, distinguished from the others by the addition of the name of the river on which it lies.

Villeneuve-sur-Lot. *Town, southwestern France.* The town's basic name, found elsewhere in France, means "new town," from Medieval Latin *Villanova*, a name given to a commune formed on the merger of existing settlements. The places so called are distinguished by means of a suffix, in this case for the town's location on the **Lot** River.

Villeurbanne. *City, east central France.* The city, now a suburb of Lyons, had the Medieval Latin name of *Villa Orbana*, from *villa*, "town," and either *urbana*, "urban," or the female personal name *Urbana*. The latter seems more likely.

Villingen-Schwenningen. *Town, southwestern Germany.* The twin city was formed in 1972 on the union of the formerly independent towns of *Villingen in Schwarzwald*, in the **Black Forest**, and *Schwenningen am Neckar*, on the **Neckar** River. Their names derive from those of their Alemannic founders, and respectively mean "(settlement of) *Filo*'s people" and "(settlement of) *Swano*'s people."

Vilnius. *Capital of Lithuania.* The city takes its name from the *Viliya* River on which it lies. The river name itself is said to derive from Lithuanian *vilnis*, "wave."

Vincennes. *Town, northern France.* The town, now a suburb of Paris, probably takes its name from the Gaulish personal name *Vilicus*, of uncertain meaning.

Vindhya Range. *Hill range, central India.* The range, forming a natural dividing line between north and south India, has a name meaning "split," "cleft," referring to its many ravines and gorges.

Vineland. *City, eastern United States.* The

New Jersey city was founded in 1861 by Charles K. Landis, who is said to have named it for the abundance of grapes here. *Cp*. **Vinland**.

Vinland. *Historic region, eastern North America*. The name is that given to a portion of the east coast of North America by Leif Eriksson and other Norsemen in the early 11th century. The literal meaning is "wine land," possibly referring to the wild grapes that grew here, although it has been suggested that the "grapes" found by the visitors were really cranberries. The region itself has been variously located from Labrador, Canada, to New Jersey, USA.

Vinnitsa. *City, west central Ukraine*. The city's name is ultimately based on Ukrainian *vino*, "wine." Vinnitsa is in the heart of a major agricultural region. The Ukrainian form of the name is *Vinnytsya*.

Virginia. *State, eastern United States*. The state, the site of the first permanent English settlement in North America (at Jamestown in 1607), is named for Queen Elizabeth (1533–1603), the "*Virgin* Queen." There is evidence to suggest that the name was given by Elizabeth herself, as much to refer to the newly claimed "virgin land" as to represent her own epithet. The state of *West Virginia* was set off from Virginia in 1861, its name describing its location relative to the now reduced original state.

Virginia Beach. *City and resort, eastern United States*. **Virginia**'s largest city is named for its state and the *beach* on the Atlantic coast where it was founded in 1887.

Virgin Islands. *Island group, eastern Caribbean Sea*. The islands, divided between Britain and the United States as the *British Virgin Islands* and *Virgin Islands of the United States*, were sighted by Columbus in 1493, when he named them *Santa Ursula y las Once Mil Virgenes* ("St. Ursula and the Eleven Thousand Virgins"), in honor of St. Ursula and her legendary 11,000 martyred companions.

Virovitica. *Town, northern Croatia*. The town bases its name on Slavic *vir*, "whirlpool," and the Serbo-Croat adjectival suffix *-ovit* denoting the presence of the named object, i.e. "abounding in whirlpools." (The final *-ica* is an Old Slavonic suffix common in river names.)

Virunga. *Mountain range, east central Africa*. The volcanic range, extending along the borders of the Democratic Republic of Congo, Rwanda, and Uganda, has a Swahili name meaning "volcanoes." This name has gained precedence over the earlier name *Mfumbiro*, "that which cooks," although this is still the preferred name in Uganda.

Visayas. *Island group, central Philippines*. The name is that of the islands' indigenous people, itself of unknown origin. An alternate spelling is *Bisayas*.

Visby. *Town, southeastern Sweden*. The final Scandinavian *-by* of the name, found also in German and English placenames, means "village." The first part of the name is said to mean "sacred" (*cp*. **Viborg**), referring to pagan worship here, although another possible derivation is in *vith*, "forest."

Vishakhapatnam. *City and port, southern India*. The city, in Andhra Pradesh state, has a name meaning "city of *Vishakh*," from *Vishakh*, a name of Skanda, the Hindu war god, with *-patnam* representing Hindi *pattan*, "town."

Vistula. *River, Poland*. Poland's chief river probably derives its name from the Indoeuropean root element *viso*, "water." The German form of the name is *Weichsel*. The *Vistula Lagoon*, entered by the Vistula on the Baltic coast, has the German name *Frisches Haff*, "freshwater lagoon," while the *Vistula Spit*, separating the lagoon from the Gulf of Gdańsk, is *Frische Nehrung*, "freshwater spit."

Vitebsk. *City, northeastern Belarus*. The city takes its name from the *Vit'ba* River on which it stands. The river's own name is believed to come from a local word meaning "marsh," "damp place."

Viti Levu. *Island, Fiji, southwestern Pacific*. Fiji's largest island has a name meaning "great **Fiji**."

Vitoria. *City, northeastern Spain*. The city, in the Basque Country, had the Medieval Latin name of *Victoriacum*, "place of victory," referring to the victory of Leovigild, king of the Visigoths, over the Basques in 581. Its Basque name is *Gazteiz*, based on *gazte*, "young."

Vitry-le-François. *Town, northeastern France*. The town had the Medieval Latin name of *Vitriacum*, representing the Roman personal name *Victorius* and the Gallo-Roman suffix *-acum*. The second part of the name is that of *Francis* I of France, who founded it in 1545 to replace the former *Vitry-en-Perthois* ("Vitry-in-Perthois"), or earlier *Vitry-le-Brûlé* ("Vitry-the-burned"), which was burned down by Louis VII in 1142 and, although later rebuilt, destroyed by Charles V in 1544. The second part of the name distinguishes this town from others identically named, such as **Vitry-sur-Seine**.

Vitry-sur-Seine. *City, northern France*. The city, now a suburb of Paris, had the Medieval Latin name of *Vitriacum*, from the Roman personal name *Victorius* and the Gallo-Roman suffix

-*acum*. The second part of the name, indicating its location on the **Seine**, distinguishes it from identically named towns, such as **Vitry-le-François**.

Vittoria. *Town, southern Italy*. The town, in southeastern Sicily, was founded in 1607 by *Vittoria* Colonna, daughter of Marco Antonio Colonna (1535–1584), viceroy of Sicily, and wife of Luigi III Enriquez, count of Modica, and is named for her.

Vittoriosa. *Town, eastern Malta*. The medieval town was originally known as *Birgu*. Its present name, meaning "victorious," was given to commemorate the *victory* of the Knights Hospitalers over the Turks in the Great Siege of Malta (1565).

Vittorio Veneto. *Town, northeastern Italy*. The town, until 1921 known simply as *Vittorio*, was formed in 1866 by the union of two urban districts and named for *Victor* Emmanuel II (1820–1878), king of Italy. The second word locates it in the region of **Veneto**.

Vizianagaram. *Town, southern India*. The town, in Andhra Pradesh state, derives its name from the **Vijayanagar** empire, the Hindu dynasty that resisted Muslim expansion in southern India in the 14th and 15th centuries.

Vlaardingen. *City and port, southwestern Netherlands*. The name is of uncertain origin. It may derive from a family or river name.

Vladikavkaz. *City, southwestern Russia*. The city was founded in 1784 as a military fortress. Its name means "possessing the Caucasus," from the root of Russian *vladet'*, "to possess," and *Kavkaz*, "Caucasus." The fort was designed to protect the Georgian Military Highway, one of the key routes over the Caucasus. The name was devised by the soldier and statesman Grigory Potyomkin, favorite of Catherine the Great. In 1931 the city was renamed *Ordzhonikidze*, for the Georgian Communist leader and revolutionary Grigory *Ordzhonikidze* (1886–1937), who in the Civil War led the defense of the town against counterrevolutionaries and who helped bring Georgia under Soviet rule. From 1944 to 1954 it was further renamed *Dzaudzhikau*, from a personal name and *kau*, "village." The city reverted to its original name in 1990. **Vladivostok** has a name directly based on that of Vladikavkaz.

Vladimir. *City, western Russia*. The city was founded in 1108 by *Vladimir* Monomakh (1053–1125), grand prince of Kiev, and is named for him. His own name, popularly interpreted as "possessing the world" (really "famous ruler"), may have served as a template for **Vladikavkaz** and **Vladivostok**.

Vladimir-Volynsky. *City, northwestern Ukraine*. The city, first mentioned in 988, was founded in the reign of the Kievan prince *Vladimir* Svyatoslavovich. Hence the main name. The addition distinguishes the city from **Vladimir**, Russia, by locating it in **Volynia**. The Ukrainian form of the name is *Volodymyr-Volyns'kyy*.

Vladivostok. *City and port, southeastern Russia*. The city was founded as a military base in 1860 and given a name based on that of **Vladikavkaz**. It means "possessing the east," from the root of Russian *vladet'*, "to possess," and *vostok*, "east." Vladivostok is the principal Russian Pacific port.

Vlissingen *see* **Flushing**

Vlorë. *City and port, southwestern Albania*. The town was founded as the Greek colony of *Aulon*, apparently from the identical Greek word meaning "valley," although possibly a reinterpretation of an existing pre–Greek name. The present name evolved as a corruption of this.

Vltava. *River, Czech Republic*. The river, a tributary of the Elbe, has a name of Germanic origin, from *Wilthahwa*, "wild water," representing *wilth*, "wild," and *ahwa*, "water." The reference is to the strong current. The river's present German name is *Moldau*, a corruption of an earlier variant form *Voltava*.

Vobarno. *Town, northern Italy*. The town, on the Chiese River, has a name of Celtic origin meaning "hidden stream," referring to a stream hidden in a wood, from a word related to Irish *fobhar*, "well," "underground river passage."

Vogtland. *Region, southeastern Germany*. The region takes its name from its ruler under the Hohenstaufen dynasty of Holy Roman emperors (1138–1254), an imperial official known as a *Vogt* (from Medieval Latin *vocatus*, "elected"), who had his castle in Plauen, the region's main city.

Vojvodina. *Province, northern Serbia*. The name means "land of the *voivode*," this being originally the title of an army leader but subsequently that of the governor of a province. The title itself derives from Slavic words related to Russian *vojsko*, "army," and *vodit'*, "to lead."

Volga. *River, western Russia*. The name of Russia's principal river, rising northwest of Moscow to flow generally southeastward into the Caspian Sea, has so far defied any definitive interpretation. It probably derives from a root element meaning simply "damp," "wet," related to modern Russian *vlaga*, "moisture," although some sources prefer to relate it to modern Russian *velikij*, "great."

Volgograd. *City and river port, southwestern*

Russia. The city's name means "**Volga** town," denoting its location on this river. It was founded in 1589 and until 1925 was known as *Tsaritsyn*, from Turkish *sarışın*, "yellowish," from the color of the river's waters. Inevitably, the name came to be associated with Russian *tsar'*, "czar." From 1925 through 1961 it was *Stalingrad*, "*Stalin*'s town," a name complementing that of *Leningrad* (now again ¹**St. Petersburg**).

Volhynia *see* **Volynia**

Völklingen. *City, western Germany*. The city, near the French border, has a name meaning "(settlement of) *Folko*'s people."

Vologda. *City, northwestern Russia*. The city takes its name from the river on which it lies. The river's name is of Finno-Ugric origin and means "white," referring to its waters, as for modern Finnish *valkea*, Estonian *valge*, and Hungarian *világ*.

Volta. *River, Ghana*. The chief river of Ghana was originally named *Rio da Volta* by Portuguese explorers here in the 15th century. This means "river of return" or "river of the bend," either because it marked the limit of their expedition, the point where they turned back, or with reference to the many bends in its lower reaches.

Volta Redonda. *City, eastern Brazil*. The city was founded in 1941 in a broad bend of the Paraíba River. Hence its name, Portuguese for "complete curve."

Volynia. *Historic region, northwestern Ukraine*. The region was originally larger than now, and extended over much of eastern Europe. The origin of its name is uncertain. It probably derives from the extinct city of *Volin'* (otherwise *Velin'*), said to have stood on the Western Bug River. Popular etymology takes it from the Latin root *vol*, "to wish," supposedly because local rulers had their wishes or commands fulfilled here. The name is also spelled *Volhynia*.

Vorarlberg. *State, western Austria*. The state derives its name from German *vor*, "before," "in front of," and **Arlberg**, the mountain region that separates it from the Tyrol and the rest of Austria.

Vorkuta. *City, northwestern Russia*. The city takes its name from the river on which it lies. The river is said to take its name from Nenets *varkuta*, "abounding in bears," from *vark*, "bear." Bears have been seen in living memory foraging for cloudberries in the tundra here.

Voronezh. *City, western Russia*. The city is named for the river on which it lies. The river's Slavic name means "black," describing its waters, from a word related to modern Russian *voron*, "crow."

Voroshilovgrad *see* **Lugansk**
Voroshilovsk *see* **Stavropol**

Vosges. *Mountain range, eastern France*. The range has a name of Celtic origin, perhaps based on *vos*, "peak," or deriving from the name of a Celtic god. The German form of the name is *Vogesen*.

Vratsa. *City, northwestern Bulgaria*. The city's name was recorded in the 13th century as *Vratitsa*, representing a source in Old Slavonic *vrata*, "gate." The fortress here guarded an important route through a mountain pass. It is also possible that the "gate" is the point where the Leva River emerges from a narrow gorge here.

Vršac. *City, northeastern Serbia*. The city's name represents Slavic *v'rkh*, "upper," denoting the elevated terrain here. The German form of the name is *Werschetz*.

Vsetín. *Town, eastern Czech Republic*. The town derives its name from the personal name *Vseta* followed by the Slavic possessive suffix *-in*.

Vukovar. *Town, eastern Croatia*. The town takes its name from the *Vuka* River, a tributary of the Danube, on which it lies. The river's own name apparently means "wolf," but may be a popular interpretation of a non–Slavic name. The second part of the name is Hungarian *vár*, "fort," "town."

Vyatka. *City, western Russia*. The city is named for the river on which it lies. The river's own name probably gave that of the *Votyak* people of this region, and is itself based on Votyak *vu*, "water." From 1934 through 1991 Vyatka was known as *Kirov*, for the Soviet Communist leader Sergei *Kirov* (1886–1934), who was born near here. *See also* **Udmurtia**.

Vyborg. *City and port, northwestern Russia*. The city has a name of Swedish origin meaning "holy fort," from *vi*, "holy," and *borg*, "fort." The name, as *Viborg*, originally applied to the Swedish fortress built here in 1293. The city passed to Russia in 1710. When part of Finland from 1918 through 1940, it was known as *Viipuri*, a Finnish form of the name. *Cp.* **Viborg**.

Vyshny Volochyok. *City, western Russia*. The city arose on a portage (Russian *volok*) between the Msta and Tvertsa rivers. The first word denotes that it must have been higher (*vyshny*, "upper") than some other.

Waco. *City, southern United States*. The Texas city was founded in 1849 on the site of a *Waco* (*Hueco*) Native American village and is named for these people. The origin of their own name is disputed.

Wagga Wagga. *City, southeastern Australia*.

The city, in New South Wales, has an Aboriginal name said to mean "(place of) many crows." The repeated word denotes the plural, and the word itself probably represents the bird's cry.

Wagram. *Town, northeastern Austria.* The town, now properly *Deutsch-Wagram*, "German *Wagram*," derives its name from Middle High German *wāch-rein*, "bank of the pool."

Wahiawa. *City, northwestern Hawaii, United States.* The city, on Oahu Island, has a Hawaiian name meaning "place of noise," alluding to its location between the two branches of the Kaukonahua Stream.

Waialeale, Mt. *Mountain, northwestern Hawaii, United States.* The mountain, on Kauai Island, has a Hawaiian name meaning "rippling water," alluding to its heavy annual rainfall.

Waiblingen. *Town, southwestern Germany.* The town, now a district of Stuttgart, has a name meaning either "(place of) those under the officer of the court," from Old High German *weibil*, "officer of the court," or "(place of) *Weibilo*'s people." The name is said to have given that of the *Ghibellines*, supporters of the Hohenstaufen emperors against the Guelphs. Waiblingen was a Hohenstaufen town.

Waikaremoana, Lake. *Lake, northeastern New Zealand.* The lake, in eastern North Island, has a Maori name meaning "sea of rippling water."

Waikato. *Region, northern New Zealand.* The local government region, in northern North Island, takes its name from the river here, the longest in New Zealand. Its own name is Maori for "flowing water."

Waikiki. *Resort area, northwestern Hawaii, United States.* The resort with its famous beach, a suburb of Honolulu, has a Hawaiian name meaning "gushing water."

Wailuku. *City, central Hawaii, United States.* The city, on northern Maui Island, has a Hawaiian name meaning "water of destruction." The reference is to the Battle of Kepaniwai in 1790, when the Iao Stream here was blocked with corpses.

Waimea. *Town, northwestern Hawaii, United States.* The town, on Kauai Island, takes its name from the river here. Its own name is Hawaiian for "reddish water."

Wairarapa. *Region, central New Zealand.* The local government region, in southeastern North Island, has a Maori name meaning "glistening waters."

Wakatipu Lake. *Lake, southern New Zealand.* The lake, in south central South Island, has a Maori name said to mean "water springs dug by

Rakaihaitu," although a more likely origin is in a local legend about a goblin living in its waters.

Wakayama. *City and port, southern Japan.* The city, in the island of Honshu, derives its name from Japanese *wa*, "peace," "harmony," *ka*, "song," "singing," and *yama*, "mountain."

Wakefield. *City, northern England.* The name of the former West Yorkshire city refers to the *wakes* (festivities) that were held here, perhaps as a forerunner of the famous medieval mystery plays. Many towns in northern England had an annual wake or holiday when factories and schools closed for one or two weeks. The word itself derives from Old English *wacu*, "watch," "wake." Wakefield would have been an ideal site for such festivities, with the "field" (Old English *feld*) being the open land between the Calder River in the south and the extensive wood of Outwood in the north.

Wake Island. *Island, north central Pacific.* The atoll, claimed by the United States in 1898, takes its name from the English sailor William *Wake*, who visited it in 1796.

Walachia. *Historic region, southeastern Europe.* The former principality, now part of Romania, derives its name from its indigenous people, the *Walachians* or *Vlachs*, i.e. the Romanians proper, who claimed descent from the ancient Romans. They were so named by their Slav neighbors, who regarded them as "strangers" or "foreigners," and who thus designated them by a Slavic form of the Germanic word *walho* in this sense. *Cp.* **Walcheren**, **Wales**.

Wałbrzych. *City, southwestern Poland.* The city, in the Sudeten mountains, has a Germanic name meaning "forest town," as more readily seen in its German name of *Waldenburg*.

Walcheren. *Historic island, southeastern Netherlands.* The former island in the Scheldt estuary, now joined to the mainland, derives its name from Old German *walho*, "stranger," referring to its original inhabitants, who were not Germanic in origin. *Cp.* **Walachia**, **Wales**.

Waldeck. *Town, central Germany.* The town arose in the 13th century around a castle of the same name belonging to the counts of Schwalenburg, who had called themselves after it. It is a typical castle name, denoting a fortified place on a projecting piece of land, here overlooking the Eder reservoir. It thus derives from early forms of German *Wald*, "forest," and *Ecke*, "corner," the latter word (from Old High German *ekka*) meaning literally "edge." The name is also that of a former principality here.

Wales. *Country, western Great Britain.* The principality takes its name from Old English *walh*, "stranger," "foreigner," "Celt." The term was applied by Anglo-Saxon settlers in Britain to the "native" Celts, who were alien to them in many ways, speaking a different language and with different traditions and social customs. The Medieval Latin name for Wales was *Cambria*, representing the Welsh people's name for themselves, *Cymry*, "Welsh," literally "compatriots," "fellow countrymen." The Welsh name for Wales is thus *Cymru*. *See also* **Cumbria**.

Wallachia *see* **Walachia**

Walla Walla. *City, northwestern United States*. The Washington city, originally named *Steptoeville*, takes its regular name from the river on which the fort from which it arose was built in 1856. The river's Native American name means "little rapid rivers."

Wallis and Futuna Islands. *Island groups, southwestern Pacific*. The French island territory takes its first name from the English navigator Samuel *Wallis* (1728–1795), who discovered the archipelago in 1767. The islands were occupied by the French in 1842 and joined with the *Futuna* Islands in 1887. The latter name is an old one of indigenous origin and uncertain meaning.

Wallonia. *Region, southern Belgium*. The name is that of the French-speaking part of Belgium, so called for the *Walloons* who are its indigenous people. Their own name represents Germanic *walhon*, "stranger," "foreigner." (*Cp.* **Wales**.) They are so named because they speak French, unlike their Flemish neighbors, who speak a Germanic language.

Wallsend. *Town and river port, northeastern England*. The Tyneside town is named for its location at the eastern *end* of Hadrian's *Wall*, the Roman defensive embankment protecting England from raids from the north. The Roman name of the station here was *Segedunum*, "strong fort." *Cp.* **Rodez**.

Walnut Creek. *City, southwestern United States*. The California city was settled in 1849 during the gold rush and was at first known as *The Corners*. It was renamed as now in 1860 for the abundance of *walnut* trees here.

Walsall. *Town, west central England*. The town, near Birmingham, has an Old English name meaning "*Walh*'s little valley," with the Anglo-Saxon personal name (probably denoting a Celt, as for **Wales**), followed by *halh*, "small valley."

Waltham. *City, northeastern United States*. The Massachusetts city was settled in the 1630s and named for *Waltham Abbey*, Essex, England, from where many of the settlers had come.

Walvis Bay. *Town and port, western Namibia*. The town, a former exclave of South Africa, has a name representing Afrikaans *Walvisbaai*, from *walvis*, "whale" (literally "whale fish"), and *baai*, "bay." The port was at one time a noted whaling center.

Wanaka Lake. *Lake, southwestern New Zealand*. The lake, in west central South Island, derives its name from Maori *oanaka*, "place of Anaka," the name of an early Maori chief.

Wandsworth. *Borough of London, southeastern England*. The name is of Old English origin and means "*Wændel*'s enclosure," with the same Anglo-Saxon personal name as that for **Wellingborough**.

Wanganui. *City and port, north central New Zealand*. The city, in southwestern North Island, was founded in 1841 and originally named *Petre*. It was renamed as now in 1844, from Maori words meaning "big harbor," referring to the mouth of the river of the same name on which the city stands.

Wan-hsien. *City and river port, central China*. The city, in Szechwan province, derives its name from Chinese *wàn*, "ten thousand," and *xiàn*, "district."

Warner Robins. *City, southeastern United States*. The Georgia city was originally a small village called *Wellston*. It developed after the establishment in 1940 of *Robins* Air Force Base, and was named for Brigadier General Augustine *Warner Robins* (1882–1940), a pioneer of the US Army Air Corps.

[1]**Warren**. *City, northern United States*. The Michigan city, now a suburb of Detroit, was organized in 1837 as *Hickory Township* and was called *Aba* in 1838 before receiving its present name in 1839 for General Joseph *Warren* (1741–1775), killed at the Battle of Bunker Hill.

[2]**Warren**. *City, northern United States*. The Ohio city was settled in 1799 and named for the surveyor Moses *Warren*, one of its founders.

Warrington. *Town, northwestern England*. The former Cheshire town has an Old English name meaning "settlement by a weir," referring to a dam at one time on the Mersey River here. The first part of the name represents *wering*, a conjectural Old English derivative of *wer*, "weir."

Warrnambool. *City, southeastern Australia*. The city, on Lady Bay in Victoria, has an Aboriginal name meaning either "much water" or "running swamps."

Warsaw. *Capital of Poland*. The source of the city's name has not been finally established. It may have derived from *Warsz*, the name of a landowner here at some time, so that the overall meaning is "territory of *Warsz.*" The Polish form of the name is *Warszawa.* The lack of a definitive origin has generated the usual folk etymologies, as the king who found baby twins here and named them *War* and *Sawa,* or the raftsmen on the Vistula River who called to their cook, "*Warz, Ewa!*" ("Broth, Eve!").

Wartburg. *Castle, central Germany.* The castle, on a hill southwest of Erfurt, derives its name from Old High German *warta,* "watch," "lookout," and *berg,* "hill," or *burg,* "fort." The castle is famous in German history and legend, and is the best-known example of the name, found elsewhere in Germany.

¹Warwick. *Town, central England.* The town, in the county of the same name, has a name meaning "dwellings by the weir," referring to a former dam on the Avon River here. The first part of the name derives from the basic Old English word that gave the name of **Warrington.**

²Warwick. *City, northeastern United States.* The Rhode Island city, now a suburb of Providence, was first settled in 1642 and named for the English colonial administrator Robert Rich, 2d Earl of *Warwick* (1587–1658).

Wash, The. *Sea inlet, eastern England.* The shallow bay of the North Sea, partly in Lincolnshire and partly in Norfolk, was originally known as *The Washes,* referring to the sandbanks here that were alternately covered and exposed or "washed" by the sea.

¹Washington. *Town, northeastern England.* The former Co. Durham town, designated a New Town in 1964, has an Old English name that means "estate named after *Wassa.*" It was this town that gave the family name of George *Washington* and so that of **²Washington,** DC, and **³Washington** state, as well as of many other places in the USA.

²Washington. *Capital of the United States.* The city, in the District of Columbia, was founded in 1791 on a site chosen by George *Washington* (1732–1799), 1st president of the United States, and named for him. *See also* **¹Washington.**

³Washington. *State, northwestern United States.* The region here was organized as *Washington* Territory in 1853 and named for George *Washington* (1732–1799), 1st president of the United States, despite objections at the time that his name was already borne by several places in the country.

Wasit. *Province, central Iraq.* The province has a name meaning "medial," from Arabic *wasţ,* "middle," describing its geographical location.

Waterbury. *City, northeastern United States.*

The Connecticut city, established as *Mattatuck Plantation* in 1674, was incorporated in 1686 under its present name, referring to the ease of drainage here.

Waterford. *City and port, southeastern Ireland.* The city, in the county of the same name, has a name of Scandinavian origin meaning "wether inlet," from Old Norse *vethr,* "wether" (uncastrated ram), and *fjorthr,* "inlet," "fjord." The town arose at the point on the Suir River where wethers were loaded onto boats for shipping to other ports. The present form of the name has been influenced by unrelated English words. The city's Irish name is *Port Láirge,* "port of the haunch," referring to the rounded contour of the river bank here.

¹Waterloo. *Town, central Belgium.* The town, now a suburb of Brussels, derives its name from Flemish *water,* "water," and *loo,* "sacred wood."

²Waterloo. *City, southeastern Canada.* The Ontario city, on the Grand River, was settled in the 1800s and named for the Battle of **¹Waterloo** (1815).

³Waterloo. *City, north central United States.* The Iowa city was settled in 1845 on the Cedar River and was initially known as *Prairie Rapids.* It took its present name in 1851, when a petition was made for a post office. The choice may have been random, and taken from a postal directory, although there could have been a deliberate intention to commemorate the Battle of **¹Waterloo.**

Watford. *Town, southeastern England.* The Hertfordshire town has an Old English name meaning "hunters' ford," from *wāth,* "hunting," and *ford,* "ford." The reference is to a ford over the Colne River where hunters would have crossed on horseback.

Watling Street. *Roman road, England.* The ancient military road, running from London to Wroxeter, Shropshire, in a general northwesterly direction, takes its name from the Anglo-Saxon name of **St. Albans,** through which it passed. This was *Wæclingaceaster,* as if "Watlingchester," from the people known as the *Wæclingas,* named after one *Wæcel.*

Wattrelos. *Town, northern France.* The town, on the border with Belgium, probably derives its name from Flemish *water,* "water," and *lo,* "sacred wood," exactly as for **¹Waterloo.**

Watts. *Town, southwestern United States.* The California town, now a district of Los Angeles, was originally known as *Mud Town.* It was renamed in 1900 for C. H. *Watts,* a Pasadena realtor who opened a ranch here, and was annexed to Los Angeles in 1926.

Waukegan. *City, northern United States*. The Illinois city, on a bluff above Lake Michigan, stands on a site marked as *Little Fort* on 18th-century maps. In 1849 the settlement that had developed was incorporated as a village and renamed as now, from a Potawatomi word meaning likewise "little fort."

Waukesha. *City, northern United States*. The Wisconsin city, on the Fox River, was settled in 1834 under the name *Prairieville*. It was subsequently renamed as now from the Potawatomi word meaning "by the little *Fox*," referring to the river.

Wausau. *City, northern United States*. The Wisconsin city, on the Wisconsin River, was settled in 1839 and was at first known as *Big Bull Falls*. In 1872 it received its present name, from a Chippewa word meaning "remote place."

Wavre. *Town, central Belgium*. The name means "quagmire," "morass," from a Germanic word related to English *waver*, describing swampy terrain that may be firm or soft. The town, chartered in 1222, arose as a trading center at a crossing of the Dyle River.

Wazirabad. *City, eastern Pakistan*. The city is said to have been founded in the 18th century by *Wazir* Khan and is thus named for him, with Iranian *ābād*, "inhabited place," "town," added. (The title *Wazir* is English *vizier*.)

Waziristan. *Region, northern Pakistan*. The region is named for the *Wazir* people, also known as the Darwish, who with the Mahsud are its main indigenous inhabitants. Iranian *ostān*, "country," was added to their name.

Weald, The. *Region, southeastern England*. The former well-wooded region between the North Downs and South Downs, mainly in Kent, takes its name from Old English *wald*, "forest," or more precisely the Kentish dialect form of this, *weald*. The term came to designate a specifically upland forest. The Anglo-Saxon word was reintroduced by the English antiquary William Lambarde in *A Perambulation of Kent* (1576), the earliest English county history known:

> Nowe then we are come to the Weald of Kent, which (after the common opinion of men of our time) is conteined within very streight and narrowe limits, notwithstanding that in times paste, it was reputed of suche exceeding bignesse, that it was thought to extende into Sussex, Surrey, and Hamshyre.

Weddell Sea. *Sea, South Atlantic*. The Antarctic sea, southeast of the Antarctic Peninsula, is named for the English sealer and explorer James *Weddell* (1787–1834), who in 1823 penetrated farther south here than anyone before him. Weddell himself called it *George IV Sea*, for the reigning monarch, and this name remained in use until 1900, when it was decided that the sea should be more fittingly named for the man who had discovered it.

Weeki Wachee Spring. *Spring, southeastern United States*. The Florida spring, forming a river that wends its way through the marshes of the same name to the Gulf of Mexico, derives its name from Creek *wekiwa*, "spring," and *chee*, "little."

Wei. *River, northeastern China*. The river, a tributary of the **Huang Ho** in Kansu and Shensi provinces, derives its name from Chinese *wèi*, a name with no particular meaning.

Weiden. *City, southeastern Germany*. The city derives its name from an early form of German *Weide*, "willow," a tree that would have grown by the Naab River here. The city's full formal name is *Weiden in der Oberpfalz*, from its location in the *Oberpfalz* (Upper Palatinate). *See* **Pfalz**.

Wei-fang. *City, northeastern China*. The city, in Shantung province, derives its name from Chinese *wéi*, the **Wei** River, and *fāng*, "neighborhood," "vicinity."

Wei-hai. *City and port, northeastern China*. The city, in Shantung province, derives its name from Chinese *wēi*, "majestic," "imposing," and *hǎi*, "sea." It is also known as *Wei-hai-wei*, the added *wèi* meaning "to defend," "to protect." From 1898 through 1930 the port was leased to the British under the name *Port Edward*, for King *Edward* VII (1841–1910).

Weimar. *City, southern Germany*. The city's name ultimately goes back to Old High German *wīh*, "holy," and *mari*, "lake," "spring." The meaning is thus "holy lake" or "holy spring," referring to some local legend.

Weinheim. *City, southwestern Germany*. The city happens to produce a well-known local wine, but this is not the origin of the name, which means "*Wino*'s abode," with a Old German personal name.

Weissenfels. *City, eastern Germany*. The city, on the Saale River, takes its name from that of a medieval castle here, its own name meaning "white cliff," from the light-colored sandstone cliff on which it was built.

Weisshorn. *Mountain, southwestern Switzerland*. The mountain has a German name meaning "white peak," from *weiß*, "white," and *Horn*, "horn," "peak." The reference is to its snowy summit.

Welkom. *Town, central South Africa*. The Free

State town has an Afrikaans name meaning "welcome." It arose in 1948 on a farm where gold had been discovered, and the name was thus propitious, for the *welcome* riches that would ensue.

Welland Ship Canal. *Waterway, southeastern Canada*. The canal, linking Lake Erie with Lake Ontario, is named for the *Welland* River formerly here. It was itself named by John G. Simcoe, first lieutenant governor of Upper Canada, for the *Welland* River in Lincolnshire, England, only a few miles from his Northamptonshire birthplace.

Wellesley Islands. *Island group, northern Australia*. The islands, off the northwest coast of Queensland, were charted by the English navigator Matthew Flinders in 1802 and named for Richard Colley *Wellesley*, Marquess Wellesley (1760–1842), then governor general of India.

Wellingborough. *Town, central England*. The Northamptonshire town has an Old English name meaning "*Wændel's* fortified place." *Cp.* **Wandsworth**.

¹**Wellington**. *Town, western England*. The Shropshire town has an Old English name of disputed meaning. A formerly favored interpretation was "farm by the grove of the shrine," from *wēoh*, "idol," "shrine," referring to a heathen temple, *lēah*, "wood," and *tūn*, "farm." But for various topological and linguistic reasons this has now been generally rejected. The first part of the name could instead represent Old English *walu*, "ridge," "bank," referring to some kind of ditch or enbankment, perhaps connected with Watling Street, which runs through the town.

²**Wellington**. *Town, southwestern England*. The name of the Somerset town is of partly obscure origin. It may mean "farm associated with *Wēola*" or else "farm with a trap," from conjectural Old English *wēol*, "artifice."

³**Wellington**. *Capital of New Zealand*. The city, in southern North Island, was founded in 1840 and named for Arthur Wellesley, 1st Duke of *Wellington* (1769–1852), whose title came from ²**Wellington**, Somerset, England. The name commemorated not so much the duke's victory at Waterloo (1815) as the generous aid he gave to the New Zealand Company, whose colonizing members had arrived the previous year with the task of finding a suitable site for their proposed settlement. Wellington replaced Auckland as the country's capital in 1865.

Wells. *City, southwestern England*. The Somerset town has a self-explanatory name, referring to the natural springs or *wells* that have long existed here and that still flow to the southeast of the cathedral.

Wels. *City, north central Austria*. The city, on the Traun River, evolved its name from its Roman name of *Ovilava*, itself from a pre–Celtic river name based on the Indoeuropean root element *ab*, "water," "current."

Welshpool. *Town, eastern Wales*. The town, in Powys, has a name that means what it says, referring to a *pool* (in the Severn River) that is on the *Welsh* side of the border, not the English. The Welsh name of Welshpool is *Y Trallwng*, "the very wet swamp," referring to the same pool.

Welwyn Garden City. *City, east central England*. The Hertfordshire city, designated a New Town in 1948, takes its name from the old town of *Welwyn* immediately north of it. Its own name means "(place) at the willows," from the dative plural of Old English *welig*, "willow tree." The New Town is the only one in Britain to incorporate the title *Garden City*, a term (and concept) imported to England from the United States.

Wembley. *District of London, southeastern England*. The district has an Old English name meaning "*Wemba's* clearing," with the personal name followed by *lēah*, "clearing."

Wen-chou. *City and port, eastern China*. The city, in Chekiang province, derives its name from Chinese *wēn*, "mild," "temperate," and *zhōu*, "region."

Werdau. *City, eastern Germany*. The name derives from Middle High German *wert* (dative *werde*), "river island," "raised land between streams." Werdau is on the Pleisse River. *Cp.* **Bischofswerda**.

Wernigerode. *City, central Germany*. The city, dating from the 11th century, has a name meaning "(settlement in the) clearing of *Werin's* people," with an early form of German *Rodung*, "clearing."

Wesel. *City, northwestern Germany*. The city, at the mouth of the Lippe River, has a name that is probably of Germanic origin, perhaps from Old High German *wise*, "meadow."

Weser. *River, northwestern Germany*. The river's name ultimately goes back to the Indoeuropean root elements *ueis*, "to flow," and *aha*, "water."

Wessex. *Historic region, southern England*. The name of the former Anglo-Saxon kingdom denotes that it was the territory of the *West Saxons*, as distinct from the South Saxons of **Sussex** and the East Saxons of **Essex**. It applied to too large an area to become a county name, as the other two did. The name gained a literary revival from the novels of Thomas Hardy, which are largely set in the region it occupied, but with fictitious placenames mostly replacing the real ones.

West Bank. *Territory, Palestine*. The former British-mandated territory of Palestine lies on and beyond the *west bank* of the Jordan River. Hence its name. It was occupied by Israel in 1967 and within Israel is also known by its biblical names of **Judaea** (in the south) and **Samaria** (in the north). Many familiar biblical places lie within the West Bank, such as ¹**Bethlehem**, **Hebron**, and **Jericho**.

West Bromwich. *Town, west central England*. The town, near Birmingham, derives the main word of its name from the Old English words for "broom farm," i.e. "farm where broom grows." The first word distinguishes the town from the smaller *Castle Bromwich*, now a suburb of Birmingham.

Westchester. *County, eastern United States*. The New York county, formed in 1683, is named for **Chester**, England, and (obviously) lies to the *west* of that city.

West Covina. *City, southwestern United States*. The main name of the California city is said to mean "place of vines." The first word indicates its location with regard to the smaller city of *Covina*.

Western Australia. *State, western Australia*. The prosaic descriptive name was given in 1829 when this part of Australia was annexed as a colony by Britain. The earlier European name for this region was *New Holland*, a consequence of the exploration of Australia's west coast by Dutch navigators in the 17th century, beginning with Dirck Hartog in 1616. Western Australia is the only Australian state not to have been set off from New South Wales, and this may explain its unoriginal name. (The other states had to have a *new* name, to be distinguished from New South Wales, whereas Western Australia had its official name from the first.)

Western Samoa *see* **Samoa**

West Indies. *Island groups, Caribbean Sea*. The islands, between North and South America, were discovered by Columbus in 1492 and are so named (*las Indias Occidentales*) because he believed he had reached **India** and the east (the Indies) by a western route, as he had planned. He thought that Haiti was "Cipango" (Japan), that Cuba was China, and that Costa Rica was Malacca. The name came into use in the 16th century following the discovery of the real (East) Indies by Vasco da Gama in 1497, who reached them by sailing an eastern route around the Cape of Good Hope. The West Indies gave the name "Indian" to the indigenous peoples of the Americas now usually known as Native Americans.

Westmeath. *County, north central Ireland*. The county's name indicates its geographical location with regard to that of **Meath**, from which it was set off in 1542.

Westminster. *Borough of London, southeastern England*. The borough is so named for its former *minster*, which stood on a site to the *west* of the City of London. The present Westminster Abbey was built on the same site in the 13th century.

Westmorland. *Historic county, northwestern England*. The name of the former county denotes a region inhabited by people who lived on the *west moorland*, i.e. on the moors to the west of the Pennines. Together with its neighbor, Cumberland, it is now represented by the county of Cumbria.

Westphalia. *Region, western Germany*. The former province of northwestern Prussia has a name that means "western *Phalia*," to distinguish it from the now historic *Ostphalia*, "eastern *Phalia*," which lay on the other side of the Weser River. The basic name, that of the people who inhabited the region, may relate to Swedish *fala*, "plain," "heath." The German form of the name is *Westfalen*.

West Virginia *see* **Virginia**

Wetterhorn. *Mountain, south central Switzerland*. The mountain has a name meaning effectively "weather peak," since its summit is always shrouded in clouds that indicate the weather to come.

Wetzlar. *City, west central Germany*. The city's name is based on that of the *Wetzbach*, a tributary of the Lahn River here, to which is added conjectural Old High German *lar*, "hurdle," "pen." The name as a whole can be understood as "enclosure by the *Wetzbach*."

Wexford. *County, southeastern Ireland*. The county takes its name from its main town. Its own name is of part Irish, part Scandinavian origin, from Old Irish *escir*, "sandbank," "ridge," and Old Norse *fjorthr*, "inlet," "fjord." The overall sense is thus "inlet by the sandbank," relating to its location at the mouth of the Slaney River. The town's Irish name is *Loch Garman*, referring to a pool (*loch*) also at the mouth of the Slaney, whose earlier name was *Garma*, from Irish *garma*, "headland."

Whangarei. *City and port, northern New Zealand*. The city, with its natural harbor, has a Maori name said to mean "cherished harbor," from *whanga*, "harbor," and *rei*, "cherished possession."

Wheeling. *City, northern United States*. The name of the Ohio city, settled in 1769, is said to derive from a Delaware word meaning "head" or "skull," referring to the beheading of a group of settlers.

Whitby. *Town and resort, northeastern England.* The North Yorkshire town has a Scandinavian name meaning "*Hvíti*'s village," with the personal name meaning "white one," probably referring to a light-haired or pale-faced person.

Whitehaven. *Town and port, northwestern England.* The original form of the Cumbria town's name was the equivalent of *Whitehead Haven*, from Old Norse *hvít*, "white," *hofuth*, "head," and *hofn*, "harbor." The word for "head" was later dropped for ease of pronunciation. The reference is to the headland of white stone that forms one side of the natural harbor here.

Whitehorse. *City, northwestern Canada.* The capital of the Yukon Territory takes its name from the nearby *Whitehorse* Rapids on the Yukon River, themselves so called because the falling water suggested the flowing mane of a white horse. The rapids are now submerged in a lake created by a dam.

White Nile *see* **Nile**

White Russia *see* **Belarus**

White Sea. *Sea, northwestern Russia.* The sea, an inlet of the Arctic Ocean, is probably so named for its frequent snow and ice, or for the color of its waters, which reflect these. But one theory interprets "white" here as "west," just as the **Black Sea** can be regarded as the "north" sea, and the **Red Sea** as the "south" sea. The White Sea is in fact the westernmost inlet on Russia's northern seaboard.

Whitney, Mt. *Mountain, southwestern United States.* The California peak is named for the American geologist Josiah D. *Whitney* (1819–1896), who in 1864 led the expedition that discovered it.

Whitstable. *Town and resort, southeastern England.* The Kent town has an Old English name meaning "white post," from *hwīt*, "white," and *stapol*, "post." The original "white post" may have been a marker at the meeting place of the local hundred (county subdivision), or have indicated a landing place on the English Channel coast here.

Whittier. *City, southwestern United States.* The California city was founded in 1887 as a Quaker community and named for the Quaker poet and abolitionist John Greenleaf *Whittier* (1807–1892).

Whyalla. *City and port, southern Australia.* The city, in South Australia, was founded in 1901 as an iron-ore tramway terminus with the name *Hummock Hill*. In 1920 it was renamed as now

from an Aboriginal word meaning "place of deep water."

Wichita. *City, south central United States.* The Kansas city was founded in 1864 on the site of a village of the *Wichita* Native Americans, and is named for them. Their name probably means simply "person," "man."

Wick. *Town and port, northeastern Scotland.* The town has a Scandinavian name representing Old Norse *vík*, "bay." The reference is to *Wick* Bay, on which the town stands.

Wicklow. *County, eastern Ireland.* The county takes its name from the town here, its own name being Scandinavian in origin and meaning "Vikings' meadows," from Old Norse *víkingr*, "Viking," and *ló*, "meadow." The town's Irish name is *Cill Mhantáin*, "St. *Mantan*'s church." The named saint is said to have built a church here in the 5th century.

Wiener Neustadt. *City, northeastern Austria.* The city, founded in 1194, has a basic name meaning "new town," from early forms of German *neu*, "new," and *Stadt*, "town." The first word denotes its proximity to *Vienna* (German *Wien*), and distinguishes this "new town" from the many others.

Wiesbaden. *City and resort, western Germany.* The city derives its name from Old High German *wisa*, "meadow," "pasture," and *bada*, "to bathe," the latter referring to the hot springs here, familiar since Roman times, when the place was known as *Aquae Mattiacae*, "springs of the *Mattiaci*."

Wigan. *Town, northwestern England.* The name of the town, near Manchester, is traditionally explained as a shortening of a Welsh name *Tref Wigan*, from Welsh *tref*, "village," and a personal name. A more recent theory derives it from Old English *wīcum*, "(place) at the dwellings," as probably for **High Wycombe**.

Wight, Isle of. *Island, southern England.* The island county was known by the Roman name of *Vectis*, and this probably came from a Celtic word related to modern Welsh *gwaith*, "work," "time." The sense can probably be best interpreted as "division," "watershed," referring to the location of the island in the fork of the Solent, forming a division of the waters. The name does not thus mean "white island," as popularly explained, referring to the white cliffs at the western end and the chalk ridge that traverses the island from east to west.

Wild Coast. *Coastal region, southeastern Africa.* The section of the Atlantic seaboard between the mouths of the Great Kei and Mtamvuna rivers is so named both for its rugged terrain and for the rocky outcrops and reefs extending into the sea, the latter a constant hazard to mariners.

Just after 4:30 on the morning of August 4, 1782, the *Grosvenor*, East Indiaman, homeward bound, fully laden with goods and passengers, ran aground during a storm on the Wild Coast of south-east Africa [James Kelly, review of Stephen Taylor, *The Caliban Shore*, *Times Literary Supplement*, August 6, 2004].

Wilhelmshaven. *City and port, northwestern Germany.* Germany's biggest oil port was founded as a naval base in 1856 and named in 1869 for the German emperor *Wilhelm* I (1797–1888). The second part of the name is a Low German form of *Hafen*, "port."

Wilkes-Barre. *City, eastern United States.* The Pennsylvania city was first settled in 1769 by a group of Connecticut colonists and named for the British politicians John *Wilkes* (1725–1797) and Isaac *Barré* (1726–1802), who supported the American colonies in Parliament.

Wilkes Land. *Region, Antarctica.* The region, south of Australia, takes its name from the American naval officer and explorer Charles *Wilkes* (1798–1877), who discovered the coast here in his expedition of 1838–42.

Willemstad. *Capital of Netherlands Antilles.* The city and port, in southern Curaçao, has a Dutch name meaning "*William*'s town," given in honor of *William* (Dutch *Willem*) the Silent (1533–1584), prince of Orange and count of Nassau, the first stadholder of the United Provinces of the Netherlands.

Williamsburg. *City, eastern United States.* The former state capital of Virginia was settled in 1633 and originally named *Middle Plantation*. On being made capital in 1699 it was renamed in honor of King *William* III (1650–1702). The capital was moved to Richmond in 1780.

[1]**Wilmington.** *City, eastern United States.* The Delaware city was settled by Swedish colonists in 1638 and initially called *Fort Christina*, for Queen *Christina* of Sweden (1626–1689). It was captured by the Dutch in 1655 and renamed by them *Altena*, for the city of this name, now in western Germany. In 1739 it was renamed as now by Thomas Penn for his friend Spencer Compton, Earl of *Wilmington* (1673–1743), favorite of George II.

[2]**Wilmington.** *City and port, eastern United States.* The North Carolina city was formed in the 1730s from New Liverpool and New Carthage and named for the British politician Spencer Compton, Earl of *Wilmington* (1673–1743), favorite of George II.

Wilson, Mt. *Mountain, southwestern United States.* The California mountain is named for Benjamin Davis *Wilson*, who blazed a trail to the summit in 1864.

Wiltshire. *County, southern England.* The county takes its name from the town of *Wilton*, in its southern part, on which it was at one time dependent. The town's name comes from that of the *Wylye* River on which it lies, the river's name itself being of uncertain meaning.

Wimbledon. *District of London, southeastern England.* The Old English name means "*Wynnman*'s hill," with the *-don* related to modern English *down*. The personal name has altered under Norman influence. The Normans found *Wynnman* difficult to pronounce, and the present *Wimble-* (via *Wimen-* and *Wimel-*) is the result of their compromise.

Winchester. *City, southern England.* The Hampshire city has the *-chester* that shows it to have been a Roman station, from Old English *ceaster*, a borrowing from Latin *castrum*, "camp." The initial *Win-* is of pre–Celtic and possibly Indoeuropean origin with a meaning something like "place," implying the most important locality in a region, such as a trading center. It is represented in the city's Roman name, which was *Venta Belgarum*, "*Venta* of the *Belgae*," the latter being the people who gave the name of **Belgium**. *Cp.* **Gwent**.

Windermere. *Lake, northwestern England.* The largest lake in the **Lake District**, Cumbria, has a name meaning "*Vinand*'s lake," with the Germanic personal name followed by Old English *mere*, "lake."

Windhoek. *Capital of Namibia.* The city has an Afrikaans name meaning literally "wind corner." It can hardly be a descriptive name, since winds are rare here. The name was originally made known in the 19th century by the Khoikhoin (Hottentot) chief Jonker Afrikaner, and it may well derive from the South African village of *Winterhoek*, where he spent his childhood. Its own name derives from the *Winterhoek* Mountains, called "winter corner" for their snow-covered peaks in winter.

Windisch. *Town, northern Switzerland.* The Roman name of the town was *Vindonissa*, from a Celtic word meaning "white," as for **Vienna**.

[1]**Windsor.** *Town, southern England.* The former Berkshire town has an Old English name that means "bank with a windlass," from *windels*, "windlass," and *ōra*, "shore," "bank." The reference is probably to a winding mechanism that was used to assist carts up the muddy hill from the edge of the Thames River here,

rather than for actually hauling boats out of the water.

²**Windsor.** *City, southwestern Canada.* The city, on the Detroit River in Ontario, was settled as *The Ferry* soon after 1701 and was subsequently known as *Richmond* before acquiring its present name in 1836. It was adopted from its English namesake, not only because both towns are on a river, but because the Canadian Thames River (named in turn for its English original in 1792) enters Lake St. Clair to the east of Windsor.

Windward Islands. *Island group, southwestern West Indies.* The islands are so named because they lie in the path of the northeastern trade winds. *See also* **Leeward Islands**.

Winnipeg. *City, southern Canada.* The capital of Manitoba takes its name from Lake *Winnipeg,* some 40 miles (65 km) to the north. Its own name comes from Cree *win-nipi,* "muddy water." The city was founded in 1738 and was known successively as *Fort Rouge* (for the *Red* River here), *Fort Gibraltar* (for **Gibraltar**), and *Fort Garry* (for an officer of the Hudson's Bay Company) before gaining its present name in 1873, when it was incorporated. *See also* **Winnipegosis, Lake**.

Winnipegosis, Lake. *Lake, southern Canada.* The Manitoba lake, west of Lake Winnipeg, derives its name from a Cree term meaning "little muddy water." *Cp.* **Winnipeg**.

Winston-Salem. *City, eastern United States.* The North Carolina city was formed in 1913 on the merger of the two towns of *Winston* and *Salem,* originally a mile apart. *Winston* was founded in 1849 and named for Major General Joseph *Winston* (1746–1815), a Revolutionary War soldier. *Salem* was laid out in 1766 by Moravian colonists and given a biblical name meaning "peace." *See also* ³**Salem**.

Winterthur. *Town, northern Switzerland.* The name of the town evolved from its Roman name of *Vitudurum,* itself either from a Celtic personal name *Vitu* or *Vetu* or a Gaulish word meaning "willow" (German *Weide*) and Gaulish *duron,* "fort."

Wirral. *Peninsula, northwestern England.* The name of the Cheshire peninsula, between the Dee and Mersey estuaries, has been explained as deriving from Old English *wīr,* "bog myrtle," and *halh,* "corner." But this poses problems. First, the broad peninsula is hardly a "corner." Second, bog myrtle, as its name implies, grows in damp places, although the Wirral is mostly a high, dry ridge.

Wisconsin. *State, northern United States.* The state is named for the river that rises in it, as a tributary of the Mississippi. The river's own name represents Ojibwa *mesconsing,* perhaps meaning either "gathering place of the waters" or simply "long river."

Wismar. *City and port, northern Germany.* The city, on an inlet of the Baltic Sea, arose in the 13th century on the site of a pre–Slavic fishing and trading settlement. Its name is said to have originally applied to the inlet, now known as the *Wismarbucht,* from Germanic *wisu,* "good," and *mari,* "sea."

Witten. *City, northwestern Germany.* The city, on the Ruhr River, probably derives its name from Middle Low German *wit,* "white," as for **Wittenberg**, but the actual reference is uncertain.

Wittenberg. *City, north central Germany.* The city, first mentioned in 1160, derives its name from Middle Low German *wit,* "white," "shining," and Old High German *berg,* "hill," giving a sense "(town built on the) bright hill," for its origin as a castle built by a ford over the Elbe River. (Old High German *berg,* "hill," and *burg,* "fort," are interrelated, their common meaning being "raised place.")

Wittenberge. *City, eastern Germany.* The city, which arose on the site of a Slavic fort, has a name of the same origin as **Wittenberg**, but for distinction has retained the *-e* of the dative (locative) ending.

Witwatersrand. *Rocky ridge, northeastern South Africa.* The ridge has an Afrikaans name meaning "ridge of white water," from *wit,* "white," *water,* "water," and *rand,* "ridge," "bank." The reference is to the watershed between the Vaal and Limpopo rivers. The ridge is colloquially known as *The Rand*.

Woëvre. *Region, northeastern France.* The plateau region, formerly known as *Voivre,* may derive its name from Gaulish *vobero,* "gully," "hidden stream." If so it could also be related to English *wyvern* and *viper,* referring to a stream that "snakes" by winding its way unseen across the country.

Woking. *Town, southern England.* The name of the Surrey town means "(territory of) *Wocc*'s people." The same people gave the name of the town of *Wokingham,* some 15 miles (24 km) away.

Wolfenbüttel. *City, northwestern Germany.* The city takes its name from the site of the 11th-century castle around which it developed. The meaning is "*Wolfher*'s estate," with the second half of the name ultimately from Germanic *bhu-,* "to build," "to live" (and thus not from German *Büttel,* "bailiff").

Wolfsburg. *City, northern Germany*. The city was founded in 1938 as the headquarters of the Volkswagen automobile company, as which it was originally named *Stadt des KdF-Wagens*, "town of the *Kraft durch Freude* (Strength through Joy) car." In 1946 it took the old name *Wolfsburg* from a medieval castle here, its own name meaning "wolf castle."

Wollongong. *City, southeastern Australia*. The city, in New South Wales, has a name of Aboriginal origin but uncertain meaning. It is popularly said to represent the exclamation *nwool- yarngungli*, "see, the monster comes," made by Aborigines as a expression of combined wonder and alarm on first sighting a ship in full sail. An alternate derivation takes the name from *woolyunyah*, variously interpreted as "five islands" or "dry land near water."

Wolverhampton. *City, west central England*. The city, near Birmingham, has a name that means "*Wulfrūn*'s high farm," the Anglo-Saxon personal name being that of the lady to whom the manor here was granted by King Ethelred in 985. The *-hampton* is not as for **Northampton** but represents Old English *hēan*, dative of *hēah*, "high," with *tūn*, "farm."

Wonsan. *City, southeastern North Korea*. The city derives its name from Korean *wŏn*, "won" (the basic monetary unit of both Koreas), and *san*, from Chinese *shān*, "mountain."

Woodbridge. *City, eastern United States*. The New Jersey city was founded in the 17th century and apparently named for the English town of *Woodbridge*, Suffolk.

Woodstock. *City, southeastern Canada*. The Ontario city was founded in 1834 by the British naval officer Henry Vansittart who named it for the English town of *Woodstock*, Oxfordshire. The Canadian city is itself the seat of Oxford county.

Woolwich. *District of London, southeastern England*. The district has an Old English name meaning "wool port," with the *-wich* as for **Greenwich**. The reference is to a place where wool was traded or was loaded onto or off boats on the Thames River here.

Woomera. *Town, southern Australia*. The town, in South Australia, has a name of Aboriginal origin meaning "throwing stick." The name is coincidentally appropriate for a place that became the site of a rocket range.

Woonsocket. *City, northeastern United States*. The Rhode Island city, founded in 1666, has a name of Algonquian origin said to mean "at a steep spot."

¹**Worcester**. *City, west central England*. The city, in the county of the same name, has the *-cester* that shows it to have been a Roman station, from Old English *ceaster*, a borrowing from Latin *castrum*, "camp." The first part of the name probably derives from the *Weogoran*, the Celtic people formerly here. Their own name is of uncertain origin. It may derive from a former river name.

²**Worcester**. *City, northeastern United States*. The Massachusetts city, originally settled in 1673, was incorporated as a town in 1722 and named for ¹**Worcester**, England.

Workington. *Town and port, northwestern England*. The Cumbria town has an Old English name meaning "estate associated with *Wyrc*." The Anglo-Saxon personal name is the same as that behind **Worksop**, though almost certainly not the same man.

Worksop. *Town, north central England*. The Nottinghamshire town has an Old English name meaning "*Wyrc*'s valley," with the Anglo-Saxon personal name (the same as for **Workington**) followed by Old English *hop*, "valley." It is not certain which particular valley is meant.

Worms. *City, southwestern Germany*. The present name has evolved from a Celtic original *Borbetomagus*, from *Borbeta*, perhaps an earlier name of the Pfrimm River here, and *magos*, "field."

Worthing. *Town and resort, southern England*. The West Sussex town has an Old English name meaning "(place of) *Weorth*'s people."

Wounded Knee. *Creek, north central United States*. The name of the South Dakota creek translates a Sioux name that itself alludes to some incident in which a Sioux was *wounded* in the *knee*.

Wrangel Island. *Island, northeastern Russia*. The island, in the Arctic Ocean, is named for the Russian explorer of Swedish descent, Ferdinand Petrovich *Wrangel* (1797–1870), who determined the location of the island from indigenous Siberians but who did not land there during his mapping of northeastern Siberia in the early 1820s. (It was subsequently discovered in 1867 by American whalers.)

Wrexham. *Town, northern Wales*. The Denbighshire town is near enough to the English border to have an English name. It means "*Wryhtel*'s pasture," with the Old English personal name followed by *hamm*, "riverside land." There is no obvious river at Wrexham now, but there clearly once was, as testified by such street names as Watery Road, Brook Street, and Rivulet Road. The Welsh form of the name is *Wrecsam*.

Wrocław. *City, southwestern Poland*. The city has a name of exactly the same origin as that of

Bratislava, Slovakia, so represents the same Slav people. It is known to German speakers as *Breslau*.

Wu-ch'ang. *City, east central China*. The capital of Hupei province derives its name from Chinese *wŭ*, "military," and *chāng*, "prosperous," "flourishing." *See also* **Wu-han**.

Wu-chou. *City, southeastern China*. The city, in Kwangsi Chuan autonomous district, derives its name from Chinese *wú*, "sterculia" (a shrub related to the mallows), and *zhōu*, "region."

Wu-han. *City, east central China*. The city, in Hupei province, was formed in 1950 from the amalgamation of the three adjacent cities **Wu-ch'ang**, **Han-k'ou**, and **Han-yang** and takes its name from the first elements of their own names.

Wu-hsi. *City, eastern China*. The city, in Kiangsu province, derives its name from Chinese *wú*, "nothing," "without," and *xī*, "tin." The region was originally a source of tin but the deposits were exhausted as early as the 3d century B.C.

Wu-hu. *City and river port, eastern China*. The city, in Anhwei province, derives its name from Chinese *wú*, the name of a lake, and *hú*, "lake."

Wu-lan-hao-te *see* **Ulanhot**

Wuppertal. *City, western Germany*. The city was formed in 1929 on the amalgamation of **Barmen** and **Elberfeld** with other towns, and was thus at first known as *Barmen-Elberfeld*. In January 1930 it took its present name, meaning "*Wupper* valley," from the river here. Its own name derives from New High German *wippen*, "to leap," "to vault" (related to English *whip*).

Württemberg *see* **Baden-Württemberg**

Würzburg. *City, south central Germany*. The city derives its name from Old High German *wirz*, "herb," and Germanic *berg*, "hill," or *burg*, "fort," meaning "hill (fort) where herbs grow." The Roman name of the settlement here was correspondingly *Herbipolis*, as if "herb city."

Wu-t'ai, Mt. *Mountain, northeastern China*. The mountain, in Shansi province, has a name meaning "five terraces," from Chinese *wŭ*, "five," and *tái*, "platform," "terrace," referring to its five flat-topped peaks at different levels.

Wyoming. *State, west central United States*. The state has a name of Delaware origin representing *maugh-wau-wamei*, "broad meadows."

Xai-Xai. *Town and port, southern Mozambique*. The town's name is said to be a reduplicated (plural) form of Portuguese *cheia*, "flood," referring to the formerly frequent floods at the mouth of the Limpopo River here. But the origin is more likely to be in an indigenous word

or phrase. A meaning "kill, kill," has been suggested, with reference to some battle here. The town's earlier name was *João Belo*, for *João Belo* (1876–1928), the Portuguese ship's captain who held various posts in Mozambique following his arrival there as a midshipman in 1896.

Xankändi. *City, southwestern Azerbaijan*. The city was founded after the 1917 Russian Revolution on the site of the village of *Khankendy*, "town of the khan." In 1923 it was renamed *Stepanakert* for the Baku Communist leader *Stepan* Shaumyan (1878–1918), who engaged in revolutionary activities in the Caucasus but who was executed by counterrevolutionaries during the Civil War. The second part of the name is Armenian *kert*, "town." The Azerbaijanis resumed the original name in its indigenous form on gaining independence in 1991, although Armenians continued to call the city *Stepanakert*.

Xenia. *City, north central United States*. The Ohio city was founded in 1803 and give a Greek name intended to mean "hospitality." (Greek *xenos* is "guest.")

Xianggang *see* **Hong Kong**

Xochimilco. *Town, southern central Mexico*. The suburb of Mexico City has a Native American name meaning "plantation of flowers," referring to the *chinampas* (garden plots) in Lake Xochimilco on which the Aztecs grew vegetables and flowers to be shipped to the capital in pre-Hispanic times.

Xylocastron. *Town and port, southern Greece*. The name means "wooden castle," from modern Greek *xulo*, "wood," and *kastro*, "castle," describing the original fortress here. *Cp*. **Sidiro-kastron**.

Yablonovy Mountains. *Mountain range, eastern Russia*. The Siberian range might seem to have a name deriving from Russian *yablonya*, "apple tree." It is actually an alteration of a Buryat original *Yableni daba*, "foot crossing," referring to a path across the mountains here.

Yad Mordechai. *Kibbutz, eastern Israel*. The kibbutz, at the northern end of the Gaza Strip, was founded in 1943 with a Hebrew name meaning "monument to *Mordechai*," for *Mordechai* Anielewicz (1919–1943), Polish leader of the revolt in the Warsaw Ghetto during World War II.

Yad Rambam. *Settlement, central Israel*. The cooperative settlement was founded in 1955 by religious Jews from Fez, Morocco, and given a Hebrew name meaning "monument to *Rambam*," for the Spanish scholar, physician, and philosopher Maimonides (Moses ben-Maimon) (1135–1204), known as *Rambam*.

Yakima. *City, northwestern United States*. The

Washington city was founded in 1886 (originally as *North Yakima*) and named for the *Yakima* Native Americans. Their own name is said to mean "runaway," but the relevance of this is not clear.

Yakutsk. *City, eastern Russia.* The Siberian city takes its name from its indigenous people, the *Yakut*, who in the 17th century adopted their Evenki name of *yekot*, the plural of *yeko*, "stranger," as they were in relation to the namers. For their own name for themselves, *see* **Sakha.**

Yalta. *Town and resort, southern Ukraine.* The town, in the southern Crimea, has a name recorded in the 12th century as *Djalita*. This is believed to represent modern Greek *gialos*, "shore," a word that evolved from classical Greek *ialtos*, "sent," "despatched." The Greeks are said to have settled on the coast here when driven from the northern and central Crimea by the Turks.

Yalu. *River, northeastern China.* The river, forming the border between China (Manchuria) and North Korea, derives its name from Chinese *yā*, "duck," and *lù*, "greenish blue," comparing the color of its waters with that of some species of duck that inhabits it.

Yamagata. *City, northern Japan.* The city, in the island of Honshu, derives its name from Japanese *yama*, "mountain," and *kata*, "shape," with reference to the region's mountainous nature.

Yamaguchi. *City, southwestern Japan.* The city, in the island of Honshu, derives its name from Japanese *yama*, "mountain," and *kuchi*, "mouth," referring to the peninsular nature of the region here.

Yamanashi. *Prefecture, north central Japan.* The prefecture, in the island of Honshu, has a name representing Japanese *yama*, "mountain," and *nashi*, "shape," alluding to its mountainous terrain.

Yamato. *Historic province, west central Japan.* The region, in the island of Honshu, corresponding to the modern Naru prefecture, is the site of the original settlement of the imperial clan, so that in early times the Japanese were known as the "people of *Yamato*." The characters that comprise the name, taken separately, are pronounced quite differently, as *tai*, "big," "great," and *wa*, "peace," "harmony."

Yamoussoukro. *Capital designate of Côte d'Ivoire.* The city derives its name from that of *Yamusa* (in French spelling *Yamoussou*), its founder, and the local (Baule) word *kro*, "village." Yamoussoukro replaced Abidjan as capital in 1983, although the transfer is not yet complete.

Yang-chou. *City, eastern China.* The city, in Kiangsu province, derives its name from Chinese *yáng*, "abundant," "prosperous," and *zhōu*, "region." It has long been a flourishing trading center.

Yang-ch'üan. *City, northeastern China.* The city, in Shansi province, derives its name from Chinese *yáng*, "sun," "male," and *quán*, "source."

Yangon. *Capital of Myanmar.* The city, familiar until 1989 as *Rangoon*, derives its name from Burmese *yangun*, "peaceful," "end of conflict." The name was given the city in 1756, when Alaungpaya, king of Burma, captured it from the Mons, who had known it as *Dagon*. This name itself derives from Burmese *takun*, "tree trunk." The focal point of the city is the *Shwe Dagon* pagoda, the center of Burmese religious life.

Yangtze. *River, China.* China's principal river, also known as the *Yangtze Kiang*, "Yangtze river," derives its name from Chinese *yáng*, "abundant," "prosperous," and *zǐ*, "son," "child." Its alternate Chinese name is *Chang Jiang*, "long river." Its former European name was *Blue River*, apparently given by Jesuit missionaries to distinguish it from the **Huang Ho** (Yellow River).

Yaoundé. *Capital of Cameroon.* The city's name represents that of the *Yaunde* (*Ewondo*) people here. Their own name is of uncertain meaning. The form of the name is due to French influence.

Yarkand. *City, western China.* The city, in the Uighur Autonomous Region of Sinkiang, derives its name from Turkish *yar*, "precipice," or Iranian *yār*, "friend," and Sogdian *kand*, "town." Its Chinese name is *Sha-ch'e*, from *suō*, "reed," "rush," and *chē*, "vehicle." The city gave the name of the *Yarkand* River here.

Yarmouth. *Town and port, eastern England.* The Norfolk town takes its name from the *Yare* River at the mouth of which it stands. The river's name is of uncertain origin but has been associated with the Indoeuropean root element *gar*, "shout" (English *garrulous*), supposedly referring to its noisy current. But the Yare is actually a slow-flowing river in a flat terrain, and this meaning is hardly appropriate. The town is also known as *Great Yarmouth*.

Yaroslavl. *City, western Russia.* The city is named for *Yaroslav* the Wise (978–1054), grand prince of Kiev, who founded it in 1026. *Cp.* **Jarosław.**

Yarqon. *River, west central Israel.* The river's name derives from Hebrew *yaroq*, "green," referring to the color of its waters, mostly by reflecting the foliage along its banks. Its former Arabic name was *nahr el-'auja*, "the crooked river."

Yasinya. *Town, western Ukraine.* The town derives its name from Ukrainian *yasen'*, "ash tree." Its corresponding Hungarian name is *Kőrösmező*, from a dialect form of *kőrisfa*, "ash tree," and *mező*, "field."

Yasodharapura *see* **Angkor**

Yaxchilán. *Archaeological site, southeastern Mexico.* The Classic Maya site, noted for its carved stone stelas, has a Nahuatl name meaning "green stones."

Yazd. *City, central Iran.* The city, an important Zoroastrian center, derives its name from Iranian *yazdān*, "god," "light," another name of Mazda (Ahura Mazda), the Persian god of light, the one true god preached by Zarathustra, founder of Zoroastrianism. The name is also spelled *Yezd*.

Yazılıkaya. *Archaeological site, eastern Turkey.* The Hittite monument has a name meaning "inscribed rock," from Turkish *yazılı*, "written," and *kaya*, "rock." The reference is to the portrayals of Hittite gods carved in relief on the rock face.

Yazoo. *River, southern United States.* The river, a tributary of the Mississippi, takes its name from that of a Native American people. The origin and meaning of their name are unknown.

Yekaterinburg. *City, western Russia.* The city was founded in 1722 as a fortified settlement and named for *Yekaterina*, otherwise *Catherine* I (1684–1727), the future empress of Russia and wife of Peter the Great, with *-burg* the Germanic word for "fort," as was then the fashion for new foundations (*cp.* **St. Petersburg**). From 1924 through 1991 the city was renamed *Sverdlovsk*, for Yakov Mikhailovich *Sverdlov* (1885–1919), the Russian Communist leader who had engaged in revolutionary activities here.

Yellowknife. *Town, northwestern Canada.* The capital of the Northwest Territories, on Great Slave Lake, takes its name from a local Native American people who used *knives* made from *yellow* copper. The town arose in 1934 following the discovery of gold here.

Yellow River *see* **Huang Ho**

Yellow Sea *see* **Huang Hai**

Yellowstone National Park. *National park, north central United States.* The oldest and largest national park in the United States, mostly in Wyoming, takes its name from the *Yellowstone* River here. Its own name is an English translation of its earlier French name, *Roche Jaune*, in turn a rendering of its Native American name, *missi-a-dazi*, "river of yellow stones."

Yemen. *Republic, southwestern Asia.* The country, in the southern Arabian Peninsula, derives its name from Arabic *al-yamīn*, "the right." In the Arabic world, the right has always been regarded as the lucky or fortunate side, as against the left, which is unfortunate or unlucky. Yemen is "right" (to the east) from the point of view of a Muslim in Egypt facing Mecca, just as Syria is "left" (to the west).

Yenakiyevo. *City, eastern Ukraine.* The city arose as a mining settlement in 1883 and was presumably named for an original landowner or mining boss. It was twice renamed. From c.1928 through 1935 it was known as *Rykovo*, for the Soviet Communist official Aleksey *Rykov* (1881–1938), a victim of the Great Purge. Then from 1935 through 1943 it was *Ordzhonikidze*, for the Georgian Communist leader Grigory *Ordzhonikidze* (1886–1937). When he fell from favor following a suspected suicide, the original name was readopted. The Ukrainian form of the name is *Yenakiyeve*.

Yeniköy. *District of Istanbul, northwestern Turkey.* The district of Istanbul had the ancient Greek name of *Neapolis*, "new city." The present name is a virtual equivalent, from Turkish *yeni*, "new," and *köy*, "village." The name is found elsewhere in Turkey.

Yenisei. *River, eastern Russia.* The Siberian river is believed to derive its name from local words *ientaiea* or *iondessi*, meaning simply "big river."

Yen-t'ai. *City and port, northeastern China.* The city, in Shantung province, derives its name from Chinese *yān*, "smoke," and *tái*, "platform." The reference is to the lookout beacon built on the coast here in the 15th century as part of the city's defense system against Japanese pirates.

Yerevan. *Capital of Armenia.* The city has an ancient name of uncertain origin. It is probably that of a people who once inhabited this region. The name has been popularly but not very convincingly associated with that of Mt. **Ararat**, barely 30 miles (48 km) away.

Yeşilırmak. *River, northern Turkey.* The name means "green river," from Turkish *yeşil*, "green," and *ırmak*, "river." *Cp.* **Kızıl Irmak**.

Yevpatoriya. *City and port, southern Ukraine.* The city, in the western Crimea, arose from the ancient Greek colony of *Eupatoria*, said to have been named for Mithridates *Eupator*, king of Pontus, who died in 63 B.C. (His byname means "(born of a) noble father.") The Tatars captured the town in the 14th century and renamed it *Göslöwi*. When the Crimea became part of Russia in 1783 this name was russified as *Kozlov*, a name used in parallel with the Greek one down to the 19th century.

Yin-ch'uan. *City, north central China*. The capital of Ningsia autonomous region has a name meaning "silver river," from Chinese *yín*, "silver," and *chuān*, "river." It is actually on the Yellow River (Huang Ho).

Ying-k'ou. *City and port, northeastern China*. The city, In Liaoning province, derives its name from Chinese *yíng*, "camp," and *kŏu*, "mouth," denoting its location near the mouth of the Hun River.

Yirka. *Township, northeastern Israel*. The Druze township may derive its name from that of Hushai the *Archite*, a friend and confidant of King David (1 Chronicles 27:33, etc.).

Yogyakarta. *City, southern Indonesia*. The city, in southern Java, is said to have a Javan name meaning "flourishing fortress," although some authorities interpret it as "peaceful," "safe." The actual origin remains disputed. The name was formerly spelled *Jogjakarta*.

Yokkaichi. *City and port, central Japan*. The city, in the island of Honshu, derives its name from Japanese *yo*, "four," *ka*, "day," and *ichi*, "market," referring to the date of a regular monthly market.

Yokohama. *City and port, central Japan*. The city, on Tokyo Bay in the island of Honshu, derives its name from Japanese *yoko*, "side," and *hama*, "shore," "beach," denoting its location.

Yokosuka. *City and port, central Japan*. The city, on Tokyo Bay in the island of Honshu, derives its name from Japanese *yoko*, "side," the syllable *su*, and *ga*, "compliments."

Yonkers. *City, eastern United States*. The New York city arose in 1646 on land granted to the Dutchman Adriaen van der Donck, familiarly (and presumably also punningly) known as *de jonkheer*, a title roughly equivalent to "squire," and its present name is a corruption of the latter.

York. *City, northern England*. The name of the Yorkshire city has undergone several changes of form and meaning over the centuries. Ptolemy recorded it in the 2d century A.D. as *Eborakon*. This represents a Celtic personal name *Eburos*, which probably meant "yew man," from a word that eventually gave modern English *yew*. The name presumably denoted the owner of an estate of yew trees. The Anglo-Saxons took the name to represent *eofor*, "wild boar," to which they added *wīc*, "settlement," giving a name *Eoforwic*, as if meaning "settlement where boars are found." The Vikings then arrived and in turn took the *wīc* to be Old Norse *vík*, "bay," although York is inland, and has no bay. The name was now *Jórvik*, adopted in modern times for the

city's popular Jorvik Viking Centre. By the 14th century this had been eroded to the present *York*.

York, Cape. *Peninsula, northern Australia*. The northernmost point of Australia, in Queensland, was so named by Captain Cook in 1770 "in honour of his late Royal Highness, the Duke of York." This was Edward Augustus, Duke of *York* and Albany (1739–1767), a brother of George III.

Yorktown. *Historic town, eastern United States*. The Virginia town was settled in 1631 and named for Charles, Duke of *York* (1600–1649), the future Charles I of England.

Yosemite National Park. *National park, western United States*. The national park, in central California, takes its name from a former Native American people here, with their own name meaning "grizzly bear."

Yoshkar-Ola. *City, western Russia*. The city was founded in 1584 by order of Czar Fyodor I Ivanovich following Russia's acquisition of Mari territory here. (It is now the Mari El capital.) Its original name was thus *Tsarev gorod na Kokshayke*, "czar's town on the *Kokshaga* (River)." This lengthy name was subsequently smoothed to *Tsaryovokokshaysk*. In 1919, after the Russian Revolution, the czarist element was replaced with Russian *Krasno-*, "red" (in the revolutionary sense), to give *Krasnokokshaysk*. In 1927 it took the Mari equivalent, from *yoshkar*, "red," and *ola*, "town."

Youngstown. *City, northeastern United States*. The Ohio city is named for John *Young*, a surveyor from New York, who purchased land here in 1797 and laid out a town (originally known as *Young's town*).

Youth, Isle of *see* **Juventud, Isla de la**

Ypacaraí. *Lake, southern Paraguay*. The lake has a Guaraní name meaning "water of God."

Ypres. *Town, western Belgium*. The town ultimately derives its name from Gaulish *ivo*, "yew." The Flemish form of the name is *Ieper*.

Ypsilanti. *City, northern United States*. The Michigan city, originally known as *Woodruff's Grove*, was renamed in 1833 for the Greek patriot Demetrios *Ypsilanti* (1793–1832), whose monument stands here.

Yubari. *City, northern Japan*, The city, in the island of Hokkaido, derives its name from Japanese *yū*, "evening," and *bari*, "mode," "manner."

Yucatán. *State, southeastern Mexico*. The name, that of the peninsula here, is said to derive from a local word meaning "massacre," representing *yuka*, "to kill," and *yetá*, "many." It was perhaps on this peninsula that the Maya were exterminated. A popular account tells how Spanish explorers asked local people what the name of the region was and received the reply *yucatan*, "I don't understand."

Yugoslavia. *Historic republic, southeastern Europe.* The name means "southern Slavs," from Serbo-Croat *jug*, "south," and the ethnic-based name. The name *Yugoslavia* was officially adopted only in 1929. The earlier name, given in 1918 when the country was formed following the collapse of Austro-Hungary, was *Kingdom of the Serbs, Croats, and Slovenes* (Serbo-Croat, *Kraljevina Serba, Hrvata i Slovenaca*). Until 1991 federal Yugoslavia had six republics: Bosnia-Hercegovina, Croatia, Macedonia, Montenegro, Serbia, and Slovenia. Four of these then declared their independence, leaving just Serbia and Montenegro to form a "rump" Yugoslavia, which in turn in 2003 became the union republic of *Serbia and Montenegro.*

Yukon. *Territory, northwestern Canada.* The territory takes its name from the river here. Its own name represents Native American *yu-kun-ah*, "big river."

Yü-men. *City, northern China.* The city, in Kansu province, has a name meaning "jade gate," from Chinese *yù*, "jade," and *mén*, "gate."

Yunnan. *Province, southwestern China.* The province derives its name from Chinese *yún*, "cloud," and *nán*, "south," referring to its location south of the *Yün-ling* ("cloudy mountain") range.

Yuzhno-Sakhalinsk. *City, eastern Russia.* The city, at the southern end of Sakhalin Island, has a name denoting its location, from Russian *yuzhno-*, "southern," and the name of **Sakhalin**. Its Japanese name from 1905 through 1945 was *Toyohara*, "eastern plain."

Yvelines. *Department, northern France.* The name is that of the forest here, part of the Forest of Rambouillet. Its Medieval Latin name had various forms, ranging from *Aequalina silva* to *Egilina silva*, and it is only in the 13th century that *Yvelina* appears. All the early forms probably go back to a Celtic original meaning "water." There are many streams here.

Yverdon. *City, western Switzerland.* The city had the Roman name *Eburodunum*, based either on a Gaulish personal name *Eburo*, meaning "yew," or on an ethnic name *Eburones*, people for whom the yew was a totemic tree or who used its wood to make bows in battle (*see* Évreux), with Gaulish *dunon*, "height," "fort," added. The German form of the name is *Iferten*.

Zaanstad. *City and port, western Netherlands.* The city was formed in 1974 as a merger of seven existing towns and villages and took a name

based on that of the *Zaan* River that was already a component of the names of four of these. Dutch *stad*, "town," was added to the river name, which itself represents Old Dutch *saden*, "marshland."

Zabrze. *City, southern Poland.* The city has a Slavic name meaning "behind the wood" (Russian *za*, "behind," and *bor*, "(coniferous) forest"). In 1913, when in Prussia, it was renamed *Hindenburg* for the German field marshal Paul von *Hindenburg* (1847–1934). (His name was an existing placename, meaning "*Hinta*'s stronghold," so needed no addition.) The original name was restored when the city was ceded to Poland in 1945.

Zacatecas. *City, north central Mexico.* The city, founded in 1548, has a local name meaning "place of *zacate*," this being a type of grass.

Zagorsk *see* **Sergiyev Posad**

Zagreb. *Capital of Croatia.* The city's name means "beyond the bank," from Old Croat *za*, "beyond," and *grebom*, the instrumental case (required after *za*) of *greb*, "bank," "embankment," "ditch." The name relates to the original site here, above the Sava River. The Germans knew the city as *Agram*, explained as representing Old German *am graben*, "by the ditch," but more likely to be a corruption of the Slavic name (less its initial *Z*-).

Zagros. *Mountain range, southwestern Iran.* The range takes its name from Iranian *zāj*, "alum," and *ros*, "clay," for constituents of its formation.

Zaire. *Historic republic, south central Africa.* The name derives from an earlier alternate name of the **Congo** River here, from Kikongo *nzai*, a dialect form of *nzadi*, "river." The name Zaire was in use for the country from 1971 through 1997, when it became the *Democratic Republic of Congo.* Previous names also included that of the river: *Congo Free State* (1885–1908), *Belgian Congo* (1908–60), and *Democratic Republic of the Congo* (1960–71).

Zakinthos. *Island, Ionian Islands, Greece.* The southernmost of the Ionian Islands has a Mediterranean name of uncertain origin. A Phoenician base meaning "height" has been suggested, referring to the high cliffs on its south coast. The final *-nthos*, as for **Corinth**, is non–Indoeuropean.

Zakopane. *City and resort, south central Poland.* The city, in the Carpathian Mountains, has a Slavic name meaning "beyond the clearing," describing a place cleared of trees and stumps, from *za*, "beyond," and a word related to Russian *kopat*', "to dig up," "to dig out."

Zalaegerszeg. *City, southwestern Hungary.* The first part of the city's name is that of the *Zala* River on which it lies, its own name of uncertain origin. The rest means "alder corner," from Hungarian *eger*, a dialect form of *égerfa*, "alder tree," and *szeg*, "corner."

Zalaszentgrót. *Town, western Hungary.* The town is on the *Zala* River, its own name of uncertain origin. The second part of the name is a dedication to "*St. Gerold*" (Hungarian *szent*, "saint"), better known as St. *Gerard*, 11th-century bishop of Csanád.

Zambezi. *River, central and eastern Africa.* The river derives its name from the same root word, *za*, "river," that gave the name of **Zaire**.

Zambia. *Republic, central Africa.* The country takes its name from the **Zambezi** River that rises near its northern border and that flows south to form part of its southern border with Zimbabwe. Until 1964, when it gained independence, it was known as *Northern Rhodesia* (*see* **Zimbabwe**).

Zamboanga. *City, southern Philippines.* The city, in western Mindanao, has a name representing Malay *jambangan*, "place of flowers." The roads here are lined with bougainvillea, orchids, and other tropical flowers.

Zamora. *City, northwestern Spain.* The city's name is probably of Arabic origin, representing *zamurrud*, "emerald," referring to the exploitation of this gemstone by Arabs here from the 8th century.

Zamość. *City, east central Poland.* The city was founded in 1579 on the estates of the Polish chancellor Jan *Zamoyski* (1542–1605), who named it for the estate bought by his predecessors in the 15th century. His name thus comes from the original estate, with its own Slavic name meaning "beyond the bridge."

Zanzibar. *Island, western Indian Ocean.* The island, off the east coast of Africa, derives its name from that of the *Zengi* or *Zengj*, a local people, their own name meaning "black," to which is added Arabic *barr*, "coast," "shore." The first syllable of the name now forms part of the name of **Tanzania**.

Zaporozhye. *City, southeastern Ukraine.* The city, on the Dnieper River, has a name meaning "beyond the rapids," from Russian *za*, "beyond," and *porog*, "rapids." There are no rapids here now, but there were before the construction of the Dneproges dam in 1932. The city has had its present name since 1921. Its earlier name was *Aleksandrovsk*, for the Russian general *Aleksandr* Golytsin (1718–1783), who commanded an army stationed in southern Ukraine at the time of the town's foundation in 1770. The Ukrainian form of the name is *Zaporizhzhya*.

Zaragoza *see* **Saragossa**

Zaria. *City and historic kingdom, northern Nigeria.* The city was founded in c.1536 and became the capital of the Hausa state of *Zazzau*, both city and state being named for Queen *Zaria* (late 16th century), younger sister and successor of Queen Amina, the state's ruler. The state itself traditionally dates from the 11th century.

Zbuba. *Village, northern West Bank.* The name of the Arab village has been tentatively linked with the biblical *Beelzebub*, "the prince of the devils" (Matthew 12:24, etc).

Zealand *see* **Sjælland**

Zeebrugge. *Town and port, northwestern Belgium.* The town is linked by canal with **Bruges** and is the North Sea port for that city. Hence its name, which means literally "sea *Bruges*," from Flemish *zee*, "sea," and *Brugge*, "Bruges."

Zeeland. *Province, southwestern Netherlands.* The name means "sea land," from Dutch *zee*, "sea," and *land*, "land." Zeeland has many islands and is located on the North Sea coast. *See also* **New Zealand**.

Zeitz. *City, east central Germany.* The city arose in the 10th century on the site of a Slavic settlement, and may have a Slavic name, from Old Sorbian *sit*, "rush," giving a sense "place where rushes grow." But the name may really be pre–Slavic and of unknown meaning.

Zeravshan. *River, central Asia.* The river, in Tajikistan and Uzbekistan, is said to derive its name from Tajik *zer*, "gold," and *rekhtan*, "to scatter," alluding to its importance in irrigation. But there could be a link with real gold, which was at one time panned in its upper reaches. In its course past Samarkand the Zeravshan divides into two: the *Akdarya*, "white river," and *Karadarya*, "black river." These then reunite, and in its lower reaches it is known as the *Karakuldarya*, "black lake river."

Zerbst. *City, east central Germany.* The city, first mentioned in 948, has a name of Slavic origin based on *cherv'*, "worm," perhaps referring to the collection of scale-insect larvae for the manufacture of red dye here.

Zermatt. *Village and resort, southern Switzerland.* The village derives its name from German *zur Matte*, "(place) at the pasture," describing its location in the Pennine Alps.

Zerufa. *Settlement, northwestern Israel.* The settlement has a Hebrew name meaning "sown land," referring to the biblical passage: "Thou wentest after me in the wilderness, in a land that was not sown" (Jeremiah 2:2).

Zgorzelec *see* **Görlitz**

Zhitomir. *City, west central Ukraine.* The city, founded in the second half of the 9th century, probably derives its name from a personal name, perhaps that of a local landowner. Legend identifies him as a favorite of the Kievan princes Askold and Dir, who no longer wished to serve Prince Oleg. The Ukrainian form of the name is *Zhytomyr.*

Zhob. *Town, western Pakistan.* The town was originally known as *Apozai*, a name still in local use. In 1889 it was renamed *Fort Sandeman*, for the British army officer and colonial administrator Sir Robert *Sandeman* (1835–1892). It assumed its present name, a form of the original, in the 1970s.

Zielona Góra. *City, west central Poland.* The city's name means "green hill," seen more readily in its German name of *Grünberg.* It lies in a hollow of the hills here, rather than actually on such a hill.

Zikhron Ya'aqov. *Village, northern Israel.* The Jewish village was founded on Mt. Carmel in 1882 by Romanian pioneers with the backing of the French philanthropist Baron Edmond de Rothschild. Hence its name, Hebrew for "memory of *Jacob*," for Edmond's father, *James* Rothschild (1792–1868).

Žilina. *Town, northwestern Slovakia.* The town probably derives its name from the Slavic personal name *Zhila*, although there could also be a source in a root word related to Russian *zhit'*, "to live," or *zhil'yo*, "residence." The German form of the name is *Sillein.*

Zimbabwe. *Republic, southeastern Africa.* The country takes its name from that of a large complex of ruins, the remains of an ancient city, in its southeastern part, itself from Bantu *zimba we bahwe*, "houses of stones," from *zimba*, the plural of *imba*, "house," and *bahwe*, "stones." Zimbabwe was known as *Southern Rhodesia* until 1964 and as *Rhodesia* from then until 1980. *Northern Rhodesia* became **Zambia** in 1964, and previous to that *Rhodesia* was the unified name for both territories. It derives from that of the British colonial administrator and financier Cecil John *Rhodes* (1853–1902), whose name first appeared on the map of Africa in 1895. (For some reason the name came to be pronounced in three syllables, "Rho-*deez*-ia," instead of two, "*Rhodes*-ia." It may have been influenced by classical names such as *Magnesia*.)

Zion. *Hill, southwestern Jordan.* The name for various aspects of Jerusalem and Israel, mentioned frequently in the Bible (2 Samuel 5:7 has "the strong hold of Zion," while "mount Zion" and "daughters of Zion" often occur), is of obscure origin and meaning. It is probably a pre–Israelite Canaanite name. Suggested meanings include "rock," "stronghold," "dry place," and "flowing water." The name is now applied to the hill south of the southwestern portion of the old city of Jerusalem.

Zittau. *City, eastern Germany.* The city arose on the site of a Slavic settlement with a name recorded in Latin form as *Sitauia* in 1238. The origin is in Old Sorbian *zhito*, "corn," "cereal."

Zlatni Pyasŭtsi. *Resort, northeastern Bulgaria.* The Black Sea resort, developing from the 1950s, has a descriptively promotional name meaning "golden sands." As such, it often appears in translated form in tourist literature (*see* **Slŭnchev Bryag**).

Zlatoust. *Town, west central Russia.* The town arose in 1754 and took its name from its church, dedicated to St. *John Chrysostom* (347–407), known in Russian as *Ioann Zlatoust* ("golden-mouthed"), so nicknamed for his fine oratory.

Zlín. *City, southeastern Czech Republic.* The city's name is probably based on the Slavic personal name *Zla*, although it could also derive from a river name. (Zlín itself is on the Dřevnice.) From 1948 through 1990 it was renamed *Gottwaldov*, for the Czech Communist leader Klement *Gottwald* (1896–1953), president of Czechoslovakia from 1948.

Znojmo. *City, southern Czech Republic.* The city, originating as a fortress in the 11th century, derives its name from Slavic *znoj*, "heat," "warmth," referring to a stretch of land cleared by burning. Its German name is *Znaim.*

Zomba. *City, southern Malawi.* The former capital of Malawi was founded in 1885 on the slopes of Mt. *Zomba* and is named for this mountain. Its own name represents a Nyanja word meaning "locust," probably because these insects are common here. *Cp.* **Albert, Lake.**

Zonguldak. *City and port, northwestern Turkey.* The city, on the Black Sea coast, is said to derive its name from an altered form of Turkish *zongalık*, "place of reeds."

Zug. *Canton, north central Switzerland.* The canton takes its name from that of a lake here, with its own name perhaps representing Celtic *tug*, "roof," referring to its lofty location, at an altitude of 1,368 feet (417 m).

Zuider Zee *see* **IJsselmeer**

Zululand *see* **KwaZulu**

Zürich. *City, northeastern Switzerland.* The name of the city ultimately derives from the Celtic root element *dur*, "water," referring to its location on Lake *Zürich*, itself named for it.

Zutphen. *Town, east central Netherlands*. The town was founded in the 11th century as *Zuid-veen*, a name meaning "southern peat marsh," from Middle Dutch words related to English *south* and *fen*.

Zuyder Zee *see* **IJsselmeer**

Zvenigorod. *Town, western Russia*. The town, first mentioned in 1339, appears to take its name from Russian *zvenet'*, "to ring," and *gorod*, "town," presumably with reference to the bells of a church or a watchtower, in the latter (or even the former) case warning of the approach of an enemy. According to one authority, however, the allusion is to the "purling" of the Moskva River here.

Zvishavane. *Town, south central Zimbabwe*. The town derives its name from Sindebele *shavani*, said to mean eaither "finger millet" or "trading together." The earlier form of the name was *Shabani*.

Zweibrücken. *City, southwestern Germany*. The city had the Medieval Latin name of *Bipontium*, and in French it is today known as *Deux-Ponts*. All three names mean "two bridges," referring to the bridges on an old road over an island in the Schwarz River here.

Zwelitsha. *Town, southern South Africa*. The former capital of Ciskei was founded in 1948 as a residential settlement for textile workers and was given a Xhosa name meaning "new world."

Zwickau. *City, eastern Germany*. The name, probably of Old Sorbian origin but uncertain meaning, appears to have been influenced by Middle High German *zwic*, "nail," "bolt," "wedge-shaped object."

Zwolle. *City, north central Netherlands*. The city is said to be so called because it stands at the "swell" (Dutch *zwellen*) of the waters, i.e. at the point where the Zwarte Water enters the IJssel River and the Vecht River enters the Zwarte Water.

Żyrardów. *Town, east central Poland*. The town is named for Philippe de *Girard* (1775–1845), French inventor of a flax-spinning machine, who emigrated to Poland and founded a factory here. The town grew up around the factory and adopted its name. The final *-ów* is the Slavic possessive suffix.

Appendix 1:
Common Placename Words and Elements

This appendix gives some of the commoner words and elements found as the first part of a non–English placename. Grammatical details regarding gender (masculine, feminine, neuter) or number (singular, plural) are kept to a minimum as it is the meaning that really matters.

Names in **bold** have their own entries. Names in *italic* are followed by their meanings.

Abu: Arabic, "father of." **Abu Dhabi**

Aïn: Arabic, "spring." **Aïn Beïda**

Al(-): Arabic, "the." **Al-Hammada al-Hamra'**

Alto: Italian, Spanish, Portuguese, "upper (place)." *Alto de Inca*, Chile ("height of the Inca")

An: Arabic, "the" (before N-). **An-Nafud**

Ar: Arabic, "the" (before R-). **Er Rif**

As: Arabic, "the" (before S-). *As-Sukhna*, Syria ("the hot")

Ash: Arabic, "the" (before Sh-). *Ash-Sharqi*, Lebanon ("the east")

Áyios: Greek, "holy," "saint." *Áyios Pétros*, Greece ("St. Peter")

Bad: German, "bath," "spa." **Bad Godesberg**

Bahr: Arabic, "sea," "lake," "river." **Bahr al-Ghazal**

Ban: Thai, Laotian, "village." *Ban Nong*, Laos ("village by the lake")

Bandar: Arabic, Farsi, "port," "harbor." **Bandar Abbas**

Barra: Spanish, Portuguese, "sandbank." *Barra de Navidad*, Mexico ("Christmas sandbank")

Beit: Hebrew, "house." **Beit Zayit**

Ben: Gaelic, "mountain." **Ben Nevis**

Beni. Arabic, "sons of." **Beni Isguene**

Bir: Arabic, "well." **Bir Hacheim**

Boca: Spanish, Portuguese, "mouth," "inlet." **Boca Raton**

Cabo: Spanish, Portuguese, "cape," "point." *Cabo Blanco*, Argentina ("white cape")

Campo: Italian, Spanish, Portuguese, "field," "plain." **Campo Grande**

Cap: French, "cape, "point." **Cap-de-la-Madeleine**

Cerro: Spanish, "hill," "mountain." *Cerro Azul*, Mexico ("blue mountain")

Ciudad: Spanish, "town," "city." **Ciudad Bolívar**

Coronel. Spanish, "colonel." *Coronel Suárez*, Argentina ("Colonel Suárez")

Côte: French, (1) "coast"; (2) "hill," "slope." (1) **Côte d'Azur**; (2) **Côte d'Or**

Da: Vietnamese, "river." **Da Nang**

Dar: Arabic, "house." **Dar es Salaam**

El: (1) Spanish, "the"; (2) Arabic, "the" (as **Al-**). (1) **El Banco**; (2) **El Aaiún**

Fuente: Spanish, "spring," "well." **Fuente Obejuna**

General: Spanish, "general." **General Santos**

Gross: German, "big," "great." **Gross-Gerau**

Haute: French, "high," "upper." *Haute-Marne*, France ("upper Marne")

Hohen-: German, "high." **Hohenstaufen**

Huang: Chinese, "yellow." **Huang Ho**

Île: French, "island." **Île-de-France**

Isla: Spanish, "island." *Isla Verde*, Argentina ("green island")

Kafr: Arabic, "village." **Kafr Misr**

Kara-: Turkic, "black." **Karakol**

Kato: Greek, "lower." *Káto Akhaïa*, Greece ("lower **Achaea**")

Kfar: Hebrew, "village." **Kfar Habad**

Kis: Hungarian, "little." **Kiskunhalas**

Klein: German, "little." *Klein-Gerau*, Germany (*see* **Gross-Gerau**)

Koh: Iranian, "mountain." **Koh-i-Baba**
Kota: Malay, "fort." **Kota Kinabalu**
Krasno-: Russian, "red" (earlier, "beautiful"). **Krasnoyarsk**
Kyzyl: Turkic, "red." **Kyzyl Kum**
La: French, Italian, Spanish, "the" (feminine). **La Paz**
Las: Spanish, "the" (feminine plural). **Las Vegas**
Le: French, "the" (masculine). **Le Havre**
Llan-: Welsh, "church (site)." **Llandudno**
Los: Spanish, "the" (masculine plural). **Los Angeles**
Mont: French, "hill," "mountain." **Mont Blanc**
Monte: Italian, Spanish, "hill," "mountain." **Monte Carlo**
Nakhon: Thai, "town." **Nakhon Pathom**
Nagy: Hungarian, "big," "great." **Nagykáta**
Nan: Chinese, "south." **Nan-ch'ang**
Nizhny: Russian, "lower." **Nizhny Novgorod**
Nova: Portuguese, "new." *Nova* **Iguaçu**, Brazil
Nová: Czech, Slovak, "new." *Nova Dubnica*, Slovakia (*cp.* **Dubno**)
Novi: Bulgarian, Croatian, Serbian, "new." **Novi Pazar**
Novo: Portuguese, "new." **Porto-Novo**
Novo-: Russian, "new." **Novocherkassk**
Novy: Russian, "new." *Novy Afon*, Georgia ("new Athos")
Novy: Czech, "new." *Novy Bor*, Czech Republic ("new pinewood")
Nowa: Polish, "new." **Nowa Huta**
Nowy: Polish, "new." *Nowy Targ*, Poland ("new market")
Nueva: Spanish, "new." **Nueva Gerona**
Nuevo: Spanish "new." **Nuevo León**
Oum: French spelling of **Umm**
Paso: Spanish, "pass." **Paso de los Libres**
Pico: Spanish, "peak." **Pico**
Pointe: French, "cape," "point." **Pointe-Noire**
Pont-: French, "bridge." **Pontoise**
Port: French, "port," "harbor." **Port Louis**
Porto: Portuguese, "port," "harbor." **Porto-Novo**
Pôrto: Brazilian Portuguese, "port," "harbor." **Pôrto Velho**
Puebla: Spanish, "town." **Puebla**
Pueblo: Spanish, "village," "(small) town." **Pueblo**
Puente: Spanish, "bridge." **Puente-Genil**
Puerto: Spanish, "port," "harbor." **Puerto Cabello**
Punta: Spanish, "cape," "point." **Punta Arenas**

Qiryat: Hebrew, "town." **Qiryat Bialik**
Ras: Arabic, "cape," "point." **Ras Asir**
Rio: Portuguese, "river." **Rio Branco**
Río: Spanish, "river." **Río de Oro**
San: Italian, Spanish, "saint." **San Francisco**
Sankt: German, "saint." **Sankt Augustin**
Santa: Italian, Spanish, Portuguese, "saint" (feminine). **Santa Barbara**
Santo: Italian, Spanish, Portuguese, "saint" (masculine). **Santo Domingo** (*cp.* **Santiago**)
São: Portuguese, "saint" (masculine, before name beginning with consonant). **São Luís**
Sidi: Arabic, "Sir." **Sidi Bel Abbès**
Sierra: Spanish, "mountain range." **Sierra Madre**
Stara: Slavic, "old." **Stara Zagora**
Staro-: Russian, "old." *Starodub*, Russia ("old oak")
Stary: Russian, "old." **Stary Oskol**
Sveti: Serbian, Croatian, "saint" (masculine). **Sveti Konstantín**
Szent-: Hungarian, "saint." **Szentendre**
Tel: Hebrew, "hill." **Tel Aviv**
Tell: Arabic, "hill." **Tell el-Amarna**
Terre: French, "land." **Terre Haute**
Tierra: Spanish, "land." **Tierra del Fuego**
Torre: Italian, Spanish, "tower." **Torre Annunziata**
Tres: Spanish, "three." **Tres Marías**
Três: Portuguese, "three." *Três Rios*, Brazil ("three rivers")
Új: Hungarian, "new." *Újfehértó* ("new white lake")
Umm: Arabic, "mother of." **Oum er-Rabi'**
Ust-: Russian, "river mouth." **Ust-Kamenogorsk**
Val: French, "valley." **Val-d'Or**
Valle: Spanish, "valley." *Valle de la Pascua*, Venezuela ("valley of Easter")
Velikaya: Russian, "big," "great." *Velikaya*, Russia (river name)
Veliki: Croatian, Serbian: "big," "great." *Veliki Kanal*, Serbia ("great canal")
Velikiye: Russian, "big," "great." **Velikiye Luki**
Velké. Czech, "big," "great." *Velké Karlovice*, Czech Republic (*cp.* **Karlovac**)
Verkhne-: Russian, "upper." *Verkhneudinsk* (*see* **Ulan-Ude**)
Vila: Portuguese, "(small) town." **Vila Real**
Villa: Spanish, "town." **Villa Obregón**
Yeni: Turkish, "new." **Yeniköy**

Appendix 2:
Major Placenames in European Languages

Geographical names can vary slightly or significantly in their different languages. The selection below is both for interest and reference, since many maps and atlases now give prominence to the indigenous name of a place rather than its familiar English or Western form. One thus finds *Lisboa* not Lisbon in Portugal, *Athina* not Athens in Greece, *Napoli* not Naples in Italy, and *Moskva* not Moscow in Russia. Language abbreviations are (F) for French, (G) for German, (I) for Italian, and (S) for Spanish. More languages could have been given, but these four give a fair indication of the situation. Names in other languages are sometimes included in individual entries in the main sequence of this work anyway, as the Turkish name for **Poland** or the Finnish name for **Finland**. The cities in Part B are mostly those with significantly differing names in the four languages.

Grammatical indications regarding gender or number are not included, mainly because the gender of geographical names in different languages can be a complex matter, as any language student will testify. Thus, French names of countries ending in *-e* are usually feminine, but *Mexique* is masculine, while most German country names are neuter, but *Schweiz* is feminine. Similarly, the way one says "in" a particular country can vary within a single language, as French *en France* but *au Canada*.

In general, if a name can be literally translated, it will be, as for *Ivory Coast* and *Netherlands*. Otherwise, it usually a matter of adaptation to the norms of the language in question.

A. Countries, Continents, and Regions

Afghanistan: (F) Afghanistan (G) Afghanistan (I) Afganistan (S) Afganistán

Africa: (F) Afrique (G) Afrika (I) Africa (S) África

Albania: (F) Albanie (G) Albanien (I) Albania (S) Albania

Algeria: (F) Algérie (G) Algerien (I) Algeria (S) Argelia

America: (F) Amérique (G) Amerika (I) America (S) América

Angola: (F) Angola (G) Angola (I) Angola (S) Angola

Argentina: (F) Argentine (G) Argentinien (I) Argentina (S) Argentina

Armenia: (F) Arménie (G) Armenien (I) Armenia (S) Armenia

Asia: (F) Asie (G) Asien (I) Asia (S) Asia

Australia: (F) Australie (G) Australien (I) Australia (S) Australia

Austria: (F) Autriche (G) Österreich (I) Austria (S) Austria

Azerbaijan: (F) Azerbaïdjan (G) Aserbaidschan (I) Azerbaijian (S) Azerbaiyán

Bangladesh: (F) Bangladesh (G) Bangladesh (I) Bangladesh (S) Bangladesh

Belarus: (F) Biélorussie (G) Belorußland (I) Bielorussia (S) Bielorrusia

Belgium: (F) Belgique (G) Belgien (I) Belgio (S) Bélgica

Benin: (F) Bénin (G) Benin (I) Benin (S) Benin

Bolivia: (F) Bolivie (G) Bolivien (I) Bolivia (S) Bolivia

Bosnia-Hercegovina: (F) Bosnie-Herzégovine (G) Bosnien-Herzegowina (I) Bosnia-Erzegovina (S) Bosnia Herzegovina

Brazil: (F) Brésil (G) Brasilien (I) Brasile (S) Brasilia

Brittany: (F) Bretagne (G) Bretagne (I) Bretagna (S) Bretaña

Bulgaria: (F) Bulgarie (G) Bulgarien (I) Bulgaria (S) Bulgaria

Burkina Faso: (F) Burkina (G) Burkina Faso (I) Burkina Faso (S) Burkina-Faso

Burma: (F) Birmanie (G) Birma (I) Birmania (S) Birmania (*see also* **Myanmar**)

Cambodia: (F) Cambodge (G) Kambodscha (I) Cambogia (S) Camboya

Cameroon: (F) Cameroun (G) Kamerun (I) Camerun (S) Camerún

Canada: (F) Canada (G) Kanada (I) Canada (S) Canadá

Cape Verde: (F) Cap-Vert (G) Kapverden (I) Capo Verde (S) Cabo Verde

Central African Republic: (F) République Centrafricaine (G) Zentralafrikanische Republik (I) Repubblica Centrafricana (S) República Centroafricana

Chad: (F) Tchad (G) Tschad (I) Ciad (S) Chad

Chile: (F) Chili (G) Chile (I) Cile (S) Chile

China: (F) Chine (G) China (I) Cina (S) China

Colombia: (F) Colombie (G) Kolumbien (I) Colombia (S) Colombia

Congo: (F) Congo (G) Kongo (I) Congo (S) Congo

Corsica: (F) Corse (G) Korsika (I) Corsica (S) Córcega

Costa Rica: (F) Costa Rica (G) Costa Rica (I) Costa Rica (S) Costa Rica

Côte d'Ivoire *see* **Ivory Coast**

Crete: (F) Crète (G) Kreta (I) Creta (S) Creta

Croatia: (F) Croatie (G) Kroatien (I) Croazia (S) Croacia

Cuba: (F) Cuba (G) Kuba (I) Cuba (S) Cuba

Cyprus: (F) Chypre (G) Zypern (I) Cipro (S) Chipre

Czech Republic: (F) République Tchèque (G) Tschechische Republik (I) Repubblica Ceca (S) República Checa

Democratic Republic of Congo: (F) République démocratique du Congo (G) Demokratische Republik Kongo (I) Repubblica Democratica del Congo (S) República democrática del Congo

Denmark: (F) Danemark (G) Dänemark (I) Danimarca (S) Dinamarca

Dominica: (F) Dominique (G) Dominika (I) Dominica (S) Dominica

Dominican Republic: (F) République Dominicaine (G) Dominikanische Republik (I) Repubblica Dominicana (S) República Dominicana

Ecuador: (F) Équateur (G) Ecuador (I) Ecuador (S) Ecuador

Egypt: (F) Égypte (G) Ägypten (I) Egitto (S) Egipto

El Salvador: (F) Salvador (G) El Salvador (I) El Salvador (S) El Salvador

England: (F) Angleterre (G) England (I) Inghilterra (S) Inglaterra

Ethiopia: (F) Éthiopie (G) Äthiopien (I) Etiopia (S) Etiopía

Europe: (F) Europe (G) Europa (I) Europa (S) Europa

Finland: (F) Finlande (G) Finnland (I) Finlandia (S) Finlandia

France: (F) France (G) Frankreich (I) Francia (S) Francia

French Guiana: (F) Guyane Française (G) Französisch-Guayana (I) Guayana Francese (S) Guayana Francesa

Georgia: (F) Géorgie (G) Georgien (I) Georgia (S) Georgia

Germany: (F) Allemagne (G) Deutschland (I) Germania (S) Alemania

Gibraltar: (F) Gibraltar (G) Gibraltar (I) Gibilterra (S) Gibraltar

Ghana: (F) Ghana (G) Ghana (I) Gana (S) Ghana

Great Britain: (F) Grande-Bretagne (G) Großbritannien (I) Gran Bretagna (S) Gran Bretana

Greece: (F) Grèce (G) Griechenland (I) Grecia (S) Grecia

Greenland: (F) Groenland (G) Grönland (I) Groenlandia (S) Groenlandia

Grenada: (F) Grenade (G) Grenada (I) Grenada (S) Granada

Guatemala: (F) Guatemala (G) Guatemala (I) Guatemala (S) Guatemala

Guinea: (F) Guinée (G) Guinea (I) Guinea (S) Guinea

Guyana: (F) Guyana (G) Guyana (I) Guyana (S) Guyana

Haiti: (F) Haïti (G) Haiti (I) Haiti (S) Haití

Honduras: (F) Honduras (G) Honduras (I) Honduras (S) Honduras

Hungary: (F) Hongrie (G) Ungarn (I) Ungheria (S) Hungría

Iceland: (F) Islande (G) Island (I) Islanda (S) Islandia

India: (F) Inde (G) Indien (I) India (S) India

Indonesia: (F) Indonésie (G) Indonesien (I) Indonesia (S) Indonesia

Iran: (F) Iran (G) Iran (I) Iran (S) Irán

Iraq: (F) Iraq (G) Irak (I) Iraq (S) Irak

Ireland: (F) Irlande (G) Irland (I) Irlanda (S) Irlanda

Israel: (F) Israël (G) Israel (I) Israele (S) Israel

Italy: (F) Italie (G) Italien (I) Italia (S) Italia

Ivory Coast: (F) Côte d'Ivoire (G) Elfenbein-küste (I) Costa d'Avorio (S) Costa de Marfil

Jamaica: (F) Jamaïque (G) Jamaika (I) Giamaica (S) Jamaica

Japan: (F) Japon (G) Japan (I) Giappone (S) Japón

Jordan: (F) Jordanie (G) Jordanien (I) Giordania (S) Jordania

Kazakhstan: (F) Kazakhstan (G) Kasachstan (I) Kazakhstan (S) Kadsastán

Kenya: (F) Kenya (G) Kenia (I) Kenia (S) Kenia

Korea *See* (1) **North Korea;** (2) **South Korea**

Kyrgyzstan: (F) Kirghizistan (G) Kirgistan (I) Kirgizistan (S) Kirguidstán

Latvia: (F) Lettonie (G) Lettland (I) Lettonia (S) Letonia

Lebanon: (F) Liban (G) Libanon (I) Libano (S) Líbano

Liberia: (F) Liberia (G) Liberia (I) Liberia (S) Liberia

Libya: (F) Libye (G) Libyen (I) Libia (S) Libia

Liechtenstein: (F) Liechtenstein (G) Liechten-stein (I) Liechtenstein (S) Liechtenstein

Lithuania: (F) Lituanie (G) Litauen (I) Lituania (S) Lituania

Luxembourg: (F) Luxembourg (G) Luxemburg (I) Lussemburgo (S) Luxemburgo

Macedonia: (F) Macédoine (G) Makedonien (I) Macedonia (S) Macedonia

Madagascar: (F) Madagascar (G) Madagaskar (I) Madagascar (S) Madagascar

Madeira: (F) Madère (G) Madeira (I) Madera (S) Madera

Malawi: (F) Malawi (G) Malawi (I) Malawi (S) Malawi

Malaysia: (F) Malaisie (G) Malaysia (I) Malaysia (S) Malasia

Maldives: (F) Maldives (G) Malediven (I) Maldive (S) Maldivas

Mali: (F) Mali (G) Mali (I) Mali (S) Mali

Malta: (F) Malte (G) Malta (I) Malta (S) Malta

Mauritania: (F) Mauritanie (G) Mauritanien (I) Mauritania (S) Mauritania

Mauritius: (F) Maurice (G) Mauritius (I) Maurizio (S) Mauricio

Mexico: (F) Mexique (G) Mexiko (I) Messico (S) Méjico

Moldova: (F) Moldavie (G) Moldawien (I) Moldavia (S) Moldavia

Monaco: (F) Monaco (G) Monaco (I) Monaco (S) Mónaco

Mongolia: (F) Mongolie (G) Mongolei (I) Mongolia (S) Mongolia

Morocco: (F) Maroc (G) Marokko (I) Marocco (S) Marruecos

Mozambique: (F) Mozambique (G) Mosambik (I) Mozambico (S) Mozambique

Myanmar: (F) Myanmar (G) Myanmar (I) Myanmar (S) Myanmar (*see also* **Burma**)

Namibia: (F) Namibie (G) Namibia (I) Namibia (S) Namibia

Nepal: (F) Népal (G) Nepal (I) Nepal (S) Nepal

Netherlands: (F) Pays-Bas (G) Niederlande (I) Paesi Bassi (S) Países Bajos

New Caledonia: (F) Nouvelle-Calédonie (G) Neukaledonien (I) Nuova Caledonia (S) Nueva Caledonia

Newfoundland: (F) Terre-Neuve (G) Neufund-land (I) Terranova (S) Terranova

New Zealand: (F) Nouvelle-Zélande (G) Neuseeland (I) Nuova Zelanda (S) Nueva Zelanda

Nicaragua: (F) Nicaragua (G) Nicaragua (I) Nicaragua (S) Nicaragua

Niger: (F) Niger (G) Niger (I) Niger (S) Niger

Nigeria: (F) Nigeria (G) Nigeria (I) Nigeria (S) Nigeria

Normandy: (F) Normandie (G) Normandie (I) Normandia (S) Normandía

North Korea: (F) Corée du Nord (G) Nordkorea (I) Corea del Nord (S) Corea del Norte

Norway: (F) Norvège (G) Norwegen (I) Norvegia (S) Noruega

Nova Scotia: (F) Nouvelle-Écosse (G) Neuschottland (I) Nuova Scozia (S) Nueva Escocia

Pakistan: (F) Pakistan (G) Pakistan (I) Pakistan (S) Pakistán

Panama: (F) Panamá (G) Panama (I) Panamá (S) Panamá

Paraguay: (F) Paraguay (G) Paraguay (I) Paraguay (S) Paraguay

Peru: (F) Pérou (G) Peru (I) Perú (S) Perú

Philippines: (F) Philippines (G) Philippinen (I) Filippine (S) Filipinas

Poland: (F) Pologne (G) Polen (I) Polonia (S) Polonia

Portugal: (F) Portugal (G) Portugal (I) Portogallo (S) Portugal

Puerto Rico: (F) Porto Rico (G) Puerto Rico (I) Portorico (S) Puerto Rico

Romania: (F) Roumanie (G) Rumänien (I) Romania (S) Rumania

Russia: (F) Russie (G) Russland (I) Russia (S) Rusia

San Marino: (F) Saint-Marin (G) San Marino (I) San Marino (S) San Marino

Sardinia: (F) Sardaigne (G) Sardinien (I) Sardegna (S) Cerdeña

Saudi Arabia: (F) Arabie Saoudite (G) Saudi-Arabien (I) Arabia Saudita (S) Arabia Saudita

Scotland: (F) Écosse (G) Schottland (I) Scozia (S) Escocia

Senegal: (F) Sénégal (G) Senegal (I) Senegal (S) Senegal

Seychelles: (F) Seychelles (G) Seychellen (I) Seicelle (S) Seychelles

Sierra Leone: (F) Sierra Leone (G) Sierra Leone (I) Sierra Leone (S) Sierra Leona

Singapore: (F) Singapour (G) Singapur (I) Singapore (S) Singapur

Slovakia: (F) Slovaquie (G) Slowakei (I) Slovacchia (S) Eslovaquia

Slovenia: (F) Slovénie (G) Slowenien (I) Slovenia (S) Eslovenia

Somalia: (F) Somalie (G) Somalia (I) Somalia (S) Somalia

South Africa: (F) Afrique du Sud (G) Südafrika (I) Sudafrica (S) África del Sur

South Korea: (F) Corée du Sud (G) Südkorea (I) Corea del Sud (S) Corea del Sur

Spain: (F) Espagne (G) Spanien (I) Spagna (S) España

Sri Lanka: (F) Sri Lanka (G) Sri Lanka (I) Sri Lanka (S) Sri Lanka

Sudan: (F) Soudan (G) Sudan (I) Sudan (S) Sudán

Surinam: (F) Suriname (G) Surinam (I) Suriname (S) Suriname

Sweden: (F) Suède (G) Schweden (I) Svezia (S) Suecia

Switzerland: (F) Suisse (G) Schweiz (I) Svizzera (S) Suiza

Syria: (F) Syrie (G) Syrien (I) Siria (S) Siria

Taiwan: (F) Taïwan (G) Taiwan (I) Taiwan (S) Taiwán

Tajikistan: (F) Tadjikistan (G) Tadschikistan (I) Tagikistan (S) Tajikistán

Tanzania: (F) Tanzanie (G) Tansania (I) Tanzania (S) Tanzania

Thailand: (F) Thaïlande (G) Thailand (I) Tailandia (S) Tailandia

Tierra del Fuego: (F) Terre de Feu (G) Feuerland (I) Terra del Fuoco (S) Tierra del Fuego

Togo: (F) Togo (G) Togo (I) Togo (S) Togo

Tunisia: (F) Tunisie (G) Tunesien (I) Tunisia (S) Túnez

Turkey: (F) Turquie (G) Türkei (I) Turchia (S) Turquía

Turkmenistan: (F) Turkménistan (G) Turkmenistan (I) Turkmenistan (S) Turkmenistán

Uganda: (F) Ouganda (G) Uganda (I) Uganda (S) Uganda

Ukraine: (F) Ukraine (G) Ukraine (I) Ucraina (S) Ucrania

Uruguay: (F) Uruguay (G) Uruguay (I) Uruguay (S) Uruguay

Uzbekistan: (F) Ouzbékistan (G) Usbekistan (I) Uzbekistan (S) Usbiekistán

Vatican: (F) Vatican (G) Vatikan (I) Vaticano (S) Vaticano

Venezuela: (F) Venezuela (G) Venezuela (I) Venezuela (S) Venezuela

Vietnam: (F) Viêt Nam (G) Vietnam (I) Vietnam (S) Vietnam

Wales: (F) Pays de Galles (G) Wales (I) Galles (S) País de Gales

Yemen: (F) Yémen (G) Jemen (I) Yemen (S) Yemen

Zambia: (F) Zambie (G) Sambia (I) Zambia (S) Zambia

Zimbabwe: (F) Zimbabwe (G) Simbabwe (I) Zimbabwe (S) Zimbabue

B. Cities

Aachen: (F) Aix-la-Chapelle (G) Aachen (I) Aquisgrana (S) Aquisgrán

Alexandria: (F) Alexandrie (G) Alexandria (I) Alessandria (S) Alejandría

Algiers: (F) Alger (G) Algier (I) Algeri (S) Argel

Antwerp: (F) Anvers (G) Antwerpen (I) Anversa (S) Amberes

Athens: (F) Athènes (G) Athen (I) Atene (S) Atenas

Basel: (F) Bâle (G) Basel (I) Basilea (S) Basilea

Beijing: (F) Pékin (G) Peking (I) Pechino (S) Pekín

Bern: (F) Berne (G) Bern (I) Berna (S) Berna

Brussels: (F) Bruxelles (G) Brüssel (I) Bruxelles (S) Bruselas

Cairo: (F) Le Caire (G) Kairo (I) Il Cairo (S) El Cairo

Cape Town: (F) Le Cap (G) Kapstadt (I) Città del Capo (S) El Cabo

Cologne: (F) Cologne (G) Köln (I) Colonia (S) Colonia

Copenhagen: (F) Copenhague (G) Kopenhagen (I) Copenaghen (S) Copenhague

Cracow: (F) Cracovie (G) Krakau (I) Cracovia (S) Cracovia

Damascus: (F) Damas (G) Damaskus (I) Damasco (S) Damasco

Dunkirk: (F) Dunkerque (G) Dünkirchen (I) Dunkerque (S) Dunquerque

Edinburgh: (F) Édimbourg (G) Edinburgh (I) Edimburgo (S) Edimburgo

Florence: (F) Florence (G) Florenz (I) Firenze (S) Florencia

Frankfurt: (F) Francfort (G) Frankfurt (I) Francoforte (S) Francoforte

Geneva: (F) Genève (G) Genf (I) Ginevra (S) Ginebra

Genoa: (F) Gênes (G) Genua (I) Genova (S) Génova

Ghent: (F) Gand (G) Gent (I) Gand (S) Gante

Granada: (F) Grenade (G) Granada (I) Granada (S) Granada

Hague, The: (F) La Haye (G) Den Haag (I) L'Aia (S) La Haya

Hamburg: (F) Hamboug (G) Hamburg (I) Amburgo (S) Hamburgo

Havana: (F) La Havane (G) Havanna (I) L'Avana (S) La Habana

Jerusalem: (F) Jérusalem (G) Jerusalem (I) Gerusalemme (S) Jerusalén

Lisbon: (F) Lisbonne (G) Lissabon (I) Lisbona (S) Lisboa

London: (F) Londres (G) London (I) Londra (S) Londres

Mecca: (F) La Mecque (G) Mekka (I) La Mecca (S) La Meca

Mexico City: (F) Mexico (G) Mexiko City (I) Città di Messico (S) México

Milan: (F) Milan (G) Mailand (I) Milano (S) Milán

Moscow: (F) Moscou (G) Moskau (I) Mosca (S) Moscú

Munich: (F) Munich (G) München (I) Monaco (S) Munich

Naples: (F) Naples (G) Neapel (I) Napoli (S) Nápoles

New Orleans: (F) La Nouvelle-Orléans (G) New Orleans (I) New Orleans (S) New Orleans

New York: (F) New York (G) New York (I) New York (S) Nueva York

Nuremberg: (F) Nuremberg (G) Nürnberg (I) Norimberga (S) Nuremberg

Paris: (F) Paris (G) Paris (I) Parigi (S) París

Prague: (F) Prague (G) Prag (I) Praga (S) Praga

Rome: (F) Rome (G) Rom (I) Roma (S) Roma

St. Petersburg: (F) St-Pétersbourg (G) St. Petersburg (I) San Pietroburgo (S) San Petersburgo

Santiago (de Compostela): (F) Saint-Jacques (G) Santiago (I) Santiago (S) Santiago

Seville: (F) Séville (G) Sevilla (I) Siviglia (S) Sevilla

Sofia: (F) Sofia (G) Sofia (I) Sofia (S) Sofía

Stockholm: (F) Stockholm (G) Stockholm (I) Stoccolma (S) Estocolmo

Venice: (F) Venise (G) Venedig (I) Venezia (S) Venecia

Vienna: (F) Vienne (G) Wien (I) Vienna (S) Viena

Warsaw: (F) Varsovie (G) Warschau (I) Varsavia (S) Varsovia

C. European Rivers

Danube: (F) Danube (G) Donau (I) Danubio (S) Danubio

Ebro: (F) Èbre (G) Ebro (I) Ebro (S) Ebro

Meuse: (F) Meuse (G) Maas (I) Mosa (S) Mosa

Rhine: (F) Rhin (G) Rhein (I) Reno (S) Rin

Rhône: (F) Rhône (G) Rhone (I) Rodano (S) Ródano

Scheldt: (F) Escaut (G) Scheldt (I) Schelda (S) Schelda

Seine: (F) Seine (G) Seine (I) Senna (S) Sena

Tagus: (F) Tage (G) Tagus (I) Tago (S) Tajo

Thames: (F) Tamise (G) Themse (I) Tamigi (S) Támesis

Tiber: (F) Tibre (G) Tiber (I) Tevere (S) Tíber

Vistula: (F) Vistule (G) Weichsel (I) Vistola (S) Vístola

Volga: (F) Volga (G) Wolga (I) Volga (S) Volga

Appendix 3:
Chinese Names of
Countries and Capitals

The selection of Chinese equivalents below is given for the interest of the general reader, not simply for Sinophiles, and no knowledge of Chinese is required to appreciate the presentation.

Most Chinese names of non–Chinese places are transliterations, given here in their Roman equivalent. Some are recognisably close to the original, as *dákǎ* for *Dhaka*, *lìmǎ* for *Lima*. Others are approximations, allowing for the particularities of the Chinese language. Any name with *r*, for example, will usually have this letter rendered as *l*, as *ānkǎlā* for *Ankara*, *luōmǎ* for *Rome*. This results from the so-called "flied lice" syndrome, occasioned by the absence of *r* in Chinese. In other cases, consonants are simply omitted, as *dānmài* for *Denmark*, *āijí* for *Egypt*. In some instances the name consists of a shortened form of the non–Chinese place-name, usually that of the accented syllable, followed by a Chinese word. A well-known example is *měizhōu* for *America*, where *měi* is the stressed syllable of the name followed by Chinese *zhōu*, "continent." By contrast, the name of the *United States of America* is *měiguó*, with *měi* followed by *guó*, "country," "nation." Chinese *guó* is found in other names, such as *yīngguó* for *England*, *fǎguó* for *France* (note the omitted *r*.) Other "continent" names on the lines of *měizhōu* are *fēizhōu* for *Africa*, *yàzhōu* for *Asia*, and *ōuzhōu* for *Europe*.

The Chinese ideograms used for transliteration purposes usually have a meaning of their own, although this is not understood in the placename. Thus, the *měi* of *America* happens to mean "beautiful," and the *fēi* of *Africa* means "wrong." In *niǔyuē*, the Chinese rendering of *New York*, *niǔ* properly means "button," while *yuē* is "to make an appointment," and in *bālí*, the transliteration of *Paris* (with *l* for *r*), *bā* properly means "to hope earnestly," while *lí* is "multitude." If taken literally, some of the Chinese meanings are hardly complimentary. *America* can be literally interpreted as "beautiful continent," but by the same token *Asia* could be understood as "inferior continent," since Chinese *yà* means "inferior," "second."

Some names of non–Chinese places have fully translated forms, such as *nán-jízhōu*, "south pole continent" for *Antarctica*, and *tàipíngyáng*, "peace ocean," for *Pacific Ocean*. Where a country name has "republic," this is of course also translated, as *gònghéguó*, literally "common peace country."

Certain Chinese names do not transliterate a general international name but a particular indigenous one. The Chinese name of *Korea*, for example, is *cháoxiān*, transliterating the Korean name, *chosŏn*, as does the country's Japanese name, *chosen*. Translated literally, the two ideograms *cháo* and *xiān* that form the Chinese name respectively mean "dynasty" and "fresh," "bright."

Accra : ākèlā
Addis Ababa : yàdìsǐyàbèibā
Aden : yàdīngchéng
Afghanistan : āfùhán
Africa : fēizhōu
Alaska : ālāsījiā
Albania : ā'ěrbāníyà
Algeria : ā'ěrjílìyá
Algiers : ā'ěrjí'ěr
Al-Kuwayt : kēwēitèchéng
America : měizhōu
Amsterdam : āmǔsītèdān
Angola : āngēlā
Ankara : ānkǎlā
Antarctica : nánjízhōu
Arctic Ocean : běibīngyáng
Arctic Regions : běijídìdài
Argentina : āgēntíng
Asia : yàzhōu
Asunción : yàsōgsēn
Athens : yǎdiǎn
Atlantic Ocean : dàxīyáng
Australia : àodàlìyà
Austria : àodìlì
Baghdad : bāgédá
Baltic Sea : bōluódìhǎi
Bamako : bāmǎkē
Bangkok : màngǔ
Bangladesh : mèngjiālā
Bangui : bānjí
Beirut : bèilǔtè
Belgium : bǐlìshí
Belgrade : bèi'ěrgéláidé
Benghazi : bānjiāxī
Berlin : bólín
Berne : bó'ěrní
Bhutan : bùdān
Black Sea : hēihǎi
Bogotá: bōgēdà
Bolivia : bōlìwéiyà
Bombay (Mumbai) : mèngmǎi
Bonn : bō'ēn
Brasília : bāxīlìyà
Brazil : bāxī
Brazzaville : bùlācháiwéi'ěr
Brussels : bùlǔsài'ěr
Bucharest : bùjiālèsītè
Budapest : bùdápèisī
Buenos Aires : bùyínuòsī àilìsī
Bujumbura : bùqióngbùlā
Bulgaria : bǎojiālìyà
Burma (Myanmar) : miǎndiàn
Burundi : bùlóngdí
Cairo : kāiluó
Calcutta : jiā'ěrgèdā
Cambodia: jiǎnpǔzhài

Cameroon : kāmàilóng
Canada : jiānádà
Canberra : kānpéilā
Caracas : jiālājiāsī
Caucasus : gāojiāsuǒ
Central African Republic : zhōngfēi gònghéguó
Chad : zhàdé
Chile : zhìlì
Colombia : gēlúnbǐyà
Colombo : kēlúnpō
Conakry : kēnàkèlǐ
Congo : gāngguǒ
Copenhagen : gēběnhāgēn
Costa Rica : gēsīdálíjiā
Cuba : gǔbā
Cyprus : sàipǔlùsī
Czech Republic: jiékè gònghéguó
Dakar : dáka'ěr
Damascus : dàmǎshìgē
Danube : duōnǎohé
Dar es Salaam : dálèisī sàlāmǔ
Delhi : délǐ
Denmark : dānmài
Dhaka : dákǎ
Dominican Republic : duōmǐníjiā gònghéguó
Dublin : dūbǎilín
Ecuador : èguāduō'ěr
Egypt : āijí
England : yīngguó
English Channel : yīngjílì hǎixiá
Ethiopia : āisàiébǐyà
Europe : ōuzhōu
Far East : yuǎndōng
Finland : fēnlán
France : fǎguó
Gabon : jiāpéng
Gambia: gāngběyà
Ganges : hénghé
Geneva : rìnèiwǎ
Germany : déyìzhì
Ghana : jiānà
Gibraltar : zhíbùluótuó
Great Britain : dàbùlièdiān
Greece : xīlà
Guatemala : wēidìmǎlā
Guinea : jǐnèiyà
Hague, The : hǎiyá
Haiti : hǎidì
Havana : hāwǎnà
Helsinki : hè'ěrxīnjī
Himalayas : xǐmǎlāyǎshān
Hiroshima : guǎngdǎo
Honduras : hóngdūlāsī
Hungary : xiōngyálì
Iceland : bīngdǎo
India : yìndù

Indonesia : yìndùníxīyà
Iran : yīlǎng
Iraq : yīlākè
Ireland : àiěrlán
Islamabad : yīsīlánbǎo
Israel : yǐsèliè
Italy : yìdàlì
Jakarta : yǎjiādá
Japan : rìběn
Jordan : yuēdàn
Kabul : kābù'ěr
Kampala : kǎnpàlā
Karachi : kǎlāqí
Kashmir : kèshímǐ'ěr
Kathmandu : jiādémǎndū
Kenya : kěnníyà
Khartoum : kātǔmù
Kinshasa : jīnshāsà
Korea : cháoxiān
Kuala Lumpur : jílóngpō
Kuwait : kēwēitè
Lagos: lāgèsī
Laos : lǎowō
La Paz : lābāsī
Lebanon : líbānùn
Lhasa : lāsàshì
Liberia : lìbǐlǐyà
Libreville : lìbówéi'ěr
Libya : lìbǐyà
Lima : lìmǎ
Lisbon : lǐsīběn
Lomé : luòměi
London : lúndūn
Luanda : luó'āndá
Lusaka : lúsàkǎ
Luxembourg : lúsēnbǎo
Madrid : mǎdélǐ
Mali : mǎlǐ
Malaysia : mǎláixīyà
Malta : mǎ'ěrtā
Managua : mǎnàguā
Manila : mǎnílā
Mediterranean Sea : dìzhōnghǎi
Mexico : mòxīgē
Mexico City : mòxīgēchéng
Mogadishu : mójiādíshā
Mongolia : měnggǔ
Monrovia : měngluówéiyà
Montevideo : měngdéwéidìyà
Morocco : móluògē
Moscow : mòsīkē
Mozambique : mòsānbígěi
Nairobi : nèiluóbì
Nepal: níbó'ěr
Netherlands : hélán
New York : niǔyuē

New Zealand : xīnxīlán
Niamey : níyàměi
Nicaragua : níjiālāguā
Nicosia : níkēxīyà
Niger : nírì'ěr
Nigeria : nírìlìyà
Norway : nuówēi
Oceania : dàyángzhōu
Oslo : àosīlù
Ottawa : wòtàihuā
Pacific Ocean : tàipíngyáng
Pakistan : bājīsītán
Palestine : bālēsītǎn
Panama : bānámǎ
Panama Canal : bānámǎ yùnhé
Panama City : bānámǎchéng
Paraguay : bālāguī
Paris : bālí
Peru : mìlǔ
Philippines : fěilǜbìn
Phnom Penh : jīnbiān
Port-au-Prince : tàizǐgǎng
Porto-Novo : bōduōnuòfú
Portugal : pútǎoyá
Prague : bùlāgé
Pretoria : bǐlētuólìyà
Puerto Rico : bōduōlígè
Quito: jíduō
Rabat : lābātè
Reykjavík : léikèyǎwèikè
Riyadh : lìyǎdé
Rome : luōmǎ
Russia : éluósī
Rwanda : lúwàngdá
Sana : sànà
San José : shèngyuēsè
San Juan : shènghú'ān
San Salvador : shèngsà'ěrwǎduō
Santiago : shèngdìyàgē
Santo Domingo : shèngduōmínggè
Saudi Arabia : shātè ālābó
Senegal : sàinèijiā'ěr
Seoul : hànchéng
Siberia : xībólìyà
Singapore : xīnjiāpō
Slovakia : sīluòfákè
Sofia : suǒfēiyà
Somalia : suǒmǎlǐ
South Africa : nánfēi
Spain : xībānyá
Sri Lanka : sīlǐ lánkǎ
Stockholm : sīdégē'ěrmó
Sudan : sūdān
Sweden : ruìdiǎn
Switzerland : ruìshì
Syria : xùlìyà

Taiwan : táiwān
Tanzania : tǎnsāngníyà
Tegucigalpa : tègǔxījiā'ěrbā
Tehran : déhēilán
Tel-Aviv : táilāwéifū
Thailand : tàiguó
Tibet : xīzàng
Tiranë : dìlānà
Togo : duōgē
Tokyo : dōngjīng
Tunis : tūnísī
Tunisia : tūnísī
Turkey : tǔ'ěrgí
Uganda : wūgàndá
Ulan Bator: wūlánbātuō
United States of America : měiguó

Uruguay : wūlāguī
Valetta : wǎláitǎ
Venezuela : wěinèiruìlā
Vienna : wéiyěnà
Vientiane : wànxiàng
Vietnam : yuènán
Vladivostok : fúlādíwòsītuōkè
Volga : fú'ěrjiāhé
Warsaw : huāshā
Washington : huāshèngdùn
Wellington : huìlíngdùn
Yangon (Rangoon) : yǎnguāng
Yaoundé : yǎwēndé
Yemen : yěmén
Zambia : zànbǐyà

Select Bibliography

The bibliography below does not include placename dictionaries of administrative areas within a particular country, such as American states or Russian republics. There are simply too many to list. This does not mean, of course, that such resources were not used during work on the present book.

Nor, with one exception, does it include the titles of the various foreign-language dictionaries consulted. They deserve mention, however, and recourse was made as necessary to dictionaries of the following languages: Arabic, Chinese, Finnish, French, German, Greek (classical and modern), Hebrew, Hindi, Hungarian, Irish, Italian, Japanese, Latin, Polish, Portuguese, Russian, Sanskrit, Spanish, Turkish, and Welsh. The exception is the Gaulish dictionary by Xavier Delamarre, which not only translates Gaulish words and elements but incorporates personal names and placenames containing them.

The significance of the notations [!] and [!!] against certain titles is explained below. Some bibliographies might have omitted such titles, but they are not entirely valueless, if used with care.

English translations of foreign titles are given in brackets.

Ageyeva, R.A. *Strany i narody: Proiskhozhdeniye nazvaniy* (Countries and peoples: The origins of names). Moscow: Nauka, 1990.

Appleton, Richard, and Barbara Appleton. *The Cambridge Dictionary of Australian Places.* Cambridge: Cambridge University Press, 1992.

Armstrong, G.H. *The Origin and Meaning of Place Names in Canada.* Toronto: Macmillan Company of Canada, 1930.

Arousseau, M. *The Rendering of Geographical Names.* London: Hutchinson University Library, 1957.

Batowski, Henryk. *Słownik nazv miejscowych Europy Środkowej i Wschodniej XIX i XX wieku* (Dictionary of placenames of Central and Eastern Europe of the 19th and 20th centuries). Warsaw: Państwowe Wydawnictwo Naukowe, 1964.

Berger, Dieter. *Geographische Namen in Deutschland* (Geographical names in Germany). Mannheim: Duden, 1993.

Blackie, Christine. *Etymological Geography.* 2d ed. London: Dalby, Isbister, 1876 [!!].

Cabral, António. *Dicionário de Nomes Geográficos de Moçambique* (Dictionary of the geographical names of Mozambique). Lourenço Marques: Impresa Moderna, 1975.

Cameron, Kenneth. *English Place Names.* New ed. London: Batsford, 1996.

Cherpillod, André. *Dictionnaire étymologique des noms géographiques* (Etymological dictionary of geographical names). 2d ed. Paris: Masson, 1991.

Cohen, Saul B., ed. *The Columbia Gazetteer of the World.* 3 vols. New York, NY: Columbia University Press, 1998.

_____, and Nurit Kliot, "Israel's Place-Names as Reflection of Continuity and Change in Nation-Building." *Names: Journal of the American Name Society,* Vol. 29, No. 3, September 1981.

Darton, Mike. *The Dictionary of Place Names in Scotland.* New ed. Orpington: Eric Dobb, 1994.

Dauzat, A., and Ch. Rostaing. *Dictionnaire étymologique des noms de lieux en France* (Etymological dictionary of placenames in France). 2d ed. Paris: Guénégaud, 1978.

[!] = consult with caution; [!!] = consult with extreme caution.

Delamarre, Xavier. *Dictionnaire de la langue gauloise* (Dictionary of the Gaulish language). 2d rev. and enl. ed. Paris: Éditions Errance, 2003.

Dubrovin, L.I., and M.A. Preobrazhenskaya. *O chyom govorit karta Antarktiki* (What the map of the Antarctic has to tell). Leningrad: Gidrometeoizdat, 1987.

Everett-Heath, John. *Place Names of the World*. New York, NY: St. Martin's Press, 2000.

Farmer, Austin. *Place-Name Correspondences*. London: David Nutt, 1904 [!!].

_____. *Place-Name Synonyms Classified*. London: David Nutt, 1904 [!!].

Field, John. *Place-Names of Great Britain and Ireland*. Newton Abbot: David & Charles, 1980.

Flanagan, Deirdre, and Laurence Flanagan. *Irish Place Names*. Dublin: Gill & Macmillan, 1994.

Freedman, David Noel, ed. in chief. *Eerdmans Dictionary of the Bible*. Grand Rapids, MI: Wm. B. Eerdmans, 2000.

Graesse, Johann Gustav Theodor, and Friedrich Benedict. *Orbis latinus, oder Verzeichnis der wichtigsten lateinischen Orts- under Ländernamen* (The Latin world, or a register of the most important Latin names of places and countries). Berlin: Transpress, 1980.

Grimal, Pierre. *Dictionnaire de la Mythologie Grecque et Romaine* (Dictionary of Greek and Roman mythology). 6th ed. Paris: Presses Universitaires de France, 1979.*

Hamilton, William B. *The Macmillan Book of Canadian Place Names*. Toronto: Macmillan of Canada, 1978.

Hanks, Patrick, and Flavia Hodges. *A Dictionary of Surnames*. Oxford: Oxford University Press, 1988.

Harder, Kelsie B., ed. *Illustrated Dictionary of Place Names, United States and Canada*. New York, NY: Van Nostrand Reinhold, 1976.

Hattersley-Smith, G. *The History of Place-Names in the Falkland Islands Dependencies (South Georgia and the South Sandwich Islands)*. British Antarctic Survey Scientific Report No. 101. Cambridge: British Antarctic Survey, 1980.

_____. *The History of Place-Names in the British Antarctic Territory*. British Antarctic Survey Scientific Report No. 113 (Parts I and II). Cambridge: British Antarctic Survey, 1991.

Hazlitt, William. *The Classical Gazetteer: A Dictionary of Ancient Sites*. London: Whittaker, 1851 [!!].

Hornblower, Simon, and Antony Spawforth, eds. *The Oxford Classical Dictionary*. 3d ed. Oxford: Oxford University Press, 1996.

Joyce, P.W. *Irish Names of Places*. 3 vols. Dublin: Phoenix Publishing, 1869–1913.

Kálmán, Béla. *The World of Names: A Study in Hungarian Onomatology*. Budapest: Akadémiai Kiadó, 1978.

Kirchherr, Eugene C. *Place Names of Africa, 1935–1986: A Political Gazetteer*. Metuchen, NJ: Scarecrow Press, 1987.

Losique, Serge. *Dictionnaire étymologique des noms de pays et de peuples* (Etymological dictionary of the names of countries and peoples). Paris: Klincksieck, 1971.

Louda, Jiří. *European Civic Coats of Arms*, trans. from the Czech by Alice Denesová, ed. by Dermot Morrah. London: Paul Hamlyn, 1966.

McKay, Patrick. *A Dictionary of Ulster Place-Names*. Belfast: Institute of Irish Studies, 1999.

Maori Place Names and Their Meanings. Wellington: A.H. & A.W. Reed, 1950.

Matthews, C.M. *Place Names of the English-speaking World*. London: Weidenfeld & Nicolson, 1972.

Merriam-Webster's New Geographical Dictionary. 3d ed. Springfield, MA: Merriam-Webster, 1997.

Mills, A.D. *A Dictionary of British Place-Names*. Oxford: Oxford University Press, 2004.

_____. *A Dictionary of London Place-Names*. Oxford: Oxford University Press, 2001.

Nelson, Derek. *Off the Map: The Curious Histories of Place-Names*. New York: Kodansha, 1997.

The New Encyclopædia Britannica. 30 vols. 15th ed. Chicago, IL: Encyclopædia Britannica, 2002.

Nicolaisen, W.F.H. *Scottish Place-Names*. New ed. Edinburgh: John Donald, 2001.

_____, Margaret Gelling, and Melville Richards. *The Names of Towns and Cities in Britain*. London: Batsford, 1970.

Nikonov, V.A. *Kratkij toponimicheskij slovar'* (Concise toponymical dictionary). Moscow: Mysl', 1966.

Odelain, O., and R. Séguineau. *Dictionnaire des noms propres de la Bible* (Dictionary of proper names in the Bible). Paris: Éditions du Cerf, 1978.

Owen, Hywel Wyn. *The Place-Names of Wales*. Cardiff: University of Wales Press, 1998.

*An English translation by A.R. Maxwell-Hyslop, *The Dictionary of Classical Mythology, *was published in 1985 by Basil Blackwell, Oxford.*

Raper, P.E. *A Dictionary of Southern African Place Names.* 2d ed. Johannesburg: Jonathan Ball, 1989.

Reader's Digest World Atlas. London: The Reader's Digest Association, 2004.

Reed, A.W. *Place Names of Australia.* Sydney: Reed Books, 1973.

Rivet, A.L.F., and Colin Smith. *The Place-Names of Roman Britain.* London: Batsford, 1979.

Room, Adrian. *African Placenames.* Jefferson, NC: McFarland, 1994.

_____. *A Dictionary of Irish Place-Names.* Rev. ed. Belfast: Appletree Press, 1994.

_____. *Dictionary of Place-Names in the British Isles.* London: Bloomsbury, 1988.

_____. *Dictionary of World Place Names Derived from British Names.* London: Routledge, 1989.

_____. *Place-Name Changes: 1900–1991.* 2d ed. Metuchen, NJ: Scarecrow Press, 1993.

_____. *Placenames of France.* Jefferson, NC: McFarland, 2004.

_____. *Placenames of Russia and the Former Soviet Union.* Jefferson, NC: McFarland, 1996.

_____. *Place-Names of the World.* Newton Abbot: David & Charles, 1974.

Smith, William. *A Dictionary of the Bible.* Rev. and ed. by F.N. and M.A. Peloubet. Nashville, TN: Nelson, 1986.

Stewart, George R. *Names on the Land.* 3d ed. Boston, MA: Houghton Mifflin, 1967.

_____. *American Place-Names.* New York, NY: Oxford University Press, 1970.

_____. *Names on the Globe.* New York, NY: Oxford University Press, 1975.

Stewart, John. *African States and Rulers.* Jefferson, NC: McFarland, 1989.

Sturmfels, Wilhelm, and Heinz Bischof. *Unsere Ortsnamen* (Our placenames). Bonn: Dümmler, 1961 [!].

Tapsell, R.F., comp. *Monarchs, Rulers, Dynasties, and Kingdoms of the World.* London: Thames and Hudson, 1983.

Taylor, Isaac. *Names and Their Histories.* London: Rivington, Percival, 1896 [!].

_____. *Words and Places.* Edited with corrections and additions by A. Smythe Palmer. London: Routledge, 1909 [!].

The Times Comprehensive Atlas of the World. 11th ed. London: Times Books, 2003.

Treharne, R.F., and Harold Fullard, eds. *Muir's Historical Atlas: Ancient and Classical.* 6th ed. London: George Philip and Son, 1963.

Watts, Victor. *The Cambridge Dictionary of English Place-Names.* Cambridge: Cambridge University Press, 2004.

Wolk, Allan. *The Naming of America.* Nashville, TN: Thomas Nelson, 1977.

Wright, F.A. *Lemprière's Classical Dictionary of Proper Names Mentioned in Ancient Authors.* New ed., rev. with additions. London: Routledge & Kegan Paul, 1949.

Zhuchkevich, V.A. *Kratkiy toponimicheskiy slovar' Belorussii* (Concise toponymical dictionary of Belorussia). Minsk: Izdatel'stvo BGU im. V.I. Lenina, 1974.

The following Internet site provides links to the names of 68 Israeli kibbutzim:

<http://judaism.about.com/cs/kibbutzdirectory/index.htm>